The Self Assesment Library:
Insights Into Your Skills, Abilities and Interests

VERSION 2.0

Stephen P. Robbins; San Diego State University; © 2003
PRINT ISBN: 0-13-035293-4; CD-ROM ISBN: 0-13-045449-4

What Time of Day Am I Most Productive?

How Good Am I at Personal Planning?

How Good Are My Listening Skills?

Students will learn the answers to these questions and many
more! Steve Robbins' *Self-Assessment Library** is a unique instrument
that allows students to assess their knowledge, beliefs, feelings, and
actions in regard to a wide range of personal skills, abilities, and interests.
Automatically graded, self-scoring exercises generate immediate, individual
analysis, which can be printed out or e-mailed to the instructor. Forty-nine research-based
instruments are provided in a single volume to offer students one source from which to learn more
about themselves.

*Available in both print and CD-ROM formats.

NEW FEATURES

- Professors can now relate tests to
  management and organizational
  behavior topics with the addition
  of a convenient new matrix.

- Help students better understand
  the meaning of their results with
  new approximate quantitative
  cut-off scores, and improve areas
  of weakness with added remedial
  actions or references.

- Eight new tests have been added to
  provide students with additional self-
  assessment instruments.

SUPPLEMENTS
Instructor's Manual

CONTENTS
I. WHAT ABOUT ME?
  A. Personality Insights
  B. Values and Attitude Insights
  C. Motivation Insights
  D. Decision Making Insights
  E. Other

II. WORKING WITH OTHERS.
  A. Communication Skills
  B. Leadership and Team Skills
  C. Power and Conflict Skills

III. LIFE IN ORGANIZATIONS.
  A. Jobs
  B. Organization Structure
  C. Careers
  D. Change and Stress

Organizational Behavior

10th Edition

Stephen P. Robbins

San Diego State University

Prentice Hall

Upper Saddle River, New Jersey 07458

Library of Congress Cataloging-in-Publication Data

Robbins, Stephen P.
    Organizational behavior/Stephen P. Robbins.--10th ed.
      p. cm.
    Includes bibliographical references and index.
    ISBN 0-13-100069-1
     1. Organizational behavior. I. Title.

HD58.7 .R62 2003
658.3--dc21 2002070204

Acquisitions Editor: Michael Ablassmeir
Editor-in-Chief: Jeff Shelstad
Managing Editor (Editorial): Jennifer Glennon
Assistant Editor: Melanie Olsen
Editorial Assistant: Kevin Glynn
Media Project Manager: Michele Faranda
Senior Marketing Manager: Shannon Moore
Marketing Assistant: Christine Genneken
Managing Editor (Production): Judy Leale
Production Editor: Cindy Spreder
Permissions Supervisor: Suzanne Grappi
Associate Director, Manufacturing: Vincent Scelta
Production Manager: Arnold Vila
Manufacturing Buyer: Diane Peirano
Design Manager: Maria Lange
Art Director: Pat Smythe
Cover Design: Laura Ospanik
Designer: John Romer
Illustrator (Interior): Amanda Kavanaugh
Manager, Print Production: Karen Goldsmith
Composition: Carlisle Communications
Full-Service Project Management: Lynn Steines, Carlisle Communications
Printer/Binder: Quebecor

Credits and acknowledgments borrowed from other sources and reproduced, with permission, in this textbook appear on the appropriate page within text .

Pearson Education LTD.
Pearson Education Australia PTY, Limited
Pearson Education Singapore, Pte. Ltd
Pearson Education North Asia Ltd
Pearson Education, Canada, Ltd
Pearson Educación de Mexico, S.A. de C.V.
Pearson Education–Japan
Pearson Education Malaysia, Pte. Ltd

10 9 8 7 6 5 4 3
ISBN 0-13-100069-1

This book is dedicated to my family support team:

Laura Ospanik

Dana, Jim, and Mallory Murray

Jennifer Robbins

Judi and David Robman

Gert and Lad Ospanik

Stephen P. Robbins received his Ph.D. from the University of Arizona and has taught at the University of Nebraska at Omaha, Concordia University in Montreal, the University of Baltimore, Southern Illinois University at Edwardsville, and San Diego State University. Dr. Robbins' research interests have focused on conflict, power, and politics in organizations, as well as on the development of effective interpersonal skills. His articles on these and other topics have appeared in journals such as *Business Horizons*, the *California Management Review*, *Business and Economic Perspectives*, *International Management*, *Management Review*, *Canadian Personnel and Industrial Relations*, and *The Journal of Management Education*.

In recent years, Dr. Robbins has been spending most of his professional time writing textbooks. These include *Essentials of Organizational Behavior*, 7th ed. (Prentice Hall, 2003); *Training in InterPersonal Skills*, 3rd ed., with Phillip Hunsaker (Prentice Hall, 2003); *Management*, 7th ed. with Mary Coulter (Prentice Hall, 2002); *Human Resource Management*, 7th ed., with David DeCenzo (Wiley, 2002); *The Self-Assessment Library* 2.0 (Prentice Hall, 2002); *Fundamentals of Management*, 3rd ed., with David DeCenzo (Prentice Hall, 2001); *Supervision Today!*, 3rd ed., with David DeCenzo (Prentice Hall, 2001); *Business Today* (Harcourt, 2001); *Managing Today!* 2nd ed. (Prentice Hall, 2000); and *Organization Theory*, 3rd ed. (Prentice Hall, 1990).

In Dr. Robbins' "other life," he participates in masters' track competition. Since turning 50 in 1993, he has set numerous indoor and outdoor age-group world sprint records; won more than a dozen indoor and outdoor U.S. championships at 60, 100, 200, and 400 meters; and captured seven gold medals at the World Masters Championships. Most recently, he won gold medals at 100 and 200 meters and as the anchor on the U.S. 4 × 100 relay in the Men's 55–59 age group at the 2001 World Championships in Brisbane, Australia.

CONTENTS IN BRIEF

CONTENTS

PREFACE

Since it was first published in 1979, this book has been read by more than 900,000 students. The previous edition was used by students at more than a thousand colleges and universities worldwide. If there's such a thing as a "global textbook," this book probably has earned that label. It's the number-one selling organizational behavior (OB) textbook in the United States, Canada, Mexico, Central America, South America, Australia, Hong Kong, Singapore, Thailand, the Philippines, Taiwan, South Korea, Malaysia, Indonesia, India, China, Sweden, Finland, Denmark, and Greece. There are also translations available in German, Chinese, Japanese, Korean, Thai, Spanish, Portuguese, and Indonesian; and adaptations with country-specific examples and content for the Australian and Canadian markets.

Features Still Around After Nearly a Quarter of a Century

As much as the field of OB has changed since 1979 and, with it, the contents of this textbook, a number of features still remain from the first edition. It is these features, in fact, that I think largely explain this book's success. These include the conversational writing style, the cutting-edge content, the extensive use of current examples, the three-level integrative model, the point-counterpoint dialogues, the end-of-chapter pedagogy, and the comprehensive supplement package. Let me elaborate on each of these points.

- **Writing style.** This book is most often singled out for the writing style. Reviewers and users regularly tell me that it's "conversational," "interesting," "student-friendly," and "very clear and understandable." I believe this revision maintains that tradition.
- **Cutting-edge content.** This book was the first OB textbook to have a chapter on power and politics, a chapter on conflict, a chapter on organizational culture, and two chapters on motivation. The book continues to provide cutting-edge content that is often missing in other OB books. A list of contemporary topics new to this edition is included later in this Preface.
- **Examples, examples, examples.** My teaching experience tells me that students may not remember a concept, but they'll remember an example. Moreover, a good example goes a long way in helping students to better understand a concept. So, as with the previous editions, you'll find this revision packed full of recent real-world examples drawn from a variety of organizations—business and not-for-profit, large and small, and local and international.
- **The three-level model of analysis.** Since its first edition, this book has presented OB at three levels of analysis. It begins with individual behavior and then moves to group behavior. Finally, it adds the organization system to capture the full complexity of organizational behavior. Students seem to find this approach logical and straightforward.
- **"Point–Counterpoint" dialogues.** These focused arguments allow students to see two sides of an OB controversy and to stimulate their critical thinking. Faculty tell me they find these dialogues to be excellent devices

for stimulating class discussion and getting students to think critically about OB issues in the workplace. Some of these 19 dialogues are now in this edition.

- **Pedagogy.** This edition continues the tradition of providing the most complete assortment of in-text pedagogy available in any OB book. This includes review and critical-thinking questions, team exercises, ethical dilemma exercises, and case applications.
- **Supplement package.** This text provides the most comprehensive teaching and learning support package available. It is described in detail in the latter part of this Preface.

Features Added in Recent Editions

A number of features that were added in recent editions continue to receive positive comments from students and faculty alike. These, too, have been retained. They include the integration of globalization, diversity, and ethics, and the "Myth or Science?" boxes.

- **Integration of globalization, diversity, and ethics.** As seen in Exhibit P-1, the topics of globalization and cross-cultural differences, workforce diversity, and ethics are discussed throughout this book. Rather than presented in stand-alone chapters, they have been woven into the context of relevant issues. I have found that this integrative approach makes these issues more fully part of OB and reinforces their importance. In this edition, I've expanded the number of end-of-chapter "Ethical Dilemma" exercises from 5 to 12.
- **"Myth or Science?" boxes.** This feature presents a commonly accepted "fact" about human behavior, followed by confirming or disproving research evidence. Some examples include "You Can't Teach an Old Dog New Tricks"; "Happy Workers are Productive Workers"; and "It's Not What You Know, It's Who You Know." These boxes provide repeated evidence that common sense can often lead you astray in the attempt to understand human behavior, and that behavioral research offers a means for testing the validity of common-sense notions. These boxes are meant to help you to see how the field of OB, built on a large body of research evidence, can provide valuable insights toward understanding and explaining human behavior at work.

What's New in This 10th Edition?

Users of the previous edition will find that the most obvious changes in this revision are the inclusion of an additional chapter on leadership and the broadly expanded coverage of skills.

The additional chapter on leadership reflects the increasing awareness of the important role this concept plays in achieving effective organizational performance and the rapidly expanding body of leadership-related research findings.

By going from one chapter to two, I've been able to bring in new leadership-related material such as framing issues, mentoring, self-leadership, online leadership, and the GLOBE studies on cross-cultural leadership.

Previous editions had a box theme on "From Concepts to Skills." The expressed desire by both students and faculty for increased skill coverage led me to create the Skill-Building Modules in this edition. These modules have been integrated into

Integrative Topics (with specific page references)

EXHIBIT

P-1

what I call the KSS Program. KSS refers to the three elements in building effective OB skills: Knowing the concepts, Self-awareness, and Skill applications. KSS proposes that the skill modules are best used when combined with text content and the Self-Assessment CD-ROM that is included in the back of this book.

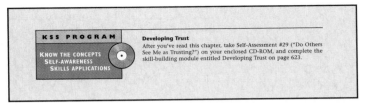

Specifically, students can build and improve their interpersonal and behavioral skills by reading a chapter, completing the relevant self-assessment(s), and then reading and practicing the appropriate skill module(s) in the back of the book.

A more careful review of this new edition will also reveal that Chapter 10 on communication has been reorganized and rewritten. This was undertaken to improve the flow of what I find to be a widely encompassing and eclectic topic of study.

I hear and I forget. I see and I remember. I do and I understand.
—Confucius

This section on skill-building has been added to help readers apply and use OB concepts. The 16 skills selected were chosen because of their relevance to developing competence in interpersonal skills and their linkage to one or more of the topic areas in this book.

To maximize the learning of skills, we suggest combining text content and self-assessment feedback with the skill-building modules in this section. The self-assessments are available on the CD-ROM includ-ed with this book. Exhibit SB-1 provides a matrix indicating the relevant self-assessment and skill-module for Chapters 2 through 19 in your textbook.

For each of the 16 skills, we provide the following. (1) A brief interpretation of what your self-assessment results mean. (2) A review of basic skill concepts and specific behaviors associated with developing competence in the skill. (3) A short scenario designed to pro-vide you with an opportunity to practice the behaviors associated with the skill. (4) Several reinforcement activities to give you additional opportunities to prac-tice and learn the behaviors associated with the skill.

Exhibit SB-1 From Knowledge to Skills

Skill-Building Chapter/Topic	Self-Assessment	Module
2. Individual Behavior	Feedback Skills (#26)	Effective Disciplining
3. Values and Attitudes	Job Satisfaction (#11)	Changing Attitudes
4. Personality and Emotions	EI Score (#20)	Reading Emotions
5. Perception and Decisions	How Creative Am I? (#8)	Creative Problem-Solving
6/7. Motivation	Personal Planning (#22)	Setting Goals
8/9. Groups and Teams	Leading a Team (#30)	Creating Effective Teams
10. Communication	Listening Skills (#25)	Active Listening
11. Basic Leadership	Leadership Style (#27)	Choosing a Leadership Style
12. Contemporary Leadership	Trusting? (#29)	Developing Trust
13. Power and Politics	Power Orientation (#31)	Becoming Politically Adept
14. Conflict and Negotiation	Conflict Style (#34)	Negotiating
15. Organization Structure	Willingness to Delegate (#40)	Delegating Authority
16. Technology and Work Design	JCM (#37)	Designing Motivating Jobs
17. HR Policies and Practices	D-M Style (#17)	Selection Interviewing
18. Organizational Culture	Right Culture? (#42)	Reading an Organization's Culture
19. Organizational Change	Response to Change (#47)	Managing Resistance to Change

1 EFFECTIVE DISCIPLINING

Self-Assessment Interpretation

Complete the self-assessment (#26) on feedback skills. This instrument assesses how good you are at providing feedback to others.

Strong feedback skills are an important part of disciplinary actions. If your strength/weakness ratio was 6/2 or higher, you already know a considerable amount about behaviors associated with effective disciplining.

Skills Concepts and Behaviors

If an employee's performance regularly isn't up to par or if an employee consistently ignores the orga-nization's standards and regulations, a manager may have to use discipline as a way to control behavior. What exactly is *discipline*? It's actions taken by a manager to enforce the organization's expectations, standards, and rules. The most common types of dis-cipline problems managers have to deal with include attendance (absenteeism, tardiness, abuse of sick leave), on-the-job behaviors (failure to meet per-formance goals, disobedience, failure to use safety devices, alcohol or drug abuse), and dishonesty (theft, lying to managers).

The essence of effective disciplining can be summarized by the following eight behaviors.[12]

1. *Respond immediately.* The more quickly a dis-ciplinary action follows an offense, the more likely it is that the employee will associate the discipline with the offense rather than with you as the dispenser of the discipline. It's best to begin the disciplinary process as soon as possible after you notice a violation.
2. *Provide a warning.* You have an obligation to warn an employee before initiating discipli-nary action. This means that the employee must be aware of the organization's rules and accept its standards of behavior. Disciplinary action is more likely to be interpreted by employees as fair when they have received a clear warning that a given violation will lead to discipline and when they know what that dis-cipline will be.
3. *State the problem specifically.* Give the date, time, place, individuals involved, and any mit-igating circumstances surrounding the viola-tion. Be sure to define the violation in exact terms instead of just reciting company regula-tions or terms from a union contract. It's not the violation of the rules per se about which you want to convey concern. It's the effect that the rule violation has on the work unit's per-formance. Explain why the behavior can't be continued by showing how it specifically affects the employee's job performance, the unit's effectiveness, and the employee's col-leagues.
4. *Allow the employee to explain his or her position.* Regardless of what facts you have uncovered, due process demands that you give the employee the opportunity to explain his or her position. From the employee's perspective, what happened? Why did it happen? What was his or her perception of the rules, regula-tions, and circumstances?

5. *Keep the discussion impersonal.* Penalties should be connected with a given violation, not with the personality of the individual vio-lator. That is, discipline should be directed at what the employee has done, not at the employee.
6. *Be consistent.* Fair treatment of employees demands that disciplinary action be consis-tent. If you enforce rule violations in an incon-sistent manner, the rules will lose their impact, morale will decline, and employees will likely question your competence. Consistency, how-ever, need not result in treating everyone exactly alike; doing that would ignore mitigat-ing circumstances. It's reasonable to modify the severity of penalties to reflect the employ-ee's past history, job performance record, and the like. But the responsibility is yours to clear-ly justify disciplinary actions that might appear inconsistent to employees.
7. *Take progressive action.* Choose a punishment that's appropriate to the crime. Penalties should get progressively stronger if, or when, an offense is repeated. Typically, progressive disciplinary action begins with a verbal warn-ing and then proceeds through a written repri-mand, suspension, a demotion or pay cut, and finally, in the most serious cases, dismissal.
8. *Obtain agreement on change.* Disciplining should include guidance and direction for cor-recting the problem. Let the employee state what he or she plans to do in the future to ensure that the violation won't be repeated.

Practicing the Skill

Read through the following scenario, then practice your skill in a role-play conducted either in front of the class or in groups of two.

You're a team leader in the customer services department at Mountain View Microbrewery. Sandy is the newest member of your 10-person team, hav-ing been there only six weeks. Sandy came to Mountain View with good recommendations from his/her previous job as a customer support repre-sentative at a car dealership. However, not long after joining your team, Sandy was late in issuing an important purchasing order. When you talked

---

The GLOBE Framework for Assessing Cultures Hofstede's cultural dimensions have become the basic framework for differentiating among national cultures. This is in spite of the fact that the data on which it's based comes from a single company and is nearly 30 years old. Since these data were originally gathered, a lot has hap-pened on the world scene. Some of the most obvious include the fall of the Soviet Union, the merging of East and West Germany, the end of apartheid in South Africa, and the rise of China as a global power. All this suggests the need for an updated as-sessment of cultural dimensions. The GLOBE study provides such an update.[15]

Begun in 1993, the Global Leadership and Organizational Behavior Effectiveness (GLOBE) research program is an ongoing cross-cultural investigation of leadership and national culture. Using data from 825 organizations in 62 countries, the GLOBE team identified nine dimensions on which national cultures differ (see Exhibit 3-4 on page 70 for examples of country ratings on each of the dimensions).

- *Assertiveness.* The extent to which a society encourages people to be tough, con-frontational, assertive, and competitive versus modest and tender. This is essen-tially equivalent to Hofstede's quantity-of-life dimension.
- *Future orientation.* The extent to which a society encourages and rewards future-oriented behaviors such as planning, investing in the future, and delaying gratifi-cation. This is essentially equivalent to Hofstede's long-term/short-term orienta-tion.
- *Gender differentiation.* The extent to which a society maximizes gender role differences.
- *Uncertainty avoidance.* As identified by Hofstede, the GLOBE team defined this term as a society's reliance on social norms and procedures to alleviate the unpre-dictability of future events.
- *Power distance.* As did Hofstede, the GLOBE team defined this as the degree to which members of a society expect power to be unequally shared.
- *Individualism/collectivism.* Again, this term was defined as was Hofstede's as the degree to which individuals are encouraged by societal institutions to be integrat-ed into groups within organizations and society.
- *In-group collectivism.* In contrast to focusing on societal institutions, this dimen-sion encompasses the extent to which members of a society take pride in mem-bership in small groups, such as their family and circle of close friends, and the organizations in which they are employed.

This book continues to lead the field in coverage of contem-porary OB issues. New to this edition is material on:

Customer service (Chapters 1, 3, 4, and 18)
Work/life balance (Chapters 1, 17, and 19)
Multiple intelligences (Chapter 2)
Evolutionary psychology and hardwired behavior (Chapter 2)
GLOBE measures of national cultural attributes (Chapter 3)
Motivation as flow (Chapter 6)
Thomas's intrinsic motivation model (Chapter 6)
Deviant workplace behavior (Chapter 8)
Silence as communication (Chapter 10)
Employee response to organizational politics (Chapter 13)
Mass customization (Chapter 16)
OB in an e-World (Chapter 16)
Feng Shui and workplace design (Chapter 16)
Creating ethical organizational cultures (Chapter 18)
Spirituality in organizations (Chapter 18)
Knowledge management (Chapter 19)
Appreciative inquiry (Chapter 19)

Of course, the entire book's research base has been revised and updated for this edition.

This includes recent events—specifically the terrorists attacks of 9/11, the col-lapse of Enron, and the misdeeds of senior executives at companies like WorldCom

Leaders are visionaries with a poorly developed sense of fear and no concept of the odds against them.
—R. Jarvik

Contemporary Issues in Leadership

chapter **12**

R udolph W. Giuliani (see photo) was elected mayor of New York City in 1993 on a law-and-order platform. And he did successfully bring law and order to the city. For instance, by the end of his second term, in 2001, he had overseen a 57 percent decline in felony crimes and a 68 percent reduction in the city's murder rate. In a city that many said was ungovernable, Giuliani had turned around New York's fortunes. He boosted property values, redeveloped large parts of Manhattan, brought tourists back, and restored the city's spirit. But he stepped on a lot of toes in the process. His arrogant, self-serving, and combative style rubbed a lot of people the wrong way. He became known more for his uncontrollable temper and vindictiveness than for his success in improving life in New York City. However, any negative perceptions of Giuliani essentially disappeared on September 11, 2001.[1]

On September 11th, the worst crime ever committed on American soil took place in New York City—terrorists flew two hijacked commercial jets into the World Trade Center, killing almost 3,000 people. As shock and then fear gripped the nation, Rudy Giuliani stepped up and led the city and nation through the crisis. Within minutes after the first plane hit, Giuliani was on the scene directing operations. Without regard for his own safety, he established a makeshift command center and a temporary morgue, found a million pairs of gloves and dust masks and respirators, threw up protections against another attack, and tamed the mobs that wanted vengeance. One of the public's strongest memories of that first day was of Giuliani, on the streets of New York, trying to give the public reassurance with his hair and suit still covered in the silt from the falling buildings.

In the weeks that followed, Giuliani provided the leadership that the public so craved. Day after day, his mastery of the details of rescue and recovery plus his calm explanations of awful news helped to reassure a

Nation tional leader. He consoled widows, widowers, and survivors; he attended close to 200 funerals, wakes, and memorial services; he revisited the attack site to mingle with rescue workers; he urged residents to dine out; and he reached out to tourists to come back to the city. In addition to the decisiveness and honesty he had always displayed, he now showed traits that the public had rarely seen in him before—compassion, fearlessness, calmness, and openness. He put in 20-hour days and showed an uncanny ability to be consistently visible. Maybe most importantly, Giuliani was able to find the words and tap into emotions to help people better cope with the tragedy. He conveyed optimism and created, as one writer put it, "an illusion that we were bound to win." For instance, on that first day following the attack, he said, "Tomorrow New York is going to be here. And we're going to rebuild, and we're going to be stronger than we were before . . . I want the people of New York to be an example to the rest of the country, and the rest of the world, that terrorism can't stop us." Within days, Giuliani almost unilaterally managed to create the sense that New York City was getting back to normalcy.

Time magazine may have summarized Giuliani's leadership role best when, in naming him its 2001 Person of the Year, said: ". . . for having more faith in us than we had in ourselves, for being brave when required and rude where appropriate and tender without being trite, for not sleeping and not quitting and not shrinking from the pain all around him."

F ormer Mayor Guiliani is a 21st century leader. He called upon his experience, charisma, and ability to create meaning out of tragedy and to help a city and nation recover. In this chapter, we address contemporary leadership topics such as charisma and the ability to create meaning in new or difficult

LEARNING OBJECTIVES

AFTER STUDYING THIS CHAPTER, YOU SHOULD BE ABLE TO:

1. Identify the five dimensions of trust.

2. Define the qualities of a charismatic leader.

3. Contrast transformational with transactional leadership.

4. Identify the skills that visionary leaders exhibit.

5. Explain how framing influences leadership effectiveness.

6. Identify the four roles that team leaders perform.

7. Explain the role of a mentor.

8. Describe how on-line leadership differs from face-to-face leadership.

9. Identify when leadership may not be necessary.

1

---

and Tyco International—that influence organizational behavior. These events are discussed as they relate to values, ethics, employee stereotyping and profiling, trust, leadership, organizational culture, anxiety and stress, and managing change. For instance, on pages 334–35 we describe the transformational leadership displayed by Rudolph Giuliani following 9/11; and on page 539 we explain how Enron's culture played a major part in the company's downfall.

I'm particularly enthusiastic about the new material on customer service and satisfaction. We all know the critical role that the customer plays in the success or failure of any organization—whether it's profit or nonprofit. Authors of OB textbooks, however, have tended to leave everything that has to do with the customer to our friends in marketing. That has been a mistake of omission. There is an increasing body of research demonstrating that customer satisfaction is linked to organizational performance and that employee attitudes and behavior are positively related to customer satisfaction. This edition shows why OB should be concerned with the customer, the role of displayed emotions in friendly and helpful service, how employee attitudes and behavior shape an organization's "customer culture," and what management can do to make an organization more customer-oriented.

Teaching and Learning Package

The supplements package for this new edition offers a comprehensive teaching and learning package.

- **Instructor's Manual.** The Instructor's Manual has been thoroughly updated, and includes Teaching Tips and additional Internet exercises to supplement student learning. The Instructor's Manual also includes comprehensive information about the BusinessNOW video cases, which are new to this edition.
- **Test Item File.** The test item file has also been thoroughly updated, and includes both essay and scenario-based questions. The Test Item File is also available in electronic format via the Prentice Hall Test Manager software.
- **Self-Assessment Library 2.0.** The latest version of this CD-ROM includes 49 self-scoring individual assessment questionnaires that provide students with insights into their skills, abilities, and interests.

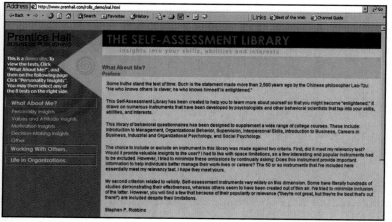

- **PowerPoints.** The PowerPoints include text outlines and figures from the text, and are available on both the Instructor's Resource CD-ROM and via the Internet at www.prenhall.com/robbins.
- **Instructor's Resource CD-ROM.** All of the resources for your text are available in one place! On the IRCD, you will find the electronic files for the Instructor's Manual, the Prentice Hall Test Manager software, and the complete set of PowerPoints.
- **MyCW Companion Website.** The format of our Web sites has been updated, and includes the same great features in a more user-friendly format. Here you will find password-protected instructor's resources, as well as a student section, which features sample true/false, multiple choice, and Internet essay questions. The Web site for Robbins' *Organizational Behavior,* 10/e, can be found at www.prenhall.com/robbins.

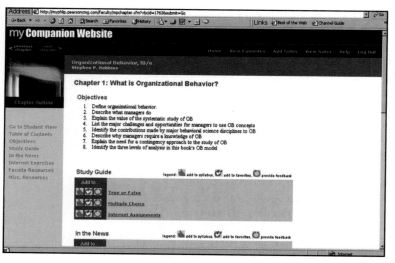

- **WebCT Course.** With the increasing popularity of Internet-based courses, WebCT has become one of the market-leading course management software applications that helps professors and students create an e-learning experience and transform their educational experience.
- **BusinessNOW Video Cases.** Brand new to this edition, Prentice Hall is pleased to offer exciting new BusinessNOW video cases. BusinessNOW is a fast-paced television news magazine that takes viewers on location and behind closed doors to look at America's most interesting companies and the corporate executives who run them. These videos offer interesting, up-to-date content pertaining to the topics raised in *Organizational Behavior,* 10/e, and were chosen specifically for their tie-ins to organizational behavior-related topics. Some of the companies featured

on the BusinessNOW video include Quova and DuPont, and topics featured include leadership challenges, motivating employees, managing conflicts, and cultural diversity.

- ■ **It's as easy as 1, 2, 3...** *Keep current with our new course packing option!* Prentice Hall and XanEdu have teamed up to create a CompletePack that complements *Organizational Behavior,* 10th edition, chapter-by-chapter. This course pack is available in print and digital formats and can be wrapped with the text for a 10% discount. You have the option of using our CompletePack, or easily customizing by adding content from one of the largest copyright-cleared commercial and scholarly archives of journals, periodicals, newspapers, primary literature works, and academic collections in the world. Developmental editors can work with you to help craft your own custom CoursePack. Contact your local Prentice Hall representative for more details or visit: www.prenhall.com/custombusiness.

Acknowledgments

Getting this book into your hands was a team effort. It took faculty reviewers and a talented group of designers and production specialists, editorial personnel, and marketing and sales staff.

Let me begin my acknowledgments by thanking a number of faculty for providing suggestions on how the previous edition could be improved and/or reviewing this revision. This text is an immensely better book because of the comments of Kathleen Edwards, University of Texas, Austin; Leslie A Korb, University of Nebraska at Kearney; Timothy A. Matherly, Florida State University; Janice Miller, University of Wisconsin-Milwaukee; Clint Relyea, Arkansas State University; Stuart Sidle, DePaul University; and William D. Tudor, Ohio State University.

On the design and production side, I want to thank Cindy Spreder, Amanda Kavanaugh (interior designer), and my wife Laura Ospanik. Cindy did a superb job of "mothering" this book through the production process. Thanks Cindy for putting your heart and soul into this project and for tolerating my continual barrage of phone calls and e-mails. And a very loving "thank you" goes to my wife Laura. In addition to being the greatest wife in the world, she is also an extremely talented graphic artist. She designed the cover for the previous edition (which I'm proud to say won numerous design awards) as well as this one. She also helped to modify the interior design, create the exhibits, find advertisements, and rapidly solve computer problems that regularly surfaced during the revision. Thanks, honey, for your love and support.

I also want to thank Shannon Moore, Kevin Glynn, Jennifer Glennon, and Judy Leale at Prentice Hall. Finally, let me thank the Prentice-Hall sales staff, who have been selling my books for more than a quarter of a century: Thank you for the attention you've given this book through its many editions.

Stephen P. Robbins

PART ONE

INTRODUCTION

Meet Michael Bowser (pictured in center of photo). He has a degree in geology with a minor in chemistry from Elizabeth City State University in North Carolina and has spent the past 14 years working for the U.S. Department of Defense. For the past three and a half of those years, Michael has been a supervisor/team chief in a mapping unit, overseeing 13 to 18 people.

"My prior experience was as a systems engineer so I have a technical background," says Bowser. "The people on my team are technical specialists—regional analysts, geospatial analysts, cartographers, and the like. My job, as a supervisor, is more 'people-centered' than technical. I have to understand the different needs of my people. Some, for instance, readily accept change. Some fight it. Some people don't want to make decisions. Others enjoy jumping in and participating. I've had to learn to use different approaches to motivate these varied types of people. I've had to enhance my skills in communication. I've learned that communication is key in dealing with my workers and with the politics inside our organization."

Michael Bowser has learned what most managers learn very quickly: A large part of the success in any management job is developing good interpersonal, or people, skills. Managers need to be technically competent in their area of expertise. But technical knowledge isn't enough. Successful managers and entrepreneurs also need interpersonal skills in order to work with others.[1]

Although practicing managers have long understood the importance of interpersonal skills to managerial effectiveness, business schools were slower to get the message. Until the late 1980s, business school curricula focused almost singularly on the

What Is Organizational Behavior?

technical aspects of management, emphasizing courses in economics, accounting, finance, and quantitative techniques. Course work in human behavior and people skills received minimal attention relative to the technical aspects of management. Over the past decade and a half, however, business faculty have come to realize the importance that an understanding of human behavior plays in determining a manager's effectiveness, and required courses on people skills have been widely added to the curriculum.

Recognition of the importance of developing managers' interpersonal skills is closely tied to the need for organizations to get and keep high-performing employees. This becomes particularly crucial in a tight labor market.[2] Companies with reputations as a good place to work—such as Lincoln Electric, Southwest Airlines, SAS Institute, Whole Food Markets, and Starbucks—have a big advantage. A national study of the U.S. workforce found that wages and fringe benefits are not the reasons people like their jobs or stay with an employer. Far more important is the quality of the employees' jobs and the supportiveness of their work environments.[3] So having managers with good interpersonal skills is likely to make the workplace more pleasant, which, in turn, makes it easier to hire and keep qualified people.

We have come to understand that technical skills are necessary, but insufficient, for succeeding in management. In today's increasingly competitive and demanding workplace, managers can't succeed on their technical skills alone. They also have to have good people skills. This book has been written to help both managers and potential managers develop those people skills.

LEARNING OBJECTIVES

AFTER STUDYING THIS CHAPTER, YOU SHOULD BE ABLE TO:

1. Define *organizational behavior (OB)*.

2. Describe what managers do.

3. Explain the value of the systematic study of OB.

4. List the major challenges and opportunities for managers to use OB concepts.

5. Identify the contributions made by major behavioral science disciplines to OB.

6. Describe why managers require a knowledge of OB.

7. Explain the need for a contingency approach to the study of OB.

8. Identify the three levels of analysis in this book's OB model.

WHAT MANAGERS DO

Let's begin by briefly defining the terms *manager* and the place where managers work—the *organization*. Then let's look at the manager's job; specifically, what do managers do?

managers

Individuals who achieve goals through other people.

organization

A consciously coordinated social unit, composed of two or more people, that functions on a relatively continuous basis to achieve a common goal or set of goals.

Managers get things done through other people. They make decisions, allocate resources, and direct the activities of others to attain goals. Managers do their work in an **organization**. This is a consciously coordinated social unit, composed of two or more people, that functions on a relatively continuous basis to achieve a common goal or set of goals. On the basis of this definition, manufacturing and service firms are organizations and so are schools, hospitals, churches, military units, retail stores, police departments, and local, state, and federal government agencies. The people who oversee the activities of others and who are responsible for attaining goals in these organizations are managers (although they're sometimes called *administrators*, especially in not-for-profit organizations).

Management Functions

In the early part of the 20th century, a French industrialist by the name of Henri Fayol wrote that all managers perform five management functions: They plan, organize, command, coordinate, and control.[4] Today, we have condensed these to four: planning, organizing, leading, and controlling.

Since organizations exist to achieve goals, someone has to define those goals and the means by which they can be achieved. Management is that someone. The **planning** function encompasses defining an organization's goals, establishing an overall strategy for achieving those goals, and developing a comprehensive hierarchy of plans to integrate and coordinate activities.

Managers are also responsible for designing an organization's structure. We call this function **organizing**. It includes the determination of what tasks are to be done, who is to do them, how the tasks are to be grouped, who reports to whom, and where decisions are to be made.

Every organization contains people, and it is management's job to direct and coordinate those people. This is the **leading** function. When managers motivate employees, direct the activities of others, select the most effective communication channels, or resolve conflicts among members, they are engaging in leading.

The final function managers perform is **controlling**. To ensure that things are going as they should, management must monitor the organization's performance. Actual performance must be compared with the previously set goals. If there are any significant deviations, it's management's job to get the organization back on track. This monitoring, comparing, and potential correcting is what is meant by the controlling function.

So, using the functional approach, the answer to the question, What do managers do? is that they plan, organize, lead, and control.

Management Roles

In the late 1960s, a graduate student at MIT, Henry Mintzberg, undertook a careful study of five executives to determine what these managers did on their jobs. On the basis of his observations of these managers, Mintzberg

In our definition of organizations we include hospitals, churches, colleges, and schools, though their "managers" are more likely to go by the title "administrator." They perform all the management functions, and the concepts of organizational behavior apply to them, their staffs, and their colleagues.

concluded that managers perform 10 different, highly interrelated roles, or sets of behaviors attributable to their jobs.[5] As shown in Exhibit 1-1 on page 6, these 10 roles can be grouped as being primarily concerned with interpersonal relationships, the transfer of information, and decision making.

Interpersonal Roles   All managers are required to perform duties that are ceremonial and symbolic in nature. When the president of a college hands out diplomas at commencement or a factory supervisor gives a group of high school students a tour of the plant, he or she is acting in a *figurehead* role. All managers also have a *leadership* role. This role includes hiring, training, motivating, and disciplining employees. The third role within the interpersonal grouping is the *liaison* role. Mintzberg described this activity as contacting outsiders who provide the manager with information. These may be individuals or groups inside or outside the organization. The sales manager who obtains information from the quality-control manager in his or her own company has an internal liaison relationship. When that sales manager has contacts with other sales executives through a marketing trade association, he or she has an outside liaison relationship.

Informational Roles   All managers, to some degree, collect information from organizations and institutions outside their own. Typically, they get information by reading magazines and talking with other people to learn of changes in the public's tastes, what competitors may be planning, and the like. Mintzberg called this the *monitor* role. Managers also act as a conduit to transmit information to organizational members. This is the *disseminator* role. In addition, managers perform a *spokesperson* role when they represent the organization to outsiders.

Decisional Roles   Finally, Mintzberg identified four roles that revolve around the making of choices. In the *entrepreneur* role, managers initiate and oversee new projects that will improve their organization's performance. As *disturbance handlers*, managers take corrective action in response to unforeseen problems. As *resource allocators*, managers are responsible for allocating human, physical, and monetary resources. Last, managers perform a *negotiator* role, in which they discuss issues and bargain with other units to gain advantages for their own unit.

Management Skills

Still another way of considering what managers do is to look at the skills or competencies they need to achieve their goals. Robert Katz has identified three essential management skills: technical, human, and conceptual.[6]

Technical Skills   **Technical skills** encompass the ability to apply specialized knowledge or expertise. When you think of the skills held by professionals such as civil engineers or oral surgeons, you typically focus on their technical skills. Through extensive formal education, they have learned the special knowledge and practices of their field. Of course, professionals don't have a monopoly on technical skills, and not all technical skills have to be learned in schools or formal training programs. All jobs require some specialized expertise, and many people develop their technical skills on the job.

Human Skills   The ability to work with, understand, and motivate other people, both individually and in groups, describes **human skills**. Many people are

planning
A process that includes defining goals, establishing strategy, and developing plans to coordinate activities.

organizing
Determining what tasks are to be done, who is to do them, how the tasks are to be grouped, who reports to whom, and where decisions are to be made.

leading
A function that includes motivating employees, directing others, selecting the most effective communication channels, and resolving conflicts.

controlling
Monitoring activities to ensure they are being accomplished as planned and correcting any significant deviations.

technical skills
The ability to apply specialized knowledge or expertise.

human skills
The ability to work with, understand, and motivate other people, both individually and in groups.

EXHIBIT

1-1

Mintzberg's Managerial Roles

Role	Description	Example
Interpersonal		
Figurehead	Symbolic head; required to perform a number of routine duties of a legal or social nature	Ceremonies, status requests, solicitations
Leader	Responsible for the motivation and direction of employees	Virtually all managerial activities involving employees
Liaison	Maintains a network of outside contacts who provide favors and information	Acknowledges mail, external board work
Informational		
Monitor	Receives wide variety of information; serves as nerve center of internal and external information of the organization	Handling all mail and contacts categorized as concerned primarily with receiving information
Disseminator	Transmits information received from outsiders or from other employees to members of the organization	Forwarding mail into organization for informational purposes; verbal contacts involving information flow to subordinates such as review sessions
Spokesperson	Transmits information to outsiders on organization's plans, policies, actions, and results; serves as expert on organization's industry	Board meetings; handles contacts involving transmission of information to outsiders
Decisional		
Entrepreneur	Searches organization and its environment for opportunities and initiates projects to bring about change	Strategy and review sessions involving initiation or design of improvement projects
Disturbance handler	Responsible for corrective action when organization faces important, unexpected disturbances	Strategy and review sessions involving disturbances and crises
Resource allocator	Makes or approves significant organizational decisions	Scheduling; requests for authorization; budgeting; the programming of employees' work
Negotiator	Responsible for representing the organization at major negotiations	Contract negotiation

Source: Adapted from *The Nature of Managerial Work* by H. Mintzberg. Copyright © 1973 by H. Mintzberg. Reprinted by permission of Pearson Education.

technically proficient but interpersonally incompetent. They might be poor listeners, unable to understand the needs of others, or have difficulty managing conflicts. Since managers get things done through other people, they must have good human skills to communicate, motivate, and delegate.

conceptual skills

The mental ability to analyze and diagnose complex situations.

Conceptual Skills Managers must have the mental ability to analyze and diagnose complex situations. These tasks require **conceptual skills**. Decision making, for instance, requires managers to spot problems, identify alternatives that can correct them, evaluate those alternatives, and select the best one. Managers can be technically and interpersonally competent yet still fail because of an inability to rationally process and interpret information.

Effective Versus Successful Managerial Activities

Fred Luthans and his associates looked at the issue of what managers do from a somewhat different perspective.[7] They asked the question: Do managers who move up most quickly in an organization do the same activities and with the same emphasis as managers who do the best job? You would tend to think that the managers who were the most effective in their jobs would also be the ones who were promoted fastest. But that's not what appears to happen.

Luthans and his associates studied more than 450 managers. What they found was that these managers all engaged in four managerial activities:

1. *Traditional management.* Decision making, planning, and controlling
2. *Communication.* Exchanging routine information and processing paperwork
3. *Human resource management.* Motivating, disciplining, managing conflict, staffing, and training
4. *Networking.* Socializing, politicking, and interacting with outsiders

The "average" manager in the study spent 32 percent of his or her time in traditional management activities, 29 percent communicating, 20 percent in human resource management activities, and 19 percent networking. However, the amount of time and effort that different managers spent on those four activities varied a great deal. Specifically, as shown in Exhibit 1-2, managers who were *successful* (defined in terms of the speed of promotion within their organization) had a very different emphasis than managers who were *effective* (defined in terms of the quantity and quality of their performance and the satisfaction and commitment of their employees). Among successful managers, networking made the largest relative contribution to success, and human resource management activities made the least relative contribution. Among effective managers, communication made the largest relative contribution

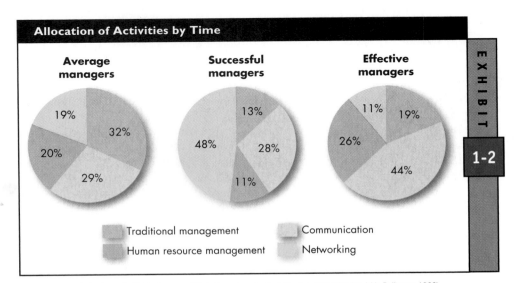

Allocation of Activities by Time

Average managers

Successful managers

Effective managers

EXHIBIT

1-2

Traditional management Communication
Human resource management Networking

Source: Based on F. Luthans, R. M. Hodgetts, and S. A. Rosenkrantz, *Real Managers* (Cambridge, MA: Ballinger, 1988).

and networking the least. A more recent study of Australian managers further confirms the importance of networking.[8] Australian managers who actively networked received more promotions and enjoyed other rewards associated with career success.

This research adds important insights to our knowledge of what managers do. On average, managers spend approximately 20 to 30 percent of their time on each of the four activities: traditional management, communication, human resource management, and networking. However, successful managers don't give the same emphasis to each of those activities as do effective managers. In fact, their emphases are almost the opposite. This finding challenges the historical assumption that promotions are based on performance, vividly illustrating the importance that social and political skills play in getting ahead in organizations.

A Review of the Manager's Job

One common thread runs through the functions, roles, skills, and activities approaches to management: Each recognizes the paramount importance of managing people. Regardless of whether it is called "the leading function," "interpersonal roles," "human skills," or "human resource management, communication, and networking activities," it's clear that managers need to develop their people skills if they're going to be effective and successful.

ENTER ORGANIZATIONAL BEHAVIOR

We've made the case for the importance of people skills. But neither this book nor the discipline on which it is based is called People Skills. The term that is widely used to describe the discipline is *Organizational Behavior*.

organizational behavior (OB)

A field of study that investigates the impact that individuals, groups, and structure have on behavior within organizations, for the purpose of applying such knowledge toward improving an organization's effectiveness.

Organizational behavior (often abbreviated as OB) is a field of study that investigates the impact that individuals, groups, and structure have on behavior within organizations for the purpose of applying such knowledge toward improving an organization's effectiveness. That's a lot of words, so let's break it down.

Organizational behavior is a field of study. This statement means that it is a distinct area of expertise with a common body of knowledge. What does it study? It studies three determinants of behavior in organizations: individuals, groups, and structure. In addition, OB applies the knowledge gained about individuals, groups, and the effect of structure on behavior in order to make organizations work more effectively.

To sum up our definition, OB is concerned with the study of what people do in an organization and how that behavior affects the performance of the organization. And because OB is concerned specifically with employment-related situations, you should not be surprised to find that it emphasizes behavior as related to concerns such as jobs, work, absenteeism, employment turnover, productivity, human performance, and management.

There is increasing agreement as to the components or topics that constitute the subject area of OB. Although there is still considerable debate as to the relative importance of each, there appears to be general agreement that OB includes the core topics of motivation, leader behavior and power, interpersonal communication, group structure and processes, learning, attitude development and perception, change processes, conflict, work design, and work stress.[9]

Replacing Intuition with Systematic Study

Each of us is a student of behavior. Since our earliest years, we have watched the actions of others and have attempted to interpret what we see. Whether or not you've explicitly thought about it before, you've been "reading" people almost all your life. You watch what others do and try to explain to yourself why they have engaged in their behavior. In addition, you've attempted to predict what they might do under different sets of conditions. Unfortunately, your casual or commonsense approach to reading others can often lead to erroneous predictions. However, you can improve your predictive ability by replacing your intuitive opinions with a more systematic approach.

The systematic approach used in this book will uncover important facts and relationships and will provide a base from which more-accurate predictions of behavior can be made. Underlying this systematic approach is the belief that behavior is not random. It stems from and is directed toward some end that the individual believes, rightly or wrongly, is in his or her best interest.

Communication in organizations is one of the core topics of OB, along with areas of study such as power, group processes, learning, motivation, perception, conflict, and stress.

> Behavior generally is predictable if we know how the person perceived the situation and what is important to him or her. While people's behavior may not appear to be rational to an outsider, there is reason to believe it usually is intended to be rational and it is seen as rational by them. An observer often sees behavior as nonrational because the observer does not have access to the same information or does not perceive the environment in the same way.[10]

Certainly there are differences between individuals. Placed in similar situations, all people don't act exactly alike. However, there are certain fundamental consistencies underlying the behavior of all individuals that can be identified and then modified to reflect individual differences.

These fundamental consistencies are very important. Why? Because they allow predictability. When you get into your car, you make some definite and usually highly accurate predictions about how other people will behave. In North America, for instance, you would predict that other drivers will stop at stop signs and red lights, drive on the right side of the road, pass on your left, and not cross the solid double line on mountain roads. Notice that your predictions about the behavior of people behind the wheels of their cars are almost always correct. Obviously, the rules of driving make predictions about driving behavior fairly easy.

What may be less obvious is that there are rules (written and unwritten) in almost every setting. Therefore, it can be argued that it's possible to predict behavior (undoubtedly, not always with 100 percent accuracy) in supermarkets, classrooms, doctors' offices, elevators, and in most structured situations. For instance, do you turn around and face the doors when you get into an elevator? Almost everyone does. But did you ever read that you're supposed to do this? Probably not! Just as I make predictions about automobile drivers (for which there are definite rules of the road), I can make predictions about the behavior of people in elevators (where there are few written rules). In a class of 60 students, if you wanted to ask a question of the instructor, I predict that you would raise your hand. Why don't you clap, stand up, raise your leg, cough, or yell "Hey, over here!"? The reason is that you have learned that raising your hand is appropriate behavior in school. These examples support a major contention in this textbook: Behavior is generally predictable, and the *systematic study* of behavior is a means to making reasonably accurate predictions.

When we use the phrase **systematic study**, we mean looking at relationships, attempting to attribute causes and effects, and basing our conclusions on scientific evidence—that is, on data gathered under controlled conditions and measured and interpreted in a reasonably rigorous manner. (See Appendix B for a basic review of research methods used in studies of organizational behavior.)

Systematic study replaces **intuition**, or those "gut feelings" about "why I do what I do" and "what makes others tick." Of course, a systematic approach does not mean that the things you have come to believe in an unsystematic way are necessarily incorrect. Some of the conclusions we make in this text, based on reasonably substantive research findings, will only support what you always knew was true. But you'll also be exposed to research evidence that runs counter to what you may have thought was common sense. One of the objectives of this text is to encourage you to move away from your intuitive views of behavior toward a systematic analysis, in the belief that such analysis will improve your accuracy in explaining and predicting behavior.

systematic study

Looking at relationships, attempting to attribute causes and effects, and drawing conclusions based on scientific evidence.

intuition

A feeling not necessarily supported by research.

OR **SCIENCE** **?**

MYTH

Preconceived Notions Versus Substantive Evidence

Assume you signed up to take an introductory college course in calculus. On the first day of class your instructor asks you to take out a piece of paper and answer the following question: "Why is the sign of the second derivative negative when the first derivative is set equal to zero, if the function is concave from below?" It's unlikely you'd be able to answer that question. Your reply to that instructor would probably be something like, "How am I suppose to know? That's why I'm taking this course!"

Now, change the scenerio. You're in an introductory course in organizational behavior. On the first day of class your instructor asks you to write the answer to the following question: "Why are employees not as motivated at work today as they were 30 years ago?"

You might feel a bit of reluctance, but I'd guess you'd begin writing. You'd have no problem coming up with an explanation to this question of motivation.

The previous scenarios were meant to demonstrate one of the challenges of teaching a course in OB. You enter an OB course with a lot of *preconceived notions* that you accept as *facts*. You think you already know a lot about human behavior.[11] Typically that is not true in calculus, physics, chemistry, or even accounting. So, in contrast to many other disciplines, OB

not only introduces you to a comprehensive set of concepts and theories, it has to deal with a lot of commonly accepted "facts" about human behavior and organizations that you've acquired over the years. Some examples might include: "You can't teach an old dog new tricks;" "happy workers are productive workers;" and "two heads are better than one." But these "facts" aren't necessarily true. So one of the objectives of a course in organizational behavior is to *replace* popularly held notions, often accepted without question, with science-based conclusions.

As you'll see in this book, the field of OB is built on decades of research. This research provides a body of substantive evidence that is able to replace preconceived notions. Throughout this book, we've included boxes entitled "Myth or Science?" They call your attention to some of the more popular of these notions or myths about organizational behavior. We use the boxes to show how OB research has disproved them or, in some cases, shown them to be true. We hope that you'll find these boxes interesting. But more importantly, they should help remind you that the study of human behavior at work is a science and that you need to be vigilant about "seat of the pants" explanations of work-related behaviors.

CONTRIBUTING DISCIPLINES TO THE OB FIELD

Organizational behavior is an applied behavioral science that is built on contributions from a number of behavioral disciplines. The predominant areas are psychology, sociology, social psychology, anthropology, and political science. As we shall learn, psychology's contributions have been mainly at the individual or micro level of analysis, while the other four disciplines have contributed to our understanding of macro concepts such as group processes and organization. Exhibit 1-3 is an overview of the major contributions to the study of organizational behavior.

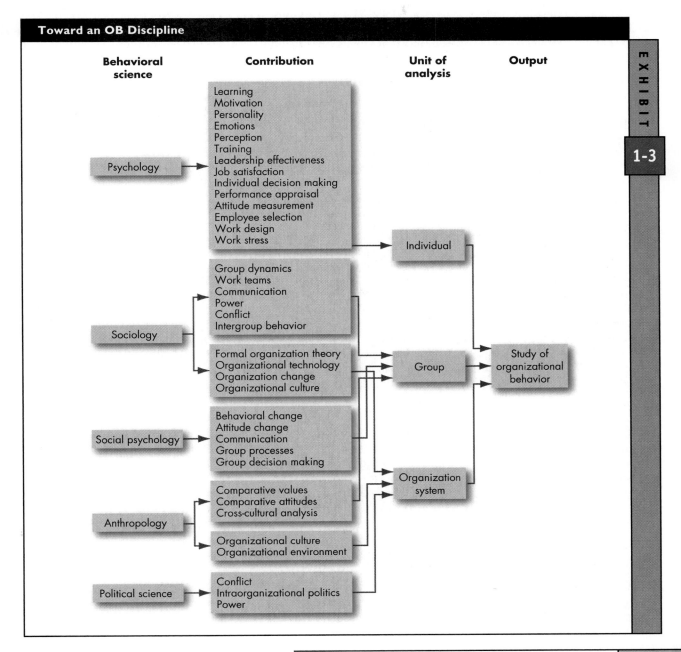

Toward an OB Discipline

Behavioral science	Contribution	Unit of analysis	Output
Psychology	Learning / Motivation / Personality / Emotions / Perception / Training / Leadership effectiveness / Job satisfaction / Individual decision making / Performance appraisal / Attitude measurement / Employee selection / Work design / Work stress	Individual	Study of organizational behavior
Sociology	Group dynamics / Work teams / Communication / Power / Conflict / Intergroup behavior	Group	
	Formal organization theory / Organizational technology / Organization change / Organizational culture		
Social psychology	Behavioral change / Attitude change / Communication / Group processes / Group decision making		
Anthropology	Comparative values / Comparative attitudes / Cross-cultural analysis	Organization system	
	Organizational culture / Organizational environment		
Political science	Conflict / Intraorganizational politics / Power		

EXHIBIT 1-3

Psychology

Psychology is the science that seeks to measure, explain, and sometimes change the behavior of humans and other animals. Psychologists concern themselves with studying and attempting to understand individual behavior. Those who have contributed and continue to add to the knowledge of OB are learning theorists, personality theorists, counseling psychologists, and, most important, industrial and organizational psychologists.

Early industrial/organizational psychologists concerned themselves with the problems of fatigue, boredom, and other factors relevant to working conditions that could impede efficient work performance. More recently, their contributions have been expanded to include learning, perception, personality, emotions, training, leadership effectiveness, needs and motivational forces, job satisfaction, decision-making processes, performance appraisals, attitude measurement, employee selection techniques, work design, and job stress.

psychology

The science that seeks to measure, explain, and sometimes change the behavior of humans and other animals.

Sociology

While psychologists focus their attention on the individual, sociologists study the social system in which individuals fill their roles; that is, **sociology** studies people in relation to their fellow human beings. Specifically, sociologists have made their greatest contribution to OB through their study of group behavior in organizations, particularly formal and complex organizations. Some of the areas within OB that have received valuable input from sociologists are group dynamics, design of work teams, organizational culture, formal organization theory and structure, organizational technology, communications, power, and conflict.

sociology

The study of people in relation to their fellow human beings.

Social Psychology

Social psychology is an area within psychology, blending concepts from both psychology and sociology. It focuses on the influence of people on one another. One of the major areas receiving considerable investigation from social psychologists has been *change*—how to implement it and how to reduce barriers to its acceptance. In addition, we find social psychologists making significant contributions in the areas of measuring, understanding, and changing attitudes; communication patterns; building trust; the ways in which group activities can satisfy individual needs; and group decision-making processes.

social psychology

An area within psychology that blends concepts from psychology and sociology and that focuses on the influence of people on one another.

Anthropology

Anthropology is the study of societies to learn about human beings and their activities. For instance, anthropologists' work on cultures and environments has helped us understand differences in fundamental values, attitudes, and behavior between people in different countries and within different organizations. Much of our current understanding of organizational culture, organizational environments, and differences between national cultures is the result of the work of anthropologists or those using their methods.

anthropology

The study of societies to learn about human beings and their activities.

Political Science

Although frequently overlooked, the contributions of political scientists are significant to the understanding of behavior in organizations. **Political science** studies the behavior of individuals and groups within a political environment. Specific topics of concern here include the structuring of conflict, allocation of power, and how people manipulate power for individual self-interest.

political science

The study of the behavior of individuals and groups within a political environment.

THERE ARE FEW ABSOLUTES IN OB

There are few, if any, simple and universal principles that explain organizational behavior. There are laws in the physical sciences—chemistry, astronomy, physics—that are consistent and apply in a wide range of situations. They allow scientists to generalize about the pull of gravity or to be confident about sending astronauts into space to repair satellites. But as one noted behavioral researcher aptly concluded, "God gave all the easy problems to the physicists." Human beings are complex. Because they are not alike, our ability to make simple, accurate, and sweeping generalizations is limited. Two people often act very differently in the same situation, and the same person's behavior changes in different situations. For instance, not everyone is motivated by money, and you behave differently at church on Sunday than you did at a beer party the night before.

That doesn't mean, of course, that we can't offer reasonably accurate explanations of human behavior or make valid predictions. However, it does mean that OB concepts must reflect situational, or contingency, conditions. We can say that x leads to y, but only under conditions specified in z (the **contingency variables**). The science of OB was developed by using general concepts and then altering their application to the particular situation. So, for example, OB scholars would avoid stating that effective leaders should always seek the ideas of their followers before making a decision. Rather, we shall find that in some situations a participative style is clearly superior, but, in other situations, an autocratic decision-making style is more effective. In other words, the effectiveness of a particular leadership style is contingent on the situation in which it's used.

contingency variables

Situational factors: variables that moderate the relationship between two or more other variables and improve the correlation.

As you proceed through this book, you will encounter a wealth of research-based theories about how people behave in organizations. But don't expect to find a lot of straightforward cause-and-effect relationships. There aren't many! Organizational behavior theories mirror the subject matter with which they deal. People are complex and complicated, and so too must be the theories developed to explain their actions.

CHALLENGES AND OPPORTUNITIES FOR OB

Understanding organizational behavior has never been more important for managers. A quick look at a few of the dramatic changes now taking place in organizations supports this claim. For instance, the typical employee is getting older; more and more women and nonwhites are in the workplace; corporate downsizing and the heavy use of temporary workers are severing the bonds of loyalty that historically tied many employees to their employers; and global competition is requiring employees to become more flexible and to learn to cope with rapid change.

In short, there are a lot of challenges and opportunities today for managers to use OB concepts. In this section, we review some of the more critical issues confronting managers for which OB offers solutions—or at least some meaningful insights toward solutions.

Responding to Globalization

Organizations are no longer constrained by national borders. Burger King is owned by a British firm, and McDonald's sells hamburgers in Moscow. ExxonMobil, a so-called American company, receives almost 75 percent of its revenues from sales outside the United States. New employees at Finland-based phone maker Nokia are increasingly being recruited from India, China, and other developing countries—with non-Finns now outnumbering Finns at Nokia's renowned research center in Helsinki. And all major automobile manufacturers now build cars outside their borders; for instance, Honda builds cars in Ohio; Ford in Brazil; and both Mercedes and BMW in South Africa. These examples illustrate that the world has become a global village. In turn, managers have to become capable of working with people from different cultures.

Globalization affects a manager's people skills in at least two ways. First, if you're a manager, you're increasingly likely to find yourself in a foreign assignment. You may be transferred to your employer's operating division or subsidiary in another country. Once there, you'll have to manage a work force that is likely to be very different in needs, aspirations, and attitudes from those you were used to back home. Second, even in your own country, you're going to find yourself working with bosses, peers, and other employees who were born and raised in different cultures. What motivates you may not motivate them. Or your style of communication may be straightforward and open, but they may find this approach uncomfortable and threatening. To work effectively with these people, you'll need to understand their culture, how it has shaped them, and how to adapt your management style to their differences. As we discuss OB concepts throughout this book, we'll frequently address how cultural differences might require managers to modify their practices.

Managing Workforce Diversity

One of the most important and broad-based challenges currently facing organizations is adapting to people who are different. The term we use for describing this challenge is workforce diversity. While globalization focuses on differences between people *from* different countries, workforce diversity addresses differences among people *within* given countries.

Workforce diversity means that organizations are becoming more heterogeneous in terms of gender, race, and ethnicity. But the term encompasses anyone who varies from the so-called norm. In addition to the more obvious groups— women, African Americans, Latinos, Asian Americans—it also includes the physically disabled, gays and lesbians, and the elderly. Moreover, it's an issue in Canada, Australia, South Africa, Japan, and Europe as well as the United States. Managers in Canada and Australia, for instance, are having to adjust to large influxes of Asian workers. The "new" South Africa is increasingly characterized by blacks' holding important technical and managerial jobs. Women, long confined to low-paying temporary jobs in Japan, are moving into managerial positions. And the European Union cooperative trade arrangement, which opened up borders throughout much of western Europe, has increased workforce diversity in organizations that operate in countries such as Germany, Portugal, Italy, and France.

We used to take a melting-pot approach to differences in organizations, assuming people who were different would somehow automatically want to assimilate. But we now recognize that employees don't set aside their cultural values and lifestyle preferences when they come to work. The challenge for organizations, therefore, is to make themselves more accommodating to diverse groups of people by addressing their different lifestyles, family needs, and work styles. The melting-pot assumption is being replaced by one that recognizes and values differences.[12]

Haven't organizations always included members of diverse groups? Yes, but they were a small percentage of the workforce and were, for the most part, ignored by large organizations. Moreover, it was assumed that these minorities would seek to blend in and assimilate. For instance, the bulk of the pre-1980s U.S. workforce were male Caucasians working full-time to support a nonemployed wife and school-aged children. Now such employees are the true minority![13] Currently, 47 percent of the U.S. labor force are women. Minorities and immigrants make up 23 percent.[14] And an increasing proportion of workers are unmarried, with no children.

Workforce diversity has important implications for management practice. Managers have to shift their philosophy from treating everyone alike to recognizing differences and responding to those differences in ways that ensure employee retention and greater productivity while, at the same time, not discriminating. This shift includes, for instance, providing diversity training and revamping benefits programs to accommodate the different needs of different employees.

Xerox values diversity and is consistently rated among the best companies for women, Asians, blacks, and Hispanics to work for.

workforce diversity

The concept that organizations are becoming more heterogeneous in terms of gender, race, ethnicity and inclusion of other diverse groups.

Diversity, if positively managed, can increase creativity and innovation in organizations as well as improve decision making by providing different perspectives on problems.[15] When diversity is not managed properly, there is a potential for higher turnover, more-difficult communication, and more interpersonal conflicts.

Improving Quality and Productivity

Peter Wood manages in a very competitive business. He's manufacturing-systems manager at the Oak Creek, Wisconsin, plant for Delphi Automotive Systems. The plant makes catalytic converters for more than 40 automobile manufacturers. In 1997, Wood recognized that customers increasingly wanted customized products and they weren't willing to wait three weeks for delivery. So Wood led a complete overhaul of the Oak Creek plant.[16] Assembly lines were replaced with team work cells, employees were given total responsibility for quality, and hundreds of wasteful processes were cut from the production system. The overhaul worked. Within two years, productivity at Oak Creek has increased by more than 25 percent, quality has improved, and delivery time has been cut to four days.

More and more managers are confronting the challenges that Peter Wood is facing. They are having to improve their organization's productivity and the quality of the products and services they offer. Toward improving quality and productivity, they are implementing programs such as quality management and process reengineering—programs that require extensive employee involvement.

As Exhibit 1-5 describes, **quality management (QM)** is driven by the constant attainment of customer satisfaction through the continuous improvement of all organizational processes.[17] It has implications for OB because it requires employees to rethink what they do and become more involved in workplace decisions.

In times of rapid and dramatic change, it's sometimes necessary to approach improving quality and productivity from the perspective of "How would we do things around here if we were starting from scratch?" That, in essence, is the approach of **process reengineering**. It asks managers to reconsider how work would be done and their organization structured if they were starting over.[18] The actions that Peter Wood took at Delphi's Oak Creek plant illustrate process reengi-

quality management (QM)

The constant attainment of customer satisfaction through the continuous improvement of all organizational processes.

process reengineering

Reconsidering how work would be done and an organization structured if it were starting over.

EXHIBIT 1-5

What Is Quality Management?

1. *Intense focus on the customer.* The customer includes not only outsiders who buy the organization's products or services but also internal customers (such as shipping or accounts payable personnel) who interact with and serve others in the organization.
2. *Concern for continuous improvement.* QM is a commitment to never being satisfied. "Very good" is not good enough. Quality can always be improved.
3. *Improvement in the quality of everything the organization does.* QM uses a very broad definition of quality. It relates not only to the final product but also to how the organization handles deliveries, how rapidly it responds to complaints, how politely the phones are answered, and the like.
4. *Accurate measurement.* QM uses statistical techniques to measure every critical performance variable in the organization's operations. These performance variables are then compared against standards or benchmarks to identify problems, the problems are traced to their roots, and the causes are eliminated.
5. *Empowerment of employees.* QM involves the people on the line in the improvement process. Teams are widely used in QM programs as empowerment vehicles for finding and solving problems.

neering. Instead of merely making incremental changes in the basic production processes, Wood reinvented the plant's whole production system. Every process was evaluated in terms of its contribution to the plant's goals. Inefficient processes were thrown out. Entire new systems were introduced. And most employees found themselves undergoing training to do entirely new jobs. Rather than try to make small improvements in a system that was too rigid and inflexible to meet changing customer needs, Wood completely revamped his plant's production system and the jobs of individual employees. For instance, Oak Creek employees now check for quality, help establish productivity standards, and actively participate in introducing work-flow innovations.

Today's managers understand that the success of any effort at improving quality and productivity must include their employees. These employees will not only be a major force in carrying out changes but increasingly will actively participate in planning those changes. OB offers important insights into helping managers work through these changes.

Responding to the Labor Shortage

Economic ups and downs are difficult to predict. The world economy in the late 1990s, for instance, was generally quite robust and labor markets were tight. Most employers found it difficult to find skilled workers to fill vacancies. Then, in 2001, most developed countries suffered an economic recession. Layoffs were widespread and the supply of skilled workers became much more plentiful. In contrast, demographic trends are much more predictable. And we're facing one that has direct implications for OB: Barring some unforeseeable economic or political calamity, there will be a labor shortage for at least another 10 to 15 years. [19] We'll discuss the problem using U.S. statistics, but this shortage of skilled labor is also likely to be just as prevalent in most of Europe due to a graying population and a declining birth rate.

The U.S. labor shortage is a function of two factors—birth rates and labor participation rates. From the late 1960s through the late 1980s, American employers benefited from the large number of Baby Boomers (those born between 1946 and 1965) entering the workforce. Specifically, there are 76 million Baby Boomers in the workforce. But there are 10 million fewer Gen-Xers to replace them when they retire. Some Boomers have already retired early. The problem becomes severe in around 2006, when the major exodus of Boomers from the workplace begins. Importantly, in spite of continued increases in immigration, new entrants to the workforce from foreign countries will not do much to correct the supply shortage.

The labor shortage problem is compounded by the fact that the latter part of the 20th century benefited from a huge increase in the number of women entering the workforce. That provided a new supply of talented and skilled workers. This source has now been tapped. Moreover, there is declining interest by older workers to stay in the labor force. In 1950, nearly 80 percent of all 62-year-old men were still working. Today, only slightly more than half are. Improved pension plans, expanded Social Security benefits, and a healthy stock market has led many workers to retire early, especially those whose jobs were stressful or unchallenging. So the combination of the smaller Generation X population, the already high participation rate of women in the work force, and early retirements will lead to a significantly smaller future labor pool from which employers can hire.

In times of labor shortage, good wages and benefits aren't going to be enough to get and keep skilled employees. Managers will need sophisticated recruitment and retention strategies. And OB can help managers create these. In tight labor markets, managers who don't understand human behavior and fail to treat their employees properly, risk having no one to manage!

Improving Customer Service

American Express recently turned Joan Weinbel's worst nightmare into a non-event. It was 10 P.M. Joan was home in New Jersey, packing for a week-long trip, when she suddenly realized she had left her AmEx Gold Card at a restaurant in New York City earlier in the evening. The restaurant was 30 miles away. She had a flight to catch at 7:30 the next morning and she wanted her card for the trip. She called American Express. The phone was quickly answered by a courteous and helpful AmEx customer service representative. He told Ms. Weinbel not to worry. He asked her a few questions and told her "help was on the way." To say Joan was flabbergasted would be an understatement when her doorbell rang at 11:45 P.M.—less than 2 hours after she had called AmEx. At her door was a courier with a new card. How the company was able to produce the card and get it to her so quickly still puzzles Joan. But she said the experience made her a customer for life.

Today, the majority of employees in developed countries work in service jobs. For instance, 80 percent of the U.S. labor force is employed in service industries. In Australia, 73 percent work in service industries. In the United Kingdom, Germany, and Japan the percentages are 69, 68, and 65, respectively. Examples of these service jobs include technical support representatives, fast-food counter workers, sales clerks, teachers, waiters or waitresses, nurses, automobile repair technicians, consultants, credit representatives, financial planners, and flight attendants. The common characteristic of these jobs is that they require substantial interaction with an organization's customers. And since an organization can't exist without customers—whether that organization is DaimlerChrysler, Merrill Lynch, L.L. Bean, a law firm, a museum, a school, or a government agency—management needs to ensure that employees do what it takes to please its customers. OB can help in that task.

An analysis of a Qantas Airways' passenger survey confirms the role that employees play in satisfying customers. Passengers were asked to rate their "essential needs" in air travel. Almost every factor listed by passengers were directly influenced by the actions of Qantas' employees—from prompt baggage delivery, to courteous and efficient cabin crews, to assistance with connections, to quick and friendly airport check-ins.[20]

Except for OB researchers' interest in customer satisfaction through improvements in quality, the field of OB has generally ignored the customer. Focusing on the customer was thought to be the concern of people who study and practice marketing. But OB can contribute to improving an organization's performance by showing managers how employee attitudes and behavior are associated with customer satisfaction. Many an organization has failed because its employees failed to please the customer. So management needs to create a customer-responsive culture. And OB can provide considerable guidance in helping managers create such cultures—cultures in which employees are friendly and courteous, accessible, knowledgeable, prompt in responding to customer needs, and willing to do what's necessary to please the customer.[21]

Improving People Skills

We opened this chapter by demonstrating how important people skills are to managerial effectiveness. We said that "this book has been written to help both managers and potential managers develop those people skills."

As you proceed through this book, we'll present relevant concepts and theories that can help you explain and predict the behavior of people at work. In addition, you'll also gain insights into specific people skills that you can use on the job. For instance, you'll learn ways to design motivating jobs, techniques for improving your listening skills, and how to create more effective teams.

Empowering People

If you pick up any popular business periodical nowadays, you'll read about the reshaping of the relationship between managers and those they're supposedly responsible for managing. You'll find managers being called coaches, advisers, sponsors, or facilitators. In some organizations, employees are now called associates. And there's a blurring between the roles of managers and workers. Decision making is being pushed down to the operating level, where workers are being given the freedom to make choices about schedules and procedures and to solve work-related problems.[22] In the 1980s, managers were encouraged to get their employees to participate in work-related decisions. Now, managers are going considerably further by allowing employees full control of their work. An increasing number of organizations are using self-managed teams, in which workers operate largely without bosses.

Empowered employees, whether they work individually or in teams like this one at Carbon Five, need the tools and training to take responsibility for their work. Teams at Carbon Five have a great deal of freedom to make decisions, while their managers act as advisors and coaches.

What's going on? What's going on is that managers are **empowering employees**. They are putting employees in charge of what they do. And in so doing, managers are having to learn how to give up control, and employees are having to learn how to take responsibility for their work and make appropriate decisions. In later chapters, we'll show how empowerment is changing leadership styles, power relationships, the way work is designed, and the way organizations are structured.

empowering employees
Putting employees in charge of what they do.

Coping with "Temporariness"

Managing used to be characterized by long periods of stability, interrupted occasionally by short periods of change. Managing today would be more accurately described as long periods of ongoing change, interrupted occasionally by short periods of stability. The world that most managers and employees face today is one of permanent temporariness. The actual jobs that workers perform are in a permanent state of flux, so workers need to update their knowledge and skills continually to perform new job requirements. For example, production employees at companies such as Caterpillar, Ford, and Alcoa now need to know how to operate computerized production equipment. That was not part of their job descriptions 20 years ago. Work groups are also increasingly in a state of flux. In the past, employees were assigned to a specific work group, and that assignment was relatively permanent. There was a considerable amount of security in working with the same people day in and day out. That predictability has been replaced by temporary work groups, teams that include members from different departments and whose members change all the time, and the increased use of employee rotation to fill constantly changing work assignments. Finally, organizations themselves are in a state of flux. They continually reorganize their various divisions, sell off poor-performing businesses, downsize operations, subcontract noncritical services and operations to other organizations, and replace permanent employees with temporary workers.

Today's managers and employees must learn to cope with temporariness. They have to learn to live with flexibility, spontaneity, and unpredictability. The study of OB can provide important insights into helping you better understand a work world of continual change, how to overcome resistance to change, and how best to create an organizational culture that thrives on change.

Stimulating Innovation and Change

Whatever happened to Montgomery Ward, Woolworth, Smith Corona, and Eastern Airlines? All these giants went bust. Why have other giants, such as Sears, Boeing, and Lucent Technologies implemented huge cost-cutting programs and eliminated thousands of jobs? To avoid going bust.

Today's successful organizations must foster innovation and master the art of change or they'll become candidates for extinction. Victory will go to the organizations that maintain their flexibility, continually improve their quality, and beat their competition to the marketplace with a constant stream of innovative products and services. Domino's single-handedly brought on the demise of thousands of small pizza parlors whose managers thought they could continue doing what they had been doing for years. Amazon.com is putting a lot of independent bookstores out of business as it proves you can successfully sell books from an Internet Web site. Fox Television successfully stole a major portion of the under-25 viewing audience from their larger network rivals through innovative programming such as *The Simpsons* and *The X-Files*.

An organization's employees can be the impetus for innovation and change or they can be a major stumbling block. The challenge for managers is to stimulate their employees' creativity and tolerance for change. The field of OB provides a wealth of ideas and techniques to aid in realizing these goals.

The terrorist attacks of September 11 on New York City and Washington, DC changed many workplaces. For instance, employee security can no longer be taken for granted, many employees display signs of post-terrorist attack anxiety, and some now fear working in skyscrapers.

Helping Employees Balance Work/Life Conflicts

The typical employee in the 1960s or 1970s showed up at the workplace Monday through Friday and did his or her job in 8- or 9-hour chunks of time. The workplace and hours were clearly specified. That's no longer true for a large segment of today's workforce. Employees are increasingly complaining that the line between work and nonwork time has become blurred, creating personal conflicts and stress.[23]

A number of forces have contributed to blurring the lines between employees' work life and personal life. First, the creation of global organizations means their world never sleeps. At any time and on any day, for instance, thousands of General Electric employees are working somewhere. The need to consult with colleagues or customers 8 or 10 time zones away means that many employees of global firms are "on call" 24 hours a day. Second, communication technology allows employees to do their work at home, in their cars, or on the beach in Tahiti. This lets many people in technical and professional jobs do their work any time and from any place. Third, organizations are asking employees to put in longer hours. For instance, between 1977 and 1997, the average American workweek increased from 43 to 47 hours; and the number of people working 50 or more hours a week jumped from 24 percent to 37 percent. Finally, fewer families have only a single breadwinner. Today's married employee is typically part of a dual-career couple. This makes it increasingly diffi-

OB in the News

America's World-Class Workaholics

From the late 1970s to the late 1990s, the average workweek among salaried Americans increased from 43 hours to 47. Over the same years, the number of workers putting in 50 or more hours a week jumped from 24 percent to 37 percent. The United States has now moved past Japan to become the longest-working nation in the advanced industrial world. Who works the longest hours? Managers and professionals. And part of the reason that average weekly work hours have increased is that more Americans—34 percent in 1999, compared with 27 percent in

1997—are holding managerial and professional jobs.

These statistics are in stark contrast to many other places on the globe. For instance, in Norway and Sweden, ordinary workers get 4 to 6 weeks of vacation and up to a year of paid parental leave. In France, a 35-hour maximum workweek is the law of the land. Compared to the average Western European, Americans have a right to complain. The Americans are working an average of 8 weeks a year longer than their European counterparts.

One exception in Western Europe is Britain. Eighty-one percent of managers in Britain work more than 40 hours a week, and over 30 percent put in more than 50 hours a week. Seventy-one percent of these

managers complain about the impact of long hours on their health; and 68 percent say overwork is affecting their relationships with their children and their spouses.

These statistics lead us to two conclusions. First, relative to much of the world, Americans are overworked. And this is making it harder for them to balance work and family responsibilities. Second, the problem is most prevalent among managers and professionals. Given the changing make-up of the workforce—with technology expanding the number of professional jobs—we can expect an increasing proportion of the labor force to be complaining of long hours and difficulty in handling work/life conflicts.

Source: "America's World-Class Workaholics," *Manpower Argus,* April 2000, pp. 4–5.

cult for married employees to find the time to fulfill commitments to home, spouse, children, parents, and friends.

Employees are increasingly recognizing that work is squeezing out personal lives and they're not happy about it. For example, recent studies suggest that employees want jobs that give them flexibility in their work schedules so they can better manage work/life conflicts.[24] In addition, the next generation of employees is likely to show similar concerns.[25] A majority of college and university students say that attaining a balance between personal life and work is a primary career goal. They want "a life" as well as a job. Organizations that don't help their people achieve work/life balance will find it increasingly hard to attract and retain the most capable and motivated employees.

As you'll see in later chapters, the field of OB offers a number of suggestions to guide managers in designing workplaces and jobs that can help employees deal with work/life conflicts.

Improving Ethical Behavior

In an organizational world characterized by cutbacks, expectations of increasing worker productivity, and tough competition in the marketplace, it's not altogether surprising that many employees feel pressured to cut corners, break rules, and engage in other forms of questionable practices.

Members of organizations are increasingly finding themselves facing **ethical dilemmas**, situations in which they are required to define right and wrong conduct. For example, should they "blow the whistle" if they uncover illegal activities taking place in their company? Should they follow orders with which they don't

ethical dilemmas
Situations in which individuals are required to define right and wrong conduct.

personally agree? Do they give an inflated performance evaluation to an employee whom they like, knowing that such an evaluation could save that employee's job? Do they allow themselves to "play politics" in the organization if it will help their career advancement?

What constitutes good ethical behavior has never been clearly defined. And, in recent years, the line differentiating right from wrong has become even more blurred. Employees see people all around them engaging in unethical practices—elected officials are indicted for padding their expense accounts or taking bribes; successful executives use insider information for personal financial gain; university administrators "look the other way" when a winning coach verbally abuses his athletes; and even the President of the United States distorts the truth under oath. They hear people, when caught, giving excuses such as "everyone does it," or "you have to seize every advantage nowadays," or "I never thought I'd get caught."

Managers and their organizations are responding to this problem from a number of directions.[26] They're writing and distributing codes of ethics to guide employees through ethical dilemmas. They're offering seminars, workshops, and similar training programs to try to improve ethical behaviors. They're providing in-house advisors who can be contacted, in many cases anonymously, for assistance in dealing with ethical issues. And they're creating protection mechanisms for employees who reveal internal unethical practices.

Today's manager needs to create an ethically healthy climate for his or her employees, where they can do their work productively and confront a minimal degree of ambiguity regarding what constitutes right and wrong behaviors. In upcoming chapters, we'll discuss the kinds of actions managers can take to create an ethically healthy climate and to help employees sort through ethically ambiguous situations. We'll also present a number of exercises that will allow you to think through ethical issues and assess how you would handle them.

COMING ATTRACTIONS: DEVELOPING AN OB MODEL

We conclude this chapter by presenting a general model that defines the field of OB, stakes out its parameters, and identifies its primary dependent and independent variables. The end result will be a "coming attraction" of the topics making up the remainder of this book.

An Overview

model

An abstraction of reality. A simplified representation of some real-world phenomenon.

A **model** is an abstraction of reality, a simplified representation of some real-world phenomenon. A mannequin in a retail store is a model. So, too, is the accountant's formula: Assets + Liabilities = Owners' Equity. Exhibit 1-6 presents the skeleton on which we will construct our OB model. It proposes that there are three levels of analysis in OB and that, as we move from the individual level to the organization systems level, we add systematically to our understanding of behavior in organizations. The

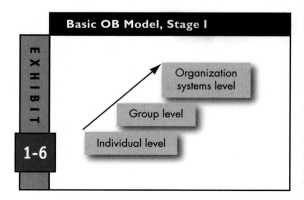

EXHIBIT 1-6

Basic OB Model, Stage I

Organization systems level

Group level

Individual level

three basic levels are analogous to building blocks; each level is constructed on the previous level. Group concepts grow out of the foundation laid in the individual section; we overlay structural constraints on the individual and group in order to arrive at organizational behavior.

The Dependent Variables

Dependent variables are the key factors that you want to explain or predict and that are affected by some other factor. What are the primary dependent variables in OB? Scholars have historically tended to emphasize productivity, absenteeism, turnover, and job satisfaction. More recently, a fifth variable—organizational citizenship—has been added to this list. Let's briefly review each of these variables to ensure that we understand what they mean and why they've achieved their level of distinction.

dependent variable
A response that is affected by an independent variable.

Productivity   An organization is productive if it achieves its goals and does so by transferring inputs to outputs at the lowest cost. As such, **productivity** implies a concern for both **effectiveness** and **efficiency**.

productivity
A performance measure that includes effectiveness and efficiency.

A hospital, for example, is *effective* when it successfully meets the needs of its clientele. It is *efficient* when it can do so at a low cost. If a hospital manages to achieve higher output from its present staff by reducing the average number of days a patient is confined to a bed or by increasing the number of staff–patient contacts per day, we say that the hospital has gained productive efficiency. A business firm is effective when it attains its sales or market share goals, but its productivity also depends on achieving those goals efficiently. Popular measures of organizational efficiency include return on investment, profit per dollar of sales, and output per hour of labor.

effectiveness
Achievement of goals.

efficiency
The ratio of effective output to the input required to achieve it.

We can also look at productivity from the perspective of the individual employee. Take the cases of Mike and Al, who are both long-distance truckers. If Mike is supposed to haul his fully loaded rig from New York to its destination in Los Angeles in 75 hours or less, he is effective if he makes the 3,000-mile trip within that time period. But measures of productivity must take into account the costs incurred in reaching the goal. That's where efficiency comes in. Let's assume that Mike made the New York to Los Angeles run in 68 hours and averaged 7 miles per gallon. Al, on the other hand, made the trip in 68 hours also but averaged 9 miles per gallon (rigs and loads are identical). Both Mike and Al were effective—they accomplished their goal—but Al was more efficient than Mike because his rig consumed less gas and, therefore, he achieved his goal at a lower cost.

Organizations in service industries need to include additionally "attention to customer needs and requirements" in assessing their effectiveness. Why? Because in these types of businesses, there is a clear chain of cause-and-effect running from employee attitudes and behavior to customer attitudes and behavior to an organization's revenues and profits. Sears, in fact, has carefully documented this chain.[27] The company's management found that a 5 percent improvement in employee attitudes leads to a 1.3 percent increase in customer satisfaction, which in turn translated into a 0.5 percent improvement in revenue growth. More specifically, Sears found that by training employees to improve the employee–customer interaction, it was able to improve customer satisfaction by 4 percent over a 12-month period, which generated an estimated $200 million in additional revenues.

In summary, one of OB's major concerns is productivity. We want to know what factors will influence the effectiveness and efficiency of individuals, of groups, and of the overall organization.

absenteeism

The failure to report to work.

Absenteeism **Absenteeism** is the failure to report to work. Its annual cost has been estimated at over $40 billion for U.S. organizations and $12 billion for Canadian firms.[28] In Germany, absences cost industrial firms more than 31 billion euros (approximately U.S. $31 billion) each year.[29] At the job level, a one-day absence by a clerical worker can cost a U.S. employer several hundred dollars in reduced efficiency and increased supervisory workload. These figures indicate the importance to an organization of keeping absenteeism low.

It's obviously difficult for an organization to operate smoothly and to attain its objectives if employees fail to report to their jobs. The work flow is disrupted, and often important decisions must be delayed. In organizations that rely heavily on assembly-line production, absenteeism can be considerably more than a disruption; it can result in a drastic reduction in the quality of output, and, in some cases, it can bring about a complete shutdown of the production facility. But levels of absenteeism beyond the normal range in any organization have a direct impact on that organization's effectiveness and efficiency.

Are *all* absences bad? Probably not. Although most absences have a negative impact on the organization, we can conceive of situations in which the organization may benefit by an employee's voluntarily choosing not to come to work. For instance, illness, fatigue, or excess stress can significantly decrease an employee's productivity. In jobs in which an employee needs to be alert—surgeons and airline pilots are obvious examples—it may well be better for the organization if the employee does not report to work rather than show up and perform poorly. The cost of an accident in such jobs could be prohibitive. Even in managerial jobs, where mistakes are less spectacular, performance may be improved when managers absent themselves from work rather than make a poor decision under stress. But these examples are clearly atypical. For the most part, we can assume that organizations benefit when employee absenteeism is low.

turnover

The voluntary and involuntary permanent withdrawal from an organization.

Turnover **Turnover** is the voluntary and involuntary permanent withdrawal from an organization. A high turnover rate results in increased recruiting, selection, and training costs. What are those costs? They're higher than you might think. For instance, the cost for a typical information-technology company in the United States to replace a programmer or systems analyst has been put at $34,100; and the cost of a retail store to replace a lost sales clerk has been calculated at $10,445.[30] In addition, a high rate of turnover can disrupt the efficient running of an organization when knowledgeable and experienced personnel leave and replacements must be found and prepared to assume positions of responsibility.

All organizations, of course, have some turnover. In fact, if the "right" people are leaving the organization—the marginal and submarginal employees—turnover can be positive. It may create the opportunity to replace an underperforming individual with someone who has higher skills or motivation, open up increased opportunities for promotions, and add new and fresh ideas to the organization.[31] In today's changing world of work, reasonable levels of employee-initiated turnover facilitate organizational flexibility and employee independence, and they can lessen the need for management-initiated layoffs.

But turnover often involves the loss of people the organization doesn't want to lose. For instance, one study covering 900 employees who had resigned their jobs found that 92 percent earned performance ratings of "satisfactory" or better from their superiors.[32] So when turnover is excessive, or when it involves valuable performers, it can be a disruptive factor, hindering the organization's effectiveness.

Organizational Citizenship **Organizational citizenship** is discretionary behavior that is not part of an employee's formal job requirements, but that nevertheless promotes the effective functioning of the organization.[33]

Successful organizations need employees who will do more than their usual job duties—who will provide performance that is *beyond* expectations. In today's dynamic workplace, where tasks are increasingly done in teams and where flexibility is critical, organizations need employees who'll engage in "good citizenship" behaviors such as making constructive statements about their work group and the organization, helping others on their team, volunteering for extra job activities, avoiding unnecessary conflicts, showing care for organizational property, respecting the spirit as well as the letter of rules and regulations, and gracefully tolerating the occasional work-related impositions and nuisances.

Organizations want and need employees who will do those things that aren't in any job description. And the evidence indicates that the organizations that have such employees outperform those that don't.[34] As a result, OB is concerned with organizational citizenship behavior (OCB) as a dependent variable.

Job Satisfaction The final dependent variable we will look at is **job satisfaction**, which we define simply, at this point, as an individual's general attitude toward his or her job. (We expand considerably on that definition in Chapter 3.) Unlike the previous four variables, job satisfaction represents an attitude rather than a behavior. Why, then, has it become a primary dependent variable? For two reasons: its demonstrated relationship to performance factors and the value preferences held by many OB researchers.

The belief that satisfied employees are more productive than dissatisfied employees has been a basic tenet among managers for years. Although much evidence questions that assumed causal relationship, it can be argued that advanced societies should be concerned not only with the quantity of life—that is, concerns such as higher productivity and material acquisitions—but also with its quality. Those researchers with strong humanistic values argue that satisfaction is a legitimate objective of an organization. Not only is satisfaction negatively related to absenteeism and turnover, but, they argue, organizations have a responsibility to provide employees with jobs that are challenging and intrinsically rewarding. Therefore, although job satisfaction represents an attitude rather than a behavior, OB researchers typically consider it an important dependent variable.

The Independent Variables

What are the major determinants of productivity, absenteeism, turnover, OCB, and job satisfaction? Our answer to that question brings us to the **independent variables**. Consistent with our belief that organizational behavior can best be understood when viewed essentially as a set of increasingly complex building blocks, the base, or first level, of our model lies in understanding individual behavior.

Individual-Level Variables It has been said that "managers, unlike parents, must work with used, not new, human beings—human beings whom others have gotten to first."[35] When individuals enter an organization, they are a bit like used cars. Each is different. Some are "low-mileage"—they have been treated carefully and have had only limited exposure to the realities of the elements. Others are "well worn," having been driven over some rough roads. This metaphor indicates that people enter organizations with certain characteristics that will influence their behavior at work. The more obvious of these are personal or biographical characteristics such as age, gender, and marital status; personality characteristics; an inherent emotional framework; values and attitudes; and basic ability levels. These characteristics are essentially intact when an individual enters the workforce, and, for the most part, there is little management can do to alter them. Yet they have a very real impact on employee behavior. Therefore, each of these factors—biographical characteristics, ability, values, attitudes, personality, and emotions—will be discussed as independent variables in Chapters 2 through 4.

There are four other individual-level variables that have been shown to affect employee behavior: perception, individual decision making, learning, and motivation. Those topics will be introduced and discussed in Chapters 2, 5, 6, and 7.

Group-Level Variables   The behavior of people in groups is more than the sum total of all the individuals acting in their own way. The complexity of our model is increased when we acknowledge that people's behavior when they are in groups is different from their behavior when they are alone. Therefore, the next step in the development of an understanding of OB is the study of group behavior.

Chapter 8 lays the foundation for an understanding of the dynamics of group behavior. That chapter discusses how individuals in groups are influenced by the patterns of behavior they are expected to exhibit, what the group considers to be acceptable standards of behavior, and the degree to which group members are attracted to each other. Chapter 9 translates our understanding of groups to the design of effective work teams. Chapters 10 through 14 demonstrate how communication patterns, leadership, power and politics, and levels of conflict affect group behavior.

Organization Systems Level Variables   Organizational behavior reaches its highest level of sophistication when we add formal structure to our previous knowledge of individual and group behavior. Just as groups are more than the sum of their individual members, so are organizations more than the sum of their member groups. The design of the formal organization, work processes, and jobs; the organization's human resource policies and practices (that is, selection processes, training programs, performance evaluation methods); and the internal culture all have an impact on the dependent variables. These are discussed in detail in Chapters 15 through 18.

Toward a Contingency OB Model

Our final model is shown in Exhibit 1-7. It shows the five key dependent variables and a large number of independent variables, organized by level of analysis, that research indicates have varying effects on the former. As complicated as this model is, it still does not do justice to the complexity of the OB subject matter, but it should help explain why the chapters in this book are arranged as they are and help you to explain and predict the behavior of people at work.

For the most part, our model does not explicitly identify the vast number of contingency variables because of the tremendous complexity that would be involved in such a diagram. Rather, throughout this book we will introduce important contingency variables that will improve the explanatory linkage between the independent and dependent variables in our OB model.

Note that we have included the concepts of change and stress in Exhibit 1-7, acknowledging the dynamics of behavior and the fact that work stress is an individual, group, and organizational issue. Specifically, in Chapter 19 we will discuss the change

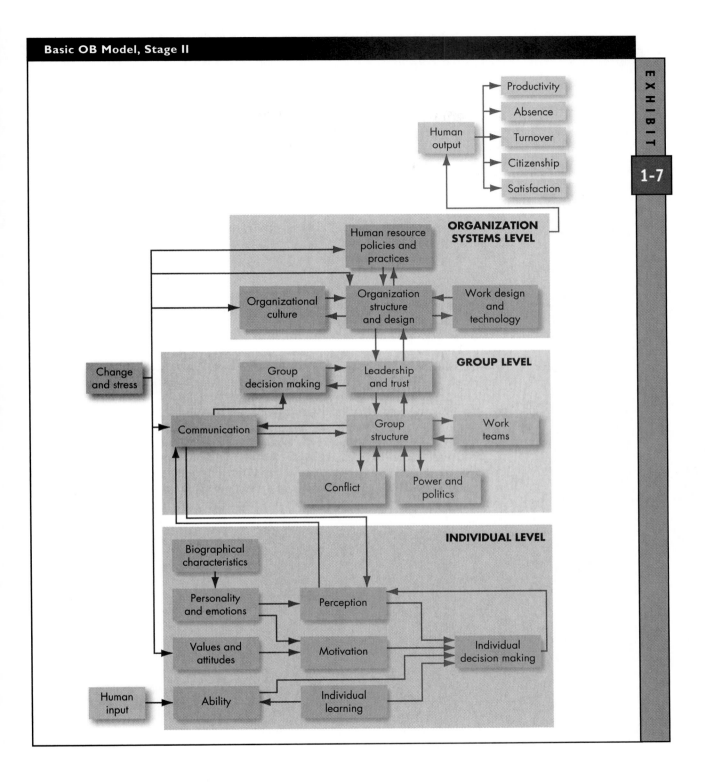

process, ways to manage organizational change, key change issues currently facing managers, consequences of work stress, and techniques for managing stress.

Also note that Exhibit 1-7 includes linkages between the three levels of analysis. For instance, organizational structure is linked to leadership. This link is meant to convey that authority and leadership are related; management exerts its influence on group behavior through leadership. Similarly, communication is the means by which individuals transmit information; thus, it is the link between individual and group behavior.

SUMMARY AND IMPLICATIONS FOR MANAGERS

Managers need to develop their interpersonal or people skills if they are going to be effective in their jobs. Organizational behavior (OB) is a field of study that investigates the impact that individuals, groups, and structure have on behavior within an organization, and then it applies that knowledge to make organizations work more effectively. Specifically, OB focuses on how to improve productivity, reduce absenteeism and turnover, and increase employee citizenship and job satisfaction.

We all hold generalizations about the behavior of people. Some of our generalizations may provide valid insights into human behavior, but many are erroneous. Organizational behavior uses systematic study to improve predictions of behavior that would be made from intuition alone. But, because people are different, we need to look at OB in a contingency framework, using situational variables to moderate cause-and-effect relationships.

Organizational behavior offers both challenges and opportunities for managers. It offers specific insights to improve a manager's people skills. It recognizes differences and helps managers to see the value of workforce diversity and practices that may need to be changed when managing in different countries. It can improve quality and employee productivity by showing managers how to empower their people, design and implement change programs, and help employees balance work/life conflicts. It provides suggestions for helping managers meet chronic labor shortages. It can help managers to cope in a world of temporariness and to learn ways to stimulate innovation. Finally, OB can offer managers guidance in creating an ethically healthy work climate.

Successful Organizations Put People First

Timberland does it. So does W.L. Gores & Associates, SAS Institute, Southwest Airlines, Goldman Sachs, Johnson & Johnson, Lincoln Electric, and Starbucks. What is *it*? These companies pursue "people-first" strategies.

There is an increasing amount of evidence that successful organizations put people first.[a] Why? Astute managers have come to learn that their organization's employees are its only true competitive advantage. Competitors can match most organization's products, processes, locations, distribution channels, and the like. What's far more difficult to emulate is a workforce made up of highly knowledgeable and motivated people. The characteristic that differentiates successful companies from their less successful counterparts in almost every industry is the quality of the people they're able to get and keep.

What kind of practices differentiate people-first organizations? We can list at least four: (1) They value cultural diversity. They actively seek a diverse workforce based on age, gender, and race. (2) They are family-friendly. They help employees balance work and personal responsibilities through programs such as flexible work schedules and on-site child care facilities. (3) They invest in employee training. These organizations spend heavily to make sure employee skill levels are kept current. This not only ensures that employees can handle the latest technologies and processes for the organization but that employees will be marketable to other employers. (4) People-first organizations empower their employees. They push authority and responsibility down to the lowest levels.

Organizations that put people first have a more dedicated and committed workforce. This, in turn, converts into higher employee productivity and satisfaction. These employees are willing to put forth the extra effort—to do whatever is necessary to see that their jobs are done properly and completely. People-first strategies also lead to organizations being able to recruit smarter, more conscientious, and more loyal employees.

---

[a]See, for instance, J. Pfeffer, *The Human Equation: Building Profits by Putting People First* (Boston: Harvard Business School Press, 1998); and P. Drucker, "They're Not Employees, They're People," *Harvard Business Review*, February 2002, pp. 70–77.

Putting "people first" is easy to say. And it's currently politically correct. What manager, in his or her right mind, is going to admit publicly that employees take a back seat to cost cutting or profitability? It's important, however, not to confuse talk with action.

Putting people first is not necessarily consistent with long-term competitiveness. Managers recognize this fact and are increasingly acting on it. Today's organizations are more typically pursuing a "labor-cost-minimization" strategy rather than a people-first strategy.

When you look beyond what managers say, you find most business firms place profits over people. To stay competitive in a global economy, they look for cost-cutting measures. They reengineer processes and cut the size of their permanent workforce. They move jobs to countries with lower costs. And they substitute temporary workers for full-time permanent staff.

Organizations with problems typically look to staffing cuts as a first response. And organizations *without* problems are regularly reviewing their staffing needs to identify redundancies and overstaffing. Their goal is to keep themselves "lean and mean." In today's competitive environment, few organizations have the luxury to be able to provide workers with implied "permanent employment" or to offer anything more than minimal job security.

For almost all organizations today, employees are a variable cost. Staffing levels are kept to a minimum and employees are continually added or removed as needed.

Interestingly, the labor-cost-minimization strategy appears to be spreading worldwide. It began in the United States in the early 1990s. Now it has become the model for companies in countries such as Japan, South Korea, and Thailand—places that historically protected their employees in good times and bad. Many firms in these countries have abandoned their permanent-employment, people-first policies. Why? Because such policies are inconsistent with aggressive, low-cost, global competition.

Points in this argument are based on N. Nicholson, "How Hardwired Is Human Behavior?" *Harvard Business Review*, July–August 1998, pp. 135–47; and B. D. Pierce and R. White, "The Evolution of Social Structure: Why Biology Matters," *Academy of Management Review*, October 1999, pp. 843–53.

1. How are OB concepts addressed in management functions, roles, and skills?

2. Define *organizational behavior*. Relate it to *management*.

3. What is an organization? Is the family unit an organization? Explain.

4. Identify and contrast the three general management roles.

5. What is a "contingency approach" to OB?

6. Contrast psychology and sociology's contribution to OB.

7. "Behavior is generally predictable, so there is no need to formally study OB." Why is that statement wrong?

8. What are the three levels of analysis in our OB model? Are they related? If so, how?

9. If job satisfaction is not a behavior, why is it considered an important dependent variable?

10. What are effectiveness and efficiency, and how are they related to organizational behavior?

1. Contrast the research comparing effective managers with successful managers. What are the implications from the research for practicing managers?

2. Why do you think the subject of OB might be criticized as being "only common sense," when one would rarely hear such a criticism of a course in physics or statistics?

3. Millions of workers have lost their jobs due to downsizing. At the same time, many organizations are complaining that they cannot find qualified people to fill vacancies. How do you explain this apparent contradiction?

4. On a 1 to 10 scale measuring the sophistication of a scientific discipline in predicting phenomena, mathematical physics would probably be a 10. Where do you think OB would fall on the scale? Why?

5. What do you think is the single most critical "people" problem facing managers today? Give specific support for your position.

Team Exercise   Workforce Diversity

Purpose: To learn about the different needs of a diverse workforce.

Time required: Approximately 40 minutes.

Participants and roles: Divide the class into six groups of approximately equal size. Each group is assigned one of the following roles:

Nancy is 28 years old. She is a divorced mother of three children, aged 3, 5, and 7. She is the department head. She earns $40,000 a year on her job and receives another $3,600 a year in child support from her ex-husband.

Ethel is a 72-year-old widow. She works 25 hours a week to supplement her $8,000 annual pension. Including her hourly wage of $8.50, she earns $19,000 a year.

John is a 34-year-old black male born in Trinidad who is now a U.S. resident. He is married and the father of two small children. John attends college at night and is within a year of earning his bachelor's degree. His salary is $27,000 a year. His wife is an attorney and earns approximately $50,000 a year.

Lu is a 26-year-old physically impaired male Asian American. He is single and has a master's degree in education. Lu is paralyzed and confined to a wheelchair as a result of an auto accident. He earns $32,000 a year.

Maria is a single 22-year-old Hispanic woman. Born and raised in Mexico, she came to the United States only three months ago. Maria's English needs considerable improvement. She earns $20,000 a year.

Mike is a 16-year-old white male high school sophomore who works 15 hours a week after school and during vacations. He earns $7.20 an hour, or approximately $5,600 a year.

The members of each group are to assume the character consistent with their assigned role.

Background: Our six participants work for a company that has recently installed a flexible benefits program. Instead of the traditional "one benefit package fits all," the company is allocating an additional 25 percent of each employee's annual pay to be used for discretionary benefits. Those benefits and their annual cost are listed below.

- Supplementary health care for employee:

  Plan A (no deductible and pays 90%) = $3,000
  Plan B ($200 deductible and pays 80%) = $2,000
  Plan C ($1,000 deductible and pays 70%) = $500

- Supplementary health care for dependents (same deductibles and percentages as above):

  Plan A = $2,000
  Plan B = $1,500
  Plan C = $500

- Supplementary dental plan = $500

- Life insurance:

  Plan A ($25,000 coverage) = $500
  Plan B ($50,000 coverage) = $1,000
  Plan C ($100,000 coverage) = $2,000
  Plan D ($250,000 coverage) = $3,000

- Mental health plan = $500

- Prepaid legal assistance = $300

- Vacation = 2% of annual pay for each week, up to 6 weeks a year

- Pension at retirement equal to approximately 50% of final annual earnings = $1,500

- Four-day workweek during the three summer months (available only to full-time employees) = 4% of annual pay

- Day-care services (after company contribution) = $2,000 for all of an employee's children, regardless of number

- Company-provided transportation to and from work = $750

- College tuition reimbursement = $1,000

- Language class tuition reimbursement = $500

The Task:

1. Each group has 15 minutes to develop a flexible benefits package that consumes 25 percent (and no more!) of their character's pay.

2. After completing step 1, each group appoints a spokesperson who describes to the entire class the benefits package they have arrived at for their character.

3. The entire class then discusses the results. How did the needs, concerns, and problems of each participant influence the group's decision? What do the results suggest for trying to motivate a diverse workforce?

Special thanks to Professor Penny Wright (San Diego State University) for her suggestions during the development of this exercise.

Ethical Dilemma	What's the Right Balance Between Work and Personal Life?

When you think of work/life conflicts, you probably tend to think of people in lower levels of organizations. But a recent survey of 179 CEOs revealed that many of them are struggling with this issue. Thirty-one percent, for instance, said they have a high level of stress in their lives; 47 percent admitted that they would sacrifice some compensation for more personal time; and 16 percent considered changing jobs in the past 6 months to reduce stress or sacrifices made in their personal lives.

Most of these surveyed executives conceded that they had given up, and continue to give up, a lot to get to the top in their organizations. They're often tired from the extensive and exhausting travel their jobs demand, not to mention an average 60-hour workweek. Yet most feel the climb to the CEO position was worth whatever sacrifices they have had to make.

Jean Stone, while not representative of the group, indicates the price that some of these executives have had to pay. As CEO and president of Dukane Corp., an Illinois-based manufacturer of electronic communications equipment, Stone describes herself as highly achievement-oriented. She has an intense focus on her job and admits to having lost sight of her personal life. Recently divorced after a 10-year marriage, she acknowledges that "career and work pressures were a factor in that."

How much emphasis on work is *too much*? What's the right balance between work and personal life? How much would you be willing to give up to be CEO of a major company? And if you were a CEO, what ethical responsibilities, if any, do you think you have to help your employees balance their work/family obligations?

Source: Based on M.J. Critelli, "Striking a Balance," *Industry Week*, November 20, 2000, pp. 26–36.

Great Plains Software in Fargo, North Dakota, is a success story. Begun in 1983, today it employs 2,200 people, generates sales of $195 million, and was recently bought by Microsoft for $1 billion. Management attributes much of its success to the company's people-first strategy.

The company's CEO, Doug Burgum, says that the company's growth and success can be attributed to three guiding principles. First, make the company such a great place to work that people not only won't want to leave, they'll knock down the door to get in. Second, give employees ownership at every level. And third, let people grow—as professionals and as individuals.

What does Great Plains do to facilitate its people-first culture? Managers point to the company's structure, perks, and its commitment to helping employees develop their skills and leadership. Great Plains has a flat organization structure with a minimal degree of hierarchy. Work is done mostly in teams, and there are no traditional status accouterments such as executive parking spaces or corner office suites. Perks include stock options for everyone, casual dress standards, an on-site child-care center, and daily extracurricular classes in everything from aerobics to personal finance. But management is most proud of its commitment to the development of its people. The company offers a long list of training and educational opportunities to its employees. These are run on site and designed to help employees build their skill level. Great Plains' premier training program is called Leadership is Everywhere. It's designed to ensure that the company will have people who can assume new leadership roles in a continuously changing environment. The company reinforces class training by placing its workers in departmental teams. At the helm of these teams are "team leaders," whose job is to help foster their charges' ideas and projects. They are also expected to provide one-on-one job coaching and career planning advice. Nearly all Great Plains employees are given the opportunity to become team leaders.

Burgum has more than just increased revenues to support his belief that his people-first strategy works. It has also succeeded in keeping employees contented. Turnover, for instance, is a minuscule 5 percent a year—far below the information-technology average of 18 to 25 percent.

Questions

1. Putting people first has worked for Great Plains. If it's so effective, why do you think all firms haven't adopted these practices?

2. Do you think a people-first approach is more applicable to certain businesses or industries than others? If so, what might they be? Why?

3. What downside, if any, do you see in working at a company like Great Plains?

4. What downside, if any, do you see in managing at a company like Great Plains?

5. Some critics have argued that "People-first policies don't lead to high profits. High profits allow people-first policies." Do you agree? Explain your position.

Source: Based on S. Boehle, "From Humble Roots," *Training*, October 2000, pp. 106–13.

Endnotes

1. See, for instance, R. A. Baron and G. D. Markman, "Beyond Social Capital: How Social Skills Can Enhance Entrepreneurs' Success," *Academy of Management Executive*, February 2000, pp. 106–16.

2. D. Foust, "Wooing the Worker," *Business Week*, May 22, 2000, pp. 44–46.

3. *The 1997 National Study of the Changing Workforce* (New York: Families and Work Institute, 1997).

4. H. Fayol, *Industrial and General Administration* (Paris: Dunod, 1916).

5. H. Mintzberg, *The Nature of Managerial Work* (Upper Saddle River, NJ: Prentice Hall, 1973).

6. R. L. Katz, "Skills of an Effective Administrator," *Harvard Business Review*, September–October 1974, pp. 90–102.

7. F. Luthans, "Successful vs. Effective Real Managers," *Academy of Management Executive*, May 1988, pp. 127–32; and F. Luthans, R. M. Hodgetts, and S. A. Rosenkrantz, *Real Managers* (Cambridge, MA: Ballinger, 1988).

8. P. H. Langford, "Importance of Relationship Management for the Career Success of Australian Managers," *Australian Journal of Psychology*, December 2000, pp. 163–69.

9. See, for instance, J. E. Garcia and K. S. Keleman, "What Is Organizational Behavior Anyhow?" paper presented at the 16th Annual Organizational Behavior Teaching Conference, Columbia, MO, June 1989; and C. Heath and S. B. Sitkin, "Big-B Versus Big-O: What Is *Organizational* about Organizational Behavior?" *Journal of Organizational Behavior*, February 2001, pp. 43–58.

10. E. E. Lawler III and J. G. Rhode, *Information and Control in Organizations* (Pacific Palisades, CA: Goodyear, 1976), p. 22.

11. See F. D. Richard, C. F. Bond, Jr., and J. J. Stokes-Zoota, "'That is Completely Obvious . . . and Important': Lay Judgments of Social Psychological Findings," *Personality and Social Psychological Bulletin*, April 2001, pp. 497–505.

12. O. C. Richard, "Racial Diversity, Business Strategy, and Firm Performance: A Resource-Based View," *Academy of Management Journal*, April 2000, pp. 164–77.

13. "Bye-Bye, Ozzie and Harriet," *American Demographics*, December 2000, p. 59.

14. U.S. Department of Labor, Women's Bureau, 2002; and U.S. Census Bureau, 2002.

15. See, for instance, E. E. Kossek and S. A. Lobel (eds.), *Managing Diversity* (Cambridge, MA: Blackwell, 1996); "Building a Competitive Workforce: Diversity—The Bottom Line," *Forbes*, April 3, 2000, pp. 181–94; and O. C. Richard, "Racial Diversity, Business Strategy, and Firm Performance."

16. D. Dorsey, "Change Factory," *Fast Company*, June 2000, pp. 215–24.

17. See, for instance, W. J. Kolarik, *Creating Quality: Process Design for Results* (New York: McGraw Hill, 2000); and D. Bell, et al, *Managing Quality*, 2nd ed. (Woburn, MA: Butterworth-Heinemann, 2002).

18. See, for instance, C. M. Khoong, *Reengineering in Action* (London: Imperial College Press, 1999); and J. A. Champy, *X-Engineering the Corporation* (New York: Warner Books, 2002).

19. This section is based on M. Bolch, "The Coming Crunch," *Training*, April 2001, pp. 54–58; P. Nyhan, "As Baby Boomers Retire, They'll Leave Big Gap in the Work Force, Chao Warns," *Seattle Post-Intelligencer*, August 24, 2001, p. C1; G. M. McEvoy and M. J. Blahna, "Engagement or Disengagement? Older Workers and the Looming Labor Shortage," *Business Horizons*, September–October 2001, pp. 46–52; P. Francese, "Looming Labor Shortages," *American Demographics*, November 2001, pp. 34–35; and D. Eisenberg, "The Coming Job Boom," *Time*, May 6, 2002, pp. 40–44.

20. Cited in E. Naumann and D. W. Jackson, Jr., "One More Time: How Do You Satisfy Customers?" *Business Horizons*, May–June 1999, p. 73.

21. See, for instance, M. D. Hartline and O. C. Ferrell, "The Management of Customer-Contact Service Employees: An Empirical Investigation," *Journal of Marketing*, October 1996, pp. 52–70; E. Naumann and D. W. Jackson, Jr., "One More Time: How Do You Satisfy Customers?" pp. 71–76; W-C. Tsai, "Determinants and Consequences of Employee Displayed Positive Emotions," *Journal of Management* vol. 27, no. 4, 2001, pp. 497–512; and S. D. Pugh, "Service with a Smile: Emotional Contagion in the Service Encounter," *Academy of Management Journal*, October 2001, pp. 1018–27.

22. J. Flaherty, "Suggestions Rise from the Floors of U.S. Factories," *New York Times*, April 18, 2001, p. C1.

23. See, for instance, P. Cappelli, J. Constantine, and C. Chadwick, "It Pays to Value Family: Work and Family Tradeoffs Reconsidered," *Industrial Relations*, April 2000, pp. 175–98; M. A. Verespej, "Balancing Act," *Industry Week*, May 15, 2000, pp, 81–85; and R. C. Barnett and D. T. Hall, "How to Use Reduced Hours to Win the War for Talent," *Organizational Dynamics*, vol. 29, no. 3, 2001, pp. 192–210.

24. M. Conlin, "9 to 5 Isn't Working Anymore," *Business Week*, September 20, 1999, p. 94; and "The New World of Work: Flexibility Is the Watchword," *Business Week*, January 10, 2000, p. 36.

25. S. Shellenbarger, "What Job Candidates Really Want to Know: Will I Have a Life?" *Wall Street Journal*, November 17, 1999, p. B1; and "U.S. Employers Polish Image to Woo a Demanding New Generation," *Manpower Argus*, February 2000, p. 2.

26. See, for instance, G. R. Weaver, L. K. Trevino, and P. L. Cochran, "Corporate Ethics Practices in the Mid-1990's: An Empirical Study of the Fortune 1000," *Journal of Business Ethics*, February 1999, pp. 283–94.

27. A. J. Rucci, S. P. Kirn, and R. T. Quinn, "The Employee-Customer-Profit Chain at Sears," *Harvard Business Review*, January–February 1998, pp. 83–97.

28. S. R. Rhodes and R. M. Steers, *Managing Employee Absenteeism* (Reading, MA: Addison–Wesley, 1990). For a full review of the direct and indirect costs of absenteeism, see D. A. Harrison and J. J. Martocchio, "Time for Absenteeism: A 20-Year Review of Origins, Offshoots, and Outcomes," *Journal of Management*, vol. 24, no. 3, 1998, pp. 305–50.

29. Cited in J. Schmid, "'Sick' German Workers Get Corporate Medicine," *International Herald Tribune*, September 28–29, 1996, p. 1.

30. "Employee Turnover Costs in the U.S.," *Manpower Argus*, January 2001, p. 5.

31. See, for example, D. R. Dalton and W. D. Todor, "Functional Turnover: An Empirical Assessment," *Journal of Applied Psychology*, December 1981, pp. 716–21; G. M. McEvoy and W. F. Cascio, "Do Good or Poor Performers Leave? A Meta-Analysis of the Relationship between Performance and Turnover," *Academy of Management Journal*, December 1987, pp. 744–62; S. Lorge, "When Turnover Isn't So Bad," *Sales & Marketing Management*, September 1999, p. 13; and M. C. Sturman and C. O. Trevor, "The Implications of Linking the Dynamic Performance and Turnover Literatures," *Journal of Applied Psychology*, August 2001, pp. 684–96.

32. Cited in "You Often Lose the Ones You Love," *Industry Week*, November 21, 1988, p. 5.

33. D. W. Organ, *Organizational Citizenship Behavior: The Good Soldier Syndrome* (Lexington, MA: Lexington Books, 1988), p. 4. See also J. A. LePine, A. Erez, and D. E. Johnson, "The Nature and Dimensionality of Organizational Citizenship Behavior: A Critical Review and Meta-Analysis," *Journal of Applied Psychology*, February 2002, pp. 52–65.

34. P. M. Podsakoff, S. B. MacKenzie, J. B. Paine, and D. G. Bachrach, "Organizational Citizenship Behaviors: A Critical Review of the Theoretical and Empirical Literature and Suggestions for Future Research," *Journal of Management*, vol. 26, no. 3, 2000, pp. 543–48.

35. H. J. Leavitt, *Managerial Psychology*, rev. ed. (Chicago: University of Chicago Press, 1964), p. 3.

PART TWO

THE
INDIVIDUAL

Kevin Nguyen, a Continental Airlines flight attendant, thought he'd done something wrong when he was called into the cockpit on a flight from Newark to Las Vegas.[1] To his surprise, Nguyen was told that Continental's chairman, Gordon Bethune, was on the line. But Bethune had good news. Mr. Nguyen had won a new Ford Explorer, one of eight that Continental awards twice a year to workers with perfect job attendance for the previous 6 months. "I couldn't believe it," said Mr. Nguyen, who has worked at Continental since 1997. Fred Miller, a 757 pilot for Continental, also won an Explorer on the same day as Nguyen. His comment? "All I did was come to work like I'm supposed to, and they gave me a car!"

Continental's attendance-reward program is working. Since the program's inception, the company has given away 83 Ford sport utility vehicles, costing about $3 million. But it has saved the company more than $20 million by reducing the airline's rate of absenteeism. For instance, more than 14,000 or about one-third of Continental's employees qualified for the Explorer giveaway by having had perfect attendance records during the most recent 6-month period.

In addition to improving attendance, the Explorer reward program has had other benefits. Specifically, it has improved employee motivation and produced more contented passengers. Continental now has the highest on-time rankings of any major U.S. airline and is ranked first in the latest customer satisfaction survey conducted by J.D. Power and Associates. All of this is helping to solidify Continental's financial performance. After filing for bankruptcy twice in the 1980s and early 1990s, Bethune was hired in 1994 to turn the company around. He immediately introduced a number of programs—like rewarding attendance—to make Continental a better place to work. And employees responded. Under Bethune's leadership, Continental has been consistently profitable.

Foundations of Individual Behavior

Continental's program of giving out cars to employees as a reward for not missing work encourages attendance. In this chapter, we'll discuss how rewards shape behaviors like attendance through learning. First, however, we'll look at how biographical characteristics (such as gender and age) and ability effect employee performance and satisfaction.

BIOGRAPHICAL CHARACTERISTICS

As discussed in Chapter 1, this textbook is essentially concerned with finding and analyzing the variables that have an impact on employee productivity, absence, turnover, and satisfaction. The list of those variables—as shown in Exhibit 1-7—is long and contains some complicated concepts. Many of the concepts—motivation, say, or power and politics or organizational culture—are hard to assess. It might be valuable, then, to begin by looking at factors that are easily definable and readily available; data that can be obtained, for the most part, simply from information available in an employee's personnel file. What factors would these be? Obvious characteristics would be an employee's age, gender, marital status, and length of service with an organization. Fortunately, there is a sizable amount of research that has specifically analyzed many of these **biographical characteristics**.

Age

The relationship between age and job performance is likely to be an issue of increasing importance during the next decade. Why? There are at least three reasons. First, there is a widespread belief that job performance declines with increasing age. Regardless of whether it's true or not, a lot of people believe it and act on it.

AFTER STUDYING THIS CHAPTER, YOU SHOULD BE ABLE TO:

1. Define the key biographical characteristics.
2. Identify two types of ability.
3. Shape the behavior of others.
4. Distinguish between the four schedules of reinforcement.
5. Clarify the role of punishment in learning.
6. Practice self-management.

Second, as noted in Chapter 1, is the reality that the workforce is aging. Workers 55 and older are currently the fastest-growing sector of the labor force.[2] The third reason is U.S. legislation that, for all intents and purposes, outlaws mandatory retirement. Most U.S. workers today no longer have to retire at the age of 70.

What is the perception of older workers? Evidence indicates that employers hold mixed feelings.[3] They see a number of positive qualities that older workers bring to their jobs: specifically, experience, judgment, a strong work ethic, and commitment to quality. But older workers are also perceived as lacking flexibility and as being resistant to new technology. And in a time when organizations actively seek individuals who are adaptable and open to change, the negatives associated with age clearly hinder the initial hiring of older workers and increase the likelihood that they will be let go during cutbacks. Now let's take a look at the evidence. What effect does age actually have on turnover, absenteeism, productivity, and satisfaction?

The older you get, the less likely you are to quit your job. That conclusion is based on studies of the age–turnover relationship.[4] Of course, this shouldn't be too surprising. As workers get older, they have fewer alternative job opportunities. In addition, older workers are less likely to resign than are younger workers because their long tenure tends to provide them with higher wage rates, longer paid vacations, and more-attractive pension benefits.

It's tempting to assume that age is also inversely related to absenteeism. After all, if older workers are less likely to quit, won't they also demonstrate higher stability by coming to work more regularly? Not necessarily. Most studies do show an inverse relationship, but close examination finds that the age–absence relationship is partially a function of whether the absence is avoidable or unavoidable.[5] In general, older employees have lower rates of avoidable absence than do younger employees. However, they have higher rates of unavoidable absence, probably due to the poorer health associated with aging and the longer recovery period that older workers need when injured.

How does age affect productivity? There is a widespread belief that productivity declines with age. It is often assumed that an individual's skills—particularly speed, agility, strength, and coordination—decay over time and that prolonged job boredom and lack of intellectual stimulation all contribute to reduced productivity. The evidence, however, contradicts that belief and those assumptions. For instance, during a three-year period, a large hardware chain staffed one of its stores solely with employees over 50 and compared its results with those of five stores with younger employees. The store staffed by the over-50 employees was significantly more productive (measured in terms of sales generated against labor costs) than two of the other stores and held its own with the other three.[6] Other reviews of the research find that age and job performance are unrelated.[7] Moreover, this finding seems to be true for almost all types of jobs, professional and nonprofessional. The natural conclusion is that the demands of most jobs, even those with heavy manual labor requirements, are not extreme enough for any declines in physical skills attributable

McDonald's relies heavily on older workers to fill job vacancies. The company finds seniors to be highly productive and dependable employees.

to age to have an impact on productivity; or, if there is some decay due to age, it is offset by gains due to experience.[8]

Our final concern is the relationship between age and job satisfaction. On this issue, the evidence is mixed. Most studies indicate a positive association between age and satisfaction, at least up to age 60.[9] Other studies, however, have found a U-shaped relationship.[10] Several explanations could clear up these results, the most plausible being that these studies are intermixing professional and nonprofessional employees. When the two types are separated, satisfaction tends to continually increase among professionals as they age, whereas it falls among nonprofessionals during middle age and then rises again in the later years.

Gender

Few issues initiate more debates, misconceptions, and unsupported opinions than whether women perform as well on jobs as men do. In this section, we review the research on that issue.

The evidence suggests that the best place to begin is with the recognition that there are few, if any, important differences between men and women that will affect their job performance. There are, for instance, no consistent male–female differences in problem-solving ability, analytical skills, competitive drive, motivation, sociability, or learning ability.[11] Psychological studies have found that women are more willing to conform to authority and that men are more aggressive and more likely than women to have expectations of success, but those differences are minor. Given the significant changes that have taken place in the past 30 years in terms of increasing female participation rates in the workforce and rethinking what constitutes male and female roles, you should operate on the assumption that there is no significant difference in job productivity between men and women. Similarly, there is no evidence indicating that an employee's gender affects job satisfaction.[12]

One issue that does seem to differ between genders, especially when the employee has preschool-age children, is preference for work schedules.[13] Working mothers are more likely to prefer part-time work, flexible work schedules, and telecommuting in order to accommodate their family responsibilities.

But what about absence and turnover rates? Are women less stable employees than men? First, on the question of turnover, the evidence indicates no significant differences.[14] Women's quit rates are similar to those for men. The research on absence, however, consistently indicates that women have higher rates of absenteeism than men do.[15] The most logical explanation for this finding is that the research was conducted in North America, and North American culture has historically placed home and family responsibilities on the woman. When a child is ill or someone needs to stay home to wait for the plumber, it has been the woman who has traditionally taken time off from work. However, this research is undoubtedly time-bound.[16] The historical role of the woman in caring for children and as secondary breadwinner has definitely changed in the past generation, and a large proportion of men nowadays are as interested in day care and the problems associated with child care in general as are women.

Marital Status

There are not enough studies to draw any conclusions about the effect of marital status on productivity. But research consistently indicates that married employees have fewer absences, undergo less turnover, and are more satisfied with their jobs than are their unmarried coworkers.[17]

Marriage imposes increased responsibilities that may make a steady job more valuable and important. But the question of causation is not clear. It may very well be that conscientious and satisfied employees are more likely to be married. Another offshoot of this issue is that research has not pursued statuses other than single or married. Does being divorced or widowed have an impact on an employee's performance and satisfaction? What about couples who live together without being married? These are questions in need of investigation.

Tenure

The last biographical characteristic we'll look at is tenure. With the exception of the issue of male–female differences, probably no issue is more subject to misconceptions and speculations than the impact of seniority on job performance.

Extensive reviews of the seniority–productivity relationship have been conducted.[18] If we define seniority as time on a particular job, we can say that the most recent evidence demonstrates a positive relationship between seniority and job productivity. So tenure, expressed as work experience, appears to be a good predictor of employee productivity.

The research relating tenure to absence is quite straightforward. Studies consistently demonstrate seniority to be negatively related to absenteeism.[19] In fact, in terms of both frequency of absence and total days lost at work, tenure is the single most important explanatory variable.[20]

Tenure is also a potent variable in explaining turnover. The longer a person is in a job, the less likely he or she is to quit.[21] Moreover, consistent with research that suggests that past behavior is the best predictor of future behavior,[22] evidence indicates that tenure on an employee's previous job is a powerful predictor of that employee's future turnover.[23]

The evidence indicates that tenure and satisfaction are positively related.[24] In fact, when age and tenure are treated separately, tenure appears to be a more consistent and stable predictor of job satisfaction than is chronological age.

ABILITY

Contrary to what we were taught in grade school, we weren't all created equal. Most of us are to the left of the median on some normally distributed ability curve. Regardless of how motivated you are, it is unlikely that you can act as well as Meryl Streep, play golf as well as Tiger Woods, write horror stories as well as Stephen King, or sing as well as Whitney Houston. Of course, just because we aren't all equal in abilities does not imply that some individuals are inherently inferior to others. What we are acknowledging is that everyone has strengths and weaknesses in terms of ability that make him or her relatively superior or inferior to others in performing certain tasks or activities.[25] From management's standpoint, the issue is not whether people differ in terms of their abilities. They clearly do. The issue is knowing how people differ in abilities and using that knowledge to increase the likelihood that an employee will perform his or her job well.

ability

An individual's capacity to perform the various tasks in a job.

What does ability mean? As we will use the term, **ability** refers to an individual's capacity to perform the various tasks in a job. It is a current assessment of what one can do. An individual's overall abilities are essentially made up of two sets of factors: intellectual and physical abilities.

Intellectual Abilities

intellectual ability

The capacity to do mental activities.

Intellectual abilities are those needed to perform mental activities. Intelligence quotient (IQ) tests, for example, are designed to ascertain one's general intellectual abilities. So, too, are popular college admission tests such as the SAT and ACT and

Dimensions of Intellectual Ability

EXHIBIT

2-1

Dimension	Description	Job Example
Number aptitude	Ability to do speedy and accurate arithmetic	Accountant: Computing the sales tax on a set of items
Verbal comprehension	Ability to understand what is read or heard and the relationship of words to each other	Plant manager: Following corporate policies
Perceptual speed	Ability to identify visual similarities and differences quickly and accurately	Fire investigator: Identifying clues to support a charge of arson
Inductive reasoning	Ability to identify a logical sequence in a problem and then solve the problem	Market researcher: Forecasting demand for a product in the next time period
Deductive reasoning	Ability to use logic and assess the implications of an argument	Supervisor: Choosing between two different suggestions offered by employees
Spatial visualization	Ability to imagine how an object would look if its position in space were changed	Interior decorator: Redecorating an office
Memory	Ability to retain and recall past experiences	Salesperson: Remembering the names of customers

graduate admission tests in business (GMAT), law (LSAT), and medicine (MCAT). The seven most frequently cited dimensions making up intellectual abilities are number aptitude, verbal comprehension, perceptual speed, inductive reasoning, deductive reasoning, spatial visualization, and memory.[26] Exhibit 2-1 describes those dimensions.

Jobs differ in the demands they place on incumbents to use their intellectual abilities. Generally speaking, the more information-processing demands that exist in a job, the more general intelligence and verbal abilities will be necessary to perform the job successfully.[27] Of course, a high IQ is not a prerequisite for all jobs. In fact, for many jobs—in which employee behavior is highly routine and there are little or no opportunities to exercise discretion—a high IQ may be unrelated to performance. On the other hand, a careful review of the evidence demonstrates that tests that assess verbal, numerical, spatial, and perceptual abilities are valid predictors of job proficiency at all levels of jobs.[28] Therefore, tests that measure specific dimensions of intelligence have been found to be strong predictors of future job performance. This explains why a company like Microsoft emphasizes assessing candidates' intelligence as a key element in its interview process.

The major dilemma faced by employers who use mental ability tests for selection, promotion, training, and similar personnel decisions is that they may have a negative impact on racial and ethnic groups.[29] The evidence indicates that some minority groups score, on the average, as much as one standard deviation lower than whites on verbal, numerical, and spatial ability tests.

In the past decade, researchers have begun to expand the meaning of intelligence beyond mental abilities. The most recent evidence suggests that intelligence can be better understood by breaking it down into four subparts: cognitive, social, emotional, and cultural.[30] Cognitive intelligence encompasses the aptitudes that have long been tapped by traditional intelligence tests. Social intelligence is a person's ability to relate effectively to others. Emotional intelligence is the ability to identify, understand, and manage emotions. And cultural intelligence is awareness of cross-cultural differences and the ability to function successfully in cross-cultural situations. Although this line of inquiry—toward **multiple intelligences**—is in its infancy, it does hold considerable promise. For instance, it may be able to help us explain why so-called smart people—those with high cognitive intelligence—don't necessarily adapt well to everyday life, work well with others, or succeed when placed in leadership roles.

multiple intelligences

Intelligence contains four subparts: cognitive, social, emotional, and cultural.

Physical Abilities

To the same degree that intellectual abilities play a larger role in complex jobs with demanding information-processing requirements, specific **physical abilities** gain importance for successfully doing less-skilled and more-standardized jobs. For example, jobs in which success demands stamina, manual dexterity, leg strength, or similar talents require management to identify an employee's physical capabilities.

physical ability

The capacity to do tasks demanding stamina, dexterity, strength, and similar characteristics.

Research on the requirements needed in hundreds of jobs has identified nine basic abilities involved in the performance of physical tasks.[31] These are described in Exhibit 2-2. Individuals differ in the extent to which they have each of these abilities. Not surprisingly, there is also little relationship between them: A high score on one is no assurance of a high score on others. High employee performance is likely to be achieved when management has ascertained the extent to which a job requires each of the nine abilities and then ensures that employees in that job have those abilities.

EXHIBIT 2-2	Nine Basic Physical Abilities	
	Strength Factors	
	1. Dynamic strength	Ability to exert muscular force repeatedly or continuously over time
	2. Trunk strength	Ability to exert muscular strength using the trunk (particularly abdominal) muscles
	3. Static strength	Ability to exert force against external objects
	4. Explosive strength	Ability to expend a maximum of energy in one or a series of explosive acts
	Flexibility Factors	
	5. Extent flexibility	Ablity to move the trunk and back muscles as far as possible
	6. Dynamic flexibility	Ability to make rapid, repeated flexing movements
	Other Factors	
	7. Body coordination	Ability to coordinate the simultaneous actions of different parts of the body
	8. Balance	Ability to maintain equilibrium despite forces pulling off balance
	9. Stamina	Ability to continue maximum effort requiring prolonged effort over time

Source: Reprinted with permission of *HRMagazine* published by the Society for Human Resource Management, Alexandria, VA.

The Ability–Job Fit

Our concern is with explaining and predicting the behavior of people at work. In this section, we have demonstrated that jobs make differing demands on people and that people differ in the abilities they possess. Therefore, employee performance is enhanced when there is a high ability–job fit.

The specific intellectual or physical abilities required for adequate job performance depend on the ability requirements of the job. So, for example, airline pilots need strong spatial-visualization abilities; beach lifeguards need both strong spatial-visualization abilities and body coordination; senior executives need verbal abilities; high-rise construction workers need balance; and journalists with weak reasoning abilities would likely have difficulty meeting minimum job-performance standards. Directing attention at only the employee's abilities or only the ability requirements of the job ignores the fact that employee performance depends on the interaction of the two.

What predictions can we make when the fit is poor? As alluded to previously, if employees lack the required abilities, they are likely to fail. If you are hired as a word processor and you cannot meet the job's basic keyboard typing requirements, your performance is going to be poor irrespective of your positive attitude or your high level of motivation. When the ability–job fit is out of sync because the employee has abilities that far exceed the requirements of the job, our predictions would be very different. Job performance is likely to be adequate, but there will be organizational inefficiencies and possible declines in employee satisfaction. Given that pay tends to reflect the highest skill level that employees possess, if an employee's abilities far exceed those necessary to do the job, management will be paying more than it needs to. Abilities significantly above those required can also reduce the employee's job satisfaction when the employee's desire to use his or her abilities is particularly strong and is frustrated by the limitations of the job.

LEARNING

All complex behavior is learned. If we want to explain and predict behavior, we need to understand how people learn. In this section, we define learning, present three popular learning theories, and describe how managers can facilitate employee learning.

A Definition of Learning

What is **learning**? A psychologist's definition is considerably broader than the layperson's view that "it's what we did when we went to school." In actuality, each of us is continuously "going to school." Learning occurs all the time. Therefore, a generally accepted definition of learning is *any relatively permanent change in behavior that occurs as a result of experience*.[32] Ironically, we can say that changes in behavior indicate that learning has taken place and that learning is a change in behavior.

Obviously, the foregoing definition suggests that we shall never see someone "learning." We can see changes taking place but not the learning itself. The concept is theoretical and, hence, not directly observable:

> You have seen people in the process of learning, you have seen people who behave in a particular way as a result of learning and some of you (in fact, I guess the majority of you) have "learned" at some time in your life. In other words, we infer that learning has taken place if an individual behaves, reacts, responds as a result of experience in a manner different from the way he formerly behaved.[33]

learning

Any relatively permanent change in behavior that occurs as a result of experience.

Our definition has several components that deserve clarification. First, learning involves change. Change may be good or bad from an organizational point of view. People can learn unfavorable behaviors—to hold prejudices or to restrict their output, for example—as well as favorable behaviors. Second, the change must be relatively permanent. Temporary changes may be only reflexive and may not represent learning. Therefore, the requirement that learning must be relatively permanent rules out behavioral changes caused by fatigue or temporary adaptations. Third, our definition is concerned with behavior. Learning takes place when there is a change in actions. A change in an individual's thought processes or attitudes, if not accompanied by a change in behavior, would not be learning. Finally, some form of experience is necessary for learning. Experience may be acquired directly through observation or practice, or it may be acquired indirectly, as through reading. The crucial test still remains: Does this experience result in a relatively permanent change in behavior? If the answer is Yes, we can say that learning has taken place.

Theories of Learning

How do we learn? Three theories have been offered to explain the process by which we acquire patterns of behavior. These are classical conditioning, operant conditioning, and social learning.

Classical Conditioning **Classical conditioning** grew out of experiments to teach dogs to salivate in response to the ringing of a bell, conducted at the turn of the century by Russian physiologist Ivan Pavlov.[34] A simple surgical procedure allowed Pavlov to measure accurately the amount of saliva secreted by a dog. When Pavlov presented the dog with a piece of meat, the dog exhibited a noticeable increase in salivation. When Pavlov withheld the presentation of meat and merely rang a bell, the dog did not salivate. Then Pavlov proceeded to link the meat and the ringing of the bell. After repeatedly hearing the bell before getting the food, the dog began to salivate as soon as the bell rang. After a while, the dog would salivate merely at the sound of the bell, even if no food was offered. In effect, the dog had learned to respond—that is, to salivate—to the bell. Let's review this experiment to introduce the key concepts in classical conditioning.

The meat was an *unconditioned stimulus*; it invariably caused the dog to react in a specific way. The reaction that took place whenever the unconditioned stimulus occurred was called the *unconditioned response* (or the noticeable increase in salivation, in this case). The bell was an artificial stimulus, or what we call the *conditioned stimulus*. Although it was originally neutral, after the bell was paired with the meat (an unconditioned stimulus), it eventually produced a response when presented alone. The last key concept is the *conditioned response*. This describes the behavior of the dog; it salivated in reaction to the bell alone.

Using these concepts, we can summarize classical conditioning. Essentially, learning a conditioned response involves building up an association between a conditioned stimulus and an unconditioned stimulus. When the stimuli, one compelling and the other one neutral, are paired, the neutral one becomes a conditioned stimulus and, hence, takes on the properties of the unconditioned stimulus.

Classical conditioning can be used to explain why Christmas carols often bring back pleasant memories of childhood; the songs are associated with the festive Christmas spirit and evoke fond memories and feelings of euphoria. In an organizational setting, we can also see classical conditioning operating. For example, at one manufacturing plant, every time the top executives from the head office

Learning occurs throughout life. Patrick Bernhardt is becoming a teacher after changing careers. He not only learns on the job but also attends evening classes three times a week. "This is the hardest thing I've ever done," he says, "but the sense of satisfaction is great."

classical conditioning

A type of conditioning in which an individual responds to some stimulus that would not ordinarily produce such a response.

THE FAR SIDE® By GARY LARSON

© 1993 FarWorks, Inc. All Rights Reserved/Dist. by Creators Syndicate

Larson

Unbeknownst to most students of psychology, Pavlov's first experiment was to ring a bell and cause his dog to attack Freud's cat.

were scheduled to make a visit, the plant management would clean up the administrative offices and wash the windows. This went on for years. Eventually, employees would turn on their best behavior and look prim and proper whenever the windows were cleaned—even in those occasional instances when the cleaning was not paired with the visit from the top brass. People had learned to associate the cleaning of the windows with a visit from the head office.

Classical conditioning is passive. Something happens and we react in a specific way. It is elicited in response to a specific, identifiable event. As such, it can explain simple reflexive behaviors. But most behavior—particularly the complex behavior of individuals in organizations—is emitted rather than elicited. It is voluntary rather than reflexive. For example, employees choose to arrive at work on time, ask their boss for help with problems, or "goof off" when no one is watching. The learning of those behaviors is better understood by looking at operant conditioning.

Operant Conditioning **Operant conditioning** argues that behavior is a function of its consequences. People learn to behave to get something they want or to avoid something they don't want. Operant behavior means voluntary or learned behavior in contrast to reflexive or unlearned behavior. The tendency to repeat such behavior is influenced by the reinforcement or lack of reinforcement brought about by the consequences of the behavior. Therefore, reinforcement strengthens a behavior and increases the likelihood that it will be repeated.

operant conditioning

A type of conditioning in which desired voluntary behavior leads to a reward or prevents a punishment.

What Pavlov did for classical conditioning, the Harvard psychologist B. F. Skinner did for operant conditioning.[35] Building on earlier work in the field, Skinner's research extensively expanded our knowledge of operant conditioning. Even his staunchest critics, who represent a sizable group, admit that his operant concepts work.

Behavior is assumed to be determined from without—that is, learned—rather than from within—reflexive, or unlearned. Skinner argued that creating pleasing consequences to follow specific forms of behavior would increase the frequency of that behavior. People will most likely engage in desired behaviors if they are positively reinforced for doing so. Rewards are most effective if they immediately follow the desired response. In addition, behavior that is not rewarded, or is punished, is less likely to be repeated.

You see illustrations of operant conditioning everywhere. For example, any situation in which it is either explicitly stated or implicitly suggested that reinforcements are contingent on some action on your part involves the use of operant learning. Your instructor says that if you want a high grade in the course you must supply correct answers on the test. A commissioned salesperson wanting to earn a sizable income finds that doing so is contingent on generating high sales in her territory. Of course, the linkage can also work to teach the individual to engage in behaviors that work against the best interests of the organization. Assume that your boss tells you that if you will work overtime during the next three-week busy season, you will be compensated for it at the next performance appraisal. However, when performance appraisal time comes, you find that you are given no positive reinforcement for your overtime work. The next time your boss asks you to work overtime, what will you do? You'll probably decline! Your behavior can be explained by operant conditioning: If a behavior fails to be positively reinforced, the probability that the behavior will be repeated declines.

Social Learning Individuals can also learn by observing what happens to other people and just by being told about something, as well as by direct experiences. So, for example, much of what we have learned comes from watching models— parents, teachers, peers, motion picture and television performers, bosses, and so forth. This view that we can learn through both observation and direct experience has been called **social-learning theory**.[36]

Although social-learning theory is an extension of operant conditioning— that is, it assumes that behavior is a function of consequences—it also acknowledges the existence of observational learning and the importance of perception in learning. People respond to how they perceive and define consequences, not to the objective consequences themselves.

The influence of models is central to the social-learning viewpoint. Four processes have been found to determine the influence that a model will have on an individual. As we will show later in this chapter, the inclusion of the following processes when management sets up employee-training programs will significantly improve the likelihood that the programs will be successful:

1. *Attentional processes.*   People learn from a model only when they recognize and pay attention to its critical features. We tend to be most influenced by models that are attractive, repeatedly available, important to us, or similar to us in our estimation.
2. *Retention processes.*   A model's influence will depend on how well the individual remembers the model's action after the model is no longer readily available.

social-learning theory

People can learn through observation and direct experience.

M Y T H

"You Can't Teach an Old Dog New Tricks!"

This statement is false. It reflects the widely held stereotype that older workers have difficulties in adapting to new methods and techniques. Studies consistently demonstrate that older employees are *perceived* as being relatively inflexible, resistant to change, and less trainable than their younger counterparts, particularly with respect to information technology skills.[37] But these perceptions are wrong.

The evidence indicates that older workers (typically defined as people aged 50 and over) want to learn and are just as capable of learning as any other employee group. Older workers do seem to be somewhat less efficient in acquiring complex or de-manding skills. That is, they may take longer to train. But once trained, they perform at levels comparable to those of younger workers.[38]

The ability to acquire the skills, knowledge, or behavior necessary to perform a job at a given level—that is, trainability—has been the subject of much research. And the evidence indicates that there are differences between people in their trainability. A number of individual-difference factors (such as ability, motivational level, and personality) have been found to significantly influence learning and training outcomes.[39] However, age has not been found to influence these outcomes.

---

3. *Motor reproduction processes.* After a person has seen a new behavior by observing the model, the watching must be converted to doing. This process then demonstrates that the individual can perform the modeled activities.

4. *Reinforcement processes.* Individuals will be motivated to exhibit the modeled behavior if positive incentives or rewards are provided. Behaviors that are positively reinforced will be given more attention, learned better, and performed more often.

Shaping: A Managerial Tool

Because learning takes place on the job as well as prior to it, managers will be concerned with how they can teach employees to behave in ways that most benefit the organization. When we attempt to mold individuals by guiding their learning in graduated steps, we are **shaping behavior**.

Consider the situation in which an employee's behavior is significantly different from that sought by management. If management rewarded the individual only when he or she showed desirable responses, there might be very little reinforcement taking place. In such a case, shaping offers a logical approach toward achieving the desired behavior.

We *shape* behavior by systematically reinforcing each successive step that moves the individual closer to the desired response. If an employee who has chronically been a half-hour late for work comes in only 20 minutes late, we can reinforce that improvement. Reinforcement would increase as responses more closely approximated the desired behavior.

shaping behavior
Systematically reinforcing each successive step that moves an individual closer to the desired response.

Methods of Shaping Behavior There are four ways in which to shape behavior: through positive reinforcement, negative reinforcement, punishment, and extinction.

Following a response with something pleasant is called *positive reinforcement*. This would describe, for instance, the boss who praises an employee for a job well done. Following a response by the termination or withdrawal of something unpleasant is called *negative reinforcement*. If your college instructor asks a question and you don't know the answer, looking through your lecture notes is likely to preclude your being called on. This is a negative reinforcement because you have learned that looking busily through your notes prevents the instructor from calling on you. *Punishment* is causing an unpleasant condition in an attempt to eliminate an undesirable behavior. Giving an employee a two-day suspension from work without pay for showing up drunk is an example of punishment. Eliminating any reinforcement that is maintaining a behavior is called *extinction*. When the behavior is not reinforced, it tends to be gradually extinguished. College instructors who wish to discourage students from asking questions in class can eliminate this behavior in their students by ignoring those who raise their hands to ask questions. Hand-raising will become extinct when it is invariably met with an absence of reinforcement.

Both positive and negative reinforcement result in learning. They strengthen a response and increase the probability of repetition. In the preceding illustrations, praise strengthens and increases the behavior of doing a good job because praise is desired. The behavior of "looking busy" is similarly strengthened and increased by its terminating the undesirable consequence of being called on by the teacher. However, both punishment and extinction weaken behavior and tend to decrease its subsequent frequency.

Reinforcement, whether it is positive or negative, has an impressive record as a shaping tool. Our interest, therefore, is in reinforcement rather than in punish-

---

OB in the News

The High-Tech Stock Bubble and Reinforcement Schedules

The Nasdaq stock index, which is heavily laden with the stocks of high-tech and Internet-related companies, soared to over 5000 in March 2000. In 1998 and 1999, this index had been rising at better than 80 percent per year. In spite of stratospheric price-earnings ratios (many of the fastest-rising stocks, in fact, had no earnings and were losing tens of millions of dollars a month), most stock analysts continued to recommend that investors buy stocks in companies such as Cisco Systems, Oracle, Pets.com, and Amazon.com because of the analysts' belief that the price of these stocks would go a whole lot higher. They were wrong (in the summer of 2002, the Nasdaq index was below 1400), but millions of investors bought into the analysts' irrational exuberance.

With the rally in technology stocks in the late 1990s came a change in the way that many people looked at their investment portfolios. Instead of passively handing their money over to a traditional stockbroker and pursuing a long-term strategy, many people became aggressive traders. They opened up online brokerage accounts and relied on real-time quotes and CNBC to provide them with a day-long supply of market news and stock recommendations. They actively bought and sold stocks, in some cases selling a stock within minutes of buying it if they could lock in a quick profit.

In retrospect, the explosive run-up in the Nasdaq index was an example of the power of intermittent reinforcement schedules. Many of the investors who bid up Internet shares were happy to admit they knew nothing about business or technology or valuation theories. Like a slot-machine addict in Las Vegas, they just wanted in on the game. Ironically, for many traders during 1998 and 1999, trading in technology stocks actually looked more like continuous reinforcement than intermittent. Everything they bought went up in price. A large number of investors who stood on the sidelines, chastising the foolishness of buying "Internet dreams," eventually began to consider themselves fools for not playing the game. Why stand on the sidelines, watching everyone else make money, when they could play too? By spring 2000, millions of historically conservative investors had been sucked into the high-tech bubble and ended up losing a large part of their savings and retirement portfolios.

Source: Based on *Wall Street Journal* editorial, March 7, 2001, p. A23.

ment or extinction. A review of research findings on the impact of reinforcement upon behavior in organizations concluded that

1. Some type of reinforcement is necessary to produce a change in behavior.
2. Some types of rewards are more effective than others for use in organizations.
3. The speed with which learning takes place and the permanence of its effects will be determined by the timing of reinforcement.[40]

Point 3 is extremely important and deserves considerable elaboration.

Schedules of Reinforcement The two major types of reinforcement schedules are *continuous* and *intermittent*. A **continuous reinforcement** schedule reinforces the desired behavior each and every time it is demonstrated. Take, for example, the case of someone who has historically had trouble arriving at work on time. Every time he is not tardy his manager might compliment him on his desirable behavior. In an intermittent schedule, on the other hand, not every instance of the desirable behavior is reinforced, but reinforcement is given often enough to make the behavior worth repeating. This latter schedule can be compared to the workings of a slot machine, which people will continue to play even when they know that it is adjusted to give a considerable return to the gambling house. The intermittent payoffs occur just often enough to reinforce the behavior of slipping in coins and pulling the handle. Evidence indicates that the intermittent, or varied, form of reinforcement tends to promote more resistance to extinction than does the continuous form.[41]

An **intermittent reinforcement** can be of a ratio or interval type. *Ratio schedules* depend on how many responses the subject makes. The individual is reinforced after giving a certain number of specific types of behavior. *Interval schedules* depend on how much time has passed since the previous reinforcement. With interval schedules, the individual is reinforced on the first appropriate behavior after a particular time has elapsed. A reinforcement can also be classified as fixed or variable.

When rewards are spaced at uniform time intervals, the reinforcement schedule is of the **fixed-interval** type. The critical variable is time, and it is held constant. This is the predominant schedule for most salaried workers in North America. When you get your paycheck on a weekly, semimonthly, monthly, or other predetermined time basis, you are rewarded on a fixed-interval reinforcement schedule.

If rewards are distributed in time so that reinforcements are unpredictable, the schedule is of the **variable-interval** type. When an instructor advises her class that pop quizzes will be given during the term (the exact number of which is unknown to the students) and the quizzes will account for 20 percent of the term grade, she is using a variable-interval schedule. Similarly, a series of randomly timed unannounced visits to a company office by the corporate audit staff is an example of a variable-interval schedule.

This Boeing manager (center) makes it a point to visit production areas on a random or irregular schedule. This kind of variable-interval inspection tour is designed to keep employees on their toes.

continuous reinforcement

A desired behavior is reinforced each time it is demonstrated.

intermittent reinforcement

A desired behavior is reinforced often enough to make the behavior worth repeating but not every time it is demonstrated.

fixed-interval schedule

Rewards are spaced at uniform time intervals.

variable-interval schedule

Rewards are initiated after a fixed or constant number of responses.

EXHIBIT

2-4

Schedules of Reinforcement

Reinforcement Schedule	Nature of Reinforcement	Effect on Behavior	Example
Continuous	Reward given after each desired behavior	Fast learning of new behavior but rapid extinction	Compliments
Fixed-interval	Reward given at fixed time intervals	Average and irregular performance with rapid extinction	Weekly paychecks
Variable-interval	Reward given at variable times	Moderately high and stable performance with slow extinction	Pop quizzes
Fixed-ratio	Reward given at fixed amounts of output	High and stable performance attained quickly but also with rapid extinction	Piece-rate pay
Variable-ratio	Reward given at variable amounts of output	Very high performance with slow extinction	Commissioned sales

fixed-ratio schedule

Rewards are initiated after a fixed or constant number of responses.

In a **fixed-ratio** schedule, after a fixed or constant number of responses are given, a reward is initiated. For example, a piece-rate incentive plan is a fixed-ratio schedule; the employee receives a reward based on the number of work pieces generated. If the piece rate for a zipper installer in a dressmaking factory is $5.00 a dozen, the reinforcement (money in this case) is fixed to the number of zippers sewn into garments. After every dozen is sewn in, the installer has earned another $5.00.

variable-ratio schedule

The reward varies relative to the behavior of the individual.

When the reward varies relative to the behavior of the individual, he or she is said to be reinforced on a **variable-ratio** schedule. Salespeople on commission are examples of individuals on such a reinforcement schedule. On some occasions, they may make a sale after only two calls on a potential customer. On other occasions, they might need to make 20 or more calls to secure a sale. The reward, then, is variable in relation to the number of successful calls the salesperson makes. Exhibit 2-4 summarizes the schedules of reinforcement.

Reinforcement Schedules and Behavior   Continuous reinforcement schedules can lead to early satiation, and under this schedule behavior tends to weaken rapidly when reinforcers are withheld. However, continuous reinforcers are appropriate for newly emitted, unstable, or low-frequency responses. In contrast, intermittent reinforcers preclude early satiation because they don't follow every response. They are appropriate for stable or high-frequency responses.

In general, variable schedules tend to lead to higher performance than fixed schedules (see Exhibit 2-5). For example, as noted previously, most employees in organizations are paid on fixed-interval schedules. But such a schedule does not clearly link performance and rewards. The reward is given for time spent on the job rather than for a specific response (performance). In contrast, variable-interval schedules generate high rates of response and more stable and consistent behavior because of a high correlation between performance and reward and because of the uncertainty involved—the employee tends to be more alert because there is a surprise factor.

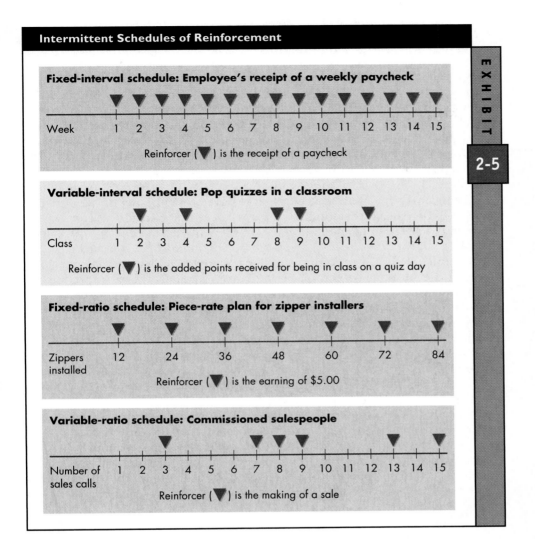

EXHIBIT

2-5

Intermittent Schedules of Reinforcement

Fixed-interval schedule: Employee's receipt of a weekly paycheck

Week   1 2 3 4 5 6 7 8 9 10 11 12 13 14 15

Reinforcer (▼) is the receipt of a paycheck

Variable-interval schedule: Pop quizzes in a classroom

Class   1 2 3 4 5 6 7 8 9 10 11 12 13 14 15

Reinforcer (▼) is the added points received for being in class on a quiz day

Fixed-ratio schedule: Piece-rate plan for zipper installers

Zippers   12   24   36   48   60   72   84
installed

Reinforcer (▼) is the earning of $5.00

Variable-ratio schedule: Commissioned salespeople

Number of   1 2 3 4 5 6 7 8 9 10 11 12 13 14 15
sales calls

Reinforcer (▼) is the making of a sale

Behavior Modification   There is a now-classic study that took place a number of years ago with freight packers at Emery Air Freight (now part of FedEx).[42] Emery's management wanted packers to use freight containers for shipments whenever possible because of specific economic savings. When packers were asked about the percentage of shipments contained, the standard reply was 90 percent. An analysis by Emery found, however, that the actual container utilization rate was only 45 percent. In order to encourage employees to use containers, management established a program of feedback and positive reinforcements. Each packer was instructed to keep a checklist of his or her daily packings, both containerized and noncontainerized. At the end of each day, the packer computed his or her container utilization rate. Almost unbelievably, container utilization jumped to more than 90 percent on the first day of the program and held at that level. Emery reported that this simple program of feedback and positive reinforcements saved the company $2 million over a three-year period.

This program at Emery Air Freight illustrates the use of behavior modification, or what has become more popularly called **OB Mod**.[43] It represents the application of reinforcement concepts to individuals in the work setting.

OB Mod

The application of reinforcement concepts to individuals in the work setting.

The typical OB Mod program follows a five-step problem-solving model: (1) identifying critical behaviors; (2) developing baseline data; (3) identifying behavioral consequences; (4) developing and implementing an intervention strategy; and (5) evaluating performance improvement.[44]

Everything an employee does on his or her job is not equally important in terms of performance outcomes. The first step in OB Mod, therefore, is to identify the critical behaviors that make a significant impact on the employee's job performance. These are those 5 to 10 percent of behaviors that may account for up to 70 or 80 percent of each employee's performance. Using containers whenever possible by freight packers at Emery Air Freight is an example of a critical behavior.

The second step requires the manager to develop some baseline performance data. This is obtained by determining the number of times the identified behavior is occurring under present conditions. In our freight packing example at Emery, this would have revealed that 45 percent of all shipments were containerized.

The third step is to perform a functional analysis to identify the behavioral contingencies or consequences of performance. This tells the manager the antecedent cues that emit the behavior and the consequences that are currently maintaining it. At Emery Air Freight, social norms and the greater difficulty in packing containers were the antecedent cues. This encouraged the practice of packing items separately. Moreover, the consequences for continuing the behavior, prior to the OB Mod intervention, were social acceptance and escaping more demanding work.

This office worker handles a number of tasks—answering phones, filing, copying, keyboarding—but only a few behaviors will account for about 70 to 80 percent of her performance. Determining what those critical behaviors are is the first step in designing an OB Mod program to reinforce desired behaviors.

Once the functional analysis is complete, the manager is ready to develop and implement an intervention strategy to strengthen desirable performance behaviors and weaken undesirable behaviors. The appropriate strategy will entail changing some elements of the performance–reward linkage—structure, processes, technology, groups, or the task—with the goal of making high-level performance more rewarding. In the Emery example, the work technology was altered to require the keeping of a checklist. The checklist plus the computation, at the end of the day, of a container utilization rate acted to reinforce the desirable behavior of using containers.

The final step in OB Mod is to evaluate performance improvement. In the Emery intervention, the immediate improvement in the container utilization rate demonstrated that behavioral change took place. That it rose to 90 percent and held at that level further indicates that learning took place. That is, the employees underwent a relatively permanent change in behavior.

OB Mod has been used by a number of organizations to improve employee productivity, to reduce errors, absenteeism, tardiness, accident rates, and to improve friendliness toward customers.[45] For instance, a clothing manufacturer saved $60,000 in one year from fewer absences. A packing firm improved productivity 16 percent, cut errors by 40 percent, and reduced accidents by more than 43 percent—resulting in savings of over $1 million. A bank successfully used OB Mod to increase the friendliness of its tellers, which led to a demonstrable improvement in customer satisfaction.

Some Specific Organizational Applications

We have alluded to a number of situations in which learning theory could be helpful to managers. For instance, we opened this chapter by showing how Continental Airlines used a variable-ratio schedule to reward employees for good attendance. In this section, we will briefly look at four specific applications: substituting well pay for sick pay, disciplining problem employees, developing effective employee training programs, and applying learning theory to self-management.

Well Pay Versus Sick Pay Most organizations provide their salaried employees with paid sick leave as part of the employee's benefit program. But, ironically, organizations with paid sick leave programs experience almost twice the absenteeism of organizations without such programs.[46] The reality is that sick leave programs reinforce the wrong behavior—absence from work. When employees receive 10 paid sick days a year, it's the unusual employee who isn't sure to use them all up, regardless of whether he or she is sick. Organizations should reward *attendance* not *absence*.

As a case in point, one Midwest organization implemented a well-pay program that paid a bonus to employees who had no absence for any given four-week period and then paid for sick leave only after the first eight hours of absence.[47] Evaluation of the well-pay program found that it produced increased savings to the organization, reduced absenteeism, increased productivity, and improved employee satisfaction.

Forbes magazine used the same approach to cut its health care costs.[48] It rewarded employees who stayed healthy and didn't file medical claims by paying them the difference between $500 and their medical claims, then doubling the amount. So if someone submitted no claims in a given year, he or she would receive $1,000 ($500 × 2). By rewarding employees for good health, *Forbes* cut its major medical and dental claims by over 30 percent.

Employee Discipline Every manager will, at some time, have to deal with an employee who drinks on the job, is insubordinate, steals company property, arrives consistently late for work, or engages in similar problem behaviors. Managers will respond with disciplinary actions such as oral reprimands, written warnings, and temporary suspensions. But our knowledge about punishment's effect on behavior indicates that the use of discipline carries costs. It may provide only a short-term solution and result in serious side effects.

Disciplining employees for undesirable behaviors tells them only what *not* to do. It doesn't tell them what alternative behaviors are preferred. The result is that this form of punishment frequently leads to only short-term suppression of the undesirable behavior rather than its elimination. Continued use of punishment, rather than positive reinforcement, also tends to produce a fear of the manager. As the punishing agent, the manager becomes associated in the employee's mind with adverse consequences. Employees respond by "hiding" from their boss. Hence, the use of punishment can undermine manager–employee relations.

Discipline does have a place in organizations. In practice, it tends to be popular because of its ability to produce fast results in the short run. Moreover, managers are reinforced for using discipline because it produces an immediate change in the employee's behavior.

Developing Training Programs Most organizations have some type of systematic training program. More specifically, U.S. corporations with 100 or more employees spent in excess of $58 billion in one recent year on formal training for 47.3 million workers.[49] Can these organizations draw from our discussion of learning in order to improve the effectiveness of their training programs? Certainly.

Social-learning theory offers such a guide. It tells us that training should offer a model to grab the trainee's attention; provide motivational properties; help the trainee to file away what he or she has learned for later use; provide opportunities to practice new behaviors; offer positive rewards for accomplishments; and, if the training has taken place off the job, allow the trainee some opportunity to transfer what he or she has learned to the job.[50]

Self-Management   Organizational applications of learning concepts are not restricted to managing the behavior of others. These concepts can also be used to allow individuals to manage their own behavior and, in so doing, reduce the need for managerial control. This is called **self-management**.[51]

self-management

Learning techniques that allow individuals to manage their own behavior so that less external management control is necessary.

Self-management requires an individual to deliberately manipulate stimuli, internal processes, and responses to achieve personal behavioral outcomes. The basic processes involve observing one's own behavior, comparing the behavior with a standard, and rewarding oneself if the behavior meets the standard.

So how might self-management be applied? Here's an illustration. A group of state government blue-collar employees received eight hours of training in which they were taught self-management skills.[52] They were then shown how the skills could be used for improving job attendance. They were instructed on how to set specific goals for job attendance, in both the short and intermediate term. They learned how to write a behavioral contract with themselves and to identify self-chosen reinforcers. Finally, they learned the importance of self-monitoring their attendance behavior and administering incentives when they achieved their goals. The net result for these participants was a significant improvement in job attendance.

SUMMARY AND IMPLICATIONS FOR MANAGERS

This chapter looked at three individual variables—biographical characteristics, ability, and learning. Let's now try to summarize what we found and consider their importance for the manager who is trying to understand organizational behavior.

Biographical Characteristics   Biographical characteristics are readily available to managers. For the most part, they include data that are contained in almost every employee's personnel file. The most important conclusions we can draw after our review of the evidence are that age seems to have no relationship to productivity; older workers and those with longer tenure are less likely to resign; and married employees have fewer absences, less turnover, and report higher job satisfaction than do unmarried employees. But what value can this information have for managers? The obvious answer is that it can help in making choices among job applicants.

Ability   Ability directly influences an employee's level of performance and satisfaction through the ability–job fit. Given management's desire to get a compatible fit, what can be done?

First, an effective selection process will improve the fit. A job analysis will provide information about jobs currently being done and the abilities that individuals need to perform the jobs adequately. Applicants can then be tested, interviewed, and evaluated on the degree to which they possess the necessary abilities.

Second, promotion and transfer decisions affecting individuals already in the organization's employ should reflect the abilities of candidates. As with new employees, care should be taken to assess critical abilities that incumbents will need in the job and to match those requirements with the organization's human resources.

Third, the fit can be improved by fine-tuning the job to better match an incumbent's abilities. Often, modifications can be made in the job that, while not having a significant impact on the job's basic activities, better adapts it to the specific talents of a given employee. Examples would be to change some of the equipment used or to reorganize tasks within a group of employees.

A final alternative is to provide training for employees. This is applicable to both new workers and job incumbents. Training can keep the abilities of incumbents current or provide new skills as times and conditions change.

Learning Any observable change in behavior is prima facie evidence that learning has taken place. What we want to do, of course, is to ascertain if learning concepts provide us with any insights that would allow us to explain and predict behavior.

Positive reinforcement is a powerful tool for modifying behavior. By identifying and rewarding performance-enhancing behaviors, management increases the likelihood that they will be repeated.

Our knowledge about learning further suggests that reinforcement is a more effective tool than punishment. Although punishment eliminates undesired behavior more quickly than negative reinforcement does, punished behavior tends to be only temporarily suppressed rather than permanently changed. And punishment may produce unpleasant side effects such as lower morale and higher absenteeism or turnover. In addition, the recipients of punishment tend to become resentful of the punisher. Managers, therefore, are advised to use reinforcement rather than punishment.

Finally, managers should expect that employees will look to them as models. Managers who are constantly late to work, or take two hours for lunch, or help themselves to company office supplies for personal use should expect employees to read the message they are sending and model their behavior accordingly.

All Human Behavior Is Learned

Human beings are essentially blank slates that are shaped by their environment. B. F. Skinner, in fact, summarized his belief in the power of the environment to shape behavior when he said, "Give me a child at birth and I can make him into anything you want."

We have numerous societal mechanisms that exist because of this belief in the power of learned behavior. Let me identify some of them:

Role of parenting. We place a great deal of importance on the role of mothers and fathers in the raising of children. We believe, for instance, that children raised without fathers will be hindered by their lack of a male role model. And parents who have continual run-ins with the law risk having government authorities take their children from them. The latter action is typically taken because society believes that irresponsible parents don't provide the proper learning environment for their children.

Importance of education. Most advanced societies invest heavily in the education of their young. They typically provide 10 or more years of free education. And in countries such as the United States, going on to college after finishing high school has become the norm rather than the exception. This investment in education is undertaken because it is seen as a way for young people to learn knowledge and skills.

Job training. For individuals who don't go onto college, most will pursue job-training programs to develop specific work-related skills. They'll take courses to become proficient as auto mechanics, medical assistants, and the like. Similarly, people who seek to become skilled trades workers will pursue apprenticeships as carpenters, electricians, or pipe fitters. In addition, business firms invest billions of dollars each year in training and education to keep current employees' skills up to date.

Manipulating of rewards. Complex compensation programs are designed by organizations to reward employees fairly for their work performance. But these programs are also designed with the intention to motivate employees. They're designed to encourage employees to engage in behaviors that management desires and to extinguish behaviors that management wants to discourage. Salary levels, for instance, typically reward employee loyalty, encourage the learning of new skills, and motivate individuals to assume greater responsibilities in the organization.

The above mechanisms all exist and flourish because organizations and society believe that people can learn and change their behavior.

While people can learn and can be influenced by their environment, far too little attention has been paid to the role that evolution has played in shaping human behavior. Evolutionary psychology tells us that human beings are basically hardwired at birth. We arrive on Earth with ingrained traits, honed and adapted over millions of years, that shape and limit our behavior.

All living creatures are "designed" by specific combinations of genes. As a result of natural selection, genes that produce faulty design features are eliminated. Characteristics that help a species survive tend to endure and get passed on to future generations. In the case of human beings, many of the characteristics that helped our early *Homo sapiens* ancestors survive live on today and influence the way we behave. Here are a few examples:

Emotions. Stone Age people, at the mercy of wild predators and natural disasters, learned to trust their instincts. Those with the best instincts survived. Today, emotions remain the first screen to all information we receive. We know we're supposed to act rationally but our emotions can never be fully suppressed.

Risk avoidance. Ancient hunter-gatherers who survived weren't big risk takers. They were cautious. Today, when we're comfortable with the status quo, we typically see any change as risky and, thus, tend to resist it.

Stereotyping. To prosper in a clan society, Early Man had to become expert at making judicious alliances. He had to quickly "size-up" who he could trust and who he couldn't. Those who could do this quickly were more likely to survive. Today, like our ancestors, we naturally stereotype people based on very small pieces of evidence, mainly their looks and a few readily apparent behaviors.

Male competitiveness. Males in early human societies frequently had to engage in games or battles in which there were clear winners and losers. Winners attained high status, were viewed as more attractive mates, and were more likely to reproduce. The ingrained male desire to do public battle and display virility and competence persists today.

Evolutionary psychology challenges the notion that people are free to change their behavior if trained or motivated. It doesn't say that we can't engage in learning or exercise free will. What it does say is that nature predisposes us to act and interact in particular ways in particular circumstances. As a result, we find that people in organizational settings often behave in ways that don't appear to be beneficial to themselves or their employers.

Points in this argument are based on N. Nicholson, "How Hardwired Is Human Behavior?" *Harvard Business Review*, July–August 1998, pp. 135–47; and B. D. Pierce and R. White, "The Evolution of Social Structure: Why Biology Matters," *Academy of Management Review*, October 1999, pp. 843–53.

Questions for Review

1. Which biographical characteristics best predict productivity? Absenteeism? Turnover? Satisfaction?

2. Assess the validity of using intelligence scores for selecting new employees.

3. Describe the specific steps you would take to ensure that an individual has the appropriate abilities to satisfactorily do a given job.

4. Explain classical conditioning.

5. Contrast classical conditioning, operant conditioning, and social learning.

6. How might employees actually learn unethical behaviors on their jobs?

7. Describe the four types of intermittent reinforcers.

8. What are the five steps in behavior modification?

9. If you had to take disciplinary action against an employee, how, specifically, would you do it?

10. Describe the four processes in successful social learning.

Questions for Critical Thinking

1. "All organizations would benefit from hiring the smartest people they can get." Do you agree or disagree with this statement? Support your answer.

2. What do you think is more likely to lead to success on a job—a good *ability–job* fit or *personality–organization* fit? Explain.

3. In addition to past work history and an employee's job performance, what other mitigating factors do you think a manager should use in applying discipline? And does not the mere attempt to use mitigating circumstances turn disciplinary action into a political process?

4. What abilities do you think are especially important for success in senior-level management positions?

5. What have you learned about "learning" that could help you to explain the behavior of students in a classroom if: (a) The instructor gives only one test—a final examination at the end of the course? (b) The instructor gives four exams during the term, all of which are announced on the first day of class? (c) The student's grade is based on the results of numerous exams, none of which are announced by the instructor ahead of time?

Team Exercise | Positive Reinforcement Versus Punishment

Exercise Overview (Steps 1–4)

This 10-step exercise takes approximately 20 minutes.

1. Two volunteers are selected to receive reinforcement or punishment from the class while performing a particular task. The volunteers leave the room.

2. The instructor identifies an object for the student volunteers to locate when they return to the room. (The object should be unobstructed but clearly visible to the class. Examples that have worked well include a small triangular piece of paper that was left behind when a notice was torn off a classroom bulletin board, a smudge on the chalkboard, and a chip in the plaster of a classroom wall.)

3. The instructor specifies the actions that will be in effect when the volunteers return to the room. For punishment, students should hiss or boo when the first volunteer is moving away from the object. For positive reinforcement, they should cheer and applaud when the second volunteer is getting closer to the object.

4. The instructor should assign a student to keep a record of the time it takes each of the volunteers to locate the object.

Volunteer 1 (Steps 5 and 6)

5. Volunteer 1 is brought back into the room and is told, "Your task is to locate and touch a particular object in the room and the class has agreed to help you. You cannot use words or ask questions. Begin."

6. Volunteer 1 continues to look for the object until it is found, while the class engages in the punishing behavior.

Volunteer 2 (Steps 7 and 8)

7. Volunteer 2 is brought back into the room and is told, "Your task is to locate and touch a particular object in the room and the class has agreed to help you. You cannot use words or ask questions. Begin."

8. Volunteer 2 continues to look for the object until it is found, while the class assists by giving positive reinforcement.

Class Review (Steps 9 and 10)

9. The timekeeper will present the results on how long it took each volunteer to find the object.

10. The class will discuss: What was the difference in behavior of the two volunteers? What are the implications of this exercise to shaping behavior in organizations?

Source: Adapted from an exercise developed by Larry Michaelson of the University of Oklahoma. With permission.

| Ethical Dilemma | Is OB Mod a Form of Manipulation? |

Two questions: Is OB Mod a form of manipulation? And if it is, is it unethical for managers to manipulate the behavior of employees?

Critics of OB Mod say that it manipulates employees. They argue that when managers purposely select consequences to control employee behavior, they rob workers of their individuality and freedom of choice. For instance, an auto parts plant in Kentucky reinforces safe working conditions through a game called safety bingo. Every day that the plant has no accidents, employees can draw a number for their bingo card. The first employee to fill a bingo card wins a television set. This program, critics might argue, pressures employees to behave in ways they might not otherwise engage in. It makes these human beings little different from the seal at the circus who, every time it does its assigned trick, is given a fish by its trainer. Only instead of getting a fish, some employee walks off with a television.

On the question regarding the ethics of manipulation, the answer typically surrounds what the term "manipulation" means to you. Some people believe the term has a negative connotation. To manipulate is to be devious or conniving. Others, however, would argue that manipulation is merely the thoughtful effort to control outcomes. In fact, one can say that "management *is* manipulation" because it's concerned with planned efforts to get people to do what management wants them to do.

What do you think?

| Case Incident | Bonne Bell Factory Employees Average Age 70 |

The morning shift at the Bonne Bell plant in Lakewood, Ohio—composed of 86 assembly-line workers—packed and boxed 10,800 tubes of lipstick. Anything over 10,000 is considered good. But in addition to meeting their production goals, what's unique on this assembly line is that the average age of these workers is 70. The oldest just turned 90.

This seniors-only production department was launched in 1997, not as some grand social experiment, but as a practical business decision. The company needed workers, labor markets were tight, and seniors were available. The company's president, who himself was 76, suggested the idea. His executives in charge of manufacturing and packaging were skeptical. They thought older workers would be too slow and costly or be misfits in a high-tech world. They worried that seniors would complain they couldn't do the work or that they needed breaks or weren't feeling well. The company's president refused to accept these stereotypes. Although he didn't know of any other company that had a senior department, he said, "Let's try it and see if it works."

And work it did. Retirees now account for close to 20 percent of Bonne Bell's workforce of 500. The group handles work that once was outsourced, saving the company more than $1 million in its first four years and effectively silencing the skeptics. Shipment goals are set and met. Turnover is almost nil. And the company has a sizable waiting list of seniors who are interested in taking jobs when they become available. Seniors have proven to be an ideal source for new employees.

Not only have seniors proven to be productive and loyal, they also help keep costs down. Since most receive Social Security, they don't rely on their jobs to fully support themselves. They don't need $15 or $20 an hour jobs to make ends meet. They seem more than happy to accept pay rates that start at $7.50 an hour and move to $8 after a year. In addition, the company saves by providing these employees with no health benefits. Most of these workers are covered by a spouse's medical plan or Medicare and say they don't need extra coverage.

Questions

1. How do the facts in this case align with research on age in the chapter?

2. Is this factory engaging in reverse age-discrimination?

3. Do you think these older workers would perform as well if they were integrated into a department with younger workers? Support your position.

4. Do you think the success that Bonne Bell has had with hiring older workers is transferable to other companies? Why or why not?

Source: Based on C. Ansberry, "Averaging Age 70, Staff in This Cosmetics Plant Retires Old Stereotypes," *Wall Street Journal*, February 5, 2001, p. A1.

KSS PROGRAM

KNOW THE CONCEPTS
SELF-AWARENESS
SKILLS APPLICATIONS

Developing Effective Disciplining Skills

After you've read this chapter, take Self-Assessment #26 (How Good Am I at Giving Feedback?) on your enclosed CD-ROM, and complete the skill-building module entitled "Effective Disciplining" on page 614.

Endnotes

1. Based on L. Zuckerman, "Happy Skies of Continental," *Continental Magazine*, July 2001, pp. 51–53; and S. McCartney, "Continental Airlines Keeps Little Things, and It Pays Off Big," *Wall Street Journal*, February 4, 2002, p. A1.
2. M. Bolch, "The Changing Face of the Workforce," *Training*, December 2000, pp. 73–78.
3. "American Business and Older Workers: A Road Map to the 21st Century," a report prepared for the American Association of Retired Persons by DYG Inc., 1995; "Valuing Older Workers: A Study of Costs and Productivity," a report prepared for the American Association of Retired Persons by ICF Inc., 1995; and W. C. K. Chiu, A. W. Chan, E. Snape, and T. Redman, "Age Stereotypes and Discriminatory Attitudes towards Older Workers: An East–West Comparison," *Human Relations*, May 2001, pp. 629–61.
4. S. R. Rhodes, "Age-Related Differences in Work Attitudes and Behavior: A Review and Conceptual Analysis," *Psychological Bulletin*, March 1983, pp. 328–67; J. L. Cotton and J. M. Tuttle, "Employee Turnover: A Meta-Analysis and Review with Implications for Research," *Academy of Management Review*, January 1986, pp. 55–70; and D. R. Davies, G. Matthews, and C. S. K. Wong, "Ageing and Work," in C. L. Cooper and I. T. Robertson (eds.), *International Review of Industrial and Organizational Psychology*, vol. 6 (Chichester, England: Wiley, 1991), pp. 183–87.
5. Rhodes, "Age-Related Differences in Work Attitudes and Behavior," pp. 347–49; R. D. Hackett, "Age, Tenure, and Employee Absenteeism," *Human Relations*, July 1990, pp. 601–19; and Davies, Matthews, and Wong, "Ageing and Work," pp. 183–87.
6. Cited in K. Labich, "The New Unemployed," *Fortune*, March 8, 1993, p. 43.
7. See G. M. McEvoy and W. F. Cascio, "Cumulative Evidence of the Relationship between Employee Age and Job Performance," *Journal of Applied Psychology*, February 1989, pp. 11–17; and F. L. Schmidt and J. E. Hunter, "The Validity and Utility of Selection Methods in Personnel Psychology: Practical and Theoretical Implications of 85 Years of Research Findings," *Psychological Bulletin*, September 1998, pp. 262–74.
8. See, for instance, F. J. Landy, et al, *Alternatives to Chronological Age in Determining Standards of Suitability for Public Safety Jobs* (University Park, PA: Center for Applied Behavioral Sciences, Pennsylvania State University, 1992).
9. A. L. Kalleberg and K. A. Loscocco, "Aging, Values, and Rewards: Explaining Age Differences in Job Satisfaction," *American Sociological Review*, February 1983, pp. 78–90; R. Lee and E. R. Wilbur, "Age, Education, Job Tenure, Salary, Job Characteristics, and Job Satisfaction: A Multivariate Analysis," *Human Relations*, August 1985, pp. 781–91; and Davies, Matthews, and Wong, "Ageing and Work," pp. 176–83.
10. K. M. Kacmar and G. R. Ferris, "Theoretical and Methodological Considerations in the Age-Job Satisfaction Relationship," *Journal of Applied Psychology*, April 1989, pp. 201–07; G. Zeitz, "Age and Work Satisfaction in a Government Agency: A Situational Perspective," *Human Relations*, May 1990, pp. 419–38; and G. Koretz, "Yes, Workers Are Grumpier," *Business Week*, November 13, 2000, p. 42.
11. See, for example, A. H. Eagly and L. L. Carli, "Sex Researchers and Sex-Typed Communications as Determinants

of Sex Differences in Influenceability: A Meta-Analysis of So-cial Influence Studies," *Psychological Bulletin*, August 1981, pp. 1–20; J. S. Hyde, "How Large Are Cognitive Gender Dif-ferences?" *American Psychologist*, October 1981, pp. 892–901; and P. Chance, "Biology, Destiny, and All That," *Across the Board*, July–August 1988, pp. 19–23.

12. R. P. Quinn, G. L. Staines, and M. R. McCullough, *Job Sat-isfaction: Is There a Trend?* Document 2900-00195 (Wash-ington, DC: Government Printing Office, 1974).

13. See, for example, B. Kantrowitz, P. Wingert, and K. Robins, "Advocating a 'Mommy Track,'" *Newsweek*, March 13, 1989, p. 45; and S. Shellenbarger, "More Job Seekers Put Family Needs First," *Wall Street Journal*, November 15, 1991, p. B1.

14. R. W. Griffeth, P. W. Hom, and S. Gaertner, "A Meta-Analysis of Antecedents and Correlates of Employee Turnover: Update, Moderator Tests, and Research Impli-cations for the Next Millennium," *Journal of Management*, vol. 26, no. 3, 2000, pp. 463–88.

15. See, for instance, J. P. Leigh, "Sex Differences in Absen-teeism," *Industrial Relations*, Fall 1983, pp. 349–61; K. D. Scott and E. L. McClellan, "Gender Differences in Absen-teeism," *Public Personnel Management*, Summer 1990, pp. 229–53; and A. VandenHeuvel and M. Wooden, "Do Explanations of Absenteeism Differ for Men and Women?" *Human Relations*, November 1995, pp. 1309–29.

16. See, for instance, M. Tait, M. Y. Padgett, and T. T. Baldwin, "Job and Life Satisfaction: A Reevaluation of the Strength of the Relationship and Gender Effects as a Function of the Date of the Study," *Journal of Applied Psychology*, June 1989, pp. 502–07; and M. B. Grover, "Daddy Stress," *Forbes*, September 6, 1999, pp. 202–08.

17. K. R. Garrison and P. M. Muchinsky, "Attitudinal and Bi-ographical Predictors of Incidental Absenteeism," *Journal of Vocational Behavior*, April 1977, pp. 221–30; C. J. Wat-son, "An Evaluation and Some Aspects of the Steers and Rhodes Model of Employee Attendance," *Journal of Ap-plied Psychology*, June 1981, pp. 385–89; R. T. Keller, "Pre-dicting Absenteeism from Prior Absenteeism, Attitudinal Factors, and Nonattitudinal Factors," *Journal of Applied Psychology*, August 1983, pp. 536–40; J. M. Federico, P. Fed-erico, and G. W. Lundquist, "Predicting Women's Turnover as a Function of Extent of Met Salary Expecta-tions and Biodemographic Data," *Personnel Psychology*, Winter 1976, pp. 559–66; R. Marsh and H. Mannari, "Or-ganizational Commitment and Turnover: A Predictive Study," *Administrative Science Quarterly*, March 1977, pp. 57–75; and D. R. Austrom, T. Baldwin, and G. J. Macy, "The Single Worker: An Empirical Exploration of Attitudes, Behavior, and Well-Being," *Canadian Journal of Administrative Sciences*, December 1988, pp. 22–29.

18. M. E. Gordon and W. J. Fitzgibbons, "Empirical Test of the Validity of Seniority as a Factor in Staffing Decisions," *Journal of Applied Psychology*, June 1982, pp. 311–19; M. E. Gordon and W. A. Johnson, "Seniority: A Review of Its Le-gal and Scientific Standing," *Personnel Psychology*, Summer 1982, pp. 255–80; M. A. McDaniel, F. L. Schmidt, and J. E. Hunter, "Job Experience Correlates of Job Performance," *Journal of Applied Psychology*, May 1988, pp. 327–30; and M. A. Quinones, J. K. Ford, and M. S. Teachout, "The Re-lationship between Work Experience and Job Perfor-

mance: A Conceptual and Meta-Analytic Review," *Personnel Psychology*, Winter 1995, pp. 887–910.

19. Garrison and Muchinsky, "Attitudinal and Biographical Predictors of Incidental Absenteeism"; N. Nicholson, C. A. Brown, and J. K. Chadwick-Jones, "Absence from Work and Personal Characteristics," *Journal of Applied Psychology*, June 1977, pp. 319–27; and R. T. Keller, "Predicting Ab-senteeism from Prior Absenteeism, Attitudinal Factors, and Nonattitudinal Factors," *Journal of Applied Psychology*, August 1983, pp. 536–40.

20. P. O. Popp and J. A. Belohlav, "Absenteeism in a Low Sta-tus Work Environment," *Academy of Management Journal*, September 1982, p. 681.

21. R. W. Griffeth, P. W. Hom, and S. Gaertner, "A Meta-Analysis of Antecedents and Correlates of Employee Turnover."

22. R. D. Gatewood and H. S. Field, *Human Resource Selection* (Chicago: Dryden Press, 1987).

23. J. A. Breaugh and D. L. Dossett, "The Effectiveness of Bio-data for Predicting Turnover," paper presented at the Na-tional Academy of Management Conference, New Orleans, August 1987.

24. A. G. Bedeian, G. R. Ferris, and K. M. Kacmar, "Age, Tenure, and Job Satisfaction: A Tale of Two Perspectives," *Journal of Vocational Behavior,* February 1992, pp. 33–48.

25. K. R. Murphy (ed.), *Individual Differences and Behavior in Organizations* (San Francisco: Jossey-Bass, 1996).

26. M. D. Dunnette, "Aptitudes, Abilities, and Skills," in M. D. Dunnette (ed.), *Handbook of Industrial and Organizational Psychology* (Chicago: Rand McNally, 1976), pp. 478–83.

27. D. Lubinski and R. V. Dawis, "Aptitudes, Skills, and Profi-ciencies," in M. D. Dunnette and L. M. Hough (eds.), *Handbook of Industrial & Organizational Psychology*, vol. 3, 2nd ed. (Palo Alto, CA: Consulting Psychologists Press, 1992), pp. 30–33.

28. See, for instance, J. E. Hunter and R. F. Hunter, "Validity and Utility of Alternative Predictors of Job Performance," *Psychological Bulletin*, January 1984, pp. 72–98; J. E. Hunter, "Cognitive Ability, Cognitive Aptitudes, Job Knowledge, and Job Performance," *Journal of Vocational Behavior*, December 1986, pp. 340–62; W. M. Coward and P. R. Sackett, "Linear-ity of Ability–Performance Relationships: A Reconfirma-tion," *Journal of Applied Psychology*, June 1990, pp. 297–300; M. J. Ree, J. A. Earles, and M. S. Teachout, "Predicting Job Per-formance: Not Much More Than *g*," *Journal of Applied Psy-chology*, August 1994, pp. 518–24; and F. L. Schmidt and J. E. Hunter, "The Validity and Utility of Selection Methods in Personnel Psychology."

29. P. Bobko, P. L. Roth, and D. Potosky, "Derivation and Impli-cations of a Meta-Analytic Matrix Incorporating Cognitive Ability, Alternative Predictors, and Job Performance," *Personnel Psychology*, Autumn 1999, pp. 561–89.

30. This section is based on R. E. Riggio, S. E. Murphy, and F. J. Pirozzolo (eds.), *Multiple Intelligences and Leadership* (Mahwah, NJ: Lawrence Erlbaum, 2002).

31. E. A. Fleishman, "Evaluating Physical Abilities Required by Jobs," *Personnel Administrator*, June 1979, pp. 82–92.

32. See, for instance, H. M. Weiss, "Learning Theory and In-dustrial and Organizational Psychology," in M. D. Dun-nette and L. M. Hough, eds., *Handbook of Industrial & Organizational Psychology*, 2nd ed., vol. 1 (Palo Alto: Con-sulting Psychologists Press, 1990), pp. 172–73.

33. W. McGehee, "Are We Using What We Know about Training? Learning Theory and Training," *Personnel Psychology*, Spring 1958, p. 2.

34. I. P. Pavlov, *The Work of the Digestive Glands*, trans. W. H. Thompson (London: Charles Griffin, 1902). See also the special issue of *American Psychologist* (September 1997, pp. 933–72) commemorating Pavlov's work.

35. B. F. Skinner, *Contingencies of Reinforcement* (East Norwalk, CT: Appleton-Century-Crofts, 1971).

36. A. Bandura, *Social Learning Theory* (Upper Saddle River, NJ: Prentice Hall, 1977).

37. See literature review in D. R. Davies, G. Matthews, and C. S. K. Wong, "Ageing and Work," in C. L. Cooper and I. T. Robertson (eds.), *International Review of Industrial and Organizational Psychology*, vol. 6 (Chichester, England: Wiley, 1991), pp. 159–60.

38. Ibid, p. 165.

39. M. E. Gordon and S. L. Cohen, "Training Behavior as a Predictor of Trainability," *Personnel Psychology*, Summer 1973, pp. 261–72; and I. Robertson and S. Downs, "Learning and the Prediction of Performance: Development of Trainability Testing in the United Kingdom," *Journal of Applied Psychology*, February 1979, pp. 42–50.

40. T. W. Costello and S. S. Zalkind, *Psychology in Administration* (Englewood Cliffs, NJ: Prentice Hall, 1963), p. 193.

41. F. Luthans and R. Kreitner, *Organizational Behavior Modification and Beyond*, 2nd ed. (Glenview, IL: Scott, Foresman, 1985); and A. D. Stajkovic and F. Luthans, "A Meta-Analysis of the Effects of Organizational Behavior Modification on Task Performance, 1975–95," *Academy of Management Journal*, October 1997, pp. 1122–49.

42. "At Emery Air Freight: Positive Reinforcement Boosts Performance," *Organizational Dynamics*, Winter 1973, pp. 41–50.

43. F. Luthans and R. Kreitner, *Organizational Behavior Modification and Beyond: An Operant and Social Learning Approach* (Glenview, IL: Scott, Foresman, 1985); and A. D. Stajkovic and F. Luthans, "A Meta-Analysis of the Effects of Organizational Behavior Modification on Task Performance, 1975–95," *Academy of Management Journal*, October 1997, pp. 1122–49.

44. A. D. Stajkovic and F. Luthans, "A Meta-Analysis of the Effects of Organizational Behavior Modification on Task Performance," p. 1123.

45. See, for instance, L. W. Frederiksen, *Handbook of Organizational Behavior Management* (New York: Wiley, 1982); B. Sulzer-Azarof, B. Loafman, R. J. Merante, and A. C. Hlavacek, "Improving Occupational Safety in a Large Industrial Plant: A Systematic Replication," *Journal of Organizational Behavior Management*, vol. 11, no. 1, 1990, pp. 99–120; J. C. Landau, "The Impact of a Change in an Attendance Control System on Absenteeism and Tardiness," *Journal of Organizational Behavior Management*, vol. 13, no. 2, 1993, pp. 51–70; C. S. Brown and B. Sulzer-Azaroff, "An Assessment of the Relationship Between Customer Satisfaction and Service Friendliness," *Journal of Organizational Behavior Management*, vol. 14, no. 2 1994, pp. 55–75; and F. Luthans and A. D. Stajkovic, "Reinforce for Performance: The Need to Go Beyond Pay and Even Rewards," *Academy of Management Executive*, May 1999, pp. 49–57.

46. D. Willings, "The Absentee Worker," *Personnel and Training Management,* December 1968, pp. 10–12.

47. B. H. Harvey, J. F. Rogers, and J. A. Schultz, "Sick Pay vs. Well Pay: An Analysis of the Impact of Rewarding Employees for Being on the Job," *Public Personnel Management Journal*, Summer 1983, pp. 218–24.

48. M. S. Forbes Jr., "There is a Better Way," *Forbes*, April 26, 1993, p. 23.

49. Cited in *Training*, October 2001, p. 40.

50. See, for instance, S. J. Simon and J. M. Werner, "Computer Training Through Behavior Modeling, Self-Paced, and Instructional Approaches: A Field Experiment," *Journal of Applied Psychology*, December 1996, pp. 648–59; and D. Stamps, "Learning is Social. Training Is Irrelevant?" *Training*, February 1997, pp. 34–42.

51. See, for instance, S. E. Markham and I. S. Markham, "Self-Management and Self-Leadership Reexamined: A Levels-of-Analysis Perspective," *Leadership Quarterly*, Fall 1995, pp. 343–60; and C. A. Frayne and J. M. Geringer, "Self-Management Training for Improving Job Performance: A Field Experiment Involving Salespeople," *Journal of Applied Psychology*, June 2000, pp. 361–72.

52. G. P. Latham and C. A. Frayne, "Self-Management Training for Increasing Job Attendance: A Follow-up and a Replication," *Journal of Applied Psychology*, June 1989, pp. 411–16.

*How can I know what I
think til I see what I say?*
—E.M. Forster

PART TWO

THE
INDIVIDUAL

Tammy Savage has an interesting job. The 30-year-old Microsoft employee heads up a group that is trying to figure out what the Nexters generation—people born after 1977—thinks and wants.[1] She hopes to use this information to help Microsoft better understand its future employees and customers. After all, this is the first generation that never knew a world without computers and the Internet—something in which Microsoft has an obvious interest.

Savage is using a number of approaches to tap into the values of Nexters. For instance, on one recent July morning, she invited 10 of the company's 500-plus summer interns to talk about their lives and dreams over coffee in a Seattle restaurant. A question was posed: "What's most important to you in your ideal job?" At first, the interns' replies were predictable: good people, a balance between work and life, flexible hours. Then the interns became more passionate. They talked about integrity, teamwork and moral support, responsibility, and freedom to pursue their visions. When one pounded the table and yelled, "I don't ever, ever want to lose the kid-like view that I can change the world!" the rest of the interns cheered. This comment had hit a button. But Tammy wasn't really surprised. Her research, and that of others who are studying Nexters, confirms that these young people want to work for a company that understands their generation, provides a work climate that supports their needs, and where they can have a significant influence in shaping society. More specifically, and good news for Microsoft, Nexters see technology and the Internet as a major force for changing the world.

Values, Attitudes, and Job Satisfaction

chapter

3

In this chapter, we look at values, how they've changed from generation to generation, and what these changes mean for managing people of different ages. We'll also review research on the topic of attitudes, demonstrate the link between attitudes and behavior, and look at factors that shape employees' satisfaction with their jobs.

VALUES

Is capital punishment right or wrong? If a person likes power, is that good or bad? The answers to these questions are value-laden. Some might argue, for example, that capital punishment is right because it is an appropriate retribution for crimes like murder and treason. However, others might argue, just as strongly, that no government has the right to take anyone's life.

Values represent basic convictions that "a specific mode of conduct or end-state of existence is personally or socially preferable to an opposite or converse mode of conduct or end-state of existence."[2] They contain a judgmental element in that they carry an individual's ideas as to what is right, good, or desirable. Values have both content and intensity attributes. The content attribute says that a mode of conduct or end-state of existence is *important*. The intensity attribute specifies *how important* it is. When we rank an individual's values in terms of their intensity, we obtain that person's **value system**. All of us have a hierarchy of values that forms our value system. This system is identified by the relative importance we assign to values such as freedom, pleasure, self-respect, honesty, obedience, and equality.

LEARNING OBJECTIVES

AFTER STUDYING THIS CHAPTER, YOU SHOULD BE ABLE TO:

1. Contrast terminal and instrumental values.
2. List the dominant values in today's workforce.
3. Identify Hofstede's five value dimensions of national culture.
4. Contrast the three components of an attitude.
5. Summarize the relationship between attitudes and behavior.
6. Identify the role consistency plays in attitudes.
7. State the relationship between job satisfaction and behavior.
8. Identify four employee responses to dissatisfaction.

63

values

Basic convictions that a specific mode of conduct or end-state of existence is personally or socially preferable to an opposite or converse mode of conduct or end-state of existence.

value system

A hierarchy based on a ranking of an individual's values in terms of their intensity.

Are values fluid and flexible? Generally speaking, No. Values tend to be relatively stable and enduring.[3] A significant portion of the values we hold is established in our early years—from parents, teachers, friends, and others. As children, we are told that certain behaviors or outcomes are always desirable or always undesirable. There were few gray areas. You were told, for example, that you should be honest and responsible. You were never taught to be just a little bit honest or a little bit responsible. It is this absolute or "black-or-white" learning of values that more or less ensures their stability and endurance. The process of questioning our values, of course, may result in a change. We may decide that these underlying convictions are no longer acceptable. More often, our questioning merely acts to reinforce the values we hold.

Importance of Values

Values are important to the study of organizational behavior because they lay the foundation for the understanding of attitudes and motivation and because they influence our perceptions. Individuals enter an organization with preconceived notions of what "ought" and what "ought not" to be. Of course, these notions are not value free. On the contrary, they contain interpretations of right and wrong. Furthermore, they imply that certain behaviors or outcomes are preferred over others. As a result, values cloud objectivity and rationality.

Values generally influence attitudes and behavior.[4] Suppose that you enter an organization with the view that allocating pay on the basis of performance is right, while allocating pay on the basis of seniority is wrong or inferior. How are you going to react if you find that the organization you have just joined rewards seniority and not performance? You're likely to be disappointed—and this can lead to job dissatisfaction and the decision not to exert a high level of effort since "it's probably not going to lead to more money, anyway." Would your attitudes and behavior be different if your values aligned with the organization's pay policies? Most likely.

Types of Values

Can we classify values? The answer is: Yes. In this section, we review two approaches to developing value typologies.

Rokeach Value Survey   Milton Rokeach created the Rokeach Value Survey (RVS).[5] The RVS consists of two sets of values, with each set containing 18 individual value items. One set, called **terminal values**, refers to desirable end-states of existence. These are the goals that a person would like to achieve during his or her lifetime. The other set, called **instrumental values**, refers to preferable modes of behavior, or means of achieving the terminal values. Exhibit 3-1 gives common examples for each of these sets.

Several studies confirm that the RVS values vary among groups.[6] People in the same occupations or categories (e.g., corporate managers, union members, parents, students) tend to hold similar values. For instance, one study compared corporate executives, members of the steelworkers' union, and members of a community activist group. Although a good deal of overlap was found among the three groups,[7] there were also some very significant differences (see Exhibit 3-2). The activists had value preferences that were quite different from those of the other two groups. They ranked "equality" as their most important terminal value; executives and union

terminal values

Desirable end-states of existence; the goals that a person would like to achieve during his or her lifetime.

instrumental values

Preferable modes of behavior or means of achieving one's terminal values.

Terminal and Instrumental Values in Rokeach Value Survey

Terminal Values	Instrumental Values
A comfortable life (a prosperous life)	Ambitious (hardworking, aspiring)
An exciting life (a stimulating, active life)	Broad-minded (open-minded)
A sense of accomplishment (lasting contribution)	Capable (competent, effective)
A world at peace (free of war and conflict)	Cheerful (lighthearted, joyful)
A world of beauty (beauty of nature and the arts)	Clean (neat, tidy)
Equality (brotherhood, equal opportunity for all)	Courageous (standing up for your beliefs)
Family security (taking care of loved ones)	Forgiving (willing to pardon others)
Freedom (independence, free choice)	Helpful (working for the welfare of others)
Happiness (contentedness)	Honest (sincere, truthful)
Inner harmony (freedom from inner conflict)	Imaginative (daring, creative)
Mature love (sexual and spiritual intimacy)	Independent (self-reliant, self-sufficient)
National security (protection from attack)	Intellectual (intelligent, reflective)
Pleasure (an enjoyable, leisurely life)	Logical (consistent, rational)
Salvation (saved, eternal life)	Loving (affectionate, tender)
Self-respect (self-esteem)	Obedient (dutiful, respectful)
Social recognition (respect, admiration)	Polite (courteous, well-mannered)
True friendship (close companionship)	Responsible (dependable, reliable)
Wisdom (a mature understanding of life)	Self-controlled (restrained, self-disciplined)

EXHIBIT 3-1

Source: M. Rokeach, *The Nature of Human Values* (New York: The Free Press, 1973).

members ranked this value 12 and 13, respectively. Activists ranked "helpful" as their second-highest instrumental value. The other two groups both ranked it 14. These differences are important, because executives, union members, and activists all have a vested interest in what corporations do. "When corporations and critical stakeholder groups such as these [other] two come together in negotiations or contend with one another over economic and social policies, they are likely to begin with these built-in differences in personal value preferences. . . . Reaching agreement on any specific issue or policy where these personal values are importantly implicated might prove to be quite difficult."[8]

Mean Value Ranking of Executives, Union Members, and Activists (Top Five Only)

Executives		Union Members		Activists	
Terminal	Instrumental	Terminal	Instrumental	Terminal	Instrumental
1. Self-respect	1. Honest	1. Family security	1. Responsible	1. Equality	1. Honest
2. Family security	2. Responsible	2. Freedom	2. Honest	2. A world of peace	2. Helpful
3. Freedom	3. Capable	3. Happiness	3. Courageous	3. Family security	3. Courageous
4. A sense of accomplishment	4. Ambitious	4. Self-respect	4. Independent	4. Self-respect	4. Responsible
5. Happiness	5. Independent	5. Mature love	5. Capable	5. Freedom	5. Capable

EXHIBIT 3-2

Source: Based on W. C. Frederick and J. Weber, "The Values of Corporate Managers and Their Critics: An Empirical Description and Normative Implications," in W. C. Frederick and L. E. Preston (eds.), *Business Ethics: Research Issues and Empirical Studies* (Greenwich, CT: JAI Press, 1990), pp. 123–44.

Dominant Work Values in Today's Workforce

EXHIBIT 3-3

Cohort	Entered the Workforce	Approximate Current Age	Dominant Work Values
Veterans	1950s or early 1960s	60+	Hard working, conservative, conforming; loyalty to the organization
Boomers	1965–1985	40–60	Success, achievement, ambition, dislike of authority; loyalty to career
Xers	1985–2000	25–40	Work/life balance, team-oriented, dislike of rules; loyalty to relationships
Nexters	2000 to present	Under 25	Confident, financial success, self-reliant but team-oriented; loyalty to both self and relationships

Contemporary Work Cohorts I have integrated several recent analyses of work values into four groups that attempt to capture the unique values of different cohorts or generations in the U.S. workforce.[9] (No assumption is made that this framework would apply universally across all cultures.[10]) Exhibit 3-3 proposes that employees can be segmented by the era in which they entered the workforce. Because most people start work between the ages of 18 and 23, the eras also correlate closely with the chronological age of employees.

Workers who grew up influenced by the Great Depression, World War II, the Andrews Sisters, and the Berlin blockade entered the workforce through the 1950s and early 1960s believing in hard work, the status quo, and authority figures. We call them *Veterans*. Once hired, Veterans tended to be loyal to their employer. In terms of the terminal values on the RVS, these employees are likely to place the greatest importance on a comfortable life and family security.

Boomers entered the workforce from the mid-1960s through the mid-1980s. This cohort were influenced heavily by the civil rights movement, women's lib, the Beatles, the Vietnam war, and baby-boom competition. They brought with them a large measure of the "hippie ethic" and distrust of authority. But they place a great deal of emphasis on achievement and material success. They're pragmatists who believe that ends can justify means. Boomers see the organizations that employ them merely as vehicles for their careers. Terminal values such as a sense of accomplishment and social recognition rank high with them.

Xers lives have been shaped by globalization, two-career parents, MTV, AIDS, and computers. They value flexibility, life options, and the achievement of job satisfaction. Family and relationships are very important to this cohort. They also enjoy team-oriented work. Money is important as an indicator of career performance, but Xers are willing to trade off salary increases, titles, security, and promotions for increased leisure time and expanded lifestyle options. In search of balance in their lives, Xers are less willing to make personal sacrifices for the sake of their employer than previous generations were. On the RVS, they rate high on true friendship, happiness, and pleasure.

After 9/11, American Workers Rethink Priorities

Values are relatively permanent. But dramatic shocks can realign them. And the terrorists' attacks on September 11 may have significantly reprioritized many Americans' values.

The initial response to the terrorists attacks for many people was a reevaluation of choices related to jobs, family, and career success. In some cases, this led to a rethinking of career paths, cutting back on grueling schedules, and deciding to pursue work that might pay less but seem more meaningful. For instance, in California, young workers who once talked of dot-com millions are now asking: "Is it worth it?" Some employees appear less concerned about putting in face time, making deadlines, and getting on the fast track. They seem more concerned about family and worry less about time at the office. CEOs say some of their employees are talking more earnestly about work/life balance, mortality, and other questions once considered taboo in the office. Said one consultant, "The event de-emphasized what most people value— the money and the luxuries. People are questioning what's really important; they're questioning work. It's happening across the board."

It's now been more than a year since the terrorist attacks on New York and Washington. That provides a more meaningful perspective on whether this event has had long-term implications on workplace values. Or whether any reprioritizing was merely a knee-jerk reaction to a traumatic event, followed by a return to "business as usual." Do you think a significant portion of Americans have permanently reprioritized their values as a result of 9/11?

Source: Based on S. Armour, "American Workers Rethink Priorities," *USA Today*, October 4, 2001, p. 1B.

The most recent entrants to the workforce, the *Nexters*, grew up during prosperous times. They tend to have high expectations, believe in themselves, and are confident about their ability to succeed. They seem to be on a never-ending search for the ideal job, see nothing wrong with constant job hopping, and continually look for meaning in their work. Nexters are at ease with diversity and are the first generation to take technology for granted. They've lived most of their lives with CD players, VCRs, cellular phones, and the Internet. This generation is very money-oriented and desirous of the things that money can buy. They seek financial success. Like Xers, they enjoy teamwork but they're also highly self-reliant. They tend to emphasize terminal values such as freedom and a comfortable life.

An understanding that individuals' values differ but tend to reflect the societal values of the period in which they grew up can be a valuable aid in explaining and predicting behavior. Employees in their 60s, for instance, are more likely to accept authority than their coworkers who are 10 or 15 years younger. And workers in their 30s are more likely than their parents to balk at having to work weekends and more prone to leave a job in mid-career to pursue another that provides more leisure time.

Values, Loyalty, and Ethical Behavior

Has there been a decline in business ethics? While the issue is debatable, a lot of people think ethical standards began to erode in the late 1970s.[11] If there has been a decline in ethical standards, perhaps we should look to our work cohorts model (see Exhibit 3-3) for a possible explanation. After all, managers consistently report that the action of their bosses is the most important factor influencing ethical and unethical behavior in their organizations.[12] Given this fact, the values of those in middle and upper management should have a significant bearing on the entire ethical climate within an organization.

UK
Relaxed

THAILAND
Rude

Never underestimate the
importance of local knowledge.

HSBC ◆X▶

Issued by HSBC Holdings plc   The world's local bank

Never underestimate the power of cultural differences. A behavior that may be perfectly acceptable in one culture may be rude in another.

Through the mid-1970s, the managerial ranks were dominated by Veterans, whose loyalties were to their employers. When faced with ethical dilemmas, their decisions were made in terms of what was best for their organization. Beginning in the mid-to-late 1970s, Boomers began to rise into the upper levels of management. By the early 1990s, a large portion of middle and top management positions in business organizations were held by Boomers.

The loyalty of Boomers is to their careers. Their focus is inward and their primary concern is with looking out for "Number One." Such self-centered values would be consistent with a decline in ethical standards. Could this help explain the alleged decline in business ethics beginning in the late 1970s?

The potential good news in this analysis is that Xers are now in the process of moving into middle-management slots and soon will be rising into top management. Since their loyalty is to relationships, they are more likely to consider the ethical implications of their actions on others around them. The result? We might look forward to an uplifting of ethical standards in business over the next decade or two merely as a result of changing values within the managerial ranks.

Values Across Cultures

In Chapter 1, we described the new global village and said "managers have to become capable of working with people from different cultures." Because values differ across cultures, an understanding of these differences should be helpful in explaining and predicting behavior of employees from different countries.

Hofstede's Framework for Assessing Cultures   One of the most widely referenced approaches for analyzing variations among cultures has been done by Geert Hofstede.[13] He surveyed more than 116,000 IBM employees in 40 countries about their work-related values. He found that managers and employees vary on five value dimensions of national culture. They are listed and defined as follows:

- **Power distance**. The degree to which people in a country accept that power in institutions and organizations is distributed unequally. Ranges from relatively equal (low power distance) to extremely unequal (high power distance).
- **Individualism** versus **collectivism**. Individualism is the degree to which people in a country prefer to act as individuals rather than as members of groups. Collectivism is the equivalent of low individualism.
- **Quantity of life** versus **quality of life**. Quantity of life is the degree to which values such as assertiveness, the acquisition of money and material goods, and competition prevail. Quality of life is the degree to which people value relationships, and show sensitivity and concern for the welfare of others.[14]

power distance

A national culture attribute describing the extent to which a society accepts that power in institutions and organizations is distributed unequally.

individualism

A national culture attribute describing the degree to which people prefer to act as individuals rather than as member of groups.

collectivism

A national culture attribute that describes a tight social framework in which people expect others in groups of which they are a part to look after them and protect them.

quantity of life

A national culture attribute describing the extent to which societal values are characterized by assertiveness and materialism.

- **Uncertainty avoidance**. The degree to which people in a country prefer structured over unstructured situations. In countries that score high on uncertainty avoidance, people have an increased level of anxiety, which manifests itself in greater nervousness, stress, and aggressiveness.
- **Long-term** versus **short-term orientation**. People in cultures with long-term orientations look to the future and value thrift and persistence. A short-term orientation values the past and present and emphasizes respect for tradition and fulfilling social obligations.

What did Hofstede's research conclude? Here are a few highlights. China and West Africa scored high on power distance; the United States and the Netherlands scored low. Most Asian countries were more collectivist than individualistic; the United States ranked highest among all countries on individualism. Germany and Hong Kong rated high on quantity of life; Russia and the Netherlands rated low. On uncertainty avoidance, France and Russia were high; Hong Kong and the United States were low. And China and Hong Kong had a long-term orientation, whereas France and the United States had a short-term orientation.

The GLOBE Framework for Assessing Cultures Hofstede's cultural dimensions have become the basic framework for differentiating among national cultures. This is in spite of the fact that the data on which it's based comes from a single company and is nearly 30 years old. Since these data were originally gathered, a lot has happened on the world scene. Some of the most obvious include the fall of the Soviet Union, the merging of East and West Germany, the end of apartheid in South Africa, and the rise of China as a global power. All this suggests the need for an updated assessment of cultural dimensions. The GLOBE study provides such an update.[15]

Begun in 1993, the Global Leadership and Organizational Behavior Effectiveness (GLOBE) research program is an ongoing cross-cultural investigation of leadership and national culture. Using data from 825 organizations in 62 countries, the GLOBE team identified nine dimensions on which national cultures differ (see Exhibit 3-4 on page 70 for examples of country ratings on each of the dimensions).

- *Assertiveness.* The extent to which a society encourages people to be tough, confrontational, assertive, and competitive versus modest and tender. This is essentially equivalent to Hofstede's quantity-of-life dimension.
- *Future orientation.* The extent to which a society encourages and rewards future-oriented behaviors such as planning, investing in the future, and delaying gratification. This is essentially equivalent to Hofstede's long-term/short-term orientation.
- *Gender differentiation.* The extent to which a society maximizes gender role differences.
- *Uncertainty avoidance.* As identified by Hofstede, the GLOBE team defined this term as a society's reliance on social norms and procedures to alleviate the unpredictability of future events.
- *Power distance.* As did Hofstede, the GLOBE team defined this as the degree to which members of a society expect power to be unequally shared.
- *Individualism/collectivism.* Again, this term was defined as was Hofstede's as the degree to which individuals are encouraged by societal institutions to be integrated into groups within organizations and society.
- *In-group collectivism.* In contrast to focusing on societal institutions, this dimension encompasses the extent to which members of a society take pride in membership in small groups, such as their family and circle of close friends, and the organizations in which they are employed.

quality of life
A national culture attribute that emphasizes relationships and concern for others.

uncertainty avoidance
A national culture attribute describing the extent to which a society feels threatened by uncertain and ambiguous situations and tries to avoid them.

long-term orientation
A national culture attribute that emphasizes the future, thrift, and persistence.

short-term orientation
A national culture attribute that emphasizes the past and present, respect for tradition, and fulfilling social obligations.

EXHIBIT 3-4

Dimension	Countries Rating Low	Countries Rating Moderate	Countries Rating High
Assertiveness	Sweden New Zealand Switzerland	Egypt Ireland Philippines	Spain U.S. Greece
Future orientation	Russia Argentina Poland	Slovenia Egypt Ireland	Denmark Canada Netherlands
Gender differentiation	Sweden Denmark Slovenia	Italy Brazil Argentina	South Korea Egypt Morocco
Uncertainty avoidance	Russia Hungary Bolivia	Israel U.S. Mexico	Austria Denmark Germany
Power distance	Denmark Netherlands South Africa	England France Brazil	Russia Spain Thailand
Individualism/collectivism*	Denmark Singapore Japan	Hong Kong U.S. Egypt	Greece Hungary Germany
In-group collectivism	Denmark Sweden New Zealand	Japan Israel Qatar	Egypt China Morocco
Performance orientation	Russia Argentina Greece	Sweden Israel Spain	U.S. Taiwan New Zealand
Humane orientation	Germany Spain France	Hong Kong Sweden Taiwan	Indonesia Egypt Malaysia

*A low score is synonymous with collectivism.

Source: M. Javidan and R. J. House, "Cultural Acumen for the Global Manager: Lessons from Project GLOBE," *Organizational Dynamics,* Spring 2001, pp. 289–305.

- *Performance orientation.* This refers to the degree to which a society encourages and rewards group members for performance improvement and excellence.
- *Humane orientation.* This is defined as the degree to which a society encourages and rewards individuals for being fair, altruistic, generous, caring, and kind to others. This closely approximates Hofstede's quality-of-life dimension.

A comparison of the GLOBE dimensions against those identified by Hofstede suggest that the former has extended Hofstede's work rather than replaced it. The GLOBE study confirms that Hofstede's five dimensions are still valid. However, it has added some additional dimensions and provides us with an updated measure of where countries rate on each dimension. For instance, while the United States led the world in individualism in the 1970s, today it scores in the mid-ranks of countries. We can expect future cross-cultural studies of human behavior and organizational practices to increasingly use the GLOBE dimensions to assess differences between countries.

Implications for OB   Most of the concepts that currently make up the body of knowledge we call *organizational behavior* have been developed by Americans using American subjects within domestic contexts. A comprehensive study, for instance, of more than 11,000 articles published in 24 management and organizational behavior journals over a 10-year period revealed that approximately 80 percent of the studies were done in the United States and had been conducted by Americans.[16] Follow-up studies continue to confirm the lack of cross-cultural considerations in management and OB research,[17] although the past half-dozen years has seen some improvement. What this means is that (1) not all OB theories and concepts are universally applicable to managing people around the world, especially in countries where work values are considerably different from those in the United States; and (2) you should take into consideration cultural values when trying to understand the behavior of people in different countries. To help you with this second point, we'll regularly stop to consider the generalizability of theories and concepts presented in this book to different cultures.

ATTITUDES

Attitudes are evaluative statements—either favorable or unfavorable—concerning objects, people, or events. They reflect how one feels about something. When I say "I like my job," I am expressing my attitude about work.

Attitudes are not the same as values, but the two are interrelated. You can see this by looking at the three components of an attitude: cognition, affect, and behavior.[18]

The belief that "discrimination is wrong" is a value statement. Such an opinion is the **cognitive component** of an attitude. It sets the stage for the more critical part of an attitude—its **affective component**. Affect is the emotional or feeling segment of an attitude and is reflected in the statement "I don't like Jon because he discriminates against minorities." Finally, and we'll discuss this issue at considerable length later in this section, affect can lead to behavioral outcomes. The **behavioral component** of an attitude refers to an intention to behave in a certain way toward someone or something. So, to continue our example, I might choose to avoid Jon because of my feeling about him.

Viewing attitudes as made up of three components—cognition, affect, and behavior—is helpful in understanding their complexity and the potential relationship between attitudes and behavior. But for clarity's sake, keep in mind that the term *attitude* essentially refers to the affect part of the three components.

Also keep in mind that, in contrast to values, your attitudes are less stable. Advertising messages, for example, attempt to alter your attitudes toward a certain product or service: If the people at Ford can get you to hold a favorable feeling toward their cars, that attitude may lead to a desirable behavior (for them)—your purchase of a Ford product.

In organizations, attitudes are important because they affect job behavior. If workers believe, for example, that supervisors, auditors, bosses, and time-and-motion engineers are all in conspiracy to make employees work harder for the same or less money, then it makes sense to try to understand how these attitudes were formed, their relationship to actual job behavior, and how they might be changed.

attitudes
Evaluative statements or judgments concerning objects, people, or events.

cognitive component of an attitude
The opinion or belief segment of an attitude.

affective component of an attitude
The emotional or feeling segment of an attitude.

behavioral component of an attitude
An intention to behave in a certain way toward someone or something.

Types of Attitudes

A person can have thousands of attitudes, but OB focuses our attention on a very limited number of work-related attitudes. These work-related attitudes tap positive or negative evaluations that employees hold about aspects of their work environment. Most of the research in OB has been concerned with three attitudes: job satisfaction, job involvement, and organizational commitment.[19]

Job Satisfaction The term *job satisfaction* refers to an individual's general attitude toward his or her job. A person with a high level of job satisfaction holds positive attitudes about the job, while a person who is dissatisfied with his or her job holds negative attitudes about the job. When people speak of employee attitudes, more often than not they mean job satisfaction. In fact, the two are frequently used interchangeably. Because of the high importance OB researchers have given to job satisfaction, we'll review this attitude in considerable detail later in this chapter.

Job Involvement The term **job involvement** is a more recent addition to the OB literature.[20] While there isn't complete agreement over what the term means, a workable defini-

In a desperate effort to save their firm following its implications in the bankruptcy of energy-trading giant Enron, Inc., these employees of the accounting firm Arthur Andersen voiced support for their company outside a federal courthouse. Their strong organizational commitment led them to identify with their beleaguered firm.

job involvement

The degree to which a person identifies with his or her job, actively participates in it, and considers his or her performance important to self-worth.

tion states that job involvement measures the degree to which a person identifies psychologically with his or her job and considers his or her perceived performance level important to self-worth.[21] Employees with a high level of job involvement strongly identify with and really care about the kind of work they do.

High levels of job involvement have been found to be related to fewer absences and lower resignation rates.[22] However, it seems to more consistently predict turnover than absenteeism, accounting for as much as 16 percent of the variance in the former.[23]

organizational commitment

The degree to which an employee identifies with a particular organization and its goals, and wishes to maintain membership in the organization.

Organizational Commitment The third job attitude we will discuss is **organizational commitment**, which is defined as a state in which an employee identifies with a particular organization and its goals, and wishes to maintain membership in the organization.[24] So, high job involvement means identifying with one's specific job, while high organizational commitment means identifying with one's employing organization.

As with job involvement, the research evidence demonstrates negative relationships between organizational commitment and both absenteeism and turnover.[25] In fact, studies demonstrate that an individual's level of organizational commitment is a better indicator of turnover than the far more frequently used job satisfaction predictor, explaining as much as 34 percent of the variance.[26] Organizational commitment is probably a better predictor because it is a more global and enduring response to the organization as a whole than is job satisfaction.[27] An employee may be dissatisfied with his or her particular job and consider it a temporary condition, yet not be dissatisfied with the organization as a whole. But when dissatisfaction spreads to the organization itself, individuals are more likely to consider resigning.

The previous evidence, most of which was drawn more than two decades ago, needs to be qualified to reflect the changing employee–employer relationship. The unwritten loyalty contract that existed 20 years ago between employees and employers has been seriously damaged; and the notion of an employee staying with a single organization for most of his or her career has become increasingly obsolete. As such, "measures of employee–firm attachment, such as commitment, are problematic for new employment relations."[28] This suggests that *organizational* commitment is probably less important as a work-related attitude than it once was. In its place we might expect something akin to *occupational* commitment to become a more relevant variable because it better reflects today's fluid workforce.[29]

Attitudes and Consistency

Did you ever notice how people change what they say so it doesn't contradict what they do? Perhaps a friend of yours has consistently argued that the quality of American cars isn't up to that of the imports and that he'd never own anything but a foreign import. But his dad gives him a late-model American-made car, and suddenly they're not so bad. Or, when going through sorority rush, a new freshman believes that sororities are good and that pledging a sorority is important. If she fails to make a sorority, however, she may say, "I recognized that sorority life isn't all it's cracked up to be, anyway."

Research has generally concluded that people seek consistency among their attitudes and between their attitudes and their behavior.[30] This means that individuals seek to reconcile divergent attitudes and align their attitudes and behavior so they appear rational and consistent. When there is an inconsistency, forces are initiated to return the individual to an equilibrium state in which attitudes and behavior are again consistent. This can be done by altering either the attitudes or the behavior, or by developing a rationalization for the discrepancy. Tobacco executives provide an example.[31] How, you might wonder, do these people cope with the ongoing barrage of data linking cigarette smoking and negative health outcomes? They can deny that any clear causation between smoking and cancer, for instance, has been established. They can brainwash themselves by continually articulating the benefits of tobacco. They can acknowledge the negative consequences of smoking but rationalize that people are going to smoke and that tobacco companies merely promote freedom of choice. They can accept the research evidence and begin actively working to make more healthy cigarettes or at least reduce their availability to more vulnerable groups, such as teenagers. Or they can quit their job because the dissonance is too great.

These tobacco company executives probably experienced cognitive dissonance after testifying before Congress that nicotine was not addictive, when evidence suggests they had long known of its harmful effects.

Cognitive Dissonance Theory

Can we also assume from this consistency principle that an individual's behavior can always be predicted if we know his or her attitude on a subject? If Mr. Jones views the company's pay level as too low, will a substantial increase in his pay change his behavior, that is, make him work harder? The answer to this question is, unfortunately, more complex than merely a "Yes" or "No."

cognitive dissonance

Any incompatibility between two or more attitudes or between behavior and attitudes.

In the late 1950s, Leon Festinger proposed the theory of **cognitive dissonance**.[32] This theory sought to explain the linkage between attitudes and behavior. *Dissonance* means an inconsistency. *Cognitive dissonance* refers to any incompatibility that an individual might perceive between two or more of his or her attitudes, or between his or her behavior and attitudes. Festinger argued that any form of inconsistency is uncomfortable and that individuals will attempt to reduce the dissonance and, hence, the discomfort. Therefore, individuals will seek a stable state, in which there is a minimum of dissonance.

Of course, no individual can completely avoid dissonance. You know that cheating on your income tax is wrong, but you "fudge" the numbers a bit every year, and hope you're not audited. Or you tell your children to brush after every meal, but *you* don't. So how do people cope? Festinger would propose that the desire to reduce dissonance would be determined by the *importance* of the elements creating the dissonance, the degree of *influence* the individual believes he or she has over the elements, and the *rewards* that may be involved in dissonance.

If the elements creating the dissonance are relatively unimportant, the pressure to correct this imbalance will be low. However, say that a corporate manager—Mrs. Smith—believes strongly that no company should pollute the air or water. Unfortunately, Mrs. Smith, because of the requirements of her job, is placed in the position of having to make decisions that would trade off her company's profitability against her attitudes on pollution. She knows that dumping the company's sewage into the local river (which we shall assume is legal) is in the best economic interest of her firm. What will she do? Clearly, Mrs. Smith is experiencing a high degree of cognitive dissonance. Because of the importance of the elements in this example, we cannot expect Mrs. Smith to ignore the inconsistency. There are several paths she can follow to deal with her dilemma. She can change her behavior (stop polluting the river). Or she can reduce dissonance by concluding that the dissonant behavior is not so important after all ("I've got to make a living, and in my role as a corporate decision maker, I often have to place the good of my company above that of the environment or society."). A third alternative would be for Mrs. Smith to change her attitude ("There is nothing wrong with polluting the river."). Still another choice would be to seek out more consonant elements to outweigh the dissonant ones ("The benefits to society from manufacturing our products more than offset the cost to society of the resulting water pollution.").

The degree of influence that individuals believe they have over the elements will have an impact on how they will react to the dissonance. If they perceive the dissonance to be an uncontrollable result—something over which they have no choice—they are less likely to be receptive to attitude change. If, for example, the dissonance-producing behavior is required as a result of the boss's directive, the pressure to reduce dissonance would be less than if the behavior was performed voluntarily. While dissonance exists, it can be rationalized and justified.

Rewards also influence the degree to which individuals are motivated to reduce dissonance. High rewards accompanying high dissonance tend to reduce the tension inherent in the dissonance. The rewards act to reduce dissonance by increasing the consistency side of the individual's balance sheet.

These moderating factors suggest that just because individuals experience dissonance they will not necessarily move directly toward consistency, that is, toward reduction of this dissonance. If the issues underlying the dissonance are of minimal importance, if an individual perceives that the dissonance is externally imposed and is substantially uncontrollable by him or her, or if rewards are significant enough to offset the dissonance, the individual will not be under great tension to reduce the dissonance.

What are the organizational implications of the theory of cognitive dissonance? It can help to predict the propensity to engage in attitude and behavioral change. For example, if individuals are required by the demands of their job to say or do things that contradict their personal attitude, they will tend to modify their attitude in order to make it compatible with the cognition of what they have said or done. In addition, the greater the dissonance—after it has been moderated by importance, choice, and reward factors—the greater the pressures to reduce it.

Measuring the A–B Relationship

We have maintained throughout this chapter that attitudes affect behavior. Early research on attitudes assumed that they were causally related to behavior; that is, the attitudes that people hold determine what they do. Common sense, too, suggests a relationship. Is it not logical that people watch television programs that they say they like or that employees try to avoid assignments they find distasteful?

However, in the late 1960s, this assumed relationship between attitudes and behavior (A–B) was challenged by a review of the research.[33] Based on an evaluation of a number of studies that investigated the A–B relationship, the reviewer concluded that attitudes were unrelated to behavior or, at best, only slightly related.[34] More recent research has demonstrated that attitudes significantly predict future behavior and confirmed Festinger's original belief that the relationship can be enhanced by taking moderating variables into account.[35]

Moderating Variables   The most powerful moderators have been found to be the *importance* of the attitude, its *specificity*, its *accessibility*, whether there exist *social pressures*, and whether a person has *direct experience* with the attitude.[36]

Important attitudes are ones that reflect fundamental values, self-interest, or identification with individuals or groups that a person values. Attitudes that individuals consider important tend to show a strong relationship to behavior.

The more specific the attitude and the more specific the behavior, the stronger the link between the two. For instance, asking someone specifically about her intention to stay with the organization for the next 6 months is likely to better predict turnover for that person than if you asked her how satisfied she was with her pay.

Attitudes that are easily remembered are more likely to predict behavior than attitudes that are not accessible in memory. Interestingly, you're more likely to remember attitudes that are frequently expressed. So the more you talk about your attitude on a subject, the more you're likely to remember it, and the more likely it is to shape your behavior.

Discrepancies between attitudes and behavior are more likely to occur when social pressures to behave in certain ways hold exceptional power. This tends to characterize behavior in organizations. This may explain why an employee who holds strong anti-union attitudes attends pro-union organizing meetings; or why tobacco executives, who are not smokers themselves and who tend to believe the research linking smoking and cancer, don't actively discourage others from smoking in their offices.

Finally, the attitude–behavior relationship is likely to be much stronger if an attitude refers to something with which the individual has direct personal experience. Asking college students with no significant work experience how they would respond to working for an authoritarian supervisor is far less likely to predict actual behavior than asking that same question of employees who have worked for such an individual.

Self-Perception Theory Although most A–B studies yield positive results, researchers have achieved still higher correlations by pursuing another direction—looking at whether or not behavior influences attitudes. This view, called **self-perception theory**, has generated some encouraging findings. Let's briefly review the theory.[37]

When asked about an attitude toward some object, individuals recall their behavior relevant to that object and then infer their attitude from their past behavior. So if an employee were asked about her feelings about being a training specialist at Marriott, she would likely think, "I've had this same job with Marriott as a trainer for 10 years. Nobody forced me to stay on this job. So I must like it!" Self-perception theory, therefore, argues that attitudes are used, after the fact, to make sense out of an action that has already occurred rather than as devices that precede and guide action. And contrary to cognitive dissonance theory, attitudes are just casual verbal statements. When people are asked about their attitudes, and they don't have strong convictions or feelings, self-perception theory says they tend to create plausible answers.

Self-perception theory has been well supported.[38] While the traditional attitude–behavior relationship is generally positive, the behavior–attitude relationship is stronger. This is particularly true when attitudes are vague and ambiguous. When you have had few experiences regarding an attitude issue or given little previous thought to it, you'll tend to infer your attitudes from your behavior. However, when your attitudes have been established for a while and are well defined, those attitudes are likely to guide your behavior.

Home Depot encourages its employees to take part in community service projects like this one—building homes for Habitat for Humanity. Consistent with self-perception theory, volunteer work can be a powerful force in shaping attitudes about community service and helping others.

self-perception theory
Attitudes are used after the fact to make sense out of an action that has already occurred.

An Application: Attitude Surveys

The preceding review indicates that a knowledge of employee attitudes can be helpful to managers in attempting to predict employee behavior. But how does management get information about employee attitudes? The most popular method is through the use of **attitude surveys**.[39]

Exhibit 3-5 illustrates what an attitude survey might look like. Typically, attitude surveys present the employee with a set of statements or questions. Ideally, the items are tailored to obtain the specific information that management desires. An attitude score is achieved by summing up responses to individual questionnaire items. These scores can then be averaged for work groups, departments, divisions, or the organization as a whole.

attitude surveys
Eliciting responses from employees through questionnaires about how they feel about their jobs, work groups, supervisors, and the organization.

Results from attitude surveys can frequently surprise management. For instance, managers at the Heavy-Duty Division of Springfield Remanufacturing thought everything was great.[40] Because employees were actively involved in division decisions and profitability was the highest within the entire company, management assumed morale was high. To confirm their beliefs, they conducted a short attitude survey. Employees were asked if they agreed or disagreed with the following statements: (1) At work, your opinions count; (2) those of you who want to be a leader in this company have the opportunity to become one; and (3) in the past six months, someone has talked to you about your personal development. In the

Sample Attitude Survey

E X H I B I T

3-5

Please answer each of the following statements using the following rating scale:

5 = Strongly agree
4 = Agree
3 = Undecided
2 = Disagree
1 = Strongly disagree

Statement	Rating
1. This company is a pretty good place to work.	_____
2. I can get ahead in this company if I make the effort.	_____
3. This company's wage rates are competitive with those of other companies.	_____
4. Employee promotion decisions are handled fairly.	_____
5. I understand the various benefits the company offers.	_____
6. My job makes the best use of my abilities.	_____
7. My workload is challenging but not burdensome.	_____
8. I have trust and confidence in my boss.	_____
9. I feel free to tell my boss what I think.	_____
10. I know what my boss expects of me.	_____

survey, 43 percent disagreed with the first statement, 48 percent with the second, and 62 percent with the third. Management was astounded. How could this be? The division had been holding shop floor meetings to review the numbers every week for more than 12 years. And most of the managers had come up through the ranks. Management responded by creating a committee made up of representatives from every department in the division and all three shifts. The committee quickly found that there were lots of little things the division was doing that was alienating employees. Out of this committee came a large number of suggestions that after implementation, significantly improved employees' perception of their decision-making influence and their career opportunities in the division.

Using attitude surveys on a regular basis provides managers with valuable feedback on how employees perceive their working conditions. Policies and practices that management views as objective and fair may be seen as inequitable by employees in general or by certain groups of employees. If distorted perceptions lead to negative attitudes about the job and organization, it's important for management to know about it. Why? Because employee behaviors are based on perceptions, not reality. Remember, the employee who quits because she believes she is underpaid—when, in fact, management has objective data to support that her salary is highly competitive—is just as gone as if she had actually been underpaid. The use of regular attitude surveys can alert management to potential problems and employees' intentions early so that action can be taken to prevent repercussions.[41]

Attitudes and Workforce Diversity

Managers are increasingly concerned with changing employee attitudes to reflect shifting perspectives on racial, gender, and other diversity issues. A comment to a co-worker of the opposite sex, which 20 years ago might have been taken as a compliment, can today become a career-limiting episode. As such, organizations are investing in training to help reshape the attitudes of employees.

The majority of large U.S. employers and a substantial proportion of medium-sized and smaller ones sponsor some sort of diversity training.[42] Some examples: Police officers in Escondido, California, receive 36 hours of diversity training each year. Pacific Gas & Electric Co. requires a minimum of 4 hours of training for its 12,000 employees. The Federal Aviation Administration sponsors a mandatory 8-hour diversity seminar for employees of its Western Pacific region.

What do these diversity programs look like and how do they address attitude change?[43] They almost all include a self-evaluation phase. People are pressed to examine themselves and to confront ethnic and cultural stereotypes they might hold. Then participants typically take part in group discussions or panels with representatives from diverse groups. So, for instance, a Hmong man might describe his family's life in Southeast Asia, and explain why they resettled in California; or a lesbian might describe how she discovered her sexual identity, and the reaction of her friends and family when she came out.

Additional activities designed to change attitudes include arranging for people to do volunteer work in community or social service centers in order to meet face to face with individuals and groups from diverse backgrounds and using exercises that let participants feel what it's like to be different. For example, when participants see the film *Eye of the Beholder,* in which people are segregated and stereotyped according to their eye color, participants see what it's like to be judged by something over which they have no control.

JOB SATISFACTION

We have already discussed job satisfaction briefly—earlier in this chapter as well as in Chapter 1. In this section, we want to dissect the concept more carefully. How do we measure job satisfaction? How satisfied are employees in their jobs? What's the effect of job satisfaction on employee productivity, absenteeism, and turnover rates?

Measuring Job Satisfaction

We've previously defined job satisfaction as an individual's general attitude toward his or her job. This definition is clearly a very broad one.[44] Yet this is inherent in the concept. Remember, a person's job is more than just the obvious activities of shuffling papers, writing programming code, waiting on customers, or driving a truck. Jobs require interaction with co-workers and bosses, following organizational rules and policies, meeting performance standards, living with working conditions that are often less than ideal, and the like.[45] This means that an employee's assessment of how satisfied or dissatisfied he or she is with his or her job is a complex summation of a number of discrete job elements. How, then, do we measure the concept?

The two most widely used approaches are a *single global rating* and a *summation score* made up of a number of job facets. The single global rating method is nothing more than asking individuals to respond to one question, such as "All things considered, how satisfied are you with your job?" Respondents then reply by circling a number between one and five that corresponds to answers from "highly satisfied" to "highly dissatisfied." The other approach—a summation of job facets—is more sophisticated. It identifies key elements in a job and asks for the employee's feelings about each. Typical factors that would be included are the nature of the work, supervision, present pay, promotion opportunities, and relations with co-workers.[46] These factors are rated on a standardized scale and then added up to create an overall job satisfaction score.

Is one of the foregoing approaches superior to the other? Intuitively, it would seem that summing up responses to a number of job factors would achieve a more accurate evaluation of job satisfaction. The research, however, doesn't support this intuition.[47] This is one of those rare instances in which simplicity seems to work as well as complexity. Comparisons of one-question global ratings with the more lengthy summation-of-job-factors method indicate that the former is essentially as valid as the latter. The best explanation for this outcome is that the concept of job satisfaction is inherently so broad that the single question captures its essence.

How Satisfied Are People in Their Jobs?

Are most people satisfied with their jobs? The answer seems to be a qualified "yes" in the United States and in most developed countries. Independent studies, conducted among U.S. workers over the past 30 years, generally indicate that the majority of workers are satisfied with their jobs.[48] While the percentage range is pretty wide—from the low 50s to the high 70s—more people report that they're satisfied than not. Moreover, these results are generally applicable to other developed countries. For instance, comparable studies among workers in Canada, Mexico, and Europe indicate more positive than negative results.[49]

In spite of the generally positive results, recent trends are not encouraging. The evidence indicates a marked decline in job satisfaction since the early 1990s. A Conference Board study found that 58.6 percent of Americans were satisfied with their jobs in 1995. By the year 2000, that percentage was down to 50.7.[50] This intuitively seems surprising since those five years were ones of economic expansion, increased incomes, and a strong labor market. Apparently, economic prosperity doesn't necessarily translate into higher job satisfaction. And even though all income groups in the Conference Board study indicated lower job satisfaction in 2000 than in 1995, money did seem to buy some happiness. Job satisfaction increased directly with pay for every income category in both 1995 and 2000.

What factors might explain this recent drop in job satisfaction? Experts suggest it might be due to employers' efforts at trying to increase productivity through heavier employee workloads and tighter deadlines. Another contributing factor may be a feeling, increasingly reported by workers, that they have less control over their work.[51] But does the fact that job satisfaction increases with pay mean that money can buy happiness? Not necessarily. While it's possible that higher pay alone translates into higher job satisfaction, an alternative explanation is that higher pay is reflecting different types of jobs.[52] Higher-paying jobs generally require higher skills, give incumbents greater responsibilities, are more stimulating and provide more challenges, and allow workers more control. So it may be that the reports of higher satisfaction among better-paid workers reflects the greater challenge and freedom they have in their jobs rather than the pay itself.

The Effect of Job Satisfaction on Employee Performance

Managers' interest in job satisfaction tends to center on its effect on employee performance. Researchers have recognized this interest, so we find a large number of studies that have been designed to assess the impact of job satisfaction on employee productivity, absenteeism, and turnover. Let's look at the current state of our knowledge.

"Happy Workers Are Productive Workers"

This statement is generally false. The myth that "happy workers are productive workers" developed in the 1930s and 1940s, largely as a result of findings drawn by researchers conducting the Hawthorne studies at Western Electric. Based on those conclusions, managers began efforts to make their employees happier by engaging in practices such as laissez-faire leadership, improving working conditions, expanding health and family benefits such as insurance and college tuition-reimbursement, providing company picnics and other informal get-togethers, and offering counseling services for employees.

But these paternalistic practices were based on questionable findings. Reviews of the research indicate that, if there is a positive relationship between happi- ness (i.e., satisfaction) and productivity, the correlation is in the low-to-moderate range—somewhere between +.17 and +.30. This means that no more than 3 to 9 percent of the variance in output can be accounted for by employee satisfaction.[53]

Based on the evidence, a more accurate conclusion is actually the reverse—productive workers are likely to be happy workers. That is, productivity leads to satisfaction rather than the other way around.[54] If you do a good job, you intrinsically feel good about it. In addition, assuming that the organization rewards productivity, your higher productivity should increase verbal recognition, your pay level, and probabilities for promotion. These rewards, in turn, increase your level of satisfaction with the job.

Satisfaction and Productivity As the "Myth or Science?" box concludes, happy workers aren't necessarily productive workers. At the individual level, the evidence suggests the reverse to be more accurate—that productivity is likely to lead to satisfaction.

Interestingly, if we move from the individual level to that of the organization, there is renewed support for the original satisfaction–performance relationship.[55] When satisfaction and productivity data are gathered for the organization as a whole, rather than at the individual level, we find that organizations with more satisfied employees tend to be more effective than organizations with fewer satisfied employees. It may well be that the reason we haven't gotten strong support for the satisfaction-causes-productivity thesis is that studies have focused on individuals rather than on the organization and that individual-level measures of productivity don't take into consideration all the interactions and complexities in the work process. So while we might not be able to say that a happy *worker* is more productive, it might be true that happy *organizations* are more productive.

Satisfaction and Absenteeism We find a consistent negative relationship between satisfaction and absenteeism, but the correlation is moderate—usually less than +.40.[56] While it certainly makes sense that dissatisfied employees are more likely to miss work, other factors have an impact on the relationship and reduce the correlation coefficient. For example, remember our discussion of sick pay versus well pay in Chapter 2? Organizations that provide liberal sick leave benefits are encouraging all their employees—including those who are highly satisfied—to take days off. Assuming that you have a reasonable number of varied interests, you can find work satisfying and yet still take off work to enjoy a three-day weekend or tan yourself on a warm summer day if those days come free with no penalties.

An excellent illustration of how satisfaction directly leads to attendance, when there is a minimum impact from other factors, is a study done at Sears, Roebuck.[57] Satisfaction data were available on employees at Sears's two headquarters in Chicago and New York. In addition, it is important to note that Sears's policy was not to permit employees to be absent from work for avoidable reasons without penalty. The occurrence of a freak April 2 snowstorm in Chicago created the opportunity to compare employee attendance at the Chicago office with attendance in New York, where the weather was quite nice. The interesting dimension in this study is that the snowstorm gave the Chicago employees a built-in excuse not to come to work. The storm crippled the city's transportation, and individuals knew they could miss work this day with no penalty. This natural experiment permitted the comparison of attendance records for satisfied and dissatisfied employees at two locations—one where you were expected to be at work (with normal pressures for attendance) and the other where you were free to choose with no penalty involved. If satisfaction leads to attendance, when there is an absence of outside factors, the more satisfied employees should have come to work in Chicago, while dissatisfied employees should have stayed home. The study found that on this particular April 2, absenteeism rates in New York were just as high for satisfied groups of workers as for dissatisfied groups. But in Chicago, the workers with high satisfaction scores had much higher attendance than did those with lower satisfaction levels. These findings are exactly what we would have expected if satisfaction is negatively correlated with absenteeism.

Satisfaction and Turnover Satisfaction is also negatively related to turnover, but the correlation is stronger than what we found for absenteeism.[58] Yet, again, other factors such as labor-market conditions, expectations about alternative job opportunities, and length of tenure with the organization are important constraints on the actual decision to leave one's current job.[59]

Evidence indicates that an important moderator of the satisfaction–turnover relationship is the employee's level of performance.[60] Specifically, level of satisfaction is less important in predicting turnover for superior performers. Why? The organization typically makes considerable efforts to keep these people. They get pay raises, praise, recognition, increased promotional opportunities, and so forth. Just the opposite tends to apply to poor performers. Few attempts are made by the organization to retain them. There may even be subtle pressures to encourage them to quit. We would expect, therefore, that job satisfaction is more important in influencing poor performers to stay than superior performers. Regardless of level of satisfaction, the latter are more likely to remain with the organization because the receipt of recognition, praise, and other rewards gives them more reasons for staying.

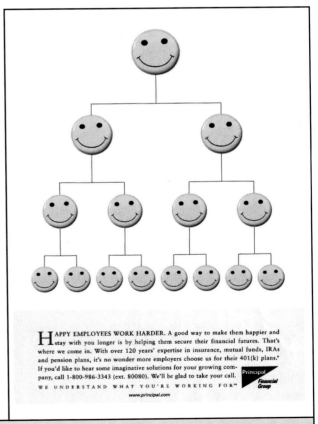

This Principal Financial Group ad accepts the widespread belief that happy workers are more productive workers.

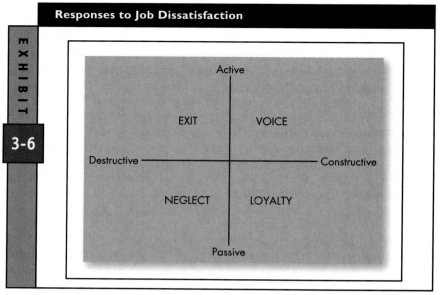

Source: C. Rusbult and D. Lowery, "When Bureaucrats Get the Blues," *Journal of Applied Social Psychology*, vol. 15, no. 1, 1985, p. 83. Reprinted with permission.

How Employees Can Express Dissatisfaction

Employee dissatisfaction can be expressed in a number of ways.[61] For example, rather than quit, employees can complain, be insubordinate, steal organizational property, or shirk a part of their work responsibilities. Exhibit 3-6 offers four responses that differ from one another along two dimensions: constructive/destructive and active/passive. They are defined as follows:[62]

- **Exit**: Behavior directed toward leaving the organization, including looking for a new position as well as resigning.
- **Voice**: Actively and constructively attempting to improve conditions, including suggesting improvements, discussing problems with superiors, and some forms of union activity.
- **Loyalty**: Passively but optimistically waiting for conditions to improve, including speaking up for the organization in the face of external criticism and trusting the organization and its management to "do the right thing."
- **Neglect**: Passively allowing conditions to worsen, including chronic absenteeism or lateness, reduced effort, and increased error rate.

Exit and neglect behaviors encompass our performance variables—productivity, absenteeism, and turnover. But this model expands employee response to include voice and loyalty—constructive behaviors that allow individuals to tolerate unpleasant situations or to revive satisfactory working conditions. It helps us to understand situations, such as those sometimes found among unionized workers, for whom low job satisfaction is coupled with low turnover.[63] Union members often express dissatisfaction through the grievance procedure or through formal contract negotiations. These voice mechanisms allow union members to continue in their jobs while convincing themselves that they are acting to improve the situation.

Job Satisfaction and OCB

It seems logical to assume that job satisfaction should be a major determinant of an employee's organizational citizenship behavior (OCB).[64] Satisfied employees would

exit

Dissatisfaction expressed through behavior directed toward leaving the organization.

voice

Dissatisfaction expressed through active and constructive attempts to improve conditions.

loyalty

Dissatisfaction expressed by passively waiting for conditions to improve.

neglect

Dissatisfaction expressed through allowing conditions to worsen.

seem more likely to talk positively about the organization, help others, and go beyond the normal expectations in their job. Moreover, satisfied employees might be more prone to go beyond the call of duty because they want to reciprocate their positive experiences. Consistent with this thinking, early discussions of OCB assumed that it was closely linked with satisfaction.[65] More recent evidence, however, suggests that satisfaction influences OCB, but through perceptions of fairness.

There is a modest overall relationship between job satisfaction and OCB.[66] But satisfaction is unrelated to OCB when fairness is controlled for.[67] What does this mean? Basically, job satisfaction comes down to conceptions of fair outcomes, treatment, and procedures.[68] If you don't feel like your supervisor, the organization's procedures, or pay policies are fair, your job satisfaction is likely to suffer significantly. However, when you perceive organizational processes and outcomes to be fair, trust is developed. And when you trust your employer, you're more willing to voluntarily engage in behaviors that go beyond your formal job requirements.

Employees at Office Depot obsess on pleasing their customers. Here, at an Office Depot store in Santa Rosa, California, employee Greg Scherer helps customer Chantal Vogel find the office supplies she's looking for during one of California's power blackouts in the winter of 2001.

Job Satisfaction and Customer Satisfaction

As we noted in Chapter 1, employees in service jobs often interact with customers. Since the management of service organizations should be concerned with pleasing those customers, it is reasonable to ask: Is employee satisfaction related to positive customer outcomes? For frontline employees who have regular contact with customers, the answer is "Yes."

The evidence indicates that satisfied employees increase customer satisfaction and loyalty.[69] Why? In service organizations, customer retention and defection are highly dependent on how front-line employees deal with customers. Satisfied employees are more likely to be friendly, upbeat, and responsive—which customers appreciate. And because satisfied employees are less prone to turnover, customers are more likely to encounter familiar faces and receive experienced service. These qualities build customer satisfaction and loyalty. In addition, the relationship seems to apply in reverse: Dissatisfied customers can increase an employee's job dissatisfaction. Employees who have regular contact with customers report that rude, thoughtless, or unreasonably demanding customers adversely effect the employees' job satisfaction.[70]

A number of companies are acting on this evidence. Service-oriented businesses such as FedEx, Southwest Airlines, American Express, and Office Depot obsess about pleasing their customers. Toward that end, they also focus on building employee satisfaction—recognizing that employee satisfaction will go a long way toward contributing to their goal of having happy customers. These firms seek to hire upbeat and friendly employees, they train employees in the importance of customer service, they reward customer service, they provide positive employee work climates, and they regularly track employee satisfaction through attitude surveys.

SUMMARY AND IMPLICATIONS FOR MANAGERS

Why is it important to know an individual's values? Although they don't have a direct impact on behavior, values strongly influence a person's attitudes. So knowledge of an individual's value system can provide insight into his or her attitudes.

Given that people's values differ, managers can use the Rokeach Value Survey to assess potential employees and determine if their values align with the dominant values of the organization. An employee's performance and satisfaction are likely to be higher if his or her values fit well with the organization. For instance, the person who places high importance on imagination, independence, and freedom is likely to be poorly matched with an organization that seeks conformity from its employees. Managers are more likely to appreciate, evaluate positively, and allocate rewards to employees who "fit in," and employees are more likely to be satisfied if they perceive that they do fit in. This argues for management to strive during the selection of new employees to find job candidates who not only have the ability, experience, and motivation to perform, but also a value system that is compatible with the organization's.

Managers should be interested in their employees' attitudes because attitudes give warnings of potential problems and because they influence behavior. Satisfied and committed employees, for instance, have lower rates of turnover and absenteeism. Given that managers want to keep resignations and absences down—especially among their more productive employees—they will want to do the things that will generate positive job attitudes.

Managers should also be aware that employees will try to reduce cognitive dissonance. More important, dissonance can be managed. If employees are required to engage in activities that appear inconsistent to them or that are at odds with their attitudes, the pressures to reduce the resulting dissonance are lessened when the employee perceives that the dissonance is externally imposed and is beyond his or her control or if the rewards are significant enough to offset the dissonance.

Managers Can Create Satisfied Employees

A review of the evidence has identified four factors conducive to high levels of employee job satisfaction: mentally challenging work, equitable rewards, supportive working conditions, and supportive colleagues.[a] Importantly, each of these factors is controllable by management.

Mentally challenging work. People prefer jobs that give them opportunities to use their skills and abilities and offer a variety of tasks, freedom, and feedback on how well they're doing. These characteristics make work mentally challenging.

Equitable rewards. Employees want pay systems and promotion policies that they perceive as being just, unambiguous, and in line with their expectations. When pay is seen as fair based on job demands, individual skill level, and community pay standards, satisfaction is likely to result. Similarly, employees seek fair promotion policies and practices. Promotions provide opportunities for personal growth, more responsibilities, and increased social status. Individuals who perceive that promotion decisions are made in a fair and just manner, therefore, are likely to experience satisfaction from their jobs.

Supportive working conditions. Employees are concerned with their work environment for both personal comfort and facilitating doing a good job. Studies demonstrate that employees prefer physical surroundings that are not dangerous or uncomfortable. In addition, most employees prefer working relatively close to home, in clean and relatively modern facilities, and with adequate tools and equipment.

Supportive colleagues. People get more out of work than merely money or tangible achievements. For most employees, work also fills the need for social interaction. Not surprisingly, therefore, having friendly and supportive co-workers leads to increased job satisfaction. The behavior of one's boss is also a major determinant of satisfaction. Studies generally find that employee satisfaction is increased when the immediate supervisor is understanding and friendly, offers praise for good performance, listens to employees' opinions, and shows a personal interest in them.

[a]E. A. Locke, "The Nature and Causes of Job Satisfaction," in M. D. Dunnette (ed.), *Handbook of Industrial and Organizational Psychology* (Chicago: Rand McNally, 1976), pp. 1319–28.

The notion that managers and organizations can control the level of employee job satisfaction is inherently attractive. It fits nicely with the view that managers directly influence organizational processes and outcomes. Unfortunately there is a growing body of evidence that challenges the notion that managers control the factors that influence employee job satisfaction. The most recent findings indicate that employee job satisfaction is largely genetically determined.[b]

Whether a person is happy or not is essentially determined by his or her gene structure. Approximately 80 percent of people's differences in happiness, or subjective well-being, has been found to be attributable to their different genes.

Analysis of satisfaction data for a selected sample of individuals over a 50-year period found that individual results were consistently stable over time, even when these people changed employers and occupations. This and other research suggests that an individual's disposition toward life—positive or negative—is established by his or her genetic make-up, holds over time, and carries over into his or her disposition toward work.

Given these findings, there is probably little that most managers can do to influence employee satisfaction. In spite of the fact that managers and organizations go to extensive lengths to try to improve employee job satisfaction through actions such as manipulating job characteristics, working conditions, and rewards, these actions are likely to have little effect. The only place where managers will have any significant influence will be through their control of the selection process. If managers want satisfied workers, they need to make sure their selection process screens out the negative, maladjusted, trouble-making fault-finders who derive little satisfaction in anything about their jobs.

[b]See, for instance, R. D. Arvey, B. McCall, T. J. Bouchard, Jr., and P. Taubman, "Genetic Influences on Job Satisfaction and Work Values," *Personality and Individual Differences*, July 1994, pp. 21–33; D. Lykken and A. Tellegen, "Happiness is a Stochastic Phenomenon," *Psychological Science*, May 1996, pp. 186–89; and T. A. Judge, E. A. Locke, C. C. Durham, and A. N. Kluger, "Dispositional Effects on Job and Life Satisfaction: The Role of Core Evaluations," *Journal of Applied Psychology*, February 1998, pp. 17–34.

1. Contrast the Veteran, Boomers, Xers, and Nexters classifications with the terminal values identified in the Rokeach Value Survey.

2. Contrast the cognitive and affective components of an attitude.

3. What is cognitive dissonance and how is it related to attitudes?

4. What is self-perception theory? How does it increase our ability to predict behavior?

5. What contingency factors can improve the statistical relationship between attitudes and behavior?

6. What explains the recent declines in employee job satisfaction?

7. Are happy workers productive workers?

8. What is the relationship between job satisfaction and absenteeism? Turnover? Which is the stronger relationship?

9. How can managers get employees to more readily accept working with colleagues who are different from themselves?

10. Contrast exit, voice, loyalty, and neglect as employee responses to job dissatisfaction.

Questions for Critical Thinking

1. "Thirty-five years ago, young employees we hired were ambitious, conscientious, hardworking, and honest. Today's young workers don't have the same values." Do you agree or disagree with this manager's comments? Support your position.

2. Do you think there might be any positive and significant relationship between the possession of certain personal values and successful career progression in organizations like Merrill Lynch, the AFL-CIO, and the city of Cleveland's police department? Discuss.

3. "Managers should do everything they can to enhance the job satisfaction of their employees." Do you agree or disagree? Support your position.

4. Discuss the advantages and disadvantages of using regular attitude surveys to monitor employee job satisfaction.

5. When employees are asked whether they would again choose the same work or whether they would want their children to follow in their footsteps, typically less than half answer in the affirmative. What, if anything, do you think this implies about employee job satisfaction?

Team Exercise | Challenges in Negotiating with Chinese Executives

Form into teams of three to five members each. All your team's members work for a company in the midwestern part of the United States that manufactures bathroom fixtures such as sinks, toilets, and bathtubs. Your company's senior management has decided to make a serious effort to expand sales of its fixtures into the Chinese market. And to begin the process, your team has been chosen to make a 10-day trip to Beijing and Shanghai to meet with purchasing executives at half-a-dozen Chinese residential and commercial real estate construction developers.

Your team will be leaving for its trip in a week. You will have a translator in both cities, but your team wants to do whatever it can to make a good impression on the Chinese executives they will be meeting. Unfortunately, the members of your team have a relatively limited knowledge of Chinese culture. To help with the trip, one of your team members has found a brochure that summarizes some of the unique characteristics of the Chinese and that might prove valuable in opening negotiations. The highlights of that brochure included:

- China is a group-oriented society and any negotiations must cover the interests of many different parties.
- Emphasis is placed on trust and mutual connections.
- The Chinese are interested in long-term benefits.
- Chinese seem to have a compelling need to dwell on the subject of friendship.
- Initial business meetings are devoted to pleasantries—such as serving tea and chit chat.
- So as not to lose face, Chinese prefer to negotiate through an intermediary.
- Chinese expect reciprocal invitations—if a banquet is given in the honor of your team, they expect you to give a banquet for their team.

- The Chinese are sensitive about foreigners' comments on Chinese politics.

- The Chinese are punctual and expect others will arrive promptly on time for each meeting.

- The Chinese are well aware of Americans' reputation for impatience. They will often take their time in decision making to gain an advantage in negotiations.

- The Chinese do not like to be touched or slapped on the back or even to shake hands. A slight bow and a brief shake of the hands are more appropriate.

- The Chinese generally believe that foreign business persons will be highly qualified technically in their specific area of expertise.

- Chinese posture becomes rigid whenever they feel their goals are being compromised.

- Very often, several visits are necessary to consummate any business transaction.

- Foreigners should not focus on the individual Chinese person but rather on the group of individuals who are working for a particular goal.

- Telephone calls and fax machines are a vital part of Chinese business but they think important business is conducted only face to face.

- In negotiations with the Chinese, nothing should be considered final until it has been actually realized.

Your team has 30 minutes to rough out a strategy for meeting with the Chinese purchasing executives. Be as specific as possible. When finished, be prepared to present your strategy to the entire class.

This exercise is based on information in R. Harris and R. T. Moran, *Managing Cultural Differences*, 4th ed. (Houston, TX: Gulf Publishing, 1996), pp. 252–57.

Ethical Dilemma | Is It a Bribe or a Gift?

The Foreign Corrupt Practices Act prohibits U.S. firms from making payments to foreign government officials with the aim of gaining or maintaining business. But payments are acceptable if they don't violate local laws. For instance, payments to officers working for foreign corporations are legal. Most other countries don't have such legal guidelines.

Bribery is a common way of doing business in many underdeveloped countries. Government jobs there often don't pay very well, so it's tempting for officials to supplement their income with bribes. In addition, in many countries, the penalties for demanding and receiving bribes is little or nonexistent.

You are an American who works for a large European multinational computer manufacturer. You are currently working to sell a $3 million system to a government agency in Nigeria. The Nigerian official who heads up the team that will decide who gets this contract has asked you for a payment of $20,000. He said this payment won't guarantee you get the order but without it he couldn't be very encouraging. Your company's policy is very flexible on the issue of "gifts" to facilitate sales. Your boss says that it's OK to pay the $20,000, but only if you can be relatively assured of the order.

You're not sure what you should do. The Nigerian official has told you specifically that any payment to him is not to be mentioned to anyone else on the Nigerian team. You know for certain that three other companies are also negotiating to get this contract. You've heard through the grapevine, but it's unconfirmed, that two of those companies have turned down the payment request.

What would you do?

This exercise is based on M. Allen, "Here Comes the Bribe," *Entrepreneur*, October 2000, p. 48.

Case Incident | Trilogy Software

Few industries have undergone as much turbulence in the past few years as those in Internet-related businesses. One of the leaders in this industry is Trilogy Software, based in Austin, Texas. Trilogy, founded in 1989, creates software to help e-businesses handle procurement, customer service, relationship management, and data integration. Its 1500 employees serve an impressive client base that includes Ford, FedEx, Land's End, Charles Schwab, and Motorola.

Trilogy's president and CEO, Joe Liemandt, seeks to hire and keep employees who can flourish in a chaotic environment, who are willing to take risks, and aren't afraid of working long hours. Liemandt has fashioned a strategy for Trilogy that encompasses maintaining the high energy of a start-up with the experience of an established company. An important part of that strategy is continually recruiting "only the best"— bright, dynamic individuals from the best universities, business schools, and industries. By hiring great people and giving them significant responsibilities from day one, Liemandt hopes his firm will be able to respond to competitive challenges, keep its entrepreneurial spirit alive, and achieve its goal of being a high-impact company.

New recruits are wooed to Austin with dinners, cultural and recreational outings, and competitive salaries. Once there, the recruits go through "boot camp"—an intensive training program conducted to turn rookies into Trilogians. In classes led by Liemandt and other Trilogy veterans, the first week is spent learning about programming languages, product plans, and marketing. Classes start at 8 A.M. and, in the first month at least, last until midnight. During the second week, the new hires are divided into small teams and given three weeks to complete projects ranging from making an existing Trilogy product run faster to creating new products from scratch. Their performance on these projects will affect where the new hires are eventually placed and also determines whether they'll be rewarded with a trip to Las Vegas at the end of boot camp.

This boot camp introduction to Trilogy is designed to instill the company's values and shape new employees' expectations. Recruits are told that effort won't be enough. In a presentation given by Liemandt about the team projects, the recruits are shown a slide that says, "No Reward for Trying." He flatly states, "If you set a hard goal and don't make it, you don't win any points." Some recruits fall out during this boot camp. But for those who survive, life at Trilogy can be very rewarding and satisfying.

The company's atmosphere combines work and play. Trilogy gives employees ambitious responsibilities and the freedom and resources to fulfill them. The firm's culture encourages maximizing employee passion, energy, and commitment. And the company generously rewards its employees for their performance. Company benefits are intended to keep employees motivated and excited. For instance, it offers fully stocked kitchens, company trips, discounted memberships at local gyms, the use of company ski boats on two Austin lakes, and an on-site concierge service to take care of personal errands.

Questions

1. Design an employee attitude survey that Trilogy's managers might use. Remember to tailor it to tap the attitudes that Trilogy is looking for in its employees.

2. What predictions, if any, could you make about job satisfaction at Trilogy? How might job satisfaction affect work outcomes at Trilogy?

3. How might the collapse of many dot-com businesses since 2000 affect the attitudes of Trilogy employees? What, if anything, could management do to shape those attitudes positively?

Based on www.trilogy.com, March 6, 2002; E. Ramstad, "High Rollers," *Wall Street Journal*, September 21, 1998, p. A1; and N. M. Tichy, "No Ordinary Boot Camp," *Harvard Business Review*, April 2001, pp. 63–70.

KSS PROGRAM

KNOW THE CONCEPTS
SELF-AWARENESS
SKILLS APPLICATIONS

Changing Attitudes

After you've read this chapter, take Self-Assessment #11 (How Satisfied Am I with My Job?) on your enclosed CD-ROM, and complete the skill-building module "Changing Attitudes" on p. 616.

Endnotes

1. C. Y. Chen, "Chasing the Net Generation," *Fortune*, September 4, 2000, pp. 295–98.
2. M. Rokeach, *The Nature of Human Values* (New York: Free Press, 1973), p. 5.
3. M. Rokeach and S. J. Ball-Rokeach, "Stability and Change in American Value Priorities, 1968–1981," *American Psychologist*, May 1989, pp. 775–84; and B. M. Meglino and E. C. Ravlin, "Individual Values in Organizations: Concepts, Controversies, and Research," *Journal of Management*, vol. 24, no. 3, 1998, p. 355.
4. See, for instance, Meglino and Ravlin, "Individual Values in Organizations," pp. 351–89.
5. Rokeach, *The Nature of Human Values*, p. 6.
6. J. M. Munson and B. Z. Posner, "The Factorial Validity of a Modified Rokeach Value Survey for Four Diverse Samples," *Educational and Psychological Measurement*, Winter 1980, pp. 1073–79; and W. C. Frederick and J. Weber, "The Values of Corporate Managers and Their Critics: An Empirical Description and Normative Implications," in W. C. Frederick and L. E. Preston (eds.), *Business Ethics: Re-*

search Issues and Empirical Studies (Greenwich, CT: JAI Press, 1990), pp. 123–44.

7. Frederick and Weber, "The Values of Corporate Managers and Their Critics."

8. Ibid., p. 132.

9. See, for example R. Zemke, C. Raines, and B. Filipczak, *Generations at Work: Managing the Clash of Veterans, Boomers, Xers, and Nexters in Your Workplace* (New York: AMACOM, 1999); C. Penttila, "Generational Gyrations," *Entrepreneur*, April 2001, pp. 102–05; R. Zemke, "Here Come the Millennials," *Training*, July 2001, pp. 44–49; J. Pruitt, "The Generational Blur," *Training*, January 2002, p. 64; and P. Paul, "Global Generation Gap," *American Demographics*, March 2002, pp. 18–19.

10. As noted to your author by R. Volkema and R. L. Neal, Jr., of American University, this model may also be limited in its application to minority populations and recent immigrants to North America.

11. R. E. Hattwick, Y. Kathawala, M. Monipullil, and L. Wall, "On the Alleged Decline in Business Ethics," *Journal of Behavioral Economics*, Summer 1989, pp. 129–43.

12. B. Z. Posner and W. H. Schmidt, "Values and the American Manager: An Update Updated," *California Management Review*, Spring 1992, p. 86.

13. G. Hofstede, *Culture's Consequences: International Differences in Work Related Values* (Beverly Hills, CA: Sage, 1980); G. Hofstede, *Cultures and Organizations: Software of the Mind* (London: McGraw-Hill, 1991); G. Hofstede, "Cultural Constraints in Management Theories," *Academy of Management Executive*, February 1993, pp. 81–94; G. Hofstede and M. F. Peterson, "National Values and Organizational Practices," in N. M. Ashkanasy, C. M. Wilderom, and M. F. Peterson (eds.), *Handbook of Organizational Culture and Climate* (Thousand Oaks, CA: Sage, 2000), pp. 401–16. For criticism of this research, see B. McSweeney, "Hofstede's Model of National Cultural Differences and Their Consequences: A Triumph of Faith—a Failure of Analysis," *Human Relations*, January 2002, pp. 89–118.

14. Hofstede called this dimension masculinity versus femininity, but we have changed his terms because of their strong sexist connotation.

15. M. Javidan and R. J. House, "Cultural Acumen for the Global Manager: Lessons from Project GLOBE," *Organizational Dynamics*, Spring 2001, pp. 289–305.

16. N. J. Adler, "Cross-Cultural Management Research: The Ostrich and the Trend," *Academy of Management Review*, April 1983, pp. 226–32.

17. L. Godkin, C. E. Braye, and C. L. Caunch, "U.S.-Based Cross Cultural Management Research in the Eighties," *Journal of Business and Economic Perspectives*, vol. 15 (1989), pp. 37–45; and T. K. Peng, M. F. Peterson, and Y. Shyi, "Quantitative Methods in Cross-National Management Research: Trends and Equivalence Issues," *Journal of Organizational Behavior*, vol. 12 (1991), pp. 87–107.

18. S. J. Breckler, "Empirical Validation of Affect, Behavior, and Cognition as Distinct Components of Attitude," *Journal of Personality and Social Psychology*, May 1984, pp. 1191–1205; and S. L. Crites, Jr., L. R. Fabrigar, and R. E. Petty, "Measuring the Affective and Cognitive Properties of Attitudes: Conceptual and Methodological Issues," *Personality and Social Psychology Bulletin*, December 1994, pp. 619–34.

19. P. P. Brooke Jr., D. W. Russell, and J. L. Price, "Discriminant Validation of Measures of Job Satisfaction, Job Involvement, and Organizational Commitment," *Journal of Applied Psychology*, May 1988, pp. 139–45; and R. T. Keller, "Job Involvement and Organizational Commitment as Longitudinal Predictors of Job Performance: A Study of Scientists and Engineers," *Journal of Applied Psychology*, August 1997, pp. 539–45.

20. See, for example, S. Rabinowitz and D. T. Hall, "Organizational Research in Job Involvement," *Psychological Bulletin*, March 1977, pp. 265–88; G. J. Blau, "A Multiple Study Investigation of the Dimensionality of Job Involvement," *Journal of Vocational Behavior*, August 1985, pp. 19–36; and N. A. Jans, "Organizational Factors and Work Involvement," *Organizational Behavior and Human Decision Processes*, June 1985, pp. 382–96.

21. Based on G. J. Blau and K. R. Boal, "Conceptualizing How Job Involvement and Organizational Commitment Affect Turnover and Absenteeism," *Academy of Management Review*, April 1987, p. 290.

22. G. J. Blau, "Job Involvement and Organizational Commitment as Interactive Predictors of Tardiness and Absenteeism," *Journal of Management*, Winter 1986, pp. 577–84; and K. Boal and R. Cidambi, "Attitudinal Correlates of Turnover and Absenteeism: A Meta Analysis," paper presented at the meeting of the American Psychological Association, Toronto, Canada, 1984.

23. G. Farris, "A Predictive Study of Turnover," *Personnel Psychology*, Summer 1971, pp. 311–28.

24. Blau and Boal, "Conceptualizing," p. 290.

25. See, for instance, W. Hom, R. Katerberg, and C. L. Hulin, "Comparative Examination of Three Approaches to the Prediction of Turnover," *Journal of Applied Psychology*, June 1979, pp. 280–90; H. Angle and J. Perry, "Organizational Commitment: Individual and Organizational Influence," *Work and Occupations*, May 1983, pp. 123–46; and J. L. Pierce and R. B. Dunham, "Organizational Commitment: Pre-Employment Propensity and Initial Work Experiences," *Journal of Management*, Spring 1987, pp. 163–78.

26. Hom, Katerberg, and Hulin, "Comparative Examination"; and R. T. Mowday, L. W. Porter, and R. M. Steers, *Employee Organization Linkages: The Psychology of Commitment, Absenteeism, and Turnover* (New York: Academic Press, 1982).

27. L. W. Porter, R. M. Steers, R. T. Mowday, and V. Boulian, "Organizational Commitment, Job Satisfaction, and Turnover among Psychiatric Technicians," *Journal of Applied Psychology*, October 1974, pp. 603–09.

28. D. M. Rousseau, "Organizational Behavior in the New Organizational Era," in J. T. Spence, J. M. Darley, and D. J. Foss (eds.), *Annual Review of Psychology*, vol. 48 (Palo Alto, CA: Annual Reviews, 1997), p. 523.

29. Ibid.

30. See, for instance, A. J. Elliot and G. Devine, "On the Motivational Nature of Cognitive Dissonance: Dissonance as Psychological Discomfort," *Journal of Personality and Social Psychology*, September 1994, pp. 382–94.

31. See R. Rosenblatt, "How Do Tobacco Executives Live with Themselves?" *The New York Times Magazine*, March 20, 1994, pp. 34–41; and J. A. Byrne, "Philip Morris: Inside America's Most Reviled Company," *U.S. News & World Report*, November 29, 1999, pp. 176–92.

32. L. Festinger, *A Theory of Cognitive Dissonance* (Stanford, CA: Stanford University Press, 1957).

33. A. W. Wicker, "Attitude versus Action: The Relationship of Verbal and Overt Behavioral Responses to Attitude Objects," *Journal of Social Issues*, Autumn 1969, pp. 41–78.

34. Ibid., p. 65.

35. See S. J. Kraus, "Attitudes and the Prediction of Behavior: A Meta-Analysis of the Empirical Literature," *Personality and Social Psychology Bulletin*, January 1995, pp. 58–75; I. Ajzen, "The Directive Influence of Attitudes on Behavior," in M. Gollwitzer and J. A. Bargh (eds.), *The Psychology of Action: Linking Cognition and Motivation to Behavior* (New York: Guilford, 1996), pp. 385–403; and I. Ajzen, "Nature and Operation of Attitudes," in S. T. Fiske, D. L. Schacter, and C. Zahn-Waxler (eds.), *Annual Review of Psychology*, vol. 52 (Palo Alto, CA: Annual Reviews, Inc., 2001), pp. 27–58.

36. Ibid.

37. D. J. Bem, "Self-Perception Theory," in L. Berkowitz (ed.), *Advances in Experimental Social Psychology*, vol. 6 (New York: Academic Press, 1972), pp. 1–62.

38. See C. A. Kiesler, R. E. Nisbett, and M. Zanna, "On Inferring One's Belief from One's Behavior," *Journal of Personality and Social Psychology*, April 1969, pp. 321–27; S. E. Taylor, "On Inferring One's Attitudes from One's Behavior: Some Delimiting Conditions," *Journal of Personality and Social Psychology*, January 1975, pp. 126–31; and A. M. Tybout and C. A. Scott, "Availability of Well-Defined Internal Knowledge and the Attitude Formation Process: Information Aggregation Versus Self-Perception," *Journal of Personality and Social Psychology*, March 1983, pp. 474–91.

39. See, for example, B. Fishel, "A New Perspective: How to Get the Real Story from Attitude Surveys," *Training*, February 1998, pp. 91–94.

40. J. Stack, "Measuring Morale," *INC.*, January 1997, pp. 29–30.

41. See S. Shellenbarger, "Companies Are Finding It Really Pays to Be Nice to Employees," *Wall Street Journal*, July 22, 1998, p. B1.

42. See Society for Human Resource Management, "Impact of Diversity on the Bottom Line," www.fortune.com/sections, August 31, 2001, pp. 5–12; and M. Bendick, Jr., M. L. Egan, and S. M. Lofhjelm, "Workforce Diversity Training: From Anti-Discrimination Compliance to Organizational Development," *Human Resource Planning*, vol. 24, no. 2, 2001, pp. 10–25.

43. This section is based on A. Rossett and T. Bickham, "Diversity Training: Hope, Faith and Cynicism," *Training*, January 1994, pp. 40–46.

44. For problems with the concept of job satisfaction, see R. Hodson, "Workplace Behaviors," *Work and Occupations*, August 1991, pp. 271–90; and H. M. Weiss and R. Cropanzano, "Affective Events Theory: A Theoretical Discussion of the Structure, Causes and Consequences of Affective Experiences at Work," in B. M. Staw and L. L. Cummings (eds), *Research in Organizational Behavior*, vol. 18 (Greenwich, CT: JAI Press, 1996), pp. 1–3.

45. The Wyatt Company's 1989 national WorkAmerica study identified 12 dimensions of satisfaction: work organization, working conditions, communications, job performance and performance review, co-workers, supervision, company management, pay, benefits, career development and training, job content and satisfaction, and company image and change.

46. See E. Spector, *Job Satisfaction: Application, Assessment, Causes, and Consequences* (Thousand Oaks, CA: Sage, 1997), p. 3.

47. J. Wanous, A. E. Reichers, and M. J. Hudy, "Overall Job Satisfaction: How Good Are Single-Item Measures?" *Journal of Applied Psychology*, April 1997, pp. 247–52.

48. A. F. Chelte, J. Wright, and C. Tausky, "Did Job Satisfaction Really Drop During the 1970s?" *Monthly Labor Review*, November 1982, pp. 33–36; "Job Satisfaction High in America, Says Conference Board Study," *Monthly Labor Review*, February 1985, p. 52; C. Hartman and S. Pearlstein, "The Joy of Working," *INC.*, November 1987, pp. 61–66; E. Graham, "Work May Be a Rat Race, but It's Not a Daily Grind," *Wall Street Journal*, September 19, 1997, p. R1; and J. L. Seglin, "Americans @ Work," *INC.*, June 1998, pp. 91–94.

49. L. Grant, "Unhappy in Japan," *Fortune*, January 13, 1997, p. 142; "Survey Finds Satisfied Workers in Canada," *Manpower Argus*, January 1997, p. 6; and T. Mudd, "Europeans Generally Happy in the Workplace," *Industry Week*, October 4, 1999, pp. 11–12.

50. Conference Board study of job satisfaction; www.consumerresearchcenter.org; October 2000.

51. Ibid; and R. Gardyn, "Happiness Grows on Trees," *American Demographics*, May 2001, pp. 18–21.

52. R. Gardyn, "Happiness Grows on Trees."

53. M. T. Iaffaldano and M. Muchinsky, "Job Satisfaction and Job Performance: A Meta-Analysis," *Psychological Bulletin*, March 1985, pp. 251–73; and T. A. Judge, C. J. Thoresen, J. E. Bono, and G. K. Patton, "The Job Satisfaction-Job Performance Relationship: A Qualitative and Quantitative Review," *Psychological Bulletin*, May 2001, pp. 376–407.

54. C. N. Greene, "The Satisfaction-Performance Controversy," *Business Horizons*, February 1972, pp. 31–41; E. E. Lawler III, *Motivation in Organizations* (Monterey, CA: Brooks/Cole, 1973); and M. M. Petty, G. W. McGee, and J. W. Cavender, "A Meta-Analysis of the Relationship Between Individual Job Satisfaction and Individual Performance," *Academy of Management Review*, October 1984, pp. 712–21.

55. C. Ostroff, "The Relationship between Satisfaction, Attitudes, and Performance: An Organizational Level Analysis," *Journal of Applied Psychology*, December 1992, pp. 963–74; and A. M. Ryan, M. J. Schmit, and R. Johnson, "Attitudes and Effectiveness: Examining Relations at an Organizational Level," *Personnel Psychology*, Winter 1996, pp. 853–82.

56. E. A. Locke, "The Nature and Causes of Job Satisfaction," in M. D. Dunnette (ed.), *Handbook of Industrial and Organizational Psychology* (Chicago: Rand McNally, 1976), p. 1331; S. L. McShane, "Job Satisfaction and Absenteeism: A Meta-Analytic Re-Examination," *Canadian Journal of Administrative Science*, June 1984, pp. 61–77; R. D. Hackett and R. M. Guion, "A Reevaluation of the Absenteeism–Job Satisfaction Relationship," *Organizational Behavior and Human Decision Processes*, June 1985, p. 340–81; K. D. Scott and G. S. Taylor, "An Examination of Conflicting Findings on the Relationship between Job Satisfaction and Absenteeism: A Meta-Analysis," *Academy of Management Journal*, September 1985, pp. 599–612; R. D. Hackett, "Work Attitudes and Employee Absenteeism: A Synthesis of the Literature," paper presented at 1988 National Academy of Management Conference, Anaheim, CA, August 1988; and R. Steel and J. R. Rentsch, "Influence of Cumulation Strategies on the Long-

Range Prediction of Absenteeism," *Academy of Management Journal*, December 1995, pp. 1616–34.

57. F. J. Smith, "Work Attitudes as Predictors of Attendance on a Specific Day," *Journal of Applied Psychology*, February 1977, pp. 16–19.

58. W. Hom and R. W. Griffeth, *Employee Turnover* (Cincinnati, OH: Southwestern, 1995); and R. W. Griffeth, P. W. Hom, and S. Gaertner, "A Meta-Analysis of Antecedents and Correlates of Employee Turnover: Update, Moderator Tests, and Research Implications for the Next Millennium," *Journal of Management*, vol. 26, no. 3, 2000, p. 479.

59. See, for example, C. L. Hulin, M. Roznowski, and D. Hachiya, "Alternative Opportunities and Withdrawal Decisions: Empirical and Theoretical Discrepancies and an Integration," *Psychological Bulletin*, July 1985, pp. 233–50; and J. M. Carsten and P. E. Spector, "Unemployment, Job Satisfaction, and Employee Turnover: A Meta-Analytic Test of the Muchinsky Model," *Journal of Applied Psychology*, August 1987, pp. 374–81.

60. D. G. Spencer and R. M. Steers, "Performance as a Moderator of the Job Satisfaction–Turnover Relationship," *Journal of Applied Psychology*, August 1981, pp. 511–14.

61. S. M. Puffer, "Prosocial Behavior, Noncompliant Behavior, and Work Performance among Commission Salespeople," *Journal of Applied Psychology*, November 1987, pp. 615–21; J. Hogan and R. Hogan, "How to Measure Employee Reliability," *Journal of Applied Psychology*, May 1989, pp. 273–79; and C. D. Fisher and E. A. Locke, "The New Look in Job Satisfaction Research and Theory," in C. J. Cranny, P. C. Smith, and E. F. Stone (eds.), *Job Satisfaction* (New York: Lexington Books, 1992), pp. 165–94.

62. See D. Farrell, "Exit, Voice, Loyalty, and Neglect as Responses to Job Dissatisfaction: A Multidimensional Scaling Study," *Academy of Management Journal*, December 1983, pp. 596–606; C. E. Rusbult, D. Farrell, G. Rogers, and A. G. Mainous III, "Impact of Exchange Variables on Exit, Voice, Loyalty, and Neglect: An Integrative Model of Responses to Declining Job Satisfaction," *Academy of Management Journal*, September 1988, pp. 599–627; M. J. Withey and W. H. Cooper, "Predicting Exit, Voice, Loyalty, and Neglect," *Administrative Science Quarterly*, December 1989, pp. 521–39; and J. Zhou and J. M. George, "When Job Dissatisfaction Leads to Creativity: Encouraging the Expression of Voice," *Academy of Management Journal*, August 2001, pp. 682–96.

63. R. B. Freeman, "Job Satisfaction as an Economic Variable," *American Economic Review*, January 1978, pp. 135–41.

64. P. E. Spector, *Job Satisfaction*, pp. 57–58.

65. See T. S. Bateman and D. W. Organ, "Job Satisfaction and the Good Soldier: The Relationship between Affect and Employee 'Citizenship,'" *Academy of Management Journal*, December 1983, pp. 587–95; C. A. Smith, D. W. Organ, and J. Near, "Organizational Citizenship Behavior: Its Nature and Antecedents," *Journal of Applied Psychology*, October 1983, pp. 653–63; A. P. Brief, *Attitudes in and around Organizations* (Thousand Oaks, CA: Sage, 1998), pp. 44–45; and M. Podsakoff, S. B. MacKenzie, J. B. Paine, and D. G. Bachrach, "Organizational Citizenship Behaviors: A Critical Review of the Theoretical and Empirical Literature and Suggestions for Future Research," *Journal of Management*, vol. 26, no. 3, 2000, pp. 513–63.

66. D. W. Organ and K. Ryan, "A Meta-Analytic Review of Attitudinal and Dispositional Predictors of Organizational Citizenship Behavior," *Personnel Psychology*, Winter 1995, p. 791; and J. A. LePine, A. Erez, and D. E. Johnson, "The Nature and Dimensionality of Organizational Citizenship Behavior: A Critical Review and Meta-Analysis," *Journal of Applied Psychology*, February 2002, pp. 52–65.

67. J. Fahr, P. M. Podsakoff, and D. W. Organ, "Accounting for Organizational Citizenship Behavior: Leader Fairness and Task Scope Versus Satisfaction," *Journal of Management*, December 1990, pp. 705–22; R. H. Moorman, "Relationship between Organization Justice and Organizational Citizenship Behaviors: Do Fairness Perceptions Influence Employee Citizenship?" *Journal of Applied Psychology*, December 1991, pp. 845–55; and M. A. Konovsky and D. W. Organ, "Dispositional and Contextual Determinants of Organizational Citizenship Behavior," *Journal of Organizational Behavior*, May 1996, pp. 253–66.

68. D. W. Organ, "Personality and Organizational Citizenship Behavior," *Journal of Management*, Summer 1994, p. 466.

69. See, for instance, B. Schneider and D. E. Bowen, "Employee and Customer Perceptions of Service in Banks: Replication and Extension," *Journal of Applied Psychology*, August 1985, pp. 423–33; W. W. Tornow and J. W. Wiley, "Service Quality and Management Practices: A Look at Employee Attitudes, Customer Satisfaction, and Bottom-line Consequences," *Human Resource Planning*, vol. 4, no. 2, 1991, pp. 105–16; E. Naumann and D. W. Jackson, Jr., "One More Time: How Do You Satisfy Customers?" *Business Horizons*, May–June 1999, pp. 71–76; D. J. Koys, "The Effects of Employee Satisfaction, Organizational Citizenship Behavior, and Turnover on Organizational Effectiveness: A Unit-Level, Longitudinal Study," *Personnel Psychology*, Spring 2001, pp. 101–14; and J. Griffith, "Do Satisfied Employees Satisfy Customers? Support-Services Staff Morale and Satisfaction among Public School Administrators, Students, and Parents," *Journal of Applied Social Psychology*, August 2001, pp. 1627–58.

70. M. J. Bitner, B. H. Booms, and L. A. Mohr, "Critical Service Encounters: The Employee's Viewpoint," *Journal of Marketing*, October 1994, pp. 95–106.

PART TWO

THE INDIVIDUAL

The terms often used to describe Charles B. Wang (see photo) aren't very complimentary. He's been frequently described as a mercenary brute, ruthless, authoritarian, defiant, volatile, blunt, tactless, and isolated.[1] So who is Charles Wang and what makes him so tough and aggressive?

Wang emigrated to New York City from Shanghai in 1952, when he was eight years old. He attended Queens College in New York and obtained a degree in mathematics. In 1976 he founded a company called Computer Associates. Today, Computer Associates is the third largest software company in the United States, behind Microsoft and Oracle, and Wang is its chairman. The highly successful company has made Wang a billionaire. But if you want insights into Wang's personality and behavior, you need to understand the experiences that shaped them.

Unlike Microsoft co-founder and fellow billionaire Bill Gates, Wang didn't grow up rich. Wang's view of the world as tough and ruthless was forged by the harshness of his early immigrant experience. "I know what it is to go hungry," Wang says. "[Bill Gates] doesn't." Wang was always keenly aware that he was a Chinese immigrant in New York City. When he, his parents, and brothers settled in Queens in the early 1950s, the borough was not the multi-ethnic mosaic that it is today. The Wang boys were the only Chinese kids at grade school and on their Little League baseball teams. Incidents of blatant racism were rare but the family abandoned its first attempt at exchanging their walk-up apartment for a house after neighbors-to-be circulated an anti-Chinese petition. Growing up being different made Wang highly sensitive to slights. In fact, in Computer Associates' early years, Wang would become irate if anyone disrespected his company. Even today, revenge still seems to matter to Wang. Managers who resign are treated as traitors. Anyone who isn't Wang's and Computer Associates' friend seems to automatically be its enemy.

Personality and Emotions

Today, Wang, his wife, and three children live a secluded life on a large estate near Oyster Bay on Long Island. Unlike other software moguls such as Gates and Oracle's Lawrence Ellison, who are outgoing and play to the media, Wang has recreated (only in a deluxe fashion) the isolation he experienced in his formative years in New York City. That may have been nearly 50 years ago, but Wang hasn't forgotten. The isolated and angry man of today has been largely forged by his early family experiences.

C harles Wang isn't unique. *All* our behavior is somewhat shaped by our personalities. In the first half of this chapter, we review the research on personality and its relationship to behavior. In the latter half, we look at how emotions shape many of our work-related behaviors.

PERSONALITY

Why are some people quiet and passive, while others are loud and aggressive? Are certain personality types better adapted for certain job types? Before we can answer these questions, we need to address a more basic one: What is personality?

What Is Personality?

When we talk of personality, we don't mean that a person has charm, a positive attitude toward life, a smiling face, or is a finalist for "Happiest and Friendliest" in this year's Miss America contest. When psychologists talk of personality, they mean a dynamic concept describing the growth and development of a person's whole psychological system. Rather than looking at parts of the person, personality looks at some aggregate whole that is greater than the sum of the parts.

The most frequently used definition of personality was produced by Gordon Allport more than 65 years ago. He said personality is "the dynamic organization within the individual of those psychophysical systems that determine his unique adjustments to his environment."[2] For our purposes, you should think of **personality** as the sum total of ways in which an individual reacts to and interacts with others. It is most often described in terms of measurable traits that a person exhibits.

personality

The sum total of ways in which an individual reacts and interacts with others.

Personality Determinants

An early debate in personality research centered on whether an individual's personality was the result of heredity or of environment. Was the personality predetermined at birth, or was it the result of the individual's interaction with his or her environment? Clearly, there is no simple black-and-white answer. Personality appears to be a result of both influences. In addition, today we recognize a third factor—the situation. Thus, an adult's personality is now generally considered to be made up of both hereditary and environmental factors, moderated by situational conditions.

Heredity *Heredity* refers to those factors that were determined at conception. Physical stature, facial attractiveness, gender, temperament, muscle composition and reflexes, energy level, and biological rhythms are characteristics that are generally considered to be either completely or substantially influenced by who your parents are; that is, by their biological, physiological, and inherent psychological makeup. The heredity approach argues that the ultimate explanation of an individual's personality is the molecular structure of the genes, located in the chromosomes.

Three different streams of research lend some credibility to the argument that heredity plays an important part in determining an individual's personality. The first looks at the genetic underpinnings of human behavior and temperament among young children. The second addresses the study of twins who were separated at birth. The third examines the consistency in job satisfaction over time and across situations.

Recent studies of young children lend strong support to the power of heredity.[3] Evidence demonstrates that traits such as shyness, fear, and distress are most likely caused by inherited genetic characteristics. This finding suggests that some personality traits may be built into the same genetic code that affects factors such as height and hair color.

Researchers have studied more than 100 sets of identical twins who were separated at birth and raised separately.[4] If heredity played little or no part in determining personality, you would expect to find few similarities between the separated twins. But the researchers found a lot in common. For almost every behavioral trait, a significant part of the variation between the twins turned out to be associated with genetic factors. For instance, one set of twins who had been separated for 39 years and raised 45 miles apart were found to drive the same model and color car, chain-smoked the same brand of cigarette, owned dogs with the same name, and regularly vacationed within three blocks of each other in a beach community 1,500 miles away. Researchers have found that genetics accounts for about 50 percent of the personality differences and more than 30 percent of the variation in occupational and leisure interests.

Further support for the importance of heredity can be found in studies of individual job satisfaction, which we discussed in the previous chapter. Individual job satisfaction is found to be remarkably stable over time. This result is consistent with what you would expect if satisfaction is determined by something inherent in the person rather than by external environmental factors.

If personality characteristics were *completely* dictated by heredity, they would be fixed at birth and no amount of experience could alter them. If you were relaxed and easygoing as a child, for example, that would be the result of your genes, and it would not be possible for you to change those characteristics. But personality characteristics are not completely dictated by heredity.

Environment Among the factors that exert pressures on our personality formation are the culture in which we are raised; our early conditioning; the norms among our family, friends, and social groups; and other influences that we experience. These environmental factors play a substantial role in shaping our personalities.

Early training and the culture in which we are raised are important environmental factors that shape our personalities. Other influences are family norms and memberships in social groups.

For example, culture establishes the norms, attitudes, and values that are passed along from one generation to the next and create consistencies over time. An ideology that is intensely fostered in one culture may have only moderate influence in another. For instance, North Americans have had the themes of industriousness, success, competition, independence, and the Protestant work ethic constantly instilled in them through books, the school system, family, and friends. North Americans, as a result, tend to be ambitious and aggressive relative to individuals raised in cultures that have emphasized getting along with others, cooperation, and the priority of family over work and career.

Careful consideration of the arguments favoring either heredity or environment as the primary determinant of personality forces the conclusion that both are important. Heredity sets the parameters or outer limits, but an individual's full potential will be determined by how well he or she adjusts to the demands and requirements of the environment.

Situation A third factor, the situation, influences the effects of heredity and environment on personality. An individual's personality, although generally stable and consistent, does change in different situations. The different demands of different situations call forth different aspects of one's personality. So we shouldn't look at personality patterns in isolation.[5]

It seems only logical to suppose that situations will influence an individual's personality, but a neat classification scheme that would tell us the impact of various types of situations has so far eluded us. However, we do know that certain situations are more relevant than others in influencing personality.

What is of interest taxonomically is that situations seem to differ substantially in the constraints they impose on behavior. Some situations—e.g., church, an employment interview—constrain many behaviors; other situations—e.g., a picnic in a public park—constrain relatively few.[6]

Furthermore, although certain generalizations can be made about personality, there are significant individual differences. As we shall see, the study of individual differences has come to receive greater emphasis in personality research, which originally sought out more general, universal patterns.

Source: Peanuts reprinted with permission of United Features Syndicate, Inc.

Personality Traits

The early work in the structure of personality revolved around attempts to identify and label enduring characteristics that describe an individual's behavior. Popular characteristics include shy, aggressive, submissive, lazy, ambitious, loyal, and timid. Those characteristics, when they are exhibited in a large number of situations, are called **personality traits**.[7] The more consistent the characteristic and the more frequently it occurs in diverse situations, the more important that trait is in describing the individual.

personality traits

Enduring characteristics that describe an individual's behavior.

Early Search for Primary Traits   Efforts to isolate traits have been hindered because there are so many of them. In one study, 17,953 individual traits were identified.[8] Obviously, it's virtually impossible to predict behavior when such a large number of traits must be taken into account. As a result, attention has been directed toward reducing these thousands to a more manageable number.

One researcher isolated 171 traits but concluded that they were superficial and lacking in descriptive power.[9] What he sought was a reduced set of traits that would identify underlying patterns. The result was the identification of 16 personality factors, which he called the *source*, or *primary*, *traits*. They are shown in Exhibit 4-2. These 16 traits have been found to be generally steady and constant sources of behavior, allowing prediction of an individual's behavior in specific situations by weighing the characteristics for their situational relevance.

Myers-Briggs Type Indicator (MBTI)

A personality test that taps four characteristics and classifies people into 1 of 16 personality types.

The Myers–Briggs Type Indicator   One of the most widely used personality frameworks is called the **Myers-Briggs Type Indicator (MBTI)**.[10] It is essentially a 100-question personality test that asks people how they usually feel or act in particular situations.

On the basis of the answers individuals give to the test, they are classified as extroverted or introverted (E or I), sensing or intuitive (S or N), thinking or feeling (T or F), and perceiving or judging (P or J). These classifications are then combined into 16 personality types. (These types are different from the 16 primary traits in Exhibit 4-2.) To illustrate, let's take several examples. INTJs are visionaries. They usually have original minds and great drive for their own ideas and purposes. They are characterized as skeptical, critical, independent, determined, and often stubborn. ESTJs are organizers. They are realistic, logical, analytical, and decisive and have a natural head for business or mechanics. They like to organize and run activities. The ENTP type is a conceptualizer. He or she is innovative, individualistic, versatile, and attracted to entrepreneurial ideas. This person tends to be resourceful in solving challenging problems but may neglect routine assignments. A recent book that profiled 13 contemporary businesspeople who created supersuccessful firms including

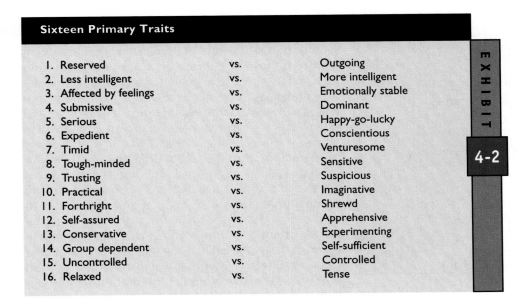

			EXHIBIT 4-2
1. Reserved	vs.	Outgoing	
2. Less intelligent	vs.	More intelligent	
3. Affected by feelings	vs.	Emotionally stable	
4. Submissive	vs.	Dominant	
5. Serious	vs.	Happy-go-lucky	
6. Expedient	vs.	Conscientious	
7. Timid	vs.	Venturesome	
8. Tough-minded	vs.	Sensitive	
9. Trusting	vs.	Suspicious	
10. Practical	vs.	Imaginative	
11. Forthright	vs.	Shrewd	
12. Self-assured	vs.	Apprehensive	
13. Conservative	vs.	Experimenting	
14. Group dependent	vs.	Self-sufficient	
15. Uncontrolled	vs.	Controlled	
16. Relaxed	vs.	Tense	

Apple Computer, Federal Express, Honda Motors, Microsoft, and Sony found that all 13 are intuitive thinkers (NTs).[11] This result is particularly interesting because intuitive thinkers represent only about five percent of the population.

More than two million people a year take the MBTI in the United States alone. Organizations using the MBTI include Apple Computer, AT&T, Citigroup, GE, 3M Co., plus many hospitals, educational institutions, and even the U.S. Armed Forces.

Ironically, there is no hard evidence that the MBTI is a valid measure of personality. But lack of evidence doesn't seem to deter its use in a wide range of organizations.

The Big Five Model   MBTI may lack for valid supporting evidence, but that can't be said for the five-factor model of personality—more typically called the "Big Five."[12] In recent years, an impressive body of research supports that five basic dimensions underlie all others and encompass most of the significant variation in human personality. The Big Five factors are:

- **Extroversion**.   This dimension captures one's comfort level with relationships. Extroverts tend to be gregarious, assertive, and sociable. Introverts tend to be reserved, timid, and quiet.
- **Agreeableness**.   This dimension refers to an individual's propensity to defer to others. Highly agreeable people are cooperative, warm, and trusting. People who score low on agreeableness are cold, disagreeable, and antagonistic.
- **Conscientiousness**.   This dimension is a measure of reliability. A highly conscientious person is responsible, organized, dependable, and persistent. Those who score low on this dimension are easily distracted, disorganized, and unreliable.
- **Emotional stability**.   This dimension taps a person's ability to withstand stress. People with positive emotional stability tend to be calm, self-confident, and secure. Those with high negative scores tend to be nervous, anxious, depressed, and insecure.
- **Openness to experience**.   The final dimension addresses one's range of interests and fascination with novelty. Extremely open people are creative, curious, and artistically sensitive. Those at the other end of the openness category are conventional and find comfort in the familiar.

extroversion

A personality dimension describing someone who is sociable, gregarious, and assertive.

agreeableness

A personality dimension that describes someone who is good-natured, cooperative, and trusting.

conscientiousness

A personality dimension that describes someone who is responsible, dependable, persistent, and organized.

emotional stability

A personality dimension that characterizes someone as calm, self-confident, secure (positive) versus nervous, depressed, and insecure (negative).

openness to experience

A personality dimension that characterizes someone in terms of imagination, sensitivity, and curiosity.

In addition to providing a unifying personality framework, research on the Big Five also has found important relationships between these personality dimensions and job performance.[13] A broad spectrum of occupations were looked at: professionals (including engineers, architects, accountants, attorneys), police, managers, salespeople, and semiskilled and skilled employees. Job performance was defined in terms of performance ratings, training proficiency (performance during training programs), and personnel data such as salary level. The results showed that conscientiousness predicted job performance for all occupational groups. "The preponderance of evidence shows that individuals who are dependable, reliable, careful, thorough, able to plan, organized, hardworking, persistent, and achievement-oriented tend to have higher job performance in most if not all occupations."[14] In addition, employees who score higher in conscientiousness develop higher levels of job knowledge, probably because highly conscientious people exert greater levels of effort on their jobs. The higher levels of job knowledge then contribute to higher levels of job performance. Consistent with these findings, evidence also finds a relatively strong and consistent relationship between conscientiousness and organizational citizenship behavior.[15] This, however, seems to be the only personality dimension that predicts OCB.

Extroversion is one of the dimensions in the Big Five Model of personality. Extroverts are gregarious and sociable, while introverts tend to be reserved and quiet.

For the other personality dimensions, predictability depended on both the performance criterion and the occupational group. For instance, extroversion predicted performance in managerial and sales positions. This finding makes sense because those occupations involve high social interaction. Similarly, openness to experience was found to be important in predicting training proficiency, which, too, seems logical. What wasn't so clear was why positive emotional stability wasn't related to job performance. Intuitively, it would seem that people who are calm and secure would do better on almost all jobs than people who are anxious and insecure. The answer might be that only people who score fairly high on emotional stability retain their jobs. So the range on this dimension among those people studied, all of whom were employed, would tend to be quite small.

Major Personality Attributes Influencing OB

In this section, we want to more carefully evaluate specific personality attributes that have been found to be powerful predictors of behavior in organizations. The first is related to where one perceives the locus of control in one's life. The others are Machiavellianism, self-esteem, self-monitoring, propensity for risk taking, and Type A personality. In this section, we shall briefly introduce these attributes and summarize what we know about their ability to explain and predict employee behavior.

Locus of Control   Some people believe that they are masters of their own fate. Other people see themselves as pawns of fate, believing that what happens to them in their lives is due to luck or chance. The first type, those who believe that they control their destinies, have been labeled **internals**, whereas the latter, who see their lives as being controlled by outside forces, have been called **externals**.[16] A person's perception of the source of his or her fate is termed **locus of control**.

internals

Individuals who believe that they control what happens to them.

externals

Individuals who believe that what happens to them is controlled by outside forces such as luck or chance.

locus of control

The degree to which people believe they are masters of their own fate.

A large amount of research comparing internals with externals has consistently shown that individuals who rate high in externality are less satisfied with their jobs, have higher absenteeism rates, are more alienated from the work setting, and are less involved on their jobs than are internals.[17] Externals are also less likely to initially get a job. Why? In contrast to externals, internals exhibit more motivation and willingness to take action in their initial interviews, which has been shown to relate to significantly more second interviews.[18]

Why are externals more dissatisfied? The answer is probably that they perceive themselves as having little control over the organizational outcomes that are important to them. Internals, facing the same situation, attribute organizational outcomes to their own actions. If the situation is unattractive, they believe that they have no one else to blame but themselves. Also, the dissatisfied internal is more likely to quit a dissatisfying job.

The impact of locus of control on absence is an interesting one. Internals believe that health is substantially under their own control through proper habits, so they take more responsibility for their health and have better health habits. Consequently, their incidences of sickness and, hence, of absenteeism, are lower.[19]

We shouldn't expect any clear relationship between locus of control and turnover because there are opposing forces at work. "On the one hand, internals tend to take action and thus might be expected to quit jobs more readily. On the other hand, they tend to be more successful on the job and more satisfied, factors associated with less individual turnover."[20]

The overall evidence indicates that internals generally perform better on their jobs, but that conclusion should be moderated to reflect differences in jobs. Internals search more actively for information before making a decision, are more motivated to achieve, and make a greater attempt to control their environment. Externals, however, are more compliant and willing to follow directions. Therefore, internals do well on sophisticated tasks—which include most managerial and professional jobs—that require complex information processing and learning. In addition, internals are more suited to jobs that require initiative and independence of action. Almost all successful sales people, for instance, are internals. Why? Because it's pretty difficult to succeed in sales if you don't believe you can effectively influence outcomes. In contrast, externals should do well on jobs that are well structured and routine and in which success depends heavily on complying with the direction of others.

Machiavellianism The personality characteristic of **Machiavellianism** (Mach) is named after Niccolo Machiavelli, who wrote in the sixteenth century on how to gain and use power. An individual high in Machiavellianism is pragmatic, maintains emotional distance, and believes that ends can justify means. "If it works, use it" is consistent with a high-Mach perspective.

A considerable amount of research has been directed toward relating high- and low-Mach personalities to certain behavioral outcomes.[21] High Machs manipulate more, win more, are persuaded less, and persuade others more than do low Machs.[22] Yet these high Mach outcomes are moderated by situational factors. It has been found that high Machs flourish (1) when they interact face to face with others rather than indirectly; (2) when the situation has a minimum number of rules and regulations, thus allowing latitude for improvisation; and (3) when emotional involvement with details irrelevant to winning distracts low Machs.[23]

Should we conclude that high Machs make good employees? That answer depends on the type of job and whether you consider ethical implications in evaluating performance. In jobs that require bargaining skills (such as labor negotiation) or that

Machiavellianism

Degree to which an individual is pragmatic, maintains emotional distance, and believes that ends can justify means.

offer substantial rewards for winning (as in commissioned sales), high Machs will be productive. But if ends can't justify the means, if there are absolute standards of behavior, or if the three situational factors noted in the preceding paragraph are not in evidence, our ability to predict a high Mach's performance will be severely curtailed.

Self-Esteem   People differ in the degree to which they like or dislike themselves. This trait is called **self-esteem**.[24] The research on self-esteem (SE) offers some interesting insights into organizational behavior. For example, self-esteem is directly related to expectations for success. High SEs believe that they possess the ability they need to succeed at work.

Individuals with high self-esteem will take more risks in job selection and are more likely to choose unconventional jobs than people with low self-esteem.

The most generalizable finding on self-esteem is that low SEs are more susceptible to external influence than are high SEs. Low SEs are dependent on the receipt of positive evaluations from others. As a result, they are more likely to seek approval from others and more prone to conform to the beliefs and behaviors of those they respect than are high SEs. In managerial positions, low SEs will tend to be concerned with pleasing others and, therefore, are less likely to take unpopular stands than are high SEs.

Not surprisingly, self-esteem has also been found to be related to job satisfaction. A number of studies confirm that high SEs are more satisfied with their jobs than are low SEs.

Self-Monitoring   A personality trait that has recently received increased attention is called **self-monitoring**.[25] It refers to an individual's ability to adjust his or her behavior to external, situational factors.

Individuals high in self-monitoring show considerable adaptability in adjusting their behavior to external situational factors. They are highly sensitive to external cues and can behave differently in different situations. High self-monitors are capable of presenting striking contradictions between their public persona and their private self. Low self-monitors can't disguise themselves in that way. They tend to display their true dispositions and attitudes in every situation; hence, there is high behavioral consistency between who they are and what they do.

The research on self-monitoring is in its infancy, so predictions must be guarded. However, preliminary evidence suggests that high self-monitors tend to pay closer attention to the behavior of others and are more capable of conforming than are low self-monitors.[26] In addition, high self-monitoring managers tend to be more mobile in their careers, receive more promotions (both internal and cross-organizational), and are more likely to occupy central positions in an organization.[27] We might also hypothesize that high self-monitors will be more successful in managerial positions in which individuals are required to play multiple, and even contradicting, roles. The high self-monitor is capable of putting on different "faces" for different audiences.

Risk Taking   Donald Trump stands out for his willingness to take risks. He started with almost nothing in the 1960s. By the mid-1980s, he had made a fortune by betting on a resurgent New York City real estate market. Then, trying to capitalize on his previous successes, Trump overextended himself. By 1994, he had a *negative* net worth of $850 million. Never fearful of taking chances, "The Donald" leveraged the few assets he had left on several New York, New Jersey, and Caribbean real estate ventures. He hit it big again. In 2001, *Forbes* estimated his net worth at over $2 billion.

People differ in their willingness to take chances. This propensity to assume or avoid risk has been shown to have an impact on how long it takes managers to make a decision and how much information they require before making their choice. For instance, 79 managers worked on simulated personnel exercises that required them to make hiring decisions.[28] High risk-taking managers made more rapid decisions and used less information in making their choices than did the low risk-taking managers. Interestingly, the decision accuracy was the same for both groups.

In general, managers in large organizations tend to be risk averse, especially in contrast to growth-oriented entrepreneurs who actively manage small businesses.[29] For the work population as a whole, there are also differences in risk propensity.[30] As a result, it makes sense to recognize these differences and even to consider aligning risk-taking propensity with specific job demands. For instance, a high risk-taking propensity may lead to more effective performance for a stock trader in a brokerage firm because that type of job demands rapid decision making. On the other hand, a willingness to take risks might prove a major obstacle to an accountant who performs auditing activities. The latter job might be better filled by someone with a low risk-taking propensity.

Donald Trump personifies the risk-taking personality. He thrives in situations that most others would find perilous and stressful.

Type A Personality Do you know people who are excessively competitive and always seem to be experiencing a sense of time urgency? If you do, it's a good bet that those people have a **Type A personality**. A person with a Type A personality is "aggressively involved in a chronic, incessant struggle to achieve more and more in less and less time, and, if required to do so, against the opposing efforts of other things or other persons."[31] In the North American culture, such characteristics tend to be highly prized and positively associated with ambition and the successful acquisition of material goods.

Type A personality

Aggressive involvement in a chronic, incessant struggle to achieve more and more in less and less time and, if necessary, against the opposing efforts of other things or other people.

Type A's
1. are always moving, walking, and eating rapidly;
2. feel impatient with the rate at which most events take place;
3. strive to think or do two or more things at once;
4. cannot cope with leisure time;
5. are obsessed with numbers, measuring their success in terms of how many or how much of everything they acquire.

In contrast to the Type A personality is the Type B, who is exactly opposite. Type B's are "rarely harried by the desire to obtain a wildly increasing number of things or participate in an endless growing series of events in an ever-decreasing amount of time."[32]

Type B's
1. never suffer from a sense of time urgency with its accompanying impatience;
2. feel no need to display or discuss either their achievements or accomplishments unless such exposure is demanded by the situation;
3. play for fun and relaxation, rather than to exhibit their superiority at any cost;
4. can relax without guilt.

Type A's operate under moderate to high levels of stress. They subject themselves to more or less continuous time pressure, creating for themselves a life of deadlines. These characteristics result in some rather specific behavioral outcomes. For example, Type A's are fast workers, because they emphasize quantity over quality. In managerial positions, Type A's demonstrate their competitiveness by working long hours and, not infrequently, making poor decisions because they make them too fast. Type A's are also rarely creative. Because of their concern with quantity and speed, they rely on past experiences when faced with problems. They will not allocate the time necessary to develop unique solutions to new problems. They rarely vary in their responses to specific challenges in their milieu; hence, their behavior is easier to predict than that of Type B's.

Do Type A's differ from Type B's in their ability to get hired? The answer appears to be "yes."[33] Type A's do better in job interviews because they are more likely to be judged as having desirable traits such as high drive, competence, aggressiveness, and success motivation. Are Type A's or Type B's more successful in organizations? Despite the Type A's hard work, the Type B's are the ones who appear to make it to the top. Great salespersons are usually Type A's; senior executives are usually Type B's. Why? The answer lies in the tendency of Type A's to trade off quality of effort for quantity. Promotions in corporate and professional organizations "usually go to those who are wise rather than to those who are merely hasty, to those who are tactful rather than to those who are hostile, and to those who are creative rather than to those who are merely agile in competitive strife."[34]

Personality and National Culture

Do personality frameworks, like the Big Five model, transfer across cultures? Are dimensions like locus of control and the Type A personality relevant in all cultures? Let's try to answer these questions.

The five personality factors identified in the Big Five model appear in almost all cross-cultural studies.[35] This includes a wide variety of diverse cultures—such as China, Israel, Germany, Japan, Spain, Nigeria, Norway, Pakistan, and the United States. Differences tend to surface by the emphasis on dimensions. Chinese, for example, use the category of conscientiousness more often and use the category of agreeableness less often than do Americans. But there is a surprisingly high amount of agreement, especially among individuals from developed countries. As a case in point, a comprehensive review of studies covering people from the 15-nation European Community found that conscientiousness was a valid predictor of performance across jobs and occupational groups.[36] This is exactly what U.S. studies have found.

There are no common personality types for a given country. You can, for instance, find high and low risk-takers in almost any culture. Yet a country's culture influences the dominant personality characteristics of its population. We can see this by looking at locus of control and the Type A personality.

There is evidence that cultures differ in terms of people's relationship to their environment.[37] In some cultures, such as those in North America, people believe that they can dominate their environment. People in other societies, such as Middle Eastern countries, believe that life is essentially preordained. Note the close parallel to internal and external locus of control.[38] We should expect, therefore, a larger proportion of internals in the American and Canadian workforce than in the Saudi Arabian or Iranian workforce.

The prevalence of Type A personalities will be somewhat influenced by the culture in which a person grows up. There are Type A's in every country, but there will be more in capitalistic countries, where achievement and material success are highly valued. For instance, it is estimated that about 50 percent of the North American population is Type A.[39] This percentage shouldn't be too surprising. The United States and Canada both have a high emphasis on time management and efficiency. Both have cultures that stress accomplishments and acquisition of money and material goods. In cultures such as Sweden and France, where materialism is less revered, we would predict a smaller proportion of Type A personalities.

"Deep Down, People Are All Alike"

This statement is essentially false. Only in the broadest sense can we say that "people are all alike." For instance, it's true that people all have values, attitudes, likes and dislikes, feelings, goals, and similar general attributes. But individual differences are far more illuminating.[40] People differ in intelligence, personality, abilities, ambition, motivations, emotional display, values, priorities, expectations, and the like. If we want to understand, explain, or predict human behavior accurately, we need to focus on individual differences. Your ability to predict behavior will be severely limited if you constantly assume that all people are alike or that everyone is like you.

As an illustration, consider the task of selecting among job applicants. Managers regularly use information about a candidate's personality (in addition to experience, knowledge, skill level, and intellectual abilities) to help make their hiring decisions. Recognizing that jobs differ in terms of demands and requirements, managers interview and test applicants to (1) categorize them by specific traits, (2) assess job tasks in terms of the type of personality best suited for effectively completing those tasks, and (3) match applicants and job tasks to find an appropriate fit. So by using an individual-difference variable—in this case, personality—managers improve the likelihood of identifying and hiring high-performing employees.

Achieving Personality Fit

Twenty years ago, organizations were concerned with personality primarily because they wanted to match individuals to specific jobs. That concern still exists. But, in recent years, interest has expanded to include the individual–organization fit. Why? Because managers today are less interested in an applicant's ability to perform a *specific* job than with his or her *flexibility* to meet changing situations.

The Person-Job Fit   In the discussion of personality attributes, our conclusions were often qualified to recognize that the requirements of the job moderated the relationship between possession of the personality characteristic and job performance. This concern with matching the job requirements with personality characteristics is best articulated in John Holland's **personality–job fit theory**.[41] The theory is based on the notion of fit between an individual's personality characteristics and his or her occupational environment. Holland presents six personality types and proposes that satisfaction and the propensity to leave a job depend on the degree to which individuals successfully match their personalities to an occupational environment.

Each one of the six personality types has a congruent occupational environment. Exhibit 4-3 on page 104 describes the six types and their personality characteristics and gives examples of congruent occupations.

Holland has developed a Vocational Preference Inventory questionnaire that contains 160 occupational titles. Respondents indicate which of these occupations they like or dislike, and their answers are used to form personality profiles. Using this procedure, research strongly supports the hexagonal diagram shown in Exhibit 4-4 on page 104.[42] This figure shows that the closer two fields or orientations are in the hexagon, the more compatible they are. Adjacent categories are quite similar, whereas those diagonally opposite are highly dissimilar.

What does all this mean? The theory argues that satisfaction is highest and turnover lowest when personality and occupation are in agreement. Social individuals should be in social jobs, conventional people in conventional jobs, and so forth. A realistic person in a realistic job is in a more congruent situation than is a

personality–job fit theory

Identifies six personality types and proposes that the fit between personality type and occupational environment determines satisfaction and turnover.

Holland's Typology of Personality and Congruent Occupations

EXHIBIT 4-3

Type	Personality Characteristics	Congruent Occupations
Realistic: Prefers physical activities that require skill, strength, and coordination	Shy, genuine, persistent, stable, conforming, practical	Mechanic, drill press operator, assembly-line worker, farmer
Investigative: Prefers activities that involve thinking, organizing, and understanding	Analytical, original, curious, independent	Biologist, economist, mathematician, news reporter
Social: Prefers activities that involve helping and developing others	Sociable, friendly, cooperative, understanding	Social worker, teacher, counselor, clinical psychologist
Conventional: Prefers rule-regulated, orderly, and unambiguous activities	Conforming, efficient, practical, unimaginative, inflexible	Accountant, corporate manager, bank teller, file clerk
Enterprising: Prefers verbal activities in which there are opportunities to influence others and attain power	Self-confident, ambitious, energetic, domineering	Lawyer, real estate agent, public relations specialist, small business manager
Artistic: Prefers ambiguous and unsystematic activities that allow creative expression	Imaginative, disorderly, idealistic, emotional, impractical	Painter, musician, writer, interior decorator

realistic person in an investigative job. A realistic person in a social job is in the most incongruent situation possible. The key points of this model are that (1) there do appear to be intrinsic differences in personality among individuals, (2) there are different types of jobs, and (3) people in job environments congruent with their personality types should be more satisfied and less likely to voluntarily resign than should people in incongruent jobs.

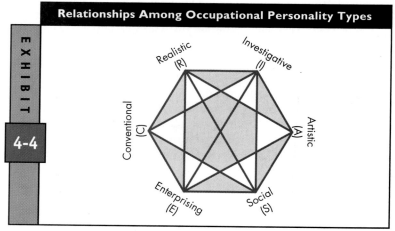

EXHIBIT 4-4

Relationships Among Occupational Personality Types

Realistic (R) · Investigative (I) · Conventional (C) · Artistic (A) · Enterprising (E) · Social (S)

Source: Reprinted by special permission of the publisher, Psychological Assessment Resources, Inc. from *Making Vocational Choices*, Copyright 1973, 1985, 1992 by Psychological Assessment Resources, Inc. All rights reserved.

The Person–Organization Fit As previously noted, attention in recent years has expanded to include matching people to *organizations* as well as *jobs*. To the degree that an organization faces a dynamic and changing environment and requires employees who are able to readily change tasks and move fluidly between teams, it's probably more important that employees' personalities fit with the overall organization's culture than with the characteristics of any specific job.

The person–organization fit essentially argues that people leave jobs that are not compatible with their personalities.[43] Using the Big Five terminology, for instance, we could expect that people high on extroversion fit better with aggressive and team-oriented cultures; that people high on agreeableness will match up better with a supportive organizational climate than one that focuses on aggressiveness; and that people high on openness to experience fit better into organizations that emphasize innovation rather than standardization.[44] Following these guidelines at the time of hiring should lead to selecting new employees who fit better with the organization's culture, which, in turn, should result in higher employee satisfaction and reduced turnover.

EMOTIONS

On December 26, 2000, Michael McDermott, a 42-year-old software tester at a Boston-area Internet consulting firm, walked into his place of work. Armed with an AK-47 assault rifle, a shotgun, and a semiautomatic handgun, he killed seven of his co-workers. Why? He was purportedly angry over his employer's plans to comply with an Internal Revenue Service request to withhold a portion of his pay because of back taxes he owed.[45] For McDermott, anger had led to violence.

Going on a shooting rampage at work is an extreme example but it does dramatically illustrate the theme of this section: Emotions are a critical factor in employee behavior.

Given the obvious role that emotions play in our everyday life, it might surprise you to learn that, until very recently, the topic of emotions had been given little or no attention within the field of OB.[46] How could this be? We can offer two possible explanations. The first is the *myth of rationality*.[47] Since the late

When his employer planned to withhold part of his pay to satisfy back taxes he owed, Michael McDermott allowed his emotions to turn to violence, resulting in his killing seven of his Boston co-workers.

nineteenth century and the rise of scientific management, organizations have been specifically designed with the objective of trying to control emotions. A well-run organization was one that successfully eliminated frustration, fear, anger, love, hate, joy, grief and similar feelings. Such emotions were the antithesis of rationality. So while researchers and managers knew that emotions were an inseparable part of everyday life, they tried to create organizations that were emotion-free. That, of course, was not possible. The second factor that acted to keep emotions out of OB was the belief that *emotions of any kind were disruptive*.[48] When emotions were considered, the discussion focused on strong negative emotions—especially anger—that interfered with an employee's ability to do his or her job effectively. Emotions were rarely viewed as being constructive or able to stimulate performance-enhancing behaviors.

Certainly some emotions, particularly when exhibited at the wrong time, can reduce employee performance. But this doesn't change the reality that employees bring an emotional component with them to work everyday and that no study of OB could be comprehensive without considering the role of emotions in workplace behavior.

What Are Emotions?

Although we don't want to obsess on definitions, before we can proceed with our analysis, we need to clarify three terms that are closely intertwined: *affect*, *emotions*, and *moods*.

Affect is a generic term that covers a broad range of feelings that people experience. It's an umbrella concept that encompasses both emotions and moods.[49] **Emotions** are intense feelings that are directed at someone or something.[50] Finally, **moods** are feelings that tend to be less intense than emotions and which lack a contextual stimulus.[51]

Emotions are reactions to an object, not a trait. They're object-specific. You show your emotions when you're "happy about something, angry at someone, afraid of something."[52] Moods, on the other hand, aren't directed at an object. Emotions can turn into moods when you lose focus on the contextual object. So when a work colleague criticizes you for the way you spoke to a client, you might become angry at him. That is, you show emotion (anger) toward a specific object (your colleague). But later in the day, you might find yourself just generally dispirited. You can't attribute this feeling to any single event; you're just not your normal, upbeat self. This affect state describes a mood.

A related affect-term that is gaining increasing importance in organizational behavior is *emotional labor*. Every employee expends physical and mental labor when they put their bodies and cognitive capabilities, respectively, into their job. But most jobs also require **emotional labor**. This is when an employee expresses organizationally desired emotions during interpersonal transactions.[53] The concept of emotional labor originally developed in relation to service jobs. Airline flight attendants, for instance, are expected to be cheerful, funeral counselors sad, and doctors emotionally neutral. But today, the concept of emotional labor seems relevant to almost every job. You're expected, for example, to be courteous and not hostile in interactions with co-workers. And leaders are expected to draw on emotional labor to "charge the troops." Almost every great speech, for instance, contains a strong emotional component that stirs feelings in others. As we proceed in this section, you'll see that it's because of the increasing importance of emotional labor as a key component of effective job performance that an understanding of emotion has gained heightened relevance within the field of OB.

Felt Versus Displayed Emotions

Emotional labor creates dilemmas for employees when their job requires them to exhibit emotions that are incongruous with their actual feelings. Not surprisingly, this is a frequent occurrence. There are people with whom you have to work toward whom you find it very difficult to be friendly. Maybe you consider their personality abrasive. Maybe you know they've said negative things about you behind your back. Regardless, your job requires you to interact with these people on a regular basis. So you're forced to feign friendliness. Or you're a sales clerk in a retail store. Management expects you to smile and be friendly with customers. But there are days when you just don't feel like smiling and being friendly.

It can help you to better understand emotions if you separate them into *felt* versus *displayed*.[54] **Felt emotions** are an individual's actual emotions. In contrast, **displayed emotions** are those that are organizationally-required and considered

---

affect

A broad range of feelings that people experience.

emotions

Intense feelings that are directed at someone or something.

moods

Feelings that tend to be less intense than emotions and that lack a contextual stimulus.

emotional labor

A situation in which an employee expresses organizationally desired emotions during interpersonal transactions.

felt emotions

An individual's actual emotions.

displayed emotions

Emotions that are organizationally required and considered appropriate in a given job.

appropriate in a given job. They're not innate; they're learned. "The ritual look of delight on the face of the first runner-up as the new Miss America is announced is a product of the display rule that losers should mask their sadness with an expression of joy for the winner."[55] Similarly, most of us know that we're expected to act sad at funerals regardless of whether we consider the person's death to be a loss; and to pretend to be happy at weddings even if we don't feel like celebrating.[56] Effective managers have learned to be serious when giving an employee a negative performance evaluation and to cover-up their anger when they've been passed over for promotion. And the salesperson who hasn't learned to smile and appear friendly, regardless of his or her true feelings at the moment, isn't typically going to last long on most sales jobs.

The key point here is that felt and displayed emotions are often different. In fact, many people have problems working with others simply because they naively assume that the emotions they see others display is what those others actually feel. This is particularly true in organizations, where role demands and situations often require people to exhibit emotional behaviors that mask their true feelings. In addition, jobs today increasingly require employees to interact with customers. And customers aren't always easy to deal with. They often complain, behave rudely, and make unrealistic demands. In such instances, an employee's felt emotions may need to be disguised. Employees who aren't able to project a friendly and helpful demeanor in such situations are likely to alienate customers and are unlikely to be effective in their jobs.

Flight attendants at many airlines are selected largely for their ability to exhibit positive emotions and an upbeat personality. A major portion of a flier's impression of the airline's overall service is formed by interaction with gate agents and flight attendants.

Emotion Dimensions

How many emotions are there? In what ways do they vary? We'll answer these questions in this section.

Variety There are dozens of emotions. They include anger, contempt, enthusiasm, envy, fear, frustration, happiness, hate, hope, jealousy, joy, love, pride, surprise, and sadness. One way to classify them is by whether they are positive or negative.[57] Positive emotions—like happiness and hope—express a favorable evaluation or feeling. Negative emotions—like anger or hate—express the opposite. And keep in mind that emotions can't be neutral. Being neutral is nonemotional.[58] Importantly, negative emotions seem to have a greater affect on individuals. People reflect on and think about events inducing strong negative emotions five times as long as they do about events inducing strong positive ones.[59] So we should expect people to recall negative experiences more readily than positive ones.

There have been numerous efforts to limit and define the dozens of emotions into a fundamental or basic set of emotions.[60] Research has identified six universal emotions: anger, fear, sadness, happiness, disgust, and surprise.[61]

One factor that has strongly shaped what is and isn't listed in this basic set is the manner in which they were identified. Researchers tended to look for universally identified facial expressions and then convert them into categories (see Exhibit 4-5 on page 108). Emotions that couldn't be readily identified by others through facial expressions, or that were considered a subset of one of the basic six, were not selected.

Facial Expressions Convey Emotions

EXHIBIT 4-5

Each picture portrays a different emotion. Try to identify them before looking at the answers. (Top, left to right: neutral, surprise, happiness. Bottom: fear, sadness, anger.)

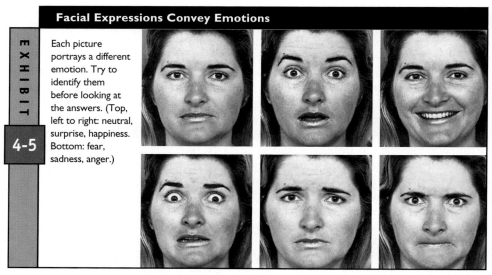

Source: S. E. Taylor, L. A. Peplan, and D. O. Sears, *Social Psychology*, 9th ed. (Upper Saddle River, NJ: Prentice Hall, 1997), p. 98. Photographs by Paul Eikman, Ph.D. Used with permission.

Exhibit 4-6 illustrates that the six emotions can be conceptualized as existing along a continuum.[62] The closer any two emotions are to each other on this continuum, the more people are likely to confuse them. For instance, happiness and surprise are frequently mistaken for each other, while happiness and disgust are rarely confused. In addition, as we'll elaborate later in this section, cultural factors can also influence interpretations.

Do these six basic emotions surface in the workplace? Absolutely. I get *angry* after receiving a poor performance appraisal. I *fear* that I could be laid off as a result of a company cutback. I'm *sad* about one of my co-workers leaving to take a new job in another city. I'm *happy* after being selected as employee-of-the-month. I'm *disgusted* with the way my supervisor treats the women on our team. And I'm *surprised* to find out that management plans a complete restructuring of the company's retirement program.

Intensity People give different responses to identical emotion-provoking stimuli. In some cases this can be attributed to the individual's personality. Other times it is a result of the job requirements.

Emotion Continuum

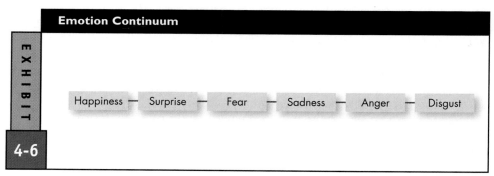

Happiness — Surprise — Fear — Sadness — Anger — Disgust

EXHIBIT 4-6

Source: Based on R. D. Woodworth, *Experimental Psychology* (New York: Holt, 1938).

People vary in their inherent ability to express intensity. You undoubtedly know individuals who almost never show their feelings. They rarely get angry. They never show rage. In contrast, you probably also know people who seem to be on an emotional roller coaster. When they're happy, they're ecstatic. When they're sad, they're deeply depressed. And two people can be in the exact same situation—one showing excitement and joy, the other remaining calm and collected.

Jobs make different intensity demands in terms of emotional labor. For instance, air traffic controllers and trial judges are expected to be calm and controlled, even in stressful situations. Conversely, the effectiveness of television evangelists, public-address announcers at sporting events, and lawyers can depend on their ability to alter their displayed emotional intensity as the need arises.

Frequency and Duration   How often does an emotion need to be exhibited? And for how long?

Sean Wolfson is basically a quiet and reserved person. He loves his job as a financial planner. He doesn't enjoy, however, having to give speeches in order to increase his visibility and to promote his programs. But he still has to give speeches occasionally. "If I had to speak to large audiences every day, I'd quit this business," he says. "I think this works for me because I can fake excitement and enthusiasm for an hour, a couple of times a month."

Emotional labor that requires high frequency or long durations is more demanding and requires more exertion by employees. So whether an employee can successfully meet the emotional demands of a given job depends not only on what emotions need to be displayed and their intensity, but also on how frequently and for how long the effort has to be made.

Can People Be Emotion*less*?

Some people seem outwardly calm or apathetic in situations in which others are clearly emotionally charged. Are the former without feeling? Can people be emotion*less*?

Some people have severe difficulty in expressing their emotions and understanding the emotions of others. Psychologists call this *alexithymia* (which is Greek for "lack of emotion").[63] People who suffer from alexithymia rarely cry and are often seen by others as bland and cold. Their own feelings make them uncomfortable, and they're not able to discriminate among their different emotions. In addition, they're often at a complete loss to understand what others around them feel.

Does this inability to express emotions and read others mean that people who suffer from alexithymia are poor work performers? Not necessarily. Consistent with our discussion on matching personality types with appropriate jobs, people who lack emotion need to be in jobs that require little or no emotional labor. These people are not well suited to sales and managerial positions. But they might very well be effective performers, for instance, in a job writing program code or in any work that is confined exclusively to computer interaction.

Gender and Emotions

It's widely assumed that women are more "in touch" with their feelings than men—that they react more emotionally and are better able to read emotions in others. Is there any truth to these assumptions?

The evidence does confirm differences between men and women when it comes to emotional reactions and ability to read others. In contrasting the genders, women show greater emotional expression than men[64]; they experience emotions more intensely; and they display more frequent expressions of both positive and negative emotions, except anger.[65] In contrast to men, women also report more comfort in expressing emotions. Finally, women are better at reading nonverbal and paralinguistic cues than are men.[66]

What explains these differences? Three possible answers have been suggested. One explanation is the different ways men and women have been socialized.[67] Men are taught to be tough and brave; and showing emotion is inconsistent with this image. Women, on the other hand, are socialized to be nurturing. This may account for the perception that women are generally warmer and friendlier than men. For instance, women are expected to express more positive emotions on the job (shown by smiling) than men, and they do.[68] A second explanation is that women may have more innate ability to read others and present their emotions than do men.[69] Thirdly, women may have a greater need for social approval and, thus, a higher propensity to show positive emotions, such as happiness.

External Constraints on Emotions

An emotion that is acceptable on the athletic playing field may be totally unacceptable when exhibited at the workplace. Similarly, what's appropriate in one country is often inappropriate in another. These facts illustrate the role that external constraints play in shaping displayed emotions.

Every organization defines boundaries that identify what emotions are acceptable and the degree to which they can be expressed. The same applies in different cultures. In this section, we look at organizational and cultural influences on emotions.

Organizational Influences   If you can't smile and appear happy, you're unlikely to have much of a career working at a Disney amusement park. And a manual produced by McDonald's states that its counter personnel "must display traits such as sincerity, enthusiasm, confidence, and a sense of humor."[70]

There is no single emotional "set" sought by all organizations. However, at least in the United States, the evidence indicates that there's a bias against negative and intense emotions. Expressions of negative emotions such as fear, anxiety, and anger tend to be unacceptable except under fairly specific conditions.[71] For instance, one such condition might be a high-status member of a group conveying impatience with a low-status member.[72] Moreover, expressions of intense emotion, whether negative or positive, tend to be typically unacceptable because they're seen as undermining routine task performance.[73] Again, there are exceptional conditions in which this isn't true—for example, a brief grieving over the sudden death of a company's CEO or the celebration of a record year of profits. But for the most part, consistent with the myth of rationality, well-managed organizations are expected to be essentially emotion-free.

Cultural Influences   Cultural norms in the United States dictate that employees in service organizations should smile and act friendly when interacting with customers.[74] But this norm doesn't apply worldwide. In Israel, smiling by supermarket cashiers is seen as a sign of inexperience, so cashiers are encouraged to look somber.[75] In Moslem cultures, smiling is frequently taken as a sign of sexual attraction, so women are socialized not to smile at men.[76] And Wal-Mart has found that its emphasis on employee friendliness, which has won them a loyal following among U.S. shoppers, doesn't work in Germany. Accustomed to a culture where "the customer traditionally comes last," serious German shoppers have been turned off by Wal-Mart's friendly greeters and helpful personnel.[77]

The above examples illustrate the need to consider cultural factors as influencing what is or isn't considered as emotionally appropriate.[78] What's acceptable in one culture may seem extremely unusual or even dysfunctional in another. And cultures differ in terms of the interpretation they give to emotions.

There tends to be high agreement on what emotions mean *within* cultures but not between. For instance, one study asked Americans to match facial expressions with the six basic emotions.[79] The range of agreement was between 86 and 98 percent. When a group of Japanese were given the same task, they correctly labeled only surprise (with 97 percent agreement). On the other five emotions, their accuracy ranged from only 27 to 70 percent. In addition, studies indicate that some cultures lack words for standard emotions such as *anxiety*, *depression*, or *guilt*. Tahitians, as a case in point, don't have a word directly equivalent to *sadness*. When Tahitians are sad, their peers typically attribute their state to a physical illness.[80]

OB Applications

We conclude our discussion of emotions by considering their application to several topics in OB. In this section, we assess how an understanding of emotions can improve our ability to explain and predict the selection process in organizations, decision making, motivation, leadership, interpersonal conflict, and deviant workplace behaviors.

Ability and Selection   People who know their own emotions and are good at reading others' emotions may be more effective in their jobs. That, in essence, is the theme underlying recent research on *emotional intelligence*.[81]

Emotional intelligence (EI) refers to an assortment of noncognitive skills, capabilities, and competencies that influence a person's ability to succeed in coping with environmental demands and pressures. It's composed of five dimensions:

People don't leave their emotions at the front door when they come to work.

Self-awareness. Being aware of what you're feeling.
Self-management. The ability to manage one's own emotions and impulses.
Self-motivation. The ability to persist in the face of setbacks and failures.
Empathy. The ability to sense how others are feeling.
Social skills. The ability to handle the emotions of others.

Several studies suggest that EI may play an important role in job performance. For instance, one study looked at the characteristics of Lucent Technologies' engineers who were rated as stars by their peers. The researchers concluded that stars were better at relating to others. That is, it was EI, not IQ, that characterized high performers. A study of U.S. Air Force recruiters generated similar findings. Top-performing recruiters exhibited high levels of EI. Using these findings, the Air Force revamped its selection criteria. A follow-up investigation found that future hires who had high EI scores were 2.6 times more successful than those who didn't. By using EI in selection, the Air Force was able to cut turnover among new recruiters in one year by more than 90 percent and save nearly $3 million in hiring and training costs. Another illuminating study looked at the successes and failures of 11 American presidents—from Franklin Roosevelt to Bill Clinton. They were evaluated on six qualities—communication, organization, political skill, vision, cognitive style, and emotional intelligence. It was found that the key quality that differentiated the successful (like Roosevelt, Kennedy, and Reagan) from the unsuccessful (like Johnson, Carter, and Nixon) was emotional intelligence.

The implications from the initial evidence on EI is that employers should consider it as a factor in selection, especially in jobs that demand a high degree of social interaction.

emotional intelligence

An assortment of noncognitive skills, capabilities, and competencies that influence a person's ability to succeed in coping with environmental demands and pressures.

Decision Making As you will see in Chapter 5, traditional approaches to the study of decision making in organizations has emphasized rationality. They have downplayed, or even ignored, the role of anxiety, fear, frustration, happiness, envy, and similar emotions. Yet it's naive to assume that decision choices aren't influenced by one's feelings at a particular moment.[82] Given the same objective data, we should expect that people may make different choices when they are angry and stressed out than when they're calm and collected.

Negative emotions can result in a limited search for new alternatives and a less vigilant use of information. On the other hand, positive emotions can increase problem-solving skills and facilitate the integration of information.[83]

You can improve your understanding of decision making by considering "the heart" as well as "the head." People use emotions as well as rational and intuitive processes in making decisions. Failure to incorporate emotions into the study of decision processes will result in an incomplete (and often inaccurate) view of the process.

Motivation We'll discuss motivation thoroughly in Chapters 6 and 7. At this point, we want merely to introduce the idea that, like decision making, the dominant approaches to the study of motivation reflect an overrationalized view of individuals.[84]

Motivation theories basically propose that individuals "are motivated to the extent that their behavior is expected to lead to desired outcomes. The image is that of rational exchange: the employee essentially trades effort for pay, security, promotions, and so forth."[85] But people aren't cold, unfeeling machines. Their perceptions and calculations of situations are filled with emotional content that significantly influences how much effort they exert. Moreover, when you see people who are highly motivated in their jobs, they're emotionally committed. People who are engaged in their work "become physically, cognitively, *and* emotionally immersed in the experience of activity, in the pursuit of a goal."[86]

Are all people emotionally engaged in their work? No. But many are. And if we focus only on rational calculations of inducements and contributions, we fail to be able to explain behaviors such as the individual who forgets to have dinner and works late into the night, lost in the thrill of her work.[87]

Leadership The ability to lead others is a fundamental quality sought by organizations. We'll discuss the topic of leadership, in depth, in Chapters 11 and 12. Here, however, we briefly introduce how emotions can be an integral part of leadership.

Effective leaders almost all rely on the expression of feelings to help convey their messages.[88] In fact, the expression of emotions in speeches are often the critical element that results in individuals accepting or rejecting a leader's message. "When leaders feel excited, enthusiastic, and active, they may be more likely to energize their subordinates and convey a sense of efficacy, competence, optimism, and enjoyment."[89] Politicians, as a case in point, have learned to show enthusiasm when talking about their chances for winning an election, even when polls suggest otherwise.

Corporate executives know that emotional content is critical if employees are to buy into their vision of their company's future and accept change. When new visions are offered, especially when they contain distant or vague goals, change is often difficult to accept. So when effective leaders want to implement significant changes, they rely on "the evocation, framing, and mobilization of *emotions*."[90] By arousing emotions and linking them to an appealing vision, leaders increase the likelihood that managers and employees alike will accept change.

Interpersonal Conflict   Few issues are more intertwined with emotions than the topic of interpersonal conflict. Whenever conflicts arise, you can be fairly certain that emotions are also surfacing. A manager's success in trying to resolve conflicts, in fact, is often largely attributable to his or her ability to identify the emotional elements in the conflict and to get the conflicting parties to work through their emotions. And the manager who ignores the emotional elements in conflicts, focusing singularly on rational and task-focused concerns, is unlikely to be very effective in resolving those conflicts.

Deviant Workplace Behaviors   Negative emotions can lead to a number of deviant workplace behaviors.

Anyone who has spent much time in an organization realizes that people often engage in voluntary actions that violate established norms and which threaten the organization, its members, or both. These actions are called **employee deviance**.[91] These deviant behaviors can be violent or nonviolent and fall into categories such as production (i.e., leaving early, intentionally working slowly); property (theft, sabotage); political (i.e., gossiping, blaming co-workers); and personal aggression (i.e., sexual harassment, verbal abuse).[92] Many of these deviant behaviors can be traced to negative emotions.

For instance, envy is an emotion that occurs when you resent someone for having something that you don't, and which you strongly desire—such as a better work assignment, larger office, or higher salary.[93] It can lead to malicious deviant behaviors. Envy, for example, has been found to be associated with hostility, "backstabbing" and other forms of political behavior, negatively distorting others' successes, and positively distorting one's own accomplishments.[94]

employee deviance
Voluntary actions that violate established norms and that threaten the organization, its members, or both.

OB in the News

The Increasing Popularity of Anger-Management Classes

Anger-management classes have become a trendy solution for dealing with people who have difficulty controlling their tempers. Prosecutors across the United States, for instance, are sending thousands of criminals for anger-management instruction each year. Men who menace their wives or girlfriends are finding that a frequent legal solution is for them to attend anger-management classes. Hotheaded celebrities such as Mike Tyson, Tommy Lee, Sean "Puffy" Combs, Latrell Sprewell, Shannon Doherty, and Courtney Love have been required to take these classes to help them cool their tempers. And companies are increasingly sending short-tempered employees to these classes to help them manage their negative emotions.

Courses in anger management tend to be similar in content. Participants share their stories that have led them to the class; then they are told to think about the consequences of what they do when they get worked up. They're taught how to look at the big picture, how not to let small things bother them, how to be a good listener, how to accept someone else's opinion without going ballistic, and the like.

Mental-health professionals say that anger-management classes can be beneficial. They say that making mature decisions is a skill that can be taught. But it requires committed students over a long period. Unfortunately, many people who suffer from anger problems aren't willing to admit they have a problem and are even less willing to put in the effort—one expert says her clients typically need about a year to overcome their anger issues—to try to control it. But studies of anger-management programs find little to support their effectiveness. This may be due to several factors. It may reflect a lack of commitment by participants. It may be that many people in these programs actually need other kinds of therapy. Anger management is designed to deal with spontaneous rage, yet many of the individuals taking these courses are just cold, calculating people. Or it may well be that it's not possible to change a basic personality that includes the tendency to exhibit spontaneous rage when angered or frustrated.

Source: Based on J. Cloud, "Classroom for Hotheads," Time, April 10, 2000, pp. 53–54.

SUMMARY AND IMPLICATIONS FOR MANAGERS

Personality

A review of the personality literature offers general guidelines that can lead to effective job performance. As such, it can improve hiring, transfer, and promotion decisions. Because personality characteristics create the parameters for people's behavior, they give us a framework for predicting behavior. For example, individuals who are shy, introverted, and uncomfortable in social situations would probably be ill-suited as salespeople. Individuals who are submissive and conforming might not be effective as advertising "idea" people.

Can we predict which people will be high performers in sales, research, or assembly-line work on the basis of their personality characteristics alone? The answer is No. Personality assessment should be used in conjunction with other information such as skills, abilities, and experience.[95] But a knowledge of an individual's personality can aid in reducing mismatches, which, in turn, can lead to reduced turnover and higher job satisfaction.

We can look at certain personality characteristics that tend to be related to job success, test for those traits, and use the data to make selection more effective. A person who accepts rules, conformity, and dependence, for instance, is likely to feel more comfortable in, say, a structured assembly-line job, as an admittance clerk in a hospital, or as an administrator in a large public agency than as a researcher or an employee whose job requires a high degree of creativity.

Emotions

Can managers control the emotions of their colleagues and employees? No. Emotions are a natural part of an individual's make-up. Where managers err is if they ignore the emotional elements in organizational behavior and assess individual behavior as if it were completely rational. As one consultant aptly put it, "You can't divorce emotions from the workplace because you can't divorce emotions from people."[96] Managers who understand the role of emotions will significantly improve their ability to explain and predict individual behavior.

Do emotions affect job performance? Yes. They can *hinder* performance, especially negative emotions. That's probably why organizations, for the most part, try to extract emotions out of the workplace. But emotions can also *enhance* performance. How? Two ways.[97] First, emotions can increase arousal levels, thus acting as motivators to higher performance. Second, emotional labor recognizes that feelings can be part of a job's required behavior. So, for instance, the ability to effectively manage emotions in leadership, sales, and customer-interface positions may be critical to success in those positions.

What differentiates functional from dysfunctional emotions at work? While there is no precise answer to this, it's been suggested that the critical moderating variable is the complexity of the individual's task.[98] The more complex a task, the lower the level of arousal that can be tolerated without interfering with performance. While a certain minimal level of arousal is probably necessary for good performance, very high levels interfere with the ability to function, especially if the job requires calculative and detailed cognitive processes. Given that the trend is toward jobs becoming more complex, you can see why organizations are likely to go to considerable efforts to discourage the overt display of emotions—especially intense ones—in the workplace.

Traits Are Powerful Predictors of Behavior

The essence of trait approaches in OB is that employees possess stable personality characteristics that significantly influence their attitudes toward, and behavioral reactions to, organizational settings. People with particular traits tend to be relatively consistent in their attitudes and behavior over time and across situations.[a]

Of course, trait theorists recognize that all traits are not equally powerful. They tend to put them into one of three categories. *Cardinal traits* are those so strong and generalized that they influence every act a person performs. *Primary traits* are generally consistent influences on behavior, but they may not show up in all situations. Finally, *secondary traits* are attributes that do not form a vital part of the personality but come into play only in particular situations. For the most part, trait theories have focused on the power of primary traits to predict employee behavior.

Trait theorists do a fairly good job of meeting the average person's face-validity test. Think of friends, relatives, and acquaintances you have known for a number of years. Do they have traits that have remained essentially stable over time? Most of us would answer that question in the affirmative. If Cousin Anne was shy and nervous when we last saw her 10 years ago, we would be surprised to find her outgoing and relaxed now.

Managers seem to have a strong belief in the power of traits to predict behavior. If managers believed that situations determined behavior, they would hire people almost at random and structure the situation properly. But the employee selection process in most organizations places a great deal of emphasis on how applicants perform in interviews and on tests. Assume you're an interviewer and ask yourself: What am I looking for in job candidates? If you answered with terms such as *conscientious*, *hardworking*, *persistent*, *confident*, and *dependable*, you're a trait theorist.

Few people would dispute that there are some stable individual attributes that affect reactions to the workplace. But trait theorists go beyond that generality and argue that individual behavior consistencies are widespread and account for much of the differences in behavior among people.[b]

There are two important problems with using traits to explain a large proportion of behavior in organizations. First, organizational settings are strong situations that have a large impact on employee behavior. Second, individuals are highly adaptive and personality traits change in response to organizational situations.

It has been well known for some time that the effects of traits are likely to be strongest in relatively weak situations and weakest in relatively strong situations. Organizational settings tend to be strong situations because they have rules and other formal regulations that define acceptable behavior and punish deviant behavior; and they have informal norms that dictate appropriate behaviors. These formal and informal constraints minimize the effects of personality traits.

By arguing that employees possess stable traits that lead to cross-situational consistencies in behaviors, trait theorists are implying that individuals don't really adapt to different situations. But there is a growing body of evidence that an individual's traits are changed by the organizations that that individual participates in. If the individual's personality changes as a result of exposure to organizational settings, in what sense can that individual be said to have traits that persistently and consistently affect his or her reactions to those very settings? Moreover, people typically belong to multiple organizations that often include very different kinds of members. And they adapt to those different situations. Instead of being the prisoners of a rigid and stable personality framework as trait theorists propose, people regularly adjust their behavior to reflect the requirements of various situations.

[a]Some of the points in this argument are from R. J. House, S. A. Shane, and D. M. Herold, "Rumors of the Death of Dispositional Research Are Vastly Exaggerated," *Academy of Management Review*, January 1996, pp. 203–24.

[b]Based on A. Davis-Blake and J. Pfeffer, "Just a Mirage: The Search for Dispositional Effects in Organizational Research," *Academy of Management Review*, July 1989, pp. 385–400.

1. What is *personality*?

2. What behavioral predictions might you make if you knew that an employee had (a) an external locus of control? (b) a low Mach score? (c) low self-esteem? (d) a Type A personality?

3. What is the Myers–Briggs Type Indicator?

4. Describe the factors in the Big Five model. Which factor shows the greatest value in predicting behavior? Why does it?

5. What were the six personality types identified by Holland?

6. Do people from the same country have a common personality type? Explain.

7. Why might managers today pay more attention to the person–organization fit than the person–job fit?

8. What is *emotional labor,* and why is it important to understanding OB?

9. How does national culture influence expressed emotions?

10. What is *emotional intelligence* and why is it important?

Questions for Critical Thinking

1. "Heredity determines personality." (a) Build an argument to support this statement. (b) Build an argument against this statement.

2. "The type of job an employee does moderates the relationship between personality and job productivity." Do you agree or disagree with this statement? Discuss.

3. One day your boss comes in and he is nervous, edgy, and argumentative. The next day he is calm and relaxed. Does this behavior suggest that personality traits are not consistent from day to day?

4. What, if anything, can managers do to *manage* emotions?

5. Give some examples of situations in which the overt expression of emotions might enhance job performance.

Team Exercise | What is a "Team Personality"?

It's the unusual organization today that isn't using work teams. But not everybody is a good team player. This prompts the questions: What individual personality characteristics enhance a team's performance? And what characteristics might hinder team performance?

Break into groups of five or six. Based on the research presented in this chapter, each group should (a) identify personality characteristics they think are associated with high-performance teams and justify their choices, (b) identify personality characteristics they think hinder high-performance teams and justify their choices, and (c) resolve whether it is better to have teams composed of individuals with similar or dissimilar traits.

Each group should select an individual who will present his or her group's findings to the class.

Ethical Dilemma | Managing Emotions at Work

Our understanding of emotions at work has increased rapidly in the past decade. We are now at the point at which we are capable of, or close to being able to, managing the emotions of employees. For instance, companies that want to create open and friendly work places are using the selection process to "select out" job applicants who aren't outgoing and enthusiastic and are providing training to teach employees how to smile and appear cheerful. Some organizations are going further in attempting to create "emotionally humanistic" work environments by not only shaping the emotions that workers evoke in their daily contacts with customers but also by selecting employee applicants with high emotional intelligence, controlling the emotional atmosphere of teams and work groups, and similar emotion-management practices.

Groucho Marx once joked that "the secret of success in show business is honesty and sincerity. Once you learn how to fake that, you've got it made." In many service organizations today, Groucho's remark is being applied. For instance, telephone-sales staff in a number of insurance companies are trained to invoke positive feelings from customers—to make it easy for them to say "yes." Employees are taught to avoid words with negative connotations and replace them with upbeat and confidence-building words such as "certainly," "rest assured," "immediate," and "great." Moreover, employees are taught to convey these "scripts" in a way that seems natural and spontaneous. To ensure that these "authentic" positive feelings are consistently evoked, the phone calls of these sales people are often monitored.

Organizations like McDonalds, Disney, and Starbucks select and program employees to be upbeat and friendly. They allow employees no choices. Moreover, these organizations export their emotional expectations to everywhere in the world in which they locate. When the hamburgers or lattes come to town, the typical grimace of the Moscovite or shyness of the Finnish employee are subject to a similar genre of smile-training.

Is asking people to feign specific job-related emotions unethical if it conflicts with their basic personality? Is exporting standardized emotional "rule books" to alien cultures unethical? What do you think?

This dilemma is based on S. Fineman, "Managing Emotions at Work: Some Political Reflections;" paper presented at a symposium at the Academy of Management Conference; Washington, DC, August 2001.

Case Incident	Roustabouts Need Understanding Too!

If you were to walk around one of Transocean Sedco Forex's oil rigs, off the New Orleans' coast, you'd see something that might puzzle you. Most of the workers have three stickers on their hard hats. One says "Start to Understand Me." The other two are colored dots. What's this all about? The colored dots are there to tell co-workers about the personality under the hat. The company believes that workers are better able to understand each other and get along if they know the personalities of the people with whom they have to work.

Transocean has hired an outside consulting firm to provide personality assessment to its 8,300 workers worldwide. For instance, employees are presented with 28 sets of four words. Each worker picks a word that describes him best and a word that describes him least. A typical set: fussy, obedient, firm, playful. Employees then are shown how to score their test and find out their two dominant colors. For instance, reds are driven. Yellows are emotional, talkative, and have a fondness for people. Greens are cautious and serious. Reds are strong-willed and decisive. And blues dislike change and can be a little wishy-washy. Rig workers wear their dots on their hats, while land-based employees post theirs outside their office doors. No one is forced to display their colors and some think the program may be too intrusive. Tim Callais, a Transocean adviser for operational safety, says those who question the program's credibility are "probably blue people."

A number of employees seem to find the dots helpful. Thom Keeton, a red–green rig manager, keeps a color chart under the glass covering his desk for quick reference. Tom Watkins, a senior rig hand on a drilling ship who is also a red–green, thinks the colors correctly reflect his personality: blunt, to the point, and not liking to talk much. David Gray, a blue–yellow, says the colored dots help him deal with high-strung red–greens now that he's figured out that he just has to get to the point more quickly.

This program is not being applied only at Transocean. Similar personality-based coding systems are being put into place with a number of blue-collar employees. Assembly-line workers in Kentucky are using the system. So are police officers in Kansas, electricians in Texas, construction crews in Florida, and carpenters and plumbers in New York City.

Questions

1. Are you surprised that oil-rig workers would buy into a program like this?

2. How valid do you think color-coded personality ratings are?

3. Do you think having employees "wear their personalities on their hats" is a personal intrusion? Is it unethical?

4. Transocean's CEO supports the program but says, "I can be whatever color I want to be." Do you agree with him? Explain.

Based on C. Cummins, "Workers Wear Feelings on Their Hard Hats and Show True Colors," *Wall Street Journal*, November 7, 2000, p. A1.

Reading Emotions

After you've read this chapter, take Self-Assessment #20 (What's My Emotional Intelligence Score?) on your enclosed CD-ROM, and complete the skill-building module entitled "Reading Emotions" on page 617.

Endnotes

1. Based on A. Bianco, "Software's Tough Guy," *Business Week*, March 6, 2000, pp. 133–44; and www.askmen.com/men/business, October 1, 2001.

2. G. W. Allport, *Personality: A Psychological Interpretation* (New York: Holt, Rinehart & Winston, 1937), p. 48.

3. Reported in R. L. Hotz, "Genetics, Not Parenting, Key to Temperament, Studies Say," *Los Angeles Times*, February 20, 1994, p. A1.

4. See R. D. Arvey and T. J. Bouchard, Jr., "Genetics, Twins, and Organizational Behavior," in B. M. Staw and L. L. Cummings (eds.), *Research in Organizational Behavior*, vol. 16 (Greenwich, CT: JAI Press, 1994), pp. 65–66; D. Lykken and A. Tellegen, "Happiness is a Stochastic Phenomenon," *Psychological Science*, May 1996, pp. 186–89; and W. Wright, *Born That Way: Genes, Behavior, Personality* (New York: Knopf, 1998).

5. R. C. Carson, "Personality," in M. R. Rosenzweig and L. W. Porter (eds.), *Annual Review of Psychology*, vol. 40 (Palo Alto, CA: Annual Reviews, 1989), pp. 228–29.

6. W. Mischel, "The Interaction of Person and Situation," in D. Magnusson and N. S. Endler, eds., *Personality at the Crossroads: Current Issues in Interactional Psychology* (Hillsdale, NJ: Erlbaum, 1977), pp. 166–207.

7. See A. H. Buss, "Personality as Traits," *American Psychologist*, November 1989, pp. 1378–88; R. R. McCrae, "Trait Psychology and the Revival of Personality and Culture Studies," *American Behavioral Scientist*, September 2000, pp. 10–31; and L. R. James and M. D. Mazerolle, *Personality in Work Organizations* (Thousand Oaks, CA: Sage, 2002).

8. G. W. Allport and H. S. Odbert, "Trait Names, A Psycholexical Study," *Psychological Monographs*, no. 47 (1936).

9. R. B. Cattell, "Personality Pinned Down," *Psychology Today*, July 1973, pp. 40–46.

10. See R. R. McCrae and T. Costa, Jr., "Reinterpreting the Myers–Briggs Type Indicator from the Perspective of the Five Factor Model of Personality," *Journal of Personality*, March 1989, pp. 17–40; and N. L. Quenk, *Essentials of Myers-Briggs Type Indicator Assessment* (New York: Wiley, 2000).

11. G. N. Landrum, *Profiles of Genius* (New York: Prometheus, 1993).

12. See, for example, J. M. Digman, "Personality Structure: Emergence of the Five-Factor Model," in M. R. Rosenzweig and L. W. Porter (eds.), *Annual Review of Psychology*, vol. 41 (Palo Alto, CA: Annual Reviews, 1990), pp. 417–40; R. R. McCrae, "Special Issue: The Five-Factor Model: Issues and Applications," *Journal of Personality*, June 1992; P. H. Raymark, M. J. Schmit, and R. M. Guion, "Identifying Potentially Useful Personality Constructs for Employee Se-

lection," *Personnel Psychology*, Autumn 1997, pp. 723–36; and D. B. Smith, P. J. Hanges, and M. W. Dickson, "Personnel Selection and the Five-Factor Model: Reexamining the Effects of Applicant's Frame of Reference," *Journal of Applied Psychology*, April 2001, pp. 304–15.

13. See, for instance, M. R. Barrick and M. K. Mount, "The Big Five Personality Dimensions and Job Performance: A Meta-Analysis," *Personnel Psychology* 44 (1991), pp. 1–26; R. P. Tett, D. N. Jackson, and M. Rothstein, "Personality Measures as Predictors of Job Performance: A Meta-Analytic Review, *Personnel Psychology*, Winter 1991, pp. 703–42; O. Behling, "Employee Selection: Will Intelligence and Conscientiousness Do the Job?" *Academy of Management Executive*, February 1998, pp. 77–86; A. J. Vinchur, J. S. Schippmann, F. S. Switzer III and P. L. Roth, "A Meta-Analytic Review of Predictors of Job Performance for Salespeople," *Journal of Applied Psychology*, August 1998, pp. 586–97; G. M. Hurtz and J. J. Donovan, "Personality and Job Performance: The Big Five Revisited," *Journal of Applied Psychology*, December 2000, pp. 869–79; and T. A. Judge and J. E. Bono, "Relationship of Core Self-Evaluations Traits—Self-Esteem, Generalized Self-Efficacy, Locus of Control, and Emotional Stability—With Job Satisfaction and Job Performance: A Meta-Analysis," *Journal of Applied Psychology*, February 2001, pp. 80–92.

14. M. K. Mount, M. R. Barrick, and J. P. Strauss, "Validity of Observer Ratings of the Big Five Personality Factors," *Journal of Applied Psychology*, April 1994, p. 272. Additionally confirmed by G. M. Hurtz and J. J. Donovan, "Personality and Job Performance: The Big Five Revisited."

15. D. W. Organ, "Personality and Organizational Citizenship Behavior," *Journal of Management*, Summer 1994, pp. 465–78; D. W. Organ and K. Ryan, "A Meta-Analytic Review of Attitudinal and Dispositional Predictors of Organizational Citizenship Behavior," *Personnel Psychology*, Winter 1995, pp. 775–802; M. A. Konovsky and D. W. Organ, "Dispositional and Contextual Determinants of Organizational Citizenship Behavior," *Journal of Organizational Behavior*, May 1996, pp. 253–66; and P. M. Podsakoff, S. B. MacKenzie, J. B. Paine, and D. G. Bachrach, "Organizational Citizenship Behaviors: A Critical Review of the Theoretical and Empirical Literature and Suggestions for Future Research," *Journal of Management*, vol. 6, no. 3, 2000, pp. 513–63.

16. J. B. Rotter, "Generalized Expectancies for Internal versus External Control of Reinforcement," *Psychological Monographs*, 80, no. 609 (1966).

17. See P. E. Spector, "Behavior in Organizations as a Function of Employee's Locus of Control," *Psychological Bulletin*,

May 1982, pp. 482–97; and G. J. Blau, "Locus of Control as a Potential Moderator of the Turnover Process," *Journal of Occupational Psychology*, Fall 1987, pp. 21–29.

18. K. W. Cook, C. A. Vance, and P. E. Spector, "The Relation of Candidate Personality with Selection-Interview Outcomes," *Journal of Applied Social Psychology*, April 2000, pp. 867–85.

19. R. T. Keller, "Predicting Absenteeism from Prior Absenteeism, Attitudinal Factors, and Nonattitudinal Factors, *Journal of Applied Psychology*, August 1983, pp. 536–40.

20. Spector, "Behavior in Organizations as a Function of Employee's Locus of Control,"p. 493.

21. R. G. Vleeming, "Machiavellianism: A Preliminary Review," *Psychological Reports*, February 1979, pp. 295–310.

22. R. Christie and F. L. Geis, *Studies in Machiavellianism* (New York: Academic Press, 1970), p. 312; and N. V. Ramanaiah, A. Byravan, and F. R. J. Detwiler, "Revised Neo Personality Inventory Profiles of Machiavellian and Non-Machiavellian People," *Psychological Reports*, October 1994, pp. 937–38.

23. Christie and Geis, *Studies in Machiavellianism*.

24. See J. Brockner, *Self-Esteem at Work* (Lexington, MA: Lexington Books, 1988); and N. Branden, *Self-Esteem at Work* (San Francisco: Jossey-Bass, 1998).

25. See M. Snyder, *Public Appearances/Private Realities: The Psychology of Self-Monitoring* (New York: W. H. Freeman, 1987); and D. V. Day, D. J. Schleicher, A. L. Unckless, and N. J. Hiller, "Self-Monitoring Personality at Work: A Meta-Analytic Investigation of Construct Validity," *Journal of Applied Psychology*, April 2002, pp. 390–401.

26. M. Snyder, *Public Appearances/Private Realities*.

27. M. Kilduff and D. V. Day, "Do Chameleons Get Ahead? The Effects of Self-Monitoring on Managerial Careers," *Academy of Management Journal*, August 1994, pp. 1047–60; and A. Mehra, M. Kilduff, and D. J. Brass, "The Social Networks of High and Low Self-Monitors: Implications for Workplace Performance," *Administrative Science Quarterly*, March 2001, pp. 121–46.

28. R. N. Taylor and M. D. Dunnette, "Influence of Dogmatism, Risk-Taking Propensity, and Intelligence on Decision-Making Strategies for a Sample of Industrial Managers," *Journal of Applied Psychology*, August 1974, pp. 420–23.

29. I. L. Janis and L. Mann, *Decision Making: A Psychological Analysis of Conflict, Choice, and Commitment* (New York: Free Press, 1977); and W. H. Stewart, Jr., and L. Roth, "Risk Propensity Differences Between Entrepreneurs and Managers: A Meta-Analytic Review," *Journal of Applied Psychology*, February 2001, pp. 145–53.

30. N. Kogan and M. A. Wallach, "Group Risk Taking as a Function of Members' Anxiety and Defensiveness," *Journal of Personality*, March 1967, pp. 50–63.

31. M. Friedman and R. H. Rosenman, *Type A Behavior and Your Heart* (New York: Alfred A. Knopf, 1974), p. 84 (emphasis in original).

32. Ibid., pp. 84–85.

33. K. W. Cook, C. A. Vance, and E. Spector, "The Relation of Candidate Personality with Selection-Interview Outcomes."

34. M. Friedman and R. H. Rosenman, *Type A Behavior and Your Heart*, p. 86.

35. See, for instance, G. W. M. Ip and M. H. Bond, "Culture, Values, and the Spontaneous Self-Concept," *Asian Journal of Psychology*, vol. 1, 1995, pp. 30–36; J. E. Williams, J. L. Saiz, D. L. FormyDuval, M. L. Munick, E. E. Fogle, A. Adom, A. Haque, F. Neto, and J. Yu, "Cross-Cultural Variation in the Importance of Psychological Characteristics: A Seven-Country Study," *International Journal of Psychology*, October 1995, pp. 529–50; V. Benet and N. G. Waller, "The Big Seven Factor Model of Personality Description: Evidence for Its Cross-Cultural Generalizability in a Spanish Sample," *Journal of Personality and Social Psychology*, October 1995, pp. 701–18; R. R. McCrae and P. T. Costa Jr., "Personality Trait Structure as a Human Universal," *American Psychologist*, 1997, pp. 509–16; and M. J. Schmit, J. A. Kihm, and C. Robie, "Development of a Global Measure of Personality," *Personnel Psychology*, Spring 2000, pp. 153–93.

36. J. F. Salgado, "The Five Factor Model of Personality and Job Performance in the European Community," *Journal of Applied Psychology*, February 1997, pp. 30–43.

37. F. Kluckhohn and F. L. Strodtbeck, *Variations in Value Orientations* (Evanston, IL: Row Peterson, 1961).

38. P. B. Smith, F. Trompenaars, and S. Dugan, "The Rotter Locus of Control Scale in 43 Countries: A Test of Cultural Relativity, " *International Journal of Psychology*, June 1995, pp. 377–400.

39. Friedman and Rosenman, *Type A Behavior and Your Heart*, p. 86.

40. P. L. Ackerman and L. G. Humphreys, "Individual Differences Theory in Industrial and Organizational Psychology," in M. D. Dunnette and L. M. Hough, eds., *Handbook of Industrial & Organizational Psychology*, 2nd ed., vol. 1 (Palo Alto: Consulting Psychologists, 1990), pp. 223–82.

41. J. L. Holland, *Making Vocational Choices: A Theory of Vocational Personalities and Work Environments* (Odessa, FL: Psychological Assessment Resources, 1997).

42. See, for example, A. R. Spokane, "A Review of Research on Person-Environment Congruence in Holland's Theory of Careers," *Journal of Vocational Behavior*, June 1985, pp. 306–43; J. L. Holland and G. D. Gottfredson, "Studies of the Hexagonal Model: An Evaluation (or, The Perils of Stalking the Perfect Hexagon)," *Journal of Vocational Behavior*, April 1992, pp. 158–70; T. J. Tracey and J. Rounds, "Evaluating Holland's and Gati's Vocational-Interest Models: A Structural Meta-Analysis," *Psychological Bulletin*, March 1993, pp. 229–46; and F. De Fruyt and I. Mervielde, "RIASEC Types and Big Five Traits as Predictors of Employment Status and Nature of Employment," *Personnel Psychology*, Autumn 1999, pp. 701–27.

43. See B. Schneider, "The People Make the Place," *Personnel Psychology*, Autumn 1987, pp. 437–53; D. E. Bowen, G. E. Ledford, Jr., and B. R. Nathan, "Hiring for the Organization, Not the Job," *Academy of Management Executive*, November 1991, pp. 35–51; B. Schneider, H. W. Goldstein, and D. B. Smith, "The ASA Framework: An Update," *Personnel Psychology*, Winter 1995, pp. 747–73; A. L. Kristof, "Person-Organization Fit: An Integrative Review of Its Conceptualizations, Measurement, and Implications," *Personnel Psychology*, Spring 1996, pp. 1–49; and B. Schneider, D. B. Smith, S. Taylor, and J. Fleenor, "Personality and Organizations: A Test of the Homogeneity of Personality Hypothesis," *Journal of Applied Psychology*, June 1998, pp. 462–70.

44. Based on T. A. Judge and D. M. Cable, "Applicant Personality, Organizational Culture, and Organization Attraction," *Personnel Psychology*, Summer 1997, pp. 359–94.

45. C. Goldberg, "7 Die in Rampage at Company; Co-Worker of Victims Arrested," *New York Times*, December 27, 2000, p. A1.

46. See, for instance, C. D. Fisher and N. M. Ashkanasy, "The Emerging Role of Emotions in Work Life: An Introduction," *Journal of Organizational Behavior*, Special Issue 2000, pp. 123–29; and N. M. Ashkanasy, C. E. J. Hartel, and W. J. Zerbe, eds., *Emotions in the Workplace: Research, Theory, and Practice* (Westport, CT: Quorum Books, 2000).

47. See, for example, L. L. Putnam and D. K. Mumby, "Organizations, Emotion and the Myth of Rationality," in S. Fineman (ed.), *Emotion in Organizations* (Thousand Oaks, CA: Sage, 1993), pp. 36–57; and J. Martin, K. Knopoff, and C. Beckman, "An Alternative to Bureaucratic Impersonality and Emotional Labor: Bounded Emotionality at the Body Shop," *Administrative Science Quarterly*, June 1998, pp. 429–69.

48. B. E. Ashforth and R. H. Humphrey, "Emotion in the Workplace: A Reappraisal," *Human Relations*, February 1995, pp. 97–125.

49. J. M. George, "Trait and State Affect," in K. R. Murphy (ed.), *Individual Differences and Behavior in Organizations* (San Francisco: Jossey-Bass, 1996), p. 145.

50. See N. H. Frijda, "Moods, Emotion Episodes and Emotions," in M. Lewis and J. M. Haviland (eds.), *Handbook of Emotions* (New York: Guilford Press, 1993), pp. 381–403.

51. H. M. Weiss and R. Cropanzano, "Affective Events Theory," in B. M. Staw and L. L. Cummings, *Research in Organizational Behavior*, vol. 18 (Greenwich, CT: JAI Press, 1996), pp. 17–19.

52. N. H. Frijda, "Moods, Emotion Episodes and Emotions," p. 381.

53. See J. A. Morris and D. C. Feldman, "Managing Emotions in the Workplace," *Journal of Managerial Issues*, vol. 9, no. 3, 1997, pp. 257–74; and S. M. Kruml and D. Geddes, "Catching Fire without Burning Out: Is There an Ideal Way to Perform Emotion Labor?" in N. M. Ashkansay, C. E. J. Hartel, and W. J. Zerbe, *Emotions in the Workplace*, pp. 177–88.

54. A. R. Hochschild, "Emotion Work, Feeling Rules, and Social Structure," *American Journal of Sociology*, November 1979, pp. 551–75; and S. Mann, *Hiding What We Feel, Faking What We Don't* (Shaftesbury, Dorset, UK: Element, 1999).

55. B. M. DePaulo, "Nonverbal Behavior and Self-Presentation," *Psychological Bulletin*, March 1992, pp. 203–43.

56. C. S. Hunt, "Although I Might Be Laughing Loud and Hearty, Deep Inside I'm Blue: Individual Perceptions Regarding Feeling and Displaying Emotions at Work," paper presented at the Academy of Management Conference; Cincinnati, August 1996, p. 3.

57. D. Watson, L. A. Clark, and A. Tellegen, "Development and Validation of Brief Measures of Positive and Negative Affect: The PANAS Scales," *Journal of Personality and Social Psychology*, 1988, pp. 1063–70.

58. A. Ben-Ze'ev, *The Subtlety of Emotions* (Cambridge, MA: MIT Press, 2000), p. 94.

59. Cited in Ibid., p. 99

60. See, for example, P. Shaver, J. Schwartz, D. Kirson, and C. O'Connor, "Emotion Knowledge: Further Exploration of a Prototype Approach," *Journal of Personality and Social Psychology*, June 1987, pp. 1061–86; P. Ekman, "An Argument for Basic Emotions," *Cognition and Emotion*, May/July 1992, pp. 169–200; C. E. Izard, "Basic Emotions, Relations among Emotions, and Emotion–Cognition Relations," *Psychological Bulletin*, November 1992, pp. 561–65; and

R. Plutchik, *The Psychology and Biology of Emotion* (New York: HarperCollins, 1994).

61. H. M. Weiss and R. Cropanzano, "Affective Events Theory," pp. 20–22.

62. Cited in R. D. Woodworth, *Experimental Psychology* (New York: Holt, 1938).

63. See, for instance, J. K. Salminen, S. Saarijanvi, E. Aairela, and T. Tamminen, "Alexithymia: State or Trait? One-Year Follow-up Study of General Hospital Psychiatric Consultation Outpatients," *Journal of Psychosomatic Research*, July 1994, pp. 681–85; and M. F. R. Kets de Vries, "Organizational Sleepwalkers: Emotional Distress at Midlife," *Human Relations*, November 1999, pp. 1377–1401.

64. K. Deaux, "Sex Differences," in M. R. Rosenzweig and L. W. Porter (eds.), *Annual Review of Psychology*, vol. 26 (Palo Alto, CA: Annual Reviews, 1985), pp. 48–82; M. LaFrance and M. Banaji, "Toward a Reconsideration of the Gender-Emotion Relationship," in M. Clark (ed.), *Review of Personality and Social Psychology*, vol. 14 (Newbury Park, CA: Sage, 1992), pp. 178–97; and A. M. Kring and A. H. Gordon, "Sex Differences in Emotion: Expression, Experience, and Physiology," *Journal of Personality and Social Psychology*, March 1998, pp. 686–703.

65. L. R. Brody and J. A. Hall, "Gender and Emotion," in M. Lewis and J. M. Haviland (eds.), *Handbook of Emotions* (New York: Guilford Press, 1993), pp. 447–60; and M. Grossman and W. Wood, "Sex Differences in Intensity of Emotional Experience: A Social Role Interpretation," *Journal of Personality and Social Psychology*, November 1992, pp. 1010–22.

66. J. A. Hall, *Nonverbal Sex Differences: Communication Accuracy and Expressive Style* (Baltimore: Johns Hopkins Press, 1984).

67. N. James, "Emotional Labour: Skill and Work in the Social Regulations of Feelings," *Sociological Review*, February 1989, pp. 15–42; A. Hochschild, *The Second Shift* (New York: Viking, 1989); and F. M. Deutsch, "Status, Sex, and Smiling: The Effect of Role on Smiling in Men and Women," *Personality and Social Psychology Bulletin*, September 1990, pp. 531–40.

68. A. Rafaeli, "When Clerks Meet Customers: A Test of Variables Related to Emotional Expression on the Job," *Journal of Applied Psychology*, June 1989, pp. 385–93; and M. LaFrance and M. Banaji, "Toward a Reconsideration of the Gender-Emotion Relationship."

69. L. W. Hoffman, "Early Childhood Experiences and Women's Achievement Motives," *Journal of Social Issues*, vol. 28, no. 2, 1972, pp. 129–55.

70. M. Boas and S. Chain, *Big Mac: The Unauthorized Story of McDonald's* (New York: Dutton, 1976), p. 84.

71. B. E. Ashforth and R. H. Humphrey, "Emotion in the Workplace," p. 104.

72. G. L. Flett, K. R. Blankstein, P. Pliner, and C. Bator, "Impression-Management and Self-Deception Components of Appraised Emotional Experience," *British Journal of Social Psychology*, January 1988, pp. 67–77.

73. B. E. Ashforth and R. H. Humphrey, "Emotion in the Workplace," p. 104.

74. A. Rafaeli and R. I. Sutton, "The Expression of Emotion in Organizational Life," in L. L. Cummings and B. M. Staw, eds., *Research in Organizational Behavior*, vol. 11 (Greenwich, CT: JAI Press, 1989), p. 8.

75. A. Rafaeli, "When Cashiers Meet Customers: An Analysis of Supermarket Cashiers," *Academy of Management Journal*, June 1989, pp. 245–73.

76. Ibid.
77. D. Rubin, "Grumpy German Shoppers Distrust the Wal-Mart Style," *Seattle Times*, December 30, 2001, p. A15.
78. B. Mesquita and N. H. Frijda, "Cultural Variations in Emotions: A Review," *Psychological Bulletin*, September 1992, pp. 179–204; and B. Mesquita, "Emotions in Collectivist and Individualist Contexts," *Journal of Personality and Social Psychology*, January 2001, pp. 68–74.
79. Described in S. Emmons, "Emotions at Face Value," *Los Angeles Times*, January 9, 1998, p. E1.
80. R. I. Levy, *Tahitians: Mind and Experience in the Society Islands* (Chicago: University of Chicago Press, 1973).
81. This section is based on Daniel Goleman, *Emotional Intelligence* (New York: Bantam, 1995); J. D. Mayer and G. Geher, "Emotional Intelligence and the Identification of Emotion," *Intelligence*, March–April 1996, pp. 89–113; R. K. Cooper, "Applying Emotional Intelligence in the Workplace," *Training & Development*, December 1997, pp. 31–38; "HR Pulse: Emotional Intelligence," *HRMagazine*, January 1998, p. 19; M. Davies, L. Stankov, and R. D. Roberts, "Emotional Intelligence: In Search of an Elusive Construct," *Journal of Personality and Social Psychology*, October 1998, pp. 989–1015; D. Goleman, *Working with Emotional Intelligence* (New York: Bantam, 1999); R. Bar-On and J. D. A. Parker, eds. *The Handbook of Emotional Intelligence: Theory, Development, Assessment, and Application at Home, School, and in the Workplace* (San Francisco: Jossey-Bass, 2000); T. Schwartz, "How Do You Feel?" *Fast Company*, June 2000, pp. 297–313; and F I. Greenstein, *The Presidential Difference* (Princeton, NJ: Princeton University Press, 2001).
82. Fineman, "Emotional Arenas Revisited," in S. Fineman, ed., *Emotion in Organizations*, 2nd ed. (Thousand Oaks, CA: Sage, 2000), p. 11.
83. See, for example, K. Fiedler, "Emotional Mood, Cognitive Style, and Behavioral Regulation," in K. Fiedler and J. Forgas (eds.), *Affect, Cognition, and Social Behavior* (Toronto: Hogrefe International, 1988), pp. 100–19; M. Luce, J. Bettman, and J. W. Payne, "Choice Processing in Difficult Decisions," *Journal of Experimental Psychology: Learning, Memory, and Cognition*, vol. 23, 1997, pp. 384–405; and A. M. Isen, "Positive Affect and Decision Making," in M. Lewis and J. M. Haviland-Jones (eds.), *Handbook of Emotions*, 2nd ed. (New York: Guilford, 2000), pp. 261–77.
84. B. E. Ashforth and R. H. Humphrey, "Emotion in the Workplace," p. 109; and M. G. Seo, "The Role of Emotion in Motivation," paper presented at the Annual Academy of Management Conference, Toronto, Canada; August 2000.
85. B. E. Ashforth and R. H. Humphrey, "Emotion in the Workplace," p. 109.
86. Ibid., p. 110.
87. Ibid.
88. K. M. Lewis, "When Leaders Display Emotion: How Followers Respond to Negative Emotional Expression of Male and Female Leaders," *Journal of Organizational Behavior*, March 2000, pp. 221–34; and J. M. George, "Emotions and Leadership: The Role of Emotional Intelligence," *Human Relations*, August 2000, pp. 1027–55.
89. J. M. George, "Trait and State Affect," 162.
90. B. E. Ashforth and R. H. Humphrey, "Emotion in the Workplace," p. 116.
91. See S. L. Robinson and R. J. Bennett, "A Typology of Deviant Workplace Behaviors: A Multidimensional Scaling Study," *Academy of Management Journal*, April 1995, p. 556; and R. J. Bennett and S. L. Robinson, "Development of a Measure of Workplace Deviance," *Journal of Applied Psychology*, June 2000, pp. 349–60.
92. R. W. Griffin, A. O'Leary-Kelly, and J. M. Collins, eds., *Dysfunctional Behavior in Organizations* (Parts A & B), vol. 23 (Stamford, CT: JAI Press, 1998).
93. A. G. Bedeian, "Workplace Envy," *Organizational Dynamics*, Spring 1995, p. 50; and A. Ben-Ze'ev, *The Subtlety of Emotions*, pp. 281–326.
94. A. G. Bedeian, "Workplace Envy," p. 54.
95. R. Hogan, J. Hogan, and B. W. Roberts, "Personality Measurement and Employment Decisions," *American Psychologist*, May 1996, p. 475.
96. S. Nelton, "Emotions in the Workplace," *Nation's Business*, February 1996, p. 25.
97. H. M. Weiss and R. Cropanzano, "Affective Events Theory," p. 55.
98. See the Yerkes–Dodson law cited in D. O. Hebb, "Drives and the CNS (Conceptual Nervous System)," *Psychological Review*, July 1955, pp. 243–54.

> We don't see things
> as they are, we see
> things as we are.
> —A. Nin

PART TWO

THE INDIVIDUAL

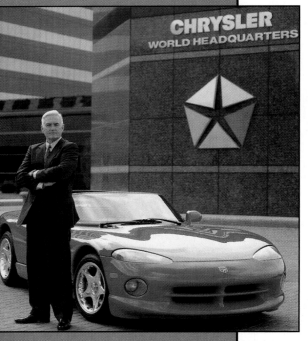

A decision that Bob Lutz made in the late 1980s is interesting for at least two reasons. It reshaped the public's perception of Chrysler Corp. (now part of DaimlerChrysler). And the process that Lutz used at arriving at this decision followed none of the rational logic that economists and management experts propose should be used for optimal decision making.[1]

At the time, Lutz was Chrysler's president. (He's now head of product development at General Motors and chairman of GM North America.) It was a warm weekend day in 1988, and Lutz was out taking his classic Cobra roadster for a spin. He wanted to get his mind off of what critics were saying about Chrysler—that the company was brain-dead, technologically dated, and building cars that were uninspiring. And there had to be some irony in the fact that the president of Chrysler was enjoying himself driving a Ford product. The guilt got him thinking: "What if I replaced the Cobra's V-8 engine with one from Chrysler?" But he quickly realized that Chrysler didn't have a V-8 engine that was up to snuff. Lutz's mind was now racing. Didn't Chrysler have a powerful 10-cylinder engine in development for its new Dodge pickup truck? And wasn't his company also building a five-speed, heavy-duty manual transmission for that truck? Why not use those parts as ingredients to create a sexy, two-seat concept sports car that would be as revolutionary as his Cobra had been in the 1960s? Maybe this would silence some of Chrysler's critics.

That Monday, Lutz got the ball rolling. He instructed his design people to create a high-powered sports car built on the V-10 engine being developed by the truck group. Not that this decision was met with strong enthusiasm at the company. His financial people, for instance, argued that the $80 million investment could be better spent on paying down the company's debt or refurbishing plants. And his marketing executives questioned whether Dodge dealers, who were used to selling conservative vehicles that sold for under $20,000, could effectively sell a $50,000 sports car. They were also

Perception and Individual Decision Making

concerned that neither Lutz nor they had any market research to support this decision.

Ignoring others' concerns, Lutz pushed the project forward with unwavering commitment. Even though he had no tangible evidence to support his belief that this car would be successful and give Chrysler the lift it needed, his intuition told him this was right. He was going with his gut instincts. And his instincts proved to be correct. The Dodge Viper (pictured in photo with Lutz) single-handedly changed the public's perception of Chrysler, dramatically boosted company morale, and ultimately spurred the company's turnaround in the 1990s.

M aking decisions is a critical element of organizational life. And as the Bob Lutz example illustrates, those decisions don't always follow a carefully formulated rational process. In this chapter, we'll describe how decisions in organizations are made. But first, we discuss perceptual processes and show how they are linked to individual decision making.

WHAT IS PERCEPTION, AND WHY IS IT IMPORTANT?

Perception is a process by which individuals organize and interpret their sensory impressions in order to give meaning to their environment. However, what one perceives can be substantially different from objective reality. It need not be, but there is often disagreement. For example, it's possible that all employees in a firm may view it as a great place to work—favorable working conditions, interesting job assignments, good pay, an understanding and responsible management—but, as most of us know, it's very unusual to find such agreement.

LEARNING OBJECTIVES

AFTER STUDYING THIS CHAPTER, YOU SHOULD BE ABLE TO:

1. Explain how two people can see the same thing and interpret it differently.

2. List the three determinants of attribution.

3. Describe how shortcuts can assist in or distort our judgment of others.

4. Explain how perception affects the decision-making process.

5. Outline the six steps in the rational decision-making model.

6. Describe the actions of the boundedly rational decision maker.

7. Identify the conditions in which individuals are most likely to use intuition in decision making.

8. Describe four styles of decision making.

9. Define heuristics and explain how they bias decisions.

10. Contrast the three ethical decision criteria.

perception

A process by which individuals organize and interpret their sensory impressions in order to give meaning to their environment.

Why is perception important in the study of OB? Simply because people's behavior is based on their perception of what reality is, not on reality itself. *The world as it is perceived is the world that is behaviorally important.*

FACTORS INFLUENCING PERCEPTION

How do we explain that individuals may look at the same thing, yet perceive it differently? A number of factors operate to shape and sometimes distort perception. These factors can reside in the *perceiver*, in the object or *target* being perceived, or in the context of the *situation* in which the perception is made (see Exhibit 5-1).

When an individual looks at a target and attempts to interpret what he or she sees, that interpretation is heavily influenced by the personal characteristics of the individual perceiver. Personal characteristics that affect perception include a person's attitudes, personality, motives, interests, past experiences, and expectations. For instance, if you expect police officers to be authoritative, young people to be unambitious, or individuals holding public office to be unscrupulous, you may perceive them as such regardless of their actual traits.

Characteristics of the target being observed can affect what is perceived. Loud people are more likely to be noticed in a group than quiet ones. So, too, are extremely attractive or unattractive individuals. Because targets are not looked at in isolation, the relationship of a target to its background also influences perception, as does our tendency to group close things and similar things together. For instance, women, African Americans, or members of any other group that has clearly distinguishable characteristics in terms of features or color are often perceived as alike in other, unrelated characteristics as well.

The context in which we see objects or events is also important. The time at which an object or event is seen can influence attention, as can location, light, heat, or any number of situational factors. I may not notice a 22-year-old female

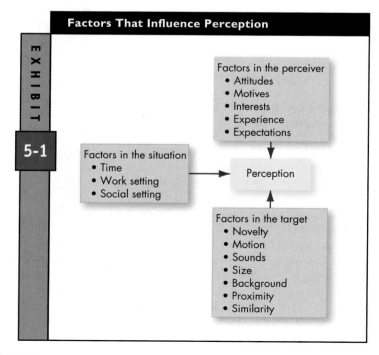

EXHIBIT 5-1

Factors That Influence Perception

Factors in the perceiver
- Attitudes
- Motives
- Interests
- Experience
- Expectations

Factors in the situation
- Time
- Work setting
- Social setting

Perception

Factors in the target
- Novelty
- Motion
- Sounds
- Size
- Background
- Proximity
- Similarity

in an evening gown and heavy make-up at a nightclub on Saturday night. Yet that same woman so attired for my Monday morning management class would certainly catch my attention (and that of the rest of the class). Neither the perceiver nor the target changed between Saturday night and Monday morning, but the situation is different.

PERSON PERCEPTION: MAKING JUDGMENTS ABOUT OTHERS

Now we turn to the most relevant application of perception concepts to OB. This is the issue of *person perception*.

Attribution Theory

Our perceptions of people differ from our perceptions of inanimate objects such as desks, machines, or buildings because we make inferences about the actions of people that we don't make about inanimate objects. Nonliving objects are subject to the laws of nature, but they have no beliefs, motives, or intentions. People do. The result is that when we observe people, we attempt to develop explanations of why they behave in certain ways. Our perception and judgment of a person's actions, therefore, will be significantly influenced by the assumptions we make about that person's internal state.

Attribution theory has been proposed to develop explanations of the ways in which we judge people differently, depending on what meaning we attribute to a given behavior.[2] Basically, the theory suggests that when we observe an individual's behavior, we attempt to determine whether it was internally or externally caused. That determination, however, depends largely on three factors: (1) distinctiveness, (2) consensus, and (3) consistency. First, let's clarify the differences between internal and external causation and then we will elaborate on each of the three determining factors.

Internally caused behaviors are those that are believed to be under the personal control of the individual. *Externally* caused behavior is seen as resulting from outside causes; that is, the person is seen as having been forced into the behavior by the situation. If one of your employees is late for work, you might attribute his lateness to his partying into the wee hours of the morning and then oversleeping. This would be an internal attribution. But if you attribute his arriving late to an automobile accident that tied up traffic on the road that this employee regularly uses, then you would be making an external attribution.

Distinctiveness refers to whether an individual displays different behaviors in different situations. Is the employee who arrives late today also the source of complaints by co-workers for being a "goof-off"? What we want to know is whether this behavior is unusual. If it is, the observer is likely to give the behavior an external attribution. If this action is not unusual, it will probably be judged as internal.

If everyone who is faced with a similar situation responds in the same way, we can say the behavior shows *consensus*. The behavior of the employee discussed above would meet this criterion if all employees who took the same route to work were also late. From an attribution perspective, if consensus is high, you would be expected to give an external attribution to the employee's tardiness, whereas if other employees who took the same route made it to work on time, your conclusion as to causation would be internal.

Finally, an observer looks for *consistency* in a person's actions. Does the person respond the same way over time? Coming in 10 minutes late for work is not perceived in the same way for the employee for whom it is an unusual case (she

attribution theory

When individuals observe behavior, they attempt to determine whether it is internally or externally caused.

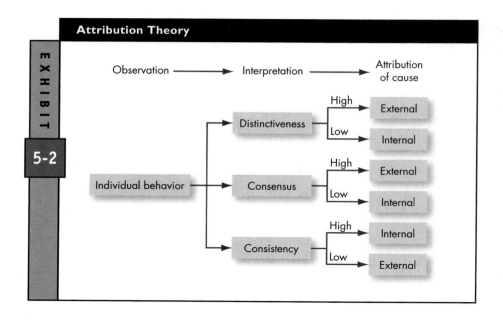

EXHIBIT 5-2

Attribution Theory

Observation ⟶ Interpretation ⟶ Attribution of cause

Individual behavior

Distinctiveness
- High → External
- Low → Internal

Consensus
- High → External
- Low → Internal

Consistency
- High → Internal
- Low → External

hasn't been late for several months) as it is for the employee for whom it is part of a routine pattern (she is late two or three times a week). The more consistent the behavior, the more the observer is inclined to attribute it to internal causes.

Exhibit 5-2 summarizes the key elements in attribution theory. It would tell us, for instance, that if your employee—Kim Randolph—generally performs at about the same level on other related tasks as she does on her current task (low distinctiveness), if other employees frequently perform differently—better or worse—than Kim does on that current task (low consensus), and if Kim's performance on this current task is consistent over time (high consistency), you or anyone else who is judging Kim's work is likely to hold her primarily responsible for her task performance (internal attribution).

One of the more interesting findings from attribution theory is that there are errors or biases that distort attributions. For instance, there is substantial evidence that when we make judgments about the behavior of other people, we have a tendency to underestimate the influence of external factors and overestimate the influence of internal or personal factors.[3] This is called the **fundamental attribution error** and can explain why a sales manager is prone to attribute the poor performance of her sales agents to laziness rather than to the innovative product line introduced by a competitor. There is also a tendency for individuals to attribute their own successes to internal factors such as ability or effort while putting the blame for failure on external factors such as bad luck or unproductive co-workers. This is called the **self-serving bias**.[4] During the high-tech stock market rally between 1996 and early 2000, investors were quick to brag about their expertise and take credit for their investing smarts. However, when that market imploded in the spring of 2000 and eventually declined more than 70 percent, most of those same investors were looking for external sources to blame—the investment analysts who kept hyping technology stocks because they had a vested interest in pumping up their prices, their brokers being too aggressive, the Federal Reserve for not cutting rates fast enough, and the like.

Are these errors or biases that distort attributions universal across different cultures? We can't answer that question definitively, but there is some preliminary

fundamental attribution error

The tendency to underestimate the influence of external factors and overestimate the influence of internal factors when making judgments about the behavior of others.

self-serving bias

The tendency for individuals to attribute their own successes to internal factors while putting the blame for failures on external factors.

evidence that indicates cultural differences.[5] For instance, a study of Korean managers found that, contrary to the self-serving bias, they tended to accept responsibility for group failure "because I was not a capable leader" instead of attributing it to group members.[6] Attribution theory was developed largely based on experiments with Americans and Western Europeans. But the Korean study suggests caution in making attribution theory predictions in non-Western societies, especially in countries with strong collectivist traditions.

Frequently Used Shortcuts in Judging Others

We use a number of shortcuts when we judge others. Perceiving and interpreting what others do is burdensome. As a result, individuals develop techniques for making the task more manageable. These techniques are frequently valuable—they allow us to make accurate perceptions rapidly and provide valid data for making predictions. However, they are not foolproof. They can and do get us into trouble. An understanding of these shortcuts can be helpful in recognizing when they can result in significant distortions.

Many day traders credited the gains they made in high-tech stocks between 1996 and early 2000 to their personal skills. But they blamed external sources for the losses they incurred when the prices of high-tech stocks took a nose dive.

Selective Perception Any characteristic that makes a person, object, or event stand out will increase the probability that it will be perceived. Why? Because it is impossible for us to assimilate everything we see—only certain stimuli can be taken in. This tendency explains why, as we noted earlier, you are more likely to notice cars like your own or why some people may be reprimanded by their boss for doing something that, when done by another employee, goes unnoticed. Since we can't observe everything going on about us, we engage in **selective perception**. A classic example shows how vested interests can significantly influence which problems we see.

selective perception
People selectively interpret what they see on the basis of their interests, background, experience, and attitudes.

Dearborn and Simon performed a perceptual study in which 23 business executives read a comprehensive case describing the organization and activities of a steel company.[7] Of the 23 executives, 6 were in sales, 5 in production, 4 in accounting, and 8 in miscellaneous functions. Each manager was asked to write down the most important problem he found in the case. Eighty-three percent of the sales executives rated sales important; only 29 percent of the others did so. This, along with other results of the study, led the researchers to conclude that the participants perceived aspects of a situation that were specifically related to the activities and goals of the unit to which they were attached. A group's perception of organizational activities is selectively altered to align with the vested interests they represent. In other words, when the stimuli are ambiguous, as in the steel company case, perception tends to be influenced more by an individual's base of interpretation (that is, attitudes, interests, and background) than by the stimulus itself.

But how does selectivity work as a shortcut in judging other people? Since we cannot assimilate all that we observe, we take in bits and pieces. But those bits and pieces are not chosen randomly; rather, they are selectively chosen according to our interests, background, experience, and attitudes. Selective perception allows us to "speed-read" others, but not without the risk of drawing an inaccurate picture. Because we see what we want to see, we can draw unwarranted conclusions from an ambiguous situation.

Halo Effect   When we draw a general impression about an individual on the basis of a single characteristic, such as intelligence, sociability, or appearance, a **halo effect** is operating.[8] This phenomenon frequently occurs when students appraise their classroom instructor. Students may give prominence to a single trait such as enthusiasm and allow their entire evaluation to be tainted by how they judge the instructor on that one trait. Thus, an instructor may be quiet, assured, knowledgeable, and highly qualified, but if his style lacks zeal, those students would probably give him a low rating.

The reality of the halo effect was confirmed in a classic study in which subjects were given a list of traits such as intelligent, skillful, practical, industrious, determined, and warm and were asked to evaluate the person to whom those traits applied.[9] When those traits were used, the person was judged to be wise, humorous, popular, and imaginative. When the same list was modified—cold was substituted for warm—a completely different set of perceptions was obtained. Clearly, the subjects were allowing a single trait to influence their overall impression of the person being judged.

The propensity for the halo effect to operate is not random. Research suggests that it is likely to be most extreme when the traits to be perceived are ambiguous in behavioral terms, when the traits have moral overtones, and when the perceiver is judging traits with which he or she has had limited experience.[10]

Contrast Effects   There is an old adage among entertainers who perform in variety shows: Never follow an act that has kids or animals in it. Why? The common belief is that audiences love children and animals so much that you'll look bad in comparison. This example demonstrates how **contrast effects** can distort perceptions. We don't evaluate a person in isolation. Our reaction to one person is influenced by other persons we have recently encountered.

An illustration of how contrast effects operate is an interview situation in which one sees a pool of job applicants. Distortions in any given candidate's evaluation can occur as a result of his or her place in the interview schedule. A candidate is likely to receive a more favorable evaluation if preceded by mediocre applicants and a less favorable evaluation if preceded by strong applicants.

Projection   It's easy to judge others if we assume that they're similar to us. For instance, if you want challenge and responsibility in your job, you assume that others want the same. Or, you're honest and trustworthy, so you take it for granted that other people are equally honest and trustworthy. This tendency to attribute one's own characteristics to other people—which is called **projection**—can distort perceptions made about others.

People who engage in projection tend to perceive others according to what they themselves are like rather than according to what the person being observed is really like. When managers engage in projection, they compromise their ability to respond to individual differences. They tend to see people as more homogeneous than they really are.

Stereotyping   When we judge someone on the basis of our perception of the group to which he or she belongs, we are using the shortcut called **stereotyping**.[11] F. Scott Fitzgerald engaged in stereotyping in his reported conversation with Ernest

halo effect

Drawing a general impression about an individual on the basis of a single characteristic.

contrast effects

Evaluation of a person's characteristics that are affected by comparisons with other people recently encountered who rank higher or lower on the same characteristics.

projection

Attributing one's own characteristics to other people.

stereotyping

Judging someone on the basis of one's perception of the group to which that person belongs.

Hemingway when he said, "The very rich are different from you and me." Hemingway's reply, "Yes, they have more money," indicated that he refused to generalize characteristics about people on the basis of their wealth.

Generalization, of course, is not without advantages. It's a means of simplifying a complex world, and it permits us to maintain consistency. It's less difficult to deal with an unmanageable number of stimuli if we use stereotypes. As an example, assume you're a sales manager looking to fill a sales position in your territory. You want to hire someone who is ambitious and hard working and who can deal well with adversity. You've had success in the past by hiring individuals who participated in athletics during college. So you focus your search by looking for candidates who participated in collegiate athletics. In so doing, you have cut down considerably on your search time. Furthermore, to the extent that athletes are ambitious, hard working, and able to deal with adversity, the use of this stereotype can improve your decision making. The problem, of course, is when we inaccurately stereotype.[12] All college athletes are *not necessarily* ambitious, hard working, or good at dealing with adversity.

In organizations, we frequently hear comments that represent stereotypes based on gender, age, race, ethnicity, and even weight[13]: "Women won't relocate for a promotion"; "men aren't interested in child care"; "older workers can't learn new skills"; "Asian immigrants are hard working and conscientious"; "overweight people lack discipline." From a perceptual standpoint, if people expect to see these stereotypes, that is what they will perceive, whether or not they are accurate.

Obviously, one of the problems of stereotypes is that they are widespread, despite the fact that they may not contain a shred of truth or that they may be irrelevant. Their being widespread may mean only that many people are making the same inaccurate perception on the basis of a false premise about a group.

What occupational stereotypes do you hold about firefighters? How do you think they were formed?

Specific Applications in Organizations

People in organizations are always judging each other. Managers must appraise their employees' performances. We evaluate how much effort our co-workers are putting into their jobs. When a new person joins a work team, he or she is immediately "sized up" by the other team members. In many cases, these judgments have important consequences for the organization. Let's briefly look at a few of the more obvious applications.

Employment Interview A major input into who is hired and who is rejected in any organization is the employment interview. It's fair to say that few people are hired without an interview. But the evidence indicates that interviewers make perceptual judgments that are often inaccurate. In addition, agreement among interviewers is often poor; that is, different interviewers see different things in the same candidate and thus arrive at different conclusions about the applicant.

Interviewers generally draw early impressions that become very quickly entrenched. If negative information is exposed early in the interview, it tends to be more heavily weighted than if that same information comes out later.[14] Studies indicate that most interviewers' decisions change very little after the first four or five minutes of the interview. As a result, information elicited early in the interview carries greater weight than does information elicited later, and a "good applicant" is probably characterized more by the absence of unfavorable characteristics than by the presence of favorable characteristics.

Importantly, who you think is a good candidate and who I think is one may differ markedly. Because interviews usually have so little consistent structure and interviewers vary in terms of what they are looking for in a candidate, judgments about the same candidate can vary widely. If the employment interview is an important input into the hiring decision—and it usually is—you should recognize that perceptual factors influence who is hired and eventually the quality of an organization's labor force.

Performance Expectations   There is an impressive amount of evidence that demonstrates that people will attempt to validate their perceptions of reality, even when those perceptions are faulty.[15] This characteristic is particularly relevant when we consider performance expectations on the job.

self-fulfilling prophecy

A situation in which one person inaccurately perceives a second person and the resulting expectations cause the second person to behave in ways consistent with the original perception.

The terms **self-fulfilling prophecy**, or *pygmalion effect*, have evolved to characterize the fact that people's expectations determine their behavior. In other words, if a manager expects big things from his people, they're not likely to let him down. Similarly, if a manager expects people to perform minimally, they'll tend to behave so as to meet those low expectations. The result then is that the expectations become reality.

An interesting illustration of the self-fulfilling prophecy is a study undertaken with 105 soldiers in the Israeli Defense Forces who were taking a 15-week combat command course.[16] The four course instructors were told that one third of the specific incoming trainees had high potential, one-third had normal potential, and the potential of the rest was unknown. In reality, the trainees were randomly placed into those categories by the researchers. The results confirmed the existence of a self-fulfilling prophecy. The trainees whom instructors were told had high potential scored significantly higher on objective achievement tests, exhibited more positive attitudes, and held their leaders in higher regard than did the other two groups. The instructors of the supposedly high-potential trainees got better results from them because the instructors expected it.

Performance Evaluation   Although the impact of performance evaluations on behavior will be discussed fully in Chapter 17, it should be pointed out here that an employee's performance appraisal is very much dependent on the perceptual process.[17] An employee's future is closely tied to his or her appraisal—promotions, pay raises, and continuation of employment are among the most obvious outcomes. The performance appraisal represents an assessment of an employee's work. Although the appraisal can be objective (for example, a salesperson is appraised on how many dollars of sales she generates in her territory), many jobs are evaluated in subjective terms. Subjective measures are easier to implement, they provide managers with greater discretion, and many jobs do not readily lend themselves to objective measures. Subjective measures are, by definition, judgmental. The evaluator forms a general impression of an employee's work. To the degree that managers use subjective measures in appraising employees, what the evaluator perceives to be good or bad employee characteristics or behaviors will significantly influence the outcome of the appraisal.

Employee Effort   An individual's future in an organization is usually not dependent on performance alone. In many organizations, the level of an employee's effort is given high importance. Just as teachers frequently consider how hard you try in a course as well as how you perform on examinations, so, often, do managers. An assessment of an individual's effort is a subjective judgment susceptible to perceptual distortions and bias.

THE LINK BETWEEN PERCEPTION AND INDIVIDUAL DECISION MAKING

Individuals in organizations make **decisions**. That is, they make choices from among two or more alternatives. Top managers, for instance, determine their organization's goals, what products or services to offer, how best to finance operations, or where to locate a new manufacturing plant. Middle- and lower-level managers determine production schedules, select new employees, and decide how pay raises are to be allocated. Of course, making decisions is not the sole province of managers. Nonmanagerial employees also make decisions that affect their jobs and the organizations for which they work. The more obvious of these decisions might include whether or not to come to work on any given day, how much effort to put forth once at work, and whether or not to comply with a request made by the boss. In addition, an increasing number of organizations in recent years have been empowering their nonmanagerial employees with job-related decision-making authority that historically was reserved for managers alone. Individual decision making, therefore, is an important part of organizational behavior. But how individuals in organizations make decisions and the quality of their final choices are largely influenced by their perceptions.

Decision making occurs as a reaction to a **problem**.[18] That is, there is a discrepancy between some current state of affairs and some desired state, requiring the consideration of alternative courses of action. So if your car breaks down and you rely on it to get to work, you have a problem that requires a decision on your part. Unfortunately, most problems don't come neatly packaged with a label "problem" clearly displayed on them. One person's *problem* is another person's *satisfactory state of affairs*. One manager may view her division's two percent decline in quarterly sales to be a serious problem requiring immediate action on her part. In contrast, her counterpart in another division of the same company, who also had a two percent sales decrease, may consider that percentage quite acceptable. So the awareness that a problem exists and that a decision needs to be made is a perceptual issue.

Moreover, every decision requires the interpretation and evaluation of information. Data are typically received from multiple sources and they need to be screened, processed, and interpreted. Which data, for instance, are relevant to the decision and which are not? The perceptions of the decision maker will answer that question. Alternatives will be developed, and the strengths and weaknesses of each will need to be evaluated. Again, because alternatives don't come with "red flags" identifying them as such or with their strengths and weaknesses clearly marked, the individual decision maker's perceptual process will have a large bearing on the final outcome.

HOW SHOULD DECISIONS BE MADE?

Let's begin by describing how individuals should behave in order to maximize or optimize a certain outcome. We call this the *rational decision-making process*.

The Rational Decision-Making Process

The optimizing decision maker is **rational**. That is, he or she makes consistent, value-maximizing choices within specified constraints.[19] These choices are made

---

decisions

The choices made from among two or more alternatives.

problem

A discrepancy between some current state of affairs and some desired state.

John Toner runs Belfast's Europa Hotel. One of his most vivid lessons in defining a problem came early in his career when a terrorist bomb destroyed the reception desk of a hotel in Newcastle where he worked. The hotel owner's response was, "Well, John, this gives us the opportunity to change the reception area."

rational

Making consistent, value-maximizing choices within specified constraints.

	Steps in the Rational Decision-Making Model
EXHIBIT 5-3	1. Define the problem.
	2. Identify the decision criteria.
	3. Allocate weights to the criteria.
	4. Develop the alternatives.
	5. Evaluate the alternatives.
	6. Select the best alternative.

rational decision-making model

A decision-making model that describes how individuals should behave in order to maximize some outcome.

following a six-step **rational decision-making model**.[20] Moreover, specific assumptions underlie this model.

The Rational Model   The six steps in the rational decision-making model are listed in Exhibit 5-3.

The model begins by *defining the problem*. As noted previously, a problem exists when there is a discrepancy between an existing and a desired state of affairs.[21] If you calculate your monthly expenses and find you're spending $50 more than you allocated in your budget, you have defined a problem. Many poor decisions can be traced to the decision maker overlooking a problem or defining the wrong problem.

Once a decision maker has defined the problem, he or she needs to *identify the decision criteria* that will be important in solving the problem. In this step, the decision maker determines what is relevant in making the decision. This step brings the decision maker's interests, values, and similar personal preferences into the process. Identifying criteria is important because what one person thinks is relevant another person may not. Also keep in mind that any factors not identified in this step are considered irrelevant to the decision maker.

The criteria identified are rarely all equal in importance. So the third step requires the decision maker to *weight the previously identified criteria* in order to give them the correct priority in the decision.

The fourth step requires the decision maker to *generate possible alternatives* that could succeed in resolving the problem. No attempt is made in this step to appraise these alternatives, only to list them.

Once the alternatives have been generated, the decision maker must critically analyze and evaluate each one. This is done by *rating each alternative on each criterion*. The strengths and weaknesses of each alternative become evident as they are compared with the criteria and weights established in the second and third steps.

The final step in this model requires *computing the optimal decision*. This is done by evaluating each alternative against the weighted criteria and selecting the alternative with the highest total score.

Assumptions of the Model   The rational decision-making model we just described contains a number of assumptions.[22] Let's briefly outline those assumptions.

1. *Problem clarity.*   The problem is clear and unambiguous. The decision maker is assumed to have complete information regarding the decision situation.
2. *Known options.*   It is assumed the decision maker can identify all the relevant criteria and can list all the viable alternatives. Furthermore, the decision maker is aware of all the possible consequences of each alternative.

3. *Clear preferences.* Rationality assumes that the criteria and alternatives can be ranked and weighted to reflect their importance.
4. *Constant preferences.* It's assumed that the specific decision criteria are constant and that the weights assigned to them are stable over time.
5. *No time or cost constraints.* The rational decision maker can obtain full information about criteria and alternatives because it's assumed that there are no time or cost constraints.
6. *Maximum payoff.* The rational decision maker will choose the alternative that yields the highest perceived value.

Improving Creativity in Decision Making

The rational decision maker needs **creativity**, that is, the ability to produce novel and useful ideas.[23] These are ideas that are different from what's been done before but that are also appropriate to the problem or opportunity presented. Why is creativity important to decision making? It allows the decision maker to more fully appraise and understand the problem, including seeing problems others can't see. However, creativity's most obvious value is in helping the decision maker identify all viable alternatives.

Creative Potential Most people have creative potential that they can use when confronted with a decision-making problem. But to unleash that potential, they have to get out of the psychological ruts many of us get into and learn how to think about a problem in divergent ways.

We can start with the obvious. People differ in their inherent creativity. Einstein, Edison, Picasso, and Mozart were individuals of exceptional creativity. Not surprisingly, exceptional creativity is scarce. A study of the lifetime creativity of 461 men and women found that fewer than 1 percent were exceptionally creative.[24] But 10 percent were highly creative and about 60 percent were somewhat creative. This suggests that most of us have creative potential; we just need to learn to unleash it.

Three-Component Model of Creativity Given that most people have the capacity to be at least moderately creative, what can individuals and organizations do to stimulate employee creativity? The best answer to this question lies in the **three-component model of creativity**.[25] Based on an extensive body of research, this model proposes that individual creativity essentially requires expertise, creative-thinking skills, and intrinsic task motivation (see Exhibit 5-4 on page 134). Studies confirm that the higher the level of each of these three components, the higher the creativity.

Expertise is the foundation for all creative work. Picasso's understanding of art and Einstein's knowledge of physics were necessary conditions for them to be able to make creative contributions to their fields. And you wouldn't expect someone with a minimal knowledge of programming to be very creative as a software engineer. The potential for creativity is enhanced when individuals have abilities, knowledge, proficiencies, and similar expertise in their field of endeavor.

The second component is *creative-thinking skills*. This encompasses personality characteristics associated with creativity, the ability to use analogies, as well as the talent to see the familiar in a different light. For instance, the following individual traits have been found to be associated with the development of creative ideas: intelligence, independence, self-confidence, risk-taking, an internal locus of control, tolerance for ambiguity, and perseverance in the face of frustration.[26] The effective use of analogies allows decision makers to apply an idea from one context to

creativity
The ability to produce novel and useful ideas.

three-component model of creativity
Proposition that individual creativity requires expertise, creative-thinking skills, and intrinsic task motivation.

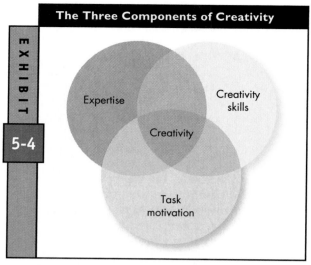

The Three Components of Creativity

EXHIBIT 5-4

Expertise

Creativity skills

Creativity

Task motivation

Source: T. M. Amabile, "Motivating Creativity in Organizations," *California Management Review*, Fall 1997, p. 43

another. One of the most famous examples in which analogy resulted in a creative breakthrough was Alexander Graham Bell's observation that it might be possible to take concepts that operate in the ear and apply them to his "talking box." He noticed that the bones in the ear are operated by a delicate, thin membrane. He wondered why, then, a thicker and strong piece of membrane shouldn't be able to move a piece of steel. Out of that analogy, the telephone was conceived. Of course, some people have developed their skill at being able to see problems in a new way. They're able to make the strange familiar and the familiar strange.[27] For instance, most of us think of hens laying eggs. But how many of us have considered that a hen is only an egg's way of making another egg?

The final component in our model is *intrinsic task motivation*. This is the desire to work on something because it's interesting, involving, exciting, satisfying, or personally challenging. This motivational component is what turns creativity *potential* into *actual* creative ideas. It determines the extent to which individuals fully engage their expertise and creative skills. So creative people often love their work, to the point of seeming obsessed. Importantly, an individual's work environment can have a significant effect on intrinsic motivation. Work-environment stimulants that have been found to foster creativity include a culture that encourages the flow of ideas, fair and constructive judgment of ideas, and rewards and recognizes creative work; sufficient financial, material, and information resources; freedom to decide what work is to be done and how to do it; a supervisor who communicates effectively, shows confidence in others, and supports the work group; and work-group members who support and trust each other.[28]

Glenn McQueen's job, as an animator at Pixar, provides strong intrinsic task motivation and inspires his creativity.

HOW ARE DECISIONS ACTUALLY MADE IN ORGANIZATIONS?

Are decision makers in organizations rational? Do they carefully assess problems, identify all relevant criteria, use their creativity to identify all viable alternatives, and painstakingly evaluate every alternative to find an optimal choice? For novice decision makers with little experience, decision makers faced with simple problems that have few alternative courses of action, or when the cost of searching out and evaluating alternatives is low, the rational model provides a fairly accurate description of the decision process.[29] But such situations are the exception. Most decisions in the real world don't follow the rational model. For instance, people are usually content to find an acceptable or reasonable solution to their problem rather than an optimal one. As such, decision makers generally make limited use of their creativity. Choices tend to be confined to the neighborhood of the problem symptom and to the neighborhood of the current alternative. As one expert in decision making put it: "Most significant decisions are made by judgment, rather than by a defined prescriptive model."[30]

The following reviews a large body of evidence to provide you with a more accurate description of how most decisions in organizations are actually made.[31]

Bounded Rationality

When you considered which college to attend, did you look at *every* viable alternative? Did you carefully identify *all* the criteria that were important in your decision? Did you evaluate *each* alternative against the criteria in order to find the optimal college? I expect the answers to these questions is probably "No." Well, don't feel bad. Few people made their college choice this way. Instead of optimizing, you probably satisficed.

When faced with a complex problem, most people respond by reducing the problem to a level at which it can be readily understood. This is because the limited information-processing capability of human beings makes it impossible to assimilate and understand all the information necessary to optimize. So people *satisfice*; that is, they seek solutions that are satisfactory and sufficient.

Because the capacity of the human mind for formulating and solving complex problems is far too small to meet the requirements for full rationality, individuals operate within the confines of **bounded rationality**. They construct simplified models that extract the essential features from problems without capturing all their complexity.[32] Individuals can then behave rationally within the limits of the simple model.

How does bounded rationality work for the typical individual? Once a problem is identified, the search for criteria and alternatives begins. But the list of criteria is likely to be far from exhaustive. The decision maker will identify a limited list made up of the more conspicuous choices. These are the choices that are easy to find and that tend to be highly visible. In most cases, they will represent familiar criteria and previously tried-and-true solutions. Once this limited set of alternatives is identified, the decision maker will begin reviewing them. But the review will not be comprehensive—not all the alternatives will be carefully evaluated. Instead, the decision maker will begin with alternatives that differ only in a relatively small degree from the choice currently in effect. Following along familiar and well-worn paths, the decision maker proceeds to review alternatives only until he or she identifies an alternative that is "good enough"—one that meets an acceptable level of performance. The first alternative that meets the "good enough" criterion ends the search. So the final solution represents a satisficing choice rather than an optimal one.

bounded rationality

Individuals make decisions by constructing simplified models that extract the essential features from problems without capturing all their complexity.

One of the more interesting aspects of bounded rationality is that the order in which alternatives are considered is critical in determining which alternative is selected. Remember, in the fully rational decision-making model, all alternatives are eventually listed in a hierarchy of preferred order. Because all alternatives are considered, the initial order in which they are evaluated is irrelevant. Every potential solution would get a full and complete evaluation. But this isn't the case with bounded rationality. Assuming that a problem has more than one potential solution, the satisficing choice will be the first *acceptable* one the decision maker encounters. Since decision makers use simple and limited models, they typically begin by identifying alternatives that are obvious, ones with which they are familiar, and those not too far from the status quo. The solutions that depart least from the status quo and meet the decision criteria are those most likely to be selected. A unique and creative alternative may present an optimizing solution to the problem; however, it's unlikely to be chosen because an acceptable solution will be identified well before the decision maker is required to search very far beyond the status quo.

Intuition

Joe Garcia has just committed his corporation to spend in excess of $40 million to build a new plant in Atlanta to manufacture electronic components for satellite communication equipment. As vice president of operations for his firm, Joe had before him a comprehensive analysis of five possible plant locations developed by a site-location consulting firm he had hired. This report ranked the Atlanta location third among the five alternatives. After carefully reading the report and its conclusions, Joe decided against the consultant's recommendation. When asked to explain his decision, Joe said, "I looked the report over very carefully. But in spite of its recommendation, I felt that the numbers didn't tell the whole story. Intuitively, I just sensed that Atlanta would prove to be the best bet over the long run."

intuitive decision making

An unconscious process created out of distilled experience.

Intuitive decision making, like that used by Joe Garcia, has recently come out of the closet and into some respectability. Experts no longer automatically assume that using intuition to make decisions is irrational or ineffective.[33] There is growing recognition that rational analysis has been overemphasized and that, in certain instances, relying on intuition can improve decision making.

What do we mean by intuitive decision making? There are a number of ways to conceptualize intuition.[34] For instance, some consider it a form of extrasensory power or sixth sense, and some believe it is a personality trait with which a limited number of people are born. For our purposes, we define **intuitive decision making** as an unconscious process created out of distilled experience. It doesn't necessarily operate independently of rational analysis; rather, the two complement each other.

Research on chess playing provides an excellent example of how intuition works.[35] Novice chess players and grand masters were shown an actual, but unfamiliar, chess game with about 25 pieces on the board. After 5 or 10 seconds, the pieces were removed and each was asked to reconstruct the pieces by position. On average, the grand master could put 23 or 24 pieces in their correct squares, while the novice was

Experience with a situation allows experts, such as master chess players, to make quick decisions.

able to replace only 6. Then the exercise was changed. This time the pieces were placed randomly on the board. Again, the novice got only about 6 correct, but so did the grand master! The second exercise demonstrated that the grand master didn't have any better memory than the novice. What he did have was the ability, based on the experience of having played thousands of chess games, to recognize patterns and clusters of pieces that occur on chessboards in the course of games. Studies further show that chess professionals can play 50 or more games simultaneously, in which decisions often must be made in only seconds, and exhibit only a moderately lower level of skill than when playing one game under tournament conditions, where decisions take half an hour or longer. The expert's experience allows him or her to recognize the pattern in a situation and draw on previously learned information associated with that pattern to arrive at a decision choice quickly. The result is that the intuitive decision maker can decide rapidly based on what appears to be very limited information.

When are people most likely to use intuitive decision making? Eight conditions have been identified: (1) when a high level of uncertainty exists; (2) when there is little precedent to draw on; (3) when variables are less scientifically predictable; (4) when "facts" are limited; (5) when facts don't clearly point the way; (6) when analytical data are of little use; (7) when there are several plausible alternative solutions from which to choose, with good arguments for each; and (8) when time is limited and there is pressure to come up with the right decision.[36]

OB in the News

Firefighters Use Intuition to Make the Right Choices

Do fire commanders use the rational model to make life-and-death decisions? No. They rely on their intuition, built on years of experience. And intuition begins with recognition. The following illustrates how that recognition process works.

A Cleveland, Ohio, fire commander and his crew encountered a fire at the back of a house. The commander led his hose team into the building. Standing in the living room, they blasted water onto the smoke and flames that appeared to be consuming the kitchen. But the fire roared back and continued to burn. The men doused the fire again, and the flames briefly subsided. But then they flared up again with an even greater intensity. As the firefighters retreated and regrouped, the commander was gripped by an uneasy feeling. He ordered everyone to leave. Just as the crew reached the street, the living-room floor caved in. Had the men stayed in the house, they would have plunged into a blazing basement.

Why did the commander give the order to leave? Because the fire's behavior didn't match his expectations. Much of the fire was burning underneath the living-room floor, so it was unaffected by the firefighters' attack. Also, the rising heat made the room extremely hot—too hot for such a seemingly small fire. Another clue that this was not just a small kitchen fire was that the sounds it emitted were strangely quiet. Hot fires are loud. The commander was intuitively sensing that the floor was muffling the roar of the flames that were raging below.

Veteran firefighters have accumulated a storehouse of experiences and they subconsciously categorize fires according to how they should react to them. They look for cues or patterns in situations that direct them to take one action over another.

Experienced people whose jobs require quick decisions—firefighters, intensive-care nurses, jet-fighter pilots, SWAT team members—see a different world than novices in those same jobs do. And what they see tells them what they should do. Ultimately, intuition is all about perception. The formal rules of decision making are almost incidental.

Source: Based on B. Breen, "What's Your Intuition?" Fast Company, September 2000, pp. 290–300.

Although intuitive decision making has gained in respectability, don't expect people—especially in North America, Great Britain, and other cultures in which rational analysis is the approved way of making decisions—to acknowledge they are using it. People with strong intuitive abilities don't usually tell their colleagues how they reached their conclusions. Since rational analysis is considered more socially desirable, intuitive ability is often disguised or hidden. As one top executive commented, "Sometimes one must dress up a gut decision in 'data clothes' to make it acceptable or palatable, but this fine-tuning is usually after the fact of the decision."[37]

Problem Identification

As suggested earlier, problems don't come with flashing neon lights to identify themselves. And one person's *problem* is another person's *acceptable status quo*. So how do decision makers identify and select problems?

Problems that are visible tend to have a higher probability of being selected than ones that are important.[38] Why? We can offer at least two reasons. First, visible problems are more likely to catch a decision maker's attention. This explains why politicians are more likely to talk about the "crime problem" than the "illiteracy problem." Second, remember we're concerned with decision making in organizations. Decision makers want to appear competent and "on top of problems." This motivates them to focus attention on problems that are visible to others.

Don't ignore the decision maker's self-interest. If a decision maker faces a conflict between selecting a problem that is important to the organization and one that is important to the decision maker, self-interest tends to win out.[39] This also ties in with the issue of visibility. It's usually in a decision maker's best interest to attack high-profile problems. It conveys to others that things are under control. Moreover, when the decision maker's performance is later reviewed, the evaluator is more likely to give a high rating to someone who has been aggressively attacking visible problems than to someone whose actions have been less obvious.

Alternative Development

Because decision makers rarely seek an optimal solution, but rather a satisficing one, we should expect to find a minimal use of creativity in the search for alternatives. And that expectation is generally on target.

Efforts will be made to try to keep the search process simple. It will tend to be confined to the neighborhood of the current alternative. More complex search behavior, which includes the development of creative alternatives, will be resorted to only when a simple search fails to uncover a satisfactory alternative.

Rather than formulating new and unique problem definitions and alternatives, with frequent journeys into unfamiliar territory, the evidence indicates that decision making is incremental rather than comprehensive.[40] This means decision makers avoid the difficult task of considering all the important factors, weighing their relative merits and drawbacks, and calculating the value for each alternative. Instead, they make successive limited comparisons. This simplifies decision choices by comparing only the alternatives that differ in relatively small degrees from the choice currently in effect.

The picture that emerges is one of a decision maker who takes small steps toward his or her objective. Acknowledging the noncomprehensive nature of choice selection, decision makers make successive comparisons because decisions are never made forever and written in stone, but rather decisions are made and remade endlessly in small comparisons between narrow choices.

Making Choices

In order to avoid information overload, decision makers rely on **heuristics**, or judgmental shortcuts, in decision making.[41] There are two common categories of heuristics—availability and representativeness. Each creates biases in judgment. Another bias that decision makers often have is the tendency to escalate commitment to a failing course of action.

Availability Heuristic Many more people suffer from fear of flying than fear of driving in a car. The reason is that many people think flying is more dangerous. It isn't, of course. With apologies ahead of time for this graphic example, if flying on a commercial airline was as dangerous as driving, the equivalent of two 747s filled to capacity would have to crash every week, killing all aboard, to match the risk of being killed in a car accident. But the media give a lot more attention to air accidents, so we tend to overstate the risk of flying and understate the risk of driving.

This illustrates an example of the **availability heuristic**, which is the tendency for people to base their judgments on information that is readily available to them. Events that evoke emotions, that are particularly vivid, or that have occurred more recently tend to be more available in our memory. As a result, we tend to be prone to overestimating unlikely events like an airplane crash. The availability heuristic can also explain why managers, when doing annual performance appraisals, tend to give more weight to recent behaviors of an employee than those behaviors of six or nine months ago.

Representative Heuristic Literally millions of inner-city African-American boys in the United States talk about the goal of playing basketball in the NBA. In reality, they have a far better chance of becoming medical doctors than they do of playing in the NBA, but these kids are suffering from a **representative heuristic**. They tend to assess the likelihood of an occurrence by trying to match it with a preexisting category. They hear about a boy from their neighborhood 10 years ago who went on to play professional basketball. Or they watch NBA games on television and think that those players are like them. We all are guilty of using this heuristic at times. Managers, for example, frequently predict the performance of a new product by relating it to a previous product's success. Or if three graduates from the same college were hired and turned out to be poor performers, managers may predict that a current job applicant from the same college will not be a good employee.

The representative heuristic is a rule of thumb by which we try to match a new circumstance with a preexisting category. For example, many inner-city African-American youths may hope to play basketball in the NBA, although their individual chances of achieving this goal are slim.

Escalation of Commitment Another bias that creeps into decisions in practice is a tendency to escalate commitment when a decision stream represents a series of decisions.[42] **Escalation of commitment** refers to staying with a decision even when there is clear evidence that it's wrong. For example, a friend of mine had been dating a woman for about four years. Although he admitted that things weren't going too well in the relationship, he informed me that he was going to

heuristics

Judgmental shortcuts in decision making.

availability heuristic

The tendency for people to base their judgments on information that is readily available to them.

representative heuristic

Assessing the likelihood of an occurrence by drawing analogies and seeing identical situations in which they don't exist.

escalation of commitment

An increased commitment to a previous decision in spite of negative information.

marry the woman. A bit surprised by his decision, I asked him why. He responded: "I have a lot invested in the relationship!"

It has been well documented that individuals escalate commitment to a failing course of action when they view themselves as responsible for the failure. That is, they "throw good money after bad" to demonstrate that their initial decision wasn't wrong and to avoid having to admit they made a mistake. Escalation of commitment is also congruent with evidence that people try to appear consistent in what they say and do. Increasing commitment to previous actions conveys consistency.

Escalation of commitment has obvious implications for managerial decisions. Many an organization has suffered large losses because a manager was determined to prove his or her original decision was right by continuing to commit resources to what was a lost cause from the beginning. In addition, consistency is a characteristic often associated with effective leaders. So managers, in an effort to appear effective, may be motivated to be consistent when switching to another course of action may be preferable. In actuality, effective managers are those who are able to differentiate between situations in which persistence will pay off and situations in which it will not.

Individual Differences: Decision-Making Styles

Put Chad and Sean into the same decision situation and Chad almost always seems to take longer to come to a solution. Chad's final choices aren't necessarily always better than Sean's, he's just slower in processing information. In addition, if there's an obvious risk dimension in the decision, Sean seems to consistently prefer a riskier option than does Chad. What this illustrates is that all of us bring our individual style to the decisions we make.

Research on decision styles has identified four different individual approaches to making decisions.[43] This model was designed to be used by managers and aspiring managers, but its general framework can be used with any individual decision maker.

The basic foundation of the model is the recognition that people differ along two dimensions. The first is their way of *thinking*. Some people are logical and rational. They process information serially. In contrast, some people are intuitive and creative. They perceive things as a whole. Note that these differences are above and beyond general human limitations such as those we described regarding bounded rationality. The other dimension addresses a person's *tolerance for ambiguity*. Some people have a high need to structure information in ways that minimize ambiguity, while others are able to process many thoughts at the same time. When these two dimensions are diagrammed, they form four styles of decision making (see Exhibit 5-5). These are: directive, analytic, conceptual, and behavioral.

People using the *directive* style have a low tolerance for ambiguity and seek rationality. They are efficient and logical, but their efficiency concerns result in decisions made with minimal information and with few alternatives assessed. Directive types make decisions fast and they focus on the short run.

The *analytic* type has a much greater tolerance for ambiguity than do directive decision makers. This leads to the desire for more information and consideration of more alternatives than is true for directives. Analytic managers would be best characterized as careful decision makers with the ability to adapt to or cope with novel and unexpected situations.

Individuals with a *conceptual* style tend to use data from multiple sources and consider many alternatives. Their focus is long range, and they are very good at finding creative solutions to problems.

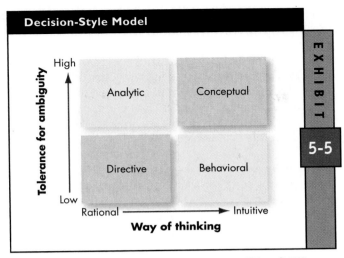

Decision-Style Model

High

Tolerance for ambiguity

Analytic   Conceptual

Directive   Behavioral

Low

Rational ⟶ Intuitive

Way of thinking

EXHIBIT

5-5

Source: A. J. Rowe and J. D. Boulgarides, Managerial Decision Making, © 1992 Prentice Hall, Upper Saddle River, NJ, p. 29.

The final category—the *behavioral* style—characterizes decision makers who have a strong concern for the people in the organization and their development. They're concerned with the well-being of their subordinates and are receptive to suggestions from others. They tend to focus on the short term and to downplay the use of data in their decision making. This type of manager tries to avoid conflict and seeks acceptance.

Although these four categories are distinct, most managers have characteristics that fall into more than one. It's probably best to think in terms of a manager's dominant style and his or her backup styles. Some managers rely almost exclusively on their dominant style, however, more flexible managers can make shifts depending on the situation.

American business students, lower-level managers, and top executives tend to score highest in the analytic style. That's not surprising given the emphasis that formal education, particularly business education, gives to developing rational thinking. For instance, courses in accounting, statistics, and finance all stress rational analysis. In contrast, evidence indicates that managers in China and Japan tend to rely more on directive and behavioral styles, respectively.[44] This may be explained by the Chinese emphasis on maintaining social order and the Japanese's strong sense of collectivism in the workplace.

In addition to providing a framework for looking at individual differences, focusing on decision styles can be useful for helping you to understand how two equally intelligent people, with access to the same information, can differ in the ways they approach decisions and the final choices they make. It can also help you understand how individuals from different cultures might approach a decision problem.

Organizational Constraints

The organization itself constrains decision makers. Managers, for instance, shape their decisions to reflect the organization's performance evaluation and reward system, to comply with the organization's formal regulations, and to meet organizationally imposed time constraints. Previous organizational decisions also act as precedents to constrain current decisions.

Performance Evaluation Managers are strongly influenced in their decision making by the criteria by which they are evaluated. If a division manager believes that the manufacturing plants under his responsibility are operating best when he hears nothing negative, we shouldn't be surprised to find his plant managers spending a good part of their time ensuring that negative information doesn't reach the division boss. Similarly, if a college dean believes that an instructor should never fail more than 10 percent of her students—to fail more reflects on the instructor's ability to teach—we should expect that instructors who want to receive favorable evaluations will decide not to fail too many students.

Reward Systems The organization's reward system influences decision makers by suggesting to them what choices are preferable in terms of personal payoff. For example, if the organization rewards risk aversion, managers are more likely to make conservative decisions. From the 1930s through the mid-1980s, General Motors consistently gave out promotions and bonuses to managers who kept a low profile, avoided controversy, and were good team players. The result was that GM managers became very adept at dodging tough issues and passing controversial decisions on to committees.

Formal Regulations David Gonzalez, a shift manager at a Taco Bell restaurant in San Antonio, Texas, describes constraints he faces on his job: "I've got rules and regulations covering almost every decision I make—from how to make a burrito to how often I need to clean the restrooms. My job doesn't come with much freedom of choice."

David's situation is not unique. All but the smallest of organizations create rules, policies, procedures, and other formalized regulations in order to standardize the behavior of their members. By programming decisions, organizations are able to get individuals to achieve high levels of performance without paying for the years of experience that would be necessary in the absence of regulations. And of course, in so doing, they limit the decision maker's choices.

System-Imposed Time Constraints Organizations impose deadlines on decisions. For instance, department budgets need to be completed by next Friday. Or the report on new-product development has to be ready for the executive committee to review by the first of the month. A host of decisions must be made quickly in order to stay ahead of the competition and keep customers satisfied. And almost all important decisions come with explicit deadlines. These conditions create time pressures on decision makers and often make it difficult, if not impossible, to gather all the information they might like to have before making a final choice.

Historical Precedents Decisions aren't made in a vacuum. They have a context. In fact, individual decisions are more accurately characterized as points in a stream of decisions.

Decisions made in the past are ghosts that continually haunt current choices. For instance, commitments made in the past constrain current

The same formal rules that regulate nearly every aspect of managing a franchise restaurant like a Taco Bell constrain the decision maker's ability to choose. But they also help achieve standardization and consistency.

options. To use a social situation as an example, the decision you might make after meeting "Mr. or Ms. Right" is more complicated if you're already married than if you're single. Prior commitments—in this case, having chosen to get married—constrain your options. Government budget decisions also offer an illustration of our point. It's common knowledge that the largest determining factor of the size of any given year's budget is last year's budget.[45] Choices made today, therefore, are largely a result of choices made over the years.

Cultural Differences

The rational model makes no acknowledgment of cultural differences. But Arabs, for instance, don't necessarily make decisions the same way that Canadians do. Therefore, we need to recognize that the cultural background of the decision maker can have significant influence on his or her selection of problems, depth of analysis, the importance placed on logic and rationality, or whether organizational decisions should be made autocratically by an individual manager or collectively in groups.[46]

Cultures, for example, differ in terms of time orientation, the importance of rationality, their belief in the ability of people to solve problems, and their preference for collective decision making. Differences in time orientation help us understand why managers in Egypt will make decisions at a much slower and more deliberate pace than their American counterparts. Whereas rationality is valued in North America, that's not true everywhere in the world. A North American manager might make an important decision intuitively, but he or she knows that it's important to appear to proceed in a rational fashion. This is because rationality is highly valued in the West. In countries such as Iran, where rationality is not deified, efforts to appear rational are not necessary.

Some cultures emphasize solving problems, while others focus on accepting situations as they are. The United States falls in the former category; Thailand and Indonesia are examples of cultures that fall into the latter category. Because problem-solving managers believe they can and should change situations to their benefit, American managers might identify a problem long before their Thai or Indonesian counterparts would choose to recognize it as such.

Decision making by Japanese managers is much more group-oriented than in the United States. The Japanese value conformity and cooperation. So before Japanese CEOs make an important decision, they collect a large amount of information, which is then used in consensus-forming group decisions.

WHAT ABOUT ETHICS IN DECISION MAKING?

No contemporary discussion of decision making would be complete without inclusion of ethics because ethical considerations should be an important criterion in organizational decision making. In this final section, we present three different ways to frame decisions ethically and look at how ethical standards vary across national cultures.

Three Ethical Decision Criteria

An individual can use three different criteria in making ethical choices.[47] The first is the *utilitarian* criterion, in which decisions are made solely on the basis of their outcomes or consequences. The goal of **utilitarianism** is to provide the greatest good for the greatest number. This view tends to dominate business decision making. It is consistent with goals like efficiency, productivity, and high profits. By maximizing profits, for instance, a business executive can argue he is securing the

utilitarianism

Decisions are made to provide the greatest good for the greatest number.

greatest good for the greatest number—as he hands out dismissal notices to 15 percent of his employees.

Another ethical criterion is to focus on *rights*. This calls on individuals to make decisions consistent with fundamental liberties and privileges as set forth in documents like the Bill of Rights. An emphasis on rights in decision making means respecting and protecting the basic rights of individuals, such as the right to privacy, to free speech, and to due process. For instance, use of this criterion would protect **whistle-blowers**—individuals who report unethical or illegal practices by their employer to outsiders—when they reveal unethical practices by their organization to the press or government agencies on the grounds of their right to free speech.

A third criterion is to focus on *justice*. This requires individuals to impose and enforce rules fairly and impartially so that there is an equitable distribution of benefits and costs. Union members typically favor this view. It justifies paying people the same wage for a given job, regardless of performance differences, and using seniority as the primary determination in making layoff decisions.

Each of these three criteria has advantages and liabilities. A focus on utilitarianism promotes efficiency and productivity, but it can result in ignoring the rights of some individuals, particularly those with minority representation in the organization. The use of rights as a criterion protects individuals from injury and is consistent with freedom and privacy, but it can create an overly legalistic work environment that hinders productivity and efficiency. A focus on justice protects the interests of the underrepresented and less powerful, but it can encourage a sense of entitlement that reduces risk taking, innovation, and productivity.

Decision makers, particularly in for-profit organizations, tend to feel safe and comfortable when they use utilitarianism. A lot of questionable actions can be justified when framed as being in the best interests of "the organization" and stockholders. But many critics of business decision makers argue that this perspective needs to change.[48] Increased concern in society about individual rights and social justice suggests the need for managers to develop ethical standards based on nonutilitarian criteria. This presents a solid challenge to today's managers because

whistle-blowers

Individuals who report unethical practices by their employer to outsiders.

OR SCIENCE ?

MYTH

"Ethical People Don't Do Unethical Things"

This statement is mostly true. People with high ethical standards are less likely to engage in unethical practices, even in organizations or situations in which there are strong pressures to conform.

The essential issue that this statement addresses is whether ethical behavior is more a function of the individual or the situational context. The evidence indicates that people with high ethical principles will follow them in spite of what others do or the dictates of organizational norms.[49] But when an individual's ethical and moral development are not of the highest level, he or she is more likely to be influenced by strong cultures. This is true even when those cultures encourage questionable practices.

Because ethical people essentially avoid unethical practices, managers should be encouraged to screen job candidates (through testing and background investigations) to determine their ethical standards. By seeking out people with integrity and strong ethical principles, the organization increases the likelihood that employees will act ethically. Of course, unethical practices can be further minimized by providing individuals with a supportive work climate.[50] This would include clear job descriptions, a written code of ethics, positive management role models, the evaluating and rewarding of means as well as ends, and a culture that encourages individuals to openly challenge questionable practices.

making decisions using criteria such as individual rights and social justice involves far more ambiguities than using utilitarian criteria such as effects on efficiency and profits. This helps to explain why managers are increasingly criticized for their actions. Raising prices, selling products with questionable effects on consumer health, closing down inefficient plants, laying off large numbers of employees, moving production overseas to cut costs, and similar decisions can be justified in utilitarian terms. But that may no longer be the single criterion by which good decisions should be judged.

Ethics and National Culture

What is seen as an ethical decision in China may not be seen as such in Canada. The reason is that there are no global ethical standards.[51] Contrasts between Asia and the West provide an illustration.[52] Because bribery is commonplace in countries such as China, a Canadian working in China might face the dilemma: Should I pay a bribe to secure business if it is an accepted part of that country's culture? Or how about this for a shock? A manager of a large U.S. company operating in China caught an employee stealing. Following company policy, she fired him and turned him over to the local authorities. Later, she was horrified to learn that the employee had been summarily executed.[53]

Although ethical standards may seem ambiguous in the West, criteria defining right and wrong are actually much clearer in the West than in Asia. Few issues are black and white there; most are gray. The need for global organizations to establish ethical principles for decision makers in countries such as India and China, and modifying them to reflect cultural norms, may be critical if high standards are to be upheld and if consistent practices are to be achieved.

SUMMARY AND IMPLICATIONS FOR MANAGERS

Perception

Individuals behave in a given manner based not on the way their external environment actually is but, rather, on what they see or believe it to be. It is the employee's perception of a situation that becomes the basis for his or her behavior. Whether or not a job is actually interesting or challenging is irrelevant. Whether or not a manager successfully plans and organizes the work of his or her employees and actually helps them to structure their work more efficiently and effectively is far less important than how employees perceive the manager's efforts. Similarly, issues such as fair pay for work performed, the validity of performance appraisals, and the adequacy of working conditions are not judged by employees in a way that ensures common perceptions; nor can we be assured that individuals will interpret conditions about their jobs in a favorable light. Therefore, to be able to influence productivity, it's necessary to assess how workers perceive their jobs.

Absenteeism, turnover, and job satisfaction are also reactions to the individual's perceptions. Dissatisfaction with working conditions or the belief that there is a lack of promotion opportunities in the organization are judgments based on attempts to make some meaning out of one's job. The employee's conclusion that a job is good or bad is an interpretation. Managers must spend time understanding how each individual interprets reality and, when there is a significant difference between what is seen and what exists, try to eliminate the distortions. Failure to deal with the differences when individuals perceive the job in negative terms will result in increased absenteeism and turnover and lower job satisfaction.

Individual Decision Making

Individuals think and reason before they act. It is because of this that an understanding of how people make decisions can be helpful for explaining and predicting their behavior.

Under some decision situations, people follow the rational decision-making model. But for most people, and most nonroutine decisions, this is probably more the exception than the rule. Few important decisions are simple or unambiguous enough for the rational model's assumptions to apply. So we find individuals looking for solutions that satisfice rather than optimize, injecting biases and prejudices into the decision process, and relying on intuition.

Given the evidence we've described on how decisions are actually made in organizations, what can managers do to improve their decision making? We offer five suggestions.

First, analyze the situation. Adjust your decision-making style to the national culture you're operating in and to the criteria your organization evaluates and rewards. For instance, if you're in a country that doesn't value rationality, don't feel compelled to follow the rational decision-making model or even to try to make your decisions appear rational. Similarly, organizations differ in terms of the importance they place on risk, the use of groups, and the like. Adjust your decision style to ensure that it's compatible with the organization's culture.

Second, be aware of biases. We all bring biases to the decisions we make. If you understand the biases influencing your judgment, you can begin to change the way you make decisions to reduce those biases.

Third, combine rational analysis with intuition. These are not conflicting approaches to decision making. By using both, you can actually improve your decision-making effectiveness. As you gain managerial experience, you should feel increasingly confident in imposing your intuitive processes on top of your rational analysis.

Fourth, don't assume that your specific decision style is appropriate for every job. Just as organizations differ, so too do jobs within organizations. And your effectiveness as a decision maker will increase if you match your decision style to the requirements of the job. For instance, if your decision-making style is directive, you'll be more effective working with people whose jobs require quick action. This style might match well with managing stockbrokers. An analytic style, on the other hand, might be more effective in managing accountants, market researchers, or financial analysts.

Finally, try to enhance your creativity. Overtly look for novel solutions to problems, attempt to see problems in new ways, and use analogies. In addition, try to remove work and organizational barriers that might impede your creativity.

When Hiring Employees, Emphasize the Positive

Hiring new employees requires managers to become salespeople. They have to emphasize the positive, even if it means failing to mention the negative aspects in the job. While there is a real risk of setting unrealistic expectations about the organization and about the specific job, that's a risk managers have to take. As in dealing with any salesperson, it is the job applicant's responsibility to follow the dictum *caveat emptor*—let the buyer beware.

Why should managers emphasize the positive when discussing a job with a prospective candidate? They have no choice. First, there is a dwindling supply of qualified applicants for many job vacancies; and second, this approach is necessary to meet the competition.

Corporate layoffs have received a lot of attention in recent years. What has often been overlooked in this process is the growing shortage of qualified applicants for literally millions of jobs. Through the foreseeable future, managers will find it increasingly difficult to get qualified people who can fill jobs such as legal secretary, nurse, accountant, maintenance mechanic, computer-repair specialist, software programmer, social worker, physical therapist, environmental engineer, and telecommunications specialist. But managers will also find it harder to get qualified people to fill entry-level, minimum-wage jobs. There may be no shortage of physical bodies, but finding individuals who can read, write, perform basic mathematical calculations, and have the proper work habits to effectively perform these jobs isn't so easy. There is a growing gap between the skills workers have and the skills employers require. So managers need to *sell* jobs to the limited pool of applicants. And this means presenting the job and the organization in the most favorable light possible.

Another reason management is forced to emphasize the positive with job candidates is that this is what the competition is doing. Other employers also face a limited applicant pool. As a result, to get people to join their organizations, they are forced to put a positive "spin" on their descriptions of their organizations and the jobs they seek to fill. In this competitive environment, any employer who presents jobs realistically to applicants—that is, openly provides the negative aspects of a job along with the positive—risks losing many of the most desirable candidates.

Regardless of labor-market conditions, managers who treat the recruiting and hiring of candidates as if the applicants must be sold on the job and exposed to only positive aspects set themselves up to have a workforce that is dissatisfied and prone to high turnover.[a]

Every applicant acquires, during the selection process, a set of expectations about the organization and about the specific job he or she hopes to be offered. When the information an applicant receives is excessively inflated, a number of things happen that have potentially negative effects on the organization. First, mismatched applicants who will probably become dissatisfied with the job and soon quit are less likely to select themselves out of the search process. Second, the absence of negative information builds unrealistic expectations. And these unrealistic expectations often lead to premature resignations. Third, new hires are prone to become disillusioned and less committed to the organization when they come face-to-face with the negatives in the job. Employees who feel they were tricked or misled during the hiring process are unlikely to be satisfied workers.

To increase job satisfaction among employees and reduce turnover, applicants should be given a realistic job preview—provided both unfavorable and favorable information—before an offer is made. For example, in addition to positive comments, the candidate might be told that there are limited opportunities to talk with co-workers during work hours, or that erratic fluctuations in workloads create considerable stress on employees during rush periods.

Research indicates that applicants who have been given a realistic job preview hold lower and more realistic expectations about the job they'll be doing and are better prepared for coping with the job and its frustrating elements. The result is fewer unexpected resignations by new employees. Remember that retaining qualified people is as critical as hiring them in the first place. Presenting only the positive aspects of a job to a recruit may initially entice him or her to join the organization, but it may be a marriage that both parties will quickly regret.

Source: [a]Information in this argument comes from J. M. Phillips, "Effects of Realistic Job Previews on Multiple Organizational Outcomes: A Meta-Analysis," *Academy of Management Journal*, December 1998, pp. 673–90; and J. A. Breaugh and M. Starke, "Research on Employee Recruitment: So Many Studies, So Many Remaining Questions," *Journal of Management*, vol. 26, no. 3, 2000, pp. 415–17.

Questions for Review

1. Define *perception*.

2. What is attribution theory? What are its implications for explaining organizational behavior?

3. How are our perceptions of our own actions different from our perceptions of the actions of others?

4. How does selectivity affect perception? Give an example of how selectivity can create perceptual distortion.

5. What is stereotyping? Give an example of how stereotyping can create perceptual distortion.

6. Give some positive results of using shortcuts when judging others.

7. What is the rational decision-making model? Under what conditions is it applicable?

8. Describe organizational factors that might constrain decision makers.

9. What role does intuition play in effective decision making? When is it likely to be most effective?

10. Are unethical decisions more a function of the individual decision maker or the decision maker's work environment? Explain.

Questions for Critical Thinking

1. How might the differences in the experiences of students and instructors affect their perceptions of students' written work and class comments?

2. An employee does an unsatisfactory job on an assigned project. Explain the attribution process that this person's manager will use to form judgments about this employee's job performance.

3. "For the most part, individual decision making in organizations is an irrational process." Do you agree or disagree? Discuss.

4. What factors do you think differentiate good decision makers from poor ones? Relate your answer to the six-step rational model.

5. Have you ever increased your commitment to a failed course of action? If so, analyze the follow-up decision to increase your commitment and explain why you behaved as you did.

Team Exercise | Biases in Decision Making

Step 1.   Answer each of the following problems.

1. The following 10 corporations were ranked by *Fortune* magazine to be among the 500 largest United States-based firms according to sales volume for 2001:

   Group A: Apple Computer, Hershey Foods, Mattel, Maytag, Levi Strauss

   Group B: Conagra, Ingram Micro, Delphi, Cardinal Health, American International Group

   Which group of five organizations listed (A or B) had the larger total sales volume? By what percentage (10%, 50%, 100%, or ?) do you think the higher group's sales exceeded the lower group's?

2. The best student in my introductory MBA class this past semester writes poetry and is rather shy and small in stature. What was the student's undergraduate major: Chinese studies or psychology?

3. Which of the following causes more deaths in the United States each year:
   a. Stomach cancer
   b. Motor vehicle accidents

4. Which would you choose?
   a. A sure gain of $240
   b. A 25 percent chance of winning $1,000 and a 75 percent chance of winning nothing.

5. Which would you choose?
   a. A sure loss of $750
   b. A 75 percent chance of losing $1,000 and a 25 percent chance of losing nothing.

6. Which would you choose?
   a. A sure loss of $3,000
   b. An 80 percent chance of losing $4,000 and a 20 percent chance of losing nothing.

Step 2.   Break into groups of 3 to 5. Compare your answers. Explain why you chose the answers that you did.

Step 3.   Your instructor will give you the correct answers to each problem. Now discuss the accuracy of your decisions; the biases evident in the decisions you reached; and how you might improve your decision making to make it more accurate.

Source: These problems are based on examples provided in M. H. Bazerman, *Judgment in Managerial Decision Making*, 3rd ed. (New York: Wiley, 1994).

Ethical Dilemma	Five Ethical Decisions: What Would You Do?

Assume you're a middle manager in a company with about a thousand employees. How would you respond to each of the following situations?

1. You're negotiating a contract with a potentially very large customer whose representative has hinted that you could almost certainly be assured of getting his business if you gave him and his wife an all-expense-paid cruise to the Caribbean. You know the representative's employer wouldn't approve of such a "payoff," but you have the discretion to authorize such an expenditure. What would you do?

2. You have the opportunity to steal $100,000 from your company with absolute certainty that you would not be detected or caught. Would you do it?

3. Your company policy on reimbursement for meals while traveling on company business is that you will be repaid for your out-of-pocket costs, not to exceed $60 a day. You don't need receipts for these expenses—the company will take your word. When traveling, you tend to eat at fast-food places and rarely spend in excess of $15 a day. Most of your colleagues put in reimbursement requests in the range of $45 to $50 a day regardless of what their actual expenses are. How much would you request for your meal reimbursements?

4. Another executive, who is part of a small planning team in which you're a member, frequently has the smell of alcohol on his breath. You've noticed that his work hasn't been up to standard lately and is

hurting your team's performance. This executive happens to be the son-in-law of the company's owner and is held in very high regard by the owner. What would you do?

5. You've discovered that one of your closest friends at work has stolen a large sum of money from the company. Would you: Do nothing? Go directly to an executive to report the incident before talking about it with the offender? Confront the individual before taking action? Make contact with the individual with the goal of persuading that person to return the money?

| Case Incident | John Neill at Unipart |

While most part suppliers for the United Kingdom's automobile industry struggle, one company is doing just fine—Unipart. This 2.3 billion-euro company has done well largely because of the decisions made by its CEO, John Neill.

In 1974, at the youthful age of 29, John Neill was made managing director of the Unipart division of British Leyland (BL). He immediately began to ruffle feathers of conservative BL executives by developing innovative marketing campaigns and focusing company attention on the parts business (in contrast to its cars and trucks). He increased the division's marketing budget sixfold, created a retail shop program, altered the packaging, and began promoting the division's parts on television. His "parts first" pitch didn't go down well with his bosses, who saw it as an attack on the viability of BL itself. But it was too late for BL's top management to do much about it. Neill had created a viable business, while the rest of the company (which later became part of the Rover Group) labored along, losing market share every year.

Almost from the beginning, Neill envisioned making Unipart independent from BL. In 1987, he did just that. He negotiated a 89.5 million euro management buyout of Unipart from BL. He then immediately began taking actions that would allow Unipart to stand on its own two feet. "We knew the future would be worse," Neill recalls, "because today's market share was smaller than yesterday's. So the parts business would go down unless we did something dramatically different." That "something" was to move away from providing original parts for Rover. Instead, Unipart would commit to creating a strong consumer brand built around replacement parts. Today, Unipart has become a highly recognizable consumer brand in the United Kingdom. It has also diversified into a range of other businesses. Producing and selling automotive parts is still the company's main activity but it also runs a successful warehouse, a logistics business, and has created an Internet trading platform.

In 1987, when Unipart became independent, sales to Rover represented 90 percent of its business. It's now down to 3 percent. No longer are Unipart's fortunes tied singularly to Rover. In fact, one of Unipart's most profitable current businesses is running Jaguar's entire parts operation on a fee basis.

Despite Neill's success since the buy-out, Unipart faces tough times ahead. The U.K. auto industry suffers from massive overcapacity. Intensive downward pricing pressure on suppliers is likely to eat away at Unipart's profits. In response, Neill has expanded Unipart's logistic business by paying 292 million euros for auto parts distributor Partco. This acquisition makes Unipart the biggest automotive parts distributor in the United Kingdom. Neill is also diversifying beyond Unipart's automotive parts roots, especially on the e-commerce front.

Questions

1. "John Neill isn't smart; he's just lucky." Do you agree or disagree? Explain.

2. Did intuition play a role in Neill's decisions? Discuss.

3. Contrast the major strategic decisions at Unipart and British Leyland.

4. Do you think John Neill would have been equally successful if, back in 1987, he had been made head of BL? Explain.

Source: Based on T. Rubython and A. Sibillin, "The Reality Man," *EuroBusiness*, October 2000, pp. 76–78.

Endnotes

1. Based on A. M. Hayahsi, "When To Trust Your Gut," *Harvard Business Review*, February 2001, pp. 59–60.

2. H. H. Kelley, "Attribution in Social Interaction," in E. Jones et al. (eds.), *Attribution: Perceiving the Causes of Behavior* (Morristown, NJ: General Learning Press, 1972).

3. See L. Ross, "The Intuitive Psychologist and His Shortcomings," in L. Berkowitz (ed.), *Advances in Experimental Social Psychology*, vol. 10 (Orlando, FL: Academic Press, 1977), pp. 174–220; and A. G. Miller and T. Lawson, "The Effect of an Informational Option on the Fundamental Attribution Error," *Personality and Social Psychology Bulletin*, June 1989, pp. 194–204.

4. See, for instance, G. Johns, "A Multi-Level Theory of Self-Serving Behavior in and by Organizations," in R. I. Sutton and B. M. Staw (eds.), *Research in Organizational Behavior*, vol. 21 (Stamford, CT: JAI Press, 1999), pp. 1–38; and N. Epley and D. Dunning, "Feeling 'Holier Than Thou': Are Self-Serving Assessments Produced by Errors in Self- or Social Prediction?" *Journal of Personality and Social Psychology*, December 2000, pp. 861–75.

5. See, for instance, G. R. Semin, "A Gloss on Attribution Theory," *British Journal of Social and Clinical Psychology*, November 1980, pp. 291–30; and M. W. Morris and K. Peng, "Culture and Cause: American and Chinese Attributions for Social and Physical Events," *Journal of Personality and Social Psychology*, December 1994, pp. 949–71.

6. S. Nam, "Cultural and Managerial Attributions for Group Performance," unpublished doctoral dissertation; University of Oregon. Cited in R. M. Steers, S. J. Bischoff, and L. H. Higgins, "Cross-Cultural Management Research," *Journal of Management Inquiry*, December 1992, pp. 325–26.

7. D. C. Dearborn and H. A. Simon, "Selective Perception: A Note on the Departmental Identification of Executives," *Sociometry*, June 1958, pp. 140–44. Some of the conclusions in this classic study have recently been challenged in J. Walsh, "Selectivity and Selective Perception: An Investigation of Managers' Belief Structures and Information Processing," *Academy of Management Journal*, December 1988, pp. 873–96; M. J. Waller, G. Huber, and W. H. Glick, "Functional Background as a Determinant of Executives'

Selective Perception," *Academy of Management Journal*, August 1995, pp. 943–74; and J. M. Beyer, P. Chattopadhyay, E. George, W. H. Glick, D. T. Ogilvie, and D. Pugliese, "The Selective Perception of Managers Revisited," *Academy of Management Journal*, June 1997, pp. 716–37.

8. See K. R. Murphy and R. L. Anhalt, "Is Halo a Property of the Rater, the Ratees, or the Specific Behaviors Observed?" *Journal of Applied Psychology*, June 1992, pp. 494–500; and K. R. Murphy, R. A. Jako, and R. L. Anhalt, "Nature and Consequences of Halo Error: A Critical Analysis," *Journal of Applied Psychology*, April 1993, pp. 218–25.

9. S. E. Asch, "Forming Impressions of Personality," *Journal of Abnormal and Social Psychology*, July 1946, pp. 258–90.

10. J. S. Bruner and R. Tagiuri, "The Perception of People," in E. Lindzey (ed.), *Handbook of Social Psychology* (Reading, MA: Addison–Wesley, 1954), p. 641.

11. J. L. Hilton and W. von Hippel, "Stereotypes," in J. T. Spence, J. M. Darley, and D. J. Foss (eds.), *Annual Review of Psychology*, vol. 47 (Palo Alto, CA: Annual Reviews Inc., 1996), pp. 237–71.

12. See, for example, C. M. Judd and B. Park, "Definition and Assessment of Accuracy in Social Stereotypes," *Psychological Review*, January 1993, pp. 109–28.

13. See, for example, S. T. Fiske, D. N. Beroff, E. Borgida, K. Deaux, and M. E. Heilman, "Use of Sex Stereotyping Research in Price Waterhouse vs. Hopkins," *American Psychologist*, October 1991, pp. 1049–60; G. N. Powell, "The Good Manager: Business Students' Stereotypes of Japanese Managers versus Stereotypes of American Managers," *Group & Organizational Management*, March 1992, pp. 44–56; and W. C. K. Chiu, A. W. Chan, E. Snape, and T. Redman, "Age Stereotypes and Discriminatory Attitudes Towards Older Workers: An East-West Comparison," *Human Relations*, May 2001, pp. 629–61.

14. See, for example, E. C. Webster, *Decision Making in the Employment Interview* (Montreal: McGill University, Industrial Relations Center, 1964).

15. See, for example, D. Eden, *Pygmalion in Management* (Lexington, MA: Lexington, 1990); D. Eden, "Leadership and Expectations: Pygmalion Effects and Other Self-Fulfilling

Prophecies," *Leadership Quarterly*, Winter 1992, pp. 271–305; D. B. McNatt, "Ancient Pygmalion Joins Contemporary Management: A Meta-Analysis of the Result," *Journal of Applied Psychology*, April 2000, pp. 314–22; and O. B. Davidson and D. Eden, "Remedial Self-Fulfilling Prophecy: Two Field Experiments to Prevent Golem Effects Among Disadvantaged Women," *Journal of Applied Psychology*, June 2000, pp. 386–98.

16. D. Eden and A. B. Shani, "Pygmalion Goes to Boot Camp: Expectancy, Leadership, and Trainee Performance," *Journal of Applied Psychology*, April 1982, pp. 194–99.

17. See, for example, R. D. Bretz, Jr., G. T. Milkovich, and W. Read, "The Current State of Performance Appraisal Research and Practice: Concerns, Directions, and Implications," *Journal of Management*, June 1992, pp. 323–24; and P. M. Swiercz, M. L. Icenogle, N. B. Bryan, and R. W. Renn, "Do Perceptions of Performance Appraisal Fairness Predict Employee Attitudes and Performance?" in D. P. Moore (ed.), *Proceedings of the Academy of Management* (Atlanta: Academy of Management, 1993), pp. 304–08.

18. R. Sanders, *The Executive Decisionmaking Process: Identifying Problems and Assessing Outcomes* (Westport, CT: Quorum, 1999).

19. See H. A. Simon, "Rationality in Psychology and Economics," *Journal of Business*, October 1986, pp. 209–24; and A. Langley, "In Search of Rationality: The Purposes Behind the Use of Formal Analysis in Organizations," *Administrative Science Quarterly*, December 1989, pp. 598–631.

20. For a review of the rational model, see E. F. Harrison, *The Managerial Decision-Making Process*, 5th ed. (Boston: Houghton Mifflin, 1999), pp. 75–102.

21. W. Pounds, "The Process of Problem Finding," *Industrial Management Review*, Fall 1969, pp. 1–19.

22. J. G. March, *A Primer on Decision Making* (New York: Free Press, 1994), pp. 2–7.

23. T. M. Amabile, "A Model of Creativity and Innovation in Organizations," in B. M. Staw and L. L. Cummings (eds.), *Research in Organizational Behavior*, vol. 10 (Greenwich, CT: JAI Press, 1988), p. 126; and T. M. Amabile, "Motivating Creativity in Organizations," *California Management Review*, Fall 1997, p. 40.

24. Cited in C. G. Morris, *Psychology: An Introduction*, 9th ed. (Upper Saddle River, NJ: Prentice Hall, 1996), p. 344.

25. This section is based on T. M. Amabile, "Motivating Creativity in Organizations," pp. 42–52.

26. R. W. Woodman, J. E. Sawyer, and R. W. Griffin, "Toward a Theory of Organizational Creativity," *Academy of Management Review*, April 1993, p. 298.

27. W. J. J. Gordon, *Synectics* (New York: Harper & Row, 1961).

28. See T .M. Amabile, *KEYS: Assessing the Climate for Creativity* (Greensboro, NC: Center for Creative Leadership, 1995).

29. D. L. Rados, "Selection and Evaluation of Alternatives in Repetitive Decision Making," *Administrative Science Quarterly*, June 1972, pp. 196–206; and G. Klein, *Sources*

of Power: How People Make Decisions (Cambridge, MA: MIT Press, 1998).

30. M. Bazerman, *Judgment in Managerial Decision Making*, 3rd ed. (New York: Wiley, 1994), p. 5.

31. See, for instance, L. R. Beach, *The Psychology of Decision Making* (Thousand Oaks, CA: Sage, 1997).

32. See H. A. Simon, *Administrative Behavior*, 4th ed. (New York: Free Press, 1997); and M. Augier, "Simon Says: Bounded Rationality Matters," *Journal of Management Inquiry*, September 2001, pp. 268–75.

33. W. H. Agor (ed.), *Intuition in Organizations* (Newbury Park, CA: Sage Publications, 1989); O. Behling and N. L. Eckel, "Making Sense Out of Intuition," *Academy of Management Executive*, February 1991, pp. 46–47; L. A. Burke and M. K. Miller, "Taking the Mystery out of Intuitive Decision Making," *Academy of Management Executive*, November 1999, pp. 91–99; and N. Khatri and H. A. Ng, "The Role of Intuition in Strategic Decision Making," *Human Relations*, January 2000, pp. 57–86.

34. Behling and Eckel, "Making Sense out of Intuition," pp. 46–54.

35. As described in H. A. Simon, "Making Management Decisions: The Role of Intuition and Emotion," *Academy of Management Executive*, February 1987, pp. 59–60.

36. Agor, *Intuition in Organizations*, p. 9.

37. Ibid., p. 15.

38. See, for example, M. D. Cohen, J. G. March, and J. P. Olsen, "A Garbage Can Model of Organizational Choice," *Administrative Science Quarterly*, March 1972, pp. 1–25.

39. See J. G. Thompson, *Organizations in Action* (New York: McGraw-Hill, 1967), p. 123.

40. C. E. Lindholm, "The Science of 'Muddling Through,'" *Public Administration Review*, Spring 1959, pp. 79–88.

41. A. Tversky and K. Kahneman, "Judgment under Uncertainty: Heuristics and Biases," *Science*, September 1974, pp. 1124–31; and J. S. Hammond, R. L. Keeney, and H. Raiffa, "The Hidden Traps in Decision Making," *Harvard Business Review*, September–October 1998, pp. 47–58.

42. See B. M. Staw, "The Escalation of Commitment to a Course of Action," *Academy of Management Review*, October 1981, pp. 577–87; and H. Moon, "Looking Forward and Looking Back: Integrating Completion and Sunk-Cost Effects within an Escalation-of-Commitment Progress Decision," *Journal of Applied Psychology*, February 2001, pp. 104–13.

43. A. J. Rowe and J. D. Boulgarides, *Managerial Decision Making* (Englewood Cliffs, NJ: Prentice Hall, 1992).

44. M. G. Martinsons, "Comparing the Decision Styles of American and Asian Business Leaders," paper presented at the 61st annual meeting of the Academy of Management, Washington, DC, August 2001.

45. A. Wildavsky, *The Politics of the Budgetary Process* (Boston: Little Brown, 1964).

46. N. J. Adler, *International Dimensions of Organizational Behavior*, 4th ed. (Cincinnati, OH: Southwestern, 2002), pp. 182–89.

47. G. F. Cavanagh, D. J. Moberg, and M. Valasquez, "The Ethics of Organizational Politics," *Academy of Management Journal*, June 1981, pp. 363–74.

48. See, for example, T. Machan, ed., *Commerce and Morality* (Totowa, NJ: Rowman and Littlefield, 1988).

49. L. Kohlberg, "Stage and Sequence: The Cognitive-Developmental Approach to Socialization," in D. A. Goslin (ed.), *Handbook of Socialization Theory and Research* (Chicago: Rand McNally, 1969), pp. 347–480.

50. See, for instance, B. Victor and J. B. Cullen, "The Organizational Bases of Ethical Work Climates," *Administrative Science Quarterly*, March 1988, pp. 101–25; and J. C. Wimbush, "The Effect of Cognitive Moral Development and Supervisory Influence on Subordinates' Ethical Behavior," *Journal of Business Ethics*, February 1999, pp. 383–95.

51. T. Jackson, "Cultural Values and Management Ethics: A 10-Nation Study," *Human Relations*, October 2001, pp. 1267–302.

52. W. Chow Hou, "To Bribe or Not to Bribe?" *Asia, Inc.*, October 1996, p. 104.

53. P. Digh, "Shades of Gray in the Global Marketplace," *HRMagazine*, April 1997, p. 91.

Set me anything to do as a task, and it is inconceivable the desire I have to do something else.
—**G. B. Shaw**

PART TWO

THE INDIVIDUAL

Motivation is a problem and organizations keep looking for a solution. A recent Gallup poll, for instance, found that a majority of U.S. employees—55 percent to be exact—have no enthusiasm for their work.[1] That's a pretty startling statistic!

Management has used a number of approaches to improve employee motivation. They've tried traditional approaches like increasing pay and improving benefits. They've also tried some more bizarre ideas. For instance, data storage giant EMC is among a number of companies that are having employees walk on 1,500-degree coals.[2] Why? Management believes that once employees have faced fear, they're ready to tackle the impossible in their jobs. EMC vice president Jeff Goldberg, a three-time fire walker, admits that he doesn't have any concrete proof that walking across hot coals increases accomplishment by snuffing out workplace fear. But he says there is plenty of anecdotal evidence. Jan Gunneson (see photo), an EMC district sales manager, says that sales agents who have walked on coals are more likely to aggressively call on CEOs and other senior executives, going over the heads of more traditional, lower-level contacts, in efforts to get new business. And Gunneson believes that the motivation derived from fire walking is permanent. "I'm sure that 50 years from now, if I'm talking with my grandkids, this is an experience I will remember and share with them." Is the secret to employee motivation to get them to walk on coals? Probably not.

Motivation is one of the most frequently researched topics in OB.[3] In spite of the facts that managers continue to search for innovative ways to motivate their employees and that a significant proportion of today's workers seem to be unmotivated, we actually know a great deal about how to improve employee motivation. In this chapter and the following one, we'll review

Basic Motivation Concepts

the basics of motivation, assess a number of motivation theories, provide an integrative model that shows how the best of these theories fit together, and offer some guidelines for designing effective motivation programs.

DEFINING MOTIVATION

What is motivation? Maybe the place to begin is to say what motivation isn't. Many people incorrectly view motivation as a personal trait—that is, some have it and others don't. In practice, inexperienced managers often label employees who seem to lack motivation as lazy. Such a label assumes that an individual is always lazy or is lacking in motivation. Our knowledge of motivation tells us that this just isn't true. What we know is that motivation is the result of the interaction of the individual and the situation. Certainly, individuals differ in their basic motivational drive. But the same student who finds it difficult to read a textbook for more than 20 minutes may devour a Harry Potter book in one afternoon. For this student, the change in motivation is driven by the situation. So as we analyze the concept of motivation, keep in mind that the level of motivation varies both between individuals and within individuals at different times.

We'll define **motivation** as the processes that account for an individual's intensity, direction, and persistence of effort toward attaining a goal.[4] While general motivation is concerned with effort toward *any* goal, we'll narrow the focus to *organizational* goals in order to reflect our singular interest in work-related behavior.

The three key elements in our definition are intensity, direction, and persistence. *Intensity* is concerned with how hard a person tries. This is the element most of us focus on when we talk about motivation. However, high intensity is unlikely to lead to favorable

LEARNING OBJECTIVES

AFTER STUDYING THIS CHAPTER, YOU SHOULD BE ABLE TO:

1. Outline the motivation process.
2. Describe Maslow's need hierarchy.
3. Contrast Theory X and Theory Y.
4. Differentiate motivators from hygiene factors.
5. List the characteristics that high achievers prefer in a job.
6. Summarize the types of goals that increase performance.
7. State the impact of underrewarding employees.
8. Clarify the key relationships in expectancy theory.
9. Explain how the contemporary theories of motivation complement each other.

motivation

The processes that account for an individual's intensity, direction, and persistence of effort toward attaining a goal.

job-performance outcomes unless the effort is channeled in a *direction* that benefits the organization. Therefore, we have to consider the quality of effort as well as its intensity. Effort that is directed toward, and consistent with, the organization's goals is the kind of effort that we should be seeking. Finally, motivation has a *persistence* dimension. This is a measure of how long a person can maintain their effort. Motivated individuals stay with a task long enough to achieve their goal.

EARLY THEORIES OF MOTIVATION

The 1950s were a fruitful period in the development of motivation concepts. Three specific theories were formulated during this period, which although heavily attacked and now questionable in terms of validity, are probably still the best-known explanations for employee motivation. These are the hierarchy of needs theory, Theories X and Y, and the two-factor theory. As you'll see later in this chapter, we have since developed more valid explanations of motivation, but you should know these early theories for at least two reasons: (1) They represent a foundation from which contemporary theories have grown, and (2) practicing managers still regularly use these theories and their terminology in explaining employee motivation.

Hierarchy of Needs Theory

It's probably safe to say that the most well-known theory of motivation is Abraham Maslow's **hierarchy of needs**.[5] He hypothesized that within every human being there exists a hierarchy of five needs. These needs are:

hierarchy of needs theory

There is a hierarchy of five needs—physiological, safety, social, esteem, and self-actualization; as each need is substantially satisfied, the next need becomes dominant.

self-actualization

The drive to become what one is capable of becoming.

1. *Physiological:* Includes hunger, thirst, shelter, sex, and other bodily needs
2. *Safety:* Includes security and protection from physical and emotional harm
3. *Social:* Includes affection, belongingness, acceptance, and friendship
4. *Esteem:* Includes internal esteem factors such as self-respect, autonomy, and achievement; and external esteem factors such as status, recognition, and attention
5. **Self-actualization**: The drive to become what one is capable of becoming; includes growth, achieving one's potential, and self-fulfillment

As each of these needs becomes substantially satisfied, the next need becomes dominant. In terms of Exhibit 6-1, the individual moves up the steps of the hierarchy. From the standpoint of motivation, the theory would say that although no need is ever fully gratified, a substantially satisfied need no longer motivates. So if you want to motivate someone, according to Maslow, you need to understand

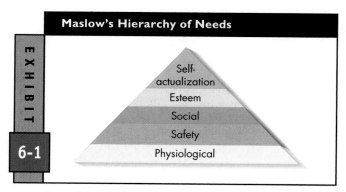

Source: *Motivation and Personality*, 2nd ed., by A. H. Maslow, 1970. Reprinted by permission of Prentice Hall, Inc., Upper Saddle River, New Jersey.

what level of the hierarchy that person is currently on and focus on satisfying the needs at or above that level.

Maslow separated the five needs into higher and lower orders. Physiological and safety needs were described as **lower-order** and social, esteem, and self-actualization as **higher-order needs**. The differentiation between the two orders was made on the premise that higher-order needs are satisfied internally (within the person), whereas lower-order needs are predominantly satisfied externally (by things such as pay, union contracts, and tenure).

Maslow's need theory has received wide recognition, particularly among practicing managers. This can be attributed to the theory's intuitive logic and ease of understanding. Unfortunately, however, research does not generally validate the theory. Maslow provided no empirical substantiation, and several studies that sought to validate the theory found no support for it.[6]

Old theories, especially ones that are intuitively logical, apparently die hard. Although the need hierarchy theory and its terminology have remained popular with practicing managers, it has minimal empirical support for its predictions.[7] More specifically, there is little evidence that need structures are organized along the dimensions proposed by Maslow, that unsatisfied needs motivate, or that a satisfied need activates movement to a new need level.[8]

lower-order needs

Needs that are satisfied externally; physiological and safety needs.

higher-order needs

Needs that are satisfied internally; social, esteem, and self-actualization needs.

Theory X and Theory Y

Douglas McGregor proposed two distinct views of human beings: one basically negative, labeled **Theory X**, and the other basically positive, labeled **Theory Y**.[9] After viewing the way in which managers dealt with employees, McGregor concluded that a manager's view of the nature of human beings is based on a certain grouping of assumptions and that he or she tends to mold his or her behavior toward employees according to these assumptions.

Under Theory X, the four assumptions held by managers are:

1. Employees inherently dislike work and, whenever possible, will attempt to avoid it.
2. Since employees dislike work, they must be coerced, controlled, or threatened with punishment to achieve goals.
3. Employees will avoid responsibilities and seek formal direction whenever possible.
4. Most workers place security above all other factors associated with work and will display little ambition.

In contrast to these negative views about the nature of human beings, McGregor listed the four positive assumptions that he called Theory Y:

1. Employees can view work as being as natural as rest or play.
2. People will exercise self-direction and self-control if they are committed to the objectives.
3. The average person can learn to accept, even seek, responsibility.
4. The ability to make innovative decisions is widely dispersed throughout the population and is not necessarily the sole province of those in management positions.

Theory X

The assumption that employees dislike work, are lazy, dislike responsibility, and must be coerced to perform.

Theory Y

The assumption that employees like work, are creative, seek responsibility, and can exercise self-direction.

What are the motivational implications if you accept McGregor's analysis? The answer is best expressed in the framework presented by Maslow. Theory X assumes that lower-order needs dominate individuals. Theory Y assumes that higher-order needs dominate individuals. McGregor himself held to the belief that Theory Y assumptions were more valid than Theory X. Therefore, he proposed such ideas as participative decision making, responsible and challenging jobs, and good group relations as approaches that would maximize an employee's job motivation.

MYTH

"People Are Inherently Lazy"

This statement is false on two levels. *All* people are not inherently lazy; and "laziness" is more a function of the situation than an inherent individual characteristic.

If this statement is meant to imply that *all* people are inherently lazy, the evidence strongly indicates the contrary.[10] Many people today suffer from the opposite affliction—they're overly busy, overworked, and suffer from overexertion. Whether externally motivated or internally driven, a good portion of the labor force is anything *but* lazy.

Managers frequently draw the conclusion that people are lazy from watching some of their employees, who may be lazy at work. But these same employees are often quite industrious in one or more

activities *off* the job. People's need structures differ.[11] As Exhibit 6-2 illustrates, evidence indicates that work needs differ by gender, age, income level, job type, and level in the organization.

Unfortunately for employers, work often ranks low in its ability to satisfy individual needs. So the same employee who shirks responsibility on the job may work obsessively on reconditioning an antique car, maintaining an award-winning garden, perfecting bowling skills, or selling Amway products on weekends. Very few people are perpetually lazy. They merely differ in terms of the activities they most enjoy doing. And because work isn't important to everyone, they may appear lazy.

EXHIBIT 6-2

What Workers Want, Ranked by Subgroups*

	All Employees	Sex		Age				Income Level				Job Type				Organization Level		
		Men	Women	Under 30	31–40	41–50	Over 50	Under $25,000	$25,001–$40,000	$40,001–$50,000	Over $50,000	Blue-Collar Unskilled	Blue-Collar Skilled	White-Collar Unskilled	White-Collar Skilled	Lower Nonsupervisory	Middle Nonsupervisory	Higher Nonsupervisory
Interesting work	1	1	2	4	2	3	1	5	2	1	1	2	1	1	2	3	1	1
Full appreciation of work done	2	2	1	5	3	2	2	4	3	3	2	1	6	3	1	4	2	2
Feeling of being in on things	3	3	3	6	4	1	3	6	1	2	4	5	2	5	4	5	3	3
Job security	4	5	4	2	1	4	7	2	4	4	3	4	3	7	5	2	4	6
Good wages	5	4	5	1	5	5	8	1	5	6	8	3	4	6	6	1	6	8
Promotion and growth in organization	6	6	6	3	6	8	9	3	6	5	7	6	5	4	3	6	5	5
Good working conditions	7	7	10	7	7	7	4	8	7	7	6	9	7	2	7	7	7	4
Personal loyalty to employees	8	8	8	9	9	6	5	7	8	8	5	8	9	9	8	8	8	7
Tactful discipline	9	9	9	8	10	9	10	10	9	9	10	7	10	10	9	9	9	10
Sympathetic help with personal problems	10	10	7	10	8	10	6	9	10	10	9	10	8	8	10	10	10	9

*Ranked from 1 (highest) to 10 (lowest).

Source: Courtesy of Prof. K. A. Kovach, George Mason University. Results are from a study of 1,000 employees conducted in 1995.

Unfortunately, there is no evidence to confirm that either set of assumptions is valid or that accepting Theory Y assumptions and altering one's actions accordingly will lead to more motivated workers. As will become evident later in this chapter, either Theory X or Theory Y assumptions may be appropriate in a particular situation.

Two-Factor Theory

The **two-factor theory** (sometimes also called *motivation-hygiene theory*) was proposed by psychologist Frederick Herzberg.[12] In the belief that an individual's relation to work is basic and that one's attitude toward work can very well determine success or failure, Herzberg investigated the question, "What do people want from their jobs?" He asked people to describe, in detail, situations in which they felt exceptionally *good* or *bad* about their jobs. These responses were then tabulated and categorized.

From the categorized responses, Herzberg concluded that the replies people gave when they felt good about their jobs were significantly different from the replies given when they felt bad. As seen in Exhibit 6-3, certain characteristics tend to be consistently related to job satisfaction and others to job dissatisfaction.

two-factor theory

Intrinsic factors are related to job satisfaction, while extrinsic factors are associated with dissatisfaction.

Comparison of Satisfiers and Dissatisfiers

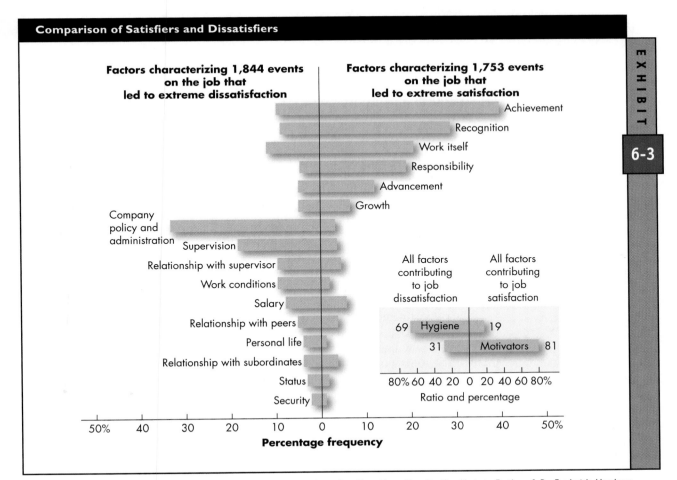

EXHIBIT 6-3

EXHIBIT 6-4 Contrasting Views of Satisfaction and Dissatisfaction

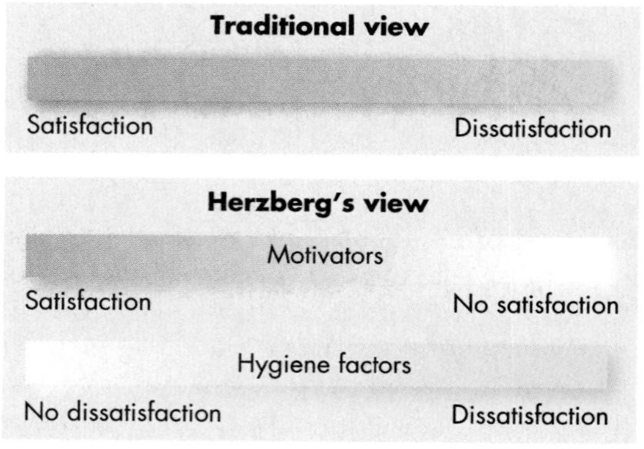

Traditional view

Satisfaction ——————————————— Dissatisfaction

Herzberg's view

Motivators

Satisfaction ——————————————— No satisfaction

Hygiene factors

No dissatisfaction ——————————————— Dissatisfaction

Intrinsic factors, such as advancement, recognition, responsibility, and achievement seem to be related to job satisfaction. Respondents who felt good about their work tended to attribute these factors to themselves. On the other hand, dissatisfied respondents tended to cite extrinsic factors, such as supervision, pay, company policies, and working conditions.

The data suggest, said Herzberg, that the opposite of satisfaction is not dissatisfaction, as was traditionally believed. Removing dissatisfying characteristics from a job does not necessarily make the job satisfying. As illustrated in Exhibit 6-4, Herzberg proposed that his findings indicated the existence of a dual continuum: The opposite of "Satisfaction" is "No Satisfaction," and the opposite of "Dissatisfaction" is "No Dissatisfaction."

According to Herzberg, the factors leading to job satisfaction are separate and distinct from those that lead to job dissatisfaction. Therefore, managers who seek to eliminate factors that can create job dissatisfaction may bring about peace but not necessarily motivation. They will be placating their workforce rather than motivating them. As a result, conditions surrounding the job such as quality of supervision, pay, company policies, physical working conditions, relations with others, and job security were characterized by Herzberg as **hygiene factors**. When they're adequate, people will not be dissatisfied; neither will they be satisfied. If we want to motivate people on their jobs, Herzberg suggested emphasizing factors associated with the work itself or to outcomes directly derived from it, such as promotional opportunities, opportunities for personal growth, recognition, responsibility, and achievement. These are the characteristics that people find intrinsically rewarding.

The two-factor theory is not without detractors.[13] The criticisms of the theory include the following:

1. The procedure that Herzberg used is limited by its methodology. When things are going well, people tend to take credit themselves. Contrarily, they blame failure on the extrinsic environment.
2. The reliability of Herzberg's methodology is questioned. Raters have to make interpretations, so they may contaminate the findings by interpreting one response in one manner while treating a similar response differently.
3. No overall measure of satisfaction was utilized. A person may dislike part of his or her job yet still think the job is acceptable.

hygiene factors

Factors—such as company policy and administration, supervision, and salary—that, when adequate in a job, placate workers. When these factors are adequate, people will not be dissatisfied.

4. The theory is inconsistent with previous research. The two-factor theory ignores situational variables.

5. Herzberg assumed a relationship between satisfaction and productivity, but the research methodology he used looked only at satisfaction not at productivity. To make such research relevant, one must assume a strong relationship between satisfaction and productivity.

Regardless of criticisms, Herzberg's theory has been widely read and few managers are unfamiliar with his recommendations. The popularity over the past 35 years of vertically expanding jobs to allow workers greater responsibility in planning and controlling their work can probably be attributed largely to Herzberg's findings and recommendations.

CONTEMPORARY THEORIES OF MOTIVATION

The previous theories are well known but, unfortunately, have not held up well under close examination. However, all is not lost. There are a number of contemporary theories that have one thing in common—each has a reasonable degree of valid supporting documentation. Of course, this doesn't mean that the theories we are about to introduce are unquestionably right. We call them "contemporary theories" not because they necessarily were developed recently, but because they represent the current state of the art in explaining employee motivation.

ERG Theory

Clayton Alderfer of Yale University has reworked Maslow's need hierarchy to align it more closely with the empirical research. His revised need hierarchy is labeled **ERG theory**.[14]

Alderfer argues that there are three groups of core needs—existence, relatedness, and growth—hence, the label: ERG theory. The *existence* group is concerned with providing our basic material existence requirements. They include the items that Maslow considered to be physiological and safety needs. The second group of needs are those of *relatedness*—the desire we have for maintaining important interpersonal relationships. These social and status desires require interaction with others if they are to be satisfied, and they align with Maslow's social need and the external component of Maslow's esteem classification. Finally, Alderfer isolates *growth* needs—an intrinsic desire for personal development. These include the intrinsic component from Maslow's esteem category and the characteristics included under self-actualization.

Aside from substituting three needs for five, how does Alderfer's ERG theory differ from Maslow's? In contrast to the hierarchy of needs theory, the ERG theory demonstrates that (1) more than one need may be operative at the same time, and (2) if the gratification of a higher-level need is stifled, the desire to satisfy a lower-level need increases.

Maslow's need hierarchy follows a rigid, steplike progression. ERG theory does not assume that there exists a rigid hierarchy in which a lower need must be substantially gratified before one can move on. A person can, for instance, be working on growth even though existence or relatedness needs are unsatisfied; or all three need categories could be operating at the same time.

ERG theory also contains a frustration-regression dimension. Maslow, you'll remember, argued that an individual would stay at a certain need level until that need was satisfied. ERG theory counters by noting that when a higher-order need level is frustrated, the individual's desire to increase a lower-level need takes place.

ERG theory
There are three groups of core needs: existence, relatedness, and growth.

Employees with strong relatedness needs seek friendship and interaction with others at work.

Inability to satisfy a need for social interaction, for instance, might increase the desire for more money or better working conditions. So frustration can lead to a regression to a lower need.

In summary, ERG theory argues, like Maslow's theory, that satisfied lower-order needs lead to the desire to satisfy higher-order needs; but multiple needs can be operating as motivators at the same time, and frustration in attempting to satisfy a higher-level need can result in regression to a lower-level need.

ERG theory is more consistent with our knowledge of individual differences among people. Variables such as education, family background, and cultural environment can alter the importance or driving force that a group of needs holds for a particular individual. The evidence demonstrating that people in other cultures rank the need categories differently—for instance, natives of Spain and Japan place social needs before their physiological requirements[15]—would be consistent with ERG theory. Several studies have supported ERG theory,[16] but there is also evidence that it doesn't work in some organizations.[17] Overall, however, ERG theory represents a more valid version of the need hierarchy.

McClelland's Theory of Needs

You have one beanbag and there are five targets set up in front of you. Each one is progressively farther away and, hence, more difficult to hit. Target A is a cinch. It sits almost within arm's reach of you. If you hit it, you get $2. Target B is a bit farther out, but about 80 percent of the people who try can hit it. It pays $4. Target C pays $8, and about half the people who try can hit it. Very few people can hit Target D, but the payoff is $16 if you do. Finally, Target E pays $32, but it's almost impossible to achieve. Which target would you try for? If you selected C, you're likely to be a high achiever. Why? Read on.

McClelland's theory of needs was developed by David McClelland and his associates.[18] The theory focuses on three needs: achievement, power, and affiliation. They are defined as follows:

- **Need for achievement**: The drive to excel, to achieve in relation to a set of standards, to strive to succeed
- **Need for power**: The need to make others behave in a way that they would not have behaved otherwise
- **Need for affiliation**: The desire for friendly and close interpersonal relationships

Some people have a compelling drive to succeed. They're striving for personal achievement rather than the rewards of success per se. They have a desire to do something better or more efficiently than it has been done before. This drive is the achievement need (*nAch*). From research into the achievement need, McClelland found that high achievers differentiate themselves from others by their desire to do things better.[19] They seek situations in which they can attain personal responsibility for finding solutions to problems, in which they can receive rapid feedback on their performance so they can determine easily whether they are improving or not, and in which they can set moderately challenging goals. High achievers are not gamblers; they dis-

McClelland's theory of needs

Achievement, power, and affiliation are three important needs that help explain motivation.

need for achievement

The drive to excel, to achieve in relation to a set of standards, to strive to succeed.

need for power

The need to make others behave in a way that they would not have behaved otherwise.

need for affiliation

The desire for friendly and close interpersonal relationships.

like succeeding by chance. They prefer the challenge of working at a problem and accepting the personal responsibility for success or failure rather than leaving the outcome to chance or the actions of others. Importantly, they avoid what they perceive to be very easy or very difficult tasks. They prefer tasks of intermediate difficulty.

High achievers perform best when they perceive their probability of success as being 0.5, that is, when they estimate that they have a 50–50 chance of success. They dislike gambling with high odds because they get no achievement satisfaction from happenstance success. Similarly, they dislike low odds (high probability of success) because then there is no challenge to their skills. They like to set goals that require stretching themselves a little.

The need for power (nPow) is the desire to have impact, to be influential, and to control others. Individuals high in nPow enjoy being "in charge," strive for influence over others, prefer to be placed into competitive and status-oriented situations, and tend to be more concerned with prestige and gaining influence over others than with effective performance.

The third need isolated by McClelland is affiliation (nAff). This need has received the least attention from researchers. Individuals with a high affiliation motive strive for friendship, prefer cooperative situations rather than competitive ones, and desire relationships that involve a high degree of mutual understanding.

How do you find out if someone is, for instance, a high achiever? There are questionnaires that tap this motive,[20] but most research uses a projective test in which subjects respond to pictures.[21] Each picture is briefly shown to the subject and then he or she writes a story based on the picture. As an example, the picture may show a male sitting at a desk in a pensive position, looking at a photograph of a woman and two children that sits at the corner of the desk. The subject will then be asked to write a story describing what is going on, what preceded this situation, what will happen in the future, and the like. The stories become, in effect, projective tests that measure unconscious motives. Each story is scored and a subject's ratings on each of the three motives is obtained.

Relying on an extensive amount of research, some reasonably well-supported predictions can be made based on the relationship between achievement need and job performance. Although less research has been done on power and affiliation needs, there are consistent findings here, too.

First, as shown in Exhibit 6-5, individuals with a high need to achieve prefer job situations with personal responsibility, feedback, and an intermediate degree of risk. When these characteristics are prevalent, high achievers will be strongly motivated. The evidence consistently demonstrates, for instance, that high achievers are successful in entrepreneurial activities such as running their own businesses and managing a self-contained unit within a large organization.[22]

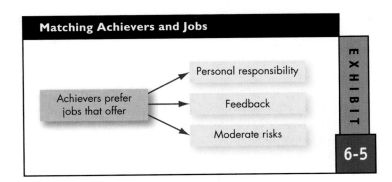

Matching Achievers and Jobs

Achievers prefer jobs that offer → Personal responsibility

→ Feedback

→ Moderate risks

EXHIBIT 6-5

Second, a high need to achieve does not necessarily lead to being a good manager, especially in large organizations. People with a high achievement need are interested in how well they do personally and not in influencing others to do well. High-nAch salespeople do not necessarily make good sales managers, and the good general manager in a large organization does not typically have a high need to achieve.[23]

Third, the needs for affiliation and power tend to be closely related to managerial success. The best managers are high in their need for power and low in their need for affiliation.[24] In fact, a high power motive may be a requirement for managerial effectiveness.[25] Of course, what the cause is and what the effect is are arguable. It has been suggested that a high power need may occur simply as a function of one's level in a hierarchical organization.[26] The latter argument proposes that the higher the level an individual rises to in the organization, the greater is the incumbent's power motive. As a result, powerful positions would be the stimulus to a high power motive.

Finally, employees have been successfully trained to stimulate their achievement need. Trainers have been effective in teaching individuals to think in terms of accomplishments, winning, and success, and then helping them to learn how to *act* in a high achievement way by preferring situations in which they have personal responsibility, feedback, and moderate risks. So if the job calls for a high achiever, management can select a person with a high nAch or develop its own candidate through achievement training.[27]

Cognitive Evaluation Theory

cognitive evaluation theory

Allocating extrinsic rewards for behavior that had been previously intrinsically rewarding tends to decrease the overall level of motivation.

In the late 1960s, one researcher proposed that the introduction of extrinsic rewards, such as pay, for work effort that had been previously intrinsically rewarding due to the pleasure associated with the content of the work itself would tend to decrease the overall level of motivation.[28] This proposal—which has come to be called the **cognitive evaluation theory**—has been extensively researched, and a large number of studies have been supportive.[29] As we'll show, the major implications for this theory relate to the way in which people are paid in organizations.

Historically, motivation theorists generally assumed that intrinsic motivations such as achievement, responsibility, and competence were independent of extrinsic motivators such as high pay, promotions, good supervisor relations, and pleasant working conditions. That is, the stimulation of one would not affect the other. But the cognitive evaluation theory suggests otherwise. It argues that when extrinsic rewards are used by organizations as payoffs for superior performance, the intrinsic rewards, which are derived from individuals doing what they like, are reduced. In other words, when extrinsic rewards are given to someone for performing an interesting task, it causes intrinsic interest in the task itself to decline.

Why would such an outcome occur? The popular explanation is that the individual experiences a loss of control over his or her own behavior so that the previous intrinsic motivation diminishes. Furthermore, the elimination of extrinsic rewards can produce a shift—from an external to an internal explanation—in an individual's perception of causation of why he or she works on a task. If you're reading a novel a week because your English literature instructor requires you to, you can attribute your reading behavior to an external source. However, after the course is over, if you find yourself continuing to read a novel a week, your natural inclination is to say, "I must enjoy reading novels because I'm still reading one a week."

If the cognitive evaluation theory is valid, it should have major implications for managerial practices. It has been a truism among compensation specialists for years that if pay or other extrinsic rewards are to be effective motivators, they should be made contingent on an individual's performance. But, cognitive evaluation theorists would argue that this will only tend to decrease the internal satisfaction that the individual receives from doing the job. We have substituted an external stimulus for an internal stimulus. In fact, if cognitive evaluation theory is correct, it would make sense to make an individual's pay noncontingent on performance in order to avoid decreasing intrinsic motivation.

We noted earlier that the cognitive evaluation theory has been supported in a number of studies. Yet it has also met with attacks, specifically on the methodology used in these studies[30] and in the interpretation of the findings.[31] But where does this theory stand today? Can we say that when organizations use extrinsic motivators such as pay and promotions to stimulate workers' performance they do so at the expense of reducing intrinsic interest and motivation in the work being done? The answer is not a simple "Yes" or "No."

Although further research is needed to clarify some of the current ambiguity, the evidence does lead us to conclude that the interdependence of extrinsic and intrinsic rewards is a real phenomenon.[32] However, its impact on employee motivation at work, in contrast to motivation in general, may be considerably less than originally thought. First, many of the studies testing the theory were done with students, not paid organizational employees. The researchers would observe what happens to a student's behavior when a reward that had been allocated is stopped. This is interesting, but it doesn't represent the typical work situation. In the real world, when extrinsic rewards are stopped, it usually means the individual is no longer part of the organization. Second, evidence indicates that very high intrinsic motivation levels are strongly resistant to the detrimental impacts of extrinsic rewards.[33] Even when a job is inherently interesting, there still exists a powerful norm for extrinsic payment.[34] At the other extreme, on dull tasks extrinsic rewards appear to increase intrinsic motivation.[35] Therefore, the theory may have limited applicability to work organizations because most low-level jobs are not inherently satisfying enough to foster high intrinsic interest and many managerial and professional positions offer intrinsic rewards. Cognitive evaluation theory may be relevant to that set of organizational jobs that falls in between—those that are neither extremely dull nor extremely interesting.

If cognitive evaluation theory is correct in proposing that extrinsic rewards such as pay reduce intrinsic motivations, it seems to be less true for jobs that are inherently interesting, such as a concert violinist.

Goal-Setting Theory

Gene Broadwater, coach of the Hamilton High School cross-country team, gave his squad these last words before they approached the line for the league championship race: "Each one of you is physically ready. Now, get out there and do your best. No one can ever ask more of you than that."

You've heard the phrase a number of times yourself: "Just do your best. That's all anyone can ask for." But what does "do your best" mean? Do we ever know if we've achieved that vague goal? Would the cross-country runners have recorded faster times if Coach Broadwater had given each a specific goal to shoot for? Might you have done better in your high school English class if your parents had said, "You should strive for 85 percent or higher on all your work in English" rather

EXHIBIT

6-6

"What do you *mean* money isn't everything? This is a bank!"

Source: From the *Wall Street Journal*, February 8, 1995. Reprinted with permission of Cartoon Features Syndicate.

goal-setting theory

The theory that specific and difficult goals, with feedback, lead to higher performance.

than telling you to "do your best"? The research on **goal-setting theory** addresses these issues, and the findings, as you will see, are impressive in terms of the effect that goal specificity, challenge, and feedback have on performance.

In the late 1960s, Edwin Locke proposed that intentions to work toward a goal are a major source of work motivation.[36] That is, goals tell an employee what needs to be done and how much effort will need to be expended.[37] The evidence strongly supports the value of goals. More to the point, we can say that specific goals increase performance; that difficult goals, when accepted, result in higher performance than do easy goals; and that feedback leads to higher performance than does nonfeedback.[38]

Specific hard goals produce a higher level of output than does the generalized goal of "do your best." The specificity of the goal itself acts as an internal stimulus. For instance, when a trucker commits to making 12 round-trip hauls between Toronto and Buffalo, New York, each week, this intention gives him a specific objective to try to attain. We can say that, all things being equal, the trucker with a specific goal will outperform his or her counterpart operating with no goals or the generalized goal of "do your best."

If factors such as ability and acceptance of the goals are held constant, we can also state that the more difficult the goal, the higher the level of performance. However, it's logical to assume that easier goals are more likely to be accepted. But once an employee accepts a hard task, he or she will exert a high level of effort until it is achieved, lowered, or abandoned.

People will do better when they get feedback on how well they are progressing toward their goals because feedback helps to identify discrepancies between what they have done and what they want to do; that is, feedback acts to guide behavior. But all feedback is not equally potent. Self-generated feedback—for which the employee is able to monitor his or her own progress—has been shown to be a more powerful motivator than externally generated feedback.[39]

If employees have the opportunity to participate in the setting of their own goals, will they try harder? The evidence is mixed regarding the superiority of participative over assigned goals.[40] In some cases, participatively set goals elicited superior performance, while in other cases, individuals performed best when assigned goals by their boss. But a major advantage of participation may be in increasing acceptance of the goal itself as a desirable one toward which to work.[41] As we noted, resistance is greater when goals are difficult. If people participate in goal setting, they are more likely to accept even a difficult goal than if they are arbitrarily assigned it by their boss. The reason is that individuals are more committed to choices in which they have a part. Thus, although participative goals may have no superiority over assigned goals when acceptance is taken as a given, participation does increase the probability that more difficult goals will be agreed to and acted on.

Are there any contingencies in goal-setting theory or can we take it as a universal truth that difficult and specific goals will always lead to higher performance? In addition to feedback, four other factors have been found to influence the goals–performance relationship. These are goal commitment, adequate self-efficacy, task characteristics, and national culture. Goal-setting theory presupposes that an individual is committed to the goal; that is, is determined not to lower or abandon the goal. This is most likely to occur when goals are made public, when the individual has an internal locus of control, and when the goals are self-set rather than assigned.[42] **Self-efficacy** refers to an individual's belief that he or she is capable of performing a task.[43] The higher your self-efficacy, the more confidence you have in your ability to succeed in a task. So, in difficult situations, we find that people with low self-efficacy are more likely to lessen their effort or give up altogether, while those with high self-efficacy will try harder to master the challenge.[44] In addition, individuals high in self-efficacy seem to respond to negative feedback with increased effort and motivation, while those low in self-efficacy are likely to lessen their effort when given negative feedback.[45]

Research indicates that individual goal setting doesn't work equally well on all tasks. The evidence suggests that goals seem to have a more substantial effect on performance when tasks are simple rather than complex, well-learned rather than novel, and independent rather than interdependent.[46] On interdependent tasks, group goals are preferable. Finally, goal-setting theory is culture bound. It's well adapted to countries like the United States and Canada because its key components align reasonably well with North American cultures. It assumes that employees will be reasonably independent (not too high a score on power distance), that managers and employees will seek challenging goals (low in uncertainty avoidance), and that performance is considered important by both (high in quantity of life). So don't expect goal setting to necessarily lead to higher employee performance in countries such as Portugal or Chile, where the opposite conditions exist.

Our overall conclusion is that intentions—as articulated in terms of hard and specific goals—are a potent motivating force. Under the proper conditions, they can lead to higher performance. However, there is no evidence that such goals are associated with increased job satisfaction.[47]

Reinforcement Theory

A counterpoint to goal-setting theory is **reinforcement theory**. The former is a cognitive approach, proposing that an individual's purposes direct his or her action. In reinforcement theory, we have a behavioristic approach, which argues that reinforcement conditions behavior. The two are clearly at odds

self-efficacy
The individual's belief that he or she is capable of performing a task.

reinforcement theory
Behavior is a function of its consequences.

philosophically. Reinforcement theorists see behavior as being environmentally caused. You need not be concerned, they would argue, with internal cognitive events; what controls behavior are reinforcers—any consequence that, when immediately following a response, increases the probability that the behavior will be repeated.

Reinforcement theory ignores the inner state of the individual and concentrates solely on what happens to a person when he or she takes some action. Because it does not concern itself with what initiates behavior, it is not, strictly speaking, a theory of motivation. But it does provide a powerful means of analysis of what controls behavior, and it is for this reason that it is typically considered in discussions of motivation.[48]

We discussed the reinforcement process in detail in Chapter 2. We showed how using reinforcers to condition behavior gives us considerable insight into how people learn. Yet we cannot ignore the fact that reinforcement has a wide following as a motivational device. In its pure form, however, reinforcement theory ignores feelings, attitudes, expectations, and other cognitive variables that are known to impact behavior. In fact, some researchers look at the same experiments that reinforcement theorists use to support their position and interpret the findings in a cognitive framework.[49]

Reinforcement is undoubtedly an important influence on behavior, but few scholars are prepared to argue that it is the only influence. The behaviors you engage in at work and the amount of effort you allocate to each task are affected by the consequences that follow from your behavior. If you are consistently reprimanded for outproducing your colleagues, you will likely reduce your productivity. But your lower productivity may also be explained in terms of goals, inequity, or expectancies.

Flow and Intrinsic Motivation Theory

The "flow" experience arises more often at work than during leisure. It is characterized by intense concentration and motivation that centers on the process more than on the goal. Chef Benjamin Ford experiences "the flow" as he prepares a flaming dish at Chadwick's in Los Angeles.

Can you think of times in your life when you've been so deeply involved in something that nothing else seems to matter? The task consumes you totally and you lose track of time. Most people can. It's likely to occur when you're doing a favorite activity: running, skiing, dancing, reading a novel, playing a computer game, listening to music, cooking an elegant meal. Athletes commonly refer to it as being "in the zone." But as we'll show, it can also occur at work. Motivation researchers call this state of absolute concentration *flow*.[50]

The Flow Experience A key element of the flow experience is that its motivation is unrelated to end goals. The activity people are pursuing when they achieve the timelessness feeling of flow comes from the process of the activity itself rather than trying to reach a goal. So when a person experiences flow, he or she is completely intrinsically motivated.

Do people typically feel happy when they're experiencing flow? The answer, which might surprise you, is No. They're too consumed in deep concentration. But when the flow task is completed, and the person looks back on what has happened, he or she is flooded with feelings of gratitude for the experience. It's then that the satisfaction received from the experience is realized. And it's the desire to repeat the experience that creates continued motivation.

Are there conditions that are likely to produce flow? Yes. When people have described flow experiences, they talked about common characteristics in the tasks they were doing. The tasks were challenging and required using a high level of skills. They were goal-directed and had feedback on how well they were performing. The tasks demanded total concentration and creativity. And the tasks were so consuming that people had no attention left over to think about anything irrelevant or to worry about problems. Note again, though, that although the task was goal-directed, it wasn't the goal that provided the motivation. It was the task.

One of the most surprising research findings related to flow is that it's not associated with leisure. The flow experience, in fact, is rarely reported by people when they're doing leisure activities such as watching television or relaxing. Another surprise is that it's more likely to be experienced at work than at home.

If you ask people if they'd like to work less, the answer is almost always Yes. People link leisure with happiness. They think if they had more free time, they'd be happier. Studies of thousands of people suggests that people are generally wrong in this belief. When people spend time at home, for instance, they often lack a clear purpose, don't know how well they're doing, get distracted, and feel that their skills are underused. They frequently describe themselves as bored. But work has many of the properties that stimulate flow. It usually has clear goals. It provides people with feedback on how well they're doing—either from the work process itself or through a boss's evaluation. People's skills are typically matched to their jobs, which provides challenge. And jobs usually encourage concentration and prevent distractions.

A Model of Intrinsic Motivation   A clearer understanding of flow has been offered in Ken Thomas's model of intrinsic motivation.[51] This extension of the flow concept identifies the key elements that create intrinsic motivation.

Thomas describes employees as intrinsically motivated when they genuinely care about their work, look for better ways to do it, and are energized and fulfilled by doing it well. As with flow, the rewards an employee gets from intrinsic motivation comes from the work itself rather than from external factors like increases in pay or compliments from the boss.

Thomas's model proposes that intrinsic motivation is achieved when people experience feelings of choice, competence, meaningfulness, and progress. He defines these components as follows:

Choice is the opportunity to be able to select task activities that make sense to you and to perform them in ways that seem appropriate.

Competence is the accomplishment you feel in skillfully performing task activities you've chosen.

Meaningfulness is the opportunity to pursue a worthy task purpose; a purpose that matters in the larger scheme of things.

Progress is feeling that you're making significant advancement in achieving the task's purpose.

Thomas reports a number of studies demonstrating that these four components of intrinsic motivation are significantly related to improved job satisfaction and increased performance as rated by supervisors.[52] However, almost all the studies reported by Thomas were done with professional and managerial employees. Whether these four components will predict intrinsic motivation with, for example, rank-and-file blue-collar workers, is currently unclear.

Note how Thomas's four intrinsic-motivation components link with the concept of flow. When a task is *meaningful*, people find themselves resenting the time they have to spend on other, less meaningful tasks. They're totally absorbed in the intrinsic task, thinking about it all the time. We should even expect them to borrow time from other activities in order to devote more time to something that's meaningful. When a task provides a flow experience, a person typically is free to *choose* to work on that task in contrast to others. *Competence* also stimulates the flow experience. We tend to be "most engaged in a task when we are performing activities most competently—having all our attention on meeting the challenge of the activities we are performing."[53] Finally, *progress* enhances feelings that our time and efforts are paying off. You feel enthusiastic about the task and are eager to keep investing your time and effort in it.

Equity Theory

Jane Pearson graduated last year from the State University with a degree in accounting. After interviews with a number of organizations on campus, she accepted a position with one of the nation's largest public accounting firms and was assigned to their Boston office. Jane was very pleased with the offer she received: challenging work with a prestigious firm, an excellent opportunity to gain valuable experience, and the highest salary any accounting major at State was offered last year—$4,550 a month. But Jane was the top student in her class; she was ambitious and articulate and fully expected to receive a commensurate salary.

Twelve months have passed since Jane joined her employer. The work has proved to be as challenging and satisfying as she had hoped. Her employer is extremely pleased with her performance; in fact, she recently received a $200-a-month raise. However, Jane's motivational level has dropped dramatically in the past few weeks. Why? Her employer has just hired a fresh college graduate out of State University, who lacks the one-year experience Jane has gained, for $4,800 a month—$50 more than Jane now makes! It would be an understatement to describe Jane in any other terms than irate. Jane is even talking about looking for another job.

Jane's situation illustrates the role that equity plays in motivation. Employees make comparisons of their job inputs (i.e., effort, experience, education, competence) and outcomes (i.e., salary levels, raises, recognition) relative to those of others. We perceive what we get from a job situation (outcomes) in relation to what we put into it (inputs), and then we compare our outcome-input ratio with the outcome-input ratio of relevant others. This is shown in Exhibit 6-7. If we perceive our ratio to be equal to that of the relevant others with whom we compare our-

EXHIBIT 6-7	Equity Theory	
	Ratio Comparisons*	**Perception**
	$O/I_A < O/I_B$	Inequity due to being underrewarded
	$O/I_A = O/I_B$	Equity
	$O/I_A > O/I_B$	Inequity due to being overrewarded

*Where O/I_A represents the employee; and O/I_B represents relevant others.

selves, a state of equity is said to exist. We perceive our situation as fair—that justice prevails. When we see the ratio as unequal, we experience equity tension. When we see ourselves as underrewarded, the tension creates anger; when overrewarded, the tension creates guilt. J. Stacy Adams has proposed that this negative tension state provides the motivation to do something to correct it.[54]

The referent that an employee selects adds to the complexity of **equity theory**. Evidence indicates that the referent chosen is an important variable in equity theory.[55] There are four referent comparisons that an employee can use:

1. *Self-inside:*   An employee's experiences in a different position inside his or her current organization
2. *Self-outside:*   An employee's experiences in a situation or position outside his or her current organization
3. *Other-inside:*   Another individual or group of individuals inside the employee's organization
4. *Other-outside:*   Another individual or group of individuals outside the employee's organization

Employees might compare themselves to friends, neighbors, co-workers, or colleagues in other organizations or compare their present job with past jobs they themselves have had. Which referent an employee chooses will be influenced by the information the employee holds about referents as well as by the attractiveness of the referent. This has led to focusing on four moderating variables—gender, length of tenure, level in the organization, and amount of education or professionalism.[56] Research shows that both men and women prefer same-sex comparisons. The research also demonstrates that women are typically paid less than men in comparable jobs and have lower pay expectations than men for the same work. So a woman who uses another woman as a referent tends to calculate a lower comparative standard. This leads us to conclude that employees in jobs that are not sex segregated will make more cross-sex comparisons than those in jobs that are either male- or female-dominated. This also suggests that if women are tolerant of lower pay, it may be due to the comparative standard they use.

Employees with short tenure in their current organizations tend to have little information about others inside the organization, so they rely on their own personal experiences. On the other hand, employees with long tenure rely more heavily on co-workers for comparison. Upper-level employees, those in the professional ranks, and those with higher amounts of education tend to be more cosmopolitan and have better information about people in other organizations. Therefore, these types of employees will make more other-outside comparisons.

Based on equity theory, when employees perceive an inequity, they can be predicted to make one of six choices[57]:

1. Change their inputs (for example, don't exert as much effort)
2. Change their outcomes (for example, individuals paid on a piece-rate basis can increase their pay by producing a higher quantity of units of lower quality)
3. Distort perceptions of self (for example, "I used to think I worked at a moderate pace but now I realize that I work a lot harder than everyone else.")
4. Distort perceptions of others (for example, "Mike's job isn't as desirable as I previously thought it was.")
5. Choose a different referent (for example, "I may not make as much as my brother-in-law, but I'm doing a lot better than my Dad did when he was my age.")
6. Leave the field (for example, quit the job)

equity theory
Individuals compare their job inputs and outcomes with those of others and then respond to eliminate any inequities.

Pedro Martinez, star pitcher for the Boston Red Sox, missed six days of team drills in February 2001 because of a salary dispute. Although he was scheduled to make $12.5 million for the season, the future Hall of Famer with two back-to-back Cy Young awards wanted more money. As the top pitcher in baseball, Martinez was frustrated that he was not earning more than many pitchers with far less impressive statistics.

The theory establishes the following propositions relating to inequitable pay:

A. *Given payment by time, overrewarded employees will produce more than will equitably paid employees.* Hourly and salaried employees will generate high quantity or quality of production in order to increase the input side of the ratio and bring about equity.

B. *Given payment by quantity of production, overrewarded employees will produce fewer, but higher-quality, units than will equitably paid employees.* Individuals paid on a piece-rate basis will increase their effort to achieve equity, which can result in greater quality or quantity. However, increases in quantity will only increase inequity, since every unit produced results in further overpayment. Therefore, effort is directed toward increasing quality rather than increasing quantity.

C. *Given payment by time, underrewarded employees will produce less or poorer quality of output.* Effort will be decreased, which will bring about lower productivity or poorer-quality output than equitably paid subjects.

D. *Given payment by quantity of production, underrewarded employees will produce a large number of low-quality units in comparison with equitably paid employees.* Employees on piece-rate pay plans can bring about equity because trading off quality of output for quantity will result in an increase in rewards with little or no increase in contributions.

These propositions have generally been supported, with a few minor qualifications.[58] First, inequities created by overpayment do not seem to have a very significant impact on behavior in most work situations. Apparently, people have a great deal more tolerance of overpayment inequities than of underpayment inequities, or are better able to rationalize them.[59] Second, not all people are equity sensitive. For example, there is a small part of the working population who actually prefer that their outcome-input ratio be less than the referent comparison. Predictions from equity theory are not likely to be very accurate with these "benevolent types."

It's also important to note that while most research on equity theory has focused on pay, employees seem to look for equity in the distribution of other organizational rewards. For instance, it has been shown that the use of high-status job titles as well as large and lavishly furnished offices may function as outcomes for some employees in their equity equation.[60]

Finally, recent research has been directed at expanding what is meant by equity or fairness.[61] Historically, equity theory focused on **distributive justice** or the perceived fairness of the *amount and allocation* of rewards among individuals. But equity should also consider **procedural justice**—the perceived fairness of the *process* used to determine the distribution of rewards. The evidence indicates that distributive justice has a greater influence on employee satisfaction than procedural justice, while procedural justice tends to affect an employee's organizational commitment, trust in his or her boss, and intention to quit.[62] As a result, managers should consider openly sharing information on how allocation decisions are made, following consistent and unbiased procedures, and engaging in similar practices to increase the perception of procedural justice. By increasing the perception of procedural fairness, employees are likely to view their bosses and the organization as positive even if they are dissatisfied with pay, promotions, and other personal outcomes. Moreover, as noted in Chapter 3, organizational citizenship behavior is significantly influenced by perceptions of fairness. Specifically, evidence indicates that although distributive justice issues such as pay are impor-

distributive justice

Perceived fairness of the amount and allocation of rewards among individuals.

procedural justice

The perceived fairness of the process used to determine the distribution of rewards.

tant, perceptions of procedural justice are particularly relevant to OCB.[63] So another plus from employees' perceptions of fair treatment is that they will be more satisfied and reciprocate by volunteering for extra job activities, helping others, and engaging in similar positive behaviors.

In conclusion, equity theory demonstrates that, for most employees, motivation is influenced significantly by relative rewards as well as by absolute rewards, but some key issues are still unclear.[64] For instance, how do employees handle conflicting equity signals, such as when unions point to other employee groups who are substantially *better off*, while management argues how much things have *improved*? How do employees define inputs and outcomes? How do they combine and weigh their inputs and outcomes to arrive at totals? When and how do the factors change over time? Yet, regardless of these problems, equity theory continues to offer us some important insights into employee motivation.

Expectancy Theory

Currently, one of the most widely accepted explanations of motivation is Victor Vroom's **expectancy theory**.[65] Although it has its critics,[66] most of the evidence is supportive of the theory.[67]

Expectancy theory argues that the strength of a tendency to act in a certain way depends on the strength of an expectation that the act will be followed by a given outcome and on the attractiveness of that outcome to the individual. In more practical terms, expectancy theory says that an employee will be motivated to exert a high level of effort when he or she believes that effort will lead to a good performance appraisal; that a good appraisal will lead to organizational rewards such as a bonus, a salary increase, or a promotion; and that the rewards will satisfy the employee's personal goals. The theory, therefore, focuses on three relationships (see Exhibit 6-8).

expectancy theory

The strength of a tendency to act in a certain way depends on the strength of an expectation that the act will be followed by a given outcome and on the attractiveness of that outcome to the individual.

1. *Effort–performance relationship.* The probability perceived by the individual that exerting a given amount of effort will lead to performance.
2. *Performance–reward relationship.* The degree to which the individual believes that performing at a particular level will lead to the attainment of a desired outcome.
3. *Rewards–personal goals relationship.* The degree to which organizational rewards satisfy an individual's personal goals or needs and the attractiveness of those potential rewards for the individual.[68]

Expectancy theory helps explain why a lot of workers aren't motivated on their jobs and do only the minimum necessary to get by. This is evident when we look at the theory's three relationships in a little more detail. We present them as questions employees need to answer in the affirmative if their motivation is to be maximized.

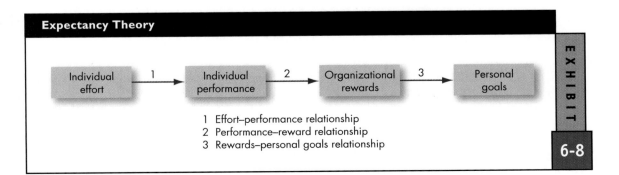

Expectancy Theory

Individual effort → 1 → Individual performance → 2 → Organizational rewards → 3 → Personal goals

1 Effort–performance relationship
2 Performance–reward relationship
3 Rewards–personal goals relationship

EXHIBIT 6-8

First, *if I give a maximum effort, will it be recognized in my performance appraisal?* For a lot of employees, the answer is No. Why? Their skill level may be deficient, which means that no matter how hard they try, they're not likely to be a high performer. The organization's performance appraisal system may be designed to assess nonperformance factors such as loyalty, initiative, or courage, which means more effort won't necessarily result in a higher evaluation. Still another possibility is that the employee, rightly or wrongly, perceives that her boss doesn't like her. As a result, she expects to get a poor appraisal regardless of her level of effort. These examples suggest that one possible source of low employee motivation is the belief by the employee that no matter how hard she works, the likelihood of getting a good performance appraisal is low.

Second, *if I get a good performance appraisal, will it lead to organizational rewards?* Many employees see the performance–reward relationship in their job as weak. The reason, as we elaborate on in the next chapter, is that organizations reward a lot of things besides just performance. For example, when pay is allocated to employees based on factors such as seniority, being cooperative, or for "kissing up" to the boss, employees are likely to see the performance–reward relationship as being weak and demotivating.

Finally, *if I'm rewarded, are the rewards ones that I find personally attractive*? The employee works hard in hope of getting a promotion but gets a pay raise instead. Or the employee wants a more interesting and challenging job but receives only a few words of praise. Or the employee puts in extra effort to be relocated to the company's Paris office but instead is transferred to Singapore. These examples illustrate the importance of the rewards being tailored to individual employee needs. Unfortunately, many managers are limited in the rewards they can distribute, which makes it difficult to individualize rewards. Moreover, some managers incorrectly assume that all employees want the same thing, thus overlooking the motivational effects of differentiating rewards. In either case, employee motivation is submaximized.

In summary, the key to expectancy theory is the understanding of an individual's goals and the linkage between effort and performance, between performance and rewards, and, finally, between the rewards and individual goal satisfaction. As a contingency model, expectancy theory recognizes that there is no universal principle for explaining everyone's motivations. In addition, just because we understand what needs a person seeks to satisfy does not ensure that the individual perceives high performance as necessarily leading to the satisfaction of these needs.

Does expectancy theory work? Attempts to validate the theory have been complicated by methodological, criterion, and measurement problems. As a result, many published studies that purport to support or negate the theory must be viewed with caution. Importantly, most studies have failed to replicate the methodology as it was originally proposed. For example, the theory proposes to explain different levels of effort from the same person under different circumstances, but almost all replication studies have looked at different people. Correcting for this flaw has greatly improved support for the validity of expectancy theory.[69] Some critics suggest that the theory has only limited use, arguing that it tends to be more valid for predicting in situations in which effort–performance and performance–reward linkages are clearly perceived by the individual.[70] Because few individuals perceive a high correlation between performance and rewards in their jobs, the theory tends to be idealistic. If organizations actually rewarded individuals for performance rather than according to such criteria as seniority, effort, skill level, and job difficulty, then the theory's validity might be considerably greater. However, rather than invalidating expectancy theory, this criticism can be used in support of the theory, because it explains why a significant segment of the workforce exerts low levels of effort in carrying out job responsibilities.

Don't Forget Ability and Opportunity

Robin and Chris both graduated from college a couple of years ago with their degrees in elementary education. They each took jobs as first-grade teachers, but in different school districts. Robin immediately confronted a number of obstacles on the job: a large class (42 students), a small and dingy classroom, and inadequate supplies. Chris's situation couldn't have been more different. He had only 15 students in his class, plus a teaching aide for 15 hours each week, a modern and well-lighted room, a well-stocked supply cabinet, six iMac computers for students to use, and a highly supportive principal. Not surprisingly, at the end of their first school year, Chris had been considerably more effective as a teacher than had Robin.

Earl Berg (right), a manager at the Trane division of plumbing-supply manufacturer American Standard, applies the expectancy theory of motivation with team leader Perry Gilbert. Gilbert has told Berg about his desire to achieve a promotion. Berg, as shown here, clarifies to Gilbert his performance expectations that will lead to this reward.

The preceding episode illustrates an obvious but often overlooked fact. Success on a job is facilitated or hindered by the existence or absence of support resources.

A popular, although arguably simplistic, way of thinking about employee performance is as a function (f) of the interaction of ability (A) and motivation (M); that is, performance = $f(A \times M)$. If either is inadequate, performance will be negatively affected. This helps to explain, for instance, the hard-working athlete or student with modest abilities who consistently outperforms his or her more gifted, but lazy, rival. So, as we noted in Chapter 2, an individual's intelligence and skills (subsumed under the label *ability*) must be considered in addition to motivation if we are to be able to accurately explain and predict employee performance. But a piece of the puzzle is still missing. We need to add **opportunity to perform** (O) to our equation performance = $f(A \times M \times O)$.[71] Even though an individual may be willing and able, there may be obstacles that constrain performance. This is shown in Exhibit 6-9 on page 176.

opportunity to perform
High levels of performance are partially a function of an absence of obstacles that constrain the employee.

When you attempt to assess why an employee may not be performing to the level that you believe he or she is capable of, take a look at the work environment to see if it's supportive. Does the employee have adequate tools, equipment, materials, and supplies? Does the employee have favorable working conditions, helpful co-workers, supportive work rules and procedures, sufficient information to make job-related decisions, adequate time to do a good job, and the like? If not, performance will suffer.

INTEGRATING CONTEMPORARY THEORIES OF MOTIVATION

We've looked at a lot of motivation theories in this chapter. The fact that a number of these theories have been supported only complicates the matter. How simple it would have been if, after presenting several theories, only one was found

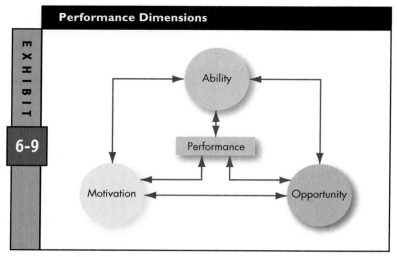

Performance Dimensions

EXHIBIT 6-9

Ability

Performance

Motivation

Opportunity

Source: Adapted from M. Blumberg and C. D. Pringle, "The Missing Opportunity in Organizational Research: Some Implications for a Theory of Work Performance," *Academy of Management Review* (October 1982), p. 565.

valid. But these theories are not all in competition with one another. Because one is valid doesn't automatically make the others invalid. In fact, many of the theories presented in this chapter are complementary. The challenge is now to tie these theories together to help you understand their interrelationships.[72]

Exhibit 6-10 presents a model that integrates much of what we know about motivation. Its basic foundation is the expectancy model shown in Exhibit 6-8. Let's work through Exhibit 6-10.

We begin by explicitly recognizing that opportunities can aid or hinder individual effort. The individual effort box also has another arrow leading into it. This arrow flows out of the person's goals. Consistent with goal-setting theory, this goals–effort loop is meant to remind us that goals direct behavior.

Expectancy theory predicts that an employee will exert a high level of effort if he or she perceives that there is a strong relationship between effort and performance, performance and rewards, and rewards and satisfaction of personal goals. Each of these relationships, in turn, is influenced by certain factors. For effort to lead to good performance, the individual must have the requisite ability to perform, and the performance appraisal system that measures the individual's performance must be perceived as being fair and objective. The performance–reward relationship will be strong if the individual perceives that it is performance (rather than seniority, personal favorites, or other criteria) that is rewarded. If cognitive evaluation theory were fully valid in the actual workplace, we would predict here that basing rewards on performance should decrease the individual's intrinsic motivation. The final link in expectancy theory is the rewards–goals relationship. ERG theory would come into play at this point. Motivation would be high to the degree that the rewards an individual received for his or her high performance satisfied the dominant needs consistent with his or her individual goals.

A closer look at Exhibit 6-10 will also reveal that the model considers the achievement need, intrinsic motivation, and reinforcement and equity theories. The high achiever is not motivated by the organization's assessment of his or her performance or organizational rewards, hence, the jump from effort to personal goals for those with a high nAch. Remember, high achievers are internally driven

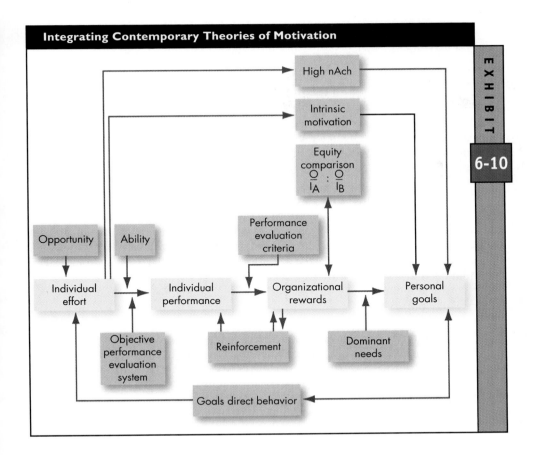

EXHIBIT

6-10

as long as the jobs they are doing provide them with personal responsibility, feedback, and moderate risks. They are not concerned with the effort–performance, performance–rewards, or rewards–goal linkages. Similarly, if tasks create intrinsic motivation as a result of providing choice, competence, meaningfulness, and progress, then individual effort should be internally driven toward goals.

Reinforcement theory enters our model by recognizing that the organization's rewards reinforce the individual's performance. If management has designed a reward system that is seen by employees as "paying off" for good performance, the rewards will reinforce and encourage continued good performance. Rewards also play the key part in equity theory. Individuals will compare the rewards (outcomes) they receive from the inputs they make with the outcome-input ratio of relevant others ($O/I_A:O/I_B$), and inequities may influence the effort expended.

CAVEAT EMPTOR: MOTIVATION THEORIES ARE CULTURE-BOUND

In our discussion of goal setting, we said that care needs to be taken in applying this theory because it assumes cultural characteristics that are not universal. This is true for many of the theories presented in this chapter. Most current motivation theories were developed in the United States by Americans and about Americans.[73] Maybe the most blatant pro-American characteristic inherent in these theories is the strong emphasis on what we defined in Chapter 3 as individualism and quantity of life. For

Motivation is culture-bound. Maslow's social needs, for instance, would be at the top of the need hierarchy in the Netherlands, whereas self-actualization is at the top in the United States.

instance, both goal-setting and expectancy theories emphasize goal accomplishment as well as rational and individual thought. Let's take a look at several motivation theories and consider their cross-cultural transferability.

Maslow's need hierarchy argues that people start at the physiological level and then move progressively up the hierarchy in this order: physiological, safety, social, esteem, and self-actualization. This hierarchy, if it has any application at all, aligns with American culture. In countries like Japan, Greece, and Mexico, where uncertainty avoidance characteristics are strong, security needs would be on top of the need hierarchy. Countries that score high on quality-of-life characteristics—Denmark, Sweden, Norway, the Netherlands, and Finland—would have social needs on top.[74] We would predict, for instance, that group work will motivate employees more when the country's culture scores high on the quality criterion.

Another motivation concept that clearly has an American bias is the achievement need. The view that a high achievement need acts as an internal motivator presupposes two cultural characteristics—a willingness to accept a moderate degree of risk (which excludes countries with strong uncertainty avoidance characteristics) and a concern with performance (which applies almost singularly to countries with strong quantity-of-life characteristics). This combination is found in Anglo-American countries like the United States, Canada, and Great Britain.[75] On the other hand, these characteristics are relatively absent in countries such as Chile and Portugal.

Equity theory has gained a relatively strong following in the United States. That's not surprising since U.S.-style reward systems are based on the assumption that workers are highly sensitive to equity in reward allocations. And in the United States, equity is meant to closely tie pay to performance. However, recent evidence suggests that in collectivist cultures, especially in the former socialist countries of Central and Eastern Europe, employees expect rewards to reflect their individual needs as well as their performance.[76] Moreover, consistent with a legacy of communism and centrally planned economies, employees exhibited an entitlement attitude—that is, they expected outcomes to be *greater* than their inputs.[77] These findings suggest that U.S.-style pay practices may need modification, especially in Russia and former communist countries, in order to be perceived as fair by employees.

But don't assume there are *no* cross-cultural consistencies. For instance, the desire for interesting work seems important to almost all workers, regardless of their national culture. In a study of seven countries, employees in Belgium, Britain, Israel, and the United States ranked "interesting work" number one among 11 work goals. And this factor was ranked either second or third in Japan, the Netherlands, and Germany.[78] Similarly, in a study comparing job-preference outcomes among graduate students in the United States, Canada, Australia, and Singapore, growth, achievement, and responsibility were rated the top three and had identical rankings.[79] Both of these studies suggest some universality to the importance of intrinsic factors in the two-factor theory.

SUMMARY AND IMPLICATIONS FOR MANAGERS

The theories we've discussed in this chapter address different outcome variables. Some, for instance, are directed at explaining turnover, while others emphasize productivity. The theories also differ in their predictive strength. In this section, we (1) review the most established motivation theories to determine their relevance in explaining our dependent variables, and (2) assess the predictive power of each.[80]

Need Theories   We introduced four theories that focused on needs. These were Maslow's hierarchy, two-factor, ERG, and McClelland's needs theories. The strongest of these is probably the last, particularly regarding the relationship between achievement and productivity. If the other three have any value at all, that value relates to explaining and predicting job satisfaction.

Goal-Setting Theory   There is little dispute that clear and difficult goals lead to higher levels of employee productivity. This evidence leads us to conclude that goal-setting theory provides one of the more powerful explanations of this dependent variable. The theory, however, does not address absenteeism, turnover, or satisfaction.

Reinforcement Theory   This theory has an impressive record for predicting factors like quality and quantity of work, persistence of effort, absenteeism, tardiness, and accident rates. It does not offer much insight into employee satisfaction or the decision to quit.

Equity Theory   Equity theory deals with all four dependent variables. However, it is strongest when predicting absence and turnover behaviors and weak when predicting differences in employee productivity.

Expectancy Theory   Our final theory focused on performance variables. It has proved to offer a relatively powerful explanation of employee productivity, absenteeism, and turnover. But expectancy theory assumes that employees have few constraints on their decision discretion. It makes many of the same assumptions that the rational model makes about individual decision making (see Chapter 5). This acts to restrict its applicability.

For major decisions, like accepting or resigning from a job, expectancy theory works well because people don't rush into decisions of this nature. They're more prone to take the time to carefully consider the costs and benefits of all the alternatives. However, expectancy theory is not a very good explanation for more typical types of work behavior, especially for individuals in lower-level jobs, because such jobs come with considerable limitations imposed by work methods, supervisors, and company policies. We would conclude, therefore, that expectancy theory's power in explaining employee productivity increases when the jobs being performed are more complex and higher in the organization (where discretion is greater).

Money Motivates!

Behavioral scientists tend to downplay money as a motivator. They prefer to emphasize the importance of challenging jobs, goals, participative decision making, feedback, cohesive work teams, and other nonmonetary factors. We argue otherwise here—that is, money is *the* critical incentive to work motivation.

Money is important to employees because it's a medium of exchange. People may not work *only* for money, but take the money away and how many people would come to work? A study of nearly 2,500 employees found that although these people disagreed over what was their number-one motivator, they unanimously chose money as their number two.[a]

As equity theory suggests, money has symbolic value in addition to its exchange value. We use pay as the primary outcome against which we compare our inputs to determine if we are being treated equitably. That an organization pays one executive $80,000 a year and another $95,000 means more than the latter's earning $15,000 a year more. It's a message, from the organization to both employees, of how much it values the contribution of each.

In addition to equity theory, both reinforcement and expectancy theories attest to the value of money as a motivator.[b] In the former, if pay is contingent on performance, it will encourage workers to generate high levels of effort. Consistent with expectancy theory, money will motivate to the extent that it is seen as being able to satisfy an individual's personal goals and is perceived as being dependent on performance criteria.

However, maybe the best case for money is a review of studies that looked at four methods of motivating employee performance: money, goal setting, participative decision making, and redesigning jobs to give workers more challenge and responsibility. The average improvement from money was consistently higher than with any of the other methods.[c]

Money can motivate *some* people under *some* conditions, so the issue isn't really whether or not money can motivate. The answer to that is: "It can!" The more relevant question is: Does money motivate most employees in the workforce today? The answer to this question, we'll argue, is No.

For money to motivate an individual's performance, certain conditions must be met. First, money must be important to the individual. But money isn't important to everybody. High achievers, for instance, are intrinsically motivated. Money would have little impact on these people.

Second, money must be perceived by the individual as being a direct reward for performance. Unfortunately, performance and pay are poorly linked in most organizations. Pay increases are far more often determined by non–performance factors such as experience, community pay standards, or company profitability.

Third, the marginal amount of money offered for the performance must be perceived by the individual as being significant. Research indicates that merit raises must be at least 7 percent of base pay for employees to perceive them as motivating. Unfortunately, recent data indicates average merit increases are only in the 3.9 to 4.4 percent range.[d]

Finally, management must have the discretion to reward high performers with more money. But unions and organizational compensation policies constrain managerial discretion. Where unions exist, that discretion is almost zero. In nonunionized environments, traditional limited compensation grades create severe restrictions on pay increases. For example, in one organization, a Systems Analyst IV's pay grade ranges from $4,775 to $5,500 a month. No matter how good a job that analyst does, her boss cannot pay her more than $5,500 a month. Similarly, no matter how poorly she performs, she will not earn less than $4,775. So money might be theoretically capable of motivating employee performance, but most managers aren't given enough flexibility to do much about it.

[a]S. Caudron, "Motivation? Money's Only No. 2," *Industry Week*, November 15, 1993, p. 33.

[b]T. R. Mitchell and A. E. Mickel, "The Meaning of Money: An Individual-Difference Perspective," *Academy of Management Review*, July 1999, p. 570.

[c]E. A. Locke et al., "The Relative Effectiveness of Four Methods of Motivating Employee Performance," in K. D. Duncan, M. M. Gruenberg, and D. Wallis (eds.), *Changes in Working Life* (London: Wiley, 1980), pp. 363–83.

[d]A. Mitra, N. Gupta, and G. D. Jenkins Jr., "The Case of the Invisible Merit Raise: How People See Their Pay Raises," *Compensation & Benefits Review*, May–June 1995, pp. 71–76; and Hewitt Associates Salary Survey, 2000.

1. Does motivation come from within a person or is it a result of the situation? Explain.

2. What are the implications of Theories X and Y for motivation practices?

3. Compare and contrast Maslow's hierarchy of needs theory with (a) Alderfer's ERG theory and (b) Herzberg's two-factor theory.

4. Describe the three needs isolated by McClelland. How are they related to worker behavior?

5. Explain cognitive evaluation theory. How applicable is it to management practice?

6. What is the role of self-efficacy in goal setting?

7. Contrast distributive and procedural justice. What implications might they have for designing pay systems in different countries?

8. Identify the variables in expectancy theory.

9. Explain the formula: Performance $= f(A \times M \times O)$ and give an example.

10. What consistencies among motivation concepts, if any, apply cross-culturally?

Questions for Critical Thinking

1. "The cognitive evaluation theory is contradictory to reinforcement and expectancy theories." Do you agree or disagree? Explain.

2. "Managers should be able, through proper selection and job design, to have every employee experience flow in his or her job." Do you agree or disagree? Discuss.

3. Analyze the application of Maslow's and Herzberg's theories to an African or Caribbean nation where more than a quarter of the population is unemployed.

4. Can an individual be too motivated, so that his or her performance declines as a result of excessive effort? Discuss.

5. Identify three activities you really enjoy (for example, playing tennis, reading a novel, going shopping). Next, identify three activities you really dislike (for example, going to the dentist, cleaning the house, staying on a restricted-calorie diet). Using the expectancy model, analyze each of your answers to assess why some activities stimulate your effort while others do not.

Team Exercise   What Do People Want from Their Jobs?

Each class member begins by completing the following questionnaire:

Rate the following 12 job factors according to how important each is to you. Place a number on a scale of 1 to 5 on the line before each factor.

Very important		Somewhat important		Not important
5	4	3	2	1

_____ 1. An interesting job
_____ 2. A good boss
_____ 3. Recognition and appreciation for the work I do
_____ 4. The opportunity for advancement
_____ 5. A satisfying personal life
_____ 6. A prestigious or status job
_____ 7. Job responsibility
_____ 8. Good working conditions
_____ 9. Sensible company rules, regulations, procedures, and policies
_____ 10. The opportunity to grow through learning new things
_____ 11. A job I can do well and succeed at
_____ 12. Job security

This questionnaire taps the dimensions in Herzberg's two-factor theory. To determine if hygiene or motivating factors are important to you, place the numbers 1–5 that represent your answers below.

Hygiene factors score	Motivational factors score
2. _____	1. _____
5. _____	3. _____
6. _____	4. _____
8. _____	7. _____
9. _____	10. _____
12. _____	11. _____
Total points _____	Total points _____

Add up each column. Did you select hygiene or motivating factors as being most important to you?

Now break into groups of five or six and compare your questionnaire results. (a) How similar are your scores? (b) How close did your group's results come to those found by Herzberg? (c) What motivational implications did your group arrive at based on your analysis?

Source: This exercise is based on R. N. Lussier, *Human Relations in Organizations: A Skill Building Approach*, 2nd ed. Homewood, IL: Irwin, 1993. Reprinted with permission.

Case Incident | **What Drives Employees at Microsoft?**

The reality of software development in a huge company like Microsoft—it employs more than 48,000 people—is that a substantial portion of your work involves days of boredom punctuated by hours of tedium. You basically spend your time in an isolated office writing code and sitting in meetings during which you participate in looking for and evaluating hundreds of bugs and potential bugs. Yet Microsoft has no problem in finding and retaining software programmers. Their programmers work horrendously long hours and obsess on the goal of shipping product.

From the day new employees begin work at Microsoft, they know they're special and that their employer is special. New hires all have one thing in common—they're smart. The company prides itself on putting all recruits through a grueling "interview loop," during which they confront a barrage of brain-teasers by future colleagues to see how well they think. Only the best and the brightest survive to become employees. The company does this because Microsofties truly believe that their company is special. For instance, it has a high tolerance for nonconformity. Would you believe that one software tester comes to work every day

dressed in extravagant Victorian outfits? But the underlying theme that unites Microsofties is the belief that the firm has a manifest destiny to change the world. The least consequential decision by a programmer can have an outsized importance when it can effect a new release that might be used by 50 million people.

Microsoft employees are famous for putting in long hours. One program manager said, "In my first five years, I was the Microsoft stereotype. I lived on caffeine and vending-machine hamburgers and free beer and 20-hour workdays. . . . I had no life. . . . I considered everything outside the building as a necessary evil." More recently, things have changed. There are still a number of people who put in 80-hour weeks, but 60- and 70-hour weeks are more typical and some even are doing their jobs in only 40 hours.

No discussion of employee life at Microsoft would be complete without mentioning the company's lucrative stock option program. Microsoft created more millionaire employees, faster, than any company in American history—more than 10,000 by the late-1990s. While the company is certainly more than a place to get rich, executives still realize that money matters. One former manager claims that the human resources' department actually kept a running chart of employee satisfaction versus the company's stock price. "When the stock was up, human resources could turn off the ventilation and everybody would say they were happy. When the stock was down, we could give people massages and they would tell us that the massages were too hard." In the go-go 1990s, when Microsoft stock was doubling every few months and yearly stock splits were predictable, employees not only got to participate in Microsoft's manifest destiny, they could get rich in the process. By the spring of 2002, with the world in a recession, stock prices down, and the growth for Microsoft products slowing, it wasn't so clear what was driving its employees to continue the company's dominance of the software industry.

Questions

1. If you were a programmer, would you want to work at Microsoft? Why or why not?

2. How many activities in this case can you tie into specific motivation theories? List the activities, the motivation theories, and how they apply.

3. As Microsoft continues to get larger and its growth rate flattens, do you think management will have to modify any of its motivation practices? Elaborate.

Source: Based on M. Gimein, "Smart Is Not Enough!" *Fortune*, January 8, 2001, pp. 124–36.

Endnotes

1. Cited in D. Jones, "Firms Spend Billions to Fire Up Workers—With Little Luck," *USA Today*, May 10, 2001, p. 1A.
2. Ibid.
3. C. A. O'Reilly III, "Organizational Behavior: Where We've Been, Where We're Going," in M. R. Rosenzweig and L. W. Porter (eds.), *Annual Review of Psychology*, vol. 42 (Palo Alto, CA: Annual Reviews, Inc., 1991), p. 431. See also M. L. Ambrose and C. T. Kulik, "Old Friends, New Faces: Motivation Research in the 1990s," *Journal of Management*, vol. 25, no. 3, 1999, pp. 231–92.
4. See, for instance, T. R. Mitchell, "Matching Motivational Strategies with Organizational Contexts," in L. L. Cummings and B. M. Staw (eds.), *Research in Organizational Behavior*, vol. 19 (Greenwich, CT: JAI Press, 1997), pp. 60–62.
5. A. Maslow, *Motivation and Personality* (New York: Harper & Row, 1954).
6. See, for example, E. E. Lawler III and J. L. Suttle, "A Causal Correlation Test of the Need Hierarchy Concept," *Organizational Behavior and Human Performance*, April 1972, pp. 265–87; D. T. Hall and K. E. Nougaim, "An Examination of Maslow's Need Hierarchy in an Organizational Setting," *Organizational Behavior and Human Performance*, February 1968, pp. 12–35; and J. Rauschenberger, N. Schmitt, and J. E. Hunter, "A Test of the Need Hierarchy Concept by a Markov Model of Change in Need Strength," *Administrative Science Quarterly*, December 1980, pp. 654–70.
7. A. K. Korman, J. H. Greenhaus, and I. J. Badin, "Personnel Attitudes and Motivation," in M. R. Rosenzweig and L. W. Porter (eds.), *Annual Review of Psychology* (Palo Alto, CA: Annual Reviews, 1977), pp. 178–79.
8. M. A. Wahba and L. G. Bridwell, "Maslow Reconsidered: A Review of Research on the Need Hierarchy Theory," *Organizational Behavior and Human Performance*, April 1976, pp. 212–40.
9. D. McGregor, *The Human Side of Enterprise* (New York: McGraw-Hill, 1960). For an updated analysis of Theory X and Theory Y constructs, see R. J. Summers and S. F. Cronshaw, "A Study of McGregor's Theory X, Theory Y and the Influence of Theory X, Theory Y Assumptions on Causal Attributions for Instances of Worker Poor Performance," in S. L. McShane (ed.), Organizational Behavior, *ASAC 1988 Conference Proceedings*, vol. 9, Part 5. Halifax, Nova Scotia, 1988, pp. 115–23.
10. See, for example, E. E. Lawler III, *Motivation in Work Organizations* (Belmont, CA: Brooks/Cole, 1973); B. Weiner, *Human Motivation* (New York: Holt, Rinehart, and Winston, 1980); and K. W. Thomas, *Intrinsic Motivation at Work* (San Francisco: Berrett-Koehler, 2000).
11. See, for instance, K. A. Kovach, "What Motivates Employees? Workers and Supervisors Give Different Answers," *Business Horizons*, September–October 1987, p. 61. This research was updated in 1995 and reported in a paper by K. A. Kovach, "Employee Motivation: Addressing a Crucial Factor in Your Organization's Performance," Fairfax, VA: George Mason University.
12. F. Herzberg, B. Mausner, and B. Snyderman, *The Motivation to Work* (New York: Wiley, 1959).
13. R. J. House and L. A. Wigdor, "Herzberg's Dual-Factor Theory of Job Satisfaction and Motivations: A Review of the Evidence and Criticism," *Personnel Psychology*, Winter

1967, pp. 369–89; D. P. Schwab and L. L. Cummings, "Theories of Performance and Satisfaction: A Review," *Industrial Relations*, October 1970, pp. 403–30; R. J. Caston and R. Braito, "A Specification Issue in Job Satisfaction Research," *Sociological Perspectives*, April 1985, pp. 175–97; and J. Phillipchuk and J. Whittaker, "An Inquiry into the Continuing Relevance of Herzberg's Motivation Theory," *Engineering Management Journal*, vol. 8, 1996, pp. 15–20.

14. C. P. Alderfer, "An Empirical Test of a New Theory of Human Needs," *Organizational Behavior and Human Performance*, May 1969, pp. 142–75.

15. M. Haire, E. E. Ghiselli, and L. W. Porter, "Cultural Patterns in the Role of the Manager," *Industrial Relations*, February 1963, pp. 95–117.

16. C. P. Schneider and C. P. Alderfer, "Three Studies of Measures of Need Satisfaction in Organizations," *Administrative Science Quarterly*, December 1973, pp. 489–505; and I. Borg and M. Braun, "Work Values in East and West Germany: Different Weights, But Identical Structures," *Journal of Organizational Behavior*, vol. 17, special issue, 1996, pp. 541–55.

17. J. P. Wanous and A. Zwany, "A Cross-Sectional Test of Need Hierarchy Theory," *Organizational Behavior and Human Performance*, May 1977, pp. 78–97.

18. D. C. McClelland, *The Achieving Society* (New York: Van Nostrand Reinhold, 1961); J. W. Atkinson and J. O. Raynor, *Motivation and Achievement* (Washington, D.C.: Winston, 1974); D. C. McClelland, *Power: The Inner Experience* (New York: Irvington, 1975); and M. J. Stahl, *Managerial and Technical Motivation: Assessing Needs for Achievement, Power, and Affiliation* (New York: Praeger, 1986).

19. McClelland, *The Achieving Society*.

20. See, for example, A. Mehrabian, "Measures of Achieving Tendency," *Educational and Psychological Measurement*, Summer 1969, pp. 445–51; H. J. M. Hermans, "A Questionnaire Measure of Achievement Motivation," *Journal of Applied Psychology*, August 1970, pp. 353–63; and J. M. Smith, "A Quick Measure of Achievement Motivation," *British Journal of Social and Clinical Psychology*, June 1973, pp. 137–43.

21. See W. D. Spangler, "Validity of Questionnaire and TAT Measures of Need for Achievement: Two Meta-Analyses," *Psychological Bulletin*, July 1992, pp. 140–54.

22. D. C. McClelland and D. G. Winter, *Motivating Economic Achievement* (New York: Free Press, 1969); and J. B. Miner, N. R. Smith, and J. S. Bracker, "Role of Entrepreneurial Task Motivation in the Growth of Technologically Innovative Firms: Interpretations from Follow-up Data," *Journal of Applied Psychology*, October 1994, pp. 627–30.

23. D. C. McClelland, *Power*; D. C. McClelland and D. H. Burnham, "Power Is the Great Motivator," *Harvard Business Review*, March–April 1976, pp. 100–10; and R. E. Boyatzis, "The Need for Close Relationships and the Manager's Job," in D. A. Kolb, I. M. Rubin, and J. M. McIntyre, *Organizational Psychology: Readings on Human Behavior in Organizations*, 4th ed. (Upper Saddle River, NJ: Prentice Hall, 1984), pp. 81–86.

24. D. G. Winter, "The Motivational Dimensions of Leadership: Power, Achievement, and Affiliation," in R. E. Riggio, S. E. Murphy, and F. J. Pirozzolo (eds.), *Multiple Intelligences and Leadership* (Mahwah, NJ: Lawrence Erlbaum, 2002), pp. 119–38.

25. J. B. Miner, *Studies in Management Education* (New York: Springer, 1965).

26. D. Kipnis, "The Powerholder," in J. T. Tedeschi (ed.), *Perspectives in Social Power* (Chicago: Aldine, 1974), pp. 82–123.

27. D. McClelland, "Toward a Theory of Motive Acquisition," *American Psychologist*, May 1965, pp. 321–33; and D. Miron and D. C. McClelland, "The Impact of Achievement Motivation Training on Small Businesses," *California Management Review*, Summer 1979, pp. 13–28.

28. R. de Charms, *Personal Causation: The Internal Affective Determinants of Behavior* (New York: Academic Press, 1968).

29. E. L. Deci, *Intrinsic Motivation* (New York: Plenum, 1975); J. Cameron and W. D. Pierce, "Reinforcement, Reward, and Intrinsic Motivation: A Meta-Analysis," *Review of Educational Research*, Fall 1994, pp. 363–423; and S. Tang and V. C. Hall, "The Overjustification Effect: A Meta-Analysis," *Applied Cognitive Psychology*, October 1995, pp. 365–404.

30. W. E. Scott, "The Effects of Extrinsic Rewards on 'Intrinsic Motivation': A Critique," *Organizational Behavior and Human Performance*, February 1976, pp. 117–19; B. J. Calder and B. M. Staw, "Interaction of Intrinsic and Extrinsic Motivation: Some Methodological Notes," *Journal of Personality and Social Psychology*, January 1975, pp. 76–80; and K. B. Boal and L. L. Cummings, "Cognitive Evaluation Theory: An Experimental Test of Processes and Outcomes," *Organizational Behavior and Human Performance*, December 1981, pp. 289–310.

31. G. R. Salancik, "Interaction Effects of Performance and Money on Self-Perception of Intrinsic Motivation," *Organizational Behavior and Human Performance*, June 1975, pp. 339–51; and F. Luthans, M. Martinko, and T. Kess, "An Analysis of the Impact of Contingency Monetary Rewards on Intrinsic Motivation," *Proceedings of the Nineteenth Annual Midwest Academy of Management*, St. Louis, 1976, pp. 209–21.

32. J. B. Miner, *Theories of Organizational Behavior* (Hinsdale, IL: Dryden Press, 1980), p. 157.

33. H. J. Arnold, "Effects of Performance Feedback and Extrinsic Reward upon High Intrinsic Motivation," *Organizational Behavior and Human Performance*, December 1976, pp. 275–88.

34. B. M. Staw, "Motivation in Organizations: Toward Synthesis and Redirection," in B. M. Staw and G. R. Salancik (eds.), *New Directions in Organizational Behavior* (Chicago: St. Clair, 1977), p. 76.

35. B. J. Calder and B. M. Staw, "Self-Perception of Intrinsic and Extrinsic Motivation," *Journal of Personality and Social Psychology*, April 1975, pp. 599–605.

36. E. A. Locke, "Toward a Theory of Task Motivation and Incentives," *Organizational Behavior and Human Performance*, May 1968, pp. 157–89.

37. P. C. Earley, P. Wojnaroski, and W. Prest, "Task Planning and Energy Expended: Exploration of How Goals Influence Performance," *Journal of Applied Psychology*, February 1987, pp. 107–14.

38. G. P. Latham and G. A. Yukl, "A Review of Research on the Application of Goal Setting in Organizations," *Academy of Management Journal*, December 1975, pp. 824–45; E. A. Locke, K. N. Shaw, L. M. Saari, and G. P. Latham, "Goal Setting and Task Performance," *Psychological Bulletin*, January

1981, pp. 125–52; A. J. Mento, R. P. Steel, and R. J. Karren, "A Meta-Analytic Study of the Effects of Goal Setting on Task Performance: 1966–1984," *Organizational Behavior and Human Decision Processes*, February 1987, pp. 52–83; M. E. Tubbs "Goal Setting: A Meta-Analytic Examination of the Empirical Evidence," *Journal of Applied Psychology*, August 1986, pp. 474–83; E. A. Locke and G. P. Latham, *A Theory of Goal Setting and Task Performance* (Upper Saddle River, NJ: Prentice Hall, 1990); J. C. Wofford, V. L. Goodwin, and S. Premack, "Meta-Analysis of the Antecedents of Personal Goal Level and of the Antecedents and Consequences of Goal Commitment," *Journal of Management*, vol. 18, no. 3, 1992, pp. 595–615; and E. A. Locke, "Motivation through Conscious Goal Setting," *Applied and Preventive Psychology*, vol. 5, 1996, pp. 117–24.

39. J. M. Ivancevich and J. T. McMahon, "The Effects of Goal Setting, External Feedback, and Self-Generated Feedback on Outcome Variables: A Field Experiment," *Academy of Management Journal*, June 1982, pp. 359–72; and E. A. Locke, "Motivation through Conscious Goal Setting."

40. See, for example, G. P. Latham, M. Erez, and E. A. Locke, "Resolving Scientific Disputes by the Joint Design of Crucial Experiments by the Antagonists: Application to the Erez-Latham Dispute Regarding Participation in Goal Setting," *Journal of Applied Psychology*, November 1988, pp. 753–72; T. D. Ludwig and E. S. Geller, "Assigned versus Participative Goal Setting and Response Generalization: Managing Injury Control among Professional Pizza Deliverers," *Journal of Applied Psychology*, April 1997, pp. 253–61; and S. G. Harkins and M. D. Lowe, "The Effects of Self-Set Goals on Task Performance," *Journal of Applied Social Psychology*, January 2000, pp. 1–40.

41. M. Erez, P. C. Earley, and C. L. Hulin, "The Impact of Participation on Goal Acceptance and Performance: A Two-Step Model," *Academy of Management Journal*, March 1985, pp. 50–66.

42. J. R. Hollenbeck, C. R. Williams, and H. J. Klein, "An Empirical Examination of the Antecedents of Commitment to Difficult Goals," *Journal of Applied Psychology,* February 1989, pp. 18–23. See also J. C. Wofford, V. L. Goodwin, and S. Premack, "Meta-Analysis of the Antecedents of Personal Goal Level and of the Antecedents and Consequences of Goal Commitment," *Journal of Management*, September 1992, pp. 595–615; and M. E. Tubbs, "Commitment as a Moderator of the Goal-Performance Relation: A Case for Clearer Construct Definition," *Journal of Applied Psychology*, February 1993, pp. 86–97.

43. A. Bandura, *Self-Efficacy: The Exercise of Control* (New York: Freeman, 1997).

44. E. A. Locke, E. Frederick, C. Lee, and P. Bobko, "Effect of Self-Efficacy, Goals, and Task Strategies on Task Performance," *Journal of Applied Psychology*, May 1984, pp. 241–51; M. E. Gist and T. R. Mitchell, "Self-Efficacy: A Theoretical Analysis of Its Determinants and Malleability," *Academy of Management Review*, April 1992, pp. 183–211; and A. D. Stajkovic and F. Luthans, "Self-Efficacy and Work-Related Performance: A Meta-Analysis," *Psychological Bulletin*, September 1998, pp. 240–61.

45. A. Bandura and D. Cervone, "Differential Engagement in Self-Reactive Influences in Cognitively-Based Motivation," *Organizational Behavior and Human Decision Processes*, August 1986, pp. 92–113.

46. See R. E. Wood, A. J. Mento, and E. A. Locke, "Task Complexity as a Moderator of Goal Effects: A Meta Analysis," *Journal of Applied Psychology*, August 1987, pp. 416–25; R. Kanfer and P. L. Ackerman, "Motivation and Cognitive Abilities: An Integrative/Aptitude-Treatment Interaction Approach to Skill Acquisition," *Journal of Applied Psychology (monograph)*, vol. 74, 1989, pp. 657–90; T. R. Mitchell and W. S. Silver, "Individual and Group Goals When Workers Are Interdependent: Effects on Task Strategies and Performance," *Journal of Applied Psychology*, April 1990, pp. 185–93; and A. M. O'Leary-Kelly, J. J. Martocchio, and D. D. Frink, "A Review of the Influence of Group Goals on Group Performance," *Academy of Management Journal*, October 1994, pp. 1285–301.

47. See J. C. Anderson and C. A. O'Reilly, "Effects of an Organizational Control System on Managerial Satisfaction and Performance," *Human Relations*, June 1981, pp. 491–501; and J. P. Meyer, B. Schacht-Cole, and I. R. Gellatly, "An Examination of the Cognitive Mechanisms by Which Assigned Goals Affect Task Performance and Reactions to Performance," *Journal of Applied Social Psychology*, vol. 18, no. 5, 1988, pp. 390–408.

48. J. L. Komaki, T. Coombs, and S. Schepman, "Motivational Implications of Reinforcement Theory," in R. M. Steers, L. W. Porter, and G. Bigley (eds.), *Motivation and Work Behavior*, 6th ed. (New York: McGraw-Hill, 1996), pp. 87–107.

49. E. A. Locke, "Latham vs. Komaki: A Tale of Two Paradigms," *Journal of Applied Psychology*, February 1980, pp. 16–23.

50. M. Csikszentmihalyi, *Flow: The Psychology of Optimal Experience* (New York: HarperCollins, 1990); M. Csikszentmihalyi, *Finding Flow* (New York: Basic Books, 1997); and C. Mainemelis, "When the Muse Takes It All: A Model for the Experience of Timelessness in Organizations," *Academy of Management Review*, October 2001, pp. 548–65.

51. This section is based on K. W. Thomas, *Intrinsic Motivation at Work*; and K. W. Thomas, "Intrinsic Motivation and How It Works," *Training*, October 2000, pp. 130–35.

52. As reported in K. W. Thomas and W. G. Tymon, Jr., "Bridging the Motivation Gap in Total Quality," *Quality Management Journal*, vol. 4, no. 2, 1997, p. 89.

53. K. W. Thomas, *Intrinsic Motivation at Work*, p. 79.

54. J. S. Adams, "Inequity in Social Exchanges," in L. Berkowitz (ed.), *Advances in Experimental Social Psychology* (New York: Academic Press, 1965), pp. 267–300.

55. P. S. Goodman, "An Examination of Referents Used in the Evaluation of Pay," *Organizational Behavior and Human Performance*, October 1974, pp. 170–95; S. Ronen, "Equity Perception in Multiple Comparisons: A Field Study," *Human Relations*, April 1986, pp. 333–46; R. W. Scholl, E. A. Cooper, and J. F. McKenna, "Referent Selection in Determining Equity Perception: Differential Effects on Behavioral and Attitudinal Outcomes," *Personnel Psychology*, Spring 1987, pp. 113–27; and T. P. Summers and A. S. DeNisi, "In Search of Adams' Other: Reexamination of Referents Used in the Evaluation of Pay," *Human Relations*, June 1990, pp. 497–511.

56. C. T. Kulik and M. L. Ambrose, "Personal and Situational Determinants of Referent Choice," *Academy of Management Review*, April 1992, pp. 212–37.

57. See, for example, E. Walster, G. W. Walster, and W. G. Scott, *Equity: Theory and Research* (Boston: Allyn & Bacon, 1978); and J. Greenberg, "Cognitive Reevaluation of Outcomes in Response to Underpayment Inequity," *Academy of Management Journal*, March 1989, pp. 174–84.

58. P. S. Goodman and A. Friedman, "An Examination of Adams' Theory of Inequity," *Administrative Science Quarterly*, September 1971, pp. 271–88; R. P. Vecchio, "An Individual-Differences Interpretation of the Conflicting Predictions Generated by Equity Theory and Expectancy Theory," *Journal of Applied Psychology*, August 1981, pp. 470–81; J. Greenberg, "Approaching Equity and Avoiding Inequity in Groups and Organizations," in J. Greenberg and R. L. Cohen (eds.), *Equity and Justice in Social Behavior* (New York: Academic Press, 1982), pp. 389–435; R. T. Mowday, "Equity Theory Predictions of Behavior in Organizations," in R. Steers, L. W. Porter, and G. Bigley (eds.), *Motivation and Work Behavior*, 6th ed. (New York: McGraw-Hill, 1996), pp. 111–31; S. Werner and N. P. Mero, "Fair or Foul? The Effects of External, Internal, and Employee Equity on Changes in Performance of Major League Baseball Players," *Human Relations*, October 1999, pp. 1291–1312; and R. W. Griffeth and S. Gaertner, "A Role for Equity Theory in the Turnover Process: An Empirical Test," *Journal of Applied Social Psychology*, May 2001, pp. 1017–37.

59. See, for example, K. S. Sauley and A. G. Bedeian, "Equity Sensitivity: Construction of a Measure and Examination of Its Psychometric Properties," *Journal of Management*, vol. 26, no. 5, 2000, pp. 885–910; and M. N. Bing and S. M. Burroughs, "The Predictive and Interactive Effects of Equity Sensitivity in Teamwork-Oriented Organizations," *Journal of Organizational Behavior*, May 2001, pp. 271–90.

60. J. Greenberg and S. Ornstein, "High Status Job Title as Compensation for Underpayment: A Test of Equity Theory," *Journal of Applied Psychology*, May 1983, pp. 285–97; and J. Greenberg, "Equity and Workplace Status: A Field Experiment," *Journal of Applied Psychology*, November 1988, pp. 606–13.

61. See, for instance, J. Greenberg, *The Quest for Justice on the Job* (Thousand Oaks, CA: Sage, 1996); R. Cropanzano and J. Greenberg, "Progress in Organizational Justice: Tunneling through the Maze," in C. L. Cooper and I. T. Robertson (eds.), *International Review of Industrial and Organizational Psychology*, vol. 12 (New York: Wiley, 1997); and J. A. Colquitt, D. E. Conlon, M. J. Wesson, C. O. L. H. Porter, and K. Y. Ng, "Justice at the Millennium: A Meta-Analytic Review of the 25 Years of Organizational Justice Research," *Journal of Applied Psychology*, June 2001, pp. 425–45.

62. See, for example, R. C. Dailey and D. J. Kirk, "Distributive and Procedural Justice as Antecedents of Job Dissatisfaction and Intent to Turnover," *Human Relations*, March 1992, pp. 305–16; D. B. McFarlin and P. D. Sweeney, "Distributive and Procedural Justice as Predictors of Satisfaction with Personal and Organizational Outcomes," *Academy of Management Journal*, August 1992, pp. 626–37; and M. A. Konovsky, "Understanding Procedural Justice and Its Impact on Business Organizations," *Journal of Management*, vol. 26, no. 3, 2000, pp. 489–511.

63. R. H. Moorman, "Relationship Between Justice and Organizational Citizenship Behaviors: Do Fairness Perceptions Influence Employee Citizenship?" *Journal of Applied Psychology*, December 1991, pp. 845–55.

64. P. S. Goodman, "Social Comparison Process in Organizations," in B. M. Staw and G. R. Salancik (eds.), *New Directions in Organizational Behavior* (Chicago: St. Clair, 1977), pp. 97–132; and J. Greenberg, "A Taxonomy of Organizational Justice Theories," *Academy of Management Review*, January 1987, pp. 9–22.

65. V. H. Vroom, *Work and Motivation* (New York: John Wiley, 1964).

66. See, for example, H. G. Heneman III and D. P. Schwab, "Evaluation of Research on Expectancy Theory Prediction of Employee Performance," *Psychological Bulletin*, July 1972, pp. 1–9; T. R. Mitchell, "Expectancy Models of Job Satisfaction, Occupational Preference and Effort: A Theoretical, Methodological and Empirical Appraisal," *Psychological Bulletin*, November 1974, pp. 1053–77; and L. Reinharth and M. A. Wahba, "Expectancy Theory as a Predictor of Work Motivation, Effort Expenditure, and Job Performance," *Academy of Management Journal*, September 1975, pp. 502–37.

67. See, for example, L. W. Porter and E. E. Lawler III, *Managerial Attitudes and Performance* (Homewood, IL: Irwin, 1968); D. F. Parker and L. Dyer, "Expectancy Theory as a Within-Person Behavioral Choice Model: An Empirical Test of Some Conceptual and Methodological Refinements," *Organizational Behavior and Human Performance*, October 1976, pp. 97–117; H. J. Arnold, "A Test of the Multiplicative Hypothesis of Expectancy-Valence Theories of Work Motivation," *Academy of Management Journal*, April 1981, pp. 128–41; and W. Van Eerde and H. Thierry, "Vroom's Expectancy Models and Work-Related Criteria: A Meta-Analysis," *Journal of Applied Psychology*, October 1996, pp. 575–86.

68. Vroom refers to these three variables as expectancy, instrumentality, and valence, respectively.

69. P. M. Muchinsky, "A Comparison of Within- and Across-Subjects Analyses of the Expectancy-Valence Model for Predicting Effort," *Academy of Management Journal*, March 1977, pp. 154–58.

70. R. J. House, H. J. Shapiro, and M. A. Wahba, "Expectancy Theory as a Predictor of Work Behavior and Attitudes: A Re-evaluation of Empirical Evidence," *Decision Sciences*, January 1974, pp. 481–506.

71. L. H. Peters, E. J. O'Connor, and C. J. Rudolf, "The Behavioral and Affective Consequences of Performance-Relevant Situational Variables," *Organizational Behavior and Human Performance*, February 1980, pp. 79–96; M. Blumberg and C. D. Pringle, "The Missing Opportunity in Organizational Research: Some Implications for a Theory of Work Performance," *Academy of Management Review*, October 1982, pp. 560–69; D. A. Waldman and W. D. Spangler, "Putting Together the Pieces: A Closer Look at the Determinants of Job Performance," *Human Performance*, vol. 2, 1989, pp. 29–59; and J. Hall, "Americans Know How to Be Productive If Managers Will Let Them," *Organizational Dynamics*, Winter 1994, pp. 33–46.

72. For other examples of models that seek to integrate motivation theories, see H. J. Klein, "An Integrated Control Theory Model of Work Motivation," *Academy of Management Review,* April 1989, pp. 150–72; E. A. Locke, "The Motivation Sequence, the Motivation Hub, and the Motivation Core," *Organizational Behavior and Human Decision Processes*, December 1991, pp. 288–99; and T. R. Mitchell, "Matching Motivational Strategies with Organizational Contexts," in *Research in Organizational Behavior.*

73. N. J. Adler, *International Dimensions of Organizational Behavior*, 4th ed. (Cincinnati, OH: Southwestern, 2002), p. 174.

74. G. Hofstede, "Motivation, Leadership, and Organization: Do American Theories Apply Abroad?" *Organizational Dynamics*, Summer 1980, p. 55.

75. Ibid.

76. J. K. Giacobbe-Miller, D. J. Miller, and V. I. Victorov, "A Comparison of Russian and U.S. Pay Allocation Decisions, Distributive Justice Judgments, and Productivity under Different Payment Conditions," *Personnel Psychology*, Spring 1998, pp. 137–63.

77. S. L. Mueller and L. D. Clarke, "Political-Economic Context and Sensitivity to Equity: Differences between the United States and the Transition Economies of Central and Eastern Europe," *Academy of Management Journal*, June 1998, pp. 319–29.

78. I. Harpaz, "The Importance of Work Goals: An International Perspective," *Journal of International Business Studies*, First Quarter 1990, pp. 75–93.

79. G. E. Popp, H. J. Davis, and T. T. Herbert, "An International Study of Intrinsic Motivation Composition," *Management International Review*, January 1986, pp. 28–35.

80. This section is based on F. J. Landy and W. S. Becker, "Motivation Theory Reconsidered," in L. L. Cummings and B. M. Staw (eds.), *Research in Organizational Behavior*, vol. 9 (Greenwich, CT: JAI Press, 1987), pp. 24–35.

PART TWO

THE INDIVIDUAL

In 1983, when Ricardo Semler's father handed him control of the family's small Brazilian company, Semco, a maker of industrial machinery, the business was on the verge of bankruptcy.[1] While only 22 years old and short on experience, Semler (see photo) recognized he had to take some drastic steps if he was to save the company. Ironically, his youth and naiveté may have worked to his advantage. He wasn't bogged down with traditional notions of how a business was supposed to be run.

What Semler proceeded to do was downright radical for the time. He fired most of the company's top managers, cut out almost all of the firm's bureaucratic overhead, and eliminated nearly all job titles. In place of a hierarchical structure, he basically turned the company over to his employees. He allowed people to interview and select their own coworkers. He told employees to set their own salaries and work schedules. He opened up the company's books and encouraged workers to learn how to read the firm's financial statements. And he allowed workers to choose their managers by vote, to evaluate them regularly, and to post the evaluations on bulletin boards for everyone to see. Today, although Semler owns the company, he likes to boast that he hasn't made a decision in 10 years and hasn't had his own office in 14 years. The job of CEO at Semco is transitory—with half-a-dozen senior managers trading the title every 6 months.

Semler's radical approach has been an overwhelming success. In the 20 years since he took over, sales have grown at a 24 percent annual rate. Since 1996 alone, profits have tripled and employment has gone from 350 to 2,500. The annual turnover of employees averages less than one percent—against an industry average closer to 20 percent. When Semler is asked to what he attributes Semco's success, he quickly responds that he's taken top management out of managing the company. He's used employee involvement to stimulate motivation and to create a place where people want to

Motivation: From Concepts to Applications

come to work in the morning. "It's hard to attract people away from us," says Semler. "If you can set your own vacation, go to the beach on a Wednesday if you want, and take part in decision making about the company budget, why would you do a nine-to-five job for 20 percent more?"

In this chapter, we want to focus on how to apply motivation concepts. We want to link theories to practices such as employee involvement. For it's one thing to be able to regurgitate motivation theories. It's often another to see how, as a manager, you could use them.

In the following pages, we review a number of motivation techniques and programs that have gained varying degrees of acceptance in practice. And for each of the techniques and programs we review, we specifically address how they build on one or more of the motivation theories covered in the previous chapter.

MANAGEMENT BY OBJECTIVES

Goal-setting theory has an impressive base of research support. But as a manager, how do you make goal setting operational? The best answer to that question is: Install a management by objectives (MBO) program. MTW Corp., a provider of software services mainly for insurance companies and state governments, has an MBO-type program.[2] Management attributes this program with unlocking its workers' potential, helping the company average an astonishing 50 percent a year growth rate between 1996 and 2001, and cutting employee turnover to one fifth of the industry norm.

EXHIBIT

7-1

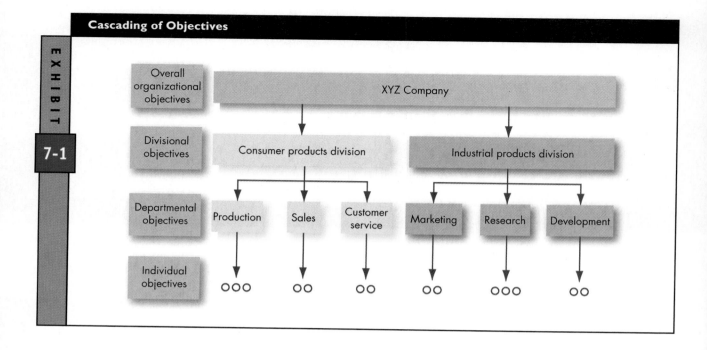

Overall organizational objectives	XYZ Company
Divisional objectives	Consumer products division	Industrial products division
Departmental objectives	Production	Sales	Customer service	Marketing	Research	Development
Individual objectives	OOO	OO	OO	OO	OOO	OO

What Is MBO?

management by objectives (MBO)

A program that encompasses specific goals, participatively set, for an explicit time period, with feedback on goal progress.

Management by objectives emphasizes participatively set goals that are tangible, verifiable, and measurable. It's not a new idea. In fact, it was originally proposed 50 years ago as a means of using goals to motivate people rather than to control them.[3] Today, no introduction to basic management concepts would be complete without a discussion of MBO.

MBO's appeal undoubtedly lies in its emphasis on converting overall organizational objectives into specific objectives for organizational units and individual members. MBO operationalizes the concept of objectives by devising a process by which objectives cascade down through the organization. As depicted in Exhibit 7-1, the organization's overall objectives are translated into specific objectives for each succeeding level (that is, divisional, departmental, individual) in the organization. But because lower-unit managers jointly participate in setting their own goals, MBO works from the "bottom up" as well as from the "top down." The result is a hierarchy that links objectives at one level to those at the next level. And for the individual employee, MBO provides specific personal performance objectives.

There are four ingredients common to MBO programs. These are goal specificity, participative decision making, an explicit time period, and performance feedback.[4]

The objectives in MBO should be concise statements of expected accomplishments. It's not adequate, for example, to merely state a desire to cut costs, improve service, or increase quality. Such desires have to be converted into tangible objectives that can be measured and evaluated. To cut departmental costs *by seven percent*, to improve service by ensuring that all telephone orders are processed *within 24 hours of receipt*, or to increase quality *by keeping returns to less than one percent of sales* are examples of specific objectives.

The objectives in MBO are not unilaterally set by the boss and then assigned to employees. MBO replaces imposed goals with participatively determined goals. The manager and employee jointly choose the goals and agree on how they will be measured.

Each objective has a specific time period in which it is to be completed. Typically the time period is three months, six months, or a year. So managers and employees have specific objectives and stipulated time periods in which to accomplish them.

The final ingredient in an MBO program is feedback on performance. MBO seeks to give continuous feedback on progress toward goals. Ideally, this is accomplished by giving ongoing feedback to individuals so they can monitor and correct their own actions. This is supplemented by periodic managerial evaluations, when progress is reviewed.

Linking MBO and Goal-Setting Theory

Goal-setting theory demonstrates that hard goals result in a higher level of individual performance than do easy goals, that specific hard goals result in higher levels of performance than do no goals at all or the generalized goal of "do your best," and that feedback on one's performance leads to higher performance. Compare these findings with MBO.

MBO directly advocates specific goals and feedback. MBO implies, rather than explicitly states, that goals must be perceived as feasible. Consistent with goal setting, MBO would be most effective when the goals are difficult enough to require the person to do some stretching.

The only area of possible disagreement between MBO and goal-setting theory relates to the issue of participation—MBO strongly advocates it, while goal-setting theory demonstrates that assigning goals to subordinates frequently works just as well. The major benefit to using participation, however, is that it appears to induce individuals to establish more difficult goals.

MBO in Practice

How widely used is MBO? Reviews of studies that have sought to answer this question suggest that it's a popular technique. You'll find MBO programs in many business, health-care, educational, government, and nonprofit organizations.[5]

MBO's popularity should not be construed to mean that it always works. There are a number of documented cases in which MBO has been implemented but failed to meet management's expectations.[6] A close look at these cases, however, indicates that the problems rarely lie with MBO's basic components. Rather, the culprits tend to be factors such as unrealistic expectations regarding results, lack of commitment by top management, and an inability or unwillingness by management to allocate rewards based on goal accomplishment. Failures can also arise out of cultural incompatibilities, as noted in the previous chapter. For instance, Fujitsu recently scrapped its MBO-type program because management found it didn't fit well with the Japanese culture's emphasis on minimizing risk and long-term goals.

EMPLOYEE RECOGNITION PROGRAMS

Laura Schendell makes only $7.50 an hour working at her fast-food job in Pensacola, Florida, and the job isn't very challenging or interesting. Yet Laura talks enthusiastically about her job, her boss, and the company that employs her. "What I like is the fact that Guy [her supervisor] appreciates the effort I make. He compliments me regularly in front of the other people on my shift, and I've been chosen "Employee of the Month" twice in the past six months. Did you see my picture on that plaque on the wall?"

Organizations are increasingly recognizing what Laura Schendell is acknowledging: Recognition can be a potent motivator.

What Are Employee Recognition Programs?

Employee recognition programs consist of personal attention, expressing interest, approval, and appreciation for a job well done.[7] They can take numerous forms. For instance, Nichols Foods Ltd., a British bottler of soft drinks and syrups, has a comprehensive recognition program.[8] The central hallway in its production area is lined with "bragging boards," where the accomplishments of various individuals and teams are regularly updated. Monthly awards are presented to people who have been nominated by peers for extraordinary effort on the job. And monthly award winners are eligible for further recognition at an annual off-site meeting for all employees. In contrast, most managers use a far more informal approach. As a case in point, Julia Stewart, president of Applebee's restaurants, frequently leaves sealed notes on the chairs of employees after everyone has gone home.[9] These notes explain how critical Stewart thinks the person's work is or how much she appreciates the completion of a recent project. Stewart also relies heavily on voice mail messages left after office hours to tell employees how appreciative she is for a job well done.

Linking Recognition Programs and Reinforcement Theory

A few years back, 1,500 employees were surveyed in a variety of work settings to find out what they considered to be the most powerful workplace motivator. Their response? Recognition, recognition, and more recognition![10]

Consistent with reinforcement theory, rewarding a behavior with recognition immediately following that behavior is likely to encourage its repetition. Recognition can take many forms. You can personally congratulate an employee in private for a good job. You can send a handwritten note or an e-mail message acknowledging something positive that the employee has done. For employees with a strong need for social acceptance, you can publicly recognize accomplishments. To enhance group cohesiveness and motivation, you can celebrate team successes. For instance, you can throw a team pizza party to celebrate a team's accomplishments. Or, as illustrated in Exhibit 7-3 on page 194, you can also let customers provide recognition.

Employee Recognition Programs in Practice

In today's highly competitive global economy, most organizations are under severe cost pressures. That makes recognition programs particularly attractive. In contrast to most other motivators, recognizing an employee's superior performance often costs little or no money.[11] Maybe that's why a recent Conference Board study found that 85 percent of companies surveyed reported that they use recognition programs to reward and motivate employees—with a new emphasis on job performance rather than the historical criterion of career milestones (i.e., 20 years of service).[12]

One of the most well-known and widely used recognition devices is the use of suggestion systems. Employees offer suggestions for improving processes or cutting costs and are recognized with small cash awards. The Japanese have been especially effective at making suggestion systems work. For instance, a typical high-performing Japanese plant in the auto components business generates 47 suggestions per employee a year and pays approximately the equivalent of U.S. $35 per suggestion. In contrast, a comparable Western factory generates about one suggestion per employee per year, but pays out $90 per suggestion.[13]

EXHIBIT 7-2

Source: S. Adams, *Share the Whales*, p. 66.

EMPLOYEE INVOLVEMENT PROGRAMS

At the Bic Corporation plant in Milford, Connecticut, which makes pens, razors, and cigarette lighters, production employees meet every week to review offerings from the employee suggestion box. Whenever a group voices its support for a proposal, it is immediately passed on to the appropriate supervisor, who has 10 days to put the change in place.[14] At General Electric's aircraft-engine assembly facility in Durham, North Carolina, the plant's 170 employees essentially manage themselves. Jet engines are produced by nine teams of people and they are given just one basic directive: the day that their next engine must be loaded onto a truck. All other decisions are made within the teams. Childress Buick, an automobile dealer in Phoenix, allows its salespeople to negotiate and finalize deals with customers without any approval from management. The laws of Germany, France, Denmark, Sweden, and Austria require companies to have elected representatives from their employee groups as members of their boards of directors.

The common theme throughout the preceding examples is that they all illustrate employee involvement programs. In this section, we clarify what we mean by employee involvement, describe some of the various forms that it takes, consider the motivational implications of these programs, and show some applications.

EXHIBIT

7-3

Nomination Ballot

EMPLOYEE
RECOGNITION
PROGRAM

SERVICE PLUS ★

Fairmont Hotels & Resorts is committed to providing you with a level of personal attention, courtesy and comfort that outshines your every expectation.

We're also committed to a company-wide program that recognizes employees who truly excel in serving you: the *Service Plus* Program.

If one of our employees has done something extra for you, something truly outstanding, please take a moment to nominate that person as our Star **Employee of the Month.**

Simply complete this ballot and deposit it in the *Service Plus* ballot box.

We value your patronage and look forward to seeing you again.

I would like to recognize:

EMPLOYEE NAME (PLEASE PRINT)

DEPARTMENT   DATE

FOR (please be specific):

GUEST NAME

What Is Employee Involvement?

Employee involvement has become a convenient catchall term to cover a variety of techniques.[15] For instance, it encompasses popular ideas such as employee participation or participative management, workplace democracy, empowerment, and employee ownership. Our position is, although each of these ideas has some unique characteristics, they all have a common core—that of employee involvement.

employee involvement program

A participative process that uses the entire capacity of employees and is designed to encourage increased commitment to the organization's success.

What specifically do we mean by **employee involvement**? We define it as a participative process that uses the entire capacity of employees and is designed to encourage increased commitment to the organization's success.[16] The underlying logic is that by involving workers in the decisions that affect them and by increasing their autonomy and control over their work lives, employees will become more motivated, more committed to the organization, more productive, and more satisfied with their jobs.[17]

Does that mean that participation and employee involvement are synonyms for each other? No. Participation is a more limited term. It's a subset within the larger framework of employee involvement. All of the employee involvement programs we describe include some form of employee participation but the term *participation*, per se, is too narrow and too limiting.

Examples of Employee Involvement Programs

In this section we review four forms of employee involvement: participative management, representative participation, quality circles, and employee stock ownership plans.

Participative Management   The distinct characteristic common to all **participative management** programs is the use of joint decision making. That is, subordinates actually share a significant degree of decision-making power with their immediate superiors.

Participative management has, at times, been promoted as a panacea for poor morale and low productivity. Some authors have even proposed that participative management is an ethical imperative.[18] But participative management is not appropriate for every organization or every work unit. For it to work, the issues in which employees get involved must be relevant to their interests so they'll be motivated, employees must have the competence and knowledge to make a useful contribution, and there must be trust and confidence between all parties involved.[19]

Why would management want to share its decision-making power with subordinates? There are a number of good reasons. As jobs have become more complex, managers often don't know everything their employees do. Thus, participation allows those who know the most to contribute. The result can be better decisions. The interdependence in tasks that employees often do today also requires consultation with people in other departments and work units. This increases the need for teams, committees, and group meetings to resolve issues that affect them jointly. Participation additionally increases commitment to decisions. People are less likely to undermine a decision at the time of its implementation if they shared in making that decision. Finally, participation provides intrinsic rewards for employees. It can make their jobs more interesting and more meaningful.

Dozens of studies have been conducted on the participation–performance relationship. The findings, however, are mixed.[20] When the research is reviewed carefully, it appears that participation typically has only a modest influence on variables such as employee productivity, motivation, and job satisfaction. Of course, that doesn't mean that the use of participative management can't be beneficial under the right conditions. What it says, however, is that the use of participation is no sure means for improving employee performance.

Representative Participation   Almost every country in Western Europe has some type of legislation requiring companies to practice **representative participation**. That is, rather than participate directly in decisions, workers are represented by a small group of employees who actually participate. Representative participation has been called "the most widely legislated form of employee involvement around the world."[21]

The goal of representative participation is to redistribute power within an organization, putting labor on a more equal footing with the interests of management and stockholders.

An amateur soccer team from Helsinki allows 300 of its fans to provide input to some of its games every season via cell phone text messages. Owner Jussi Rautavirta and coach Janne Viljamaa limit the shared decisions to very simple ones, however, and they offer limited choices, because fans are not as familiar with the game or the team's strategy. The team finished first in its division after implementing the new policy.

participative management

A process in which subordinates share a significant degree of decision-making power with their immediate superiors.

representative participation

Workers participate in organizational decision making through a small group of representative employees.

The two most common forms which representative participation takes are works councils and board representatives.[22] **Works councils** link employees with management. They are groups of nominated or elected employees who must be consulted when management makes decisions involving personnel. For example, in the Netherlands, if a Dutch company is taken over by another firm, the former's works council must be informed at an early stage, and if the council objects, it has 30 days to seek a court injunction to stop the takeover.[23] **Board representatives** are employees who sit on a company's board of directors and represent the interests of the firm's employees. In some countries, large companies may be legally required to make sure that employee representatives have the same number of board seats as stockholder representatives.

The overall influence of representative participation on working employees seems to be minimal.[24] For instance, the evidence suggests that works councils are dominated by management and have little impact on employees or the organization. And while this form of employee involvement might increase the motivation and satisfaction of the individuals who are doing the representing, there is little evidence that this trickles down to the operating employees whom they represent. Overall, "the greatest value of representative participation is symbolic. If one is interested in changing employee attitudes or in improving organizational performance, representative participation would be a poor choice."[25]

Quality Circles   The quality circle concept is frequently mentioned as one of the techniques that Japanese firms use that has allowed them to make high-quality products at low costs. Originally begun in the United States and exported to Japan in the 1950s, the quality circle became quite popular in North America and Europe during the 1980s.[26]

What is a **quality circle**? It's a work group of 8 to 10 employees and supervisors who have a shared area of responsibility. They meet regularly—typically once a week, on company time and on company premises—to discuss their quality problems, investigate causes of the problems, recommend solutions, and take corrective actions. They take over the responsibility for solving quality problems, and they generate and evaluate their own feedback. But management typically retains control over the final decision regarding implementation of recommended solutions. Of course, it is not presumed that employees inherently have this ability to analyze and solve quality problems. Therefore, part of the quality circle concept includes teaching participating employees group communication skills, various quality strategies, and measurement and problem analysis techniques. Exhibit 7-4 describes a typical quality circle process.

Do quality circles improve employee productivity and satisfaction? A review of the evidence indicates that they are much more likely to positively affect productivity. They tend to show little or no effect on employee satisfaction; and although many studies report positive results from quality circles on productivity, these results are by no means guaranteed.[27] The failure of many quality circle programs to produce measurable benefits has also led to a large number of them being discontinued.

One author has gone as far as to say that although quality circles were the management fad of the 1980s, they've "become a flop."[28] He offers two possible explanations for their disappointing results. First is the little bit of time that actually deals with employee involvement. "At most, these programs operate for one hour per week, with the remaining 39 hours unchanged. Why should changes in 2.5 percent of a person's job have a major impact?"[29] Second, the ease of implementing quality circles often worked against them. They were seen as a simple device that could be added on to the organization with few changes required outside

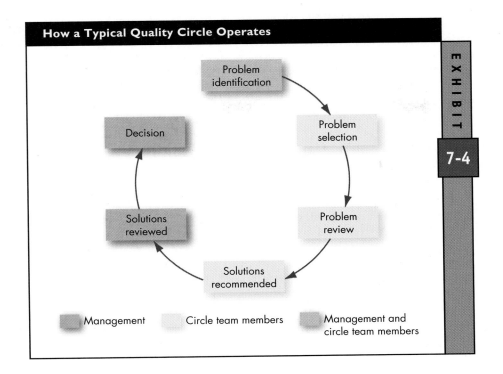

How a Typical Quality Circle Operates

Problem identification → Problem selection → Problem review → Solutions recommended → Solutions reviewed → Decision

Management | Circle team members | Management and circle team members

EXHIBIT

7-4

the program itself. In many cases, the only significant involvement by management was funding the program. So quality circles became an easy way for management to get on the employee involvement bandwagon. And, unfortunately, the lack of planning and commitment of top management often contributed to the failure of quality circles.

Employee Stock Ownership Plans   The final employee involvement approach we'll discuss is **employee stock ownership plans (ESOPs)**.[30]

Employee ownership can mean any number of things, from employees owning some stock in the company at which they work to the individuals working in the company owning and personally operating the firm. Employee stock ownership plans are company-established benefit plans in which employees acquire stock as part of their benefits. Companies as varied as United Airlines, Publix Supermarkets, Graybar Electric, and W.L. Gore & Associates are now over 50 percent employee-owned.[31]

In the typical ESOP, an employee stock ownership trust is created. Companies contribute either stock or cash to buy stock for the trust and allocate the stock to employees. While employees hold stock in their company, they usually cannot take physical possession of their shares or sell them as long as they're still employed at the company.

The research on ESOPs indicates that they increase employee satisfaction.[32] But their impact on performance is less clear. For instance, one study compared 45 ESOPs against 238 conventional companies.[33] The ESOPs outperformed the conventional firms both in terms of employment and sales growth. Another study found that ESOPs had total shareholder returns that averaged 6.9 percentage points higher over the four years after the ESOP was set up than market returns of similar companies without an ESOP.[34] But other studies have shown disappointing results.[35]

employee stock ownership plans (ESOPs)

Company-established benefit plans in which employees acquire stock as part of their benefits.

ESOPs have the potential to increase employee job satisfaction and work motivation. But for this potential to be realized, employees need to psychologically experience ownership.[36] That is, in addition to merely having a financial stake in the company, employees need to be kept regularly informed on the status of the business and also have the opportunity to exercise influence over the business. The evidence consistently indicates that it takes ownership and a participative style of management to achieve significant improvements in an organization's performance.[37]

Linking Employee Involvement Programs and Motivation Theories

Employee involvement draws on a number of the motivation theories discussed in the previous chapter. For instance, Theory Y is consistent with participative management, while Theory X aligns with the more traditional autocratic style of managing people. In terms of two-factor theory, employee involvement programs could provide employees with intrinsic motivation by increasing opportunities for growth, responsibility, and involvement in the work itself. Similarly, the opportunity to make and implement decisions, and then seeing them work out, can help satisfy an employee's needs for responsibility, achievement, recognition, growth, and enhanced self-esteem. So employee involvement is compatible with ERG theory and efforts to stimulate the achievement need. And extensive employee involvement programs clearly have the potential to increase employee intrinsic motivation in work tasks and create a flow experience.

Employee Involvement Programs in Practice

Germany, France, Holland, and the Scandinavian countries have firmly established the principle of industrial democracy in Europe, and other nations, including Japan and Israel, have traditionally practiced some form of representative participation for decades. Participative management and representative participation were much slower to gain ground in North American organizations. But nowadays, employee involvement programs that stress participation have become the norm.

A study comparing the acceptance of employee involvement programs in four countries, including the United States and India, confirmed the importance of modifying practices to reflect national culture.[38] Specifically, while American employees readily accepted these programs, managers in India who tried to empower their employees were rated low by those employees; and the use of empowerment also negatively affected employee satisfaction. These reactions are consistent with India's high power–distance culture, which accepts and expects differences in authority.

What about quality circles? How popular are they in practice? The names of companies that have used quality circles reads like a *Who's Who of Corporate America*: Hewlett-Packard, General Electric, Texas Instruments, Inland Steel, Xerox, Eastman Kodak, Polaroid, Procter & Gamble, Control Data, General Motors, Ford, IBM, Motorola, American Airlines, and TRW.[39] But, as we noted, the success of quality circles has been far from overwhelming. They were popular in the 1980s, largely because they were easy to implement. In more recent years, many organizations have dropped their quality circles and replaced them with more comprehensive team-based structures (which we discuss in Chapter 8).

What about ESOPs? They've grown from just a handful in the mid-1970s to around 11,500 now, covering approximately 10 million employees.[40] Many large, well-known companies have implemented ESOPs, but most tend to be small, private firms. And the emphasis among small firms is likely to increase because a recent change in U.S. laws now allows S-corporations—which encompasses mostly small businesses—to establish ESOPs.[41]

VARIABLE PAY PROGRAMS

"Why should I put any extra effort into this job?" asked Anne Garcia, a fourth-grade elementary school teacher in Denver, Colorado. "I can excel or I can do the bare minimum. It makes no difference. I get paid the same. Why do anything above the minimum to get by?"

Comments similar to Anne's have been voiced by school teachers for decades because pay increases were tied to seniority. Recently, however, a number of school districts have begun revamping their compensation systems to motivate people like Anne to strive for excellence in their jobs.[42] Teachers in several U.S. cities, including Denver, Minneapolis, and Columbus, Ohio, are having their pay tied to the performance of the students in their classrooms. In Denver, for instance, teachers whose students improve on standardized tests can earn a $1,500 increase in salary.

A number of organizations—business firms as well as school districts and other government agencies—are moving away from paying people based solely on credentials or length of service toward variable-pay programs.

What Are Variable-Pay Programs?

Piece-rate plans, wage incentives, profit sharing, bonuses, and gainsharing are all forms of **variable-pay programs**. What differentiates these forms of compensation from more traditional programs is that instead of paying a person only for time on the job or seniority, a portion of an employee's pay is based on some individual and/or organizational measure of performance. Unlike more traditional base-pay programs, variable pay is not an annuity. There is no guarantee that just because you made $60,000 last year that you'll make the same amount this year. With variable pay, earnings fluctuate up and down with the measure of performance.[43]

It is precisely the fluctuation in variable pay that has made these programs attractive to management. It turns part of an organization's fixed labor costs into a variable cost, thus reducing expenses when performance declines. So when the U.S. economy entered a recession in the spring of 2001, companies with variable pay were able to reduce their labor costs much faster than companies that had maintained non-performance-based compensation systems.[44] In addition, by tying pay to performance, earnings recognize contribution rather than being a form of entitlement. Low performers find, over time, that their pay stagnates, while high performers enjoy pay increases commensurate with their contribution.

Four of the more widely used variable-pay programs are piece-rate wages, bonuses, profit sharing, and gainsharing.

Piece-rate wages have been around for nearly a century. They have long been popular as a means for compensating production workers. In **piece-rate pay plans** workers are paid a fixed sum for each unit of production completed. When an employee gets no base salary and is paid only for what he or she produces, this is a pure piece-rate plan. People who work ball parks selling peanuts and soda pop frequently are paid this way. They might get to keep $.75 for every bag of peanuts they sell. If they sell 200 bags during a game, they make $150. If they sell only 40 bags, their take is only $30. The harder they work and the more peanuts they sell, the more they earn. Many organizations use a modified piece-rate plan, in which employees

variable-pay programs
A portion of an employee's pay is based on some individual and/or organizational measure of performance.

piece-rate pay plans
Workers are paid a fixed sum for each unit of production completed.

People who sell peanuts and soda at ball games are usually paid no base salary but instead earn a percentage of what they sell. This is a pure piece-rate pay plan.

earn a base hourly wage plus a piece-rate differential. So a medical transcriber might be paid $7 an hour plus 20 cents per page. Such modified plans provide a floor under an employee's earnings, while still offering a productivity incentive.

Bonuses can be paid exclusively to executives or to all employees. For instance, annual bonuses in the millions of dollars are not uncommon in American corporations. Apple Computer's CEO Steve Jobs, for example, received a $90 million bonus in 2000 for his success in reenergizing the company.[45] Increasingly, bonus plans are taking on a larger net within organizations to include lower-ranking employees.[46] Many companies now routinely reward production employees with bonuses in the thousands of dollars when company profits improve.

Profit-sharing plans are organization-wide programs that distribute compensation based on some established formula designed around a company's profitability. These can be direct cash outlays or, particularly in the case of top managers, allocated as stock options.

profit-sharing plans

Organizationwide programs that distribute compensation based on some established formula designed around a company's profitability.

gainsharing

An incentive plan in which improvements in group productivity determine the total amount of money that is allocated.

When you read about executives like Sanford Weill, the CEO at Citigroup, earning over $200 million in one year, almost all of this comes from cashing in stock options previously granted based on company profit performance.

The variable-pay program that has gotten the most attention in recent years is undoubtedly **gainsharing**.[47] This is a formula-based group incentive plan. Improvements in group productivity—from one period to another—determine the total amount of money that is to be allocated. The division of productivity savings can be split between the company and employees in any number of ways, but 50–50 is pretty typical.

Isn't gainsharing the same thing as profit sharing? They're similar but not the same thing. By focusing on productivity gains rather than on profits, gain-sharing rewards specific behaviors that are less influenced by external factors. Employees in a gainsharing plan can receive incentive awards even when the organization isn't profitable.

Do variable-pay programs work? Do they increase motivation and productivity? The answer is a qualified Yes. For example, studies generally support that organizations with profit-sharing plans have higher levels of profitability than those without them.[48] Similarly, gainsharing has been found to improve productivity in a majority of cases and often has a positive impact on employee attitudes.[49] An American Management Association study of 83 companies that used gainsharing found, on average, that grievances dropped 83 percent, absences fell 84 percent, and lost-time accidents decreased by 69 percent.[50] The downside of variable pay, from an employee's perspective, is its unpredictability. With a straight base salary, employees know what they'll be earning. Adding in merit and cost-of-living increases, they can make fairly accurate predictions about what they'll be making next year and the year after that. They can finance cars and homes based on reasonably solid assumptions. That's more difficult to do with variable pay. Your group's performance might slip this year or a recession might undermine your company's profits. Depending on how your variable pay is determined, these can cut your income. Moreover, people begin to take repeated annual performance bonuses for granted. A 15 or 20 percent bonus, received three years in a row, begins to become expected in the fourth year. If it doesn't materialize, management will find itself with some disgruntled employees on its hands.

Linking Variable-Pay Programs and Expectancy Theory

Variable pay is probably most compatible with expectancy theory predictions. Specifically, individuals should perceive a strong relationship between their performance and the rewards they receive if motivation is to be maximized. If rewards are allocated completely on nonperformance factors—such as seniority or job title—then employees are likely to reduce their effort.

The evidence supports the importance of this linkage, especially for operative employees working under piece-rate systems. For example, one study of 400 manufacturing firms found that companies with wage incentive plans achieved 43 to 64 percent greater productivity than those without such plans.[51]

Group and organization-wide incentives reinforce and encourage employees to sublimate personal goals for the best interests of their department or the organization. Group-based performance incentives are also a natural extension for organizations that are trying to build a strong team ethic. By linking rewards to team performance, employees are encouraged to make extra efforts to help their team succeed.

Variable-Pay Programs in Practice

Variable pay is a concept that is rapidly replacing the annual cost-of-living raise. One reason, as cited earlier, is its motivational power—but don't ignore the cost implications. Bonuses, gainsharing, and other variable-based reward programs avoid the fixed expense of permanent salary boosts. Variable-pay, for instance, allowed the management of many companies in 2001 and 2002 to cushion profits (or cut losses) during times of economic recession.

Pay for performance has been "in" for compensating managers for more than a decade. The new trend has been expanding this practice to nonmanagerial employees. IBM, Wal-Mart, Pizza Hut, Cigna Corp., and John Deere are just a few examples of companies using variable-pay with rank-and-file employees.[52] Today, 78 percent of U.S. companies have some form of variable-pay plan for nonexecutives; up from 47 percent in 1990.[53]

Variable pay also seems to be gaining in global popularity. For instance, a recent survey found that 21.8 percent of Japanese companies now are now using such pay systems. The rate was less than 10 percent in the 1980s.[54]

Gainsharing's popularity seems to be narrowly focused among large, unionized manufacturing companies such as American Safety Razor, Champion Spark Plug, Cincinnati Milacron, Hooker Chemical, and Mead Paper. For instance, among Fortune 1000 firms, approximately 45 percent have implemented gainsharing plans.[55]

Among firms that haven't introduced performance-based compensation programs, common concerns tend to surface.[56] Managers fret over what should constitute performance and how it should be measured. They have to overcome the historical attachment to cost-of-living adjustments and the belief that they have an obligation to keep all employees' pay in step with inflation. Other barriers include salary scales keyed to what the competition is paying, traditional compensation systems that rely heavily on specific pay grades and relatively narrow pay ranges, and performance appraisal practices that produce inflated evaluations and expectations of full rewards. Of course, from the employees' standpoint, the major concern is a potential drop in earnings. Pay for performance means employees have to share in the risks as well as the rewards of their employer's business.

Pay for Performance at Siebel Systems

Executives at Siebel Systems, the sales-automation software firm headquartering in San Mateo, California, understand how rewards shape behavior. So they've scrapped their traditional system of rewarding their sales people solely on the basis of how well they achieve their sales targets. They've replaced it with a new motivation system that broadens the definition of sales performance to include building long-term customer satisfaction.

Siebel considers building long-term customer relationships to be its top priority. Says the company's vice president of technical services, Steve Mankoff: "[If reps] close a contract with a customer, continue to follow up with that customer, and make sure that customer is successful, chances are that customer will come back for more. In any given quarter, 45 to 60 percent of our business is from repeat customers."

So now nearly 40 percent of each salesperson's incentive compensation is based on their customer's reported satisfaction with service and implementation of the products they've purchased. To determine how well its salespeople are doing, Siebel regularly surveys customers on the responsiveness of its sales organization, the sales consultant's ability to integrate a customer's requirements with Siebel's software solutions, the rep's knowledge of the products and of the customer's project, and ease of purchasing and contracting.

By broadening pay for performance from just generating sales to also including customer satisfaction, Siebel is getting its sales force to focus on the needs of its customers. "It works," says Mankoff. "Our loyalty rate among customers is in the 96 to 99 percent range."

Source: E. Zimmerman, "Quota Busters," *Sales & Marketing Management*, January 2001, pp. 59–63.

SKILL-BASED PAY PLANS

Organizations hire people for their skills, then typically put them in jobs and pay them based on their job title or rank. For example, the director of operations earns $180,000 a year, the regional operations managers make $125,000, and plant operations managers get $85,000. But if organizations hire people because of their competencies, why don't they pay them for those same competencies? Some organizations do.[57] For instance, production and maintenance workers at JLG Industries in Pennsylvania earn an extra 30 cents an hour for each new skill they acquire within a specific family of job activities. Employees at American Steel & Wire can boost their annual salaries by up to $12,480 by acquiring as many as 10 skills. And Frito-Lay Corporation ties its compensation for front-line operations managers to developing their skills in leadership, workforce development, and functional excellence.

What Are Skill-Based Pay Plans?

skill-based pay plans

Pay levels are based on how many skills employees have or how many jobs they can do.

Skill-based pay is an alternative to job-based pay. Rather than having an individual's job title define his or her pay category, **skill-based pay** (also sometimes called *competency-based or knowledge-based pay*) sets pay levels on the basis of how many skills employees have or how many jobs they can do.[58]

What's the appeal of skill-based pay plans? From management's perspective: flexibility. Filling staffing needs is easier when employee skills are interchangeable. This is particularly true today, as many organizations cut the size of their workforce. Downsized organizations require more generalists and fewer specialists. While skill-based pay encourages employees to acquire a broader range of skills, there are also other benefits. It facilitates communication across the organization because people gain a better understanding of others' jobs. It lessens dysfunctional "protection of territory" behavior. Where skill-based pay exists, you're less likely to hear the phrase, "It's not my job!" In addition, skill-based pay helps meet the needs of ambitious employees who confront minimal advancement opportunities. These people can increase their earnings and knowledge without a promotion in job title. Finally, skill-based pay appears to lead to performance improvements. A broad-based survey of Fortune 1000 firms found that 60 percent of those with skill-based pay plans rated their plans as successful or very successful in increasing organizational performance, while only 6 percent considered them unsuccessful or very unsuccessful.[59]

What about the downside of skill-based pay? People can "top out"—learning all the skills the program calls for them to learn. This can frustrate employees after they've become challenged by an environment of learning, growth, and continual pay raises. Skills can become obsolete. When this happens, what should management do? Cut employee pay or continue to pay for skills that are no longer relevant? There is also the problem created by paying people for acquiring skills for which there may be no immediate need. This happened at IDS Financial Services.[60] The company found itself paying people more money even though there was little immediate use for their new skills. IDS eventually dropped its skill-based pay plan and replaced it with

Frito-Lay Corp., uses a skill-based pay plan to link managers' compensation to their acquisition of leadership, group process, and communication skills.

one that equally balances individual contribution and gains in work-team productivity. Finally, skill-based plans don't address the level of performance. They deal only with the issue of whether or not someone can perform the skill. For some skills, such as checking quality or leading a team, level of performance may be equivocal. Although it's possible to assess how well employees perform each of the skills and combine that with a skill-based plan, that is not an inherent part of skill-based pay.

Linking Skill-Based Pay Plans to Motivation Theories

Skill-based pay plans are consistent with several motivation theories. Because they encourage employees to learn, expand their skills, and grow, they are consistent with ERG theory. Among employees whose lower-order needs are substantially satisfied, the opportunity to experience growth can be a motivator.

Paying people to expand their skill levels is also consistent with research on the achievement need. High achievers have a compelling drive to do things better or more efficiently. By learning new skills or improving the skills they already hold, high achievers will find their jobs more challenging.

There is also a link between reinforcement theory and skill-based pay. Skill-based pay encourages employees to develop their flexibility, to continue to learn, to cross-train, to be generalists rather than specialists, and to work cooperatively with others in the organization. To the degree that management wants employees to demonstrate such behaviors, skill-based pay should act as a reinforcer.

In addition, skill-based pay may have equity implications. When employees make their input-outcome comparisons, skills may provide a fairer input criterion for determining pay than factors such as seniority or education. To the degree that employees perceive skills as the critical variable in job performance, the use of skill-based pay may increase the perception of equity and help optimize employee motivation.

Skill-Based Pay in Practice

A number of studies have investigated the use and effectiveness of skill-based pay. The overall conclusion, based on these studies, is that skill-based pay is expanding and that it generally leads to higher employee performance, satisfaction, and perceptions of fairness in pay systems.[61]

Research has also identified some interesting trends. The increased use of skills as a basis for pay appears particularly strong among organizations facing aggressive foreign competition and companies with shorter product life cycles and speed-to-market concerns.[62] Also, skill-based pay is moving from the shop floor to the white-collar workforce, and sometimes as far as the executive suite.[63]

Skilled-based pay appears to be an idea whose time has come. As one expert noted, "Slowly, but surely, we're becoming a skill-based society where your market value is tied to what you can do and what your skill set is. In this new world where skills and knowledge are what really counts, it doesn't make sense to treat people as jobholders. It makes sense to treat them as people with specific skills and to pay them for those skills."[64]

FLEXIBLE BENEFITS

Todd Evans and Allison Murphy both work for PepsiCo, but they have very different needs in terms of employee benefits. Todd is married, has three young children, and a wife who is at home full time. Allison, too, is married, but her husband has a high-paying job with the federal government, and they have no children. Todd is concerned about having a good medical plan and enough life insurance to support his family if he weren't around. In contrast, Allison's husband already has her medical needs covered on his plan, and life insurance is a low priority for both her and her husband. Allison is more interested in extra vacation time and long-term financial benefits such as a tax-deferred savings plan.

A standardized benefit package for all employees at PepsiCo would be unlikely to meet the optimal needs of both Todd and Allison. They could, however, optimize their needs if PepsiCo offered flexible benefits.

What Are Flexible Benefits?

flexible benefits

Employees tailor their benefit program to meet their personal needs by picking and choosing from a menu of benefit options.

Flexible benefits allow employees to pick benefits that most meet their needs. The idea is to allow each employee to choose a benefit package that is individually tailored to his or her own needs and situation. It replaces the traditional "one-benefit-plan-fits-all" programs that dominated organizations for more than 50 years.[65]

The average organization provides fringe benefits worth approximately 40 percent of an employee's salary. Traditional benefit programs were designed for the typical employee of the 1950s—a male with a wife and two children at home. Less than 10 percent of employees now fit this stereotype. While 25 percent of today's employees are single, a third are part of two-income families with no children. As such, these traditional programs don't tend to meet the needs of today's more diverse workforce. Flexible benefits, however, do meet these diverse needs. They can be uniquely tailored to reflect differences in employee needs based on age, marital status, spouses' benefit status, number and age of dependents, and the like.

The three most popular type of benefit plans are modular plans, core-plus options, and flexible spending accounts.[66] *Modular plans* are predesigned packages of benefits, with each module put together to meet the needs of a specific group of employees. So a module designed for single employees with no dependents might include only essential benefits. Another, designed for single parents, might have additional life insurance, disability insurance, and expanded health coverage. *Core-plus plans* consist of a core of essential benefits and a menu-like selection of other benefit options from which employees can select and add to the core. Typically, each employee is given "benefit credits," which allow the "purchase" of additional benefits that uniquely meet his or her needs. *Flexible spending plans* allow employees to set aside up to the dollar amount offered in the plan to pay for particular services. It's a convenient way, for example, for employees to pay for health-care and dental premiums. Flexible spending accounts can increase employee take-home pay because employees don't have to pay taxes on the dollars they spend out of these accounts.

Linking Flexible Benefits and Expectancy Theory

Giving all employees the same benefits assumes that all employees have the same needs. Of course, we know this assumption is false. Thus, flexible benefits turn the benefits' expenditure into a motivator.

Consistent with expectancy theory's thesis that organizational rewards should be linked to each individual employee's goals, flexible benefits individualize rewards by allowing each employee to choose the compensation package that best satisfies his or her current needs. The fact that flexible benefits can turn the traditional homogeneous benefit program into a motivator was demonstrated at one company when 80 percent of the organization's employees changed their fixed benefit packages when a flexible plan was put into effect.[67]

Flexible Benefits in Practice

Approximately 13 percent of large- and medium-sized U.S. companies have flexible benefit plans in place. This includes TRW Systems, Educational Testing Services, DaimlerChrysler, and Verizon.[68] In the future, we can probably expect this percentage to increase to reflect the expanding diversity among employees.

The stereotype of the 1950s employee, a married man with wife and two children at home, now describes less than 10 percent of employees. Today, when 25 percent of employees are single and a third are part of two-income households with no children, a standardized benefit program will not meet the majority of employees' needs.

Now, let's look at the benefits and drawbacks. For employees, flexibility is attractive because they can tailor their benefits and levels of coverage to their own needs. The major drawback, from the employee's standpoint, is that the costs of optional benefits often go up, so fewer total benefits can be purchased. From the organization's standpoint, the good news is that flexible benefits often produce savings. Many organizations use the introduction of flexible benefits to raise deductibles and premiums. Moreover, once in place, costly increases in things like health insurance premiums often have to be substantially absorbed by the employee. The bad news for the organization is that these plans are more cumbersome for management to oversee, and administering the programs is often expensive.

SPECIAL ISSUES IN MOTIVATION

Various groups provide specific challenges in terms of motivation. In this section we look at some of the unique problems faced in trying to motivate professional employees, contingent workers, the diverse workforce, low-skilled service workers, and people doing highly repetitive tasks.

Motivating Professionals

In contrast to a generation ago, the typical employee today is more likely to be a highly trained professional with a college degree than a blue-collar factory worker. These professionals receive a great deal of intrinsic satisfaction from their work. They tend to be well paid. So what, if any, special concerns should you be aware of when trying to motivate a team of engineers at Intel, a software designer at Microsoft, or a group of CPAs at PricewaterhouseCoopers?

Professionals are typically different from nonprofessionals.[69] They have a strong and long-term commitment to their field of expertise. Their loyalty is more often to their profession than to their employer. To keep current in their field, they need to update their knowledge regularly, and their commitment to their profession means they rarely define their work week in terms of 8 to 5 and five days a week.

What motivates professionals? Money and promotions typically are low on their priority list. Why? They tend to be well paid and they enjoy what they do. In contrast, job challenge tends to be ranked high. They like to tackle problems and find solutions. Their chief reward in their job is the work itself. Professionals also value support. They want others to think what they're working on is important. Although this may be true for all employees, because professionals tend to be more focused on their work as their central life interest, nonprofessionals typically have other interests outside of work that can compensate for needs not met on the job. And professionals place a high level of importance on having skill-development opportunities.

The foregoing description implies a few guidelines to keep in mind if you're trying to motivate professionals. Provide them with ongoing challenging projects. Give them autonomy to follow their interests and allow them to structure their work in ways that they find productive. Reward them with educational opportunities—training, workshops, attending conferences—that allow them to keep current in their field. Also reward them with recognition, and ask questions and engage in other actions that demonstrate to them you're sincerely interested in what they're doing.

An increasing number of companies are creating alternative career paths for their professional/technical people, allowing employees to earn more money and status, without assuming managerial responsibilities. At Merck & Co., IBM, and AT&T, the best scientists, engineers, and researchers gain titles such as fellow and senior scientist. Their pay and prestige are comparable to those of managers but without the corresponding authority or responsibility.

Motivating Contingent Workers

We noted in Chapter 1 that one of the more comprehensive changes taking place in organizations is the addition of temporary or contingent employees. As downsizing has eliminated millions of "permanent" jobs, an increasing number of new openings are for "nonpermanent" workers. For instance, approximately six million Americans, or 4.9 percent of those with jobs, consider themselves to be part of the contingent workforce.[70] These include part-timers, on-call workers, short-term hires, temps, day laborers, independent contractors, and leased workers. The common denominator among these contingent employees is that they don't have the security or stability that permanent employees have. As such, they don't identify with the organization or display the commitment that other employees do. Temporary workers also are typically provided with little or no health care, pensions, or similar benefits.[71]

There is no simple solution for motivating contingent employees. For those who prefer the freedom of their temporary status—many students, working mothers, seniors, and professionals who don't want the demands of a permanent job—the lack of stability may not be an issue. Interestingly, this seems to be considerably more people than originally thought. Recent estimates indicate that 35 to 40 percent of contingent workers have chosen this status voluntarily.[72] The challenge, however, is in dealing with temporary employees who are in this status involuntarily.

What will motivate involuntarily contingent employees? An obvious answer is the opportunity for permanent status. In cases in which permanent employees are selected from the pool of temporaries, temporaries will often work hard in hopes of becoming permanent. A less obvious answer is the opportunity for training. The ability of a contingent employee to find a new job is largely dependent on his or her skills. If the employee sees that the job he or she is doing for you can help develop salable skills, then motivation is increased. From an equity standpoint, you should also consider the repercussions of mixing permanent and contingent workers where pay

Kim Drake, an intern at Embassy Suites, is among the millions of students in the United States that do contingent or nonpermanent work.

differentials are significant.[73] For instance, when temps work alongside permanent employees who earn more, and get benefits too, for doing the same job, the performance of temps is likely to suffer. Separating such employees or converting all employees to a variable-pay or skill-based pay plan might help lessen this problem.

Motivating the Diversified Workforce

Not everyone is motivated by money. Not everyone wants a challenging job. The needs of women, singles, immigrants, the physically disabled, senior citizens, and others from diverse groups are not the same as a married white American male with three dependents. A couple of examples can make this point clearer. Employees who are attending college typically place a high value on flexible work schedules. Such individuals may be attracted to organizations that offer flexible work hours, job sharing, or temporary assignments. Similarly, a father may prefer to work the midnight to 8 A.M. shift in order to spend time with his children during the day when his wife is at work.

If you're going to maximize your employees' motivation, you've got to understand and respond to this diversity. How? The key word to guide you should be *flexibility*. Be ready to design work schedules, compensation plans, benefits, physical work settings, and the like to reflect your employees' varied needs. This might include offering child and elder care, flexible work hours, and job sharing for employees with family responsibilities. It also might include offering flexible leave policies for immigrants who want occasionally to make extensive return trips to their homelands, or creating work teams for employees who come from countries with a strong collectivist orientation, or allowing employees who are going to school to vary their work schedules from semester to semester.

Motivating Low-Skilled Service Workers

One of the most challenging motivation problems in industries such as retailing and fast food is: How do you motivate individuals who are making very low wages and who have little opportunity to significantly increase their pay in either their current jobs or through promotions? These jobs are typically filled with people who have limited education and skills, and pay levels are little above minimum wage.

Traditional approaches for motivating these people have focused on providing more flexible work schedules and filling these jobs with teenagers and retirees whose financial needs are less. This has met with less than enthusiastic results. For instance, turnover rates of 200 percent or more are not uncommon for businesses like McDonald's. Taco Bell has tried to make some of its service jobs more interesting and challenging but with limited results.[74] It has experimented with incentive pay and stock options for cashiers and cooks. These employees also have been given broader responsibility for inventory, scheduling, and hiring. But over a four-year period, this experiment has only reduced annual turnover from 223 percent to 160 percent.

What choices are left? Unless pay and benefits are significantly increased, high turnover probably has to be expected in these jobs. This can be somewhat offset by widening the recruiting net, making these jobs more appealing, and raising pay levels.

Motivating People Doing Highly Repetitive Tasks

Our final category considers employees who do standardized and repetitive jobs. For instance, working on an assembly line or transcribing court reports are jobs that workers often find boring and even stressful.

Motivating individuals in these jobs can be made easier through careful selection. People vary in their tolerance for ambiguity. Many individuals prefer jobs that have a minimal amount of discretion and variety. Such individuals are obviously a better match to standardized jobs than individuals with strong needs for growth and autonomy. Standardized jobs should also be the first considered for automation. This helps explain management's motivation to install ATMs at banks, self-service soda machines in fast-food restaurants, and customer-operated check-in kiosks at airports.

Many standardized jobs, especially in the manufacturing sector, pay well. This makes it relatively easy to fill vacancies. While high pay can ease recruitment problems and reduce turnover, it doesn't necessarily lead to highly motivated workers. And realistically, there are jobs that don't readily lend themselves to being made more challenging and interesting or to being redesigned. Some tasks, for instance, are just far more efficiently done on assembly lines than in teams. This leaves limited options. You may not be able to do much more than try to make a bad situation tolerable by creating a pleasant work climate. This might include providing clean and attractive work surroundings, ample work breaks, the opportunity to socialize with colleagues during these breaks, and empathetic supervisors.

SUMMARY AND IMPLICATIONS FOR MANAGERS

We've presented a number of motivation theories and applications in this and the previous chapter. While it's always dangerous to synthesize a large number of complex ideas into a few simple guidelines, the following suggestions summarize the essence of what we know about motivating employees in organizations.

Recognize Individual Differences   Employees have different needs. Don't treat them all alike. Moreover, spend the time necessary to understand what's important to each employee. This will allow you to individualize goals, level of involvement, and rewards to align with individual needs.

Use Goals and Feedback   Employees should have hard, specific goals, as well as feedback on how well they are faring in pursuit of those goals.

Allow Employees to Participate in Decisions that Affect Them   Employees can contribute to a number of decisions that affect them: setting work goals, choosing their own benefits packages, solving productivity and quality problems, and the like. This can increase employee productivity, commitment to work goals, motivation, and job satisfaction.

Link Rewards to Performance   Rewards should be contingent on performance. Importantly, employees must perceive a clear linkage. Regardless of how closely rewards are actually correlated to performance criteria, if individuals perceive this relationship to be low, the results will be low performance, a decrease in job satisfaction, and an increase in turnover and absenteeism.

Check the System for Equity   Rewards should also be perceived by employees as equating with the inputs they bring to the job. At a simplistic level, this should mean that experience, skills, abilities, effort, and other obvious inputs should explain differences in performance and, hence, pay, job assignments, and other obvious rewards.

The Power of Stock Options as a Motivator

S tock options are being used as incentives for booksellers at Borders, clerks at Wal-Mart, box packers at Pfizer, chemical-plant operators at Monsanto, baggage handlers at Delta Air Lines, and part-time espresso servers at Starbucks.[a]

Approximately 10 million U.S. employees currently receive options, roughly a 10-fold jump since 1992. One study found that 39 percent of large U.S. companies now have stock option plans that cover all or a majority of employees—from the CEO down to operatives. And while plans vary, most are allocated as a percentage of annual income and allow employees to buy their employer's stock at a price below the fair market value.

Proponents of broad-based stock offer a long list of reasons to explain these plans' popularity: They help to: create a company-wide "ownership" culture by focusing employees' attention on the employers' financial performance; create a pay-for-performance climate; foster pride of ownership; raise morale; encourage retention of employees; attract new employees; and motivate front-line employees who interact with customers.

Starbucks' experience provides insights into the power of stock options as a motivator. Their program began in 1991. Each employee was awarded stock options worth 12 percent of his or her annual base pay. Every October since then, high profits have allowed Starbucks to raise the grant to 14 percent of base pay. An employee making $20,000 a year in 1991 could have recently cashed in his 1991 options alone for more than $70,000.

Starbucks' management believes stock options allow employees to share both the ownership of the company and the rewards of financial success. And management contends that it's working. The company's CEO says, "People started coming up with innovative ideas about how to cut costs, to increase sales, to create value. Most important, they could speak to our customers from the heart, as partners in the business."

---

[a]This is based on "Starbucks' Secret Weapon," *Fortune*, September 29, 1997, p. 268; "Stock Options for the Ranks," *Business Week*, September 7, 1998, p. 22; and E. Ackerman, "Optionnaires, Beware!" *U.S. News & World Report*, March 6, 2000, pp. 36–38.

B road-based stock options sound terrific in theory. Motivation increases because employees see themselves as owners, rather than merely workers. And these options create the opportunity for moderately-paid employees to accumulate substantial savings. What's wrong with the theory? Several things.[b]

First is the fact that options tend to be disproportionately allocated to managers. Because options are typically distributed as a percent of base pay, managers get more of them because they make more money. Senior executives also tend to get additional options based on company profitability or stock performance. This is how someone like Gerald Levin, when he was CEO of AOL Time Warner, could make $152 million in one year alone from his options. Such huge payoffs make the few thousand dollars a low-level AOL Time Warner employee gets from her options seem like "chump change." This comparison is just as likely to anger or frustrate nonmanagerial employees as it is to motivate them.

Second, stock options are poor motivators because they offer a weak link between employee effort and rewards. How much impact can the average worker really have on the company's stock price? Very little! The decline in the price of high-tech stocks in 2000 and 2001 made a majority of stock options at these firms worthless, yet this was a time when many employees of these high-tech firms were working harder than ever to try to keep their companies alive.

Finally, stock options are great when a company is growing rapidly or during bull markets in stocks. Starbucks's plan proved very profitable for employees between 1991 and 2000 because the company grew rapidly. But all companies aren't growing, nor do stock markets go up forever. Stock options issued to employees at companies like Cisco Systems, Amazon.com, Oracle, and eToys in the mid-1990s were essentially worthless in the summer of 2002. When high-tech stocks imploded, so did thousands of employees' dreams of wealth and early retirement. Stock options may actually become demotivators when employees realize that they are like a lottery, with very few big winners.

---

[b]This is based on K. Capell, "Options for Everyone," *Business Week*, July 22, 1996, pp. 80–84; P. Coy, "The Drawbacks of Stock-Option Fever," *Business Week*, December 13, 1999, p. 204; and D. Henry and M. Conlin, "Too Much of a Good Incentive?" *Business Week*, March 4, 2002, pp. 38–39.

1. Relate goal-setting theory to the MBO process. How are they similar? Different?

2. What is an ESOP? How might it positively influence employee motivation?

3. Explain the roles of employees and management in quality circles.

4. What are the pluses of variable-pay programs from an employee's viewpoint? From management's viewpoint?

5. Contrast job-based and skill-based pay.

6. What is gainsharing? What explains its recent popularity?

7. What motivates professional employees?

8. What motivates contingent employees?

9. Is it possible to motivate low-skilled service workers? Discuss.

10. What can you do, as a manager, to increase the likelihood that your employees will exert a high level of effort?

Questions for Critical Thinking

1. Identify five different criteria by which organizations can compensate employees. Based on your knowledge and experience, do you think performance is the criterion most used in practice? Discuss.

2. "Recognition may be motivational for the moment but it doesn't have any staying power. It's an empty reinforcer. Why? Because when you go to the grocery store, they don't take recognition as a form of payment!" Do you agree or disagree? Discuss.

3. "Performance can't be measured, so any effort to link pay with performance is a fantasy. Differences in performance are often caused by the system, which means the organization ends up rewarding the circumstances. It's the same thing as reward-ing the weather forecaster for a pleasant day." Do you agree or disagree with this statement? Support your position.

4. It's an indisputable fact that there has been an explosive increase in the difference between the average U.S. worker's income and those of senior executives. In 1980 the average CEO made 42 times the average blue-collar worker's pay. In 1990 it was 85 times. In 2000 it had risen to 531 times. What are the implications of this trend for motivation in organizations?

5. This book argues for recognizing individual differences. It also suggests paying attention to members of diversity groups. Is this contradictory? Discuss.

Team Exercise   Goal-Setting Task

Purpose

This exercise will help you learn how to write tangible, verifiable, measurable, and relevant goals as might evolve from an MBO program.

Time

Approximately 20 to 30 minutes.

Instructions

1. Break into groups of three to five.

2. Spend a few minutes discussing your class instructor's job. What does he or she do? What defines good performance? What behaviors will lead to good performance?

3. Each group is to develop a list of five goals that, although not established partic-ipatively with your instructor, you believe might be developed in an MBO pro-gram at your college. Try to select goals that seem most critical to the effective performance of your instructor's job.

4. Each group will select a leader who will share his or her group's goals with the entire class. For each group's goals, class discussion should focus on their: (a) specificity, (b) ease of measurement, (c) importance, and (d) motivational properties.

Ethical Dilemma | Are American CEOs Paid Too Much?

Critics have described the astronomical pay packages given to American CEO's as "rampant greed." They note, for instance, that during the 1990s, corporate profits rose 108 percent. During this same period, workers' pay rose only 28 percent. Yet CEO pay rose 481 percent! In the year 2000, the average CEO of a major American corporation made 531 times as much as the average factory worker. If the average production workers' pay had increased at the same rate as CEO pay during this period, worker pay would be $110,399 today rather than $29,267.

High levels of executive compensation seem to be widely spread in the United States. In 2000, for instance, John Chambers of Cisco Systems took home $157.3 million; General Electric's Jack Welch was paid $122.6 million; and Coca-Cola's Douglas Daft earned $91.7 million. These figures were for pay and exercised stock options only. They do *not* include potentially hundreds of millions more from appreciated value of unexercised stock options. Twenty-five years ago, an executive who earned a million dollars a year made headlines. Now it's "routine" for a senior executive at a large U.S. corporation to earn more than $1 million in compensation.

How do you explain these astronomical pay packages? Some say this represents a classic economic response to a situation in which the demand is great for high-quality top executive talent and the supply is low. Ira Kay, a compensation consultant, says: "It's not fair to compare [executives] with hourly workers. Their market is the global market for executives." Other arguments in favor of paying executives $1 million a year or more are: the need to compensate people for the tremendous responsibilities and stress that go with such jobs, the motivating potential that seven- and eight-figure annual incomes provide to senior executives and those who might aspire to be, the need to

keep the best and the brightest in the corporate world rather than being enticed into investment banking or venture capital firms, and the influence that senior executives have on a company's bottom line.

Contrary to the global argument, executive pay is considerably higher in the United States than in most other countries. In 1998, the most recent year for which data is available, American CEOs of industrial companies with annual revenues of $250 million to $500 million made, on average, $1,072,400. Comparable figures for Britain, France, Canada, Mexico, and Japan were, respectively, $645,540, $520,389, $498,118, $456,902, and $420,855. All evidence suggests that this gap between American CEOs and those from other countries has only grown since these data were calculated.

Critics of executive pay practices in the United States argue that CEOs choose board members whom they can count on to support ever-increasing pay (including lucrative bonus and stock-option plans) for top management. If board members fail to "play along," they risk losing their positions, their fees, and the prestige and power inherent in board membership.

Is high compensation of U.S. executives a problem? If so, does the blame for the problem lie with CEOs or with the shareholders and boards that knowingly allow the practice? Are American CEO's greedy? Are these CEO's acting unethically? What do you think?

Source: Towers, Perrin, *Worldwide Total Rewards 1998* (April 1998), p. 21; J. Greenfield, "Study Finds Inequities in CEO Pay, Worker Pay, Profits," *The Working Stiff Journal*, October 1999; L. Lavelle, "Executive Pay," *Business Week*, April 16, 2001, pp. 76–80; and R. C. Longworth, "CEO Pay 531 Times That of Workers; Study: Gap Grows Despite Downturn," *Chicago Tribune*, August 28, 2001.

For Ted Sims, it was a double whammy. First, Sims had 60 percent of his 401(k) retirement account in his employer's stock, Lucent Technologies. Between 1996 and 1999, Lucent stock rose 10-fold to $80 a share, boosting his retirement nest egg to about $70,000. Then the stock's price collapsed. In the fall of 2001, his Lucent "nest egg" was worth around $31,000. If that weren't bad enough news, Sims lost his job in one of the many job cuts Lucent made following the meltdown in the telecommunications industry in 2000.

Ted Sims isn't alone in his suffering. He has plenty of sympathy from former Enron employees like Marie Thibaut. She spent 15 years as an administrative assistant at Enron in Houston. She dutifully put 15 percent of her salary into a 401(k) plan, investing the entire amount in the company's stock. When the company collapsed in the winter of 2000, so did the 61-year-old divorcee's retirement plans. The value of her Enron stock, which had been worth close to $500,000, dropped to just $22,000.

Having a majority of one's retirement savings in an employer's stock is no longer unusual. Procter & Gamble, Coca-Cola, Dell Computer, and McDonald's are all firms at which more than 70 percent of employees' 401(k) assets are held in company stock. And the price of these companies' shares fell between 21 percent and 56 percent from April 2000 to April 2001.

Thirty years ago, this issue was irrelevant. Then, most employers offered defined benefit pension plans. So, for instance, an employee retired from AT&T at age 65, with 30 years of service, making $55,000 a year, and the company provided him with a guaranteed annual pension of around $24,000 for the rest of his life. This changed in the early-1980s, with the creation of 401(k) programs—retirement savings plans that are funded by employee contributions and (often) matching contributions from the employer. Most employers dropped their pension plans and replaced with them 401(k) programs. The major benefits of these programs, in addition to allowing funds to grow tax-free until they are withdrawn, was that they could be carried from employer to employer should a participant change jobs and they allowed the employee some discretion in how the funds were invested. Today, approximately 80 percent of eligible American workers participate in 401(k)s.

While financial planners routinely advise against putting more than 10 percent of one's portfolio in one stock, millions of employees routinely invest a much larger portion of their 401(k) assets in their employer's stock. Currently, for instance, 41 percent of 401(k) assets are invested in the stock of participants' employers. Why this lack of diversification? There seem to be at least four reasons. First, many employers give matching contributions only in company stock. Second, companies often set age or tenure requirements that employees must meet before they can sell company stock from matching contributions. Third, many employees believe that because they work at a company, they are in a better position to predict its stock performance. And fourth, employees often feel that investing in their employer's stock is a way of showing company loyalty.

As long as a company's stock was appreciating rapidly, putting "all your eggs in one basket" proved to be an effective strategy. But in times of economic uncertainty, when major corporations like IBM, Polaroid, Eastman Kodak, and Gillette can have their stock prices drop by 50 percent or more, employees who have a disproportionate amount of their 401(k) assets in their employer's stock, risk absorbing large declines in their retirement funds. One 52-year-old AT&T employee summed up his experience this way: "I put my retirement money in AT&T stock because I knew the company and its record of dependability. They didn't call it Ma Bell for nothing. Now I've watched my retirement assets decline by more than 65 percent. I had planned on retiring early—at age 55. It's looking more like at least 62 now."

Questions

1. Consider the effects of having 40 percent or more of an employee's retirement funds in the company's stock on his or her work motivation.

2. What are the advantages and disadvantages for companies having the bulk of their employees' 401(k) funds tied up in the company's stock?

3. What ethical implications, if any, are there in a company matching an employee's retirement contribution with company stock?

Source: This case is based on P. J. Lim, "The 401(k) Blues Have Some Investors Rethinking Strategy," *U.S. News & World Report*, April 2, 2001, pp. 52–54; "Don't Bank 401(k) on Employer's Stock," *USA Today.com*, August 4, 2000; and J. Kahn, "When 401(k)s are KO'd," *Fortune*, January 7, 2002, p. 104.

Endnotes

1. Based on G. Dyer, "A Renaissance Maverick," *Financial Times*, October 18, 2001, pp. 10–11; and G. Colvin, "The Anti-Control Freak," *Fortune*, November 26, 2001, p. 60.
2. E. O. Welles, "Great Expectations," *INC.*, March 2001, pp. 68–73.
3. P. F. Drucker, *The Practice of Management* (New York: Harper & Row, 1954).
4. See, for instance, S. J. Carroll and H. L. Tosi, *Management by Objectives: Applications and Research* (New York, Macmillan, 1973); and R. Rodgers and J. E. Hunter, "Impact of Management by Objectives on Organizational Productivity," *Journal of Applied Psychology*, April 1991, pp. 322–36.
5. See, for instance, R. C. Ford, F. S. MacLaughlin, and J. Nixdorf, "Ten Questions about MBO," *California Management Review*, Winter 1980, p. 89; T. J. Collamore, "Making MBO Work in the Public Sector," *Bureaucrat*, Fall 1989, pp. 37–40; G. Dabbs, "Nonprofit Businesses in the 1990s: Models for Success," *Business Horizons*, September–October 1991, pp. 68–71; R. Rodgers and J. E. Hunter, "A Foundation of Good Management Practice in Government: Management by Objectives," *Public Administration Review*, January–February 1992, pp. 27–39; T. H. Poister and G. Streib, "MBO in Municipal Government: Variations on a Traditional Management Tool," *Public Administration Review*, January/February 1995, pp. 48–56; and C. Garvey, "Goalsharing Scores," *HRMagazine*, April 2000, pp. 99–106.
6. See, for instance, C. H. Ford, "MBO: An Idea Whose Time Has Gone?" *Business Horizons*, December 1979, p. 49; R. Rodgers and J. E. Hunter, "Impact of Management by Objectives on Organizational Productivity," *Journal of Applied Psychology*, April 1991, pp. 322–36; R. Rodgers, J. E. Hunter , and D. L. Rogers, "Influence of Top Management Commitment on Management Program Success," *Journal of Applied Psychology*, February 1993, pp. 151–55; and M. Tanikawa, "Fujitsu Decides to Backtrack on Performance-Based Pay," *New York Times*, March 22, 2001, p. W1.
7. F. Luthans and A. D. Stajkovic, "Provide Recognition for Performance Improvement," in E. A. Locke (ed.), *Principles of Organizational Behavior* (Oxford, England: Blackwell, 2000), pp. 166–80.
8. D. Drickhamer, "Best Plant Winners: Nichols Foods Ltd.," *Industry Week*, October 1, 2001, pp. 17–19.
9. M. Littman, "Best Bosses Tell All," *Working Woman*, October 2000, p. 54.
10. Cited in S. Caudron, "The Top 20 Ways to Motivate Employees," *Industry Week*, April 3, 1995, pp. 15–16. See also B. Nelson, "Try Praise," *INC.*, September 1996, p. 115.
11. A. D. Stajkovic and F. Luthans, "Differential Effects of Incentive Motivators on Work Performance," *Academy of Management Journal*, June 2001, p. 587.
12. B. Leonard, "Performance Is the Key to Reforming Reward Programs," *HRMagazine,* May 2000, p. 20.
13. Cited in *Asian Business*, December 1994, p. 3.
14. Several of these examples come from C. Fishman, "Engines of Democracy," *Fast Company*, October 1999, pp. 174–202; and J. Flaherty, "Suggestions Rise From the Floors of U.S. Factories," *New York Times*, April 18, 2001, p. C1.
15. J. L. Cotton, *Employee Involvement* (Newbury Park, CA: Sage, 1993), pp. 3, 14.
16. Ibid., p. 3.
17. See, for example, the increasing body of literature on empowerment such as R. C. Ford and M. D. Fottler, "Empowerment: A Matter of Degree," *The Academy of Management Executive*, August 1995, pp. 21–31; K. Blanchard, J. P. Carlos, and W. A. Randolph, *The 3 Keys to Empowerment: Release the Power within People for Astonishing Results* (San Francisco: Berrett-Koehler, 1999); W. A. Randolph, "Re-Thinking Empowerment: Why Is It So Hard to Achieve?" *Organizational Dynamics*, vol. 29, no. 2, 2000,

pp. 94–107; and D. P. Ashmos, D. Duchon, R. R. McDaniel, Jr., and J. W. Huonker, "What a Mess! Participation as a Simple Managerial Rule to 'Complexify' Organizations," *Journal of Management Studies*, March 2002, pp. 189–206.

18. See M. Sashkin, "Participative Management Is an Ethical Imperative," *Organizational Dynamics*, Spring 1984, pp. 5–22; and D. Collins, "The Ethical Superiority and Inevitability of Participatory Management as an Organizational System," *Organization Science*, September–October 1997, pp. 489–507.

19. F. Heller, E. Pusic, G. Strauss, and B. Wilpert, *Organizational Participation: Myth and Reality* (Oxford: Oxford University Press, 1998).

20. K. L. Miller and P. R. Monge, "Participation, Satisfaction, and Productivity: A Meta-Analytic Review," *Academy of Management Journal*, December 1986, pp. 727–53; J. A. Wagner III and R. Z. Gooding, "Shared Influence and Organizational Behavior: A Meta-Analysis of Situational Variables Expected to Moderate Participation–Outcome Relationships," *Academy of Management Journal*, September 1987, pp. 524–41; J. A. Wagner III, "Participation's Effects on Performance and Satisfaction: A Reconsideration of Research Evidence," *Academy of Management Review*, April 1994, pp. 312–30; C. Doucouliagos, "Worker Participation and Productivity in Labor-Managed and Participatory Capitalist Firms: A Meta-Analysis," *Industrial and Labor Relations Review*, October 1995, pp. 58–77; J. A. Wagner III, C. R. Leana, E. A. Locke, and D. M. Schweiger, "Cognitive and Motivational Frameworks in U.S. Research on Participation: A Meta-Analysis of Primary Effects," *Journal of Organizational Behavior*, vol. 18, 1997, pp. 49–65; J. S. Black and H. B. Gregersen, "Participative Decision-Making: An Integration of Multiple Dimensions," *Human Relations*, July 1997, pp. 859–78; and E. A. Locke, M. Alavi, and J. A. Wagner III, "Participation in Decision Making: An Information Exchange Perspective," in G. R. Ferris (ed.), *Research in Personnel and Human Resource Management*, vol. 15 (Greenwich, CT: JAI Press, 1997), pp. 293–331.

21. J. L. Cotton, *Employee Involvement*, p. 114.

22. See, for example, M. Poole, "Industrial Democracy: A Comparative Analysis," *Industrial Relations*, Fall 1979, pp. 262–72; IDE International Research Group, *European Industrial Relations* (Oxford, UK: Clarendon, 1981); E. M. Kassalow, "Employee Representation on U.S., German Boards," *Monthly Labor Review*, September 1989, pp. 39–42; T. H. Hammer, S. C. Currall, and R. N. Stern, "Worker Representation on Boards of Directors: A Study of Competing Roles," *Industrial and Labor Relations Review*, Winter 1991, pp. 661–80; and P. Kunst and J. Soeters, "Works Council Membership and Career Opportunities," *Organization Studies*, vol. 12, no. 1, 1991, pp. 75–93.

23. J. D. Kleyn and S. Perrick, "Netherlands," *International Financial Law Review*, February 1990, pp. 51–56.

24. J. L. Cotton, *Employee Involvement*, pp. 129–30, 139–40.

25. Ibid., p. 140.

26. See, for example, G. W. Meyer and R. G. Stott, "Quality Circles: Panacea or Pandora's Box?" *Organizational Dynamics*, Spring 1985, pp. 34–50; E. E. Lawler III and S. A. Mohrman, "Quality Circles: After the Honeymoon," *Organizational Dynamics*, Spring 1987, pp. 42–54; T. R. Miller, "The Quality Circle Phenomenon: A Review and Appraisal," *SAM Advanced Management Journal*, Winter 1989, pp. 4–7; K. Buch and R. Spangler, "The Effects of Quality Circles on Performance and Promotions," *Human Relations*, June 1990, pp. 573–82; P. R. Liverpool, "Employee Participation in Decision-Making: An Analysis of the Perceptions of Members and Nonmembers of Quality Circles," *Journal of Business and Psychology*, Summer 1990, pp. 411–22, and E. E. Adams, Jr., "Quality Circle Performance," *Journal of Management*, March 1991, pp. 25–39.

27. J. L. Cotton, *Employee Involvement*, p. 76.

28. Ibid., p. 78.

29. Ibid., p. 87.

30. See K. M. Young (ed.), *The Expanding Role of ESOPs in Public Companies* (New York: Quorum, 1990); J. L. Pierce and C. A. Furo, "Employee Ownership: Implications for Management," *Organizational Dynamics*, Winter 1990, pp. 32–43; A. A. Buchko, "The Effects of Employee Ownership on Employee Attitudes: An Integrated Causal Model and Path Analysis," *Journal of Management Studies*, July 1993, pp. 633–56; and J. McDonald, "The Boom in Employee Ownership," *INC.*, August 2000, pp. 106–112.

31. "The Employee Ownership 100," www.nceo.org; December 2001.

32. A. A. Buchko, "The Effects of Employee Ownership on Employee Attitudes."

33. C. M. Rosen and M. Quarrey, "How Well Is Employee Ownership Working?" *Harvard Business Review*, September–October 1987, pp. 126–32.

34. Cited in "ESOP Benefits Are No Fables," *Business Week*, September 6, 1999, p. 26.

35. W. N. Davidson and D. L. Worrell, "ESOP's Fables: The Influence of Employee Stock Ownership Plans on Corporate Stock Prices and Subsequent Operating Performance," *Human Resource Planning*, January 1994, pp. 69–85.

36. Pierce and Furo, "Employee Ownership."

37. See data in D. Stamps, "A Piece of the Action," *Training*, March 1996, p. 66.

38. C. Robert, T. M. Probst, J. J. Martocchio, R. Drasgow, and J. J. Lawler, "Empowerment and Continuous Improvement in the United States, Mexico, Poland, and India: Predicting Fit on the Basis of the Dimensions of Power Distance and Individualism," *Journal of Applied Psychology*, October 2000, pp. 643–58.

39. Pierce and Furo, "Employee Ownership," p. 32; and S. Kaufman, "ESOPs' Appeal on the Increase," *Nation's Business*, June 1997, p. 43.

40. M. Arndt, "From Milestone to Millstone?" *Business Week*, March 20, 2000, pp. 120–22.

41. C. Farrell, "Now, More Can Join the ESOP Game," *Business Week*, May 25, 1998, pp. ENT20–22.

42. "Denver Teachers Accept Plan Linking Pay to Performance," *New York Times*, September 12, 1999, p. Y25; and T. Henry, "States to Tie Teacher Pay to Results," *USA Today*, September 30, 1999, p. 1A.

43. Based on J. R. Schuster and P. K. Zingheim, "The New Variable Pay: Key Design Issues," *Compensation & Benefits Review*, March–April 1993, p. 28; and K. S. Abosch, "Variable Pay: Do We Have the Basics in Place?" *Compensation & Benefits Review*, July–August 1998, pp. 12–22.

44. B. Wysocki, Jr, "Chilling Reality Awaits Even the Employed," *Wall Street Journal*, November 5, 2001, p. A1.

45. L. Lavelle, "Executive Pay," *Business Week*, April 16, 2001, p. 77.

46. R. Balu, "Bonuses Aren't Just for the Bosses," *Fast Company*, December 2000, pp. 74–76; and M. Conlin, "A Little Less in the Envelope This Week," *Business Week*, February 18, 2002, pp. 64–66.

47. See, for instance, S. E. Gross and D. Duncan, "Case Study: Gainsharing Plans Spurs Record Productivity and Payouts at AmeriSteel," *Compensation and Benefits Review*, November–December 1998, pp. 46–50; J. B. Arthur and G. S. Jelf, "The Effects of Gainsharing on Grievance Rates and Absenteeism," *Journal of Labor Research*, vol. 20, 1999, pp. 133–45; and L. R. Gomez-Mejia, T. M. Welbourne, and R. M. Wiseman, "The Role of Risk Sharing and Risk Taking Under Gainsharing," *Academy of Management Review*, July 2000, pp. 492–507.

48. C. G. Hanson and W. D. Bell, *Profit Sharing and Profitability: How Profit Sharing Promotes Business Success* (London: Kogan Page, 1987); and M. Magnan and S. St-Onge, "Profit-Sharing and Firm Performance: A Comparative and Longitudinal Analysis," paper presented at the 58th annual meeting of the Academy of Management, San Diego, August 1998.

49. T. M. Welbourne and L. R. Gomez-Mejia, "Gainsharing: A Critical Review and a Future Research Agenda," *Journal of Management*, vol. 21, no. 3, 1995, pp. 559–609.

50. See J. L. Cotton, *Employee Involvement*, pp. 89–113; and W. Imberman, "Boosting Plant Performance with Gainsharing," *Business Horizons*, November–December 1992, p. 79.

51. M. Fein, "Work Measurement and Wage Incentives," *Industrial Engineering*, September 1973, pp. 49–51. For an updated review of the effect of pay on performance, see G. D. Jenkins, Jr., N. Gupta, A. Mitra, and J. D. Shaw, "Are Financial Incentives Related to Performance? A Meta-Analytic Review of Empirical Research," *Journal of Applied Psychology*, October 1998, pp. 777–87.

52. W. Zellner, "Trickle-Down Is Trickling Down at Work," *Business Week*, March 18, 1996, p. 34; and "Linking Pay to Performance is Becoming a Norm in the Workplace," *Wall Street Journal*, April 6, 1999, p. A1.

53. G. Koretz, "Pay Perks Cloud the Crystal Ball," *Business Week*, September 10, 2001, p. 34; and "As Bonuses Evaporate, a Reluctant Consumer," *New York Times*, December 10, 2001, p. C5.

54. "More Than 20 Percent of Japanese Firms Use Pay Systems Based on Performance," *Manpower Argus*, May 1998, p. 7.

55. "U.S. Wage and Productivity Growth Attainable Through Gainsharing," Employment Policy Foundation; www.epf.org; May 10, 2000.

56. See, for example, R. Ganzel, "What's Wrong with Pay for Performance?" *Training*, December 1998, pp. 34–40.

57. See "Skilled-Based Pay Boosts Worker Productivity and Morale," *Wall Street Journal*, June 23, 1992, p. A1; L. Wiener, "No New Skills? No Raise," *U.S. News & World Report*, October 26, 1992, p. 78; and M. A. Verespej, "New Responsibilities? New Pay!" *Industry Week*, August 15, 1994, p. 14; and "Skill-Based Pay Program," www.bmpoc.org, June 29, 2001.

58. G. E. Ledford, Jr., "Paying for the Skills, Knowledge, and Competencies of Knowledge Workers," *Compensation & Benefits Review*, July–August 1995, pp. 55–62; and B. Murray and B. Gerhart, "An Empirical Analysis of a Skill-Based Pay Program and Plant Performance Outcomes," *Academy of Management Journal*, February 1998, pp. 68–78.

59. E. E. Lawler III, G. E. Ledford, Jr., and L. Chang, "Who Uses Skill-Based Pay, and Why," *Compensation & Benefits Review*, March–April 1993, p. 22.

60. "Tensions of a New Pay Plan," *New York Times*, May 17, 1992, p. F5.

61. E. E. Lawler III, S. A. Mohrman, and G. E. Ledford, Jr., *Creating High Performance Organizations: Practices and Results in the Fortune 1000* (San Francisco: Jossey-Bass, 1995); C. Lee, K. S. Law, and P. Bobko, "The Importance of Justice Perceptions on Pay Effectiveness: A Two-Year Study of a Skill-Based Pay Plan," *Journal of Management*, vol. 25, no. 6, 1999, pp. 851–73; A. Podolske, "Seven-Year Update on Skill-Based Pay Plans," www.ioma.com, July 1999.

62. E. E. Lawler III, G. E. Ledford, Jr., and L. Chang, "Who Uses Skill-Based Pay, and Why."

63. M. Rowland, "It's What You Can Do That Counts," *New York Times*, June 6, 1993, p. F17.

64. Ibid.

65. See, for instance, M. W. Barringer and G. T. Milkovich, "A Theoretical Exploration of the Adoption and Design of Flexible Benefit Plans: A Case of Human Resource

Innovation," *Academy of Management Review*, April 1998, pp. 305–24; J. A. Fraser, "Stretching Your Benefits Dollar," *INC.*, March 2000, pp. 123–26; and J. J. Meyer, "The Future of Flexible Benefit Plans," *Employee Benefits Journal*, June 2000, pp. 3–7.

66. D. A. DeCenzo and S. P. Robbins, *Human Resource Management*, 7th ed. (New York: Wiley, 2002), pp. 346–48.

67. E. E. Lawler III, "Reward Systems," in J. R. Hackman and J. L. Suttle (eds.), *Improving Life at Work* (Santa Monica, CA: Goodyear, 1977), p. 182.

68. L. Alderman and S. Kim, "Get the Most from Your Company Benefits," *Money*, January 1996, pp. 102–06.

69. See, for instance, C. Meyer, "What Makes Workers Tick?" *INC.*, December 1997, pp. 74–81; N. Munk, "The New Organization Man," *Fortune*, March 16, 1998, pp. 62–74; D. Levy, "Net Elite: 'It's Not About Money,'" *USA Today*, February 22, 1999, p. B1; and M. W. Walsh, "Money Isn't Everything," *New York Times*, January 30, 2001, p. E10.

70. "Six Million Americans Say Jobs Are Temporary," *Manpower Argus*, November 1995, p. 2; and "What Contingent Work Is," www.fairjobs.org, November 2001.

71. A. Penzias, "New Paths to Success," *Fortune*, June 12, 1995, pp. 90–94; and S. Greenhouse, "Equal Work, Less-Equal Perks," *New York Times*, March 30, 1998, p. C1.

72. U.S. Bureau of Labor Statistics, "Employed Contingent Workers By Their Preference for Contingent or Noncontingent Work Arrangements, February 2001," U.S. Department of Labor; www.bls.gov.

73. B. Filipczak, "Managing a Mixed Work Force," *Training*, October 1997, pp. 96–103.

74. D. Hage and J. Impoco, "Jawboning the Jobs," *U.S. News & World Report*, August 9, 1993, p. 53.

PART THREE
THE GROUP

Many of us like to think that status isn't as important as it was a generation or two ago. We can point to Equal Rights legislation, open office
designs, casual work dress, and employee empowerment as examples of
forces that have made organizations more egalitarian. The reality is that we
continue to live in an essentially class-structured society.

Despite all attempts to make it more egalitarian, we have made little
progress toward a classless society. Even the smallest group will develop
roles, rights, and rituals to differentiate its members. We're even finding that
New Economy organizations adapt mechanisms to create status differences.
Take, for instance, e-mail. Here is a communication tool that its proponents
claim democratizes organizations. It allows people to communicate up and
down hierarchical lines, unimpeded by gatekeepers and protocols. It allows,
for example, people low in the organization to directly communicate with
higher-ups without going through traditional authority channels. But you
know what? Status differences have creeped into the e-mail process. A recent study of some 30,000 e-mail messages at a New Economy firm that
didn't use job titles, was organized around teams, and prided itself on
democratic decision making provides interesting insights.[1]

In spite of e-mails' egalitarian intentions, employees in this company had
found ways to use it and still create social distinctions. For instance, high-
status employees tended to send short, curt messages, in part to minimize
contact with lower-status workers but also to convey comfort with their
own authority. In contrast, midstatus employees tended to produce long, argumentative messages loaded with jargon or overexplained answers to simple questions. And low-status employees' e-mails would contain non–work-
related elements such as forwarded jokes or happy-face "emoticons." In
addition, the study found that senior managers would take the longest to reply, had the poorest spelling, and the worst grammar—which all conveyed
that they have better things to do with their time.

Foundations of Group Behavior

The creation of status differences is just one of a number of naturally occurring actions in groups. Along with concepts like roles and norms, an understanding of status can help you better explain and predict the behavior of people in groups. The objectives of this and the following chapter are to provide you with a foundation for understanding how groups work and to show you how to create effective teams. Let's begin by defining groups and explaining why people join them.

DEFINING AND CLASSIFYING GROUPS

A **group** is defined as two or more individuals, interacting and interdependent, who have come together to achieve particular objectives. Groups can be either formal or informal. By **formal groups**, we mean those defined by the organization's structure, with designated work assignments establishing tasks. In formal groups, the behaviors that one should engage in are stipulated by and directed toward organizational goals. The six members making up an airline flight crew are an example of a formal group. In contrast, **informal groups** are alliances that are neither formally structured nor organizationally determined. These groups are natural formations in the work environment that appear in response to the need for social contact. Three employees from different departments who regularly eat lunch together are an example of an informal group.

It's possible to further subclassify groups as command, task, interest, or friendship groups.[2] Command and task groups are dictated by the formal organization, while interest and friendship groups are informal alliances.

LEARNING OBJECTIVES

AFTER STUDYING THIS CHAPTER, YOU SHOULD BE ABLE TO:

1. Differentiate between formal and informal groups.

2. Compare two models of group development.

3. Explain how group interaction can be analyzed.

4. Identify the key factors in explaining group behavior.

5. Explain how role requirements change in different situations.

6. Describe how norms exert influence on an individual's behavior.

7. Define social loafing and its effect on group performance.

8. Identify the benefits and disadvantages of cohesive groups.

9. List the strengths and weaknesses of group decision making.

10. Contrast the effectiveness of interacting, brainstorming, nominal, and electronic meeting groups.

group

Two or more individuals, interacting and interdependent, who have come together to achieve particular objectives.

formal group

A designated work group defined by the organization's structure.

informal group

A group that is neither formally structured nor organizationally determined; appears in response to the need for social contact.

command group

A group composed of the individuals who report directly to a given manager.

task group

Those working together to complete a job task.

interest group

Those working together to attain a specific objective with which each is concerned.

friendship group

Those brought together because they share one or more common characteristics.

five-stage group-development model

Groups go through five distinct stages: forming, storming, norming, performing, and adjourning.

forming stage

The first stage in group development, characterized by much uncertainty.

A **command group** is determined by the organization chart. It is composed of the individuals who report directly to a given manager. An elementary school principal and her 18 teachers form a command group, as do the director of postal audits and his five inspectors.

Task groups, also organizationally determined, represent those working together to complete a job task. However, a task group's boundaries are not limited to its immediate hierarchical superior. It can cross command relationships. For instance, if a college student is accused of a campus crime, it may require communication and coordination among the dean of academic affairs, the dean of students, the registrar, the director of security, and the student's advisor. Such a formation would constitute a task group. It should be noted that all command groups are also task groups, but because task groups can cut across the organization, the reverse need not be true.

People who may or may not be aligned into common command or task groups may affiliate to attain a specific objective with which each is concerned. This is an **interest group**. Employees who band together to have their vacation schedules altered, to support a peer who has been fired, or to seek improved working conditions represent the formation of a united body to further their common interest.

Groups often develop because the individual members have one or more common characteristics. We call these formations **friendship groups**. Social alliances, which frequently extend outside the work situation, can be based on similar age or ethnic heritage, support for Notre Dame football, or the holding of similar political views, to name just a few such characteristics.

Informal groups provide a very important service by satisfying their members' social needs. Because of interactions that result from the close proximity of workstations or task interactions, we find workers often do things together—like play golf, commute to work, take lunch, and chat during coffee breaks. We must recognize that these types of interactions among individuals, even though informal, deeply affect their behavior and performance.

There is no single reason why individuals join groups. Because most people belong to a number of groups, it's obvious that different groups provide different benefits to their members. Exhibit 8-1 summarizes the most popular reasons people have for joining groups.

STAGES OF GROUP DEVELOPMENT

Groups generally pass through a standardized sequence in their evolution. We call this sequence the five-stage model of group development. Recent studies, however, indicate that temporary groups with task-specific deadlines follow a very different pattern. In this section, we describe the five-stage general model and an alternative model for temporary groups with deadlines.

The Five-Stage Model

As shown in Exhibit 8-2, the **five-stage group-development model** characterizes groups as proceeding through five distinct stages: forming, storming, norming, performing, and adjourning.[3]

The first stage, **forming**, is characterized by a great deal of uncertainty about the group's purpose, structure, and leadership. Members are "testing the waters" to determine what types of behavior are acceptable. This stage is complete when members have begun to think of themselves as part of a group.

The **storming** stage is one of intragroup conflict. Members accept the existence of the group, but there is resistance to the constraints that the group imposes on individuality. Furthermore, there is conflict over who will control the group. When this stage is complete, there will be a relatively clear hierarchy of leadership within the group.

The third stage is one in which close relationships develop and the group demonstrates cohesiveness. There is now a strong sense of group identity and camaraderie. This **norming** stage is complete when the group structure solidifies and the group has assimilated a common set of expectations of what defines correct member behavior.

The fourth stage is **performing**. The structure at this point is fully functional and accepted. Group energy has moved from getting to know and understand each other to performing the task at hand.

For permanent work groups, performing is the last stage in their development. However, for temporary committees, teams, task forces, and similar groups that

storming stage

The second stage in group development, characterized by intragroup conflict.

norming stage

The third stage in group development, characterized by close relationships and cohesiveness.

performing stage

The fourth stage in group development, when the group is fully functional.

Stages of Group Development

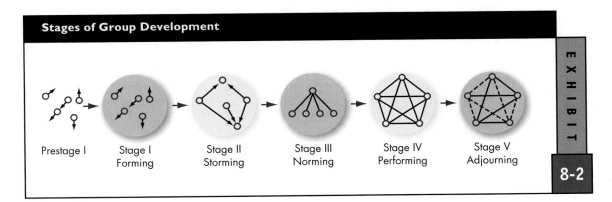

| Prestage I | Stage I Forming | Stage II Storming | Stage III Norming | Stage IV Performing | Stage V Adjourning |

EXHIBIT 8-2

adjourning stage

The final stage in group development for temporary groups, characterized by concern with wrapping up activities rather than task performance.

have a limited task to perform, there is an **adjourning** stage. In this stage, the group prepares for its disbandment. High task performance is no longer the group's top priority. Instead, attention is directed toward wrapping up activities. Responses of group members vary in this stage. Some are upbeat, basking in the group's accomplishments. Others may be depressed over the loss of camaraderie and friendships gained during the work group's life.

Many interpreters of the five-stage model have assumed that a group becomes more effective as it progresses through the first four stages. Although this assumption may be generally true, what makes a group effective is more complex than this model acknowledges. Under some conditions, high levels of conflict are conducive to high group performance. So we might expect to find situations in which groups in Stage II outperform those in Stage III or IV. Similarly, groups do not always proceed clearly from one stage to the next. Sometimes, in fact, several stages go on simultaneously, as when groups are storming and performing at the same time. Groups even occasionally regress to previous stages. Therefore, even the strongest proponents of this model do not assume that all groups follow its five-stage process precisely or that Stage IV is always the most preferable.

Another problem with the five-stage model, in terms of understanding work-related behavior, is that it ignores organizational context.[4] For instance, a study of a cockpit crew in an airliner found that, within ten minutes, three strangers assigned to fly together for the first time had become a high-performing group. What allowed for this speedy group development was the strong organizational context surrounding the tasks of the cockpit crew. This context provided the rules, task definitions, information, and resources needed for the group to perform. They didn't need to develop plans, assign roles, determine and allocate resources, resolve conflicts, and set norms the way the five-stage model predicts.

An Alternative Model: For Temporary Groups with Deadlines

punctuated-equilibrium model

Temporary groups go through transitions between inertia and activity.

Temporary groups with deadlines don't seem to follow the previous model. Studies indicate that they have their own unique sequencing of actions (or inaction): (1) Their first meeting sets the group's direction; (2) this first phase of group activity is one of inertia; (3) a transition takes place at the end of this first phase, which occurs exactly when the group has used up half its allotted time; (4) a transition initiates major changes; (5) a second phase of inertia follows the transition; and (6) the group's last meeting is characterized by markedly accelerated activity.[5] This pattern is called the **punctuated-equilibruim model** and is shown in Exhibit 8-3.

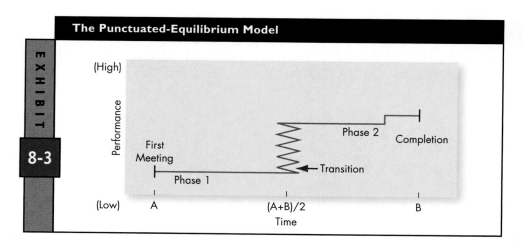

EXHIBIT 8-3

The Punctuated-Equilibrium Model

The first meeting sets the group's direction. A framework of behavioral patterns and assumptions through which the group will approach its project emerges in this first meeting. These lasting patterns can appear as early as the first few seconds of the group's life.

Once set, the group's direction becomes "written in stone" and is unlikely to be reexamined throughout the first half of the group's life. This is a period of inertia—that is, the group tends to stand still or become locked into a fixed course of action. Even if it gains new insights that challenge initial patterns and assumptions, the group is incapable of acting on these new insights in Phase 1.

One of the more interesting discoveries made in these studies was that each group experienced its transition at the same point in its calendar—precisely halfway between its first meeting and its official deadline—despite the fact that some groups spent as little as an hour on their project while others spent six months. It was as if the groups universally experienced a midlife crisis at this point. The midpoint appears to work like an alarm clock, heightening members' awareness that their time is limited and that they need to "get moving."

This transition ends Phase 1 and is characterized by a concentrated burst of changes, dropping of old patterns, and adoption of new perspectives. The transition sets a revised direction for Phase 2.

Phase 2 is a new equilibrium or period of inertia. In this phase, the group executes plans created during the transition period.

The group's last meeting is characterized by a final burst of activity to finish its work.

In summary, the punctuated-equilibrium model characterizes groups as exhibiting long periods of inertia interspersed with brief revolutionary changes triggered primarily by their members' awareness of time and deadlines. Keep in mind, however, that this model doesn't apply to all groups. It's essentially limited to temporary task groups who are working under a time-constrained completion deadline.[6]

TOWARD EXPLAINING WORK-GROUP BEHAVIOR

Why are some group efforts more successful than others? The answer to that question is complex, but it includes variables such as the ability of the group's members, the size of the group, the level of conflict, and the internal pressures on members to conform to the group's norms. Exhibit 8-4 presents the major components that determine group performance and satisfaction.[7] The following discussions are based on this model.

Group-Behavior Model

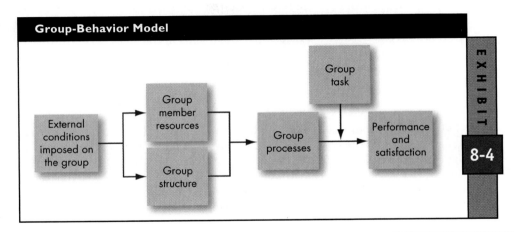

EXHIBIT 8-4

EXTERNAL CONDITIONS IMPOSED ON THE GROUP

To begin understanding the behavior of a work group, you need to view it as a subsystem embedded in a larger system.[8] Work groups don't exist in isolation. They're part of a larger organization. A research team in Dow's plastic products division, for instance, must live within the rules and policies dictated by the division's headquarters and Dow's corporate offices. So every work group is influenced by external conditions imposed from outside it. These external conditions include the organization's overall strategy, its authority structures, formal regulations, resources, employee selection process, performance evaluation and reward systems, culture, and physical work setting.

An *organization's overall strategy*, typically put into place by top management, outlines the organization's goals and the means for attaining these goals. It might, for example, direct the organization toward reducing costs, improving quality, expanding market share, or shrinking the size of its overall operations. The strategy that an organization is pursuing, at any given time, will influence the power of various work groups, which, in turn, will determine the resources that the organization's top management is willing to allocate to it for performing its tasks. To illustrate, an organization that is retrenching through selling off or closing down major parts of its business is going to have work groups with a shrinking resource base, increased member anxiety, and the potential for heightened intragroup conflict.[9]

Organizations have *authority structures* that define who reports to whom, who makes decisions, and what decisions individuals or groups are empowered to make. This structure typically determines where a given work group is placed in the organization's hierarchy, the formal leader of the group, and formal relationships between groups. So while a work group might be led by someone who emerges informally from within the group, the formally designated leader—appointed by management—has authority that others in the group don't have.

Organizations create rules, procedures, policies, job descriptions, and other forms of *formal regulations* to standardize employee behavior. Because McDonald's has standard operating procedures for taking orders, making hamburgers, and cooking fries, the discretion of work-group members to set independent standards of behavior is severely limited. The more formal regulations that the organization imposes on all its employees, the more the behavior of work group members will be consistent and predictable.

Some organizations are large and profitable, with an abundance of resources. Their employees, for instance, will have modern, high-quality tools and equipment to do their jobs. Other organizations aren't as fortunate. When organizations have limited resources, so do their work groups. What a group actually accomplishes is, to a large degree, determined by what it is capable of accomplishing. The presence or absence of *resources* such as money, time, raw materials, and equipment—which are allocated to the group by the organization—have a large bearing on the group's behavior.

Members of any work group are, first, members of the organization of which the group is a part. Members of a cost-reduction task force at Boeing first had to be hired as employees of the company. So the criteria that an organization uses in its *selection process* will determine the kinds of people that will be in its work groups.

Another organizationwide variable that affects all employees is the *performance evaluation and reward system*.[10] Does the organization provide employees with challenging, specific performance objectives? Does the organization reward the accomplishment of individual or group objectives? Since work groups are part of the larger organizational system, group members' behavior will be influenced by how the organization evaluates performance and what behaviors are rewarded.

Every organization has an unwritten culture that defines standards of acceptable and unacceptable behavior for employees. After a few months, most employees understand their *organization's culture*. They know things like how to dress for work, whether or not rules are rigidly enforced, what kinds of questionable behaviors are sure to get them into trouble and which are likely to be overlooked, the importance of honesty and integrity, and the like. While many organizations have subcultures—often created around work groups—with an additional or modified set of standards, they still have a dominant culture that conveys to all employees the values the organization holds dearest. Members of work groups have to accept the standards implied in the organization's dominant culture if they are to remain in good standing.

Finally, the *physical work setting* that is imposed on the group by external parties has an important bearing on work-group behavior.[11] Architects, industrial engineers, and office designers make decisions regarding the size and physical layout of an employee's work space, the arrangement of equipment, illumination levels, and the need for acoustics to cut down on noise distractions. These create both barriers and opportunities for work group interaction. It's obviously a lot easier for employees to talk or "goof off" if their work stations are close together, there are no physical barriers between them, and their supervisor is in an enclosed office 50 meters away.

Separated work stations, such as these at a Hong Kong toy factory, inhibit work group interactions.

GROUP MEMBER RESOURCES

A group's potential level of performance is, to a large extent, dependent on the resources that its members individually bring to the group. In this section, we want to look at two general resources that have received the greatest amount of attention: knowledge, skills, and abilities; and personality characteristics.

Knowledge, Skills, and Abilities

Part of a group's performance can be predicted by assessing the knowledge, skills, and abilities of its individual members. It's true that we occasionally read about the athletic team composed of mediocre players who, because of excellent coaching, determination, and precision teamwork, beats a far more talented group of players. But such cases make the news precisely because they represent an aberration. As the old saying goes, "The race doesn't always go to the swiftest nor the battle to the strongest, but that's the way to bet." A group's performance is not merely the summation of its individual members' abilities. However, these abilities set parameters for what members can do and how effectively they will perform in a group.

A review of the evidence has found that interpersonal skills consistently emerge as important for high performance by work groups.[12] These include conflict management and resolution, collaborative problem solving, and communication.

For instance, members need to be able to recognize the type and source of conflict confronting the group and to implement an appropriate conflict-resolution strategy; to identify situations requiring participative group problem solving and to utilize the proper degree and type of participation; and to listen nonevaluatively and to appropriately use active listening techniques.

Personality Characteristics

There has been a great deal of research on the relationship between personality traits and group attitudes and behavior. The general conclusion is that attributes that tend to have a positive connotation in our culture tend to be positively related to group productivity, morale, and cohesiveness. These include traits such as sociability, initiative, openness, and flexibility. In contrast, negatively evaluated characteristics such as authoritarianism, dominance, and unconventionality tend to be negatively related to the dependent variables.[13] These personality traits affect group performance by strongly influencing how the individual will interact with other group members.

Is any one personality characteristic a good predictor of group behavior? The answer to that question is No. The magnitude of the effect of any single characteristic is small, but taking personality characteristics together, the consequences for group behavior are of major significance.

GROUP STRUCTURE

Work groups are not unorganized mobs. They have a structure that shapes the behavior of members and makes it possible to explain and predict a large portion of individual behavior within the group as well as the performance of the group itself. What are some of these structural variables? They include formal leadership, roles, norms, status, group size, composition of the group, and the degree of group cohesiveness.

Formal Leadership

Almost every work group has a formal leader. He or she is typically identified by titles such as unit or department manager, supervisor, foreman, project leader, task force head, or committee chair. This leader can play an important part in the group's success—so much so, in fact, that we have devoted two entire chapters to the topic of leadership. In Chapters 11 and 12, we review the research on leadership and the effect that leaders have on individual and group performance variables.

Roles

role

A set of expected behavior patterns attributed to someone occupying a given position in a social unit.

Shakespeare said, "All the world's a stage, and all the men and women merely players." Using the same metaphor, all group members are actors, each playing a **role**. By this term, we mean a set of expected behavior patterns attributed to someone occupying a given position in a social unit. The understanding of role behavior would be dramatically simplified if each of us chose one role and "played it out" regularly and consistently. Unfortunately, we are required to play a number of diverse roles, both on and off our jobs. As we shall see, one of the tasks in understanding behavior is grasping the role that a person is currently playing.

For example, Bill Patterson is a plant manager with Electrical Industries, a large electrical equipment manufacturer in Phoenix. He has a number of roles that he fulfills on that job—for instance, Electrical Industries employee, member of middle management, electrical engineer, and the primary company spokesperson in the community. Off the job, Bill Patterson finds himself in still more roles: husband, father, Catholic, Rotarian, tennis player, member of the Thunderbird Country Club, and president of his homeowners' association. Many of these roles are compatible; some create conflicts. For instance, how does his religious involvement influence his managerial decisions regarding layoffs, expense account padding, and providing accurate information to government agencies? A recent offer of promotion requires Bill to relocate, yet his family very much wants to stay in Phoenix. Can the role demands of his job be reconciled with the demands of his husband and father roles?

The issue should be clear: Like Bill Patterson, we all are required to play a number of roles, and our behavior varies with the role we are playing. Bill's behavior when he attends church on Sunday morning is different from his behavior on the golf course later that same day. So different groups impose different role requirements on individuals.

Role Identity   There are certain attitudes and actual behaviors consistent with a role, and they create the **role identity**. People have the ability to shift roles rapidly when they recognize that the situation and its demands clearly require major changes. For instance, when union stewards were promoted to supervisory positions, it was found that their attitudes changed from pro-union to pro-management within a few months of their promotion. When these promotions had to be rescinded later because of economic difficulties in the firm, it was found that the demoted supervisors had once again adopted their pro-union attitudes.[14]

role identity

Certain attitudes and behaviors consistent with a role.

Role Perception   One's view of how one is supposed to act in a given situation is a **role perception**. Based on an interpretation of how we believe we are supposed to behave, we engage in certain types of behavior.

Where do we get these perceptions? We get them from stimuli all around us—friends, books, movies, television. Many current law enforcement officers learned their roles from reading Joseph Wambaugh novels, while many of tomorrow's lawyers will be influenced by watching the actions of attorneys in *Law and Order* or *The Practice*. Of course, the primary reason that apprenticeship programs exist in many trades and professions is to allow beginners to watch an "expert," so that they can learn to act as they are supposed to.

role perception

An individual's view of how he or she is supposed to act in a given situation.

Role Expectations   **Role expectations** are defined as how others believe you should act in a given situation. How you behave is determined to a large extent by the role defined in the context in which you are acting. For instance, the role of a U.S. federal judge is viewed as having propriety and dignity, while a football coach is seen as aggressive, dynamic, and inspiring to his players.

In the workplace, it can be helpful to look at the topic of role expectations through the perspective of the **psychological contract**. There is an unwritten agreement that exists between employees and their employer. This psychological contract sets out mutual expectations—what management expects from workers, and vice versa.[15] In effect, this contract defines the behavioral expectations that go with every role. Management is expected to treat employees justly, provide acceptable working conditions, clearly communicate what is a fair day's work, and give feedback on how well the employee is doing. Employees are expected to respond by demonstrating a good attitude, following directions, and showing loyalty to the organization.

What happens when role expectations as implied in the psychological contract are not met? If management is derelict in keeping up its part of the bargain, we can expect negative repercussions on employee performance and satisfaction. When employees fail to live up to expectations, the result is usually some form of disciplinary action up to and including firing.

role expectations

How others believe a person should act in a given situation.

psychological contract

An unwritten agreement that sets out what management expects from the employee, and vice versa.

Role Conflict   When an individual is confronted by divergent role expectations, the result is **role conflict**. It exists when an individual finds that compliance with one role requirement may make it more difficult to comply with another.[16] At the extreme, it would include situations in which two or more role expectations are mutually contradictory.

Our previous discussion of the many roles Bill Patterson had to deal with included several role conflicts—for instance, Bill's attempt to reconcile the expectations placed on him as a husband and father with those placed on him as an executive with Electrical Industries. The former, as you will remember, emphasizes stability and concern for the desire of his wife and children to remain in Phoenix. Electrical Industries, on the other hand, expects its employees to be responsive to the needs and requirements of the company. Although it might be in Bill's financial and career interests to accept a relocation, the conflict comes down to choosing between family and career role expectations.

An Experiment: Zimbardo's Simulated Prison   One of the more illuminating role experiments was done by Stanford University psychologist Philip Zimbardo and his associates.[17] They created a "prison" in the basement of the Stanford psychology building; hired at $15 a day two dozen emotionally stable, physically healthy, law-abiding students who scored "normal average" on extensive personality tests; randomly assigned them the role of either "guard" or "prisoner"; and established some basic rules.

To get the experiment off to a "realistic" start, Zimbardo got the cooperation of the City of Palo Alto Police Department. They went, unannounced, to each future prisoners' home, arrested and handcuffed them, put them in a squad car in front of friends and neighbors, and took them to police headquarters, where they were booked and fingerprinted. From there, they were taken to the Stanford prison.

At the start of the planned two-week experiment, there were no measurable differences between the individuals assigned to be guards and those chosen to be prisoners. In addition, the guards received no special training in how to be prison guards. They were told only to "maintain law and order" in the prison and not to take any nonsense from the prisoners. Physical violence was forbidden. To simulate further the realities of prison life, the prisoners were allowed visits from relatives and friends. And although the mock guards worked eight-hour shifts, the mock prisoners were kept in their cells around the clock and were allowed out only for meals, exercise, toilet privileges, head-count lineups, and work details.

It took the "prisoners" little time to accept the authority positions of the guards, or the mock guards to adjust to their new authority roles. After the guards crushed a rebellion attempt on the second day, the prisoners became increasingly passive. Whatever the guards "dished out," the prisoners took. The prisoners actually began to believe and act as if they were, as the guards constantly reminded them, inferior and powerless. And every guard, at some time during the simulation, engaged in abusive, authoritative behavior. For example, one guard said, "I was surprised at myself. . . . I made them call each other names and clean the toilets out with their bare hands. I practically considered the prisoners cattle, and I kept thinking: 'I have to watch out for them in case they try something.'" Another guard added, "I was tired of seeing the prisoners in their rags and smelling the strong odors of their bodies that filled the cells. I watched them tear at each other on orders given by us. They didn't see it as an experiment. It was real and they were fighting to keep their identity. But we were always there to show them who was boss." Surprisingly, during the entire experiment—even after days of abuse—not one prisoner said, "Stop this. I'm a student like you. This is just an experiment!"

The simulation actually proved too successful in demonstrating how quickly individuals learn new roles. The researchers had to stop the experiment after only six days because of the pathological reactions that the participants were demonstrating. And remember, these were individuals chosen precisely for their normalcy and emotional stability.

What should you conclude from this prison simulation? The participants in this experiment had, like the rest of us, learned stereotyped conceptions of guard and prisoner roles from the mass media and their own personal experiences in power and powerlessness relationships gained at home (parent–child), in school (teacher–student), and in other situations. This, then, allowed them easily and rapidly to assume roles that were very different from their inherent personalities. In this case, we saw that people with no prior personality pathology or training in their roles could execute extreme forms of behavior consistent with the roles they were playing.

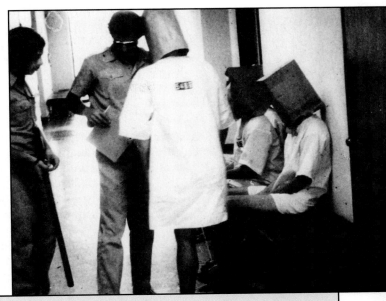

Students at Stanford University played roles of "guard" and "prisoner" in a simulated prison experiment. The experiment demonstrated how quickly individuals can learn new roles different from their personalities and without any special training.

Norms

Did you ever notice that golfers don't speak while their partners are putting on the green or that employees don't criticize their bosses in public? Why? The answer is: "Norms!"

All groups have established **norms**, that is, acceptable standards of behavior that are shared by the group's members. Norms tell members what they ought and ought not to do under certain circumstances. From an individual's standpoint, they tell what is expected of you in certain situations. When agreed to and accepted by the group, norms act as a means of influencing the behavior of group members with a minimum of external controls. Norms differ among groups, communities, and societies, but they all have them.[18]

norms

Acceptable standards of behavior within a group that are shared by the group's members.

Common Classes of Norms A work group's norms are like an individual's fingerprints—each is unique. Yet there are still some common classes of norms that appear in most work groups.[19]

Probably the most common class of norms is *performance norms*. Work groups typically provide their members with explicit cues on how hard they should work, how to get the job done, their level of output, appropriate levels of tardiness, and the like.[20] These norms are extremely powerful in affecting an individual employee's performance—they are capable of significantly modifying a performance prediction that was based solely on the employee's ability and level of personal motivation.

A second category encompasses *appearance norms*. This includes things like appropriate dress, loyalty to the work group or organization, when to look busy, and when it's acceptable to goof off. Some organizations have formal dress codes. However, even in their absence, norms frequently develop to dictate the kind of clothing that should be worn to work. Similarly, presenting the appearance of loyalty is important, especially among professional employees and those in the executive ranks. So it's often considered inappropriate to be openly looking for another job.

Another category concerns *social arrangement norms*. These norms come from informal work groups and primarily regulate social interactions within the group.

With whom group members eat lunch, friendships on and off the job, social games, and the like are influenced by these norms.

A final category relates to *allocation of resources norms*. These norms can originate in the group or in the organization and cover things like pay, assignment of difficult jobs, and allocation of new tools and equipment.

Conformity   As a member of a group, you desire acceptance by the group. Because of your desire for acceptance, you are susceptible to conforming to the group's norms. There is considerable evidence that groups can place strong pressures on individual members to change their attitudes and behaviors to conform to the group's standard.[21]

Do individuals conform to the pressures of all the groups to which they belong? Obviously not, because people belong to many groups and their norms vary. In some cases, they may even have contradictory norms. So what do people do? They conform to the important groups to which they belong or hope to belong. The important groups have been referred to as **reference groups** and are characterized as ones in which the person is aware of the others; the person defines himself or herself as a member, or would like to be a member; and the person feels that the group members are significant to him or her.[22] The implication, then, is that all groups do not impose equal conformity pressures on their members.

The impact that group pressures for **conformity** can have on an individual member's judgment and attitudes was demonstrated in the now-classic studies by Solomon Asch.[23] Asch made up groups of seven or eight people, who sat around a table and were asked to compare two cards held by the experimenter. One card had one line, the other had three lines of varying length. As shown in Exhibit 8-5, one of the lines on the three-line card was identical to the line on the one-line card. Also as shown in Exhibit 8-5, the difference in line length was quite obvious; under ordinary conditions, subjects made fewer than 1 percent errors. The object was to announce aloud which of the three lines matched the single line. But what happens if the members in the group begin to give incorrect answers? Will the pressures to conform result in an unsuspecting subject (USS) altering his or her answer to align with the others? That was what Asch wanted to know. So he arranged the group so that only the USS was unaware that the experiment was "fixed." The seating was prearranged: The USS was placed so as to be one of the last to announce his or her decision.

The experiment began with several sets of matching exercises. All the subjects gave the right answers. On the third set, however, the first subject gave an obviously wrong answer—for example, saying "C" in Exhibit 8-5. The next subject gave the same wrong answer, and so did the others until it got to the unknowing sub-

reference groups

Important groups to which individuals belong or hope to belong and with whose norms individuals are likely to conform.

conformity

Adjusting one's behavior to align with the norms of the group.

Examples of Cards Used in Asch's Study

EXHIBIT 8-5

ject. He knew "B" was the same as "X," yet everyone had said "C." The decision confronting the USS was this: Do you publicly state a perception that differs from the preannounced position of the others in your group? Or do you give an answer that you strongly believe is incorrect in order to have your response agree with that of the other group members?

The results obtained by Asch demonstrated that over many experiments and many trials, 75 percent of the subjects gave at least one answer that conformed—that is, that they knew was wrong but that was consistent with the replies of other group members—and the average for conformers was 37 percent. What meaning can we draw from these results? They suggest that there are group norms that press us toward conformity. That is, we desire to be one of the group and avoid being visibly different.

The above conclusions are based on research that was conducted 50 years ago. Has time altered their validity? And should we consider these findings generalizable across cultures? The evidence indicates that there have been changes in the level of conformity over time; and Asch's findings are culture-bound.[24] Specifically, levels of conformity have steadily declined since Asch's studies in the early 1950s. In addition, conformity to social norms is higher in collectivist cultures than in individualistic cultures. Nevertheless, even in individualistic countries such as the United States, you should consider conformity to norms to still be a powerful force in groups.

Deviant Workplace Behavior   Ted Vowinkel is frustrated by a co-worker who constantly spreads malicious and unsubstantiated rumors about him. Debra Hundley is tired of a member of her work team who, when confronted with a problem, takes out his frustration by yelling and screaming at her and other work team members. And Rhonda Lieberman recently quit her job as a dental hygienist after being constantly sexually harassed by her employer.

What do these three episodes have in common? They represent employees being exposed to acts of **deviant workplace behavior**.[25] This term covers a full range of antisocial actions by organizational members that intentionally violate established norms and that result in negative consequences for the organization, its members, or both. Exhibit 8-6 on page 232 provides a typology of deviant workplace behaviors with examples of each.

Few organizations will admit to creating or condoning conditions that encourage and maintain deviant norms. Yet they exist. Employees report, for example, an increase in rudeness and disregard toward others by bosses and co-workers in recent years. And nearly half of employees who have suffered this incivility report that it has led them to think about changing jobs, with 12 percent actually quitting because of it.[26]

As with norms in general, individual employees' antisocial actions are shaped by the group context within which they work. Evidence demonstrates that the antisocial behavior exhibited by a work group is a significant predictor of an individual's antisocial behavior at work.[27] In other words, deviant workplace behavior is likely to flourish where it's supported by group norms. What this means for managers is that when deviant workplace norms surface, employee cooperation, commitment, and motivation is likely to suffer. This, in turn, can lead to reduced employee productivity and job satisfaction, and increased turnover.

Status

While teaching a college course on adolescence, the instructor asked the class to list things that contributed to status when they were in high school. The list was long and included being an athlete or a cheerleader and being able to cut class

deviant workplace behavior

Antisocial actions by organizational members that intentionally violate established norms and that result in negative consequences for the organization, its members, or both.

Typology of Deviant Workplace Behavior	
Category	**Examples**
Production	Leaving early
	Intentionally working slow
	Wasting resources
Property	Sabotage
	Lying about hours worked
	Stealing from the organization
Political	Showing favoritism
	Gossiping and spreading rumors
	Blaming coworkers
Personal Aggression	Sexual harassment
	Verbal abuse
	Stealing from coworkers

EXHIBIT 8-6

Source: Adapted from S. L. Robinson and R. J. Bennett, "A Typology of Deviant Workplace Behaviors: A Multidimensional Scaling Study," *Academy of Management Journal,* April 1995, p. 565.

without getting caught. Then the instructor asked the students to list things that didn't contribute to status. Again, it was easy for the students to create a long list: getting straight A's, having your mother drive you to school, and so forth. Finally, the students were asked to develop a third list—those things that didn't matter one way or the other. There was a long silence. At last one student in the back row volunteered, "In high school, nothing didn't matter."[28]

status

A socially defined position or rank given to groups or group members by others.

Status—that is, a socially defined position or rank given to groups or group members by others—permeates society far beyond the walls of high school. It would not be extravagant to rephrase the preceding quotation to read, "In the status hierarchy of life, nothing doesn't matter." Despite all attempts to make it more egalitarian, we have made little progress toward a classless society. Even the smallest group will develop roles, rights, and rituals to differentiate its members. Status is an important factor in understanding human behavior because it is a significant motivator and has major behavioral consequences when individuals perceive a disparity between what they believe their status to be and what others perceive it to be.

Status and Norms Status has been shown to have some interesting effects on the power of norms and pressures to conform. For instance, high-status members of groups often are given more freedom to deviate from norms than are other group members.[29] High-status people also are better able to resist conformity pressures than their lower-status peers. An individual who is highly valued by a group but who doesn't much need or care about the social rewards the group provides is particularly able to pay minimal attention to conformity norms.[30]

The previous findings explain why many star athletes, celebrities, top-performing salespeople, and outstanding academics seem oblivious to appearance or social norms that constrain their peers. As high-status individuals, they're given a wider range of discretion. But this is true only as long as the high-status person's activities aren't severely detrimental to group goal achievement.[31]

Status Equity   It is important for group members to believe that the status hierarchy is equitable. When inequity is perceived, it creates disequilibrium, which results in various types of corrective behavior.[32]

The concept of equity presented in Chapter 6 applies to status. People expect rewards to be proportionate to costs incurred. If Dana and Anne are the two finalists for the head nurse position in a hospital, and it is clear that Dana has more seniority and better preparation for assuming the promotion, Anne will view the selection of Dana to be equitable. However, if Anne is chosen because she is the daughter-in-law of the hospital director, Dana will believe an injustice has been committed.

The trappings that go with formal positions are also important elements in maintaining equity. When we believe there is an inequity between the perceived ranking of an individual and the status accouterments that person is given by the organization, we are experiencing status incongruence. An example of this kind of incongruence is the more desirable office location being held by a lower-ranking individual. Pay incongruence has long been a problem in the insurance industry, where top sales agents often earn two to five times more than senior corporate executives. The result is that it is very hard for insurance companies to entice successful agents into management positions. Our point is that employees expect the things an individual has and receives to be congruent with his or her status.

Groups generally agree within themselves on status criteria and, hence, there is usually high concurrence in group rankings of individuals. However, individuals can find themselves in a conflict situation when they move between groups whose status criteria are different or when they join groups whose members have heterogeneous backgrounds. For instance, business executives may use personal income or the growth rate of their companies as determinants of status. Government bureaucrats may use the size of their budgets. Blue-collar workers may use years of seniority. In groups made up of heterogeneous individuals or when heterogeneous groups are forced to be interdependent, status differences may initiate conflict as the group attempts to reconcile and align the differing hierarchies. As we'll see in the next chapter, this can be a particular problem when management creates teams made up of employees from across varied functions within the organization.

Status and Culture Before we leave the topic of status, we should briefly address the issue of cross-culture transferability. Do cultural differences affect status? The answer is a resounding Yes.[33]

The importance of status does vary between cultures. The French, for example, are highly status conscious. Also, countries differ on the criteria that create status. For instance, status for Latin Americans and Asians tends to be derived from family position and formal roles held in organizations. In contrast, while status is still important in countries like the United States and Australia, it tends to be less "in your face." And it tends to be bestowed more on accomplishments than on titles and family trees.

The message here is make sure you understand who and what holds status when interacting with people from a culture different from your own. An American manager who doesn't understand that office size is no measure of a Japanese executive's position or who fails to grasp the importance that the British place on family genealogy and social class is likely to unintentionally offend his Japanese or British counterpart and, in so doing, lessen his interpersonal effectiveness.

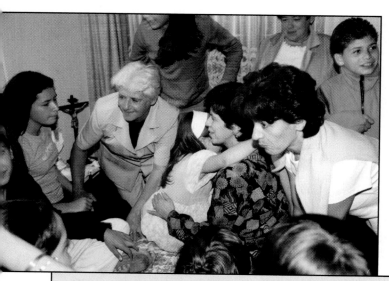

Cultural differences mean that status arises from different factors in different countries. In many Latin American cultures, for instance, status derives from one's position in the family.

Size

Does the size of a group affect the group's overall behavior? The answer to this question is a definite Yes, but the effect depends on what dependent variables you look at.[34]

The evidence indicates, for instance, that smaller groups are faster at completing tasks than are larger ones. However, if the group is engaged in problem solving, large groups consistently get better marks than their smaller counterparts. Translating these results into specific numbers is a bit more hazardous, but we can offer some parameters. Large groups—with a dozen or more members—are good for gaining diverse input. So if the goal of the group is fact finding, larger groups should be more effective. On the other hand, smaller groups are better at doing something productive with that input. Groups of approximately seven members, therefore, tend to be more effective for taking action.

social loafing

The tendency for individuals to expend less effort when working collectively than when working individually.

One of the most important findings related to the size of a group has been labeled **social loafing**. Social loafing is the tendency for individuals to expend less effort when working collectively than when working individually.[35] It directly challenges the logic that the productivity of the group as a whole should at least equal the sum of the productivity of each individual in that group.

A common stereotype about groups is that the sense of team spirit spurs individual effort and enhances the group's overall productivity. In the late 1920s, a German psychologist named Max Ringelmann compared the results of individual and group performance on a rope-pulling task.[36] He expected that the group's effort would be equal to the sum of the efforts of individuals within the group. That is, three people pulling together should exert three times as much pull on the rope as one person, and eight people should exert eight times as much pull. Ringelmann's results, however, didn't confirm his expectations. One person pulling on a rope alone exerted an average of 63 kilograms of force. In groups of three, per-person force dropped to 53 kilograms. And in groups of eight, it fell to only 31 kilograms per person.

Replications of Ringelmann's research with similar tasks have generally supported his findings.[37] Group performance increases with group size, but the addition of new members to the group has diminishing returns on productivity. So more may be better in the sense that the total productivity of a group of four is greater than that of three people, but the individual productivity of each group member declines.

What causes this social loafing effect? It may be due to a belief that others in the group are not carrying their fair share. If you see others as lazy or inept, you can reestablish equity by reducing your effort. Another explanation is the dispersion of responsibility. Because the results of the group cannot be attributed to any single person, the relationship between an individual's input and the group's output is clouded. In such situations, individuals may be tempted to become "free riders" and coast on the group's efforts. In other words, there will be a reduction in efficiency when individuals think that their contribution cannot be measured.

The implications for OB of this effect on work groups are significant. When managers use collective work situations to enhance morale and teamwork, they must also provide means by which individual efforts can be identified. If this isn't done, management must weigh the potential losses in productivity from using groups against any possible gains in worker satisfaction.[38] However, this conclusion has a Western bias. It's consistent with individualistic cultures, like the United States and Canada, that are dominated by self-interest. It is not consistent with collective societies, in which individuals are motivated by in-group goals. For instance, in studies comparing employees from the United States with employees from the People's Republic of China and Israel (both collectivist societies), the Chinese and Israelis showed no propensity to engage in social loafing. In fact, the Chinese and Israelis actually performed better in a group than when working alone.[39]

The research on group size leads us to two additional conclusions: (1) Groups with an odd number of members tend to be preferable to those with an even number; and (2) groups made up of five or seven members do a pretty good job of exercising the best elements of both small and large groups.[40] Having an odd number of members eliminates the possibility of ties when votes are taken. And groups made up of five or seven members are large enough to form a majority and allow for diverse input, yet small enough to avoid the negative outcomes often associated with large groups, such as domination by a few members, development of subgroups, inhibited participation by some members, and excessive time taken to reach a decision.

Composition

Most group activities require a variety of skills and knowledge. Given this requirement, it would be reasonable to conclude that heterogeneous groups—those composed of dissimilar individuals—would be more likely to have diverse abilities and information and should be more effective. Research studies generally substantiate this conclusion, especially on cognitive, creativity-demanding tasks.[41]

When a group is diverse in terms of personality, gender, age, education, functional specialization, and experience, there is an increased probability that the group will possess the needed characteristics to complete its tasks effectively.[42] The group

Although racial and national diversity can impede group processes at first, difficulties often disappear quickly as groups work through disagreements and differences in problem-solving methods.

may be more conflict-laden and less expedient as varied positions are introduced and assimilated, but the evidence generally supports the conclusion that heterogeneous groups perform more effectively than do those that are homogeneous. Essentially, diversity promotes conflict, which stimulates creativity, which leads to improved decision making.

But what about diversity created by racial or national differences? The evidence indicates that these elements of diversity interfere with group processes, at least in the short term.[43] Cultural diversity seems to be an asset for tasks that call for a variety of viewpoints. But culturally heterogeneous groups have more difficulty in learning to work with each other and in solving problems. The good news is that these difficulties seem to dissipate with time. Although newly formed culturally diverse groups underperform newly formed culturally homogeneous groups, the differences disappear after about three months. The reason is that it takes diverse groups a while to learn how to work through disagreements and different approaches to solving problems.

An offshoot of the composition issue has recently received a great deal of attention by group researchers. This is the degree to which members of a group share a common demographic attribute, such as age, sex, race, educational level, or length of service in the organization, and the impact of this attribute on turnover. We call this variable **group demography**.

group demography

The degree to which members of a group share a common demographic attribute, such as age, sex, race, educational level, or length of service in the organization, and the impact of this attribute on turnover.

cohorts

Individuals who, as part of a group, hold a common attribute.

We discussed individual demographic factors in Chapter 2. Here we consider the same type of factors, but in a group context. That is, it's not whether a person is male or female or has been employed with the organization for a year rather than ten years that concerns us now, but rather the individual's attribute in relationship to the attributes of others with whom he or she works. Let's work through the logic of group demography, review the evidence, and then consider the implications.

Groups and organizations are composed of **cohorts**, which we define as individuals who hold a common attribute. For instance, everyone born in 1960 is of the same age. This means they also have shared common experiences. People born in 1970 have experienced the information revolution, but not the Korean conflict. People born in 1945 shared the Vietnam War, but not the Great Depression. Women in U.S. organizations today who were born before 1945 matured prior to the women's movement and have had substantially different experiences from women born after 1960. Group demography, therefore, suggests that attributes such as age or the date that someone joins a specific work group or organization should help us to predict turnover. Essentially, the logic goes like this: Turnover will be greater among those with dissimilar experiences because communication is more difficult. Conflict and power struggles are more likely, and more severe when they occur. The increased conflict makes group membership less attractive, so employees are more likely to quit. Similarly, the losers in a power struggle are more apt to leave voluntarily or to be forced out.

Several studies have sought to test this thesis, and the evidence is quite encouraging.[44] For example, in departments or separate work groups in which a large portion of members entered at the same time, there is considerably more turnover among those outside this cohort. Also, when there are large gaps between cohorts, turnover is higher. People who enter a group or an organization together, or at approximately the same time, are more likely to associate with one another, have a similar perspective on the group or organization, and thus be more likely to stay. On the other hand, discontinuities or bulges in the group's date-of-entry distribution are likely to result in a higher turnover rate within that group.

The implication of this line of inquiry is that the composition of a group may be an important predictor of turnover. Differences per se may not predict turnover. But large differences within a single group will lead to turnover. If everyone is moderately dissimilar from everyone else in a group, the feelings of being an outsider are reduced. So, it's the degree of dispersion on an attribute, rather than the level, that matters most.

Cohesiveness

Groups differ in their **cohesiveness**, that is, the degree to which members are attracted to each other and are motivated to stay in the group.[45] For instance, some work groups are cohesive because the members have spent a great deal of time together, or the group's small size facilitates high interaction, or the group has experienced external threats that have brought members close together. Cohesiveness is important because it has been found to be related to the group's productivity.[46]

Studies consistently show that the relationship of cohesiveness and productivity depends on the performance-related norms established by the group. If performance-related norms are high (for example, high output, quality work, cooperation with individuals outside the group), a cohesive group will be more productive than will a less cohesive group. But if cohesiveness is high and performance norms are low, productivity will be low. If cohesiveness is low and performance norms are high, productivity increases, but less than in the high-cohesiveness/high-norms situation. When cohesiveness and performance-related norms are both low, productivity will tend to fall into the low-to-moderate range. These conclusions are summarized in Exhibit 8-7.

What can you do to encourage group cohesiveness? You might try one or more of the following suggestions: (1) Make the group smaller. (2) Encourage agreement with group goals. (3) Increase the time members spend together. (4) Increase the status of the group and the perceived difficulty of attaining membership in the

cohesiveness

Degree to which group members are attracted to each other and are motivated to stay in the group.

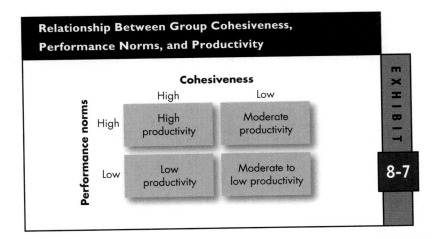

Relationship Between Group Cohesiveness, Performance Norms, and Productivity

Performance norms		Cohesiveness	
		High	Low
	High	High productivity	Moderate productivity
	Low	Low productivity	Moderate to low productivity

EXHIBIT 8-7

group. (5) Stimulate competition with other groups. (6) Give rewards to the group rather than to individual members. (7) Physically isolate the group.[47]

GROUP PROCESSES

The next component of our group behavior model considers the processes that go on within a work group—the communication patterns used by members for information exchanges, group decision processes, leader behavior, power dynamics, conflict interactions, and the like. Chapters 10 through 14 elaborate on many of these processes.

Why are processes important to understanding work-group behavior? One way to answer this question is to return to the topic of social loafing. We found that $1 + 1 + 1$ doesn't necessarily add up to three. In group tasks for which each member's contribution is not clearly visible, there is a tendency for individuals to decrease their effort. Social loafing, in other words, illustrates a process loss as a result of using groups. But group processes can also produce positive results. That is, groups can create outputs greater than the sum of their inputs. The development of creative alternatives by a diverse group would be one such instance. Exhibit 8-8 illustrates how group processes can have an impact on a group's actual effectiveness.[48]

synergy

An action of two or more substances that results in an effect that is different from the individual summation of the substances.

Synergy is a term used in biology that refers to an action of two or more substances that results in an effect that is different from the individual summation of the substances. We can use the concept to better understand group processes.

Social loafing, for instance, represents negative synergy. The whole is less than the sum of its parts. On the other hand, research teams are often used in research laboratories because they can draw on the diverse skills of various individuals to produce more meaningful research as a group than could be generated by all of the researchers working independently. That is, they produce positive synergy. Their process gains exceed their process losses.

Another line of research that helps us to better understand group processes is the social facilitation effect.[49] Have you ever noticed that performing a task in front of others can have a positive or negative effect on your performance? For instance, you privately practice a complex springboard dive at your home pool for weeks. Then you do the dive in front of a group of friends and you do it better than ever. Or you practice a speech in private and finally get it down perfect, but you "bomb" when you have to give the speech in public.

social facilitation effect

The tendency for performance to improve or decline in response to the presence of others.

The **social facilitation effect** refers to this tendency for performance to improve or decline in response to the presence of others. While this effect is not entirely a group phenomenon—people can work in the presence of others and not

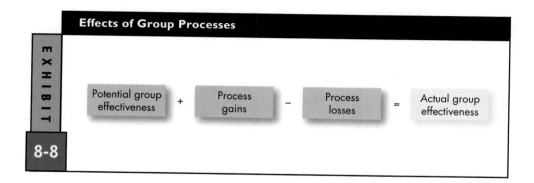

EXHIBIT 8-8

Effects of Group Processes

Potential group effectiveness + Process gains − Process losses = Actual group effectiveness

be members of a group—the group situation is more likely to provide the conditions for social facilitation to occur. The research on social facilitation tells us that the performance of simple, routine tasks tends to be speeded up and made more accurate by the presence of others. When the work is more complex, requiring closer attention, the presence of others is likely to have a negative effect on performance.[50] So what are the implications of this research in terms of managing process gains and losses? The implications relate to learning and training. People seem to perform better on a task in the presence of others if that task is very well learned, but poorer if it is not well learned. So process gains will be maximized by training people for simple tasks in groups, and training people for complex tasks in individual private practice sessions.

GROUP TASKS

Imagine, for a moment, that there are two groups at a major oil company. The job of the first is to consider possible locations for a new refinery. The decision is going to affect people in many areas of the company—production, engineering, marketing, distribution, purchasing, real estate development, and the like—so key people from each of these areas will need to provide input into the decision. The job of the second group is to coordinate the building of the refinery after the site has been selected, the design finalized, and the financial arrangements completed. Research on group effectiveness tells us that management would be well advised to use a larger group for the first task than for the second.[51] The reason is that large groups facilitate pooling of information. The addition of a diverse perspective to a problem-solving committee typically results in a process gain. But when a group's task is coordinating and implementing a decision, the process loss created by each additional member's presence is likely to be greater than the process gain he or she makes. So the size–performance relationship is moderated by the group's task requirements.

The preceding conclusions can be extended: The impact of group processes on the group's performance and member satisfaction is also moderated by the tasks that the group is doing. The evidence indicates that the complexity and interdependence of tasks influence the group's effectiveness.[52]

Tasks can be generalized as either simple or complex. Complex tasks are ones that tend to be novel or nonroutine. Simple ones are routine and standardized. We would hypothesize that the more complex the task, the more the group will benefit from discussion among members on alternative work methods. If the task is simple, group members don't need to discuss such alternatives. They can rely on standardized operating procedures for doing the job. Similarly, if there is a high degree of interdependence among the tasks that group members must perform, they'll need to interact more. Effective communication and minimal levels of conflict, therefore, should be more relevant to group performance when tasks are interdependent.

These conclusions are consistent with what we know about information-processing capacity and uncertainty.[53] Tasks that have higher uncertainty—those that are complex and interdependent—require more information processing. This, in turn, puts more importance on group processes. So just because a group is characterized by poor communication, weak leadership, high levels of conflict, and the like, it doesn't necessarily mean that it will be low performing. If the group's tasks are simple and require little interdependence among members, the group still may be effective.

GROUP DECISION MAKING

The belief—characterized by juries—that two heads are better than one has long been accepted as a basic component of North American and many other countries' legal systems. This belief has expanded to the point that, today, many decisions in organizations are made by groups, teams, or committees. In this section, we want to review group decision making.

Groups Versus the Individual

Decision-making groups may be widely used in organizations, but does that imply that group decisions are preferable to those made by an individual alone? The answer to this question depends on a number of factors. Let's begin by looking at the strengths and weaknesses of groups.[54]

At Pret A Manger, a British sandwich shop chain, job applicants spend a trial day working at a shop, after which the shop's team of employees decide whether the applicant would make a good addition to the staff.

Strengths of Group Decision Making Groups generate *more complete information and knowledge*. By aggregating the resources of several individuals, groups bring more input into the decision process. In addition to more input, groups can bring heterogeneity to the decision process. They offer *increased diversity of views*. This opens up the opportunity for more approaches and alternatives to be considered. The evidence indicates that a group will almost always outperform even the best individual. So groups generate *higher-quality decisions*. Finally, groups lead to increased *acceptance of a solution*. Many decisions fail after the final choice is made because people don't accept the solution. Group members who participated in making a decision are likely to enthusiastically support the decision and encourage others to accept it.

Weaknesses of Group Decision Making In spite of the pluses noted, group decisions have their drawbacks. They're *time consuming*. They typically take more time to reach a solution than would be the case if an individual were making the decision alone. There are *conformity pressures in groups*. The desire by group members to be accepted and considered an asset to the group can result in squashing any overt disagreement. Group discussion can be *dominated by one or a few members*. If this dominant coalition is composed of low- and medium-ability members, the group's overall effectiveness will suffer. Finally, group decisions suffer from *ambiguous responsibility*. In an individual decision, it's clear who is accountable for the final outcome. In a group decision, the responsibility of any single member is watered down.

Effectiveness and Efficiency Whether groups are more effective than individuals depends on the criteria you use for defining effectiveness. In terms of *accuracy*, group decisions will tend to be more accurate. The evidence indicates that, on the average, groups make better-quality decisions than individuals.[55] However, if decision effectiveness is defined in terms of *speed*, individuals are superior. If *creativity* is important, groups tend to be more effective than individuals. And if effectiveness means the degree of *acceptance* the final solution achieves, the nod again goes to the group.[56]

But effectiveness cannot be considered without also assessing efficiency. In terms of efficiency, groups almost always stack up as a poor second to the individual decision maker. With few exceptions, group decision making consumes more work hours than if an individual were to tackle the same problem alone. The exceptions tend to be the instances in which, to achieve comparable quantities of diverse input, the single decision maker must spend a great deal of time reviewing files and talking to people. Because groups can include members from diverse areas, the time spent searching for information can be reduced. However, as we noted, these advantages in efficiency tend to be the exception. Groups are generally less efficient than individuals. In deciding whether to use groups, then, consideration should be given to assessing whether increases in effectiveness are more than enough to offset the losses in efficiency.

Summary   In summary, groups offer an excellent vehicle for performing many of the steps in the decision-making process. They are a source of both breadth and depth of input for information gathering. If the group is composed of individuals with diverse backgrounds, the alternatives generated should be more extensive and the analysis more critical. When the final solution is agreed on, there are more people in a group decision to support and implement it. These pluses, however, can be more than offset by the time consumed by group decisions, the internal conflicts they create, and the pressures they generate toward conformity.

Groupthink and Groupshift

Two byproducts of group decision making have received a considerable amount of attention by researchers in OB. As we'll show, these two phenomena have the potential to affect the group's ability to appraise alternatives objectively and to arrive at quality decision solutions.

The first phenomenon, called **groupthink**, is related to norms. It describes situations in which group pressures for conformity deter the group from critically

groupthink
Phenomenon in which the norm for consensus overrides the realistic appraisal of alternative courses of action.

OR SCIENCE ?

MYTH

"Two Heads Are Better Than One"

This statement is mostly true if "better" means that two people will come up with more original and workable answers to a problem than one person working alone.

The evidence generally confirms the superiority of groups over individuals in terms of decision-making quality.[57] Groups usually produce more and better solutions to problems than do individuals working alone. And the choices groups make will be more accurate and creative. Why is this? Groups bring more complete information and knowledge to a decision, so they generate more ideas. In addition, the give and take that typically takes place in group decision processes provides diversity of opinion and increases the likelihood that weak alternatives will be identified and abandoned.

Research indicates that certain conditions favor groups over individuals.[58] These conditions include: (1) Diversity among members. The benefits of "two heads" requires that they differ in relevant skills and abilities. (2) The group members must be able to communicate their ideas freely and openly. This requires an absence of hostility and intimidation. (3) The task being undertaken is complex. Relative to individuals, groups do better on complex rather than simple tasks.

groupshift

A change in decision risk between the group's decision and the individual decision that members within the group would make; can be either toward conservatism or greater risk.

appraising unusual, minority, or unpopular views. Groupthink is a disease that attacks many groups and can dramatically hinder their performance. The second phenomenon we shall review is called **groupshift**. It indicates that in discussing a given set of alternatives and arriving at a solution, group members tend to exaggerate the initial positions that they hold. In some situations, caution dominates, and there is a conservative shift. More often, however, the evidence indicates that groups tend toward a risky shift. Let's look at each of these phenomena in more detail.

Groupthink   Have you ever felt like speaking up in a meeting, classroom, or informal group, but decided against it? One reason may have been shyness. On the other hand, you may have been a victim of groupthink, the phenomenon that occurs when group members become so enamored of seeking concurrence that the norm for consensus overrides the realistic appraisal of alternative courses of action and the full expression of deviant, minority, or unpopular views. It describes a deterioration in an individual's mental efficiency, reality testing, and moral judgment as a result of group pressures.[59]

We have all seen the symptoms of the groupthink phenomenon:

1. Group members rationalize any resistance to the assumptions they have made. No matter how strongly the evidence may contradict their basic assumptions, members behave so as to reinforce those assumptions continually.
2. Members apply direct pressures on those who momentarily express doubts about any of the group's shared views or who question the validity of arguments supporting the alternative favored by the majority.
3. Members who have doubts or hold differing points of view seek to avoid deviating from what appears to be group consensus by keeping silent about misgivings and even minimizing to themselves the importance of their doubts.
4. There appears to be an illusion of unanimity. If someone doesn't speak, it's assumed that he or she is in full accord. In other words, abstention becomes viewed as a Yes vote.[60]

In studies of historic American foreign policy decisions, these symptoms were found to prevail when government policy-making groups failed—unpreparedness at Pearl Harbor in 1941, the U.S. invasion of North Korea, the Bay of Pigs fiasco, and the escalation of the Vietnam War.[61] More recently, the *Challenger* space shuttle disaster and the failure of the main mirror on the *Hubble* telescope have been linked to decision processes at NASA in which groupthink symptoms were evident.[62]

Groupthink appears to be closely aligned with the conclusions Asch drew in his experiments with a lone dissenter. Individuals who hold a position that is different from that of the dominant majority are under pressure to suppress, withhold, or modify their true feelings and beliefs. As members of a group, we find it more pleasant to be in agreement—to be a positive part of the group—than to be a disruptive force, even if disruption is necessary to improve the effectiveness of the group's decisions.

Does groupthink attack all groups? No. It seems to occur most often when there is a clear group identity, where members hold a positive image of their group that they want to protect, and when the group perceives a collective threat to this positive image.[63] So groupthink is not a dissenter-suppression mechanism as much as it's a means for a group to protect its positive image. In the cases of the *Challenger* and *Hubble* fiascos, it was NASA's attempt to confirm its identity as "the elite organization that could do no wrong."[64]

What can managers do to minimize groupthink?[65] One thing is to monitor group size. People grow more intimidated and hesitant as group size increases and, although there is no magic number that will eliminate groupthink, individuals are likely to feel less personal responsibility when groups get larger than about ten. Managers should also encourage group leaders to play an impartial role. Leaders should actively seek input from all members and avoid expressing their own opinions, especially in the early stages of deliberation. Another thing is to appoint one group member to play the role of devil's advocate. This member's role is to overtly challenge the majority position and offer divergent perspectives. Still another suggestion is to use exercises that stimulate active discussion of diverse alternatives without threatening the group and intensifying identity protection. One such exercise is to have group members talk about dangers or risks involved in a decision and delaying discussion of any potential gains. By requiring members to first focus on the negatives of a decision alternative, the group is less likely to stifle dissenting views and more likely to gain an objective evaluation.

Groupshift   In comparing group decisions with the individual decisions of members within the group, evidence suggests that there are differences.[66] In some cases, the group decisions are more conservative than the individual decisions. More often, the shift is toward greater risk.[67]

What appears to happen in groups is that the discussion leads to a significant shift in the positions of members toward a more extreme position in the direction in which they were already leaning before the discussion. So conservative types become more cautious and the more aggressive types take on more risk. The group discussion tends to exaggerate the initial position of the group.

The groupshift can be viewed as actually a special case of groupthink. The decision of the group reflects the dominant decision-making norm that develops during the group's discussion. Whether the shift in the group's decision is toward greater caution or more risk depends on the dominant prediscussion norm.

The greater occurrence of the shift toward risk has generated several explanations for the phenomenon.[68] It's been argued, for instance, that the discussion creates familiarization among the members. As they become more comfortable with each other, they also become more bold and daring. Another argument is that most first-world societies value risk, that we admire individuals who are willing to take risks, and that group discussion motivates members to show that they are at least as willing as their peers to take risks. The most plausible explanation of the shift toward risk, however, seems to be that the group diffuses responsibility. Group decisions free any single member from accountability for the group's final choice. Greater risk can be taken because even if the decision fails, no one member can be held wholly responsible.

So how should you use the findings on groupshift? You should recognize that group decisions exaggerate the initial position of the individual members, that the shift has been shown more often to be toward greater risk, and that whether or not a group will shift toward greater risk or caution is a function of the members' prediscussion inclinations.

GROUP DECISION-MAKING TECHNIQUES

The most common form of group decision-making takes place in **interacting groups**. In these groups, members meet face-to-face and rely on both verbal and nonverbal interaction to communicate with each other. But as our discussion of groupthink demonstrated, interacting groups often censor themselves and pressure individual members toward conformity of opinion. Brainstorming, the nominal group technique, and electronic meetings have been proposed as ways to reduce many of the problems inherent in the traditional interacting group.

interacting groups

Typical groups, in which members interact with each other face-to-face.

EXHIBIT

8-9

Source: S. Adams, *Build a Better Life by Stealing Office Supplies* (Kansas City, MO: Andrews & McMeal, 1991), p. 31. DILBERT reprinted with permission of United Feature Syndicate, Inc.

brainstorming

An idea-generation process that specifically encourages any and all alternatives, while withholding any criticism of those alternatives.

nominal group technique

A group decision-making method in which individual members meet face-to-face to pool their judgments in a systematic but independent fashion.

Brainstorming is meant to overcome pressures for conformity in the interacting group that retard the development of creative alternatives.[69] It does this by utilizing an idea-generation process that specifically encourages any and all alternatives, while withholding any criticism of those alternatives.

In a typical brainstorming session, a half-dozen to a dozen people sit around a table. The group leader states the problem in a clear manner so that it is understood by all participants. Members then "free-wheel" as many alternatives as they can in a given length of time. No criticism is allowed, and all the alternatives are recorded for later discussion and analysis. That one idea stimulates others and that judgments of even the most bizarre suggestions are withheld until later encourage group members to "think the unusual." Brainstorming, however, is merely a process for generating ideas. The following two techniques go further by offering methods of actually arriving at a preferred solution.[70]

The **nominal group technique** restricts discussion or interpersonal communication during the decision-making process, hence, the term *nominal*. Group members are all physically present, as in a traditional committee meeting, but members operate independently. Specifically, a problem is presented and then the following steps take place:

1. Members meet as a group but, before any discussion takes place, each member independently writes down his or her ideas on the problem.
2. After this silent period, each member presents one idea to the group. Each member takes his or her turn, presenting a single idea until all ideas have been presented and recorded. No discussion takes place until all ideas have been recorded.
3. The group now discusses the ideas for clarity and evaluates them.
4. Each group member silently and independently rank-orders the ideas. The idea with the highest aggregate ranking determines the final decision.

The chief advantage of the nominal group technique is that it permits the group to meet formally but does not restrict independent thinking, as does the interacting group.

The most recent approach to group decision making blends the nominal group technique with sophisticated computer technology.[71] It's called the computer-assisted group or **electronic meeting**. Once the technology is in place, the concept is simple. Up to 50 people sit around a horseshoe-shaped table, empty except for a series of computer terminals. Issues are presented to participants and they type their responses onto their computer screen. Individual comments, as well as aggregate votes, are displayed on a projection screen.

The major advantages of electronic meetings are anonymity, honesty, and speed. Participants can anonymously type any message they want and it flashes on the screen for all to see at the push of a participant's board key. It also allows people to be brutally honest without penalty. And it's fast because chitchat is eliminated, discussions don't digress, and many participants can "talk" at once without stepping on one another's toes. The future of group meetings undoubtedly will include extensive use of this technology.

Each of these four group decision techniques has its own set of strengths and weaknesses. The choice of one technique over another will depend on what criteria you want to emphasize and the cost–benefit trade-off. For instance, as Exhibit 8-10 on page 246 indicates, the interacting group is good for building group cohesiveness, brainstorming keeps social pressures to a minimum, the nominal group technique is an inexpensive means for generating a large number of ideas, and electronic meetings process ideas fast.

electronic meeting

A meeting in which members interact on computers, allowing for anonymity of comments and aggregation of votes.

SUMMARY AND IMPLICATIONS FOR MANAGERS

We've covered a lot of territory in this chapter. Since we essentially organized our discussion around the group behavior model in Exhibit 8-4, let's use this model to summarize our findings regarding performance and satisfaction.

Performance

Any predictions about a group's performance must begin by recognizing that work groups are part of a larger organization and that factors such as the organization's strategy, authority structure, selection procedures, and reward system can provide a favorable or unfavorable climate within which the group can operate. For example, if an organization is characterized by distrust between management and workers, it is more likely that work groups in that organization will develop norms to restrict effort and output than will work groups in

EXHIBIT

8-10

Evaluating Group Effectiveness

Effectiveness Criteria	Type of Group			
	Interacting	Brainstorming	Nominal	Electronic
Number of ideas	Low	Moderate	High	High
Quality of ideas	Low	Moderate	High	High
Social pressure	High	Low	Moderate	Low
Money costs	Low	Low	Low	High
Speed	Moderate	Moderate	Moderate	High
Task orientation	Low	High	High	High
Potential for interpersonal conflict	High	Low	Moderate	Low
Feelings of accomplishment	High to low	High	High	High
Commitment to solution	High	Not applicable	Moderate	Moderate
Development of group cohesiveness	High	High	Moderate	Low

Source: Based on J. K. Murnighan, "Group Decision Making: What Strategies Should You Use?" *Management Review*, February 1981, p. 61.

an organization in which trust is high. So managers shouldn't look at any group in isolation. Rather, they should begin by assessing the degree of support provided to the group by external conditions. It is obviously a lot easier for any work group to be productive when the overall organization of which it is a part is growing and it has both top management's support and abundant resources. Similarly, a group is more likely to be productive when its members have the requisite skills to do the group's tasks and the personality characteristics that facilitate working well together.

A number of structural factors show a relationship to performance. Among the more prominent are role perception, norms, status inequities, the size of the group, its demographic make-up, the group's task, and cohesiveness.

There is a positive relationship between role perception and an employee's performance evaluation.[72] The degree of congruence that exists between an employee and his or her boss in the perception of the employee's job influences the degree to which that employee will be judged as an effective performer by the boss. To the extent that the employee's role perception fulfills the boss's role expectations, the employee will receive a higher performance evaluation.

Norms control group member behavior by establishing standards of right and wrong. If managers know the norms of a given group, it can help to explain the behaviors of its members. When norms support high output, managers can expect individual performance to be markedly higher than when group norms aim to restrict output. Similarly, norms that support antisocial behavior increase the likelihood that individuals will engage in deviant workplace activities.

Status inequities create frustration and can adversely influence productivity and the willingness to remain with an organization. Among individuals who are equity-sensitive, incongruence is likely to lead to reduced motivation and an increased search for ways to bring about fairness (i.e., taking another job).

The impact of size on a group's performance depends on the type of task in which the group is engaged. Larger groups are more effective at fact-finding activities. Smaller groups are more effective at action-taking tasks. Our knowledge of social loafing suggests that if management uses larger groups, efforts should be made to provide measures of individual performance within the group.

We found the group's demographic composition to be a key determinant of individual turnover. Specifically, the evidence indicates that group members who share a common age or date of entry into the work group are less prone to resign.

We also found that cohesiveness can play an important function in influencing a group's level of productivity. Whether or not it does depends on the group's performance-related norms.

The primary contingency variable moderating the relationship between group processes and performance is the group's task. The more complex and interdependent the tasks, the more inefficient processes will lead to reduced group performance.

Satisfaction

As with the role perception–performance relationship, high congruence between a boss and employee, as to the perception of the employee's job, shows a significant association with high employee satisfaction.[73] Similarly, role conflict is associated with job-induced tension and job dissatisfaction.[74]

Most people prefer to communicate with others at their own status level or a higher one rather than with those below them.[75] As a result, we should expect satisfaction to be greater among employees whose job minimizes interaction with individuals who are lower in status than themselves.

The group size–satisfaction relationship is what one would intuitively expect: Larger groups are associated with lower satisfaction.[76] As size increases, opportunities for participation and social interaction decrease, as does the ability of members to identify with the group's accomplishments. At the same time, having more members also prompts dissension, conflict, and the formation of subgroups which all act to make the group a less pleasant entity of which to be a part.

All Jobs Should Be Designed Around Groups

G roups, not individuals, are the ideal building blocks for an organization. There are at least six reasons for designing all jobs around groups.[a]

First, small groups are good for people. They can satisfy social needs and they can provide support for employees in times of stress and crisis.

Second, groups are good problem-finding tools. They are better than individuals in promoting creativity and innovation.

Third, in a wide variety of decision situations, groups make better decisions than individuals do.

Fourth, groups are very effective tools for implementation. Groups gain commitment from their members so that group decisions are likely to be willingly and more successfully carried out.

Fifth, groups can control and discipline individual members in ways that are often extremely difficult through impersonal quasi-legal disciplinary systems. Group norms are powerful control devices.

Sixth, groups are a means by which large organizations can fend off many of the negative effects of increased size. Groups help to prevent communication lines from growing too long, the hierarchy from growing too steep, and the individual from getting lost in the crowd.

Given the above argument for the value of group-based job design, what would an organization look like that was truly designed around group functions? This might best be considered by merely taking the things that organizations do with individuals and applying them to groups. Instead of hiring individuals, they'd hire groups. Similarly, they'd train groups rather than individuals, pay groups rather than individuals, promote groups rather than individuals, fire groups rather than individuals, and so on.

The rapid growth of team-based organizations over the past decade suggests we may well be on our way toward the day when almost all jobs are designed around groups.

[a]Based on H. J. Leavitt, "Suppose We Took Groups Seriously," in E. L. Cass and F. G. Zimmer (eds.), *Man and Work in Society* (New York: Van Nostrand Reinhold, 1975), pp. 67–77.

D esigning jobs around groups is consistent with socialistic doctrine. It might have worked well in the former Soviet Union or Eastern European countries. But capitalistic countries like the United States, Canada, Australia, and the United Kingdom value the individual. Designing jobs around groups is inconsistent with the economic values of these countries. Moreover, as capitalism and entrepreneurship have spread throughout Eastern Europe, we should expect to see *less* emphasis on groups and *more* on the individual in workplaces throughout the world. Let's look at the United States to see how cultural and economic values shape employee attitudes toward groups.

America was built on the ethic of the individual. Americans strongly value individual achievement. They praise competition. Even in team sports, they want to identify individuals for recognition. Americans enjoy being part of a group in which they can maintain a strong individual identity. They don't enjoy sublimating their identity to that of the group.

The American worker likes a clear link between his or her individual effort and a visible outcome. It is not by chance that the United States, as a nation, has a considerably larger proportion of high achievers than exists in most of the world. America breeds achievers, and achievers seek personal responsibility. They would be frustrated in job situations in which their contribution is commingled and homogenized with the contributions of others.

Americans want to be hired, evaluated, and rewarded on their individual achievements. Americans believe in an authority and status hierarchy. They accept a system in which there are bosses and subordinates. They are not likely to accept a group's decision on such issues as their job assignments and wage increases. It's harder yet to imagine that they would be comfortable in a system in which the sole basis for their promotion or termination would be the performance of their group.

1. Compare and contrast command, task, interest, and friendship groups.

2. What might motivate you to join a group?

3. Describe the five-stage group-development model.

4. What is the relationship between a work group and the organization of which it is a part?

5. What are the implications of Zimbardo's prison experiment for OB?

6. Explain the implications from the Asch experiments.

7. How are status and norms related?

8. When do groups make better decisions than individuals?

9. How can a group's demography help you to predict turnover?

10. What is groupthink? What is its effect on decision-making quality?

Questions for Critical Thinking

1. How could you use the punctuated-equilibrium model to better understand group behavior?

2. Identify five roles you play. What behaviors do they require? Are any of these roles in conflict? If so, in what way? How do you resolve these conflicts?

3. "High cohesiveness in a group leads to higher group productivity." Do you agree or disagree? Explain.

4. What effect, if any, do you expect that workforce diversity has on a group's performance and satisfaction?

5. If group decisions consistently achieve better-quality outcomes than those achieved by individuals, how did the phrase "a camel is a horse designed by a committee" become so popular and ingrained in the culture?

Team Exercise   Assessing Occupational Status

Rank the following 20 occupations from most prestigious (1) to least prestigious (20):

_____ Accountant
_____ Air traffic controller
_____ Coach of a college football team
_____ Coach of a college women's basketball team
_____ Criminal defense attorney
_____ Electrical engineer
_____ Environmental scientist
_____ Firefighter
_____ Investment banker
_____ Manager of a U.S. automobile plant

_____ Mayor of a large city
_____ Minister
_____ Pharmacist
_____ Physician
_____ Plumber
_____ Real estate salesperson
_____ Sports agent
_____ Teacher in a public elementary school
_____ U.S. Army colonel
_____ Used car salesperson

Now form into groups of three to five students each. Answer the following questions:

a. How closely did your top five choices (1–5) match?

b. How closely did your bottom five choices (16–20) match?

c. What occupations were generally easiest to rate? Which were most difficult? Why?

d. What does this exercise tell you about criteria for assessing status?

e. What does this exercise tell you about stereotypes?

Less than two months after the terrorist attacks on the World Trade Center and the Pentagon, security officials at FedEx's sorting center at Newark Airport became alarmed when they heard a rumor that one of the company's contract mechanics, Osama Sweilan, had been periodically disappearing into the company's flight-simulator room. The security men quickly set up an interrogation at an off-site location. The Egyptian-born 35-year-old Sweilan nervously explained how he sometimes would slip into the room to make sure a pipe he'd fixed wasn't leaking. He also made a few quick calls to his wife. Sometimes he even prayed. The FedEx people pressed him further, asking about his beliefs regarding politics and Osama bin Laden. Afterward, they confiscated his ID and told his outsourcing firm that he was no longer wanted in his 16-month-old job.

Organizations have a responsibility to know who is working for them. But how far does that responsibility allow management to go? Although it's illegal for employers to discriminate, how should FedEx managers have responded to the heightened wariness that many employees and customers felt toward anyone from the Arab world after the terrorist attack? What can managers do if one or more of their employees is discriminating against an Arab-American co-worker?

Source: This dilemma is based on M. Conlin, "Taking Precautions—Or Harassing Workers?" *Business Week*, December 3, 2001, p. 84.

In the spring of 2000, Time Warner was finalizing its merger with America Online. With critics claiming that this merger would create an unruly monopoly, you would have thought that Time Warner management would have been particularly sensitive to its public image. But it made a decision on April 30 that would sorely tarnish that image.

Time Warner was in the process of renegotiating its contract with Walt Disney to determine how much Time Warner would pay for the use of three of Disney's cable channels and whether Disney would renew Time Warner's right to carry the ABC network (ABC is owned by Disney). Negotiations had begun more than five months earlier but were going nowhere. Deadlines had been extended seven times. Animosities were escalating between Time Warner and Disney negotiators. By late April, face-to-face talks had ceased. Communication had come down to the exchanges of nasty faxes.

On April 26, five days before the latest negotiating deadline, when Time Warner's rights to carry the ABC network were to expire, ABC faxed a terse letter to Time Warner notifying it that Disney expected Time Warner to continue to carry the ABC signal through May 24 after the end of the sweeps period, when stations measure audiences to determine what to charge advertisers. Time Warner had been insisting on an eight-month extension. The tone of the fax set off the tempers of some Time Warner executives. They felt ABC was negotiating by fiat.

Within Time Warner, executives began considering blocking ABC's signal to the 3.5 million homes that Time Warner's cable serviced. Some saw blocking the signal as a real risk. Given that cable companies aren't popular with the public and often seen as charging monopolistic prices, several Time Warner execs feared that they would take the blame rather than Disney. Others argued that Disney, itself a huge conglomerate, might take just as much blame, if not more, if Time Warner put its message out effectively. And they doubted ABC would take the chance of losing up to $3 million a day in advertising revenues. They figured the threat of blocking ABC's signal might finally bring Disney to agree to Time Warner's terms.

By Sunday, April 30, still no agreement had been reached. More terse faxes went back and forth. Neither side would budge from its demands. By 8:30 P.M., Disney executives began to sense that Time Warner's threat to pull the ABC signal was real, though they still found it hard to believe. Meanwhile, Time Warner executives were convinced that they had Disney cornered. "It's clear they didn't think we would drop, and we didn't think they would let us drop," said Fred Dessler, a senior vice president at Time Warner and head of its negotiating team.

Finally, with no compromise offer from Disney, Time Warner executives felt there was no turning back. Time Warner Cable's president called the company's CEO, Gerald Levin, and told him he was about to order his engineers to block the ABC signal. Levin supported the decision. At 12:01 on Monday May 1, the ABC screen went briefly to static, then the phrase "Disney has taken ABC away from you" appeared in bright yellow letters on a blue screen.

Within 24 hours, the mayor of New York attacked Time Warner as a predatory monopoly. Disney dispatched its lawyers to the Washington offices of the U.S. Federal Communications Commission, where they requested that the commission force Time Warner to transmit its signals. Time Warner executives went to Washington to plead their case before the FCC. It quickly became clear that the commission was siding with Disney in this dispute. The next day, Tuesday, The *New York Times* published an editorial that said the threat to Disney by a combined AOL and Time Warner was real. It now was becoming increasingly clear to Time Warner executives that they were losing the public relations war.

Tuesday afternoon, after only 39 hours of blocking ABC's signal, Time Warner called a news conference and announced that it had offered Disney a six month extension of the negotiations. The following day the FCC ruled that Time Warner had violated the law by blocking ABC from its system during a sweeps month.

Time Warner executives admitted afterward that they erred. They say they made a legal miscalculation and also incorrectly assumed that Disney would back down. "Why did we decide to take a stand now?" asked Dessler. "We thought it was the right time. They were just pushing us and pushing us."

Questions

1. What does this case say about the role of emotions in decision making?

2. How did "group forces" shape this decision?

3. What, if anything, could senior Time-Warner executives have done to have achieved a more effective outcome in this process?

Source: Based on J. Rutenberg, "Reconstructing the Genesis of a Blunder," *New York Times*, May 8, 2000, p. C20.

Endnotes

1. This section is based on B. Headlam, "How to E-Mail Like a C.E.O.," *New York Times Magazine*, April 8, 2001, pp. 7–8.
2. L. R. Sayles, "Work Group Behavior and the Larger Organization," in C. Arensburg, et al. (eds.), *Research in Industrial Relations* (New York: Harper & Row, 1957), pp. 131–45.
3. B. W. Tuckman, "Developmental Sequences in Small Groups," *Psychological Bulletin*, June 1965, pp. 384–99; B. W. Tuckman and M. C. Jensen, "Stages of Small-Group Development Revisited," *Group and Organizational Studies*, December 1977, pp. 419–27; and M. F. Maples, "Group Development: Extending Tuckman's Theory," *Journal for Specialists in Group Work*, Fall 1988, pp. 17–23.
4. R. C. Ginnett, "The Airline Cockpit Crew," in J. R. Hackman (ed.), *Groups That Work (and Those That Don't)* (San Francisco: Jossey-Bass, 1990).
5. C. J. G. Gersick, "Time and Transition in Work Teams: Toward a New Model of Group Development," *Academy of Management Journal*, March 1988, pp. 9–41; C. J. G. Gersick, "Marking Time: Predictable Transitions in Task Groups," *Academy of Management Journal*, June 1989, pp. 274–309; and M. J. Waller, J. M. Conte, C. B. Gibson, and M. A. Carpenter, "The Effect of Individual Perceptions of Deadlines on Team Performance," *Academy of Management Review*, October 2001, pp. 586–600.
6. A. Seers and S. Woodruff, "Temporal Pacing in Task Forces: Group Development or Deadline Pressure?" *Journal of Management*, vol. 23, no. 2, 1997, pp. 169–87.
7. This model is based on the work of P. S. Goodman, E. Ravlin, and M. Schminke, "Understanding Groups in Organizations," in L. L. Cummings and B. M. Staw (eds.), *Research in Organizational Behavior*, Vol. 9 (Greenwich, CT: JAI Press, 1987), pp. 124–28; J. R. Hackman, "The Design of Work Teams," in J. W. Lorsch (ed.), *Handbook of Organizational Behavior* (Englewood Cliffs, NJ: Prentice Hall, 1987), pp. 315–42; G. R. Bushe and A. L. Johnson, "Contextual and Internal Variables Affecting Task Group Outcomes in Organizations," *Group and Organization Studies*, December 1989, pp. 462–82; M. A. Campion,

G. J. Medsker, and A. C. Higgs, "Relations Between Work Group Characteristics and Effectiveness: Implications for Designing Effective Work Groups," *Personnel Psychology*, Winter 1993, pp. 823–50; D. E. Hyatt and T. M. Ruddy, "An Examination of the Relationship Between Work Group Characteristics and Performance: Once More into the Breach," *Personnel Psychology*, Autumn 1997, pp. 553–85; and P. E. Tesluk and J. E. Mathieu, "Overcoming Roadblocks to Effectiveness: Incorporating Management of Performance Barriers into Models of Work Group Effectiveness," *Journal of Applied Psychology*, April 1999, pp. 200–17.

8. F. Friedlander, "The Ecology of Work Groups," in J. W. Lorsch (ed.), *Handbook of Organizational Behavior*, pp. 301–14; P. B. Paulus and D. Nagar, "Environmental Influences on Groups," in P. Paulus (ed.), *Psychology of Group Influence*, 2nd ed. (Hillsdale, NJ: Erlbaum, 1989); and E. Sundstrom and I. Altman, "Physical Environments and Work-Group Effectiveness," in L. L. Cummings and B. M. Staw (eds.), *Research in Organizational Behavior*, vol. 11 (Greenwich, CT: JAI Press, 1989), pp. 175–209.

9. See, for example, J. Krantz, "Group Processes Under Conditions of Organizational Decline," *Journal of Applied Behavioral Science*, vol. 21, no. 1, 1985, pp. 1–17.

10. Hackman, "The Design of Work Teams," pp. 325–26.

11. See, for instance, R. A. Baron, "The Physical Environment of Work Settings: Effects on Task Performance, Interpersonal Relations, and Job Satisfaction," in B. M. Staw and L. L. Cummings (eds.), *Research in Organizational Behavior*, vol. 16 (Greenwich, CT: JAI Press, 1994), pp. 1–46; and M. Rich, "Shut Up So We Can Do Our Jobs!" *Wall Street Journal*, August 29, 2001, p. B1.

12. M. J. Stevens and M. A. Campion, "The Knowledge, Skill, and Ability Requirements for Teamwork: Implications for Human Resource Management," *Journal of Management*, Summer 1994, pp. 503–30.

13. M. E. Shaw, *Contemporary Topics in Social Psychology* (Morristown, NJ: General Learning Press, 1976); and D. C. Kinlaw, *Developing Superior Work Teams: Building Quality and the Competitive Edge* (San Diego, CA: Lexington, 1991).

14. S. Lieberman, "The Effects of Changes in Roles on the Attitudes of Role Occupants," *Human Relations*, November 1956, pp. 385–402.

15. See D. M. Rousseau, *Psychological Contracts in Organizations: Understanding Written and Unwritten Agreements* (Thousand Oaks, CA: Sage, 1995); and D. Rousseau and R. Schalk (eds.), *Psychological Contracts in Employment: Cross-Cultural Perspectives* (San Francisco: Jossey-Bass, 2000).

16. See M. F. Peterson, et al., "Role Conflict, Ambiguity, and Overload: A 21-Nation Study," *Academy of Management Journal*, April 1995, pp. 429–52.

17. P. G. Zimbardo, C. Haney, W. C. Banks, and D. Jaffe, "The Mind Is a Formidable Jailer: A Pirandellian Prison," *New York Times*, April 8, 1973, pp. 38–60; and C. Haney and P. G. Zimbardo, "Social Roles and Role-Playing: Observa-

tions from the Stanford Prison Study," *Behavioral and Social Science Teacher*, January 1973, pp. 25–45.

18. For a review of the research on group norms, see J. R. Hackman, "Group Influences on Individuals in Organizations," in M. D. Dunnette and L. M. Hough (eds.), *Handbook of Industrial & Organizational Psychology*, 2nd ed., vol. 3 (Palo Alto, CA: Consulting Psychologists Press, 1992), pp. 235–50.

19. Adapted from Goodman, Ravlin, and Schminke, "Understanding Groups in Organizations," p. 159.

20. See, for instance, G. Blau, "Influence of Group Lateness on Individual Lateness: A Cross-Level Examination," *Academy of Management Journal*, October 1995, pp. 1483–96.

21. C. A. Kiesler and S. B. Kiesler, *Conformity* (Reading, MA: Addison-Wesley, 1969).

22. Ibid, p. 27.

23. S. E. Asch, "Effects of Group Pressure upon the Modification and Distortion of Judgments," in H. Guetzkow (ed.), *Groups, Leadership and Men* (Pittsburgh: Carnegie Press, 1951), pp. 177–90; and S. E. Asch, "Studies of Independence and Conformity: A Minority of One Against a Unanimous Majority," *Psychological Monographs: General and Applied*, vol. 70, no. 9, 1956, pp. 1–70.

24. R. Bond and P. B. Smith, "Culture and Conformity: A Meta-Analysis of Studies Using Asch's (1952, 1956) Line Judgment Task," *Psychological Bulletin*, January 1996, pp. 111–37.

25. See S. L. Robinson and R. J. Bennett, "A Typology of Deviant Workplace Behaviors: A Multidimensional Scaling Study," *Academy of Management Journal*, April 1995, pp. 555–72; S. L. Robinson and J. Greenberg, "Employees Behaving Badly: Dimensions, Determinants, and Dilemmas in the Study of Workplace Deviance," in D. M. Rousseau and C. Cooper (eds.), *Trends in Organizational Behavior*, vol. 5 (New York: Wiley, 1998); S. L. Robinson and A. M. O'Leary-Kelly, "Monkey See, Monkey Do: The Influence of Work Groups on the Antisocial Behavior of Employees," *Academy of Management Journal*, December 1998, pp. 658–72; and C. M. Pearson, L. M. Andersson, and C. L. Porath, "Assessing and Attacking Workplace Incivility," *Organizational Dynamics*, vol. 29, no. 2, 2000, pp. 123–37.

26. C. M. Pearson, L. M. Andersson, and C. L. Porath, "Assessing and Attacking Workplace Civility," p. 130.

27. S. L. Robinson and A. M. O'Leary-Kelly, "Monkey See, Monkey Do."

28. R. Keyes, *Is There Life After High School?* (New York: Warner Books, 1976).

29. Cited in J. R. Hackman, "Group Influences on Individuals in Organizations," p. 236.

30. O. J. Harvey and C. Consalvi, "Status and Conformity to Pressures in Informal Groups," *Journal of Abnormal and Social Psychology*, Spring 1960, pp. 182–87.

31. J. A. Wiggins, F. Dill, and R. D. Schwartz, "On 'Status-Liability,'" *Sociometry*, April–May 1965, pp. 197–209.

32. J. Greenberg, "Equity and Workplace Status: A Field Experiment," *Journal of Applied Psychology*, November 1988, pp. 606–13.

33. This section is based on P. R. Harris and R. T. Moran, *Managing Cultural Differences*, 4th ed. (Houston: Gulf Publishing, 1996).

34. E. J. Thomas and C. F. Fink, "Effects of Group Size," *Psychological Bulletin*, July 1963, pp. 371–84; A. P. Hare, *Handbook of Small Group Research* (New York: Free Press, 1976); and M. E. Shaw, *Group Dynamics: The Psychology of Small Group Behavior*, 3rd ed. (New York: McGraw-Hill, 1981).

35. See D. R. Comer, "A Model of Social Loafing in Real Work Groups," *Human Relations*, June 1995, pp. 647–67.

36. W. Moede, "Die Richtlinien der Leistungs-Psychologie," *Industrielle Psychotechnik*, vol. 4 (1927), pp. 193–207. See also D. A. Kravitz and B. Martin, "Ringelmann Rediscovered: The Original Article," *Journal of Personality and Social Psychology*, May 1986, pp. 936–41.

37. See, for example, J. A. Shepperd, "Productivity Loss in Performance Groups: A Motivation Analysis," *Psychological Bulletin*, January 1993, pp. 67–81; and S. J. Karau and K. D. Williams, "Social Loafing: A Meta-Analytic Review and Theoretical Integration," *Journal of Personality and Social Psychology*, October 1993, pp. 681–706.

38. S. G. Harkins and K. Szymanski, "Social Loafing and Group Evaluation," *Journal of Personality and Social Psychology*, December 1989, pp. 934–41.

39. See P. C. Earley, "Social Loafing and Collectivism: A Comparison of the United States and the People's Republic of China," *Administrative Science Quarterly*, December 1989, pp. 565–81; and P. C. Earley, "East Meets West Meets Mideast: Further Explorations of Collectivistic and Individualistic Work Groups," *Academy of Management Journal*, April 1993, pp. 319–48.

40. Thomas and Fink, "Effects of Group Size"; Hare, *Handbook*; Shaw, *Group Dynamics*; and P. Yetton and P. Bottger, "The Relationships Among Group Size, Member Ability, Social Decision Schemes, and Performance," *Organizational Behavior and Human Performance*, October 1983, pp. 145–59.

41. See, for example, R. A. Guzzo and G. P. Shea, "Group Performance and Intergroup Relations in Organizations," in M. D. Dunnette and L. M. Hough, eds., *Handbook of Industrial & Organizational Psychology*, 2nd ed., vol. 3 (Palo Alto, CA: Consulting Psychologists Press, 1992), pp. 288–90; S. E. Jackson, K. E. May, and K. Whitney, "Understanding the Dynamics of Diversity in Decision-Making Teams," in R. A. Guzzo and E. Salas (eds.), *Team Effectiveness and Decision Making in Organizations* (San Francisco: Jossey-Bass, 1995), pp. 204–61; K. Y. Williams and C. A. O'Reilly III, "Demography and Diversity in Organizations: A Review of 40 Years of Research," in B. M. Staw and L. L. Cummings (eds.), *Research in Organizational Behavior*, vol. 20 (Greenwich, CT: JAI Press, 1998), pp. 77–140; and F. Linnehan and A. M. Konrad, "Diluting Diversity: Implications for Intergroup Inequality in Organizations," *Journal of Management Inquiry*, December 1999, pp. 399–414.

42. Shaw, *Contemporary Topics*, p. 356.

43. W. E. Watson, K. Kumar, and L. K. Michaelsen, "Cultural Diversity's Impact on Interaction Process and Performance: Comparing Homogeneous and Diverse Task Groups," *Academy of Management Journal*, June 1993, pp. 590–602; and P. C. Earley and E. Mosakowski, "Creating Hybrid Team Cultures: An Empirical Test of Transnational Team Functioning," *Academy of Management Journal*, February 2000, pp. 26–49.

44. W. G. Wagner, J. Pfeffer, and C. A. O'Reilly III, "Organizational Demography and Turnover in Top-Management Groups," *Administrative Science Quarterly*, March 1984, pp. 74–92; J. Pfeffer and C. A. O'Reilly III, "Hospital Demography and Turnover among Nurses," *Industrial Relations*, Spring 1987, pp. 158–73; C. A. O'Reilly III, D. F. Caldwell, and W. P. Barnett, "Work Group Demography, Social Integration, and Turnover," *Administrative Science Quarterly*, March 1989, 21–37; S. E. Jackson, J. F. Brett, V. I. Sessa, D. M. Cooper, J. A. Julin, and K. Peyronnin, "Some Differences Make a Difference: Individual Dissimilarity and Group Heterogeneity as Correlates of Recruitment, Promotions, and Turnover," *Journal of Applied Psychology*, August 1991, pp. 675–89; M. F. Wiersema and A. Bird, "Organizational Demography in Japanese Firms: Group Heterogeneity, Individual Dissimilarity, and Top Management Team Turnover," *Academy of Management Journal*, October 1993, pp. 996–1025; F. J. Milliken and L. L. Martins, "Searching for Common Threads: Understanding the Multiple Effects of Diversity in Organizational Groups," *Academy of Management Review*, April 1996, pp. 402–33; and B. Lawrence, "The Black Box of Organizational Demography," *Organizational Science*, February 1997, pp. 1–22 .

45. For some of the controversy surrounding the definition of cohesion, see J. Keyton and J. Springston, "Redefining Cohesiveness in Groups," *Small Group Research*, May 1990, pp. 234–54.

46. C. R. Evans and K. L. Dion, "Group Cohesion and Performance: A Meta-Analysis," *Small Group Research*, May 1991, pp. 175–86; B. Mullen and C. Cooper, "The Relation between Group Cohesiveness and Performance: An Integration," *Psychological Bulletin*, March 1994, pp. 210–27; and P. M. Podsakoff, S. B. MacKenzie, and M. Ahearne, "Moderating Effects of Goal Acceptance on the Relationship Between Group Cohesiveness and Productivity," *Journal of Applied Psychology*, December 1997, pp. 974–83

47. Based on J. L. Gibson, J. M. Ivancevich, and J. H. Donnelly, Jr., *Organizations*, 8th ed. (Burr Ridge, IL: Irwin, 1994), p. 323.

48. I. D. Steiner, *Group Process and Productivity* (New York: Academic Press, 1972).

49. R. B. Zajonc, "Social Facilitation," *Science*, March 1965, pp. 269–74.

50. C. F. Bond, Jr., and L. J. Titus, "Social Facilitation: A Meta-Analysis of 241 Studies," *Psychological Bulletin*, September 1983, pp. 265–92.

51. V. F. Nieva, E. A. Fleishman, and A. Rieck, "Team Dimensions: Their Identity, Their Measurement, and Their Relationships." Final Technical Report for Contract No. DAHC 19-C-0001. Washington, DC: Advanced Research Resources Organizations, 1978.

52. See, for example, J. R. Hackman and C. G. Morris, "Group Tasks, Group Interaction Process and Group Performance Effectiveness: A Review and Proposed Integration," in L. Berkowitz (ed.), *Advances in Experimental Social Psychology* (New York: Academic Press, 1975), pp. 45–99; R. Saavedra, P. C. Earley, and L. Van Dyne, "Complex Interdependence in Task-Performing Groups," *Journal of Applied Psychology*, February 1993, pp. 61–72; and K. A. Jehn, G. B. Northcraft, and M. A. Neale, "Why Differences Make a Difference: A Field Study of Diversity, Conflict, and Performance in Workgroups," *Administrative Science Quarterly*, December 1999, pp. 741–63.

53. J. Galbraith, *Organizational Design* (Reading, MA: Addison-Wesley, 1977).

54. See N. R. F. Maier, "Assets and Liabilities in Group Problem Solving: The Need for an Integrative Function," *Psychological Review*, April 1967, pp. 239–49; G. W. Hill, "Group Versus Individual Performance: Are N+1 Heads Better Than One?" *Psychological Bulletin*, May 1982, pp. 517–39; and A. E. Schwartz and J. Levin, "Better Group Decision Making," *Supervisory Management*, June 1990, p. 4.

55. See, for example, R. A. Cooke and J. A. Kernaghan, "Estimating the Difference Between Group versus Individual Performance on Problem-Solving Tasks," *Group & Organization Studies*, September 1987, pp. 319–42; and L. K. Michaelsen, W. E. Watson, and R. H. Black, "A Realistic Test of Individual versus Group Consensus Decision Making," *Journal of Applied Psychology*, October 1989, pp. 834–39.

56. See, for example, W. C. Swap and Associates, *Group Decision Making* (Newbury Park, CA: Sage, 1984).

57. See G. W. Hill, "Group versus Individual Performance"; and L. K. Michaelsen, W. E. Watson, and R. H. Black, "A Realistic Test of Individual versus Group Consensus Decision Making."

58. J. H. Davis, *Group Performance* (Reading, MA: Addison-Wesley, 1969); J. P. Wanous and M. A. Youtz, "Solution Diversity and the Quality of Group Decisions," *Academy of Management Journal*, March 1986, pp. 149–59; and R. Libby, K. T. Trotman, and I. Zimmer, "Member Variation, Recognition of Expertise, and Group Performance," *Journal of Applied Psychology*, February 1987, pp. 81–87.

59. I. L. Janis, *Groupthink* (Boston: Houghton Mifflin, 1982); W. Park, "A Review of Research on Groupthink," *Journal of Behavioral Decision Making*, July 1990, pp. 229–45; C. P. Neck and G. Moorhead, "Groupthink Remodeled: The Importance of Leadership, Time Pressure, and Methodical Decision-Making Procedures," *Human Relations*, May

1995, pp. 537–58; and J. N. Choi and M. U. Kim, "The Organizational Application of Groupthink and Its Limits in Organizations," *Journal of Applied Psychology*, April 1999, pp. 297–306.

60. Janis, *Groupthink*.

61. Ibid.

62. G. Moorhead, R. Ference, and C. P. Neck, "Group Decision Fiascos Continue: Space Shuttle Challenger and a Revised Groupthink Framework," *Human Relations*, May 1991, pp. 539–50; and E. J. Chisson, *The Hubble Wars* (New York: HarperPerennial, 1994).

63. M. E. Turner and A. R. Pratkanis, "Mitigating Groupthink by Stimulating Constructive Conflict," in C. De Dreu and E. Van de Vliert (eds.), *Using Conflict in Organizations* (London: Sage, 1997), pp. 53–71.

64. Ibid., p. 68.

65. See N. R. F. Maier, *Principles of Human Relations* (New York: Wiley, 1952); I. L. Janis, *Groupthink: Psychological Studies of Policy Decisions and Fiascoes*, 2nd ed. (Boston: Houghton Mifflin, 1982); C. R. Leana, "A Partial Test of Janis' Groupthink Model: Effects of Group Cohesiveness and Leader Behavior on Defective Decision Making," *Journal of Management*, Spring 1985, pp. 5–17; and L. Thompson, *Making the Team: A Guide for Managers* (Upper Saddle River, NJ: Prentice Hall, 2000), pp. 116–18.

66. See D. J. Isenberg, "Group Polarization: A Critical Review and Meta-Analysis," *Journal of Personality and Social Psychology*, December 1986, pp. 1141–51; J. L. Hale and F. J. Boster, "Comparing Effect Coded Models of Choice Shifts," *Communication Research Reports*, April 1988, pp. 180–86; and P. W. Paese, M. Bieser, and M. E. Tubbs, "Framing Effects and Choice Shifts in Group Decision Making," *Organizational Behavior and Human Decision Processes*, October 1993, pp. 149–65.

67. See, for example, N. Kogan and M. A. Wallach, "Risk Taking as a Function of the Situation, the Person, and the Group," in *New Directions in Psychology*, vol. 3 (New York: Holt, Rinehart and Winston, 1967); and M. A. Wallach, N. Kogan, and D. J. Bem, "Group Influence on Individual Risk Taking," *Journal of Abnormal and Social Psychology*, vol. 65 (1962), pp. 75–86.

68. R. D. Clark III, "Group-Induced Shift Toward Risk: A Critical Appraisal," *Psychological Bulletin*, October 1971, pp. 251–70.

69. A. F. Osborn, *Applied Imagination: Principles and Procedures of Creative Thinking*, 3rd ed. (New York: Scribner, 1963). See also T. Rickards, "Brainstorming Revisited: A Question of Context," *International Journal of Management Reviews*, March 1999, pp. 91–110.

70. See A. L. Delbecq, A. H. Van deVen, and D. H. Gustafson, *Group Techniques for Program Planning: A Guide to Nominal and Delphi Processes* (Glenview, IL: Scott, Foresman, 1975); and P. B. Paulus and H.-C. Yang, "Idea Generation in

Groups: A Basis for Creativity in Organizations," *Organizational Behavior and Human Decision Processing*, May 2000, pp. 76–87.

71. See, for instance, R. B. Gallupe and W. H. Cooper, "Brainstorming Electronically," *Sloan Management Review*, Fall 1993, pp. 27–36; A. B. Hollingshead and J. E. McGrath, "Computer-Assisted Groups: A Critical Review of the Empirical Research," in R. A. Guzzo and E. Salas (eds.), *Team Effectiveness and Decision Making in Organizations*, pp. 46–78; and M. Stepanek, "Using the Net for Brainstorming," *Business Week e.biz*, December 13, 1999, pp. EB55–57.

72. T. P. Verney, "Role Perception Congruence, Performance, and Satisfaction," in D. J. Vredenburgh and R. S. Schuler (eds.), *Effective Management: Research and Application*, Proceedings of the 20th Annual Eastern Academy of Management, Pittsburgh, PA, May 1983, pp. 24–27.

73. Ibid.

74. M. Van Sell, A. P. Brief, and R. S. Schuler, "Role Conflict and Role Ambiguity: Integration of the Literature and Directions for Future Research," *Human Relations*, January 1981, pp. 43–71; and A. G. Bedeian and A. A. Armenakis, "A Path-Analytic Study of the Consequences of Role Conflict and Ambiguity," *Academy of Management Journal*, June 1981, pp. 417–24.

75. Shaw, *Group Dynamics*.

76. B. Mullen, C. Symons, L. Hu, and E. Salas, "Group Size, Leadership Behavior, and Subordinate Satisfaction," *Journal of General Psychology*, April 1989, pp. 155–70.

PART THREE

THE GROUP

Steve Blake, president of Wes-Tex Printing in Brownwood, Texas, was getting frustrated with his lack of success at reducing the seven days' time it took his company to deliver on orders of business cards.[1] So he decided to try something he'd never done before. A take-charge, autocratic decision-maker by nature, he turned over the task of speeding up production to his 130 employees (some are shown in photo).

The employees decided to use teams as a way to attack the problem. A team of workers from each step in the production process came together to pinpoint the bottlenecks. Then team leaders, using charts of the production process, assessed the entire process in reverse. They began at the loading dock, where finished boxes of business cards are picked up by United Parcel Service at 6 P.M. weekdays to be shipped to neighborhood printing shops around the country. They traced every step back to the time that orders arrived in the morning mail. Their analysis led them to the conclusion that, with a number of changes, repeat orders could be turned around in two days and all products could go out within four days. The individual teams then went about creating ideas for change and implementing them in their areas. For instance, they cut out delays in the production process and readjusted work schedules. Lo and behold, they dramatically reduced delivery times—achieving their two-day/four-day goal.

After this success, the turnaround-time team recommended the setting up of a new team to improve work flow. This new team decided to try an experiment in which three workers from different but related departments were thrown together to teach each other their jobs and jointly solve problems. This would allow orders that used to sit in baskets going back and forth between departments for changes or fixes to be acted on immediately. Again, the team approach resulted in a significant improvement in efficiency and better service for customers.

Understanding Work Teams

Steve Blake has become sold on the value of teams. And success with the team concept was a major factor leading to Wes-Tex winning the 2001 RIT/USA TODAY Quality Cup for small business.

Wes-Tex is at the cutting edge of a major trend. Teams are increasingly becoming the primary means for organizing work in contemporary business firms.

WHY HAVE TEAMS BECOME SO POPULAR?

Twenty-five years ago, when companies like W. L. Gore, Volvo, and General Foods introduced teams into their production processes, it made news because no one else was doing it. Today, it's just the opposite. It's the organization that *doesn't* use teams that has become newsworthy. Currently, 80 percent of Fortune 500 companies have half or more of their employees on teams. And 68 percent of small U.S. manufacturers are using teams in their production areas.[2]

How do we explain the current popularity of teams? The evidence suggests that teams typically outperform individuals when the tasks being done require multiple skills, judgment, and experience.[3] As organizations have restructured themselves to compete more effectively and efficiently, they have turned to teams as a way to use employee talents better. Management has found that teams are more flexible and responsive to changing events than are traditional departments or other forms of permanent groupings. Teams have the capability to quickly assemble, deploy, refocus, and disband.

LEARNING OBJECTIVES

AFTER STUDYING THIS CHAPTER, YOU SHOULD BE ABLE TO:

1. Explain the growing popularity of teams in organizations.

2. Contrast teams with groups.

3. Identify four types of teams.

4. Describe conditions when teams are preferred over individuals.

5. Specify the characteristics of effective teams.

6. Explain how organizations can create team players.

7. Describe the advantages and disadvantages of diversity for work teams.

8. Explain how management can keep teams from becoming stagnant and rigid.

But don't overlook the motivational properties of teams. Consistent with our discussion in Chapter 7 of the role of employee involvement as a motivator, teams facilitate employee participation in operating decisions. For instance, some assembly-line workers at John Deere are part of sales teams that call on customers.[4] These workers know the products better than any traditional salesperson; and by traveling and speaking with farmers, these hourly workers develop new skills and become more involved in their jobs. So another explanation for the popularity of teams is that they are an effective means for management to democratize their organizations and increase employee motivation.

TEAMS VERSUS GROUPS: WHAT'S THE DIFFERENCE?

Groups and teams are not the same thing. In this section, we want to define and clarify the difference between a work group and a work team.[5]

In the previous chapter, we defined a *group* as two or more individuals, interacting and interdependent, who have come together to achieve particular objectives. A **work group** is a group that interacts primarily to share information and to make decisions to help each member perform within his or her area of responsibility.

Work groups have no need or opportunity to engage in collective work that requires joint effort. So their performance is merely the summation of each group member's individual contribution. There is no positive synergy that would create an overall level of performance that is greater than the sum of the inputs.

A **work team** generates positive synergy through coordinated effort. Their individual efforts results in a level of performance that is greater than the sum of those individual inputs. Exhibit 9-1 highlights the differences between work groups and work teams.

These definitions help clarify why so many organizations have recently restructured work processes around teams. Management is looking for that positive synergy that will allow their organizations to increase performance. The extensive use of teams creates the *potential* for an organization to generate greater outputs with no increase in inputs. Notice, however, we said "potential." There is nothing inherently magical in the creation of teams that ensures the achievement of this positive synergy. Merely calling a *group* a *team* doesn't automatically increase its

work group

A group that interacts primarily to share information and to make decisions to help each group member perform within his or her area of responsibility.

work team

A group whose individual efforts result in a performance that is greater than the sum of the individual inputs.

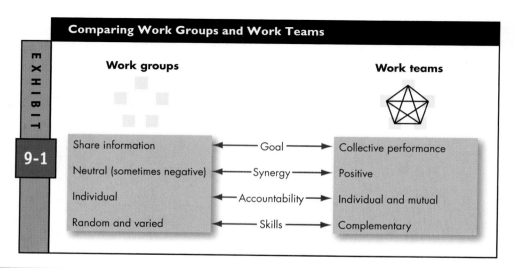

EXHIBIT 9-1

Comparing Work Groups and Work Teams

Work groups		Work teams
Share information	← Goal →	Collective performance
Neutral (sometimes negative)	← Synergy →	Positive
Individual	← Accountability →	Individual and mutual
Random and varied	← Skills →	Complementary

performance. As we show later in this chapter, effective teams have certain common characteristics. If management hopes to gain increases in organizational performance through the use of teams, it will need to ensure that its teams possess these characteristics.

TYPES OF TEAMS

Teams can do a variety of things. They can make products, provide services, negotiate deals, coordinate projects, offer advice, and make decisions.[6] In this section we'll describe the four most common types of teams you're likely to find in an organization: *problem-solving teams*, *self-managed work teams*, *cross-functional teams*, and *virtual teams* (see Exhibit 9-2).

Problem-Solving Teams

If we look back 20 years or so, teams were just beginning to grow in popularity, and most of those teams took similar form. These were typically composed of 5 to 12 hourly employees from the same department who met for a few hours each week to discuss ways of improving quality, efficiency, and the work environment.[7] We call these **problem-solving teams**.

In problem-solving teams, members share ideas or offer suggestions on how work processes and methods can be improved. Rarely, however, are these teams given the authority to unilaterally implement any of their suggested actions.

One of the most widely practiced applications of problem-solving teams during the 1980s was quality circles.[8] As described in Chapter 7, these are work teams of eight to ten employees and supervisors who have a shared area of responsibility and meet regularly to discuss their quality problems, investigate causes of the problems, recommend solutions, and take corrective actions.

> **problem-solving teams**
> Groups of 5 to 12 employees from the same department who meet for a few hours each week to discuss ways of improving quality, efficiency, and the work environment.

Self-Managed Work Teams

Problem-solving teams were on the right track but they didn't go far enough in getting employees involved in work-related decisions and processes. This led to experimentation with truly autonomous teams that could not only solve problems but implement solutions and take full responsibility for outcomes.

Self-managed work teams are groups of employees (typically 10 to 15 in number) who perform highly related or interdependent jobs and take on many of the responsibilities of their former supervisors.[9] Typically, this includes planning and scheduling of work, assigning tasks to members, collective control over the pace of work, making operating decisions, taking action on problems, and working with suppliers and customers. Fully self-managed work teams even select their own

> **self-managed work teams**
> Groups of 10 to 15 people who take on responsibilities of their former supervisors.

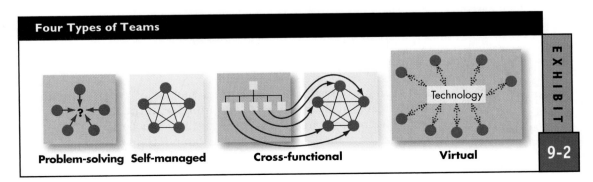

Four Types of Teams

Problem-solving   Self-managed   Cross-functional   Technology   Virtual

EXHIBIT 9-2

members and have the members evaluate each other's performance. As a result, supervisory positions take on decreased importance and may even be eliminated.

A factory at Eaton Corp's Aeroquip Global Hose Division provides an example of how self-managed teams are being used in industry.[10] Located in the heart of Arkansas' Ozark Mountains, this factory makes hydraulic hose that is used in trucks, tractors, and other heavy equipment. In 1994, to improve quality and productivity, Eaton-Aeroquip's management threw out the assembly line and organized the plant's 285 workers into more than 50 self-managed teams. Workers were suddenly free to participate in decisions that were previously reserved solely for management—for instance, the teams set their own schedules, selected new members, negotiated with suppliers, made calls on customers, and disciplined members who created problems. And the results? Between 1993 and 1999, response time to customer concerns improved 99 percent; productivity and manufacturing output both increased by more than 50 percent; and accident rates dropped by more than half.

Xerox, General Motors, Coors Brewing, PepsiCo, Hewlett-Packard, Honeywell, M&M/Mars, Aetna Life, and Industrial Light & Magic are just a few familiar names that have implemented self-managed work teams. Estimates suggest that about 30 percent of U.S. employers now use this form of team; and among large firms, the number is probably closer to 50 percent.[11]

Business periodicals have been chock full of articles describing successful applications of self-managed teams. But a word of caution needs to be offered. Some organizations have been disappointed with the results from self-managed teams. For instance, they don't seem to work well during organizational downsizing. Employees often view cooperating with the team concept as an exercise in assisting one's own executioner.[12] The overall research on the effectiveness of self-managed work teams has not been uniformly positive.[13] Moreover, although individuals on these teams do tend to report higher levels of job satisfaction, they also sometimes have higher absenteeism and turnover rates. Inconsistency in findings suggests that the effectiveness of self-managed teams is situationally dependent.[14] In addition to downsizing, factors such as the strength and make-up of team norms, the type of tasks the team undertakes, and the reward structure can significantly influence how well the team performs. Finally, care needs to be taken when introducing self-managed teams globally. For instance, evidence suggests that these types of teams have not fared well in Mexico largely due to that culture's low tolerance of ambiguity and uncertainty and employees' strong respect for hierarchical authority.[15]

Cross-Functional Teams

Custom Research Inc., a Minneapolis-based market-research firm, had been historically organized around functional departments, but senior management concluded that these functional departments weren't meeting the changing needs of the firm's clients. So management reorganized Custom Research's 100 employees into account teams.[16] The idea behind the teams was to have every aspect of a client's work handled within one team rather than by separate departments. The goal was to improve communication and tracking of work, which would lead to increased productivity and more satisfied clients.

Custom Research's reorganization illustrates the use of **cross-functional teams**. These are teams made up of employees from about the same hierarchical level, but from different work areas, who come together to accomplish a task.

Many organizations have used horizontal, boundary-spanning groups for decades. For example, IBM created a large task force in the 1960s—made up of employees from across departments in the company—to develop its highly successful

cross-functional teams

Employees from about the same hierarchical level, but from different work areas, who come together to accomplish a task.

Teams Help Boeing Save Its 717 Program

The Boeing 717 is a 100-seat, short-range jet designed basically for the commuter market. It's one of four planes manufactured at Boeing's Long Beach, California, facility.

In 1996, Boeing was at a crossroads. The company saw a growing market for a short-range plane like the 717 but orders were slow to come in and the project was losing money at a high rate. The choice was either to kill the project or drastically improve efficiencies in producing the plane. Management chose the latter.

Management decided that to make the plane profitable, they would focus on three areas: implement a team-based organization, provide employees with improved training, and introduce lean-manufacturing techniques. Employee training included learning labor savings techniques and financial concepts like in-

ternal return-on-investment and shareholder value. Lean-manufacturing efforts emphasized ways to improve work flow and cut costs. For instance, more than five million square feet of space at the facility was sold and personnel working on the 717 were moved into a single space—a 600,000 square foot factory.

To open lines of communication and eliminate waste, functionally aligned, self-managing work teams were created, grouping employees according to their function, not their titles. For example, instead of housing all the engineers in a separate building, they grouped them in teams around specific tasks. Members in all functions—from finance and labor unions to engineering and product support—were grouped together according to specific tasks such as interior design, final assembly, propulsion, and product delivery. The work-flow process was redesigned so employees work side by side on a full-moving production

line—a first for a commercial airplane. As described by a Boeing executive, "In this environment the person who designs the seat is next to the person who builds them, and he's next to the person who installs them." Support teams are located within a few feet of the assembly positions. They're equipped with everything they need to help keep airplanes moving, including specialists who inspect work while it's being done.

These changes helped turn the 717 project from a money-loser to a major success. Although the company expected to sell fewer than 200 of the planes during its lifetime, Boeing now has orders for more than 300. The time required to manufacture a 717 plane has been cut from six days to four. Other costs have been significantly cut. And the plane is now trouncing its competition. In the year 2000, for instance, Boeing sold 19 of the 717s, while Airbus Industries sold only three of its comparably-sized A318s.

Source: Based on S. F. Gale, "The Little Airplane That Could," *Training*, December 2000, pp. 60–67.

System 360. And a *task force* is really nothing other than a temporary cross-functional team. Similarly, *committees* composed of members from across departmental lines are another example of cross-functional teams. But the popularity of cross-discipline work teams exploded in the late 1980s. For instance, all the major automobile manufacturers—including Toyota, Honda, Nissan, BMW, GM, Ford, and DaimlerChrysler—currently use this form of team to coordinate complex projects. Harley-Davidson relies on specific cross-functional teams to manage each line of its motorcycles. These teams include Harley employees from design, manufacturing, and purchasing, as well as representatives from key outside suppliers.[17] And IBM still makes use of temporary cross-functional teams. Between November 1999 and June 2000, for instance, IBM's senior management pulled together 21 employees from among its 100,000 information technology staff to come up with recommendations on how the company can speed up projects and bring products to market faster.[18] The 21 members were selected because they had one common characteristic—they had all successfully led fast-moving projects. The Speed Team, as they came to be known, spent eight months sharing experiences, examining differences between fast-moving projects and slow ones, and eventually generated recommendations on how to speed up IBM projects.

Cross-functional teams are an effective means for allowing people from diverse areas within an organization (or even between organizations) to exchange information, develop new ideas and solve problems, and coordinate complex projects. Of course, cross-functional teams are no picnic to manage. Their early stages of development are often very time consuming as members learn to work with diversity and complexity. It takes time to build trust and teamwork, especially among people from different backgrounds with different experiences and perspectives.

Virtual Teams

virtual teams

Teams that use computer technology to tie together physically dispersed members in order to achieve a common goal.

The previous types of teams do their work face-to-face. **Virtual teams** use computer technology to tie together physically dispersed members in order to achieve a common goal.[19] They allow people to collaborate online—using communication links like wide-area networks, video conferencing, or e-mail—whether they're only a room away or continents apart.

Virtual teams can do all the things that other teams do—share information, make decisions, complete tasks. And they can include members from the same organization or link an organization's members with employees from other organizations (i.e., suppliers and joint partners). They can convene for a few days to solve a problem, a few months to complete a project, or exist permanently.[20]

The three primary factors that differentiate virtual teams from face-to-face teams are: (1) the absence of paraverbal and nonverbal cues; (2) limited social context; and (3) the ability to overcome time and space constraints. In face-to-face conversation, people use paraverbal (tone of voice, inflection, voice volume) and nonverbal (eye movement, facial expression, hand gestures, and other body language) cues. These help clarify communication by providing increased meaning, but aren't available in online interactions. Virtual teams often suffer from less social rapport and less direct interaction among members. They aren't able to duplicate the normal give and take of face-to-face discussion. Especially when members haven't personally met, virtual teams tend to be more task-oriented and exchange less social–emotional information. Not surprisingly, virtual team members report less satisfaction with the group interaction process than do face-to-face teams. Finally, virtual teams are able to do their work even if members are thousands of miles apart and separated by a dozen or more time zones. It allows people to work together who might otherwise never be able to collaborate.

Companies like Hewlett-Packard, Boeing, Ford, VeriFone, and Royal Dutch/Shell have become heavy users of virtual teams. VeriFone, for instance, is a California-based maker of computerized swipe machines that read credit card information. Yet the use of virtual teams allows its 3,000 employees, who are located all around the globe, to work together on design projects, marketing plans, and making sales presentations. Moreover, VeriFone has found that virtual teams provide strong recruiting inducements. Says a VeriFone vice president, "We don't put relocation requirements on people. If a person enjoys living in Colorado and can do the job in virtual space, we're not intimidated by that."[21]

BEWARE! TEAMS AREN'T ALWAYS THE ANSWER

Teamwork takes more time and often more resources than individual work. Teams, for instance, have increased communication demands, conflicts to be managed, and meetings to be run. So the benefits of using teams have to exceed the costs. And that's not always the case. In the excitement to enjoy the benefits of teams, some managers have introduced them into situations in which the work is better done by individuals. So before you rush to implement teams, you should carefully assess whether the work requires or will benefit from a collective effort.

How do you know if the work of your group would be better done in teams? It's been suggested that three tests be applied to see if a team fits the situation.[22] First, can the work be done better by more than one person? A good indicator is the complexity of the work and the need for different perspectives. Simple tasks that don't require diverse input are probably better left to individuals. Second, does the work create a common purpose or set of goals for the people in the group that is more than the aggregate of individual goals? For instance, many new-car dealer service departments have introduced teams that link customer service personnel, mechanics, parts specialists, and sales representatives. Such teams can better manage collective responsibility for ensuring that customer needs are properly met. The final test to assess whether teams fit the situation is: Are the members of the group interdependent? Teams make sense when there is interdependence between tasks; when the success of the whole depends on the success of each one *and* the success of each one depends on the success of the others. Soccer, for instance, is an obvious *team* sport. Success requires a great deal of coordination between interdependent players. Conversely, except possibly for relays, swim teams are not really teams. They're groups of individuals, performing individually, whose total performance is merely the aggregate summation of their individual performances.

CREATING EFFECTIVE TEAMS

There is no shortage of efforts at trying to identify factors related to team effectiveness.[23] However, recent studies have taken what was once a "veritable laundry list of characteristics"[24] and organized them into a relatively focused model.[25] Exhibit 9-3 on page 264 summarizes what we currently know about what makes teams effective. As you'll see, it builds on many of the group concepts introduced in the previous chapter.

The following discussion is based on the model in Exhibit 9-3. Keep in mind two caveats before we proceed. First, teams differ in form and structure. Since the model we present attempts to generalize across all varieties of teams, you need to be careful not to rigidly apply the model's predictions to all teams.[26] The model should be used as a guide, not as an inflexible prescription. Second, the model assumes that it's already been determined that teamwork is preferable over individual work. Creating "effective" teams in situations in which individuals can do the job better is equivalent to solving the wrong problem perfectly.

The key components making up effective teams can be subsumed into four general categories. The first category is *work design*. The second relates to the team's *composition*. Third is the resources and other *contextual* influences that make teams effective. Finally, *process* variables reflect those things that go on in the team that influences effectiveness.

What does *team effectiveness* mean in this model? Typically this has included objective measures of the team's productivity, managers' ratings of the team's performance, and aggregate measures of member satisfaction.

Work Design

Effective teams need to work together and take collective responsibility to complete significant tasks. They must be more than a "team-in-name-only."[27] The work-design category includes variables like freedom and autonomy, the opportunity to use different skills and talents, the ability to complete a whole and identifiable task

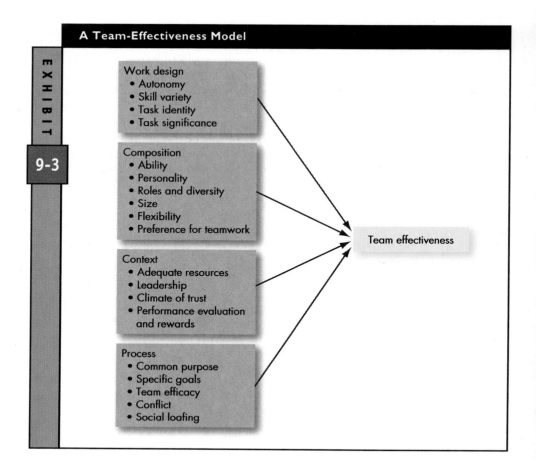

EXHIBIT 9-3

A Team-Effectiveness Model

Work design
• Autonomy
• Skill variety
• Task identity
• Task significance

Composition
• Ability
• Personality
• Roles and diversity
• Size
• Flexibility
• Preference for teamwork

Context
• Adequate resources
• Leadership
• Climate of trust
• Performance evaluation and rewards

Process
• Common purpose
• Specific goals
• Team efficacy
• Conflict
• Social loafing

Team effectiveness

or product, and working on a task or project that has a substantial impact on others. The evidence indicates that these characteristics enhance member motivation and increase team effectiveness.[28] These work-design characteristics motivate because they increase members' sense of responsibility and ownership over the work and because they make the work more interesting to perform.[29]

Composition

This category includes variables that relate to how teams should be staffed. In this section, we'll address the ability and personality of team members, allocating roles and diversity, size of the team, member flexibility, and members' preference for team work.

Abilities of Members To perform effectively, a team requires three different types of skills. First, it needs people with *technical expertise*. Second, it needs people with the *problem-solving and decision-making skills* to be able to identify problems, generate alternatives, evaluate those alternatives, and make competent choices. Finally, teams need people with good listening, feedback, conflict resolution, and other *interpersonal skills*.[30]

No team can achieve its performance potential without developing all three types of skills. The right mix is crucial. Too much of one at the expense of others will result in lower team performance. But teams don't need to have all the complementary skills in place at their beginning. It's not uncommon for one or more members to take responsibility to learn the skills in which the group is deficient, thereby allowing the team to reach its full potential.

Personality We demonstrated in Chapter 4 that personality has a significant influence on individual employee behavior. This can also be extended to team behavior. Many of the dimensions identified in the Big Five personality model have been shown to be relevant to team effectiveness. Specifically, teams that rate higher in mean levels of extroversion, agreeableness, conscientiousness, and emotional stability tend to receive higher managerial ratings for team performance.[31]

Very interestingly, the evidence indicates that the variance in personality characteristics may be more important than the mean.[32] So, for example, while higher mean levels of conscientiousness on a team is desirable, mixing both conscientious and not-so-conscientious members tends to lower performance. "This may be because, in such teams, members who are highly conscientious not only must perform their own tasks but also must perform or re-do the tasks of low-conscientious members. It may also be because such diversity leads to feelings of contribution inequity."[33] Another interesting finding related to personality is that "one bad apple can spoil the barrel." A single team member who lacks a minimal level of, say, agreeableness, can negatively affect the whole team's performance. So including just one person who is low on agreeableness, conscientiousness, or extroversion can result in strained internal processes and decreased overall performance.[34]

Effective teams need to possess three different kinds of skills, including interpersonal skills like listening and feedback. Those skills helped this inventory-reduction team at plastics manufacturer Spartech Polycom dramatically reduce the company's finished goods inventory and win an award in the process.

Allocating Roles and Diversity Teams have different needs, and people should be selected for a team to ensure that there is diversity and that all various roles are filled. We can identify nine potential team roles (see Exhibit 9-4 on page 266). Successful work teams have people to fill all these roles and have selected people to play in these roles based on their skills and preferences.[35] (On many teams, individuals will play multiple roles.) Managers need to understand the individual strengths that each person can bring to a team, select members with their strengths in mind, and allocate work assignments that fit with members' preferred styles. By matching individual preferences with team role demands, managers increase the likelihood that the team members will work well together.

Size of Teams The president of AOL Technologies says the secret to a great team is: "Think small. Ideally, your team should have seven to nine people."[36] His advice is supported by evidence.[37] Generally speaking, the most effective teams have fewer than 10 members. And experts suggest using the smallest number of people who can do the task. Unfortunately, there is a pervasive tendency for managers to err on the side of making teams too large. While a minimum of four or five may be necessary to develop diversity of views and skills, managers seem to seriously underestimate how coordination problems can geometrically increase as team members are added. When teams have excess members, cohesiveness and mutual accountability declines, social loafing increases, and more and more people do less

EXHIBIT

9-4

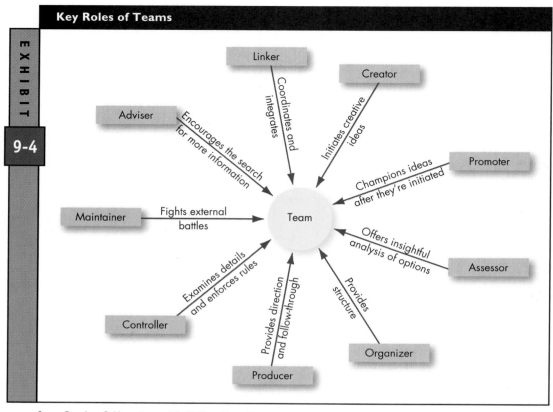

Source: Based on C. Margerison and D. McCann, *Team Management: Practical New Approaches* (London: Mercury Books, 1990).

talking relative to others. So in designing effective teams, managers should try to keep them under 10. If a natural working unit is larger and you want a team effort, consider breaking the group into subteams.

Member Flexibility   Teams made up of flexible individuals have members who can complete each other's tasks. This is an obvious plus to a team because it greatly improves its adaptability and makes it less reliant on any single member.[38] So selecting members who themselves value flexibility, then cross-training them to be able to do each other's jobs, should lead to higher team performance over time.

Member Preferences   Not every employee is a team player. Given the option, many employees will select themselves *out* of team participation. When people who would prefer to work alone are required to team-up, there is a direct threat to the team's morale and to individual member satisfaction.[39] This suggests that, when selecting team members, individual preferences should be considered as well as abilities, personalities, and skills. High-performing teams are likely to be composed of people who prefer working as part of a group.

Context

The four contextual factors that appear to be most significantly related to team performance are the presence of adequate resources, effective leadership, a climate of trust, and a performance evaluation and reward system that reflects team contributions.

Adequate Resources In our work-group model in the previous chapter, we acknowledged that a work group is part of a larger organization system. As such, all work teams rely on resources outside the group to sustain it. And a scarcity of resources directly reduces the ability of the team to perform its job effectively. As one set of researchers concluded, after looking at 13 factors potentially related to group performance, "perhaps one of the most important characteristics of an effective work group is the support the group receives from the organization."[40] This support includes timely information, technology, adequate staffing, encouragement, and administrative assistance. Teams must receive the necessary support from management and the larger organization if they are going to succeed in achieving their goals.

Leadership and Structure Team members must agree on who is to do what and ensure that all members contribute equally in sharing the workload. In addition, the team needs to determine how schedules will be set, what skills need to be developed, how the group will resolve conflicts, and how the group will make and modify decisions. Agreeing on the specifics of work and how they fit together to integrate individual skills requires team leadership and structure. This, incidentally, can be provided directly by management or by the team members themselves as they fulfill promoter, organizer, producer, maintainer, and linker roles (refer back to Exhibit 9-4).

Leadership, of course, isn't always needed. For instance, the evidence indicates that self-managed work teams often perform better than teams with formally appointed leaders.[41] And leaders can obstruct high performance when they interfere with self-managing teams.[42] On self-managed teams, team members absorb many of the duties typically assumed by managers.

On traditionally managed teams, we find that two factors seem to be important in influencing team performance—the leader's expectations and his or her mood. Leaders who expect good things from their team are more likely to get them. For instance, military platoons under leaders who held high expectations performed significantly better in training than control platoons.[43] In addition, studies have found that leaders who exhibit positive mood get better team performance and lower turnover.[44]

Climate of Trust Members of effective teams trust each other. And they also exhibit trust in their leaders.[45] Interpersonal trust among team members facilitates cooperation, reduces the need to monitor each others' behavior, and bonds members around the belief that others on the team won't take advantage of them. Team members, for instance, are more likely to take risks and expose vulnerabilities when they believe they can trust others on their team. Similarly, as we'll show in Chapter 12, trust is the foundation of leadership. Trust in leadership is important in that it allows the team to be willing to accept and commit to their leader's goals and decisions.

Performance Evaluation and Reward Systems How do you get team members to be both individually and jointly accountable? The traditional, individually oriented evaluation and reward system must be modified to reflect team performance.[46]

Individual performance evaluations, fixed hourly wages, individual incentives, and the like are not consistent with the development of high-performance teams. So in addition to evaluating and rewarding employees for their individual contributions, management should consider group-based appraisals, profit sharing, gainsharing, small-group incentives, and other system modifications that will reinforce team effort and commitment.

Process

The final category related to team effectiveness is process variables. These include member commitment to a common purpose, establishment of specific team goals, team efficacy, a managed level of conflict, and minimizing social loafing.

A Common Purpose Effective teams have a common and meaningful purpose that provides direction, momentum, and commitment for members.[47] This purpose is a vision. It's broader than specific goals.

Members of successful teams put a tremendous amount of time and effort into discussing, shaping, and agreeing on a purpose that belongs to them both collectively and individually. This common purpose, when accepted by the team, becomes the equivalent of what celestial navigation is to a ship captain—it provides direction and guidance under any and all conditions.

Annie Morita, senior vice president of marketing for Columbia Tristar, is responsible for creating a sense of common purpose among the members of her team. Says Morita, "My job is to encourage people to work together to market TV shows and feature films to broadcasters around the world."

Specific Goals Successful teams translate their common purpose into specific, measurable, and realistic performance goals. Just as we demonstrated in Chapter 6 how goals lead individuals to higher performance, goals also energize teams. These specific goals facilitate clear communication. They also help teams maintain their focus on getting results.

Also, consistent with the research on individual goals, team goals should be challenging. Difficult goals have been found to raise team performance on those criteria for which they're set. So, for instance, goals for quantity tend to raise quantity, goals for speed tend to raise speed, goals for accuracy raise accuracy, and so on.[48]

Team Efficacy Effective teams have confidence in themselves. They believe they can succeed. We call this *team efficacy*.[49]

Success breeds success. Teams that have been successful raise their beliefs about future success, which, in turn, motivates them to work harder.

What, if anything, can management do to increase team efficacy? Two possible options are helping the team to achieve small successes and skill training. Small successes build team confidence. As a team develops an increasingly stronger performance record, it also increases the collective belief that future efforts will lead to success. In addition, managers should consider providing training to improve members' technical and interpersonal skills. The greater the abilities of team members, the greater the likelihood that the team will develop confidence and the capability to deliver on that confidence.

Conflict Levels Conflict on a team isn't necessarily bad. As we'll elaborate in Chapter 14, teams that are completely void of conflict are likely to become apathetic and stagnant. So conflict can actually improve team effectiveness.[50] But not all types of conflict. Relationship conflicts—those based on interpersonal incompatibilities, tension, and animosity toward others—are almost always dysfunctional. However, on teams performing nonroutine activities, disagreements among members about task content (called task conflicts) is not detrimental. In fact, it is often beneficial because it lessens the likelihood of groupthink. Task conflicts stimulate discussion, promote critical assessment of problems and options, and can lead to better team decisions. So effective teams will be characterized by an appropriate level of conflict.

Social Loafing   We learned in the previous chapter that individuals can hide inside a group. They can engage in social loafing and coast on the group's effort because their individual contributions can't be identified. Effective teams undermine this tendency by holding themselves accountable at both the individual and team level.

Successful teams make members individually and jointly accountable for the team's purpose, goals, and approach.[51] They are clear on what they are individually responsible for and what they are jointly responsible for.

TURNING INDIVIDUALS INTO TEAM PLAYERS

To this point, we've made a strong case for the value and growing popularity of teams. But many people are not inherently team players. They're loners or people who want to be recognized for their individual achievements. There are also many organizations that have historically nurtured individual accomplishments. They have created competitive work environments in which only the strong survive. If these organizations adopt teams, what do they do about the selfish, "I've-got-to-look-out-for-me" employees that they've created? Finally, as we discussed in Chapter 3, countries differ in terms of how they rate on individualism and collectivism. Teams fit well with countries that score high on collectivism.[52] But what if an organization wants to introduce teams into a work population that is made up largely of individuals born and raised in a highly individualistic society? As one writer so aptly put it, in describing the role of teams in the United States: "Americans don't grow up learning how to function in teams. In school we never receive a team report card or learn the names of the team of sailors who traveled with Columbus to America."[53] This limitation would obviously be just as true of Canadians, British, Australians, and others from individualistic societies.

The Challenge

The previous points are meant to dramatize that one substantial barrier to using work teams is individual resistance. An employee's success is no longer defined in terms of individual performance. To perform well as team members, individuals must be able to communicate openly and honestly, to confront differences and resolve conflicts, and to sublimate personal goals for the good of the team. For many employees, this is a difficult—sometimes impossible—task. The challenge of creating team players will be greatest when (1) the national culture is highly individualistic and (2) the teams are being introduced into an established organization that has historically valued individual achievement. This describes, for instance, what faced managers at AT&T, Ford, Motorola, and other large U.S.-based companies. These firms prospered by hiring and rewarding corporate stars, and they bred a competitive climate that encouraged individual achievement and recognition. Employees in these types of firms can be jolted by this sudden shift to the importance of team play.[54] A veteran employee of a large company, who had done well working alone, described the experience of joining a team: "I'm learning my lesson. I just had my first negative performance appraisal in 20 years."[55]

On the other hand, the challenge for management is less demanding when teams are introduced where employees have strong collectivist values—such as in Japan or Mexico—or in new organizations that use teams as their initial form for structuring work. Saturn Corp., for instance, is an American organization owned by General Motors. The company was designed around teams from its inception. Everyone at Saturn was hired with the knowledge that they would be working in teams. The ability to be a good team player was a basic hiring qualification that had to be met by all new employees.

Shaping Team Players

The following summarizes the primary options managers have for trying to turn individuals into team players.

Training in problem solving and conflict management often improves the performance of individual team members and of the team as a whole. Such training is, in fact, critical to the success of process-improvement teams like this one at Honeywell.

Selection Some people already possess the interpersonal skills to be effective team players. When hiring team members, in addition to the technical skills required to fill the job, care should be taken to ensure that candidates can fulfill their team roles as well as technical requirements.[56]

Many job candidates don't have team skills. This is especially true for those socialized around individual contributions. When faced with such candidates, managers basically have three options. The candidates can undergo training to "make them into team players." If this isn't possible or doesn't work, the other two options are to transfer the individual to another unit within the organization, without teams (if this possibility exists); or don't hire the candidate. In established organizations that decide to redesign jobs around teams, it should be expected that some employees will resist being team players and may be untrainable. Unfortunately, such people typically become casualties of the team approach.

Training On a more optimistic note, a large proportion of people raised on the importance of individual accomplishments can be trained to become team players. Training specialists conduct exercises that allow employees to experience the satisfaction that teamwork can provide. They typically offer workshops to help employees improve their problem-solving, communication, negotiation, conflict-management, and coaching skills. Employees also learn the five-stage group development model described in Chapter 8. At Verizon, for example, trainers focus on how a team goes through various stages before it finally gels. And employees are reminded of the importance of patience—because teams take longer to make decisions than if employees were acting alone.[57]

Emerson Electric's Specialty Motor Division in Missouri, for instance, has achieved remarkable success in getting its 650-member workforce not only to accept, but to welcome, team training.[58] Outside consultants were brought in to give workers practical skills for working in teams. After less than a year, employees have enthusiastically accepted the value of teamwork.

Rewards The reward system needs to be reworked to encourage cooperative efforts rather than competitive ones.[59] For instance, Hallmark Cards, Inc., added an annual bonus based on achievement of team goals to its basic individual-incentive system. Trigon Blue Cross Blue Shield changed its system to reward an even split between individual goals and teamlike behaviors.[60]

Promotions, pay raises, and other forms of recognition should be given to individuals for how effective they are as a collaborative team member. This doesn't mean individual contributions are ignored; rather, they are balanced with selfless contributions to the team. Examples of behaviors that should be rewarded include training new colleagues, sharing information with teammates, helping to resolve team conflicts, and mastering new skills that the team needs but in which it is deficient.

Lastly, don't forget the intrinsic rewards that employees can receive from teamwork. Teams provide camaraderie. It's exciting and satisfying to be an integral part of a successful team. The opportunity to engage in personal development and to help teammates grow can be a very satisfying and rewarding experience for employees.

CONTEMPORARY ISSUES IN MANAGING TEAMS

In this section, we address three issues related to managing teams: (1) How do teams facilitate the adoption of quality management? (2) What are the implications of workforce diversity on team performance? and (3) How does management reenergize stagnant teams?

Teams and Quality Management

One of the central characteristics of quality management (QM) is the use of teams. But why are teams an essential part of QM?

The essence of QM is process improvement, and employee involvement is the linchpin of process improvement. In other words, QM requires management to give employees the encouragement to share ideas and act on what they suggest. As one author put it, "None of the various [quality management] processes and techniques will catch on and be applied except in work teams. All such techniques and processes require high levels of communication and contact, response and adaptation, and coordination and sequencing. They require, in short, the environment that can be supplied only by superior work teams."[61]

Teams provide the natural vehicle for employees to share ideas and to implement improvements. As stated by Gil Mosard, a QM specialist at Boeing: "When your measurement system tells you your process is out of control, you need teamwork for structured problem solving. Not everyone needs to know how to do all kinds of fancy control charts for performance tracking, but everybody does need to know where their process stands so they can judge if it is improving."[62] Examples from Ford Motor Co. and Amana Refrigeration, Inc., illustrate how teams are being used in QM programs.[63]

Ford began its QM efforts in the early 1980s with teams as the primary organizing mechanism. "Because this business is so complex, you can't make an impact on it without a team approach," noted one Ford manager. In designing its quality problem-solving teams, Ford's management identified five goals. The teams should (1) be small enough to be efficient and effective; (2) be properly trained in the skills their members will need; (3) be allocated enough time to work on the problems they plan to address; (4) be given the authority to resolve the problems

Teamwork leads to quality on the basketball floor as well as the production floor. For instance, teams that stay together longer tend to play better. A recent study of 23 National Basketball Association teams found that "shared experience"—tenure on the team and time on court—tended to boost win–loss performance significantly.

and implement corrective action; and (5) each have a designated "champion" whose job it is to help the team get around roadblocks that arise.

At Amana, cross-functional task forces made up of people from different levels within the company are used to deal with quality problems that cut across departmental lines. The various task forces each have a unique area of problem-solving responsibility. For instance, one handles in-plant products, another deals with items that arise outside the production facility, and still another focuses its attention specifically on supplier problems. Amana claims that the use of these teams has improved vertical and horizontal communication within the company and substantially reduced both the number of units that don't meet company specifications and the number of service problems in the field.

Teams and Workforce Diversity

Managing diversity on teams is a balancing act (see Exhibit 9-5). Diversity typically provides fresh perspectives on issues but it makes it more difficult to unify the team and reach agreements.

The strongest case for diversity on work teams is when these teams are engaged in problem-solving and decision-making tasks.[64] Heterogeneous teams bring multiple perspectives to the discussion, thus increasing the likelihood that the team will identify creative or unique solutions. In addition, the lack of a common perspective usually means diverse teams spend more time discussing issues, which decreases the chances that a weak alternative will be chosen. However, keep in mind that the positive contribution that diversity makes to decision-making teams undoubtedly declines over time. As we pointed out in the previous chapter, diverse groups have more difficulty working together and solving problems, *but this dissipates with time.* Expect the value-added component of diverse teams to decrease as members become more familiar with each other and the team becomes more cohesive.

Studies tell us that members of cohesive teams have greater satisfaction, lower absenteeism, and lower attrition from the group.[65] Yet cohesiveness is likely to be lower on diverse teams.[66] So here is a potential negative of diversity: It is detrimental to group cohesiveness. But again, referring to the previous chapter, we found that the relationship between cohesiveness and group productivity was moderated by performance-related norms. We suggest that if the norms of the

EXHIBIT 9-5

Advantages and Disadvantages of Diversity

Advantages	Disadvantages
Multiple perspectives	Ambiguity
Greater openness to new ideas	Complexity
Multiple interpretations	Confusion
Increased creativity	Miscommunication
Increased flexibility	Difficulty in reaching a single agreement
Increased problem-solving skills	Difficulty in agreeing on specific actions

Source: Adapted from *International Dimensions of Organizational Behavior,* 4th ed., by N. J. Adler. Copyright © 2002 (pg. 109). By permission of South-Western College Publishing, a division of International Thomson Publishing, Inc., Cincinnati, OH 45227.

team are supportive of diversity, then a team can maximize the value of heterogeneity while, at the same time, achieving the benefits of high cohesiveness.[67] This makes a strong case for team members to participate in diversity training.

Reinvigorating Mature Teams

Just because a team is performing well at a given point in time is no assurance that it will continue to do so.[68] Effective teams can become stagnant. Initial enthusiasm can give way to apathy. Time can diminish the positive value from diverse perspectives as cohesiveness increases.

In terms of the five-stage development model introduced in the previous chapter, teams don't automatically stay at the "performing stage." Familiarity breeds apathy. Success can lead to complacency. And maturity brings less openness to novel ideas and innovation.

Mature teams are particularly prone to suffer from groupthink. Members begin to believe they can read everyone's mind so they assume they know what everyone is thinking. As a result, team members become reluctant to express their thoughts and less likely to challenge each other.

Another source of problems for mature teams is that their early successes are often due to having taken on easy tasks. It's normal for new teams to begin by taking on issues and problems that they can handle most easily. But as time passes, the easy problems become solved and the team has to begin to confront more difficult issues. At this point, the team has typically developed entrenched processes and routines, and members are reluctant to change the "perfect" system they've already worked out. The results can often be disastrous. Internal team processes no longer work smoothly. Communication bogs down. Conflicts increase because problems are less likely to have obvious solutions. And team performance can drop dramatically.

What can be done to reinvigorate mature teams? We offer four suggestions: (1) *Prepare members to deal with the problems of maturity*. Remind team members that they're not unique—all successful teams have to confront maturity issues. They shouldn't feel let down or lose their confidence in the team concept when the initial euphoria subsides and conflicts surface. (2) *Offer refresher training*. When teams get into ruts, it may help to provide them with refresher training in communication, conflict resolution, team processes, and similar skills. This can help members regain confidence and trust in one another. (3) *Offer advanced training*. The skills that worked with easy problems may be insufficient for more difficult ones. So mature teams can often benefit from advanced training to help members develop stronger problem-solving, interpersonal, and technical skills. (4) *Encourage teams to treat their development as a constant learning experience*. Like quality management, teams should approach their own development as part of a search for continuous improvement. Teams should look for ways to improve, to confront member fears and frustrations, and to use conflict as a learning opportunity.

SUMMARY AND IMPLICATIONS FOR MANAGERS

Few trends have influenced employee jobs as much as the massive movement to introduce teams into the workplace. The shift from working alone to working on teams requires employees to cooperate with others, share information, confront differences, and sublimate personal interests for the greater good of the team.

Effective teams have been found to have common characteristics. The work that members do should provide freedom and autonomy, the opportunity to use different skills and talents, the ability to complete a whole and identifiable task or product, and work that has a substantial impact on others. The teams require individuals with technical expertise, as well as problem-solving, decision-making, and interpersonal skills; and high scores on the personality characteristics of extroversion, agreeableness, conscientiousness, and emotional stability. Effective teams tend to be small—with fewer than 10 people. They have members who fill role demands, are flexible, and who prefer to be part of a group. They also have adequate resources, effective leadership, a climate of trust, and a performance evaluation and reward system that reflects team contributions. Finally, effective teams have members committed to a common purpose, specific team goals, members who believe in the team's capabilities, a manageable level of conflict, and a minimal degree of social loafing.

Because individualistic organizations and societies attract and reward individual accomplishments, it is more difficult to create team players in these environments. To make the conversion, management should try to select individuals with the interpersonal skills to be effective team players, provide training to develop teamwork skills, and reward individuals for cooperative efforts.

Once teams are mature and performing effectively, management's job isn't over. Mature teams can become stagnant and complacent. Managers need to support mature teams with advice, guidance, and training if these teams are to continue to improve.

Sports Teams Are Good Models for Workplace Teams

Studies from football, soccer, basketball, hockey, and baseball have found a number of elements that successful sports teams have that can be extrapolated to successful work teams.

Successful teams integrate cooperation and competition. Effective team coaches get athletes to help one another but also push one another to perform at their best. Sports teams with the best win–loss record had coaches who promoted a strong spirit of cooperation and a high level of healthy competition among their players.

Successful teams score early wins. Early successes build teammates' faith in themselves and their capacity as a team. For instance, research on hockey teams of relatively equal ability found that 72 percent of the time the team that was ahead at the end of the first period went on to win the game. So managers should provide teams with early tasks that are simple and provide "easy wins."

Successful teams avoid losing streaks. Losing can become a self-fulfilling prophecy. A couple of failures can lead to a downward spiral if a team becomes demoralized and believes it is helpless to end its losing streak. Managers need to instill confidence in team members that they can turn things around when they encounter setbacks.

Practice makes perfect. Successful sport teams execute on game day but learn from their mistakes in practice. Practice should be used to try new things and fail. A wise manager carves out time and space in which work teams can experiment and learn.

Successful teams use half-time breaks. The best coaches in basketball and football use half-time during a game to reassess what is working and what isn't. Managers of work teams should similarly build in assessments at the approximate halfway point in a team project to evaluate what it can do to improve.

Winning teams have a stable membership. Stability improves performance. For instance, studies of professional basketball teams have found that the more stable a team's membership, the more likely the team is to win. The more time teammates have together, the more able they are to anticipate one another's moves and the clearer they are about one another's roles.

Successful teams debrief after failures and successes. The best sports teams study the game video. Similarly, work teams need to take time to routinely reflect on both their successes and failures and to learn from them.

There are flaws in using sports as a model for developing effective work teams. Here are just four caveats.

All sport teams aren't alike. In baseball, for instance, there is little interaction among teammates. Rarely are more than two or three players directly involved in a play. The performance of the team is largely the sum of the performance of its individual players. In contrast, basketball has much more interdependence among players. Geographic distribution is dense. Usually all players are involved in every play, team members have to be able to switch from offense to defense at a moment's notice, and there is continuous movement by all, not just the player with the ball. The performance of the team is more than the sum of its individual players. So when using sports teams as a model for work teams, you have to make sure you're making the correct comparison.

Work teams are more varied and complex. In an athletic league, the design of the task, the design of the team, and the team's context vary relatively little from team to team. But these variables can vary tremendously between work teams. As a result, coaching plays a much more significant part of a sports' teams performance than a work team. Performance of work teams is more a function of getting the team's structural and design variables right. So, in contrast to sports, managers of work teams should focus more on getting the team set up for success than coaching.

A lot of employees can't relate to sports metaphors. Not everyone on work teams is conversant in sports. Women, for instance, often are not as interested in sports as men and aren't as savvy about sports terminology. And team members from different cultures may not know the sports metaphors you're using. Most Americans, for instance, are unfamiliar with the rules and terminology of Australian Rules football.

Work team outcomes aren't easily defined in terms of wins and losses. Sports teams typically measure success in terms of wins and losses. Such measures of success are rarely as clear for work teams. When managers try to define success in wins and losses it tends to infer that the workplace is ethically no more complex than the playing field, which is rarely true.

Source: Both of these arguments are based on N. Katz, "Sports Teams as a Model for Workplace Teams: Lessons and Liabilities," *Academy of Management Executive*, August 2001, pp. 56–67.

Questions for Review

1. Contrast self-managed and cross-functional teams.

2. Contrast virtual and face-to-face teams.

3. List and describe nine team roles.

4. How do effective teams minimize social loafing?

5. How do effective teams minimize groupthink?

6. List and describe the process variables associated with effective team performance.

7. Under what conditions will the challenge of creating team players be greatest?

8. What role do teams play in quality management?

9. Contrast the pros and cons of having diverse teams.

10. How can management invigorate stagnant teams?

Questions for Critical Thinking

1. Don't teams create conflict? Isn't conflict bad? Why, then, would management support the concept of teams?

2. Are there factors in the Japanese society that make teams more acceptable in the workplace than in the United States or Canada? Explain.

3. What problems might surface in teams at each stage in the five-stage group development model?

4. How do you think member expectations might affect team performance?

5. Would you prefer to work alone or as part of a team? Why? How do you think your answer compares with others in your class?

Team Exercise | Building Effective Work Teams

Objective

This exercise is designed to allow class members to (a) experience working together as a team on a specific task and (b) analyze this experience.

Time

Teams will have 90 minutes to engage in Steps 2 and 3 below. Another 45–60 minutes will be used in class to critique and evaluate the exercise.

Procedure

1. Class members are assigned to teams of about six people.

2. Each team is required to:
   a. Determine a team name
   b. Compose a team song

3. Each team is to try to find the following items on its scavenger hunt:
   a. A picture of a team
   b. A newspaper article about a group or team
   c. A piece of apparel with the college name or logo
   d. A set of chopsticks
   e. A ball of cotton
   f. A piece of stationery from a college department
   g. A bottle of Liquid Paper
   h. A floppy disk
   i. A cup from McDonald's
   j. A dog leash
   k. A utility bill
   l. A calendar from last year
   m. A book by Ernest Hemingway
   n. An ad brochure for a Ford product

o. A test tube
p. A pack of gum
q. An ear of corn
r. A Garth Brooks tape or CD

4. After 90 minutes, all teams are to be back in the classroom. (A penalty, determined by the instructor, will be imposed on late teams.) The team with the most items on the list will be declared the winner. The class and instructor will determine whether or not the items meet the requirements of the exercise.

5. Debriefing of the exercise will begin by having each team engage in self-evaluation. Specifically, it should answer the following:

   a. What was the team's strategy?
   b. What roles did individual members perform?
   c. How effective was the team?
   d. What could the team have done to be more effective?

6. Full class discussion will focus on issues such as:

   a. What differentiated the more effective teams from the less effective teams?
   b. What did you learn from this experience that is relevant to the design of effective teams?

Source: Adapted from M. R. Manning and P. J. Schmidt, "Building Effective Work Teams: A Quick Exercise Based on a Scavenger Hunt," *Journal of Management Education*, August 1995, pp. 392–98. With permission.

Case Incident	A Virtual Team at T.A. Stearns

T.A. Stearns is a national tax accounting firm whose main business is tax preparation services for individuals. Stearns' superior reputation is based on the high quality of its advice and the excellence of its service. Key to the achievement of its reputation is the state-of-the-art computer databases and analysis tools that its people use when counseling clients. These programs were developed by highly trained individuals.

The programs that these individuals produce are highly technical, both in terms of the tax laws they cover and the code in which they are written. Perfecting them requires high levels of programming skill as well as the ability to understand the law. New laws and interpretations of existing laws have to be integrated quickly and flawlessly into the existing regulations and analysis tools.

The creation of these programs is carried out in a virtual environment by four programmers in the greater Boston area. The four work at home and are connected to each other and to the company by email, telephone, and conference software. Formal, onsite meetings among all of the programmers take place only a few times a year, although the workers sometimes meet informally outside of these scheduled occasions. Here's some background on the four:

Tom Andrews is a tax lawyer, a graduate of the University of Maine and a former hockey player there. At 35, Tom has worked on the programs for six years and is the longest-standing member of the team. Along with his design responsibilities, Tom is the primary liaison with Stearns. He is also responsible for training new team members. Single, Tom works out of his farm in Southern New Hampshire where, in his spare time, he enjoys hunting and fishing.

Cy Crane, a tax accountant and computer science graduate of the University of Massachusetts, is 32 years old, married, with two children ages 4 and 6. His wife works full time in a law firm in downtown Boston. In his spare time, Cy enjoys biking and fishing.

Marge Dector, a tax lawyer, graduated from Penn State University, is 38 years old, married, with two children ages 8 and 10. Her husband works full time as an electrical engineer at a local defense contractor. Marge's hobbies include golf and skiing.

Megan Harris, tax accountant and graduate of Indiana University, is 26 years old and single. She recently relocated to Boston and works out of her apartment in the Back Bay area.

These four people exchange e-mail messages many times every day. In fact, it's not unusual for them to step away from guests or family to log on and check in with the others. Often their e-mails are amusing as well as work-related. Sometimes, for instance, when they were facing a deadline and one of Marge's kids is home sick, they help each other with the work. Tom has occasionally invited the others to visit his farm; and Marge and Cy have gotten their families together several times for dinner. About once a month the whole group gets together for lunch.

All four of these Stearns employees are on salary, which, consistent with company custom, is negotiated separately and secretly with management. Although each is required to check in regularly during every work day, they were told when they were hired they could work wherever they wanted. Clearly, flexibility is one of the pluses of these jobs. When the four get together, they often joke about the managers and workers who are tied to the office, referring to them as "face timers" and to themselves as "free agents."

When the programmers were asked to make a major program change, they often developed programming tools called macros that would help them to do their work more efficiently. These macros greatly enhanced the speed at which a change could be written into the programs. Cy, in particular, really enjoyed hacking around with macros. On one recent project, for instance, he became obsessed with the prospect of creating a shortcut that could save him a huge amount of time. One week after he turned in his code and his release notes to the company, Cy bragged to Tom that he created a new macro that had saved him eight hours of work that week. Tom was skeptical of the shortcut, but after trying it out, he found that it actually saved him many hours too.

Stearns has an employee suggestion program that rewards employees for innovations that save the company money. The program gives an employee five percent of the savings generated by their innovation over a period of three months. The company also has a profit-sharing plan. Tom and Cy felt that the small amount of money that would be generated by a company reward would not offset the free time that they gained using their new macro. They wanted the time for leisure or consulting work. They also feared their group might suffer if management learned about the innovation. It would allow three people to do the work of four, which could mean one might lose their job. So they didn't share their innovative macro with management.

Although Tom and Cy wouldn't share the innovation with management, they were concerned that they were entering their busy season and knew everyone on the team would be stressed by the heavy workload. They decided to distribute the macro to the other members of their team and swore them to secrecy.

Over lunch one day, the team set for itself a level of production that it felt would not arouse management's suspicion. Several months passed and they used some of their extra time to push the quality of their work even higher. But they also now had more time to pursue their own personal interests.

Dave Regan, the in-house manager of the work team, picked up on the innovation several weeks after it was first implemented. He had wondered why production time had gone down a bit, while quality had shot up, and he got his first inkling of an answer when he saw an e-mail from Marge to Cy thanking him for saving her so much time with his "brilliant mind." Not wanting to embarrass his group of employees, the manager hinted to Tom that he wanted to know what was happening, but he got nowhere. He did not tell his own manager about his suspicions, reasoning that since both quality and productivity were up he did not really need to pursue the matter further.

Dave has just learned that Cy has boasted about his trick to a member of another virtual work team in the company. Suddenly, the situation seems to have gotten out of control. Dave decided to take Cy to lunch. During the meal, Dave asked Cy to explain what was happening. Cy told him about the innovation, but he insisted the team's actions had been justified to protect itself.

Dave knew that his own boss would soon hear of the situation and that he would be looking for answers—from him.

Questions

1. Why is this group a team?

2. Has anyone in this case acted unethically?

3. What, if any, characteristics of groupthink are manifested in the work team?

4. Has Dave been an effective team leader? Explain your position.

5. What should Dave do now?

Source: Adapted from "The Virtual Environment Work Team," a case prepared by R. Andre, professor, Northeastern University. With permission.

KSS PROGRAM

KNOW THE CONCEPTS
SELF-AWARENESS
SKILLS APPLICATIONS

Creating Effective Teams

After you've read Chapter 8 and this chapter, take Self-Assessment #30 (How Good Am I at Building and Leading a Team?) on your enclosed CD-ROM, and complete the skill-building module entitled Creating Effective Teams on page 620.

1. C. Woodyard, "Teams of Employees Search and Destroy Bottlenecks," *USA Today*, May 9, 2001, p. 3B.
2. Cited in C. Joinson, "Teams at Work," *HRMagazine*, May 1999, p. 30; and P. Strozniak, "Teams at Work," *Industry Week*, September 18, 2000, p. 47.
3. See, for example, S. A. Mohrman, S. G. Cohen, and A. M. Mohrman, Jr., *Designing Team-Based Organizations* (San Francisco: Jossey-Bass, 1995); P. MacMillan, *The Performance Factor: Unlocking the Secrets of Teamwork* (Nashville, TN: Broadman & Holman, 2001); and E. Salas, C. A. Bowers, and E. Edens (eds.), *Improving Teamwork in Organizations: Applications of Resource Management Training* (Mahwah, NJ: Lawrence Erlbaum, 2002).
4. K. Kelly, "The New Soul of John Deere," *Business Week*, January 31, 1994, pp. 64–66.
5. This section is based on J. R. Katzenbach and D. K. Smith, *The Wisdom of Teams* (Cambridge, MA: Harvard University Press, 1993), pp. 21, 45, and 85; and D. C. Kinlaw, *Developing Superior Work Teams* (Lexington, MA: Lexington Books, 1991), pp. 3–21.
6. See, for instance, E. Sunstrom, K. DeMeuse, and D. Futrell, "Work Teams: Applications and Effectiveness," *American Psychologist*, February 1990, pp. 120–33.
7. J. H. Shonk, Team-Based Organizations (Homewood, IL: Business One Irwin, 1992); and M. A. Verespej, "When Workers Get New Roles," *Industry Week*, February 3, 1992, p. 11.
8. M. L. Marks, P. H. Mirvis, E. J. Hackett, and J. F. Grady, Jr., "Employee Participation in a Quality Circle Program: Impact on Quality of Work Life, Productivity, and Absenteeism," *Journal of Applied Psychology*, February 1986, pp. 61–69; T. R. Miller, "The Quality Circle Phenomenon: A Review and Appraisal," *SAM Advanced Management Journal*, Winter 1989, pp. 4–7; and E. E. Adams, Jr., "Quality Circle Performance," *Journal of Management*, March 1991, pp. 25–39.
9. See, for example, S. G. Cohen, G. E. Ledford, Jr., and G. M. Spreitzer, "A Predictive Model of Self-Managing Work Team Effectiveness," *Human Relations*, May 1996, pp. 643–76; D. E. Yeats and C. Hyten, *High-Performing Self-Managed Work Teams: A Comparison of Theory to Practice* (Thousand Oaks, CA: Sage, 1998); and C. E. Nicholls, H. W. Lane, and M. Brehm Brechu, "Taking Self-Managed Teams to Mexico," *Academy of Management Executive*, August 1999, pp. 15–27.
10. W. Royal, "Team-Centered Success," *Industry Week*, October 18, 1999, pp. 56–58.
11. "Teams," *Training*, October 1996, p. 69; and C. Joinson, "Teams at Work," p. 30.
12. R. Zemke, "Rethinking the Rush to Team Up," *Training*, November 1993, pp. 55–61.
13. See, for instance, T. D. Wall, N. J. Kemp, P. R. Jackson, and C. W. Clegg, "Outcomes of Autonomous Workgroups: A Long-Term Field Experiment," *Academy of Management Journal*, June 1986, pp. 280–304; and J. L. Cordery, W. S. Mueller, and L. M. Smith, "Attitudinal and Behavioral Effects of Autonomous Group Working: A Longitudinal Field Study," *Academy of Management Journal*, June 1991, pp. 464–76.
14. J. R. Barker, "Tightening the Iron Cage: Concertive Control in Self-Managing Teams," *Administrative Science Quarterly*, September 1993, pp. 408–37; S. G. Cohen and G. E. Ledford Jr., "The Effectiveness of Self-Managing Teams: A Field Experiment, *Human Relations*, January 1994, pp. 13–43; and C. Smith and D. Comer, "Self-Organization in Small Groups: A Study of Group Effectiveness Within Non-Equilibrium Conditions," *Human Relations*, May 1994, pp. 553–81.
15. C. E. Nicholls, H. W. Lane, and M. Brehm Brechu, "Taking Self-Managed Teams to Mexico."
16. R. Maynard, "A Client-Centered Firm's Lessons in Teamwork," *Nation's Business*, March 1997, p. 32.
17. M. Brunelli, "How Harley-Davidson Uses Cross-Functional Teams," *Purchasing Online*; November 4, 1999; www.manufacturing.net/magazine/purchasing/archives/1999.
18. S. Kirsner, "Faster Company," *Fast Company*, May 2000, pp. 162–72.
19. See, for example, A. M. Townsend, S. M. DeMarie, and A. R. Hendrickson, "Virtual Teams: Technology and the Workplace of the Future," *Academy of Management Executive*, August 1998, pp. 17–29; D. Duarte and N. T. Snyder, *Mastering Virtual Teams: Strategies, Tools, and Techniques* (San Francisco: Jossey-Bass, 1999); M. L. Maznevski and K. M. Chudoba, "Bridging Space over Time: Global Virtual Team Dynamics and Effectiveness," *Organization Science*, September–October 2000, pp. 473–92; and J. Katzenbach and D. Smith, "Virtual Teaming," *Forbes*, May 21, 2001, pp. 48–51.
20. K. Kiser, "Working on World Time," *Training*, March 1999, p. 30.
21. Ibid.
22. A. B. Drexler and R. Forrester, "Teamwork—Not Necessarily the Answer," *HRMagazine*, January 1998, pp. 55–58.
23. See, for instance, D. L. Gladstein, "Groups in Context: A Model of Task Group Effectiveness," *Administrative Science Quarterly*, December 1984, pp. 499–517; J. R. Hackman, "The Design of Work Teams," in J. W. Lorsch (ed.), *Handbook of Organizational Behavior* (Upper Saddle River, NJ: Prentice Hall, 1987), pp. 315–42; M. A. Campion, G. J. Medsker, and C. A. Higgs, "Relations Between Work Group Characteristics and Effectiveness: Implications for Designing Effective Work Groups," *Personnel Psychology*, Winter 1993, pp. 823–50; and R. A. Guzzo and M. W. Dickson, "Teams in Organizations: Recent Research on Performance and Effectiveness," in J. T. Spence, J. M. Darley, and D. J. Foss, *Annual Review of Psychology*, vol. 47, pp. 307–38.
24. D. E. Hyatt and T. M. Ruddy, "An Examination of the Relationship between Work Group Characteristics and Performance: Once More into the Breech," *Personnel Psychology*, Autumn 1997, p. 555.
25. This model is based on M. A. Campion, E. M. Papper, and G. J. Medsker, "Relations between Work Team Characteristics and Effectiveness: A Replication and Extension," *Personnel Psychology*, Summer 1996, pp. 429–52; D. E. Hyatt and T. M. Ruddy, "An Examination of the Relationship between Work Group Characteristics and Performance," pp. 553–85; S. G. Cohen and D. E. Bailey, "What Makes Teams Work: Group Effectiveness Research from the Shop Floor to the Executive Suite," *Journal of Management*, vol. 23,

no. 3, 1997, pp. 239–90; G. A. Neuman and J. Wright, "Team Effectiveness: Beyond Skills and Cognitive Ability," *Journal of Applied Psychology*, June 1999, pp. 376–89; L. Thompson, *Making the Team* (Upper Saddle River, NJ: Prentice Hall, 2000), pp. 18–33.

26. See M. Mattson, T. V. Mumford, and G. S. Sintay, "Taking Teams to Task: A Normative Model for Designing or Recalibrating Work Teams," paper presented at the National Academy of Management Conference; Chicago, August 1999; and G. L. Stewart and M. R. Barrick, "Team Structure and Performance: Assessing the Mediating Role of Intrateam Process and the Moderating Role of Task Type," *Academy of Management Journal*, April 2000, pp. 135–48.

27. R. Wageman, "Critical Success Factors for Creating Superb Self-Managing Teams," *Organizational Dynamics*, Summer 1997, p. 55.

28. M. A. Campion, E. M. Papper, and G. J. Medsker, "Relations between Work Team Characteristics and Effectiveness," p. 430; and B. L. Kirkman and B. Rosen, "Powering Up Teams," *Organizational Dynamics*, Winter 2000, pp. 48–66.

29. M. A. Campion, E. M. Papper, and G. J. Medsker, "Relations between Work Team Characteristics and Effectiveness," p. 430.

30. For a more detailed breakdown on team skills, see M. J. Stevens and M. A. Campion, "The Knowledge, Skill, and Ability Requirements for Teamwork: Implications for Human Resource Management," *Journal of Management*, Summer 1994, pp. 503–30.

31. M. R. Barrick, G. L. Stewart, M. J. Neubert, and M. K. Mount, "Relating Member Ability and Personality to Work-Team Processes and Team Effectiveness," *Journal of Applied Psychology*, June 1998, pp. 377–91; and G. A. Neuman and J. Wright, "Team Effectiveness: Beyond Skills and Cognitive Ability," *Journal of Applied Psychology*, June 1999, pp. 376–89.

32. M. R. Barrick, G. L. Stewart, M. J. Neubert, and M. K. Mount, "Relating Member Ability and Personality to Work-Team Processes and Team Effectiveness."

33. Ibid., p. 388.

34. Ibid.

35. C. Margerison and D. McCann, *Team Management: Practical New Approaches* (London: Mercury Books, 1990).

36. J. Katzenbach, "What Makes Teams Work?" *Fast Company*, November 2000, p. 110.

37. The evidence in this section is described in L. Thompson, *Making the Team*, pp. 65–67.

38. E. Sundstrom, K. P. Meuse, and D. Futrell, "Work Teams: Applications and Effectiveness," *American Psychologist*, February 1990, pp. 120–33.

39. D. E. Hyatt and T. M. Ruddy, "An Examination of the Relationship between Work Group Characteristics and Performance;" and J. D. Shaw, M. K. Duffy, and E. M. Stark, "Interdependence and Preference for Group Work: Main and Congruence Effects on the Satisfaction and Performance of Group Members," *Journal of Management*, vol. 26, no. 2, 2000, pp. 259–79.

40. Ibid., p. 577. See also J. W. Bishop, K. D. Scott, and S. M. Burroughs, "Support, Commitment, and Employee Outcomes in a Team Environment," *Journal of Management*, vol. 26, no. 6, 2000, pp. 1113–32.

41. R. I. Beekun, "Assessing the Effectiveness of Sociotechnical Interventions: Antidote or Fad?" *Human Relations*, August 1989, pp. 877–97.

42. S. G. Cohen, G. E. Ledford, and G. M. Spreitzer, "A Predictive Model of Self-Managing Work Team Effectiveness."

43. D. Eden, "Pygmalion without Interpersonal Contrast Effects: Whole Groups Gain from Raising Manager Expectations," *Journal of Applied Psychology*, August 1990, pp. 394–98.

44. J. M. George and K. Bettenhausen, "Understanding Prosocial Behavior, Sales, Performance, and Turnover: A Group-Level Analysis in a Service Context," *Journal of Applied Psychology*, October 1990, pp. 698–709; and J. M. George, "Leader Positive Mood and Group Performance: The Case of Customer Service," *Journal of Applied Social Psychology*, December 1995, pp. 778–94.

45. K. T. Dirks, "Trust in Leadership and Team Performance: Evidence from NCAA Basketball," *Journal of Applied Psychology*, December 2000, pp. 1004–12; and M. Williams, "In Whom We Trust: Group Membership as an Affective Context for Trust Development," *Academy of Management Review*, July 2001, pp. 377–96.

46. See S. T. Johnson, "Work Teams: What's Ahead in Work Design and Rewards Management," *Compensation & Benefits Review*, March–April 1993, pp. 35–41; and L. N. McClurg, "Team Rewards: How Far Have We Come?" *Human Resource Management*, Spring 2001, pp. 73–86.

47. K. Hess, *Creating the High-Performance Team* (New York: Wiley, 1987); J. R. Katzenbach and D. K. Smith, *The Wisdom of Teams*, pp. 43–64; and K. D. Scott and A. Townsend, "Teams: Why Some Succeed and Others Fail," *HRMagazine*, August 1994, pp. 62–67.

48. E. Weldon and L. R. Weingart, "Group Goals and Group Performance," *British Journal of Social Psychology*, Spring 1993, pp. 307–34.

49. R. A. Guzzo, P. R. Yost, R. J. Campbell, and G. P. Shea, "Potency in Groups: Articulating a Construct," *British Journal of Social Psychology*, March 1993, pp. 87–106; S. J. Zaccaro, V. Blair, C. Peterson, and M. Zazanis, "Collective Efficacy," in J. E. Maddux (ed.), *Self-Efficacy, Adaptation and Adjustment: Theory, Research and Application* (New York: Plenum, 1995), pp. 308–30; and D. L. Feltz and C. D. Lirgg, "Perceived Team and Player Efficacy in Hockey," *Journal of Applied Psychology*, August 1998, pp. 557–64.

50. K. A. Jehn, "A Qualitative Analysis of Conflict Types and Dimensions in Organizational Groups," *Administrative Science Quarterly*, September 1997, pp. 530–57.

51. K. Hess, *Creating the High-Performance Team*.

52. See, for instance, B. L. Kirkman and D. L. Shapiro, "The Impact of Cultural Values on Employee Resistance to Teams: Toward a Model of Globalized Self-Managing Work Team Effectiveness," *Academy of Management Review*, July 1997, pp. 730–57; and B. L. Kirkman, C. B. Gibson, and D. L. Shapiro, "'Exporting' Teams: Enhancing the Implementation and Effectiveness of Work Teams in Global Affiliates," *Organizational Dynamics*, vol. 30, no. 1, 2001, pp. 12–29.

53. D. Harrington-Mackin, *The Team Building Tool Kit* (New York: AMACOM, 1994), p. 53.

54. T. D. Schellhardt, "To Be a Star among Equals, Be a Team Player," *Wall Street Journal*, April 20, 1994, p. B1.

55. Ibid.

56. See, for instance, J. Prieto, "The Team Perspective in Selection and Assessment," in H. Schuler, J. L. Farr, and M. Smith (eds.), *Personnel Selection and Assessment: Industrial and Organizational Perspectives* (Hillsdale, NJ: Erlbaum, 1994); R. Klimoski

and R. G. Jones, "Staffing for Effective Group Decision Making: Key Issues in Matching People and Teams," in R. A. Guzzo and E. Salas (eds.), *Team Effectiveness and Decision Making in Organizations* (San Francisco: Jossey-Bass, 1995), pp. 307-26; and C. Hymowitz, "How to Avoid Hiring the Prima Donnas Who Hate Teamwork," *Wall Street Journal*, February 15, 2000, p. B1.

57. T. D. Schellhardt, "To Be a Star among Equals, Be a Team Player."

58. "Teaming Up for Success," *Training*, January 1994, p. S41.

59. J. S. DeMatteo, L. T. Eby, and E. Sundstrom, "Team-Based Rewards: Current Empirical Evidence and Directions for Future Research," in B. M. Staw and L. L. Cummings (eds.), *Research in Organizational Behavior*, vol. 20 (Greenwich, CT: JAI Press, 1998), pp. 141–83.

60. B. Geber, "The Bugaboo of Team Pay," *Training*, August 1995, pp. 27, 34.

61. D. C. Kinlaw, Developing Superior Work Teams, p. 43.

62. B. Krone, "Total Quality Management: An American Odyssey," *The Bureaucrat*, Fall 1990, p. 37.

63. *Profiles in Quality: Blueprints for Action from 50 Leading Companies* (Boston: Allyn & Bacon, 1991), pp. 71–72, 76–77.

64. See the review of the literature in S. E. Jackson, V. K. Stone, and E. B. Alvarez, "Socialization Amidst Diversity: The Impact of Demographics on Work Team Oldtimers and Newcomers," in L. L. Cummings and B. M. Staw (eds.), *Research in Organizational Behavior*, vol. 15 (Greenwich, CT: JAI Press, 1993), p. 64.

65. R. M. Stogdill, "Group Productivity, Drive, and Cohesiveness," *Organizational Behavior and Human Performance*, February 1972, pp. 36–43. See also M. Mayo, J. C. Pastor, and J. R. Meindl, "The Effects of Group Heterogeneity on the Self-Perceived Efficacy of Group Leaders," *Leadership Quarterly*, Summer 1996, pp. 265–84.

66. J. E. McGrath, *Groups: Interaction and Performance* (Englewood Cliffs, NJ: Prentice Hall, 1984).

67. This idea is proposed in S. E. Jackson, V. K. Stone, and E. B. Alvarez, "Socialization Amidst Diversity," p. 68.

68. This section is based on M. Kaeter, "Repotting Mature Work Teams," *Training*, April 1994 (Supplement), pp. 4–6.

PART THREE
THE GROUP

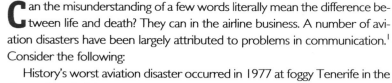

Can the misunderstanding of a few words literally mean the difference between life and death? They can in the airline business. A number of aviation disasters have been largely attributed to problems in communication.[1] Consider the following:

History's worst aviation disaster occurred in 1977 at foggy Tenerife in the Canary Islands. The captain of a KLM flight thought the air traffic controller had cleared him to take off. But the controller intended only to give departure instructions. Although the language spoken between the Dutch KLM captain and the Spanish controller was English, confusion was created by heavy accents and improper terminology. The KLM Boeing 747 hit a Pan Am 747 at full throttle on the runway, killing 583 people.

In 1990, Colombian Avianca pilots, after several holding patterns caused by bad weather, told controllers as they neared New York Kennedy Airport that their Boeing 707 was "running low on fuel." Controllers hear those words all the time, so they took no special action. While the pilots knew there was a serious problem, they failed to use a key phrase—"fuel emergency"—which would have obligated controllers to direct the Avianca flight ahead of all others and clear it to land as soon as possible. The people at Kennedy never understood the true nature of the pilots' problem. The jet ran out of fuel and crashed 16 miles from Kennedy. Seventy-three people died.

In 1993, Chinese pilots flying a U.S.-built MD-80 tried to land in heavy fog at Urumqi, in northwest China. They were baffled by an audio alarm from the jet's ground proximity warning system. Just before impact, the cockpit recorder picked up one crew member saying to the other in Chinese: "What does 'pull up' mean?" The plane hit power lines and crashed, killing 12.

On December 20, 1995, American Airlines Flight 965 was approaching the Cali, Colombia airport. The pilot expected to hear either the words "cleared as filed" (meaning follow the flight plan filed before leaving Miami) or "cleared direct" (meaning fly straight from where you are to Cali, a slightly different route from the flight plan). But the pilot heard neither. The

Communication

controller intended to clear him "as filed" but said "cleared to Cali." The pilot interpreted that as a direct clearance. When he checked back, the controller said "affirmative." Both were obviously confused. The plane crashed, killing 160 people.

In November 1996, there was a mid-air collision near New Delhi of a Saudia 747 and a Kazakhstan Airlines cargo plane. Investigators placed blame for the collision on poor communications between the Kazakh pilot and the Indian air-traffic controller. The crash killed 349 people.

In September 1997, a Garuda Airlines jetliner crashed into a jungle, just 20 miles south of the Medan Airport on the island of Sumatra. All 234 aboard were killed. The cause of this disaster was the pilot and the air traffic controller confusing the words "left" and "right" as the plane approached the airport under poor visibility conditions.

The preceding examples tragically illustrate how miscommunication can have deadly consequences. In this chapter, we'll show (obviously not in as dramatic a fashion) that good communication is essential to any group's or organization's effectiveness.

Research indicates that poor communication is probably the most frequently cited source of interpersonal conflict.[2] Because individuals spend nearly 70 percent of their waking hours communicating—writing, reading, speaking, listening—it seems reasonable to conclude that one of the most inhibiting forces to successful group performance is a lack of effective communication.

No group can exist without communication: the transference of meaning among its members. It is only through transmitting meaning from one person to another that information and ideas can be conveyed. Communication, however, is more than merely

LEARNING OBJECTIVES

AFTER STUDYING THIS CHAPTER, YOU SHOULD BE ABLE TO:

1. Describe the communication process.

2. Contrast the advantages and disadvantages of oral versus written communication.

3. Compare the effectiveness of the chain, wheel, and all-channel networks.

4. Identify the factors affecting the use of the grapevine.

5. Discuss how computer-aided technology is changing organizational communication.

6. Explain the importance of channel richness to improving communication effectiveness.

7. Identify common barriers to effective communication.

8. Contrast the meaning of talk for men versus women.

9. Describe the potential problems in cross-cultural communication.

imparting meaning. It must also be understood. In a group in which one member speaks only German and the others do not know German, the individual speaking German will not be fully understood. Therefore, **communication** must include both the *transference and the understanding of meaning*.

An idea, no matter how great, is useless until it is transmitted and understood by others. Perfect communication, if there were such a thing, would exist when a thought or an idea was transmitted so that the mental picture perceived by the receiver was exactly the same as that envisioned by the sender. Although elementary in theory, perfect communication is never achieved in practice, for reasons we shall expand on later in the chapter.

Before making too many generalizations concerning communication and problems in communicating effectively, we need to review briefly the functions that communication performs and describe the communication process.

FUNCTIONS OF COMMUNICATION

Communication serves four major functions within a group or organization: control, motivation, emotional expression, and information.[3]

Communication acts to *control* member behavior in several ways. Organizations have authority hierarchies and formal guidelines that employees are required to follow. When employees, for instance, are required to first communicate any job-related grievance to their immediate boss, to follow their job description, or to comply with company policies, communication is performing a control function. But informal communication also controls behavior. When work groups tease or harass a member who produces too much (and makes the rest of the group look bad), they are informally communicating with, and controlling, the member's behavior.

Communication fosters *motivation* by clarifying to employees what is to be done, how well they are doing, and what can be done to improve performance if it's subpar. We saw this operating in our review of goal-setting and reinforcement theories in Chapter 6. The formation of specific goals, feedback on progress toward the goals, and reinforcement of desired behavior all stimulate motivation and require communication.

For many employees, their work group is a primary source for social interaction. The communication that takes place within the group is a fundamental mechanism by which members show their frustrations and feelings of satisfaction. Communication, therefore, provides a release for the *emotional expression* of feelings and for fulfillment of social needs.

The final function that communication performs relates to its role in facilitating decision making. It provides the *information* that individuals and groups need to make decisions by transmitting the data to identify and evaluate alternative choices.

No one of these four functions should be seen as being more important than the others. For groups to perform effectively, they need to maintain some form of control over members, stimulate members to perform, provide a means for emotional expression, and make decision choices. You can assume that almost every communication interaction that takes place in a group or organization performs one or more of these four functions.

THE COMMUNICATION PROCESS

Before communication can take place, a purpose, expressed as a message to be conveyed, is needed. It passes between a source (the sender) and a receiver. The message is encoded (converted to a symbolic form) and passed by way of some medium

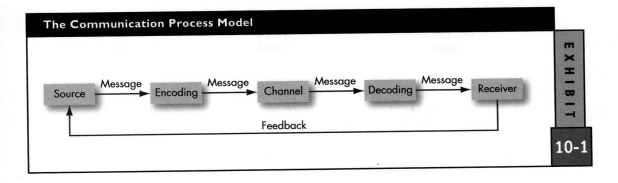

The Communication Process Model

EXHIBIT

10-1

(channel) to the receiver, who retranslates (decodes) the message initiated by the sender. The result is a transference of meaning from one person to another.[4]

Exhibit 10-1 depicts this **communication process**. This model is made up of seven parts: (1) the communication source, (2) encoding, (3) the message, (4) the channel, (5) decoding, (6) the receiver, and (7) feedback.

The *source* initiates a message by encoding a thought. The *message* is the actual physical product from the source *encoding*. When we speak, the speech is the message. When we write, the writing is the message. When we gesture, the movements of our arms and the expressions on our faces are the message. The *channel* is the medium through which the message travels. It is selected by the source, who must determine whether to use a formal or informal channel. Formal channels are established by the organization and transmit messages that are related to the professional activities of members. They traditionally follow the authority chain within the organization. Other forms of messages, such as personal or social, follow the informal channels in the organization. The *receiver* is the object to whom the message is directed. But before the message can be received, the symbols in it must be translated into a form that can be understood by the receiver. This step is the *decoding* of the message. The final link in the communication process is a feedback loop. *Feedback* is the check on how successful we have been in transferring our messages as originally intended. It determines whether understanding has been achieved.

communication process

The steps between a source and a receiver that result in the transference and understanding of meaning.

DIRECTION OF COMMUNICATION

Communication can flow vertically or laterally. The vertical dimension can be further divided into downward and upward directions.[5]

Downward

Communication that flows from one level of a group or organization to a lower level is a downward communication. When we think of managers communicating with employees, the downward pattern is the one we are usually thinking of. It's used by group leaders and managers to assign goals, provide job instructions, inform employees of policies and procedures, point out problems that need attention, and offer feedback about performance. But downward communication doesn't have to be oral or face-to-face contact. When management sends letters to employees' homes to advise them of the organization's new sick leave policy, it's using downward communication. So is an e-mail from a team leader to the members of her team, reminding them of an upcoming deadline.

Upward

Upward communication flows to a higher level in the group or organization. It's used to provide feedback to higher-ups, inform them of progress toward goals, and relay current problems. Upward communication keeps managers aware of how employees feel about their jobs, co-workers, and the organization in general. Managers also rely on upward communication for ideas on how things can be improved.

Some organizational examples of upward communication are performance reports prepared by lower management for review by middle and top management, suggestion boxes, employee attitude surveys, grievance procedures, superior–subordinate discussions, and informal "gripe" sessions in which employees have the opportunity to identify and discuss problems with their boss or representatives of higher management. For example, FedEx prides itself on its computerized upward communication program. All its employees annually complete climate surveys and reviews of management. This program was cited as a key human resources strength by the Malcolm Baldrige National Quality Award examiners when FedEx won the honor.

Lateral

When communication takes place among members of the same work group, among members of work groups at the same level, among managers at the same level, or among any horizontally equivalent personnel, we describe it as lateral communications.

Why would there be a need for horizontal communications if a group or organization's vertical communications are effective? The answer is that horizontal communications are often necessary to save time and facilitate coordination. In some cases, these lateral relationships are formally sanctioned. More often, they are informally created to short-circuit the vertical hierarchy and expedite action. So lateral communications can, from management's viewpoint, be good or bad. Since strict adherence to the formal vertical structure for all communications can impede the efficient and accurate transfer of information, lateral communications can be beneficial. In such cases, they occur with the knowledge and support of superiors. But they can create dysfunctional conflicts when the formal vertical channels are breached, when members go above or around their superiors to get things done, or when bosses find out that actions have been taken or decisions made without their knowledge.

INTERPERSONAL COMMUNICATION

How do group members transfer meaning between and among each other? There are three basic methods. People essentially rely on oral, written, and non-verbal communication.

Oral Communication

The chief means of conveying messages is oral communication. Speeches, formal one-on-one and group discussions, and the informal rumor mill or grapevine are popular forms of oral communication.

The advantages of oral communication are speed and feedback. A verbal message can be conveyed and a response received in a minimal amount of time. If the receiver is unsure of the message, rapid feedback allows for early detection by the sender and, hence, allows for early correction.

The major disadvantage of oral communication surfaces in organizations or whenever the message has to be passed through a number of people. The more people a message must pass through, the greater the potential distortion. If you ever played the game "telephone" at a party, you know the problem. Each person interprets the message in his or her own way. The message's content, when it reaches its destination, is often very different from that of the original. In an organization, where decisions and other communiqués are verbally passed up and down the authority hierarchy, there are considerable opportunities for messages to become distorted.

Written Communication

Written communications include memos, letters, electronic mail, fax transmissions, organizational periodicals, notices placed on bulletin boards, or any other device that is transmitted via written words or symbols.

Why would a sender choose to use written communications? They're tangible and verifiable. Typically, both the sender and receiver have a record of the communication. The message can be stored for an indefinite period. If there are questions concerning the content of the message, it is physically available for later reference. This feature is particularly important for complex and lengthy communications. The marketing plan for a new product, for instance, is likely to contain a number of tasks spread out over several months. By putting it in writing, those who have to initiate the plan can readily refer to it over the life of the plan. A final benefit of written communication comes from the process itself. You're usually more careful with the written word than the oral word. You're forced to think more thoroughly about what you want to convey in a written message than in a spoken one. Thus, written communications are more likely to be well thought out, logical, and clear.

Of course, written messages have their drawbacks. They're time consuming. You could convey far more information to a college instructor in a one-hour oral exam than in a one-hour written exam. In fact, you could probably say the same thing in 10 to 15 minutes that it would take you an hour to write. So, although writing may be more precise, it also consumes a great deal of time. The other major disadvantage is feedback, or lack of it. Oral communication allows the receiver to respond rapidly to what he thinks he hears. Written communication, however, does not have a built-in feedback mechanism. The result is that the mailing of a memo is no assurance it has been received, and, if received, there is no guarantee the recipient will interpret it as the sender intended. The latter point is also relevant in oral communiqués, except it's easy in such cases merely to ask the receiver to summarize what you've said. An accurate summary presents feedback evidence that the message has been received and understood.

Nonverbal Communication

Every time we verbally give a message to someone, we also impart a nonverbal message. In some instances, the nonverbal component may stand alone. For example, in a singles bar, a glance, a stare, a smile, a frown, and a provocative body movement all convey meaning. As such, no discussion of communication would be complete without consideration of *nonverbal communication*—which includes body movements, the intonations or emphasis we give to words, facial expressions, and the physical distance between the sender and receiver.

It can be argued that every *body movement* has a meaning and no movement is accidental. For example, through body language we say, "Help me, I'm lonely"; "Take me, I'm available"; "Leave me alone, I'm depressed." And rarely do we send our messages consciously. We act out our state of being with nonverbal body language. We lift one eyebrow for disbelief. We rub our noses for puzzlement. We clasp our arms to isolate ourselves or to protect ourselves. We shrug our shoulders for indifference, wink one eye for intimacy, tap our fingers for impatience, slap our forehead for forgetfulness.[6]

The two most important messages that body language conveys are (1) the extent to which an individual likes another and is interested in his or her views and (2) the relative perceived status between a sender and receiver.[7] For instance, we're more likely to position ourselves closer to people we like and touch them more often. Similarly, if you feel that you're higher status than another, you're more likely to display body movements—such as crossed legs or a slouched seating position—that reflect a casual and relaxed manner.

Body language adds to, and often complicates, verbal communication. A body position or movement does not by itself have a precise or universal meaning, but when it is linked with spoken language, it gives fuller meaning to a sender's message.

If you read the verbatim minutes of a meeting, you wouldn't grasp the impact of what was said in the same way you would if you had been there or saw the meeting on video. Why? There is no record of nonverbal communication. The emphasis given to words or phrases is missing. Exhibit 10-2 illustrates how *intonations* can change the meaning of a message.

Facial expressions also convey meaning. A snarling face says something different from a smile. Facial expressions, along with intonations, can show arrogance, aggressiveness, fear, shyness, and other characteristics that would never be communicated if you read a transcript of what had been said.

The way individuals space themselves in terms of *physical distance* also has meaning. What is considered proper spacing is largely dependent on cultural norms. For example, what is considered a businesslike distance in some European countries would be viewed as intimate in many parts of North America. If someone stands closer to you than is considered appropriate, it may indicate aggres-

Change your tone and you change your meaning:

Placement of the emphasis	What it means
Why don't I take **you** to dinner tonight?	I was going to take someone else.
Why don't **I** take you to dinner tonight?	Instead of the guy you were going with.
Why **don't** I take you to dinner tonight?	I'm trying to find a reason why I shouldn't take you.
Why don't I take you to dinner tonight?	Do you have a problem with me?
Why don't I **take** you to dinner tonight?	Instead of going on your own.
Why don't I take you to **dinner** tonight?	Instead of lunch tomorrow.
Why don't I take you to dinner **tonight**?	Not tomorrow night.

EXHIBIT

10-2

Source: Based on M. Kiely, "When 'No' Means 'Yes'," *Marketing*, October 1993, pp. 7–9. Reproduced in A. Huczynski and D. Buchanan, *Organizational Behaviour*, 4th ed. (Essex, England: Pearson Education, 2001), p. 194.

siveness or sexual interest; if farther away than usual, it may mean disinterest or displeasure with what is being said.

It's important for the receiver to be alert to these nonverbal aspects of communication. You should look for nonverbal cues as well as listen to the literal meaning of a sender's words. You should particularly be aware of contradictions between the messages. Your boss may say she is free to talk to you about a pressing budget problem, but you may see nonverbal signals suggesting that this is not the time to discuss the subject. Regardless of what is being said, an individual who frequently glances at her wristwatch is giving the message that she would prefer to terminate the conversation. We misinform others when we express one message verbally, such as trust, but nonverbally communicate a contradictory message that reads, "I don't have confidence in you."

MYTH *OR* **SCIENCE** **?**

"It's Not What You *Say*, It's What You *Do*"

This statement is mostly true. Actions DO speak louder than words.[8] When faced with inconsistencies between words and actions, people tend to give greater credence to actions. It's behavior that counts. The implications of this is that managers and leaders are role models. Employees will imitate their behaviors and attitudes. They will, for example, watch what their boss does and then imitate or adapt what they do. This conclusion doesn't mean that words fall on deaf ears. Words can influence others.[9] But when words and actions diverge, people focus most on what they see in terms of behavior.

There is an obvious exception to the previous conclusion. An increasing number of leaders (and their associates) have developed the skill of shaping words and putting the proper "spin" on situations so that others focus on the leader's words rather than the behavior. Successful politicians seem particularly adept at this skill. Why people believe these spins when faced with conflicting behavioral evidence is not clear. Do we want to believe that our leaders would not lie to us? Do we want to believe what politicians say, especially when we hold them in high regard? Do we give high-status people, for whom we've previously given our vote, the benefit of the doubt when confronted with their negative behavior? Additional research is necessary to clarify these questions.

ORGANIZATIONAL COMMUNICATION

In this section we move from interpersonal communication to organizational communication. Our focus here will be on formal networks, the grapevine, and computer-aided mechanisms used by organizations to facilitate communication.

Formal Small-Group Networks

Formal organizational networks can be very complicated. They can, for instance, include hundreds of people and a half-dozen or more hierarchical levels. To simplify our discussion, we've condensed these networks into three common small groups of five people each (see Exhibit 10-3). These three networks are the chain, wheel, and all-channel. Although these three networks have been extremely simplified, they do allow us to describe the unique qualities of each.

The *chain* rigidly follows the formal chain of command. This network approximates the communication channels you might find in a rigid three-level organization. The *wheel* relies on a central figure to act as the conduit for all the group's communication. It simulates the communication network you would find on a team with a strong leader. The *all-channel* network permits all group members to actively communicate with each other. The all-channel network is most often characterized in practice by self-managed teams, in which all group members are free to contribute and no one person takes on a leadership role.

As Exhibit 10-4 demonstrates, the effectiveness of each network depends on the dependent variable you're concerned about. For instance, the structure of the wheel facilitates the emergence of a leader, the all-channel network is best if you are concerned with having high member satisfaction, and the chain is best if accuracy is most important. Exhibit 10-4 leads us to the conclusion that no single network will be best for all occasions.

The Grapevine

The formal system is not the only communication network in a group or organization. There is also an informal one, which is called the **grapevine**.[10] And although the grapevine may be informal, this doesn't mean it's not an important source of information. For instance, a survey found that 75 percent of employees hear about matters first through rumors on the grapevine.[11]

The grapevine has three main characteristics.[12] First, it is not controlled by management. Second, it is perceived by most employees as being more believable

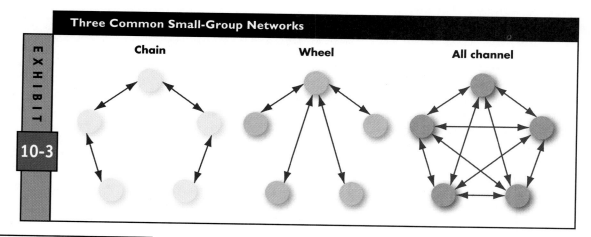

EXHIBIT 10-3

Three Common Small-Group Networks

Chain   Wheel   All channel

Small-Group Networks and Effectiveness Criteria

	Networks		
Criteria	Chain	Wheel	All Channel
Speed	Moderate	Fast	Fast
Accuracy	High	High	Moderate
Emergence of a leader	Moderate	High	None
Member satisfaction	Moderate	Low	High

EXHIBIT 10-4

and reliable than formal communiqués issued by top management. And third, it is largely used to serve the self-interests of the people within it.

One of the most famous studies of the grapevine investigated the communication pattern among 67 managerial personnel in a small manufacturing firm.[13] The basic approach used was to learn from each communication recipient how he or she first received a given piece of information and then trace it back to its source. It was found that, while the grapevine was an important source of information, only 10 percent of the executives acted as liaison individuals, that is, passed the information on to more than one other person. For example, when one executive decided to resign to enter the insurance business, 81 percent of the executives knew about it, but only 11 percent transmitted this information to others.

Two other conclusions from this study are also worth noting. Information on events of general interest tended to flow between the major functional groups (production, sales) rather than within them. Also, no evidence surfaced to suggest that any one group consistently acted as liaisons; rather, different types of information passed through different liaison persons.

An attempt to replicate this study among employees in a small state government office also found that only 10 percent act as liaison individuals.[14] This finding is interesting, because the replication contained a wider spectrum of employees, including operative as well as managerial personnel. But the flow of information in the government office took place within, rather than between, functional groups. It was proposed that this discrepancy might be due to comparing an executive-only sample against one that also included operative workers. Managers, for example, might feel greater pressure to stay informed and thus cultivate others outside their immediate functional group. Also, in contrast to the findings of the original study, the replication found that a consistent group of individuals acted as liaisons by transmitting information in the government office.

Is the information that flows along the grapevine accurate? The evidence indicates that about 75 percent of what is carried is accurate.[15] But what conditions foster an active grapevine? What gets the rumor mill rolling?

The grapevine is so pervasive as a means of communication in organizations that Web sites to confirm or deny popular rumors now exist.

EXHIBIT

10-5

Suggestions for Reducing the Negative Consequences of Rumors

1. Announce timetables for making important decisions.
2. Explain decisions and behaviors that may appear inconsistent or secretive.
3. Emphasize the downside, as well as the upside, of current decisions and future plans.
4. Openly discuss worst-case possibilities—it is almost never as anxiety provoking as the unspoken fantasy.

Source: Adapted from L. Hirschhorn, "Managing Rumors," in L. Hirschhorn (ed.), *Cutting Back* (San Francisco: Jossey-Bass, 1983), pp. 54–56. With permission.

It is frequently assumed that rumors start because they make titillating gossip. This is rarely the case. Rumors emerge as a response to situations that are *important* to us, when there is *ambiguity*, and under conditions that arouse *anxiety*.[16] The fact that work situations frequently contain these three elements explains why rumors flourish in organizations. The secrecy and competition that typically prevail in large organizations—around issues such as the appointment of new bosses, the relocation of offices, downsizing decisions, and the realignment of work assignments—create conditions that encourage and sustain rumors on the grapevine. A rumor will persist either until the wants and expectations creating the uncertainty underlying the rumor are fulfilled or until the anxiety is reduced.

What can we conclude from the preceding discussion? Certainly the grapevine is an important part of any group or organization's communication network and is well worth understanding.[17] It identifies for managers the confusing issues that employees consider important and that create anxiety. It acts, therefore, as both a filter and a feedback mechanism, picking up the issues that employees consider relevant. For employees, the grapevine is particularly valuable for translating formal communications into their group's own jargon. Maybe more important, again from a managerial perspective, it seems possible to analyze grapevine information and to predict its flow, given that only a small set of individuals (approximately 10 percent) actively pass on information to more than one other person. By assessing which liaison individuals will consider a given piece of information to be relevant, we can improve our ability to explain and predict the pattern of the grapevine.

Can management entirely eliminate rumors? No. What management should do, however, is minimize the negative consequences of rumors by limiting their range and impact. Exhibit 10-5 offers a few suggestions for minimizing those negative consequences.

Computer-Aided Communication

Communication in today's organizations is enhanced and enriched by computer-aided technologies. These include electronic mail, intranet and extranet links, and videoconferencing. Electronic mail, for instance, has dramatically reduced the number of memos, letters, and phone calls that employees historically used to communicate among themselves and with suppliers, customers, or other outside stakeholders.

E-Mail Electronic mail (or e-mail) uses the Internet to transmit and receive computer-generated text and documents. Its growth has been spectacular. Most

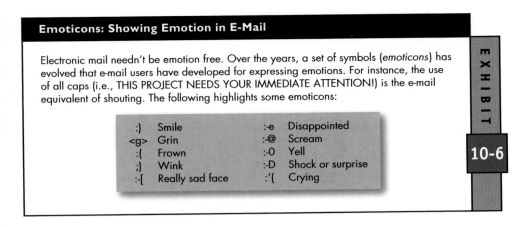

Emoticons: Showing Emotion in E-Mail

Electronic mail needn't be emotion free. Over the years, a set of symbols (*emoticons*) has evolved that e-mail users have developed for expressing emotions. For instance, the use of all caps (i.e., THIS PROJECT NEEDS YOUR IMMEDIATE ATTENTION!) is the e-mail equivalent of shouting. The following highlights some emoticons:

:)	Smile	:-e	Disappointed
<g>	Grin	:-@	Scream
:(	Frown	:-O	Yell
;)	Wink	:-D	Shock or surprise
:-[	Really sad face	:'(	Crying

white-collar employees now regularly use e-mail. In fact, a recent study found that the average U.S. employee receives 31 e-mail messages a day.[18] And organizations are recognizing the value of e-mail for all workers. Ford Motor Co., for instance, recently made a computer, modem, printer, and e-mail account available for $5 a month to all of its more than 300,000 employees worldwide.[19]

As a communication tool, e-mail has a long list of benefits. E-mail messages can be quickly written, edited, and stored. They can be distributed to one person or thousands with a click of a mouse. They can be read, in their entirety, at the convenience of the recipient. And the cost of sending formal e-mail messages to employees is a fraction of what it would cost to print, duplicate, and distribute a comparable letter or brochure.

E-mail, of course, is not without its drawbacks. At the top of the list is information overload. It's not unusual for employees to get a hundred or more e-mails a day. Reading, absorbing, and responding to such an inflow can literally consume an employee's entire day. In essence, e-mail's ease of use has become its biggest negative. Employees are finding it increasingly difficult to distinguish important e-mails from junk mail and irrelevant messages. Another drawback of e-mails is that they lack emotional content. The nonverbal cues in a face-to-face message or the tone of voice from a phone call convey important information that doesn't come across in e-mail, although efforts have been made to create emotional icons (see Exhibit 10-6). Finally, e-mail tends to be cold and impersonal. As such, it's not the ideal means to convey information like layoffs, plant closings, or other messages that might evoke emotional responses and require empathy or social support.

Intranet and Extranet Links   *Intranets* are private, organization-wide information networks that look and act like a Web site but to which only people in an organization have access. Intranets are rapidly becoming the preferred means for employees within companies to communicate with each other. IBM, as a case in point, recently brought together 52,000 of its employees online for what it called WorldJam.[20] Using the company's intranet, IBMers everywhere swapped ideas on everything from how to retain employees to how to work faster without undermining quality.

In addition, organizations are creating *extranet* links that connect internal employees with selected suppliers, customers, and strategic partners. For instance, an extranet allows GM employees to send electronic messages and documents to its steel and rubber suppliers as well as to communicate with its dealers. Similarly, all Wal-Mart vendors are linked into its extranet system, allowing Wal-Mart buyers to easily communicate with its suppliers and for suppliers to monitor the inventory status of its products at Wal-Mart stores.

Videoconferencing   *Videoconferencing* is an extension of intranet or extranet systems. It permits employees in an organization to have meetings with people at different locations. Live audio and video images of members allow them to see, hear, and talk with each other. Videoconferencing technology, in effect, allows employees to conduct interactive meetings without the necessity of all physically being in the same location.

In the late 1990s, videoconferencing was basically conducted from special rooms equipped with television cameras, located at company facilities. More recently, cameras and microphones are being attached to individual computers, allowing people to participate in videoconferences without leaving their desks. As the cost of this technology drops in price, videoconferencing is likely to be increasingly seen as an alternative to expensive and time-consuming travel.

Summary   Computer-aided communications are reshaping the way we communicate in organizations. Specifically, it's no longer necessary for employees to be at their work station or desk to be "available." Pagers, cellular phones, and personal communicators allow employees to be reached when they're in a meeting, during a lunch break, while visiting a customer across town, or during a golf game on Saturday morning. The line between an employee's work and non-work life is no longer distinct. In the electronic age, all employees can theoretically be "on call" 24 hours a day, 7 days a week.

Organizational boundaries become less relevant as a result of computer-aided communications. Networked computers allow employees to jump vertical levels within the organization, work full-time at home or someplace other than an organizationally operated facility, and conduct ongoing communications with people in other organizations. The market researcher who wants to discuss an issue with the vice president of marketing (who is three levels up in the hierarchy), can bypass the people in between and send an e-mail message directly. And in so doing, the traditional status hierarchy, largely determined by level and access, becomes essentially negated. Or that same market researcher may choose to live in the Cayman Islands and work at home via telecommuting rather than do his or her job in the company's Chicago office. And when an employee's computer is linked to suppliers' and customers' computers, the boundaries separating organizations become further blurred. As a case in point, because Levi Strauss' and Wal-Mart's computers are linked, Levi is able to monitor Wal-Mart's inventory of its jeans and to replace merchandise as needed, clouding the distinction between Levi and Wal-Mart employees.

CHOICE OF COMMUNICATION CHANNEL

Neal L. Patterson, CEO at medical-software maker Cerner Corp. likes e-mail. Maybe too much so. Upset with his staff's work ethic, he recently sent a seething e-mail to his firm's 400 managers.[21] Here are some of that e-mail's highlights:

"Hell will freeze over before this CEO implements ANOTHER EMPLOYEE benefit in this Culture. . . . We are getting less than 40 hours of work from a large number of our Kansas City-based employees. The parking lot is sparsely used at 8 A.M.; likewise at 5 P.M. As managers—you either do not know what your EMPLOYEES are doing; or YOU do not CARE. . . . You have a problem and you will fix it or I will replace you. . . . What you are doing, as managers, with this company makes me SICK."

Patterson's e-mail additionally suggested that managers schedule meetings at 7 A.M., 6 P.M., and Saturday mornings; promised a staff reduction of five percent and institution of a time-clock system, and Patterson's intention to charge unapproved absences to employees' vacation time.

Within hours of this e-mail, copies of it had made its way onto a Yahoo! Web site. And within three days, Cerner's stock price had plummeted 22 percent. Although one can argue about whether such harsh criticism should be communicated at all, one thing is certainly clear: Patterson erred by selecting the wrong channel for his message. Such an emotional and sensitive message would likely have been better received in a face-to-face meeting.

Why do people choose one channel of communication over another—for instance, a phone call instead of a face-to-face talk? Is there any general insight we might be able to provide regarding choice of communication channel? The answer to the latter question is a qualified "Yes." A model of media richness has been developed to explain channel selection among managers.[22]

Research has found that channels differ in their capacity to convey information. Some are rich in that they have the ability to (1) handle multiple cues simultaneously, (2) facilitate rapid feedback, and (3) be very personal. Others are lean in that they score low on these three factors. As Exhibit 10-7 illustrates, face-to-face conversation scores highest in terms of **channel richness** because it provides for the maximum amount of information to be transmitted during a communication episode. That is, it offers multiple information cues (words, postures, facial expressions, gestures, intonations), immediate feedback (both verbal and nonverbal), and the personal touch of "being there." Impersonal written media such as formal reports and bulletins rate lowest in richness.

The choice of one channel over another depends on whether the message is routine or nonroutine. The former types of messages tend to be straightforward and have a minimum of ambiguity. The latter are likely to be complicated and have the potential for misunderstanding. Managers can communicate routine

channel richness

The amount of information that can be transmitted during a communication episode.

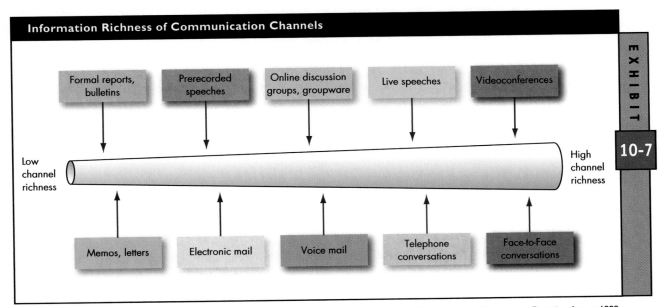

Information Richness of Communication Channels

Formal reports, bulletins • Prerecorded speeches • Online discussion groups, groupware • Live speeches • Videoconferences

Low channel richness ——————————— High channel richness

Memos, letters • Electronic mail • Voice mail • Telephone conversations • Face-to-Face conversations

EXHIBIT 10-7

Source: Based on R. H. Lengel and D. L. Daft, "The Selection of Communication Media as an Executive Skill," *Academy of Management Executive*, August 1988, pp. 225–32; and R. L. Daft and R. H. Lengel, "Organizational Information Requirements, Media Richness, and Structural Design," *Managerial Science*, May 1996, pp. 554–72. Reproduced from R. L. Daft and R. A. Noe, *Organizational Behavior* (Fort Worth, TX: Harcourt, 2001), p. 311.

Don't Push E-Mail Beyond Its Limits

E-mail is fine for some communications but it has its limitations. And, unfortunately, many people are using it to convey messages that are best expressed in other ways.

Relationships can suffer when people use e-mail as a substitute for face-to-face conversation or a phone call. For instance, one writer tells of communicating with an editor by e-mail about an article he had written. The relationship turned sour because each was taking the other's comments as far more critical than intended. "We had to get offline and apologize," says the writer.

An expert on communication says, "There's a tremendous overreliance on e-mail, which is leading to a lot of confusion, misunderstanding, anger, and frustration." The "overreliance" factor is due to the popularity of the technology—for instance, in the United States, 55 percent of adults now use e-mail. The negative responses to e-mail are due to its inherent limitations and misuse. These include:

Low feedback. Conversation is a give-and-take exchange, but e-mail allows one to "talk" at length without any response.

Reduced social cues. When we talk, we can hear the tone of a joke that might come across as stern on a computer screen. And emoticons can hint that something is meant lightly but can't replace voice or visual cues.

Excess attention. E-mail allows people to create carefully worded messages that can be interpreted as more formal than verbal messages. The same words expressed off-handedly in a verbal conversation often take on greater meaning and importance when read in an e-mail.

Wordiness. E-mail allows the writer to go on forever, often confusing the receiver as to what's important and what isn't. In face-to-face contact, senders get verbal and nonverbal cues—interruptions, quizzical looks, glassy eyes—indicating the message is getting too long.

Source: Based on J. Kornblum, "E-Mail's Limits Create Confusion, Hurt Feelings," *USA Today*, February 5, 2002, p. 6D.

messages efficiently through channels that are lower in richness. However, they can communicate nonroutine messages effectively only by selecting rich channels. Referring back to our opening example at Cerner Corp., it appears that Neal Patterson's problem was using a channel relatively low in richness (e-mail) to convey a message that, because of its nonroutine nature and complexity, should have been conveyed using a rich communication medium.

Evidence indicates that high-performing managers tend to be more media-sensitive than low-performing managers.[23] That is, they're better able to match appropriate media richness with the ambiguity involved in the communication.

The media richness model is consistent with organizational trends and practices during the past decade. It is not just coincidence that more and more senior managers have been using meetings to facilitate communication and regularly leaving the isolated sanctuary of their executive offices to manage by walking around. These executives are relying on richer channels of communication to transmit the more ambiguous messages they need to convey. The past decade has been characterized by organizations closing facilities, imposing large layoffs, restructuring, merging, consolidating, and introducing new products and services at an accelerated pace—all nonroutine messages high in ambiguity and requiring the use of channels that can convey a large amount of information. It is not surprising, therefore, to see the most effective managers expanding their use of rich channels.

BARRIERS TO EFFECTIVE COMMUNICATION

A number of barriers can retard or distort effective communication. In this section, we highlight the more important of these barriers.

Filtering

Filtering refers to a sender's purposely manipulating information so it will be seen more favorably by the receiver. For example, when a manager tells his boss what he feels his boss wants to hear, he is filtering information.

The major determinant of filtering is the number of levels in an organization's structure. The more vertical levels in the organization's hierarchy, the more opportunities there are for filtering. But you can expect some filtering to occur wherever there are status differences. Factors such as fear of conveying bad news and the desire to please one's boss often lead employees to tell their superiors what they think those superiors want to hear, thus distorting upward communications.

Selective Perception

We have mentioned selective perception before in this book. It appears again here because the receivers in the communication process selectively see and hear based on their needs, motivations, experience, background, and other personal characteristics. Receivers also project their interests and expectations into communications as they decode them. The employment interviewer who expects a female job applicant to put her family ahead of her career is likely to see that in female applicants, regardless of whether the applicants feel that way or not. As we said in Chapter 5, we don't see reality; we interpret what we see and call it reality.

filtering

A sender's manipulation of information so that it will be seen more favorably by the receiver.

Bonnie Reitz, senior vice president for sales and distribution at Continental Airlines, doesn't want employees to filter information when they communicate with her. "If something's not going well," she says, "tell us so that we can deal with it."

Information Overload

Individuals have a finite capacity for processing data. As noted in our previous discussion of e-mail, when the information we have to work with exceeds our processing capacity, the result is **information overload**. And with e-mails, phone calls, faxes, meetings, and the need to keep current in one's field, more and more managers and professionals are complaining that they're suffering overload.

What happens when individuals have more information than they can sort out and use? They tend to select out, ignore, pass over, or forget information. Or they may put off further processing until the overload situation is over. Regardless, the result is lost information and less effective communication.

information overload

A condition in which information inflow exceeds an individual's processing capacity.

Emotions

How the receiver feels at the time of receipt of a communication will influence how he or she interprets it. The same message received when you're angry or distraught is often interpreted differently from when you're happy. Extreme emotions such as jubilation or depression are most likely to hinder effective communication. In such instances, we are most prone to disregard our rational and objective thinking processes and substitute emotional judgments.

Language

Words mean different things to different people. Age, education, and cultural background are three of the more obvious variables that influence the language a person uses and the definitions he or she gives to words.

EXHIBIT

10-8

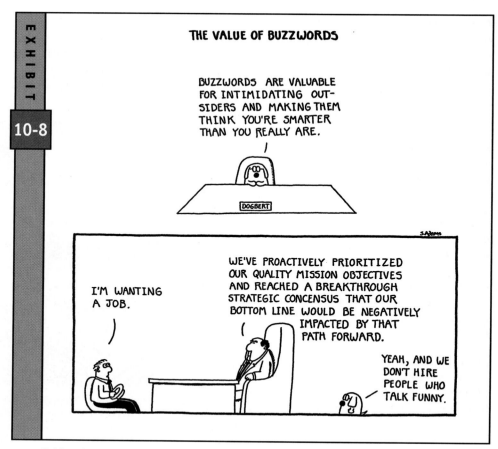

S. Adams, *Dogbert's Big Book of Business*. DILBERT reprinted by permission of United Feature Syndicate, Inc.

In an organization, employees usually come from diverse backgrounds. Further, the grouping of employees into departments creates specialists who develop their own "buzzwords" or technical jargon. In large organizations, members are also frequently widely dispersed geographically—even operating in different countries— and individuals in each locale will use terms and phrases that are unique to their area. The existence of vertical levels can also cause language problems. For instance, differences in meaning with regard to words such as *incentives* and *quotas* have been found at different levels in management. Top managers often speak about the need for incentives and quotas, yet these terms imply manipulation and create resentment among many lower managers.

The point is that although you and I probably speak a common language— English—our use of that language is far from uniform. If we knew how each of us modified the language, communication difficulties would be minimized. The problem is that members in an organization usually don't know how those with whom they interact have modified the language. Senders tend to assume that the words and terms they use mean the same to the receiver as they do to them. This assumption is often incorrect.

Communication Apprehension

Another major barrier to effective communication is that some people—an estimated 5 to 20 percent of the population[24]—suffer from debilitating

communication apprehension or anxiety. Although lots of people dread speaking in front of a group, communication apprehension is a more serious problem because it affects a whole category of communication techniques. People who suffer from it experience undue tension and anxiety in oral communication, written communication, or both.[25] For example, oral apprehensives may find it extremely difficult to talk with others face to face or become extremely anxious when they have to use the telephone. As a result, they may rely on memos or faxes to convey messages when a phone call would be not only faster but more appropriate.

Studies demonstrate that oral-communication apprehensives avoid situations that require them to engage in oral communication.[26] We should expect to find some self-selection in jobs so that such individuals don't take positions, such as teacher, for which oral communication is a dominant requirement.[27] But almost all jobs require some oral communication. And of greater concern is the evidence that high-oral-communication apprehensives distort the communication demands of their jobs in order to minimize the need for communication.[28] So we need to be aware that there is a set of people in organizations who severely limit their oral communication and rationalize this practice by telling themselves that more communication isn't necessary for them to do their job effectively.

communication apprehension

Undue tension and anxiety about oral communication, written communication, or both.

CURRENT ISSUES IN COMMUNICATION

In this section, we discuss four current issues related to communication in organizations: Why do men and women often have difficulty communicating with each other? What role does silence play in communication? What are the implications of the "politically correct" movement on communications in organizations? And how can individuals improve their cross-cultural communications?

Communication Barriers Between Women and Men

Research by Deborah Tannen provides us with some important insights into the differences between men and women in terms of their conversational styles.[29] In particular, she has been able to explain why gender often creates oral communication barriers.

The essence of Tannen's research is that men use talk to emphasize status, whereas women use it to create connection. Her conclusion, of course, doesn't apply to *every* man or *every* woman. As she puts it, her generalization means "a larger percentage of women or men *as a group* talk in a particular way, or individual women and men *are more likely* to talk one way or the other."[30]

Tannen states that communication is a continual balancing act, juggling the conflicting needs for intimacy and independence. Intimacy emphasizes closeness and commonalities. Independence emphasizes separateness and differences. But here's the kick: Women speak and hear a language of connection and intimacy; men speak and hear a language of status, power, and independence. So, for many men, conversations are primarily a means to preserve independence and maintain status in a hierarchical social order. For many women, conversations are negotiations for closeness in which people try to seek and give confirmation and support. A few examples will illustrate Tannen's thesis:

Men frequently complain that women talk on and on about their problems. Women criticize men for not listening. What's happening is that when men hear a problem, they frequently assert their desire for independence and control by offering solutions. Many women, on the other hand, view telling a problem as a means to promote closeness. The women present the problem to gain support and connection, not to get the man's

Research indicates that men and women use talk differently. Women use language to create connection. Men, in contrast, use language to emphasize status and power.

advice. Mutual understanding is symmetrical. But giving advice is asymmetrical—it sets up the advice giver as more knowledgeable, more reasonable, and more in control. This contributes to distancing men and women in their efforts to communicate.

Men are often more direct than women in conversation. A man might say, "I think you're wrong on that point." A woman might say, "Have you looked at the marketing department's research report on that point?" (the implication being that the report will show the error). Men frequently see female indirectness as "covert" or "sneaky," but women are not as concerned as men with the status and one-upmanship that directness often creates.

Women tend to be less boastful than men. They often downplay their authority or accomplishments to avoid appearing as braggarts and to take the other person's feelings into account. However, men can frequently misinterpret this and incorrectly conclude that a woman is less confident and competent than she really is.

Finally, men often criticize women for seeming to apologize all the time. Men tend to see the phrase "I'm sorry" as a weakness because they interpret the phrase to mean the woman is accepting blame, when he knows she's not to blame. The woman also knows she's not to blame. The problem is that women frequently use "I'm sorry" to express regret and restore balance to a conversation: "I know you must feel bad about this; I do, too." For many women, "I'm sorry" is an expression of understanding and caring about the other person's feelings rather than an apology.

Silence as Communication

Sherlock Holmes once solved a murder mystery based not on what happened but on what *didn't* happen. Holmes remarked to his assistant, Dr. Watson, about "the curious incident of the dog in the nighttime." Watson, surprised, responds, "But the dog did nothing in the nighttime." To which Holmes replied, "That was the curious incident." Holmes concluded the crime had to be committed by someone with whom the dog was familiar because the watchdog didn't bark.

The dog that didn't bark in the night is often used as a metaphor for an event that is significant by reason of its absence. That story is also an excellent illustration of the importance of silence in communication.

Silence—defined here as an absence of speech or noise—has been generally ignored as a form of communication in OB because it represents *in*action or nonbehavior. But it's not necessarily inaction. Nor is silence, as many believe, a failure to communicate. It can, in fact, be a powerful form of communication.[31] It can mean someone is thinking or contemplating a response to a question. It can mean a person is anxious and fearful of speaking. It can signal agreement, dissent, frustration, or anger.

In terms of OB, we can see several links between silence and work-related behavior. For instance, silence is a critical element of groupthink, in which it implies agreement with the majority. It can be a way for employees to express dissatisfaction, as when they "suffer in silence." It can be a sign that someone is upset, as when a typically talkative person suddenly says nothing—"What's the matter with him? Is he all right?" It's a powerful tool used by managers to signal disfavor by shunning or ignoring employees with "silent insults." And, of course, it's a crucial element of group decision making, allowing individuals to think over and contemplate what others have said.

Failing to pay close attention to the silent portion of a conversation can result in missing a vital part of the message. Astute communicators watch for gaps, pauses, and hesitations. They hear and interpret silence. They treat pauses, for instance, as analogous to a flashing yellow light at an intersection—they pay attention to what comes next. Is the person thinking, deciding how to frame an answer? Is the person suffering from communication apprehension? Sometimes the real message in a communication is buried in the silence.

"Politically Correct" Communication

What words do you use to describe a colleague who is wheelchair-bound? What terms do you use in addressing a female customer? How do you communicate with a brand-new client who is not like you? Your answers can mean the difference between losing a client, an employee, a lawsuit, a harassment claim, or a job.[32]

Most of us are acutely aware of how our vocabulary has been modified to reflect political correctness. For instance, most of us have cleansed the words *handicapped*, *blind*, and *elderly* from our vocabulary—and replaced them with terms like *physically challenged*, *visually impaired*, and *senior*. The *Los Angeles Times*, for instance, allows its journalists to use the term *old age* but cautions that the onset of old age varies from "person to person," so a group of 75-year-olds aren't necessarily all old.[33]

EXHIBIT

10-9

THE FAR SIDE® BY GARY LARSON

Larson 6-9   © 1994 FarWorks, Inc./Dist. by Universal Press Syndicate

"Well, actually, Doreen, I rather resent being called a 'swamp thing.' ... I prefer the term 'wetlands-challenged mutant.'"

We must be sensitive to others' feelings. Certain words can and do stereotype, intimidate, and insult individuals. In an increasingly diverse workforce, we must be sensitive to how words might offend others. But there's a downside to political correctness. It's complicating our vocabulary and making it more difficult for people to communicate. To illustrate, you probably know what these four terms mean: *death, garbage, quotas,* and *women.* But each of these words also has been found to offend one or more groups. They've been replaced with terms like *negative patient outcome, postconsumer waste materials, educational equity,* and *people of gender.* The problem is that this latter group of terms is much less likely to convey a uniform message than the words they replaced. You know what death means; I know what death means; but can you be sure that "negative patient outcome" will be consistently defined as synonymous with death? No. For instance, the phrase could also mean a longer stay than expected in the hospital or notification that your insurance company won't pay your hospital bill.

Some critics, for humor's sake, enjoy carrying political correctness to the extreme. Even those of us with thinning scalps, who aren't too thrilled at being labeled "bald," have to smirk when we're referred to as "folliclely challenged." But our concern here is with how politically correct language is contributing a new barrier to effective communication.

Words are the primary means by which people communicate. When we eliminate words from use because they're politically incorrect, we reduce our options for conveying messages in the clearest and most accurate form. For the most part, the larger the vocabulary used by a sender and a receiver, the greater the opportunity to accurately transmit messages. By removing certain words from our vocabulary, we make it harder to communicate accurately. When we further replace these words with new terms whose meanings are less well understood, we have reduced the likelihood that our messages will be received as we had intended them.

We must be sensitive to how our choice of words might offend others. But we also have to be careful not to sanitize our language to the point at which it clearly restricts clarity of communication. There is no simple solution to this dilemma. However, you should be aware of the trade-offs and the need to find a proper balance.

Cross-Cultural Communication

Effective communication is difficult under the best of conditions. Cross-cultural factors clearly create the potential for increased communication problems. This is illustrated in Exhibit 10-10. A gesture that is well understood and acceptable in one culture can be meaningless or lewd in another.[34]

Cultural Barriers   One author has identified four specific problems related to language difficulties in cross-cultural communications.[35]

First, there are *barriers caused by semantics.* As we've noted previously, words mean different things to different people. This is particularly true for people from different national cultures. Some words, for instance, don't translate between cultures. Understanding the word *sisu* will help you in communicating with people from Finland, but this word is untranslatable into English. It means something akin to "guts" or "dogged persistence." Similarly, the new capitalists in Russia may have difficulty communicating with their British or Canadian counterparts because English terms such as *efficiency, free market,* and *regulation* are not directly translatable into Russian.

Second, there are *barriers caused by word connotations.* Words imply different things in different languages. Negotiations between Americans and Japanese exec-

Hand Gestures Mean Different Things in Different Countries

EXHIBIT

10-10

The A-OK Sign

In the United States, this is just a friendly sign for "All right!" or "Good going." In Australia and Islamic countries, it is equivalent to what generations of high school students know as "flipping the bird."

The "Hook'em Horns" Sign

This sign encourages University of Texas athletes, and it's a good luck gesture in Brazil and Venezuela. In parts of Africa it is a curse. In Italy, it is signaling to another that "your spouse is being unfaithful."

"V" for Victory Sign

In many parts of the world, this means "victory" or "peace." In England, if the palm and fingers face inward, it means "Up yours!" especially if executed with an upward jerk of the fingers.

Finger-Beckoning Sign

This sign means "come here" in the United States. In Malaysia, it is used only for calling animals. In Indonesia and Australia, it is used for beckoning "ladies of the night."

Source: "What's A-O-K in the U.S.A. Is Lewd and Worthless Beyond," *New York Times*, August 18, 1996, p. E7. From Roger E. Axtell, *GESTURES: The Do's and Taboos of Body Language Around the World.* Copyright © 1991. This material is used by permission of John Wiley & Sons, Inc.

utives, for instance, are made more difficult because the Japanese word *hai* translates as "yes," but its connotation may be "yes, I'm listening," rather than "yes, I agree."

Third are *barriers caused by tone differences*. In some cultures, language is formal, in others it's informal. In some cultures, the tone changes depending on the context: people speak differently at home, in social situations, and at work. Using a personal, informal style in a situation in which a more formal style is expected can be embarrassing and off-putting.

Fourth, there are *barriers caused by differences among perceptions*. People who speak different languages actually view the world in different ways. Eskimos perceive snow differently because they have many words for it. Thais perceive "no" differently than do Americans because the former have no such word in their vocabulary.

Cultural Context   A better understanding of these cultural barriers and their implications for communicating across cultures can be achieved by considering the concepts of high- and low-context cultures.[36]

Cultures tend to differ in the importance to which context influences the meaning that individuals take from what is actually said or written in light of who the other person is. Countries like China, Korea, Japan, and Vietnam are

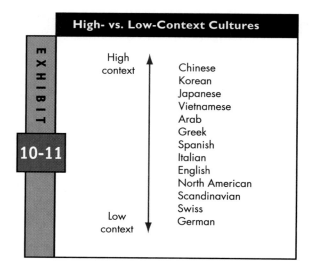

EXHIBIT 10-11

High- vs. Low-Context Cultures

High context

Chinese
Korean
Japanese
Vietnamese
Arab
Greek
Spanish
Italian
English
North American
Scandinavian
Swiss
German

Low context

high-context cultures

Cultures that rely heavily on nonverbal and subtle situational cues in communication.

low-context cultures

Cultures that rely heavily on words to convey meaning in communication.

high-context cultures. They rely heavily on nonverbal and subtle situational cues when communicating with others. What is *not* said may be more significant than what *is* said. A person's official status, place in society, and reputation carry considerable weight in communications. In contrast, people from Europe and North America reflect their **low-context cultures**. They rely essentially on words to convey meaning. Body language or formal titles are secondary to spoken and written words (see Exhibit 10-11).

What do these contextual differences mean in terms of communication? Actually, quite a lot. Communication in high-context cultures implies considerably more trust by both parties. What may appear, to an outsider, as casual and insignificant conversations is important because it reflects the desire to build a relationship and create trust. Oral agreements imply strong commitments in high-context cultures. And who you are—your age, seniority, rank in the organization—is highly valued and heavily influence your credibility. But in low-context cultures, enforceable contracts will tend to be in writing, precisely worded, and highly legalistic. Similarly, low-context cultures value directness. Managers are expected to be explicit and precise in conveying intended meaning. It's quite different in high-context cultures, in which managers tend to "make suggestions" rather than give orders.

A Cultural Guide   When communicating with people from a different culture, what can you do to reduce misperceptions, misinterpretations, and misevaluations? You can begin by trying to assess the cultural context. You're likely to have fewer difficulties if these people come from a similar cultural context to you. In addition, the following four rules can be helpful:[37]

1. *Assume differences until similarity is proven.* Most of us assume that others are more similar to us than they actually are. But people from different countries often are very different from us. So you are far less likely to make an error if you assume others are different from you rather than assuming similarity until difference is proven.

2. *Emphasize description rather than interpretation or evaluation.* Interpreting or evaluating what someone has said or done, in contrast to description, is based more on the observer's culture and background than on the observed situation. As a result, delay judgment until you've had sufficient time to observe and interpret the

situation from the differing perspectives of all the cultures involved.

3. *Practice empathy.* Before sending a message, put yourself in the recipient's shoes. What are his or her values, experiences, and frames of reference? What do you know about his or her education, upbringing, and background that can give you added insight? Try to see the other person as he or she really is.

4. *Treat your interpretations as a working hypothesis.* Once you've developed an explanation for a new situation or think you empathize with someone from a foreign culture, treat your interpretation as a hypothesis that needs further testing rather than as a certainty. Carefully assess the feedback provided by recipients to see if it confirms your hypothesis. For important decisions or communiqués, you can also check with other foreign and home-country colleagues to make sure that your interpretations are on target.

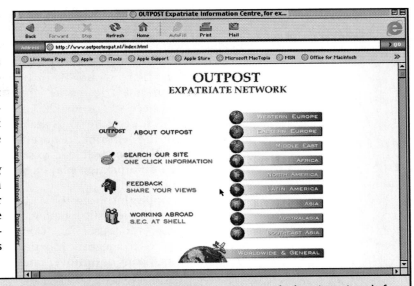

Cultural differences in communication can hinder even the best-intentioned efforts. To assist employees posted abroad as they make their way in a new culture, Shell International operates a Web site called Outpost that provides practical information to Shell expatriates and their families.

SUMMARY AND IMPLICATIONS FOR MANAGERS

A careful review of this chapter finds a common theme regarding the relationship between communication and employee satisfaction: the less the uncertainty, the greater the satisfaction. Distortions, ambiguities, and incongruities all increase uncertainty and, hence, they have a negative impact on satisfaction.[38]

The less distortion that occurs in communication, the more that goals, feedback, and other management messages to employees will be received as they were intended.[39] This, in turn, should reduce ambiguities and clarify the group's task. Extensive use of vertical, lateral, and informal channels will increase communication flow, reduce uncertainty, and improve group performance and satisfaction. We should also expect incongruities between verbal and nonverbal communiqués to increase uncertainty and to reduce satisfaction.

Findings in the chapter further suggest that the goal of perfect communication is unattainable. Yet, there is evidence that demonstrates a positive relationship between effective communication (which includes factors such as perceived trust, perceived accuracy, desire for interaction, top-management receptiveness, and upward information requirements) and worker productivity.[40] Choosing the correct channel, being an effective listener, and using feedback may, therefore, make for more effective communication. But the human factor generates distortions that can never be fully eliminated. The communication process represents an exchange of messages, but the outcome is meanings that may or may not approximate those that the sender intended. Whatever the sender's expectations, the decoded message in the mind of the receiver represents his or her reality. And it is this "reality" that will determine performance, along with the individual's level of motivation and his or her degree of satisfaction. The issue of motivation is critical, so we should briefly review how communication is central in determining an individual's degree of motivation.

You will remember from expectancy theory that the degree of effort an individual exerts depends on his or her perception of the effort–performance, performance–reward, and reward–goal satisfaction links. If individuals are not given the data necessary to make the perceived probability of these links high, motivation will suffer. If rewards are not made clear, if the criteria for determining and measuring performance are ambiguous, or if individuals are not relatively certain that their effort will lead to satisfactory performance, then effort will be reduced. So communication plays a significant role in determining the level of employee motivation.

A final implication from the communication literature relates to predicting turnover. The use of realistic job previews acts as a communication device for clarifying role expectations (see the "Counterpoint" in Chapter 5). Employees who have been exposed to a realistic job preview have more accurate information about that job. Comparisons of turnover rates between organizations that use the realistic job preview versus either no preview or presentation of only positive job information show that those not using the realistic preview have, on average, almost 29 percent higher turnover.[41] This makes a strong case for managers to convey honest and accurate information about a job to applicants during the recruiting and selection process.

Open-Book Management Improves the Bottom Line

pen-book management (OBM) seeks to get every employee to think and behave like an owner.[a] It throws out the notion that bosses run things and employees do what they're told. In the open-book approach, employees are given the information that historically was strictly kept within the management ranks.

There are three key elements to any OBM program. First, management opens the company's books and shares detailed financial and operating information with employees. If employees don't know how the company makes money, how can they be expected to make the firm more successful? Second, employees need to be taught to understand the company's financial statements. This means management must provide employees with a "basic course" in how to read and interpret income statements, balance sheets, and cash flow statements. And third, management needs to show employees how their work influences financial results. Showing employees the impact of their jobs on the bottom line makes financial-statement analysis relevant.

Who is using OBM? More than 3,500 organizations, including Springfield Remanufacturing Corp., Allstate Insurance, Amoco Canada, Rhino Foods, and Sprint's Government Systems division.

Why should it work? Access to detailed financial information, and the ability to understand that information, makes employees think like owners. And this leads to them making decisions that are best for the organization, not just for themselves.

Does it work? Most firms that have introduced OBM offer evidence that it has significantly helped the business. For instance, Springfield Remanufacturing was losing $61,000 on sales of $16 million. Management attributes much of the company's current success—profits of $6 million a year on sales of $100 million—to OBM. Similarly, Allstate's Business Insurance Group used OBM to boost return-on-equity from 2.9 percent to 16.5 percent in just three years.

[a]Based on J. Case, "The Open-Book Revolution," *INC*, June 1995, pp. 26–50; J. P. Schuster, J. Carpenter, and M. P. Kane, *The Power of Open-Book Management* (New York: John Wiley, 1996); and R. Aggarwal and B. J. Simkins, "Open Book Management—Optimizing Human Capital," *Business Horizons*, September–October 2001, pp. 5–13.

he owners of Optics 1 Inc., an optical-engineering company in southern California, with 23 employees and sales of less than $10 million a year implemented an OBM program. After a short time, the program was discontinued. Said one of the co-owners, "Employees used the information against me. When we made a profit, they demanded bigger bonuses and new computers. When I used profits to finance a new product line, everybody said, 'That's nice, but what's in it for me?' . . . If your employees misinterpret financial information, it's more damaging than their not having access at all. I gave them general and administrative rates. Next thing I knew they were backing out everyone's salaries, and I'd hear, 'You're paying that guy $86,000? I contribute more.'"

As the preceding illustrates, part of the downside to OBM is that employees may misuse or misinterpret the information they get against management.[b] Another potential problem is leaking of confidential information to competitors. In the hands of the competition, detailed information on the company's operations and financial position may undermine a firm's competitive advantage.

When OBM succeeds, two factors seem to exist. First, the organization or unit in which it's implemented tends to be small. It's a lot easier to introduce OBM in a small, start-up company than in a large, geographically dispersed company that has operated for years with closed books and little employee involvement. Second, there needs to be a mutually trusting relationship between management and workers. In organizational cultures in which management doesn't trust employees to act selflessly or in which managers and accountants have been trained to keep information under lock and key, OBM isn't likely to work. Nor will it succeed when employees believe any new change program is only likely to further manipulate or exploit them for management's advantage.

[b]Based on S. L. Gruner, "Why Open the Books?" *INC.*, November 1996, p. 95; and T. R. V. Davis, "Open-Book Management: Its Promise and Pitfalls," *Organizational Dynamics*, Winter 1997, pp. 7–20.

1. Describe the functions that communication provides within a group or organization. Give an example of each.

2. Contrast encoding and decoding.

3. Contrast downward with upward communication.

4. What is nonverbal communication? Does it aid or hinder verbal communication?

5. What conditions stimulate the emergence of rumors?

6. What are the advantages and disadvantages of e-mail?

7. What can managers do to improve their skills at providing performance feedback?

8. What does the phrase "sometimes the real message in a communication is buried in the silence" mean?

9. Describe how political correctness can hinder effective communication.

10. Contrast high- and low-context cultures.

Questions for Critical Thinking

1. "Ineffective communication is the fault of the sender." Do you agree or disagree? Discuss.

2. What can you do to improve the likelihood that your communiqués will be received and understood as you intend?

3. How might managers use the grapevine for their benefit?

4. Using the concept of channel richness, give examples of messages best conveyed by e-mail, by face-to-face communication, and on the company bulletin board.

5. Why do you think so many people are poor listeners?

Team Exercise | The Impact of Attentive Listening Skills

The objective of this exercise is to show the importance of listening skills to interpersonal success.

Form groups by counting off by sixes. There should be a minimum of three students to a group and a maximum of seven.

Each group has 30 minutes to address the four questions below. The groups should begin by brainstorming answers, then narrow their selections to the three most significant answers. Appoint one member of the group to transcribe answers on the board and another to tell the class why the group selected these answers.

1. How do you know when a person is listening to you?

2. Describe a situation in which you exhibited outstanding listening behavior. How did it influence the speaker's subsequent communication behaviors?

3. How do you know when a person is ignoring you?

4. Describe a situation in which you ignored someone. What impact did it have on that person's subsequent communication behaviors?

Source: Adapted from T. Clark, "Sharing the Importance of Attentive Listening Skills," *Journal of Management Education,* April 1999, pp. 216–23.

Ethical Dilemma | Is It Wrong to Tell a Lie?

When we were children, our parents told us, "It's wrong to tell a lie." Yet we all have told lies at one time or another. If most of us agree that telling lies is wrong, how do we justify continuing to do it? The answer is: Most of us differentiate between "real lies" and "little white lies"—the latter being an acceptable, even necessary, part of social interaction.

A recent survey of 10,000 people 18 to 50 years old provides some insights into people's attitudes toward lying. Eighty percent described honesty as important but nearly one-quarter said that they would lie to an employer "if necessary." More than 15 percent admitted to lying on a resume or job application. And more than 45 percent said he or she would happily tell you a "little white lie."

Since lying is so closely intertwined with interpersonal communication, let's look at an issue many managers confront: Does a sound purpose justify intentionally distorting information? Consider the following situation.

An employee who works for you asks you about a rumor she's heard that your department and all its employees will be transferred from New York City to Dallas.

You know the rumor is true, but you would rather not let the information out just yet. You're fearful it could hurt departmental morale and lead to premature resignations. What do you say to your employee? Do you lie, evade the question, distort your answer, or tell the truth?

In a larger context, where do *you* draw the line between the truth and lying? And if you're in a managerial position, how does your answer to the previous question fit with your desire to be trusted by those who work for you?

Source: Cited in "Who's Lying Now?" *Training*, October 2000, p. 34.

Case Incident	Do We Have a Communication Problem Here?

"I don't want to hear your excuses. Just get those planes in the air," Jim Tuchman was screaming at his gate manager. As head of American Airlines' operations at the Mexico City airport, Tuchman has been consistently frustrated by the attitude displayed by his native employees. Transferred from Dallas to Mexico City only three months ago, Tuchman was having difficulty adjusting to the Mexican style of work. "Am I critical of these people? You bet I am! They don't listen when I talk. They think things are just fine and fight every change I suggest. And they have no appreciation for the importance of keeping on schedule."

If Tuchman is critical of his Mexico City staff, it's mutual. They universally dislike him. Here's a few anonymous comments made about their boss: "He's totally insensitive to our needs." "He thinks if he yells and screams, that things will improve. We don't see it that way." "I've been working here for four years.

Before he came here, this was a good place to work. Not anymore. I'm constantly in fear of being chewed out. I feel stress all the time, even at home. My husband has started commenting on it a lot."

Tuchman was brought in specifically to tighten up the Mexico City operation. High on his list of goals is improving American's on-time record in Mexico City, increasing productivity, and improving customer service. When Tuchman was asked if he thought he had any problems with his staff, he replied, "Yep. We just can't seem to communicate."

Questions

1. Does Jim Tuchman have a communication problem? Explain.

2. What suggestions, if any, would you make to Jim to help him improve his managerial effectiveness?

KSS PROGRAM	Active Listening Skills

KNOW THE CONCEPTS
SELF-AWARENESS
SKILLS APPLICATIONS

Active Listening Skills

After you've read this chapter, take Self-Assessment #25 (How Good Are My Listening Skills?) on your enclosed CD-ROM, and complete the skill-building module entitled Active Listening on page 621.

1. This opening section is based on S. Cushing, *Fatal Words: Communication Clashes and Aircraft Crashes* (Chicago: University of Chicago Press, 1997); and "Pilot Communication Risks Flight Safety," www.abc.net.au, March 21, 2001.

2. See, for example, K. W. Thomas and W. H. Schmidt, "A Survey of Managerial Interests with Respect to Conflict," *Academy of Management Journal*, June 1976, p. 317.

3. W. G. Scott and T. R. Mitchell, *Organization Theory: A Structural and Behavioral Analysis* (Homewood, IL: Richard D. Irwin, 1976).

4. D. K. Berlo, *The Process of Communication* (New York: Holt, Rinehart & Winston, 1960), pp. 30–32.

5. R. L. Simpson, "Vertical and Horizontal Communication in Formal Organizations," *Administrative Science Quarterly*, September 1959, pp. 188–96; B. Harriman, "Up and Down the Communications Ladder," *Harvard Business Review*, September–October 1974, pp. 143–51; and A. G. Walker and J. W. Smither, "A Five-Year Study of Upward Feedback: What Managers Do With Their Results Matter," *Personnel Psychology*, Summer 1999, pp. 393–424.

6. J. Fast, *Body Language* (Philadelphia: M. Evan, 1970), p. 7.

7. A. Mehrabian, *Nonverbal Communication* (Chicago: Aldine-Atherton, 1972).

8. A. Bandura, *Social Learning Theory* (Englewood Cliffs, NJ: Prentice Hall, 1977).

9. An example is assigned goals. See E. A. Locke and G. P. Latham, *A Theory of Goal Setting and Task Performance* (Upper Saddle River, NJ: Prentice Hall, 1990).

10. See, for example, N. B. Kurland and L. H. Pelled, "Passing the Word: Toward a Model of Gossip and Power in the Workplace," *Academy of Management Review*, April 2000, pp. 428–38; and N. Nicholson, "The New Word on Gossip," *Psychology Today*, June 2001, pp. 41–45.

11. Cited in "Heard It Through the Grapevine," *Forbes*, February 10, 1997, p. 22.

12. See, for instance, J. W. Newstrom, R. E. Monczka, and W. E. Reif, "Perceptions of the Grapevine: Its Value and Influence," *Journal of Business Communication*, Spring 1974, pp. 12–20; and S. J. Modic, "Grapevine Rated Most Believable," *Industry Week*, May 15, 1989, p. 14.

13. K. Davis, "Management Communication and the Grapevine," *Harvard Business Review*, September–October 1953, pp. 43–49.

14. H. Sutton and L. W. Porter, "A Study of the Grapevine in a Governmental Organization," *Personnel Psychology*, Summer 1968, pp. 223–30.

15. K. Davis, cited in R. Rowan, "Where Did That Rumor Come From?" *Fortune*, August 13, 1979, p. 134.

16. R. L. Rosnow and G. A. Fine, *Rumor and Gossip: The Social Psychology of Hearsay* (New York: Elsevier, 1976).

17. See, for instance, J. G. March and G. Sevon, "Gossip, Information and Decision Making" in J. G. March (ed.), *Decisions and Organizations* (Oxford: Blackwell, 1988), pp. 429–42; M. Noon and R. Delbridge, "News from Behind My Hand: Gossip in Organizations," *Organization Studies*, vol. 14, no. 1, 1993, pp. 23–36; and N. DiFonzo, P. Bordia, and R. L. Rosnow, "Reining in Rumors," *Organizational Dynamics*, Summer 1994, pp. 47–62.

18. S. Amour, "Boss: It's in the E-Mail," *USA Today*, August 10, 1999, p. 3B.

19. "Ford to Offer Employees Home PCs for $5 a Month," www.ifnormationweek.com; February 3, 2000.

20. G. Anders, "Inside Job," *Fast Company*, September 2001, p. 178.

21. T. M. Burton and R. E. Silverman, "Lots of Empty Spaces in Cerner Parking Lot Get CEO Riled Up," *Wall Street Journal*, March 30, 2001, p. B3; and E. Wong, "A Stinging Office Memo Boomerangs," *New York Times*, April 5, 2001, p. C1.

22. See R. L. Daft and R. H. Lengel, "Information Richness: A New Approach to Managerial Behavior and Organization Design," in B. M. Staw and L. L. Cummings (eds.), *Research in Organizational Behavior*, vol. 6 (Greenwich, CT: JAI Press, 1984), pp. 191–233; R. L. Daft and R. H. Lengel, "Organizational Information Requirements, Media Richness, and Structural Design," *Managerial Science*, May 1986, pp. 554–72; R. E. Rice, "Task Analyzability, Use of New Media, and Effectiveness," *Organization Science*, November 1992, pp. 475–500; S. G. Straus and J. E. McGrath, "Does the Medium Matter? The Interaction of Task Type and Technology on Group Performance and Member Reaction," *Journal of Applied Psychology*, February 1994, pp. 87–97; and L. K. Trevino, J. Webster, and E. W. Stein, "Making Connections: Complementary Influences on Communication Media Choices, Attitudes, and Use," *Organization Science*, March-April 2000, pp. 163–82.

23. R. L. Daft, R. H. Lengel, and L. K. Trevino, "Message Equivocality, Media Selection, and Manager Performance: Implications for Information Systems," *MIS Quarterly*, September 1987, pp. 355–68.

24. J. C. McCroskey, J. A. Daly, and G. Sorenson, "Personality Correlates of Communication Apprehension," *Human Communication Research*, Spring 1976, pp. 376–80.

25. B. H. Spitzberg and M. L. Hecht, "A Competent Model of Relational Competence," *Human Communication Research*, Summer 1984, pp. 575–99.

26. See, for example, L. Stafford and J. A. Daly, "Conversational Memory: The Effects of Instructional Set and Recall Mode on Memory for Natural Conversations," *Human Communication Research*, Spring 1984, pp. 379–402.

27. J. A. Daly and J. C. McCrosky, "Occupational Choice and Desirability as a Function of Communication Apprehension," paper presented at the annual meeting of the International Communication Association, Chicago, 1975.

28. J. A. Daly and M. D. Miller, "The Empirical Development of an Instrument of Writing Apprehension," *Research in the Teaching of English*, Winter 1975, pp. 242–49.

29. See D. Tannen, *You Just Don't Understand: Women and Men in Conversation* (New York: Ballentine Books, 1991); and D. Tannen, *Talking from 9 to 5* (New York: William Morrow, 1995).

30. D. Tannen, *Talking from 9 to 5*, p. 15.
31. This section is largely based on C. G. Pinder and K. P. Harlos, "Silent Organizational Behavior," paper presented at the Western Academy of Management Conference; March 2000; and P. Mornell, "The Sounds of Silence," *INC.*, February 2001, pp. 117–18.
32. M. L. LaGanga, "Are There Words That Neither Offend Nor Bore?" *Los Angeles Times*, May 18, 1994, p. II–27; and J. Leo, "Language in the Dumps," *U.S. News & World Report*, July 27, 1998, p. 16.
33. Cited in J. Leo, "Falling for Sensitivity," *U.S. News & World Report*, December 13, 1993, p. 27.
34. R. E. Axtell, *Gestures: The Do's and Taboos of Body Language Around the World* (New York: Wiley, 1991).
35. See M. Munter, "Cross-Cultural Communication for Managers," *Business Horizons*, May–June 1993, pp. 75–76.
36. See E. T. Hall, *Beyond Culture* (Garden City, NY: Anchor Press/Doubleday, 1976); E. T. Hall, "How Cultures Collide," *Psychology Today*, July 1976, pp. 67–74; E. T. Hall and M. R. Hall, *Understanding Cultural Differences* (Yarmouth, ME: Intercultural Press, 1990); and R. E. Dulek, J. S. Fielden, and J. S. Hill, "International Communication: An Executive Primer," *Business Horizons*, January–February 1991, pp. 20–25.
37. N. Adler, *International Dimensions of Organizational Behavior*, 4th ed. (Cincinnati, OH: Southwestern, 2002), p. 94.
38. See, for example. R. S. Schuler, "A Role Perception Transactional Process Model for Organizational Communication-Outcome Relationships," *Organizational Behavior and Human Performance*, April 1979, pp. 268–91.
39. J. P. Walsh, S. J. Ashford, and T. E. Hill, "Feedback Obstruction: The Influence of the Information Environment on Employee Turnover Intentions," *Human Relations*, January 1985, pp. 23–46.
40. S. A. Hellweg and S. L. Phillips, "Communication and Productivity in Organizations: A State-of-the-Art Review," in *Proceedings of the 40th Annual Academy of Management Conference*, Detroit, 1980, pp. 188–92.
41. R. R. Reilly, B. Brown, M. R. Blood, and C. Z. Malatesta, "The Effects of Realistic Previews: A Study and Discussion of the Literature," *Personnel Psychology*, Winter 1981, pp. 823–34.

PART THREE

THE GROUP

Can one person make a difference in an organization's performance? Andrea Jung, chairman and CEO of Avon (see photo), is proving one can.[1] Jung joined Avon in 1994 after working for retailers such as Neiman Marcus and Bloomingdale's. Her original task at Avon was to create a global brand. And that's what she did. Jung integrated and standardized the company's logo, packaging, and ads to create a uniform image; and she pushed for the current corporate slogan, "The company for women." Based on her success in improving Avon's marketing focus, the company's board appointed her chairman and CEO in 1999.

The company that Jung took over was in deep trouble. The day of the "Avon Lady" seemed to have passed. Fewer women were signing on as Avon reps and sales were sagging. But after only four weeks in her new job, Jung had a turnaround plan worked out. Avon would launch an entirely new line of businesses, develop blockbuster products, and begin selling Avon products in retail stores—something it had never done in its long history. She added 46 percent to Avon's research-and-development budget to get blockbusters to market faster. This led to the launching of Retroactive, an anti-aging skin cream that has become a runaway hit, and new lines of vitamins and therapy oils. She also reduced the number of Avon suppliers from 300 to 75, saving the company $60 million a year. Maybe most importantly, Jung has breathed new life into the ranks of the "Avon Ladies." To rebuild the company's sales force, she created a multilevel marketing program that rewards current sales people for signing up new reps. One saleswoman in East Rockaway, New York, for instance, brought in 350 new reps in just 18 months.

After two years on the job, Jung's leadership has truly made a difference in Avon's performance. Sales growth climbed from 1.5 percent a year to 6 percent; operating profits grew from 4 percent to 7 percent; and the company's stock was up 70 percent.

Basic Approaches to Leadership

As Andrea Jung is demonstrating at Avon, leaders can make a difference. In this chapter, we'll look at three basic approaches to determining what makes an effective leader and what differentiates leaders from nonleaders. First, we'll present trait theories. They dominated the study of leadership up to the late 1940s. Then we'll discuss behavioral theories, which were popular until the late 1960s. Finally, we'll introduce contingency theories, which is currently the dominant approach to the field of leadership. But before we review these three approaches, let's first clarify what we mean by the term *leadership*.

WHAT IS LEADERSHIP?

Leadership and *management* are two terms that are often confused. What's the difference between them?

John Kotter of the Harvard Business School argues that management is about coping with complexity.[2] Good management brings about order and consistency by drawing up formal plans, designing rigid organization structures, and monitoring results against the plans. Leadership, in contrast, is about coping with change. Leaders establish direction by developing a vision of the future; then they align people by communicating this vision and inspiring them to overcome hurdles.

Robert House of the Wharton School at the University of Pennsylvania basically concurs when he says that managers use the authority inherent in their designated formal rank to obtain compliance from organizational members.[3] Management consists of implementing the vision and strategy provided by leaders, coordinating and staffing the organization, and handling day-to-day problems.

LEARNING OBJECTIVES

AFTER STUDYING THIS CHAPTER, YOU SHOULD BE ABLE TO:

1. Contrast leadership and management.
2. Summarize the conclusions of trait theories.
3. Identify the limitations of behavioral theories.
4. Describe Fiedler's contingency model.
5. Explain Hersey and Blanchard's situational theory.
6. Summarize leader-member exchange theory.
7. Describe the path-goal theory.
8. Identify the situational variables in the leader-participation model.

Although Kotter and House provide separate definitions of the two terms, both researchers and practicing managers frequently make no such distinctions. So we need to present leadership in a way that can capture how it is used in theory and practice.

leadership

The ability to influence a group toward the achievement of goals.

We define **leadership** as the ability to influence a group toward the achievement of goals. The source of this influence may be formal, such as that provided by the possession of managerial rank in an organization. Since management positions come with some degree of formally designated authority, a person may assume a leadership role simply because of the position he or she holds in the organization. But not all leaders are managers; nor, for that matter, are all managers leaders. Just because an organization provides its managers with certain formal rights is no assurance that they will be able to lead effectively. We find that non-sanctioned leadership—that is, the ability to influence that arises outside the formal structure of the organization—is often as important or more important than formal influence. In other words, leaders can emerge from within a group as well as by formal appointment to lead a group.

You should note that our definition makes no specific mention of a vision, even though both Kotter and House use the term in their efforts to differentiate leadership and management. This omission is purposeful. While most contemporary discussions of the leadership concept (see Chapter 12) include articulating a common *vision*,[4] almost all work on leadership conducted prior to the 1980s made no reference to this concept. So in order for our definition to encompass both historical and contemporary approaches to leadership, we make no explicit reference to vision.

One last comment before we move on: Organizations need strong leadership and strong management for optimal effectiveness. In today's dynamic world, we need leaders to challenge the status-quo, to create visions of the future, and to inspire organizational members to want to achieve the visions. We also need managers to formulate detailed plans, create efficient organizational structures, and oversee day-to-day operations.

TRAIT THEORIES

When Margaret Thatcher was prime minister of Great Britain, she was regularly singled out for her leadership. She was described in terms such as confident, iron-willed, determined, and decisive. These terms are traits and, whether Thatcher's advocates and critics recognized it at the time, when they described her in such terms they became trait-theorist supporters.

trait theories of leadership

Theories that consider personal qualities and characteristics that differentiate leaders from nonleaders.

The media has long been a believer in **trait theories of leadership**—differentiating leaders from nonleaders by focusing on personal qualities and characteristics. The media identify people like Margaret Thatcher, South Africa's Nelson Mandela, Virgin Group CEO Richard Branson, Apple co-founder Steve Jobs, former New York mayor Rudolph Giuliani, and American Express' chairman Ken Chenault as leaders, then describe them in terms such as *charismatic, enthusiastic,* and *courageous*. Well the media isn't alone. The search for personality, social, physical, or intellectual attributes that would describe leaders and differentiate them from nonleaders goes back to the 1930s.

Research efforts at isolating leadership traits resulted in a number of dead ends. For instance, a review of 20 different studies identified nearly 80 leadership traits, but only five of these traits were common to four or more of the investigations.[5] If the search was intended to identify a set of traits that would always differentiate leaders from followers and effective from ineffective leaders, the search failed. Perhaps it was a bit optimistic to believe that there could be consistent and unique traits that would apply universally to all effective leaders, no matter whether they were in charge of DaimlerChrysler, the Mormon Tabernacle Choir, Ted's Malibu Surf Shop, the Brazilian national soccer team, or Oxford University.

If, however, the search was intended to identify traits that were consistently associated with leadership, the results can be interpreted in a more impressive light. For example, six traits on which leaders tend to differ from nonleaders are ambition and energy, the desire to lead, honesty and integrity, self-confidence, intelligence, and job-relevant knowledge.[6] In addition, more recent research provides strong evidence that people who are high self-monitors—that is, are highly flexible in adjusting their behavior in different situations—are much more likely to emerge as leaders in groups than low self-monitors.[7] Overall, the cumulative findings from more than half a century of research lead us to conclude that some traits increase the likelihood of success as a leader, but none of the traits *guarantee* success.[8]

When leaders like Steve Jobs at Apple Computer are described as charismatic or enthusiastic, these adjectives reflect the trait theory of leadership, which seeks to identify specific personal qualities and characteristics of leaders to explain their success.

But the trait approach has at least four limitations. First, there are no universal traits that predict leadership in all situations. Rather, traits appear to predict leadership in *selective* situations.[9] Second, traits predict behavior more in "weak" situations than in "strong" situations.[10] Strong situations are those in which there are strong behavioral norms, strong incentives for specific types of behaviors, and clear expectations as to what behaviors are rewarded and punished. Such strong situations create less opportunity for leaders to express their inherent dispositional tendencies. Since highly formalized organizations and those with strong cultures fit the description of strong situations, the power of traits to predict leadership in many organizations is probably limited. Third, the evidence is unclear in separating cause from effect. For example, does self-confidence create leadership, or does success as a leader build self-confidence? Finally, traits do a better job at predicting the appearance of leadership than in actually distinguishing between *effective* and *ineffective* leaders.[11] The facts that an individual exhibits the traits and others consider that person to be a leader does not necessarily mean that the leader is successful at getting his or her group to achieve its goals.

These limitations have led researchers to look in other directions. Although there has been a resurgent interest in traits during the past 20 years, a major movement away from traits began as early as the 1940s. Leadership research from the late 1940s through the late 1960s emphasized the preferred behavioral styles that leaders demonstrated.

BEHAVIORAL THEORIES

The inability to strike "gold" in the trait "mines" led researchers to look at the behaviors exhibited by specific leaders. They wondered if there was something unique in the way that effective leaders behave. For example, Titan International CEO Morry Taylor and Siebel Systems' CEO Tom Siebel both have been very successful in leading their companies through difficult times.[12] And they both rely on a common leadership style—tough-talking, intense, autocratic. Does this suggest that autocratic behavior is a preferred style for all leaders? In this section, we look at four different **behavioral theories of leadership** in order to answer that question. First, however, let's consider the practical implications of the behavioral approach.

If the behavioral approach to leadership were successful, it would have implications quite different from those of the trait approach. If trait research had been successful, it would have provided a basis for *selecting* the "right" persons to assume formal positions in groups and organizations requiring leadership. In contrast, if behavioral studies were to turn up critical behavioral determinants of leadership, we could *train* people to be leaders. The difference between trait and behavioral theories, in terms of application, lies in their underlying assumptions. If trait theories were valid, then leaders are born rather than made. On the other hand, if there were specific behaviors that identified leaders, then we could teach leadership—we could design programs that implanted these behavioral patterns in individuals who desired to be effective leaders. This was surely a more exciting avenue, for it meant that the supply of leaders could be expanded. If training worked, we could have an infinite supply of effective leaders.

Ohio State Studies

The most comprehensive and replicated of the behavioral theories resulted from research that began at Ohio State University in the late 1940s.[13] These researchers sought to identify independent dimensions of leader behavior. Beginning with over a thousand dimensions, they eventually narrowed the list to two categories that substantially accounted for most of the leadership behavior described by employees. They called these two dimensions *initiating structure* and *consideration*.

Initiating structure refers to the extent to which a leader is likely to define and structure his or her role and those of employees in the search for goal attainment. It includes behavior that attempts to organize work, work relationships, and goals. The leader characterized as high in initiating structure could be described as someone who "assigns group members to particular tasks," "expects workers to maintain definite standards of performance," and "emphasizes the meeting of deadlines." Morry Taylor and Tom Siebel exhibit high initiating structure behavior.

Consideration is described as the extent to which a person is likely to have job relationships that are characterized by mutual trust, respect for employees' ideas, and regard for their feelings. He or she shows concern for followers' comfort, well-being, status, and satisfaction. A leader high in consideration could be described as one who helps employees with personal problems, is friendly and approachable, and treats all employees as equals. AOL Time Warner's CEO, Richard Parsons, rates high on consideration behavior. His leadership style is very people-oriented, emphasizing cooperation and consensus-building.[14]

With a leadership style that is people-oriented and that focuses on cooperation and consensus, Richard Parsons (left in photo), CEO of AOL Time Warner, can be described as a leader high in the leadership dimension of consideration.

Extensive research, based on these definitions, found that leaders high in initiating structure and consideration (a "high–high" leader) tended to achieve high employee performance and satisfaction more frequently than those who rated low on consideration, initiating structure, or both. However, the "high–high" style did not always result in positive consequences. For example, leader behavior characterized as high on initiating structure led to greater rates of grievances, absenteeism, and turnover and lower levels of job satisfaction for workers performing routine tasks. Other studies found that high consideration was negatively related to performance ratings of the leader by his or her superior. In conclusion, the Ohio State studies suggested that the "high–high" style generally resulted in positive outcomes, but enough exceptions were found to indicate that situational factors needed to be integrated into the theory.

University of Michigan Studies

Leadership studies undertaken at the University of Michigan's Survey Research Center, at about the same time as those being done at Ohio State, had similar research objectives: to locate behavioral characteristics of leaders that appeared to be related to measures of performance effectiveness.

The Michigan group also came up with two dimensions of leadership behavior that they labeled **employee-oriented** and **production-oriented**.[15] Leaders who were employee-oriented were described as emphasizing interpersonal relations; they took a personal interest in the needs of their employees and accepted individual differences among members. The production-oriented leaders, in contrast, tended to emphasize the technical or task aspects of the job—their main concern was in accomplishing their group's tasks, and the group members were a means to that end.

The conclusions arrived at by the Michigan researchers strongly favored the leaders who were employee-oriented in their behavior. Employee-oriented leaders were associated with higher group productivity and higher job satisfaction. Production-oriented leaders tended to be associated with low group productivity and lower job satisfaction.

employee-oriented leader

Emphasizing interpersonal relations; taking a personal interest in the needs of employees and accepting individual differences among members.

production-oriented leader

One who emphasizes technical or task aspects of the job.

The Managerial Grid

A graphic portrayal of a two-dimensional view of leadership style was developed by Blake and Mouton.[16] They proposed a **managerial grid** (sometimes also now called the *leadership grid)* based on the styles of "concern for people" and "concern for production," which essentially represent the Ohio State dimensions of consideration and initiating structure or the Michigan dimensions of employee-oriented and production-oriented.

The grid, depicted in Exhibit 11-1 on page 318, has nine possible positions along each axis, creating 81 different positions in which the leader's style may fall. The grid does not show results produced but, rather, the dominating factors in a leader's thinking in regard to getting results.

Based on the findings of Blake and Mouton, managers were found to perform best under a 9,9 style, as contrasted, for example, with a 9,1 (authority type) or 1,9 (laissez-faire type) style.[17] Unfortunately, the grid offers a better framework for conceptualizing leadership style than for presenting any tangible new information in clarifying the leadership quandary, because there is little substantive evidence to support the conclusion that a 9,9 style is most effective in all situations.[18]

managerial grid

A nine-by-nine matrix outlining 81 different leadership styles.

Scandinavian Studies

The three behavioral approaches we've just reviewed were essentially developed between the late 1940s and early 1960s. These approaches evolved during a time

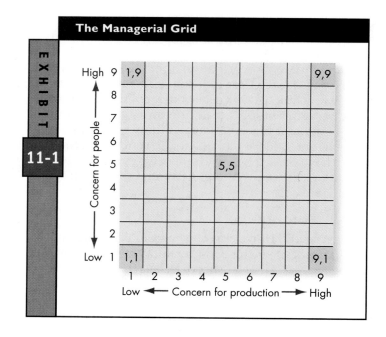

The Managerial Grid

EXHIBIT

11-1

High 9 [1,9] . . . . [9,9]
8
7
6
5 [5,5]
4
3
2
Low 1 [1,1] . . . . [9,1]

1 2 3 4 5 6 7 8 9

Low ◄— Concern for production —► High

(Vertical axis: Concern for people)

when the world was a far more stable and predictable place. In the belief that these studies fail to capture the more dynamic realities of today, researchers in Finland and Sweden have been reassessing whether there are only two dimensions that capture the essence of leadership behavior.[19] Their basic premise is that in a changing world, effective leaders would exhibit **development-oriented** behavior. These are leaders who value experimentation, seek new ideas, and generate and implement change.

development-oriented leader

One who values experimentation, seeks new ideas, and generates and implements change.

For instance, these Scandinavian researchers reviewed the original Ohio State data. They found that the Ohio State people included development items such as "pushes new ways of doing things," "originates new approaches to problems," and "encourages members to start new activities." But these items, at the time, didn't explain much toward effective leadership. It could be, the Scandinavian researchers proposed, that this was because developing new ideas and implementing change were not critical in those days. In today's dynamic environment, this may no longer be true. So the Scandinavian researchers have been conducting new studies looking to see if there is a third dimension—development orientation—that is related to leader effectiveness.

The early evidence is positive. Using samples of leaders in Finland and Sweden, the researchers have found strong support for development-oriented leader behavior as a separate and independent dimension. That is, the previous behavioral approaches that focused in on only two behaviors may not appropriately capture leadership in the twenty-first century. Moreover, while initial conclusions need to be guarded without more confirming evidence, it also appears that leaders who demonstrate development-oriented behavior have more satisfied employees and are seen as more competent by those employees.

Summary of Behavioral Theories

The behavioral theories have had modest success in identifying consistent relationships between leadership behavior and group performance. What seems to be missing is consideration of the situational factors that influence success or failure.

Leadership Styles: Little Change over Time

A consensus-building style among managers still has a way to go. That was the conclusion from a national 15-year study that assessed the leadership style of 41,000 middle- and upper-level managers.

The results showed that managers are only slightly more likely to be inclusive in decisions made in 1999 than they were in 1985. Specifically, 35 percent of managers in 1985 preferred an autocratic style versus 31 percent of managers surveyed in 1999. For situations in which consensus was more appropriate, 21 percent of managers in 1985 selected the most inclusive style versus 24 percent in 1999. And when faced with a vague problem, more than 30 percent of the contemporary managers tended to select a leadership style that didn't allow for clarifying input from others.

This evidence suggests that, in spite of all the attention that consultants, academics, and the media have given to the new workplace and the changing role of manager from boss to coach or advisor, it appears that many managers continue to rely on an autocratic style of leadership.

Source: "The Tyranny of Managers," *Training*, January 2002, p. 19.

For example, it seems unlikely that Martin Luther King, Jr., would have been a great civil-rights leader at the turn of the twentieth century; yet he was in the 1950s and 1960s. Would Ralph Nader have risen to lead a consumer activist group had he been born in 1834 rather than 1934, or in Costa Rica rather than Connecticut? It seems quite unlikely, yet the behavioral approaches we have described could not clarify these situational factors.

CONTINGENCY THEORIES

Linda Wachner had a reputation as being a very tough boss. And for a number of years, this style worked. In 1987, Wachner became CEO of Warnaco, a struggling $425-million-a-year apparel company. Over a 14-year period, she transformed Warnaco into a $2.2 billion company whose products ranged from Calvin Klein jeans to Speedo swimsuits. In spite of an abrasive style that included frequently humiliating employees in front of their peers, and led to rapid turnover among top managers, Wachner's style worked for most of the 1990s. In fact, in 1993, *Fortune* magazine anointed her "America's most successful businesswoman." But times change and Wachner didn't.[20] Beginning in 1998, the company's business began to unravel, hurt by a reduction in demand for its products and a fast-eroding market share. Wachner's headstrong approach and brash tactics, which had driven off many competent executives, was now alienating creditors and licensers as well as employees. In June 2001, Warnaco was forced to file for bankruptcy protection. Five months later, the restructuring committee of Warnaco's board of directors fired Wachner.

Linda Wachner's rise and fall illustrates what became increasingly clear to those studying the leadership phenomenon decades earlier: Predicting leadership success is more complex than isolating a few traits or preferable behaviors. In Wachner's case, what worked in 1990 didn't work in 2000. The failure by researchers to obtain consistent results led to a focus on situational influences. The relationship between leadership style and effectiveness suggested that under condition a, style x would be appropriate, whereas style y would be more suitable for condition b, and

How much do circumstances account for a leader's success? As CEO of apparel company Warnaco, Linda Wachner was an abrasive but successful manager in the 1990s but was fired in 2001 after the company filed for bankruptcy. Contingency theory would argue that while Wachner's production-oriented style worked at Warnaco in the early 1990s, conditions changed, making this style ineffective at the end of the decade.

style *z* for condition *c*. But what were the conditions *a*, *b*, *c*, and so forth? It was one thing to say that leadership effectiveness was dependent on the situation and another to be able to isolate those situational conditions.

Several approaches to isolating key situational variables have proven more successful than others and, as a result, have gained wider recognition. We shall consider five of these: the Fiedler model, Hersey and Blanchard's situational theory, leader-member exchange theory, and the path-goal and leader-participation models.

Fiedler Model

The first comprehensive contingency model for leadership was developed by Fred Fiedler.[21] The **Fiedler contingency model** proposes that effective group performance depends on the proper match between the leader's style and the degree to which the situation gives control to the leader.

Identifying Leadership Style   Fiedler believes a key factor in leadership success is the individual's basic leadership style. So he begins by trying to find out what that basic style is. Fiedler created the **least preferred co-worker (LPC) questionnaire** for this purpose; it purports to measure whether a person is task- or relationship-oriented. The LPC questionnaire contains sets of 16 contrasting adjectives (such as pleasant–unpleasant, efficient–inefficient, open–guarded, supportive–hostile). It asks respondents to think of all the co-workers they have ever had and to describe the one person they *least enjoyed* working with by rating him or her on a scale of 1 to 8 for each of the 16 sets of contrasting adjectives. Fiedler believes that based on the respondents' answers to this LPC questionnaire, he can determine their basic leadership style. If the least preferred co-worker is described in relatively positive terms (a high LPC score), then the respondent is primarily interested in good personal relations with this co-worker. That is, if you essentially describe the person you are least able to work with in favorable terms, Fiedler would label you *relationship-oriented*. In contrast, if the least preferred co-worker is seen in relatively unfavorable terms (a low LPC score), the respondent is primarily interested in productivity and thus would be labeled *task-oriented*. About 16 percent of respondents score in the middle range.[22] Such individuals cannot be classified as either relationship-oriented or task-oriented and thus fall outside the theory's predictions. The rest of our discussion, therefore, relates to the 84 percent who score in either the high or low range of the LPC.

Fiedler assumes that an individual's leadership style is fixed. As we'll show below, this is important because it means that if a situation requires a task-oriented leader and the person in that leadership position is relationship-oriented, either the situation has to be modified or the leader replaced if optimal effectiveness is to be achieved.

Defining the Situation   After an individual's basic leadership style has been assessed through the LPC, it is necessary to match the leader with the situation. Fiedler has identified three contingency dimensions that, he argues, define the key situational factors that determine leadership effectiveness. These are leader–member relations, task structure, and position power. They are defined as follows:

1. **Leader-member relations:** The degree of confidence, trust, and respect members have in their leader
2. **Task structure:** The degree to which the job assignments are procedurized (that is, structured or unstructured)
3. **Position power:** The degree of influence a leader has over power variables such as hiring, firing, discipline, promotions, and salary increases

Fiedler contingency model

The theory that effective groups depend on a proper match between a leader's style of interacting with subordinates and the degree to which the situation gives control and influence to the leader.

least preferred co-worker (LPC) questionnaire

An instrument that purports to measure whether a person is task- or relationship-oriented.

leader-member relations

The degree of confidence, trust, and respect subordinates have in their leader.

task structure

The degree to which the job assignments are procedurized.

position power

Influence derived from one's formal structural position in the organization; includes power to hire, fire, discipline, promote, and give salary increases.

The next step in the Fiedler model is to evaluate the situation in terms of these three contingency variables. Leader-member relations are either good or poor, task structure is either high or low, and position power is either strong or weak.

Fiedler states the better the leader-member relations, the more highly structured the job, and the stronger the position power, the more control the leader has. For example, a very favorable situation (in which the leader would have a great deal of control) might involve a payroll manager who is well respected and whose employees have confidence in her (good leader-member relations), for which the activities to be done—such as wage computation, check writing, report filing—are specific and clear (high task structure), and the job provides considerable freedom for her to reward and punish her employees (strong position power). On the other hand, an unfavorable situation might be the disliked chairperson of a voluntary United Way fund-raising team. In this job, the leader has very little control. Altogether, by mixing the three contingency variables, there are potentially eight different situations or categories in which leaders could find themselves.

Matching Leaders and Situations With knowledge of an individual's LPC and an assessment of the three contingency variables, the Fiedler model proposes matching them up to achieve maximum leadership effectiveness.[23] Based on his research, Fiedler concluded that task-oriented leaders tend to perform better in situations that were very favorable to them and in situations that were very unfavorable (see Exhibit 11-2). So Fiedler would predict that when faced with a category I, II, III, VII, or VIII situation, task-oriented leaders perform better. Relationship-oriented leaders, however, perform better in moderately favorable situations—categories IV through VI. In recent years, Fiedler has condensed these eight situations down to three.[24] He now says that task-oriented leaders perform best in

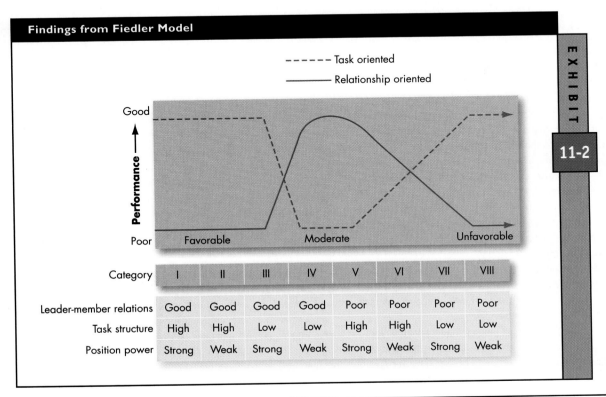

Findings from Fiedler Model

EXHIBIT 11-2

situations of high and low control, while relationship-oriented leaders perform best in moderate control situations.

Given Fiedler's findings, how would you apply them? You would seek to match leaders and situations. Individuals' LPC scores would determine the type of situation for which they were best suited. That "situation" would be defined by evaluating the three contingency factors of leader-member relations, task structure, and position power. But remember that Fiedler views an individual's leadership style as being fixed. Therefore, there are really only two ways in which to improve leader effectiveness.

First, you can change the leader to fit the situation—as in a baseball game, a manager can put a right-handed pitcher or a left-handed pitcher into the game, depending on the situational characteristics of the hitter. So, for example, if a group situation rates as highly unfavorable but is currently led by a relationship-oriented manager, the group's performance could be improved by replacing that manager with one who is task-oriented. The second alternative would be to change the situation to fit the leader. That could be done by restructuring tasks or increasing or decreasing the power that the leader has to control factors such as salary increases, promotions, and disciplinary actions.

Evaluation As a whole, reviews of the major studies that tested the overall validity of the Fiedler model lead to a generally positive conclusion. That is, there is considerable evidence to support at least substantial parts of the model.[25] If predictions from the model use only three categories rather than the original eight,

OR **SCIENCE** **?**

MYTH

"It's Experience That Counts!"

The belief in the value of experience as a predictor of leadership effectiveness is very strong and widespread. Unfortunately, experience alone is generally a poor predictor of leadership.[26]

Organizations carefully screen outside candidates for senior management positions on the basis of their experience. Similarly, organizations usually require several years of experience at one managerial level before a person can be considered for promotions. For that matter, have you ever filled out an employment application that *didn't* ask about previous experience or job history? Clearly, management believes that experience counts. But the evidence doesn't support this view. Studies of military officers, research and development teams, shop supervisors, post office administrators, and school principals tell us that experienced managers tend to be no more effective than the managers with little experience.

One flaw in the "experience counts" logic is the assumption that length of time on a job is actually a measure of experience. This says nothing about the quality of experience. The fact that one person has 20 years' experience while another has two years' doesn't necessarily mean that the former has had 10 times as many meaningful experiences. Too often, 20 years of experience is nothing more than one year of experience repeated 20 times! In even the most complex jobs, real learning typically ends after about two years. By then, almost all new and unique situations have been experienced. So one problem with trying to link experience with leadership effectiveness is not paying attention to the quality and diversity of the experience.

A second problem is that there is variability between situations that influence the transferability or relevance of experience. Situations in which experience is obtained is rarely comparable to new situations. Jobs differ, support resources differ, organizational cultures differ, follower characteristics differ, and so on. So another reason that leadership experience isn't strongly related to leadership performance is undoubtedly due to variability of situations.

there is ample evidence to support Fiedler's conclusions.[27] But there are problems with the LPC and the practical use of the model that need to be addressed. For instance, the logic underlying the LPC is not well understood and studies have shown that respondents' LPC scores are not stable.[28] Also, the contingency variables are complex and difficult for practitioners to assess. It's often difficult in practice to determine how good the leader–member relations are, how structured the task is, and how much position power the leader has.[29]

Cognitive Resource Theory   More recently, Fiedler and an associate, Joe Garcia, reconceptualized the former's original theory.[30] Specifically, they focused on the role of stress as a form of situational unfavorableness and how a leader's intelligence and experience influence his or her reaction to stress. They call this reconceptualization **cognitive resource theory**.

cognitive resource theory

A theory of leadership that states that stress unfavorably affects a situation and that intelligence and experience can lessen the influence of stress on the leader.

The essence of the new theory is that stress is the enemy of rationality. It's difficult for leaders (or anyone else, for that matter) to think logically and analytically when they're under stress. Moreover, the importance of a leader's intelligence and experience to his or her effectiveness differs under low- and high-stress situations. Fiedler and Garcia found that a leader's intellectual abilities correlate positively with performance under low stress but negatively under high stress. And, conversely, a leader's experience correlates negatively with performance under low stress but positively under high stress. So, according to Fiedler and Garcia, it's the level of stress in the situation that determines whether an individual's intelligence and experience will contribute to leadership performance.

In spite of its newness, cognitive resource theory is developing a solid body of research support.[31] That is, in high-stress situations, bright individuals perform worse in the leadership role than their less intelligent counterparts. When stress is low, more experienced individuals perform worse than do less experienced people.

Research evidence suggests that the emphasis military units place on leadership training and experienced-based promotions are well founded. Battle conditions are highly stressful. As cognitive resource theory demonstrates, experience (achieved through training and on-the-job practice) is important to success under high-stress conditions.

Hersey and Blanchard's Situational Theory

Paul Hersey and Ken Blanchard have developed a leadership model that has gained a strong following among management development specialists.[32] This model—called **situational leadership theory (SLT)**—has been incorporated into leadership training programs at over 400 of the Fortune 500 companies; and over one million managers a year from a wide variety of organizations are being taught its basic elements.[33]

situational leadership theory (SLT)

A contingency theory that focuses on followers' readiness.

Situational leadership is a contingency theory that focuses on the followers. Successful leadership is achieved by selecting the right leadership style, which Hersey and Blanchard argue is contingent on the level of the followers' readiness. Before we proceed, we should clarify two points: Why focus on the followers? and What do they mean by the term *readiness*?

The emphasis on the followers in leadership effectiveness reflects the reality that it is the followers who accept or reject the leader. Regardless of what the leader does, effectiveness depends on the actions of his or her followers. This is an important dimension that has been overlooked or underemphasized in most leadership theories. The term *readiness*, as defined by Hersey and Blanchard, refers to the extent to which people have the ability and willingness to accomplish a specific task.

SLT essentially views the leader-follower relationship as analogous to that between a parent and a child. Just as a parent needs to relinquish control as a child becomes more mature and responsible, so too should leaders. Hersey and Blanchard identify four specific leader behaviors—from highly directive to highly laissez-faire. The most effective behavior depends on a followers' ability and motivation. So SLT says if a follower is *unable* and *unwilling* to do a task, the leader needs to give clear and specific directions; if followers are *unable* and *willing*, the leader needs to display high task orientation to compensate for the followers' lack of ability and high relationship orientation to get the follower to "buy into" the leader's desires; if followers are *able* and *unwilling*, the leader needs to use a supportive and participative style; and if the employee is both *able* and *willing*, the leader doesn't need to do much.

SLT has an intuitive appeal. It acknowledges the importance of followers and builds on the logic that leaders can compensate for ability and motivational limitations in their followers. Yet research efforts to test and support the theory have generally been disappointing.[34] Why? Possible explanations include internal ambiguities and inconsistencies in the model itself as well as problems with research methodology in tests of the theory. So in spite of its intuitive appeal and wide popularity, at least at this time, any enthusiastic endorsement has to be cautioned against.

Leader-Member Exchange Theory

For the most part, the leadership theories we've covered to this point have largely assumed that leaders treat all their followers in the same manner. That is, they assume leaders use a fairly homogeneous style with all of the people in their work unit. But think about your experiences in groups. Did you notice that leaders often act very differently toward different people? Did the leader tend to have favorites who made up his or her "in-group"? If you answered "Yes" to both these questions, you're acknowledging the foundation of leader-member exchange theory.[35]

David Lein, a manager at Autodesk, considers employee Mary Morse (and her dog) in his in-group. Based on LMX theory, we would predict that his favoritism would lead to higher performance ratings and job satisfaction for Morse.

leader-member exchange (LMX) theory

Leaders create in-groups and out-groups, and subordinates with in-group status will have higher performance ratings, less turnover, and greater job satisfaction.

The **leader-member exchange (LMX) theory** argues that because of time pressures, leaders establish a special relationship with a small group of their followers. These individuals make up the in-group—they are trusted, get a disproportionate amount of the leader's attention, and are more likely to receive special privileges. Other followers fall into the out-group. They get less of the leader's time, fewer of the preferred rewards that the leader controls, and have leader-follower relations based on formal authority interactions.

The theory proposes that early in the history of the interaction between a leader and a given follower, the leader implicitly categorizes the follower as an "in" or an "out" and that relationship is relatively stable over time.[36] Just precisely how the leader chooses who falls into each category is unclear, but there is evidence

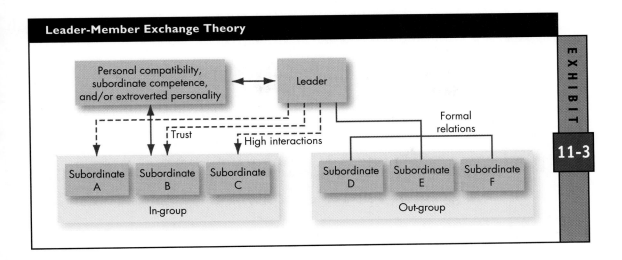

EXHIBIT

11-3

Leader-Member Exchange Theory

Personal compatibility, subordinate competence, and/or extroverted personality

Leader

Formal relations

Trust

High interactions

| Subordinate A | Subordinate B | Subordinate C |

In-group

| Subordinate D | Subordinate E | Subordinate F |

Out-group

that leaders tend to choose in-group members because they have attitude and personality characteristics that are similar to the leader's or a higher level of competence than out-group members[37] (see Exhibit 11-3). A key point to note here is that even though it is the leader who is doing the choosing, it is the follower's characteristics that are driving the leader's categorizing decision.

Research to test LMX theory has been generally supportive. More specifically, the theory and research surrounding it provide substantive evidence that leaders do differentiate among followers; that these disparities are far from random; and that followers with in-group status will have higher performance ratings, lower turnover intentions, greater satisfaction with their superior, and higher overall satisfaction than will the out-group.[38] These positive findings for in-group members shouldn't be totally surprising given our knowledge of the self-fulfilling prophesy (see Chapter 5). Leaders invest their resources with those they expect to perform best. And "knowing" that in-group members are the most competent, leaders treat them as such and unwittingly fulfill their prophecy.[39]

Path-Goal Theory

Currently, one of the most respected approaches to leadership is the path-goal theory. Developed by Robert House, path-goal theory is a contingency model of leadership that extracts key elements from the Ohio State leadership research on initiating structure and consideration and the expectancy theory of motivation.[40]

The essence of the **path-goal theory** is that it's the leader's job to assist followers in attaining their goals and to provide the necessary direction and/or support to ensure that their goals are compatible with the overall objectives of the group or organization. The term *path-goal* is derived from the belief that effective leaders clarify the path to help their followers get from where they are to the achievement of their work goals and to make the journey along the path easier by reducing roadblocks.

House identified four leadership behaviors. The *directive leader* lets followers know what is expected of them, schedules work to be done, and gives specific guidance as to how to accomplish tasks. The *supportive leader* is friendly and shows concern for the needs of followers. The *participative leader* consults with followers and uses their suggestions before making a decision. The *achievement-oriented leader* sets challenging goals and expects followers to perform

path-goal theory

The theory that it is the leader's job to assist followers in attaining their goals and to provide the necessary direction and/or support to ensure that their goals are compatible with the overall objectives of the group or organization.

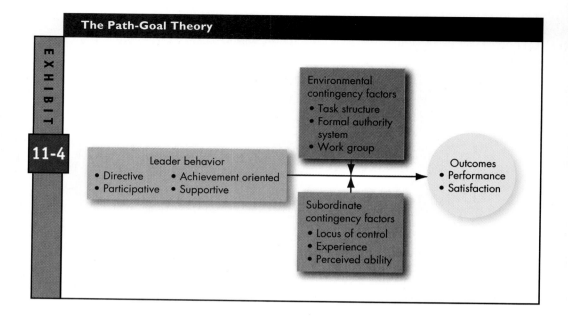

The Path-Goal Theory

EXHIBIT 11-4

Leader behavior
- Directive   • Achievement oriented
- Participative   • Supportive

Environmental contingency factors
- Task structure
- Formal authority system
- Work group

Subordinate contingency factors
- Locus of control
- Experience
- Perceived ability

Outcomes
- Performance
- Satisfaction

at their highest level. In contrast to Fiedler, House assumes leaders are flexible and that the same leader can display any or all of these behaviors depending on the situation.

As Exhibit 11-4 illustrates, path-goal theory proposes two classes of situational or contingency variables that moderate the leadership behavior–outcome relationship—those in the environment that are outside the control of the employee (task structure, the formal authority system, and the work group) and those that are part of the personal characteristics of the employee (locus of control, experience, and perceived ability). Environmental factors determine the type of leader behavior required as a complement if follower outcomes are to be maximized, while personal characteristics of the employee determine how the environment and leader behavior are interpreted. So the theory proposes that leader behavior will be ineffective when it is redundant with sources of environmental structure or incongruent with employee characteristics. For example, the following are illustrations of predictions based on path-goal theory:

- Directive leadership leads to greater satisfaction when tasks are ambiguous or stressful than when they are highly structured and well laid out.
- Supportive leadership results in high employee performance and satisfaction when employees are performing structured tasks.
- Directive leadership is likely to be perceived as redundant among employees with high perceived ability or with considerable experience.
- Employees with an internal locus of control will be more satisfied with a participative style.
- Achievement-oriented leadership will increase employees' expectancies that effort will lead to high performance when tasks are ambiguously structured.

The research evidence generally supports the logic underlying the path-goal theory.[41] That is, employee performance and satisfaction are likely to be positively influenced when the leader compensates for things lacking in either the employee or the work setting. However, the leader who spends time explaining tasks when those tasks are already clear or when the employee has the ability and experience to handle them without interference is likely to be ineffective because the employee will see such directive behavior as redundant or even insulting.

Leader-Participation Model

Victor Vroom and Phillip Yetton developed a **leader-participation model** that related leadership behavior and participation in decision making.[42] Recognizing that task structures have varying demands for routine and nonroutine activities, these researchers argued that leader behavior must adjust to reflect the task structure. Vroom and Yetton's model was normative—it provided a sequential set of rules that should be followed in determining the form and amount of participation in decision making, as determined by different types of situations. The model was a decision tree incorporating seven contingencies (whose relevance could be identified by making "yes" or "no" choices) and five alternative leadership styles.

More recent work by Vroom and Arthur Jago has resulted in a revision of this model.[43]

During the crisis aboard *Apollo 13* that cut short the space craft's mission to the moon and jeopardized its return to Earth, flight director Gene Kranz had to redirect the efforts of everyone in the *Apollo* command center toward a new mission, that of getting the crew home alive. Path-goal theory helps explain how Kranz's clarifying the new goal and supporting the team's efforts to achieve it resulted in the craft's safe return.

The new model retains the same five alternative leadership styles—from the leader's making the decision completely by himself or herself to sharing the problem with the group and developing a consensus decision—but adds a set of problem types and expands the contingency variables to 12. The 12 contingency variables are listed in Exhibit 11-5.

Research testing both the original and revised leader-participation models has been encouraging.[44] Criticism has tended to focus on variables that have been omitted and on the model's overall complexity.[45] Other contingency theories demonstrate that stress, intelligence, and experience are important situational variables. Yet the leader-participation model fails to include them. But more importantly, at least from a practical point of view, is the fact that the model is far too

leader-participation model

A leadership theory that provides a set of rules to determine the form and amount of participative decision making in different situations.

Contingency Variables in the Revised Leader-Participation Model

1. Importance of the decision
2. Importance of obtaining follower commitment to the decision
3. Whether the leader has sufficient information to make a good decision
4. How well structured the problem is
5. Whether an autocratic decision would receive follower commitment
6. Whether followers "buy into" the organization's goals
7. Whether there is likely to be conflict among followers over solution alternatives
8. Whether followers have the necessary information to make a good decision
9. Time constraints on the leader that may limit follower involvement
10. Whether costs to bring geographically dispersed members together is justified
11. Importance to the leader of minimizing the time it takes to make the decision
12. Importance of using participation as a tool for developing follower decision skills

EXHIBIT 11-5

complicated for the typical manager to use on a regular basis. While Vroom and Jago have developed a computer program to guide managers through all the decision branches in the revised model, it's not very realistic to expect practicing managers to consider 12 contingency variables, eight problem types, and five leadership styles in trying to select the appropriate decision process for a specific problem.

We obviously haven't done justice in this discussion to the model's sophistication. So what can you gain from this brief review? Additional insights into relevant contingency variables. Vroom and his associates have provided us with some specific, empirically-supported contingency variables that you should consider when choosing your leadership style.

SUMMARY AND IMPLICATIONS FOR MANAGERS

Leadership plays a central part in understanding group behavior, for it's the leader who usually provides the direction toward goal attainment. Therefore, a more accurate predictive capability should be valuable in improving group performance.

The original search for a set of universal leadership traits failed. At best, we can say that individuals who are ambitious; have high energy, a desire to lead, self-confidence, and intelligence; hold job-relevant knowledge; are perceived as honest and trustworthy; and are flexible are more likely to succeed as leaders than individuals without these traits.

The behavioral approach's major contribution was narrowing leadership into task-oriented and people-oriented styles. But no one style was found to be effective in all situations.

A major breakthrough in our understanding of leadership came when we recognized the need to develop contingency theories that included situational factors. At present, the evidence indicates that relevant situational variables would include the task structure of the job; level of situational stress; level of group support; the leader's intelligence and experience; and follower characteristics such as personality, experience, ability, and motivation.

The Perils of Leadership Training

Organizations spend billions of dollars on leadership training every year. They send managers and manager-wannabes to a wide range of leadership training activities—formal MBA programs, leadership seminars, weekend retreats, and even outward-bound adventures. They appoint mentors. They establish "fast tracks" for high-potential individuals in order for them to gain a variety of the "right kinds of experience." We propose that much of this effort to train leaders is probably a waste of money. And we base our position by looking at two very basic assumptions that underlie leadership training.[a]

The first assumption is that we know what leadership is. We don't. Experts can't agree if it's a trait, a characteristic, a behavior, a role, a style, or an ability. They further can't even agree on whether leaders really make a difference in organizational outcomes. Some experts have persuasively argued that leadership is merely an attribution made to explain organizational successes and failures, which themselves occur by chance. Leaders are the people who get credit for successes and take the blame for failures, but they may actually have little influence over organizational outcomes.

The second basic assumption is that we can train people to lead. The evidence here is not very encouraging. We do seem to be able to teach individuals *about leadership*. Unfortunately, findings indicate we aren't so good at teaching people *to lead*. There are several possible explanations. To the degree that personality is a critical element in leadership effectiveness, some people may not have been born with the right personality traits.[b] A second explanation is that there is no evidence that individuals can substantially alter their basic leadership style.[c] A third possibility is that, even if certain theories could actually guide individuals in leadership situations and even if individuals could alter their style, the complexity of those theories make it nearly impossible for any normal human being to assimilate all the variables and be capable of enacting the right behaviors in every situation.

Leadership training exists, and is a multi-billion-dollar industry, because it works. Decision makers are, for the most part, rational. Would a company like General Electric spend literally tens-of-millions of dollars each year on leadership training if it didn't expect a handsome return? We don't think so! And the ability to lead successfully is why corporations like Disney willingly pay a Michael Eisner $100 million a year or more. By his ability to lead, Eisner has increased the value of Disney stock by 30-fold.

While there are certainly disagreements over the exact definition of leadership, most academics and business people agree that leadership is an influence process whereby an individual, by his or her actions, facilitates the movement of a group of people toward the achievement of a common goal.

Do leaders affect organizational outcomes? Of course they do. Successful leaders anticipate change, vigorously exploit opportunities, motivate their followers to higher levels of productivity, correct poor performance, and lead the organization toward its objectives. A review of the leadership literature, in fact, led two academics to conclude that the research shows "a consistent effect for leadership explaining 20 to 45 percent of the variance on relevant organizational outcomes."[d]

What about the effectiveness of leadership programs? They vary. And well they should since the programs themselves are so diverse. Moreover, people learn in different ways. Since some leadership programs are better than others and because some people participate in programs that are poorly matched to their needs and learning style, we should expect leadership-training effectiveness to have a spotty record. So decision makers need to be careful in choosing leadership-training experiences for their managers. But they shouldn't conclude that all leadership training is a waste of money.

[a]See R. A. Barker, "How Can We Train Leaders If We Do Not Know What Leadership Is?" *Human Relations*, April 1997, pp. 343–62.

[b]N. Nicholson, *Executive Instinct* (New York: Crown, 2001).

[c]R. J. House and R. N. Aditya, "The Social Scientific Study of Leadership: Quo Vadis?" *Journal of Management*, vol. 23, no. 3, 1997, pp. 460–61.

[d]D. V. Day and R. G. Lord, "Executive Leadership and Organizational Performance: Suggestions for a New Theory and Methodology," *Journal of Management*, Fall 1988, pp. 453–64.

Questions for Review

1. Trace the development of leadership research.

2. Describe the strengths and weaknesses in the trait approach to leadership.

3. What is *initiating structure*? *Consideration*?

4. What is the managerial grid? Contrast its approach to leadership with the approaches of the Ohio State and Michigan groups.

5. What was the contribution of the Scandinavian studies to the behavioral theories?

6. What are Fiedler's three contingency variables?

7. What contribution does cognitive resource theory make to leadership?

8. What are its implications of LMX theory for leadership practice?

9. What are the contingency variables in the path-goal theory?

10. What are the implications if leaders are inflexible in adjusting their style?

Questions for Critical Thinking

1. Review trait theories in the context of the "nature versus nurture" debate.

2. If you were a manager, how would you assess a situation in terms of Fiedler's three contingency variables?

3. Develop an example in which you operationalize the Fiedler model.

4. Develop an example in which you operationalize the path-goal theory.

5. Develop an example in which you operationalize SLT.

Team Exercise   Debate: Do Leaders Really Matter?

Break the class into groups of two. One group member will argue "Leaders are the primary determinant of an organization's success or failure." The other group member will argue "Leaders don't really matter because most of the things that affect an organization's success or failure are outside a leader's control." Take 10 minutes to develop your arguments; then you have 10 minutes to conduct your debate.

After the dyad debates, form into teams of six. Three from each of these groups should have taken the "pro" argument on leadership and three should have taken the "con" side. The teams have 15 minutes to reconcile their arguments and to develop a unified position. When the 15 minutes are up, each team should be prepared to make a brief presentation to the class, summarizing their unified position.

Case Incident   Can a Leader's Means Justify the Ends?

By any objective measure, Jack Welch's 20-year reign as CEO of General Electric would have to be called an overwhelming success. When Welch took over the head job at GE, the company had a market value of $13 billion. When he retired in 2001, the company was worth $400 billion. Its profits in 2000 of $12.7 billion were more than eight times the $1.5 billion it earned in 1980. And Welch's performance paid off for stockholders. Including dividends, the value of GE shares rose an average of 21.3 percent a year since he took over. This compared with about 14.3 percent for the S&P 500 during the same period.

How did Welch achieve such success? On a strategic level, he redefined GE's objectives for every business in which it operated. He said GE would either be No. 1 or No. 2 in all businesses or get out of them. He dropped those with low growth prospects, like small appliances and TVs, while expanding fast-growth businesses such as financial services and broadcasting. During his tenure as CEO, Welch oversaw 933 acquisitions and the sale of 408 businesses. He was obsessed with improving efficiency, cutting costs, and improving performance. To achieve these ends, Welch completely remolded GE in his style—impatient, aggressive, and competitive.

In the 1980s, as Welch began his remaking of GE, he picked up the nickname of "Neutron Jack." A play off of the neutron bomb—that kills people but leaves buildings standing—Welch cut more than 100,000 jobs—a fourth of GE's workforce—through mass layoffs, divestitures, forced retirements, and relocating U.S. jobs to overseas locations with cheaper labor. He pressured his managers and the employees who remained to drive themselves to meet ever-more-demanding efficiency standards. And he was blatantly impatient when things didn't move very rapidly. For instance, a former technical worker at a GE plant that makes industrial drives says his unit set aggressive goals every year. "We would meet and beat those goals, but it was never good enough. It was always, 'We could have done more.' We felt the philosophy at General Electric was that they could replace us in a heartbeat." To reinforce the competitive environment, Welch established a comprehensive performance evaluation and ranking system for managers. Outstanding managers were highly rewarded while those at the bottom of the annual rankings were routinely fired.

Welch's demanding goals and penchant for closing down poor-performing units upended the lives of thousands of employees and severely strained the bonds between the company and many of the communities in which it operated. There were also a number of scandals that surfaced under Welch's watch at GE. These ranged from the company's 1985 admission that it had submitted time cards for too much overtime on government contracts to the 1994 bond-trading scandal at its former Kidder Peabody & Co. investment-banking unit.

Welch's style was a blend of restlessness, bluntness, sarcasm, emotional volatility, and teasing humor. As one former GE vice chairman said about Welch, "even when he has fun, he's driving himself. He won't give up till he has won, whatever he does." Welch regularly put in days of 12 hours or more but he expected the same kind of dedication from his employees. And when he got angry, he could lash out with personal attacks that sometimes left shamed managers hurt and speechless.

Questions

1. Describe Welch's leadership style using (a) the Ohio State dimensions, (b) the managerial grid, and (c) LMX theory.

2. Assess Welch's leadership effectiveness as assessed by (a) stockholders, (b) GE managers, (c) GE employees, and (d) communities where GE operations are located.

3. Would you describe Jack Welch as a successful leader at GE? Explain.

4. How would you rate the ethics of Welch's leadership?

5. Would you have wanted to work for Jack Welch? Why or why not?

Based on M. Murray, "Why Jack Welch's Brand of Leadership Matters," *Wall Street Journal*, September 5, 2001, p. B1.

KSS PROGRAM

KNOW THE CONCEPTS
SELF-AWARENESS
SKILLS APPLICATIONS

Choosing the Right Leadership Style

After you've read this chapter, take Self-Assessment #27 (What's My Leadership Style?) on your enclosed CD-ROM, and complete the skill-building module entitled Choosing an Effective Leadership Style on page 622.

ENDNOTES

1. Based on K. Brooker, "It Took a Lady to Save Avon," *Fortune*, October 15, 2001, pp. 203–08.

2. J. P. Kotter, "What Leaders Really Do," *Harvard Business Review*, May–June 1990, pp. 103–11; and J. P. Kotter, *A Force for Change: How Leadership Differs from Management* (New York: Free Press, 1990).

3. R. J. House and R. N. Aditya, "The Social Scientific Study of Leadership: Quo Vadis?" *Journal of Management*, vol. 23, no. 3, 1997, p. 445.

4. See, for instance, W. B. Snavely, "Organizational Leadership: An Alternative View and Implications for Managerial Education," paper presented at the Midwest Academy of Management Conference; Toledo, OH; April 2001.

5. J. G. Geier, "A Trait Approach to the Study of Leadership in Small Groups," *Journal of Communication*, December 1967, pp. 316–23.

6. S. A. Kirkpatrick and E. A. Locke, "Leadership: Do Traits Matter?" *Academy of Management Executive*, May 1991, pp. 48–60.

7. G. H. Dobbins. W. S. Long, E. J. Dedrick, and T. C. Clemons, "The Role of Self-Monitoring and Gender on Leader Emergence: A Laboratory and Field Study," *Journal of Management*, September 1990, pp. 609–18; and S. J. Zaccaro,

R. J. Foti, and D. A. Kenny, "Self-Monitoring and Trait-Based Variance in Leadership: An Investigation of Leader Flexibility across Multiple Group Situations," *Journal of Applied Psychology*, April 1991, pp. 308–15.

8. G. Yukl and D. D. Van Fleet, "Theory and Research on Leadership in Organizations," in M. D. Dunnette and L. M. Hough (eds.), *Handbook of Industrial & Organizational Psychology*, 2nd ed., vol. 3 (Palo Alto, CA: Consulting Psychologists Press, 1992), p. 150.

9. B. Schneider, "Interactional Psychology and Organizational Behavior," in L. L. Cummings and B. M. Staw (eds.), *Research in Organizational Behavior*, vol. 5 (Greenwich, CT: JAI Press, 1983), pp. 1–31.

10. See W. Mischel, "Toward a Cognitive Social Learning Reconceptualization of Personality," *Psychological Review*, July 1973, pp. 252–83; and M. R. Barrick and M. K. Mount, "Autonomy as a Moderator of the Relationship between the Big Five Personality Dimensions and Job Performance," *Journal of Applied Psychology*, February 1993, pp. 111–18.

11. R. G. Lord, C. L. DeVader, and G. M. Alliger, "A Meta-Analysis of the Relation between Personality Traits and Leadership Perceptions: An Application of Validity Generalization Procedures," *Journal of Applied Psychology*, August 1986, pp. 402–10; and J. A. Smith and R. J. Foti, "A Pattern Approach to the Study of Leader Emergence," *Leadership Quarterly*, Summer 1998, pp. 147–60.

12. See C. Palmeri, "The Grizz Gets Grizzly," *Forbes*, November 16, 1998, p. 196; and M. Warner, "Confessions of a Control Freak," *Fortune*, September 4, 2000, pp. 130–40.

13. R. M. Stogdill and A. E. Coons (eds.), *Leader Behavior: Its Description and Measurement*, Research Monograph no. 88 (Columbus: Ohio State University, Bureau of Business Research, 1951). This research is updated in C. A. Schriesheim, C. C. Cogliser, and L. L. Neider, "Is It 'Trustworthy'? A Multiple-Levels-of-Analysis Reexamination of an Ohio State Leadership Study, with Implications for Future Research," *Leadership Quarterly*, Summer 1995, pp. 111–45.

14. H. Yen, "Richard Parsons, AOL Time Warner's New CEO, Known as Consensus-Builder," www.tbo.com, December 6, 2001.

15. R. Kahn and D. Katz, "Leadership Practices in Relation to Productivity and Morale," D. Cartwright and A. Zander (eds.), *Group Dynamics: Research and Theory*, 2nd ed. (Elmsford, NY: Row, Paterson, 1960).

16. R. R. Blake and J. S. Mouton, *The Managerial Grid* (Houston: Gulf, 1964).

17. See, for example, R. R. Blake and J. S. Mouton, "A Comparative Analysis of Situationalism and 9,9 Management by Principle," *Organizational Dynamics*, Spring 1982, pp. 20–43.

18. See, for example, L. L. Larson, J. G. Hunt, and R. N. Osborn, "The Great Hi-Hi Leader Behavior Myth: A Lesson from Occam's Razor," *Academy of Management Journal*, December 1976, pp. 628–41; and P. C. Nystrom, "Managers and the Hi-Hi Leader Myth," *Academy of Management Journal*, June 1978, pp. 325–31.

19. See G. Ekvall and J. Arvonen, "Change-Centered Leadership: An Extension of the Two-Dimensional Model," *Scandinavian Journal of Management*, vol. 7, no. 1, 1991, pp. 17–26; M. Lindell and G. Rosenqvist, "Is There a Third Management Style?" *The Finnish Journal of Business Economics*, vol. 3, 1992, pp. 171–98; and M. Lindell and G. Rosen-

qvist, "Management Behavior Dimensions and Development Orientation," *Leadership Quarterly*, Winter 1992, pp. 355–77.

20. M. McDonald, "Lingerie's Iron Maiden Is Undone," *U.S. News & World Report*, June 25, 2001, p. 37; and A. D'Innocenzio, "Wachner Ousted as CEO, Chairman at Warnaco," *The Detroit News*, November 17, 2001, p. D1.

21. F. E. Fiedler, *A Theory of Leadership Effectiveness* (New York: McGraw-Hill, 1967).

22. S. Shiflett, "Is There a Problem with the LPC Score in LEADER MATCH?" *Personnel Psychology*, Winter 1981, pp. 765–69.

23. F. E. Fiedler, M. M. Chemers, and L. Mahar, *Improving Leadership Effectiveness: The Leader Match Concept* (New York: John Wiley, 1977).

24. Cited in R. J. House and R. N. Aditya, "The Social Scientific Study of Leadership," p. 422.

25. L. H. Peters, D. D. Hartke, and J. T. Pohlmann, "Fiedler's Contingency Theory of Leadership: An Application of the Meta-Analysis Procedures of Schmidt and Hunter," *Psychological Bulletin*, March 1985, pp. 274–85; C. A. Schriesheim, B. J. Tepper, and L. A. Tetrault, "Least Preferred Co-Worker Score, Situational Control, and Leadership Effectiveness: A Meta-Analysis of Contingency Model Performance Predictions," *Journal of Applied Psychology*, August 1994, pp. 561–73; and R. Ayman, M. M. Chemers, and F. Fiedler, "The Contingency Model of Leadership Effectiveness: Its Levels of Analysis," *Leadership Quarterly*, Summer 1995, pp. 147–67.

26. F. E. Fiedler, "Leadership Experience and Leadership Performance: Another Hypothesis Shot to Hell," *Organizational Behavior and Human Performance*, January 1970, pp. 1–14; F. E. Fiedler, "Time-Based Measures of Leadership Experience and Organizational Performance: A Review of Research and a Preliminary Model," *Leadership Quarterly*, Spring 1992, pp. 5–23; and M. A. Quinones, J. K. Ford, and M. S. Teachout, "The Relationship between Work Experience and Job Performance: A Conceptual and Meta-Analytic Review," *Personnel Psychology*, Winter 1995, pp. 887–910.

27. R. J. House and R. N. Aditya, "The Social Scientific Study of Leadership," p. 422.

28. See, for instance, R. W. Rice, "Psychometric Properties of the Esteem for the Least Preferred Coworker (LPC) Scale," *Academy of Management Review*, January 1978, pp. 106–18; C. A. Schriesheim, B. D. Bannister, and W. H. Money, "Psychometric Properties of the LPC Scale: An Extension of Rice's Review," *Academy of Management Review*, April 1979, pp. 287–90; and J. K. Kennedy, J. M. Houston, M. A. Korgaard, and D. D. Gallo, "Construct Space of the Least Preferred Co-Worker (LPC) Scale," *Educational & Psychological Measurement*, Fall 1987, pp. 807–14.

29. See E. H. Schein, *Organizational Psychology*, 3rd ed. (Upper Saddle River, NJ: Prentice Hall, 1980), pp. 116–17; and B. Kabanoff, "A Critique of Leader Match and Its Implications for Leadership Research," *Personnel Psychology*, Winter 1981, pp. 749–64.

30. F. E. Fiedler and J. E. Garcia, *New Approaches to Effective Leadership: Cognitive Resources and Organizational Performance* (New York: Wiley, 1987).

31. See F. W. Gibson, F. E. Fiedler, and K. M. Barrett, "Stress, Babble, and the Utilization of the Leader's Intellectual Abilities," *Leadership Quarterly*, Summer 1993, pp. 189–208; F. E. Fiedler, "Cognitive Resources and Leadership Performance," *Applied*

Psychology—An International Review, January 1995, pp. 5–28; and F. E. Fiedler, "The Curious Role of Cognitive Resources in Leadership," in R. E. Riggio, S. E. Murphy, and F. J. Pirozzolo (eds.), *Multiple Intelligences and Leadership* (Mahwah, NJ: Lawrence Erlbaum, 2002), pp. 91–104.

32. P. Hersey and K. H. Blanchard, "So You Want to Know Your Leadership Style?" *Training and Development Journal*, February 1974, pp. 1–15; and P. Hersey, K. H. Blanchard, and D. E. Johnson, *Management of Organizational Behavior: Leading Human Resources*, 8th ed. (Upper Saddle River, NJ: Prentice Hall, 2001).

33. Cited in C. F. Fernandez and R. P. Vecchio, "Situational Leadership Theory Revisited: A Test of an Across-Jobs Perspective," *Leadership Quarterly*, vol. 8, no. 1, 1997, p. 67.

34. See, for instance, *Ibid.*, pp. 67–84; and C. L. Graeff, "Evolution of Situational Leadership Theory: A Critical Review," *Leadership Quarterly*, vol. 8, no. 2, 1997, pp. 153–70.

35. R. M. Dienesch and R. C. Liden, "Leader-Member Exchange Model of Leadership: A Critique and Further Development," *Academy of Management Review*, July 1986, pp. 618–34; G. B. Graen and M. Uhl-Bien, "Relationship-Based Approach to Leadership: Development of Leader-Member Exchange (LMX) Theory of Leadership Over 25 Years: Applying a Multi-Domain Perspective," *Leadership Quarterly*, Summer 1995, pp. 219–47; R. C. Liden, R. T. Sparrowe, and S. J. Wayne, "Leader-Member Exchange Theory: The Past and Potential for the Future," in G. R. Ferris (ed.), *Research in Personnel and Human Resource Management*, vol. 15 (Greenwich, CT: JAI Press, 1997), pp. 47–119; and C. A. Schriesheim, S. L. Castro, X. Zhou, and F. J. Yammarino, "The Folly of Theorizing 'A' but Testing 'B': A Selective Level-of-Analysis Review of the Field and a Detailed Leader-Member Exchange Illustration," *Leadership Quarterly*, Winter 2001, pp. 515–51.

36. R. Liden and G. Graen, "Generalizability of the Vertical Dyad Linkage Model of Leadership," *Academy of Management Journal*, September 1980, pp. 451–65; and R. C. Liden, S. J. Wayne, and D. Stilwell, "A Longitudinal Study of the Early Development of Leader-Member Exchanges," *Journal of Applied Psychology*, August 1993, pp. 662–74.

37. D. Duchon, S. G. Green, and T. D. Taber, "Vertical Dyad Linkage: A Longitudinal Assessment of Antecedents, Measures, and Consequences," *Journal of Applied Psychology*, February 1986, pp. 56–60; R. C. Liden, S. J. Wayne, and D. Stilwell, "A Longitudinal Study on the Early Development of Leader-Member Exchanges"; R. J. Deluga and J. T. Perry, "The Role of Subordinate Performance and Ingratiation in Leader–Member Exchanges," *Group & Organization Management*, March 1994, pp. 67–86; T. N. Bauer and S. G. Green, "Development of Leader-Member Exchange: A Longitudinal Test," *Academy of Management Journal*, December 1996, pp. 1538–67; and S. J. Wayne, L. M. Shore, and R. C. Liden, "Perceived Organizational Support and Leader-Member Exchange: A Social Exchange Perspective," *Academy of Management Journal*, February 1997, pp. 82–111.

38. See, for instance, C. R. Gerstner and D. V. Day, "Meta-Analytic Review of Leader-Member Exchange Theory: Correlates and Construct Issues," *Journal of Applied Psychology*, December 1997, pp. 827–44; C. Gomez and B. Rosen, "The Leader-Member Exchange as a Link Between Managerial Trust and Employee Empowerment," *Group & Organization Management*, March 2001, pp. 53–69; and J. M. Maslyn and M. Uhl-Bien, "Leader-Member Exchange and Its Dimensions: Effects of Self-Effort and Other's Effort on Relationship Quality," *Journal of Applied Psychology*, August 2001, pp. 697–708.

39. D. Eden, "Leadership and Expectations: Pygmalion Effects and Other Self-Fulfilling Prophecies in Organizations," *Leadership Quarterly*, Winter 1992, pp. 278–79.

40. R. J. House, "A Path-Goal Theory of Leader Effectiveness," *Administrative Science Quarterly*, September 1971, pp. 321–38; R. J. House and T. R. Mitchell, "Path-Goal Theory of Leadership," *Journal of Contemporary Business*, Autumn 1974, pp. 81–97; and R. J. House, "Path-Goal Theory of Leadership: Lessons, Legacy, and a Reformulated Theory," *Leadership Quarterly*, Fall 1996, pp. 323–52.

41. J. C. Wofford and L. Z. Liska, "Path-Goal Theories of Leadership: A Meta-Analysis," *Journal of Management*, Winter 1993, pp. 857–76.

42. V. H. Vroom and P. W. Yetton, *Leadership and Decision-Making* (Pittsburgh: University of Pittsburgh Press, 1973).

43. V. H. Vroom and A. G. Jago, *The New Leadership: Managing Participation in Organizations* (Englewood Cliffs, NJ: Prentice Hall, 1988). See also V. H. Vroom and A. G. Jago, "Situation Effects and Levels of Analysis in the Study of Leader Participation," *Leadership Quarterly*, Summer 1995, pp. 169–81.

44. See, for example, R. H. G. Field, "A Test of the Vroom-Yetton Normative Model of Leadership," *Journal of Applied Psychology*, October 1982, pp. 523–32; C. R. Leana, "Power Relinquishment versus Power Sharing: Theoretical Clarification and Empirical Comparison of Delegation and Participation," *Journal of Applied Psychology*, May 1987, pp. 228–33; J. T. Ettling and A. G. Jago, "Participation Under Conditions of Conflict: More on the Validity of the Vroom-Yetton Model," *Journal of Management Studies*, January 1988, pp. 73–83; and R. H. G. Field and R. J. House, "A Test of the Vroom-Yetton Model Using Manager and Subordinate Reports," *Journal of Applied Psychology*, June 1990, pp. 362–66.

45. R. J. House and R. N. Aditya, "The Social Scientific Study of Leadership," p. 428.

PART THREE

THE GROUP

R udolph W. Giuliani (see photo) was elected mayor of New York City in 1993 on a law-and-order platform. And he did successfully bring law and order to the city. For instance, by the end of his second term, in 2001, he had overseen a 57 percent decline in felony crimes and a 68 percent reduction in the city's murder rate. In a city that many said was ungovernable, Giuliani had turned around New York's fortunes. He boosted property values, redeveloped large parts of Manhattan, brought tourists back, and restored the city's spirit. But he stepped on a lot of toes in the process. His arrogant, self-serving, and combative style rubbed a lot of people the wrong way. He became known more for his uncontrollable temper and vindictiveness than for his success in improving life in New York City. However, any negative perceptions of Giuliani essentially disappeared on September 11, 2001.[1]

On September 11th, the worst crime ever committed on American soil took place in New York City—terrorists flew two hijacked commercial jets into the World Trade Center, killing almost 3,000 people. As shock and then fear gripped the nation, Rudy Giuliani stepped up and led the city and nation through the crisis. Within minutes after the first plane hit, Giuliani was on the scene directing operations. Without regard for his own safety, he established a makeshift command center and a temporary morgue, found a million pairs of gloves and dust masks and respirators, threw up protections against another attack, and tamed the mobs that wanted vengeance. One of the public's strongest memories of that first day was of Guiliani, on the streets of New York, trying to give the public reassurance with his hair and suit still covered in the silt from the falling buildings.

In the weeks that followed, Giuliani provided the leadership that the public so craved. Day after day, his mastery of the details of rescue and recovery plus his calm explanations of awful news helped to reassure a traumatized city that the crisis was under control. He found just the right balance between being a hardnosed administrator and a caring and emo-

Contemporary Issues in Leadership

tional leader. He consoled widows, widowers, and survivors; he attended close to 200 funerals, wakes, and memorial services; he revisited the attack site to mingle with rescue workers; he urged residents to dine out; and he reached out to tourists to come back to the city. In addition to the decisiveness and honesty he had always displayed, he now showed traits that the public had rarely seen in him before—compassion, fearlessness, calmness, and openness. He put in 20-hour days and showed an uncanny ability to be consistently visible. Maybe most importantly, Giuliani was able to find the words and tap into emotions to help people better cope with the tragedy. He conveyed optimism and created, as one writer put it, "an illusion that we were bound to win." For instance, on that first day following the attack, he said, "Tomorrow New York is going to be here. And we're going to rebuild, and we're going to be stronger than we were before . . . I want the people of New York to be an example to the rest of the country, and the rest of the world, that terrorism can't stop us." Within days, Guiliani almost unilaterally managed to create the sense that New York City was getting back to normalcy.

Time magazine may have summarized Giuliani's leadership role best when, in naming him its 2001 Person of the Year, said: ". . . for having more faith in us than we had in ourselves, for being brave when required and rude where appropriate and tender without being trite, for not sleeping and not quitting and not shrinking from the pain all around him."

Former Mayor Guiliani is a 21st century leader. He called upon his experience, charisma, and ability to create meaning out of tragedy and to help a city and nation recover. In this chapter, we address contemporary leadership topics such as charisma and the ability to create meaning in new or difficult situations. We'll

LEARNING OBJECTIVES

AFTER STUDYING THIS CHAPTER, YOU SHOULD BE ABLE TO:

1. Identify the five dimensions of trust.

2. Define the qualities of a charismatic leader.

3. Contrast transformational with transactional leadership.

4. Identify the skills that visionary leaders exhibit.

5. Explain how framing influences leadership effectiveness.

6. Identify the four roles that team leaders perform.

7. Explain the role of a mentor.

8. Describe how on-line leadership differs from face-to-face leadership.

9. Identify when leadership may not be necessary.

10. Explain how to find and create effective leaders.

also discuss emotional intelligence and leadership effectiveness, contemporary leadership roles, moral leadership, and challenges to the leadership construct. First, however, we turn our attention to the topic of trust. We begin here because recent evidence indicates that trust is the foundation of leadership. Unless followers trust their leaders, they'll be unresponsive to a "leader's" influence efforts.

TRUST: THE FOUNDATION OF LEADERSHIP

Trust, or lack of trust, is an increasingly important leadership issue in today's organizations. In this section, we define *trust* and provide you with some guidelines for helping build credibility and trust.

What Is Trust?

trust

A positive expectation that another will not act opportunistically.

Trust is a positive expectation that another will not—through words, actions, or decisions—act opportunistically.[2] The two most important elements of our definition are that it implies familiarity and risk.

The phrase *positive expectation* in our definition assumes knowledge and familiarity about the other party. Trust is a history-dependent process based on relevant but limited samples of experience.[3] It takes time to form, building incrementally and accumulating. Most of us find it hard, if not impossible, to trust someone immediately if we don't know anything about them. At the extreme, in the case of total ignorance, we can gamble but we can't trust.[4] But as we get to know someone, and the relationship matures, we gain confidence in our ability to make a positive expectation.

The term *opportunistically* refers to the inherent risk and vulnerability in any trusting relationship. Trust involves making oneself vulnerable as when, for example, we disclose intimate information or rely on another's promises.[5] By its very nature, trust provides the opportunity for disappointment or to be taken advantage of.[6] But trust is not taking risk per se; rather it is a *willingness* to take risk.[7] So when I trust someone, I expect that they will not take advantage of me. This willingness to take risks is common to all trust situations.[8]

What are the key dimensions that underlie the concept of trust? Recent evidence has identified five: integrity, competence, consistency, loyalty, and openness[9] (see Exhibit 12-1).

Integrity refers to honesty and truthfulness. Of all five dimensions, this one seems to be most critical when someone assesses another's trustworthiness.[10] "Without a perception of the other's 'moral character' and 'basic honesty,' other dimensions of trust [are] meaningless."[11]

Competence encompasses an individual's technical and interpersonal knowledge and skills. Does the person know what he or she is talking about? You're unlikely to listen to or depend upon someone whose abilities you don't respect. You need to believe that the person has the skills and abilities to carry out what he or she says they will do.

Consistency relates to an individual's reliability, predictability, and good judgment in handling situations. "Inconsistencies between words and action decrease trust."[12] This dimension is particularly relevant for managers. "Nothing is noticed more quickly . . . than a discrepancy between what executives preach and what they expect their associates to practice."[13]

Loyalty is the willingness to protect and save face for another person. Trust requires that you can depend on someone not to act opportunistically.

The final dimension of trust is *openness*. Can you rely on the person to give you the full truth?

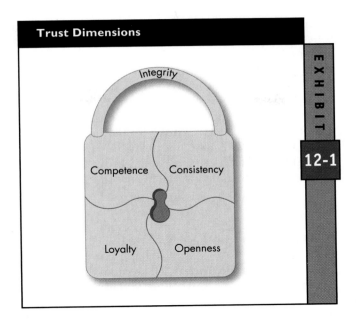

Trust Dimensions

EXHIBIT

12-1

Integrity

Competence   Consistency

Loyalty   Openness

Trust and Leadership

Morale has plummeted at Chrysler's suburban Detroit headquarters. And it's largely due to comments by DaimlerChrysler Chairman Jurgen Schrempp.[14] When Daimler-Benz and Chrysler merged, Schrempp called it "a merger of equals." But in the fall of 2000, he admitted he lied. Schrempp now says he never really intended for the combined companies to be equals. If he had been honest, he says, there would have been no deal and he couldn't have made Chrysler into just another Daimler operating unit. With these words, Schrempp has decimated any trust that he may have had with his Chrysler employees.

As the DaimlerChrysler example illustrates, trust is a primary attribute associated with leadership; and when this trust is broken, it can have serious adverse effects on a group's performance.[15] Per our discussion of traits in Chapter 11, honesty and integrity were among the six traits found to be consistently associated with leadership. It appears increasingly evident that it's impossible to lead people who don't trust you.

As one author noted: "Part of the leader's task has been, and continues to be, working with people to find and solve problems, but whether leaders gain access to the knowledge and creative thinking they need to solve problems depends on how much people trust them. Trust and trust-worthiness modulate the leader's access to knowledge and cooperation."[16]

When followers trust a leader, they are willing to be vulnerable to the leader's actions—confident that their rights and interests will not be abused.[17] People are unlikely to look up to or follow someone whom they perceive as dishonest or who is likely to take advantage of them. Honesty, for instance, consistently ranks at the top of most people's list of characteristics they admire in their leaders. "Honesty is absolutely essential to leadership. If people are going to follow someone willingly, whether it be into battle or into the boardroom, they first want to assure themselves that the person is worthy of their trust."[18]

Now, more than ever, managerial and leadership effectiveness depends on the ability to gain the trust of followers.[19] For instance, reengineering, downsizing, and the increased use of temporary employees have undermined a lot of employees' trust in management. A recent nationwide survey of U.S. employees found that only half trusted their senior managers.[20] In times of change and instability, people turn to personal relationships for guidance; and the quality of these relationships are largely determined by level of trust. Additionally, contemporary management practices such as empowerment and the use of work teams require trust to be effective. Finally, of course, has been the unprecedented revelations beginning in fall 2001 of misdeeds by senior managers in many of America's largest corporations. Leaders at Enron, Adelphia Communications, WorldCom, Dynergy, Martha Stewart, Living Omnimedia, ImClone Systems, and Tyco International were accused of engaging in an assortment of activities—from secret loans to insider trading to manipulating profit figures to evading taxes—that has shook the confidence of employees as well as investors, suppliers, and customers in the trustworthiness of these firms' senior executives.

Three Types of Trust

There are three types of trust in organizational relationships: *deterrence*-based, *knowledge*-based, and *identification*-based.[21]

deterrence-based trust

Trust based on fear of reprisal if the trust is violated.

Deterrence-Based Trust The most fragile relationships are contained in **deterrence-based trust**. One violation or inconsistency can destroy the relationship. This form of trust is based on fear of reprisal if the trust is violated. Individuals who are in this type of relationship do what they say because they fear the consequences from not following through on their obligations.

Deterrence-based trust will work only to the degree that punishment is possible, consequences are clear, and the punishment is actually imposed if the trust is violated. To be sustained, the potential loss of future interaction with the other party must outweigh the profit potential that comes from violating expectations. Moreover, the potentially harmed party must be willing to introduce harm (for example, I have no qualms about speaking badly of you if you betray my trust) to the person acting distrustingly.

Most new relationships begin on a base of deterrence. Take, as an illustration, a situation where you're selling your car to a friend of a friend. You don't know the buyer. You might be motivated to refrain from telling this buyer all the problems with the car that you know about. Such behavior would increase your chances of selling the car and securing the highest price. But you don't withhold information. You openly share the car's flaws. Why? Probably because of fear of reprisal. If the buyer later thinks you deceived him, he is likely to share this with your mutual friend. If you knew that the buyer would never say anything to the mutual friend, you might be tempted to take advantage of the opportunity. If it's clear that the buyer would tell and that your mutual friend would think considerably less of you for taking advantage of this buyer-friend, your honesty could be explained in deterrence terms.

Another example of deterrence-based trust is a new manager-employee relationship. As an employee, you typically trust a new boss even though there is little experience to base that trust on. The bond that creates this trust lies in the authority held by the boss and the punishment he or she can impose if you fail to fulfill your job-related obligations.

knowledge-based trust

Trust based on behavioral predictability that comes from a history of interaction.

Knowledge-Based Trust Most organizational relationships are rooted in **knowledge-based trust**. That is, trust is based on the behavioral predictability that comes from a history of interaction. It exists when you have adequate information about someone to understand them well enough to be able to accurately predict their behavior.

Knowledge-based trust relies on information rather than deterrence. Knowledge of the other party and predictability of his or her behavior replaces the contracts, penalties, and legal arrangements more typical of deterrence-based trust. This knowledge develops over time, largely as a function of experience that builds confidence of trustworthiness and predictability. The better you know someone, the more accurately you can predict what he or she will do. Predictability enhances trust—even if the other is predictably untrustworthy—because the ways that the other will violate the trust can be predicted! The more communication and regular interaction you have with someone else, the more this form of trust can be developed and depended upon.

Interestingly, at the knowledge-based level, trust is not necessarily broken by inconsistent behavior. If you believe you can adequately explain or understand another's apparent violation, you can accept it, forgive the person, and move on in the relationship. However, the same inconsistency at the deterrence level is likely to irrevocably break the trust.

In an organizational context, most manager-employee relationships are knowledge-based. Both parties have enough experience working with each other that they know what to expect. A long history of consistently open and honest interactions, for instance, is not likely to be permanently destroyed by a single violation.

One way to build knowledge-based trust is to keep the lines of communication open. Eze Castle Software goes one step further. Every day CEO Sean McLaughlin (far right) gathers all 90 employees together in the kitchen for an informal cookie break at which people discuss everything from work to social life to politics. McLaughlin sees the break as a way to keep the closeness and familiarity employees shared when the firm was small.

Identification-Based Trust The highest level of trust is achieved when there is an emotional connection between the parties. It allows one party to act as an agent for the other and substitute for that person in interpersonal transactions. This is called **identification-based trust**. Trust exists because the parties understand each other's intentions and appreciate the other's wants and desires. This mutual understanding is developed to the point that each can effectively act for the other.

Controls are minimal at this level. You don't need to monitor the other party because there exists unquestioned loyalty.

The best example of identification-based trust is a long-term, happily married couple. A husband comes to learn what's important to his wife and anticipates those actions. She, in turn, trusts that he will anticipate what's important to her without having to ask. Increased identification enables each to think like the other, feel like the other, and respond like the other.

You see identification-based trust occasionally in organizations among people who have worked together for long periods of time and have a depth of experience that allows them to know each other inside and out. This is also the type of trust that managers ideally seek in teams. Team members are so comfortable and trusting of each other that they can anticipate each other and freely act in each other's absence. Realistically, in the current work world, most large corporations have broken the bonds of identification trust they may have built with long-term employees. Broken promises have led to a breakdown in what was, at one time, a bond of unquestioned loyalty. It's likely to have been replaced with knowledge-based trust.

identification-based trust

Trust based on a mutual understanding of each other's intentions and appreciation of the other's wants and desires.

LEADERS AS SHAPERS OF MEANING

In the previous chapter, we depicted leadership as an influence process. More recently, leadership has increasingly become viewed as the management of meaning. That is, leaders are seen as individuals who define organizational reality through the articulation of a vision.[22] This approach of "leaders as shapers of meaning" tends to have a bias. It's directed predominantly toward leaders at the top of organizations. As such, it probably has more direct relevance to explaining the success and failures of chief executives than of first-line supervisors. However, lower-level managers can create visions to lead their units. It's just harder to define such visions and align them with the larger goals of the organization as a whole.

In this section, we present three contemporary leadership theories whose common component is that they present leaders as using words, ideas, and their physical presence to "charge the troops." To better help you understand the power of words in inspiring others, we first need to review the concept of *framing*.

Framing Issues

Martin Luther King, Jr.'s "I have a dream" speech largely shaped the civil rights movement. His words created an imagery of what a country would be like where racial prejudice no longer existed. What King did was *frame* the civil rights movement in a way so that others would see it the way he saw it.

Framing is a way to use language to manage meaning.[23] It's a way for leaders to influence how events are seen and understood. It involves the selection and highlighting of one or more aspects of a subject while excluding others.

Framing is analogous to what a photographer does. The visual world that exists is essentially ambiguous. When the photographer aims her camera and focuses on a specific shot, she frames her photo. Others then see what she wanted them to see. They see her point of view. That is precisely what leaders do when they frame an issue. They choose which aspects or portion of the subject they want others to focus on and which portions they want to be excluded.

Trial lawyers make their living by framing issues. Defense attorneys, for instance, shape their arguments so as to get the jury to see their client in the most favorable terms. They include "facts" that might help the jury find their client "not guilty." They exclude facts that might reflect unfavorably on their client. And they try to provide alternative interpretations to the "facts" that the prosecution argues makes their client guilty.

Lobbying groups also provide rich illustrations of the framing concept. The leadership of the National Rifle Association (NRA) has historically been very successful in limiting gun controls in the United States. They've done this not by focusing on shootings, deaths, or even self-defense. They've succeeded by framing gun control as a first amendment "freedom" issue. To the degree that the NRA can shape public opinion to think of gun controls as taking away a citizen's right to bear arms, they have been able to minimize gun control regulations. In a similar vein, original opponents of abortion rallied their cause by describing themselves as "anti-abortion" advocates. In response, and realizing the negative imagery from using the label "pro-abortion," supporters reframed the issue by referring to themselves as "pro-choice."

So why is framing relevant to leadership today? Because in the complex and chaotic environment in which an increasing number of leaders work, there is typically considerable manuverability with respect to "the facts." What is real is often

Martin Luther King, Jr.'s influential "I have a dream" speech, delivered on the steps of the Lincoln Memorial in 1963, succeeded in putting the civil rights movements into vivid and heartfelt terms that all could understand. King's framing statements had a profound effect on the way people saw the struggle for justice in the years that followed.

framing

A way to use language to manage meaning.

A President Who Has Perfected the Art of Framing

Effective politicians know how to frame issues to their advantage. George W. Bush, during his first year in the U.S. presidency, demonstrated his skill at framing when he successfully pushed his $1.35 trillion tax cut through Congress. In his effort to get a tax cut passed, Bush rarely spoke about a tax cut. Instead, he continually spoke about "a refund for overcharged Americans." Providing a "refund" sounds a lot better to voters than giving "a tax cut to the rich."

Bush has used language in other ways to shape arguments in his favor. School vouchers, for instance, have long been unpopular. So in his effort to enact education reform, he never used that term. Instead he speaks about "opportunity scholarships." How can anyone be against providing children, most from minority or low income families, with opportunities? Similarly, Bush's effort to repeal the estate tax made progress after he began calling it a "death tax." While the public might associate estates with the rich, who should pay taxes, a death tax sounds more egalitarian since everyone dies.

Bush shouldn't be criticized for his use of framing. Every U.S. president has engaged in the practice, some more successfully than others. Ronald Reagan, for instance, reshaped opinions when he christened the MX missile the Peacekeeper at the height of the cold war. And Bill Clinton reshaped the debate over trade with China when he dropped the elitist-sounding term "Most-Favored Nation" trade status and replaced it with the more egalitarian "Normal Trade Relations."

Source: Based on "R. S. Dunham, "When Is a Tax Cut Not a Tax Cut?" *BusinessWeek*, March 19, 2001, pp. 38–39.

what the leader says is real. What's important is what he or she chooses to say is important. Leaders can use language to influence followers' perceptions of the world, the meaning of events, beliefs about causes and consequences, and visions of the future. It's through framing that leaders determine whether people notice problems, how they understand and remember problems, and how they act upon them.[24] Thus, framing is a powerful tool by which leaders influence how others see and interpret reality.

Charismatic Leadership

John F. Kennedy, Martin Luther King, Jr., Mary Kay Ash (founder of Mary Kay Cosmetics), Steve Jobs (co-founder of Apple Computer), Ted Turner, Herb Kelleher (former CEO of Southwest Airlines), and Bill Clinton are individuals frequently cited as being charismatic leaders. What do they have in common?

What is Charismatic Leadership? According to **charismatic leadership theory**, followers make attributions of heroic or extraordinary leadership abilities when they observe certain behaviors.[25] While there have been a number of studies that have attempted to identify personal characteristics of the charismatic leader, the best documented has isolated five such characteristics—they have a vision, are willing to take risks to achieve that vision, are sensitive to both environmental constraints and follower needs, and exhibit behaviors that are out of the ordinary—that differentiate charismatic leaders from noncharismatic ones.[26] These characteristics are described in Exhibit 12-2 on page 342.

How do charismatic leaders actually influence followers? The evidence suggests a four-step process.[27] It begins by the leader articulating an appealing vision. This vision provides a sense of continuity for followers by linking the present with a better future for the organization. The leader then communicates high performance expectations and expresses confidence that followers can attain

charismatic leadership

Followers make attributions of heroic or extraordinary leadership abilities when they observe certain behaviors.

EXHIBIT

12-2

Key Characteristics of Charismatic Leaders

1. *Vision and articulation.* Has a vision—expressed as an idealized goal—that proposes a future better than the status quo; and is able to clarify the importance of the vision in terms that are understandable to others.
2. *Personal risk.* Willing to take on high personal risk, incur high costs, and engage in self-sacrifice to achieve the vision.
3. *Environmental sensitivity.* Able to make realistic assessments of the environmental constraints and resources needed to bring about change.
4. *Sensitivity to follower needs.* Perceptive of others' abilities and responsive to their needs and feelings.
5. *Unconventional behavior.* Engages in behaviors that are perceived as novel and counter to norms.

Source: Based on J. A. Conger and R. N. Kanungo, *Charismatic Leadership in Organizations* (Thousand Oaks, CA: Sage, 1998), p. 94.

them. This enhances follower self-esteem and self-confidence. Next, the leader conveys, through words and actions, a new set of values and, by his or her behavior, sets an example for followers to imitate. Finally, the charismatic leader makes self-sacrifices and engages in unconventional behavior to demonstrate courage and convictions about the vision.

What can we say about the charismatic leader's effect on his or her followers? There is an increasing body of research that shows impressive correlations between charismatic leadership and high performance and satisfaction among followers.[28] People working for charismatic leaders are motivated to exert extra work effort and, because they like and respect their leader, express greater satisfaction.

Are Charismatic Leaders Born or Made?   If charisma is desirable, can people learn to be charismatic leaders? Or are charismatic leaders born with their qualities? While a small minority still think charisma cannot be learned, most experts believe that individuals can be trained to exhibit charismatic behaviors and can thus enjoy the benefits that accrue to being labeled "a charismatic leader."[29] For instance, one set of authors proposes that a person can learn to become charismatic by following a three-step process.[30] First, an individual needs to develop the aura of charisma by maintaining an optimistic view; using passion as a catalyst for generating enthusiasm; and communicating with the whole body, not just with words. Second, an individual draws others in by creating a bond that inspires others to follow. And third, the individual brings out the potential in followers by tapping into their emotions. This approach seems to work as evidenced by researchers who've succeeded in actually scripting undergraduate business students to "play" charismatic.[31] The students were taught to articulate an overarching goal, communicate high performance expectations, exhibit confidence in the ability of followers to meet these expectations, and empathize with the needs of their followers; they learned to project a powerful, confident, and dynamic presence; and they practiced using a captivating and engaging voice tone. To further capture the dynamics and energy of charisma, the leaders were trained to evoke charismatic nonverbal characteristics: They alternated between pacing and sitting on the edges of their desks, leaned toward the subjects, maintained direct eye contact, and had relaxed postures and animated facial expressions. These researchers found that these students could learn how to project charisma. Moreover, followers of these leaders had higher task performance, task adjustment, and adjustment to the leader and to the group than did followers who worked under groups led by noncharismatic leaders.

When Charisma Is a Liability Charismatic leadership may not always be needed to achieve high levels of employee performance. Charisma appears to be most appropriate when the follower's task has an ideological component or when the environment involves a high degree of stress and uncertainty.[32] This may explain why, when charismatic leaders surface, it's more likely to be in politics, religion, wartime; or when a business firm is in its infancy or facing a life-threatening crisis. In the 1930s, Franklin D. Roosevelt offered a vision to get Americans out of the Great Depression. In the early 1970s, when Chrysler Corp. was on the brink of bankruptcy, it needed a charismatic leader with unconventional ideas like Lee Iacocca to reinvent the company. In contrast, General Motors' failure to directly address its problems in the late 1990s—such as GM's inability to launch new vehicles on time, deep-seated aversion to change, and lackluster financial performance—were frequently attributed to CEO John Smith Jr. and his *lack* of charisma.[33]

Transformational Leadership

Another stream of research has been focused on differentiating transformational leaders from transactional leaders.[34] Because transformational leaders are also charismatic, there is some overlap between this topic and our previous discussion of charismatic leadership.

Most of the leadership theories presented in the previous chapter—for instance, the Ohio State studies, Fiedler's model, path-goal theory, and the leader-participation model—have concerned **transactional leaders**. These kinds of leaders guide or motivate their followers in the direction of established goals by clarifying role and task requirements. There is also another type of leader who inspires followers to transcend their own self-interests for the good of the organization, and who is capable of having a profound and extraordinary effect on his or her followers. These are **transformational leaders** like Andrea Jung at Avon and Richard Branson of the Virgin Group. They pay attention to the concerns and developmental needs of individual followers; they change followers' awareness of issues by helping them to look at old problems in new ways; and they are able to excite, arouse, and inspire followers to put out extra effort to achieve group goals. Exhibit 12-3 on page 344 briefly identifies and defines the four characteristics that differentiate these two types of leaders.

Transactional and transformational leadership shouldn't be viewed as opposing approaches to getting things done.[35] Transformational leadership is built *on top of* transactional leadership—it produces levels of follower effort and performance that go beyond what would occur with a transactional approach alone. Moreover, transformational leadership is more than charisma. "The purely charismatic [leader] may want followers to adopt the charismatic's world view and go no further; the transformational leader will attempt to instill in followers the ability to question not only established views but eventually those established by the leader."[36]

The evidence supporting the superiority of transformational leadership over the transactional variety is overwhelmingly impressive. For instance, a number of studies with U.S., Canadian, and German military officers found, at every level, that transformational leaders were evaluated as more effective than their transactional counterparts.[37] And managers at FedEx who were rated by their followers as exhibiting more transformational leadership were evaluated by their immediate supervisors as higher performers and more promotable.[38] In summary, the overall evidence indicates that transformational leadership is more strongly correlated

transactional leaders
Leaders who guide or motivate their followers in the direction of established goals by clarifying role and task requirements.

transformational leaders
Leaders who inspire followers to transcend their own self-interests and who are capable of having a profound and extraordinary effect on followers.

E X H I B I T

12-3

Transactional Leader

Contingent Reward: Contracts exchange of rewards for effort, promises rewards for good performance, recognizes accomplishments.

Management by Exception (active): Watches and searches for deviations from rules and standards, takes corrective action.

Management by Exception (passive): Intervenes only if standards are not met.

Laissez-Faire: Abdicates responsibilities, avoids making decisions.

Transformational Leader

Charisma: Provides vision and sense of mission, instills pride, gains respect and trust.

Inspiration: Communicates high expectations, uses symbols to focus efforts, expresses important purposes in simple ways.

Intellectual Stimulation: Promotes intelligence, rationality, and careful problem solving.

Individualized Consideration: Gives personal attention, treats each employee individually, coaches, advises.

Source: B. M. Bass, "From Transactional to Transformational Leadership: Learning to Share the Vision," *Organizational Dynamics,* Winter 1990, p. 22. Reprinted by permission of the publisher. American Management Association, New York. All rights reserved.

than transactional leadership with lower turnover rates, higher productivity, and higher employee satisfaction.[39]

Visionary Leadership

The term *vision* appeared in our previous discussion of charismatic leadership. But visionary leadership goes beyond charisma. In this section, we review recent revelations about the importance of visionary leadership.

visionary leadership

The ability to create and articulate a realistic, credible, attractive vision of the future for an organization or organizational unit that grows out of and improves upon the present.

Defining Visionary Leadership   **Visionary leadership** is the ability to create and articulate a realistic, credible, attractive vision of the future for an organization or organizational unit, that grows out of and improves upon the present.[40] This vision, if properly selected and implemented, is so energizing that it "in effect jump-starts the future by calling forth the skills, talents, and resources to make it happen."[41]

A review of various definitions finds that a vision differs from other forms of direction setting in several ways: "A vision has clear and compelling imagery that offers an innovative way to improve, which recognizes and draws on traditions, and connects to actions that people can take to realize change. Vision taps people's emotions and energy. Properly articulated, a vision creates the enthusiasm that people have for sporting events and other leisure-time activities, bringing this energy and commitment to the workplace."[42]

Qualities of a Vision   The key properties of a vision seem to be inspirational possibilities that are value centered, realizable, with superior imagery and articulation.[43] Visions should be able to create possibilities that are inspirational, unique, and offer a new order that can produce organizational distinction. A vision is likely to fail if it doesn't offer a view of the future that is clearly and demonstrably better for the organization and its members. Desirable visions fit the times and circumstances and reflect the uniqueness of the organization. People in the organization must also believe that the vision is attainable. It should be perceived as challenging yet doable. Visions that have clear articulation and powerful imagery are more easily grasped and accepted.

What are some examples of visions? Rupert Murdoch had a vision of the future of the communication industry by combining entertainment and media. Through his News Corporation, Murdoch has successfully integrated a broadcast network, TV stations, movie studio, publishing, and global satellite distribution. The late Mary Kay Ash's vision of women as entrepreneurs selling products that improved their self image gave impetus to her cosmetics company. Michael Dell has created a vision of a business that allows Dell Computer to sell and deliver a finished PC directly to a customer in fewer than eight days.

Qualities of a Visionary Leader   What skills do visionary leaders exhibit? Once the vision is identified, these leaders appear to have three qualities that are related to effectiveness in their visionary roles.[44] First is the ability to explain the vision to others. The leader needs to make the vision clear in terms of required actions and aims through clear oral and written communication. Second is to be able to express the vision not just verbally but through the leader's behavior. This requires behaving in ways that continually convey and reinforce the vision. The third skill is being able to extend the vision to different leadership contexts. This is the ability to sequence activities so the vision can be applied in a variety of situations. For instance, the vision has to be as meaningful to the people in accounting as to those in marketing, and to employees in Prague as well as in Pittsburgh.

Michael Dell's vision was of a computer company whose business model included bypassing traditional retail distributors and selling customized PCs directly to consumers and firms. It was new, it was unique, and it was attainable. Dell, headquartered in Austin, Texas, was founded in 1984 and is now a $31 billion company that employs nearly 35,000 people around the globe.

EMOTIONAL INTELLIGENCE AND LEADERSHIP EFFECTIVENESS

We introduced emotional intelligence (EI) in our discussion of emotions in Chapter 4. We revisit the topic here because of recent studies indicating that EI—more than IQ, expertise, or any other single factor—is the best predictor of who will emerge as a leader.[45]

As our trait research demonstrated, leaders need basic intelligence and job-relevant knowledge. But IQ and technical skills are "threshold capabilities." They're necessary but not sufficient requirements for leadership. It's the possession of the five components of emotional intelligence—self-awareness, self-management, self-motivation, empathy, and social skills—that allows an individual to become a star performer. Without EI, a person can have outstanding training, a highly analytical mind, a long-term vision, and an endless supply of terrific ideas, but still not make a great leader. This is especially true as individuals move up in an organization. The evidence indicates that the higher the rank of a person considered to be a star performer, the more that EI capabilities surface as the reason for his or her effectiveness. Specifically, when star performers were compared with average ones in senior management positions, nearly 90 percent of the difference in their effectiveness was attributable to EI factors rather than basic intelligence.

Interestingly, it's been pointed out that the maturing of Rudolph Giuliani's leadership effectiveness closely followed the development of his emotional intelligence. For the better part of the eight years he was mayor of New York, Giuliani ruled with an iron fist. "He talked tough, picked fights, and demanded results. The result was a city that was cleaner, safer, and better governed—but also more polarized.

Critics called Giuliani a tin-eared tyrant. In the eyes of many, something important was missing from his leadership. That something, his critics acknowledged, emerged as the World Trade Center collapsed. It was a newfound compassion to complement his command: a mix of resolve, empathy, and inspiration that brought comfort to millions."[46] It's likely that Giuliani's emotional capacities and compassion for others were stimulated by a series of personal hardships—including prostate cancer and the highly visible breakup of his marriage—that had taken place less than a year before the terrorist attack on the World Trade Center.[47]

EI has shown to be positively related to job performance at all levels. But it appears to be especially relevant in jobs that demand a high degree of social interaction. And of course, that's what leadership is all about. Great leaders demonstrate their EI by exhibiting all five of its key components:

- *Self-awareness:* Exhibited by self-confidence, realistic self-assessment, and a self-deprecating sense of humor.
- *Self-management:* Exhibited by trustworthiness and integrity, comfort with ambiguity, and openness to change.
- *Self-motivation:* Exhibited by a strong drive to achieve, optimism, and high organizational commitment.
- *Empathy:* Exhibited by expertise in building and retaining talent, cross-cultural sensitivity, and service to clients and customers.
- *Social skills:* Exhibited by the ability to lead change, persuasiveness, and expertise in building and leading teams.

The recent evidence makes a strong case for concluding that EI is an essential element in leadership effectiveness. As such, it should probably be added to the list of traits associated with leadership that we described in Chapter 11.

CONTEMPORARY LEADERSHIP ROLES

What unique demands do teams place on leaders? Why are many effective leaders also active mentors? And how can leaders develop self-leadership skills in their employees? In this section, we briefly address these three leadership-role issues.

Providing Team Leadership

Leadership is increasingly taking place within a team context. As teams grow in popularity, the role of the leader in guiding team members takes on heightened importance.[48] And the role of team leader is different from the traditional leadership role performed by first-line supervisors. J. D. Bryant, a supervisor at Texas Instruments' Forest Lane plant in Dallas, found that out.[49] One day he was happily overseeing a staff of 15 circuit-board assemblers. The next day he was informed the company was moving to teams and that he was to become a "facilitator." "I'm supposed to teach the teams everything I know and then let them make their own decisions," he said. Confused about his new role, he admitted "there was no clear plan on what I was supposed to do." In this section, we consider the challenge of being a team leader and review the new roles that team leaders take on.

Many leaders are not equipped to handle the change to teams. As one prominent consultant noted, "even the most capable managers have trouble making the transition because all the command-and-control type things they were encouraged to do before are no longer appropriate. There's no reason to have any skill or sense of this."[50] This same consultant estimated that "probably 15 percent of managers are natural team leaders; another 15 percent could never lead a team because it runs counter to their personality. [They're unable to sublimate their dominating style for the good of the team.] Then there's that huge group in the middle: Team leadership doesn't come naturally to them, but they can learn it."[51]

The challenge for most managers, then, is to learn how to become an effective team leader. They have to learn skills such as the patience to share information, to trust others, to give up authority, and understanding when to intervene. Effective leaders have mastered the difficult balancing act of knowing when to leave their teams alone and when to intercede. New team leaders may try to retain too much control at a time when team members need more autonomy, or they may abandon their teams at times when the teams need support and help.[52]

A study of 20 organizations that had reorganized themselves around teams found certain common responsibilities that all leaders had to assume. These included coaching, facilitating, handling disciplinary problems, reviewing team/individual performance, training, and communication.[53] Many of these responsibilities apply to managers in general. A more meaningful way to describe the team leader's job is to focus on two priorities: managing the team's external boundary and facilitating the team process.[54] We've broken these priorities down into four specific roles.

First, team leaders are *liaisons with external constituencies*. These include upper management, other internal teams, customers, and suppliers. The leader represents the team to other constituencies, secures needed resources, clarifies others' expectations of the team, gathers information from the outside, and shares this information with team members.

Second, team leaders are *troubleshooters*. When the team has problems and asks for assistance, team leaders sit in on meetings and help try to resolve the problems. This rarely relates to technical or operation issues because the team members typically know more about the tasks being done than does the team leader. Where the leader is most likely to contribute is by asking penetrating questions, helping the team talk through problems, and by getting needed resources from external constituencies. For instance, when a team in an aerospace firm found itself short-handed, its team leader took responsibility for getting more staff. He presented the team's case to upper management and got the approval through the company's human resources department.

Third, team leaders are *conflict managers*. When disagreements surface, they help process the conflict. What's the source of the conflict? Who is involved? What are the issues? What resolution options are available? What are the advantages and disadvantages of each? By getting team members to address questions such as these, the leader minimizes the disruptive aspects of intrateam conflicts.

Source: DILBERT reprinted by permission of United Features Syndicate, Inc.

Finally, team leaders are *coaches*. They clarify expectations and roles, teach, offer support, cheerlead, and do whatever else is necessary to help team members improve their work performance.

Mentoring

Many leaders create mentoring relationships. A **mentor** is a senior employee who sponsors and supports a less-experienced employee (a protégé). The mentoring role includes coaching, counseling, and sponsorship.[55] As a coach, mentors help to develop their protégés' skills. As counselors, mentors provide support and help bolster protégés' self-confidence. And as sponsors, mentors actively intervene on behalf of their protégés, lobby to get their protégés visible assignments, and politic to get their protégés rewards such as promotions and salary increases.

Successful mentors are good teachers. They can present ideas clearly, listen well, and empathize with the problems of their protégés. They also share experiences with the protégé, act as role models, share contacts, and provide guidance through the political maze of the organization. They provide advice and guidance on how to survive and get ahead in the organization and act as a sounding board for ideas that a protégé may be hesitant to share with his or her direct supervisor. A mentor vouches for a protégé, answers for him or her in the highest circles within the organization, and makes appropriate introductions.

Some organizations have formal mentoring programs where mentors are officially assigned to new or high-potential employees. For instance, at Edward Jones, a financial services firm with 24,000 employees, mentors are assigned to new employees after recruits have completed the company's initial two-month home study program and five-day customer-service seminar.[56] The new employees shadow their mentor for three weeks to specifically learn the company's way of doing business. However, in contrast to Edward Jones' formal system, most organizations rely on informal mentoring—with senior managers personally selecting an employee and taking that employee on as a protégé.

The most effective mentoring relationships exist outside the immediate boss-subordinate interface.[57] The boss-subordinate context has an inherent conflict of interest and tension, mostly attributable to managers' directly evaluating the performance of subordinates, that limits openness and meaningful communication.

Why would a leader want to be a mentor? There are personal benefits to the leader as well as benefits for the organization. The mentor-protégé relationship gives the mentor unfiltered access to the attitudes and feelings of lower-ranking employees. Protégés can be an excellent source of potential problems by providing early warning signals. They provide timely information to upper managers that short-circuits the formal channels. So the mentor-protégé relationship is a valuable communication channel that allows mentors to have news of problems before they become common knowledge to others in upper management. In addition, in terms of leader self-interest, mentoring can provide personal satisfaction to senior executives. In the latter stages of their career, managers are often allowed the luxury of playing the part of elder statesperson. They are respected for their judgment, built up over many years and through varied experiences. The opportunity to share this knowledge with others can be personally rewarding for the mentor. From the organization's standpoint, mentoring provides a support system for high-potential employees. Where mentors exist, protégés are often more motivated, better politically grounded, and less likely to quit. For instance, one study found that where a significant mentoring relationship existed, the protégés had more favorable and frequent promotions, were paid significantly more than those who were not mentored, had a greater level of commitment to the organization, and had greater career success.[58]

Men Make Better Leaders Than Women

This statement is false. There is no evidence to support the myth that men make better leaders than women.

The evidence indicates that the similarities in leadership style between men and women tend to outweigh the differences. But where there are differences, those differences tend to favor women, not men![60] Studies show that female leaders, when rated by their peers, underlings, and bosses, score higher than their male counterparts on almost every important dimension of leadership—including goal-setting, motivating others, fostering communication, producing high-quality work, listening to others, and mentoring.

Women tend to use a more democratic leadership style. They encourage participation, share power and information, and attempt to enhance followers' self-worth. They prefer to lead through inclusion and rely on their charisma, expertise, contacts, and inter-personal skills to influence others. Men, on the other hand, are more likely to use a directive command-and-control style. They rely on the formal authority of their managerial position for their influence base.

In today's organizations, flexibility, teamwork, trust, and information sharing are replacing rigid structures, competitive individualism, control, and secrecy. The best leaders listen, motivate, and provide support to their people. That is, they display EI. And, in contrast to men, women score somewhat higher on EI. As a specific example, the expanded use of cross-functional teams in organizations means that effective leaders must become skillful negotiators. The leadership styles women typically use can make them better at negotiating, as they tend to treat negotiations in the context of a continuing relationship—trying hard to make the other party a winner in its own and others' eyes.

Are all employees in an organization equally likely to participate in a mentoring relationship? Unfortunately the answer is no.[59] Evidence indicates that minorities and women are less likely to be chosen as protégés than are white males and thus are less likely to accrue the benefits of mentorship. Mentors tend to select protégés who are similar to themselves on criteria such as background, education, gender, race, ethnicity, and religion. "People naturally move to mentor and can more easily communicate with those with whom they most closely identify."[61] In the United States, for instance, upper-management positions in most organizations have been traditionally staffed by white males, so it is hard for minorities and women to be selected as protégés. In addition, in terms of cross-gender mentoring, senior male managers may select male protégés to minimize problems such as sexual attraction or gossip. Organizations have responded to this dilemma by increasing formal mentoring programs and providing training and coaching for potential mentors of special groups such as minorities and women.

Self-Leadership

Is it possible for people to lead themselves? An increasing body of research suggests that many can.[62] Proponents of **self-leadership** propose that there are a set of processes through which individuals control their own behavior. And effective leaders (or what advocates like to call *superleaders*) help their followers to lead themselves. They do this by developing leadership capacity in others and nurturing followers so they no longer need to depend on formal leaders for direction and motivation.

How do leaders create self-leaders? The following have been suggested:[63]

self-leadership
A set of processes through which individuals control their own behavior.

1. *Model self-leadership.* Practice self-observation, setting challenging personal goals, self-direction, and self-reinforcement. Then display these behaviors and encourage others to rehearse and then produce them.

2. *Encourage employees to create self-set goals.* Having quantitative, specific goals is the most important part of self-leadership.
3. *Encourage the use of self-rewards to strengthen and increase desirable behaviors.* In contrast, self-punishment should be limited only to occasions when the employee has been dishonest or destructive.
4. *Create positive thought patterns.* Encourage employees to use mental imagery and self-talk to further stimulate self-motivation.
5. *Create a climate of self-leadership.* Redesign the work to increase the natural rewards of a job and focus on these naturally rewarding features of work to increase motivation.
6. *Encourage self-criticism.* Encourage individuals to be critical of their own performance.

The underlying assumptions behind self-leadership are that people are responsible, capable, and able to exercise initiative without the external constraints of bosses, rules, or regulations. Given the proper support, individuals can monitor and control their own behavior.

The importance of self-leadership has increased with the expanded popularity of teams. Empowered, self-managed teams need individuals who are themselves self-directed. Management can't expect individuals who have spent their organizational lives under boss-centered leadership to suddenly adjust to self-managed teams. Therefore, training in self-leadership is an excellent means to help employees make the transition from dependence to autonomy.

MORAL LEADERSHIP

The topic of leadership and ethics has surprisingly received little attention. Only recently have ethicists and leadership researchers begun to consider the ethical implications in leadership.[64] Why now? One reason may be the growing general interest in ethics throughout the field of management. Another reason may be the discovery by probing biographers that many of our past leaders—such as Martin Luther King, Jr., John F. Kennedy, and Franklin D. Roosevelt—suffered from ethical shortcomings. Certainly the impeachment hearings of American president Bill Clinton on grounds of perjury and other charges has done nothing to lessen concern about ethical leadership. And events leading to the eventual bankruptcy of Enron Corp.—where executives at Enron, its accounting firm of Arthur Andersen, and its law firm of Vinson & Elkins appear to have engaged in a multitude of unethical practices—has increased the public's and politician's concerns about ethical standards in American business.

Ethics touches on leadership at a number of junctures. Transformational leaders, for instance, have been described by one authority as fostering moral virtue when they try to change the attitudes and behaviors of followers.[65] Charisma, too, has an ethical component. Unethical leaders are more likely to use their charisma to enhance *power over* followers, directed toward self-serving ends. Ethical leaders are considered to use their charisma in a socially constructive way to serve others.[66] There is also the issue of abuse of power by leaders, for example, when they give themselves large salaries and bonuses while, at the same time, they seek to cut costs by laying off long-time employees. And, of course, the topic of trust explicitly deals with honesty and integrity in leadership.

Leadership effectiveness needs to address the *means* that a leader uses in trying to achieve goals as well as the content of those goals. For instance, Bill Gates's success in leading Microsoft to domination of the world's software business has been achieved by means of an extremely demanding work culture. Microsoft's culture demands long work hours by employees and is intolerant of individuals who want to balance work and their personal life. Microsoft's competitors and U.S. government regulators have also pinpointed this pressurized and competitive culture as the source of numerous unethical practices—from using its control of its Windows' operating system to favor Microsoft's partners and subsidiaries to encouraging its sales force to "crush" its rivals. Importantly, Microsoft's culture mirrors the personality of its chairman and co-founder, Gates. In addition, ethical leadership must address the content of a leader's goals. Are the changes that the leader seeks for the organization morally acceptable? Is a business leader effective if he or she builds an organization's success by selling products that damage the health of its users? This question, for example, might be asked of tobacco executives. Or is a military leader successful by winning a war that should not have been fought in the first place?

Leadership is not value free. Before we judge any leader to be effective, we should consider both the means used by the leader to achieve his or her goals and the moral content of those goals.

ONLINE LEADERSHIP: SOME SPECULATIVE THOUGHTS

How do you lead people who are physically separated from you and where interactions are basically reduced to written digital communications? This is a question that, so far, has received little attention from OB researchers.[67] Leadership research has been directed almost exclusively to face-to-face and verbal situations. But we can't ignore the reality that today's managers and their employees are increasingly being linked by networks rather than geographical proximity. Obvious examples include managers who regularly use e-mail to communicate with their staff, managers overseeing virtual projects or teams, and managers whose telecommuting employees are linked to the office by a computer and modem.

If leadership is important to inspiring and motivating dispersed employees, we need to offer some guidance as to how leadership in this context might function. Keep in mind, however, that the dearth of research on this topic forces us to engage in considerable speculation. The intention here is not to provide you with definitive guidelines for leading online. Rather, it's to introduce you to an increasingly important issue and get you to think about how leadership changes when relationships are defined by network interactions.

In face-to-face communications, harsh *words* can be softened by nonverbal action. A smile and comforting gestures, for instance, can lessen the blow behind strong words like *disappointed*, *unsatisfactory*, *inadequate*, or *below expectations*. That nonverbal component doesn't exist with online interactions. The *structure* of words in a digital communication also has the power to motivate or demotivate the receiver. Is the message made up of full sentences or phrases? The latter, for instance, is likely to be seen as curt and more threatening. Similarly, a message in all caps is the equivalent of shouting. The manager who inadvertently sends her message in short phrases, all in caps, may get a very different response than if she had sent that same message in full sentences, using upper and lowercase letters.

Leaders need to be sure the *tone* of their message correctly reflects the emotions they want to send. Is the message formal or informal? Does it match the verbal style of the sender? Does it convey the appropriate level of importance or urgency? The fact that many people's writing style is very different from their interpersonal style is certainly a potential problem. Your author, for instance, has observed a number of very warm and charismatic

Along with networked employees, telecommuters need leaders whose online communications are skillful and whose words and tone are well chosen. About 46 percent of small companies have telecommuters on staff, many of whom are sales representatives.

leaders who aren't comfortable with the written word and tend to make their written communications much more formal than their verbal style. This not only creates confusion for employees, it undoubtedly also hinders the leaders' overall effectiveness.

Finally, online leaders must choose a *style*. Do they use emoticons, abbreviations, jargon, and the like? Do they adapt their style to their audience? Observation suggests that some managers are having difficulty adjusting to computer-related communications. For instance, they're using the same style with their bosses that they're using with their staff, with unfortunate consequences. Or they're selectively using digital communications to "hide" when delivering bad news.

We know that messages convey more than surface information. From a leadership standpoint, messages can convey trust or lack of trust, status, task directives, or emotional warmth. Concepts such as task structure, supportive behavior, and vision can be conveyed in written form as well as verbally. It may even be possible for leaders to convey charisma through the written word. But to effectively convey on-line leadership, managers must recognize that they have choices in the words, structure, tone, and style of their digital communications. They also need to develop the skills of "reading between the lines" in the messages they receive. In the same way that EI taps an individual's ability to monitor and assess others' emotions, effective online leaders need to develop the skill of deciphering the emotional components of messages.

Any discussion of online leadership needs to also consider the possibility that the digital age can turn non-leaders into leaders. Some managers, whose face-to-face leadership skills are less than satisfactory, may shine online. Their talents may lie in their writing skills and ability to read the messages behind written communiqués. Nothing in the mainstream leadership literature addresses this unique situation.

We propose that online leaders have to think through carefully what actions they want their digital messages to initiate. Although the networked communication is a relatively new form, it's a powerful channel. When used properly, it can build and enhance an individual's leadership effectiveness. But when misused, it has the potential to undermine a great deal of what a leader has been able to achieve through his or her verbal actions.

This discussion leads us to the tentative conclusion that, for an increasing number of managers, good interpersonal skills may include the abilities to communicate warmth, emotion, trust, and leadership through written words on a computer screen and to read emotions in others' messages. In this "new world" of communications, writing skills are likely to become an extension of interpersonal skills.

CHALLENGES TO THE LEADERSHIP CONSTRUCT

A noted management expert takes issue with the omnipotent role that academicians, practicing managers, and the general public have given to the concept of leadership. He says, "In the 1500s, people ascribed all events they didn't understand to God. Why did the crops fail? God. Why did someone die? God. Now our all-purpose explanation is leadership."[68] He notes that when a company succeeds, people need someone to give the credit to. And that's typically the firm's CEO. Similarly, when a company does poorly, they need someone to blame. CEOs also play this role. But much of an organization's success or failure is due to factors outside the influence of leadership. In many cases, success or failure is just a matter of being in the right or wrong place at a given time. For instance, when the demand for microchips was growing at 60 percent or more a year, leaders at microchip makers like Intel and Motorola were considered geniuses. Similarly, the CEOs at PC makers such as Compaq and Gateway were lauded in the 1990s, when demand for PCs was exploding. But by 2001, these same leaders were being widely criticized for the decline in their company's business. And many CEOs were replaced as profits sank. The key leadership question would be: In a recession, when consumers and business are widely cutting back on technology purchases, how is firing a CEO going to increase the demand for chips and PCs? The answer is, it can't.

In this section, we present two perspectives that challenge the widely-accepted belief in the importance of leadership. The first argument proposes that leadership is more about appearances than reality. You don't have to *be* an effective leader as long as you *look* like one! The second argument directly attacks the notion that some leadership *will always* be effective *regardless* of the situation. This argument contends that in many situations, whatever actions leaders exhibit are irrelevant.

Leadership as an Attribution

We introduced attribution theory in Chapter 5. As you may remember, it deals with the ways in which people try to make sense out of cause-and-effect relationships. We said when something happens, we want to attribute it to something else. The **attribution theory of leadership** says that leadership is merely an attribution that people make about other individuals.[69] The attribution framework has shown that people characterize leaders as having such traits as intelligence, outgoing personality, strong verbal skills, aggressiveness, understanding, and industriousness.[70] Similarly, the high-high leader (high on both task and people dimensions) presented in the previous chapter has been found to be consistent with attributions of what makes a good leader.[71] That is, regardless of the situation, a high-high leadership style tends to be perceived as best. At the organizational level, the attribution framework accounts for the conditions under which people use leadership to explain organizational outcomes. Those conditions are extremes in organizational performance. When an organization has either extremely negative or extremely positive performance, people are prone to make leadership attributions to explain the performance.[72] As noted earlier, this tendency helps to account for the vulnerability of CEOs when their organizations suffer a major financial setback, regardless of whether they had much to do with it; and also accounts for why these CEOs tend to be given credit for extremely positive financial results—again, regardless of how much or how little they contributed.

Jill Barad resigned under pressure from Mattel, Inc. in February 2000 after many years as a successful marketing executive and three years as CEO. In those three years, the price of Mattel shares reached a high in the mid-40s in 1998 and then fell to about $11, where it remained at the time of Barad's departure. Despite having revived the Barbie line of toys into an almost $2 billion business before becoming CEO, Barad took the brunt of blame for a failed $3.5 billion acquisition of Learning Co., a Cambridge, Massachusetts, computer-software concern.

One of the more interesting findings in the attribution model of leadership literature is the perception that effective leaders are generally considered consistent or unwavering in their decisions.[73] One of the explanations for why Ronald Reagan (during his first term as U.S. president) was perceived as a leader was that he was fully committed, steadfast, and consistent in the decisions he made and the goals he set. Former U.S. president George Herbert Bush, in contrast, undermined the public's perception of his leadership by increasing income taxes after stating categorically during his campaign: "Read my lips. No new taxes."

Following the attribution theory of leadership, we'd say that what's important in being characterized as an "effective leader" is projecting the *appearance* of being a leader rather than focusing on *actual accomplishments*. Leader-wannabes can attempt to shape the perception that they're smart, personable, verbally adept, aggressive,

attribution theory of leadership

The idea that leadership is merely an attribution that people make about other individuals.

hard-working, and consistent in their style. And by doing so, they increase the probability that their bosses, colleagues, and employees will *view them* as an effective leader.

Substitutes and Neutralizers to Leadership

Contrary to the arguments made throughout this and the previous chapter, leadership may not always be important. Data from numerous studies collectively demonstrate that, in many situations, whatever actions leaders exhibit are irrelevant. Certain individual, job, and organizational variables can act as *substitutes* for leadership or *neutralize* the leader's effect to influence his or her followers.[74]

Neutralizers make it impossible for leader behavior to make any difference to follower outcomes. They negate the leader's influence. Substitutes, on the other hand, make a leader's influence not only impossible but also unnecessary. They act as a replacement for the leader's influence. For instance, characteristics of employees such as their experience, training, "professional" orientation, or indifference toward organizational rewards can substitute for, or neutralize the effect of, leadership. Experience and training can replace the need for a leader's support or ability to create structure and reduce task ambiguity. Jobs that are inherently unambiguous and routine or that are intrinsically satisfying may place fewer demands on the leadership variable. Organizational characteristics like explicit formalized goals, rigid rules and procedures, and cohesive work groups can also replace formal leadership (see Exhibit 12-5).

This recent recognition that leaders don't always have an impact on follower outcomes should not be that surprising. After all, we have introduced a number of variables in this text—attitudes, personality, ability, and group norms, to name but a few—that have been documented as having an effect on employee performance and satisfaction. Yet supporters of the leadership concept place an undue burden on this variable for explaining and predicting behavior. It's too simplistic to consider employees as guided to goal accomplishments solely by the actions of their leader. It is important, therefore, to recognize ex-

EXHIBIT 12-5

Substitutes and Neutralizers for Leadership

Defining Characteristics	Relationship-Oriented Leadership	Task-Oriented Leadership
Individual		
Experience/training	No effect on	Substitutes for
Professionalism	Substitutes for	Substitutes for
Indifference to rewards	Neutralizes	Neutralizes
Job		
Highly structured task	No effect on	Substitutes for
Provides its own feedback	No effect on	Substitutes for
Intrinsically satisfying	Substitutes for	No effect on
Organization		
Explicit formalized goals	No effect on	Substitutes for
Rigid rules and procedures	No effect on	Substitutes for
Cohesive work groups	Substitutes for	Substitutes for

Source: Based on S. Kerr and J. M. Jermier, "Substitutes for Leadership: Their Meaning and Measurement," *Organizational Behavior and Human Performance*, December 1978, p. 378.

plicitly that leadership is merely another independent variable in our overall OB model. In some situations, it may contribute a lot to explaining employee productivity, absence, turnover, satisfaction, and citizenship behavior, but in other situations, it may contribute little toward that end.

FINDING AND CREATING EFFECTIVE LEADERS

We have covered a lot of ground in these two chapters on leadership. But the ultimate goal of our review is to answer this question: How can organizations find or create effective leaders? Let's try to answer that question.[75]

Selection

The entire process that organizations go through to fill management positions is essentially an exercise in trying to identify individuals who will be effective leaders. Your search might begin by reviewing the specific requirements for the position to be filled. What knowledge, skills, and abilities are needed to do the job effectively? You should try to analyze the situation in order to find candidates who will make a proper match.

Testing is useful for identifying and selecting leaders. Personality tests can be used to look for traits associated with leadership—ambition and energy, desire to lead, honesty and integrity, self-confidence, intelligence, and job-relevant knowledge. Testing to find a leadership-candidate's score on self-monitoring also makes sense. High self-monitors are likely to outperform their low-scoring counterparts because the former is better at reading situations and adjusting his or her behavior accordingly. You can additionally assess candidates for emotional intelligence. Given the importance of social skills to managerial effectiveness, candidates with a high EI should have an advantage, especially in situations requiring transformational leadership.[76]

Interviews additionally provide an opportunity to evaluate leadership candidates. For instance, we know that experience is a poor predictor of leader effectiveness, but situation-specific experience is relevant. You can use the interview to determine if a candidate's prior experience fits with the situation you're trying to fill. Similarly, the interview is a reasonably good vehicle for identifying the degree to which a candidate has leadership traits such as ambition, self-confidence, a vision, the verbal skills to frame issues, or a charismatic physical presence.

We know the importance of situational factors in leadership success. And we should use this knowledge to match leaders to situations. Does the situation require a change-focused leader? If so, look for transformational qualities. If not, look for transactional qualities. You might also ask: Is leadership actually important in this specific position? There may be situational factors that substitute for or neutralize leadership. If there are, then the leader essentially performs a figurehead or symbolic role, and the importance of selecting the "right" person is not particularly crucial.

Training

Organizations, in aggregate, spend billions of dollars, yen, and euros on leadership training and development.[77] These efforts take many forms—from $50,000 executive leadership programs offered by universities such as Harvard to sailing experiences at the Outward Bound School. Although much of the money spent on training may provide dubious benefits, our review suggests that there are some things management can do to get the maximum effect from their leadership-training budgets.[78]

These participants in an Outward Bound training program are building their leadership and teamwork skills through a shared sailing experience.

First, let's recognize the obvious. People are not equally trainable. Leadership training of any kind is likely to be more successful with individuals who are high self-monitors than with low self-monitors. Such individuals have the flexibility to change their behavior.

What kinds of things can individuals learn that might be related to higher leader effectiveness? It may be a bit optimistic to believe that we can teach "vision-creation," but we can teach implementation skills. We can train people to develop "an understanding about content themes critical to effective visions."[79] We also can teach skills such as trust-building and mentoring. And leaders can be taught situational-analysis skills. They can learn how to evaluate situations, how to modify situations to make them fit better with their style, and how to assess which leader behaviors might be most effective in given situations.

On an optimistic note, there is evidence suggesting that behavioral training through modeling exercises can increase an individual's ability to exhibit charismatic leadership qualities. The success of the researchers mentioned earlier (see "Are Charismatic Leaders Born or Made?") in actually scripting undergraduate business students to "play" charismatic is a case in point.[80]

SUMMARY AND IMPLICATIONS FOR MANAGERS

Effective managers today must develop trusting relationships with those whom they seek to lead. Why? Because as organizations have become less stable and predictable, strong bonds of trust are likely to be replacing bureaucratic rules in defining expectations and relationships. Managers who aren't trusted aren't likely to be effective leaders.

Organizations are increasingly searching for managers who can exhibit transformational leadership qualities. They want leaders with visions and the charisma to carry those visions out. And while true leadership effectiveness may be a result of exhibiting the right behaviors at the right time, the evidence is quite strong that people have a relatively uniform perception of what a leader should look like. They attribute "leadership" to people who are smart, personable, verbally adept, and the like. To the degree that managers project these qualities, others are likely to deem them leaders.

For managers concerned with how to fill key positions in their organization with effective leaders, we have shown that tests and interviews help to identify people with leadership qualities. In addition to focusing on leadership selection, managers should also consider investing in leadership training. Many individuals with leadership potential can enhance their skills through formal courses, workshops, rotating job responsibilities, coaching, and mentoring.

Leadership Is Culturally-Bound

Leaders must adapt their style to different national cultures. What works in China, for instance, isn't likely to work in Canada or France. Can you imagine, for instance, executives at a large Canadian department store chain, like The Bay, being effective by humiliating their employees? But that works at the Asia Department Store in central China.[a] Executives there blatantly brag about practicing "heartless" management, requiring new employees to undergo two to four weeks of military-type training in order to increase their obedience, and conduct the store's in-house training sessions in a public place where employees can openly suffer embarrassment from their mistakes.

National culture affects leadership style by way of the follower. Leaders cannot choose their styles at will. They are constrained by the cultural conditions that their followers have come to expect. For instance, Korean leaders are expected to be paternalistic toward employees; Arab leaders who show kindness or generosity without being asked to do so are seen by other Arabs as weak; and Japanese leaders are expected to be humble and speak infrequently.[b]

Consistent with the contingency approach, leaders need to adjust their style to the unique cultural aspects of a country. For example, a manipulative or autocratic style is compatible with high power distance, and we find high power distance scores in Russia, Spain, Arab, Far Eastern, and most Latin countries. Power distance rankings should also be good indicators of employee willingness to accept participative leadership. Participation is likely to be most effective in low-power distance cultures as exist in Norway, Finland, Denmark, and Sweden.

The GLOBE research program, which we introduced in Chapter 3, has gathered data on approximately 18,000 middle managers in 825 organizations, covering 62 countries. It's the most comprehensive cross-cultural study of leadership ever undertaken. So its findings should not be quickly dismissed. It's illuminating that one of the results coming from the GLOBE program is that there are some universal aspects to leadership. Specifically, a number of the elements making up transformational leadership appear to be associated with effective leadership regardless of what country the leader is in.[c] This conclusion is very important because it flies in the face of the contingency view that leadership style needs to adapt to cultural differences.

What elements of transformational leadership appear universal? Vision, foresight, providing encouragement, trustworthiness, dynamism, positiveness, and proactiveness. The results led two members of the GLOBE team to conclude that "effective business leaders in any country are expected by their subordinates to provide a powerful and proactive vision to guide the company into the future, strong motivational skills to stimulate all employees to fulfill the vision, and excellent planning skills to assist in implementing the vision."[d]

What might explain the universal appeal of these transformational leader attributes? It's been suggested that pressures toward common technologies and management practices, as a result of global competition and multinational influences, may make some aspects of leadership universally accepted. If true, we may be able to select and train leaders in a universal style and thus significantly raise the quality of leadership worldwide.

[a]"Military-Style Management in China," *Asia Inc.*, March 1995, p. 70.

[b]R. J. House, "Leadership in the Twenty-First Century," in A. Howard (ed.), *The Changing Nature of Work* (San Francisco: Jossey-Bass, 1995), pp. 442–44; and M. F. Peterson and J. G. Hunt, "International Perspectives on International Leadership," *Leadership Quarterly*, Fall 1997, pp. 203–31.

[c]R. J. House, P. J. Hanges, S. A. Ruiz-Quintanilla, P. W. Dorfman, and Associates, "Culture Specific and Cross-Culturally Generalizable Implicit Leadership Theories: Are the Attributes of Charismatic/Transformational Leadership Universally Endorsed?" *Leadership Quarterly*, Summer 1999, pp. 219–56; and D. E. Carl and M. Javidan, "Universality of Charismatic Leadership: A Multi-Nation Study," paper presented at the National Academy of Management Conference, Washington, DC, August 2001.

[d]D. E. Carl and M. Javidan, "Universality of Charismatic Leadership," p. 29.

Questions for Review

1. Contrast the three types of trust. Relate them to your experience in personal relationships.

2. What could you do if you wanted others to perceive you as a charismatic leader?

3. When can charisma be a liability?

4. What are the qualities of a vision?

5. How does a leader increase self-leadership among his or her followers?

6. How does emotional intelligence relate to leadership effectiveness?

7. How does one become an effective team leader?

8. Why would a leader want to be a mentor?

9. How is leadership an attribution?

10. Contrast substitutes and neutralizers for leadership.

Questions for Critical Thinking

1. What role do you think training plays in an individual's ability to trust others? For instance, does the training of lawyers, accountants, law-enforcement personnel, and social workers take different approaches toward trusting others? Explain.

2. How might an understanding of knowledge-based trust explain the reluctance of a person to change jobs?

3. "It's not possible to be both a trusting boss and a politically astute leader. One requires openness and the other requires concealment." Do you agree or disagree with this statement? Explain.

4. As a new employee in an organization, why might you want to acquire a mentor? Why might women and minorities have more difficulty in finding a mentor than would white males?

5. Is there an ethical problem if leaders focus more on looking like a leader than actually being one? Discuss.

Team Exercise | Affirmation of Trust

Break into groups of 8 to 12 members each.

A. Each group has 20 minutes to discuss the following four topics:
   1. What kind of situations cause you to be afraid?
   2. What kind of situations cause you to feel insecure?
   3. What makes you happy?
   4. What makes you cry?

B. Each group member should remove a shoe and place it alongside the shoes of other members in a designated place, outside the group's meeting area. Each member should identify his or her shoe by putting his or her name on a slip of paper and putting it in front of the shoe.

C. Review the 5-item "Affirmation of Trust" listing that follows this exercise. Each member should:
   1. Write down the name of a person in your group on a slip of paper. Under his or her name, write the letters A through E in a vertical column. Next to each letter, rate your perception of that person (based on your experience in class as well as their responses to this activity) on a scale of 1 to 5 (1 being low) using the "Affirmation of Trust" listing. Sign your name to the bottom of the slip. Deposit this slip of paper in the other member's shoe.
   2. Repeat the above for all the other members of the group.

D. After all members have distributed their slips, each one retrieves his or her own shoe with the slips left in. Read each of the slips directed to you by the other members of your group and record the summary results.

E. Group members now discuss their reactions to their slips with the group. To what degree do they align with your self-perceptions? To what degree do the various statements converge and agree? What have you learned from this feedback that could help you build trust with others?

Affirmation of Trust List

A. Open

B. Speaks his or her feelings

C. Tells the truth

D. Consistent

E. Demonstrates competence

Source: Based on J. W. Pfeiffer and J. E. Jones (eds.), *A Handbook of Structured Experiences for Human Relations Training*, vol. VI (La Jolla, CA: University Associates, 1977), pp. 110–13.

Case Incident | **Three CEOs Buck the Trend**

Noel Forgeard, Edward Zore, and Andrew Taylor were bucking the trend during the 2001 recession. While their counterparts were aggressively laying off workers, these CEOs were holding the line against layoffs.

Noel Forgeard is CEO at Airbus. His company, along with Boeing, dominate the market for commercial aircraft. But while Boeing announced layoffs of up to 30,000 workers following the terror attacks of September 11, 2001, Foregeard said he wasn't firing anybody. Said an Airbus executive, "This is a bet that life will resume. There's more uncertainty now, but we decided to be optimistic. This thing will turn around, and you can't risk losing skilled people when the upturn comes."

Edward Zore is CEO at Northwestern Mutual, the largest seller of individual life insurance in the United States. Zore is no "Mr. Nice Guy." Every year his firm fires the lowest four percent of its 4,100 employees—those with the poorest performance. But it is fiercely loyal to its good ones. Zore is committed to a no-layoff policy. Why? Employee loyalty, says Zore. He believes employee loyalty breeds customer loyalty. And he may be right since Northwestern loses only about half as many customers as the industry average. Zore argues that his firm's higher customer retention rate allows Northwestern to have more money to invest longer, while spending less to replace defectors. The company can then pass the savings back to customers by lowering prices on policies.

Our final CEO, Andrew Taylor, heads up Enterprise Rent-a-Car. Taylor proudly boasts that his company has never had a layoff. This may be one reason why Enterprise is now America's largest rental car company.

In a down economy, these CEOs were running against the tide. When the economy began to slow, most corporate leaders' first reaction was to cut the size of their workforce. In 2001 alone, companies let more than one million workers go. Why? It immediately cuts operating expenses. For public companies, it sends a message to stock investors and analysts that management is serious about maintaining profits or reducing losses. A week after Boeing announced that it was laying off 20 percent of its workforce, its stock jumped 10 percent.

Questions

1. What are the arguments for and against layoffs in hard times?

2. How have the three executives in this case shown leadership?

3. Recent research indicates that stocks of companies that initiated cutbacks of 15 percent or more during an economic downturn underperformed their rivals who kept their layoffs to a minimum. Reconcile this finding with the facts in the case.

Source: Q. Hardy, "Cease Firing," *Forbes*, November 26, 2001, pp. 150–51.

KSS PROGRAM

KNOW THE CONCEPTS
SELF-AWARENESS
SKILLS APPLICATIONS

Developing Trust

After you've read this chapter, take Self-Assessment #29 ("Do Others See Me as Trusting?") on your enclosed CD-ROM, and complete the skill-building module entitled Developing Trust on page 623.

Endnotes

1. This opening vignette is based on J. Steinhauer, "In Crisis, Giuliani's Popularity Overflows City," *New York Times*, September 20, 2001, p. A1; C. Jones, "Giuliani Exits as National Icon," *USA Today*, December 28, 2001, p. 3A; D. Barry, "A Man Who Became More Than a Mayor," *New York Times*, December 31, 2001, p. A1; and E. Pooley, "Mayor of the World," *Time*, December 31, 2001–January 7, 2002.

2. Based on S. D. Boon and J. G. Holmes, "The Dynamics of Interpersonal Trust: Resolving Uncertainty in the Face of Risk," in R. A. Hinde and J. Groebel (eds.), *Cooperation and Prosocial Behavior* (Cambridge, UK: Cambridge University Press, 1991), p. 194; D. J. McAllister, "Affect- and Cognition-Based Trust as Foundations for Interpersonal Cooperation in Organizations," *Academy of Management Journal*, February 1995, p. 25; and D. M. Rousseau, S. B. Sitkin, R. S. Burt, and C. Camerer, "Not So Different After All: A Cross-Discipline View of Trust," *Academy of Management Review*, July 1998, pp. 393–404.

3. J. B. Rotter, "Interpersonal Trust, Trustworthiness, and Gullibility," *American Psychologist*, January 1980, pp. 1–7.

4. J. D. Lewis and A. Weigert, "Trust as a Social Reality," *Social Forces*, June 1985, p. 970.

5. J. K. Rempel, J. G. Holmes, and M. P. Zanna, "Trust in Close Relationships," *Journal of Personality and Social Psychology*, July 1985, p. 96.

6. M. Granovetter, "Economic Action and Social Structure: The Problem of Embeddedness," *American Journal of Sociology*, November 1985, p. 491.

7. R. C. Mayer, J. H. Davis, and F. D. Schoorman, "An Integrative Model of Organizational Trust," *Academy of Management Review*, July 1995, p. 712.

8. C. Johnson-George and W. Swap, "Measurement of Specific Interpersonal Trust: Construction and Validation of a Scale to Assess Trust in a Specific Other," *Journal of Personality and Social Psychology*, September 1982, p. 1306.

9. P. L. Schindler and C. C. Thomas, "The Structure of Interpersonal Trust in the Workplace," *Psychological Reports*, October 1993, pp. 563–73.

10. H. H. Tan and C. S. F. Tan, "Toward the Differentiation of Trust in Supervisor and Trust in Organization," *Genetic, Social, and General Psychology Monographs*, May 2000, pp. 241–60.

11. J. K. Butler Jr. and R. S. Cantrell, "A Behavioral Decision Theory Approach to Modeling Dyadic Trust in Superiors and Subordinates," *Psychological Reports*, August 1984, pp. 19–28.

12. D. McGregor, *The Professional Manager* (New York: McGraw-Hill, 1967), p. 164.

13. B. Nanus, *The Leader's Edge: The Seven Keys to Leadership in a Turbulent World* (Chicago: Contemporary Books, 1989), p. 102.

14. "Chrysler: Not Quite So Equal," *Business Week*, November 13, 2000, p. 14.

15. See, for instance, K. T. Dirks and D. L. Ferrin, "The Effects of Trust in Leadership on Employee Performance, Behavior, and Attitudes: A Meta-Analysis;" paper presented at the Academy of Management Conference; Toronto, Canada; August 2000; and J. B. Cunningham and J. MacGregor, "Trust and the Design of Work: Complementary Constructs in Satisfaction and Performance," *Human Relations*, December 2000, pp. 1575–91.

16. D. E. Zand, *The Leadership Triad: Knowledge, Trust, and Power* (New York: Oxford Press, 1997), p. 89.

17. Based on L. T. Hosmer, "Trust: The Connecting Link between Organizational Theory and Philosophical Ethics," *Academy of Management Review*, April 1995, p. 393; and R. C. Mayer, J. H. Davis, and F. D. Schoorman, "An Integrative Model of Organizational Trust," *Academy of Management Review*, July 1995, p. 712.

18. J. M. Kouzes and B. Z. Posner, *Credibility: How Leaders Gain and Lose It, and Why People Demand It* (San Francisco: Jossey-Bass, 1993), p. 14.

19. J. Brockner, P. A. Siegel, J. P. Daly, T. Tyler, and C. Martin, "When Trust Matters: The Moderating Effect of Outcome Favorability," *Administrative Science Quarterly*, September 1997, p. 558; S. Armour, "Employees' New Motto: Trust No One," *USA Today*, February 5, 2002, p. 1B; J. Scott, "Once Bitten, Twice Shy: A World of Eroding Trust," *New York Times*, April 21, 2002, p. WK5; and J. A. Byrne, "Restoring Trust in Corporate America," *Business Week*, June 24, 2002, pp. 30–35.

20. "WorkUSA 2000 Survey Finds Only Half of U.S. Workers are Committed to Employers," www.watsonwyatt.com, January 11, 2000.

21. This section is based on D. Shapiro, B. H. Sheppard, and L. Cheraskin, "Business on a Handshake," *Negotiation Journal*,

October 1992, pp. 365–77; R. J. Lewicki and B. B. Bunker, "Developing and Maintaining Trust in Work Relationships," in R. M. Kramer and T. R. Tyler (eds.), *Trust in Organizations* (Thousand Oaks, CA: Sage, 1996), pp. 119–24; and J. Child, "Trust—The Fundamental Bond in Global Collaboration," *Organizational Dynamics*, vol. 29, no. 4, 2001, pp. 274–88.

22. A. Bryman, "Leadership in Organizations," in S. R. Clegg, C. Hardy, and W. R. Nord (eds.), *Managing Organizations: Current Issues* (Thousand Oaks, CA: Sage, 1999), p. 30.

23. See R. M. Entman, "Framing: Toward Clarification of a Fractured Paradigm," *Journal of Communication*, Autumn 1993, pp. 51–58; and G. T. Fairhurst and R. A. Starr, *The Art of Framing: Managing the Language of Leadership* (San Francisco: Jossey-Bass, 1996), p. 21.

24. G. T. Fairhurst and R. A. Starr, *The Art of Framing*, p. 4.

25. J. A. Conger and R. N. Kanungo, "Behavioral Dimensions of Charismatic Leadership," in J. A. Conger, R. N. Kanungo and Associates, *Charismatic Leadership* (San Francisco: Jossey-Bass, 1988), p. 79.

26. J. A. Conger and R. N. Kanungo, *Charismatic Leadership in Organizations* (Thousand Oaks, CA: Sage, 1998); and R. Awamleh and W. L. Gardner, "Perceptions of Leader Charisma and Effectiveness: The Effects of Vision Content, Delivery, and Organizational Performance," *Leadership Quarterly*, Fall 1999, pp. 345–73.

27. B. Shamir, R. J. House, and M. B. Arthur, "The Motivational Effects of Charismatic Leadership: A Self-Concept Theory," *Organization Science*, November 1993, pp. 577–94.

28. R. J. House, J. Woycke, and E. M. Fodor, "Charismatic and Noncharismatic Leaders: Differences in Behavior and Effectiveness," in Conger and Kanungo, *Charismatic Leadership*, pp. 103–04; D. A. Waldman, B. M. Bass, and F. J. Yammarino, "Adding to Contingent-Reward Behavior: The Augmenting Effect of Charismatic Leadership," *Group & Organization Studies*, December 1990, pp. 381–94; S. A. Kirkpatrick and E. A. Locke, "Direct and Indirect Effects of Three Core Charismatic Leadership Components on Performance and Attitudes," *Journal of Applied Psychology*, February 1996, pp. 36–51; and R. J. Deluga, "American Presidential Machiavellianism: Implications for Charismatic Leadership and Rated Performance," *Leadership Quarterly*, Fall 2001, pp. 339–63.

29. J. A. Conger and R. N. Kanungo, "Training Charismatic Leadership: A Risky and Critical Task," *Charismatic Leadership*, pp. 309–23; and S. Caudron, "Growing Charisma," *Industry Week*, May 4, 1998, pp. 54–55.

30. R. J. Richardson and S. K. Thayer, *The Charisma Factor: How to Develop Your Natural Leadership Ability* (Upper Saddle River, NJ: Prentice Hall, 1993).

31. J. M. Howell and P. J. Frost, "A Laboratory Study of Charismatic Leadership," *Organizational Behavior and Human Decision Processes*, April 1989, pp. 243–69.

32. R. J. House, "A 1976 Theory of Charismatic Leadership," in J. G. Hunt and L. L. Larson (eds.), *Leadership: The Cutting Edge* (Carbondale: Southern Illinois University Press, 1977), pp. 189–207; and R. J. House and R. N. Aditya, "The Social Scientific Study of Leadership," p. 441.

33. See A. Taylor III, "Is Jack Smith the Man to Fix GM?" *Fortune*, August 3, 1998, pp. 86–92.

34. See, for instance, B. M. Bass, *Leadership and Performance Beyond Expectations* (New York: Free Press, 1985); B. M. Bass,

"From Transactional to Transformational Leadership: Learning to Share the Vision," *Organizational Dynamics*, Winter 1990, pp. 19–31; F. J. Yammarino, W. D. Spangler, and B. M. Bass, "Transformational Leadership and Performance: A Longitudinal Investigation," *Leadership Quarterly*, Spring 1993, pp. 81–102; J. C. Wofford, V. L. Goodwin, and J. L. Whittington, "A Field Study of a Cognitive Approach to Understanding Transformational and Transactional Leadership," *Leadership Quarterly*, vol. 9, no. 1, 1998, pp. 55–84; and N. M. Ashkanasy and B. Tse, "Transformational Leadership as Management of Emotion: A Conceptual Review," in N. M. Ashkanasy, C. E. J. Hartel, and W. J. Zerbe (eds), *Emotions in the Workplace: Research, Theory, and Practice* (Westport, CT: Quorum Books, 2000), pp. 221–35.

35. B. M. Bass, "Leadership: Good, Better, Best," *Organizational Dynamics*, Winter 1985, pp. 26–40; and J. Seltzer and B. M. Bass, "Transformational Leadership: Beyond Initiation and Consideration," *Journal of Management*, December 1990, pp. 693–703.

36. B. J. Avolio and B. M. Bass, "Transformational Leadership, Charisma and Beyond," working paper, School of Management, State University of New York, Binghamton, 1985, p. 14.

37. Cited in B. M. Bass and B. J. Avolio, "Developing Transformational Leadership: 1992 and Beyond," *Journal of European Industrial Training*, January 1990, p. 23.

38. J. J. Hater and B. M. Bass, "Supervisors' Evaluation and Subordinates' Perceptions of Transformational and Transactional Leadership," *Journal of Applied Psychology*, November 1988, pp. 695–702.

39. Bass and Avolio, "Developing Transformational Leadership"; K. B. Lowe, K. G. Kroeck, and N. Sivasubramaniam, "Effectiveness Correlates of Transformational and Transactional Leadership: A Meta-Analytic Review of the MLQ Literature," *Leadership Quarterly*, Fall 1996, pp. 385–425; and T. A. Judge and J. E. Bono, "Five-Factor Model of Personality and Transformational Leadership," *Journal of Applied Psychology*, October 2000, pp. 751–65.

40. This definition is based on M. Sashkin, "The Visionary Leader," in J. A. Conger and R. N. Kanungo (eds.), *Charismatic Leadership*, pp. 124–25; B. Nanus, *Visionary Leadership* (New York: Free Press, 1992), p. 8; N. H. Snyder and M. Graves, "Leadership and Vision," *Business Horizons*, January–February 1994, p. 1; and J. R. Lucas, "Anatomy of a Vision Statement," *Management Review*, February 1998, pp. 22–26.

41. B. Nanus, *Visionary Leadership*, p. 8.

42. P. C. Nutt and R. W. Backoff, "Crafting Vision," *Journal of Management Inquiry*, December 1997, p. 309.

43. Ibid., pp. 312–14.

44. Based on M. Sashkin, "The Visionary Leader," pp. 128–30; and J. R. Baum, E. A. Locke, and S. A. Kirkpatrick, "A Longitudinal Study of the Relation of Vision and Vision Communication to Venture Growth in Entrepreneurial Firms," *Journal of Applied Psychology*, February 1998, pp. 43–54.

45. This section is based on D. Goleman, *Working with Emotional Intelligence* (New York: Bantam, 1998); D. Goleman, "What Makes a Leader?" *Harvard Business Review*, November–December 1998, pp. 93–102; J. M. George, "Emotions and Leadership: The Role of Emotional

Intelligence," *Human Relations*, August 2000, pp. 1027–55; D. R. Caruso, J. D. Mayer, and P. Salovey, "Emotional Intelligence and Emotional Leadership," in R. E. Riggio, S. E. Murphy, and F. J. Pirozzolo (eds.), *Multiple Intelligences and Leadership* (Mahwah, NJ: Lawrence Erlbaum, 2002), pp. 55–74; and D. Goleman, R. E. Boyatzis, and A. McKee, *Primal Leadership: Realizing the Power of Emotional Intelligence* (Boston: Harvard Business School Press, 2002).

46. "The Secret Skill of Leaders," *U.S. News & World Report*, January 14, 2002, p. 8.

47. Ibid.

48. See, for instance, J. H. Zenger, E. Musselwhite, K. Hurson, and C. Perrin, *Leading Teams: Mastering the New Role* (Homewood, IL: Business One Irwin, 1994); M. Frohman, "Nothing Kills Teams Like Ill-Prepared Leaders," *Industry Week*, October 2, 1995, pp. 72–76; and S. Taggar, R. Hackett, and S. Saha, "Leadership Emergence in Autonomous Work Teams: Antecedents and Outcomes," *Personnel Psychology*, Winter 1999, pp. 899–926.

49. S. Caminiti, "What Team Leaders Need to Know," *Fortune*, February 20, 1995, pp. 93–100.

50. Ibid., p. 93.

51. Ibid., p. 100.

52. N. Steckler and N. Fondas, "Building Team Leader Effectiveness: A Diagnostic Tool," *Organizational Dynamics*, Winter 1995, p. 20.

53. R. S. Wellins, W. C. Byham, and G. R. Dixon, *Inside Teams* (San Francisco: Jossey-Bass, 1994), p. 318.

54. N. Steckler and N. Fondas, "Building Team Leader Effectiveness," p. 21.

55. See, for example, L. J. Zachary, *The Mentor's Guide: Facilitating Effective Learning Relationships* (San Francisco: Jossey-Bass, 2000); and M. Murray, *Beyond the Myths and Magic of Mentoring: How to Facilitate an Effective Mentoring Process*, rev. ed. (New York: Wiley, 2001).

56. K. McLaughlin, "Training Top 50: Edward Jones," *Training*, March 2001, pp. 78–79.

57. J. A. Wilson and N. S. Elman, "Organizational Benefits of Mentoring," *Academy of Management Executive*, November 1990, p. 90; and J. Reingold, "Want to Grow as a Leader? Get a Mentor?" *Fast Company*, January 2001, pp. 58–60.

58. G. F. Dreher and R. A. Ash, "A Comparative Study of Mentoring Among Men and Women in Managerial, Professional, and Technical Positions," *Journal of Applied Psychology*, October 1990, pp. 539–46.

59. See, for example, D. A. Thomas, "The Impact of Race on Managers' Experiences of Developmental Relationships: An Intra-Organizational Study," *Journal of Organizational Behavior*, November 1990, pp. 479–92; K. E. Kram and D. T. Hall, "Mentoring in a Context of Diversity and Turbulence," in E. E. Kossek and S. A. Lobel, *Managing Diversity* (Cambridge, MA: Blackwell, 1996), pp. 108–36; M. N. Ruderman and M. W. Hughes-James, "Leadership Development Across Race and Gender," in C. D. McCauley, R. S. Moxley, and E. Van Velsor (eds.), *The Center for Creative Leadership Handbook of Leadership Development* (San Francisco: Jossey-Bass, 1998), pp. 291–335; and B. R. Ragins and J. L. Cotton, "Mentor Functions and Outcomes: A Comparison of Men and Women in Formal and Informal Mentoring Relationships," *Journal of Applied Psychology*, August 1999, pp. 529–50.

60. A. H. Eagly and B. T. Johnson, "Gender and Leadership Style: A Meta-Analysis," *Psychological Bulletin*, September 1990, pp. 233–56; J. D. Mayer, D. R. Caruso, and P. Salovey, "Emotional Intelligence Meets Traditional Standards for an Intelligence," *Intelligence*, vol. 27, 1999, pp. 267–98; H. Fisher, *The First Sex: The Natural Talents of Women and How They Are Changing the World* (New York: Ballantine, 2000); and R. Sharpe, "As Leaders, Women Rule," *Business Week*, November 20, 2000, pp. 75–84.

61. J. A. Wilson and N. S. Elman, "Organizational Benefits of Mentoring," p. 90.

62. See C. C. Manz, "Self-Leadership: Toward an Expanded Theory of Self-Influence Processes in Organizations," *Academy of Management Review*, July 1986, pp. 585–600; C. C. Manz and H. P. Sims Jr., "Superleadership: Beyond the Myth of Heroic Leadership," *Organizational Dynamics*, Spring 1991, pp. 18–35; H. P. Sims Jr. and C. C. Manz, *Company of Heroes: Unleashing the Power of Self-Leadership* (New York: Wiley, 1996); M. Uhl-Bien and G. B. Graen, "Individual Self-Management: Analysis of Professionals' Self-Managing Activities in Functional and Cross-Functional Work Teams," *Academy of Management Journal*, June 1998, pp. 340–50; G. Dessler, "How to Earn Your Employees' Commitment," *Academy of Management Executive*, May 1999, pp. 58–67; and C. C. Manz and H. P. Sims Jr., *The New Superleadership: Leading Others to Lead Themselves* (San Francisco: Berrett-Koehler, 2001).

63. Based on C. C. Manz and H. P. Sims Jr, "Superleadership."

64. This section is based on R. B. Morgan, "Self- and Co-Worker Perceptions of Ethics and Their Relationships to Leadership and Salary," *Academy of Management Journal*, February 1993, pp. 200–14; E. P. Hollander, "Ethical Challenges in the Leader–Follower Relationship," *Business Ethics Quarterly*, January 1995, pp. 55–65; J. C. Rost, "Leadership: A Discussion About Ethics," *Business Ethics Quarterly*, January 1995, pp. 129–42; R. N. Kanungo and M. Mendonca, *Ethical Dimensions of Leadership* (Thousand Oaks, CA: Sage Publications, 1996); J. B. Ciulla (ed.), *Ethics: The Heart of Leadership* (New York: Praeger Publications, 1998); and J. D. Costa, *The Ethical Imperative: Why Moral Leadership Is Good Business* (Cambridge, MA: Perseus Press, 1999).

65. J. M. Burns, *Leadership* (New York: Harper & Row, 1978).

66. J. M. Howell and B. J. Avolio, "The Ethics of Charismatic Leadership: Submission or Liberation?" *Academy of Management Executive*, May 1992, pp. 43–55.

67. An exception is B. J. Avolio, S. Kahai, and G. E. Dodge, "E-Leadership: Implications for Theory, Research, and Practice," *Leadership Quarterly*, Winter 2000, pp. 615–68.

68. Comment by Jim Collins and cited in J. Useem, "Conquering Vertical Limits," *Fortune*, February 19, 2001, p. 94.

69. See, for instance, J. C. McElroy, "A Typology of Attribution Leadership Research," *Academy of Management Review*, July 1982, pp. 413–17; J. R. Meindl and S. B. Ehrlich, "The Romance of Leadership and the Evaluation of Organizational Performance," *Academy of Management Journal*, March 1987, pp. 91–109; R. G. Lord and K. J. Maher, *Leadership and Information Processing: Linking Perception and Performance* (Boston: Unwin Hyman, 1991); B. Shamir, "Attribution of Influence and Charisma to the

Leader: The Romance of Leadership Revisited," *Journal of Applied Social Psychology*, March 1992, pp. 386–407; and J. R. Meindl, "The Romance of Leadership as a Follower-Centric Theory: A Social Constructionist Approach," *Leadership Quarterly*, Fall 1995, pp. 329–41.

70. R. G. Lord, C. L. DeVader, and G. M. Alliger, "A Meta-Analysis of the Relation Between Personality Traits and Leadership Perceptions: An Application of Validity Generalization Procedures," *Journal of Applied Psychology*, August 1986, pp. 402–10.

71. G. N. Powell and D. A. Butterfield, "The 'High-High' Leader Rides Again!" *Group & Organization Studies*, December 1984, pp. 437–50.

72. J. R. Meindl, S. B. Ehrlich, and J. M. Dukerich, "The Romance of Leadership," *Administrative Science Quarterly*, March 1985, pp. 78–102.

73. B. M. Staw and J. Ross, "Commitment in an Experimenting Society: A Study of the Attribution of Leadership from Administrative Scenarios," *Journal of Applied Psychology*, June 1980, pp. 249–60; and J. Pfeffer, *Managing with Power* (Boston: Harvard Business School Press, 1992), p. 194.

74. S. Kerr and J. M. Jermier, "Substitutes for Leadership: Their Meaning and Measurement," *Organizational Behavior and Human Performance*, December 1978, pp. 375–403; P. M. Podsakoff, S. B. MacKenzie, and W. H. Bommer, "Meta-Analysis of the Relationships Between Kerr and Jermier's Substitutes for Leadership and Employee Attitudes, Role Perceptions, and Performance," *Journal of Applied Psychology*, August 1996, pp. 380–99; and J. M. Jermier and

S. Kerr, "Substitutes for Leadership: Their Meaning and Measurement—Contextual Recollections and Current Observations," *Leadership Quarterly*, vol. 8, no. 2, 1997, pp. 95–101.

75. For one prominent scholar's view on this topic, see F. E. Fiedler, "Research on Leadership Selection and Training: One View of the Future," *Administrative Science Quarterly*, June 1996, pp. 241–50.

76. B. M. Bass, "Cognitive, Social, and Emotional Intelligence of Transformational Leaders," in R. E. Riggio, S. E. Murphy, and F. J. Pirozzolo (eds.), *Multiple Intelligences and Leadership*, pp. 113–14.

77. See, for instance, R. Lofthouse, "Herding the Cats," *EuroBusiness*, February 2001, pp. 64–65; and M. Delahoussaye, "Leadership in the 21st Century," *Training*, September 2001, pp. 60–72.

78. See, for instance, A. A. Vicere, "Executive Education: The Leading Edge," *Organizational Dynamics*, Autumn 1996, pp. 67–81; J. Barling, T. Weber, and E. K. Kelloway, "Effects of Transformational Leadership Training on Attitudinal and Financial Outcomes: A Field Experiment," *Journal of Applied Psychology*, December 1996, pp. 827–32; and D. V. Day, "Leadership Development: A Review in Context," *Leadership Quarterly*, Winter 2000, pp. 581–613.

79. M. Sashkin, "The Visionary Leader," in J. A. Conger, R. N. Kanungo and Associates (eds.), *Charismatic Leadership* (San Francisco: Jossey-Bass, 1988), p. 150.

80. J. M. Howell and P. J. Frost, "A Laboratory Study of Charismatic Leadership."

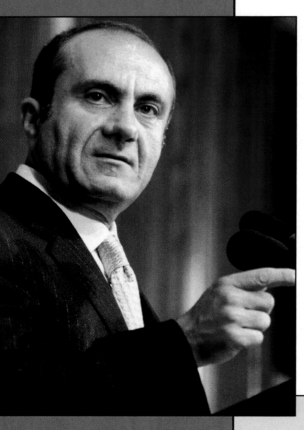

> *Sincerity is the key to success. If you can fake that, you've got it made.*
> —**G. Marx**

PART THREE

THE GROUP

Don't upset the guy who controls 40 percent of your company's stock! That's the lesson Jacques Nasser (see photo) has learned after being ousted from his position as CEO at Ford Motor Co.[1]

Nasser had spent 33 years at Ford, working his way up through the company's international division. He built his reputation as an aggressive cost cutter. That reputation, plus his vision and commitment to reinventing Ford, were the primary reasons he was appointed CEO in January 1999. But on his watch, the company's performance suffered serious setbacks. He took his eye off "the ball"—Ford's basic product line—and spent $13 billion of the company's $15 billion cash reserves to acquire Jaguar, Aston Martin, Volvo, and Land Rover. In the interim, Ford's product quality slipped badly and production efficiency seriously eroded. The company's U.S. market share fell from 28 percent to 22.6 percent. And the recall of nearly 20 million Firestone tires, linked with rollovers of Ford Explorers, cost the company in excess of $3 billion and a lot of goodwill. In three years, Nasser had burned through Ford's cash reserves, leaving the company little money to invest in the new models that are the lifeblood of the auto business.

As CEO, Nasser's style managed to anger almost every core relationship Ford Motor had. Relations with the company's unions, dealers, white-collar employees, and suppliers all suffered as he focused on them to reduce costs. By the fall of 2001, it became increasingly clear to William Clay Ford, Jr., the 44-year-old company chairman and great-grandson of the company's founder, that Nasser lacked the political skills to lead the company out of its problems. Nasser undermined relationships that the company highly valued and financial losses were mounting. He alienated many people with the decisions he made. Most importantly, he alienated Mr. Ford, whose family controlled 40 percent of the company's voting stock. On October 30, 2001, Mr. Ford called Nasser into his office and ended

Power and Politics

Nasser's 33-year career with the company. As one financial analyst concluded in assessing Nasser's demise at Ford, "This is an old school industrial company. You have to be diplomatic. This is a big organization, and there are politics you have to deal with."[2] Jacques Nasser didn't have those political skills. And he failed to maintain the support of the one person with the power to give him the boot.

*P*ower has been described as the last dirty word. It is easier for most of us to talk about money than it is to talk about power. People who have it deny it, people who want it try not to appear to be seeking it, and those who are good at getting it are secretive about how they got it.[3]

A major theme of this chapter is that power is a natural process in any group or organization. As such, you need to know how it's acquired and exercised if you're going to fully understand organizational behavior. Although you may have heard the phrase that "power corrupts, and absolute power corrupts absolutely," power is not always bad. As one author has noted, most medicines can kill if taken in the wrong amount and thousands die each year in automobile accidents, but we don't abandon chemicals or cars because of the dangers associated with them. Rather, we consider danger an incentive to get training and information that will help us to use these forces productively.[4] The same applies to power. It's a reality of organizational life and it's not going to go away. Moreover, by learning how power works in organizations, you'll be better able to use your knowledge to help you be a more effective manager.

AFTER STUDYING THIS CHAPTER, YOU SHOULD BE ABLE TO:

1. Contrast leadership and power.
2. Define the seven bases of power.
3. Clarify what creates dependency in power relationships.
4. List seven power tactics and their contingencies.
5. Explain how sexual harassment is about the abuse of power.
6. Describe the importance of a political perspective.
7. List the individual and organizational factors that stimulate political behavior.
8. Identify seven techniques for managing the impression one makes on others.
9. Explain how defensive behaviors can protect an individual's self-interest.
10. List the three questions that can help determine if a political action is ethical.

A DEFINITION OF POWER

power

A capacity that *A* has to influence the behavior of *B* so that *B* acts in accordance with *A*'s wishes.

dependency

B's relationship to *A* when *A* possesses something that *B* requires.

Power refers to a capacity that *A* has to influence the behavior of *B*, so that *B* acts in accordance with *A*'s wishes.[5] This definition implies a *potential* that need not be actualized to be effective and a *dependency* relationship.

Power may exist but not be used. It is, therefore, a capacity or potential. One can have power but not impose it.

Probably the most important aspect of power is that it is a function of **dependency**. The greater *B*'s dependence on *A*, the greater is *A*'s power in the relationship. Dependence, in turn, is based on alternatives that *B* perceives and the importance that *B* places on the alternative(s) that *A* controls. A person can have power over you only if he or she controls something you desire. If you want a college degree and have to pass a certain course to get it, and your current instructor is the only faculty member in the college who teaches that course, he or she has power over you. Your alternatives are highly limited and you place a high degree of importance on obtaining a passing grade. Similarly, if you're attending college on funds totally provided by your parents, you probably recognize the power that they hold over you. You're dependent on them for financial support. But once you're out of school, have a job, and are making a good income, your parents' power is reduced significantly. Who among us, though, has not known or heard of the rich relative who is able to control a large number of family members merely through the implicit or explicit threat of "writing them out of the will"?

CONTRASTING LEADERSHIP AND POWER

A careful comparison of our description of power with our description of leadership in the previous two chapters reveals that the concepts are closely intertwined. Leaders use power as a means of attaining group goals. Leaders achieve goals, and power is a means of facilitating their achievement.

What differences are there between the two terms? One difference relates to goal compatibility. Power does not require goal compatibility, merely dependence. Leadership, on the other hand, requires some congruence between the goals of the leader and those being led. A second difference relates to the direction of influence. Leadership focuses on the downward influence on one's followers. It minimizes the importance of lateral and upward influence patterns. Power does not. Still another difference deals with research emphasis. Leadership research, for the most part, emphasizes style. It seeks answers to questions such as: How supportive should a leader be? How much decision making should be shared with followers? In contrast, the research on power has tended to encompass a broader area and to focus on tactics for gaining compliance. It has gone beyond the individual as exerciser because power can be used by groups as well as by individuals to control other individuals or groups.

Formal power is based on an individual's position in an organization. Ken Chenault derives his power at American Express from his position as CEO.

BASES OF POWER

Where does power come from? What is it that gives an individual or a group influence over others? We answer these questions by dividing the bases or sources of power into two general groupings—formal and personal—and then breaking each of these down into more specific categories.[6]

Formal Power

Formal power is based on an individual's position in an organization. Formal power can come from the ability to coerce or reward, from formal authority, or from control of information.

Coercive Power   The **coercive power** base is dependent on fear. One reacts to this power out of fear of the negative results that might occur if one failed to comply. It rests on the application, or the threat of application, of physical sanctions such as the infliction of pain, the generation of frustration through restriction of movement, or the controlling by force of basic physiological or safety needs.

At the organizational level, A has coercive power over B if A can dismiss, suspend, or demote B, assuming that B values his or her job. Similarly, if A can assign B work activities that B finds unpleasant or treat B in a manner that B finds embarrassing, A possesses coercive power over B.

coercive power

A power base dependent on fear.

Reward Power   The opposite of coercive power is **reward power**. People comply with the wishes or directives of another because doing so produces positive benefits; therefore, one who can distribute rewards that others view as valuable will have power over those others. These rewards can be either financial—such as controlling pay rates, raises, and bonuses; or nonfinancial—including merit recognition, promotions, interesting work assignments, friendly colleagues, and preferred work shifts or sales territories.[7]

Coercive power and reward power are actually counterparts of each other. If you can remove something of positive value from another or inflict something of negative value on him or her, you have coercive power over that person. If you can give someone something of positive value or remove something of negative value, you have reward power over that person.

reward power

Compliance achieved based on the ability to distribute rewards that others view as valuable.

Legitimate Power   In formal groups and organizations, probably the most frequent access to one or more of the power bases is one's structural position. This is called **legitimate power**. It represents the formal authority to control and use organizational resources.

Positions of authority include coercive and reward powers. Legitimate power, however, is broader than the power to coerce and reward. Specifically, it includes acceptance by members in an organization of the authority of a position. When school principals, bank presidents, or army captains speak (assuming that their directives are viewed to be within the authority of their positions), teachers, tellers, and first lieutenants listen and usually comply.

legitimate power

The power a person receives as a result of his or her position in the formal hierarchy of an organization.

Information Power   The fourth source of formal power—**information power**—comes from access to and control over information. People in an organization who have data or knowledge that others need can make those others dependent on them. Managers, for instance, because of their access to privileged sales, cost, salary, profit, and similar data, can use this information to control and shape

information power

Power that comes from access to and control over information.

EXHIBIT

13-1

"I was just going to say 'Well, I don't make the rules.' But, of course, I _do_ make the rules."

Source: Drawing by Leo Cullum in the New Yorker, Copyright © 1986. The New Yorker Magazine. Reprinted by permission.

subordinates' behavior. Similarly, departments that possess information that is critical to a company's performance in times of high uncertainty—for example the legal department when a firm faces a major lawsuit or the human resources department during critical labor negotiations—will gain increased power in their organization until those uncertainties are resolved.

Personal Power

You don't have to have a formal position in an organization to have power. Many of the most competent and productive chip designers at Intel, for instance, have power, but they aren't managers and have no formal power. What they have is personal power—power that comes from an individual's unique characteristics. In this section, we look at three bases of personal power—expertise, the respect and admiration of others, and charisma.

expert power

Influence based on special skills or knowledge.

Expert Power   **Expert power** is influence wielded as a result of expertise, special skill, or knowledge. Expertise has become one of the most powerful sources of influence as the world has become more technologically oriented. As jobs become more specialized, we become increasingly dependent on experts to achieve goals. So, although it is generally acknowledged that physicians have expertise and hence expert power—most of us follow the advice that our doctor gives us—you should also recognize that computer specialists, tax accountants, economists, industrial psychologists, and other specialists are able to wield power as a result of their expertise.

Referent Power   **Referent power** is based on identification with a person who has desirable resources or personal traits. If I like, respect, and admire you, you can exercise power over me because I want to please you.

referent power

Influence based on possession by an individual of desirable resources or personal traits.

Referent power develops out of admiration of another and a desire to be like that person. It helps explain, for instance, why celebrities are paid millions of dollars to endorse products in commercials. Marketing research shows that people like Michael Jordan and Britney Spears have the power to influence your choice of athletic shoes and cola drinks. With a little practice, you and I could probably deliver as smooth a sales pitch as these celebrities, but the buying public doesn't identify with you and me.

Charismatic Power   The final base of power is charisma. **Charismatic power** is really an extension of referent power stemming from an individual's personality and interpersonal style. As we noted in the previous chapter, charismatic leaders get others to follow them because they can articulate attractive visions, take personal risks, demonstrate environmental and follower sensitivity, and are willing to engage in behavior that most others consider unconventional. But many organizations will have people with charismatic qualities who, while not in formal leadership positions, nevertheless are able to exert influence over others because of the strength of their heroic qualities.

charismatic power

An extension of referent power stemming from an individual's personality and interpersonal style.

DEPENDENCY: THE KEY TO POWER

Earlier in this chapter it was said that probably the most important aspect of power is that it is a function of dependence. In this section, we show how an understanding of dependency is central to furthering your understanding of power itself.

The General Dependency Postulate

Let's begin with a general postulate: *The greater B's dependency on A, the greater the power A has over B.* When you possess anything that others require but that you alone control, you make them dependent on you and, therefore, you gain power over them.[8] Dependency, then, is inversely proportional to the alternative sources of supply. If something is plentiful, possession of it will not increase your power. If everyone is intelligent, intelligence gives no special advantage. Similarly, among the superrich, money is no longer power. But, as the old saying goes, "In the land of the blind, the one-eyed man is king!" If you can create a monopoly by controlling information, prestige, or anything that others crave, they become dependent on you. Conversely, the more that you can expand your options, the less power you place in the hands of others. This explains, for example, why most organizations develop multiple suppliers rather than give their business to only one. It also explains why so many of us aspire to financial independence. Financial independence reduces the power that others can have over us.

What Creates Dependency?

Dependency is increased when the resource you control is important, scarce, and nonsubstitutable.[9]

Importance   If nobody wants what you've got, it's not going to create dependency. To create dependency, therefore, the thing(s) you control must be perceived as being important. Organizations, for instance, actively seek to avoid uncertainty.[10] We should, therefore, expect that the individuals or groups who can absorb an organization's uncertainty will be perceived as controlling an important resource. For instance, a study of industrial organizations found that the marketing departments in these firms were consistently rated as the most powerful.[11] It was concluded by the researcher that the most critical uncertainty facing these firms was selling their products. This might suggest that engineers, as a group, would be more powerful at Matsushita than at Procter & Gamble. These inferences appear to be generally valid. An organization such as Matsushita, which is heavily technologically oriented, is highly dependent on its engineers to maintain its products' technical advantages and quality. And, at Matsushita, engineers are clearly a powerful group. At Procter & Gamble, marketing is the name of the game, and marketers are the most powerful occupational group.

The location of power varies from organization to organization. At Matsushita, engineers like this team, which worked on the digital television and the smart refrigerator, tend to be powerful.

Scarcity   As noted previously, if something is plentiful, possession of it will not increase your power. A resource needs to be perceived as scarce to create dependency.

This can help to explain how low-ranking members in an organization who have important knowledge not available to high-ranking members gain power over the high-ranking members. Possession of a scarce resource—in this case, important knowledge—makes the high-ranking member dependent on the low-ranking member. This also helps to make sense out of behaviors of low-ranking members that otherwise might seem illogical, such as destroying the procedure manuals that describe how a job is done, refusing to train people in their jobs or even to show others exactly what they do, creating specialized language and terminology that inhibit others from understanding their jobs, or operating in secrecy so an activity will appear more complex and difficult than it really is.

The scarcity–dependency relationship can further be seen in the power of occupational categories. Individuals in occupations in which the supply of personnel is low relative to demand can negotiate compensation and benefit packages that are far more attractive than can those in occupations for which there is an abundance of candidates. College administrators have no problem today finding English instructors. The market for computer-engineering teachers, in contrast, is extremely tight, with the demand high and the supply limited. The result is that the bargaining power of computer-engineering faculty allows them to negotiate higher salaries, lighter teaching loads, and other benefits.

Nonsubstitutability   The more that a resource has no viable substitutes, the more power that control over that resource provides. Higher education again provides an excellent example. At universities in which there are strong pressures for the faculty to publish, we can say that a department head's power over a faculty member is inversely related to that member's publication record. The more recognition the faculty member receives through publication, the more mobile he or she is. That is, since other universities want faculty who are highly published and visible, there is an increased demand for his or her services. Although the concept of tenure can act to alter this relationship by restricting the department head's alternatives, faculty members who have few or no publications have the least mobility and are subject to the greatest influence from their superiors.

POWER TACTICS

power tactics

Ways in which individuals translate power bases into specific actions.

In this section we move to the topic of **power tactics** to learn how employees translate their power bases into specific actions. Recent research indicates that there are standardized ways by which powerholders attempt to get what they want.[12]

When 165 managers were asked to write essays describing an incident in which they influenced their bosses, co-workers, or employees, a total of 370 power tactics grouped into 14 categories were identified. These answers were condensed, rewritten into a 58-item questionnaire, and given to over 750 employees. These respondents were not only asked how they went about influencing others at work but also for the possible reasons for influencing the target person. The results, which are summarized here, give us considerable insight into power tactics—how managerial employees influence others and the conditions under which one tactic is chosen over another.[13]

The findings identified seven tactical dimensions or strategies:

- *Reason:* Use of facts and data to make a logical or rational presentation of ideas
- *Friendliness:* Use of flattery, creation of goodwill, acting humble, and being friendly prior to making a request
- *Coalition:* Getting the support of other people in the organization to back up the request
- *Bargaining:* Use of negotiation through the exchange of benefits or favors
- *Assertiveness:* Use of a direct and forceful approach such as demanding compliance with requests, repeating reminders, ordering individuals to do what is asked, and pointing out that rules require compliance
- *Higher authority:* Gaining the support of higher levels in the organization to back up requests
- *Sanctions:* Use of organizationally derived rewards and punishments such as preventing or promising a salary increase, threatening to give an unsatisfactory performance evaluation, or withholding a promotion

The researchers found that employees do not rely on the seven tactics equally. However, as shown in Exhibit 13-2, the most popular strategy was the use of reason, regardless of whether the influence was directed upward or downward. In addition, researchers have uncovered five contingency variables that affect the selection of a power tactic: the manager's relative power, the manager's objectives for wanting to influence, the manager's expectation of the target person's willingness to comply, the organization's culture, and cross-cultural differences.

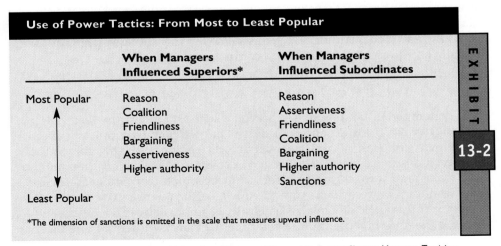

Use of Power Tactics: From Most to Least Popular

EXHIBIT 13-2

	When Managers Influenced Superiors*	When Managers Influenced Subordinates
Most Popular ↑	Reason	Reason
	Coalition	Assertiveness
	Friendliness	Friendliness
	Bargaining	Coalition
	Assertiveness	Bargaining
	Higher authority	Higher authority
↓ Least Popular		Sanctions

*The dimension of sanctions is omitted in the scale that measures upward influence.

Source: Reprinted, by permission of the publisher, from "Patterns of Managerial Influence: Shotgun Managers, Tacticians, and Bystanders," by D. Kipnis et al. *Organizational Dynamics,* Winter 1984, p. 62. © 1984 Periodicals Division, American Management Association, New York.

A manager's relative power has an impact on the selection of tactics in two ways. First, managers who control resources that are valued by others, or who are perceived to be in positions of dominance, use a greater variety of tactics than do those with less power. Second, managers with power use assertiveness with greater frequency than do those with less power. Initially, we can expect that most managers will attempt to use simple requests and reason. Assertiveness is a backup strategy, used when the target of influence refuses or appears reluctant to comply with the request. Resistance leads to managers using more directive strategies. Typically, they shift from using simple requests to insisting that their demands be met. But the manager with relatively little power is more likely to stop trying to influence others when he or she encounters resistance because he or she perceives the costs associated with assertiveness as unacceptable.

Managers vary their power tactics in relation to their objectives. When managers seek benefits from a superior, they tend to rely on kind words and the promotion of pleasant relationships; that is, they use friendliness. In comparison, managers attempting to persuade their superiors to accept new ideas usually rely on reason. This matching of tactics to objectives also holds true for downward influence. For example, managers use reason to sell ideas to employees and friendliness to obtain favors.

The manager's expectations of success guide his or her choice of tactics. When past experience indicates a high probability of success, managers use simple requests to gain compliance. When success is less predictable, managers are more tempted to use assertiveness and sanctions to achieve their objectives.

We know that cultures within organizations differ markedly—for example, some are warm, relaxed, and supportive; others are formal and conservative. The organizational culture in which a manager works, therefore, will have a significant bearing on defining which tactics are considered appropriate. Some cultures encourage the use of friendliness, some encourage reason, and still others rely on sanctions and assertiveness. So the organization itself will influence which subset of power tactics is viewed as acceptable for use by managers.

Finally, evidence indicates that people in different countries tend to prefer different power tactics. For instance, a study comparing managers in the United States and China found that the Americans perceived reason to be most effective whereas Chinese managers preferred coalition tactics and higher authority. These differences tend to be consistent with the values in these two countries. Reason is consistent with the preference of Americans for direct confrontation and the use of rational persuasion to influence others and resolve differences. Similarly, coalition tactics and higher authority are consistent with the Chinese preference for using indirect approaches for difficult or controversial requests.

POWER IN GROUPS: COALITIONS

Those "out of power" and seeking to be "in" will first try to increase their power individually. Why share the spoils if one doesn't have to? But if this proves ineffective, the alternative is to form a **coalition**—an informal group bound together by the active pursuit of a single issue.[14] The logic of a coalition? There's strength in numbers.

coalition

An informal group bound together by the active pursuit of a single issue.

The natural way to gain influence is to become a powerholder. Therefore, those who want power will attempt to build a personal power base. But, in many instances, this may be difficult, risky, costly, or impossible. In such cases, efforts will be made to form a coalition of two or more "outs" who, by joining together, can combine their resources to increase rewards for themselves.[15] Successful coalitions have been found to contain fluid membership and are able to form swiftly, achieve their target issue, and quickly disappear.[16]

What predictions can we make about coalition formation?[17] First, coalitions in organizations often seek to maximize their size. In political science theory, coalitions move the other way—they try to minimize their size. They tend to be just large enough to exert the power necessary to achieve their objectives. But legislatures are different from organizations. Specifically, decision making in organizations does not end just with selection from among a set of alternatives. The decision must also be implemented. In organizations, the implementation of and commitment to the decision is at least as important as the decision itself. It's necessary, therefore, for coalitions in organizations to seek a broad constituency to support the coalition's objectives. This means expanding the coalition to encompass as many interests as possible. This coalition expansion to facilitate consensus building, of course, is more likely to occur in organizational cultures in which cooperation, commitment, and shared decision making are highly valued. In autocratic and hierarchically controlled organizations, this search for maximizing the coalition's size is less likely to be sought.

Another prediction about coalitions relates to the degree of interdependence within the organization. More coalitions will likely be created when there is a great deal of task and resource interdependence. In contrast, there will be less interdependence among subunits and less coalition formation activity when subunits are largely self-contained or resources are abundant.

Finally, coalition formation will be influenced by the actual tasks that workers do. The more routine the task of a group, the greater the likelihood that coalitions will form. The more that the work that people do is routine, the greater their substitutability for each other and, thus, the greater their dependence. To offset this dependence, they can be expected to resort to a coalition. This helps to explain the historical appeal of labor unions, especially among low-skilled workers. Such employees are better able to negotiate improved wages, benefits, and working conditions as a united coalition than if they acted individually. A one-person "strike" has little power over management. However, if a firm's entire workforce goes on strike, management has a serious problem.

SEXUAL HARASSMENT: UNEQUAL POWER IN THE WORKPLACE

The issue of sexual harassment got increasing attention by corporations and the media in the 1980s because of the growing ranks of female employees, especially in nontraditional work environments. But it was the congressional hearings in the fall of 1991 in which law professor Anita Hill graphically accused Supreme Court nominee Clarence Thomas of sexual harassment that challenged organizations to reassess their harassment policies and practices.[18]

Sexual harassment is defined as any unwanted activity of a sexual nature that affects an individual's employment. The U.S. Supreme Court helped to clarify this definition by adding that the key test for determining if sexual harassment has occurred is whether comments or behavior in a work environment "would reasonably be perceived, and is perceived, as hostile or abusive."[19] But there continues to be disagreement as to what *specifically* constitutes sexual harassment. Organizations have generally made considerable progress in the past decade toward limiting overt forms of sexual harassment. This includes unwanted physical touching, recurring requests for dates when it is made clear the person isn't interested, and coercive threats that a person will lose his or her job if he or she refuses a sexual proposition. The problems today are likely to surface around more subtle forms of sexual harassment— unwanted looks or comments, off-color jokes, sexual artifacts like posting pin-ups in

sexual harassment

Unwelcome advances, requests for sexual favors, and other verbal or physical conduct of a sexual nature.

the workplace, or misinterpretations of where the line between "being friendly" ends and "harassment" begins.

Most studies confirm that the concept of power is central to understanding sexual harassment.[20] This seems to be true whether the harassment comes from a supervisor, a co-worker, or even an employee.

The supervisor–employee dyad best characterizes an unequal power relationship, where formal power gives the supervisor the capacity to reward and coerce. Supervisors give employees their assignments, evaluate their performance, make recommendations for salary adjustments and promotions, and even decide whether or not an employee retains his or her job. These decisions give a supervisor power. Since employees want favorable performance reviews, salary increases, and the like, it's clear supervisors control resources that most employees consider important and scarce. It's also worth noting that individuals who occupy high-status roles (like management positions) sometimes believe that sexually harassing employees is merely an extension of their right to make demands on lower-status individuals. Because of power inequities, sexual harassment by one's boss typically creates the greatest difficulty for those who are being harassed. If there are no witnesses, it is the victim's word against the harasser's. Are there others this boss has harassed and, if so, will they come forward? Because of the supervisor's control over resources, many of those who are harassed are afraid of speaking out for fear of retaliation by the supervisor.

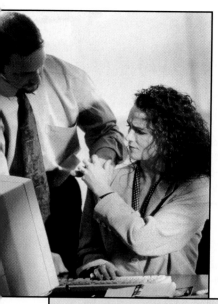

Awareness of sexual harassment has grown in recent years. More subtle forms of sexual harassment still exist, such as misinterpretation of the line between friendliness and harassment.

Although co-workers don't have legitimate power, they can have influence and use it to sexually harass peers. In fact, although co-workers appear to engage in somewhat less severe forms of harassment than do supervisors, co-workers are the most frequent perpetrators of sexual harassment in organizations. How do co-workers exercise power? Most often it's by providing or withholding information, cooperation, and support. For example, the effective performance of most jobs requires interaction and support from co-workers. This is especially true nowadays because work is often assigned to teams. By threatening to withhold or delay providing information that's necessary for the successful achievement of your work goals, co-workers can exert power over you.

Although it doesn't get nearly the attention that harassment by a supervisor does, women in positions of power can be subjected to sexual harassment from males who occupy less powerful positions within the organization. This is usually achieved by the employee devaluing the woman through highlighting traditional gender stereotypes (such as helplessness, passivity, lack of career commitment) that reflect negatively on the woman in power. An employee may engage in such practices to attempt to gain some power over the higher-ranking female or to minimize power differentials.

The topic of sexual harassment is about power. It's about an individual controlling or threatening another individual. It's wrong. And whether perpetrated against women or men, it's illegal. But you can understand how sexual harassment surfaces in organizations if you analyze it in terms of power.

POLITICS: POWER IN ACTION

When people get together in groups, power will be exerted. People want to carve out a niche from which to exert influence, to earn rewards, and to advance their careers.[21] When employees in organizations convert their power into action, we describe them as being engaged in politics. Those with good political skills have the ability to use their bases of power effectively.[22]

Definition

There has been no shortage of definitions for organizational politics. Essentially, however, they have focused on the use of power to affect decision making in the organization or on behaviors by members that are self-serving and organizationally nonsanctioned.[23] For our purposes, we shall define **political behavior** in organizations as activities that are not required as part of one's formal role in the organization, but that influence, or attempt to influence, the distribution of advantages and disadvantages within the organization.[24]

This definition encompasses key elements from what most people mean when they talk about organizational politics. Political behavior is outside one's specified job requirements. The behavior requires some attempt to use one's power bases. In addition, our definition encompasses efforts to influence the goals, criteria, or processes used for *decision making* when we state that politics is concerned with "the distribution of advantages and disadvantages within the organization." Our definition is broad enough to include varied political behaviors such as withholding key information from decision makers, joining a coalition, whistleblowing, spreading rumors, leaking confidential information about organizational activities to the media, exchanging favors with others in the organization for mutual benefit, and lobbying on behalf of or against a particular individual or decision alternative.

A final comment relates to what has been referred to as the "legitimate–illegitimate" dimension in political behavior.[25] **Legitimate political behavior** refers to normal everyday politics—complaining to your supervisor, bypassing the chain of command, forming coalitions, obstructing organizational policies or decisions through inaction or excessive adherence to rules, and developing contacts outside the organization through one's professional activities. On the other hand, there are also **illegitimate political behaviors** that violate the implied rules of the game. Those who pursue such extreme activities are often described as individuals who "play hardball." Illegitimate activities include sabotage, whistleblowing, and symbolic protests such as wearing unorthodox dress or protest buttons, and groups of employees simultaneously calling in sick.

The vast majority of all organizational political actions are of the legitimate variety. The reasons are pragmatic: The extreme illegitimate forms of political behavior pose a very real risk of loss of organizational membership or extreme sanctions against those who use them and then fall short in having enough power to ensure that they work.

The Reality of Politics

Politics is a fact of life in organizations. People who ignore this fact of life do so at their own peril. But why, you may wonder, must politics exist? Isn't it possible for an organization to be politics free? It's *possible*, but most unlikely.

Organizations are made up of individuals and groups with different values, goals, and interests.[26] This sets up the potential for conflict over resources. Departmental budgets, space allocations, project responsibilities, and salary adjustments are just a few examples of the resources about whose allocation organizational members will disagree.

Resources in organizations are also limited, which often turns potential conflict into real conflict.[27] If resources were abundant, then all the various constituencies within the organization could satisfy their goals. But because they are limited, not everyone's interests can be provided for. Furthermore, whether true or not, gains by one individual or group are often *perceived* as being at the expense of others within the organization. These forces create a competition among members for the organization's limited resources.

political behavior

Activities that are not required as part of one's formal role in the organization, but that influence, or attempt to influence, the distribution of advantages and disadvantages within the organization.

legitimate political behavior

Normal everyday politics.

illegitimate political behavior

Extreme political behavior that violates the implied rules of the game.

Whistleblowing is a form of political behavior. Sherron Watkins, formerly vice president for corporate development at Enron, was among the first to warn top management that problems were looming within the ill-fated firm.

Maybe the most important factor leading to politics within organizations is the realization that most of the "facts" that are used to allocate the limited resources are open to interpretation. What, for instance, is *good* performance? What's an *adequate* improvement? What constitutes an *unsatisfactory* job? One person's view that an act is a "selfless effort to benefit the organization" is seen by another as a "blatant attempt to further one's interest."[28] The manager of any major league baseball team knows a .400 hitter is a high performer and a .125 hitter is a poor performer. You don't need to be a baseball genius to know you should play your .400 hitter and send the .125 hitter back to the minors. But what if you have to choose between players who hit .280 and .290? Then other factors—less objective ones—come into play: fielding expertise, attitude, potential, ability to perform in a clutch, loyalty to the team, and so on. More managerial decisions resemble choosing between a .280 and a .290 hitter than deciding between a .125 hitter and a .400 hitter. It is in this large and ambiguous middle ground of organizational life—where the facts *don't* speak for themselves—that politics flourish (see Exhibit 13-3).

Finally, because most decisions have to be made in a climate of ambiguity—where facts are rarely fully objective, and thus are open to interpretation—people within organizations will use whatever influence they can to taint the facts to support their goals and interests. That, of course, creates the activities we call *politicking*.

Therefore, to answer the earlier question of whether it is possible for an organization to be politics-free, we can say: "Yes," if all members of that organization hold the same goals and interests, if organizational resources are not scarce, and if

Politics Is in the Eye of the Beholder

EXHIBIT 13-3

A behavior that one person labels as "organizational politics" is very likely to be characterized as an instance of "effective management" by another. The fact is not that effective management is necessarily political, although in some cases it might be. Rather, a person's reference point determines what he or she classifies as organizational politics. Take a look at the following labels used to describe the same phenomenon. These suggest that politics, like beauty, is in the eye of the beholder.

"Political" Label		"Effective Management" Label
1. Blaming others	vs.	Fixing responsibility
2. "Kissing up"	vs.	Developing working relationships
3. Apple polishing	vs.	Demonstrating loyalty
4. Passing the buck	vs.	Delegating authority
5. Covering your rear	vs.	Documenting decisions
6. Creating conflict	vs.	Encouraging change and innovation
7. Forming coalitions	vs.	Facilitating teamwork
8. Whistleblowing	vs.	Improving efficiency
9. Scheming	vs.	Planning ahead
10. Overachieving	vs.	Competent and capable
11. Ambitious	vs.	Career-minded
12. Opportunistic	vs.	Astute
13. Cunning	vs.	Practical-minded
14. Arrogant	vs.	Confident
15. Perfectionist	vs.	Attentive to detail

Source: Based on T. C. Krell, M. E. Mendenhall, and J. Sendry, "Doing Research in the Conceptual Morass of Organizational Politics," paper presented at the Western Academy of Management Conference, Hollywood, CA, April 1987.

MYTH

"It's Not *What* You Know, It's *Who* You Know"

This statement is somewhat true. While knowledge of *facts* is an increasingly important source of power in an information-based society, knowing the *right people* increases your chances of getting ahead.

Networking is the term usually used to refer to establishing effective relationships with key people inside and/or outside the organization. And networking has been found to be the most important activity performed by managers who were promoted the fastest.[29]

A study of general managers found that they fully understood the importance of networking.[30] They established a wide political network of key people from both inside and outside their organizations. This network provided these managers with information and established cooperative relationships that could enhance their careers. The managers did favors for these contacts, stressed the obligations of these contacts to them, and "called in" these obligations when support was needed.

Research also indicates that a person's location within an organization is an important determinant of his or her influence.[31] Being in the right place increases your ability to know "the right people." This would further support the importance of contacts over knowledge of facts in gaining influence.

The above evidence should not be interpreted as a rejection of job-relevant expertise. Rather, it indicates that "who you know" is an important *additional* factor in organizational life. And for people who want to get ahead or build their political power within an organization, they should spend time and effort in developing a network of contacts.

performance outcomes are completely clear and objective. But that doesn't describe the organizational world that most of us live in.

Factors Contributing to Political Behavior

Not all groups or organizations are equally political. In some organizations, for instance, politicking is overt and rampant, while in others, politics plays a small role in influencing outcomes. Why is there this variation? Recent research and observation have identified a number of factors that appear to encourage political behavior. Some are individual characteristics, derived from the unique qualities of the people the organization employs; others are a result of the organization's culture or internal environment. Exhibit 13-4 on page 378 illustrates how both individual and organizational factors can increase political behavior and provide favorable outcomes (increased rewards and averted punishments) for both individuals and groups in the organization.

Individual Factors   At the individual level, researchers have identified certain personality traits, needs, and other factors that are likely to be related to political behavior. In terms of traits, we find that employees who are high self-monitors, possess an internal locus of control, and have a high need for power are more likely to engage in political behavior.[32]

The high self-monitor is more sensitive to social cues, exhibits higher levels of social conformity, and is more likely to be skilled in political behavior than the low self-monitor. Individuals with an internal locus of control, because they believe they can control their environment, are more prone to take a proactive stance and attempt to manipulate situations in their favor. Not surprisingly, the Machiavellian personality—which is characterized by the will to manipulate and the desire for power—is comfortable using politics as a means to further his or her self-interest.

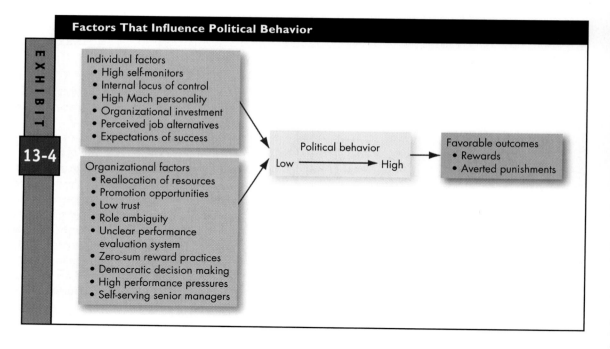

EXHIBIT 13-4

Factors That Influence Political Behavior

Individual factors
- High self-monitors
- Internal locus of control
- High Mach personality
- Organizational investment
- Perceived job alternatives
- Expectations of success

Organizational factors
- Reallocation of resources
- Promotion opportunities
- Low trust
- Role ambiguity
- Unclear performance evaluation system
- Zero-sum reward practices
- Democratic decision making
- High performance pressures
- Self-serving senior managers

Political behavior
Low ──────→ High

Favorable outcomes
- Rewards
- Averted punishments

In addition, an individual's investment in the organization, perceived alternatives, and expectations of success will influence the degree to which he or she will pursue illegitimate means of political action.[33] The more a person has invested in the organization in terms of expectations of increased future benefits, the more he or she has to lose if forced out and the less likely he or she is to use illegitimate means. The more alternative job opportunities an individual has—due to a favorable job market or the possession of scarce skills or knowledge, a prominent reputation, or influential contacts outside the organization—the more likely he or she is to risk illegitimate political actions. Finally, if an individual has a low expectation of success in using illegitimate means, it is unlikely that he or she will attempt to do so. High expectations of success in the use of illegitimate means are most likely to be the province of both experienced and powerful individuals with polished political skills and inexperienced and naive employees who misjudge their chances.

Organizational Factors   Political activity is probably more a function of the organization's characteristics than of individual difference variables. Why? Because many organizations have a large number of employees with the individual characteristics we listed, yet the extent of political behavior varies widely.

Although we acknowledge the role that individual differences can play in fostering politicking, the evidence more strongly supports that certain situations and cultures promote politics. More specifically, when an organization's resources are declining, when the existing pattern of resources is changing, and when there is opportunity for promotions, politics is more likely to surface.[34] In addition, cultures characterized by low trust, role ambiguity, unclear performance evaluation systems, zero-sum reward allocation practices, democratic decision making, high pressures for performance, and self-serving senior managers will create breeding grounds for politicking.[35]

When organizations downsize to improve efficiency, reductions in resources have to be made. Threatened with the loss of resources, people may engage in political actions to safeguard what they have. But any changes, especially those that imply significant reallocation of resources within the organization, are likely to stimulate conflict and increase politicking.

Promotion decisions have consistently been found to be one of the most political actions in organizations. The opportunity for promotions or advancement encourages people to compete for a limited resource and to try to positively influence the decision outcome.

The less trust there is within the organization, the higher the level of political behavior and the more likely that the political behavior will be of the illegitimate kind. So high trust should suppress the level of political behavior in general and inhibit illegitimate actions in particular.

Role ambiguity means that the prescribed behaviors of the employee are not clear. There are fewer limits, therefore, to the scope and functions of the employee's political actions. Because political activities are defined as those not required as part of one's formal role, the greater the role ambiguity, the more one can engage in political activity with little chance of it being visible.

The practice of performance evaluation is far from a perfect science. The more that organizations use subjective criteria in the appraisal, emphasize a single outcome measure, or allow significant time to pass between the time of an action and its appraisal, the greater the likelihood that an employee can get away with politicking. Subjective performance criteria create ambiguity. The use of a single outcome measure encourages individuals to do whatever is necessary to "look good" on that measure, but often at the expense of performing well on other important parts of the job that are not being appraised. The amount of time that elapses between an action and its appraisal is also a relevant factor. The longer the time, the more unlikely that the employee will be held accountable for his or her political behaviors.

AT&T has reduced its workforce by more than 50,000 employees in recent years. Such an uncertain climate creates the opportunity for intense political activity as people act to protect the resources they've acquired.

The more that an organization's culture emphasizes the zero-sum or win–lose approach to reward allocations, the more employees will be motivated to engage in politicking. The zero-sum approach treats the reward "pie" as fixed so that any gain one person or group achieves has to come at the expense of another person or group. If I win, you must lose! If $15,000 in annual raises is to be distributed among five employees, then any employee who gets more than $3,000 takes money away from one or more of the others. Such a practice encourages making others look bad and increasing the visibility of what you do.

In the past 25 years, there has been a general move in North America and among most developed nations toward making organizations less autocratic. Managers in these organizations are being asked to behave more democratically. They're told that they should allow employees to advise them on decisions and that they should rely to a greater extent on group input into the decision process. Such moves toward democracy, however, are not necessarily embraced by all individual managers. Many managers sought their positions in order to have legitimate power so as to be able to make unilateral decisions. They fought hard and often paid high personal costs to achieve their influential positions. Sharing their power with others runs directly against their desires. The result is that managers, especially those who began their careers in the 1950s and 1960s, may use the required committees, conferences, and group meetings in a superficial way, as arenas for maneuvering and manipulating.

The more pressure that employees feel to perform well, the more likely they are to engage in politicking. When people are held strictly accountable for outcomes, this puts great pressure on them to "look good." If a person perceives that his or her entire career is riding on next quarter's sales figures or next month's plant productivity report, there is motivation to do whatever is necessary to make sure the numbers come out favorably.

Finally, when employees see the people on top engaging in political behavior, especially when they do so successfully and are rewarded for it, a climate is created that supports politicking. Politicking by top management, in a sense, gives permission to those lower in the organization to play politics by implying that such behavior is acceptable.

How Do People Respond to Organizational Politics?

Trish O'Donnell loves her job as a writer on a weekly television comedy series but hates the internal politics. "A couple of the writers here spend more time kissing up to the executive producer than doing any work. And our head writer clearly has his favorites. While they pay me a lot and I get to really use my creativity, I'm sick of having to be on alert for backstabbers and constantly having to self-promote my contributions. I'm tired of doing most of the work and getting little of the credit."

Are Trish O'Donnell's comments typical of people who work in highly politicized workplaces? We all know of friends or relatives who regularly complain about the politics at their job. But how do people in general react to organizational politics? Let's look at the evidence.

In our discussion earlier in this chapter of factors that contribute to political behavior, we focused on the favorable outcomes for individuals who successfully engage in politicking. But for most people—who have modest political skills or are unwilling to play the politics game—outcomes tend to be predominantly negative. Exhibit 13-5 summarizes the extensive research on the relationship between the perception of organizational politics and individual outcomes.[36] There is, for instance, very strong evidence indicating that perceptions of organizational politics are negatively related to job satisfaction.[37] The perception of politics also tends to increase job anxiety or stress. This seems to be due to the perception that, by not engaging in politics, a person may be losing ground to others who are active politickers; or, conversely, because of the additional pressures individuals feel because of having entered into and competing in the political arena.[38] Not surprisingly, when politicking becomes too much to handle, it can lead to employees quitting. Finally, there is preliminary evidence suggesting that politics leads to self-reported declines in em-

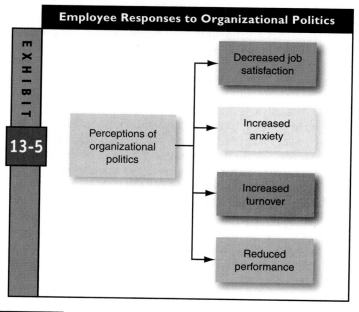

EXHIBIT 13-5

Employee Responses to Organizational Politics

Perceptions of organizational politics →
- Decreased job satisfaction
- Increased anxiety
- Increased turnover
- Reduced performance

ployee performance.[39] Perceived organizational politics appears to have a demotivating effect on individuals, thus leading to decreased performance levels.

In addition to the above conclusions, several interesting qualifiers have been noted. First, the politics–performance relationship appears to be moderated by an individual's understanding of the "hows" and "whys" of organizational politics. "An individual who has a clear understanding of who is responsible for making decisions and why they were selected to be the decision makers would have a better understanding of how and why things happen the way they do than someone who does not understand the decision-making process in the organization."[40] When both politics and understanding are high, performance is likely to increase because the individual will see political actions as an opportunity. This is consistent with what you might expect among individuals with well-honed political skills. But when understanding is low, individuals are more likely to see politics as a threat, which would have a negative effect on job performance.[41] Second, when politics is seen as a threat and consistently responded to with defensiveness, negative outcomes are almost sure to surface eventually. When people perceive politics as a threat rather than as an opportunity, they often respond with **defensive behaviors**—reactive and protective behaviors to avoid action, blame, or change[42] (Exhibit 13-6 on page 382 provides some examples of these defensive behaviors). And defensive behaviors are often associated with negative feelings toward the job and work environment.[43] In the short run, employees may find that defensiveness protects their self-interest. But in the long run, it wears them down. People who consistently rely on defensiveness find that, eventually, it is the only way they know how to behave. At that point, they lose the trust and support of their peers, bosses, employees, and clients.

Are our conclusions about responses to politics globally valid? Should we expect employees in Israel, for instance, to respond the same way to workplace politics that employees in the United States do? Almost all our conclusions on employee reactions to organizational politics are based on studies conducted in North America. The few studies that have included other countries suggest some minor modifications.[44] Israelis and Brits, for instance, seem to generally respond as do North Americans. That is, the perception of organizational politics among employees in these countries is related to decreased job satisfaction and increased turnover.[45] But in countries that are more politically unstable, like Israel, employees seem to demonstrate greater tolerance of intense political processes in the workplace. This is likely to be because people in these countries are used to power struggles and have more experience in coping with them.[46] This suggests that people from politically turbulent countries in the Middle East or Latin America might be more accepting of organizational politics, and even more willing to use aggressive political tactics in the workplace, than people from countries such as Great Britain or Switzerland.

Impression Management

We know that people have an ongoing interest in how others perceive and evaluate them. For example, North Americans spend billions of dollars on diets, health club memberships, cosmetics, and plastic surgery—all intended to make them more attractive to others.[47] Being perceived positively by others should have benefits for people in organizations. It might, for instance, help them initially to get the jobs they want in an organization and, once hired, to get favorable evaluations, superior salary increases, and more rapid promotions. In a political context, it might help sway the distribution of advantages in their favor.

The process by which individuals attempt to control the impression others form of them is called **impression management**.[48] It's a subject that has gained the attention of OB researchers only recently.[49]

defensive behaviors

Reactive and protective behaviors to avoid action, blame, or change.

impression management

The process by which individuals attempt to control the impression others form of them.

EXHIBIT

13-6

Avoiding Action

Overconforming. Strictly interpreting your responsibility by saying things like, "The rules clearly state . . ." or "This is the way we've always done it."

Buck passing. Transferring responsibility for the execution of a task or decision to someone else.

Playing dumb. Avoiding an unwanted task by falsely pleading ignorance or inability.

Stretching. Prolonging a task so that one appears to be occupied—for example, turning a two-week task into a four-month job.

Stalling. Appearing to be more or less supportive publicly while doing little or nothing privately.

Avoiding Blame

Buffing. This is a nice way to refer to "covering your rear." It describes the practice of rigorously documenting activity to project an image of competence and thoroughness.

Playing safe. Evading situations that may reflect unfavorably. It includes taking on only projects with a high probability of success, having risky decisions approved by superiors, qualifying expressions of judgment, and taking neutral positions in conflicts.

Justifying. Developing explanations that lessen one's responsibility for a negative outcome and/or apologizing to demonstrate remorse.

Scapegoating. Placing the blame for a negative outcome on external factors that are not entirely blameworthy.

Misrepresenting. Manipulation of information by distortion, embellishment, deception, selective presentation, or obfuscation.

Avoiding Change

Prevention. Trying to prevent a threatening change from occurring.

Self-protection. Acting in ways to protect one's self interest during change by guarding information or other resources.

Is everyone concerned with impression management (IM)? No! Who, then, might we predict to engage in IM? No surprise here! It's our old friend, the high self-monitor.[50] Low self-monitors tend to present images of themselves that are consistent with their personalities, regardless of the beneficial or detrimental effects for them. In contrast, high self-monitors are good at reading situations and molding their appearances and behavior to fit each situation.

Given that you want to control the impression others form of you, what techniques could you use? Exhibit 13-7 summarizes some of the more popular IM techniques and provides an example of each.

Keep in mind that IM does not imply that the impressions people convey are necessarily false (although, of course, they sometimes are).[51] Excuses, for instance, may be offered with sincerity. Referring to the example used in Exhibit 13-7, you can *actually* believe that ads contribute little to sales in your region. But misrepresentation can have a high cost. If the image claimed is false, you may be discredited.[52] If

Conformity

Agreeing with someone else's opinion in order to gain his or her approval.

Example: A manager tells his boss, "You're absolutely right on your reorganization plan for the western regional office. I couldn't agree with you more."

Excuses

Explanations of a predicament-creating event aimed at minimizing the apparent severity of the predicament.

Example: Sales manager to boss, "We failed to get the ad in the paper on time, but no one responds to those ads anyway."

Apologies

Admitting responsibility for an undesirable event and simultaneously seeking to get a pardon for the action.

Example: Employee to boss, "I'm sorry I made a mistake on the report. Please forgive me."

Self-Promotion

Highlighting one's best qualities, downplaying one's deficits, and calling attention to one's achievements.

Example: A salesperson tells his boss: "Matt worked unsuccessfully for three years to try to get that account. I sewed it up in six weeks. I'm the best closer this company has."

Flattery

Complimenting others about their virtues in an effort to make oneself appear perceptive and likable.

Example: New sales trainee to peer, "You handled that client's complaint so tactfully! I could never have handled that as well as you did."

Favors

Doing something nice for someone to gain that person's approval.

Example: Salesperson to prospective client, "I've got two tickets to the theater tonight that I can't use. Take them. Consider it a thank-you for taking the time to talk with me."

Association

Enhancing or protecting one's image by managing information about people and things with which one is associated.

Example: A job applicant says to an interviewer, "What a coincidence. Your boss and I were roommates in college."

Source: Based on B. R. Schlenker, *Impression Management* (Monterey, CA: Brooks/Cole, 1980); W. L. Gardner and M. J. Martinko, "Impression Management in Organizations," *Journal of Management*, June 1988, p. 332; and R. B. Cialdini, "Indirect Tactics of Image Management: Beyond Basking," in R. A. Giacalone and P. Rosenfeld (eds.), *Impression Management in the Organization* (Hillsdale, NJ: Lawrence Erlbaum Associates, 1989), pp. 45–71.

Augusto Matias, 25, formerly a systems administrator for a New York Internet service provider, takes the subway to a job interview. Facing a tightening job market, Matias has replaced his casual khaki-and-sport-shirt look with a suit and tie in order to impress potential employers.

you "cry wolf" once too often, no one is likely to believe you when the wolf really comes. So the impression manager must be cautious not to be perceived as insincere or manipulative.[53]

Are there *situations* in which individuals are more likely to misrepresent themselves or more likely to get away with it? Yes—situations that are characterized by high uncertainty or ambiguity provide relatively little information for challenging a fraudulent claim and reduce the risks associated with misrepresentation.[54]

Most of the studies undertaken to test the effectiveness of IM techniques have been limited to determining whether IM behavior is related to job interview success. Employment interviews make a particularly relevant area of study since applicants are clearly attempting to present positive images of themselves and there are relatively objective outcome measures (written assessments and typically a hire–don't hire recommendation).

The evidence indicates that IM behavior works.[55] In one study, for instance, interviewers felt that applicants for a position as a customer service representative who used IM techniques performed better in the interview, and they seemed somewhat more inclined to hire these people.[56] Moreover, when the researchers considered applicants' credentials, they concluded that it was the IM techniques alone that influenced the interviewers. That is, it didn't seem to matter if applicants were well or poorly qualified. If they used IM techniques, they did better in the interview.

Another employment interview study looked at whether certain IM techniques work better than others.[57] The researchers compared applicants who used IM techniques that focused the conversation on themselves (called a *controlling style*) to applicants who used techniques that focused on the interviewer (referred to as a *submissive style*). The researchers hypothesized that applicants who used the controlling style would be more effective because of the implicit expectations inherent in employment interviews. We tend to expect job applicants to use self-enhancement, self-promotion, and other active controlling techniques in an interview because they reflect self-confidence and initiative. The researchers predicted that these active controlling techniques would work better for applicants than submissive tactics like conforming their opinions to those of the interviewer and offering favors to the interviewer. The results confirmed the researchers' predictions. Applicants who used the controlling style were rated higher by interviewers on factors such as motivation, enthusiasm, and even technical skills—and they received more job offers. Another study confirmed the value of a controlling style over a submissive one.[58] Specifically, recent college graduates who used more self-promotion tactics got higher evaluations by interviewers and more follow-up job-site visits, even after adjusting for grade point average, gender, and job type.

The Ethics of Behaving Politically

We conclude our discussion of politics by providing some ethical guidelines for political behavior. Although there are no clear-cut ways to differentiate ethical from unethical politicking, there are some questions you should consider.

Exhibit 13-8 illustrates a decision tree to guide ethical actions.[59] This tree is built on the three ethical decision criteria—utilitarianism, rights, and justice—presented in Chapter 5. The first question you need to answer addresses self-interest versus organizational goals. Ethical actions are consistent with the organization's goals. Spreading untrue rumors about the safety of a new product introduced by your company, in order to make that product's design team look bad, is unethical. However,

OB in the News

Among the Politically Inept, Ignorance Is Bliss

Why are some of the most politically inept people so completely unaware of their incompetence? Why, in fact, does it often seem that the politically clueless are the most confident and self-assured about their political skills? The answer may lie with studies undertaken at Cornell University.

The researchers at Cornell have found that most incompetent people don't know they're incompetent. Actually, it's quite the opposite. Incompetents tend to be *more* confident of their abilities than people who do things well. These studies help explain why the humor-impaired persist in telling jokes that aren't funny or the politically clueless continue to give advice to others on the fine points of "getting ahead" at work. For instance, one of the findings from these studies was that college students who score *lowest* on grammar tests were the most likely to overestimate how well they had performed.

The researchers concluded that one reason that the ignorant tend to be overly self-assured is that the skills required for competence often are the same skills necessary to recognize competence. So incompetents suffer a double liability. They reach erroneous conclusions and make unfortunate choices, while their weak self-monitoring skills also rob them of the ability to realize it.

Source: E. Goode, "Among the Inept, Researchers Discover, Ignorance is Bliss," *New York Times*, January 18, 2000, p. D7.

there may be nothing unethical if a department head exchanges favors with her division's purchasing manager in order to get a critical contract processed quickly.

The second question concerns the rights of other parties. If the department head described in the previous paragraph went down to the mail room during her lunch hour and read through the mail directed to the purchasing manager—with the intent of "getting something on him" so he'll expedite your contract—she would be acting unethically. She would have violated the purchasing manager's right to privacy.

The final question that needs to be addressed relates to whether the political activity conforms to standards of equity and justice. The department head who inflates the performance evaluation of a favored employee and deflates the evaluation of a disfavored employee—and then uses these evaluations to justify giving the former a big raise and nothing to the latter—has treated the disfavored employee unfairly.

Unfortunately, the answers to the questions in Exhibit 13-8 are often argued in ways to make unethical practices seem ethical. Powerful people, for example, can become very good at explaining self-serving behaviors in terms of the organization's

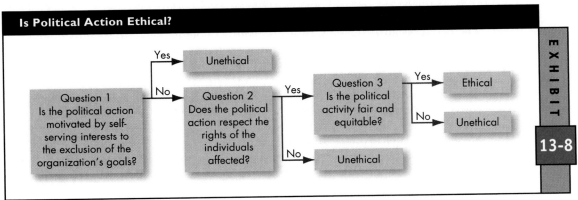

Is Political Action Ethical?

EXHIBIT 13-8

Source: Adapted from G. F. Cavanagh, D. Moberg, and M. Valasquez, "The Ethics of Organizational Politics," *Academy of Management Review,* July 1981, p. 368. Reprinted with permission.

best interests. Similarly, they can persuasively argue that unfair actions are really fair and just. Our point is that immoral people can justify almost any behavior. Those who are powerful, articulate, and persuasive are most vulnerable because they are likely to be able to get away with unethical practices successfully. When faced with an ethical dilemma regarding organizational politics, try to answer the questions in Exhibit 13-8 truthfully. If you have a strong power base, recognize the ability of power to corrupt. Remember, it's a lot easier for the powerless to act ethically, if for no other reason than they typically have very little political discretion to exploit.

SUMMARY AND IMPLICATIONS FOR MANAGERS

If you want to get things done in a group or organization, it helps to have power. As a manager who wants to maximize your power, you will want to increase others' dependence on you. You can, for instance, increase your power in relation to your boss by developing knowledge or a skill that she needs and for which she perceives no ready substitute. But power is a two-way street. You will not be alone in attempting to build your power bases. Others, particularly employees and peers, will be seeking to make you dependent on them. The result is a continual battle. While you seek to maximize others' dependence on you, you will be seeking to minimize your dependence on others. And, of course, others you work with will be trying to do the same.

Few employees relish being powerless in their job and organization. It's been argued, for instance, that when people in organizations are difficult, argumentative, and temperamental it may be because they are in positions of powerlessness; positions in which the performance expectations placed on them exceed their resources and capabilities.[60]

There is evidence that people respond differently to the various power bases.[61] Expert, referent, and charismatic forms of power are derived from an individual's personal qualities. In contrast, coercion, reward, legitimate, and information power are essentially organizationally derived. Since people are more likely to enthusiastically accept and commit to an individual whom they admire or whose knowledge they respect (rather than someone who relies on his or her position for influence), the effective use of expert, referent, and charismatic power should lead to higher employee performance, commitment, and satisfaction.[62] Competence especially appears to offer wide appeal, and its use as a power base results in high performance by group members. The message for managers seems to be: Develop and use your expert power base!

The power of your boss may also play a role in determining your job satisfaction. "One of the reasons many of us like to work for and with people who are powerful is that they are generally more pleasant—not because it is their native disposition, but because the reputation and reality of being powerful permits them more discretion and more ability to delegate to others."[63]

The effective manager accepts the political nature of organizations. By assessing behavior in a political framework, you can better predict the actions of others and use this information to formulate political strategies that will gain advantages for you and your work unit.

Some people are significantly more "politically astute" than others. Those who are good at playing politics can be expected to get higher performance evaluations and, hence, larger salary increases and more promotions than the politically naive or inept.[64] The politically astute are also likely to exhibit higher job satisfaction. For employees with modest political skills or who are unwilling to play the politics game, the perception of organizational politics is generally related to lower job satisfaction and self-reported performance, increased anxiety, and higher turnover.

Creating "Special Deals" for "Special Employees"

I n countries such as France, Belgium, and the Netherlands, terms of employment are largely mandated by law and hence highly standardized. In contrast, in countries such as the United States, Great Britain, and New Zealand, managers have considerable leeway to negotiate idiosyncratic deals with employees. And in these latter countries, managers are increasingly using this latitude to customize their treatment of "special" individuals.

Two trends help explain the growth in special deals for certain employees. First, the demand for knowledge workers with distinctive competencies in a highly competitive market means workers have greater power to negotiate employment conditions suited to their tastes and preferences. Second, the decline in unionization and the weakening of the job security–based model of organizational careers have led to less standardized conditions of employment.

In order to hire, motivate, and keep highly skilled workers, managers are negotiating special treatment for certain employees. Examples of this special treatment include higher pay than others for doing similar work, allowing an employee to work from home several days a week, permitting an employee to leave early to fulfill family obligations, upgraded travel arrangements, and allowing certain employees to spend time on personal projects during work time.

What do these employees have that allow them to make idiosyncratic arrangements? It can be unique credentials, special skills, high status, important contacts, or high marketability. But it must also include the willingness of an employee or prospective employee to speak up. These deals are typically proposed as bargaining chips when negotiating initial employment terms or after the employee has been on the job a while, built a trusting relationship with his or her manager, and become a valued performer.

These special deals have advantages for both employees and managers. They provide greater rewards for employees and allow them to tailor their job to better meet their personal needs. They also give individual managers greater latitude in motivating their employees and flexibility to adapt to changing circumstances.

Source: This is largely based on D. M. Rousseau, "The Idiosyncratic Deal: Flexibility versus Fairness?" *Organizational Dynamics*, Spring 2001, pp. 260–73.

T alk about opening up a can of worms! Making special deals with certain employees is bound to undermine whatever trust there is in an organization. Although management may desire flexibility in its relationships with employees, maintaining standardized practices is more likely to provide the appearance of fairness that is needed to create a climate of trust. And customization of employment relationships, under the guise of flexibility, only increases politics in the workplace.

There is no shortage of arguments against special deals for special employees. Here are just a few.

Special deals give too much power to managers. They allow managers to negotiate favorable treatment with employees they like. Although these employees may also be high performers, if they're not, it contributes to politicizing the work environment.

Special deals are unlikely to be perceived as fair by those who don't receive them. One person's merit is another's favoritism.

Special deals reward the wrong behaviors. They encourage employees to "kiss up" to their boss and to treat every attempt to get a raise or time off as a bargaining opportunity.

Special deals tend to go to aggressive employees, whether or not they're contributing the most. Shy, quiet, and less demanding employees who are good performers are likely to be excluded.

Special deals aren't cost free. Resources in organizations are limited. One employee's gain is often at another's expense. So allowing one employee in a department to take off two hours early every Thursday afternoon to coach his son's Little League team often means others in that department will have to take up some of his work. This has the potential to create conflicts. For instance, evidence indicates that many single and childless employees resent the "family-friendly" benefits—such as helping to find an employee's spouse employment or paid child care—that many companies offer to married workers and those with children.

Our position is that special deals undermine trust and cooperation at work. They create the appearance, if not the actuality, that those with power get favored treatment. We've spent three-quarters of a century building formalized human resource systems that ensure consistent treatment of the workforce. These systems are critical to promoting fairness, cooperation, and efficiency. Using idiosyncratic deals to supposedly enhance flexibility is a major step toward trashing these systems.

1. What is power? How do you get it?

2. Contrast power tactics with power bases. What are some of the key contingency variables that determine which tactic a powerholder is likely to use?

3. Which power bases lie with the individual? Which are derived from the organization?

4. State the general dependency postulate. What does it mean?

5. What creates dependency? Give an applied example.

6. What is a coalition? When is it likely to develop?

7. How are power and politics related?

8. Define *political behavior*. Why is politics a fact of life in organizations?

9. What factors contribute to political activity?

10. What is impression management? What type of people are most likely to engage in IM?

Questions for Critical Thinking

1. Based on the information presented in this chapter, what would you do as a recent college graduate entering a new job to maximize your power and accelerate your career progress?

2. "Politics isn't inherently bad. It's merely a way to get things accomplished within organizations." Do you agree or disagree? Defend your position.

3. You're a sales representative for an international software company. After four excellent years, sales in your territory are off 30 percent this year. Describe three defensive responses you might use to reduce the potential negative consequences of this decline in sales.

4. "Sexual harassment should not be tolerated at the workplace." "Workplace romances are a natural occurrence in organizations." Are both of these statements true? Can they be reconciled?

5. Which impression management techniques have you used? What ethical implications are there, if any, in using impression management?

Team Exercise | Understanding Power Dynamics

1. **Creation of groups**   Each student is to turn in a dollar bill (or similar value of currency) to the instructor and students are then divided into three groups based on criteria given by the instructor, assigned to their workplaces, and instructed to read the following rules and tasks. The money is divided into thirds, giving two-thirds of it to the top group, one-third to the middle group, and none to the bottom group.

2. **Conduct exercise**   Groups go to their assigned work places and have 30 minutes to complete their tasks.

     Rules

     a. Members of the top group are free to enter the space of either of the other groups and to communicate whatever they wish, whenever they wish. Members of the middle group may enter the space of the lower group when they wish but must request permission to enter the top group's space (which the top group can refuse).

Members of the lower group may not disturb the top group in any way unless specifically invited by the top. The lower group does have the right to knock on the door of the middle group and request permission to communicate with them (which can also be refused).

b. The members of the top group have the authority to make any change in the rules that they wish, at any time, with or without notice.

Tasks

a. *Top group.* To be responsible for the overall effectiveness and learning from the exercise, and to decide how to use its money.

b. *Middle group.* To assist the top group in providing for the overall welfare of the organization, and to decide how to use its money.

c. *Bottom group.* To identify its resources and to decide how best to provide for learning and the overall effectiveness of the organization.

3. Debriefing

Each of the three groups chooses two representatives to go to the front of the class and discuss the following questions:

a. Summarize what occurred within and among the three groups.

b. What are some of the differences between being in the top group versus being in the bottom group?

c. What can we learn about power from this experience?

d. How accurate do you think this exercise is to the reality of resource allocation decisions in large organizations?

Source: This exercise is adapted from L. Bolman and T. E. Deal, *Exchange*, vol. 3, no. 4, 1979, pp. 38–42. Reprinted by permission of Sage Publications, Inc.

Case Incident	Damned If You Do; Damned If You Don't

Fran Gilson has spent 15 years with the Thompson Grocery Company.* Starting out as a part-time cashier while attending college, Fran has risen up through the ranks of this 50-store grocery store chain. Today, at the age of 34, she is a regional manager, overseeing seven stores and earning approximately $95,000 a year. Fran also thinks she's ready to take on more responsibility. About five weeks ago, she was contacted by an executive-search recruiter inquiring about her interest in the position of vice president and regional manager for a national drugstore chain. She would be responsible for more than 100 stores in five states. She agreed to meet with the recruiter. This led to two meetings with top executives at the drugstore chain. The recruiter called Fran two days ago to tell her she was one of the two finalists for the job.

The only person at Thompson who knows Fran is looking at this other job is her good friend and colleague, Ken Hamilton. Ken is director of finance for the grocery chain. "It's a dream job," Fran told Ken. "It's a lot more responsibility and it's a good company to work for. The regional office is just 20 miles from here so I wouldn't have to move, and the pay is first rate. With the performance bonus, I could make nearly $200,000 a year. But best of all, the job provides terrific visibility. I'd be their only female vice president. The job would allow me to be a more visible role model for young women and give me a bigger voice in opening up doors for women and ethnic minorities in retailing management."

Since Fran considered Ken a close friend and wanted to keep the fact that she was looking at another job secret, she asked Ken last week if she could use his name as a reference. Said Ken, "Of course. I'll give you a great recommendation. We'd hate to lose you here, but you've got a lot of talent. They'd be lucky to get someone with your experience and energy." Fran passed Ken's name on to the executive recruiter as her only reference at Thompson. She made it very clear to the recruiter that Ken was the only person at Thompson who knew she was considering another job. Thompson's top management is conservative and places a high value on loyalty. If anyone heard she was talking to another company, it might seriously jeopardize her chances for promotion. But she trusted Ken completely. It's against this backdrop that this morning's incident became more than just a question of sexual harassment. It became a full-blown ethical and political dilemma for Fran.

Jennifer Chung has been a financial analyst in Ken's department for five months. Fran met Jennifer through Ken. The three have chatted together on a number of occasions in the coffee room. Fran's impression of Jennifer is quite positive. In many ways, Jennifer strikes Fran as a lot like she was ten years ago. This morning, Fran came to work around 6:30 A.M. as she usually does. It allows her to get a lot accomplished before "the troops" roll in at 8 A.M. At about 6:45, Jennifer came into Fran's office. It was immediately evident that something was wrong. Jennifer was very nervous and uncomfortable, which was most unlike her. She asked Fran if they could talk. Fran sat her down and listened to her story.

What Fran heard was hard to believe, but she had no reason to think Jennifer was lying. Jennifer said that Ken began making off-color comments to her when they were alone within a month after Jennifer joined Thompson. From there it got progressively worse. Ken would leer at her. He put his arm over her shoulder when they were reviewing reports. He patted her rear. Every time one of these occurrences happened, Jennifer would ask him to stop and not do it

again, but it fell on deaf ears. Yesterday, Ken reminded Jennifer that her six-month probationary review was coming up. "He told me that if I didn't sleep with him that I couldn't expect a very favorable evaluation." She told Fran that all she could do was go to the ladies' room and cry.

Jennifer said that she had come to Fran because she didn't know what to do or whom to turn to. "I came to you, Fran, because you're a friend of Ken's and the highest ranking woman here. Will you help me?" Fran had never heard anything like this about Ken before. About all she knew regarding his personal life was that he was in his late 30s, single, and involved in a long-term relationship.

Questions

1. Analyze Fran's situation in a purely legalistic sense. You might want to talk to friends or relatives who are in management or the legal profession for advice in this analysis.

2. Analyze Fran's dilemma in political terms.

3. Analyze Fran's situation in an ethical sense. What is the ethically right thing for her to do? Is that also the politically right thing to do?

4. If you were Fran, what would you do?

*The identity of this organization and the people described are disguised for obvious reasons.

KSS PROGRAM

KNOW THE CONCEPTS
SELF-AWARENESS
SKILLS APPLICATIONS

Building Your Power Base

After you've read this chapter, take Self-Assessment #31 (How Power-Oriented Am I?) on your enclosed CD-ROM, and complete the skill-building module entitled Becoming Politically Adept on page 625.

Endnotes

1. Based on J. B. White and N. Shirouzu, "A Stalled Revolution by Nasser Puts a Ford in the Driver's Seat," *Wall Street Journal*, October 31, 2001, p. A1; B. Yates, "It's Curtains for 'Jac the Knife,'" *Wall Street Journal*, October 31, 2001, p. A24; and D. Hakim, "Left in Nasser's Exhaust at Ford," *New York Times*, November 1, 2001, p. C4.

2. D. Hakim, "Left in Nasser's Exhaust at Ford."

3. R. M. Kanter, "Power Failure in Management Circuits," *Harvard Business Review*, July–August 1979, p. 65.

4. J. Pfeffer, "Understanding Power in Organizations," *California Management Review*, Winter 1992, p. 35.

5. Based on B. M. Bass, *Bass & Stogdill's Handbook of Leadership*, 3rd ed. (New York: Free Press, 1990).

6. J. R. P. French, Jr., and B. Raven, "The Bases of Social Power," in D. Cartwright (ed.), *Studies in Social Power* (Ann Arbor: University of Michigan, Institute for Social Research, 1959), pp. 150–67; and B. J. Raven, "The Bases of Power: Origins and Recent Developments," *Journal of Social Issues*, vol. 49, 1993, pp. 227–51.

7. E. A. Ward, "Social Power Bases of Managers: Emergence of a New Factor," *Journal of Social Psychology*, February 2001, pp. 144–47.

8. R. E. Emerson, "Power–Dependence Relations," *American Sociological Review*, vol. 27 (1962), pp. 31–41.

9. H. Mintzberg, *Power In and Around Organizations* (Upper Saddle River, NJ: Prentice Hall, 1983), p. 24.

10. R. M. Cyert and J. G. March, *A Behavioral Theory of the Firm* (Upper Saddle River, NJ: Prentice Hall, 1963).

11. C. Perrow, "Departmental Power and Perspective in Industrial Firms," in M. N. Zald (ed.), *Power in Organizations* (Nashville, TN: Vanderbilt University Press, 1970).

12. See, for example, D. Kipnis, S. M. Schmidt, C. Swaffin-Smith, and I. Wilkinson, "Patterns of Managerial Influence: Shotgun Managers, Tacticians, and Bystanders," *Organizational Dynamics*, Winter 1984, pp. 58–67; D. Kipnis and S. M. Schmidt, "Upward-Influence Styles: Relationship with Performance Evaluations, Salary, and Stress," *Administrative Science Quarterly*, December 1988, pp. 528–42; G. Yukl and C. M. Falbe, "Influence Tactics and Objectives in Upward, Downward, and Lateral Influence Attempts," *Journal of Applied Psychology*, April 1990, pp. 132–40; S. J. Wayne, R. C. Liden, I. K. Graf, and G. R. Ferris, "The Role of Upward Influence Tactics in Human Resource Decisions," *Personnel Psychology*, Winter 1997, pp. 979–1006; G. Blickle, "Influence Tactics Used by Subordinates: An Empirical Analysis of the Kipnis and Schmidt Subscales," *Psychological Reports*, February 2000, pp. 143–54; and P. P. Fu and G. Yukl, "Perceived Effectiveness of Influence Tactics in the United States and China," *Leadership Quarterly*, Summer 2000, pp. 251–66.

13. This section is adapted from Kipnis, Schmidt, Swaffin-Smith, and Wilkinson, "Patterns of Managerial Influence."

14. Based on W. B. Stevenson, J. L. Pearce, and L. W. Porter, "The Concept of 'Coalition' in Organization Theory and Research," *Academy of Management Review*, April 1985, pp. 261–63.

15. S. B. Bacharach and E. J. Lawler, "Political Alignments in Organizations," in R. M. Kramer and M. A. Neale (eds.), *Power and Influence in Organizations* (Thousand Oaks, CA: Sage, 1998), pp. 75–77.

16. J. K. Murnighan and D. J. Brass, "Intraorganizational Coalitions," in M. H. Bazerman, R. J. Lewicki, and B. H. Sheppard (eds.), *Research on Negotiation in Organizations* (Greenwich, CT: JAI Press, 1991).

17. See J. Pfeffer, *Power in Organizations* (Marshfield, MA: Pitman, 1981), pp. 155–57.

18. For recent reviews of the literature, see L. F. Fitzgerald and S. L. Shullman, "Sexual Harassment: A Research Analysis and Agenda for the 1990s," *Journal of Vocational Behavior*, February 1993, pp. 5–27; and M. L. Lengnick-Hall, "Sexual Harassment Research: A Methodological Critique," *Personnel Psychology*, Winter 1995, pp. 841–64.

19. S. Silverstein and S. Christian, "Harassment Ruling Raises Free-Speech Issues," *Los Angeles Times*, November 11, 1993, p. D2.

20. The following section is based on J. N. Cleveland and M. E. Kerst, "Sexual Harassment and Perceptions of Power: An Under-Articulated Relationship," *Journal of Vocational Behavior*, February 1993, pp. 49–67.

21. S. A. Culbert and J. J. McDonough, *The Invisible War: Pursuing Self-Interest at Work* (New York: John Wiley, 1980), p. 6.

22. Mintzberg, *Power In and Around Organizations*, p. 26. See also K. M. Kacmar and R. A. Baron, "Organizational Politics: The State of the Field, Links to Related Processes, and an Agenda for Future Research," in G. R. Ferris (ed.), *Research in Personnel and Human Resources Management*, vol. 17 (Greenwich, CT: JAI Press, 1999), pp. 1–39.

23. S. B. Bacharach and E. J. Lawler, "Political Alignments in Organizations," in R. M. Kramer and M. A. Neale, eds., *Power and Influence in Organizations*, pp. 68–69.

24. D. Farrell and J. C. Petersen, "Patterns of Political Behavior in Organizations," *Academy of Management Review*, July 1982, p. 405. For analyses of the controversies underlying the definition of organizational politics, see A. Drory and T. Romm, "The Definition of Organizational Politics: A Review," *Human Relations*, November 1990, pp. 1133–54; and R. S. Cropanzano, K. M. Kacmar, and D. P. Bozeman, "Organizational Politics, Justice, and Support: Their Differences and Similarities," in R. S. Cropanzano and K. M. Kacmar (eds.), *Organizational Politics, Justice and Support: Managing Social Climate at Work* (Westport, CT: Quorum Books, 1995), pp. 1–18.

25. Farrell and Peterson, "Patterns of Political Behavior," pp. 406–407; and A. Drory, "Politics in Organization and Its Perception Within the Organization," *Organization Studies*, vol. 9, no. 2, 1988, pp. 165–79.

26. Pfeffer, *Power in Organizations*.

27. A. Drory and T. Romm, "The Definition of Organizational Politics."

28. K. K. Eastman, "In the Eyes of the Beholder: An Attributional Approach to Ingratiation and Organizational Citizenship Behavior," *Academy of Management Journal*, October 1994, pp. 1379–91; and M. C. Bolino, "Citizenship and Impression Management: Good Soldiers or Good Actors?" *Academy of Management Review*, January 1999, pp. 82–98.

29. F. Luthans, R. M. Hodgetts, and S. A. Rosenkrantz, *Real Managers* (Cambridge, MA: Allinger, 1988).

30. J. P. Kotter, *The General Managers* (New York: The Free Press, 1982).

31. D. J. Brass, "Being in the Right Place: A Structural Analysis of Individual Influence in an Organization," *Administrative Science Quarterly*, December 1984, pp. 518–39; and N. E. Friedkin, "Structural Bases of Interpersonal Influence in Groups: A Longitudinal Case Study," *American Sociological Review*, vol. 58, 1993, pp. 861–72.

32. See, for example, G. Biberman, "Personality and Characteristic Work Attitudes of Persons with High, Moderate, and Low Political Tendencies," *Psychological Reports*, October 1985, pp. 1303–10; R. J. House, "Power and Personality in Complex Organizations," in B. M. Staw and L. L. Cummings (eds.), *Research in Organizational Behavior*, vol. 10

(Greenwich, CT: JAI Press, 1988), pp. 305–57; and G. R. Ferris, G. S. Russ, and P. M. Fandt, "Politics in Organizations," in R.A. Giacalone and P. Rosenfeld (eds.), *Impression Management in the Organization* (Hillsdale, NJ: Lawrence Erlbaum Associates, 1989), pp. 155–56.

33. Farrell and Petersen, "Patterns of Political Behavior," p. 408.

34. S. C. Goh and A. R. Doucet, "Antecedent Situational Conditions of Organizational Politics: An Empirical Investigation," paper presented at the Annual Administrative Sciences Association of Canada Conference, Whistler, B.C., May 1986; C. Hardy, "The Contribution of Political Science to Organizational Behavior," in J. W. Lorsch (ed.), *Handbook of Organizational Behavior* (Englewood Cliffs, NJ: Prentice Hall, 1987), p. 103; and G. R. Ferris and K. M. Kacmar, "Perceptions of Organizational Politics," *Journal of Management*, March 1992, pp. 93–116.

35. See, for example, Farrell and Petersen, "Patterns of Political Behavior," p. 409; P. M. Fandt and G. R. Ferris, "The Management of Information and Impressions: When Employees Behave Opportunistically," *Organizational Behavior and Human Decision Processes*, February 1990, pp. 140–58; and Ferris, Russ, and Fandt, "Politics in Organizations," p. 147.

36. G. R. Ferris, G. S. Russ, and P. M. Fandt, "Politics in Organizations," in R. A. Giacalone and P. Rosenfeld (eds.), *Impression Management in Organizations* (Newbury Park, CA: Sage, 1989), pp. 143–70; and K. M. Kacmar, D. P. Bozeman, D. S. Carlson, and W. P. Anthony, "An Examination of the Perceptions of Organizational Politics Model: Replication and Extension," *Human Relations*, March 1999, pp. 383–416.

37. K. M. Kacmar and R. A. Baron, "Organizational Politics"; and M. Valle and L. A. Witt, "The Moderating Effect of Teamwork Perceptions on the Organizational Politics-Job Satisfaction Relationship," *Journal of Social Psychology*, June 2001, pp. 379–88.

38. G. R. Ferris, D. D. Frink, M. C. Galang, J. Zhou, K. M. Kacmar, and J. L. Howard, "Perceptions of Organizational Politics: Prediction, Stress-Related Implications, and Outcomes," *Human Relations*, February 1996, pp. 233–66; and K. M. Kacmar, D. P. Bozeman, D. S. Carlson, and W. P. Anthony, "An Examination of the Perceptions of Organizational Politics Model," p. 388.

39. K. M. Kacmar, D. P. Bozeman, D. S. Carlson, and W. P. Anthony, "An Examination of the Perceptions of Organizational Politics Model."

40. Ibid, p. 389.

41. Ibid, p. 409.

42. B. E. Ashforth and R. T. Lee, "Defensive Behavior in Organizations: A Preliminary Model," *Human Relations*, July 1990, pp. 621–48.

43. M. Valle and P. L. Perrewe, "Do Politics Perceptions Relate to Political Behaviors? Tests of an Implicit Assumption and Expanded Model," *Human Relations*, March 2000, pp. 359–86.

44. See T. Romm and A. Drory, "Political Behavior in Organizations: A Cross-Cultural Comparison," *International Journal of Value Based Management*, vol. 1, 1988, pp. 97–113; and E. Vigoda, "Reactions to Organizational Politics: A Cross-Cultural Examination in Israel and Britain," *Human Relations*, November 2001, pp. 1483–1518.

45. E. Vigoda, "Reactions to Organizational Politics," p. 1512.

46. Ibid., p. 1510.

47. M. R. Leary and R. M. Kowalski, "Impression Management: A Literature Review and Two-Component Model," *Psychological Bulletin*, January 1990, pp. 34–47.

48. Ibid., p. 34.

49. See, for instance, B. R. Schlenker, *Impression Management: The Self-Concept, Social Identity, and Interpersonal Relations* (Monterey, CA: Brooks/Cole, 1980); W. L. Gardner and M. J. Martinko, "Impression Management in Organizations," *Journal of Management*, June 1988, pp. 321–38; Leary and Kowalski, "Impression Management: A Literature Review and Two-Component Model," pp. 34–47; P. R. Rosenfeld, R. A. Giacalone, and C. A. Riordan, *Impression Management in Organizations: Theory, Measurement, and Practice* (New York: Routledge, 1995); C. K. Stevens and A. L. Kristof, "Making the Right Impression: A Field Study of Applicant Impression Management During Job Interviews," *Journal of Applied Psychology*, October 1995, pp. 587–606; and D. P. Bozeman and K. M. Kacmar, "A Cybernetic Model of Impression Management Processes in Organizations," *Organizational Behavior and Human Decision Processes*, January 1997, pp. 9–30.

50. M. Snyder and J. Copeland, "Self-Monitoring Processes in Organizational Settings," in Giacalone and Rosenfeld, *Impression Management in the Organization*, p. 11; E. D. Long and G. H. Dobbins, "Self-Monitoring, Impression Management, and Interview Ratings: A Field and Laboratory Study," in J. L. Wall and L. R. Jauch, eds., *Proceedings of the 52nd Annual Academy of Management Conference*, Las Vegas, August 1992, pp. 274–78; A. Montagliani and R. A. Giacalone, "Impression Management and Cross-Cultural Adaptation," *Journal of Social Psychology*, October 1998, pp. 598–608; and W. H. Turnley and M. C. Bolino, "Achieved Desired Images While Avoiding Undesired Images: Exploring the Role of Self-Monitoring in Impression Management," *Journal of Applied Psychology*, April 2001, pp. 351–60.

51. Leary and Kowalski, "Impression Management," p. 40.

52. Gardner and Martinko, "Impression Management in Organizations," p. 333.

53. R. A. Baron, "Impression Management by Applicants During Employment Interviews: The 'Too Much of a Good Thing' Effect," in R. W. Eder and G. R. Ferris (eds.), *The Employment Interview: Theory, Research, and Practice* (Newbury Park, CA: Sage Publishers, 1989), pp. 204–15.

54. Ferris, Russ, and Fandt, "Politics in Organizations."

55. Baron, "Impression Management by Applicants During Employment Interviews"; D. C. Gilmore and G. R. Ferris, "The Effects of Applicant Impression Management Tactics on Interviewer Judgments," *Journal of Management*, December 1989, pp. 557–64; and Stevens and Kristof, "Making the Right Impression: A Field Study of Applicant Impression Management During Job Interviews."

56. Gilmore and Ferris, "The Effects of Applicant Impression Management Tactics on Interviewer Judgments."

57. K. M. Kacmar, J. E. Kelery, and G. R. Ferris, "Differential Effectiveness of Applicant IM Tactics on Employment Interview Decisions," *Journal of Applied Social Psychology*, August 16–31, 1992, pp. 1250–72.

58. Stevens and Kristof, "Making the Right Impression: A Field Study of Applicant Impression Management During Job Interviews."

59. This figure is based on G. F. Cavanagh, D. J. Moberg, and M. Valasquez, "The Ethics of Organizational Politics," *Academy of Management Journal*, June 1981, pp. 363–74.

60. R. M. Kanter, *Men and Women of the Corporation* (New York: Basic Books, 1977).

61. See, for instance, C. M. Falbe and G. Yukl, "Consequences for Managers of Using Single Influence Tactics and Combinations of Tactics," *Academy of Management Journal*, August 1992, pp. 638–52.

62. See J. G. Bachman, D. G. Bowers, and P. M. Marcus, "Bases of Supervisory Power: A Comparative Study in Five Organizational Settings," in A. S. Tannenbaum (ed.), *Control in Organizations* (New York: McGraw-Hill, 1968), p. 236; M. A. Rahim, "Relationships of Leader Power to Compliance and Satisfaction with Supervision: Evidence from a National Sample of Managers," *Journal of Management*, December 1989, pp. 545–56; and P. A. Wilson, "The Effects of Politics and Power on the Organizational Commitment of Federal Executives," *Journal of Management*, Spring 1995, pp. 101–18.

63. J. Pfeffer, *Managing with Power*, p. 137.

64. See, for example, N. Gupta and G. D. Jenkins Jr., "The Politics of Pay," *Compensation & Benefits Review*, March/April 1996, pp. 23–30.

PART THREE

THE GROUP

VIACOM

On January 30, 2002, Viacom's Board of Directors told president and chief operating officer Mel Karmazin to fulfill his employment contract, which expired at the end of 2003.[1] At the same time, the Board also instructed Karmazin and the company's CEO Sumner Redstone (see photo) to patch up their differences and concentrate on running the world's second-largest entertainment giant. Can two men with huge egos share power without driving each other crazy?[2]

Mel and Sumner have nothing on that other Odd Couple, Felix and Oscar. Karmazin, formerly CEO of CBS Corp., gained operating control of Viacom in May 2000, when the two companies merged. But Redstone owns 68 percent of Viacom's voting stock. And although he's 78 years old, Redstone created Viacom and doesn't like playing second-fiddle to anyone.

Karmazin, 58, apparently doesn't like Redstone's interference in running the company and has told the board that he would not seek to renew his employment contract with Viacom when it expires. Meanwhile, Redstone dislikes Karmazin's aggressive style and all the media attention he receives. Redstone wants Karmazin out so he can again rule Viacom. But unfortunately for Redstone, his hands are tied. The company's bylaws prevent Redstone from firing Karmazin without the approval of 14 of the board's 18 directors. That's unlikely since eight of the 18 directors are CBS appointees and loyal to Karmazin. In addition, investors and money managers think Karmazin is the better manager. There is little doubt that the company's stock would take a beating if Karmazin left.

Conflict can be a serious problem in an organization. It can create chaotic conditions that make it nearly impossible for employees to work together. On the other hand, conflict also has

Conflict and Negotiation

a less-well-known positive side. We'll explain the difference between negative and positive conflicts in this chapter and provide
a guide to help you understand how conflicts develop. We'll also
present a topic closely akin to conflict—negotiation. But first,
let's clarify what we mean by conflict.

A DEFINITION OF CONFLICT

There has been no shortage of definitions of conflict.[3] Despite the
divergent meanings the term has acquired, several common
themes underlie most definitions. Conflict must be perceived by
the parties to it; whether or not conflict exists is a perception issue. If no one is aware of a conflict, then it is generally agreed that
no conflict exists. Additional commonalities in the definitions are
opposition or incompatibility and some form of interaction.[4]
These factors set the conditions that determine the beginning
point of the conflict process.

We can define **conflict**, then, as a process that begins when
one party perceives that another party has negatively affected, or
is about to negatively affect, something that the first party cares
about.[5]

This definition is purposely broad. It describes that point in
any ongoing activity when an interaction "crosses over" to become an interparty conflict. It encompasses the wide range of conflicts that people experience in organizations—incompatibility of
goals, differences over interpretations of facts, disagreements
based on behavioral expectations, and the like. Finally, our definition is flexible enough to cover the full range of conflict levels—
from overt and violent acts to subtle forms of disagreement.

**AFTER STUDYING THIS CHAPTER,
YOU SHOULD BE ABLE TO:**

1. Define *conflict*.

2. Differentiate between the
   traditional, human relations, and
   interactionist views of conflict.

3. Contrast task, relationship, and
   process conflict.

4. Outline the conflict process.

5. Describe the five conflict-
   handling intentions.

6. Contrast distributive and
   integrative bargaining.

7. Identify the five steps in the
   negotiation process.

8. Describe cultural differences in
   negotiations.

TRANSITIONS IN CONFLICT THOUGHT

conflict

A process that begins when one party perceives that another party has negatively affected, or is about to negatively affect, something that the first party cares about.

It is entirely appropriate to say that there has been "conflict" over the role of conflict in groups and organizations. One school of thought has argued that conflict must be avoided—that it indicates a malfunctioning within the group. We call this the *traditional* view. Another school of thought, the *human relations* view, argues that conflict is a natural and inevitable outcome in any group and that it need not be evil, but rather has the potential to be a positive force in determining group performance. The third, and most recent, perspective proposes not only that conflict can be a positive force in a group but explicitly argues that some conflict is *absolutely necessary* for a group to perform effectively. We label this third school the *interactionist* approach. Let's take a closer look at each of these views.

The Traditional View

The early approach to conflict assumed that all conflict was bad. Conflict was viewed negatively, and it was used synonymously with such terms as *violence*, *destruction*, and *irrationality* to reinforce its negative connotation. Conflict, by definition, was harmful and was to be avoided.

traditional view of conflict

The belief that all conflict is harmful and must be avoided.

The **traditional** view was consistent with the attitudes that prevailed about group behavior in the 1930s and 1940s. Conflict was seen as a dysfunctional outcome resulting from poor communication, a lack of openness and trust between people, and the failure of managers to be responsive to the needs and aspirations of their employees.

The view that all conflict is bad certainly offers a simple approach to looking at the behavior of people who create conflict. Since all conflict is to be avoided, we need merely direct our attention to the causes of conflict and correct these malfunctionings in order to improve group and organizational performance. Although research studies now provide strong evidence to dispute that this approach to conflict reduction results in high group performance, many of us still evaluate conflict situations using this outmoded standard. And as we saw at Viacom, so, too, do many boards of directors.

The Human Relations View

human relations view of conflict

The belief that conflict is a natural and inevitable outcome in any group.

The **human relations** position argued that conflict was a natural occurrence in all groups and organizations. Since conflict was inevitable, the human relations school advocated acceptance of conflict. Proponents rationalized its existence: It cannot be eliminated, and there are even times when conflict may benefit a group's performance. The human relations view dominated conflict theory from the late 1940s through the mid-1970s.

The Interactionist View

interactionist view of conflict

The belief that conflict is not only a positive force in a group but that it is absolutely necessary for a group to perform effectively.

While the human relations approach accepted conflict, the **interactionist** approach encourages conflict on the grounds that a harmonious, peaceful, tranquil, and cooperative group is prone to becoming static, apathetic, and non-responsive to needs for change and innovation.[6] The major contribution of the interactionist approach, therefore, is encouraging group leaders to maintain an ongoing minimum level of conflict—enough to keep the group viable, self-critical, and creative.

Given the interactionist view—and it is the one that we shall take in this chapter—it becomes evident that to say conflict is all good or bad is inappropriate and naive. Whether a conflict is good or bad depends on the type of conflict.

FUNCTIONAL VERSUS DYSFUNCTIONAL CONFLICT

The interactionist view does not propose that all conflicts are good. Rather, some conflicts support the goals of the group and improve its performance; these are **functional**, constructive forms of conflict. In addition, there are conflicts that hinder group performance; these are **dysfunctional** or destructive forms of conflict.

What differentiates functional from dysfunctional conflict? The evidence indicates that you need to look at the *type* of conflict.[7] Specifically, there are three types: task, relationship, and process.

Task conflict relates to the content and goals of the work. **Relationship conflict** focuses on interpersonal relationships. **Process conflict** relates to how the work gets done. Studies demonstrate that relationship conflicts are almost always dysfunctional. Why? It appears that the friction and interpersonal hostilities inherent in relationship conflicts increases personality clashes and decreases mutual understanding, which hinders the completion of organizational tasks. On the other hand, low levels of process conflict and low to moderate levels of task conflict are functional. For process conflict to be productive, it must be kept low. Intense arguments about who should do what becomes dysfunctional when it creates uncertainty about task roles, increases the time to complete tasks, and leads to members working at cross purposes. Low to moderate levels of task conflict consistently demonstrate a positive effect on group performance because it stimulates discussion of ideas that help groups perform better.

functional conflict
Conflict that supports the goals of the group and improves its performance.

dysfunctional conflict
Conflict that hinders group performance.

task conflict
Conflicts over content and goals of the work.

relationship conflict
Conflict based on interpersonal relationships.

process conflict
Conflict over how work gets done.

THE CONFLICT PROCESS

conflict process

Process with five stages: potential opposition or incompatibility, cognition and personalization, intentions, behavior, and outcomes.

The **conflict process** can be seen as comprising five stages: potential opposition or incompatibility, cognition and personalization, intentions, behavior, and outcomes. The process is diagrammed in Exhibit 14-1.

Stage I: Potential Opposition or Incompatibility

The first step in the conflict process is the presence of conditions that create opportunities for conflict to arise. They *need not* lead directly to conflict, but one of these conditions is necessary if conflict is to surface. For simplicity's sake, these conditions (which also may be looked at as causes or sources of conflict) have been condensed into three general categories: communication, structure, and personal variables.[8]

Communication   Susan had worked in supply-chain management at Bristol-Myers Squibb for three years. She enjoyed her work in large part because her boss, Tim McGuire, was a great guy to work for. Then Tim got promoted six months ago and Chuck Benson took his place. Susan says her job is a lot more frustrating now. "Tim and I were on the same wavelength. It's not that way with Chuck. He tells me something and I do it. Then he tells me I did it wrong. I think he means one thing but says something else. It's been like this since the day he arrived. I don't think a day goes by when he isn't yelling at me for something. You know, there are some people you just find it easy to communicate with. Well, Chuck isn't one of those!"

Susan's comments illustrate that communication can be a source of conflict. It represents the opposing forces that arise from semantic difficulties, misunderstandings, and "noise" in the communication channels. Much of this discussion can be related back to our comments on communication in Chapter 10.

A review of the research suggests that differing word connotations, jargon, insufficient exchange of information, and noise in the communication channel are all barriers to communication and potential antecedent conditions to conflict. Evidence demonstrates that semantic difficulties arise as a result of differences in training, selective perception, and inadequate information about others. Research has further demonstrated a surprising finding: The potential for conflict increases when either too little or too much communication takes place. Apparently, an increase in communication is functional up to a point, whereupon it is possible to overcommunicate, with a resultant increase in the potential for conflict. Too much

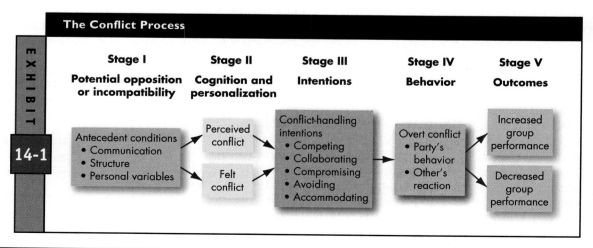

The Conflict Process

Stage I	Stage II	Stage III	Stage IV	Stage V
Potential opposition or incompatibility	Cognition and personalization	Intentions	Behavior	Outcomes

EXHIBIT 14-1

Antecedent conditions
• Communication
• Structure
• Personal variables

Perceived conflict

Felt conflict

Conflict-handling intentions
• Competing
• Collaborating
• Compromising
• Avoiding
• Accommodating

Overt conflict
• Party's behavior
• Other's reaction

Increased group performance

Decreased group performance

information as well as too little can lay the foundation for conflict. Furthermore, the channel chosen for communicating can have an influence on stimulating opposition. The filtering process that occurs as information is passed between members and the divergence of communications from formal or previously established channels offer potential opportunities for conflict to arise.

Structure   Charlotte and Teri both work at the Portland Furniture Mart—a large discount furniture retailer. Charlotte is a salesperson on the floor; Teri is the company credit manager. The two women have known each other for years and have much in common—they live within two blocks of each other, and their oldest daughters attend the same middle school and are best friends. In reality, if Charlotte and Teri had different jobs they might be best friends themselves, but these two women are consistently fighting battles with each other. Charlotte's job is to sell furniture and she does a heck of a job. But most of her sales are made on credit. Because Teri's job is to make sure the company minimizes credit losses, she regularly has to turn down the credit application of a customer with whom Charlotte has just closed a sale. It's nothing personal between Charlotte and Teri—the requirements of their jobs just bring them into conflict.

The conflicts between Charlotte and Teri are structural in nature. The term *structure* is used, in this context, to include variables such as size, degree of specialization in the tasks assigned to group members, jurisdictional clarity, member/goal compatibility, leadership styles, reward systems, and the degree of dependence between groups.

Research indicates that size and specialization act as forces to stimulate conflict. The larger the group and the more specialized its activities, the greater the likelihood of conflict. Tenure and conflict have been found to be inversely related. The potential for conflict tends to be greatest when group members are younger and when turnover is high.

The greater the ambiguity in precisely defining where responsibility for actions lies, the greater the potential for conflict to emerge. Such jurisdictional ambiguities increase intergroup fighting for control of resources and territory.

Groups within organizations have diverse goals. For instance, supply management is concerned with the timely acquisition of inputs at low prices, marketing's goals concentrate on disposing of outputs and increasing revenues, quality control's attention is focused on improving quality and ensuring that the organization's products meet standards, and production units seek efficiency of operations by maintaining a steady production flow. This diversity of goals among groups is a major source of conflict. When groups within an organization seek diverse ends, some of which—like sales and credit at Portland Furniture Mart—are inherently at odds, there are increased opportunities for conflict.

There is some indication that a close style of leadership—tight and continuous observation with general control of others' behaviors—increases conflict potential, but the evidence is not particularly strong. Too much reliance on participation may also stimulate conflict. Research tends to confirm that participation and conflict

A lot of conflicts, like this one between two department heads, are due to structural relationships created by diverse goals.

are highly correlated, apparently because participation encourages the promotion of differences. Reward systems, too, are found to create conflict when one member's gain is at another's expense. Finally, if a group is dependent on another group (in contrast to the two being mutually independent) or if interdependence allows one group to gain at another's expense, opposing forces are stimulated.

Personal Variables Did you ever meet someone to whom you took an immediate disliking? Most of the opinions they expressed, you disagreed with. Even insignificant characteristics—the sound of their voice, the smirk when they smiled, their personality—annoyed you. We've all met people like that. When you have to work with such individuals, there is often the potential for conflict.

Our last category of potential sources of conflict is personal variables. They include the individual value systems that each person has and the personality characteristics that account for individual idiosyncrasies and differences.

The evidence indicates that certain personality types—for example, individuals who are highly authoritarian and dogmatic—lead to potential conflict. Most important, and probably the most overlooked variable in the study of social conflict, is differing value systems. Value differences, for example, are the best explanation of diverse issues such as prejudice, disagreements over one's contribution to the group and the rewards one deserves, and assessments of whether this particular book is any good. That John dislikes African Americans and Dana believes John's position indicates his ignorance, that an employee thinks he is worth $55,000 a year but his boss believes him to be worth $50,000, and that Ann thinks this book is interesting to read while Jennifer views it as trash are all value judgments. And differences in value systems are important sources for creating the potential for conflict.

OR SCIENCE *?*

MYTH

"The Source of Most Conflicts Is Lack of Communication"

This statement is probably false. A popular myth in organizations is that poor communication is the primary source of conflicts. And certainly problems in the communication process do act to retard collaboration, stimulate misunderstandings, and create conflicts. But a review of the literature suggests that within organizations, structural factors and individual value differences are probably greater sources of conflict.[9]

Conflicts in organizations are frequently structurally derived. For instance, in the movie-making business, conflicts between directors and producers are often due to different goals. Directors want to create artistic films, regardless of costs. Producers want to make financially-profitable movies by minimizing costs. When people have to work together, but are pursuing diverse goals, conflicts ensue. Similarly, increased organizational size, routinization, work specialization, and zero-sum reward systems are all examples of structural factors that can lead to conflicts.

Many conflicts attributed to poor communication are, on closer examination, due to value differences. For instance, prejudice is a value-based source of conflict. When managers incorrectly treat a value-based conflict as a communication problem, the conflict is rarely eliminated. On the contrary, increased communication efforts are only likely to crystallize and reinforce differences. "Before this conversation, I thought you *might* be closed minded. Now I *know* you are!"

Lack of communication *can* be a source of conflict. But managers should first look to structural or value-based explanations because they are more prevalent in organizations.

Stage II: Cognition and Personalization

If the conditions cited in Stage I negatively affect something that one party cares about, then the potential for opposition or incompatibility becomes actualized in the second stage. The antecedent conditions can lead to conflict only when one party or more is affected by, and aware of, the conflict.

As we noted in our definition of conflict, perception is required. Therefore, one or more of the parties must be aware of the existence of the antecedent conditions. However, because a conflict is **perceived** does not mean that it is personalized. In other words, "*A* may be aware that *B* and *A* are in serious disagreement . . . but it may not make *A* tense or anxious, and it may have no effect whatsoever on *A*'s affection toward *B*."[10] It is at the **felt** level, when individuals become emotionally involved, that parties experience anxiety, tension, frustration, or hostility.

Keep in mind two points. First, Stage II is important because it's where conflict issues tend to be defined. This is the place in the process where the parties decide what the conflict is about.[11] And, in turn, this "sense making" is critical because the way a conflict is defined goes a long way toward establishing the sort of outcomes that might settle it. For instance, if I define our salary disagreement as a zero-sum situation—that is, if you get the increase in pay you want, there will be just that amount less for me— I am going to be far less willing to compromise than if I frame the conflict as a potential win–win situation (i.e., the dollars in the salary pool might be increased so that both of us could get the added pay we want). So the definition of a conflict is important, because it typically delineates the set of possible settlements. Our second point is that emotions play a major role in shaping perceptions.[12] For example, negative emotions have been found to produce oversimplification of issues, reductions in trust, and negative interpretations of the other party's behavior.[13] In contrast, positive feelings have been found to increase the tendency to see potential relationships among the elements of a problem, to take a broader view of the situation, and to develop more innovative solutions.[14]

perceived conflict

Awareness by one or more parties of the existence of conditions that create opportunities for conflict to arise.

felt conflict

Emotional involvement in a conflict creating anxiety, tenseness, frustration, or hostility.

Following the attacks of 9/11, McDonald's employee Muhammed El-Nasleh thought co-workers' comments about his "cousins" bombing the World Trade Center was just a stupid joke. But when his boss picked up on the banter and began telling him that he was going to be "checked for bombs," it was no longer funny. "I felt like I was being targeted. It was humiliating." What began as co-worker teasing escalated to a conflict, ultimately resulting in El-Nasleh being fired.

Stage III: Intentions

Intentions intervene between people's perceptions and emotions and their overt behavior. These intentions are decisions to act in a given way.[15]

Why are intentions separated out as a distinct stage? You have to infer the other's intent in order to know how to respond to that other's behavior. A lot of conflicts are escalated merely by one party attributing the wrong intentions to the other party. In addition, there is typically a great deal of slippage between intentions and behavior, so behavior does not always accurately reflect a person's intentions.

intentions

Decisions to act in a given way.

Exhibit 14-2 represents one author's effort to identify the primary conflict-handling intentions. Using two dimensions—*cooperativeness* (the degree to which one party attempts to satisfy the other party's concerns) and *assertiveness* (the degree to which one party attempts to satisfy his or her own concerns)—five conflict-handling intentions can be identified: *competing* (assertive and uncooperative),

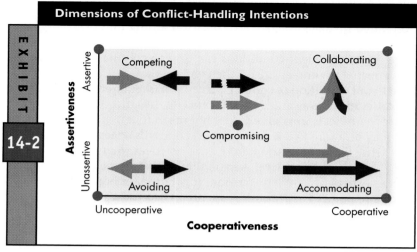

Dimensions of Conflict-Handling Intentions

Source: K. Thomas, "Conflict and Negotiation Processes in Organizations," in M. D. Dunnette and L. M. Hough (eds.), *Handbook of Industrial and Organizational Psychology*, 2nd ed., vol. 3 (Palo Alto, CA: Consulting Psychologists Press, 1992), p. 668. With permission.

collaborating (assertive and cooperative), *avoiding* (unassertive and uncooperative), *accommodating* (unassertive and cooperative), and *compromising* (midrange on both assertiveness and cooperativeness).[16]

competing

A desire to satisfy one's interests, regardless of the impact on the other party to the conflict.

Competing When one person seeks to satisfy his or her own interests, regardless of the impact on the other parties to the conflict, he or she is **competing**. Examples include intending to achieve your goal at the sacrifice of the other's goal, attempting to convince another that your conclusion is correct and that his or hers is mistaken, and trying to make someone else accept blame for a problem.

collaborating

A situation in which the parties to a conflict each desire to satisfy fully the concerns of all parties.

Collaborating When the parties to conflict each desire to fully satisfy the concerns of all parties, we have cooperation and the search for a mutually beneficial outcome. In **collaborating**, the intention of the parties is to solve the problem by clarifying differences rather than by accommodating various points of view. Examples include attempting to find a win–win solution that allows both parties' goals to be completely achieved and seeking a conclusion that incorporates the valid insights of both parties.

avoiding

The desire to withdraw from or suppress a conflict.

Avoiding A person may recognize that a conflict exists and want to withdraw from it or suppress it. Examples of **avoiding** include trying to just ignore a conflict and avoiding others with whom you disagree.

accommodating

The willingness of one party in a conflict to place the opponent's interests above his or her own.

Accommodating When one party seeks to appease an opponent, that party may be willing to place the opponent's interests above his or her own. In other words, in order for the relationship to be maintained, one party is willing to be self-sacrificing. We refer to this intention as **accommodating**. Examples are a willingness to sacrifice your goal so that the other party's goal can be attained, supporting someone else's opinion despite your reservations about it, and forgiving someone for an infraction and allowing subsequent ones.

Compromising   When each party to the conflict seeks to give up something, sharing occurs, resulting in a compromised outcome. In **compromising**, there is no clear winner or loser. Rather, there is a willingness to ration the object of the conflict and accept a solution that provides incomplete satisfaction of both parties' concerns. The distinguishing characteristic of compromising, therefore, is that each party intends to give up something. Examples might be willingness to accept a raise of $2 an hour rather than $3, to acknowledge partial agreement with a specific viewpoint, and to take partial blame for an infraction.

Intentions provide general guidelines for parties in a conflict situation. They define each party's purpose. Yet, people's intentions are not fixed. During the course of a conflict, they might change because of reconceptualization or because of an emotional reaction to the behavior of the other party. However, research indicates that people have an underlying disposition to handle conflicts in certain ways.[17] Specifically, individuals have preferences among the five conflict-handling intentions just described; these preferences tend to be relied on quite consistently, and a person's intentions can be predicted rather well from a combination of intellectual and personality characteristics. So it may be more appropriate to view the five conflict-handling intentions as relatively fixed rather than as a set of options from which individuals choose to fit an appropriate situation. That is, when confronting a conflict situation, some people want to win it all at any cost, some want to find an optimal solution, some want to run away, others want to be obliging, and still others want to "split the difference."

Stage IV: Behavior

When most people think of conflict situations, they tend to focus on Stage IV. Why? Because this is where conflicts become visible. The behavior stage includes the statements, actions, and reactions made by the conflicting parties.

These conflict behaviors are usually overt attempts to implement each party's intentions. But these behaviors have a stimulus quality that is separate from intentions. As a result of miscalculations or unskilled enactments, overt behaviors sometimes deviate from original intentions.[18]

It helps to think of Stage IV as a dynamic process of interaction. For example, you make a demand on me; I respond by arguing; you threaten me; I threaten you back; and so on. Exhibit 14-3 provides a way of visualizing conflict behavior. All

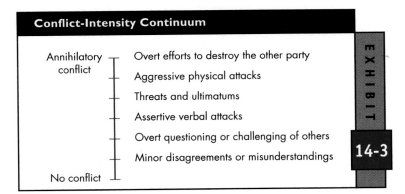

Source: Based on S. P. Robbins, *Managing Organizational Conflict: A Nontraditional Approach* (Upper Saddle River, NJ: Prentice Hall, 1974), pp. 93–97; and F. Glasi, "The Process of Conflict Escalation and the Roles of Third Parties," in G. B. J. Bomers and R. Peterson (eds.), *Conflict Management and Industrial Relations* (Boston: Kluwer-Nijhoff, 1982), pp. 119–40.

conflicts exist somewhere along this continuum. At the lower part of the continuum, we have conflicts characterized by subtle, indirect, and highly controlled forms of tension. An illustration might be a student questioning in class a point the instructor has just made. Conflict intensities escalate as they move upward along the continuum until they become highly destructive. Strikes, riots, and wars clearly fall in this upper range. For the most part, you should assume that conflicts that reach the upper ranges of the continuum are almost always dysfunctional. Functional conflicts are typically confined to the lower range of the continuum.

conflict management

The use of resolution and stimulation techniques to achieve the desired level of conflict.

If a conflict is dysfunctional, what can the parties do to de-escalate it? Or, conversely, what options exist if conflict is too low and needs to be increased? This brings us to **conflict-management** techniques. Exhibit 14-4 lists the major resolution and stimulation techniques that allow managers to control conflict levels. Note that several of the resolution techniques were described earlier as conflict-

Conflict-Management Techniques

EXHIBIT 14-4

Conflict Resolution Techniques

Problem solving	Face-to-face meeting of the conflicting parties for the purpose of identifying the problem and resolving it through open discussion.
Superordinate goals	Creating a shared goal that cannot be attained without the cooperation of each of the conflicting parties.
Expansion of resources	When a conflict is caused by the scarcity of a resource—say, money, promotion opportunities, office space—expansion of the resource can create a win-win solution.
Avoidance	Withdrawal from, or suppression of, the conflict.
Smoothing	Playing down differences while emphasizing common interests between the conflicting parties.
Compromise	Each party to the conflict gives up something of value.
Authoritative command	Management uses its formal authority to resolve the conflict and then communicates its desires to the parties involved.
Altering the human variable	Using behavioral change techniques such as human relations training to alter attitudes and behaviors that cause conflict.
Altering the structural variables	Changing the formal organization structure and the interaction patterns of conflicting parties through job redesign, transfers, creation of coordinating positions, and the like.

Conflict Stimulation Techniques

Communication	Using ambiguous or threatening messages to increase conflict levels.
Bringing in outsiders	Adding employees to a group whose backgrounds, values, attitudes, or managerial styles differ from those of present members.
Restructuring the organization	Realigning work groups, altering rules and regulations, increasing interdependence, and making similar structural changes to disrupt the status quo.
Appointing a devil's advocate	Designating a critic to purposely argue against the majority positions held by the group.

Source: Based on S. P. Robbins, *Managing Organizational Conflict: A Nontraditional Approach* (Upper Saddle River, NJ: Prentice Hall, 1974), pp. 59–89.

handling intentions. This, of course, shouldn't be surprising. Under ideal conditions, a person's intentions should translate into comparable behaviors.

Stage V: Outcomes

The action–reaction interplay between the conflicting parties results in consequences. As our model (see Exhibit 14-1) demonstrates, these outcomes may be functional in that the conflict results in an improvement in the group's performance, or dysfunctional in that it hinders group performance.

Functional Outcomes   How might conflict act as a force to increase group performance? It is hard to visualize a situation in which open or violent aggression could be functional. But there are a number of instances in which it's possible to envision how low or moderate levels of conflict could improve the effectiveness of a group. Because people often find it difficult to think of instances in which conflict can be constructive, let's consider some examples and then review the research evidence. Note how all these examples focus on task and process conflicts, and exclude the relationship variety.

Judy George, CEO of Domain Home Fashions, seeks the functional value of conflict by purposely hiring people who don't share her personality traits and then encouraging them to challenge her views.

Conflict is constructive when it improves the quality of decisions, stimulates creativity and innovation, encourages interest and curiosity among group members, provides the medium through which problems can be aired and tensions released, and fosters an environment of self-evaluation and change. The evidence suggests that conflict can improve the quality of decision making by allowing all points, particularly the ones that are unusual or held by a minority, to be weighed in important decisions.[19] Conflict is an antidote for groupthink. It doesn't allow the group to passively "rubber-stamp" decisions that may be based on weak assumptions, inadequate consideration of relevant alternatives, or other debilities. Conflict challenges the status quo and therefore furthers the creation of new ideas, promotes reassessment of group goals and activities, and increases the probability that the group will respond to change.

For an example of a company that suffered because it had too little functional conflict, you don't have to look further than automobile behemoth General Motors.[20] Many of GM's problems, from the late-1960s to the late-1990s, can be traced to a lack of functional conflict. It hired and promoted individuals who were "yes men," loyal to GM to the point of never questioning company actions. Managers were, for the most part, homogenous: conservative white males raised in the midwestern United States who resisted change—they preferred looking back to past successes rather than forward to new challenges. They were almost sanctimonious in their belief that what had worked in the past would continue to work in the future. Moreover, by sheltering executives in the company's Detroit offices and encouraging them to socialize with others inside the GM ranks, the company further insulated managers from conflicting perspectives.

Research studies in diverse settings confirm the functionality of conflict. Consider the following findings.

The comparison of six major decisions made during the administration of four different U.S. presidents found that conflict reduced the chance that groupthink would overpower policy decisions. The comparisons demonstrated that conformity among presidential advisors was related to poor decisions, whereas an atmosphere of constructive conflict and critical thinking surrounded the well-developed decisions.[21]

There is evidence indicating that conflict can also be positively related to productivity. For instance, it was demonstrated that, among established groups, performance tended to improve more when there was conflict among members than when there was fairly close agreement. The investigators observed that when groups analyzed decisions that had been made by the individual members of that group, the average improvement among the high-conflict groups was 73 percent greater than was that of those groups characterized by low-conflict conditions.[22] Others have found similar results: Groups composed of members with different interests tend to produce higher-quality solutions to a variety of problems than do homogeneous groups.[23]

The preceding leads us to predict that the increasing cultural diversity of the workforce should provide benefits to organizations. And that's what the evidence indicates. Research demonstrates that heterogeneity among group and organization members can increase creativity, improve the quality of decisions, and facilitate change by enhancing member flexibility.[24] For example, researchers compared decision-making groups composed of all-Anglo individuals with groups that also contained members from Asian, Hispanic, and black ethnic groups. The ethnically diverse groups produced more effective and more feasible ideas and the unique ideas they generated tended to be of higher quality than the unique ideas produced by the all-Anglo group.

Similarly, studies of professionals—systems analysts and research and development scientists—support the constructive value of conflict. An investigation of 22 teams of systems analysts found that the more incompatible groups were likely to be more productive.[25] Research and development scientists have been found to be most productive when there is a certain amount of intellectual conflict.[26]

Dysfunctional Outcomes   The destructive consequences of conflict on a group's or organization's performance are generally well known. A reasonable summary might state: Uncontrolled opposition breeds discontent, which acts to dissolve common ties, and eventually leads to the destruction of the group. And, of course, there is a substantial body of literature to document how conflict—the dysfunctional varieties—can reduce group effectiveness.[27] Among the more undesirable consequences are a retarding of communication, reductions in group cohesiveness, and subordination of group goals to the primacy of infighting between members. At the extreme, conflict can bring group functioning to a halt and potentially threaten the group's survival.

The demise of an organization as a result of too much conflict isn't as unusual as it might first appear. For instance, one of New York's best-known law firms, Shea & Gould, closed down solely because the 80 partners just couldn't get along.[28] As one legal consultant, familiar with the organization, said: "This was a firm that had basic and principled differences among the partners that were basically irreconcilable." That same consultant also addressed the partners at their last meeting: "You don't have an economic problem," he said. "You have a personality problem. You hate each other!"

Creating Functional Conflict   We briefly mentioned conflict stimulation as part of Stage IV of the conflict process. In this section we ask: If managers accept the interactionist view toward conflict, what can they do to encourage functional conflict in their organizations?[29]

There seems to be general agreement that creating functional conflict is a tough job, particularly in large American corporations. As one consultant put it, "A high proportion of people who get to the top are conflict avoiders. They don't like hearing negatives, they don't like saying or thinking negative things. They frequently make it up the ladder in part because they don't irritate people on the way up." Another suggests that at least seven out of ten people in American business hush up when their opinions are at odds with those of their superiors, allowing bosses to make mistakes even when they know better.

Such anticonflict cultures may have been tolerable in the past but not in today's fiercely competitive global economy. Organizations that don't encourage and support dissent may find their survival threatened. Let's look at some approaches organizations are using to encourage their people to challenge the system and develop fresh ideas.

The Walt Disney Company purposely encourages big, unruly, and disruptive meetings to create friction and stimulate creative ideas. Hewlett-Packard rewards dissenters by recognizing go-against-the-grain types, or people who stay with the ideas they believe in even when those ideas are rejected by management. Herman Miller Inc., an office-furniture manufacturer, has a formal system in which employees evaluate and criticize their bosses. IBM also has a formal system that encourages dissension. Employees can question their boss with impunity. If the disagreement can't be resolved, the system provides a third party for counsel.

Royal Dutch Shell Group, General Electric, and Anheuser-Busch build devil's advocates into the decision process. For instance, when the policy committee at Anheuser-Busch considers a major move, such as getting into or out of a business or making a major capital expenditure, it often assigns teams to make the case for each side of the question. This process frequently results in decisions and alternatives that hadn't been considered previously.

One common ingredient in organizations that successfully create functional conflict is that they reward dissent and punish conflict avoiders. The real challenge for managers, however, is when they hear news that they don't want to hear. The news may make their blood boil or their hopes collapse, but they can't show it. They have to learn to take the bad news without flinching. No tirades, no tight-lipped sarcasm, no eyes rolling upward, no gritting of teeth. Rather, managers should ask calm, even-tempered questions: "Can you tell me more about what happened?" "What do you think we ought to do?" A sincere "Thank you for bringing this to my attention" will probably reduce the likelihood that managers will be cut off from similar communications in the future.

NEGOTIATION

Negotiation permeates the interactions of almost everyone in groups and organizations. There's the obvious: Labor bargains with management. There's the not so obvious: Managers negotiate with employees, peers, and bosses; salespeople negotiate with customers; purchasing agents negotiate with suppliers. And there's the subtle: A worker agrees to answer a colleague's phone for a few minutes in exchange for some past or future benefit. In today's team-based organizations, in which members are increasingly finding themselves having to work with colleagues over whom they have no direct authority and with whom they may not even share a common boss, negotiation skills become critical.

Many employees have learned to negotiate in order to structure jobs to fit their needs. Heather Carb, bakery manager for a grocery store near Philadelphia, works weekends but has negotiated Tuesdays and Wednesdays off so she can spend time with her three children.

negotiation

A process in which two or more parties exchange goods or services and attempt to agree on the exchange rate for them.

We'll define **negotiation** as a process in which two or more parties exchange goods or services and attempt to agree on the exchange rate for them.[30] Note that we use the terms *negotiation* and *bargaining* interchangeably.

In this section, we'll contrast two bargaining strategies, provide a model of the negotiation process, ascertain the role of personality traits on bargaining, review gender and cultural differences in negotiation, and take a brief look at third-party negotiations.

Bargaining Strategies

There are two general approaches to negotiation—*distributive bargaining* and *integrative bargaining*.[31] These are compared in Exhibit 14-5.

Distributive Bargaining You see a used car advertised for sale in the newspaper. It appears to be just what you've been looking for. You go out to see the car. It's great and you want it. The owner tells you the asking price. You don't want to pay that much. The two of you then negotiate over the price. The negotiating strategy you're engaging in is called **distributive bargaining**. Its most identifying feature is that it operates under zero-sum conditions. That is, any gain I make is at your expense, and vice versa. Referring back to the used car example, every dollar you can get the seller to cut from the car's price is a dollar you save. Conversely, every dollar more the seller can get from you comes at your expense. So the essence of distributive bargaining is negotiating over who gets what share of a fixed pie.

distributive bargaining

Negotiation that seeks to divide up a fixed amount of resources; a win–lose situation.

Probably the most widely cited example of distributive bargaining is in labor–management negotiations over wages. Typically, labor's representatives come to the bargaining table determined to get as much money as possible out of management. Since every cent more that labor negotiates increases management's costs, each party bargains aggressively and treats the other as an opponent who must be defeated.

The essence of distributive bargaining is depicted in Exhibit 14-6. Parties *A* and *B* represent two negotiators. Each has a *target point* that defines what he or she would like to achieve. Each also has a *resistance point*, which marks the lowest outcome that is acceptable—the point below which they would break off negotiations rather than accept a less-favorable settlement. The area between these two points makes up each one's aspiration range. As long as there is some overlap between *A*

Distributive Versus Integrative Bargaining

Bargaining Characteristic	Distributive Characteristic	Integrative Characteristic
Available resources	Fixed amount of resources to be divided	Variable amount of resources to be divided
Primary motivations	I win, you lose	I win, you win
Primary interests	Opposed to each other	Convergent or congruent with each other
Focus of relationships	Short term	Long term

EXHIBIT 14-5

Source: Based on R. J. Lewicki and J. A. Litterer, *Negotiation* (Homewood, IL: Irwin, 1985), p. 280.

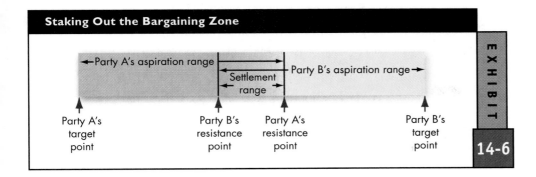

Staking Out the Bargaining Zone

EXHIBIT 14-6

←Party A's aspiration range

Settlement range

Party B's aspiration range→

Party A's target point

Party B's resistance point

Party A's resistance point

Party B's target point

and B's aspiration ranges, there exists a settlement range in which each one's aspirations can be met.

When engaged in distributive bargaining, one's tactics focus on trying to get one's opponent to agree to one's specific target point or to get as close to it as possible. Examples of such tactics are persuading your opponent of the impossibility of getting to his or her target point and the advisability of accepting a settlement near yours; arguing that your target is fair, while your opponent's isn't; and attempting to get your opponent to feel emotionally generous toward you and thus accept an outcome close to your target point.

Integrative Bargaining A sales representative for a women's sportswear manufacturer has just closed a $15,000 order from a small clothing retailer. The sales rep calls in the order to her firm's credit department. She is told that the firm can't approve credit to this customer because of a past slow-payment record. The next day, the sales rep and the firm's credit manager meet to discuss the problem. The sales rep doesn't want to lose the business. Neither does the credit manager, but he also doesn't want to get stuck with an uncollectible debt. The two openly review their options. After considerable discussion, they agree on a solution that meets both their needs: The credit manager will approve the sale, but the clothing store's owner will provide a bank guarantee that will ensure payment if the bill isn't paid within 60 days.

integrative bargaining
Negotiation that seeks one or more settlements that can create a win–win solution.

This sales–credit negotiation is an example of **integrative bargaining**. In contrast to distributive bargaining, integrative problem solving operates under the assumption that there exists one or more settlements that can create a win–win solution.

In terms of intraorganizational behavior, all things being equal, integrative bargaining is preferable to distributive bargaining. Why? Because the former builds long-term relationships and facilitates working together in the future. It bonds negotiators and allows each to leave the bargaining table feeling that he or she has achieved a victory. Distributive bargaining, on the other hand, leaves one party a loser. It tends to build animosities and deepen divisions when people have to work together on an ongoing basis.

U.S.–Russian arms-reduction negotiations have moved from distributive to integrative. Slowly but surely, as relations between the two superpowers improved over the years, negotiators became more open and candid, trusting, and sensitive to each other's needs.

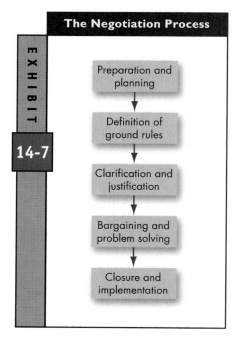

EXHIBIT

14-7

The Negotiation Process

- Preparation and planning
- Definition of ground rules
- Clarification and justification
- Bargaining and problem solving
- Closure and implementation

Why, then, don't we see more integrative bargaining in organizations? The answer lies in the conditions necessary for this type of negotiation to succeed. These include parties who are open with information and candid about their concerns, a sensitivity by both parties to the other's needs, the ability to trust one another, and a willingness by both parties to maintain flexibility.[32] Since these conditions often don't exist in organizations, it isn't surprising that negotiations often take on a win-at-any-cost dynamic.

The Negotiation Process

Exhibit 14-7 provides a simplified model of the negotiation process. It views negotiation as made up of five steps: (1) preparation and planning; (2) definition of ground rules; (3) clarification and justification; (4) bargaining and problem solving; and (5) closure and implementation.[33]

Preparation and Planning Before you start negotiating, you need to do your homework. What's the nature of the conflict? What's the history leading up to this negotiation? Who's involved and what are their perceptions of the conflict?

What do you want from the negotiation? What are *your* goals? If you're a supply manager at Dell Computer, for instance, and your goal is to get a significant cost reduction from your supplier of keyboards, make sure that this goal stays paramount in your discussions and doesn't get overshadowed by other issues. It often helps to put your goals in writing and develop a range of outcomes—from "most hopeful" to "minimally acceptable"—to keep your attention focused.

You also want to prepare an assessment of what you think the other party to your negotiation's goals are. What are they likely to ask for? How entrenched are they likely to be in their position? What intangible or hidden interests may be important to them? What might they be willing to settle on? When you can anticipate your opponent's position, you are better equipped to counter his or her arguments with the facts and figures that support your position.

The importance of sizing up the other party is illustrated by the experience of Keith Rosenbaum, a partner in a major Los Angeles law firm. "Once when we were negotiating to buy a business, we found that the owner was going through a nasty divorce. We were on good terms with the wife's attorney and we learned the seller's net worth. California is a community-property-law state, so we knew he had to pay her half of everything. We knew his time frame. We knew what he was willing to part with and what he was not. We knew a lot more about him than he would have wanted us to know. We were able to twist him a little bit, and get a better price."[34]

Once you've gathered your information, use it to develop a strategy. For example, expert chess players have a strategy. They know ahead of time how they will respond to any given situation. As part of your strategy, you should determine yours and the other side's *Best Alternative To a Negotiated Agreement* (**BATNA**).[35] Your BATNA determines the lowest value acceptable to you for a negotiated agreement. Any offer you receive that is higher than your BATNA is better than an impasse. Conversely, you shouldn't expect success in your negotiation effort unless

BATNA

The best alternative to a negotiated agreement; the lowest acceptable value to an individual for a negotiated agreement.

you're able to make the other side an offer they find more attractive than their BATNA. If you go into your negotiation having a good idea of what the other party's BATNA is, even if you're not able to meet theirs, you might be able to get them to change it.

Definition of Ground Rules   Once you've done your planning and developed a strategy, you're ready to begin defining the ground rules and procedures with the other party over the negotiation itself. Who will do the negotiating? Where will it take place? What time constraints, if any, will apply? To what issues will negotiation be limited? Will there be a specific procedure to follow if an impasse is reached? During this phase, the parties will also exchange their initial proposals or demands.

Clarification and Justification   When initial positions have been exchanged, both you and the other party will explain, amplify, clarify, bolster, and justify your original demands. This needn't be confrontational. Rather, it's an opportunity for educating and informing each other on the issues, why they are important, and how each arrived at their initial demands. This is the point at which you might want to provide the other party with any documentation that helps support your position.

Bargaining and Problem Solving   The essence of the negotiation process is the actual give-and-take in trying to hash out an agreement. It is here where concessions will undoubtedly need to be made by both parties.

Closure and Implementation   The final step in the negotiation process is formalizing the agreement that has been worked out and developing any procedures that are necessary for implementation and monitoring. For major negotiations—which would include everything from labor–management negotiations to bargaining over lease terms to buying a piece of real estate to negotiating a job offer for a senior-management position—this will require hammering out the specifics in a formal contract. For most cases, however, closure of the negotiation process is nothing more formal than a handshake.

Issues in Negotiation

We conclude our discussion of negotiation by reviewing four contemporary issues in negotiation: the role of personality traits, gender differences in negotiating, the effect of cultural differences on negotiating styles, and the use of third parties to help resolve differences.

The Role of Personality Traits in Negotiation   Can you predict an opponent's negotiating tactics if you know something about his or her personality? It's tempting to answer Yes to this question. For instance, you might assume that high risk takers would be more aggressive bargainers who make fewer concessions. Surprisingly, the evidence doesn't support this intuition.[36]

Overall assessments of the personality–negotiation relationship finds that personality traits have no significant direct effect on either the bargaining process or the negotiation outcomes. This conclusion is important. It suggests that you should concentrate on the issues and the situational factors in each bargaining episode and not on your opponent's personality.

Gender Differences in Negotiations   Do men and women negotiate differently? And does gender affect negotiation outcomes? The answer to the first question appears to be No.[37] The answer to the second is a qualified Yes.[38]

A popular stereotype held by many is that women are more cooperative and pleasant in negotiations than are men. The evidence doesn't support this belief. However, men have been found to negotiate better outcomes than women, although the difference is quite small. It's been postulated that this difference might be due to men and women placing divergent values on outcomes. "It is possible that a few hundred dollars more in salary or the corner office is less important to women than forming and maintaining an interpersonal relationship."[39]

The belief that women are "nicer" than men in negotiations is probably due to confusing gender and the lack of power typically held by women in most large organizations. The research indicates that low-power managers, regardless of gender, attempt to placate their opponents and to use softly persuasive tactics rather than direct confrontation and threats. In situations in which women and men have similar power bases, there shouldn't be any significant differences in their negotiation styles.

The evidence suggests that women's attitudes toward negotiation and toward themselves as negotiators appear to be quite different from men's. Managerial women demonstrate less confidence in anticipation of negotiating and are less satisfied with their performance after the process is complete, even when their performance and the outcomes they achieve are similar to those for men.

This latter conclusion suggests that women may unduly penalize themselves by failing to engage in negotiations when such action would be in their best interests.

Cultural Differences in Negotiations   Although there appears to be no significant direct relationship between an individual's personality and negotiation style, cultural background does seem to be relevant. Negotiating styles clearly vary across national cultures.[40]

The French like conflict. They frequently gain recognition and develop their reputations by thinking and acting against others. As a result, the French tend to take a long time in negotiating agreements and they aren't overly concerned about whether their opponents like or dislike them.[41] The Chinese also draw out negotiations but that's because they believe negotiations never end. Just when you think you've pinned down every detail and reached a final solution with a Chinese executive, that executive might smile and start the process all over again. Like the Japanese, the Chinese negotiate to develop a relationship and a commitment to work together rather than to tie up every loose end.[42] Americans are known around the world for their impatience and their desire to be liked.[43] Astute negotiators from other countries often turn these characteristics to their advantage by dragging out negotiations and making friendship conditional on the final settlement. Exhibit 14-8 offers some insights into why Americans managers might have trouble in cross-cultural negotiations.

The cultural context of the negotiation significantly influences the amount and type of preparation for bargaining, the relative emphasis on task versus interpersonal relationships, the tactics used, and even where the negotiation should be conducted. To further illustrate some of these differences, let's look at two studies that compare the influence of culture on business negotiations.

The first study compared North Americans, Arabs, and Russians.[44] Among the factors that were looked at were their negotiating style, how they responded to an opponent's arguments, their approach to making concessions, and how they handled negotiating deadlines. North Americans tried to persuade by relying on facts and appealing to logic. They countered opponents' arguments with objective facts. They made small concessions early in the negotiation to establish a relationship, and usually reciprocated opponent's concessions. North Americans treated deadlines as very important. The Arabs tried to persuade by appealing to emotion. They countered opponent's arguments with subjective feelings. They made concessions throughout the bargaining process and almost always reciprocated opponents' concessions. Arabs approached deadlines very casually. The Russians based their arguments on asserted ideals. They made few, if any, concessions. Any concession offered by an opponent was viewed as a weakness and almost never reciprocated. Finally, the Russians tended to ignore deadlines.

The second study looked at verbal and nonverbal negotiation tactics exhibited by North Americans, Japanese, and Brazilians during half-hour bargaining sessions.[45] Some of the differences were particularly interesting. For instance, the Brazilians on average said "No" 83 times, compared to five times for the Japanese and nine times for the North Americans. The Japanese displayed more than five periods of silence lasting longer than ten seconds during the 30-minute sessions. North Americans averaged 3.5 such periods; the Brazilians had none. The Japanese and North Americans interrupted their opponent about the same number of times, but the Brazilians interrupted 2.5 to 3 times more often than the North Americans and the Japanese. Finally, while the Japanese and the North Americans had no physical contact with their opponents during negotiations except for handshaking, the Brazilians touched each other almost five times every half-hour.

Third-Party Negotiations To this point, we've discussed bargaining in terms of direct negotiations. Occasionally, however, individuals or group representatives reach a stalemate and are unable to resolve their differences through direct negotiations.

Dispute resolution services exist to help companies reduce conflicts and facilitate negotiations.

mediator

A neutral third party who facilitates a negotiated solution by using reasoning, persuasion, and suggestions for alternatives.

In such cases, they may turn to a third party to help them find a solution. There are four basic third-party roles: mediator, arbitrator, conciliator, and consultant.[46]

A **mediator** is a neutral third party who facilitates a negotiated solution by using reasoning and persuasion, suggesting alternatives, and the like. Mediators are widely used in labor–management negotiations and in civil court disputes.

The overall effectiveness of mediated negotiations is fairly impressive. The settlement rate is approximately 60 percent, with negotiator satisfaction at about 75 percent. But the situation is the key to whether or not mediation will succeed; the conflicting parties must be motivated to bargain and resolve their conflict. In addition, conflict intensity can't be too high; mediation is most effective under moderate levels of conflict. Finally, perceptions of the mediator are important; to be effective, the mediator must be perceived as neutral and noncoercive.

arbitrator

A third party to a negotiation who has the authority to dictate an agreement.

An **arbitrator** is a third party with the authority to dictate an agreement. Arbitration can be voluntary (requested) or compulsory (forced on the parties by law or contract).

The authority of the arbitrator varies according to the rules set by the negotiators. For instance, the arbitrator might be limited to choosing one of the negotiator's last offers or to suggesting an agreement point that is nonbinding, or free to choose and make any judgment he or she wishes.

The big plus of arbitration over mediation is that it always results in a settlement. Whether or not there is a negative side depends on how "heavy-handed" the arbitrator appears. If one party is left feeling overwhelmingly defeated, that party is certain to be dissatisfied and unlikely to graciously accept the arbitrator's decision. Therefore, the conflict may resurface at a later time.

conciliator

A trusted third party who provides an informal communication link between the negotiator and the opponent.

A **conciliator** is a trusted third party who provides an informal communication link between the negotiator and the opponent. This role was made famous by Robert Duval in the first *Godfather* film. As Don Corleone's adopted son and a lawyer by training, Duval acted as an intermediary between the Corleone family and the other Mafioso families.

Conciliation is used extensively in international, labor, family, and community disputes. Comparing its effectiveness to mediation has proven difficult because the two overlap a great deal. In practice, conciliators typically act as more than mere communication conduits. They also engage in fact finding, interpreting messages, and persuading disputants to develop agreements.

consultant

An impartial third party, skilled in conflict management, who attempts to facilitate creative problem solving through communication and analysis.

A **consultant** is a skilled and impartial third party who attempts to facilitate problem solving through communication and analysis, aided by his or her knowledge of conflict management. In contrast to the previous roles, the consultant's role is not to settle the issues but, rather, to improve relations between the conflicting parties so that they can reach a settlement themselves. Instead of putting forward specific solutions, the consultant tries to help the parties learn to understand and work with each other. Therefore, this approach has a longer-term focus: to build new and positive perceptions and attitudes between the conflicting parties.

SUMMARY AND IMPLICATIONS FOR MANAGERS

Many people automatically assume that conflict is related to lower group and organizational performance. This chapter has demonstrated that this assumption is frequently incorrect. Conflict can be either constructive or destructive to the functioning of a group or unit. As shown in Exhibit 14-9, levels of conflict can be either too high or too low. Either extreme hinders performance. An optimal level is

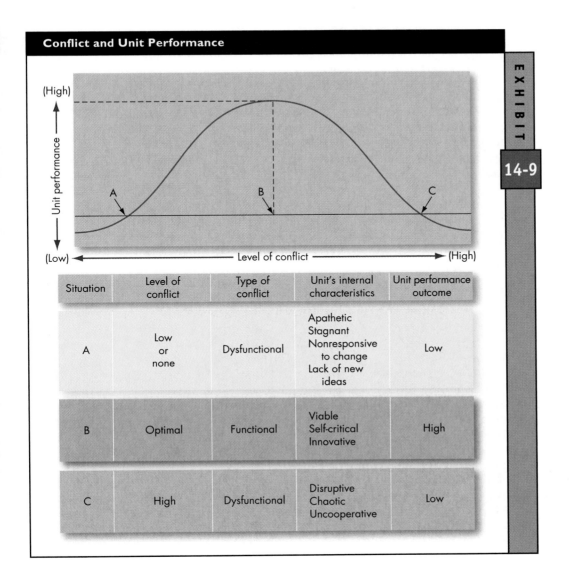

Conflict and Unit Performance

EXHIBIT 14-9

Situation	Level of conflict	Type of conflict	Unit's internal characteristics	Unit performance outcome
A	Low or none	Dysfunctional	Apathetic Stagnant Nonresponsive to change Lack of new ideas	Low
B	Optimal	Functional	Viable Self-critical Innovative	High
C	High	Dysfunctional	Disruptive Chaotic Uncooperative	Low

one at which there is enough conflict to prevent stagnation, stimulate creativity, allow tensions to be released, and initiate the seeds for change, yet not so much as to be disruptive or to deter coordination of activities.

Inadequate or excessive levels of conflict can hinder the effectiveness of a group or an organization, resulting in reduced satisfaction of group members, increased absence and turnover rates and, eventually, lower productivity. On the other hand, when conflict is at an optimal level, complacency and apathy should be minimized, motivation should be enhanced through the creation of a challenging and questioning environment with a vitality that makes work interesting, and there should be the amount of turnover needed to rid the organization of misfits and poor performers.

What advice can we give managers faced with excessive conflict and the need to reduce it? Don't assume there's one conflict-handling intention that will always be best! You should select an intention appropriate for the situation. The following provides some guidelines:[47]

Use *competition* when quick, decisive action is vital (in emergencies); on important issues, where unpopular actions need implementing (in cost cutting, enforcing unpopular rules, discipline); on issues vital to the organization's welfare when you know you're right; and against people who take advantage of noncompetitive behavior.

Use *collaboration* to find an integrative solution when both sets of concerns are too important to be compromised; when your objective is to learn; to merge insights from people with different perspectives; to gain commitment by incorporating concerns into a consensus; and to work through feelings that have interfered with a relationship.

Use *avoidance* when an issue is trivial, or more important issues are pressing; when you perceive no chance of satisfying your concerns; when potential disruption outweighs the benefits of resolution; to let people cool down and regain perspective; when gathering information supersedes immediate decision; when others can resolve the conflict more effectively; and when issues seem tangential or symptomatic of other issues.

Use *accommodation* when you find you're wrong and to allow a better position to be heard, to learn, and to show your reasonableness; when issues are more important to others than to yourself and to satisfy others and maintain cooperation; to build social credits for later issues; to minimize loss when you are outmatched and losing; when harmony and stability are especially important; and to allow employees to develop by learning from mistakes.

Use *compromise* when goals are important but not worth the effort of potential disruption of more assertive approaches; when opponents with equal power are committed to mutually exclusive goals; to achieve temporary settlements to complex issues; to arrive at expedient solutions under time pressure; and as a backup when collaboration or competition is unsuccessful.

Negotiation was shown to be an ongoing activity in groups and organizations. Distributive bargaining can resolve disputes but it often negatively affects one or more negotiators' satisfaction because it is focused on the short term and because it is confrontational. Integrative bargaining, in contrast, tends to provide outcomes that satisfy all parties and that build lasting relationships.

Conflict Benefits Organizations

L et's briefly review how stimulating conflict can provide benefits to the organization.

Conflict is a means by which to bring about radical change. It's an effective device by which management can drastically change the existing power structure, current interaction patterns, and entrenched attitudes.

Conflict facilitates group cohesiveness. Whereas conflict increases hostility between groups, external threats tend to cause a group to pull together as a unit. Intergroup conflicts raise the extent to which members identify with their own group and increase feelings of solidarity.

Conflict improves group and organizational effectiveness. The stimulation of conflict initiates the search for new means and goals and provides the stimulus for innovation. The successful solution of a conflict leads to greater effectiveness, to more trust and openness, to greater attraction of members for each other, and to depersonalization of future conflicts.

Conflict brings about a slightly higher, more constructive level of tension. When the level of tension is very low, the parties are not sufficiently motivated to do something about a conflict.

Groups or organizations devoid of conflict are likely to suffer from apathy, stagnation, groupthink, and other debilitating diseases. In fact, more organizations probably fail because they have *too little* conflict, not because they have too much. Take a look at a list of large organizations that have failed or suffered serious financial setbacks over the past decade or two. You see names like Smith Corona, Western Union, Kmart, Montgomery Ward, Morrison Knudsen, Greyhound, and Digital Computer. The common thread through these companies is that they stagnated. Their managements became complacent and unable or unwilling to facilitate change. These organizations could have benefited from functional conflict.

I t may be true that conflict is an inherent part of any group or organization. It may not be possible to eliminate it completely. However, just because conflicts exist is no reason to deify them. All conflicts are dysfunctional, and it is one of management's major responsibilities to keep conflict intensity as low as humanly possible. A few points will support this case.

The negative consequences from conflict can be devastating. The list of negatives associated with conflict are awesome. The most obvious are increased turnover, decreased employee satisfaction, inefficiencies between work units, sabotage, labor grievances and strikes, and physical aggression.

Effective managers build teamwork. A good manager builds a coordinated team. Conflict works against such an objective. A successful work group is like a successful sports team; each member knows his or her role and supports his or her teammates. When a team works well, the whole becomes greater than the sum of the parts. Management creates teamwork by minimizing internal conflicts and facilitating internal coordination.

Managers who accept and stimulate conflict don't survive in organizations. The whole argument of the value of conflict may be moot as long as the majority of senior executives in organizations view conflict from the traditional view. In the traditional view, any conflict will be seen as bad. Since the evaluation of a manager's performance is made by higher-level executives, those managers who do not succeed in eliminating conflicts are likely to be appraised negatively. This, in turn, will reduce opportunities for advancement. Any manager who aspires to move up in such an environment will be wise to follow the traditional view and eliminate any outward signs of conflict. Failure to follow this advice might result in the premature departure of the manager.

1. What are the disadvantages to conflict? What are its advantages?

2. What is the difference between functional and dysfunctional conflict? What determines functionality?

3. Under what conditions might conflict be beneficial to a group?

4. What are the components in the conflict process model? From your own experiences, give an example of how a conflict proceeded through the five stages.

5. How could a manager stimulate conflict in his or her department?

6. What defines the settlement range in distributive bargaining?

7. Why isn't integrative bargaining more widely practiced in organizations?

8. How do men and women differ, if at all, in their approaches to negotiation?

9. What problems might Americans have in negotiating with people from collectivist cultures like China and Japan?

10. What can you do to improve your negotiating effectiveness?

Questions for Critical Thinking

1. Do you think competition and conflict are different? Explain.

2. "Participation is an excellent method for identifying differences and resolving conflicts." Do you agree or disagree? Discuss.

3. From your own experience, describe a situation in which you were involved for which the conflict was dysfunctional. Describe another example, from your experience, for which the conflict was functional. Now analyze how other parties in both conflicts might have interpreted the situation in terms of whether the conflicts were functional or dysfunctional.

4. Assume a Canadian had to negotiate a contract with someone from Spain. What problems might he or she face? What suggestions would you make to help facilitate a settlement?

5. Michael Eisner, CEO at the Walt Disney Co., wants to stimulate conflict inside his firm. But he wants to minimize conflict with outside parties—agents, contractors, unions, etc. What does this say about conflict levels, functional versus dysfunctional conflict, and managing conflict?

Team Exercise | **A Negotiation Role Play**

This role play is designed to help you develop your negotiating skills. The class is to break into pairs. One person will play the role of Alex, the department supervisor. The other person will play C. J., Alex's boss. Both participants should read The Situation, The Negotiation, and then *only* their role.

The Situation: Alex and C. J. work for Nike in Portland, Oregon. Alex supervises a research laboratory. C. J. is the manager of research and development. Alex and C. J. are former college runners who have worked for Nike for more than six years. C. J. has been Alex's boss for two years.

One of Alex's employees has greatly impressed Alex. This employee is Lisa Roland. Lisa was hired 11 months ago. She is 24 years old and holds a master's degree in mechanical engineering. Her entry-level salary was $42,500 a year. She was told by Alex that, in accordance with corporation policy, she would receive an initial performance evaluation at six months and a comprehensive review after one year. Based on her performance record, Lisa was told she could expect a salary adjustment at the time of the one-year evaluation.

Alex's evaluation of Lisa after six months was very positive. Alex commented on the long hours Lisa was putting in, her cooperative spirit, the fact that others in the lab enjoyed working with her, and that she was making an immediate positive impact on the project she had been assigned. Now that Lisa's first anniversary is coming up, Alex has again reviewed Lisa's performance. Alex thinks Lisa may be the best new person the R&D group has ever hired. After only a year, Alex has ranked Lisa as the number-three performer in a department of 11.

Salaries in the department vary greatly. Alex, for instance, has a basic salary of $72,000, plus eligibility for a bonus that might add another $6,000 to $10,000 a year. The salary range of the 11 department members is $35,400 to $61,350. The lowest salary is a recent hire with a bachelor's degree in physics. The two people that Alex has rated above Lisa earn base salaries of $57,700 and $61,350. They're both 27 years old and have been at Nike for three and four years, respectively. The median salary in Alex's department is $51,660.

Alex's Role: You want to give Lisa a big raise. Although she's young, she has proven to be an excellent addition to the department. You don't want to lose her. More importantly, she knows in general what other people in the department are earning and she thinks she's underpaid. The company typically gives one-year raises of 5 percent, although 10 percent is not unusual and 20 to 30 percent increases have been approved on occasion. You'd like to get Lisa as large an increase as C. J. will approve.

C. J.'s Role: All your supervisors typically try to squeeze you for as much money as they can for their people. You understand this because you did the same thing when you were a supervisor, but your boss wants to keep a lid on costs. He wants you to keep raises for recent hires generally in the 5 to 8 percent range. In fact, he's sent a memo to all managers and supervisors saying this. However, your boss is also very concerned with equity and paying people what they're worth. You feel assured that he will support any salary recommendation you make, as long as it can be justified. Your goal, consistent with cost reduction, is to keep salary increases as low as possible.

The Negotiation: Alex has a meeting scheduled with C. J. to discuss Lisa's performance review and salary adjustment. Take a couple of minutes to think through the facts in this exercise and to prepare a strategy. Then you have up to 15 minutes to conduct your negotiation. When your negotiation is complete, the class will compare the various strategies used and pair outcomes.

Ethical Dilemma | **Is It Unethical to Lie and Deceive During Negotiations?**

In Chapter 10, we addressed lying in the context of communication. Here we return to the topic of lying but specifically as it relates to negotiation. We think this issue is important because, for many people, there is no such thing as lying when it comes to negotiating.

It's been said that the whole notion of negotiation is built on ethical quicksand: To succeed, you must deceive. Is this true? If so, how can someone maintain high ethical standards and, at the same time, deal with the daily need to negotiate with bosses, peers, staff, people from other organizations, friends, and even relatives?

We can probably agree that baldfaced lies during negotiation are wrong. At least most ethicists would probably agree. The universal dilemma surrounds the little lies—the omissions, evasions, and concealments that are often necessary to best an opponent.

During negotiations, when is a lie a *lie*? Is exaggerating benefits, downplaying negatives, ignoring flaws, or saying "I don't know" when in reality you do considered lying? Is declaring that "this is my final offer and nonnegotiable" (even when you're posturing) a lie? Is pretending to bend over backward to make meaningful concessions lying? Rather than being unethical practices, the use of these "lies" is considered by many as indicators that a negotiator is strong, smart, and savvy.

When is evasiveness and deception out of bounds? Is it naive to be completely honest and bare your soul during negotiations? Or are the rules of negotiations unique: Any tactic that will improve your chance of winning is acceptable?

Source: Based on M. Diener, "Fair Enough," *Entrepreneur*, January 2002, pp. 100–102.

Mallory Murray hadn't had much experience working as part of a team. A recent graduate of the University of Alabama, her business program had focused primarily on individual projects and accomplishments. What little exposure she'd had to teams was in her organizational behavior, marketing research, and strategy formulation courses. When she interviewed with ThinkLink, an educational software firm out of Gainesville, Florida, she wasn't much concerned by the fact that ThinkLink made extensive use of cross-functional teams. During on-site interviews, she told interviewers and managers alike that she had limited experience on teams. But she did tell them she worked well with people and thought that she could be an effective team player. Unfortunately, Mallory Murray was mistaken.

Mallory joined ThinkLink as an assistant marketing manager for the company's high school core programs. These are essentially software programs designed to help students learn algebra and geometry. Mallory's boss is Lin Chen (marketing manager). Other members of the team she is currently working with include Todd Schlotsky (senior programmer), Laura Willow (advertising), Sean Traynor (vice president for strategic marketing), Joyce Rothman (co-founder of ThinkLink, who now works only part-time in the company; formerly a high-school math teacher; the formal leader of this project), and Harlow Gray (educational consultant).

After her first week on the job, Mallory was seriously thinking about quitting. "I never imagined how difficult it would be working with people who are so opinionated and competitive. Every decision seems to be a power contest. Sean, Joyce, and Harlow are particularly troublesome. Sean thinks his rank entitles him to the last word. Joyce thinks her opinions should carry more weight because she was instrumental in creating the company. And Harlow views everyone as less knowledgeable than he is. Because he consults with a number of software firms and school districts, Harlow's a 'know-it-all.' To make things worse, Lin is passive and quiet. He rarely speaks up in meetings and appears to want to avoid any conflicts."

"What makes my job particularly difficult," Mallory went on, "is that I don't have any specific job responsibilities. It seems that someone else is always interfering with what I'm doing or telling me how to do it. Our team has seven members—six chiefs and me!"

The project team that Mallory is working on has a deadline to meet that is only six weeks away. Currently the team is at least two weeks behind schedule. Everyone is aware that there's a problem but no one seems to be able to solve it. What is especially frustrating to Mallory is that neither Lin Chen nor Joyce Rothman is showing any leadership. Lin is preoccupied with a number of other projects, and Joyce can't seem to control Sean and Harlow's strong personalities.

Questions

1. Discuss cross-functional teams in terms of their propensity to create conflict.

2. What techniques or procedures might help reduce conflict on cross-functional teams?

3. If you were Mallory, is there anything you could do to lessen the conflict on the core project? Elaborate.

KSS PROGRAM

KNOW THE CONCEPTS
SELF-AWARENESS
SKILLS APPLICATIONS

Negotiating

After you've read this chapter, take Self-Assessment #34 (What's My Preferred Conflict-Handling Style?) on your enclosed CD-ROM, and complete the skill-building module entitled Negotiating on page 626.

Endnotes

1. This vignette is based on S. Hofmeister, "Viacom's Board Tells Top Executives to Work It Out," www.latimes.com, January 31, 2002; and S. Hofmeister, "Viacom Truce Met with Skepticism," www.latimes.com, February 1, 2002.

2. With apologies to the author of the opening theme to ABC's *The Odd Couple*.

3. See, for instance, C. F. Fink, "Some Conceptual Difficulties in the Theory of Social Conflict," *Journal of Conflict Resolution*, December 1968, pp. 412–60. For an updated review of the conflict literature, see J. A. Wall, Jr., and R. R. Callister, "Conflict and Its Management," *Journal of Management*, vol. 21, no. 3, 1995, pp. 515–58.

4. L. L. Putnam and M. S. Poole, "Conflict and Negotiation," in F. M. Jablin, L. L. Putnam, K. H. Roberts, and L. W. Porter (eds.), *Handbook of Organizational Communication: An Interdisciplinary Perspective* (Newbury Park, CA: Sage, 1987), pp. 549–99.

5. K. W. Thomas, "Conflict and Negotiation Processes in Organizations," in M. D. Dunnette and L. M. Hough (eds.), *Handbook of Industrial and Organizational Psychology*, 2nd ed., vol. 3 (Palo Alto, CA: Consulting Psychologists Press, 1992), pp. 651–717.

6. For a comprehensive review of the interactionist approach, see C. De Dreu and E. Van de Vliert (eds.), *Using Conflict in Organizations* (London: Sage Publications, 1997).

7. See K. A. Jehn, "A Multimethod Examination of the Benefits and Detriments of Intragroup Conflict," *Administrative Science Quarterly*, June 1995, pp. 256–82; K. A. Jehn, "A Qualitative Analysis of Conflict Types and Dimensions in Organizational Groups," *Administrative Science Quarterly*, September 1997, pp. 530–57; K. A. Jehn and E. A. Mannix, "The Dynamic Nature of Conflict: A Longitudinal Study of Intragroup Conflict and Group Performance," *Academy of Management Journal*, April 2001, pp. 238–51; and C. K. W. De Dreu and A. E. M. Van Vianen, "Managing Relationship Conflict and the Effectiveness of Organizational Teams," *Journal of Organizational Behavior*, May 2001, pp. 309–28.

8. See S. P. Robbins, *Managing Organizational Conflict: A Nontraditional Approach* (Englewood Cliffs, NJ: Prentice Hall, 1974), pp. 31–55; and J. A. Wall, Jr., and R. R. Callister, "Conflict and Its Management," pp. 517–23.

9. S. P. Robbins, *Managing Organizational Conflict.*

10. L. R. Pondy, "Organizational Conflict: Concepts and Models," *Administrative Science Quarterly*, September 1967, p. 302.

11. See, for instance, R. L. Pinkley, "Dimensions of Conflict Frame: Disputant Interpretations of Conflict," *Journal of Applied Psychology*, April 1990, pp. 117–26; and R. L. Pinkley and G. B. Northcraft, "Conflict Frames of Reference: Implications for Dispute Processes and Outcomes," *Academy of Management Journal*, February 1994, pp. 193–205.

12. R. Kumar, "Affect, Cognition and Decision Making in Negotiations: A Conceptual Integration," in M. A. Rahim (ed.), *Managing Conflict: An Integrative Approach* (New York: Praeger, 1989), pp. 185–94.

13. Ibid.

14. P. J. D. Carnevale and A. M. Isen, "The Influence of Positive Affect and Visual Access on the Discovery of Integrative Solutions in Bilateral Negotiations," *Organizational Behavior and Human Decision Processes*, February 1986, pp. 1–13.

15. Thomas, "Conflict and Negotiation Processes in Organizations."

16. Ibid.

17. See R. J. Sternberg and L. J. Soriano, "Styles of Conflict Resolution," *Journal of Personality and Social Psychology*, July 1984, pp. 115–26; R. A. Baron, "Personality and Organizational Conflict: Effects of the Type A Behavior Pattern and Self-Monitoring," *Organizational Behavior and Human Decision Processes*, October 1989, pp. 281–96; and R. J. Volkema and T. J. Bergmann, "Conflict Styles as Indicators of Behavioral Patterns in Interpersonal Conflicts," *Journal of Social Psychology*, February 1995, pp. 5–15.

18. Thomas, "Conflict and Negotiation Processes in Organizations."

19. See, for instance, R. A. Cosier and C. R. Schwenk, "Agreement and Thinking Alike: Ingredients for Poor Decisions," *Academy of Management Executive*, February 1990, pp. 69–74; K. A. Jehn, "Enhancing Effectiveness: An Investigation of Advantages and Disadvantages of Value-Based Intragroup Conflict," *International Journal of Conflict Management*, July 1994, pp. 223–38; R. L. Priem, D. A. Harrison, and N. K. Muir, "Structured Conflict and Consensus Outcomes in Group Decision Making," *Journal of Management*, vol. 21, no. 4, 1995, pp. 691–710; and K. A. Jehn and E. A. Mannix, "The Dynamic Nature of Conflict: A Longitudinal Study of Intragroup Conflict and Group Performance," *Academy of Management Journal*, April 2001, pp. 238–51.

20. See, for instance, C. J. Loomis, "Dinosaurs?" *Fortune*, May 3, 1993, pp. 36–42.

21. I. L. Janis, *Victims of Groupthink* (Boston: Houghton Mifflin, 1972).

22. J. Hall and M. S. Williams, "A Comparison of Decision-Making Performances in Established and Ad-Hoc Groups,"

Journal of Personality and Social Psychology, February 1966, p. 217.

23. R. L. Hoffman, "Homogeneity of Member Personality and Its Effect on Group Problem-Solving," *Journal of Abnormal and Social Psychology*, January 1959, pp. 27–32; and R. L. Hoffman and N. R. F. Maier, "Quality and Acceptance of Problem Solutions by Members of Homogeneous and Heterogeneous Groups," *Journal of Abnormal and Social Psychology*, March 1961, pp. 401–07.

24. See T. H. Cox and S. Blake, "Managing Cultural Diversity: Implications for Organizational Competitiveness," *Academy of Management Executive*, August 1991, pp. 45–56; T. H. Cox, S. A. Lobel, and P. L. McLeod, "Effects of Ethnic Group Cultural Differences on Cooperative Behavior on a Group Task," *Academy of Management Journal*, December 1991, pp. 827–47; P. L. McLeod and S. A. Lobel, "The Effects of Ethnic Diversity on Idea Generation in Small Groups," paper presented at the Annual Academy of Management Conference, Las Vegas, August 1992; C. Kirchmeyer and A. Cohen, "Multicultural Groups: Their Performance and Reactions with Constructive Conflict," *Group & Organization Management*, June 1992, pp. 153–70; D. E. Thompson and L. E. Gooler, "Capitalizing on the Benefits of Diversity through Workteams," in E. E. Kossek and S. A. Lobel (eds.), *Managing Diversity: Human Resource Strategies for Transforming the Workplace* (Cambridge, MA: Blackwell, 1996), pp. 392–437; and L. H. Pelled, K. M. Eisenhardt, and K. R. Xin, "Exploring the Black Box: An Analysis of Work Group Diversity, Conflict, and Performance," *Administrative Science Quarterly*, March 1999, pp. 1–28.

25. R. E. Hill, "Interpersonal Compatibility and Work Group Performance among Systems Analysts: An Empirical Study," *Proceedings of the Seventeenth Annual Midwest Academy of Management Conference*, Kent, OH, April 1974, pp. 97–110.

26. D. C. Pelz and F. Andrews, *Scientists in Organizations* (New York: Wiley, 1966).

27. See J. A. Wall, Jr., and R. R. Callister, "Conflict and Its Management," pp. 523–26 for evidence supporting the argument that conflict is almost uniformly dysfunctional.

28. M. Geyelin and E. Felsenthal, "Irreconcilable Differences Force Shea & Gould Closure," *Wall Street Journal*, January 31, 1994, p. B1.

29. This section is based on F. Sommerfield, "Paying the Troops to Buck the System," *Business Month*, May 1990,

pp. 77–79; W. Kiechel III, "How to Escape the Echo Chamber," *Fortune*, June 18, 1990, pp. 129–30; E. Van de Vliert and C. De Dreu, "Optimizing Performance by Stimulating Conflict," *International Journal of Conflict Management*, July 1994, pp. 211–22; E. Van de Vliert, "Enhancing Performance by Conflict-Stimulating Intervention," in C. De Dreu and E. Van de Vliert (eds.), *Using Conflict in Organizations*, pp. 208–22; K. M. Eisenhardt, J. L. Kahwajy, and L. J. Bourgeois III, "How Management Teams Can Have a Good Fight," *Harvard Business Review*, July–August 1997, pp. 77–85; and S. Wetlaufer, "Common Sense and Conflict," *Harvard Business Review*, January–February 2000, pp. 114–24.

30. J. A. Wall, Jr., *Negotiation: Theory and Practice* (Glenview, IL: Scott, Foresman, 1985).

31. R. E. Walton and R. B. McKersie, *A Behavioral Theory of Labor Negotiations: An Analysis of a Social Interaction System* (New York: McGraw-Hill, 1965).

32. Thomas, "Conflict and Negotiation Processes in Organizations."

33. This model is based on R. J. Lewicki, "Bargaining and Negotiation," *Exchange: The Organizational Behavior Teaching Journal*, vol. 6, no. 2, 1981, pp. 39–40.

34. J. Lee, "The Negotiators," *Forbes*, January 11, 1999, pp. 22–24.

35. M. H. Bazerman and M. A. Neale, *Negotiating Rationally* (New York: Free Press, 1992), pp. 67–68.

36. J. A. Wall, Jr., and M. W. Blum, "Negotiations," *Journal of Management*, June 1991, pp. 278–82.

37. C. Watson and L. R. Hoffman, "Managers as Negotiators: A Test of Power versus Gender as Predictors of Feelings, Behavior, and Outcomes," *Leadership Quarterly*, Spring 1996, pp. 63–85.

38. A. E. Walters, A. F. Stuhlmacher, and L. L. Meyer, "Gender and Negotiator Competitiveness: A Meta-Analysis," *Organizational Behavior and Human Decision Processes*, October 1998, pp. 1–29; and A. F. Stuhlmacher and A. E. Walters, "Gender Differences in Negotiation Outcome: A Meta-Analysis," *Personnel Psychology*, Autumn 1999, pp. 653–77.

39. A. F. Stuhlmacher and A. E. Walters, "Gender Differences in Negotiation Outcome," p. 655.

40. See N. J. Adler, *International Dimensions of Organizational Behavior*, 4th ed. (Cincinnati, OH: Southwestern, 2002), pp. 208–56; and W. L. Adair, T. Okurmura, and J. M. Brett, "Negotiation Behavior When Cultures Collide: The

United States and Japan," *Journal of Applied Psychology*, June 2001, pp. 371–85.

41. K. D. Schmidt, *Doing Business in France* (Menlo Park, CA: SRI International, 1987).

42. S. Lubman, "Round and Round," *The Wall Street Journal*, December 10, 1993, p. R3.

43. P. R. Harris and R. T. Moran, *Managing Cultural Differences*, 4th ed. (Houston: Gulf Publishing, 1996), pp. 43–44.

44. E. S. Glenn, D. Witmeyer, and K. A. Stevenson, "Cultural Styles of Persuasion," *Journal of Intercultural Relations*, Fall 1977, pp. 52–66.

45. J. Graham, "The Influence of Culture on Business Negotiations," *Journal of International Business Studies*, Spring 1985, pp. 81–96.

46. J. A. Wall, Jr., and M. W. Blum, "Negotiations," pp. 283–87.

47. K. W. Thomas, "Toward Multidimensional Values in Teaching: The Example of Conflict Behaviors," *Academy of Management Review*, July 1977, p. 487.

*One man's red tape is
another man's system.*
—D. Waldo

PART FOUR

THE ORGANIZATION SYSTEM

It was a 10-year reunion for MBA graduates of the International Institute for Management Development (IMD) in Lausanne, Switzerland. When Andrew Bergstram and Ian Hamilton, both members of the Class of '92, began to chat at the reunion cocktail party, they found that their post-IMD lives had striking similarities. Each had taken jobs in banking—Bergstram with Sweden's Svenska Handelsbanken and Hamilton with a major bank in Canada. And each had moved up to become branch managers in major urban centers. But although they were in similar jobs in a common industry, the jobs they performed and their feelings about their work were very different.[1]

Bergstram spoke enthusiastically about his job at Handelsbanken. "I love my job! I have an amazing amount of autonomy. Our branch managers are free to choose their customers and the product mix we want to work with. We set staffing numbers and decide salary levels. And I completely control my credit portfolio. The central office keeps an eye on matters, but lending decisions are left up to me and my staff. I'm totally accountable for the performance of my branch. And so are our other 550 branch managers."

Ian Hamilton couldn't hide his envy. "I'm a branch manager but I don't have a fraction of the freedom to run my office the way you do. We're pretty bureaucratic. Lots of rules and regulations—dictated from above—govern my operations. Senior management keeps a close eye on us. And most major decisions still need to be approved by the people above me. Our company has some terrific pluses. They've been very good to me. But I've become increasingly frustrated by all the controls they put over branch managers. I'm not happy, and my friends and family are increasingly pointing that out to me. Just between you and me, I've interviewed at several other financial-service companies and I don't expect to be in this job six months from now."

Foundations of Organization Structure

As Bergstram and Hamilton's experiences indicate, organizations have different structures, and these structures have a bearing on attitudes and behavior. That's the theme of this chapter. In the following pages, we define the key components that make up an organization's structure, present half a dozen or so structural design options from which managers can choose, identify the contingency factors that make certain structural designs preferable in varying situations, and conclude by considering the different effects that various organizational designs have on employee behavior.

WHAT IS ORGANIZATIONAL STRUCTURE?

An **organizational structure** defines how job tasks are formally divided, grouped, and coordinated. There are six key elements that managers need to address when they design their organization's structure. These are: work specialization, departmentalization, chain of command, span of control, centralization and decentralization, and formalization.[2] Exhibit 15-1 presents each of these elements as answers to an important structural question. The following sections describe these six elements of structure.

Work Specialization

Early in the twentieth century, Henry Ford became rich and famous by building automobiles on an assembly line. Every Ford worker was assigned a specific, repetitive task. For instance, one person would just put on the right-front wheel and someone else would install the right-front door. By breaking jobs up into small standardized tasks, which could be performed over and over

AFTER STUDYING THIS CHAPTER, YOU SHOULD BE ABLE TO:

1. Identify the six key elements that define an organization's structure.

2. Explain the characteristics of a bureaucracy.

3. Describe a matrix organization.

4. Explain the characteristics of a virtual organization.

5. Summarize why managers want to create boundaryless organizations.

6. Contrast mechanistic and organic structural models.

7. List the factors that favor different organizational structures.

8. Explain the behavioral implications of different organizational designs.

EXHIBIT

15-1

**Key Design Questions and Answers for Designing
the Proper Organizational Structure**

The Key Question	The Answer Is Provided By
1. To what degree are tasks subdivided into separate jobs?	Work specialization
2. On what basis will jobs be grouped together?	Departmentalization
3. To whom do individuals and groups report?	Chain of command
4. How many individuals can a manager efficiently and effectively direct?	Span of control
5. Where does decision-making authority lie?	Centralization and decentralization
6. To what degree will there be rules and regulations to direct employees and managers?	Formalization

organizational structure

How job tasks are formally divided, grouped, and coordinated.

work specialization

The degree to which tasks in the organization are subdivided into separate jobs.

again, Ford was able to produce cars at the rate of one every ten seconds, while using employees who had relatively limited skills.

Ford demonstrated that work can be performed more efficiently if employees are allowed to specialize. Today we use the term **work specialization**, or *division of labor,* to describe the degree to which tasks in the organization are subdivided into separate jobs.

The essence of work specialization is that, rather than an entire job being done by one individual, it is broken down into a number of steps, with each step being completed by a separate individual. In essence, individuals specialize in doing part of an activity rather than the entire activity.

By the late 1940s, most manufacturing jobs in industrialized countries were being done with high work specialization. Management saw this as a means to make the most efficient use of its employees' skills. In most organizations, some tasks require highly developed skills and others can be performed by untrained workers. If all workers were engaged in each step of, say, an organization's manufacturing process, all would have to have the skills necessary to perform both the most demanding and the least demanding jobs. The result would be that, except when performing the most skilled or highly complex tasks, employees would be working below their skill levels. And because skilled workers are paid more than unskilled workers and their wages tend to reflect their highest level of skill, it represents an inefficient use of organizational resources to pay highly skilled workers to do easy tasks.

Managers also looked for other efficiencies that could be achieved through work specialization. Employee skills at performing a task successfully increase through repetition. Less time is spent in changing tasks, in putting away one's tools and equipment from a prior step in the work process, and in getting ready for another. Equally important, training for specialization is more efficient from the organization's perspective. It is easier and less costly to find and train workers to do specific and repetitive tasks. This is especially true of highly sophisticated and complex operations. For example, could Cessna produce one Citation jet a year if one person had to build the entire plane alone? Not likely! Finally, work specialization increases efficiency and productivity by encouraging the creation of special inventions and machinery.

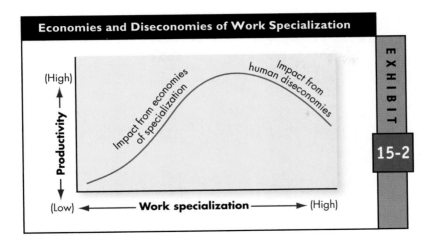

EXHIBIT

15-2

Economies and Diseconomies of Work Specialization

(High)

Productivity

(Low)

Impact from economies of specialization

Impact from human diseconomies

(Low) ← **Work specialization** → (High)

For much of the first half of the twentieth century, managers viewed work specialization as an unending source of increased productivity. And they were probably right. Because specialization was not widely practiced, its introduction almost always generated higher productivity. But by the 1960s, there came increasing evidence that a good thing can be carried too far. The point had been reached in some jobs at which the human diseconomies from specialization—which surfaced as boredom, fatigue, stress, low productivity, poor quality, increased absenteeism, and high turnover—more than offset the economic advantages (see Exhibit 15-2). In such cases, productivity could be increased by enlarging, rather than narrowing, the scope of job activities. In addition, a number of companies found that by giving employees a variety of activities to do, allowing them to do a whole and complete job, and putting them into teams with interchangeable skills, they often achieved significantly higher output, with increased employee satisfaction.

Most managers today see work specialization as neither obsolete nor an unending source of increased productivity. Rather, managers recognize the economies it provides in certain types of jobs and the problems it creates when it's carried too far. You'll find, for example, high work specialization being used by McDonald's to efficiently make and sell hamburgers and fries, and by medical specialists in most health maintenance organizations. On the other hand, companies like Saturn Corporation have had success by broadening the scope of jobs and reducing specialization.

Departmentalization

Once you've divided jobs up through work specialization, you need to group these jobs together so that common tasks can be coordinated. The basis by which jobs are grouped together is called **departmentalization**.

One of the most popular ways to group activities is by *functions* performed. A manufacturing manager might organize his or her plant by separating engineering, accounting, manufacturing, personnel, and supply specialists into common departments. Of course, departmentalization by function can be used in all types of organizations. Only the functions change to reflect the organization's objectives and activities. A hospital might have departments devoted to research, patient care, accounting, and so forth. A professional football franchise might have departments entitled Player Personnel, Ticket Sales, and Travel and Accommodations. The major

departmentalization

The basis by which jobs are grouped together.

Automatic Data Processing, Inc. (ADP™) provides an array of human-resource services to employers, each under the direction of a product or service manager.

advantage to this type of grouping is obtaining efficiencies from putting like specialists together. Functional departmentalization seeks to achieve economies of scale by placing people with common skills and orientations into common units.

Tasks can also be departmentalized by the type of *product* the organization produces. Procter & Gamble, for instance, is organized along these lines. Each major product—such as Tide, Pampers, Charmin, and Pringles—is placed under the authority of an executive who has complete global responsibility for that product. The major advantage to this type of grouping is increased accountability for product performance, since all activities related to a specific product are under the direction of a single manager. If an organization's activities are service rather than product related, each service would be autonomously grouped. For instance, Automatic Data Processing has departments for each of its employer-provided services—payroll, retirement, expense management, tax, and the like. Each offers a common array of services under the direction of a product or service manager.

Another way to departmentalize is on the basis of *geography* or territory. The sales function, for instance, may have western, southern, midwestern, and eastern regions. Each of these regions is, in effect, a department organized around geography. If an organization's customers are scattered over a large geographic area and have similar needs based on their location, then this form of departmentalization can be valuable.

At an Alcoa aluminum tubing plant in upstate New York, production is organized into five departments: casting; press; tubing; finishing; and inspecting, packing, and shipping. This is an example of *process* departmentalization because each department specializes in one specific phase in the production of aluminum tubing. The metal is cast in huge furnaces; sent to the press department, where it is extruded into aluminum pipe; transferred to the tube mill, where it is stretched into various sizes and shapes of tubing; moved to finishing, where it is cut and cleaned; and finally, arrives in the inspecting, packing, and shipping department. Since each process requires different skills, this method offers a basis for the homogeneous categorizing of activities.

Process departmentalization can be used for processing customers as well as products. If you've ever been to a state motor vehicles office to get a driver's license, you probably went through several departments before receiving your license. In one state, applicants must go through three steps, each handled by a separate department: (1) validation by motor vehicles division; (2) processing by the licensing department; and (3) payment collection by the treasury department.

A final category of departmentalization is to use the particular type of *customer* the organization seeks to reach. Microsoft, for instance, recently reorganized around four customer markets: consumers, large corporations, software developers, and small businesses. The assumption underlying customer departmentalization is that customers in each department have a common set of problems and needs that can best be met by having specialists for each.

Large organizations may use all of the forms of departmentalization that we've described. A major Japanese electronics firm, for instance, organizes each of its divisions along functional lines and its manufacturing units around processes; it departmentalizes sales around seven geographic regions, and divides each sales region into four customer groupings. Across organizations of all sizes, one strong trend has developed over the past decade. Rigid, functional departmentalization is being increasingly complemented by teams that cross over traditional departmental lines. As we described in Chapter 9, as tasks have become more complex and more diverse skills are needed to accomplish those tasks, management has turned to cross-functional teams.

Chain of Command

Thirty years ago, the chain-of-command concept was a basic cornerstone in the design of organizations. As you'll see, it has far less importance today. But contemporary managers should still consider its implications when they decide how best to structure their organizations.

The **chain of command** is an unbroken line of authority that extends from the top of the organization to the lowest echelon and clarifies who reports to whom. It answers questions for employees such as "To whom do I go if I have a problem?" and "To whom am I responsible?"

You can't discuss the chain of command without discussing two complementary concepts: *authority* and *unity of command*. **Authority** refers to the rights inherent in a managerial position to give orders and expect the orders to be obeyed. To facilitate coordination, each managerial position is given a place in the chain of command, and each manager is given a degree of authority in order to meet his or her responsibilities. The **unity-of-command** principle helps preserve the concept of an unbroken line of authority. It states that a person should have one and only one superior to whom he or she is directly responsible. If the unity of command is broken, an employee might have to cope with conflicting demands or priorities from several superiors.

Times change and so do the basic tenets of organizational design. The concepts of chain of command, authority, and unity of command have substantially less relevance today because of advancements in information technology and the trend toward empowering employees. For instance, a low-level employee today can access information in seconds that 30 years ago was available only to top managers. Similarly, networked computers increasingly allow employees anywhere in an organization to communicate with anyone else without going through formal channels. Moreover, the concepts of authority and maintaining the chain of command are increasingly less relevant as operating employees are being empowered to make decisions that previously were reserved for management. Add to this the popularity of self-managed and cross-functional teams and the creation of new structural designs that include multiple bosses, and the unity-of-command concept takes on less relevance. There are, of course, still many organizations that find they can be most productive by enforcing the chain of command. There just seem to be fewer of them nowadays.

Span of Control

How many employees can a manager efficiently and effectively direct? This question of **span of control** is important because, to a large degree, it determines the number of levels and managers an organization has. All things being equal, the

chain of command
The unbroken line of authority that extends from the top of the organization to the lowest echelon and clarifies who reports to whom.

authority
The rights inherent in a managerial position to give orders and to expect the orders to be obeyed.

unity of command
A subordinate should have only one superior to whom he or she is directly responsible.

Although Intel maintains a traditional chain of command, its newly redesigned mentoring program allows Ann Otero (left), a senior administrative assistant, to act as mentor to training manager Valerie Webb, who outranks her in the company hierarchy. The program is built around job skills, not rank.

span of control
The number of subordinates a manager can efficiently and effectively direct.

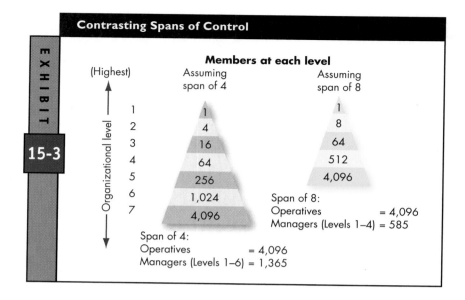

EXHIBIT

15-3

Contrasting Spans of Control

Members at each level

Organizational level	(Highest)	Assuming span of 4	Assuming span of 8
1		1	1
2		4	8
3		16	64
4		64	512
5		256	4,096
6		1,024	
7		4,096	

Span of 8:
Operatives = 4,096
Managers (Levels 1–4) = 585

Span of 4:
Operatives = 4,096
Managers (Levels 1–6) = 1,365

wider or larger the span, the more efficient the organization. An example can illustrate the validity of this statement.

Assume that we have two organizations, both of which have approximately 4,100 operative-level employees. As Exhibit 15-3 illustrates, if one has a uniform span of four and the other a span of eight, the wider span would have two fewer levels and approximately 800 fewer managers. If the average manager made $50,000 a year, the wider span would save $40 million a year in management salaries! Obviously, wider spans are more efficient in terms of cost. However, at some point wider spans reduce effectiveness. That is, when the span becomes too large, employee performance suffers because supervisors no longer have the time to provide the necessary leadership and support.

Narrow or small spans have their advocates. By keeping the span of control to five or six employees, a manager can maintain close control.[3] But narrow spans have three major drawbacks. First, as already described, they're expensive because they add levels of management. Second, they make vertical communication in the organization more complex. The added levels of hierarchy slow down decision making and tend to isolate upper management. Third, narrow spans of control encourage overly tight supervision and discourage employee autonomy.

The trend in recent years has been toward wider spans of control.[4] They're consistent with recent efforts by companies to reduce costs, cut overhead, speed up decision making, increase flexibility, get closer to customers, and empower employees. However, to ensure that performance doesn't suffer because of these wider spans, organizations have been investing heavily in employee training. Managers recognize that they can handle a wider span when employees know their jobs inside and out or can turn to their co-workers when they have questions.

Centralization and Decentralization

In some organizations, top managers make all the decisions. Lower-level managers merely carry out top management's directives. At the other extreme, there are organizations in which decision making is pushed down to the managers who are

OB in the News

Few Entrepreneurs Understand Span of Control

Pat Harpell learned a lesson that many entrepreneurs fail to learn: Having too many people report to you can undermine your effectiveness.

Harpell runs Harpell Inc, a transactive marketing services company she founded in 1982 in Maynard, Massachusetts. As her firm grew, she added managers. Eventually she had 18 people reporting

directly to her. It took her a few years but she finally recognized that she had to reduce the number of people over whom she had direct control. "I realized I was the bottleneck," Harpell says. "By limiting the number of people reporting to me, I was able to look beyond day to day and focus on building a unique brand and position for the company." Today, Harpell has only six people reporting directly to her and she has the time to focus on important issues.

Harpell's experience is not unusual among entrepreneurs. As a group they tend to want to do everything, supervise everyone, and have all decisions come through them. A study of entrepreneurs found that among two dozen popular management principles, span of control was the least appreciated. Only 23 percent of the respondents agreed that "span of control shouldn't be too large," and just 16 percent believed "top managers cannot deal with all problems personally."

Source: Based on M. Henricks, "Span Control," *Entrepreneur,* January 2001, pp. 97–98.

---

closest to the action. The former organizations are highly centralized; the latter are decentralized.

The term **centralization** refers to the degree to which decision making is concentrated at a single point in the organization. The concept includes only formal authority—that is, the rights inherent in one's position. Typically, it's said that if top management makes the organization's key decisions with little or no input from lower-level personnel, then the organization is centralized. In contrast, the more that lower-level personnel provide input or are actually given the discretion to make decisions, the more decentralization there is.

An organization characterized by centralization is an inherently different structural animal from one that is decentralized. In a decentralized organization, action can be taken more quickly to solve problems, more people provide input into decisions, and employees are less likely to feel alienated from those who make the decisions that affect their work lives.

Consistent with recent management efforts to make organizations more flexible and responsive, there has been a marked trend toward decentralizing decision making. In large companies, lower-level managers are closer to "the action" and typically have more detailed knowledge about problems than do top managers. For instance, big retailers like Sears and JC Penney have given their store managers considerably more discretion in choosing what merchandise to stock. This allows those stores to compete more effectively against local merchants.

Formalization

Formalization refers to the degree to which jobs within the organization are standardized. If a job is highly formalized, then the job incumbent has a minimum amount of discretion over what is to be done, when it is to be done, and how he or she should do it. Employees can be expected always to handle the same input in exactly the same way, resulting in a consistent and uniform output. There are explicit job descriptions, lots of organizational rules, and clearly defined procedures covering work processes in organizations in which there is

centralization
The degree to which decision making is concentrated at a single point in the organization.

formalization
The degree to which jobs within the organization are standardized.

Source: S. Adams, *Dogbert's Big Book of Business*, DILBERT reprinted by permission of United Features Syndicate, Inc.

high formalization. Where formalization is low, job behaviors are relatively nonprogrammed and employees have a great deal of freedom to exercise discretion in their work. Because an individual's discretion on the job is inversely related to the amount of behavior in that job that is preprogrammed by the organization, the greater the standardization and the less input the employee has into how his or her work is to be done. Standardization not only eliminates the possibility of employees engaging in alternative behaviors, but it even removes the need for employees to consider alternatives.

The degree of formalization can vary widely between organizations and within organizations. Certain jobs, for instance, are well known to have little formalization. College book travelers—the representatives of publishers who call on professors to inform them of their company's new publications—have a great deal of freedom in their jobs. They have no standard sales "spiel," and the extent of rules and procedures governing their behavior may be little more than the requirement that they submit a weekly sales report and some suggestions on what to emphasize for the various new titles. At the other extreme, there are clerical and editorial positions in the same publishing houses for which employees are required to be at their desks by 8:00 A.M. or be docked a half-hour's pay and, once at that desk, to follow a set of precise procedures dictated by management.

Common Organizational Designs

We now turn to describing three of the more common organizational designs found in use: the *simple structure*, the *bureaucracy*, and the *matrix structure*.

The Simple Structure

What do a small retail store, an electronics firm run by a hard-driving entrepreneur, a new Planned Parenthood office, and an airline in the midst of a company-wide pilot's strike have in common? They probably all use the **simple structure**.

The simple structure is said to be characterized most by what it is not rather than by what it is. The simple structure is not elaborated.[5] It has a low degree of departmentalization, wide spans of control, authority centralized in a single person, and little formalization. The simple structure is a "flat" organization; it usually has only two or three vertical levels, a loose body of employees, and one individual in whom the decision-making authority is centralized.

The simple structure is most widely practiced in small businesses in which the manager and the owner are one and the same. This, for example, is illustrated in Exhibit 15-5, an organization chart for a retail men's store. Jack Gold owns and manages this store. Although he employs five full-time salespeople, a cashier, and extra personnel for weekends and holidays, he "runs the show." But large companies, in times of crisis, can become simple structures for short periods. IBM, for instance, became a simple structure for more than a year back in the early 1990s.[6] When Louis Gerstner was hired as CEO in 1993, he immediately put the company into what he called "survival mode." "We had to cut $9 billion a year in expenses. We had to bring the company back, literally from the brink of death." So Gerstner implemented a highly centralized, personalized leadership and organizational style. Said Gerstner: "It was a benevolent dictatorship, with me as the dictator."

The strength of the simple structure lies in its simplicity. It's fast, flexible, and inexpensive to maintain and accountability is clear. One major weakness is that it's difficult to maintain in anything other than small organizations. It becomes increasingly inadequate as an organization grows because its low formalization and high centralization tend to create information overload at the top. As size increases, decision making typically becomes slower and can eventually come to a standstill as the single executive tries to continue making all the decisions. This often proves to be the undoing of many small businesses. When an

simple structure

A structure characterized by a low degree of departmentalization, wide spans of control, authority centralized in a single person, and little formalization.

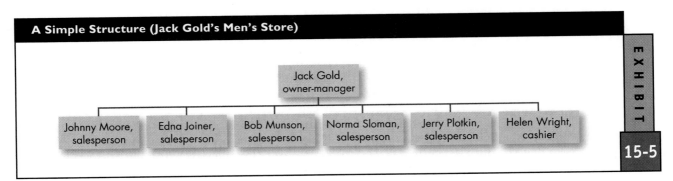

A Simple Structure (Jack Gold's Men's Store)

Jack Gold, owner-manager

Johnny Moore, salesperson | Edna Joiner, salesperson | Bob Munson, salesperson | Norma Sloman, salesperson | Jerry Plotkin, salesperson | Helen Wright, cashier

EXHIBIT 15-5

Bureaucracies rely on rules, regulation, and standardized work activities. For organizations that deal with repetitive transactions, such as an insurance company like Kaiser Permanente, this kind of structure saves time and resources.

organization begins to employ 50 or 100 people, it's very difficult for the owner-manager to make all the choices. If the structure isn't changed and made more elaborate, the firm often loses momentum and can eventually fail. The simple structure's other weakness is that it's risky—everything depends on one person. One heart attack can literally destroy the organization's information and decision-making center.

The Bureaucracy

Standardization! That's the key concept that underlies all bureaucracies. Take a look at the bank where you keep your checking account, the department store where you buy your clothes, or the government offices that collect your taxes, enforce health regulations, or provide local fire protection. They all rely on standardized work processes for coordination and control.

The **bureaucracy** is characterized by highly routine operating tasks achieved through specialization, very formalized rules and regulations, tasks that are grouped into functional departments, centralized authority, narrow spans of control, and decision making that follows the chain of command.

bureaucracy

A structure with highly routine operating tasks achieved through specialization, very formalized rules and regulations, tasks that are grouped into functional departments, centralized authority, narrow spans of control, and decision making that follows the chain of command.

The primary strength of the bureaucracy lies in its ability to perform standardized activities in a highly efficient manner. Putting like specialties together in functional departments results in economies of scale, minimum duplication of personnel and equipment, and employees who have the opportunity to talk "the same language" among their peers. Furthermore, bureaucracies can get by nicely with less talented—and, hence, less costly—middle- and lower-level managers. The pervasiveness of rules and regulations substitutes for managerial discretion. Standardized operations, coupled with high formalization, allow decision making to be centralized. There is little need, therefore, for innovative and experienced decision makers below the level of senior executives.

One of the major weaknesses of a bureaucracy is illustrated in the following dialogue between four executives in one company: "Ya know, nothing happens in this place until we *produce* something," said the production executive. "Wrong," commented the research and development manager, "nothing happens until we *design* something!" "What are you talking about?" asked the marketing executive. "Nothing happens here until we *sell* something!" Finally, the exasperated accounting manager responded, "It doesn't matter what you produce, design, or sell. No one knows what happens until we *tally up the results*!" This conversation points up the fact that specialization creates subunit conflicts. Functional unit goals can override the overall goals of the organization.

The other major weakness of a bureaucracy is something we've all experienced at one time or another when having to deal with people who work in these organizations: obsessive concern with following the rules. When cases arise that don't precisely fit the rules, there is no room for modification. The bureaucracy is efficient only as long as employees confront problems that they have previously encountered and for which programmed decision rules have already been established.

The Matrix Structure

Another popular organizational design option is the **matrix structure**. You'll find it being used in advertising agencies, aerospace firms, research and development laboratories, construction companies, hospitals, government agencies, universities, management consulting firms, and entertainment companies.[7] Essentially, the matrix combines two forms of departmentalization: functional and product.

The strength of functional departmentalization lies in putting like specialists together, which minimizes the number necessary while allowing the pooling and sharing of specialized resources across products. Its major disadvantage is the difficulty of coordinating the tasks of diverse functional specialists so that their activities are completed on time and within budget. Product departmentalization, on the other hand, has exactly the opposite benefits and disadvantages. It facilitates coordination among specialties to achieve on-time completion and meet budget targets. Furthermore, it provides clear responsibility for all activities related to a product, but with duplication of activities and costs. The matrix attempts to gain the strengths of each, while avoiding their weaknesses.

The most obvious structural characteristic of the matrix is that it breaks the unity-of-command concept. Employees in the matrix have two bosses—their functional department managers and their product managers. Therefore, the matrix has a dual chain of command.

Exhibit 15-6 shows the matrix form as used in a college of business administration. The academic departments of accounting, economics, marketing, and so forth are functional units. In addition, specific programs (that is, products) are overlaid on the functions. In this way, members in a matrix structure have a dual assignment—to their functional department and to their product groups. For instance, a professor of accounting who is teaching an undergraduate course reports to the director of undergraduate programs as well as to the chairperson of the accounting department.

matrix structure
A structure that creates dual lines of authority and combines functional and product departmentalization.

Matrix Structure for a College of Business Administration

Academic departments \ Programs	Undergraduate	Master's	Ph.D.	Research	Executive development	Community service
Accounting						
Administrative studies						
Finance						
Information and decision sciences						
Marketing						
Organizational behavior						
Quantitative methods						

EXHIBIT 15-6

The strength of the matrix lies in its ability to facilitate coordination when the organization has a multiplicity of complex and interdependent activities. As an organization gets larger, its information-processing capacity can become overloaded. In a bureaucracy, complexity results in increased formalization. The direct and frequent contact between different specialties in the matrix can make for better communication and more flexibility. Information permeates the organization and more quickly reaches the people who need to take account of it. Furthermore, the matrix reduces "bureaupathologies"—the dual lines of authority reduce the tendencies of departmental members to become so busy protecting their little worlds that the organization's overall goals become secondary.

There is another advantage to the matrix. It facilitates the efficient allocation of specialists. When individuals with highly specialized skills are lodged in one functional department or product group, their talents are monopolized and underused. The matrix achieves the advantages of economies of scale by providing the organization with both the best resources and an effective way of ensuring their efficient deployment.

The major disadvantages of the matrix lie in the confusion it creates, its propensity to foster power struggles, and the stress it places on individuals.[8] When you dispense with the unity-of-command concept, ambiguity is significantly increased, and ambiguity often leads to conflict. For example, it's frequently unclear who reports to whom, and it is not unusual for product managers to fight over getting the best specialists assigned to their products. Confusion and ambiguity also create the seeds of power struggles. Bureaucracy reduces the potential for power grabs by defining the rules of the game. When those rules are "up for grabs," power struggles between functional and product managers result. For individuals who desire security and absence from ambiguity, this work climate can produce stress. Reporting to more than one boss introduces role conflict, and unclear expectations introduce role ambiguity. The comfort of bureaucracy's predictability is absent, replaced by insecurity and stress.

NEW DESIGN OPTIONS

Over the past decade or two, senior managers in a number of organizations have been working to develop new structural options that can better help their firms to compete effectively. In this section, we'll describe three such structural designs: the *team structure*, the *virtual organization*, and the *boundaryless organization*.

The Team Structure

As described in Chapter 9, teams have become an extremely popular means around which to organize work activities. When management uses teams as its central coordination device, you have a horizontal organization or a **team structure**.[9] The primary characteristics of the team structure are that it breaks down departmental barriers and decentralizes decision making to the level of the work team. Team structures also require employees to be generalists as well as specialists.[10]

In smaller companies, the team structure can define the entire organization. For instance, Imedia, a 30-person marketing firm in New Jersey, is organized completely around teams, which have full responsibility for most operational issues and client services.[11] Whole Foods Market, Inc., the largest natural-foods grocer in the United States, is structured entirely around teams.[12] Every one of Whole Foods' stores is an autonomous profit center composed of an average of 10 self-managed teams, each with a designated team leader. The team leaders in each store are a team; store leaders in each region are a team; and the company's six regional presidents are a team.

team structure

The use of teams as the central device to coordinate work activities.

More often, particularly among larger organizations, the team structure complements what is typically a bureaucracy. This allows the organization to achieve the efficiency of bureaucracy's standardization, while gaining the flexibility that teams provide. To improve productivity at the operating level, for instance, companies like DaimlerChrysler, Saturn, Motorola, and Xerox have made extensive use of self-managed teams. On the other hand, when companies like Boeing or Hewlett-Packard need to design new products or coordinate major projects, they'll structure activities around cross-functional teams.

The Virtual Organization

Why own when you can rent? That question captures the essence of the **virtual organization** (also sometimes called the *network* or *modular* organization), typically a small, core organization that outsources major business functions.[13] In structural terms, the virtual organization is highly centralized, with little or no departmentalization.

virtual organization
A small, core organization that outsources major business functions.

The prototype of the virtual structure is today's movie-making organization. In Hollywood's golden era, movies were made by huge, vertically integrated corporations. Studios such as MGM, Warner Brothers, and 20th Century Fox owned large movie lots and employed thousands of full-time specialists—set designers, camera people, film editors, directors, and even actors. Nowadays, most movies are made by a collection of individuals and small companies who come together and make films project by project.[14] This structural form allows each project to be staffed with the talent most suited to its demands, rather than having to choose just from the people employed by the studio. It minimizes bureaucratic overhead because there is no lasting organization to maintain. And it lessens long-term risks and their costs because there is no long term—a team is assembled for a finite period and then disbanded.

Ancle Hsu and David Ji run a virtual organization. Their firm, California-based Apex Digital, is one of the world's largest producers of DVD players, yet the company neither owns a factory nor employs an engineer. They contract everything out to firms in China. With minimal investment, Apex has grown from nothing to annual sales of over $500 million in just three years.

Northwest Region President of Whole Foods, Chris Hitt, fields questions from his store leaders during a team meeting.

When large organizations use the virtual structure, they frequently use it to outsource manufacturing. Companies like Nike, Reebok, L.L. Bean, and Cisco Systems are just a few of the thousands of companies that have found that they can do hundreds of millions of dollars in business without owning manufacturing facilities. Cisco, for instance, is essentially a research and development company that uses outside suppliers and independent manufacturers to assemble the Internet routers that its engineers design. But National Steel Corp. contracts out its mail-room operations; AT&T farms out its credit-card processing; and ExxonMobil has turned over maintenance of its oil refineries to another firm.

What's going on here? A quest for maximum flexibility. These virtual organizations have created networks of relationships that allow them to contract out manufacturing, distribution, marketing, or any other business function for which management feels that others can do it better or more cheaply.

The virtual organization stands in sharp contrast to the typical bureaucracy that has many vertical levels of management and where control is sought through ownership. In such organizations, research and development are done in-house, production occurs in company-owned plants, and sales and marketing are performed by the company's own employees. To support all this, management has to employ extra staff, including accountants, human resource specialists, and

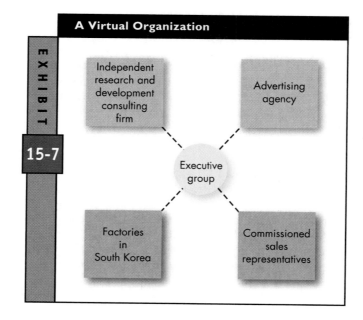

EXHIBIT 15-7

A Virtual Organization

Independent research and development consulting firm

Advertising agency

Executive group

Factories in South Korea

Commissioned sales representatives

lawyers. The virtual organization, however, outsources many of these functions and concentrates on what it does best. For most U.S. firms, that means focusing on design or marketing.

Exhibit 15-7 shows a virtual organization in which management outsources all of the primary functions of the business. The core of the organization is a small group of executives whose job is to oversee directly any activities that are done in-house and to coordinate relationships with the other organizations that manufacture, distribute, and perform other crucial functions for the virtual organization. The dotted-lines in Exhibit 15-7 represent the relationships typically maintained under contracts. In essence, managers in virtual structures spend most of their time coordinating and controlling external relations, typically by way of computer-network links.

The major advantage to the virtual organization is its flexibility. For instance, it allowed individuals with an innovative idea and little money, such as Ancle Hsu and David Ji, to successfully compete against the likes of Sony, Hitachi, and Sharp Electronics. The primary drawback to this structure is that it reduces management's control over key parts of its business.

The Boundaryless Organization

boundaryless organization

An organization that seeks to eliminate the chain of command, have limitless spans of control, and replace departments with empowered teams.

General Electric's former chairman, Jack Welch, coined the term **boundaryless organization** to describe his idea of what he wanted GE to become. Welch wanted to turn his company into a "$60 billion family grocery store."[15] That is, in spite of its monstrous size, he wanted to eliminate *vertical* and *horizontal* boundaries within GE and break down *external* barriers between the company and its customers and suppliers. The boundaryless organization seeks to eliminate the chain of command, have limitless spans of control, and replace departments with empowered teams. And because it relies so heavily on information technology, some have turned to calling this structure the *T-form* (or technology-based) organization.[16]

Although GE has not yet achieved this boundaryless state—and probably never will—it has made significant progress toward that end. So have other companies, such as Hewlett-Packard, AT&T, Motorola, and Oticon A/S. Let's take a look at what a boundaryless organization would look like and what some firms are doing to try to make it a reality.[17]

By removing vertical boundaries, management flattens the hierarchy. Status and rank are minimized. Cross-hierarchical teams (which includes top executives, middle managers, supervisors, and operative employees), participative decision-making practices, and the use of 360-degree performance appraisals (in which peers and others above and below the employee evaluate his or her performance) are examples of what GE is doing to break down vertical boundaries. At Oticon A/S, a $160 million a year Danish hearing aid manufacturer, all traces of hierarchy have disappeared. Everyone works at uniform mobile workstations. And project teams, not functions or departments, are used to coordinate work.

Functional departments create horizontal boundaries. And these boundaries stifle interaction between functions, product lines, and units. The way to reduce these barriers is to replace functional departments with cross-functional teams and to organize activities around processes. For instance, Xerox now develops new products through multidisciplinary teams that work in a single process instead of around narrow functional tasks. Similarly, some AT&T units are now doing annual budgets based not on functions or departments but on processes such as the maintenance of a worldwide telecommunications network. Another way management can cut through horizontal barriers is to use lateral transfers, rotating people into and out of different functional areas. This approach turns specialists into generalists.

When fully operational, the boundaryless organization also breaks down barriers to external constituencies (suppliers, customers, regulators, etc.) and barriers created by geography. Globalization, strategic alliances, customer-organization links, and telecommuting are all examples of practices that reduce external boundaries. Coca-Cola, for instance, sees itself as a global corporation, not as a U.S. or Atlanta company. Firms such as NEC Corp., Boeing, and Apple Computer each have strategic alliances or joint partnerships with dozens of companies. These alliances blur the distinction between one organization and another as employees work on joint projects. And some companies are allowing customers to perform functions that previously were done by management. For instance, some AT&T units are receiving bonuses based on customer evaluations of the teams that serve them. Finally, we suggest that telecommuting is blurring organizational boundaries. The security analyst with Merrill Lynch who does his job from his ranch in Montana or the software designer who works for a San Francisco company but does her job in Boulder, Colorado, are just two examples of the millions of workers who are now doing their jobs outside the physical boundaries of their employers' premises.

The one common technological thread that makes the boundaryless organization possible is networked computers. These allow people to communicate across intraorganizational and interorganizational boundaries.[18] Electronic mail, for instance, enables hundreds of employees to share information simultaneously and allows rank-and-file workers to communicate directly with senior executives. In addition, many large companies, including FedEx, AT&T, and 3M, are developing private nets or "intranets." Using the infrastructure and standards of the Internet and the World Wide Web, these private nets are internal communication systems, protected from the public Internet by special software. And interorganizational networks now make it possible for Wal-Mart suppliers such as Procter & Gamble and Levi-Strauss to monitor inventory levels of laundry soap and jeans, respectively, because P&G and Levi's computer systems are networked to Wal-Mart's system.

WHY DO STRUCTURES DIFFER?

In the previous sections, we described a variety of organizational designs ranging from the highly structured and standardized bureaucracy to the loose and amorphous boundaryless organization. The other designs we discussed tend to exist somewhere between these two extremes.

Exhibit 15-8 reconceptualizes our previous discussions by presenting two extreme models of organizational design. One extreme we'll call the **mechanistic model**. It's generally synonymous with the bureaucracy in that it has extensive departmentalization, high formalization, a limited information network (mostly downward communication), and little participation by low-level members in decision making. At the other extreme is the **organic model**. This model looks a lot like the boundaryless organization. It's flat, uses cross-hierarchical and cross-functional teams, has low formalization, possesses a comprehensive information network (using lateral and upward communication as well as downward), and involves high participation in decision making.[19]

With these two models in mind, we're now prepared to address the question: Why are some organizations structured along more mechanistic lines whereas others follow organic characteristics? What are the forces that influence the design that is chosen? In the following pages, we present the major forces that have been identified as causes or determinants of an organization's structure.[20]

Strategy

An organization's structure is a means to help management achieve its objectives. Because objectives are derived from the organization's overall strategy, it's only logical that strategy and structure should be closely linked. More specifically, structure should follow strategy. If management makes a significant change in its organization's strategy, the structure will need to be modified to accommodate and support this change.[21]

mechanistic model

A structure characterized by extensive departmentalization, high formalization, a limited information network, and centralization.

organic model

A structure that is flat, uses cross-hierarchical and cross-functional teams, has low formalization, possesses a comprehensive information network, and relies on participative decision making.

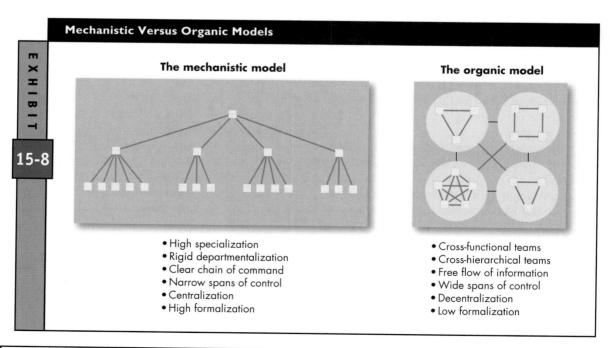

EXHIBIT 15-8

Mechanistic Versus Organic Models

The mechanistic model

- High specialization
- Rigid departmentalization
- Clear chain of command
- Narrow spans of control
- Centralization
- High formalization

The organic model

- Cross-functional teams
- Cross-hierarchical teams
- Free flow of information
- Wide spans of control
- Decentralization
- Low formalization

Most current strategy frameworks focus on three strategy dimensions—innovation, cost minimization, and imitation—and the structural design that works best with each.[22]

To what degree does an organization introduce major new products or services? An **innovation strategy** does not mean a strategy merely for simple or cosmetic changes from previous offerings but rather one for meaningful and unique innovations. Obviously, not all firms pursue innovation. This strategy may appropriately characterize 3M Co. and Apple Computer, but it's not a strategy pursued by conservative retailer Marks & Spencer.

An organization that is pursuing a **cost-minimization strategy** tightly controls costs, refrains from incurring unnecessary innovation or marketing expenses, and cuts prices in selling a basic product. This would describe the strategy pursued by Wal-Mart or the makers of generic grocery products.

Organizations following an **imitation strategy** try to capitalize on the best of both of the previous strategies. They seek to minimize risk and maximize opportunity for profit. Their strategy is to move into new products or new markets only after viability has been proven by innovators. They take the successful ideas of innovators and copy them. Manufacturers of mass-marketed fashion goods that are rip-offs of designer styles follow the imitation strategy. This label probably also characterizes well-known firms such as IBM and Caterpillar. They essentially follow their smaller and more innovative competitors with superior products, but only after their competitors have demonstrated that the market is there.

Exhibit 15-9 describes the structural option that best matches each strategy. Innovators need the flexibility of the organic structure, whereas cost minimizers seek the efficiency and stability of the mechanistic structure. Imitators combine the two structures. They use a mechanistic structure in order to maintain tight controls and low costs in their current activities, while at the same time they create organic subunits in which to pursue new undertakings.

innovation strategy
A strategy that emphasizes the introduction of major new products and services.

cost-minimization strategy
A strategy that emphasizes tight cost controls, avoidance of unnecessary innovation or marketing expenses, and price cutting.

imitation strategy
A strategy that seeks to move into new products or new markets only after their viability has already been proven.

Organization Size

There is considerable evidence to support that an organization's size significantly affects its structure.[23] For instance, large organizations—those that typically employ 2,000 or more people—tend to have more specialization, more departmentalization, more vertical levels, and more rules and regulations than do small organizations. However, the relationship isn't linear. Rather, size affects

The Strategy–Structure Relationship	
Strategy	**Structural Option**
Innovation	**Organic:** A loose structure; low specialization, low formalization, decentralized
Cost minimization	**Mechanistic:** Tight control; extensive work specialization, high formalization, high centralization
Imitation	**Mechanistic and organic:** Mix of loose with tight properties; tight controls over current activities and looser controls for new undertakings

EXHIBIT 15-9

structure at a decreasing rate. The impact of size becomes less important as an organization expands. Why is this? Essentially, once an organization has around 2,000 employees, it's already fairly mechanistic. An additional 500 employees will not have much impact. On the other hand, adding 500 employees to an organization that has only 300 members is likely to result in a significant shift toward a more mechanistic structure.

Technology

technology

How an organization transfers its inputs into outputs.

The term **technology** refers to how an organization transfers its inputs into outputs. Every organization has at least one technology for converting financial, human, and physical resources into products or services. The Ford Motor Co., for instance, predominantly uses an assembly-line process to make its products. On the other hand, colleges may use a number of instruction technologies—the ever-popular formal lecture method, the case-analysis method, the experiential exercise method, the programmed learning method, and so forth. In this section we want to show that organizational structures adapt to their technology.

Numerous studies have been carried out on the technology–structure relationship.[24] The details of those studies are quite complex, so we'll go straight to "the bottom line" and attempt to summarize what we know.

The common theme that differentiates technologies is their *degree of routineness*. By this we mean that technologies tend toward either routine or nonroutine activities. The former are characterized by automated and standardized operations. Nonroutine activities are customized. They include varied operations such as furniture restoring, custom shoemaking, and genetic research.

What relationships have been found between technology and structure? Although the relationship is not overwhelmingly strong, we find that routine tasks are associated with taller and more departmentalized structures. The relationship between technology and formalization, however, is stronger. Studies consistently show routineness to be associated with the presence of rule manuals, job descriptions, and other formalized documentation. Finally, an interesting relationship has been found between technology and centralization. It seems logical that routine technologies would be associated with a centralized structure, while nonroutine technologies, which rely more heavily on the knowledge of specialists, would be characterized by delegated decision authority. This position has met with some support. However, a more generalizable conclusion is that the technology–centralization relationship is moderated by the degree of formalization. Formal regulations and centralized decision making are both control mechanisms and management can substitute one for the other. Routine technologies should be associated with centralized control if there is a minimum of rules and regulations. However, if formalization is high, routine technology can be accompanied by decentralization. So, we would predict that routine technology would lead to centralization, but only if formalization is low.

Most college faculty members continue to rely on the popular lecture method of instruction technology.

Environment

An organization's **environment** is composed of institutions or forces outside the organization that potentially affect the organization's performance. These typically include suppliers, customers, competitors, government regulatory agencies, public pressure groups, and the like.

environment

Institutions or forces outside the organization that potentially affect the organization's performance.

Why should an organization's structure be affected by its environment? Because of environmental uncertainty. Some organizations face relatively static environments—few forces in their environment are changing. There are, for example, no new competitors, no new technological breakthroughs by current competitors, or little activity by public pressure groups to influence the organization. Other organizations face very dynamic environments—rapidly changing government regulations affecting their business, new competitors, difficulties in acquiring raw materials, continually changing product preferences by customers, and so on. Static environments create significantly less uncertainty for managers than do dynamic ones. And because uncertainty is a threat to an organization's effectiveness, management will try to minimize it. One way to reduce environmental uncertainty is through adjustments in the organization's structure.[25]

Recent research has helped clarify what is meant by environmental uncertainty. It's been found that there are three key dimensions to any organization's environment: capacity, volatility, and complexity.[26]

The *capacity* of an environment refers to the degree to which it can support growth. Rich and growing environments generate excess resources, which can buffer the organization in times of relative scarcity. Abundant capacity, for example, leaves room for an organization to make mistakes, while scarce capacity does not. In 2002, firms operating in the multimedia software business had relatively abundant environments, whereas those in the full-service brokerage business faced relative scarcity.

The degree of instability in an environment is captured in the *volatility* dimension. When there is a high degree of unpredictable change, the environment is dynamic. This makes it difficult for management to predict accurately the probabilities associated with various decision alternatives. At the other extreme is a stable environment. The accelerated changes in Eastern Europe and the demise of the Cold War had dramatic effects on the U.S. defense industry in the 1990s. This moved the environment of major defense contractors like Lockheed Martin, General Dynamics, and Northrop Grumman from relatively stable to dynamic.

Finally, the environment needs to be assessed in terms of *complexity*—that is, the degree of heterogeneity and concentration among environmental elements. Simple environments are homogeneous and concentrated. This might describe the tobacco industry, since there are relatively few players. It's easy for firms in this industry to keep a close eye on the competition. In contrast, environments characterized by heterogeneity and dispersion are called complex. This is essentially the current environment for firms competing in the Internet-connection business. Every day there seems to be another "new kid on the block" with whom current Internet access providers have to deal.

Exhibit 15-10 on page 444 summarizes our definition of the environment along its three dimensions. The arrows in this figure are meant to indicate movement toward higher uncertainty. So organizations that operate in environments characterized as scarce, dynamic, and complex face the greatest degree of uncertainty. Why? Because they have little room for error, high unpredictability, and a diverse set of elements in the environment to monitor constantly.

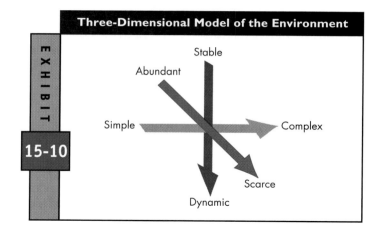

Three-Dimensional Model of the Environment

EXHIBIT

15-10

Stable

Abundant

Simple — Complex

Scarce

Dynamic

Given this three-dimensional definition of environment, we can offer some general conclusions. There is evidence that relates the degrees of environmental uncertainty to different structural arrangements. Specifically, the more scarce, dynamic, and complex the environment, the more organic a structure should be. The more abundant, stable, and simple the environment, the more the mechanistic structure will be preferred.

OR **SCIENCE** *?*

MYTH

"Bureaucracy Is Dead"

This statement is false. Some bureaucratic characteristics are in decline. And bureaucracy is undoubtedly going through changes. But it's far from dead.

Bureaucracy is characterized by specialization, formalization, departmentalization, centralization, narrow spans of control, and adherence to a chain of command. Have these characteristics disappeared from today's modern organizations? No. In spite of the increased use of empowered teams and flattened structures, certain facts remain.[27] (1) Large size prevails. Organizations that succeed and survive tend to grow to large size, and bureaucracy is efficient with large size. Small organizations and their nonbureaucratic structures are more likely to fail, so over time, small organizations may come and go but large bureaucracies stay. Moreover, while the average business today has considerably fewer employees than those 30 years ago, these smaller firms are increasingly part of a large, multilocation organization with the financial and technological resources to compete in a global marketplace. (2) Environmental turbulence can be largely managed. The impact of uncertainties in the environment on the organization are substantially reduced by management strategies such as environmental scanning, strategic alliances, advertising, and lobbying. This allows organizations facing dynamic environments to maintain bureaucratic structures and still be efficient. (3) Bureaucracy's goal of standardization can be increasingly achieved through hiring people who have undergone extensive educational training. Rational discipline, rather than that imposed by rules and regulations, is internalized by hiring professionals with college and university training. They come preprogrammed. In addition, strong cultures help achieve standardization by substituting for high formalization. (4) Finally, technology maintains control. Networked computers allow management to closely monitor the actions of employees without centralization or narrow spans of control. Technology has merely replaced some previously bureaucratic characteristics, but without any loss of management control.

In spite of some changes, bureaucracy is alive and well in many venues. It continues to be a dominant structural form in manufacturing, service firms, hospitals, schools and colleges, the military, and voluntary associations. Why? Because it's still the most efficient way to organize large-scale activities.

ORGANIZATIONAL DESIGNS AND EMPLOYEE BEHAVIOR

We opened this chapter by implying that an organization's structure can have significant effects on its members. In this section, we want to assess directly just what those effects might be.

A review of the evidence linking organizational structures to employee performance and satisfaction leads to a pretty clear conclusion—you can't generalize! Not everyone prefers the freedom and flexibility of organic structures. Some people are most productive and satisfied when work tasks are standardized and ambiguity is minimized—that is, in mechanistic structures. So any discussion of the effect of organizational design on employee behavior has to address individual differences. To illustrate this point, let's consider employee preferences for work specialization, span of control, and centralization.[28]

The evidence generally indicates that *work specialization* contributes to higher employee productivity, but at the price of reduced job satisfaction. However, this statement ignores individual differences and the type of job tasks people do.

As we noted previously, work specialization is not an unending source of higher productivity. Problems start to surface, and productivity begins to suffer, when the human diseconomies of doing repetitive and narrow tasks overtake the economies of specialization. As the workforce has become more highly educated and desirous of jobs that are intrinsically rewarding, the point at which productivity begins to decline seems to be reached more quickly than in decades past.

Some people prefer routine work tasks that are standardized, like the job of preparing flatware to be wrapped at Oneida.

Although more people today are undoubtedly turned off by overly specialized jobs than were their parents or grandparents, it would be naive to ignore the reality that there is still a segment of the workforce that prefers the routine and repetitiveness of highly specialized jobs. Some individuals want work that makes minimal intellectual demands and provides the security of routine. For these people, high work specialization is a source of job satisfaction. The empirical question, of course, is whether this represents 2 percent of the workforce or 52 percent. Given that there is some self-selection operating in the choice of careers, we might conclude that negative behavioral outcomes from high specialization are most likely to surface in professional jobs occupied by individuals with high needs for personal growth and diversity.

A review of the research indicates that it is probably safe to say there is no evidence to support a relationship between *span of control* and employee performance. Although it is intuitively attractive to argue that large spans might lead to higher employee performance because they provide more distant supervision and more opportunity for personal initiative, the research fails to support this notion. At this point it's impossible to state that any particular span of control is best for producing high performance or high satisfaction among employees. Again, the reason is probably individual differences. That is, some people like to be left alone, while others prefer the security of a boss who is quickly available at all times. Consistent with several of the contingency theories of leadership discussed in Chapter 11, we would expect factors such as employees' experiences and abilities and the degree of structure in their tasks to explain when wide or narrow spans of control are likely to contribute to their performance and job satisfaction. However, there is some evidence indicating that a manager's job satisfaction increases as the number of employees he or she supervises increases.

We find fairly strong evidence linking *centralization* and job satisfaction. In general, organizations that are less centralized have a greater amount of participative decision making. And the evidence suggests that participative decision making is positively related to job satisfaction. But, again, individual differences surface. The decentralization–satisfaction relationship is strongest with employees who have low self-esteem. Because individuals with low self-esteem have less confidence in their abilities, they place a higher value on shared decision making, which means that they're not held solely responsible for decision outcomes.

Our conclusion: To maximize employee performance and satisfaction, individual differences, such as experience, personality, and the work task, should be taken into account. In addition, national culture influences the preference for structure, so it too needs to be considered.[29] For instance, organizations that operate with people from high power distance cultures, such as those found in Greece, France, and most of Latin America, will find employees much more accepting of mechanistic structures than where employees come from low power distance countries. So you need to consider cultural differences along with individual differences when making predictions on how structure will affect employee performance and satisfaction.

One obvious insight needs to be made before we leave this topic. People don't select employers randomly. There is substantial evidence that individuals are attracted to, selected by, and stay with organizations that suit their personal characteristics.[30] Job candidates who prefer predictability, for instance, are likely to seek out and take employment in mechanistic structures, while those who want autonomy are more likely to end up in an organic structure. So the effect of structure on employee behavior is undoubtedly reduced when the selection process facilitates proper matching of individual characteristics with organizational characteristics.

SUMMARY AND IMPLICATIONS FOR MANAGERS

The theme of this chapter has been that an organization's internal structure contributes to explaining and predicting behavior. That is, in addition to individual and group factors, the structural relationships in which people work has a bearing on employee attitudes and behavior.

What's the basis for the argument that structure has an impact on both attitudes and behavior? To the degree that an organization's structure reduces ambiguity for employees and clarifies concerns such as "What am I supposed to do?" "How am I supposed to do it?" "To whom do I report?" and "To whom do I go if I have a problem?" it shapes their attitudes and facilitates and motivates them to higher levels of performance.

Of course, structure also constrains employees to the extent that it limits and controls what they do. For example, organizations structured around high levels of formalization and specialization, strict adherence to the chain of command, limited delegation of authority, and narrow spans of control give employees little autonomy. Controls in such organizations are tight, and behavior will tend to vary within a narrow range. In contrast, organizations that are structured around limited specialization, low formalization, wide spans of control, and the like provide employees greater freedom and, thus, will be characterized by greater behavioral diversity.

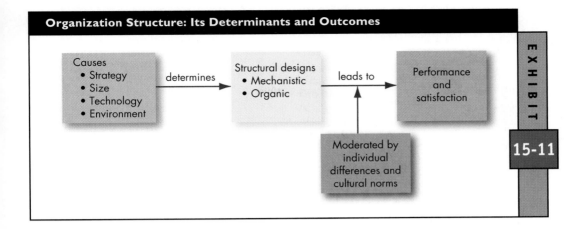

Organization Structure: Its Determinants and Outcomes

Causes
- Strategy
- Size
- Technology
- Environment

→ determines →

Structural designs
- Mechanistic
- Organic

→ leads to →

Performance and satisfaction

Moderated by individual differences and cultural norms

EXHIBIT

15-11

Exhibit 15-11 visually summarizes what we've discussed in this chapter. Strategy, size, technology, and environment determine the type of structure an organization will have. For simplicity's sake, we can classify structural designs around one of two models: mechanistic or organic. The specific effect of structural designs on performance and satisfaction is moderated by employees' individual preferences and cultural norms.

One last point: Managers need to be reminded that structural variables like work specialization, span of control, formalization, and centralization are objective characteristics that can be measured by organizational researchers. The findings and conclusions we've offered in this chapter, in fact, are directly a result of the work of these researchers. But employees don't objectively measure these structural characteristics. They observe things around them in an unscientific fashion and then form their own implicit models of what the organization's structure is like. How many people did they have to interview with before they were offered their jobs? How many people work in their departments and buildings? Is there an organization policy manual? If so, is it readily available and do people follow it closely? How is the organization and its top management described in newspapers and periodicals? Answers to questions such as these, when combined with an employee's past experiences and comments made by peers, lead members to form an overall subjective image of what their organization's structure is like. This image, though, may in no way resemble the organization's actual objective structural characteristics.

The importance of these **implicit models of organizational structure** should not be overlooked. As we noted in Chapter 5, people respond to their perceptions rather than objective reality. The research, for instance, on the relationship between many structural variables and subsequent levels of performance or job satisfaction is far from consistent. We explained some of this as being attributable to individual differences. However, an additional contributing cause to these inconsistent findings might be diverse perceptions of the objective characteristics. Researchers typically focus on actual levels of the various structural components, but these may be irrelevant if people interpret similar components differently. The bottom line, therefore, is to understand how employees interpret their organization's structure. That should prove a more meaningful predictor of their behavior than the objective characteristics themselves.

implicit models of organizational structure
Perceptions that people hold regarding structural variables formed by observing things around them in an unscientific fashion.

Technology Is Reshaping Organizations

In today's chaotic, uncertain, and high-tech world, there is essentially only one type of design that is going to survive. This is the electronically configured organic organization.[a]

We are undergoing a second Industrial Revolution and it will change every aspect of people's lives. The changes the large corporations used to take a decade to implement now occur in one to two years. Companies that are successful will be designed to thrive on change. And the structure of those organizations will have common characteristics.

Ten years from now there will be nothing but electronic organizations. Brick-and-mortar organizations won't go away, but click-and-mortar will become the only means to survival. In addition, every organization will need to keep its finger on the pulse of its customers. Customer priorities will change very rapidly. What customers will pay a premium for will become a commodity so rapidly that those who lose touch with their customers will be candidates for extinction. Consumers are gaining the ability to compare the prices of hundreds of competitors rather than just two or three. This is going to dramatically drive down prices. Consumer products in Britain, for instance, will come down 10 to 15 percent between 2000 and 2003. If firms don't improve their productivity to match these drops in prices, they'll be out of business.

Technology allows firms to stay closer to the customer, to move jobs to where costs are lowest, and to make decisions much more rapidly. For instance, executives at Cisco Systems can monitor expenses, gross margins, the supply chain, and profitability in real time. There no longer need to be surprises. Every employee can make decisions that might have had to come from the top management ranks a few years ago. At the end of a quarter, individual product managers at Cisco can see exactly what the gross margins are on his or her products, whether they are below expectations, and determine the cause of any discrepancy. Quicker decision making at lower levels will translate into higher profit margins. So instead of the CEO or chief financial officer making 50 to 100 different decisions in a quarter, managers throughout the organization can make millions of decisions. Companies that don't adjust to create this capability will be noncompetitive.

There's a saying that every generation thinks it has discovered sex. This seems to be the case with technology and how it's going to change the world completely.

Technology will transform the structure of organizations at a much slower rate than many believe.[b] For instance, it's useful to go back and ask if the railroads changed the world. There were definitely changes in how commerce and industry were arranged. But life remained the same, and the way people related to each other remained the same.

There are changes occurring that will influence the way businesses organize. But the changes have been, and will continue to be, gradual. They may accelerate some, but we're not going to see a revolution in the design of organizations. Take the case of globalization. It's significant but it is also evolutionary. Has the formation of the European Union abolished national borders in the largest continental society in the Western World? No. France is still France, and Germany is still Germany. Things have changed, but things have not changed.

The emphasis on speed has its limits. Brains don't speed up. The exchange of ideas doesn't really speed up, only the overhead that slowed down the exchange. When it comes down to the bulk of knowledge work, the twenty-first century works the same as the twentieth century: You can reach people around the clock, but they won't think any better or faster just because you've reached them faster. The give and take remains a limiting factor.

The virtual organization also has its limitations. When you farm out your data processing, manufacturing, and other functions, you make your capabilities available to your competitors. So virtualization of work diminishes competitive advantages. It leads to rapidly spreading commoditization of everything. Any function that an organization uses to achieve a competitive advantage cannot be outsourced.

Look back over the past 40 years. People haven't changed. And our fundamental organizations haven't changed. On the fringes, there is more looseness in the organization. But more hasn't changed than has. The changes we've seen have been slow and gradual. And that pace is likely to continue into the future.

[a]This argument was presented by J. Chambers, "Nothing Except E-Companies," *Business Week*, August 28, 2000, pp. 210–12.

[b]This argument was presented by A. Grove, "I'm a Little Skeptical. . . . Brains Don't Speed Up," *Business Week*, August 28, 2000, pp. 212–14.

1. Why isn't work specialization an unending source of increased productivity?

2. All things being equal, which is more efficient, a wide or narrow span of control? Why?

3. In what ways can management departmentalize?

4. What is a matrix structure? When would management use it?

5. Contrast the virtual organization with the boundaryless organization.

6. What type of structure works best with an innovation strategy? A cost-minimization strategy? An imitation strategy?

7. Summarize the size–structure relationship.

8. Define and give an example of what is meant by the term *technology*.

9. Summarize the environment–structure relationship.

10. Explain the importance of the statement: "Employees form implicit models of organizational structure."

Questions for Critical Thinking

1. How is the typical large corporation of today organized in contrast to how that same organization was probably organized in the 1960s?

2. Do you think most employees prefer high formalization? Support your position.

3. If you were an employee in a matrix structure, what pluses do you think the structure would provide? What about minuses?

4. What behavioral predictions would you make about people who worked in a "pure" boundaryless organization (if such a structure were ever to exist)?

5. AOL buys Time Warner. Alcoa purchases Reynolds Metals. Nestles S.A. merges with Ralston Purina. Each of these are recent examples of large companies combining with other large companies. Does this imply that small isn't necessarily beautiful? Are mechanistic forms winning the "survival of the fittest" battle? What are the implications of this consolidation trend for organizational behavior?

Team Exercise   Authority Figures

Purpose: To learn about one's experiences with and feelings about authority.

Time: Approximately 75 minutes.

Procedure:

1. Your instructor will separate class members into groups based on their birth order. Groups are formed consisting of "only children," "eldest," "middle," and "youngest," according to placement in families. Larger groups will be broken into smaller ones, with four or five members, to allow for freer conversation.

2. Each group member should talk about how he or she "typically reacts to the authority of others." Focus should be on specific situations that offer general information about how individuals deal with authority figures (for example, bosses, teachers, parents, or coaches). The group has 25 minutes to develop a written list of how the group generally deals with others' authority. Be sure to separate tendencies that group members share and those they do not.

3. Repeat Step 2, except this time discuss how group members "typically are as authority figures." Again make a list of shared characteristics.

4. Each group will share its general conclusions with the entire class.

5. Class discussion will focus on questions such as:

   a. What patterned differences have surfaced between the groups?

   b. What may account for these differences?

   c. What hypotheses might explain the connection between how individuals react to the authority of others and how they are as authority figures?

Source: This exercise is adapted from W. A. Kahn, "An Exercise of Authority," *Organizational Behavior Teaching Review*, vol. XIV, no. 2, 1989–90, pp. 28–42. Reprinted with permission.

Ethical Dilemma | **Can Ethical Officers Help?**

A number of organizations are creating the position of "ethical officer" to help employees deal with ethical dilemmas. One of those companies is United Technologies Corp. (UTC)—whose best known divisions include Otis Elevator, aircraft engine manufacturer Pratt & Whitney, and heating and air conditioning giant Carrier Corp.

Patrick Gnazzo is UTC's vice president for business practices and chief ethical officer. A lawyer by training, Gnazzo is responsible for his company's compliance and ethics programs. This includes managing more than 160 business-practice officers worldwide. The officers, all of whom are managers whose job descriptions have been broadened to include ethics oversight, help implement the $24 billion corporation's ethics/compliance programs for its 145,000 employees in 183 countries.

Gnazzo seeks to be eminently approachable. "We say this to our people all the time—call, call, call, call. Send e-mails. Write. I want to spend the majority of my time giving advice, not investigating [ethical breeches] after the fact." Communication at UTC is encouraged at all levels through DIALOG, a worldwide program that allows employees to ask questions, make suggestions, register complaints, and report suspected wrongdoing confidentially. Since its inception in 1986, the program has received more than 50,000 DIALOG correspondences ranging from routine maintenance and benefit questions to concerns about ethical practices.

UTC, like most large organizations, has a code of ethics. The entire document can be read over a cup of coffee. It covers all of the corporation's constituents—customers and suppliers, employees, stockholders, worldwide communities, and competitors. Basically it says, "don't lie, don't cheat, don't steal." One of the responsibilities of Gnazzo and his staff is to look at the reasonableness of a practice, in light of UTC's code of ethics, and determine what seems to be the right thing to do. With the code as a guide, Gnazzo says most ethical questions can be answered easily and a decision made. "But about once a day I get a call and say, 'This is a new one on me. Let's think this thing out.'"

Why do organizations like UTC need ethics officers and a staff if they have a code of ethics? What benefits do you think UTC's business-practice officers provide to employees? Does having a formal office and a staff responsible for ethical practices lessen the responsibility on individual employees to make good ethical decisions?

Source: Based on R. Osborne, "A Matter of Ethics," *Industry Week*, September 4, 2000, pp. 41–42.

Case Incident | **Working by the Rules**

The trend today is away from rigid rules and procedures. Flexibility is the new gospel. While these statements may be true in general, not every manager is buying into it. One in particular is Stephen Reuning, head of the New Jersey recruiting firm, Diedre Moire Corp.

New employees at Diedre Moire must copy Mr. Reuning's 244-page Standard Operating Protocol—using longhand script, three times over. This manual covers everything that's expected of company employees—from procedures on how to greet customers to how to sit during lunch to hair and grooming tips to what items should and should not be on the employee's desk. It can take 100 hours or more for new employees to make their copies. After that they still have to pass 12 oral exams over the content.

Reuning is obsessive about documenting everything. Since starting the firm 18 years ago, he has stored 45,000 pages of data on the firm's computer network. Every process, procedure, product, form, letter, brochure, and agreement used by any Diedre Moire employee is documented, cataloged and stored so it's readily available to any and all members of the firm.

Reuning's fascination with rules and control is not for everyone. According to Reuning, half of the job candidates he interviews head for the door when told about the protocol requirements. Of those who stay, about one in five lasts beyond a year. One former employee, who lasted nine months, calls the company's environment more structured than the basic training he had in the Army. "They were robotic," he says.

Those who stay make six figure incomes and say that there's a comforting efficiency about the place. Customers also seem to appreciate the result. They like that employees are well trained, systematic, and able to respond to almost any question.

Questions

1. What advantages, if any, does Reuning's system provide?

2. Why does his system work? What's its potential downside?

3. What type of employees do you think fit into Reuning's system?

Source: D. Morse, "You Think You Have an Obsessive Boss? Meet Mr. Reuning," *Wall Street Journal*, October 4, 2000, p. A1.

KSS PROGRAM:

KNOW THE CONCEPTS
SELF-AWARENESS
SKILLS APPLICATIONS

Delegating Authority/Empowerment

After you've read this chapter, take Self-Assessment #40 (How Willing Am I to Delegate?) on your enclosed CD-ROM, and complete the skill-building module entitled Delegating Authority on page 627.

Endnotes

1. This example was inspired by N. George, "Counting on the Spirit of Independent Branches," *Financial Times*, November 5, 2001, p. 10.
2. See, for instance, R. L. Daft, *Organization Theory and Design*, 7th ed. (Cincinnati, OH: Southwestern, 2001).
3. See, for instance, L. Urwick, *The Elements of Administration* (New York: Harper & Row, 1944), pp. 52–53.
4. J. Child and R. G. McGrath, "Organizations Unfettered: Organizational Form in an Information-Intensive Economy," *Academy of Management Journal*, December 2001, pp. 1135–48.
5. H. Mintzberg, *Structure in Fives: Designing Effective Organizations* (Upper Saddle River, NJ: Prentice Hall, 1983), p. 157.
6. S. Lohr, "I.B.M. Chief Gerstner Recalls Difficult Days at Big Blue," *New York Times*, July 31, 2000, p. C5.
7. K. Knight, "Matrix Organization: A Review," *Journal of Management Studies*, May 1976, pp. 111–30; L. R. Burns and D. R. Wholey, "Adoption and Abandonment of Matrix Manage-

ment Programs: Effects of Organizational Characteristics and Interorganizational Networks," *Academy of Management Journal*, February 1993, pp. 106–38; and R. E. Anderson, "Matrix Redux," *Business Horizons*, November–December 1994, pp. 6–10.
8. See, for instance, S. M. Davis and P. R. Lawrence, "Problems of Matrix Organization," *Harvard Business Review*, May–June 1978, pp. 131–42.
9. S. A. Mohrman, S. G. Cohen, and A. M. Mohrman Jr., *Designing Team-Based Organizations* (San Francisco: Jossey-Bass, 1995); F. Ostroff, *The Horizontal Organization* (New York: Oxford University Press, 1999); and R. Forrester and A. B. Drexler, "A Model for Team-Based Organization Performance," *Academy of Management Executive*, August 1999, pp. 36–49.
10. M. Kaeter, "The Age of the Specialized Generalist," *Training*, December 1993, pp. 48–53.
11. L. Brokaw, "Thinking Flat," *INC.*, October 1993, p. 88.

12. C. Fishman, "Whole Foods Is All Teams," *Fast Company*, Greatest Hits, vol. 1, 1997, pp. 102–13.

13. See, for instance, R. E. Miles and C. C. Snow, "The New Network Firm: A Spherical Structure Built on Human Investment Philosophy," *Organizational Dynamics*, Spring 1995, pp. 5–18; G. G. Dess, A. M. A. Rasheed, K. J. McLaughlin, and R. L. Priem, "The New Corporate Architecture," *Academy of Management Executive*, August 1995, pp. 7–20; D. Pescovitz, "The Company Where Everybody's a Temp," *New York Times Magazine*, June 11, 2000, pp. 94–96; W. F. Cascio, "Managing a Virtual Workplace," *Academy of Management Executive*, August 2000, pp. 81–90; and D. Lyons, "Smart and Smarter," *Forbes*, March 18, 2002, pp. 40–41.

14. J. Bates, "Making Movies and Moving On," *Los Angeles Times*, January 19, 1998, p. A1.

15. "GE: Just Your Average Everyday $60 Billion Family Grocery Store," *Industry Week*, May 2, 1994, pp. 13–18.

16. H. C. Lucas Jr., *The T-Form Organization: Using Technology to Design Organizations for the 21st Century* (San Francisco: Jossey-Bass, 1996).

17. This section is based on D. D. Davis, "Form, Function and Strategy in Boundaryless Organizations," in A. Howard (ed.), *The Changing Nature of Work* (San Francisco: Jossey-Bass, 1995), pp. 112–38; P. Roberts, "We Are One Company, No Matter Where We Are. Time and Space Are Irrelevant," *Fast Company*, April–May 1998, pp. 122–28; R. L. Cross, A. Yan, and M. R. Louis, "Boundary Activities in 'Boundaryless' Organizations: A Case Study of a Transformation to a Team-Based Structure," *Human Relations*, June 2000, pp. 841–68; and R. Ashkenas, D. Ulrich, T. Jick, and S. Kerr, *The Boundaryless Organization: Breaking the Chains of Organizational Structure*, revised and updated (San Francisco: Jossey-Bass, 2002).

18. See J. Lipnack and J. Stamps, *The TeamNet Factor* (Essex Junction, VT: Oliver Wight Publications, 1993); J. Fulk and G. DeSanctis, "Electronic Communication and Changing Organizational Forms," *Organization Science*, July–August 1995, pp. 337–49; A. Cortese, "Here Comes the Intranet," *Business Week*, February 26, 1996, pp. 76–84; and M. Hammer, *The Agenda* (New York: Crown Business, 2001).

19. T. Burns and G. M. Stalker, *The Management of Innovation* (London: Tavistock, 1961); and J. A. Courtright, G. T. Fairhurst, and L. E. Rogers, "Interaction Patterns in Organic and Mechanistic Systems," *Academy of Management Journal*, December 1989, pp. 773–802.

20. This analysis is referred to as a contingency approach to organization design. See, for instance, J. M. Pennings, "Structural Contingency Theory: A Reappraisal," in B. M. Staw and L. L. Cummings (eds.), *Research in Organizational Behavior*, vol. 14 (Greenwich, CT: JAI Press, 1992), pp. 267–309.

21. The strategy–structure thesis was originally proposed in A. D. Chandler, Jr., *Strategy and Structure: Chapters in the History of the Industrial Enterprise* (Cambridge, MA: MIT Press, 1962). For an updated analysis, see T. L. Amburgey and T. Dacin, "As the Left Foot Follows the Right? The Dynamics of Strategic and Structural Change," *Academy of Management Journal*, December 1994, pp. 1427–52.

22. See R. E. Miles and C. C. Snow, *Organizational Strategy, Structure, and Process* (New York: McGraw-Hill, 1978); D. Miller, "The Structural and Environmental Correlates of Business Strategy," *Strategic Management Journal*, January–February 1987, pp. 55–76; D. C. Galunic and K. M. Eisenhardt, "Renewing the Strategy-Structure-Performance Paradigm," in B. M. Staw and L. L. Cummings (eds.), *Research in Organizational Behavior*, vol. 16 (Greenwich, CT: JAI Press, 1994), pp. 215–55; and I. C. Harris and T. W. Ruefli, "The Strategy/Structure Debate: An Examination of the Performance Implications," *Journal of Management Studies*, June 2000, pp. 587–603.

23. See, for instance, P. M. Blau and R. A. Schoenherr, *The Structure of Organizations* (New York: Basic Books, 1971); D. S. Pugh, "The Aston Program of Research: Retrospect and Prospect," in A. H. Van de Ven and W. F. Joyce (eds.), *Perspectives on Organization Design and Behavior* (New York: John Wiley, 1981), pp. 135–66; R. Z. Gooding and J. A. Wagner III, "A Meta-Analytic Review of the Relationship Between Size and Performance: The Productivity and Efficiency of Organizations and Their Subunits," *Administrative Science Quarterly*, December 1985, pp. 462–81; and A. C. Bluedorn, "Pilgrim's Progress: Trends and Convergence in Research on Organizational Size and Environments," *Journal of Management*, Summer 1993, pp. 163–92.

24. See J. Woodward, *Industrial Organization: Theory and Practice* (London: Oxford University Press, 1965); C. Perrow, "A Framework for the Comparative Analysis of Organizations," *American Sociological Review*, April 1967, pp. 194–208; J. D. Thompson, *Organizations in Action* (New York: McGraw-Hill, 1967); J. Hage and M. Aiken, "Routine Technology, Social Structure, and Organizational Goals," *Administrative Science Quarterly*, September 1969, pp. 366–77; C. C. Miller, W. H. Glick, Y. Wang, and G. P. Huber, "Understanding Technology–Structure Relationships: Theory Development and Meta-Analytic Theory Testing," *Academy of Management Journal*, June 1991, pp. 370–99; and K. H. Roberts and M. Grabowski, "Organizations, Technology, and Structuring," in S. R. Clegg, C. Hardy, and W. R. Nord (eds.), *Managing Organizations: Current Issues* (Thousand Oaks, CA: Sage, 1999), pp. 159–71.

25. See F. E. Emery and E. Trist, "The Causal Texture of Organizational Environments," *Human Relations*, February 1965, pp. 21–32; P. Lawrence and J. W. Lorsch, *Organization and Environment: Managing Differentiation and Integration* (Boston: Harvard Business School, Division of Research, 1967); M. Yasai-Ardekani, "Structural Adaptations to Environments," *Academy of Management Review*, January 1986, pp. 9–21; and A. C. Bluedorn, "Pilgrim's Progress."

26. G. G. Dess and D. W. Beard, "Dimensions of Organizational Task Environments," *Administrative Science Quarterly*, March 1984, pp. 52–73; E. A. Gerloff, N. K. Muir, and W. D. Bodensteiner, "Three Components of Perceived Environmental Uncertainty: An Exploratory Analysis of the Effects of Aggregation," *Journal of Management*, December 1991, pp. 749–68; and O. Shenkar, N. Aranya, and T. Almor, "Construct Dimensions in the Contingency Model: An Analysis Comparing Metric and Non-Metric Multivariate Instruments," *Human Relations*, May 1995, pp. 559–80.

27. See S. P. Robbins, *Organization Theory: Structure, Design, and Applications*, 3rd ed. (Englewood Cliffs, NJ: Prentice Hall, 1990), pp. 320–25; and B. Harrison, *Lean and Mean: The Changing Landscape of Corporate Power in the Age of Flexibility* (New York: Basic Books, 1994).

28. See, for instance, L. W. Porter and E. E. Lawler III, "Properties of Organization Structure in Relation to Job Atti-

tudes and Job Behavior," *Psychological Bulletin*, July 1965, pp. 23–51; L. R. James and A. P. Jones, "Organization Structure: A Review of Structural Dimensions and Their Conceptual Relationships with Individual Attitudes and Behavior," *Organizational Behavior and Human Performance*, June 1976, pp. 74–113; D. R. Dalton, W. D. Todor, M. J. Spendolini, G. J. Fielding, and L. W. Porter, "Organization Structure and Performance: A Critical Review," *Academy of Management Review*, January 1980, pp. 49–64; W. Snizek and J. H. Bullard, "Perception of Bureaucracy and Changing Job Satisfaction: A Longitudinal Analysis," *Organizational Behavior and Human Performance*, October 1983, pp. 275–87; and D. B. Turban and T. L. Keon, "Organizational Attractiveness: An Interactionist Perspective," *Journal of Applied Psychology*, April 1994, pp. 184–93.

29. See, for example, P. R. Harris and R. T. Moran, *Managing Cultural Differences*, 4th ed. (Houston: Gulf Publishing, 1996).

30. See, for instance, B. Schneider, "The People Make the Place," *Personnel Psychology*, Autumn 1987, pp. 437–53; B. Schneider, H. W. Goldstein, and D. B. Smith, "The ASA Framework: An Update," *Personnel Psychology*, Winter 1995, pp. 747–73; and J. Schaubroeck, D. C. Ganster, and J. R. Jones, "Organization and Occupation Influences in the Attraction-Selection-Attrition Process," *Journal of Applied Psychology*, December 1998, pp. 869–91.

PART FOUR

THE ORGANIZATION SYSTEM

Net Optics Inc. and Coca-Cola are two international companies. While they're in very different businesses—one is a leading innovator in network management and security and the other the world's largest producer of soda pop—they have one thing in common. Both rely on feng shui in designing their offices.[1]

Feng shui (pronounced fung shway) has been used in China for more than 3,500 years. The term literally means "wind and water". These two elements stand as a metaphor for the power of nature and the absolute importance of respecting that power as we organize our surroundings. Feng shui uses the natural positive energy, called "chi," present in any environment to enhance surroundings. The Chinese claim that using feng shui in the design of buildings, retail stores, and offices will bring serenity, prosperity and wealth to occupants.

While feng shui may sound like "voodoo" to many Westerners, global businesses can't afford to ignore its influence. This extends to the design of offices. So Net Optics recently hired a feng shui consultant to offer advice in modifying the layout of the company's Sunnyvale, California headquarters (see photo). As a result of that consultant's advice, management made a number of changes—including rearranging office furniture and production workstations. As for the color scheme, Net Optics' founders had already made an excellent choice according to feng shui principles: green and purple, key colors for success. Similarly, Coca Cola began applying feng shui principles in its Atlanta headquarters after a group of visiting Coke bottlers from Asia pointed out some poor office layouts. "Coca-Cola is welcome in more than 200 countries because we seek out and adapt to other cultures," a Coke spokesman said. "We've done this throughout our history, and doing so made us the ultimate local brand. So we've adopted some of the design principles of feng shui to our Atlanta complex."

Work Design and Technology

I n this chapter, we'll discuss feng shui and several other work design concepts. We'll also demonstrate how technology is changing organizations and the jobs that people do, present several frameworks for analyzing jobs, and conclude by showing how management can redesign jobs and work schedules in ways that can increase employee productivity and satisfaction.

TECHNOLOGY IN THE WORKPLACE

We introduced the term *technology* in the previous chapter's discussion of why structures differ. We said it was how an organization transfers its inputs into outputs. In recent years, the term has become widely used by economists, managers, consultants, and business analysts to describe machinery and equipment that use sophisticated electronics and computers to produce those outputs.

The common theme among new technologies in the workplace is that they substitute machinery for human labor in transforming inputs into outputs. This substitution of capital for labor has been going on essentially nonstop since the Industrial Revolution in the mid-1800s. For instance, the introduction of electricity allowed textile factories to introduce mechanical looms that could produce cloth far more quickly and cheaply than was possible when the looms were powered by individuals. But it has been the computerization of equipment and machinery in the past quarter-century that has been the prime mover in reshaping today's workplace. Automated teller machines, for example, have replaced tens of thousands of human tellers in banks. Ninety-eight percent of the spot welds on new Ford Tauruses are performed by robots, not by people. Many cars now

AFTER STUDYING THIS CHAPTER, YOU SHOULD BE ABLE TO:

1. Contrast process reengineering and continuous improvement processes.

2. Describe an e-organization.

3. Summarize the implications of e-organizations on individual behavior.

4. Explain the job characteristics model.

5. Contrast the social information processing model to the job characteristics model.

6. Explain how work space design might influence employee behavior.

7. Describe how a job can be enriched.

8. Contrast flextime and job sharing.

9. Compare the benefits and drawbacks to telecommuting from the employee's point of view.

Do you remember the IBM Selectric ball? It went the way of the horse and buggy when the technology of personal computing replaced typewriters.

come equipped with on-board computers that take only seconds to diagnose problems that used to take mechanics hours to diagnose. IBM has built a plant in Austin, Texas, that can produce laptop computers without the help of a single worker; everything from the time parts arrive at the IBM plant to the final packing of finished products is completely automated.

This book is concerned with the behavior of people at work. No coverage of this topic, today, would be complete without discussing how recent advances in technology are changing the workplace and affecting the work lives of employees. In this section, we'll look at three specific issues related to technology and work. These are continuous improvement processes, process reengineering, and mass customization.

Continuous Improvement Processes

In Chapter 1, we described quality management as seeking the constant attainment of customer satisfaction through the continuous improvement of all organizational processes. This search for continuous improvement recognizes that *good* isn't *good enough* and that even excellent performance can, and should, be improved on. For instance, a 99.9 percent error-free performance sounds like a high standard of excellence. However it doesn't sound so great when you realize that this standard would result in the U.S. Post Office losing 2,000 pieces of mail an hour, U.S. doctors performing 500 incorrect surgical procedures each week, or two plane crashes a day at O'Hare Airport in Chicago.[2]

Quality-management programs seek to achieve continuous process improvements so that variability is constantly reduced. When you eliminate variations, you increase the uniformity of the product or service. Increasing uniformity, in turn, results in lower costs and higher quality. For instance, Pella Corp., the huge Iowa-based window and door manufacturer, has used continuous process improvement techniques since 1993 to streamline operations, cut inventories, speed delivery times, and significantly improve the quality of its products. These techniques have been credited as a major factor in helping the company to triple its sales over the past decade.[3]

As tens of thousands of organizations introduce continuous process improvement, how will employees be affected? They will no longer be able to rest on their previous accomplishments and successes. So some people may experience increased stress from a work climate that no longer accepts complacency with the status quo. A race with no finish line can never be won—a situation that creates constant tension. This tension may be positive for the organization (remember *functional conflict* from Chapter 14?), but the pressures from an unrelenting search for process improvements can create anxiety and stress in some employees. Probably the most significant implication for employees is that management will look to them as the prime source for improvement ideas. Employee involvement programs, therefore, are part and parcel of continuous improvement. Empowered work teams who have hands-on involvement in process improvement, for instance, are widely used in organizations that have introduced quality programs.

Process Reengineering

We also introduced process reengineering in Chapter 1. We described it as considering how you would do things if you could start all over from scratch. The term *reengineering* comes from the process of taking apart an electronic product and designing a better version. Michael Hammer applied the term to organizations. When he found companies using computers simply to automate outdated processes, rather than finding fundamentally better ways of doing things, he realized that the principles of reengineering could be applied to business. So, as applied to organizations, process reengineering means that management should start with a clean sheet of paper—rethinking and redesigning the processes by which the organization creates value and does work, ridding itself of operations that have become antiquated.[4]

Key Elements   Three key elements of process reengineering are identifying an organization's distinctive competencies, assessing core processes, and reorganizing horizontally by process. An organization's **distinctive competencies** define what it is that the organization does better than its competition. Examples might include better store locations, a more efficient distribution system, higher-quality products, more knowledgeable sales personnel, or superior technical support. Dell Computer, for instance, differentiates itself from its competitors by emphasizing high-quality hardware, comprehensive service and technical support, and low prices. Why is identifying distinctive competencies so important? Because it guides decisions regarding what activities are crucial to the organization's success.

distinctive competencies
What it is that an organization does better than its competition.

Management also needs to assess the core processes that clearly add value to the organization's distinctive competencies. These are the processes that transform materials, capital, information, and labor into products and services that the customer values. When the organization is viewed as a series of processes, ranging from strategic planning to after-sales customer support, management can determine to what degree each adds value. Not surprisingly, this process-value analysis typically uncovers a lot of activities that add little or nothing of value and whose only justification is "we've always done it this way."

Process reengineering requires management to reorganize around horizontal processes. This means using cross-functional and self-managed teams. It means focusing on processes rather than functions. So, for instance, the vice president of marketing might become the "process owner of finding and keeping customers."[5] It also means cutting out levels of middle management. As Hammer points out, "Managers are not value-added. A customer never buys a product because of the caliber of management. Management is, by definition, indirect. So if possible, less is better. One of the goals of reengineering is to minimize the necessary amount of management."[6]

Implications for Employees   Process reengineering has been popular since the early 1990s. Almost all major companies—in the United States, Asia, and Europe—have reengineered at least some of their processes. The result has been that lots of people have lost their jobs. Staff support jobs, especially middle managers, have been particularly vulnerable to process reengineering efforts. So, too, have clerical jobs in service industries.

Employees who keep their jobs after process reengineering have typically found that they aren't the same jobs. These new jobs typically require a wider range of skills, including more interaction with customers and suppliers, greater challenge, increased responsibilities, and higher pay. However, the three-to-five year period it takes to implement process reengineering is usually tough on employees. They suffer from uncertainty and anxiety associated with taking on new tasks and having to discard long-established work practices and formal social networks.

Mass Customization

The Tom Clancy or Stephen King paperbacks you find on bookstore shelves are printed on huge offset presses, then stored in hangar-size warehouses, and finally shipped to bookstores in fleets of trucks. The novels are mass-produced, with initial printings of several hundred thousand copies. Book publishers require these large print runs to keep production costs down.

New technology is completely changing this process.[7] This new technology, called print on demand, allows books to be produced and sold in small quantities—even one at a time—almost instantly. Publishers only have to digitize a book's contents and store it in a centralized computer. Then, when ordered by a customer, a single high-tech printing-and-binding machine goes into action, creating a slick, high-quality paperback. These high-tech machines can be located in bookstores, allowing a store to custom-print a book for a customer in 60 seconds or less.

From the days of Henry Ford through the late 1990s, production efficiencies demanded **mass production**. Firms used division of labor, standardization, and automated processes to manufacture products in large quantities. Economies of scale favored large quantities because that reduced costs. Industry after industry relied on mass production systems to minimize costs. Ford's Model T, McDonald's, and Levittown stand as icons to mass production.

New technologies, such as computer-aided design and manufacturing (CAD/CAM), however, are undermining the economies of mass production. And they're making possible **mass customization** like print on demand. Mass customization encompasses production processes that are flexible enough to create products and services that are individually tailored to individual customers. The future of production manufacturing is one of mass customization. Some products, like packaged foods, will probably continue to be made using traditional mass production methods. But for products for which customers want custom features, firms will be converting to "build to order" systems. And it seems that customers are increasingly seeking products that have been configured for their particular needs.[8] The Case Corp. and Levi Strauss are two examples of firms that have successfully embraced mass customization.

Case is a huge farm and construction equipment manufacturer that has converted all its products to mass customization. For instance, its $85,000 MX-series Magnum farm tractors are now made exclusively to order. Under its old system, farmers had to select from models and options that a dealer had in stock. Or they had to wait six months to get one the way they wanted it. Now buyers can make up to 28 choices on options such as engine, tires, and power train. And Case can deliver the customized tractor in five to six weeks.

Levi makes 130 styles of jeans. Still, many customers can't find a pair that is exactly what they're looking for. No problem! Levi can provide them with a custom-fitted pair, choosing from three basic models, 10 fabrics, five leg styles, and two types of fly. Although these "made to order" jeans cost a bit more (about $55), Levi uses computer technology to standardize options and cut costs.

mass production

Using division of labor, standardization, and automated processes to manufacture products in large quantities.

mass customization

Production processes that are flexible enough to create products and services that are individually tailored to individual customers.

Real estate developer Arthur Levitt revolutionized the suburbs in the period following World War II when he applied mass production technology to home construction. Levitt's firm could build 150 four-room homes a week (1 every 16 minutes).

Mass customization offers advantages to both customers and manufacturers. Customers don't have to compromise. They can have the products they want, tailored to their individual tastes and needs. For manufacturers, they create more satisfied customers while, at the same time, increasing production efficiency. Mass customization results in little or no work-in-progress or finished-goods inventories; no obsolete products gathering dust on shelves or in showrooms; and requires less working capital. Case says, for instance, that merely by reducing inventories of its finished tractors by more than half, it's saving between $1,500 and $2,000 per machine.

The downside of mass customization is that it creates increased coordination demands on management. And it typically requires employees to go through significant retraining. Mass customization usually requires the reengineering of processes and reorganizing work around teams to increase flexibility.

OB IN AN E-WORLD

No area of technology is changing organizations more than electronic technology. For instance, terms like *e-commerce* and *e-business* have become a standard part of the current lexicon. In this section, we'll define an e-organization and the affect it is having on both individual and group behavior in the workplace.

What's an e-Organization?

E-commerce refers to the sales side of electronic business. When you read about the tremendous number of people who are shopping on the Internet and how businesses can set up Web sites on which they sell goods, conduct transactions, get paid, and fulfill orders, you're hearing about e-commerce. In contrast, **e-business** is the full breadth of activities included in a successful Internet-based enterprise. It includes developing strategies for running Internet-based companies; improving communication between employees, suppliers, and customers; and collaborating with partners to electronically coordinate design and production. As such, e-commerce is really a subset of e-business. And the term **e-organization** (or *e-org*) merely refers to applications of e-business concepts to all organizations. E-orgs not only include business firms, but also hospitals, schools, museums, government agencies, and the military. For instance, the U.S. Internal Revenue Service is an e-organization because it now provides access to taxpayers over the Internet.

The best way to understand the e-organization concept is to look at its three underlying components—the Internet, intranets, and extranets. The **Internet** is a worldwide network of interconnected computers; **intranets** are an organization's private Internet; and **extranets** are extended intranets accessible only to selected employees and authorized outsiders. As Exhibit 16-1 on page 460 illustrates, an e-org is defined by the degree to which it uses global (Internet) and private (intranet and extranet) network links. Type A's are traditional organizations such as small retailers and service firms. Most organizations today fall into this category. Type B's are contemporary organizations with heavy reliance on intranets and extranets. Type C's are most small e-commerce firms. And finally, Type D's are full e-orgs. They've completely integrated global and private networks. Type D's would include firms such as eBay, Cisco Systems, Amazon.com, and Wal-Mart. Note that as an organization moves from a Type A toward a Type D, it increases the degree to which it takes on e-org properties.

The following discussion looks at how e-organizations affect employee behavior. But because e-orgs, in actuality, encompass a range of electronic technology

e-commerce
The sales side of electronic business.

e-business
The full breadth of activities included in a successful Internet-based enterprise.

e-organization
A profit or nonprofit organization that uses the Internet and private network links to facilitate activities and communication.

Internet
A worldwide network of interconnected computers.

intranets
An organization's private Internet.

extranets
Extended intranets accessible only to selected employees and authorized outsiders.

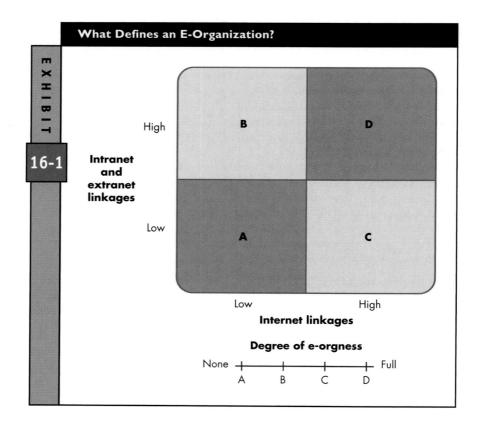

EXHIBIT

16-1

What Defines an E-Organization?

High

Intranet and extranet linkages

Low

	B		D
	A		C

Low ___ High

Internet linkages

Degree of e-orgness

None ├──────┼──────┼──────┤ Full
       A   B   C   D

applications, our observations and predictions need to be qualified: The more an organization uses global and private network links, the more our comments about e-orgs will be applicable to its employees.

Selected Implications for Individual Behavior

We could devote an entire chapter or more on detailed discussions of how e-orgs will affect individual behavior. Given our space limitations, let's look at just two selected individual topics—motivation and ethics—to get a feel for the potential impact of e-orgs.

Motivation Are there unique challenges to motivating employees in e-organizations? The answer appears to be "yes." Employees in e-orgs, for instance, are more susceptible to distractions that can undermine their work effort and reduce their productivity.

Employees have always been susceptible to distractions at work such as interruptions by colleagues or personal phone calls. The Internet, however, has significantly broadened these distractions to include surfing the Net, playing online games, stock trading, shopping at work, conducting "cyberaffairs," and searching for other jobs online. Popular sites people visit from work include the Weather Channel, Amazon.com, TheOnion.com, and eBay.

Cyberloafing refers to the act of employees using their organization's Internet access during formal work hours to surf non–job-related Web sites and to send or read personal e-mail.[9] And the evidence indicates that cyberloafing is consuming a lot of time among workers who have Internet access. Surveys indicate, for instance, that 24.5 percent of U.S. employees with Net access spend at least one

cyberloafing

The act of employees using their organization's Internet access during formal work hours to surf non–job-related Web sites and to send or read personal e-mail.

hour each workday visiting sites unrelated to their job.[10] In addition, estimates indicate that nearly one-third of employees' Internet use at work is recreational and that cyberloafing is costing U.S. employers approximately $3 million a year for every 1,000 employees with Internet access.[11]

If the work itself isn't interesting or creates excessive stress, employees are likely to be motivated to do something else. If they have easy access to the Internet, that "something else" is increasingly using the Net as a diversion. The solution to this problem includes making jobs more interesting to employees, providing formal breaks to overcome monotony, and establishing clear guidelines so employees know what online behaviors are expected. Many employers are also installing Web-monitoring software, although there is evidence that such efforts can undermine trust in the organization and adversely affect employee morale.[12]

Ethics   Electronic surveillance of employees by employers is an issue that pits an organization's desire for control against an employee's right to privacy. The development of increasingly sophisticated surveillance software only adds to the ethical dilemma of how far an organization should go in monitoring the behavior of employees who do their work on computers.[13]

For instance, the Web activity of every one of Xerox's 92,000 employees—in countries around the world—is routinely monitored by the company. The company, in fact, fired 40 of its employees because they were caught in the act of surfing forbidden Web sites. Xerox's monitoring software recorded the unauthorized visits to shopping and pornography sites, and every minute spent at those sites.[14]

Is Xerox unique? No. A recent survey found that 41.5 percent of U.S. employers actively monitor or restrict employees' Web activity.[15]

Employers argue that they need surveillance controls. These controls allow them to make sure employees are working and not goofing off; that employees are not distributing organization secrets; and to protect the organization against employees who might create a hostile environment for other employees.

> An American Management Association poll recently revealed that more than half its midsize-to-large member organizations track individual employees' Internet connections at work, and more than a third store and review employees' e-mail. What are the implications of such monitoring for employee motivation?

The surveillance dilemma is exacerbated by the blurring of workplace parameters. There seems to be little dispute that employers have the right to monitor employees at work, when using the organization's equipment, and when employees know they are being watched. But as home life and work life are increasingly intermingled—for instance, employees doing job-related work at home rather than at the office—the ethics and legality of surveillance is less clear.

Selected Implications for Group Behavior

In Chapter 12, we described how online leadership differs from face-to-face leadership. In this section, we'll show how three other group issues—specifically decision making, communication, and organizational politics—take on a different look and importance in e-organizations.

Decision Making   The traditional approach taken in OB when discussing decision making needs to be modified for e-organizations. Exactly what those modifications should be are not yet fully clear. However, we offer two projections.

First, individual decision-making models are likely to become increasingly obsolete. E-organizations are typically team-based communities. So group decision-making models will offer greater relevance.

Second, the thoughtful, rational models of decision making—which dominate the management literature (see Chapter 5)—will be replaced by action models.

There are no proven business models for e-organizations.[16] Success goes to firms that value experimentation—those that use trial and error, that are able to gather data quickly and assimilate it, and that can accept failure and learn from it.

E-organizations don't have the luxury of trying to fine-tune decisions in search of perfection. E-organizations make decisions with often very limited information and, as a result, don't fear making mistakes. Decisions in e-organizations are in a continual flux, with past choices being continually modified and even discarded. And routine decision programs are essentially useless because few of the decisions that need to be made have been encountered before. So not only do decisions in e-orgs need to be made fast, they have to be made based on little previous experience. This, of course, increases the probability of errors and the need to be able to recover fast from mistakes and move on.

Communication E-organizations are rewriting the rules of communication. Because they're designed around comprehensive, integrated information networks, traditional hierarchical levels no longer constrain communication. E-organizations allow, even encourage, individuals to communicate directly without going through channels. Employees can communicate instantly anytime, with anyone, anywhere. As noted in Chapter 10, these open communication systems break down historical status hierarchies. They make obsolete or revise interpersonal communication concepts such as the distinction between formal and informal networks, nonverbal communication, and filtering. They also redefine how activities such as meetings, negotiations, supervision, and "water cooler" talk are conducted. For instance, virtual meetings allow people in geographically dispersed locations to meet regularly. Moreover, it's now easier for employees in San Francisco and Singapore to share company gossip than those offline employees who work two cubicles apart. And employees in a number of industries even have Web sites that are becoming electronic grapevines.[17] Young lawyers are going to www.greedyassociates.com to gripe about working conditions and pay; truckers are comparing rigs and routes on www.truckinlife.com; and flight attendants share gossip at www.insidetheweb.com.

The downside of this open communication network is communication overload. E-mail, specifically, is overwhelming many employees.[18] A recent poll found that the typical employee receives between 11 and 20 work-related e-mails a day and that 25 percent of workers report getting more than 30 emails a day.[19] These frequent incoming communication interruptions cost employees valuable time, erode their ability to concentrate, and can negatively affect their work productivity.

Politics and Networking OB recognizes the political nature of organizations, the role that politics play in decision making, and the importance of networking in developing contacts both within and outside an organization. But preliminary indicators suggest that effective politicking and networking are different in e-orgs than in the more traditional offline organization.

In traditional organizations, effective politicians keep themselves visible, use impression-management techniques, and participate in activities that will put them in close contact with influential people. But these are essentially face-to-face activities that aren't likely to be as effective in e-organizations. E-politicians are likely to rely much more on cyber-schmoozing via the electronic grapevine. Internet chat rooms and message boards, for instance, open up opportunities to meet and talk with people who can help employees be more effective in their jobs and in their careers.[20]

Cyber-schmoozing isn't likely to replace the water cooler, cocktail party, university alumni get-togethers, or trade shows as places to make contacts and build political allies. But online networking will become increasingly popular and effective as a supplement to more traditional political channels.

Will e-Orgs Redefine Interpersonal Relationships?

Electronic technology has redefined workplace possibilities. Employees in e-organizations are no longer constrained by time or place in doing their work. But what are the implications of these e-orgs to interpersonal relationships?

There is substantive evidence that people generally are spending more time online today than just a few years ago. For instance, in 1997, the mean time people spent online was 4.4 hours per week. In 1999, it was 7.6 hours. In 2000, it was 8.2 hours.[21] Preliminary evidence from a Stanford University study indicated that the more time people spent online, the less time they spent in real-life relationships with friends and family.[22] About one-quarter of regular Web users reported that they were spending less time attending social activities and talking on the phone to friends and family; and 13 percent reported reduced face-to-face social interactions.[23] One of the Stanford study's co-authors, in fact, expressed concern that the Internet could become the ultimate isolating technology, promoting individual behavior over community involvement. However, data from more recent surveys suggest that the Stanford conclusions may have been premature.[24] The Internet may not be as threatening to interpersonal relationships as first thought. The latest data indicate that only a small percentage of Internet users spend less time with family and friends than before they went online. The majority of Internet users report no negative social effects from logging on. What does seem to surface is that the Internet has different effects on extroverts and introverts. Extroverts, who like making new friends, are using the Internet to widen their social network. In contrast, when introverts use the Internet, it undermines their offline social interactions.

EXHIBIT 16-2

Source: Seattle-Post Intelligencer, Saturday, September 18, 1999.

It's far too early in the development of the digital age to conclude that the Internet will undermine a sense of social community. But it clearly creates new ways to interact with work colleagues. Employees will increasingly be working on teams with people they've never met and may never meet. They'll develop "office" friendships with people thousands of miles away. And "good interpersonal skills" may increasingly mean not only the ability to interact effectively with people face to face, but may include the skills to communicate warmth, emotion, trust, and leadership through written words on a computer screen.

CONCEPTUAL FRAMEWORKS FOR ANALYZING WORK TASKS

"Every day was the same thing," Frank Greer began. "Put the right passenger seat into Jeeps as they came down the assembly line, pop in four bolts locking the seat frame to the car body, then tighten the bolts with my electric wrench. Thirty cars and 120 bolts an hour, eight hours a day. I didn't care that they were paying me $22 an hour, I was going crazy. I did it for almost a year and a half. Finally, I just said to my wife that this isn't going to be the way I'm going to spend the rest of my life. My brain was turning to Jell-O on that job. So I quit. Now I work in a print shop and I make less than $15 an hour. But let me tell you, the work I do is really interesting. It challenges me! I look forward every morning to going to work again."

Frank Greer is acknowledging two facts we all know: (1) jobs are different and (2) some are more interesting and challenging than others. These facts have not gone unnoticed by OB researchers. They have responded by developing a number of **task characteristics theories** that seek to identify task characteristics of jobs, how these characteristics are combined to form different jobs, and the relationship of these task characteristics to employee motivation, satisfaction, and performance.

There are at least seven different task characteristics theories.[25] Fortunately, there is a significant amount of overlap among them.[26] For instance, Herzberg's two-factor theory and the research on the achievement need (both discussed in Chapter 6) are essentially task characteristics theories. You'll remember that Herzberg argued that jobs that provided opportunities for achievement, recognition, responsibility, and the like would increase employee satisfaction. Similarly, McClelland demonstrated that high achievers performed best in jobs that offered personal responsibility, feedback, and moderate risks.

In this section, we review the three most important task characteristics theories—requisite task attributes theory, the job characteristics model, and the social information processing model.

Requisite Task Attributes Theory

The task characteristics approach began with the pioneering work of Turner and Lawrence in the mid-1960s.[27] They developed a research study to assess the effect of different kinds of jobs on employee satisfaction and absenteeism. They predicted that employees would prefer jobs that were complex and challenging; that is, such jobs would increase satisfaction and result in lower absence rates. They defined job complexity in terms of six task characteristics: (1) variety; (2) autonomy; (3) responsibility; (4) knowledge and skill; (5) required social interaction; and (6) optional social interaction. The higher a job scored on these characteristics, according to Turner and Lawrence, the more complex it was.

Their findings confirmed their absenteeism prediction. Employees in high-complexity tasks had better attendance records. But they found no general corre-

task characteristics theories

Theories that seek to identify task characteristics in jobs, how these characteristics are combined to form different jobs, and their relationship to employee motivation, satisfaction, and performance.

lation between task complexity and satisfaction—until they broke their data down by the background of employees. When individual differences in the form of urban-versus-rural background were taken into account, employees from urban settings were shown to be more satisfied with low-complexity jobs. Employees with rural backgrounds reported higher satisfaction in high-complexity jobs. Turner and Lawrence concluded that workers in larger communities had a variety of nonwork interests and thus were less involved and motivated by their work. In contrast, workers from smaller towns had fewer nonwork interests and were more receptive to the complex tasks of their jobs.

Turner and Lawrence's requisite task attributes theory was important for at least three reasons. First, they demonstrated that employees did respond differently to different types of jobs. Second, they provided a preliminary set of task attributes by which jobs could be assessed. And third, they focused attention on the need to consider the influence of individual differences on employees' reaction to jobs.

The Job Characteristics Model

Turner and Lawrence's requisite task attributes theory laid the foundation for what is today the dominant framework for defining task characteristics and understanding their relationship to employee motivation, performance, and satisfaction. That is Hackman and Oldham's **job characteristics model** (JCM).[28]

According to the JCM, any job can be described in terms of five core job dimensions, defined as follows:

1. **Skill variety**: The degree to which the job requires a variety of different activities so the worker can use a number of different skills and talent.
2. **Task identity**: The degree to which the job requires completion of a whole and identifiable piece of work.
3. **Task significance**: The degree to which the job has a substantial impact on the lives or work of other people.
4. **Autonomy**: The degree to which the job provides substantial freedom, independence, and discretion to the individual in scheduling the work and in determining the procedures to be used in carrying it out.
5. **Feedback**: The degree to which carrying out the work activities required by the job results in the individual obtaining direct and clear information about the effectiveness of his or her performance.

Exhibit 16-3 on page 466 offers examples of job activities that rate high and low for each characteristic.

Exhibit 16-4 on page 467 presents the model. Note how the first three dimensions—skill variety, task identity, and task significance—combine to create meaningful work. That is, if these three characteristics exist in a job, we can predict that the incumbent will view the job as being important, valuable, and worthwhile. Note, too, that jobs that possess autonomy give job incumbents a feeling of personal responsibility for the results and that, if a job provides feedback, employees will know how effectively they are performing. From a motivational standpoint, the model says that internal rewards are obtained by individuals when they learn (knowledge of results) that they personally (experienced responsibility) have performed well on a task that they care about (experienced meaningfulness).[29] The more that these three psychological states are present, the greater will be employees' motivation, performance, and satisfaction, and the lower their absenteeism and likelihood of leaving the organization. As Exhibit 16-4 shows, the links between the job dimensions and the outcomes are moderated or adjusted by the strength of the individual's growth

job characteristics model
Identifies five job characteristics and their relationship to personal and work outcomes.

skill variety
The degree to which the job requires a variety of different activities.

task identity
The degree to which the job requires completion of a whole and identifiable piece of work.

task significance
The degree to which the job has a substantial impact on the lives or work of other people.

autonomy
The degree to which the job provides substantial freedom and discretion to the individual in scheduling the work and in determining the procedures to be used in carrying it out.

feedback
The degree to which carrying out the work activities required by a job results in the individual obtaining direct and clear information about the effectiveness of his or her performance.

EXHIBIT

16-3

Examples of High and Low Job Characteristics

Skill Variety

High variety	The owner-operator of a garage who does electrical repairs, rebuilds engines, does body work, and interacts with customers
Low variety	A body shop worker who sprays paint eight hours a day

Task Identity

High identity	A cabinetmaker who designs a piece of furniture, selects the wood, builds the object, and finishes it to perfection
Low identity	A worker in a furniture factory who operates a lathe solely to make table legs

Task Significance

High significance	Nursing the sick in a hospital intensive care unit
Low significance	Sweeping hospital floors

Autonomy

High autonomy	A salesperson who schedules his or her own work for the day, makes visits without supervision, and decides on the most effective sales techniques for each particular potential customer
Low autonomy	A salesperson who is given a specific number of leads each day and is required to use a standardized sales script with each potential customer

Feedback

High feedback	An electronics factory worker who assembles a radio and then tests it to determine if it operates properly
Low feedback	An electronics factory worker who assembles a radio and then routes it to a quality-control inspector who tests it for proper operation and makes needed adjustments

Source: Adapted from G. Johns, *Organizational Behavior: Understanding and Managing Life at Work,* 4th ed. Copyright © 1996 by HarperCollins College Publishers. Reprinted by permission of Addison-Wesley Educational Publishers, Inc.

need; that is, by the employee's desire for self-esteem and self-actualization. This means that individuals with a high growth need are more likely to experience the psychological states when their jobs are enriched than are their counterparts with a low growth need. Moreover, they will respond more positively to the psychological states when they are present than will individuals with a low growth need.

The core dimensions can be combined into a single predictive index, called the **motivating potential score** (MPS). Its computation is shown in Exhibit 16-5.

motivating potential score

A predictive index suggesting the motivating potential in a job.

Jobs that are high on motivating potential must be high on at least one of the three factors that lead to experienced meaningfulness, and they must be high on both autonomy and feedback. If jobs score high on motivating potential, the model predicts that motivation, performance, and satisfaction will be positively affected, whereas the likelihood of absence and turnover will be lessened.

The job characteristics model has been well researched. Most of the evidence supports the general framework of the theory—that is, there is a multiple set of job characteristics and these characteristics impact behavioral outcomes.[30] But there is still considerable debate around the five specific core dimensions in the JCM, the

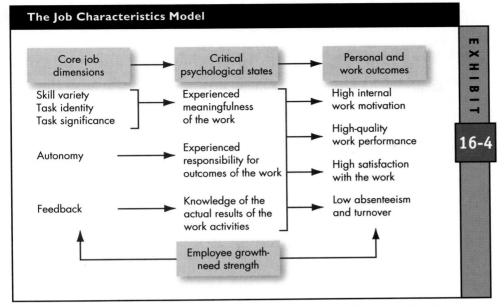

EXHIBIT

16-4

Source: J. R. Hackman and G. R. Oldham, *Work Design* (excerpted from pages 78–80) © 1980 by Addison-Wesley Publishing Co., Inc. Reprinted by permission of Addison–Wesley Longman, Inc.

multiplicative properties of the MPS, and the validity of growth-need strength as a moderating variable.

There is some question about whether task identity adds to the model's predictive ability,[31] and there is evidence suggesting that skill variety may be redundant with autonomy.[32] Furthermore, a number of studies have found that by adding all the variables in the MPS, rather than adding some and multiplying by others, the MPS becomes a better predictor of work outcomes.[33] Finally, the strength of an individual's growth needs as a meaningful moderating variable has been called into question.[34] Other variables, such as the presence or absence of social cues, perceived equity with comparison groups, and propensity to assimilate work experience,[35] may be more valid in moderating the job characteristics–outcome relationship. Given the current state of research on moderating variables, one should be cautious in unequivocally accepting growth-need strength as originally included in the JCM.

Where does this leave us? Given the current state of evidence, we can make the following statements with relative confidence: (1) People who work on jobs

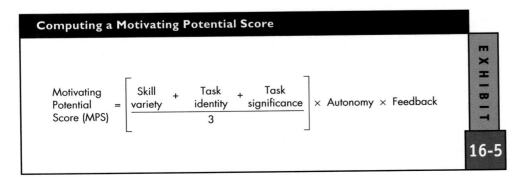

EXHIBIT

16-5

with high-core job dimensions are generally more motivated, satisfied, and productive than are those who do not; and (2) job dimensions operate through the psychological states in influencing personal and work outcome variables rather than influencing them directly.[36]

Social Information Processing Model

At the beginning of this section on task characteristics theories, do you remember Frank Greer complaining about his former job on the Jeep assembly line? Would it surprise you to know that one of Frank's best friends, Russ Wright, is still working at Jeep, doing the same job that Frank did, and that Russ thinks his job is perfectly fine? Probably not! Why? Because, consistent with our discussion of perception in Chapter 5, we recognize that people can look at the same job and evaluate it differently. The fact that people respond to their jobs as they perceive them rather than to the objective jobs themselves is the central thesis in our third task characteristics theory. It's called the **social information processing (SIP) model**.[37]

social information processing (SIP) model

People respond to their jobs as they perceive them rather than to the objective jobs themselves.

The SIP model argues that employees adopt attitudes and behaviors in response to the social cues provided by others with whom they have contact. These others can be co-workers, supervisors, friends, family members, or customers. For instance, Gary Ling got a summer job working in a British Columbia sawmill. Because jobs were scarce and this one paid particularly well, Gary arrived on his first day of work highly motivated. Two weeks later, however, his motivation was quite low. What happened was that his co-workers consistently bad-mouthed their jobs. They said the work was boring, that having to clock in and out proved management didn't trust them, and that supervisors never listened to their opinions. The objective characteristics of Gary's job had not changed in the two-week period; rather, Gary had reconstructed reality based on messages he had received from others.

MYTH OR SCIENCE?

"Everyone Wants a Challenging Job"

This statement is false. In spite of all the attention focused by the media, academicians, and social scientists on human potential and the needs of individuals, there is no evidence to support that the vast majority of workers want challenging jobs.[38] Some individuals prefer highly complex and challenging jobs; others prosper in simple, routinized work.

The individual-difference variable that seems to gain the greatest support for explaining who prefers a challenging job and who doesn't is the strength of an individual's higher-order needs.[39] Individuals with high growth needs are more responsive to challenging work. What percentage of rank-and-file workers actually desire higher-order need satisfactions and will respond positively to challenging jobs? No current data are available, but a study from the 1970s estimated the figure at about 15 percent.[40] Even after adjusting for changing work attitudes and the growth

in white-collar jobs, it seems unlikely that the number today exceeds 40 percent.

The strongest voice advocating challenging jobs has *not* been workers—it's been professors, social-science researchers, and journalists. Professors, researchers, and journalists undoubtedly made their career choices, to some degree, because they wanted jobs that gave them autonomy, identity, and challenge. That, of course, is their choice. But for them to project their needs onto the workforce in general is presumptuous.

Not every employee is looking for a challenging job. Many workers meet their higher-order needs *off* the job. There are 168 hours in every individual's week. Work rarely consumes more than 30 percent of this time. That leaves considerable opportunity, even for individuals with strong growth needs, to find higher-order need satisfaction outside the workplace.

A number of studies generally confirm the validity of the SIP model.[41] For instance, it has been shown that employee motivation and satisfaction can be manipulated by subtle actions such as a co-worker or boss commenting on the existence or absence of job features such as difficulty, challenge, and autonomy. So managers should give as much (or more) attention to employees' perceptions of their jobs as to the actual characteristics of those jobs. For instance, they might spend more time telling employees how interesting and important their jobs are. And managers should also not be surprised that newly hired employees and people transferred or promoted to a new position are more likely to be receptive to social information than are those with greater seniority.

WORK SPACE DESIGN

The 140 employees at SEI Investments in Oaks, Pennsylvania, do much of their work in teams. To enhance team flexibility and to respond to the changing nature of projects, SEI has created an office design compatible with its team focus.[42] Employees congregate in large, open rooms, with no walls or cubicle dividers separating work spaces. Each person is given a suite of minimal furniture, all on wheels. This allows members to set up their "office" with others when new teams are created. And when projects are completed, team members disband by unplugging their voice and data cords that are attached by coils to the beams overhead. Management argues that this open office design not only facilitates fluid team structures, it also eliminates the physical barriers that inhibit employees from sharing information and learning from others.

SEI Investments is not unique. Hundreds of companies—including Alcoa, Northern Telecom Ltd., Du Pont, Hewlett-Packard, 3Com, Sun Microsystems, Chiat/Day advertising, and the Greater Omaha Packing Company—have redesigned their buildings and workplaces with the intent of reshaping employee attitudes and behaviors.[43] In this section, we'll look specifically at how the amount of work space made available to employees, the arrangement or layout of that work space, and the degree of privacy it provides affect an employee's behavior.[44] In addition, we'll discuss the growing popularity of feng shui.

Kathy Faragalli works in SEI Investments' open office design. Coiled phone and data wires frame her fully mobile work space.

Size Size is defined by the square feet per employee. Historically, the most important determinant of space provided to employees was status.[45] The higher an individual was in the organization's hierarchy, the larger office he or she typically got. So at large companies, like IBM and General Motors, senior executives may have been assigned 800 square feet plus 300 square feet for a private secretary's office. A section manager may have gotten 400 square feet, a unit manager 120, and supervisors only 80 square feet. But this form of allocation is disappearing. As organizations have sought to become more egalitarian, the trends have been toward reducing the space dedicated to specific employees, lessening or eliminating space allocations based on hierarchical position, and making more space available in which groups or teams can meet.

It's been estimated that, over the past decade, the personal office space provided by organizations to administrative employees has shrunk 25 to 50 percent.[46] Part of this has been economically motivated. Space costs money and reducing space cuts costs. But a lot of this reduction can be traced to reengineering. As jobs have been redesigned and traditional hierarchies replaced with teamwork, the need for large offices has lessened.[47]

Today, when extra space is being allocated, rather than giving it to specific individuals, the trend is toward setting it aside where people can meet and teams can work. These "public spaces" can be used for socializing, small group meetings, or as places where team members can work through problems.

Arrangement   Whereas size measures the amount of space per employee, arrangement refers to the distance between people and facilities. As we'll show, the arrangement of one's workplace is important primarily because it significantly influences social interaction.

There is a sizable amount of research that supports that you're more likely to interact with individuals who are physically close.[48] An employee's work location, therefore, is likely to influence the information to which one is privy and one's inclusion or exclusion from organization events. Whether you are on a certain grapevine network or not, for instance, will be largely determined by where you are physically located in the organization.

One topic that has received a considerable amount of attention is furniture arrangements in traditional offices.[49] Unlike factory floors, individuals typically have some leeway in laying out their office furniture. And the arrangement of an office conveys nonverbal messages to visitors. For instance, a desk between two parties conveys formality and the authority of the officeholder, while setting chairs so individuals can sit at right angles to each other conveys a more natural and informal relationship.

Privacy   Privacy is in part a function of the amount of space per person and the arrangement of that space. But it also is influenced by walls, partitions, and other physical barriers. One of the most widespread work space design trends in recent years has been the phasing out of closed offices and replacing them with open office plans that have few, if any, walls or doors. Sometimes described as the cave versus cube debate, the former provides privacy whereas the latter facilitates open communication. It's estimated that 40 million Americans, or nearly 60 percent of the whole U.S. white-collar workforce, now work in cubes.[50]

Caves limit interaction. So organizations have sought to increase flexibility and employee collaboration by removing physical barriers like high walls, closed offices, and doors. Yet, while the trend is clearly toward cubes, organizations are making exceptions for employees engaged in work that requires deep concentration.[51] Companies like Microsoft, Apple Computer, and Adobe Systems, for example, continue to rely primarily on private offices for software programmers. People who write code need to cooperate with others at times, but theirs is essentially a lonely task that requires tremendous concentration. This is best achieved in a closed workplace, cut off from others.

What about individual differences? There is growing evidence that the desire for privacy is a strong one on the part of many people.[52] Yet the trend is clearly toward less privacy at the workplace. Further research is needed to determine whether organizational efforts to open work spaces and individual preferences for privacy are incompatible and result in lower employee performance and satisfaction.

Source: Non Sequitur by Wiley © Universal Press Syndicate.

Feng Shui As we introduced at the opening of this chapter, feng shui is an ancient Chinese system for arranging a person's surroundings so they are in harmony and balance with nature.[53] We include the topic here because of its growing popularity. Feng shui guides the design of most buildings and workplaces in China, Taiwan, Hong Kong, Malaysia, and Singapore. More importantly, its principles are increasingly being applied outside Asia. For instance, feng shui principles have been embraced in the United States and Britain by Donald Trump in his buildings, Universal Studios, Merrill Lynch, Marks & Spencer, and Virgin Atlantic.[54]

The single most important concept in feng shui is that of "chi" or life force. In terms of work space design, managers should layout buildings and offices so as to use this chi to gain greater strength and harmony in the workplace. Just as acupuncture has been used for thousands of years to help people attain balance and harmony in the free flow of chi through their physical bodies, feng shui works to attain the same balance and harmony with physical structures.

So how can managers attract positive chi to their workplaces? The following is a partial list of feng-shui-based suggestions. They'll give you some insights into its philosophy:[55]

1. *Office location and layout.* The manager's office should be as far as possible from the entrance to the building. The farther from the entrance, the greater the power. And never have your office across from the front door because it means your money can fly out. There should be no facing doorways because this creates rivalries and general bad feelings between people who occupy opposing offices. A screen across a front door will block evil. All protruding corners in an office should be rounded off to allow positive energy to flow.

2. *Desk position.* When seated behind his or her desk, a person must always be able to see the door. If there is no door, the desk needs to be placed so a person can see the workplace's entrance. If there is more than one door, the line of sight should be toward the door most frequently used. The desk should also be placed far inside the room to provide as much view of the room as possible because what cannot be seen cannot be controlled. Avoid placing a desk in direct line with the door. This makes a person vulnerable to noises and interruptions, and unprotected from unwelcome surprises.

3. *Water.* Water is associated with prosperity and good chi. Fish tanks and aquariums are excellent sources for bringing success and prosperity into an office. The movement and flow of water in a fish tank symbolizes positive cash flow. The popularity of fountains outside office buildings is consistent with the view that the movement and splash of flowing water encourages good chi.

4. *Plants and flowers.* Plants and flower bring good luck and happiness but they must be healthy and thriving.

5. *Reflections.* A mirror at the entrance to a building acts to repel bad things. And a mirror placed anywhere in a building will symbolically double whatever it reflects. So a mirror placed beside the cash register in a store will double income and one located next to where customers gather will double the number of customers.

Does feng shui work? To the degree that employees expect their workplace to be consistent with feng shui principles, which seems particularly true in countries with strong Chinese influence, it should make people feel comfortable and hence increase satisfaction. And although there is no hard evidence, it seems reasonable to conclude that the use of feng shui in these countries should help to attract and keep employees.

Proponents argue that positive chi is associated with health, wealth, and happiness. There is no objective evidence to support this claim. And although there are also no hard data to demonstrate that offices organized according to feng shui principles decrease stress, many of these principles would seem to be compatible with a more protected and relaxed workplace. For managers in Asian countries and those overseeing workforces with large numbers of Asian-influenced employees, we would propose giving careful consideration to adopting feng shui principles. If perception is reality, then arranging workplaces to maximize positive chi is likely to lead to higher productivity and satisfaction among its followers.

Workspace Design and Productivity   How does a redesigned work space positively affect employee productivity? Studies suggest that workspace, in and of itself, doesn't have a substantial motivational impact on people.[56] Rather, it makes certain behaviors easier or harder to perform. In this way, employee effectiveness is enhanced or reduced. More specifically, evidence indicates that work space designs that increase employee access, comfort, and flexibility are likely to influence motivation and productivity positively.[57] For instance, Amoco Corp. (now part of British Petroleum) in Denver reported a 25 percent decrease in product cycle time, a 75 percent decrease in formal meeting time, an 80 percent reduction in duplicated files, and a 44 percent reduction in overall space costs after offices were redesigned to facilitate teamwork.[58] Based on the evidence to date, we suggest an approach called "cognitive ergonomics"—which means matching the office to the brain work.[59] Jobs that are complex and require high degrees of concentration are likely to be made more difficult by noise and constant interruptions. Such jobs are best done in closed offices. But most jobs don't require quiet and privacy. In fact, quite the contrary. Jobs today increasingly require regular interaction with others to achieve maximum productivity. This is probably best achieved in an open-office setting.

WORK REDESIGN OPTIONS

What are some of the options managers have at their disposal if they want to redesign or change the makeup of employee jobs? The following discusses four options: job rotation, job enlargement, job enrichment, and team-based designs.

Job Rotation

job rotation

The periodic shifting of a worker from one task to another.

If employees suffer from overroutinization of their work, one alternative is to use **job rotation** (or what many now call *cross-training*). When an activity is no longer challenging, the employee is rotated to another job, usually at the same level, that has similar skill requirements.

In recent years, job rotation has been adopted by many manufacturing firms as a means of increasing flexibility and avoiding layoffs.[60] For instance, managers at Apex Precision Technologies, a custom-machine shop in Indiana, continually train workers on all of the company's equipment so they can be moved around in response to the requirements of incoming orders. During the 2001 recession, Cleveland-based Lincoln Electric moved some salaried workers to hourly clerical jobs and rotated production workers among various machines. This manufacturer of welding and cutting parts has been able to minimize layoffs because of its commitment to continual cross-training and moving workers wherever they're needed.

The strengths of job rotation are that it reduces boredom and increases motivation through diversifying the employee's activities. It also has indirect benefits for the organization because employees with a wider range of skills give management more flexibility in scheduling work, adapting to changes, and filling vacancies. On the other hand, job rotation is not without its drawbacks. Training costs are increased, and productivity is reduced by moving a worker into a new position just when his or her efficiency at the prior job was creating organizational economies. Job rotation also creates disruptions. Members of the work group have to adjust to the new employee. And supervisors may also have to spend more time answering questions and monitoring the work of recently rotated employees.

Job Enlargement

More than 35 years ago, the idea of expanding jobs horizontally, or what we call **job enlargement**, grew in popularity. Increasing the number and variety of tasks that an individual performed resulted in jobs with more diversity. Instead of only sorting the incoming mail by department, for instance, a mail sorter's job could be enlarged to include physically delivering the mail to the various departments or running outgoing letters through the postage meter.

job enlargement
The horizontal expansion of jobs.

Efforts at job enlargement met with less than enthusiastic results.[61] As one employee who experienced such a redesign on his job remarked, "Before I had one lousy job. Now, through enlargement, I have three!" However, there have been some successful applications of job enlargement. The job of housekeeper in some smaller hotels, for example, includes not only cleaning bathrooms, making beds, and vacuuming, but also replacing burned out light bulbs, providing turn-down service, and restocking mini-bars.

So, while job enlargement attacked the lack of diversity in overspecialized jobs, it did little to instill challenge or meaningfulness to a worker's activities. Job enrichment was introduced to deal with the shortcomings of enlargement.

Job Enrichment

Job enrichment refers to the vertical expansion of jobs. It increases the degree to which the worker controls the planning, execution, and evaluation of his or her work. An enriched job organizes tasks so as to allow the worker to do a complete activity, increases the employee's freedom and independence, increases responsibility, and provides feedback, so an individual will be able to assess and correct his or her own performance.[62]

job enrichment
The vertical expansion of jobs.

How does management enrich an employee's job? Exhibit 16-7 on page 474 offers suggested guidelines based on the job characteristics model discussed earlier in the chapter.

To illustrate job enrichment in practice, let's look at what management at Banc One in Chicago did with its international trade banking department.[63] The department's chief product is commercial letters of credit—essentially a bank

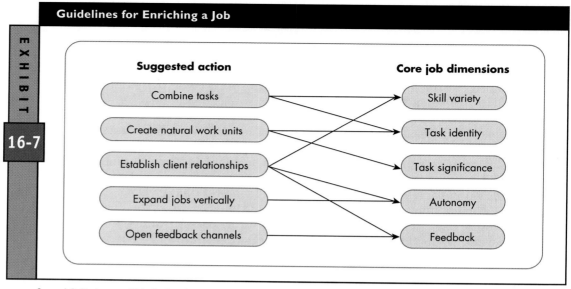

Guidelines for Enriching a Job

EXHIBIT

16-7

Suggested action

- Combine tasks
- Create natural work units
- Establish client relationships
- Expand jobs vertically
- Open feedback channels

Core job dimensions

- Skill variety
- Task identity
- Task significance
- Autonomy
- Feedback

Source: J. R. Hackman and J. L. Suttle, eds., *Improving Life at Work* (Glenview, IL: Scott, Foresman, 1977), p. 138.

guarantee to stand behind huge import and export transactions. Prior to enriching jobs, the department's 300 employees processed documents in an assembly-line fashion, with errors creeping in at each handoff. Meanwhile, employees did little to hide the boredom they were experiencing from doing narrow and specialized tasks. Management enriched these jobs by making each clerk a trade expert who was able to handle a customer from start to finish. After 200 hours of training in finance and law, the clerks became full-service advisers who could turn around documents in a day while advising clients on such arcane matters as bank procedures in Turkey and U.S. munitions' export controls. And the results? Department productivity more than tripled, employee satisfaction soared, and transaction volume rose more than 10 percent a year.

The Banc One example shouldn't be taken as a blanket endorsement of job enrichment. The overall evidence generally shows that job enrichment reduces absenteeism and turnover costs and increases satisfaction, but on the critical issue of productivity, the evidence is inconclusive.[64] In some situations, such as at Banc One, job enrichment increases productivity; in others, it decreases it. However, even when productivity goes down, there does seem to be consistently more conscientious use of resources and a higher quality of product or service.

Team-Based Work Designs Revisited

Because people are increasingly working in groups and teams, what can we say about the design of group-based work to try to improve employee performance in those groups?

We know a lot more about individual-based work design than we do about design at the group level,[65] mostly because the wide popularity of teams—specifically, assigning tasks to a group of individuals instead of to a single person—is a relatively recent phenomenon. That said, the best work in this area offers two sets of suggestions.[66]

First, the JCM recommendations seem to be as valid at the group level as they are at the individual level. Managers should expect a group to perform at a high level when (1) the group task requires members to use a variety of relatively high level skills; (2) the group task is a whole and meaningful piece of work, with a visible outcome; (3) the outcomes of the group's work on the task have significant consequences for other people; (4) the task provides group members with substantial autonomy for deciding how they do the work; and (5) work on the task generates regular, trustworthy feedback about how well the group is performing.

Second, group composition is critical to the success of the work group. Consistent with findings described in Chapter 9, managers should try to ensure that the following four conditions are met: (1) Individual members have the necessary task-relevant expertise to do their work; (2) the group is large enough to perform the work; (3) members possess interpersonal as well as task skills; and (4) membership is moderately diverse in terms of talents and perspectives.

ITT Industries, Inc., an engineering and diversified manufacturing firm based in White Plains, NY, uses teams in all its lines of business and designs aspects of its team projects to improve employee performance. Among its six "best practices" are putting projects together so that quick successes are possible because "that excites . . . and energizes people," according to Vince Fayad, an executive who serves as "head coach."

WORK SCHEDULE OPTIONS

Susan Ross is your classic "morning person." She rises each day at 5 A.M. sharp, full of energy. On the other hand, as she puts it, "I'm usually ready for bed right after the 7 P.M. news."

Susan's work schedule as a claims processor at The Hartford Financial Services Group is flexible. It allows her some degree of freedom as to when she comes to work and when she leaves. Her office opens at 6 A.M. and closes at 7 P.M. It's up to her how she schedules her eight-hour day within this 13-hour period. Because Susan is a morning person and also has a seven-year-old son who gets out of school at 3 P.M. every day, she opts to work from 6 A.M. to 3 P.M. "My work hours are perfect. I'm at the job when I'm mentally most alert, and I can be home to take care of my son after he gets out of school."

Most people work an eight-hour day, five days a week. They start at a fixed time and leave at a fixed time. And they do their work from their employer's place of business. But a number of organizations have introduced alternative work schedule options. In this section, we review some of these alternatives. The common theme among these is that they all increase flexibility for employees. In a work world where employees are increasingly complaining about being pressed for time and the difficulty of balancing work and personal responsibilities, increasing work schedule options can be a way to improve employee motivation, productivity, and satisfaction.

Flextime

Flextime is a scheduling option that allows employees, within specific parameters, to decide when to go to work. Susan Ross's work schedule at The Hartford is an example of flextime. But what specifically is flextime?

Flextime is short for flexible work hours. It allows employees some discretion over when they arrive at and leave work. Employees have to work a specific number of hours a week, but they are free to vary the hours of work within certain

flextime

Employees work during a common core time period each day but have discretion in forming their total workday from a flexible set of hours outside the core.

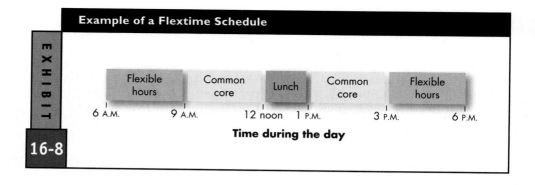

EXHIBIT

16-8

Example of a Flextime Schedule

| Flexible hours | Common core | Lunch | Common core | Flexible hours |

6 A.M.   9 A.M.   12 noon   1 P.M.   3 P.M.   6 P.M.

Time during the day

limits. As shown in Exhibit 16-8, each day consists of a common core, usually six hours, with a flexibility band surrounding the core. For example, exclusive of a one-hour lunch break, the core may be 9 A.M. to 3 P.M., with the office actually opening at 6 A.M. and closing at 6 P.M. All employees are required to be at their jobs during the common core period, but they are allowed to accumulate their other two hours before and/or after the core time. Some flextime programs allow extra hours to be accumulated and turned into a free day off each month.

Flextime has become an extremely popular scheduling option. The proportion of full-time U.S. employees on flextime almost doubled from the late 1980s to the late 1990s. Approximately 28 percent of the U.S. full-time workforce now has flexibility in their daily arrival and departure times.[67] And this is not just a U.S. phenomenon. In Germany, for instance, 29 percent of businesses have flextime for their employees.[68] But flextime isn't available to all employees equally. While 42.4 percent of U.S. managers enjoy the freedom of flextime, only 23.3 percent of manufacturing workers are offered a flexible schedule.[69]

The benefits claimed for flextime are numerous. They include reduced absenteeism, increased productivity, reduced overtime expenses, a lessening in hostility toward management, reduced traffic congestion around work sites, elimination of tardiness, and increased autonomy and responsibility for employees that may increase employee job satisfaction.[70] But beyond the claims, what's flextime's record?

Most of the performance evidence stacks up favorably. Flextime tends to reduce absenteeism and frequently improves worker productivity,[71] probably for several reasons. Employees can schedule their work hours to align with personal demands, thus reducing tardiness and absences, and employees can adjust their work activities to those hours in which they are individually more productive.

Flextime's major drawback is that it's not applicable to every job. It works well with clerical tasks for which an employee's interaction with people outside his or her department is limited. It is not a viable option for receptionists, sales personnel in retail stores, or similar jobs for which comprehensive service demands that people be at their work stations at predetermined times.

Job Sharing

job sharing

The practice of having two or more people split a 40-hour-a-week job.

A recent work scheduling innovation is **job sharing**. It allows two or more individuals to split a traditional 40-hour-a-week job. So, for example, one person might perform the job from 8 A.M. to noon, while another performs the same job from 1 P.M. to 5 P.M.; or the two could work full, but alternate, days.

Approximately 31 percent of large organizations now offer their employees job sharing.[72] Verizon (formerly Bell Atlantic) is one company that does. Sue Manix and Charlotte Schutzman, for instance, share the title of vice president of employee communications in the company's Philadelphia office.[73] Schutzman works Monday and Tuesday; Manix works Thursday and Friday; and they alternate Wednesdays. The two women have job shared for 10 years, acquiring promotions, numerous bonuses, and a 20-person staff along the way. With each having children at home, this arrangement allows them the flexibility to better balance their work and family responsibilities.

Job sharing allows the organization to draw on the talents of more than one individual in a given job. A bank manager who oversees two job sharers describes it as an opportunity to get two heads, but "pay for one."[74] It also opens up the opportunity to acquire skilled workers—for instance, women with young children and retirees—who might not be available on a full-time basis.[75] Many Japanese firms are increasingly considering job sharing—but for a very different reason.[76] Because Japanese executives are extremely reluctant to fire people, job sharing is seen as a potentially humanitarian means for avoiding layoffs due to overstaffing.

From the employee's perspective, job sharing increases flexibility. As such, it can increase motivation and satisfaction for those to whom a 40-hour-a-week job is just not practical. On the other hand, the major drawback from management's perspective is finding compatible pairs of employees who can successfully coordinate the intricacies of one job.[77]

Telecommuting

It might be close to the ideal job for many people. No commuting, flexible hours, freedom to dress as you please, and few or no interruptions from colleagues. It's called **telecommuting** and refers to employees who do their work at home at least two days a week on a computer that is linked to their office.[78] (A closely related term—*the virtual office*—is increasingly being used to describe employees who work out of their home on a relatively permanent basis.) Recent estimates indicate that between 9 million and 24 million people telecommute in the United States, depending on exactly how the term is defined.[79] This translates to about 10 percent or more of the workforce. Well-known organizations that actively encourage telecommuting include AT&T, IBM, Merrill Lynch, American Express, Hewlett-Packard, and a number of U.S. government agencies.[80] The concept is also catching on worldwide. In Finland, Sweden, Britain, and Germany, telecommuters represent 17, 15, 8, and 6 percent of their workforces, respectively.[81]

What kinds of jobs lend themselves to telecommuting? Three categories have been identified as most appropriate: routine information-handling tasks, mobile activities, and professional and other knowledge-related tasks.[82] Writers, attorneys, analysts, and employees who spend the majority of their time on computers or the telephone are natural candidates for telecommuting. For instance, telemarketers, customer-service representatives, reservation agents, and product-support specialists spend most of their time on the phone. As telecommuters, they can access information on their computer screens at home as easily as in the company's office.

telecommuting

Employees do their work at home on a computer that is linked to their office.

Telecommuting is redefining where one works or what is a "spacious corner office."

There are numerous stories of telecommuting's success.[83] For instance, 3,500 Merrill Lynch employees telecommute. And after the program was in place just a year, management reported an increase in productivity of between 15 and 20 percent among their telecommuters, 3.5 fewer sick days a year, and a six percent decrease in turnover. Putnam Investments, located in Boston, has found telecommuting to be an attractive recruitment tool. The company was having difficulty attracting new hires. But after introducing telecommuting, the number of its applicants grew by 20-fold. And Putnam's management calculates that the 12 percent of its employees who telecommute have substantially higher productivity than in-office staff and about one-tenth the attrition rate.

The potential pluses for management of telecommuting include a larger labor pool from which to select, higher productivity, less turnover, improved morale, and reduced office-space costs. The major downside for management is less direct supervision of employees. In addition, in today's team-focused workplace, telecommuting may make it more difficult for management to coordinate teamwork.[84] From the employee's standpoint, telecommuting offers a considerable increase in flexibility. But not without costs. For employees with a high social need, telecommuting can increase feelings of isolation and reduce job satisfaction. And all telecommuters potentially suffer from the "out of sight, out of mind" effect. Employees who aren't at their desks, who miss meetings, and who don't share in day-to-day informal workplace interactions may be at a disadvantage when it comes to raises and promotions. It's easy for bosses to overlook or undervalue the contribution of employees whom they see less regularly.

The long-term future of telecommuting depends on some questions for which we don't yet have definitive answers. For instance, will employees who do their work at home be at a disadvantage in office politics? And do non–work-related distractions such as children, neighbors, and the close proximity of the refrigerator significantly reduce productivity for those without superior willpower and discipline?

OB in the News

9/11 Boosts Appeal of Telecommuting

Telecommuting got a big boost following the September 11 terrorist attacks on New York and Washington. It offers a partial solution to employees who are uncomfortable working in large office complexes or who desire to cut back on air travel. A poll taken after September 11 found that more than 20 percent of American workers said that being allowed to telecommute might reduce their stress levels. Says Chuck Wilsker, executive director at Washington-based International Telework Association & Council, "A lot of people are going to want to telecommute more, and this is going to be a permanent change."

For instance, Kyle Kraus, president of IT-consulting firm LanTrax in Buffalo, is cutting back on business travel and telecommuting more. Kraus is also saving time by not undergoing hours of security checks at the airport. "At a time when threats are disrupting business so much, working at home becomes more attractive," Kraus says. "People who have the option to telecommute and feel safe will do so more often."

The terrorists strikes also seem to have made employers more willing to let staff members work from remote locations. Avaya, a New Jersey-based provider of communications software, says more firms are requesting information about the technology and systems they would have to install for letting employees work from multiple sites other than headquarters.

Source: S. Armour, "Worried Workers Turn to Telecommuting," USA Today, October 17, 2001, p. 1B.

SUMMARY AND IMPLICATIONS FOR MANAGERS

Technology is changing people's jobs and their work behavior. Quality management and its emphasis on continuous process improvement can increase employee stress as individuals find that performance expectations are constantly being increased. Process reengineering is eliminating millions of jobs and completely reshaping the jobs of those who remain. And mass customization requires employees to learn new skills.

The e-organization, with its heavy reliance on the Internet, increases potential workplace distractions. Managers need to be particularly alert to the negative effects of cyberloafing. In addition, the e-org will rely less on individual decision making and more on virtual-team decision making. But probably the most significant influence of the e-org is that it is rewriting the rules of communication. Traditional barriers are coming down, replaced by networks that cut across vertical levels and horizontal units.

An understanding of work design can help managers design jobs that positively affect employee motivation. For instance, jobs that score high in motivating potential increase an employee's control over key elements in his or her work. Therefore, jobs that offer autonomy, feedback, and similar complex task characteristics help to satisfy the individual goals of employees who desire greater control over their work. Of course, consistent with the social information processing model, the perception that task characteristics are complex is probably more important in influencing an employee's motivation than the objective task characteristics themselves. The key, then, is to provide employees with cues that suggest that their jobs score high on factors such as skill variety, task identity, autonomy, and feedback.

Work space design variables such as size, arrangement, and privacy have implications for communication, status, socializing, satisfaction, and productivity. For instance, an enclosed office typically conveys more status than an open cubicle. So employees with a high need for status might find an enclosed office increases their job satisfaction.

Alternative work schedule options such as flextime, job sharing, and telecommuting have grown in popularity in recent years. They have become an important strategic tool as organizations try to increase the flexibility their employees need in a changing workplace.

Jobs Are Becoming Obsolete

Prior to 1800, very few people had a job. People worked hard raising food or making things at home. They had no regular work hours, no job descriptions, no bosses, and no employee benefits. Instead, they put in long hours on a shifting array of tasks, in a variety of locations, on a schedule set by the weather and needs of the day. It was the industrial revolution and the creation of large manufacturing companies that brought about the concept of what we have come to think of as *jobs*.[a]

But the conditions that have created "the job" are disappearing. Customized production is pushing out mass production; most workers now handle information, not physical products; and competitive conditions are demanding rapid response to changing markets. Media people like to talk about the disappearance of jobs in certain industries or countries—such as steel and textile jobs in the United States. The reality is that *the job itself* is becoming obsolete.

In a fast-moving economy, jobs are rigid solutions to an elastic problem. When the work that needs doing changes constantly—which increasingly describes today's world—organizations can't afford the inflexibility that traditional jobs, with their limiting job descriptions, bring with them.

In the near future, very few people will have jobs as we have come to know them. In place of jobs, there will be part-time and temporary work situations. Organizations will be made up of "hired guns"—contingent employees (temporaries, part-timers, consultants, and contract workers) who join project teams created to complete a specific task. When that task is finished, the team disbands. People will work on more than one team at a time, keeping irregular hours, and relying heavily on networked computers to stay in contact with other team members. Few of these employees will be working nine-to-five at specific work spots, and they'll have little of the security that their grandfathers had.

---

[a]This argument is based on W. Bridges, *JobShift* (Reading, MA: Addison-Wesley, 1994).

The central core to any discussion of work or organizational behavior is the concept of a job. It is the aggregation of tasks that defines an individual's duties and responsibilities.

When an organization is created, managers have to determine what tasks need to be accomplished for the organization to achieve its goals and who will perform those tasks. These decisions precede the hiring of a workforce. Remember, it's the tasks that determine the need for people, not the other way around.

Can you conceive of an organization without jobs? No more than you can conceive of a car without an engine. There are no doubt changes taking place in organizations that are requiring managers to redefine what a job is. For instance, today's jobs often include extensive customer interaction as well as team responsibilities. In many cases, organizations are having to make job descriptions more flexible to reflect the more dynamic nature of work today. Because it's inefficient to rewrite job descriptions on a weekly basis, managers are rethinking what makes up a job and defining jobs in more fluid terms. But the concept of jobs continues to be a the core of any work design effort and a fundamental cornerstone to understanding formal work behavior in organizations.[b]

For those who believe that the concept of jobs is on the wane, all they need to do is look to the trade union movement and its determination to maintain clear job delineations. Labor unions have a vested interest in the status quo and will fight hard to protect the security and predictability that traditional jobs provide. Moreover, if it looked like the jobless society was to become a widespread reality, politicians would be under strong pressure to create legislation to outlaw it. Working people want the stability and predictability of jobs and, if need be, they will look to their elected representatives to protect them.

---

[b]See J. Mays, "Why We Haven't Seen 'the End of Jobs' or the End of Pay Surveys," *Compensation & Benefits Review*, July–August 1997, pp. 25–29.

1. What are the implications for employees of a continuous improvement program?

2. What are the implications for employees of a process reengineering program?

3. Contrast e-commerce with an e-organization.

4. How can managers reduce cyberloafing?

5. What are the implications of the social information processing model for predicting employee behavior?

6. How could you design an office so as to increase the opportunity for employees to be productive?

7. What is feng shui?

8. What are the advantages of flextime from an employee's perspective? From management's perspective?

9. What are the advantages of job sharing from an employee's perspective? From management's perspective?

10. From an employee's perspective, what are the pros and cons of telecommuting?

Questions for Critical Thinking

1. Process reengineering needs to be autocratically imposed in order to overcome employee resistance. This runs directly counter to the model of a contemporary manager who is a good listener, a coach, motivates through employee involvement, and possesses strong team support skills. Can these two positions be reconciled?

2. How has technology changed the manager's job over the past 20 years?

3. What effect, if any, do you think the Internet will have on the development of future employees' interpersonal skills?

4. Describe three jobs that score high on the JCM. Describe three jobs that would score low. Explain how you came to your conclusions.

5. What can management do to improve employees' perceptions that their jobs are interesting and challenging?

Team Exercise — Analyzing and Redesigning Jobs

Break into groups of five to seven members each. Each student should describe the worst job he or she has ever had. Use any criteria you want to select one of these jobs for analysis by the group.

Members of the group will analyze the job selected by determining how well it scores on the job characteristics model. Use the following scale for your analysis of each job dimension:

7 = Very high
6 = High
5 = Somewhat high
4 = Moderate
3 = Somewhat low
2 = Low
1 = Very low

Following are sample questions that can guide the group in its analysis of the job in question:

- *Skill variety:* Describe the different identifiable skills required to do this job. What is the nature of the oral, written, and/or quantitative skills needed? Physical skills? Does the jobholder get the opportunity to use all of his or her skills?

- *Task identity:* What is the product that the jobholder creates? Is he or she involved in its production from beginning to end? If not, is he or she involved in a particular phase of its production from beginning to end?

- *Task significance:* How important is the product? How important is the jobholder's role in producing it? How important is the jobholder's contribution to the people he or she works with? If the jobholder's job were eliminated, how inferior would the product be?

- *Autonomy:* How much independence does the jobholder have? Does he or she have to follow a strict schedule? How closely is he or she supervised?
- *Feedback:* Does the jobholder get regular feedback from his or her supervisor? From peers? From those below? From customers? What about intrinsic performance feedback when doing the job?

Using the formula in Exhibit 16-5, calculate the job's motivating potential. Then describe specific actions management could take to increase this job's motivating potential.

Calculate the costs to management of redesigning the job in question. Do the benefits exceed the costs?

Conclude the exercise by having a representative of each group share his or her group's analysis and redesign suggestions with the entire class. Possible topics for class discussion might include similarities in the jobs chosen, problems in rating job dimensions, and the cost–benefit assessment of design changes.

Source: This exercise is based on W. P. Ferris, "Enlivening the Job Characteristics Model," in C. Harris and C. C. Lundberg, *Proceedings of the 29th Annual Eastern Academy of Management Meeting;* Baltimore, MD; May 1992, pp. 125–28.

Ethical Dilemma | Employee Monitoring: How Far Is Too Far?

When does management's effort to control the actions of others become an invasion of privacy? Consider three cases.[85]

At Underground Service Alert, in southern California, more than 30 service representatives telecommute from home while the company keeps tabs on them. "The supervisor can monitor what the conversation is, what the keystrokes are," says the company's president. "If the customer-service representative spends 20 minutes (on a break) after taking a call, that's all monitored."

The Internal Revenue Service's internal audit group monitors a computer log that shows employee access to taxpayers' accounts. This monitoring activity allows management to check and see what employees are doing on their computers.

Versus Technology recently introduced a system that lets employers keep track of their workers' whereabouts. It deploys a series of sensors, each the size of a hockey puck, in office ceilings. They track infrared light pulses produced by personal ID tags. Workers' movements are then tracked on a Windows program, letting the boss tap in by laptop computer.

Are any of these cases—monitoring calls, computer activities, or locale—an invasion of privacy? When does management overstep the bounds of decency and privacy by silently (even covertly) scrutinizing the behavior of its employees or associates?

Managers at Underground Service and the IRS defend their practice in terms of ensuring quality, productivity, and proper employee behavior. These

organizations can point to U.S. government statistics showing that tens of millions of workers are being electronically monitored on their jobs. And silent surveillance of telephone calls can be used to help employees do their jobs better. One IRS audit of its Southeastern regional offices found that 166 employees took unauthorized looks at the tax returns of friends, neighbors, or celebrities. A product manager at Versus says his company's system doesn't watch what you do, it just knows where you are. And this can help management better distribute employees and provide customers with better service.

There are laws and ethical guidelines aimed to curb employers' rights to use electronic monitoring. For example, the Privacy for Consumers and Workers Act requires that precise notification be given to U.S. employees of when they will be monitored. Similarly, industry groups in telemarketing have established guidelines that include a recommendation that employees be given the option to be informed when they are being monitored.

When does management's need for information about employee performance cross the line and interfere with a worker's right to privacy? For instance, must employees be notified ahead of time that they will be monitored? Is it always wrong for employees to play computer games or do Internet shopping on office equipment during the workday? Does management's right to protect its interests extend to electronic monitoring of every place a worker might be—bathrooms, locker rooms, and dressing rooms?

Bob's is one of the largest fast-food chains in Latin America. Headquartered in Rio De Janeiro, more than half of this McDonald's clone's 225 outlets are located in Brazil. What's it like to work at Bob's? A day at an outlet in a mall in São Paulo provides some insights.

The most notable characteristic of this fast-food restaurant is the youth of the 12 employees. Silvana, who supervises the training of new hires, has had two promotions in her four years on the job. Yet she's only 21 years old. Levy, the short-order cook, is 20 and has been doing his job for a year. Elisangela is 21 and a Bob's employee for two years. The restaurant's manager, who has seven years at Bob's, is 23. Simone is one of the oldest employees at 25.

Bob's employees have another commonality besides their youth. They're all from a humble social background. Middle-class kids in Brazil want to avoid working in fast-food places.

The jobs at Bob's have a highly structured routine. For instance, if you're working the grill, you need to know that a Big Bob gets two slices of beef, 11 grams of lettuce and seven grams of sliced onions on a sesame seed bun; a Bob's Burger is also two slices of beef with special sauce but only a slice of tomato on a plain bun; and a Franburgao gets a chicken breast, tomato, and curry sauce on a sesame seed bun. If you're working the french fryer, you need to check the temperature of the oil, make sure it's 345 degrees Fahrenheit, put one package of fries into the bin, push it down slowly into the oil until you hear the click, wait for the machine to bring it back up, shake the bin three times and pour the fries into the steel container.

Employees seem generally content with their jobs. In spite of having to wear a silly red tie, a blue and red baseball cap and an apron that says Bob's, these people are glad to have a job in a country where as many as one in five is unemployed. Standard employees at Bob's earn 500 reais (less than $300 U.S. a month). The manager's salary is around 1300 reais a month.

Questions

1. Describe an entry-level job at Bob's in JCM terms.

2. What type of person do you think would fit well into jobs at Bob's?

3. Could jobs at Bob's be enriched or reengineered to make employees more productive?

4. How might technology change fast-food jobs over the next 10 years?

5. Could flextime work at Bob's? Explain.

Source: T. Ogier, "Life As a Burger King," _Latin Trade_, December 2000, pp. 44–47.

KSS PROGRAM:

KNOW THE CONCEPTS
SELF-AWARENESS
SKILLS APPLICATIONS

Designing Motivating Jobs
After you've read this chapter, take Self-Assessment #37 (What's My Job Motivating Potential?) on your enclosed CD-ROM, and complete the skill-building module entitled Designing Motivating Jobs on page 629.

1. See L. Elliott, "Overseas Operations Require Foreign Design, Technology," *The Business Journal*, May 3, 1999, www.milwaukee.bizjournals.com; B. McKay, "At Coke, Layoffs Inspire All Manner of Peculiar Rumors," *Wall Street Journal*, October 17, 2000, p. A1; and P. Youden, "Creating a Feng Shui Office, *The Business Journal*, February 16, 2001, www.triangle.bizjournals.com.

2. See, for example, H. S. Gitlow, *Quality Management Systems: A Practical Guide for Improvement* (Boca Raton, FL: CRC Press, 2001); and J. W. Cortada, *The Quality Yearbook 2001* (New York: McGraw-Hill, 2001).

3. P. Siekman, "Glass Act: How a Window Maker Rebuilt Itself," *Fortune*, November 13, 2000, pp. 384[C]–384[V].

4. M. Hammer and J. Champy, *Reengineering the Corporation: A Manifesto for Business Revolution* (New York: HarperBusiness, 1993).

5. R. Karlgaard, "ASAP Interview: Mike Hammer," *Forbes ASAP*, September 13, 1993, p. 70.

6. Ibid.

7. W. Kirn, "The 60-Second Book," *Time*, August 1, 1999, p. 45.

8. P. Siekman, "Where 'Build to Order' Works Best," *Fortune*, April 26, 1999, pp. 160C–160V; J. Lardner, "Your Every Command," *U.S. News & World Report*, July 5, 1999, pp. 44–46; F. Gibney Jr., "The Revolution in a Box," *Time*, July 31, 2000, pp. 30–32; and K. A. Crawford, "Customizing for the Masses," *Forbes*, October 16, 2000, p. 168.

9. V. K. G. Lim, G. L. Loo, and T. S. H. Teo, "Perceived Injustice, Neutralization, and Cyberloafing at the Workplace," paper presented at the Academy of Management Conference; Washington, DC, August 2001.

10. Cited in *Brill's Content*, December 2000/January 2001, p. 48.

11. "Internet Usage Statistics," www.n2h2.com, March 27, 2002.

12. M. Conlin, "Workers, Surf at Your Own Risk," *Business Week*, June 12, 2000, p. 106.

13. See, for instance, M. J. McCarthy, "You Assumed 'Erase' Wiped Out That Rant Against the Boss? Nope," *Wall Street Journal*, March 7, 2000, p. A1; S. Boehle, "They're Watching You: Workplace Privacy is Going . . . Going . . . ," *Training*, August 2000, pp. 50–60; K. Weisul, "How Should You Police Employees Goofing Off on the Net? Very Carefully," *Business Week Frontier*, February 5, 2001, pp. F18–20; and "Keeping Tabs on Employees Online," *Business Week*, February 19, 2001, p. 16.

14. L. Guernsey, "The Web: New Ticket to a Pink Slip," *New York Times*, December 16, 1999, p. D1+.

15. Cited in *Brill's Content*, December 2000/January 2001, p. 48.

16. J. Fonstad, "It's the Business Model, Stupid!" *Red Herring*, February 2000, pp. 70–72; and G. Dalton, "Ways of Doing Business," *The Industry Standard*, March 13, 2000, pp. 92–95.

17. A. Cohen, "Click Here for a Hot Rumor About Your Boss," *Time*, September 11, 2000, p. 48; and J. Simons, "Stop Moaning About Gripe Sites and Log On," *Fortune*, April 2, 2001, pp. 181–82.

18. E. Weinstein, "Help! I'm Drowning in E-Mail!," *Wall Street Journal*, January 10, 2002, p. B1.

19. Cited in *Training*, April 2001, p. 88.

20. D. E. Lewis, "Online Messaging, Scuttlebutt Replacing Water-Cooler Gossip," *Seattle Post-Intelligencer*, September 21, 2000, p. D2.

21. Cited in *Red Herring*, December 1999, p. 37.

22. Reported in J. Markoff, "A Newer, Lonelier Crowd Emerges in Internet Study," *New York Times*, February 16, 2000, p. A1.

23. Reported in G. Koretz, "The Web's Chilling Trend?" *Business Week*, June 5, 2000, p. 36.

24. R. Kraut, S. Kiesler, B. Boneva, J. Cummings, V. Helgeson, and A. Crawford, "Internet Paradox Revisited," *Journal of Social Issues*, Spring 2002, pp. 49-74.

25. R. M. Steers and R. T. Mowday, "The Motivational Properties of Tasks," *Academy of Management Review*, October 1977, pp. 645–58.

26. D. G. Gardner and L. L. Cummings, "Activation Theory and Job Design: Review and Reconceptualization," in B. M. Staw and L. L. Cummings (eds.), *Research in Organizational Behavior*, vol. 10 (Greenwich, CT: JAI Press, 1988), p. 100.

27. A. N. Turner and P. R. Lawrence, *Industrial Jobs and the Worker* (Boston: Harvard University Press, 1965).

28. J. R. Hackman and G. R. Oldham, "Motivation through the Design of Work: Test of a Theory," *Organizational Behavior and Human Performance*, August 1976, pp. 250–79; and J. R. Hackman and G. R. Oldham, *Work Redesign* (Reading, MA: Addison-Wesley, 1980).

29. J. R. Hackman, "Work Design," in J. R. Hackman and J. L. Suttle (eds.), *Improving Life at Work* (Santa Monica, CA: Goodyear, 1977), p. 129.

30. See "Job Characteristics Theory of Work Redesign," in J. B. Miner, *Theories of Organizational Behavior* (Hinsdale, IL: Dryden Press, 1980), pp. 231–66; B. T. Loher, R. A. Noe, N. L. Moeller, and M. P. Fitzgerald, "A Meta-Analysis of the Relation of Job Characteristics to Job Satisfaction," *Journal of Applied Psychology*, May 1985, pp. 280–89; W. H. Glick, G. D. Jenkins, Jr., and N. Gupta, "Method versus Substance: How Strong Are Underlying Relationships between Job Characteristics and Attitudinal Outcomes?" *Academy of Management Journal*, September 1986, pp. 441–64; Y. Fried and G. R. Ferris, "The Validity of the Job Characteristics Model: A Review and Meta-Analysis," *Personnel Psychology*, Summer 1987, pp. 287–322; S. J. Zaccaro and E. F. Stone, "Incremental Validity of an Empirically Based Measure of Job Characteristics," *Journal of Applied Psychology*, May 1988, pp. 245–52;

and J. R. Rentsch and R. P. Steel, "Testing the Durability of Job Characteristics as Predictors of Absenteeism over a Six-Year Period," *Personnel Psychology*, Spring 1998, pp. 165–90.

31. See R. B. Dunham, "Measurement and Dimensionality of Job Characteristics," *Journal of Applied Psychology*, August 1976, pp. 404–409; J. L. Pierce and R. B. Dunham, "Task Design: A Literature Review," *Academy of Management Review*, January 1976, pp. 83–97; D. M. Rousseau, "Technological Differences in Job Characteristics, Employee Satisfaction, and Motivation: A Synthesis of Job Design Research and Sociotechnical Systems Theory," *Organizational Behavior and Human Performance*, October 1977, pp. 18–42; and Y. Fried and G. R. Ferris, "The Dimensionality of Job Characteristics: Some Neglected Issues," *Journal of Applied Psychology*, August 1986, pp. 419–26.

32. Fried and Ferris, "The Dimensionality of Job Characteristics."

33. See, for instance, Fried and Ferris, "The Dimensionality of Job Characteristics"; and M. G. Evans and D. A. Ondrack, "The Motivational Potential of Jobs: Is a Multiplicative Model Really Necessary?" in S. L. McShane (ed.), *Organizational Behavior, ASAC Conference Proceedings*, vol. 9, part 5, Halifax, Nova Scotia, 1988, pp. 31–39.

34. R. B. Tiegs, L. E. Tetrick, and Y. Fried, "Growth Need Strength and Context Satisfactions as Moderators of the Relations of the Job Characteristics Model," *Journal of Management*, September 1992, pp. 575–93; and G. Johns, J. L. Xie, and Y. Fang, "Mediating and Moderating Effects in Jobs Design," *Journal of Management*, December 1992, pp. 657–76.

35. C. A. O'Reilly and D. F. Caldwell, "Informational Influence as a Determinant of Perceived Task Characteristics and Job Satisfaction," *Journal of Applied Psychology*, April 1979, pp. 157–65; R. V. Montagno, "The Effects of Comparison Others and Prior Experience on Responses to Task Design," *Academy of Management Journal*, June 1985, pp. 491–98; and P. C. Bottger and I. K.-H. Chew, "The Job Characteristics Model and Growth Satisfaction: Main Effects of Assimilation of Work Experience and Context Satisfaction," *Human Relations*, June 1986, pp. 575–94.

36. Hackman, "Work Design," pp. 132–33.

37. G. R. Salancik and J. Pfeffer, "A Social Information Processing Approach to Job Attitudes and Task Design," *Administrative Science Quarterly*, June 1978, pp. 224–53; J. G. Thomas and R. W. Griffin, "The Power of Social Information in the Workplace," *Organizational Dynamics*, Autumn 1989, pp. 63–75; and M. D. Zalesny and J. K. Ford, "Extending the Social Information Processing Perspective: New Links to Attitudes, Behaviors, and Perceptions," *Organizational Behavior and Human Decision Processes*, December 1990, pp. 205–46.

38. J. R. Hackman, "Work Design," in J. R. Hackman and J. L. Suttle, eds. *Improving Life at Work* (Santa Monica, CA: Goodyear, 1977), pp. 115–20.

39. J. P. Wanous, "Individual Differences and Reactions to Job Characteristics," *Journal of Applied Psychology*, October 1974, pp. 616–22; and H. P. Sims and A. D. Szilagyi, "Job Characteristic Relationships: Individual and Structural Moderators," *Organizational Behavior and Human Performance*, June 1976, pp. 211–30.

40. M. Fein, "The Real Needs and Goals of Blue-Collar Workers," *The Conference Board Record*, February 1972, pp. 26–33.

41. See, for instance, J. Thomas and R. W. Griffin, "The Social Information Processing Model of Task Design: A Review of the Literature," *Academy of Management Journal*, October 1983, pp. 672–82; and M. D. Zalesny and J. K. Ford, "Extending the Social Information Processing Perspective: New Links to Attitudes, Behaviors, and Perceptions," *Organizational Behavior and Human Decision Processes*, December 1990, pp. 205–46; G. W. Meyer, "Social Information Processing and Social Networks: A Test of Social Influence Mechanisms," *Human Relations*, September 1994, pp. 1013–45; and K. J. Klein, A. B. Conn, D. B. Smith, and J. S. Sorra, "Is Everyone in Agreement? An Exploration of Within-Group Agreement in Employee Perceptions of the Work Environment," *Journal of Applied Psychology*, February 2001, pp. 3–16.

42. T. Tetenbaum and H. Tetenbaum, "Office 2000: Tear Down the Walls," *Training*, February 2000, p. 60; and J. Sung, "Designed for Interaction," *Fortune*, January 8, 2001, p. 150.

43. See, for example, M. Milford, "Du Pont Shuts the Door on Private Offices," *New York Times*, February 23, 1997, p. 31; B. Nussbaum, "Blueprints for Business," *Business Week*, November 3, 1997, pp. 112–22; D. Bencivenga, "A Humanistic Approach to Space," *HRMagazine*, March 1998, pp. 68–78; and C. Howard, "It's the Same Job, After All," *Canadian Business*, June 26/July 10, 1998, pp. 125–26.

44. See F. Becker and F. Steele, *Workplace by Design* (San Francisco: Jossey-Bass, 1995).

45. J. Pfeffer, *Organizations and Organization Theory* (Boston: Pitman, 1982), p. 261.

46. S. Lohr, "Hey, Who Took the Office Doors?" *New York Times*, August 11, 1997, p. C7.

47. Ibid.

48. See, for example, L. S. Festinger, S. Schachter, and K. Back, *Social Pressures in Informal Groups* (Stanford, CA: Stanford University Press, 1950).

49. See, for example, R. L. Zweigenhaft, "Personal Space in the Faculty Office Desk Placement and the Student-Faculty Interaction," *Journal of Applied Psychology*, August 1976, pp. 529–32; D. E. Campbell, "Interior Office Design and Visitor Response," *Journal of Applied Psychology*, December 1979, pp. 648–53; P. C. Morrow and J. C. McElroy, "Interior Office Design and Visitor Response: A Constructive Replication," *Journal of Applied Psychology*, October 1981, pp. 646–50; and G. R. Oldham, "Effects of Changes in Workspace Partitions and Spatial Density on Employee Reactions: A Quasi-Experiment," *Journal of Applied Psychology*, May 1988, pp. 253–58.

50. S. Lohr, "Hey, Who Took the Office Doors?" p. C7.

51. Ibid. and D. Bencivenga, "A Humanistic Approach to Space"; L. Gallagher, "Get Out of My Face," *Forbes*, October 18, 1999, pp. 105–106; and M. Rich, "Shut Up So We Can Do Our Jobs!" *Wall Street Journal*, August 29, 2001, p. B1.

52. R. A. Baron, "The Physical Environment of Work Settings: Effects on Task Performance, Interpersonal Relations, and Job Satisfaction," in B. M. Staw and L. L. Cummings, eds., *Research in Organizational Behavior*, vol. 16 (Greenwich, CT: JAI Press, 1994), p. 33.

53. K. M. Lagatree, *Feng Shui at Work* (New York: Villard Books, 1998), p. 3.

54. A. Singh, "Luck Be a Stone Lion," *Time*, July 3, 2000, p. 53; and "Feng Shui and Office Space," *Manpower Argus*, October 2000, p. 10.

55. K. M. Lagatree, *Feng Shui at Work*.

56. J. I. Porras and P. J. Robertson, "Organizational Development: Theory, Practice, and Research," in M. D. Dunnette and L. M. Hough, eds., *Handbook of Industrial & Organizational Psychology*, 2nd ed., vol. 3 (Palo Alto, CA: Consulting Psychologists Press, 1992), p. 734.

57. E. Proper, "Surroundings Affect Worker Productivity," *Industry Week*, June 8, 1998, p. 14.

58. Ibid.

59. S. Lohr, "Hey, Who Took the Office Doors?" p. C7.

60. C. Ansberry, "In the New Workplace, Jobs Morph to Suit Rapid Pace of Change," *Wall Street Journal*, March 22, 2002, p. A1.

61. See, for instance, data on job enlargement described in M. A. Campion and C. L. McClelland, "Follow-up and Extension of the Interdisciplinary Costs and Benefits of Enlarged Jobs," *Journal of Applied Psychology*, June 1993, pp. 339–51.

62. J. R. Hackman and G. R. Oldham, *Work Redesign* (Reading, MA: Addison Wesley, 1980).

63. Cited in *U.S. News & World Report*, May 31, 1993, p. 63.

64. See, for example, J. R. Hackman and G. R. Oldham, *Work Redesign*; J. B. Miner, *Theories of Organizational Behavior* (Hinsdale, IL: Dryden Press, 1980), pp. 231–66; R. W. Griffin, "Effects of Work Redesign on Employee Perceptions, Attitudes, and Behaviors: A Long-Term Investigation," *Academy of Management Journal*, June 1991, pp. 425–35; and J. L. Cotton, *Employee Involvement* (Newbury Park, CA: Sage, 1993), pp. 141–72.

65. R. W. Griffin and G. C. McMahan, "Motivation Through Job Design," in J. Greenberg, ed. *Organizational Behavior: The State of the Science* (Hillsdale, NJ: Lawrence Erlbaum Associates, 1994), pp. 36–38.

66. J. R. Hackman, "The Design of Work Teams," in J. W. Lorsch, ed., *Handbook of Organizational Behavior* (Englewood Cliffs, NJ: Prentice Hall, 1987), pp. 324–27.

67. L. Rubis, "Fourth of Full-Timers Enjoy Flexible Hours," *HRMagazine*, June 1998, pp. 26–28; and T. M. Beers, "Flexible Schedules and Shift Work: Replacing the '9-to-5' Workday?" *Monthly Labor Review*, June 2000, pp. 33–40.

68. Cited in "Flextime Gains in Popularity in Germany," *Manpower Argus*, September 2000, p. 4.

69. L. Rubis, "Fourth of Full-Timers Enjoy Flexible Hours."

70. D. R. Dalton and D. J. Mesch, "The Impact of Flexible Scheduling on Employee Attendance and Turnover," *Administrative Science Quarterly*, June 1990, pp. 370–87; K. S. Kush and L. K. Stroh, "Flextime: Myth or Reality," *Business Horizons*, September–October 1994, p. 53; and L. Golden, "Flexible Work Schedules: What Are We Trading Off to Get Them?" *Monthly Labor Review*, March 2001, pp. 50–55.

71. See, for example, D. A. Ralston and M. F. Flanagan, "The Effect of Flextime on Absenteeism and Turnover for Male and Female Employees," *Journal of Vocational Behavior*, April 1985, pp. 206–17; D. A. Ralston, W. P. Anthony, and D. J. Gustafson, "Employees May Love Flextime, But What Does It Do to the Organization's Productivity?" *Journal of Applied Psychology*, May 1985, pp. 272–79; J. B. McGuire and J. R. Liro, "Flexible Work Schedules, Work Attitudes, and Perceptions of Productivity," *Public Personnel Management*, Spring 1986, pp. 65–73; P. Bernstein, "The Ultimate in Flextime: From Sweden, by Way of Volvo," *Personnel*, June 1988, pp. 70–74; and D. R. Dalton and D. J. Mesch, "The Impact of Flexible Scheduling on Employee Attendance and Turnover," *Administrative Science Quarterly*, June 1990, pp. 370–87.

72. Cited in S. Caminiti, "Fair Shares," *Working Woman*, November 1999, p. 54.

73. Ibid, pp. 52–54.

74. S. Shellenbarger, "Two People, One Job: It Can Really Work," *Wall Street Journal*, December 7, 1994, p. B1.

75. "Job-Sharing: Widely Offered, Little Used," *Training*, November 1994, p. 12.

76. C. Dawson, "Japan: Work-Sharing Will Prolong the Pain," *Business Week*, December 24, 2001, p. 46.

77. S. Shellenbarger, "Two People, One Job."

78. See, for example, T. H. Davenport and K. Pearlson, "Two Cheers for the Virtual Office," *Sloan Management Review*, Summer 1998, pp. 61–65; E. J. Hill, B. C. Miller, S. P. Weiner, and J. Colihan, "Influences of the Virtual Office on Aspects of Work and Work/Life Balance," *Personnel Psychology*, Autumn 1998, pp. 667–83; K. E. Pearlson and C. S. Saunders, "There's No Place Like Home: Managing Telecommuting Paradoxes," *Academy of Management Executive*, May 2001, pp. 117–28; and S. J. Wells, "Making Telecommuting Work," *HRMagazine*, October 2001, pp. 34–45.

79. N. B. Kurland and D. E. Bailey, "Telework: The Advantages and Challenges of Working Here, There, Anywhere, and Anytime," *Organizational Dynamics*, Autumn 1999, pp. 53–68; and S. J. Wells, "Making Telecommuting Work," p. 34.

80. See, for instance, J. D. Glater, "Telecommuting's Big Experiment," *New York Times*, May 9, 2001, p. C1; and

S. Shellenbarger, "Telework Is on the Rise, But It Isn't Just Done from Home Anymore," *Wall Street Journal*, January 23, 2001, p. B1.

81. U. Huws, "Wired in the Country," *People Management*, November 1999, pp. 46–47.

82. Cited in R. W. Judy and C. D'Amico, *Workforce 2020* (Indianapolis: Hudson Institute, 1997), p. 58.

83. Cited in S. J. Wells, "Making Telecommuting Work."

84. J. M. Stanton and J. L. Barnes-Farrell, "Effects of Electronic Performance Monitoring on Personal Control, Task Satisfaction, and Task Performance," *Journal of Applied Psychology*, December 1996, pp. 738–45; B. Pappas, "They Spy," *Forbes*, February 8, 1999, p. 47; S. Armour, "More Bosses Keep Tabs on Telecommuters," *USA Today*, July 24, 2001, p. 1B; and D. Buss, "Spies Like Us," *Training*, December 2001, pp. 44–48.

After listening to my employees, I have to conclude that I have only three types of people working for me: Stars, All-Stars, and Superstars! How is it possible for all my people to be above average?
—**An Anonymous Boss**

PART FOUR

THE ORGANIZATION SYSTEM

Employee layoffs are often a necessary evil if an organization is to maintain its competitiveness. In the United States, for instance, executives at a number of major companies—including Boeing, Sears, Aetna, WorldCom, and Lucent Technologies—have laid off thousands of employees in the past several years. But executives in France don't have the same freedom to fire employees as do their American counterparts. While much has been said about global competitiveness and the breakdown of economic barriers between countries, laws continue to vary from nation to nation. And what is an acceptable human resource management practice in one country may be totally unacceptable in another.

Take the case of French appliance-maker Moulinex.[1] The company employed 8,800 people. But it was having difficulty making money. In 2000, for instance, it lost $120 million on sales of $1.1 billion. To survive, the company needed to reduce capacity and close up several of its unprofitable factories. Yet it couldn't. Why? The French government, under pressure from the country's strong labor unions, enacted laws that make laying off workers incredibly difficult. Labor laws require companies to pursue lengthy negotiations with unions over planned job reductions and the government has a final say-so in plant closings. As Moulinex's financial status deteriorated throughout the 1990s, French authorities repeatedly blocked management's efforts to close plants. In August 2001, for instance, the government rejected Moulinex's plan to shut down a refrigerator factory and lay off 670 workers. Instead, the company was ordered to resume talks with its unions.

Unable to get its costs in line, Moulinex declared bankruptcy in October 2001. A bankruptcy court approved the sale of most of Moulinex's assets and brands to French rival SEB. However, nearly two-thirds of Moulinex's employees lost their jobs permanently.

Human Resource Policies and Practices

The message of this chapter is that human resource policies and practices—such as employee selection, training, performance evaluation, and union-management relations—influence an organization's effectiveness.[2] And as illustrated in the case of Moulinex, we'll also look at how human resource practices differ across cultures. We begin our discussion with the subject of hiring.

SELECTION PRACTICES

The objective of effective selection is to match individual characteristics (ability, experience, and so on) with the requirements of the job.[3] When management fails to get a proper match, both employee performance and satisfaction suffer. In this search to achieve the right individual–job fit, where does management begin? The answer is to assess the demands and requirements of the job. The process of assessing the activities within a job is called *job analysis*.

Job Analysis

Job analysis involves developing a detailed description of the tasks involved in a job, determining the relationship of a given job to other jobs, and ascertaining the knowledge, skills, and abilities necessary for an employee to successfully perform the job.[4]

How is this information attained? Exhibit 17-1 describes the more popular job analysis methods.

Information gathered by using one or more of the job analysis methods results in the organization being able to create

LEARNING OBJECTIVES

AFTER STUDYING THIS CHAPTER, YOU SHOULD BE ABLE TO:

1. Contrast job descriptions with job specifications.

2. List the advantages of performance simulation tests over written tests.

3. Define four general skill categories.

4. Describe how career planning has changed in the past 20 years.

5. Explain the purposes of performance evaluation.

6. Describe actions that can improve the performance-evaluation process.

7. Clarify how the existence of a union affects employee behavior.

8. Identify the content in a typical diversity-training program.

EXHIBIT

17-1

Popular Job Analysis Methods

Observation. An analyst watches employees directly or reviews videos of workers on the job.

Interviews. Selected job incumbents are extensively interviewed, and the results of a number of interviews are combined into a single job analysis.

Diaries. Job incumbents record their daily activities, and the amount of time spent on each, in a diary or log.

Questionnaires. Incumbents check or rate the items they perform in their jobs from a long list of possible task items.

job analysis
Developing a detailed description of the tasks involved in a job, determining the relationship of a given job to other jobs, and ascertaining the knowledge, skills, and abilities necessary for an employee to perform the job successfully.

job description
A written statement of what a jobholder does, how it is done, and why it is done.

job specification
A statement of the minimum acceptable qualifications that an employee must possess to perform a given job successfully.

a **job description** and **job specification**. The former is a written statement of what a jobholder does, how it is done, and why it is done. It should accurately portray job content, environment, and conditions of employment. The job specification states the minimum acceptable qualifications that an employee must possess to perform a given job successfully. It identifies the knowledge, skills, and abilities needed to do the job effectively. So job descriptions identify characteristics of the job, whereas job specifications identify characteristics of the successful job incumbent.

The job description and specification have historically been important documents for guiding the selection process. The job description can be used to describe the job to potential candidates. The job specification keeps the attention of those doing the selection on the list of qualifications necessary for an incumbent to perform a job and assists in determining whether candidates are qualified. However, there are signs that these documents may be declining in importance. Because job analysis is a static view of the job as it currently exists, job descriptions and specifications are also static documents. To facilitate flexibility, organizations are increasingly hiring for organizational needs rather than for specific individual jobs.[5] Organizations want their permanent employees to be able to do a variety of tasks and to be able to move smoothly from project to project and from one team to another. In such a climate, organizations will tend to seek new employees who, in addition to job-relevant skills, have personalities and attitudes that fit with the organization's culture and who display organizational citizenship behaviors. Traditional job analysis can identify current job-relevant skills but is inadequate for identifying these other contextual factors that managers are increasingly looking for in new employees.

Selection Devices

What do application forms, interviews, employment tests, background checks, and personal letters of recommendation have in common? Each is a device for obtaining information about a job applicant that can help the organization to determine whether the applicant's skills, knowledge, and abilities are appropriate for the job in question. In this section, we review the more important of these selection devices—interviews, written tests, and performance-simulation tests.

Interviews In Korea, Japan, and many other Asian countries, employee interviews traditionally have not been part of the selection process. Decisions were made almost entirely on the basis of exam scores, scholastic accomplishments, and letters of recommendation. This is not the case, however, throughout most of the world. It's probably correct to say that most of us don't know anyone who has gotten a job without at least one interview. You may have an acquaintance who got a part-time or summer job through a close friend or relative without having to go through an interview, but such instances are rare. Of all the selection devices that organizations use to differentiate candidates, the interview continues to be the one most frequently used.[6] Even companies in Asian countries have begun to rely on employee interviews as a screening device.[7]

Not only is the interview widely used, it also seems to carry a great deal of weight. That is, the results tend to have a disproportionate amount of influence on the selection decision. The candidate who performs poorly in the employment interview is likely to be cut from the applicant pool, regardless of his or her experience, test scores, or letters of recommendation. Conversely, "all too often, the person most polished in job-seeking techniques, particularly those used in the interview process, is the one hired, even though he or she may not be the best candidate for the position."[8]

These findings are important because of the unstructured manner in which the selection interview is frequently conducted.[9] The unstructured interview—short in duration, casual, and made up of random questions—has been proven to be an ineffective selection device.[10] The data gathered from such interviews are typically biased and often unrelated to future job performance. Without structure, a number of biases can distort results. These biases include interviewers tending to favor applicants who share their attitudes, giving unduly high weight to negative information, and allowing the order in which applicants are interviewed to influence evaluations.[11] By having interviewers use a standardized set of questions, providing interviewers with a uniform method of recording information, and standardizing the rating of the applicant's qualifications, the variability in results across applicants is reduced and the validity of the interview as a selection device is greatly enhanced.

Applicants for jobs at Southwest Airlines are screened not only for job-specific qualifications but also to determine whether their personality and attitudes fit the Southwest image.

The evidence indicates that interviews are most valuable for assessing an applicant's applied mental skills, level of conscientiousness, and interpersonal skills.[12] When these qualities are related to job performance, the validity of the interview as a selection device is increased. For example, these qualities have demonstrated relevance for performance in upper managerial positions. This may explain why applicants for senior management positions typically undergo dozens of interviews with executive recruiters, board members, and other company executives before a final decision is made. It can also explain why organizations that design work around teams may similarly put applicants through an unusually large number of interviews.

In practice, most organizations use interviews for more than a "prediction-of-performance" device.[13] Companies as diverse as Southwest Airlines, Disney, Microsoft, and Procter & Gamble use the interview to assess applicant–organization fit. So in addition to specific, job-relevant skills, organizations are looking at candidates' personality characteristics, personal values, and the like to find individuals who fit with the organization's culture and image.

Written Tests   Typical written tests are tests of intelligence, aptitude, ability, interest, and integrity. Long popular as selection devices, they suffered a decline in use between the late 1960s and mid-1980s, especially in the United States. The reason was that such tests were frequently characterized as discriminating, and many organizations had not validated such tests as being job-related. The past 20 years, however, has seen a resurgence in the use of these tests. It's been estimated, for instance, that today more than 60 percent of all U.S. organizations use some type of employment test.[14] Managers have come to recognize that there are valid tests available and that these tests can be helpful in predicting who will be successful on the job.[15]

Tests in intellectual ability, spatial and mechanical ability, perceptual accuracy, and motor ability have shown to be moderately valid predictors for many semiskilled and unskilled operative jobs in industrial organizations.[16] Intelligence tests have proven to be particularly good predictors for jobs that require cognitive complexity.[17] Japanese auto makers, when staffing plants in the United States, have relied heavily on written tests to predict candidates who will be high performers.[18] Getting a job with Toyota, for instance, can take up to three days of testing and interviewing. Written tests typically focus on skills such as reading, mathematics, mechanical dexterity, and ability to work with others.

As ethical problems have increased in organizations, integrity tests have gained in popularity. These are paper-and-pencil tests that measure factors such as dependability, carefulness, responsibility, and honesty. The evidence is impressive that these tests are powerful in predicting supervisory ratings of job performance and counterproductive employee behavior on the job such as theft, discipline problems, and excessive absenteeism.[19]

Performance-Simulation Tests   What better way is there to find out if an applicant can do a job successfully than by having him or her do it? That's precisely the logic of performance-simulation tests.

Although more complicated to develop and more difficult to administer than written tests, performance-simulation tests have increased in popularity during the past two decades. This appears to be due to the fact that they are based on job analysis data and, therefore, more easily meet the requirement of job-relatedness than do most written tests.

The two best-known performance-simulation tests are work sampling and assessment centers. The former is suited to routine jobs, while the latter is relevant for the selection of managerial personnel.

work sampling
Creating a miniature replica of a job to evaluate the performance abilities of job candidates.

Work sampling tests are hands-on simulations of part or all of the job that must be performed by applicants. By carefully devising work samples based on job analysis data, management determines the knowledge, skills, and abilities needed for each job. Then each work sample element is matched with a corresponding job performance element. Work samples are widely used in the hiring of skilled workers, such as welders, machinists, carpenters, and electricians. Job candidates for production jobs at BMW's factory in South Carolina are given work sample tests.[20] Candidates are given 90 minutes to perform a variety of typical work tasks on a specially built simulated assembly line.

The results from work sample experiments are impressive. Studies almost consistently demonstrate that work samples yield validities superior to written aptitude and personality tests.[21]

"It's First Impressions That Count"

This statement is true. When we meet someone for the first time, we notice a number of things about that person—physical characteristics, clothes, firmness of handshake, gestures, tone of voice, and the like. We then use these impressions to fit the person into ready-made categories. And this early categorization, formed quickly and on the basis of minimal information, tends to hold greater weight than impressions and information received later.

The best evidence on first impressions comes from research on employment interviews. Findings clearly demonstrate that first impressions count. For instance, the primacy effect is potent. That is, the first information presented affects later judgments more than information presented later.[22]

Research on applicant appearance confirms the power of first impressions.[23] Studies have looked at assessments made of applicants before the actual interview—that brief period in which the applicant walks into an interview room, exchanges greetings with the interviewer, sits down, and engages in minor chit-chat. The evidence indicates that the way applicants walk, talk, dress, and look can have a great impact on the interviewer's evaluation of applicant qualifications. Facial attractiveness seems to be particularly influential. Applicants who are highly attractive are evaluated as more qualified for a variety of jobs than persons who are unattractive.

A final body of confirmative research finds that interviewers' postinterview evaluations of applicants conform, to a substantial degree, to their preinterview impressions.[24] That is, those first impressions carry considerable weight in shaping the interviewers' final evaluations, regardless of what actually transpired in the interview itself. This latter conclusion assumes that the interview elicits no highly negative information.

A more elaborate set of performance simulation tests, specifically designed to evaluate a candidate's managerial potential, is administered in **assessment centers**. In assessment centers, line executives, supervisors, and/or trained psychologists evaluate candidates as they go through one to several days of exercises that simulate real problems that they would confront on the job.[25] Based on a list of descriptive dimensions that the actual job incumbent has to meet, activities might include interviews, in-basket problem-solving exercises, leaderless group discussions, and business decision games. For instance, a candidate might be required to play the role of a manager who must decide how to respond to ten memos in his or her in-basket within a two-hour period.

How valid is the assessment center as a selection device? The evidence on the effectiveness of assessment centers is impressive. They have consistently demonstrated results that predict later job performance in managerial positions.[26]

assessment centers
A set of performance-simulation tests designed to evaluate a candidate's managerial potential.

TRAINING AND DEVELOPMENT PROGRAMS

Competent employees don't remain competent forever. Skills deteriorate and can become obsolete. That's why organizations spend billions of dollars each year on formal training. For instance, it was reported that U.S. corporations with 100 or more employees spent $56.8 billion in one recent year on formal training.[27] IBM, Accenture, Ford, and Boeing alone each spend in excess of $250 million a year on employee training.[28]

Types of Training

Training can include everything from teaching employees basic reading skills to advanced courses in executive leadership. The following summarizes four general skill categories—basic literacy, technical, interpersonal, and problem solving. In addition, we briefly discuss ethics training.

Basic Literacy Skills   A recent report by the Organization of Economic Cooperation and Development found that 50 percent of the U.S. population reads below the eighth-grade level and about 90 million adults are functionally illiterate.[29] Moreover, statistics show that nearly 40 percent of the U.S. labor force and more than 50 percent of high school graduates don't possess the basic work skills needed to perform in today's workplace.[30] The National Institute of Learning estimates that this literacy problem costs corporate America about $60 billion a year in lost productivity.[31] This problem, of course, isn't unique to the United States. It's a worldwide problem—from the most developed countries to the least.[32] For many Third World countries, where few workers can read or have gone beyond the equivalent of the third grade, widespread illiteracy means there is almost no hope for these countries to compete in a global economy.

Organizations are increasingly having to provide basic reading and math skills for their employees. For instance, jobs at Springfield, Massachusetts–based Smith and Wesson have become more complex.[33] Employees need improved math skills for understanding numerical control equipment, better reading and writing skills to interpret process sheets, and better oral communication skills for working in teams. A literacy audit showed that employees needed to have at least an eighth-grade reading level to do typical workplace tasks. Yet 30 percent of the company's 676 workers with no degree scored below eighth-grade levels in either reading or math. These employees were told that they wouldn't lose their jobs but they had to take basic skill classes, paid for by the company and provided on company time. After the first round of classes, 70 percent of attendees brought their skills up to the target level. And these improved skills allowed employees to do a better job. They displayed greater ease in writing and reading charts, graphs, and bulletin boards, increased abilities to use fractions and decimals, better overall communication, and a significant increase in confidence.

Technical Skills   Most training is directed at upgrading and improving an employee's technical skills. Technical training has become increasingly important today for two reasons—new technology and new structural designs.

Jobs change as a result of new technologies and improved methods. For instance, many auto repair personnel have had to undergo extensive training to fix and maintain recent models with computer-monitored engines, electronic stabilizing systems, and other innovations. Similarly, computer-controlled equipment has required millions of production employees to learn a whole new set of skills.

In addition, technical training has become increasingly important because of changes in organization design. As organizations flatten their structures, expand their use of teams, and break down traditional departmental barriers, employees need to learn a wider variety of tasks and need an increased knowledge of how their organization operates. For instance, the restructuring of jobs at Miller Brewing Co. around empowered teams has led management to introduce a comprehensive business literacy program to help employees better understand competition, the state of the beer industry, where the company's revenues come from, how costs are calculated, and where employees fit into the company's value chain.[34]

Interpersonal Skills   Almost all employees belong to a work unit. To some degree, their work performance depends on their ability to effectively interact with their co-workers and their boss. Some employees have excellent interpersonal skills, but others require training to improve theirs. This includes learning how to be a better listener, how to communicate ideas more clearly, and how to be a more effective team player.

Problem-Solving Skills   Managers, as well as many employees who perform nonroutine tasks, have to solve problems on their jobs. When people require these skills but are deficient in them, they can participate in problem-solving training. This would include activities to sharpen their logic, reasoning, and problem-defining skills, as well as their abilities to assess causation, develop alternatives, analyze alternatives, and select solutions. Problem-solving training has become a basic part of almost every organizational effort to introduce self-managed teams or implement quality-management programs.

What About Ethics Training?   A recent survey finds that about 75 percent of employees working in the 1,000 largest U.S. corporations receive ethics training.[35] But the evidence is not clear about whether you can teach ethics.

Critics argue that ethics are based on values, and value systems are fixed at an early age. By the time employers hire people, their ethical values have already been established. The critics also claim that ethics cannot be formally "taught," but must be learned by example.

Supporters of ethics training argue that values can be learned and changed after early childhood. And even if they couldn't, ethics training would be effective because it helps employees to recognize ethical dilemmas, become more aware of the ethical issues underlying their actions, and reaffirms an organization's expectations that members will act ethically.

Training Methods

Training methods are most readily classified as formal or informal and on-the-job or off-the-job.

Historically, training meant *formal training*. It's planned in advance and has a structured format. However, recent evidence indicates that 70 percent of workplace learning is made up of *informal training*—unstructured, unplanned, and easily adapted to situations and individuals—for teaching skills and keeping employees current.[36] In reality, most informal training is nothing other than employees helping each other out. They share information and solve work-related problems with one another. Maybe the most important outcome of this trend is that many managers are now supportive of what used to be considered "idle chatter." At a Siemens plant in North Carolina, for instance, management now recognizes that people needn't be on the production line to be working.[37] Discussions around the water cooler or in the cafeteria weren't, as managers thought, about non-work topics such as sports or politics. They largely focused on solving work-related problems. So now Siemens' management encourages such casual meetings.

On-the-job training includes job rotation, apprenticeships, understudy assignments, and formal mentoring programs. But the primary drawback of these on-the-job training methods is that they often disrupt the workplace. So organizations invest in *off-the-job training*. The $57 billion figure we cited earlier for training costs was largely spent on the formal off-the-job variety. What types of training might this include? The most popular continues to be live classroom lectures. But it also encompasses videotapes, public seminars, self-study programs, Internet courses, satellite-beamed television classes, and group activities that use role plays and case studies. In recent years, the fastest-growing means for delivering training is probably computer-based or

Most formal training programs, like this one at Buckman Laboratories, continue to take place in live classrooms, using the lecture method.

e-learning.[38] Cisco Systems, for example, has created a Web site on its corporate intranet that provides a curriculum of training courses, with content organized for job titles, specific technologies, and products.[39] This system would allow, for instance, a Cisco salesperson who was making a call on a customer later in the day, to download a 20-minute chunk of information describing a new product feature and then watch it on a desktop computer.

Individualize Formal Training to Fit the Employee's Learning Style

The way that you process, internalize, and remember new and difficult material isn't necessarily the same way that I do. This fact means that effective formal training should be individualized to reflect the learning style of the employee.[40]

Some examples of different learning styles include reading, watching, listening, and participating. Some people absorb information better when they read about it. They're the kind of people who can learn to use computers by sitting in their study and reading manuals. Some people learn best by observation. They watch others and then emulate the behaviors they've seen. Such people can watch someone use a computer for a while, then copy what they've seen. Listeners rely heavily on their auditory senses to absorb information. They would prefer to learn how to use a computer, for instance, by listening to an audiotape. People who prefer a participating style learn by doing. They want to sit down, turn on the computer, and gain hands-on experience by practicing.

You can translate these styles into different learning methods. To maximize learning, readers should be given books or other reading material to review; watchers should get the opportunity to observe individuals modeling the new skills either in person or on video; listeners will benefit from hearing lectures or audiotapes; and participants will benefit most from experiential opportunities in which they can simulate and practice the new skills.

These different learning styles are obviously not mutually exclusive. In fact, good teachers recognize that their students learn differently and, therefore, provide multiple learning methods. They assign readings before class; give lectures; use visual aids to illustrate concepts; and have students participate in group projects, case analyses, role plays, and experiential learning exercises. If you know the preferred style of an employee, you can design his or her formal training program to optimize this preference. If you don't have that information, it's probably best to design the program to use a variety of learning styles. Overreliance on a single style places individuals who don't learn well from that style at a disadvantage.

CAREER DEVELOPMENT

Few human resource issues have changed as much in the past decade or two as the role of the organization in its employees' careers.[41] It has gone from paternalism—in which the organization took nearly complete responsibility for managing its employees' careers—to supporting individuals as they take personal responsibility for their future. And careers themselves have gone from a series of upward moves with increasing income, authority, status, and security to one in which people adapt quickly, learn continuously, and change their work identities over time.

For much of the twentieth century, companies recruited young workers with the intent that they would spend their entire career inside that single organization. For those with the right credentials and motivation, they created promotion paths dotted with ever-increasing responsibility. Employers would provide the training and opportunities, and employees would respond by demonstrating loyalty and

Source: Non Sequitur by Wiley. September 12, 1996. Washington Post Writers Group.

hard work. This arrangement has undergone serious decay. High uncertainty now limits the ability of organizations to accurately forecast future needs. Management seeks flexibility over permanence. Meanwhile, flattened hierarchies have reduced promotion opportunities. The result is that, today, career planning is something increasingly being done by individual employees rather than by their employers. It has become the employee's responsibility to keep his or her skills, abilities, and knowledge current and to prepare for tomorrow's new tasks.

The Organization's Responsibilities   What, if any, responsibility does the organization have for career development under these new rules? Basically, the organization's responsibility is to build employee self-reliance and to help employees maintain their marketability through continual learning.

The essence of a progressive career development program is built on providing support for employees to continually add to their skills, abilities, and knowledge. This support includes:

1. *Clearly communicating the organization's goals and future strategies.* When people know where the organization is headed, they're better able to develop a personal plan to share in that future.
2. *Creating growth opportunities.* Employees should have the opportunity to get new, interesting, and professionally challenging work experiences.
3. *Offering financial assistance.* The organization should offer tuition reimbursement to help employees keep current.
4. *Providing the time for employees to learn.* Organizations should be generous in providing paid time off from work for off-the-job training. In addition, workloads should not be so demanding that they preclude employees from having the time to develop new skills, abilities, and knowledge.

The Employee's Responsibilities   Today's employees should manage their own careers like entrepreneurs managing a small business. They should think of themselves as self-employed, even if employed in a large organization.[42] In a world of "free agency," the successful career will be built on maintaining flexibility and keeping skills and knowledge up to date. The following suggestions are consistent with the view that you, and only you, hold primary responsibility for your career.[43]

1. *Know yourself.* Know your strengths and weaknesses. What talents can you bring to an employer? Personal career planning begins by being honest with yourself.

2. *Manage your reputation.* Without appearing as a braggart, let others both inside and outside your current organization know about your achievements. Make you and your accomplishments visible.

3. *Build and maintain network contacts.* In a world of high mobility, you need to develop contacts. Join national and local professional associations, attend conferences, and network at social gatherings.

4. *Keep current.* Develop the specific skills and abilities that are in high demand. Avoid learning organization-specific skills that can't be transferred quickly to other employers.

5. *Balance your specialist and generalist competencies.* You need to stay current within your technical specialty. But you also need to develop general competencies that give you the versatility to react to an ever-changing work environment. Overemphasis in a single functional area or even in a narrow industry can limit your mobility.

6. *Document your achievements.* Employers are increasingly looking to what you've accomplished rather than the titles you've held. Seek jobs and assignments that will provide increasing challenges and that will also offer objective evidence of your competencies.

7. *Keep your options open.* Always have contingency plans prepared that you can call on when needed. You never know when your group will be eliminated, your department downsized, your project canceled, or your company acquired in a takeover. "Hope for the best but be prepared for the worst" may be cliché, but it's still not bad advice.

PERFORMANCE EVALUATION

Would you study differently or exert a different level of effort for a college course graded on a pass–fail basis than for one for which letter grades from A to F are used? When I ask that question of students, I usually get an affirmative answer. Students typically tell me that they study harder when letter grades are at stake. In addition, they tell me that when they take a course on a pass–fail basis, they tend to do just enough to ensure a passing grade.

This finding illustrates how performance evaluation systems influence behavior. Major determinants of your in-class behavior and out-of-class studying effort in college are the criteria and techniques your instructor uses to evaluate your performance. Of course, what applies in the college context also applies to employees at work. In this section, we show how the choice of a performance evaluation system and the way it's administered can be an important force influencing employee behavior.

Purposes of Performance Evaluation

Performance evaluation serves a number of purposes in organizations.[44] Management uses evaluations for general *human resource decisions.* Evaluations provide input into important decisions such as promotions, transfers, and terminations. Evaluations *identify training and development needs.* They pinpoint employee skills and competencies that are currently inadequate but for which programs can be developed to remedy. Performance evaluations can be used as a *criterion against which selection and development programs are validated.* Newly hired employees who perform poorly can be identified through performance evaluation. Similarly, the effectiveness of training and development programs can be determined by assessing how well employees who have participated do on their performance evaluation. Evaluations also fulfill the purpose of *providing feedback to employees* on how the organization views their performance. Furthermore, performance evaluations are used as the *basis for reward allocations*. Decisions as to who gets merit pay increases and other rewards are frequently determined by performance evaluations.

Each of these functions of performance evaluation is important. Yet their importance to us depends on the perspective we're taking. Several are clearly relevant to human resource management decisions. But our interest is in organizational behavior. As a result, we shall be emphasizing performance evaluation in its role as a mechanism for providing feedback and as a determinant of reward allocations.

Performance Evaluation and Motivation

In Chapter 6, considerable attention was given to the expectancy model of motivation. We argued that this model currently offers one of the best explanations of what conditions the amount of effort an individual will exert on his or her job. A vital component of this model is performance, specifically the effort–performance and performance–reward links.

But what defines *performance*? In the expectancy model, it's the individual's performance evaluation. To maximize motivation, people need to perceive that the effort they exert leads to a favorable performance evaluation and that the favorable evaluation will lead to the rewards that they value.

Following the expectancy model of motivation, if the objectives that employees are expected to achieve are unclear, if the criteria for measuring those objectives are vague, and if the employees lack confidence that their efforts will lead to a satisfactory appraisal of their performance or believe that there will be an unsatisfactory payoff by the organization when their performance objectives are achieved, we can expect individuals to work considerably below their potential.

In the real world of organizations, one explanation for why many employees may not be motivated is that the performance evaluation process is often more political than objective. Many managers will subordinate objective accuracy for self-serving ends—deliberately manipulating evaluations to get the outcomes they want.[45]

What Do We Evaluate?

The criteria or criterion that management chooses to evaluate, when appraising employee performance, will have a major influence on what employees do. Two examples illustrate this.

In a public employment agency, which served workers seeking employment and employers seeking workers, employment interviewers were appraised by the number of interviews they conducted. Consistent with the thesis that the evaluating criteria influence behavior, interviewers emphasized the *number* of interviews conducted rather than the *placements* of clients in jobs.[46]

A management consultant specializing in police research noticed that, in one community, officers would come on duty for their shift, proceed to get into their police cars, drive to the highway that cut through the town, and speed back and forth along this highway for their entire shift. Clearly, this fast cruising had little to do with good police work, but this behavior made considerably more sense once the consultant learned that the community's city council used mileage on police vehicles as an evaluative measure of police effectiveness.[47]

These examples demonstrate the importance of criteria in performance evaluation. This, of course, leads to the question: What should management evaluate?

The three most popular sets of criteria are individual task outcomes, behaviors, and traits.

Individual Task Outcomes If ends count, rather than means, then management should evaluate an employee's task outcomes. Using task outcomes, a plant manager could be judged on criteria such as quantity produced, scrap generated, and cost per unit of production. Similarly, a salesperson could be assessed on overall sales volume in his or her territory, dollar increase in sales, and number of new accounts established.

Behaviors In many cases, it's difficult to identify specific outcomes that can be directly attributable to an employee's actions. This is particularly true of personnel in advisory or support positions and individuals whose work assignments are intrinsically part of a group effort. In the latter case, the group's performance may be readily evaluated, but the contribution of each group member may be difficult or impossible to identify clearly. In such instances, it's not unusual for management to evaluate the employee's behavior. Using the previous examples, behaviors of a plant manager that could be used for performance evaluation purposes might include promptness in submitting his or her monthly reports or the leadership style that the manager exhibits. Pertinent salesperson behaviors could be the average number of contact calls made per day or sick days used per year.

Employees at Lands' End, the Dodgeville, WI, catalog retailer, are given a great deal of freedom to solve customers' problems over the phone, and they use it. Their product knowledge as well as their ability to satisfy customers who need help with, for instance, tying a bowtie or making a dog coat from children's pajamas, are among the behaviors on which their job performance is evaluated.

Note that these behaviors needn't be limited to those directly related to individual productivity.[48] As we pointed out in our previous discussion on organizational citizenship behavior (see specifically Chapters 1 and 4), helping others, making suggestions for improvements, and volunteering for extra duties make work groups and organizations more effective. So including subjective or contextual factors in a performance evaluation—as long as they contribute to organizational effectiveness—may not only make sense, they may also improve coordination, teamwork, cooperation, and overall organizational performance.

Traits The weakest set of criteria, yet one that is still widely used by organizations, is individual traits.[49] We say they're weaker than either task outcomes or behaviors because they're farthest removed from the actual performance of the job itself. Traits such as having "a good attitude," showing "confidence," being "dependable," "looking busy," or possessing "a wealth of experience" may or may not be highly correlated with positive task outcomes, but only the naive would ignore the reality that such traits are frequently used in organizations as criteria for assessing an employee's level of performance.

Who Should Do the Evaluating?

Who should evaluate an employee's performance? The obvious answer would seem to be his or her immediate boss. By tradition, a manager's authority typically has included appraising subordinates' performance. The logic behind this tradition seems to be that since managers are held responsible for their employees' performance, it only makes sense that these managers do the evaluating of that performance. But that logic may be flawed. Others may actually be able to do the job better.

Immediate Superior   The majority of performance evaluations at the lower and middle levels of organizations continue to be conducted by an employee's immediate boss.[50] Yet a number of organizations are recognizing the drawbacks to using this source of evaluation. For instance, many bosses feel unqualified to evaluate the unique contributions of each of their employees. Others resent being asked to "play God" with their employees' careers. In addition, with many of today's organizations using self-managed teams, telecommuting, and other organizing devices that distance bosses from their employees, an employee's immediate superior may not be the most reliable judge of that employee's performance.

Peers   Peer evaluations are one of the most reliable sources of appraisal data. Why? First, peers are close to the action. Daily interactions provide them with a comprehensive view of an employee's job performance. Second, using peers as raters results in a number of independent judgments. A boss can offer only a single evaluation, but peers can provide multiple appraisals. And the average of several ratings is often more reliable than a single evaluation. On the downside, peer evaluations can suffer from co-workers' unwillingness to evaluate one another and from biases based on friendship or animosity.

Self-Evaluation   Having employees evaluate their own performance is consistent with values such as self-management and empowerment. Self-evaluations get high marks from employees themselves; they tend to lessen employees' defensiveness about the appraisal process; and they make excellent vehicles for stimulating job performance discussions between employees and their superiors. However, as you might guess, they suffer from overinflated assessment and self-serving bias. Moreover, self-evaluations are often low in agreement with superiors' ratings.[51] Because of these serious drawbacks, self-evaluations are probably better suited to developmental uses than for evaluative purposes.

Immediate Subordinates   A fourth judgment source is an employee's immediate subordinates. Its proponents argue that it's consistent with recent trends toward enhancing honesty, openness, and empowerment in the workplace.

Immediate subordinates' evaluations can provide accurate and detailed information about a manager's behavior because the evaluators typically have frequent contact with the person being evaluated. The obvious problem with this form of rating is fear of reprisal from bosses who are given unfavorable evaluations. Therefore, respondent anonymity is crucial if these evaluations are to be accurate.

360-Degree Evaluations   The latest approach to performance evaluation is the use of 360-degree evaluations.[52] It provides for performance feedback from the full circle of daily contacts that an employee might have, ranging from mailroom personnel to customers to bosses to peers (see Exhibit 17-3 on page 502). The number of appraisals can be as few as three or four evaluations or as many as 25, with most organizations collecting five to ten per employee.

A recent survey shows that about 12 percent of American organizations are using full 360-degree programs, but the trend is growing.[53] Companies currently using this approach include Alcoa, Du Pont, Levi Strauss, Honeywell, UPS, Sprint, AT&T, and W.L. Gore & Associates.

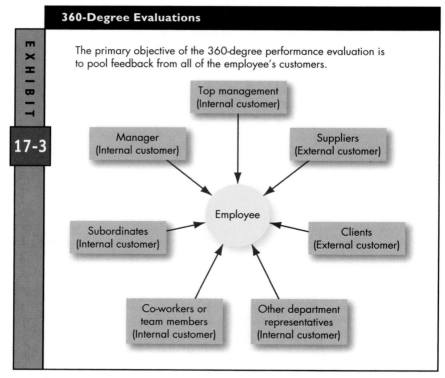

The primary objective of the 360-degree performance evaluation is to pool feedback from all of the employee's customers.

Top management
(Internal customer)

Manager
(Internal customer)

Suppliers
(External customer)

Employee

Subordinates
(Internal customer)

Clients
(External customer)

Co-workers or
team members
(Internal customer)

Other department
representatives
(Internal customer)

Source: Adapted from *Personnel Journal*, November 1994, p. 100.

What's the appeal of 360-degree evaluations? They fit well into organizations that have introduced teams, employee involvement, and quality-management programs. By relying on feedback from co-workers, customers, and subordinates, these organizations are hoping to give everyone more of a sense of participation in the review process and gain more accurate readings on employee performance. On this later point, 360-degree evaluations are consistent with evidence that employee performance varies across contexts and that people behave differently with different constituencies.[54] The use of multiple sources, therefore, is more likely to capture this variety of behavior accurately.

Methods of Performance Evaluation

The previous sections explained *what* we evaluate and *who* should do the evaluating. Now we ask: *How* do we evaluate an employee's performance? That is, what are the specific techniques for evaluation? This section reviews the major performance evaluation methods.

Written Essays   Probably the simplest method of evaluation is to write a narrative describing an employee's strengths, weaknesses, past performance, potential, and suggestions for improvement. The written essay requires no complex forms or extensive training to complete. But the results often reflect the ability of the writer. A good or bad appraisal may be determined as much by the evaluator's writing skill as by the employee's actual level of performance.

critical incidents

Evaluating the behaviors that are key in making the difference between executing a job effectively and executing it ineffectively.

Critical Incidents   **Critical incidents** focus the evaluator's attention on the behaviors that are key in making the difference between executing a job effectively and executing it ineffectively. That is, the appraiser writes down anecdotes that describe what the employee did that was especially effective or ineffective. The key here is that only specific behaviors, not vaguely defined personality traits, are cited. A list of critical incidents provides a rich set of examples from which the employee can be shown the behaviors that are desirable and those that call for improvement.

Graphic Rating Scales   One of the oldest and most popular methods of evaluation is the use of **graphic rating scales**. In this method, a set of performance factors, such as quantity and quality of work, depth of knowledge, cooperation, loyalty, attendance, honesty, and initiative, is listed. The evaluator then goes down the list and rates each on incremental scales. The scales typically specify five points, so a factor such as *job knowledge* might be rated 1 ("poorly informed about work duties") to 5 ("has complete mastery of all phases of the job").

    Why are graphic ratings scales so popular? Although they don't provide the depth of information that essays or critical incidents do, they are less time consuming to develop and administer. They also allow for quantitative analysis and comparison.

graphic rating scales
An evaluation method in which the evaluator rates performance factors on an incremental scale.

Behaviorally Anchored Rating Scales   **Behaviorally anchored rating scales** (BARS) combine major elements from the critical incident and graphic rating scale approaches: The appraiser rates the employees based on items along a continuum, but the points are examples of actual behavior on the given job rather than general descriptions or traits.

    BARS specify definite, observable, and measurable job behavior. Examples of job-related behavior and performance dimensions are found by asking participants to give specific illustrations of effective and ineffective behavior regarding each performance dimension. These behavioral examples are then translated into a set of performance dimensions, each dimension having varying levels of performance. The results of this process are behavioral descriptions, such as *anticipates*, *plans, executes, solves immediate problems, carries out orders*, and *handles emergency situations*.

behaviorally anchored rating scales (BARS)
Scales that combine major elements from the critical incident and graphic rating scale approaches: The appraiser rates the employees based on items along a continuum, but the points are examples of actual behavior on the given job rather than general descriptions or traits.

Forced Comparisons   Forced comparisons evaluate one individual's performance against the performance of another or others. It is a relative rather than an absolute measuring device. The three most popular comparisons are group order ranking, individual ranking, and paired comparisons.

    The **group order ranking** requires the evaluator to place employees into a particular classification, such as top one-fifth or second one-fifth. This method is often used in recommending students to graduate schools. Evaluators are asked whether the student ranks in the top 5 percent of the class, the next 5 percent, the next 15 percent, and so forth. But when used by managers to appraise employees, managers deal with all their subordinates. Therefore, if a rater has 20 employees, only four can be in the top fifth and, of course, four must also be relegated to the bottom fifth.

    The **individual ranking** approach rank-orders employees from best to worst. If the manager is required to appraise 30 employees, this approach assumes that the difference between the first and second employee is the same as that between the twenty-first and twenty-second. Even though some of the employees may be closely grouped, this approach allows for no ties. The result is a clear ordering of employees, from the highest performer down to the lowest.

group order ranking
An evaluation method that places employees into a particular classification, such as quartiles.

individual ranking
An evaluation method that rank-orders employees from best to worst.

Forced Rankings Gain in Popularity

It's become one of the fastest-growing trends in performance evaluation. Companies like Ford, GE, Microsoft, Sun Microsystems, and Conoco are among the 20 percent of U.S. companies that now rank their employees from best to worst and then use those rankings to determine pay and make other human resource decisions.

Many top executives became frustrated by managers who rated all their employees "above average." In addition, executives wanted to create a system that would increase the organization's competitiveness—one that would reward the very best performers and encourage poor performers to leave. So they are turning to forced rankings or what has been called "rank and yank" by its critics.

For instance, all 18,000 of Ford Motor's managers undergo this process. These managers are divided into groups of 30 to 50, then rated. For each group, 10 percent have to get an A, 80 percent a B, and 10 percent a C. Anyone receiving a C is restricted from a pay raise and two consecutive years of a C rating results in either a demotion or termination.

The most well-known "rank and yank" program is GE's "20-70-10 plan." The company forces the heads of each of its divisions to review all managers and professional employees, and to identify their top 20 percent, middle 70 percent, and bottom 10 percent. GE then does everything possible to keep and reward its top performers and fires all bottom-group performers. The company's former CEO stated, "A company that bets its future on its people must remove the lower 10 percent, and keep removing it every year—always raising the bar of performance and increasing the quality of its leadership."

Proponents see these forced rankings and elimination of weak performers as a way to continually improve an organization's workforce and to reward those who are most deserving. Critics, on the other hand, argue that these programs are harsh, arbitrary, and create a "zero-sum game" that discourages cooperation. Critics also say that these programs run counter to the belief, held by many, that almost any worker is salvageable.

Source: Based on R. Abelson, "Companies Turn to Grades, and Employees Go to Court," *New York Times*, March 19, 2001, p. A1; D. Jones, "More Firms Cut Workers Ranked at Bottom to Make Way for Talent," *USA Today*, May 30, 2001, p. 1B; and J. Greenwald, "Rank and Fire," *Time*, June 18, 2001, pp. 38–40.

paired comparison

An evaluation method that compares each employee with every other employee and assigns a summary ranking based on the number of superior scores that the employee achieves.

The **paired comparison** approach compares each employee with every other employee and rates each as either the superior or the weaker member of the pair. After all paired comparisons are made, each employee is assigned a summary ranking based on the number of superior scores he or she achieved. This approach ensures that each employee is compared against every other, but it can obviously become unwieldy when many employees are being compared.

Multiperson comparisons can be combined with one of the other methods to blend the best from both absolute and relative standards. For example, recent studies of Ivy League universities have found widespread evidence of grade inflation.[55] In one recent year, 46 percent of all undergraduate grades at Harvard were A's. At Princeton, 43 percent of all undergraduate grades were A's, with only 12 percent below the B range. One way for these universities to deal with this problem would be to require instructors to include not only an absolute letter grade but also relative data on class size and rank. So a prospective employer or graduate school could look at two students who each got an "A" in their physical geology courses and draw considerably different conclusions about each because next to one grade it says "ranked 2nd out of 26," while the other says "ranked 14th out of 30." Obviously, the former student performed better, relatively, than did the latter.

Suggestions for Improving Performance Evaluations

The performance evaluation process is a potential minefield of problems. For instance, evaluators can make leniency, halo, and similarity errors, or use the process for political purposes. They can unconsciously inflate evaluations (positive leniency), understate performance (negative leniency), or allow the assessment of one characteristic to unduly influence the assessment of other characteristics (the halo error). Some appraisers bias their evaluations by unconsciously favoring people who have qualities and traits similar to themselves (the similarity error). And, of course, some evaluators see the evaluation process as a political opportunity to overtly reward or punish employees they like or dislike. Although there are no protections that will *guarantee* accurate performance evaluations, the following suggestions can significantly help to make the process more objective and fair.

Emphasize Behaviors Rather Than Traits   Many traits often considered to be related to good performance may, in fact, have little or no performance relationship. For example, traits such as loyalty, initiative, courage, reliability, and self-expression are intuitively appealing as characteristics in employees. But the relevant question is: Are individuals who are evaluated as high on those traits higher performers than those who rate low? We can't answer this question easily. We know that there are employees who rate high on these characteristics and are poor performers. We can find others who are excellent performers but do not score well on traits such as these. Our conclusion is that traits such as loyalty and initiative may be prized by managers, but there is no evidence to support that certain traits will be adequate synonyms for performance in a large cross section of jobs.

Another weakness of trait evaluation is the judgment itself. What is "loyalty"? When is an employee "reliable"? What you consider "loyalty," I may not. So traits suffer from weak interrater agreement.

Document Performance Behaviors in a Diary   Diaries help evaluators to better organize information in their memory. The evidence indicates that by keeping a diary of specific critical incidents for each employee, evaluations tend to be more accurate and less prone to rating errors.[56] Diaries, for instance, tend to reduce leniency and halo errors because they encourage the evaluator to focus on performance-related behaviors rather than on traits.

Use Multiple Evaluators   As the number of evaluators increases, the probability of attaining more accurate information increases. If rater error tends to follow a normal curve, an increase in the number of appraisers will tend to find the majority congregating about the middle. You see this approach being used in athletic competitions in such sports as diving and gymnastics. A set of evaluators judges a performance, the highest and lowest scores are dropped, and the final performance evaluation is made up from the cumulative scores of those remaining. The logic of multiple evaluators applies to organizations as well.

If an employee has had ten supervisors, nine having rated her excellent and one poor, we can discount the value of the one poor evaluation. Therefore, by moving employees about within the organization so as to gain a number of evaluations or by using multiple assessors (as provided in 360-degree appraisals), we increase the probability of achieving more valid and reliable evaluations.

Evaluate Selectively   Appraisers should evaluate only in areas in which they have some expertise.[57] If raters make evaluations on only the dimensions on which they are in a good position to rate, we increase the interrater agreement and make the evaluation a more valid process. This approach also recognizes that different organizational levels often have different orientations toward those being rated and observe them in different settings. In general, therefore, we would recommend that appraisers should be as close as possible, in terms of organizational level, to the individual being evaluated. Conversely, the more levels that separate the evaluator and the person being evaluated, the less opportunity the evaluator has to observe the individual's behavior and, not surprisingly, the greater the possibility for inaccuracies.

Train Evaluators   If you can't *find* good evaluators, the alternative is to *make* good evaluators. There is substantial evidence that training evaluators can make them more accurate raters.[58]

Common errors such as halo and leniency have been minimized or eliminated in workshops where managers practice observing and rating behaviors. These workshops typically run from one to three days, but allocating many hours to training may not always be necessary. One case has been cited in which both halo and leniency errors were decreased immediately after exposing evaluators to explanatory training sessions lasting only five minutes.[59] But the effects of training appear to diminish over time.[60] This suggests the need for regular refresher sessions.

Provide Employees with Due Process   The concept of *due process* can be applied to appraisals to increase the perception that employees are treated fairly.[61] Three features characterize due process systems: (1) Individuals are provided with adequate notice of what is expected of them; (2) all relevant evidence to a proposed violation is aired in a fair hearing so the individuals affected can respond; and (3) the final decision is based on the evidence and free from bias.

There is considerable evidence that evaluation systems often violate employees' due process by providing them with infrequent and relatively general performance feedback, allowing them little input into the appraisal process, and knowingly introducing bias into performance ratings. However, when due process has been part of the evaluation system, employees report positive reactions to the appraisal process, perceive the evaluation results as more accurate, and express increased intent to remain with the organization.

Providing Performance Feedback

For many managers, few activities are more unpleasant than providing performance feedback to employees.[62] In fact, unless pressured by organizational policies and controls, managers are likely to ignore this responsibility.[63]

Why the reluctance to give performance feedback? There seem to be at least three reasons. First, managers are often uncomfortable discussing performance weaknesses directly with employees. Given that almost every employee could stand to improve in some areas, managers fear a confrontation when presenting negative feedback. This apparently even applies when people give negative feedback to a computer! Bill Gates reports that Microsoft conducted a project that required users to rate their experience with a computer. "When we had the computer the users had worked with ask for an evaluation of its performance, the responses tended to be positive. But when we had a second computer ask the same people to evaluate their encounters with the first machine, the people were significantly more critical. Their reluctance to criticize the first computer 'to its face' suggested that they didn't want to hurt its feelings, even though they knew it was only a machine."[64] Second, many employees tend to become defensive when their weaknesses are pointed out. Instead of accepting the feedback as constructive and a basis for improving performance, some employees challenge the evaluation by criticizing the manager or redirecting blame to someone else. A survey of 151 area managers in

Philadelphia, for instance, found that 98 percent of these managers encountered some type of aggression after giving employees negative appraisals.[65] Finally, employees tend to have an inflated assessment of their own performance. Statistically speaking, half of all employees must be below-average performers. But the evidence indicates that the average employee's estimate of his or her own performance level generally falls around the 75th percentile.[66] So even when managers are providing good news, employees are likely to perceive it as not good enough.

The solution to the performance feedback problem is not to ignore it, but to train managers in how to conduct constructive feedback sessions. An effective review—one in which the employee perceives the appraisal as fair, the manager as sincere, and the climate as constructive—can result in the employee leaving the interview in an upbeat mood, informed about the performance areas in which he or she needs to improve, and determined to correct the deficiencies.[67] In addition, the performance review should be designed more as a counseling activity than a judgment process. This can best be accomplished by allowing the review to evolve out of the employee's own self-evaluation.

What About Team Performance Evaluations?

Performance evaluation concepts have been almost exclusively developed with only individual employees in mind. This reflects the historic belief that individuals are the core building block around which organizations are built. But as we've described throughout this book, more and more organizations are restructuring themselves around teams. In organizations that use teams, how should they evaluate performance? Four suggestions have been offered for designing a system that supports and improves the performance of teams.[68]

1. *Tie the team's results to the organization's goals.* It's important to find measurements that apply to important goals that the team is supposed to accomplish.

2. *Begin with the team's customers and the work process the team follows to satisfy customers' needs.* The final product the customer receives can be evaluated in terms of the customer's requirements. The transactions between teams can be evaluated based on delivery and quality. And the process steps can be evaluated based on waste and cycle time.

3. *Measure both team and individual performance.* Define the roles of each team member in terms of accomplishments that support the team's work process. Then assess each member's contribution and the team's overall performance. Remember that individual skills are necessary for team success but are not sufficient for good team performance.[69]

4. *Train the team to create its own measures.* Having the team define its objectives and those of each member ensures that everyone understands their role on the team and helps the team to develop into a more cohesive unit.

THE UNION-MANAGEMENT INTERFACE

Labor unions are a vehicle by which employees act collectively to protect and promote their interests. Currently, in the United States, about 13 percent of the private sector workforce belongs to and is represented by a union. This number is considerably higher in other countries. For instance, the comparable figures for Canada and Australia are 37 percent and 26 percent, respectively.[70]

For employees who are members of a labor union, wage levels and conditions of employment are explicitly articulated in a contract that is negotiated, through collective bargaining, between representatives of the union and the organization's

labor union

An organization, made up of employees, that acts collectively to protect and promote employee interests.

management. Where a labor union exists, it influences a number of organizational activities.[71] Recruitment sources, hiring criteria, work schedules, job design, redress procedures, safety rules, and eligibility for training programs are examples of activities that are influenced by unions. American labor unions, having to contend with declining job markets in industries where they were historically strong—such as steel, automobiles, and rubber—have focused their attention in recent years on improving stagnant wages, discouraging corporate downsizings, minimizing the outsourcing of jobs, and coping with job obsolescence.[72]

The most obvious and pervasive area of labor's influence is wage rates and working conditions. Where unions exist, performance evaluation systems tend to be less complex because they play a relatively small part in reward decisions. Wage rates, when determined through collective bargaining, emphasize seniority and downplay performance differences.

Exhibit 17-4 shows what impact a union has on an employee's performance and job satisfaction. The union contract affects motivation through determination of wage rates, seniority rules, layoff procedures, promotion criteria, and security provisions. Unions can influence the competence with which employees perform their jobs by offering special training programs to their members, by requiring apprenticeships, and by allowing members to gain leadership experience through union organizational activities. The actual level of employee performance will be further influenced by collective bargaining restrictions placed on the amount of work produced, the speed with which work can be done, overtime allowances per worker, and the kind of tasks a given employee is allowed to perform.

The research evaluating the specific effect of unions on productivity is mixed.[73] Some studies found that unions had a positive effect on productivity as a result of improvements in labor–management relations as well as improvements in the quality of the labor force. In contrast, other studies have shown that unions have a negative impact on productivity by reducing the effectiveness of some productivity-enhancing

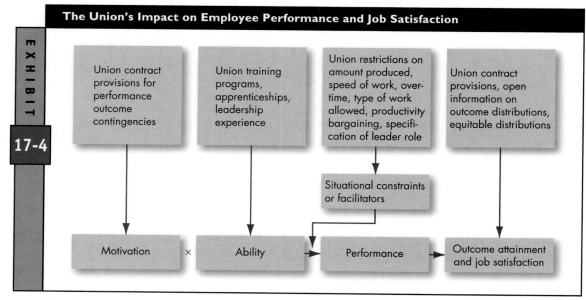

EXHIBIT 17-4

The Union's Impact on Employee Performance and Job Satisfaction

Source: T. H. Hammer, "Relationships between Local Union Characteristics and Worker Behavior and Attitudes," *Academy of Management Journal*, December 1978, p. 573

managerial practices and by contributing to a poorer labor–management climate. The evidence, then, is too inconsistent to draw any meaningful conclusions.

Are union members more satisfied with their jobs than their nonunion counterparts? The answer to this question is more complicated than a simple Yes or No. The evidence consistently demonstrates that unions have only indirect effects on job satisfaction.[74] They increase pay satisfaction but negatively affect satisfaction with the work itself (by decreasing job scope perceptions), satisfaction with co-workers and supervision (through less favorable perceptions of supervisory behavior), and satisfaction with promotions (through the lower importance placed on promotions).

INTERNATIONAL HUMAN RESOURCE PRACTICES: SELECTED ISSUES

Many of the human resource policies and practices discussed in this chapter have to be modified to reflect societal differences.[75] To illustrate this point, let's briefly look at the universality of selection practices and the importance of performance evaluation in different cultures.

Selection

A recent study of 300 large organizations in 22 countries demonstrated that selection practices differ by nation.[76] A few common procedures were found. For instance, the use of educational qualifications in screening candidates seems to be a universal practice. For the most part, however, different countries tend to emphasize different selection techniques. Structured interviews, as a case in point, were popular in some countries and nonexistent in others. The authors of the study suggested that "certain cultures may find structured interviews antithetical to beliefs about how one should conduct an interpersonal interaction or the extent to which one should trust the judgment of the interviewer."[77]

Although union membership has been declining for many years, U.S. labor unions are still powerful in many industries. These workers, on strike against Bath Iron Works, successfully closed down the company's production facility.

The above study, when combined with earlier research, tells us that there are no widely accepted universal selection practices. Moreover, global firms that attempt to implement standardized worldwide selection practices can expect to face considerable resistance from local managers. Policies and practices need to be modified to reflect culture-based norms and social values, as well as legal and economic differences.

Performance Evaluation

We previously examined the role that performance evaluation plays in motivation and in affecting behavior. Caution must be used, however, in generalizing across cultures. Why? Because many cultures are not particularly concerned with performance appraisal or, if they are, they don't look at it the same way as do managers in the United States or Canada.

Let's look at four cultural dimensions: individualism/collectivism, a person's relationship to the environment, time orientation, and focus of responsibility.

Individual-oriented cultures like the United States emphasize formal performance evaluation systems to a greater degree than informal systems. They advocate, for instance, written evaluations performed at regular intervals, the results of which are shared with employees and used in the determination of rewards. On the other hand, the collectivist cultures that dominate Asia and much of Latin America are characterized by more informal systems—downplaying formal feedback and disconnecting reward allocations from performance ratings. Japanese technology giant Fujitsu, for instance, introduced a formal, performance-based evaluation system in Japan in

Vicky Pagan-Leedy and her husband Robert moved from Indiana to Paris when she accepted a job as vice president for market research in the Paris office of Western Union. Despite being in a new environment, Ms. Pagan-Leedy can expect her annual performance evaluations during her three-year stay abroad to be conducted very much like they were at home in Evansville.

the mid-1990s. But the company recently began to dismantle it, recognizing that it "had proved flawed and a poor fit with Japanese [collectivist] business culture."[78]

U.S. and Canadian organizations hold people responsible for their actions because people in these countries believe that they can dominate their environment. In Middle Eastern countries, on the other hand, performance evaluations aren't likely to be widely used because managers in these countries tend to see people as subjugated to their environment.

Some countries, such as the United States, have a short-term time orientation. Performance evaluations are likely to be frequent in such a culture—at least once a year. In Japan, however, where people hold a long-term time frame, performance appraisals may occur only every five or ten years.

Israel's culture values group activities much more than does the culture of the United States or Canada. So, whereas North American managers emphasize the individual in performance evaluations, their counterparts in Israel are much more likely to emphasize group contributions and performance.

MANAGING DIVERSITY IN ORGANIZATIONS

David Morris and his father, Saul, started Habitat International in 1981. Located in Rossville, Georgia, the company manufacturers a grass-like indoor-outdoor carpet. From the beginning, the Morrises hired refugees from Cambodia, Bosnia, and Laos, many of whom didn't speak English. But when a social-service worker suggested in 1984 that the company hire mentally challenged people, Saul balked. Hiring someone with a condition such as Down's syndrome seemed too chancy. But David thought otherwise. He talked his dad into giving it a try.[79]

The first group of eight mentally disabled workers came in with their job coach from the social-services agency and went straight to work boxing mats. Two weeks later, says Saul, employees were coming to him and wondering why the company couldn't "hire more people like this, who care, do their work with pride, and smile?"

Today, 75 percent of Habitat's employees have some kind of disability. People with schizophrenia, for instance, are driving forklifts next to employees with autism or cerebral palsy. Meanwhile, the Morris father–son team are doing good things both for these people and for themselves. The disabled employees have enhanced self-esteem and are now self-sufficient enough to be off government aid, and the Morrises enjoy the benefits of a dedicated, hard-working labor force. "We have practically zero absenteeism and very little turnover," says David.

Habitat International illustrates the role of employee-selection in increasing diversity. But effective diversity programs go well beyond merely hiring a diverse workforce. They also include managing work/life conflicts and providing diversity training. These seem to be common characteristics among major organizations that have developed reputations as diversity leaders—including American Express, Du Pont, Johnson & Johnson, IBM, Pfizer, and Marriott International.[80]

Work/Life Conflicts

We introduced work/life balance in Chapter 1 and discussed the forces that are blurring the lines between work life and personal life. In this section we want to elaborate on this issue—specifically focusing on what organizations can do to help employees reduce conflicts.

Work/life conflicts grabbed management's attention in the 1980s, largely as a result of the growing number of women with dependent children entering the workforce. In response, most major organizations took actions to make their workplaces more family-friendly.[81] They introduced programs such as on-site child care, summer day camps, flextime, job sharing, leaves for school functions, telecommuting, and part-time employment. But organizations quickly realized that work/life conflicts were not experienced only by female employees with children. Male workers and women without children were also facing this problem. Heavy workloads and increased travel demands, for instance, were making it increasingly hard for a wide range of employees to meet both work and personal responsibilities. A Harvard study, for example, found that 82 percent of men between the ages of 20 and 39 said that a "family-friendly" schedule was their most important job criterion.[82] Even among employees who seemed to be able to "do it all," many were experiencing guilt or stress.[83]

Today's progressive workplace is being modified to accommodate the varied needs of a diverse workforce. This includes providing a wide range of scheduling options and benefits that allow employees more flexibility at work and which allows them to better balance or integrate their work and personal lives. Exhibit 17-5 on page 512 lists some examples of initiatives that organizations provide to help their employees reduce work/life conflicts.

Recent research on work/life conflicts has provided new insights for managers into what works and when. For instance, evidence indicates that time pressures aren't the primary problem underlying work/life conflicts.[84] It's the psychological interference of work into the family domain and vice versa. People are worrying about personal problems at work and thinking about work problems at home. So dad may physically make it home in time for dinner but his mind is elsewhere while he's at the dinner table. This suggests that organizations should spend less effort helping employees with time-management issues and more effort at helping them clearly segment their lives. Keeping workloads reasonable, reducing work-related travel, and offering on-site quality child-care are examples of practices that can help in this endeavor. Also, not surprisingly, people have been found to differ in their preference for scheduling options and benefits.[85] Some people prefer organizational initiatives that better segment work from their personal lives. Others prefer initiatives that facilitate integration. For instance, flextime segments because it allows employees to schedule work hours that are less likely to conflict with personal responsibilities. On the other hand, on-site child care integrates by blurring the boundaries between work and family responsibilities. People who prefer segmentation are more likely to be satisfied and committed to their work when offered options such as flextime, job sharing, and part-time hours. People who prefer integration are more likely to respond positively to options such as on-site child care, gym facilities, and company-sponsored family picnics.

Diversity Training

The centerpiece of most diversity programs is training. For instance, a relatively recent survey found that, among companies with diversity initiatives, 93 percent used training as part of their programs.[86] Diversity training programs are generally intended to provide a vehicle for increasing awareness and examining stereotypes. Participants learn to value individual differences, increase their cross-cultural understanding, and confront stereotypes.[87] In today's global economy, diversity training can be particularly helpful in accelerating cooperation in multinational work teams, facilitating group learning, and reducing cultural misunderstandings.[88]

The typical program lasts from half a day to three days and includes role-playing exercises, lectures, discussions, and sharing of experiences. For example, a training exercise at Hartford Insurance that sought to increase sensitivity to aging

EXHIBIT

17-5

Work/Life Initiatives

Strategy	Program or Policy	Example
Time-based strategies	Flextime Job sharing Part-time work Leave for new parents Telecommuting Closing plants/offices for special occasions	At Mentor Graphics, 98% of employees use flextime IBM gives parents three years of job-guaranteed leave following childbirth J. M. Smuckers shuts down plants in deer country for first day of hunting season
Information-based strategies	Intranet work/life Web site Relocation assistance Eldercare resources	Ernst & Young provides intranet work/life Web sites that include information on how to write flexible work arrangements proposals, find a job share partner, etc.
Money-based strategies	Vouchers for child care Flexible benefits Adoption assistance Discounts for child care tuition Leave with pay	At Lucent Technologies, employees with six months of service receive 52 weeks of childbirth leave at half pay
Direct services	On-site child care Emergency back-up care On-site health/beauty services Concierge services Take-out dinners	S. C. Johnson offers its employees subsidized concierge services for car maintenance, shopping, etc. AFLAC has two on-site child care centers Genentech has an on-site hair salon Stratus Technologies provides on-site mammograms and skin-cancer testing Every major location of Johnson & Johnson has a fitness center
Culture-change strategies	Training for managers to help employees deal with work/life conflicts Tie manager pay to employee satisfaction Focus on employees' actual performance, not "face time"	Lucent, Marriott, Merck, Pfizer, Prudential, and Xerox, among others, tie manager pay to employee satisfaction

Source: Based on C. A. Thompson, "Managing the Work-Life Balancing Act: An Introductory Exercise," *Journal of Management Education,* April 2002, p. 210; and R. Levering and M. Moskowitz, "The Best in the Worst of Times," *Fortune,* February 4, 2002, pp. 60–90.

asked participants to respond to the following four questions: (1) If you didn't know how old you are, how old would you guess you are? In other words, how old do you feel inside? (2) When I was 18, I thought middle age began at age ____. (3) Today, I think middle age begins at age ____. (4) What would be your first reaction if someone called you "an older worker"?[89] Answers to these questions were then used to analyze age-related stereotypes. In another program designed to raise awareness of the power of stereotypes, each participant was asked to write an anonymous paper detailing all groups—women, born-again Christians, blacks, gays, Hispanics, men—to which they had attached stereotypes.[90] They were also asked to explain why they'd had trouble working with certain groups in the past. Based on responses, guest speakers were brought into the class to shatter the stereotypes directed at each group. This was followed by extensive discussion.

SUMMARY AND IMPLICATIONS FOR MANAGERS

An organization's human resource policies and practices represent important forces for shaping employee behavior and attitudes. In this chapter, we specifically discussed the influence of selection practices, training and development programs, performance evaluation systems, and the existence of a union.

Selection Practices

An organization's selection practices will determine who gets hired. If properly designed, they will identify competent candidates and accurately match them to the job and the organization. The use of the proper selection devices will increase the probability that the right person will be chosen to fill a slot.

Although employee selection is far from a science, some organizations fail to design their selection systems so as to maximize the likelihood that the right person–job fit will be achieved. When errors are made, the chosen candidate's performance may be less than satisfactory. Training may be necessary to improve the candidate's skills. At worst, the candidate will prove unacceptable and a replacement will need to be found. Similarly, when the selection process results in the hiring of less-qualified candidates or individuals who don't fit into the organization, those chosen are likely to feel anxious, tense, and uncomfortable. This, in turn, is likely to increase dissatisfaction with the job.

Training and Development Programs

Training programs can affect work behavior in two ways. The most obvious is by directly improving the skills necessary for the employee to successfully complete his or her job. An increase in ability improves the employee's potential to perform at a higher level. Of course, whether that potential becomes realized is largely an issue of motivation.

A second benefit from training is that it increases an employee's self-efficacy. As you'll remember from Chapter 6, self-efficacy is a person's expectation that he or she can successfully execute the behaviors required to produce an outcome.[91] For employees, those behaviors are work tasks and the outcome is effective job performance. Employees with high self-efficacy have strong expectations about their abilities to perform successfully in new situations. They're confident and expect to be successful. Training, then, is a means to positively affect self-efficacy because employees may be more willing to undertake job tasks and exert a high level of effort. Or in expectancy terms (see Chapter 6), individuals are more likely to perceive their effort as leading to performance.

We also discussed career development in this chapter. We noted the significant decline in formal programs intended to guide an employee's career within a single organization. But employees still value career planning and development. So organizations can increase employee commitment, loyalty, and satisfaction by encouraging and guiding employees in developing a self-managed career plan, and by clearly communicating the organization's goals and future strategies, giving employees growth experiences, offering financial assistance to help employees keep their knowledge and skills current, and providing paid time off from work for off-the-job training.

Performance Evaluation

A major goal of performance evaluation is to assess accurately an individual's performance contribution as a basis for making reward allocation decisions. If the performance evaluation process emphasizes the wrong criteria or inaccurately appraises actual job performance, employees will be overrewarded or underrewarded. As demonstrated in Chapter 6, in our discussion of equity theory, this can lead to negative consequences such as reduced effort, increases in absenteeism, or a search for alternative job opportunities. In addition, the content of the performance evaluation has been found to influence employee performance and satisfaction.[92] Specifically, performance and satisfaction are increased when the evaluation is based on behavioral, results-oriented criteria, when career issues as well as performance issues are discussed, and when the employee has an opportunity to participate in the evaluation.

Union–Management Interface

The existence of a union in an organization adds another variable in our search to explain and predict employee behavior. The union has been found to be an important contributor to employees' perceptions, attitudes, and behavior.

The power of the union surfaces in the collective bargaining agreement that it negotiates with management. Much of what an employee can and cannot do on the job is formally stipulated in this agreement. In addition, the informal norms that union cohesiveness fosters can encourage or discourage high productivity, organizational commitment, and morale.

It's Time to Abolish Performance Evaluations

P erformance evaluations have failed us. They take up a lot of management's time and effort. And instead of providing valid and reliable information for human resource decisions, more often they do nothing other than demotivate employees. As practiced today, performance evaluations provide management with essentially worthless data and make employees angry, jealous, and cynical.

There is no shortage of good reasons why performance evaluations should be eliminated.[a] The whole process, for instance, is political. It's used by management for ulterior purposes—to cover themselves against lawsuits, to justify different levels of pay, to reward allies, and to punish enemies. Employees see the process as a sham that can be manipulated for political purposes. So most employees put little value in the process or in the final results.

Performance evaluations are subjective. In spite of efforts to formalize and systematize the process, rater errors continue to make any results highly suspicious. Evaluation results also tend to be inflated and nondifferentiating. It's typical for 80 percent or more of employees to be rated above average. This tends to overvalue most people's contribution and overlook those who are underperforming.

Employees are not immune to the influences of regular performance evaluations. Regardless of their validity, most employees still want to receive favorable evaluations. This often encourages employees to misdirect their efforts in order to look good on the criteria management has chosen to appraise. This, of course, helps to explain many behaviors that actually undermine an organization's overall performance—such as following rules that don't make any sense or engaging in practices that forgo a large payoff in the long term in order to gain a small payoff immediately.

Performance evaluations were a good fit in the management world of the 1950s and 1960s—a world of bureaucratic organizations run by command-and-control managers. In today's climate of teamwork and empowerment, performance evaluations are obsolete and should be abolished.

[a]Much of this argument is based on T. Coens and M. Jenkins, *Abolishing Performance Appraisals* (San Francisco: Berrett-Koehler, 2000).

N o knowledgeable observer can fail to acknowledge that performance evaluation has its flaws. But that's no reason to abolish the practice.

If you eliminate performance evaluations, with what do you replace it? We still need some measure of an employee's contribution. We need to hold people accountable for previous commitments they've made to their work group and organization; and employees would still need some form of feedback on how they can improve if they come up short on meeting those commitments.

Many of the negatives associated with performance evaluations can be corrected by following what we have learned that can make appraisals more valid and reliable, and by focusing on development rather than evaluation.

Much of the criticism unleashed against performance evaluations is due to the way the process is handled. For instance, having employees participate in setting their work goals and having them engage in self-evaluation makes the process more democratic and less threatening. By using comparative rankings, management can minimize the effect of inflationary ratings. And the use of multiple evaluators lessens the likelihood of political influence and increases the validity of the results.

In addition, performance appraisals should be used for more than merely evaluation. That is, they should do more than just try to identify what's wrong. They should also be used for development purposes—helping employees learn how they can improve. When the appraisal process focuses more on development than evaluation, much of the criticism aimed at the process will subside. In a developmental role, managers no longer have to play God. Rather, they become a supportive coach helping employees to improve their performance.

The arguments against performance evaluation are misdirected. The concept is solid. What needs to be abolished is the mismanagement of the process. By emphasizing development rather than evaluation, and by making sure that best practices are followed, the performance evaluation can be a valuable tool for improving both employee and organizational performance.

Questions for Review

1. What is job analysis? How is it related to those the organization hires?

2. What are assessment centers? Why do you think they might be more effective for selecting managers than traditional written tests?

3. Contrast formal and informal training.

4. What can organizations do to help employees develop their careers?

5. What can individuals do to foster their own career development?

6. Why do organizations evaluate employees?

7. What are the advantages and disadvantages of the following performance evaluation methods: (a) written essays, (b) graphic rating scales, and (c) behaviorally anchored rating scales?

8. How can management effectively evaluate individuals when they work as part of a team?

9. How can an organization's performance evaluation system affect employee behavior?

10. What impact do unions have on an organization's reward system?

Questions for Critical Thinking

1. How could the phrase "the best predictor of future behavior is past behavior" guide you in managing human resources?

2. Describe a training program you might design to help employees develop their interpersonal skills. How would that program differ from one you designed to improve employee ethical behavior?

3. What relationship, if any, is there between job analysis and performance evaluation?

4. What problems, if any, can you see developing as a result of using 360-degree evaluations?

5. GE prides itself on continually raising the performance bar by annually letting go employees who perform in the lowest 10 percent. In contrast, Cleveland-based Lincoln Electric Co. prides itself on its no-layoff policy. Lincoln Electric has provided its employees with guaranteed employment since 1958. How can two successful companies have such different approaches to employment security? How can they both work? What implications can you derive from the success of these different practices?

Team Exercise — Evaluating Performance and Providing Feedback

Objective

To experience the assessment of performance and observe the providing of performance feedback.

Time

Approximately 30 minutes.

Procedure

A class leader is to be selected. He or she may be either a volunteer or someone chosen by your instructor. The class leader will preside over the class discussion and perform the role of manager in the evaluation review.

Your instructor will leave the room. The class leader is then to spend up to 15 minutes helping the class to evaluate your instructor. Your instructor understands that this is only a class exercise and is prepared to accept criticism (and, of course, any praise you may want to convey). Your instructor also recognizes that the leader's evaluation is actually a composite of many students' input. So be open and honest in your evaluation and have confidence that your instructor will not be vindictive.

Research has identified seven performance dimensions to the college instructor's job: (1) instructor knowledge, (2) testing procedures, (3) student–teacher relations, (4) organizational skills, (5) communication skills, (6) subject relevance, and (7) utility of assignments. The discussion of your instructor's performance should focus on these seven dimensions. The leader may want to take notes for personal use but will not be required to give your instructor any written documentation.

When the 15-minute class discussion is complete, the leader will invite the instructor back into the room. The performance review will begin as soon as the instructor walks through the door, with the class leader becoming the manager and the instructor playing himself or herself.

When completed, class discussion will focus on performance evaluation criteria and how well your class leader did in providing performance feedback.

Ethical Dilemma | Is It Unethical to "Shape" Your Resume?

When does "putting a positive spin" on your accomplishments step over the line to become misrepresentation or lying? Does a resume have to be 100 percent truthful? Consider the following three situations.

Sean left a job for which his title was "credit clerk." When looking for a new job, he describes his previous title as "credit analyst." He thinks it sounds more impressive. Is this retitling of a former job wrong?

About eight years ago, Emily took nine months off between jobs to travel overseas. Afraid that people might consider her unstable or lacking in career motivation, she put down on her resume that she was en-gaged in "independent consulting activities" during the period. Was she wrong?

Michael is 50 years old with an impressive career record. He spent five years in college 30 years ago, but he never got a degree. He is being considered for a $175,000-a-year vice presidency at another firm. He knows that he has the ability and track record to do the job, but he won't get the interview if he admits to not having a college degree. He knows that the probability that anyone would check his college records, at this point in his career, is very low. Should he put on his resume that he completed his degree?

Case Incident | Is This Any Way to Run a Business?

SAS Institute Inc. is probably the least-well-known major software company in the world. The company makes statistical analysis software (hence the acronym SAS). And it's growing very rapidly. From 1,900 employees five years ago, it now has 5,400. But SAS is not your typical software company. It's not your typical *anything* company!

At its headquarters, just outside Raleigh, North Carolina, there is a 36,000-square-foot gym for employees. There's a large, hardwood aerobic floor; two full-length basketball courts; pool tables; a private, skylighted yoga room, and workout areas. Outside, there are soccer and softball fields. Massages are available several times a week, and classes are offered in golf, African dance, tennis, and tai chi. The company also operates the largest on-site day-care facility in North Carolina. To encourage families to eat lunch together, the SAS cafeteria supplies baby seats and high chairs. To encourage families to eat dinner together, the company has a seven-hour workday, five days a week. Unlike many work-obsessive software firms, most SAS employees leave the office by 5 P.M. Management likes to call its workplace culture "relaxed."

The list of employee amenities at SAS goes on and on. Unlimited soda, coffee, tea, and juice. One week paid vacation between Christmas and New Year's Day. An on-site health clinic staffed with six nurse practitioners and two physicians. Zero cost to employees for health insurance. Dirty workout clothes laundered overnight at no charge. Casual dress every day. Elder-care advice and referrals. Unlimited sick days, and use of sick days to care for sick family members.

Is this any way to run a business? Management thinks so. SAS's strategy is to make it impossible for people not to do their work. Even though the company provides no stock options and salaries no better than competitive, the company has built an unbelievably loyal workforce. Whereas competitors typically have turnover rates above 30 percent, SAS's rate has never been higher than five percent. Management claims that it saves $67 million a year just in employee replacement–related costs such as recruitment, interviews, moving costs for new hires, and lost work time. That gives it an extra $12,500 per year per employee to spend on benefits.

Just in case anyone wonders if the company makes any money, we'll add the following. SAS is owned by just two people—Jim Goodnight and John Sall. *Forbes* magazine recently listed Goodnight, with $3 billion, as number 43 on its list of the 400 richest people in America. Sall, with $1.5 billion, was number 110.

Questions

1. One critic calls SAS "a big brother approach to managing people." Is the company too paternalistic? Can a company *be* too paternalistic?

2. When, if ever, do work/life initiatives become paternalistic?

3. What negatives, if any, would you find working for SAS?

4. Are progressive HR practices like those at SAS a *cause* or a *result* of high profits? Discuss.

5. Microsoft is an unbelievably successful software company. But no one would ever call their culture relaxed. It is "frantic." Employees regularly put in 12–14 hour days, six and seven days a week. How does Microsoft keep people? Do you think SAS and Microsoft attract different types of employees? Explain.

Source: Based on C. Fishman, "Sanity Inc.," *Fast Company*, January 1999, pp. 85–96.

KSS PROGRAM:

KNOW THE CONCEPTS
SELF-AWARENESS
SKILLS APPLICATIONS

Interviewing Skills

After you've read this chapter, take Self-Assessment #17 (What's My Decision-Making Style?) on your enclosed CD-ROM, and complete the skill-building module entitled Selection Interviewing on page 630.

Endnotes

1. C. Matlack, "The High Cost of France's Aversion to Layoffs," *Business Week*, November 5, 2001, p. 56.
2. See B. Becker and B. Gerhart, "The Impact of Human Resource Management on Organizational Performance: Progress and Prospects," *Academy of Management Journal*, August 1996, pp. 779–801; J. T. Delaney and M. A. Huselid, "The Impact of Human Resource Management Practices on the Perceptions of Organizational Performance," *Academy of Management Journal*, August 1996, pp. 949–69; and M. A. Huselid, S. E. Jackson, and R. S. Schuler, "Technical and Strategic Human Resource Management Effectiveness as Determinants of Firm Performance," *Academy of Management Journal*, February 1997, pp. 171–88.
3. See, for instance, C. T. Dortch, "Job-Person Match," *Personnel Journal*, June 1989, pp. 49–57; and S. Rynes and B. Gerhart, "Interviewer Assessments of Applicant 'Fit': An Exploratory Investigation," *Personnel Psychology*, Spring 1990, pp. 13–34.
4. See, for example, J. V. Ghorpade, *Job Analysis: A Handbook for the Human Resource Director* (Englewood Cliffs, NJ: Prentice Hall, 1988).
5. D. E. Bowen, G. E. Ledford Jr., and B. R. Nathan, "Hiring for the Organization, Not the Job," *Academy of Management Executive*, November 1991, pp. 35–51; E. E. Lawler III, "From Job-Based to Competency-Based Organizations," *Journal of Organizational Behavior*, January 1994, pp. 3–15; D. M. Cable and T. A. Judge, "Interviewers' Perceptions of Person-Organization Fit and Organizational Selection Decisions," *Journal of Applied Psychology*, August 1997, pp. 546–61; and A. L. Kristof-Brown, "Perceived Applicant Fit: Distinguishing Between Recruiters' Perceptions of Person–Job and Person–Organization Fit," *Personnel Psychology*, Autumn 2000, pp. 643–71.
6. R. A. Posthuma, F. P. Moregeson, and M. A. Campion, "Beyond Employment Interview Validity: A Comprehensive Narrative Review of Recent Research and Trend Over Time," *Personnel Psychology*, Spring 2002, p. 1.
7. L. Yoo-Lim, "More Companies Rely on Employee Interviews," *Business Korea*, November 1994, pp. 22–23.
8. T. J. Hanson and J. C. Balestreri-Spero, "An Alternative to Interviews," *Personnel Journal*, June 1985, p. 114. See also T. W. Dougherty, D. B. Turban, and J. C. Callender, "Confirming First Impressions in the Employment Interview: A Field Study of Interviewer Behavior," *Journal of Applied Psychology*, October 1994, pp. 659–65.
9. K. I. van der Zee, A. B. Bakker, and P. Bakker, "Why are Structured Interviews So Rarely Used in Personnel Selection?" *Journal of Applied Psychology*, February 2002, pp. 176–84.
10. See M. A. McDaniel, D. L. Whetzel, F. L. Schmidt, and S. D. Maurer, "The Validity of Employment Interviews: A Comprehensive Review and Meta-Analysis," *Journal of Applied Psychology*, August 1994, pp. 599–616; J. M. Conway, R. A. Jako, and D. F. Goodman, "A Meta-Analysis of Interrater and Internal Consistency Reliability of Selection Interviews," *Journal of Applied Psychology*, October 1995, pp. 565–79; M. A. Campion, D. K. Palmer, and J. E. Campion, "A Review of Structure in the Selection Interview," *Personnel Psychology*, Autumn 1997, pp. 655–702; F. L. Schmidt and J. E. Hunter, "The Validity and Utility of Selection Methods in Personnel Psychology: Practical and Theoretical Implications of 85 Years of Research Findings," *Psychological Bulletin*, September 1998, pp. 262–74;

and A. I. Huffcutt and D. J. Woehr, "Further Analysis of Employment Interview Validity: A Quantitative Evaluation of Interviewer-Related Structuring Methods," *Journal of Organizational Behavior*, July 1999, pp. 549–60.

11. R. L. Dipboye, *Selection Interviews: Process Perspectives* (Cincinnati: South-Western Publishing, 1992), pp. 42–44; and R. A. Posthuma, F. P. Moregeson, and M. A. Campion, "Beyond Employment Interview Validity," pp. 1–81.

12. A. I. Huffcutt, J. M. Conway, P. L. Roth, and N. J. Stone, "Identification and Meta-Analytic Assessment of Psychological Constructs Measured in Employment Interviews," *Journal of Applied Psychology*, October 2001, p. 910.

13. See G. A. Adams, T. C. Elacqua, and S. M. Colarelli, "The Employment Interview as a Sociometric Selection Technique," *Journal of Group Psychotherapy*, Fall 1994, pp. 99–113; R. L. Dipboye, "Structured and Unstructured Selection Interviews: Beyond the Job-Fit Model," *Research in Personnel Human Resource Management*, vol. 12, 1994, pp. 79–123; and B. Schneider, D. B. Smith, S. Taylor, and J. Fleenor, "Personality and Organizations: A Test of the Homogeneity of Personality Hypothesis," *Journal of Applied Psychology*, June 1998, pp. 462–70.

14. See, for example, J. H. Prager, "Nasty or Nice: 56-Question Quiz," *Wall Street Journal*, February 22, 2000, p. A-4.

15. G. Nicholsen, "Screen and Glean: Good Screening and Background Checks Help Make the Right Match for Every Open Position," *Workforce*, October 2000, pp. 70–72.

16. E. E. Ghiselli, "The Validity of Aptitude Tests in Personnel Selection," *Personnel Psychology*, Winter 1973, p. 475.

17. R. J. Herrnstein and C. Murray, *The Bell Curve: Intelligence and Class Structure in American Life* (New York: Free Press, 1994); and M. J. Ree, J. A. Earles, and M. S. Teachout, "Predicting Job Performance: Not Much More Than g," *Journal of Applied Psychology*, August 1994, pp. 518–24.

18. J. Flint, "Can You Tell Applesauce From Pickles?" *Forbes*, October 9, 1995, pp. 106–108.

19. D. S. Ones, C. Viswesvaran, and F. L. Schmidt, "Comprehensive Meta-Analysis of Integrity Test Validities: Findings and Implications for Personnel Selection and Theories of Job Performance," *Journal of Applied Psychology*, August 1993, pp. 679–703; P. R. Sackett and J. E. Wanek, "New Developments in the Use of Measures of Honesty, Integrity, Conscientiousness, Dependability, Trustworthiness, and Reliability for Personnel Selection," *Personnel Psychology*, Winter 1996, pp. 787–829; and F. L. Schmidt and J. E. Hunter, "The Validity and Utility of Selection Methods in Personnel Psychology."

20. P. Carbonara, "Hire for Attitude, Train for Skill," *Fast Company*, Greatest Hits, vol. 1, 1997, p. 68.

21. J. J. Asher and J. A. Sciarrino, "Realistic Work Sample Tests: A Review," *Personnel Psychology*, Winter 1974, pp. 519–33; and I. T. Robertson and R. S. Kandola, "Work Sample Tests: Validity, Adverse Impact and Applicant Reaction," *Journal of Occupational Psychology*, Spring 1982, pp. 171–82.

22. R. E. Carlson, "Effect of Interview Information in Altering Valid Impressions," *Journal of Applied Psychology*, February 1971, pp. 66–72; M. London and M. D. Hakel, "Effects of Applicant Stereotypes, Order, and Information on Interview Impressions," *Journal of Applied Psychology*, April 1974, pp. 157–62; and E. C. Webster, *The Employment Interview: A Social Judgment Process* (Ontario, Canada: S.I.P., 1982).

23. N. R. Bardack and F. T. McAndrew, "The Influence of Physical Attractiveness and Manner of Dress on Success in a Simulated Personnel Decision," *Journal of Social Psychology*, August 1985, pp. 777–78; and R. Bull and N. Rumsey, *The Social Psychology of Facial Appearance* (London: Springer-Verlag, 1988).

24. T. W. Dougherty, R. J. Ebert, and J. C. Callender, "Policy Capturing in the Employment Interview," *Journal of Applied Psychology*, February 1986; and T. M. Macan and R. L. Dipboye, "The Relationship of the Interviewers' Preinterview Impressions to Selection and Recruitment Outcomes," *Personnel Psychology*, Autumn 1990, pp. 745–69.

25. See, for instance, A. C. Spychalski, M. A. Quinones, B. B. Gaugler, and K. Pohley, "A Survey of Assessment Center Practices in Organizations in the United States, *Personnel Psychology*, Spring 1997, pp. 71–90; and C. Woodruffe, *Development and Assessment Centres: Identifying and Assessing Competence* (London: Institute of Personnel and Development, 2000).

26. B. B. Gaugler, D. B. Rosenthal, G. C. Thornton, and C. Benson, "Meta-Analysis of Assessment Center Validity," *Journal of Applied Psychology*, August 1987, pp. 493–511; G. C. Thornton, *Assessment Centers in Human Resource Management* (Reading, MA: Addison-Wesley, 1992); W. Arthur Jr., D. J. Woehr, and R. Maldegen, "Convergent and Discriminant Validity of Assessment Center Dimensions: A Conceptual and Empirical Reexamination of the Assessment Center Construct-Related Validity Paradox," *Journal of Management*, vol. 26, no. 4, 2000, pp. 813–35; and P. G. W. Jansen and B. A. M. Stoop, "The Dynamics of Assessment Center Validity: Results of a 7-Year Study," *Journal of Applied Psychology*, August 2001, pp. 741–53.

27. Cited in *Training*, October 2001, p. 42.

28. Cited in *Training*, March 2002, p. 24.

29. Cited in D. Baynton, "America's $60 Billion Problem," *Training*, May 2001, p. 51.

30. "Basic Skills Training Pays Off for Employers," *HRMagazine*, October 1999, p. 32.

31. D. Baynton, "America's $60 Billion Problem," p. 51.

32. A. Bernstein, "The Time Bomb in the Workforce: Illiteracy," *Business Week*, February 25, 2002, p. 122.

33. D. Baynton, "America's $60 Billion Problem," p. 52.

34. J. Barbarian, "Mark Spear: Director of Management and Organizational Development, Miller Brewing Co.," *Training*, October 2001, pp. 34–38.

35. G. R. Weaver, L. K. Trevino, and P. L. Cochran, "Corporate Ethics Practices in the Mid-1990's: An Empirical Study of the Fortune 1000," *Journal of Business Ethics*, February 1999, pp. 283–94.

36. K. Dobbs, "The U.S. Department of Labor Estimates that 70 Percent of Workplace Learning Occurs Informally," *Sales & Marketing Management*, November 2000, pp. 94–98.

37. S. J. Wells, "Forget the Formal Training. Try Chatting at the Water Cooler," *New York Times*, May 10, 1998, p. BU-11.

38. See, for instance, K. G. Brown, "Using Computers to Deliver Training: Which Employees Learn and Why?" *Personnel Psychology*, Summer 2001, pp. 271–96; and "The Delivery: How U.S. Organizations Use Classrooms and Computers in Training," *Training*, October 2001, pp. 66–72.

39. A. Muoio, "Cisco's Quick Study," *Fast Company*, October 2000, pp. 287–95.

40. D. A. Kolb, "Management and the Learning Process," *California Management Review*, Spring 1976, pp. 21–31; and B. Filipczak, "Different Strokes: Learning Styles in the Classroom," *Training*, March 1995, pp. 43–48.

41. D. T. Hall and Associates (ed.), *The Career Is Dead—Long Live the Career* (San Francisco: Jossey-Bass, 1996); and S. E. Sullivan, "The Changing Nature of Careers: A Review and Research Agenda," *Journal of Management*, vol. 25, no. 3, 1999, pp. 457–84.

42. T. Peters, *The Brand You* (New York: Knopf, 1999).

43. Based on P. Hirsch, *Pack Your Own Parachute: How to Survive Mergers, Takeovers, and Other Corporate Disasters* (Reading, MA: Addison-Wesley, 1987); R. Henkoff, "Winning the New Career Game," *Fortune*, July 12, 1993, pp. 46–49; and H. Lancaster, "As Company Programs Fade, Workers Turn to Guild-like Groups," *Wall Street Journal*, January 16, 1996, p. B1.

44. W. F. Cascio, *Applied Psychology in Human Resource Management*, 5th ed. (Upper Saddle River, NJ: Prentice Hall, 1998), p. 59.

45. See, for instance, C. O. Longnecker, H. P. Sims, and D. A. Gioia, "Behind the Mask: The Politics of Employee Appraisal," *Academy of Management Executive*, August 1987, pp. 183–93; P. Villanova and H. Bernardin, "Impression Management in the Context of Performance Appraisal," in R. A. Giacalone and P. Rosenfeld (eds.), *Impression Management in the Organization* (Hillsdale, NJ: Lawrence Erlbaum, 1989), pp. 299–314; and P. Villanova and H. Bernardin, "Performance Appraisal: The Means, Motive, and Opportunity to Manage Impressions," in R. A. Giacalone and P. Rosenfeld (eds.), *Applied Impression Management: How Image-Making Affects Managerial Decisions* (Newbury Park, CA: Sage, 1991), pp. 81–96.

46. P. M. Blau, *The Dynamics of Bureaucracy*, rev. ed. (Chicago: University of Chicago Press, 1963).

47. "The Cop-Out Cops," *National Observer*, August 3, 1974.

48. See W. C. Borman and S. J. Motowidlo, "Expanding the Criterion Domain to Include Elements of Contextual Performance," in N. Schmitt and W. C. Borman (eds.), *Personnel Selection in Organizations* (San Francisco: Jossey-Bass, 1993), pp. 71–98; W. H. Bommer, J. L. Johnson, G. A. Rich, P. M. Podsakoff, and S. B. MacKenzie, "On the Interchangeability of Objective and Subjective Measures of Employee Performance: A Meta-Analysis," *Personnel Psychology*, Autumn 1995, pp. 587–605.

49. A. H. Locher and K. S. Teel, "Appraisal Trends," *Personnel Journal*, September 1988, pp. 139–45.

50. G. P. Latham and K. N. Wexley, *Increasing Productivity through Performance Appraisal* (Reading, MA: Addison-Wesley, 1981), p. 80.

51. See review in R. D. Bretz, Jr., G. T. Milkovich, and W. Read, "The Current State of Performance Appraisal Research and Practice: Concerns, Directions, and Implications," *Journal of Management*, June 1992, p. 326.

52. See, for instance, W. W. Tornow and M. London, eds., *Maximizing the Value of 360-Degree Feedback* (San Francisco: Jossey-Bass, 1998); J. Ghorpade, "Managing Five Paradoxes of 360-Degree Feedback," *Academy of Management Executive*, February 2000, pp. 140–50; J. D. Facteau and S. B. Craig, "Are Performance Appraisal Ratings from Different Rating Sources Compatible?" *Journal of Applied Psychology*, April 2001, pp. 215–27; J. F. Brett and L. E. Atwater, "360-Degree Feedback: Accuracy, Reactions, and Perceptions of Usefulness," *Journal of Applied Psychology*, October 2001, pp. 930–42; and C. Wingrove, "Untangling the Myths of 360: Straight Talk for Successful Outcomes," *Compensation & Benefits Review*, November–December 2001, pp. 34–37.

53. Cited in D. A. Waldman, L. E. Atwater, and D. Antonioni, "Has 360 Degree Feedback Gone Amok?" *Academy of Management Executive*, May 1998, p. 86.

54. D. V. Day, "Leadership Development: A Review in Context," *Leadership Quarterly*, Winter 2000, pp. 587–89.

55. "Ivy League Grade Inflation," *USA Today*, February 8, 2002, p. 11A.

56. A. S. DeNisi and L. H. Peters, "Organization of Information in Memory and the Performance Appraisal Process: Evidence from the Field," *Journal of Applied Psychology*, December 1996, pp. 717–37.

57. See, for instance, J. W. Hedge and W. C. Borman, "Changing Conceptions and Practices in Performance Appraisal," in A. Howard, ed., *The Changing Nature of Work* (San Francisco: Jossey-Bass, 1995), pp. 453–59.

58. See, for instance, D. E. Smith, "Training Programs for Performance Appraisal: A Review," *Academy of Management Review*, January 1986, pp. 22–40; T. R. Athey and R. M. McIntyre, "Effect of Rater Training on Rater Accuracy: Levels-of-Processing Theory and Social Facilitation Theory Perspectives," *Journal of Applied Psychology*, November 1987, pp. 567–72; and D. J. Woehr, "Understanding Frame-of-Reference Training: The Impact of Training on the Recall of Performance Information," *Journal of Applied Psychology*, August 1994, pp. 525–34.

59. H. J. Bernardin, "The Effects of Rater Training on Leniency and Halo Errors in Student Rating of Instructors," *Journal of Applied Psychology*, June 1978, pp. 301–308.

60. Ibid.; and J. M. Ivancevich, "Longitudinal Study of the Effects of Rater Training on Psychometric Error in Ratings," *Journal of Applied Psychology*, October 1979, pp. 502–508.

61. M. S. Taylor, K. B. Tracy, M. K. Renard, J. K. Harrison, and S. J. Carroll, "Due Process in Performance Appraisal: A Quasi-Experiment in Procedural Justice," *Administrative Science Quarterly*, September 1995, pp. 495–523.

62. J. S. Lublin, "It's Shape-up Time for Performance Reviews," *Wall Street Journal*, October 3, 1994, p. B1.

63. Much of this section is based on H. H. Meyer, "A Solution to the Performance Appraisal Feedback Enigma," *Academy of Management Executive*, February 1991, pp. 68–76.

64. B. Gates, *The Road Ahead* (New York: Viking, 1995), p. 86.

65. T. D. Schelhardt, "It's Time to Evaluate Your Work, and All Involved Are Groaning," *Wall Street Journal*, November 19, 1996, p. A1.

66. R. J. Burke, "Why Performance Appraisal Systems Fail," *Personnel Administration*, June 1972, pp. 32–40.

67. B. R. Nathan, A. M. Mohrman, Jr., and J. Milliman, "Interpersonal Relations as a Context for the Effects of Appraisal Interviews on Performance and Satisfaction: A Longitudinal Study," *Academy of Management Journal*, June 1991, pp. 352–69. See also B. D. Cawley, L. M. Keeping, and P. E. Levy, "Participation in the Performance Appraisal Process and Employee Reactions: A Meta-Analytic Review of Field Investigations," *Journal of Applied Psychology*, August 1998, pp. 615–33.

68. J. Zigon, "Making Performance Appraisal Work for Teams," *Training*, June 1994, pp. 58–63.

69. E. Salas, T. L. Dickinson, S. A. Converse, and S. I. Tannenbaum, "Toward an Understanding of Team Performance and Training," in R. W. Swezey and E. Salas (eds.), *Teams: Their Training and Performance* (Norwood, NJ: Ablex, 1992), pp. 3–29.

70. D. A. DeCenzo and S. P. Robbins, *Human Resource Management*, 7th ed. (New York, Wiley, 2002), p. 436.

71. Much of the material in this section was adapted from T. H. Hammer, "Relationship between Local Union Characteristics and Worker Behavior and Attitudes," *Academy of Management Journal*, December 1978, pp. 560–77.

72. See B. B. Auster and W. Cohen, "Rallying the Rank and File," *U.S. News & World Report*, April 1, 1996, pp. 26–28; and M. A. Verespej, "Wounded and Weaponless," *Industry Week*, September 16, 1996, pp. 46–58.

73. See J. B. Arthur and J. B. Dworkin, "Current Topics in Industrial and Labor Relations Research and Practice," *Journal of Management*, September 1991, pp. 530–32.

74. See, for example, C. J. Berger, C. A. Olson, and J. W. Boudreau, "Effects of Unions on Job Satisfaction: The Role of Work-Related Values and Perceived Rewards," *Organizational Behavior and Human Performance*, December 1983, pp. 289–324; and M. G. Evans and D. A. Ondrack, "The Role of Job Outcomes and Values in Understanding the Union's Impact on Job Satisfaction: A Replication," *Human Relations*, May 1990, pp. 401–18.

75. See, for instance, M. Mendonca and R. N. Kanungo, "Managing Human Resources: The Issue of Cultural Fit," *Journal of Management Inquiry*, June 1994, pp. 189–205; and N. Ramamoorthy and S. J. Carroll, "Individualism/ Collectivism Orientations and Reactions toward Alternative Human Resource Management Practices," *Human Relations*, May 1998, pp. 571–88.

76. A. M. Ryan, L. McFarland, H. Baron, and R. Page, "An International Look at Selection Practices: Nation and Culture as Explanations for Variability in Practice," *Personnel Psychology*, Summer 1999, pp. 359–92.

77. Ibid., p. 386.

78. M. Tanikawa, "Fujitsu Decides to Backtrack on Performance-Based Pay," *New York Times*, March 22, 2001, p. W1.

79. N. B. Henderson, "An Enabling Work Force," *Nation's Business*, June 1998, p. 93.

80. See L. Urresta and J. Hickman, "The Diversity Elite," *Fortune*, August 3, 1998, pp. 114–22.

81. C. Oglesby, "More Options for Moms Seeking Work-Family Balance," www.cnn.com, May 10, 2001.

82. "On the Daddy Track," *Wall Street Journal*, May 11, 2000, p. A1.

83. M. B. Grover, "Daddy Stress," *Forbes*, September 6, 1999, pp. 202–208.

84. S. D. Friedman and J. H. Greenhaus, *Work and Family— Allies or Enemies?* (New York: Oxford University Press, 2000).

85. N. P. Rothbard, T. L. Dumas, and K. W. Phillips, "The Long Arm of the Organization: Work-Family Policies and Employee Preferences for Segmentation," paper presented at the 61st Annual Academy of Management Meeting; Washington, DC, August 2001.

86. Cited in "Survey Shows 75% of Large Corporations Support Diversity Programs," *Fortune*, July 6, 1998, p. S14.

87. See, for example, S. Nelton, "Nurturing Diversity," *Nation's Business*, June 1995, pp. 25–27; J. K. Ford and S. Fisher, "The Role of Training in a Changing Workplace and Workforce: New Perspectives and Approaches," in E. E. Kossek and S. A. Lobel, eds., *Managing Diversity* (Cambridge, MA: Blackwell Publishers, 1996), pp. 164–93.

88. R. Koonce, "Redefining Diversity," *T+D*, December 2001, p. 25.

89. B. Hynes-Grace, "To Thrive, Not Merely Survive," in Textbook Authors Conference Presentations (Washington, DC: October 21, 1992), sponsored by the American Association of Retired Persons, p. 12.

90. "Teaching Diversity: Business Schools Search for Model Approaches," *Newsline*, Fall 1992, p. 21.

91. A. Bandura, "Self-Efficacy: Towards a Unifying Theory of Behavioral Change," *Psychological Review*, March 1977, pp. 191–215; and P. C. Earley, "Self or Group? Cultural Effects of Training on Self-Efficacy and Performance," *Administrative Science Quarterly*, March 1994, pp. 89–117.

92. B. R. Nathan, A. M. Mohrman, Jr., and J. Milliman, "Interpersonal Relations as a Context for the Effects of Appraisal Interviews on Performance and Satisfaction: A Longitudinal Study;" and B. D. Cawley, L. M. Keeping, and P. E. Levy, "Participation in the Performance Appraisal Process and Employee Reactions."

PART FOUR

THE ORGANIZATION SYSTEM

Nokia is a true global success story.[1] Founded in 1885 in southern Finland, the company began as a paper manufacturer. In the 1920s it added manufacturing of rubber boots, raincoats, and hunting rifles. It went into consumer electronics in the 1950s by making television sets. But it didn't find its current niche until the late 1980s, when management decided to change strategies—to transform Nokia from a traditional industrial company into a high-tech conglomerate. Management refocused Nokia on the emerging market for mobile phones and networks. Jorma Ollila (see photo), who was then the company's chief financial officer, was put in charge of the mobile phone business. He became CEO in 1992 and the rest, as they say, is history.

Management's revised strategy has proven an overwhelming success. Nokia is now the world's leading manufacturer of mobile phones. With 35 percent of the world's mobile phone market, it's annual sales have reached US$28.1 billion, with pre-tax profits of over US$3.1 billion.

Part of Nokia's success was undoubtedly due to being in the right place at the right time. But so, too, were Motorola and Ericsson. What, then, explains Nokia's remarkable performance? A major part of the answer is Nokia's strong organizational culture. Ollila has carefully shaped Nokia's culture around four core values: customer satisfaction, achievement, respect for the individual, and continuous learning.

Ollila believes Nokia has outpaced its competitors because the firm is more customer-focused, resulting in more desirable products. The company focuses on making things that are better suited to customer needs and rapidly responding as those needs change. For instance, Nokia was first to market with phones that didn't require two hands to use and with switchable covers and changeable ringing tones.

Organizational Culture

Talk with Nokia employees and they speak about similar aspects of what they like about working at the company: Respect for individual employees. Opportunities for personal growth and responsibility. Teamwork. A feeling of family. Freedom to be creative. Minimal rules and regulations. Little or no hierarchy. "You join Nokia, and no one will give you a very accurate job description," says a company market relations manager. "You don't know who your boss is. So you live in this state of confusion—it never goes away. You have to adapt to it." Nokia prides itself on attracting employees who can deal with ambiguity; then the company continually emphasizes the importance of flexibility by minimizing formalization.

To facilitate the company's desire to create a family-like environment, Nokia provides a rich array of benefits and services to facilitate work/life balance. There are on-site saunas, 24-hour gyms, cafeterias with company-subsidized meals, and a staff physician in every location. Telecommuting is also widely practiced. For instance, although Nokia's headquarters is in Finland, the company's director of communications lives in Scotland and its design director works out of Los Angeles.

A strong organizational culture like Nokia provides employees with an understanding of "the way things are done around here." It provides stability to an organization. But, for some organizations, it can also be a major barrier to change. In this chapter, we show that every organization has a culture and, depending on its strength, it can have a significant influence on the attitudes and behaviors of organization members.

LEARNING OBJECTIVES

AFTER STUDYING THIS CHAPTER, YOU SHOULD BE ABLE TO:

1. Describe institutionalization and its relationship to organizational culture.

2. Define the common characteristics making up organizational culture.

3. Contrast strong and weak cultures.

4. Identify the functional and dysfunctional effects of organizational culture on people and the organization.

5. Explain the factors determining an organization's culture.

6. List the factors that maintain an organization's culture.

7. Clarify how culture is transmitted to employees.

8. Outline the various socialization alternatives available to management.

9. Describe a customer-responsive culture.

10. Identify characteristics of a spiritual culture.

523

INSTITUTIONALIZATION: A FORERUNNER OF CULTURE

The idea of viewing organizations as cultures—where there is a system of shared meaning among members—is a relatively recent phenomenon. Until the mid-1980s, organizations were, for the most part, simply thought of as rational means by which to coordinate and control a group of people. They had vertical levels, departments, authority relationships, and so forth. But organizations are more. They have personalities too, just like individuals. They can be rigid or flexible, unfriendly or supportive, innovative or conservative. General Electric offices and people *are* different from the offices and people at General Mills. Harvard and MIT are in the same business—education—and separated only by the width of the Charles River, but each has a unique feeling and character beyond its structural characteristics. Organizational theorists now acknowledge this by recognizing the important role that culture plays in the lives of organization members. Interestingly, though, the origin of culture as an independent variable affecting an employee's attitudes and behavior can be traced back more than 50 years ago to the notion of **institutionalization**.[2]

institutionalization

When an organization takes on a life of its own, apart from any of its members, and acquires immortality.

When an organization becomes institutionalized, it takes on a life of its own, apart from its founders or any of its members. Ross Perot created Electronic Data Systems (EDS) in the early 1960s, but he left in 1987 to found a new company, Perot Systems. EDS has continued to thrive despite the departure of its founder. Sony, Eastman Kodak, Gillette, McDonald's, and Disney are examples of organizations that have existed beyond the life of their founder or any one member.

In addition, when an organization becomes institutionalized, it becomes valued for itself, not merely for the goods or services it produces. It acquires immortality. If its original goals are no longer relevant, it doesn't go out of business. Rather, it redefines itself. A classic example is the March of Dimes. It was originally created to fund the battle against polio. When polio was essentially eradicated in the 1950s, the March of Dimes didn't close down. It merely redefined its objectives as funding research for reducing birth defects and lowering infant mortality.

Institutionalization operates to produce common understandings among members about what is appropriate and, fundamentally, meaningful behavior.[3] So when an organization takes on institutional permanence, acceptable modes of behavior become largely self-evident to its members. As we'll see, this is essentially the same thing that organizational culture does. So an understanding of what makes up an organization's culture, and how it is created, sustained, and learned will enhance our ability to explain and predict the behavior of people at work.

WHAT IS ORGANIZATIONAL CULTURE?

A number of years back, I asked an executive to tell me what he thought *organizational culture* meant. He gave me essentially the same answer that a Supreme Court Justice once gave in attempting to define pornography: "I can't define it, but I know it when I see it." This executive's approach to defining organizational culture isn't acceptable for our purposes. We need a basic definition to provide a point of departure for our quest to better understand the phenomenon. In this section, we propose a specific definition and review several peripheral issues that revolve around this definition.

A Definition

There seems to be wide agreement that **organizational culture** refers to a system of shared meaning held by members that distinguishes the organization from other organizations.[4] This system of shared meaning is, on closer examination, a set of key characteristics that the organization values. The research suggests that there are seven primary characteristics that, in aggregate, capture the essence of an organization's culture.[5]

organizational culture

A system of shared meaning held by members that distinguishes the organization from other organizations.

1. *Innovation and risk taking.* The degree to which employees are encouraged to be innovative and take risks.
2. *Attention to detail.* The degree to which employees are expected to exhibit precision, analysis, and attention to detail.
3. *Outcome orientation.* The degree to which management focuses on results or outcomes rather than on the techniques and processes used to achieve those outcomes.
4. *People orientation.* The degree to which management decisions take into consideration the effect of outcomes on people within the organization.
5. *Team orientation.* The degree to which work activities are organized around teams rather than individuals.
6. *Aggressiveness.* The degree to which people are aggressive and competitive rather than easygoing.
7. *Stability.* The degree to which organizational activities emphasize maintaining the status quo in contrast to growth.

Each of these characteristics exists on a continuum from low to high. Appraising the organization on these seven characteristics, then, gives a composite picture of the organization's culture. This picture becomes the basis for feelings of shared understanding that members have about the organization, how things are done in it, and the way members are supposed to behave. Exhibit 18-1 on page 526 demonstrates how these characteristics can be mixed to create highly diverse organizations.

Culture Is a Descriptive Term

Organizational culture is concerned with how employees perceive the characteristics of an organization's culture, not with whether or not they like them. That is, it's a descriptive term. This is important because it differentiates this concept from that of job satisfaction.

Research on organizational culture has sought to measure how employees see their organization: Does it encourage teamwork? Does it reward innovation? Does it stifle initiative?

In contrast, job satisfaction seeks to measure affective responses to the work environment. It's concerned with how employees feel about the organization's expectations, reward practices, and the like. Although the two terms undoubtedly have overlapping characteristics, keep in mind that the term *organizational culture* is descriptive, while *job satisfaction* is evaluative.

Do Organizations Have Uniform Cultures?

Organizational culture represents a common perception held by the organization's members. This was made explicit when we defined culture as a system of *shared* meaning. We should expect, therefore, that individuals with different backgrounds or at different levels in the organization will tend to describe the organization's culture in similar terms.[6]

Organization A

This organization is a manufacturing firm. Managers are expected to fully document all decisions; and "good managers" are those who can provide detailed data to support their recommendations. Creative decisions that incur significant change or risk are not encouraged. Because managers of failed projects are openly criticized and penalized, managers try not to implement ideas that deviate much from the status quo. One lower-level manager quoted an often used phrase in the company: "If it ain't broke, don't fix it."

There are extensive rules and regulations in this firm that employees are required to follow. Managers supervise employees closely to ensure there are no deviations. Management is concerned with high productivity, regardless of the impact on employee morale or turnover.

Work activities are designed around individuals. There are distinct departments and lines of authority, and employees are expected to minimize formal contact with other employees outside their functional area or line of command. Performance evaluations and rewards emphasize individual effort, although seniority tends to be the primary factor in the determination of pay raises and promotions.

Organization B

This organization is also a manufacturing firm. Here, however, management encourages and rewards risk taking and change. Decisions based on intuition are valued as much as those that are well rationalized. Management prides itself on its history of experimenting with new technologies and its success in regularly introducing innovative products. Managers or employees who have a good idea are encouraged to "run with it." And failures are treated as "learning experiences." The company prides itself on being market-driven and rapidly responsive to the changing needs of its customers.

There are few rules and regulations for employees to follow, and supervision is loose because management believes that its employees are hardworking and trustworthy. Management is concerned with high productivity, but believes that this comes through treating its people right. The company is proud of its reputation as being a good place to work.

Job activities are designed around work teams and team members are encouraged to interact with people across functions and authority levels. Employees talk positively about the competition between teams. Individuals and teams have goals, and bonuses are based on achievement of these outcomes. Employees are given considerable autonomy in choosing the means by which the goals are attained.

Acknowledgment that organizational culture has common properties does not mean, however, that there cannot be subcultures within any given culture. Most large organizations have a dominant culture and numerous sets of subcultures.[7]

A **dominant culture** expresses the core values that are shared by a majority of the organization's members. When we talk about an organization's culture, we are referring to its dominant culture. It is this macro view of culture that gives an organization its distinct personality.[8] **Subcultures** tend to develop in large organizations to reflect common problems, situations, or experiences that members face. These subcultures are likely to be defined by department designations and geographical separation. The purchasing department, for example, can have a subculture that is uniquely shared by members of that department. It will include the **core values** of the dominant culture plus additional values unique to members of the purchasing department. Similarly, an office or unit of the organization that is physically separated from the organization's main operations may take on a different personality. Again, the core values are essentially retained, but they are modified to reflect the separated unit's distinct situation.

If organizations had no dominant culture and were composed only of numerous subcultures, the value of organizational culture as an independent variable would be significantly lessened because there would be no uniform interpretation

dominant culture

Expresses the core values that are shared by a majority of the organization's members.

subcultures

Minicultures within an organization, typically defined by department designations and geographical separation.

core values

The primary or dominant values that are accepted throughout the organization.

of what represented appropriate and inappropriate behavior. It is the "shared meaning" aspect of culture that makes it such a potent device for guiding and shaping behavior. That's what allows us to say that Microsoft's culture values aggressiveness and risk taking[9] and then to use that information to better understand the behavior of Microsoft executives and employees. But we cannot ignore the reality that many organizations also have subcultures that can influence the behavior of members.

Strong Versus Weak Cultures

It has become increasingly popular to differentiate between strong and weak cultures.[10] The argument here is that strong cultures have a greater impact on employee behavior and are more directly related to reduced turnover.

In a **strong culture**, the organization's core values are both intensely held and widely shared.[11] The more members who accept the core values and the greater their commitment to those values is, the stronger the culture is. Consistent with this definition, a strong culture

Nordstrom has one of the strongest service cultures in the retailing industry. Employees know in no uncertain terms what is expected of them, and these expectations go a long way toward shaping their behavior.

will have a great influence on the behavior of its members because the high degree of sharedness and intensity creates an internal climate of high behavioral control. For example, Seattle-based Nordstrom has developed one of the strongest service cultures in the retailing industry. Nordstrom employees know in no uncertain terms what is expected of them and these expectations go a long way in shaping their behavior.

One specific result of a strong culture should be lower employee turnover. A strong culture demonstrates high agreement among members about what the organization stands for. Such unanimity of purpose builds cohesiveness, loyalty, and organizational commitment. These qualities, in turn, lessen employees' propensity to leave the organization.[12]

strong culture

Culture in which the core values are intensely held and widely shared.

Culture Versus Formalization

A strong organizational culture increases behavioral consistency. In this sense, we should recognize that a strong culture can act as a substitute for formalization.

In Chapter 15, we discussed how formalization's rules and regulations act to regulate employee behavior. High formalization in an organization creates predictability, orderliness, and consistency. Our point here is that a strong culture achieves the same end without the need for written documentation. Therefore, we should view formalization and culture as two different roads to a common destination. The stronger an organization's culture, the less management need be concerned with developing formal rules and regulations to guide employee behavior. Those guides will be internalized in employees when they accept the organization's culture.

Organizational Culture Versus National Culture

Throughout this book we've argued that national differences—that is, national cultures—must be taken into account if accurate predictions are to be made about organizational behavior in different countries. But does national culture override an organization's culture? Is an IBM facility in Germany, for example, more likely to reflect German ethnic culture or IBM's corporate culture?

The research indicates that national culture has a greater impact on employees than does their organization's culture.[13] German employees at an IBM facility in Munich, therefore, will be influenced more by German culture than by IBM's culture. This means that as influential as organizational culture is in shaping employee behavior, national culture is even more influential.

The preceding conclusion has to be qualified to reflect the self-selection that goes on at the hiring stage.[14] A British multinational corporation, for example, is likely to be less concerned with hiring the "typical Italian" for its Italian operations than in hiring an Italian who fits with the corporation's way of doing things. We should expect, therefore, that the employee selection process will be used by multinationals to find and hire job applicants who are a good fit with their organization's dominant culture, even if such applicants are somewhat atypical for members of their country.

WHAT DO CULTURES DO?

We've alluded to organizational culture's impact on behavior. We've also explicitly argued that a strong culture should be associated with reduced turnover. In this section, we will more carefully review the functions that culture performs and assess whether culture can be a liability for an organization.

Culture's Functions

Culture performs a number of functions within an organization. First, it has a boundary-defining role; that is, it creates distinctions between one organization and others. Second, it conveys a sense of identity for organization members. Third, culture facilitates the generation of commitment to something larger than one's individual self-interest. Fourth, it enhances the stability of the social system. Culture is the social glue that helps hold the organization together by providing appropriate standards for what employees should say and do. Finally, culture serves as a sense-making and control mechanism that guides and shapes the attitudes and behavior of employees. It is this last function that is of particular interest to us.[15] As the following quote makes clear, culture defines the rules of the game:

> Culture by definition is elusive, intangible, implicit, and taken for granted. But every organization develops a core set of assumptions, understandings, and implicit rules that govern day-to-day behavior in the workplace. . . . Until newcomers learn the rules, they are not accepted as full-fledged members of the organization. Transgressions of the rules on the part of high-level executives or front-line employees result in universal disapproval and powerful penalties. Conformity to the rules becomes the primary basis for reward and upward mobility.[16]

The role of culture in influencing employee behavior appears to be increasingly important in today's workplace.[17] As organizations have widened spans of control, flattened structures, introduced teams, reduced formalization, and empowered employees, the *shared meaning* provided by a strong culture ensures that everyone is pointed in the same direction.

As we show later in this chapter, who receives a job offer to join the organization, who is appraised as a high performer, and who gets the promotion are strongly influenced by the individual–organization "fit"—that is, whether the applicant or employee's attitudes and behavior are compatible with the culture. It's not a coincidence that employees at Disney theme parks appear to be almost universally attractive, clean, and wholesome looking, with bright smiles. That's the image Disney seeks. The company selects employees who will maintain that image. And once on the job, a strong culture, supported by formal rules and regulations, ensures that Disney theme-park employees will act in a relatively uniform and predictable way.

Culture as a Liability

We are treating culture in a nonjudgmental manner. We haven't said that it's good or bad, only that it exists. Many of its functions, as outlined, are valuable for both the organization and the employee. Culture enhances organizational commitment and increases the consistency of employee behavior. These are clearly benefits to an organization. From an employee's standpoint, culture is valuable because it reduces ambiguity. It tells employees how things are done and what's important. But we shouldn't ignore the potentially dysfunctional aspects of culture, especially a strong one, on an organization's effectiveness.

Barrier to Change Culture is a liability when the shared values are not in agreement with those that will further the organization's effectiveness. This is most likely to occur when an organization's environment is dynamic. When an environment is undergoing rapid change, an organization's entrenched culture may no longer be appropriate. So consistency of behavior is an asset to an organization when it faces a stable environment. It may, however, burden the organization and make it difficult to respond to changes in the environment. This helps to explain the challenges that executives at organizations like Mitsubishi, Eastman Kodak, Xerox, Boeing, and the U.S. Federal Bureau of Investigation have had in recent years in adapting to upheavals in their environment.[18] These organizations have strong cultures that worked well for them in the past. But these strong cultures become barriers to change when "business as usual" is no longer effective.

Barrier to Diversity Hiring new employees who, because of race, gender, disability, or other differences, are not like the majority of the organization's members creates a paradox.[19] Management wants new employees to accept the organization's core cultural values. Otherwise, these employees are unlikely to fit in or be accepted. But at the same time, management wants to openly acknowledge and demonstrate support for the differences that these employees bring to the workplace.

Strong cultures put considerable pressure on employees to conform. They limit the range of values and styles that are acceptable. In some instances, such as the widely publicized Texaco case (which was settled on behalf of 1,400 employees for $176 million) in which senior managers made disparaging remarks about minorities, a strong culture that condones prejudice can even undermine formal corporate diversity policies.[20]

Organizations seek out and hire diverse individuals because of the alternative strengths these people bring to the workplace. Yet these diverse behaviors and strengths are likely to diminish in strong cultures as people attempt to fit in. Strong cultures, therefore, can be liabilities when they effectively eliminate the unique strengths that people of different backgrounds bring to the organization. Moreover, strong cultures can also be liabilities when they support institutional bias or become insensitive to people who are different.

Barrier to Acquisitions and Mergers Historically, the key factors that management looked at in making acquisition or merger decisions were related to financial

"Success Breeds Success"

This statement is not always true. Generally speaking, success creates positive momentum. People like being associated with a successful team or organization, which allows winning teams and organizations to get the best new recruits. Microsoft's incredible success in the 1990s made it a highly desirable place to work. They had their pick among the "best and the brightest" job applicants when filling job slots. Success led to further successes. Microsoft's experience is generalizable across decades to other companies. In the 1960s, when General Motors controlled nearly 50 percent of the U.S. automobile market, GM was the most sought-after employer by newly minted MBAs. In the early 1990s, Motorola was routinely described as one of the best-managed and successful companies in America, and it was able to attract the best and the brightest engineers and professionals.

But success often breeds failure, especially in organizations with strong cultures.[21] Organizations that have tremendous successes begin to believe in their own invulnerability. They often become arrogant. They lose their competitive edge. Their strong cultures reinforce past practices and make change difficult. "Why change? It worked in the past. If it ain't broke, don't fix it."

The corporate highway is littered with companies that let arrogance undermine previous successes. JC Penney and Sears once ruled the retail-department-store market. Their executives considered their markets immune to competition. Beginning in the mid-1970s, Wal-Mart did a pretty effective job of humbling Penney and Sears' management. General Motors executives, safe and cloistered in their Detroit headquarters, ignored the aggressive efforts by Japanese auto firms to penetrate its markets. The result? GMs' market share has been in a free fall for three decades. Motorola may have been the high-tech darling of the early 1990s, when it dominated world markets for semiconductors and analog cellular phones, but the company became arrogant. It stumbled badly in the digital market, failed to listen to the needs of its customers, and overextended itself in Asia. In the first quarter of 2001 the company lost $206 million and was in the process of cutting 22,000 jobs worldwide.[22]

---

advantages or product synergy. In recent years, cultural compatibility has become the primary concern.[23] While a favorable financial statement or product line may be the initial attraction of an acquisition candidate, whether the acquisition actually works seems to have more to do with how well the two organizations' cultures match up.

A number of acquisitions consummated in the 1990s have already failed. And the primary cause is conflicting organizational cultures.[24] For instance, AT&T's 1991 acquisition of NCR was a disaster. AT&T's unionized employees objected to working in the same building as NCR's nonunion staff. Meanwhile, NCR's conservative, centralized culture didn't take kindly to AT&T's insistence on calling supervisors "coaches" and removing executives' office doors. By the time AT&T finally sold NCR, the failure of the deal had cost AT&T more than $3 billion. In 1998, Daimler-Benz paid $36 billion for Chrysler Corp. But Daimler's culture was driven by precision engineering whereas Chrysler's strength was salesmanship. Instead of the hoped-for synergies and cost savings, the merger didn't work. It wiped out $60 billion in market value as Chrysler went from being the most-profitable car maker in the United States to its biggest money loser. Prognosticators are already forecasting hard times for the Hewlett-Packard and Compaq merger. Critics question whether Compaq's confrontational culture will clash with HP's congenial, egalitarian one.[25]

CREATING AND SUSTAINING CULTURE

An organization's culture doesn't pop out of thin air. Once established, it rarely fades away. What forces influence the creation of a culture? What reinforces and sustains these forces once they're in place? We answer both of these questions in this section.

How a Culture Begins

An organization's current customs, traditions, and general way of doing things are largely due to what it has done before and the degree of success it has had with those endeavors. This leads us to the ultimate source of an organization's culture: its founders.[26]

The founders of an organization traditionally have a major impact on that organization's early culture. They have a vision of what the organization should be. They are unconstrained by previous customs or ideologies. The small size that typically characterizes new organizations further facilitates the founders' imposition of their vision on all organizational members.

Culture creation occurs in three ways.[27] First, founders hire and keep only employees who think and feel the same way they do. Second, they indoctrinate and socialize these employees to their way of thinking and feeling. And finally, the founders' own behavior acts as a role model that encourages employees to identify with them and thereby internalize their beliefs, values, and assumptions. When the organization succeeds, the founders' vision becomes seen as a primary determinant of that success. At this point, the founders' entire personality becomes embedded in the culture of the organization.

The culture at Hyundai, the giant Korean conglomerate, is largely a reflection of its founder Chung Ju Yung. Hyundai's fierce, competitive style, and its disciplined, authoritarian nature are the same characteristics often used to describe Chung. Other contemporary examples of founders who have had an immeasurable impact on their organization's culture would include Bill Gates at Microsoft, Ingvar Kamprad at IKEA, Herb Kelleher at Southwest Airlines, Fred Smith at Federal Express, Mary Kay at Mary Kay Cosmetics, and Richard Branson at the Virgin Group.

Keeping a Culture Alive

Once a culture is in place, there are practices within the organization that act to maintain it by giving employees a set of similar experiences.[28] For example, many of the human resource practices discussed in the previous chapter reinforce the organization's culture. The selection process, performance evaluation criteria, training and career development activities, and promotion procedures ensure that those hired fit in with the culture, reward those who support it, and penalize (and even expel) those who challenge it. Three forces play a particularly important part in sustaining a culture: selection practices, the actions of top management, and socialization methods. Let's take a closer look at each.

Selection   The explicit goal of the selection process is to identify and hire individuals who have the knowledge, skills, and abilities to perform the jobs within the organization successfully. Typically, more than one candidate will be identified who meets any given job's requirements. When that point is reached, it would be naive to ignore that the final decision as to who is hired will be significantly influenced by the decision maker's judgment of how well the candidates will fit into the organization. This attempt to ensure a proper match, whether purposely or inadvertently, results in the hiring of people who have values essentially consistent with those of the organization, or at least a good portion of those values.[29] In addition, the selection process provides information to applicants about the organization. Candidates learn about the organization and, if they perceive a conflict between their values and those of the organization, they can self-select themselves out of the applicant pool. Selection, therefore, becomes a two-way street, allowing employer or applicant to abrogate a marriage if there appears to be a mismatch. In this way, the selection process sustains an organization's culture by selecting out those individuals who might attack or undermine its core values.

For instance, applicants for entry-level positions in brand management at Procter & Gamble (P&G) experience an exhaustive application and screening process. Their interviewers are part of an elite cadre who have been selected and trained extensively via lectures, videotapes, practice interviews, and role plays to identify applicants who will successfully fit in at P&G. Applicants are interviewed in depth for qualities such as their ability to "turn out high volumes of excellent work," "identify and understand problems," and "reach thoroughly substantiated and well-reasoned conclusions that lead to action." P&G values rationality and seeks applicants who think that way. College applicants receive two interviews and a general knowledge test on campus before being flown to Cincinnati for three more one-on-one interviews and a group interview at lunch. Each encounter seeks corroborating evidence of the traits that the firm believes correlate highly with "what counts" for success at P&G.[30]

Top Management   The actions of top management also have a major impact on the organization's culture.[31] Through what they say and how they behave, senior executives establish norms that filter down through the organization as to whether risk taking is desirable; how much freedom managers should give their employees; what is appropriate dress; what actions will pay off in terms of pay raises, promotions, and other rewards; and the like.

For example, Robert A. Keirlin has been called "the cheapest CEO in America."[32] Keirlin is chairman and CEO of Fastenal Co., the largest specialty retailer of nuts and bolts in the United States, with 6,500 employees. He takes a salary of only $60,000 a year. He owns only three suits, each of which he bought used. He clips grocery coupons, drives a Toyota, and stays in low-priced motels when he travels on business. Does Keirlin need to pinch pennies? No. The market value of his stock in Fastenal is worth about $300 million. But the man prefers a modest personal life style. And he prefers the same for his company. Keirlin argues that his behavior should send a message to all his employees: We don't waste things in this company. Keirlin sees himself as a role model for frugality, and employees at Fastenal have learned to follow his example.

Socialization   No matter how good a job the organization does in recruiting and selection, new employees are not fully indoctrinated in the organization's culture. Maybe most important, because they are unfamiliar with the organization's culture, new employees are potentially likely to disturb the beliefs and customs that are in place. The organization will, therefore, want to help new employees adapt to its culture. This adaptation process is called **socialization**.[33]

socialization

The process that adapts employees to the organization's culture.

All Marines must go through boot camp, where they "prove" their commitment. Of course, at the same time, the Marine trainers are indoctrinating new recruits in the "Marine way." All new employees at Starbucks, the large coffee chain, go through 24 hours of training.[34] Classes are offered on everything necessary to turn new employees into brewing consultants. They learn the Starbucks philosophy, the company jargon (including phrases such as "half-decaf double tall almond skim mocha"), and even how to help customers make decisions about beans, grind, and espresso machines. The result is employees who understand Starbucks' culture and who project an enthusiastic and knowledgeable interface with customers. For new incoming employees in the upper ranks, companies often put considerably more time and effort into the socialization process. At The Limited, newly hired vice presidents and regional directors go through an intensive one-month program, called "onboarding," designed to immerse these executives in The Limited's culture.[35] During this month they have no direct responsibilities for tasks associated with their new positions. Instead, they spend all their work time meeting with other senior leaders and mentors, working the floors of retail stores, evaluating employee and customer habits, investigating the competition, and studying The Limited's past and current operations.

As we discuss socialization, keep in mind that the most critical socialization stage is at the time of entry into the organization. This is when the organization seeks to mold the outsider into an employee "in good standing." Employees who fail to learn the essential or pivotal role behaviors risk being labeled "nonconformists" or "rebels," which often leads to expulsion. But the organization will be socializing every employee, though maybe not as explicitly, throughout his or her entire career in the organization. This further contributes to sustaining the culture.

Socialization can be conceptualized as a process made up of three stages: prearrival, encounter, and metamorphosis.[36] The first stage encompasses all the learning that occurs before a new member joins the organization. In the second stage, the new employee sees what the organization is really like and confronts the possibility that expectations and reality may diverge. In the third stage, the relatively long-lasting changes take place. The new employee masters the skills required for his or her job, successfully performs his or her new roles, and makes the adjustments to his or her work group's values and norms.[37] This three-stage process has an impact on the new employee's work productivity, commitment to the organization's objectives, and eventual decision to stay with the organization. Exhibit 18-2 depicts this process.

The **prearrival stage** explicitly recognizes that each individual arrives with a set of values, attitudes, and expectations. These cover both the work to be done and the organization. For instance, in many jobs, particularly professional work, new members will have undergone a considerable degree of prior socialization in training and in school. One major purpose of a business school, for example, is to socialize business students to the attitudes and behaviors that business firms want. If business executives believe that successful employees value the profit ethic, are loyal, will work hard, and desire to achieve, they can hire individuals out of business schools who have been premolded in this pattern. But prearrival socialization

prearrival stage

The period of learning in the socialization process that occurs before a new employee joins the organization.

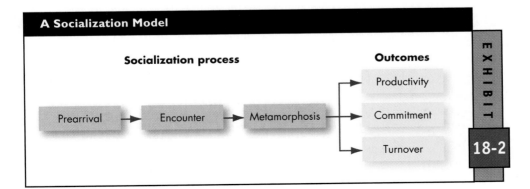

A Socialization Model

Socialization process

Prearrival → Encounter → Metamorphosis

Outcomes

Productivity

Commitment

Turnover

EXHIBIT 18-2

goes beyond the specific job. The selection process is used in most organizations to inform prospective employees about the organization as a whole. In addition, as noted previously, the selection process also acts to ensure the inclusion of the "right type"—those who will fit in. "Indeed, the ability of the individual to present the appropriate face during the selection process determines his ability to move into the organization in the first place. Thus, success depends on the degree to which the aspiring member has correctly anticipated the expectations and desires of those in the organization in charge of selection."[38]

encounter stage

The stage in the socialization process in which a new employee sees what the organization is really like and confronts the possibility that expectations and reality may diverge.

On entry into the organization, the new member enters the **encounter stage**. Here the individual confronts the possible dichotomy between her expectations—about her job, her co-workers, her boss, and the organization in general—and reality. If expectations prove to have been more or less accurate, the encounter stage merely provides a reaffirmation of the perceptions gained earlier. However, this is often not the case. Where expectations and reality differ, the new employee must undergo socialization that will detach her from her previous assumptions and replace them with another set that the organization deems desirable. At the extreme, a new member may become totally disillusioned with the actualities of her job and resign. Proper selection should significantly reduce the probability of the latter occurrence.

metamorphosis stage

The stage in the socialization process in which a new employee changes and adjusts to the job, work group, and organization.

Finally, the new member must work out any problems discovered during the encounter stage. This may mean going through changes—hence, we call this the **metamorphosis stage**. The options presented in Exhibit 18-3 are alternatives designed to bring about the desired metamorphosis. Note, for example, that the more management relies on socialization programs that are formal, collective,

---

EXHIBIT 18-3

Entry Socialization Options

Formal vs. Informal The more a new employee is segregated from the ongoing work setting and differentiated in some way to make explicit his or her newcomer's role, the more formal socialization is. Specific orientation and training programs are examples. Informal socialization puts the new employee directly into his or her job, with little or no special attention.

Individual vs. Collective New members can be socialized individually. This describes how it's done in many professional offices. They can also be grouped together and processed through an identical set of experiences, as in military boot camp.

Fixed vs. Variable This refers to the time schedule in which newcomers make the transition from outsider to insider. A fixed schedule establishes standardized stages of transition. This characterizes rotational training programs. It also includes probationary periods, such as the 8- to 10-year "associate" status used by accounting and law firms before deciding on whether or not a candidate is made a partner. Variable schedules give no advanced notice of their transition timetable. Variable schedules describe the typical promotion system, in which one is not advanced to the next stage until he or she is "ready."

Serial vs. Random Serial socialization is characterized by the use of role models who train and encourage the newcomer. Apprenticeship and mentoring programs are examples. In random socialization, role models are deliberately withheld. The new employee is left on his or her own to figure things out.

Investiture vs. Divestiture Investiture socialization assumes that the newcomer's qualities and qualifications are the necessary ingredients for job success, so these qualities and qualifications are confirmed and supported. Divestiture socialization tries to strip away certain characteristics of the recruit. Fraternity and sorority "pledges" go through divestiture socialization to shape them into the proper role.

Source: Based on J. Van Maanen, "People Processing: Strategies of Organizational Socialization," *Organizational Dynamics,* Summer 1978, pp. 19–36; and E. H. Schein, Organizational Culture," *American Psychologist,* February 1990, p. 116.

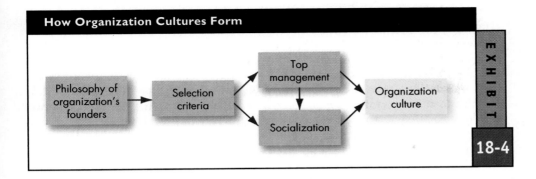

How Organization Cultures Form

Philosophy of organization's founders → Selection criteria → Top management / Socialization → Organization culture

EXHIBIT 18-4

fixed, serial, and emphasize divestiture, the greater the likelihood that newcomers' differences and perspectives will be stripped away and replaced by standardized and predictable behaviors. Careful selection by management of newcomers' socialization experiences can—at the extreme—create conformists who maintain traditions and customs, or inventive and creative individualists who consider no organizational practice sacred.

We can say that metamorphosis and the entry socialization process is complete when the new member has become comfortable with the organization and his job. He has internalized the norms of the organization and his work group, and understands and accepts these norms. The new member feels accepted by his peers as a trusted and valued individual, is confident that he has the competence to complete the job successfully, and understands the system—not only his own tasks, but the rules, procedures, and informally accepted practices as well. Finally, he knows how he will be evaluated; that is, what criteria will be used to measure and appraise his work. He knows what is expected, and what constitutes a job "well done." As Exhibit 18-2 shows, successful metamorphosis should have a positive impact on the new employee's productivity and his commitment to the organization, and reduce his propensity to leave the organization.

Summary: How Cultures Form

Exhibit 18-4 summarizes how an organization's culture is established and sustained. The original culture is derived from the founder's philosophy. This, in turn, strongly influences the criteria used in hiring. The actions of the current top management set the general climate of what is acceptable behavior and what is not. How employees are to be socialized will depend both on the degree of success achieved in matching new employees' values to those of the organization's in the selection process and on top management's preference for socialization methods.

HOW EMPLOYEES LEARN CULTURE

Culture is transmitted to employees in a number of forms, the most potent being stories, rituals, material symbols, and language.

Stories

During the days when Henry Ford II was chairman of the Ford Motor Co., one would have been hard pressed to find a manager who hadn't heard the story about Mr. Ford reminding his executives, when they got too arrogant, that "it's my name that's on the building." The message was clear: Henry Ford II ran the company!

Mike Cisco is Krispy Kreme's Minister of Culture. A key part of his job is to chronicle and transmit stories that capture the company's history and practices.

Nike has a number of senior executives who spend much of their time serving as corporate storytellers. And the stories they tell are meant to convey what Nike is about.[39] When they tell the story of how co-founder (and Oregon track coach) Bill Bowerman went to his workshop and poured rubber into his wife's waffle iron to create a better running shoe, they're talking about Nike's spirit of innovation. When new hires hear tales of Oregon running star Steve Prefontaine's battles to make running a professional sport and to attain better-performance equipment, they learn of Nike's commitment to helping athletes.

Nordstrom employees are fond of the following story. It strongly conveys the company's policy toward customer returns: When this specialty retail chain was in its infancy, a customer came in and wanted to return a set of automobile tires. The sales clerk was a bit uncertain how to handle the problem. As the customer and sales clerk spoke, Mr. Nordstrom walked by and overheard the conversation. He immediately interceded, asking the customer how much he had paid for the tires. Mr. Nordstrom then instructed the clerk to take the tires back and provide a full cash refund. After the customer had received his refund and left, the perplexed clerk looked at the boss. "But, Mr. Nordstrom, we don't sell tires!" "I know," replied the boss, "but we do whatever we need to do to make the customer happy. I mean it when I say we have a no-questions-asked return policy." Nordstrom then picked up the telephone and called a friend in the auto parts business to see how much he could get for the tires.

Stories such as these circulate through many organizations. They typically contain a narrative of events about the organization's founders, rule breaking, rags-to-riches successes, reductions in the workforce, relocation of employees, reactions to past mistakes, and organizational coping.[40] These stories anchor the present in the past and provide explanations and legitimacy for current practices. For the most part, these stories develop spontaneously. But some organizations actually try to manage this element of culture learning. For instance, Krispy Kreme, the large doughnut maker out of North Carolina, has a full time "minister of culture" whose primary responsibility is to tape interviews with customers and employees.[41] The stories these people tell are then put in the company's video magazine that describes Krispy Kreme's history and values.

Rituals

Rituals are repetitive sequences of activities that express and reinforce the key values of the organization—what goals are most important, which people are important, and which people are expendable.[42]

College faculty members undergo a lengthy ritual in their quest for permanent employment—tenure. Typically, the faculty member is on probation for six years. At the end of that period, the member's colleagues must make one of two choices: extend a tenured appointment or issue a one-year terminal contract. What does it take to obtain tenure? It usually requires satisfactory teaching performance, service to the department and university, and scholarly activity. But, of course, what satisfies the requirements for tenure in one department at one university may be appraised as inadequate in another. The key is that the tenure decision, in essence, asks those who are tenured to assess whether the candidate has demonstrated, based on six years of performance, whether he or she fits in. Colleagues who have been socialized properly will have proved themselves worthy of being granted tenure. Every year, hundreds of faculty members at colleges and universities are denied tenure. In some cases, this action is a result of poor performance across the board. More often, however, the decision can be traced to the faculty member's not doing well in the areas that the tenured faculty believe are important. The instruc-

EXHIBIT

18-5

"I don't know how it started, either. All I know is that it's part of our corporate culture."

Source: Drawing by Mick Stevens in the *New Yorker*, October 3, 1994. Copyright © 1994 by the New Yorker Magazine, Inc. Reprinted by permission.

tor who spends dozens of hours each week preparing for class and achieves outstanding evaluations by students but neglects his or her research and publication activities may be passed over for tenure. What has happened, simply, is that the instructor has failed to adapt to the norms set by the department. The astute faculty member will assess early on in the probationary period what attitudes and behaviors his or her colleagues want and will then proceed to give them what they want. And, of course, by demanding certain attitudes and behaviors, the tenured faculty have made significant strides toward standardizing tenure candidates.

One of the better-known corporate rituals is Wal-Mart's company chant. Begun by the company's founder, Sam Walton, as a way to motivate and unite his work force, "Gimme a W, gimme an A, gimme an L, gimme a squiggle, give me an M, A, R, T!" has become a company ritual that bonds Wal-Mart workers and reinforces Sam Walton's belief in the importance of his employees to the company's success. Similar corporate chants are used by IBM, Ericsson, Novell, Deutsche Bank, and Pricewaterhouse-Coopers.[43]

Material Symbols

The headquarters of Alcoa doesn't look like your typical head office operation. There are few individual offices, even for senior executives. It is essentially made up of cubicles, common areas, and meeting rooms. This informal corporate headquarters conveys to employees that Alcoa values openness, equality, creativity, and flexibility.

Some corporations provide their top executives with chauffeur-driven limousines and, when they travel by air, unlimited use of the corporate jet. Others may not get to ride in limousines or private jets but they might still get a car and air transportation paid for by the company. Only the car is a Chevrolet (with no driver) and the jet seat is in the economy section of a commercial airliner.

The layout of corporate headquarters, the types of automobiles top executives are given, and the presence or absence of corporate aircraft are a few examples of material symbols. Others include the size of offices, the elegance of furnishings, executive perks, and attire.[44] These material symbols convey to employees who is important, the degree of egalitarianism desired by top management, and the kinds of behavior (for example, risk taking, conservative, authoritarian, participative, individualistic, social) that are appropriate.

Language

Many organizations and units within organizations use language as a way to identify members of a culture or subculture. By learning this language, members attest to their acceptance of the culture and, in so doing, help to preserve it.

The following are examples of terminology used by employees at Knight-Ridder Information, a California-based data redistributor: *accession number* (a number assigned to each individual record in a database); *KWIC* (a set of key-words-in-context); and *relational operator* (searching a database for names or key terms in some order). Librarians are a rich source of terminology foreign to people outside their profession. They sprinkle their conversations liberally with acronyms like ARL (Association for Research Libraries), OCLC (a center in Ohio that does cooperative cataloging), and OPAC (for on-line patron accessing catalog). If you're a new employee at Boeing, you'll find yourself learning a whole unique vocabulary of acronyms, including: BOLD (Boeing online data); CATIA (computer-graphics-aided three-dimensional interactive application); MAIDS (manufacturing assembly and installation data system); POP (purchased outside production); and SLO (service level objectives).[45]

Organizations, over time, often develop unique terms to describe equipment, offices, key personnel, suppliers, customers, or products that relate to its business. New employees are frequently overwhelmed with acronyms and jargon that, after six months on the job, have become fully part of their language. Once assimilated, this terminology acts as a common denominator that unites members of a given culture or subculture.

CREATING AN ETHICAL ORGANIZATIONAL CULTURE

The content and strength of a culture influences an organization's ethical climate and the ethical behavior of its members.[46]

An organizational culture most likely to shape high ethical standards is one that's high in risk tolerance, low to moderate in aggressiveness, and focuses on means as well as outcomes. Managers in such a culture are supported for taking risks and innovating, are discouraged from engaging in unbridled competition, and will pay attention to *how* goals are achieved as well as to *what* goals are achieved.

A strong organizational culture will exert more influence on employees than a weak one. If the culture is strong and supports high ethical standards, it should have a very powerful and positive influence on employee behavior. Johnson & Johnson, for example, has a strong culture that has long stressed corporate obligations to customers, employees, the community, and shareholders, in that order. When poisoned Tylenol (a Johnson & Johnson product) was found on store shelves, employees at Johnson & Johnson across the United States independently pulled the product from these stores before management had even issued a statement concerning the tamperings. No one had to tell these individuals what was morally right; they knew what Johnson & Johnson would expect them to do.

What can management do to create a more ethical culture? We suggest a combination of the following practices:

Be a visible role model. Employees will look to top-management behavior as a benchmark for defining appropriate behavior. When senior management is seen as taking the ethical high-road, it provides a positive message for all employees.

Communicate ethical expectations. Ethical ambiguities can be minimized by creating and disseminating an organizational code of ethics. It should state the

Enron and the Creation of an Unethical Culture

Enron Corp., which in December 2001 became the largest-ever U.S. bankruptcy, didn't fail solely because of improper accounting practices, although that was certainly a major contributor. It also failed because it had a culture that pushed executives into unethical behavior.

During Enron's heyday in the late 1990s, the press regularly praised the company for its entrepreneurial culture: smart, sassy, creative, and risk-taking. But a post-mortem analysis reveals a different culture—an unrelenting emphasis on earnings growth and individual initiative. Instead of rewarding new ideas, the company encouraged unethical corner-cutting. How? First, it pressured executives to make their numbers. Second, it instilled lax controls over how those numbers were created. Third, it bred a "yes-man" culture among executives. People were afraid to speak out on questionable practices for fear that it would adversely affect their performance evaluations and the size of their bonuses. Fourth, bonuses and money became the Almighty God. The company sought out and rewarded people who placed a high value on money. Jeff Skilling, the CEO who created Enron's in-your-face culture, is quoted as saying "all that matters is money. You can buy loyalty with money." Fifth, although managers were supposed to be graded on teamwork, the culture was heavily built around star players, with little value attached to team-building. The organization rewarded highly competitive people who were less likely to share power, authority, or information. Finally, the company continually set itself wildly optimistic expectations for growth and then drove executives to find ways to meet them. "You've got someone at the top saying the stock price is the most important thing, which is driven by earnings," said one insider. "Whoever could provide earnings quickly would be promoted."

One former Enron employee summed up the Enron culture this way: "If your boss was [fudging], and you have never worked anywhere else, you just assume that everybody fudges earnings. Once you get there and you realized how it was, do you stand up and lose your job? It was scary. It was easy to get into 'Well, everybody else is doing it, so maybe it isn't so bad.'"

Sources: Based on W. Zellner, "Jeff Skilling: Enron's Missing Man," Business Week, February 11, 2002, pp. 38–40; and J. A. Byrne, "The Environment Was Ripe for Abuse," Business Week, February 25, 2002, pp. 118–20.

organization's primary values and the ethical rules that employees are expected to follow.

Provide ethical training. Set up seminars, workshops, and similar ethical training programs. Use these training sessions to reinforce the organization's standards of conduct; to clarify what practices are and are not permissible; and to address possible ethical dilemmas.

Visibly reward ethical acts and punish unethical ones. Performance appraisals of managers should include a point-by-point evaluation of how his or her decisions measure up against the organization's code of ethics. Appraisals must include the means taken to achieve goals as well as the ends themselves. People who act ethically should be visibly rewarded for their behavior. Just as importantly, unethical acts should be conspicuously punished.

Provide protective mechanisms. The organization needs to provide formal mechanisms so that employees can discuss ethical dilemmas and report unethical behavior without fear of reprimand. This might include creation of ethical counselors, ombudsmen, or ethical officers.

CREATING A CUSTOMER-RESPONSIVE CULTURE

French retailers have a well-established reputation for indifference to customers.[47] Sales people, for instance, routinely make it clear to customers that their phone conversations should not be interrupted. Just getting any help at all from a sales person can be a challenge. And no one in France finds it particularly surprising that the owner of a Paris store should complain that he was unable to work on his books all morning because he kept being bothered *by customers*!

Most organizations today are trying very hard to be un-French-like. They are attempting to create a customer-responsive culture because they recognize that this is the path to customer loyalty and long-term profitability. Companies that have created such cultures—like Southwest Air, FedEx, Johnson & Johnson, Nordstrom, Olive Garden, Walt Disney theme parks, and L.L. Bean—have built a strong and loyal customer base and have generally outperformed their competitors in revenue growth and financial performance. In this section, we will briefly identify the variables that shape customer-responsive cultures and offer some suggestions that management can follow for creating such cultures.

Key Variables Shaping Customer-Responsive Cultures

A review of the evidence finds that half-a-dozen variables are routinely evident in customer-responsive cultures.[48]

First is the type of employees themselves. Successful, service-oriented organizations hire employees who are outgoing and friendly. Second is low formalization. Service employees need to have the freedom to meet changing customer-service requirements. Rigid rules, procedures, and regulations make this difficult. Third is an extension of low formalization—it's the widespread use of empowerment. Empowered employees have the decision discretion to do what's necessary to please the customer. Fourth is good listening skills. Employees in customer-responsive cultures have the ability to listen to and understand messages sent by the customer. Fifth is role clarity. Service employees act as "boundary spanners" between the organization and its customers. They have to acquiesce to the demands of both their employer and the customer. This can create considerable role ambiguity and conflict, which reduces employees' job satisfaction and can hinder employee service performance. Successful customer-responsive cultures reduce employee uncertainty about the best way to perform their jobs and the importance of job activities. Finally, customer-responsive cultures have employees who exhibit organizational citizenship behavior. They are conscientious in their desire to please the customer. And they're willing to take the initiative, even when it's outside their normal job requirements, to satisfy a customer's needs.

In summary, customer-responsive cultures hire service-oriented employees with good listening skills and the willingness to go beyond the constraints of their job description to do what's necessary to please the customer. It then clarifies their roles, frees them up to meet changing customer needs by minimizing rules and regulations, and provides them with a wide range of decision discretion to do their job as they see fit.

The Olive Garden chain of Italian-style restaurants has developed a customer-responsive culture. Its slogan, "When you're here, you're family," is one part of its culture.

Managerial Action

Based on the previously identified characteristics, we can suggest a number of actions that management can take if it wants to make its culture more customer-responsive. These actions are designed to create employees with the competence, ability, and willingness to solve customer problems as they arise.

Selection   The place to start in building a customer-responsive culture is hiring service-contact people with the personality and attitudes consistent with a high service orientation. Southwest Air is a shining example of a company that has focused its hiring process on selecting out job candidates whose personalities aren't people-friendly. Job applicants go through an extensive interview process at Southwest in which company employees and executives carefully assess whether candidates have the outgoing and fun-loving personality that it wants in all its employees.

Studies show that friendliness, enthusiasm, and attentiveness in service employees positively affect customers' perceptions of service quality.[49] So managers should look for these qualities in applicants. In addition, job candidates should be screened so new hires have the patience, concern about others, and listening skills that are associated with customer-oriented employees.

Training and Socialization   Organizations that are trying to become more customer-responsive don't always have the option of hiring all new employees. More typically, management is faced with the challenge of making its current employees more customer-focused. In such cases, the emphasis will be on training rather than hiring. This describes the dilemma that senior executives at companies such as General Motors, Shell, and J.P. Morgan Chase have faced in the past decade as they have attempted to move away from their product focus. The content of these training programs will vary widely but should focus on improving product knowledge, active listening, showing patience, and displaying emotions.

In addition, even new employees who have a customer-friendly attitude may need to understand management's expectations. So all new service-contact people should be socialized into the organization's goals and values. Lastly, even the most customer-focused employees can lose direction every once in a while. This should be addressed with regular training updates in which the organization's customer-focused values are restated and reinforced.

Structural Design   Organization structures need to give employees more control. This can be achieved by reducing rules and regulations. Employees are better able to satisfy customers when they have some control over the service encounter. So management needs to allow employees to adjust their behavior to the changing needs and requests of customers. What customers *don't* want to hear are responses such as "I can't handle this. You need to talk to someone else"; or "I'm sorry but that's against our company policy."

Empowerment   Consistent with low formalization is empowering employees with the discretion to make day-to-day decisions about job-related activities. It's a necessary component of a customer-responsive culture because it allows service employees to make on-the-spot decisions to satisfy customers completely.[50]

Leadership   Leaders convey the organization's culture through both what they say and what they do. Effective leaders in customer-responsive cultures deliver by conveying a customer-focused vision and demonstrating by their continual behavior that they are committed to customers.

In almost every organization that has successfully created and maintained a strong customer-responsive culture, its chief executive officer has played a major role in championing the message. For instance, DuPont's CEO Richard Heckert led the charge to change the mentality of his company's employees from emphasizing research and product development to focusing on marketing and customer needs.[51]

Performance Evaluation   There is an impressive amount of evidence demonstrating that behavior-based performance evaluations are consistent with improved customer service.[52] Behavior-based evaluations appraise employees on the basis of how they behave or act—on criteria such as effort, commitment, teamwork, friendliness, and the ability to solve customer problems—rather than on the measurable outcomes they achieve. Why are behaviors superior to outcomes for improving service? Because it gives employees the incentive to engage in behaviors that are conducive to improved service quality and it gives employees more control over the conditions that affect their performance evaluations.[53]

In addition, a customer-responsive culture will be fostered by using 360-degree evaluations that include input from customers. Just the fact that employees know that part of their performance appraisal will include evaluations from customers is likely to make those employees more concerned with satisfying customer needs. Of course, this should only be used with employees who have direct contact with customers.

Reward Systems   Finally, if management wants employees to give good service, it has to reward good service. It needs to provide ongoing recognition to employees who have demonstrated extraordinary effort to please customers and who have been singled out by customers for "going the extra mile." And it needs to make pay and promotions contingent on outstanding customer service.

SPIRITUALITY AND ORGANIZATIONAL CULTURE

What do Southwest Airlines, Ben & Jerry's Homemade, Hewlett-Packard, Wetherill Associates, and Tom's of Maine have in common? They're among a growing number of organizations that have embraced workplace spirituality.

What Is Spirituality?

workplace spirituality

The recognition that people have an inner life that nourishes and is nourished by meaningful work that takes place in the context of community.

Workplace spirituality is *not* about organized religious practices. It's not about God or theology. **Workplace spirituality** recognizes that people have an inner life that nourishes and is nourished by meaningful work that takes place in the context of community.[54] Organizations that promote a spiritual culture recognize that people have both a mind and a spirit, seek to find meaning and purpose in their work, and desire to connect with other human beings and be part of a community.

Why Spirituality Now?

Historical models of management and organizational behavior had no room for spirituality. As we noted in our discussion of emotions in Chapter 4, the myth of rationality assumed that the well-run organization eliminated feelings. Similarly, concern about an employee's inner life had no role in the perfectly rational model. But just as we've now come to realize that the study of emotions improves our understanding of organizational behavior, an awareness of spirituality can help you to better understand employee behavior in the twenty-first century.

Of course, employees have always had an inner life. So why has the search for meaning and purposefulness in work surfaced now? There are a number of reasons. We summarize them in Exhibit 18-6.

EXHIBIT

18-6

Reasons for the Growing Interest in Spirituality

- As a counterbalance to the pressures and stress of a turbulent pace of life. Contemporary lifestyles—single-parent families, geographic mobility, the temporary nature of jobs, new technologies that create distance between people—underscore the lack of community many people feel and increases the need for involvement and connection.

- Aging baby-boomers, reaching mid-life, are looking for something in their life.

- Formalized religion hasn't worked for many people and they continue to look for anchors to replace lack of faith and to fill a growing feeling of emptiness.

- Job demands have made the workplace dominant in many people's lives yet they continue to question the meaning of work.

- The desire to integrate personal life values with one's professional life.

- In times of economic plenty, more people have the luxury to engage in a search to reach their full potential.

Characteristics of a Spiritual Organization

The concept of workplace spirituality draws on our previous discussions of topics such as values, ethics, motivation, leadership, and work/life balance. As you'll see, for instance, spiritual organizations are concerned with helping people develop and reach their full potential. This is analogous to Maslow's description of self-actualization that we discussed in relation to motiva-tion. Similarly, organizations that are concerned with spirituality are more likely to directly address problems created by work/life conflicts.

What differentiates spiritual organizations from their nonspiritual counterparts? Although research on this question is only preliminary, our review identified five cultural characteristics that tend to be evident in spiritual organizations.[55]

Strong Sense of Purpose Spiritual organizations build their cultures around a meaningful purpose. While prof-its may be important, they're not the primary values of the organization. Southwest Airlines, for instance, is strongly committed to providing the lowest airfares, on-time service, and a pleasant experience for customers. Ben & Jerry's Homemade has closely intermeshed so-cially responsible behavior into its producing and selling of ice cream. Tom's of Maine strives to sell personal care household products that are made from nat-ural ingredients and are environmentally friendly.

Tom Chappell, of Tom's of Maine, has created a spiritual cul-ture with a strong sense of purpose.

Focus on Individual Development Spiritual or-ganizations recognize the worth and value of people. They aren't just providing jobs. They seek to create cultures in which employees can continually learn and grow. Recognizing the importance of people, they also try to provide employment secu-rity. Hewlett-Packard, for instance, has gone to extremes to try to minimize the effect of economic downturns on its staff. The company has handled temporary down-turns through voluntary attrition and shortened work weeks (shared by all); and longer-term declines through early retirements and buyouts.

Trust and Openness   Spiritual organizations are characterized by mutual trust, honesty, and openness. Managers aren't afraid to admit mistakes. And they tend to be extremely up front with their employees, customers, and suppliers. The president of Wetherill Associates, a highly successful auto parts distribution firm, says: "We don't tell lies here, and everyone knows it. We are specific and honest about quality and suitability of the product for our customers' needs, even if we know they might not be able to detect any problem."[56]

Employee Empowerment   The high-trust climate in spiritual organizations, when combined with the desire to promote employee learning and growth, leads to management empowering employees to make most work-related decisions. Managers in spiritually based organizations are comfortable delegating authority to individual employees and teams. They trust their employees to make thoughtful and conscientious decisions. As a case in point, Southwest Airline employees—including flight attendants, customer service representatives, and baggage handlers—are encouraged to take whatever action they deem necessary to meet customer needs or help fellow workers, even if it means breaking company policies.

Toleration of Employee Expression   The final characteristic that differentiates spiritually based organizations is that they don't stifle employee emotions. They allow people to be themselves—to express their moods and feelings without guilt or fear of reprimand. Employees at Southwest Air, for instance, are encouraged to express their sense of humor on the job, to act spontaneously, and to make their work fun.

Criticisms of Spirituality

Critics of the spirituality movement in organizations have focused on two issues. First is the question of legitimacy. Specifically, do organizations have the right to impose spiritual values on their employees? Second is the question of economics. Are spirituality and profits compatible?

On the first question, there is clearly the potential for an emphasis on spirituality to make some employees uneasy. Critics might argue that secular institutions, especially business firms, have no business imposing spiritual values on employees. This criticism is undoubtedly valid when spirituality is defined as bringing religion and God into the workplace.[57] However, the criticism seems less stinging when the goal is limited to helping employees find meaning in their work lives. If the concerns listed in Exhibit 18-6 truly characterize a growing segment of the workforce, then maybe the time is right for organizations to help employees find meaning and purpose in their work and to use the workplace as a source of community.

The issue of whether spirituality and profits are compatible objectives is certainly relevant for managers and investors in business. The evidence, although limited, indicates that the two objectives may be very compatible. A recent research study by a major consulting firm found that companies that introduced spiritually based techniques improved productivity and significantly reduced turnover.[58] Another study found that organizations that provide their employees with opportunities for spiritual development outperformed those that didn't.[59] Other studies also report that spirituality in organizations was positively related to creativity, employee satisfaction, team performance, and organizational commitment.[60] And if you're looking for a single case to make the argument for spirituality, it's hard to beat Southwest Air. Southwest has one of the lowest employee turnover rates in the airline industry; it consistently has the lowest labor costs per miles flown of any major airline; it regularly outpaces its competitors for achieving on-time arrivals and fewest customer complaints; and it has proven itself to be the most consistently profitable airline in the United States.[61]

SUMMARY AND IMPLICATIONS FOR MANAGERS

Exhibit 18-7 depicts organizational culture as an intervening variable. Employees form an overall subjective perception of the organization based on factors such as degree of risk tolerance, team emphasis, and support of people. This overall perception becomes, in effect, the organization's culture or personality. These favorable or unfavorable perceptions then affect employee performance and satisfaction, with the impact being greater for stronger cultures.

Just as people's personalities tend to be stable over time, so too do strong cultures. This makes strong cultures difficult for managers to change. When a culture becomes mismatched to its environment, management will want to change it. But as the Point–Counterpoint debate on page 546 demonstrates, changing an organization's culture is a long and difficult process. The result, at least in the short term, is that managers should treat their organization's culture as relatively fixed.

One of the more important managerial implications of organizational culture relates to selection decisions. Hiring individuals whose values don't align with those of the organization is likely to lead to employees who lack motivation and commitment and who are dissatisfied with their jobs and the organization.[62] Not surprisingly, employee "misfits" have considerably higher turnover rates than individuals who perceive a good fit.[63]

We should also not overlook the influence socialization has on employee performance. An employee's performance depends to a considerable degree on knowing what he should or should not do. Understanding the right way to do a job indicates proper socialization. Furthermore, the appraisal of an individual's performance includes how well the person fits into the organization. Can he or she get along with co-workers? Does he or she have acceptable work habits and demonstrate the right attitude? These qualities differ between jobs and organizations. For instance, on some jobs, employees will be evaluated more favorably if they are aggressive and outwardly indicate that they are ambitious. On another job, or on the same job in another organization, such an approach may be evaluated negatively. As a result, proper socialization becomes a significant factor in influencing both actual job performance and how it's perceived by others.

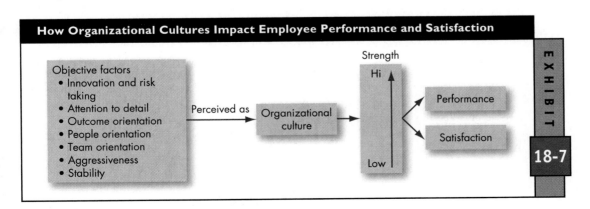

How Organizational Cultures Impact Employee Performance and Satisfaction

EXHIBIT 18-7

Organizational Cultures Can't Be Changed

An organization's culture is made up of relatively stable characteristics. It develops over many years and is rooted in deeply held values to which employees are strongly committed. In addition, there are a number of forces continually operating to maintain a given culture. These include written statements about the organization's mission and philosophy, the design of physical spaces and buildings, the dominant leadership style, hiring criteria, past promotion practices, entrenched rituals, popular stories about key people and events, the organization's historic performance evaluation criteria, and the organization's formal structure.

Selection and promotion policies are particularly important devices that work against cultural change. Employees chose the organization because they perceived their values to be a "good fit" with the organization. They become comfortable with that fit and will strongly resist efforts to disturb the equilibrium. The terrific difficulties that organizations like General Motors, AT&T, and the U.S. Postal Service have had in trying to reshape their cultures attest to this dilemma. These organizations historically tended to attract individuals who desired situations that were stable and highly structured. Those in control in organizations will also select senior managers who will continue the current culture. Even attempts to change a culture by going outside the organization to hire a new chief executive are unlikely to be effective. The evidence indicates that the culture is more likely to change the executive than the other way around.

Our argument should not be viewed as saying that culture can *never* be changed. In the unusual case in which an organization confronts a survival-threatening crisis—a crisis that is universally acknowledged as a true life-or-death situation—members of the organization will be responsive to efforts at cultural change. However, anything less than a crisis is unlikely to be effective in bringing about cultural change.

Changing an organization's culture is extremely difficult, but cultures *can* be changed. The evidence suggests that cultural change is most likely to take place when most or all of the following conditions exist:

A dramatic crisis. This is the shock that undermines the status quo and calls into question the relevance of the current culture. Examples of these crises might be a surprising financial setback, the loss of a major customer, or a dramatic technological breakthrough by a competitor.

Turnover in leadership. New top leadership, which can provide an alternative set of key values, may be perceived as more capable of responding to the crisis.

Young and small organizations. The younger the organization is, the less entrenched its culture will be. Similarly, it's easier for management to communicate its new values when the organization is small.

Weak culture. The more widely held a culture is and the higher the agreement among members on its values, the more difficult it will be to change. Conversely, weak cultures are more amenable to change than strong ones.

If the above conditions exist, the following actions may lead to change: New stories and rituals need to be set in place by top management; employees should be selected and promoted who espouse the new values; the reward system needs to be changed to support the new values; and current subcultures need to be undermined through transfers, job rotation, and terminations.

Under the best of conditions, these actions won't result in an immediate or dramatic shift in the culture. This is because, in the final analysis, cultural change is a lengthy process—measured in years rather than in months. But cultures can be changed. The success that new leadership had in turning around the cultures at companies like Harley-Davidson, IBM, Texaco, and Electronic Data Systems attests to this claim.

1. What's the difference between job satisfaction and organizational culture?

2. Can an employee survive in an organization if he or she rejects its core values? Explain.

3. What defines an organization's subcultures?

4. Contrast organizational culture with national culture.

5. How can culture be a liability to an organization?

6. How does a strong culture affect an organization's efforts to improve diversity?

7. What benefits can socialization provide for the organization? For the new employee?

8. How is language related to organizational culture?

9. How can management create an ethical culture?

10. What criticisms have been targeted against bringing spirituality to the workplace?

1. Is socialization brainwashing? Explain.

2. If management sought a culture characterized as innovative and autonomous, what might its socialization program look like?

3. Can you identify a set of characteristics that describes your college's culture? Compare them with several of your peers. How closely do they agree?

4. Today's workforce is increasingly made up of part-time or contingent employees. Is organizational culture really important if the workforce is mostly temporaries?

5. "We should be opposed to the manipulation of individuals for organizational purposes, but a degree of social uniformity enables organizations to work better." Do you agree or disagree with this statement? What are its implications for organizational culture? Discuss.

Listed here are 14 statements. Using the five-item scale (from Strongly Agree to Strongly Disagree), respond to each statement by circling the number that best represents your opinion.

	Strongly Agree	Agree	Neutral	Disagree	Strongly Disagree
1. I feel comfortable challenging statements made by my instructor.	5	4	3	2	1
2. My instructor heavily penalizes assignments that are not turned in on time.	1	2	3	4	5
3. My instructor believes that "it's final results that counts."	1	2	3	4	5

	Strongly Agree	Agree	Neutral	Disagree	Strongly Disagree
4. My instructor is sensitive to my personal needs and problems.	5	4	3	2	1
5. A large portion of my grade depends on how well I work with others in the class.	5	4	3	2	1
6. I often feel nervous and tense when I come to class.	1	2	3	4	5
7. My instructor seems to prefer stability over change.	1	2	3	4	5
8. My instructor encourages me to develop new and different ideas.	5	4	3	2	1
9. My instructor has little tolerance for sloppy thinking.	1	2	3	4	5
10. My instructor is more concerned with how I came to a conclusion than the conclusion itself.	5	4	3	2	1
11. My instructor treats all students alike.	1	2	3	4	5
12. My instructor frowns on class members helping each other with assignments.	1	2	3	4	5
13. Aggressive and competitive people have a distinct advantage in this class.	1	2	3	4	5
14. My instructor encourages me to see the world differently.	5	4	3	2	1

Calculate your total score by adding up the numbers you circled. Your score will fall between 14 and 70.

A high score (49 or above) describes an open, risk-taking, supportive, humanistic, team-oriented, easy-going, growth-oriented culture. A low score (35 or below) describes a closed, structured, task-oriented, individualistic, tense, and stability-oriented culture. Note that differences count. So a score of 60 is a more open culture than one that scores 50. Also, realize that one culture isn't preferable over the other. The "right" culture depends on you and your preferences for a learning environment.

Form teams of five to seven members each. Compare your scores. How closely do they align? Discuss and resolve discrepancies. Based on your team's analysis, what type of student do you think would perform best in this class?

Few companies have had a rougher time adapting to a changing environment than General Motors. The company is truly a textbook example of corporate entrenchment. As far back as the 1960s, the writing was on the wall that GM's way of operating—slow, deliberate decision making; layer-upon-layer of hierarchy; focus on cost-cutting rather than on new product design; and management-by-committee—was failing. From a U.S. automobile market share of nearly 50 percent in the late 1950s, the company was down to under 30 percent by the year 2000. GM's rigid and insular culture, driven by financial considerations, allowed both foreign and domestic competitors to steal away customers with new products—like fuel-efficient compacts, minivans, SUVs, and eye-catching roadsters.

A good part of GM's culture can be explained by the company's historic selection and promotion policies. It hired its future executives fresh out of school. They then shaped these recruits into the GM mentality. The company resisted ideas and innovations that were "not developed here." Executives firmly believed, to the point of arrogance, that the GM system was superior to all others. Promotions favored financial and engineering types, and individuals with these backgrounds rose to fill the company's top spots. GM rarely hired senior executives from outside the company ranks. In addition, GM encouraged its executives to socialize off the job with other GM people. This further insulated top executives and resulted in a senior management team that saw the world through similar lenses.

In the fall of 2001, GM Chief Executive Richard Wagoner hired former Chrysler executive Robert Lutz as vice chairman. His primary task? To change GM's organizational culture. Wagoner acknowledged that GM's culture—dominated by finance-types, engineers, and manufacturing personnel—was content to turn out unimaginative cars. The committee system (stacked to favor the company's accounting mentality) further hindered creative endeavors. For instance, whenever designers and engineers would disagree about a design, the engineers (and their obsession with cost minimization) would always win. This largely explained why the company's cars looked boxy and so similar. Wagoner has essentially given Lutz a free hand to do whatever he needs to change tradition-bound GM.

Lutz faces a formidable task. This is a huge company. Sales are $180 billion a year. It employs 363,000 people. This is also the place where the "GM nod" is endemic: GM lifers usually just nod at the new guy and go on doing things as they were. But Lutz has the advantage of coming to GM with a sterling reputation. He is a true "car guy," who single-handedly pushed through exciting new products at Chrysler like the Viper, the Prowler, and the PT Cruiser.

Lutz has chosen an incremental strategy for implementing change. He isn't chopping heads and bringing in loyalists. Rather, he is relying on the same designers and engineers who have been turning out duds for years. But he's giving more clout to the designers and marketing people. He's overseen a reorganization that has engineering and design divisions now reporting to just one person. He's encouraging people to question past practices, to speak out on issues, and challenge company doctrine. And GM brass is now spending more time driving competitors' cars than their own—while Lutz points out how most of them best GM.

Questions

1. Describe the "old" GM culture.

2. What specific forces created this culture?

3. Describe the new culture that Lutz is trying to create.

4. Do you think Lutz will succeed or fail in his effort to change GM's culture? Why?

Source: Parts of this case are based on R. Meredith, "Car Guy," *Forbes,* January 21, 2002, pp. 50–51.

KSS PROGRAM:

KNOW THE CONCEPTS
SELF-AWARENESS
SKILLS APPLICATIONS

Reading an Organization's Culture

After you've read this chapter, take Self-Assessment #42 (What's the Right Organizational Culture For Me?) on your enclosed CD-ROM, and complete the skill-building module entitled Reading an Organization's Culture on page 631.

1. Based on J. Fox, "Nokia's Secret Code," *Fortune*, May 1, 2000, pp. 161–74; M. Moskowitz and R. Levering, "Best Companies to Work For," *Fortune*, February 4, 2002; P. Taylor, "Nokia Goes from Humble Origins to Global Success," *Financial Times*, March 7, 2002, p. 22; and www.nokia.co.uk.

2. P. Selznick, "Foundations of the Theory of Organizations," *American Sociological Review*, February 1948, pp. 25–35.

3. See L. G. Zucker, "Organizations as Institutions," in S. B. Bacharach (ed.), *Research in the Sociology of Organizations* (Greenwich, CT: JAI Press, 1983), pp. 1–47; A. J. Richardson, "The Production of Institutional Behaviour: A Constructive Comment on the Use of Institutionalization Theory in Organizational Analysis," *Canadian Journal of Administrative Sciences*, December 1986, pp. 304–16; L. G. Zucker, *Institutional Patterns and Organizations: Culture and Environment* (Cambridge, MA: Ballinger, 1988); and R. L. Jepperson, "Institutions, Institutional Effects, and Institutionalism," in W. W. Powell and P. J. DiMaggio (eds.), *The New Institutionalism in Organizational Analysis* (Chicago: University of Chicago Press, 1991), pp. 143–63.

4. See, for example, H. S. Becker, "Culture: A Sociological View," *Yale Review*, Summer 1982, pp. 513–27; and E. H. Schein, *Organizational Culture and Leadership* (San Francisco: Jossey-Bass, 1985), p. 168.

5. This seven-item description is based on C. A. O'Reilly III, J. Chatman, and D. F. Caldwell, "People and Organizational Culture: A Profile Comparison Approach to Assessing Person–Organization Fit," *Academy of Management Journal*, September 1991, pp. 487–516; and J. A. Chatman and K. A. Jehn, "Assessing the Relationship between Industry Characteristics and Organizational Culture: How Different Can You Be?" *Academy of Management Journal*, June 1994, pp. 522–53. For a review of cultural dimensions, see N. M. Ashkanasy, C. P. M. Wilderom, and M. F. Peterson (eds.), *Handbook of Organizational Culture and Climate* (Thousand Oaks, CA: Sage, 2000), pp. 131–45.

6. The view that there will be consistency among perceptions of organizational culture has been called the "integration" perspective. For a review of this perspective and conflicting approaches, see D. Meyerson and J. Martin, "Cultural Change: An Integration of Three Different Views," *Journal of Management Studies*, November 1987, pp. 623–47; and P. J. Frost, L. F. Moore, M. R. Louis, C. C. Lundberg, and J. Martin (eds.), *Reframing Organizational Culture* (Newbury Park, CA: Sage Publications, 1991).

7. See J. M. Jermier, J. W. Slocum, Jr., L. W. Fry, and J. Gaines, "Organizational Subcultures in a Soft Bureaucracy: Resistance Behind the Myth and Facade of an Official Culture," *Organization Science*, May 1991, pp. 170–94; S. A. Sackmann, "Culture and Subcultures: An Analysis of Organizational Knowledge," *Administrative Science Quarterly*, March 1992, pp. 140–61; R. F. Zammuto, "Mapping Organizational Cultures and Subcultures: Looking Inside and Across Hospitals," paper presented at the 1995 National Academy of Management Conference, Vancouver, BC, August 1995; and G. Hofstede, "Identifying Organizational Subcultures: An Empirical Approach," *Journal of Management Studies*, January 1998, pp. 1–12.

8. T. A. Timmerman, "Do Organizations Have Personalities?" paper presented at the 1996 National Academy of Management Conference; Cincinnati, OH, August 1996.

9. S. Hamm, "No Letup—and No Apologies," *Business Week*, October 26, 1998, pp. 58–64; and C. Carlson, "Former Intel Exec Slams Microsoft Culture," eWeek.com, March 26, 2002.

10. See, for example, G. G. Gordon and N. DiTomaso, "Predicting Corporate Performance from Organizational Culture," *Journal of Management Studies*, November 1992, pp. 793–98; and J. B. Sorensen, "The Strength of Corporate Culture and the Reliability of Firm Performance," *Administrative Science Quarterly*, March 2002, pp. 70–91.

11. Y. Wiener, "Forms of Value Systems: A Focus on Organizational Effectiveness and Cultural Change and Maintenance," *Academy of Management Review*, October 1988, p. 536.

12. R. T. Mowday, L. W. Porter, and R. M. Steers, *Employee-Organization Linkages: The Psychology of Commitment, Absenteeism, and Turnover* (New York: Academic Press, 1982).

13. See N. J. Adler, *International Dimensions of Organizational Behavior*, 4th ed. (Cincinnati, OH: Southwestern, 2002), pp. 67–69.

14. S. C. Schneider, "National vs. Corporate Culture: Implications for Human Resource Management," *Human Resource Management*, Summer 1988, p. 239.

15. See C. A. O'Reilly and J. A. Chatman, "Culture as Social Control: Corporations, Cults, and Commitment," in B. M. Staw and L. L. Cummings (eds.), *Research in Organizational Behavior*, vol. 18 (Greenwich, CT: JAI Press, 1996), pp. 157–200.

16. T. E. Deal and A. A. Kennedy, "Culture: A New Look Through Old Lenses," *Journal of Applied Behavioral Science*, November 1983, p. 501.

17. J. Case, "Corporate Culture," *INC.*, November 1996, pp. 42–53.

18. See, for instance, P. L. Moore, "She's Here to Fix the Xerox," *Business Week*, August 6, 2001, pp. 47–48; and C. Ragavan, "FBI Inc.," *U.S. News & World Report*, June 18, 2001, pp. 15–21.

19. See C. Lindsay, "Paradoxes of Organizational Diversity: Living within the Paradoxes," in L. R. Jauch and J. L. Wall (eds.), *Proceedings of the 50th Academy of Management Conference* (San Francisco, 1990), pp. 374–78; T. Cox, Jr., *Cultural Diversity in Organizations: Theory, Research & Practice* (San Francisco: Berrett-Koehler, 1993), pp. 162–70; and L. Grensing-Pophal, "Hiring to Fit Your Corporate Culture," *HRMagazine*, August 1999, pp. 50–54.

20. K. Labich, "No More Crude at Texaco," *Fortune*, September 6, 1999, pp. 205–12; and "Rooting Out Racism," *Business Week*, January 10, 2000, p. 66.

21. D. Miller, "What Happens after Success: The Perils of Excellence," *Journal of Management Studies*, May 1994, pp. 11–38.

22. D. Roth, "From Poster Boy to Whipping Boy: Burying Motorola," *Fortune*, July 6, 1998, p. 28; and J. Howell-Jones, "Motorola Cuts Jobs as Profits Plummet," www.vnunet.com, April 19, 2001.

23. A. F. Buono and J. L. Bowditch, *The Human Side of Mergers and Acquisitions: Managing Collisions between People, Cultures, and Organizations* (San Francisco: Jossey-Bass, 1989); S. Cartwright and C. L. Cooper, "The Role of Culture Compatibility in Successful Organizational Marriages," *Academy of Management Executive*, May 1993, pp. 57–70; R. J. Grossman, "Irreconcilable Differences," *HRMagazine*, April 1999, pp. 42–48; J. Veiga, M. Lubatkin, R. Calori, and P. Very, "Measuring Organizational Culture Clashes: A Two-Nation Post-Hoc Analysis of a Cultural Compatibility Index," *Human Relations*, April 2000, pp. 539–57; and E. Krell, "Merging Corporate Cultures," *Training*, May 2001, pp. 68–78.

24. D. Carey and D. Ogden, "A Match Made in Heaven? Find Out Before You Merge," *Wall Street Journal*, November 30, 1998, p. A22; and M. Arndt, "Let's Talk Turkeys," *Business Week*, December 11, 2000, pp. 44–46.

25. "Carly's Last Stand?" *Business Week*, December 24, 2001, p. 65.

26. E. H. Schein, "The Role of the Founder in Creating Organizational Culture," *Organizational Dynamics*, Summer 1983, pp. 13–28.

27. E. H. Schein, "Leadership and Organizational Culture," in F. Hesselbein, M. Goldsmith, and R. Beckhard, eds., *The Leader of the Future* (San Francisco: Jossey-Bass, 1996), pp. 61–62.

28. See, for example, J. R. Harrison and G. R. Carroll, "Keeping the Faith: A Model of Cultural Transmission in Formal Organizations," *Administrative Science Quarterly*, December 1991, pp. 552–82.

29. B. Schneider, "The People Make the Place," *Personnel Psychology*, Autumn 1987, pp. 437–53; D. E. Bowen, G. E. Ledford, Jr., and B. R. Nathan, "Hiring for the Organization, Not the Job," *Academy of Management Executive*, November 1991, pp. 35–51; B. Schneider, H. W. Goldstein, and D. B. Smith, "The ASA Framework: An Update," *Personnel Psychology*, Winter 1995, pp. 747–73; A. L. Kristof, "Person-Organization Fit: An Integrative Review of Its Conceptualizations, Measurement, and Implications," *Personnel Psychology*, Spring 1996, pp. 1–49; D. M. Cable and T. A. Judge, "Interviewers' Perceptions of Person-Organization Fit and Organizational Selection Decisions," *Journal of Applied Psychology*, August 1997, pp. 546–61; J. Schaubroeck, D. C. Ganster, and J. R. Jones, "Organization and Occupation Influences in the Attraction-Selection-Attrition Process," *Journal of Applied Psychology*, December 1998, pp. 869–891; and J. Harris and J. Brannick, *Finding and Keeping Great Employees* (New York: AMACOM, 1999).

30. R. Pascale, "The Paradox of 'Corporate Culture': Reconciling Ourselves to Socialization," *California Management Review*, Winter 1985, pp. 26–27.

31. D. C. Hambrick and P. A. Mason, "Upper Echelons: The Organization as a Reflection of Its Top Managers," *Academy of Management Review*, April 1984, pp. 193–206; B. P. Niehoff, C. A. Enz, and R. A. Grover, "The Impact of Top-Management Actions on Employee Attitudes and Perceptions," *Group & Organization Studies*, September 1990, pp. 337–52; and H. M. Trice and J. M. Beyer, "Cultural Leadership in Organizations," *Organization Science*, May 1991, pp. 149–69.

32. J. S. Lublin, "Cheap Talk," *Wall Street Journal*, April 11, 2002, p. B14.

33. See, for instance, J. P. Wanous, *Organizational Entry*, 2nd ed. (New York: Addison-Wesley, 1992); G. T. Chao, A. M. O'Leary-Kelly, S. Wolf, H. J. Klein, and P. D. Gardner, "Organizational Socialization: Its Content and Consequences," *Journal of Applied Psychology*, October 1994, pp. 730–43; B. E. Ashforth, A. M. Saks, and R. T. Lee, "Socialization and Newcomer Adjustment: The Role of Organizational Context," *Human Relations*, July 1998, pp. 897–926; D. A. Major, "Effective Newcomer Socialization into High-Performance Organizational Cultures," in N. M. Ashkanasy, C. P. M. Wilderom, and M. F. Peterson (eds.), *Handbook of Organizational Culture & Climate*, pp. 355–68; and D. M. Cable and C. K. Parsons, "Socialization Tactics and Person-Organization Fit," *Personnel Psychology*, Spring 2001, pp. 1–23.

34. B. Filipczak, "Trained by Starbucks," *Training*, June 1995, pp. 73–79; and S. Gruner, "Lasting Impressions," *INC.*, July 1998, p. 126.

35. K. Rhodes, "Breaking in the Top Dogs," *Training*, February 2000, pp. 67–74.

36. J. Van Maanen and E. H. Schein, "Career Development," in J. R. Hackman and J. L. Suttle (eds.), *Improving Life at Work* (Santa Monica, CA: Goodyear, 1977), pp. 58–62.

37. D. C. Feldman, "The Multiple Socialization of Organization Members," *Academy of Management Review*, April 1981, p. 310.

38. Van Maanen and Schein, "Career Development," p. 59.
39. E. Ransdell, "The Nike Story? Just Tell It!" *Fast Company*, January–February 2000, pp. 44–46.
40. D. M. Boje, "The Storytelling Organization: A Study of Story Performance in an Office-Supply Firm," *Administrative Science Quarterly*, March 1991, pp. 106–26; and C. H. Deutsch, "The Parables of Corporate Culture," *The New York Times*, October 13, 1991, p. F25.
41. "Job Titles of the Future: Minister of Culture," *Fast Company*, September 1998, p. 64.
42. See K. Kamoche, "Rhetoric, Ritualism, and Totemism in Human Resource Management," *Human Relations*, April 1995, pp. 367–85.
43. V. Matthews, "Starting Every Day with a Shout and a Song," *Financial Times*, May 2, 2001, p. 11; and M. Gimein, "Sam Walton Made Us a Promise," *Fortune*, March 18, 2002, pp. 121–30.
44. A. Rafaeli and M. G. Pratt, "Tailored Meanings: On the Meaning and Impact of Organizational Dress," *Academy of Management Review*, January 1993, pp. 32–55.
45. "DCACronyms," April 1997, Rev. D; published by The Boeing Co.
46. See B. Victor and J. B. Cullen, "The Organizational Bases of Ethical Work Climates," *Administrative Science Quarterly*, March 1988, pp. 101–25; L. K. Trevino, "A Cultural Perspective on Changing and Developing Organizational Ethics," in W. A. Pasmore and R. W. Woodman (eds.), *Research in Organizational Change and Development*, vol. 4 (Greenwich, CT: JAI Press, 1990); and M. W. Dickson, D. B. Smith, M. W. Grojean, and M. Ehrhart, "An Organizational Climate Regarding Ethics: The Outcome of Leader Values and the Practices That Reflect Them," *Leadership Quarterly*, Summer 2001, pp. 197–217.
47. S. Daley, "A Spy's Advice to French Retailers: Politeness Pays," *New York Times*, December 26, 2000, p. A4.
48. Based on M. J. Bitner, B. H. Booms, and L. A. Mohr, "Critical Service Encounters: The Employee's Viewpoint," *Journal of Marketing*, October 1994, pp. 95–106; M. D. Hartline and O. C. Ferrell, "The Management of Customer-Contact Service Employees: An Empirical Investigation," *Journal of Marketing*, October 1996, pp. 52–70; M. L. Lengnick-Hall and Cynthia A. Lengnick-Hall, "Expanding Customer Orientation in the HR Function," *Human Resource Management*, Fall 1999, pp. 201–14; B. Schneider, D. E. Bowen, M. G. Ehrhart, and K. M. Holcombe, "The Climate for Service: Evolution of a Construct," in N. M. Ashkanasy, C. P. M. Wilderom, and M. F. Peterson (eds.), *Handbook of Organizational Culture and Climate* (Thousand Oaks, CA: Sage, 2000), pp. 21–36; M. D. Hartline, J. G. Maxham III, and D. O. McKee, "Corridors of Influence in the Dissemination of Customer-Oriented Strategy to Customer Contact Service Employees," *Journal of Marketing*, April 2000, pp. 35–50; and L. A. Bettencourt, K. P. Gwinner, and M. L. Meuter, "A Comparison of Attitude, Personality, and Knowledge Predictors of Service-Oriented Organizational Citizenship Behaviors," *Journal of Applied Psychology*, February 2001, pp. 29–41.
49. D. E. Bowen and B. Schneider, "Boundary-Spanning-Role Employees and the Service Encounter: Some Guidelines for Future Management and Research," in J. Czepiel, M. R. Solomon, and C. F. Surprenant (eds.), *The Service Encounter* (New York: Lexington Books, 1985), pp. 127–47; W.-C. Tsai, "Determinants and Consequences of Employee Displayed Positive Emotions," *Journal of Management*, vol. 27, no. 4, 2001, pp. 497–512; and S. D. Pugh, "Service with a Smile: Emotional Contagion in the Service Encounter," *Academy of Management Journal*, October 2001, pp. 1018–27.
50. M. D. Hartline and O. C. Ferrell, "The Management of Customer-Contact Service Employees," p. 56; and R. C. Ford and C. P. Heaton, "Lessons from Hospitality That Can Serve Anyone," *Organizational Dynamics*, Summer 2001, pp. 41–42.
51. E. E. Messikomer, "DuPont's 'Marketing Community,'" *Business Marketing*, October 1987, pp. 90–94.
52. See, for instance, E. Anderson and R. L. Oliver, "Perspectives on Behavior-Based Versus Outcome-Based Salesforce Control Systems," *Journal of Marketing*, October 1987, pp. 76–88; W. R. George, "Internal Marketing and Organizational Behavior: A Partnership in Developing Customer-Conscious Employees at Every Level," *Journal of Business Research*, January 1990, pp. 63–70; and K. K. Reardon and B. Enis, "Establishing a Company-Wide Customer Orientation Through Persuasive Internal Marketing," *Management Communication Quarterly*, February 1990, pp. 376–87.
53. M. D. Hartline and O. C. Ferrell, "The Management of Customer-Contact Service Employees," p. 57.
54. D. P. Ashmos and D. Duchon, "Spirituality at Work: A Conceptualization and Measure," *Journal of Management Inquiry*, June 2000, p. 139.
55. This section is based on I. A. Mitroff and E. A. Denton, *A Spiritual Audit of Corporate America: A Hard Look at Spirituality, Religion, and Values in the Workplace* (San Francisco: Jossey-Bass, 1999); J. Milliman, J. Ferguson, D. Trickett, and B. Condemi, "Spirit and Community at Southwest Airlines: An Investigation of a Spiritual Values-Based Model," *Journal of Organizational Change Management*, vol. 12, no. 3, 1999, pp. 221–33; E. H. Burack, "Spirituality in the Workplace," *Journal of Organizational Change Management*, vol. 12, no. 3, 1999, pp. 280–91; and F. Wagner-Marsh and J. Conley, "The Fourth Wave: The Spiritually-Based Firm," *Journal of Organizational Change Management*, vol. 12, no. 3, 1999, pp. 292–302.
56. Cited in F. Wagner-Marsh and J. Conley, "The Fourth Wave," p. 295.
57. M. Conlin, "Religion in the Workplace: The Growing Presence of Spirituality in Corporate America," *Business Week*, November 1, 1999, pp. 151–58; and P. Paul, "A Holier Holiday Season," *American Demographics*, December 2001, pp. 41–45.
58. Cited in M. Conlin, "Religion in the Workplace," p. 153.
59. C. P. Neck and J. F. Milliman, "Thought Self-Leadership: Finding Spiritual Fulfillment in Organizational Life," *Journal of Managerial Psychology*, vol. 9, no. 8, 1994, p. 9.

60. D. W. McCormick, "Spirituality and Management," *Journal of Managerial Psychology*, vol. 9, no. 6, 1994, p. 5; E. Brandt, "Corporate Pioneers Explore Spiritual Peace," *HRMagazine*, vol. 41, no. 4, 1996, p. 82; P. Leigh, "The New Spirit at Work," *Training and Development*, vol. 51, no. 3, 1997, p. 26; P. H. Mirvis, "Soul Work in Organizations," *Organization Science*, vol. 8, no. 2, 1997, p. 193; and J. Millman, A. Czaplewski, and J. Ferguson, "An Exploratory Empirical Assessment of the Relationship Between Spirituality and Employee Work Attitudes," paper presented at the National Academy of Management Meeting, Washington, D.C., August 2001.

61. Cited in J. Milliman, et al., "Spirit and Community at Southwest Airlines."

62. J. A. Chatman, "Matching People and Organizations: Selection and Socialization in Public Accounting Firms," *Administrative Science Quarterly*, September 1991, pp. 459–84; and B. Z. Posner, "Person–Organization Values Congruence: No Support for Individual Differences as a Moderating Influence," *Human Relations*, April 1992, pp. 351–61.

63. J. E. Sheridan, "Organizational Culture and Employee Retention," *Academy of Management Journal*, December 1992, pp. 1036–56.

PART FIVE

ORGANIZATIONAL
DYNAMICS

On June 7, 1993, Samsung's chairman, Kun-Hee Lee (see photo), officially announced his "New Management" policy. His goal? To completely overhaul the Samsung organization. Instead of focusing on producing cheap products that were copycats of stuff designed by others, Lee challenged his staff to turn Samsung into a truly innovative company, applying cutting-edge technology.[1]

In less than 10 years, Lee achieved his goal. For instance, today the South Korea–based Samsung is the world leader in memory chips, LCDs, monitors, and Braun tubes. And it has introduced a number of innovative products, including combined cell phone and handheld devices, flat-screen TVs, and ultrathin laptops.

Following his announcement, Lee faced a number of barriers in bringing about change at Samsung. Two barriers were particularly thorny. One was a lack of concern for quality. The company's historical focus on production volume encouraged employees to emphasize quantity rather than quality. So defective products were seen as just a "necessary evil" that comes from high volume. The other was employees who were afraid to speak out. The hierarchical and deferential culture of Samsung discouraged employees from questioning authority or "thinking outside the box."

To overcome these barriers and to make his New Management a reality, Lee introduced a number of radical changes. To improve quality, he implemented a Line Stop system that allows any worker to shut down production if a defect is found; adopted the Six Sigma program that establishes a goal of no more than 3.4 defects per million parts or procedures; and introduced a number of other advanced quality-control methods. To deal with his employees' complacency, Lee challenged them to "change everything except your spouses and children." To shake up Samsung's culture,

Organizational Change and Stress Management

employees in the field were empowered with much greater decision-making authority; senior managers were required to leave their offices and visit the field regularly; unnecessary or inconsistent regulations were eliminated; jobs were restructured so that engineers and designers from across the company were forced to work together on multiple projects; and breaking with the company's long-time tradition of lifetime employment, a number of senior managers were fired to make room for younger and more aggressive leaders.

While many of its major competitors—like Fujitsu, Hitachi, Matsushita, Toshiba, Ericcson, and Gateway—are losing money or barely profitable, Samsung continues to be solidly profitable. In 2002, for instance, its electronics division, which makes up less than a quarter of the company's sales, was estimating profits of $5.8 billion on sales of $30.3 billion. This success in highly competitive global markets is in no small part due to Lee's New Management and ongoing commitment to change.

This chapter is about change and stress. We describe environmental forces that are requiring managers to implement comprehensive change programs. We also consider why people and organizations often resist change and how this resistance can be overcome. We review various processes for managing organizational change. We also discuss contemporary change issues for today's managers. Then we move to the topic of stress. We elaborate on the sources and consequences of stress. Finally, we conclude this chapter with a discussion of what individuals and organizations can do to better manage stress levels.

LEARNING OBJECTIVES

AFTER STUDYING THIS CHAPTER, YOU SHOULD BE ABLE TO:

1. Describe forces that act as stimulants to change.

2. Summarize sources of individual and organizational resistance to change.

3. Summarize Lewin's three-step change model.

4. Explain the values underlying most OD efforts.

5. Identify properties of innovative organizations.

6. List characteristics of a learning organization.

7. Define knowledge management and explain its importance.

8. Describe potential sources of stress.

9. Explain individual difference variables that moderate the stress–outcome relationship.

FORCES FOR CHANGE

In January 2000, *Time* magazine described Amazon.com as a breakthrough concept and named its founder and CEO, Jeff Bezos, as the *Time* Person of the Year. Twelve months later, Amazon's stock had dropped 80 percent in value, its survival was uncertain, and Bezos himself was saying that the media had now made him the Piñata of the Year. Bezos' experience offers a chilling illustration of the rapid forces of change in the twenty-first century.

More and more organizations today face a dynamic and changing environment. This, in turn, is requiring these organizations to adapt. "Change or die!" is the rallying cry among today's managers worldwide. Exhibit 19-1 summarizes six specific forces that are acting as stimulants for change.

In a number of places in this book, we've discussed the *changing nature of the workforce*. For instance, almost every organization is having to adjust to a multicultural environment. Human resource policies and practices have to change in order to attract and keep this more diverse workforce. And many companies are having to spend large amounts of money on training to upgrade reading, math, computer, and other skills of employees.

As noted in Chapter 16, *technology* is changing jobs and organizations. For instance, computers are now commonplace in almost every organization; and cell phones and hand-held PDAs are being increasingly perceived as necessities by a large segment of the population. For the longer term, recent breakthroughs in deciphering the human genetic code offers the potential for pharmaceutical companies to produce drugs designed for specific individuals and creates serious ethical dilemmas for insurance companies as to who is insurable and who isn't.

EXHIBIT 19-1

Forces for Change

Force	Examples
Nature of the workforce	• More cultural diversity • Increase in professionals • Many new entrants with inadequate skills
Technology	• Faster and cheaper computers • New mobile communication devices • Deciphering of the human genetic code
Economic shocks	• Rise and fall of dot.com stocks • Decline in the value of the Euro • Collapse of Enron Corp.
Competition	• Global competitors • Mergers and consolidations • Growth of e-commerce
Social trends	• Internet chat rooms • Retirement of Baby Boomers • Increased interest in urban living
World politics	• Escalation of hostilities in the Middle East • Opening of markets in China • The war on terrorism following 9/11/01

We live in an "age of discontinuity." In the 1950s and 1960s, the past was a pretty good prologue to the future. Tomorrow was essentially an extended trend line from yesterday. That's no longer true. Beginning in the early 1970s, with the overnight quadrupling of world oil prices, *economic shocks* have continued to impose changes on organizations. In recent years, for instance, new dot-com businesses have been created, turned tens-of-thousands of investors into overnight millionaires, and then crashed; and the Euro has declined 20 percent against other major world currencies. The collapse of Enron Corp. in late 2001 has made executive ethics, managerial controls, responsibility of board members, manipulation of earnings, and conflicts of interest between firms and their auditors topics of concern for all corporate executives.

Competition is changing. The global economy means that competitors are as likely to come from across the ocean as from across town. Heightened competition also makes it necessary for established organizations to defend themselves against both traditional competitors who develop new products and services and small, entrepreneurial firms with innovative offerings. Successful organizations will be the ones that can change in response to the competition. They'll be fast on their feet, capable of developing new products rapidly and getting them to market quickly. They'll rely on short production runs, short product cycles, and an ongoing stream of new products. In other words, they'll be flexible. They will require an equally flexible and responsive workforce that can adapt to rapidly and even radically changing conditions.

Social trends don't remain static. For instance, in contrast to just ten years ago, people are meeting and sharing information in Internet chat rooms; Baby Boomers have begun to retire; and many Baby Boomer and Generation Xers are leaving the suburbs and moving to the cities.

Throughout this book we have argued strongly for the importance of seeing OB in a global context. Business schools have been preaching a global perspective since the early 1980s, but no one—not even the strongest proponents of globalization—could have imagined how *world politics* would change in recent years. We've seen the breakup of the Soviet Union; the opening up of South Africa and China; almost daily suicide bombings in the Middle East; and, of course, the rise of Muslim fundamentalism. The attacks on New York and Washington on September 11, and the subsequent war on terrorism, has led to changes in business practices related to the creation of backup systems, employee security, employee stereotyping and profiling, and post-terrorist-attack anxiety.

MANAGING PLANNED CHANGE

A group of housekeeping employees who work for a small hotel confronted the owner: "It's very hard for most of us to maintain rigid 7-to-4 work hours," said their spokeswoman. "Each of us has significant family and personal responsibilities. And rigid hours don't work for us. We're going to begin looking for someplace else to work if you don't set up flexible work hours." The owner listened thoughtfully to the group's ultimatum and agreed to its request. The next day the owner introduced a flextime plan for these employees.

A major automobile manufacturer spent several billion dollars to install state-of-the-art robotics. One area that would receive the new equipment was quality control. Sophisticated computer-controlled equipment would be put in place to significantly improve the company's ability to find and correct defects. Because the new equipment would dramatically change the jobs of the people working in the quality-control area, and because management anticipated considerable employee

Robotic equipment at Ford, like these spot welders, have dramatically changed the jobs for many on the company's assembly lines.

resistance to the new equipment, executives were developing a program to help people become familiar with the equipment and to deal with any anxieties they might be feeling.

Both of the previous scenarios are examples of **change**. That is, both are concerned with making things different. However, only the second scenario describes a **planned change**. Many changes in organizations are like the one that occurred at the hotel—they just happen. Some organizations treat all change as an accidental occurrence. We're concerned with change activities that are proactive and purposeful. In this chapter, we address change as an intentional, goal-oriented activity.

What are the goals of planned change? Essentially there are two. First, it seeks to improve the ability of the organization to adapt to changes in its environment. Second, it seeks to change employee behavior.

If an organization is to survive, it must respond to changes in its environment. When competitors introduce new products or services, government agencies enact new laws, important sources of supply go out of business, or similar environmental changes take place, the organization needs to adapt. Efforts to stimulate innovation, empower employees, and introduce work teams are examples of planned-change activities directed at responding to changes in the environment.

Because an organization's success or failure is essentially due to the things that its employees do or fail to do, planned change also is concerned with changing the behavior of individuals and groups within the organization. Later in this chapter, we review a number of techniques that organizations can use to get people to behave differently in the tasks they perform and in their interactions with others.

Who in organizations are responsible for managing change activities? The answer is **change agents**.[2] Change agents can be managers or nonmanagers, employees of the organization or outside consultants. For major change efforts, internal management often will hire the services of outside consultants to provide advice and assistance. Because they are from the outside, these individuals can offer an objective perspective often unavailable to insiders. Outside consultants, however, are disadvantaged because they usually have an inadequate understanding of the organization's history, culture, operating procedures, and personnel. Outside consultants also may be prone to initiating more drastic changes—which can be a benefit or a disadvantage—because they don't have to live with the repercussions after the change is implemented. In contrast, internal staff specialists or managers, when acting as change agents, may be more thoughtful (and possibly more cautious) because they have to live with the consequences of their actions.

change

Making things different.

planned change

Change activities that are intentional and goal oriented.

change agents

Persons who act as catalysts and assume the responsibility for managing change activities.

RESISTANCE TO CHANGE

One of the most well-documented findings from studies of individual and organizational behavior is that organizations and their members resist change. In a sense, this is positive. It provides a degree of stability and predictability to behavior. If there weren't some resistance, organizational behavior would take on the characteristics of chaotic randomness. Resistance to change can also be a source of functional conflict. For example, resistance to a reorganization plan or a change in a product line can stimulate a healthy debate over the merits of the idea and result in a better decision. But there is a definite downside to resistance to change. It hinders adaptation and progress.

Resistance to change doesn't necessarily surface in standardized ways. Resistance can be overt, implicit, immediate, or deferred. It's easiest for management to deal with resistance when it is overt and immediate. For instance, a change is proposed and employees quickly respond by voicing complaints, engaging in a work slowdown, threatening to go on strike, or the like. The greater challenge is managing resistance that is implicit or deferred. Implicit resistance efforts are more subtle—loss of loyalty to the organization, loss of motivation to work, increased errors or mistakes, increased absenteeism due to "sickness"—and hence are more difficult to recognize. Similarly, deferred actions cloud the link between the source of the resistance and the reaction to it. A change may produce what appears to be only a minimal reaction at the time it is initiated, but then resistance surfaces weeks, months, or even years later. Or a single change that in and of itself might have little impact becomes the straw that breaks the camel's back. Reactions to change can build up and then explode in some response that seems totally out of proportion to the change action it follows. The resistance, of course, has merely been deferred and stockpiled. What surfaces is a response to an accumulation of previous changes.

Let's look at the sources of resistance. For analytical purposes, we've categorized them by individual and organizational sources. In the real world, the sources often overlap.

Individual Resistance

Individual sources of resistance to change reside in basic human characteristics such as perceptions, personalities, and needs. The following summarizes five reasons why individuals may resist change. (See Exhibit 19-2.)

Habit   Every day, when you go to work or school, do you continually use the same route and streets? Probably. If you're like most people, you find a single route and you use it regularly.

As human beings, we're creatures of habit. Life is complex enough; we don't need to consider the full range of options for the hundreds of decisions we have to make every day. To cope with this complexity, we all rely on habits or programmed responses. But when confronted with change, this tendency to respond

Sources of Individual Resistance to Change

EXHIBIT 19-2

in our accustomed ways becomes a source of resistance. So when your department is moved to a new office building across town, it means you're likely to have to change many habits: waking up ten minutes earlier, taking a new set of streets to work, finding a new parking place, adjusting to the new office layout, developing a new lunchtime routine, and so on.

Security People with a high need for security are likely to resist change because it threatens their feelings of safety. When Ericcson announces it's laying off 17,000 people or Ford introduces new robotic equipment, many employees at these firms may fear that their jobs are in jeopardy.

Economic Factors Another source of individual resistance is concern that changes will lower one's income. Changes in job tasks or established work routines also can arouse economic fears if people are concerned that they won't be able to perform the new tasks or routines to their previous standards, especially when pay is closely tied to productivity.

Fear of the Unknown Changes substitute ambiguity and uncertainty for the known. The transition from high school to college is typically such an experience. By the time we're seniors in high school, we understand how things work. You might not have liked high school, but at least you understood the system. Then you move on to college and face a whole new and uncertain system. You have traded the known for the unknown and the fear or insecurity that goes with it.

Employees in organizations hold the same dislike for uncertainty. If, for example, the introduction of quality management means production workers will have to learn statistical process control techniques, some may fear they'll be unable to do so. They may, therefore, develop a negative attitude toward a quality-management program or behave dysfunctionally if required to use statistical techniques.

Selective Information Processing As we learned in Chapter 5, individuals shape their world through their perceptions. Once they have created this world, it resists change. So individuals are guilty of selectively processing information in order to keep their perceptions intact. They hear what they want to hear. They ignore information that challenges the world they've created. To return to the production workers who are faced with the introduction of quality management, they may ignore the arguments their managers make in explaining why a knowledge of statistics is necessary or the potential benefits the change will provide them.

EXHIBIT 19-3

Source: Dilbert by Scott Adams, August 3, 1996. DILBERT reprinted by permission of United Feature Syndicate, Inc.

Sources of Organizational Resistance to Change

Threat to established resource allocations

Structural inertia

Threat to established power relationships → Organizational resistance ← Limited focus of change

Threat to expertise

Group inertia

EXHIBIT 19-4

Organizational Resistance

Organizations, by their very nature, are conservative.[3] They actively resist change. You don't have to look far to see evidence of this phenomenon. Government agencies want to continue doing what they have been doing for years, whether the need for their service changes or remains the same. Organized religions are deeply entrenched in their history. Attempts to change church doctrine require great persistence and patience. Educational institutions, which exist to open minds and challenge established doctrine, are themselves extremely resistant to change. And the majority of business firms appear highly resistant to change.

Six major sources of organizational resistance have been identified.[4] They are shown in Exhibit 19-4.

Structural Inertia   Organizations have built-in mechanisms to produce stability. For example, the selection process systematically selects certain people in and certain people out. Training and other socialization techniques reinforce specific role requirements and skills. Formalization provides job descriptions, rules, and procedures for employees to follow.

The people who are hired into an organization are chosen for fit; they are then shaped and directed to behave in certain ways. When an organization is confronted with change, this structural inertia acts as a counterbalance to sustain stability.

Limited Focus of Change   Organizations are made up of a number of interdependent subsystems. You can't change one without affecting the others. For example, if management changes the technological processes without simultaneously modifying the organization's structure to match, the change in technology is not likely to be accepted. So limited changes in subsystems tend to get nullified by the larger system.

Group Inertia   Even if individuals want to change their behavior, group norms may act as a constraint. An individual union member, for instance, may be willing to accept changes in his job suggested by management. But if union norms dictate resisting any unilateral change made by management, he's likely to resist.

Threat to Expertise   Changes in organizational patterns may threaten the expertise of specialized groups. The introduction of decentralized personal computers, which allow managers to gain access to information directly from a company's mainframe, is an example of a change that was strongly resisted by many information systems departments in the early 1980s. Why? Because decentralized end-user computing was a threat to the specialized skills held by those in the centralized information systems departments.

Threat to Established Power Relationships   Any redistribution of decision-making authority can threaten long-established power relationships within the organization. The introduction of participative decision making or self-managed work teams is the kind of change that is often seen as threatening by supervisors and middle managers.

Threat to Established Resource Allocations   Groups in the organization that control sizable resources often see change as a threat. They tend to be content with the way things are. Will the change, for instance, mean a reduction in their budgets or a cut in their staff size? Those that most benefit from the current allocation of resources often feel threatened by changes that may affect future allocations.

Overcoming Resistance to Change

Six tactics have been suggested for use by change agents in dealing with resistance to change.[5] Let's review them briefly.

When Planned Parenthood's chief executive, Gloria Feldt, needed to institute sweeping changes to the organization, she began by setting up hundreds of meetings with its 127 affiliates to solicit their ideas and those of their staffs, volunteers, and donors. "These people had to participate," says Feldt, "or the result would turn to dust."

Education and Communication   Resistance can be reduced through communicating with employees to help them see the logic of a change. This tactic basically assumes that the source of resistance lies in misinformation or poor communication: If employees receive the full facts and get any misunderstandings cleared up, resistance will subside. Communication can be achieved through one-on-one discussions, memos, group presentations, or reports. Does it work? It does, provided that the source of resistance is inadequate communication and that management–employee relations are characterized by mutual trust and credibility. If these conditions don't exist, the change is unlikely to succeed.

Participation   It's difficult for individuals to resist a change decision in which they participated. Prior to making a change, those opposed can be brought into the decision process. Assuming that the participants have the expertise to make a meaningful contribution, their involvement can reduce resistance, obtain commitment, and increase the quality of the change decision. However, against these advantages are the negatives: potential for a poor solution and great time consumption.

Facilitation and Support   Change agents can offer a range of supportive efforts to reduce resistance. When employees' fear and anxiety are high, employee counseling and therapy, new-skills training, or a short paid leave of absence may facilitate adjustment. The drawback of this tactic is that, as with the others, it is time consuming. In addition, it's expensive, and its implementation offers no assurance of success.

Negotiation   Another way for the change agent to deal with potential resistance to change is to exchange something of value for a lessening of the resistance. For instance, if the resistance is centered in a few powerful individuals, a specific reward package can be negotiated that will meet their individual needs. Negotiation as a tactic may be necessary when resistance comes from a powerful source. Yet one cannot ignore its potentially high costs. In addition, there is the risk that, once a change agent negotiates with one party to avoid resistance, he or she is open to the possibility of being blackmailed by other individuals in positions of power.

Manipulation and Cooptation   *Manipulation* refers to covert influence attempts. Twisting and distorting facts to make them appear more attractive, withholding undesirable information, and creating false rumors to get employees to accept a change are all examples of manipulation. If corporate management threatens to close down a particular manufacturing plant if that plant's employees fail to accept an across-the-board pay cut, and if the threat is actually untrue, management is using manipulation. *Cooptation,* on the other hand, is a form of both manipulation and participation. It seeks to "buy off" the leaders of a resistance group by giving them a key role in the change decision. The leaders' advice is sought, not to seek a better decision, but to get their endorsement. Both manipulation and cooptation are relatively inexpensive and easy ways to gain the support of adversaries, but the tactics can backfire if the targets become aware that they are being tricked or used. Once discovered, the change agent's credibility may drop to zero.

Coercion   Last on the list of tactics is coercion; that is, the application of direct threats or force on the resisters. If the corporate management mentioned in the previous discussion really is determined to close a manufacturing plant if employees don't acquiesce to a pay cut, then coercion would be the label attached to its change tactic. Other examples of coercion are threats of transfer, loss of promotions, negative performance evaluations, and a poor letter of recommendation. The advantages and drawbacks of coercion are approximately the same as those mentioned for manipulation and cooptation.

The Politics of Change

No discussion of resistance to change would be complete without a brief mention of the politics of change. Because change invariably threatens the status quo, it inherently implies political activity.[6]

Internal change agents typically are individuals high in the organization who have a lot to lose from change. They have, in fact, risen to their positions of authority by developing skills and behavioral patterns that are favored by the organization. Change is a threat to those skills and patterns. What if they are no longer the ones the organization values? Change creates the potential for others in the organization to gain power at their expense.

Politics suggests that the impetus for change is more likely to come from outside change agents, employees who are new to the organization (and have less invested in the status quo), or from managers slightly removed from the main power structure. Managers who have spent their entire careers with a single organization and eventually achieve a senior position in the hierarchy are often major impediments to change. Change, itself, is a very real threat to their status and position. Yet they may be expected to implement changes to demonstrate that they're not merely caretakers. By acting as change agents, they can symbolically convey to various constituencies—stockholders, suppliers, employees, customers—that they are on top of problems and adapting to a dynamic environment. Of course, as you might guess, when forced to introduce change, these long-time power holders tend to implement incremental changes. Radical change is too threatening.

Power struggles within the organization will determine, to a large degree, the speed and quantity of change. You should expect that long-time career executives will be sources of resistance. This, incidentally, explains why boards of directors that recognize the imperative for the rapid introduction of radical change in their organizations frequently turn to outside candidates for new leadership.[7]

APPROACHES TO MANAGING ORGANIZATIONAL CHANGE

Now we turn to several popular approaches to managing change: Lewin's classic three-step model of the change process, action research, and organizational development.

Lewin's Three-Step Model

Kurt Lewin argued that successful change in organizations should follow three steps: **unfreezing** the status quo, *movement* to a new state, and **refreezing** the new change to make it permanent.[8] (See Exhibit 19-5.) The value of this model can be seen in the following example when the management of a large oil company decided to reorganize its marketing function in the western United States.

The oil company had three divisional offices in the West, located in Seattle, San Francisco, and Los Angeles. The decision was made to consolidate the divisions into a single regional office to be located in San Francisco. The reorganization meant transferring over 150 employees, eliminating some duplicate managerial positions, and instituting a new hierarchy of command. As you might guess, a move of this magnitude was difficult to keep secret. The rumor of its occurrence preceded the announcement by several months. The decision itself was made unilaterally. It came from the executive offices in New York. The people affected had no say whatsoever in the choice. For those in Seattle or Los Angeles, who may have disliked the decision and its consequences—the problems inherent in transferring to another city, pulling youngsters out of school, making new friends, having new co-workers, undergoing the reassignment of responsibilities—their only recourse was to quit. In actuality, less than 10 percent did.

The status quo can be considered to be an equilibrium state. To move from this equilibrium—to overcome the pressures of both individual resistance and group conformity—unfreezing is necessary. It can be achieved in one of three ways. (See Exhibit 19-6.) The **driving forces**, which direct behavior away from the status quo, can be increased. The **restraining forces**, which hinder movement from the existing equilibrium, can be decreased. A third alternative is to combine the first two approaches.

The oil company's management could expect employee resistance to the consolidation. To deal with that resistance, management could use positive incentives

---

unfreezing

Change efforts to overcome the pressures of both individual resistance and group conformity.

refreezing

Stabilizing a change intervention by balancing driving and restraining forces.

driving forces

Forces that direct behavior away from the status quo.

restraining forces

Forces that hinder movement from the existing equilibrium.

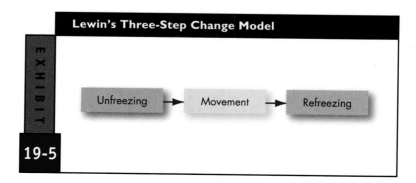

EXHIBIT 19-5

Lewin's Three-Step Change Model

Unfreezing → Movement → Refreezing

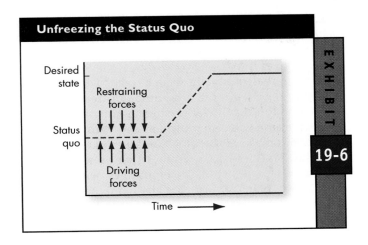

Unfreezing the Status Quo

EXHIBIT 19-6

to encourage employees to accept the change. For instance, increases in pay can be offered to those who accept the transfer. Very liberal moving expenses can be paid by the company. Management might offer low-cost mortgage funds to allow employees to buy new homes in San Francisco. Of course, management might also consider unfreezing acceptance of the status quo by removing restraining forces. Employees could be counseled individually. Each employee's concerns and apprehensions could be heard and specifically clarified. Assuming that most of the fears are unjustified, the counselor could assure the employees that there was nothing to fear and then demonstrate, through tangible evidence, that restraining forces are unwarranted. If resistance is extremely high, management may have to resort to both reducing resistance and increasing the attractiveness of the alternative if the unfreezing is to be successful.

Once the consolidation change has been implemented, if it is to be successful, the new situation needs to be refrozen so that it can be sustained over time. Unless this last step is taken, there is a very high chance that the change will be short-lived and that employees will attempt to revert to the previous equilibrium state. The objective of refreezing, then, is to stabilize the new situation by balancing the driving and restraining forces.

How could the oil company's management refreeze its consolidation change? By systematically replacing temporary forces with permanent ones. For instance, management might impose a permanent upward adjustment of salaries. The formal rules and regulations governing behavior of those affected by the change should also be revised to reinforce the new situation. Over time, of course, the work group's own norms will evolve to sustain the new equilibrium. But until that point is reached, management will have to rely on more formal mechanisms.

Action Research

Action research refers to a change process based on the systematic collection of data and then selection of a change action based on what the analyzed data indicate.[9] Their importance lies in providing a scientific methodology for managing planned change.

The process of action research consists of five steps: diagnosis, analysis, feedback, action, and evaluation. You'll note that these steps closely parallel the scientific method.

The change agent, often an outside consultant in action research, begins by gathering information about problems, concerns, and needed changes from members

action research

A change process based on systematic collection of data and then selection of a change action based on what the analyzed data indicate.

of the organization. This *diagnosis* is analogous to the physician's search to find specifically what ails a patient. In action research, the change agent asks questions, interviews employees, reviews records, and listens to the concerns of employees.

Diagnosis is followed by *analysis*. What problems do people key in on? What patterns do these problems seem to take? The change agent synthesizes this information into primary concerns, problem areas, and possible actions.

Action research includes extensive involvement of the change targets. That is, the people who will be involved in any change program must be actively involved in determining what the problem is and participating in creating the solution. So the third step—*feedback*—requires sharing with employees what has been found from steps one and two. The employees, with the help of the change agent, develop action plans for bringing about any needed change.

Now the *action* part of action research is set in motion. The employees and the change agent carry out the specific actions to correct the problems that have been identified.

The final step, consistent with the scientific underpinnings of action research, is *evaluation* of the action plan's effectiveness. Using the initial data gathered as a benchmark, any subsequent changes can be compared and evaluated.

Action research provides at least two specific benefits for an organization. First, it's problem-focused. The change agent objectively looks for problems and the type of problem determines the type of change action. While this may seem intuitively obvious, a lot of change activities aren't done this way. Rather, they're solution-centered. The change agent has a favorite solution—for example, implementing flextime, teams, or a process reengineering program—and then seeks out problems that his or her solution fits. Second, because action research so heavily involves employees in the process, resistance to change is reduced. In fact, once employees have actively participated in the feedback stage, the change process typically takes on a momentum of its own. The employees and groups that have been involved become an internal source of sustained pressure to bring about the change.

Organizational Development

No discussion of managing change would be complete without including organizational development. **Organizational development (OD)** is not an easily defined single concept. Rather, it's a term used to encompass a collection of planned-change interventions built on humanistic-democratic values that seek to improve organizational effectiveness and employee well-being.[10]

The OD paradigm values human and organizational growth, collaborative and participative processes, and a spirit of inquiry.[11] The change agent may be directive in OD; however, there is a strong emphasis on collaboration. The following briefly identifies the underlying values in most OD efforts.

organizational development (OD)

A collection of planned-change interventions, built on humanistic-democratic values, that seeks to improve organizational effectiveness and employee well-being.

1. *Respect for people.* Individuals are perceived as being responsible, conscientious, and caring. They should be treated with dignity and respect.
2. *Trust and support.* The effective and healthy organization is characterized by trust, authenticity, openness, and a supportive climate.
3. *Power equalization.* Effective organizations deemphasize hierarchical authority and control.
4. *Confrontation.* Problems shouldn't be swept under the rug. They should be openly confronted.
5. *Participation.* The more that people who will be affected by a change are involved in the decisions surrounding that change, the more they will be committed to implementing those decisions.

What are some of the OD techniques or interventions for bringing about change? In the following pages, we present six interventions that change agents might consider using.

Sensitivity Training It can go by a variety of names—**sensitivity training**, laboratory training, encounter groups, or T-groups (training groups)—but all refer to a method of changing behavior through unstructured group interaction.[12] Members are brought together in a free and open environment in which participants discuss themselves and their interactive processes, loosely directed by a professional behavioral scientist. The group is process-oriented, which means that individuals learn through observing and participating rather than being told. The professional creates the opportunity for participants to express their ideas, beliefs, and attitudes. He or she does not accept—in fact, overtly rejects—any leadership role.

The objectives of the T-groups are to provide the subjects with increased awareness of their own behavior and how others perceive them, greater sensitivity to the behavior of others, and increased understanding of group processes. Specific results sought include increased ability to empathize with others, improved listening skills, greater openness, increased tolerance of individual differences, and improved conflict-resolution skills.

If individuals lack awareness of how others perceive them, then the successful T-group can effect more realistic self-perceptions, greater group cohesiveness, and a reduction in dysfunctional interpersonal conflicts. Furthermore, it will ideally result in a better integration between the individual and the organization.

Survey Feedback One tool for assessing attitudes held by organizational members, identifying discrepancies among member perceptions, and solving these differences is the **survey feedback** approach.[13]

Everyone in an organization can participate in survey feedback, but of key importance is the organizational family—the manager of any given unit and the employees who report directly to him or her. A questionnaire is usually completed by all members in the organization or unit. Organization members may be asked to suggest questions or may be interviewed to determine what issues are relevant. The questionnaire typically asks members for their perceptions and attitudes on a broad range of topics, including decision-making practices; communication effectiveness; coordination between units; and satisfaction with the organization, job, peers, and their immediate supervisor.

The data from this questionnaire are tabulated with data pertaining to an individual's specific "family" and to the entire organization and distributed to employees. These data then become the springboard for identifying problems and clarifying issues that may be creating difficulties for people. Particular attention is given to the importance of encouraging discussion and ensuring that discussions focus on issues and ideas and not on attacking individuals.

Finally, group discussion in the survey feedback approach should result in members identifying possible implications of the questionnaire's findings. Are people listening? Are new ideas being generated? Can decision making, interpersonal relations, or job assignments be improved? Answers to questions like these, it is hoped, will result in the group agreeing on commitments to various actions that will remedy the problems that are identified.

Process Consultation No organization operates perfectly. Managers often sense that their unit's performance can be improved, but they're unable to identify what can be improved and how it can be improved. The purpose of

sensitivity training

Training groups that seek to change behavior through unstructured group interaction.

survey feedback

The use of questionnaires to identify discrepancies among member perceptions; discussion follows and remedies are suggested.

process consultation

A consultant assists a client to understand process events with which he or she must deal and identify processes that need improvement.

process consultation is for an outside consultant to assist a client, usually a manager, "to perceive, understand, and act upon process events" with which he or she must deal.[14] These might include work flow, informal relationships among unit members, and formal communication channels.

Process consultation (PC) is similar to sensitivity training in its assumption that organizational effectiveness can be improved by dealing with interpersonal problems and in its emphasis on involvement. But PC is more task-directed than is sensitivity training.

Consultants in PC are there to "give the client 'insight' into what is going on around him, within him, and between him and other people."[15] They do not solve the organization's problems. Rather, the consultant is a guide or coach who advises on the process to help the client solve his or her own problems.

The consultant works with the client in *jointly* diagnosing what processes need improvement. The emphasis is on "jointly" because the client develops a skill at analyzing processes within his or her unit that can be continually called on long after the consultant is gone. In addition, by having the client actively participate in both the diagnosis and the development of alternatives, there will be greater understanding of the process and the remedy and less resistance to the action plan chosen.

Importantly, the process consultant need not be an expert in solving the particular problem that is identified. The consultant's expertise lies in diagnosis and in developing a helping relationship. If the specific problem uncovered requires technical knowledge outside the client's and consultant's expertise, the consultant helps the client to locate such an expert and then instructs the client in how to get the most out of this expert resource.

team building

High interaction among team members to increase trust and openness.

Team Building As we've noted in numerous places throughout this book, organizations are increasingly relying on teams to accomplish work tasks. **Team building** uses high-interaction group activities to increase trust and openness among team members.[16]

Team building can be applied within groups or at the intergroup level, at which activities are interdependent. For our discussion, we emphasize the intragroup level and leave intergroup development to the next section. As a result, our interest concerns applications to organizational families (command groups), as well as to committees, project teams, self-managed teams, and task groups.

Not all group activity has interdependence of functions. To illustrate, consider a football team and a track team:

> Although members on both teams are concerned with the team's total output, they function differently. The football team's output depends synergistically on how well each player does his particular job in concert with his teammates. The quarterback's performance depends on the performance of his linemen and receivers, and ends on how well the quarterback throws the ball, and so on. On the other hand, a track team's performance is determined largely by the mere addition of the performances of the individual members.[17]

Team building is applicable to the case of interdependence, such as in football. The objective is to improve coordination efforts of members, which will result in increasing the team's performance.

The activities considered in team building typically include goal setting, development of interpersonal relations among team members, role analysis to clarify each member's role and responsibilities, and team process analysis. Of course, team building may emphasize or exclude certain activities, depending on the purpose of the development effort and the specific problems with which the team is confronted. Basically, however, team building attempts to use high interaction among members to increase trust and openness.

It may be beneficial to begin by having members attempt to define the goals and priorities of the team. This will bring to the surface different perceptions of what the team's purpose may be. Following this, members can evaluate the team's performance—how effective is the team in structuring priorities and achieving its goals? This should identify potential problem areas. This self-critique discussion of means and ends can be done with members of the total team present or, when large size impinges on a free interchange of views, may initially take place in smaller groups followed by the sharing of their findings with the total team.

Team building can also address itself to clarifying each member's role on the team. Each role can be identified and clarified. Previous ambiguities can be brought to the surface. For some individuals, it may offer one of the few opportunities they have had to think through thoroughly what their job is all about and what specific tasks they are expected to carry out if the team is to optimize its effectiveness.

Still another team-building activity can be similar to that performed by the process consultant; that is, to analyze key processes that go on within the team to identify the way work is performed and how these processes might be improved to make the team more effective.

The Winter Garden is a 10-story atrium facing the site where the World Trade Center once stood. For the architectural design team assigned the task of redesigning the eastern façade of the building by September 11, 2002, team-building processes such as setting priorities and goals had to take place relatively quickly.

Intergroup Development   A major area of concern in OD is the dysfunctional conflict that exists between groups. As a result, this has been a subject to which change efforts have been directed.

Intergroup development seeks to change the attitudes, stereotypes, and perceptions that groups have of each other. For example, in one company, the engineers saw the accounting department as composed of shy and conservative types, and the human resources department as having a bunch of "ultraliberals who are more concerned that some protected group of employees might get their feelings hurt than with the company making a profit." Such stereotypes can have an obvious negative impact on the coordination efforts between the departments.

Although there are several approaches for improving intergroup relations,[18] a popular method emphasizes problem solving.[19] In this method, each group meets independently to develop lists of its perception of itself, the other group, and how it believes the other group perceives it. The groups then share their lists, after which similarities and differences are discussed. Differences are clearly articulated, and the groups look for the causes of the disparities.

Are the groups' goals at odds? Were perceptions distorted? On what basis were stereotypes formulated? Have some differences been caused by misunderstandings of intentions? Have words and concepts been defined differently by each group? Answers to questions like these clarify the exact nature of the conflict. Once the

intergroup development
OD efforts to change the attitudes, stereotypes, and perceptions that groups have of each other.

causes of the difficulty have been identified, the groups can move to the integration phase—working to develop solutions that will improve relations between the groups.

Subgroups, with members from each of the conflicting groups, can now be created for further diagnosis and to begin to formulate possible alternative actions that will improve relations.

appreciative inquiry

Seeks to identify the unique qualities and special strengths of an organization, which can then be built on to improve performance.

Appreciative Inquiry   Most OD approaches are problem-centered. They identify a problem or set of problems, then look for a solution. **Appreciative inquiry** accentuates the positive.[20] Rather than looking for problems to fix, this approach seeks to identify the unique qualities and special strengths of an organization, which can then be built on to improve performance. That is, it focuses on an organization's successes rather than on its problems.

Advocates of appreciative inquiry (AI) argue that problem-solving approaches always ask people to look backward at yesterday's failures, to focus on shortcomings, and rarely result in new visions. Instead of creating a climate for positive change, action research and OD techniques such as survey feedback and process consultation end up placing blame and generating defensiveness. AI proponents claim it makes more sense to refine and enhance what the organization is already doing well. This allows the organization to change by playing to its strengths and competitive advantages.

The AI process essentially consists of four steps, often played out in a large-group meeting over a two- or three-day time period, and overseen by a trained change agent. The first step is one of *discovery*. The idea is to find out what people think are the strengths of the organization. For instance, employees are asked to recount times they felt the organization worked best or when they specifically felt most satisfied with their jobs. The second step is *dreaming*. The information from the discovery phase is used to speculate on possible futures for the organization. For instance, people are asked to envision the organization in five years and to describe what's different. The third step is *design*. Based on the dream articulation, participants focus on finding a common vision of how the organization will look and agree on its unique qualities. The fourth stage seeks to define the organization's *destiny*. In this final step, participants discuss how the organization is going to fulfill its dream. This typically includes the writing of action plans and development of implementation strategies.

AI has proven to be an effective change strategy in organizations such as GTE, Avon Mexico, the Cleveland Clinic, and Brazilian food wholesaler Nutrimental Foods. For instance, executives at Nutrimental Foods closed their plants and offices for a day and invited all employees, plus a large group of customers and other constituents, to meet in a vacated warehouse. After an hour of instruction by an AI consultant, the 700 participants broke into teams and interviewed each other for half a day. This generated several hundred conclusions about what the company did well. At the end of the day their work was handed off to a group of 150, who were given four days to shape the information into a new and bolder corporate vision. The process ended up generating three new strategic business initiatives. And management reports that six months after this AI exercise, company sales had increased by several million dollars and profits were up by 300 percent.[21]

CONTEMPORARY CHANGE ISSUES FOR TODAY'S MANAGERS

Talk to managers. Read the popular business periodicals. What you'll find is that three issues have risen above the rest as current change topics. They are stimulating organizational *innovation*, building a *learning organization*, and creating *knowledge-*

management systems. In the following pages, we take a look at these topics. Then we address the question: Is managing change culture-bound?

Stimulating Innovation

The relevant question is: How can an organization become more innovative? What's the secret of companies like Pfizer, Corning, GE, DuPont, 3M, and Newell Rubbermaid that consistently generate new products with very low failure rates? Although there is no guaranteed formula, certain characteristics surface again and again when researchers study innovative organizations. We've grouped them into structural, cultural, and human resource categories. Our message to change agents is that they should consider introducing these characteristics into their organization if they want to create an innovative climate. Before we look at these characteristics, however, let's clarify what we mean by innovation.

Definition   We said change refers to making things different. **Innovation** is a more specialized kind of change. Innovation is a new idea applied to initiating or improving a product, process, or service.[22] So all innovations involve change, but not all changes necessarily involve new ideas or lead to significant improvements. Innovations in organizations can range from small incremental improvements, such as Nabisco's extension of the Oreo product line to include double stuffs and chocolate-covered Oreos, up to radical break-throughs, such as Jeff Bezos' idea in 1994 to create an on-line bookstore. Keep in mind that while our examples are mostly of product innovations, the concept of innovation also encompasses new production process technologies, new structures or administrative systems, and new plans or programs pertaining to organizational members.

innovation

A new idea applied to initiating or improving a product, process, or service.

Sources of Innovation   *Structural variables* have been the most studied potential source of innovation.[23] A comprehensive review of the structure–innovation relationship leads to the following conclusions.[24] First, organic structures positively influence innovation. Because they're lower in vertical differentiation, formalization, and centralization, organic organizations facilitate the flexibility, adaptation, and cross-fertilization that make the adoption of innovations easier. Second, long tenure in management is associated with innovation. Managerial tenure apparently provides legitimacy and knowledge of how to accomplish tasks and obtain desired outcomes. Third, innovation is nurtured when there are slack resources. Having an abundance of resources allows an organization to afford to purchase innovations, bear the cost of instituting innovations, and absorb failures. Finally, interunit communication is high in innovative organizations.[25] These organizations are high users of committees, task forces, cross-functional teams, and other mechanisms that facilitate interaction across departmental lines.

One of 3M's most famous innovations was the creation and development of the Post-It. 3M has a long history of creating innovative products.

OB in the News

Innovative Concept or Harebrained Idea?

Richard Nobel has a solution to the public's mounting frustration with airline service. He's going to create an air-taxi service unlike any other. Travelers will be able to summon one of his planes, like a taxi cab, to a nearby airport and then fly straight to the local airport closest to their destination. The cost? About the same as a first-class ticket.

There are 2,071 airfields in Europe and 5,736 in North America. Yet only 3 percent are used by large commercial jets. Recognizing that there should be a large market for people who want to travel on their schedule, not the airlines, and would prefer a more direct flight,

Nobel is creating the basis for a worldwide taxi-system. It would make use of small airports. It would rely on the global-positioning system to monitor flights and guide takeoffs and landings at airports without control towers. And it would have a state-of-the-art Internet-based reservation system.

"The airlines think the solution to airport congestion is bigger planes and bigger airports, " says Nobel. "That's precisely what passengers don't want. We're coming the other way, offering point-to-point service that you schedule at your convenience."

The most innovative aspect of Nobel's idea is the development of a low-cost (under $2 million), fuel-efficient plane that would make up his taxi fleet. That plane,

dubbed the F1 Air Taxi, will be designed for trips of under 1,000 miles. Able to carry five passengers, this prop-jet would be able to meet or beat the average speed of commercial jets on short hops, get passengers closer to their destination, and avoid the congestion at big airports. The F1 is being built by Pegasus Aviation in the United Kingdom, with 18 companies providing goods and services to minimize costs.

Will the idea work? Only time will tell. But one executive at the firm that is designing Nobel's Web site and reservation system says, "This is out-of-the box thinking—a whole new approach to airline congestion. I think [Nobel] has a real market—and a small-business aircraft that could take a lot of the market from existing business planes."

Source: Based on O. Port, "Taxi! Get Me to Nebraska," *Business Week*, November 20, 2000, pp. 134–39.

Innovative organizations tend to have similar *cultures*. They encourage experimentation. They reward both successes and failures. They celebrate mistakes. At Hewlett-Packard, for instance, top management has successfully built a corporate culture that supports people who try something that doesn't work out.[26] Unfortunately, in too many organizations, people are rewarded for the absence of failures rather than for the presence of successes. Such cultures extinguish risk taking and innovation. People will suggest and try new ideas only when they feel such behaviors exact no penalties. Managers in innovative organizations recognize that failures are a natural by-product of venturing into the unknown. When Babe Ruth set his record for home runs in one season, he also led the league in strikeouts. And he is remembered for the former, not the latter.

Within the *human resources* category, we find that innovative organizations actively promote the training and development of their members so that they keep current, offer high job security so employees don't fear getting fired for making mistakes, and encourage individuals to become champions of change. Once a new idea is developed, **idea champions** actively and enthusiastically promote the idea, build support, overcome resistance, and ensure that the innovation is implemented.[27] The evidence indicates that champions have common personality characteristics: extremely high self-confidence, persistence, energy, and a tendency to take risks. Idea champions also display characteristics associated with transformational leadership. They inspire and energize others with their vision of the potential of an innovation and through their strong personal conviction in their mission. They are also good at gaining the commitment of others to support their mission. In addition, idea champions have jobs that provide considerable decision-making discretion. This autonomy helps them introduce and implement innovations in organizations.[28]

idea champions

Individuals who take an innovation and actively and enthusiastically promote the idea, build support, overcome resistance, and ensure that the idea is implemented.

Creating a Learning Organization

The learning organization has recently developed a groundswell of interest from managers and organization theorists looking for new ways to successfully respond to a world of interdependence and change.[29] In this section, we describe what a learning organization looks like and methods for managing learning.

What's A Learning Organization?   A **learning organization** is an organization that has developed the continuous capacity to adapt and change. Just as individuals learn, so too do organizations. "All organizations learn, whether they consciously choose to or not—it is a fundamental requirement for their sustained existence."[30] However, some organizations, such as Corning, FedEx, Electronic Arts, GE, Wal-Mart, and the U.S. Army, just do it better than others.

Most organizations engage in what has been called **single-loop learning**.[31] When errors are detected, the correction process relies on past routines and present policies. In contrast, learning organizations use **double-loop learning**. When an error is detected, it's corrected in ways that involve the modification of the organization's objectives, policies, and standard routines. Double-loop learning challenges deeply rooted assumptions and norms within an organization. In this way, it provides opportunities for radically different solutions to problems and dramatic jumps in improvement.

Exhibit 19-7 on page 574 summarizes the five basic characteristics of a learning organization. It's an organization in which people put aside their old ways of thinking, learn to be open with each other, understand how their organization really works, form a plan or vision that everyone can agree on, and then work together to achieve that vision.[32]

Proponents of the learning organization envision it as a remedy for three fundamental problems inherent in traditional organizations: fragmentation, competition, and reactiveness.[33] First, *fragmentation* based on specialization creates "walls" and "chimneys" that separate different functions into independent and often warring fiefdoms. Second, an overemphasis on *competition* often undermines collaboration. Members of the management team compete with one another to show who is right, who knows more, or who is more persuasive. Divisions compete with one another when they ought to cooperate and share knowledge. Team project leaders compete to show who is the best manager. And third, *reactiveness* misdirects management's attention to problem solving rather than creation. The problem solver tries to make something go away, while a creator tries to bring something new into being. An emphasis on reactiveness pushes out innovation and continuous improvement and, in its place, encourages people to run around "putting out fires."

It may help to better understand what a learning organization is if you think of it as an *ideal* model that builds on a number of previous OB concepts. No company has successfully achieved all the characteristics described in Exhibit 19-7. As such, you should think of a learning organization as an ideal to strive toward rather than a realistic description of structured activity. Note, too, how learning organizations draw on previous OB concepts such as quality management, organizational culture, the boundaryless organization, functional conflict, and transformational leadership. For instance, the learning organization adopts quality management's commitment to continuous improvement. Learning organizations are also characterized by a specific culture that values risk taking, openness, and growth. It seeks "boundarylessness" through breaking down barriers created by hierarchical levels and fragmented departmentation. A learning organization supports the importance of disagreements, constructive criticism, and other forms of

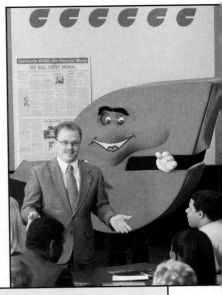

Commerce Bank in Cherry Hill, NJ, prides itself on its innovative culture and superior customer service. John Manning is vice president of the Wow Department and tells new employees about the bank's "Kill a Stupid Rule" program: "If you identify a rule that prevents you from wowing customers, we'll pay you fifty bucks."

learning organization

An organization that has developed the continuous capacity to adapt and change.

single-loop learning

Errors are corrected using past routines and present policies.

double-loop learning

Errors are corrected by modifying the organization's objectives, policies, and standard routines.

EXHIBIT

19-7

Characteristics of a Learning Organization

1. There exists a shared vision which everyone agrees on.
2. People discard their old ways of thinking and the standard routines they use for solving problems or doing their jobs.
3. Members think of all organizational processes, activities, functions, and interactions with the environment as part of a system of interrelationships.
4. People openly communicate with each other (across vertical and horizontal boundaries) without fear of criticism or punishment.
5. People sublimate their personal self-interest and fragmented departmental interests to work together to achieve the organization's shared vision.

Source: Based on P. M. Senge, *The Fifth Discipline* (New York: Doubleday, 1990).

functional conflict. And transformational leadership is needed in a learning organization to implement the shared vision.

Managing Learning How do you change an organization to make it into a continual learner? What can managers do to make their firms learning organizations?

Establish a strategy. Management needs to make explicit its commitment to change, innovation, and continuous improvement.

Redesign the organization's structure. The formal structure can be a serious impediment to learning. By flattening the structure, eliminating or combining departments, and increasing the use of cross-functional teams, interdependence is reinforced and boundaries between people are reduced.

Reshape the organization's culture. As noted earlier, learning organizations are characterized by risk taking, openness, and growth. Management sets the tone for the organization's culture both by what it says (strategy) and what it does (behavior). Managers need to demonstrate by their actions that taking risks and admitting failures are desirable traits. That means rewarding people who take chances and make mistakes. And management needs to encourage functional conflict. "The key to unlocking real openness at work," says one expert on learning organizations, "is to teach people to give up having to be in agreement. We think agreement is so important. Who cares? You have to bring paradoxes, conflicts, and dilemmas out in the open, so collectively we can be more intelligent than we can be individually."[34]

An excellent illustration of a learning organization is the U.S. Army.[35] This organization's environment has changed dramatically in the past several decades. Most significantly, the Soviet threat, which was a major justification for the army's military buildup, is largely gone. Now army soldiers are more likely to be peacekeeping in Haiti or helping to fight fires in the Pacific Northwest. In response to this new mission, the army's high command has redesigned its structure. Its formerly rigid, hierarchical, war-based command-and-control structure has been replaced with an adaptive and flexible structure to match its more varied objectives. In addition, everyone from PFCs to brigadier generals has gone through team training to make the army's culture more egalitarian. For instance, soldiers are now encouraged to question authority and have been given new skills that allow them to make decisions in the field. The "new army" is developing soldiers and officers who can adapt rapidly to different tasks and missions—fighting, peacekeeping, humanitarian rescue—and who can quickly improvise in complex and ambiguous situations.

The U.S. Army has shaped itself into a learning organization whose members can adapt to different kinds of missions, including peacekeeping and humanitarian tasks.

Knowledge Management

Siemens, the global telecommunications giant, recently won a $460,000 contract in Switzerland to build a telecommunications network for two hospitals in spite of the fact that its bid was 30 percent higher than the competition. The secret to Siemens success was its knowledge-management system.[36] This system allowed Siemens people in the Netherlands to draw on their experience and provide the Swiss sales reps with technical data that proved that the Siemens' network would be substantially more reliable than the competition's.

Siemens is one of a growing number of companies—including Cisco Systems, Ford, British Telecom, Johnson & Johnson, IBM, Whirlpool, Intel, Volkswagen, ChevronTexaco, and Royal Bank of Canada—that have realized the value of knowledge management (KM).

What is **knowledge management**? It's a process of organizing and distributing an organization's collective wisdom so the right information gets to the right people at the right time.[37] When done properly, KM provides an organization with both a competitive edge and improved organizational performance because it makes its employees smarter.

Knowledge management is increasingly important today for at least three reasons.[38] First, in many organizations, intellectual assets are now as important as physical or financial assets. Organizations that can quickly and efficiently tap into their employees' collective experience and wisdom are more likely to "outsmart" their competition. Second, as baby boomers begin to leave the workforce, there's an increasing awareness that they represent a wealth of knowledge that will be lost if there are no attempts to capture it. And third, a well-designed KM system will reduce redundancy and make the organization more efficient. For instance, when employees in a large organization undertake a new project, they needn't start from scratch. A knowledge-management system can allow them to access what previous employees have learned and cut wasteful time retracing a path that has already been traveled.

How does an organization record the knowledge and expertise of its employees and make that information easily accessible? It needs to develop computer databases of pertinent information that employees can readily access; it needs to create a culture that supports and rewards sharing; and it has to develop mechanisms that allow employees who have developed valuable expertise and insights to share them with others.

KM begins by identifying what knowledge matters to the organization.[39] As with process reengineering, management needs to review processes to identify those that provide the most value. Then it can develop computer networks and databases that can make that information readily available to the people who most need it. But KM won't work unless the culture supports sharing of information.[40] Remember, as noted in Chapter 13, information that is important and scarce can be a potent source of power. And people who hold that power are often reluctant to share it with others. So KM requires an organizational culture that promotes, values, and rewards sharing knowledge. Finally, KM must provide the mechanisms and the motivation for employees to share knowledge that employees find useful on the job and enables them to achieve better performance.[41] *More* knowledge isn't necessarily *better* knowledge. Information overload needs to be avoided by designing the system to capture only pertinent information and then organizing it so it can be quickly accessed by the people whom it can help. Royal Bank of Canada, for instance, has created a KM system with customized e-mail distribution lists carefully broken down by employees' specialty, title, and area of interest; set aside a dedicated site on the company's intranet that serves

knowledge management

A process of organizing and distributing an organization's collective wisdom so the right information gets to the right people at the right time.

as a central information repository; and created separate in-house Web sites featuring "lessons learned" summaries, where employees with various expertise can share new information with others.[42]

Managing Change: It's Culture-Bound

A number of change issues we've discussed in this chapter are culture-bound. To illustrate, let's briefly look at five questions: (1) Do people believe change is possible? (2) If it's possible, how long will it take to bring it about? (3) Is resistance to change greater in some cultures than in others? (4) Does culture influence how change efforts will be implemented? (5) Do successful idea champions do things differently in different cultures?

Do people believe change is possible? Remember that cultures vary in terms of beliefs about their ability to control their environment. In cultures in which people believe that they can dominate their environment, individuals will take a proactive view of change. This, for example, would describe the United States and Canada. In many other countries, such as Iran and Saudi Arabia, people see themselves as subjugated to their environment and thus will tend to take a passive approach toward change.

If change is possible, how long will it take to bring it about? A culture's time orientation can help us answer this question. Societies that focus on the long term, such as Japan, will demonstrate considerable patience while waiting for positive outcomes from change efforts. In societies with a short-term focus, such as the United States and Canada, people expect quick improvements and will seek change programs that promise fast results.

Is resistance to change greater in some cultures than in others? Resistance to change will be influenced by a society's reliance on tradition. Italians, as an example, focus on the past, whereas Americans emphasize the present. Italians, therefore, should generally be more resistant to change efforts than their American counterparts.

Does culture influence how change efforts will be implemented? Power distance can help with this issue. In high-power-distance cultures, such as Spain or Thailand, change efforts will tend to be autocratically implemented by top management. In contrast, low-power-distance cultures value democratic methods. We'd predict, therefore, a greater use of participation in countries such as Denmark and the Netherlands.

Finally, do successful idea champions do things differently in different cultures? The evidence indicates that the answer is Yes.[43] People in collectivist cultures, in contrast to individualistic cultures, prefer appeals for cross-functional support for innovation efforts; people in high-power-distance cultures prefer champions to work closely with those in authority to approve innovative activities before work is conducted on them; and the higher the uncertainty avoidance of a society, the more champions should work within the organization's rules and procedures to develop the innovation. These findings suggest that effective managers will alter their organization's championing strategies to reflect cultural values. So, for instance, while idea champions in Russia might succeed by ignoring budgetary limitations and working around confining procedures, champions in Austria, Denmark, Germany or other cultures high in uncertainty avoidance will be more effective by closely following budgets and procedures.

WORK STRESS AND ITS MANAGEMENT

Most of us are aware that employee stress is an increasing problem in organizations. Friends tells us they're stressed out from greater workloads and having to work longer hours because of downsizing at their company (see Exhibit 19-8). Parents talk about the lack of job stability in today's world and reminisce about a time when a job with a large company implied lifetime security. We read surveys in which employees complain about the stress created in trying to balance work and family responsibilities.[44] In this section we'll look at the causes and consequences of stress, and then consider what individuals and organizations can do to reduce it.

What Is Stress?

Stress is a dynamic condition in which an individual is confronted with an opportunity, constraint, or demand related to what he or she desires and for which the outcome is perceived to be both uncertain and important.[45] This is a complicated definition. Let's look at its components more closely.

Stress is not necessarily bad in and of itself. Although stress is typically discussed in a negative context, it also has a positive value.[46] It's an opportunity when it offers potential gain. Consider, for example, the superior performance that an athlete or stage performer gives in "clutch" situations. Such individuals often use stress positively to rise to the occasion and perform at or near their maximum. Similarly, many professionals see the pressures of heavy workloads and deadlines as positive challenges that enhance the quality of their work and the satisfaction they get from their job.

More typically, stress is associated with **constraints** and **demands**. The former prevent you from doing what you desire. The latter refers to the loss of something desired. So when you take a test at school or you undergo your annual performance review at work, you feel stress because you confront opportunities, constraints, and demands. A good performance review may lead to a promotion, greater responsibilities, and a higher salary. But a poor review may prevent you from getting the promotion. An extremely poor review might even result in your being fired.

Two conditions are necessary for potential stress to become actual stress.[47] There must be uncertainty over the outcome and the outcome must be important. Regardless of the conditions, it's only when there is doubt or uncertainty regarding whether the opportunity will be seized, the constraint removed, or the loss avoided that there is stress. That is, stress is highest for individuals who perceive that they are uncertain as to whether they will win or lose and lowest for individuals who think that winning or losing is a certainty. But importance is also critical. If winning or losing is an unimportant outcome, there is no stress. If keeping your job or earning a promotion doesn't hold any importance to you, you have no reason to feel stress over having to undergo a performance review.

stress

A dynamic condition in which an individual is confronted with an opportunity, constraint, or demand related to what he or she desires and for which the outcome is perceived to be both uncertain and important.

constraints

Forces that prevent individuals from doing what they desire.

demands

The loss of something desired.

EXHIBIT

19-9

Understanding Stress and Its Consequences

What causes stress? What are its consequences for individual employees? Why is it that the same set of conditions that creates stress for one person seems to have little or no effect on another person? Exhibit 19-10 provides a model that can help to answer questions such as these.[48]

The model identifies three sets of factors—environmental, organizational, and individual—that act as *potential* sources of stress. Whether they become *actual* stress depends on individual differences such as job experience and personality. When stress is experienced by an individual, its symptoms can surface as physiological, psychological, and behavioral outcomes.

Potential Sources of Stress

As the model in Exhibit 19-10 shows, there are three categories of potential stressors: environmental, organizational, and individual. Let's take a look at each.[49]

Environmental Factors   Just as environmental uncertainty influences the design of an organization's structure, it also influences stress levels among employees in that organization. Changes in the business cycle create *economic uncertainties*. When the economy is contracting, for example, people become increasingly anxious about their job security. *Political uncertainties* don't tend to create stress among North Americans as they do for employees in countries like Haiti or Venezuela. The obvious reason is that the United States and Canada have stable political systems, in which change is typically implemented in an orderly man-

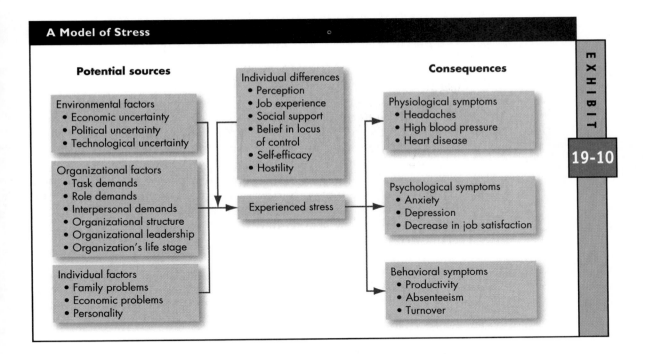

Potential sources

Environmental factors
• Economic uncertainty
• Political uncertainty
• Technological uncertainty

Organizational factors
• Task demands
• Role demands
• Interpersonal demands
• Organizational structure
• Organizational leadership
• Organization's life stage

Individual factors
• Family problems
• Economic problems
• Personality

Individual differences
• Perception
• Job experience
• Social support
• Belief in locus of control
• Self-efficacy
• Hostility

Experienced stress

Consequences

Physiological symptoms
• Headaches
• High blood pressure
• Heart disease

Psychological symptoms
• Anxiety
• Depression
• Decrease in job satisfaction

Behavioral symptoms
• Productivity
• Absenteeism
• Turnover

EXHIBIT 19-10

ner. Yet political threats and changes, even in countries like the United States and Canada, can induce stress. For instance, threats by Quebec to separate from Canada and become a distinct, French-speaking country increase stress among many Canadians, especially among Quebecers with few or no skills in the French language. *Technological uncertainty* is a third type of environmental factor that can cause stress. Because new innovations can make an employee's skills and experience obsolete in a very short time, computers, robotics, automation, and similar forms of technological innovation are a threat to many people and cause them stress. *Terrorism* is an increasing source of environmental-induced stress in the twenty-first century. Employees in Israel, for instance, have long faced this threat and have learned to cope with it. For Americans, on the other hand, 9/11 opened the door to new terrorism-related stresses—such as working in skyscrapers, flying, attending large public events, and concern about security.

Organizational Factors   There is no shortage of factors within the organization that can cause stress. Pressures to avoid errors or complete tasks in a limited time, work overload, a demanding and insensitive boss, and unpleasant co-workers are a few examples. We've categorized these factors around task, role, and interpersonal demands; organizational structure; organizational leadership; and the organization's life stage.[50]

   Task demands are factors related to a person's job. They include the design of the individual's job (autonomy, task variety, degree of automation), working conditions, and the physical work layout. Assembly lines, for instance, can put pressure on people when the line's speed is perceived as excessive. Similarly, working in an overcrowded room or in a visible location where interruptions are constant can increase anxiety and stress.

   Role demands relate to pressures placed on a person as a function of the particular role he or she plays in the organization. Role conflicts create expectations that may be hard to reconcile or satisfy. Role overload is experienced when the employee is expected to do more than time permits. Role ambiguity is created when role expectations are not clearly understood and the employee is not sure what he or she is to do.

Interpersonal demands are pressures created by other employees. Lack of social support from colleagues and poor interpersonal relationships can cause considerable stress, especially among employees with a high social need.

Organizational structure defines the level of differentiation in the organization, the degree of rules and regulations, and where decisions are made. Excessive rules and lack of participation in decisions that affect an employee are examples of structural variables that might be potential sources of stress.

Organizational leadership represents the managerial style of the organization's senior executives. Some chief executive officers create a culture characterized by tension, fear, and anxiety. They establish unrealistic pressures to perform in the short run, impose excessively tight controls, and routinely fire employees who don't "measure up."

Organizations go through a cycle. They are established, grow, become mature, and eventually decline. An *organization's life stage*—that is, where it is in this four-stage cycle—creates different problems and pressures for employees. The establishment and decline stages are particularly stressful. The former is characterized by a great deal of excitement and uncertainty, while the latter typically requires cutbacks, layoffs, and a different set of uncertainties. Stress tends to be least in the maturity stage during which uncertainties are at their lowest ebb.

Individual Factors　The typical individual works about 40 to 50 hours a week. But the experiences and problems that people encounter in those other 120-plus nonwork hours each week can spill over to the job. Our final category, then, encompasses factors in the employee's personal life. Primarily, these factors are family issues, personal economic problems, and inherent personality characteristics.

National surveys consistently show that people hold *family* and personal relationships dear. Marital difficulties, the breaking off of a relationship, and discipline troubles with children are examples of relationship problems that create stress for employees that aren't left at the front door when they arrive at work.

Economic problems created by individuals overextending their financial resources is another set of personal troubles that can create stress for employees and distract their attention from their work. Regardless of income level—people who make $80,000 a year seem to have as much trouble handling their finances as those who earn $18,000—some people are poor money managers or have wants that always seem to exceed their earning capacity.

Studies in three diverse organizations found that stress symptoms reported prior to beginning a job accounted for most of the variance in stress symptoms reported nine months later.[51] This led the researchers to conclude that some people may have an inherent tendency to accentuate negative aspects of the world in general. If this is true, then a significant individual factor that influences stress is a person's basic disposition. That is, stress symptoms expressed on the job may actually originate in the person's personality.

Stressors Are Additive　A fact that tends to be overlooked when stressors are reviewed individually is that stress is an additive phenomenon.[52] Stress builds up. Each new and persistent stressor adds to an individual's stress level. So a single stressor may be relatively unimportant in and of itself, but if it's added to an already high level of stress, it can be "the straw that breaks the camel's back." If we want to appraise the total amount of stress an individual is under, we have to sum up his or her opportunity stresses, constraint stresses, and demand stresses.

Individual Differences

Some people thrive on stressful situations, while others are overwhelmed by them. What is it that differentiates people in terms of their ability to handle stress? What individual difference variables moderate the relationship between *potential* stressors and *experienced* stress? At least six variables—perception, job experience, social support, belief in locus of control, self-efficacy, and hostility—have been found to be relevant moderators.

In Chapter 5, we demonstrated that employees react in response to their perception of reality rather than to reality itself. *Perception*, therefore, will moderate the relationship between a potential stress condition and an employee's reaction to it. For example, one person's fear that he'll lose his job because his company is laying off personnel may be perceived by another as an opportunity to get a large severance allowance and start his own business. So stress potential doesn't lie in objective conditions; it lies in an employee's interpretation of those conditions.

The evidence indicates that *experience* on the job tends to be negatively related to work stress. Why? Two explanations have been offered.[53] First is the idea of selective withdrawal. Voluntary turnover is more probable among people who experience more stress. Therefore, people who remain with the organization longer are those with more stress-resistant traits or those who are more resistant to the stress characteristics of their organization. Second, people eventually develop coping mechanisms to deal with stress. Because this takes time, senior members of the organization are more likely to be fully adapted and should experience less stress.

There is increasing evidence that *social support*—that is, collegial relationships with co-workers or supervisors—can buffer the impact of stress.[54] The logic underlying this moderating variable is that social support acts as a palliative, mitigating the negative effects of even high-strain jobs.

This photo shows Digital Fountain employees Jeff Persc and Jan Krepella playing foosball during a work break. Friendly relationships with coworkers can reduce the impact of job stress.

Locus of control was introduced in Chapter 4 as a personality attribute. Those with an internal locus of control believe they control their own destiny. Those with an external locus believe their lives are controlled by outside forces. Evidence indicates that internals perceive their jobs to be less stressful than do externals.[55] When internals and externals confront a similar stressful situation, the internals are likely to believe that they can have a significant effect on the results. They, therefore, act to take control of events. In contrast, externals are more likely to be passive and feel helpless.

Self-efficacy has also been found to influence stress outcomes. You'll remember from Chapter 5 that this term refers to an individual's belief that he or she is capable of performing a task. Recent evidence indicates that individuals with strong self-efficacy reacted less negatively to the strain created by long work hours and work overload than did those with low levels of self-efficacy.[56] That is, confidence in one's own abilities appears to decrease stress. As with an internal locus of control, strong efficacy confirms the power of self-beliefs in moderating the effect of a high-strain situation.

Some people's personality includes a high degree of hostility and anger. These people are chronically suspicious and mistrustful of others. Evidence indicates that this *hostility* significantly increases a person's stress and risk for heart disease.[57] More specifically, people who are quick to anger, maintain a persistently hostile outlook, and project a cynical mistrust of others are more likely to experience stress in situations.

Consequences of Stress

Stress shows itself in a number of ways. For instance, an individual who is experiencing a high level of stress may develop high blood pressure, ulcers, irritability, difficulty in making routine decisions, loss of appetite, accident-proneness, and the like. These can be subsumed under three general categories: physiological, psychological, and behavioral symptoms.[58]

Physiological Symptoms   Most of the early concern with stress was directed at physiological symptoms. This was predominantly due to the fact that the topic was researched by specialists in the health and medical sciences. This research led to the conclusion that stress could create changes in metabolism, increase heart and breathing rates, increase blood pressure, bring on headaches, and induce heart attacks.

The link between stress and particular physiological symptoms is not clear. There are few, if any, consistent relationships.[59] This is attributed to the complexity of the symptoms and the difficulty of objectively measuring them. But of greater relevance is the fact that physiological symptoms have the least direct relevance to students of OB. Our concern is with attitudes and behaviors. Therefore, the two other categories of symptoms are more important to us.

Psychological Symptoms   Stress can cause dissatisfaction. Job-related stress can cause job-related dissatisfaction. Job dissatisfaction, in fact, is "the simplest and most obvious psychological effect" of stress.[60] But stress shows itself in other psychological states—for instance, tension, anxiety, irritability, boredom, and procrastination.

The evidence indicates that when people are placed in jobs that make multiple and conflicting demands or in which there is a lack of clarity about the incumbent's duties, authority, and responsibilities, both stress and dissatisfaction are increased.[61] Similarly, the less control people have over the pace of their work, the greater the stress and dissatisfaction. While more research is needed to clarify the relationship, the evidence suggests that jobs that provide a low level of variety, significance, autonomy, feedback, and identity to incumbents create stress and reduce satisfaction and involvement in the job.[62]

Behavioral Symptoms   Behavior-related stress symptoms include changes in productivity, absence, and turnover, as well as changes in eating habits, increased smoking or consumption of alcohol, rapid speech, fidgeting, and sleep disorders. In dollar terms, we can not underestimate the cost of job stress. For instance, recent estimates indicate that workplace stress costs U.S. employers $200 billion annually in absenteeism, reduced productivity, employee turnover, accidents, workers' compensation, and direct medical, legal, and insurance fees.[63] Stress has also been identified as the fastest-growing reason for unscheduled work absences.[64]

There has been a significant amount of research investigating the stress–performance relationship. The most widely studied pattern in the stress–performance literature is the inverted-U relationship.[65] This is shown in Exhibit 19-11.

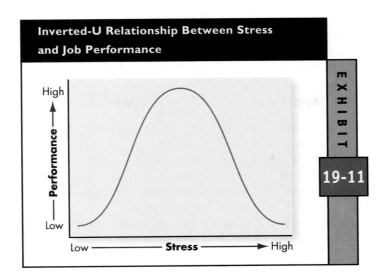

Inverted-U Relationship Between Stress and Job Performance

EXHIBIT 19-11

The logic underlying the inverted U is that low to moderate levels of stress stimulate the body and increase its ability to react. Individuals then often perform their tasks better, more intensely, or more rapidly. But too much stress places unattainable demands or constraints on a person, which result in lower performance. This inverted-U pattern may also describe the reaction to stress over time, as well as to changes in stress intensity. That is, even moderate levels of stress can have a negative influence on performance over the long term as the continued intensity of the stress wears down the individual and saps his or her energy resources. An athlete may be able to use the positive effects of stress to obtain a higher performance during every Saturday's game in the fall season, or a sales executive may be able to psych herself up for her presentation at the annual national meeting. But moderate levels of stress experienced continually over long periods, as typified by the emergency room staff in a large urban hospital, can result in lower performance. This may explain why emergency room staffs at such hospitals are frequently rotated and why it is unusual to find individuals who have spent the bulk of their career in such an environment. In effect, to do so would expose the individual to the risk of "career burnout."

In spite of the popularity and intuitive appeal of the inverted-U model, it doesn't get a lot of empirical support.[66] At this time, managers should be careful in assuming that this model accurately depicts the stress–performance relationship.

Managing Stress

From the organization's standpoint, management may not be concerned when employees experience low to moderate levels of stress. The reason, as we showed earlier, is that such levels of stress may be functional and lead to higher employee performance. But high levels of stress, or even low levels sustained over long periods, can lead to reduced employee performance and, thus, require action by management.

While a limited amount of stress may benefit an employee's performance, don't expect employees to see it that way. From the individual's standpoint, even low levels of stress are likely to be perceived as undesirable. It's not unlikely, therefore, for employees and management to have different notions of what constitutes an acceptable level of stress on the job. What management may consider to be "a positive stimulus that keeps the adrenalin running" is very likely to be seen as "excessive pressure" by the employee. Keep this in mind as we discuss individual and organizational approaches toward managing stress.[67]

Individual Approaches An employee can take personal responsibility for reducing his or her stress level. Individual strategies that have proven effective include implementing time-management techniques, increasing physical exercise, relaxation training, and expanding the social support network.

Many people manage their time poorly. The things they have to accomplish in any given day or week are not necessarily beyond completion if they manage their time properly. The well-organized employee, like the well-organized student, can often accomplish twice as much as the person who is poorly organized. So an understanding and utilization of basic *time-management* principles can help individuals better cope with tensions created by job demands.[68] A few of the more well-known time-management principles are: (1) making daily lists of activities to be accomplished; (2) prioritizing activities by importance and urgency; (3) scheduling activities according to the priorities set; and (4) knowing your daily cycle and handling the most demanding parts of your job during the high part of your cycle when you are most alert and productive.[69]

Noncompetitive physical exercise such as aerobics, walking, jogging, swimming, and riding a bicycle have long been recommended by physicians as a way to deal with excessive stress levels. These forms of *physical exercise* increase heart capacity, lower the at-rest heart rate, provide a mental diversion from work pressures, and offer a means to "let off steam."[70]

Individuals can teach themselves to reduce tension through *relaxation techniques* such as meditation, hypnosis, and biofeedback. The objective is to reach a state of deep relaxation, in which one feels physically relaxed, somewhat detached from the immediate environment, and detached from body sensations.[71] Deep relaxation for 15 or 20 minutes a day releases tension and provides a person with a pronounced sense of peacefulness. Importantly, significant changes in heart rate, blood pressure, and other physiological factors result from achieving the condition of deep relaxation.

As we noted earlier in this chapter, having friends, family, or work colleagues to talk to provides an outlet when stress levels become excessive. Expanding your *social support network*, therefore, can be a means for tension reduction. It provides you with someone to hear your problems and to offer a more objective perspective on the situation.

Organizational Approaches Several of the factors that cause stress—particularly task and role demands, and organizational structure—are controlled by management. As such, they can be modified or changed. Strategies that management might want to consider include improved personnel selection and job placement, training, use of realistic goal setting, redesigning of jobs, increased employee involvement, improved organizational communication, offering employee sabbaticals, and establishment of corporate wellness programs.

Certain jobs are more stressful than others but, as we learned earlier in this chapter, individuals differ in their response to stress situations. We know, for example, that individuals with little experience or an external locus of control tend to be more prone to stress. *Selection and placement* decisions should take these facts into consideration. Obviously, management shouldn't restrict hiring to only experienced individuals with an internal locus, but such individuals may adapt better to high-stress jobs and perform those jobs more effectively. Similarly, *training* can increase an individual's self-efficacy and thus lessen job strain.

We discussed *goal setting* in Chapter 6. Based on an extensive amount of research, we concluded that individuals perform better when they have specific and challenging goals and receive feedback on how well they are progressing toward these goals. The use of goals can reduce stress as well as provide motivation. Specific goals that are perceived as attainable clarify performance expectations. In addition, goal feedback reduces uncertainties about actual job performance. The result is less employee frustration, role ambiguity, and stress.

Redesigning jobs to give employees more responsibility, more meaningful work, more autonomy, and increased feedback can reduce stress because these factors give the employee greater control over work activities and lessen dependence on others. But as we noted in our discussion of work design, not all employees want enriched jobs. The right redesign, then, for employees with a low need for growth might be less responsibility and increased specialization. If individuals prefer structure and routine, reducing skill variety should also reduce uncertainties and stress levels. An extension of job redesign, which has received considerable recent attention, is allowing workers to take short naps during

Some organizations, like Deloitte Consulting in Pittsburgh, are creating nap rooms to let employees catch some sleep during the work day.

the work day.[72] Nap time, apparently, isn't just for pre-school kids anymore! An increasing number of companies are finding that allowing employees to catch 10 to 30 minutes of sleep in the afternoon increases productivity and makes them less prone to errors.

Role stress is detrimental to a large extent because employees feel uncertain about goals, expectations, how they'll be evaluated, and the like. By giving these employees a voice in the decisions that directly affect their job performances, management can increase employee control and reduce this role stress. So managers should consider *increasing employee involvement* in decision making.[73]

Increasing formal *organizational communication* with employees reduces uncertainty by lessening role ambiguity and role conflict. Given the importance that perceptions play in moderating the stress–response relationship, management can also use effective communications as a means to shape employee perceptions. Remember that what employees categorize as demands, threats, or opportunities are merely an interpretation, and that interpretation can be affected by the symbols and actions communicated by management.

What some employees need is an occasional escape from the frenetic pace of their work. In recent years, companies such as Charles Schwab, Du Pont, L.L. Bean, Nike, and 3Com have begun to provide extended voluntary leaves.[74] These *sabbaticals*—ranging in length from a few weeks to several months—allow employees to travel, relax, or pursue personal projects that consume time beyond normal vacation weeks. Proponents argue that these sabbaticals can revive and rejuvenate workers who might be headed for burnout.

Our final suggestion is to offer organizationally supported **wellness programs**. These programs focus on the employee's total physical and mental condition.[75] For example, they typically provide workshops to help people quit smoking, control alcohol use, lose weight, eat better, and develop a regular exercise program. The assumption underlying most wellness programs is that employees need to take personal responsibility for their physical and mental health. The organization is merely a vehicle to facilitate this end.

wellness programs

Organizationally supported programs that focus on the employee's total physical and mental condition.

Organizations, of course, aren't altruistic. They expect a payoff from their investment in wellness programs. And most of those firms that have introduced wellness programs have found significant benefits. For instance, Johnson & Johnson calculated the following annual savings in insurance premiums when an employee exchanges bad habits for healthy ones: quitting smoking ($1,110); starting to exercise ($260); lowering cholesterol from 240 to 190 milligrams ($1,200); and slimming down from obese to normal weight ($177).[76] Xerox reports that savings in medical expenses are five times the cost of its wellness programs.[77]

SUMMARY AND IMPLICATIONS FOR MANAGERS

The need for change has been implied throughout this text. "A casual reflection on change should indicate that it encompasses almost all of our concepts in the organizational behavior literature. Think about leadership, motivation, organizational environments, and roles. It is impossible to think about these and other concepts without inquiring about change."[78]

If environments were perfectly static, if employees' skills and abilities were always up to date and incapable of deteriorating, and if tomorrow were always exactly the same as today, organizational change would have little or no relevance to managers. But the real world is turbulent, requiring organizations and their members to undergo dynamic change if they are to perform at competitive levels.

Managers are the primary change agents in most organizations. By the decisions they make and their role-modeling behaviors, they shape the organization's change culture. For instance, management decisions related to structural design, cultural factors, and human resource policies largely determine the level of innovation within the organization. Similarly, management decisions, policies, and practices will determine the degree to which the organization learns and adapts to changing environmental factors.

We found that the existence of work stress, in and of itself, need not imply lower performance. The evidence indicates that stress can be either a positive or a negative influence on employee performance. For many people, low to moderate amounts of stress enable them to perform their jobs better, by increasing their work intensity, alertness, and ability to react. However, a high level of stress, or even a moderate amount sustained over a long period, eventually takes its toll, and performance declines. The impact of stress on satisfaction is far more straightforward. Job-related tension tends to decrease general job satisfaction.[79] Even though low to moderate levels of stress may improve job performance, employees find stress dissatisfying.

Managing Change Is an Episodic Activity

Organizational change is an episodic activity. That is, it starts at some point, proceeds through a series of steps, and culminates in some outcome that those involved hope is an improvement over the starting point. It has a beginning, a middle, and an end.

Lewin's three-step model represents a classic illustration of this perspective. Change is seen as a break in the organization's equilibrium. The status quo has been disturbed, and change is necessary to establish a new equilibrium state. The objective of refreezing is to stabilize the new situation by balancing the driving and restraining forces.

Some experts have argued that organizational change should be thought of as balancing a system made up of five interacting variables within the organization—people, tasks, technology, structure, and strategy. A change in any one variable has repercussions on one or more of the others. This perspective is episodic in that it treats organizational change as essentially an effort to sustain an equilibrium. A change in one variable begins a chain of events that, if properly managed, requires adjustments in the other variables to achieve a new state of equilibrium.

Another way to conceptualize the episodic view of looking at change is to think of managing change as analogous to captaining a ship. The organization is like a large ship traveling across the calm Mediterranean Sea to a specific port. The ship's captain has made this exact trip hundreds of times before with the same crew. Every once in a while, however, a storm will appear, and the crew has to respond. The captain will make the appropriate adjustments—that is, implement changes—and, having maneuvered through the storm, will return to calm waters. Like this ship's voyage, managing an organization should be seen as a journey with a beginning and an end, and implementing change as a response to a break in the status quo and needed only occasionally.

The episodic approach may be the dominant paradigm for handling organizational change, but it has become obsolete. It applies to a world of certainty and predictability. The episodic approach was developed in the 1950s and 1960s, and it reflects the environment of those times. It treats change as the occasional disturbance in an otherwise peaceful world. However, this paradigm has little resemblance to today's environment of constant and chaotic change.[a]

If you want to understand what it's like to manage change in today's organizations, think of it as equivalent to permanent white-water rafting.[b] The organization is not a large ship, but more akin to a 40-foot raft. Rather than sailing a calm sea, this raft must traverse a raging river made up of an uninterrupted flow of permanent white-water rapids. To make things worse, the raft is manned by ten people who have never worked together or traveled the river before, much of the trip is in the dark, the river is dotted by unexpected turns and obstacles, the exact destination of the raft is not clear, and at irregular intervals the raft needs to pull to shore, where some new crew members are added and others leave. Change is a natural state and managing change is a continual process. That is, managers never get the luxury of escaping the white-water rapids.

The stability and predictability characterized by the episodic perspective no longer captures the world we live in. Disruptions in the status quo are not occasional, temporary, and followed by a return to an equilibrium state. There is, in fact, no equilibrium state. Managers today face constant change, bordering on chaos. They're being forced to play a game they've never played before, governed by rules that are created as the game progresses.

---

[a]For contrasting views on episodic and continuous change, see K. E. Weick and R. E. Quinn, "Organizational Change and Development," in J. T. Spence, J. M. Darley, and D. J. Foss (eds.), *Annual Review of Psychology*, vol. 50 (Palo Alto, CA: Annual Reviews, 1999), pp. 361–86.

[b]This perspective is based on P. B. Vaill, *Managing as a Performing Art: New Ideas for a World of Chaotic Change* (San Francisco: Jossey-Bass, 1989).

Questions for Review

1. What is meant by the phrase "we live in an age of discontinuity"?

2. "Resistance to change is an irrational response." Do you agree or disagree? Explain.

3. Why is participation considered such an effective technique for lessening resistance to change?

4. Why does change so frequently become a political issue in organizations?

5. How does Lewin's three-step model of change deal with resistance to change?

6. In an organization that has a history of "following the leader," what changes can be made to foster innovation?

7. "Learning organizations attack fragmentation, competitiveness, and reactiveness." Explain this statement.

8. How does an organization build a knowledge-management system?

9. How are opportunities, constraints, and demands related to stress? Give an example of each.

10. What can organizations do to reduce employee stress?

Questions for Critical Thinking

1. How have changes in the workforce during the past 20 years affected organizational policies?

2. "Managing today is easier than at the turn of the twentieth century because the years of real change took place between the Civil War and World War I." Do you agree or disagree? Discuss.

3. Are all managers change agents? Discuss.

4. Discuss the link between learning theories discussed in Chapter 2 and the issue of organizational change.

5. Do you think napping on the job is an acceptable practice in the workplace? What negatives do you see, if any, in promoting this practice?

Team Exercise | Power and the Changing Environment

Objectives

1. To describe the forces for change influencing power differentials in organizational and interpersonal relationships.

2. To understand the effect of technological, legal/political, economic, and social changes on the power of individuals within an organization.

The Situation

Your organization manufactures golf carts and sells them to country clubs, golf courses, and consumers. Your team is faced with the task of assessing how environmental changes will affect individuals' organizational power. Read each of the five scenarios and then, for each, identify the five members in the organization whose power will increase most in light of the environmental condition(s).

(m) = male		(f) = female
Advertising expert (m)	Accountant-CPA (m)	Product designer (m)
Chief financial officer (f)	General manager (m)	In-house counsel (m)
Securities analyst (m)	Marketing manager (f)	Public relations expert (m)
Operations manager (f)	Computer programmer (f)	Human resource manager (f)
Corporate trainer (m)	Industrial engineer (m)	Chemist (m)

1. New computer-aided manufacturing technologies are being introduced in the workplace during the upcoming 2 to 18 months.

2. New federal emission standards are being legislated by the government.

3. Sales are way down; the industry appears to be shrinking.

4. The company is planning to go international in the next 12 to 18 months.

5. The U.S. Equal Employment Opportunity Commission is applying pressure to balance the male–female population in the organization's upper hierarchy by threatening to publicize the predominance of men in upper management.

The Procedure

1. Divide the class into teams of three to four students each.

2. Teams should read each scenario and identify the five members whose power will increase most in light of the external environmental condition described.

3. Teams should then address the question: Assuming that the five environmental changes are taking place at once, which five members of the organization will now have the most power?

4. After 20 to 30 minutes, representatives of each team will be selected to present and justify their conclusions to the entire class. Discussion will begin with scenario 1 and proceed through to scenario 5 and the "all at once" scenario.

Source: Adapted from J. E. Barbuto Jr., "Power and the Changing Environment," *Journal of Management Education*, April 2000, pp. 288–96.

Case Incident	Responding to the 9/11 Aftershocks

Sheryl Hicks is not a complainer. If she has a major ache, she usually suffers in silence. Although her employer, Atlantic Mutual Insurance, has an employee assistance program—to provide emotional and psychological support in the workplace—she certainly would never think to use it, even if she did have a worry on her mind. "They say it's confidential, but who really knows?" asked Ms. Hicks, an administrative assistant at the insurance company.

But Sheryl Hicks's life changed on September 11, 2001. Her office at 130 Broadway in New York City, was near the World Trade Center. "I watched the whole thing from my 33rd-floor office window."

Ms. Hicks had never seen bodies fall from high rises or planes slam into buildings and cause them to crumble. She had never been covered with jet fuel, as she was when she fled the area on that day. Nor had she ever had such vivid nightmares that forced her to relive 9/11 over and over.

"Every time I talked to people they wanted details, which made it worse for me," said Ms. Hicks. "I had so much anger about what had happened to my life and the lives of so many people and the city where I've worked for 36 years."

Two weeks after 9/11, Ms. Hicks was still suffering serious aftereffects. Even though she lives on Staten Island and Atlantic Mutual's offices have been temporarily relocated to Madison, New Jersey, not an hour goes by when she doesn't have flashbacks of her experiences on 9/11.

Questions

1. What should Atlantic Mutual's management do, if anything, to cope with the aftereffects of 9/11?

2. How long would you expect employees to be adversely effected by 9/11 if a company provided no formal assistance for dealing with anger and stress?

3. What, if anything, should management do about employees who appear to be suffering from this trauma but will neither admit it nor accept help from their employer?

4. At what point does employee assistance in dealing with this trauma step over the line and become an invasion of an employee's privacy?

Source: Based on A. Ellin, "Traumatized Workers Look for Healing on the Job," *New York Times*, September 30, 2001, p. BU-10.

Managing Resistance to Change

After you've read this chapter, take Self-Assessment #47 (How Well Do I Respond to Turbulent Change?) on your enclosed CD-ROM, and complete the skill-building module entitled Managing Resistance to Change on page 633.

Endnotes

1. Based on "New Management," www.samsung.com; W. J. Holstein, "Samsung's Golden Touch," *Fortune*, April 1, 2002, pp. 89–94; and M. Song, "Samsung Electronics Net Rises 54%," *Wall Street Journal*, April 22, 2002, p. B4.

2. See, for instance, K. H. Hammonds, "Practical Radicals," *Fast Company*, September 2000, pp. 162–74; and P. C. Judge, "Change Agents," *Fast Company*, November 2000, pp. 216–26.

3. R. H. Hall, *Organizations: Structures, Processes, and Outcomes,* 4th ed. (Upper Saddle River, NJ: Prentice Hall, 1987), p. 29.

4. D. Katz and R. L. Kahn, *The Social Psychology of Organizations*, 2nd ed. (New York: Wiley, 1978), pp. 714–15.

5. J. P. Kotter and L. A. Schlesinger, "Choosing Strategies for Change," *Harvard Business Review*, March–April 1979, pp. 106–14.

6. See J. Pfeffer, *Managing with Power: Politics and Influence in Organizations* (Boston: Harvard Business School Press, 1992), pp. 7, and 318–20; and D. Knights and D. McCabe, "When 'Life Is but a Dream': Obliterating Politics Through Business Process Reengineering?" *Human Relations*, June 1998, pp. 761–98.

7. See, for instance, W. Ocasio, "Political Dynamics and the Circulation of Power: CEO Succession in U.S. Industrial Corporations, 1960–1990," *Administrative Science Quarterly*, June 1994, pp. 285–312.

8. K. Lewin, *Field Theory in Social Science* (New York: Harper & Row, 1951).

9. See, for example, A. B. Shani and W. A. Pasmore, "Organization Inquiry: Towards a New Model of the Action Research Process," in D. D. Warrick (ed.), *Contemporary Organization Development: Current Thinking and Applications* (Glenview, IL: Scott, Foresman, 1985), pp. 438–48.

10. For a sampling of various OD definitions, see J. I. Porras and P. J. Robertson, "Organizational Development: Theory, Practice, and Research," in M. D. Dunnette and L. M. Hough (eds.), *Handbook of Industrial & Organizational Psychology*, 2nd ed., vol. 3 (Palo Alto: Consulting Psycholo-

gists Press, 1992), pp. 721–23; N. Nicholson (ed.), *Encyclopedic Dictionary of Organizational Behavior* (Malden, MA: Blackwell, 1998), pp. 359–61; and G. Farias and H. Johnson, "Organizational Development and Change Management," *Journal of Applied Behavioral Science*, September 2000, pp. 376–79.

11. See, for instance, W. A. Pasmore and M. R. Fagans, "Participation, Individual Development, and Organizational Change: A Review and Synthesis," *Journal of Management*, June 1992, pp. 375–97; T. G. Cummings and C .G. Worley, *Organization Development and Change*, 5th ed. (Minneapolis: West, 1993); and W. W. Burke, *Organization Development: A Process of Learning and Changing*, 2nd ed. (Reading, MA: Addison-Wesley, 1994).

12. R. T. Golembiewski and A. Blumberg, eds., *Sensitivity Training and the Laboratory Approach*, 2nd ed. (Itasca, IL: Peacock, 1973).

13. J. E. Edwards and M. D. Thomas, "The Organizational Survey Process: General Steps and Practical Considerations," in P. Rosenfeld, J. E. Edwards, and M. D. Thomas (eds.), *Improving Organizational Surveys: New Directions, Methods, and Applications* (Newbury Park, CA: Sage, 1993), pp. 3–28.

14. E. H. Schein, *Process Consultation: Its Role in Organizational Development*, 2nd ed. (Reading, MA: Addison-Wesley, 1988), p. 9. See also E. H. Schein, *Process Consultation Revisited: Building Helpful Relationships* (Reading, MA: Addison-Wesley, 1999).

15. Ibid.

16. W. Dyer, *Team Building: Issues and Alternatives* (Reading, MA: Addison-Wesley, 1994).

17. N. Margulies and J. Wallace, *Organizational Change: Techniques and Applications* (Glenview, IL: Scott, Foresman, 1973), pp. 99–100.

18. See, for example, E. H. Neilsen, "Understanding and Managing Intergroup Conflict," in J. W. Lorsch and P. R. Lawrence (eds.), *Managing Group and Intergroup Relations* (Homewood, IL: Irwin-Dorsey, 1972), pp. 329–43.

19. R. R. Blake, J. S. Mouton, and R. L. Sloma, "The Union–Management Intergroup Laboratory: Strategy for Resolving Intergroup Conflict," *Journal of Applied Behavioral Science*, no. 1 (1965), pp. 25–57.

20. See, for example, D. Whitney and C. Schau, "Appreciative Inquiry: An Innovative Process for Organization Change," *Employment Relations Today*, Spring 1998, pp. 11–21; R. Zemke, "Don't Fix That Company!" *Training*, June 1999, pp. 26–33; and D. L. Cooperrider and D. Whitney, *Collaborating for Change: Appreciative Inquiry* (San Francisco: Berrett-Koehler, 2000).

21. R. Zemke, "Don't Fix That Company!" p. 31.

22. See, for instance, A. Van de Ven, "Central Problems in the Management of Innovation," *Management Science*, vol. 32, 1986, pp. 590–607; and R. M. Kanter, "When a Thousand Flowers Bloom: Structural, Collective and Social Conditions for Innovation in Organizations," in B. M. Staw and L. L. Cummings (eds.), *Research in Organizational Behavior*, vol. 10 (Greenwich, CT: JAI Press, 1988), pp. 169–211.

23. F. Damanpour, "Organizational Innovation: A Meta-Analysis of Effects of Determinants and Moderators," *Academy of Management Journal*, September 1991, p. 557.

24. Ibid., pp. 555–90.

25. See also P. R. Monge, M. D. Cozzens, and N. S. Contractor, "Communication and Motivational Predictors of the Dynamics of Organizational Innovation," *Organization Science*, May 1992, pp. 250–74.

26. J. H. Sheridan, "Lew Platt: Creating a Culture for Innovation," *Industry Week*, December 19, 1994, pp. 26–30.

27. J. M. Howell and C. A. Higgins, "Champions of Change," *Business Quarterly*, Spring 1990, pp. 31–32; and D. L. Day, "Raising Radicals: Different Processes for Championing Innovative Corporate Ventures," *Organization Science*, May 1994, pp. 148–72.

28. J. M. Howell and C. A. Higgins, "Champions of Change."

29. See, for example, the special edition on organizational learning in *Organizational Dynamics*, Autumn 1998; P. Senge, *The Dance of Change: The Challenges to Sustaining Momentum in Learning Organizations* (New York: Doubleday/Currency, 1999); A. M. Webber, "Will Companies Ever Learn?" *Fast Company*, October 2000, pp. 275–82; and R. Snell, "Moral Foundations of the Learning Organization," *Human Relations*, March 2001, pp. 319–42.

30. D. H. Kim, "The Link Between Individual and Organizational Learning," *Sloan Management Review*, Fall 1993, p. 37.

31. C. Argyris and D. A. Schon, *Organizational Learning* (Reading, MA: Addison-Wesley, 1978).

32. B. Dumaine, "Mr. Learning Organization," *Fortune*, October 17, 1994, p. 148.

33. F. Kofman and P. M. Senge, "Communities of Commitment: The Heart of Learning Organizations," *Organizational Dynamics*, Autumn 1993, pp. 5–23.

34. B. Dumaine, "Mr. Learning Organization," p. 154.

35. L. Smith, "New Ideas from the Army (Really)," *Fortune*, September 19, 1994, pp. 203–12; and L. Baird, P. Holland, and S. Deacon, "Imbedding More Learning into the Performance Fast Enough to Make a Difference," *Organizational Dynamics*, Spring 1999, pp. 19–32.

36. See J. Ewing, "Sharing the Wealth," *BusinessWeek e.biz*, March 19, 2001, pp. EB36–40; and D. Tapscott, D. Ticoll, and A. Lowy, *Digital Capital: Harnessing the Power of Business Webs* (Boston: Harvard Business School Press, 2000).

37. See B. Roberts, "Pick Employees' Brains," *HRMagazine*, February 2000, p. 115; and L. Empson, "Introduction: Knowledge Management in Professional Service Firms," *Human Relations*, July 2001, pp. 811–16.

38. B. Roberts, "Pick Employees' Brains," pp. 115–16; B. Fryer, "Get Smart," *INC. Technolgy 1999*, no. 3, p. 65; and D. Zielinski, "Have You Shared a Bright Idea Today?" *Training*, July 2000, p. 65.

39. B. Fryer, "Get Smart," p. 63.

40. B. Roberts, "Pick Employees' Brains," p. 117; and D. W. DeLong and L. Fahey, "Diagnosing Cultural Barriers to Knowledge Management," *Academy of Management Executive*, November 2000, pp. 113–27.

41. J. Gordon, "Intellectual Capital and You," *Training*, September 1999, p. 33.

42. D. Zielinski, "Have You Shared a Bright Idea Today?" pp. 65–67.

43. See S. Shane, S. Venkataraman, and I. MacMillan, "Cultural Differences in Innovation Championing Strategies," *Journal of Management*, vol. 21, no. 5, 1995, pp. 931–52.

44. See, for instance, K. Slobogin, "Many U.S. Employees Feel Overworked, Stressed, Study Says," www.cnn.com; May 16, 2001.

45. Adapted from R. S. Schuler, "Definition and Conceptualization of Stress in Organizations," *Organizational Behavior and Human Performance*, April 1980, p. 189. For an updated review of definitions, see R. L. Kahn and P. Byosiere, "Stress in Organizations," in M. D. Dunnette and L. M. Hough, eds., *Handbook of Industrial and Organizational Psychology*, 2nd ed., vol. 3 (Palo Alto, CA: Consulting Psychologists Press, 1992), pp. 573–80.

46. See, for instance, M. A. Cavanaugh, W. R. Boswell, M. V. Roehling, and J. W. Boudreau, "An Empirical Examination of Self-Reported Work Stress Among U.S. Managers," *Journal of Applied Psychology*, February 2000, pp. 65–74.

47. R. S. Schuler, "Definition and Conceptualization of Stress in Organizations," p. 191.

48. This model is based on D. F. Parker and T. A. DeCotiis, "Organizational Determinants of Job Stress," *Organizational Behavior and Human Performance*, October 1983, p. 166, S. Parasuraman and J. A. Alutto, "Sources and Outcomes of Stress in Organizational Settings: Toward the Development of a Structural Model," *Academy of Management Journal*, June 1984, p. 333; and R. L. Kahn and P. Byosiere, "Stress in Organizations," p. 592.

49. This section is adapted from C. L. Cooper and R. Payne, *Stress at Work* (London: Wiley, 1978); Parasuraman and Alutto, "Sources and Outcomes of Stress in Organizational Settings," pp 330–50; and S. Cartwright and C. L. Cooper, *Managing Workplace Stress* (Thousand Oaks, CA: Sage, 1997).

50. See, for example, D. R. Frew and N. S. Bruning, "Perceived Organizational Characteristics and Personality Measures as Predictors of Stress/Strain in the Work Place," *Journal of Management*, Winter 1987, pp. 633–46; and M. L. Fox, D. J. Dwyer, and D. C. Ganster, "Effects of Stressful Job Demands and Control of Physiological and Attitudinal Outcomes in a Hospital Setting," *Academy of Management Journal*, April 1993, pp. 289–318.

51. D. L. Nelson and C. Sutton, "Chronic Work Stress and Coping: A Longitudinal Study and Suggested New Directions," *Academy of Management Journal*, December 1990, pp. 859–69.

52. H. Selye, *The Stress of Life*, rev. ed. (New York: McGraw-Hill, 1956).

53. S. J. Motowidlo, J. S. Packard, and M. R. Manning, "Occupational Stress: Its Causes and Consequences for Job Performance," *Journal of Applied Psychology*, November 1987, pp. 619–20.

54. See, for instance, R. C. Cummings, "Job Stress and the Buffering Effect of Supervisory Support," *Group & Organization Studies*, March 1990, pp. 92–104; M. R. Manning, C. N. Jackson, and M. R. Fusilier, "Occupational Stress, Social Support, and the Cost of Health Care," *Academy of Management Journal*, June 1996, pp. 738–50; and P. D. Bliese and T. W. Britt, "Social Support, Group Consensus and Stressor-Strain Relationships: Social Context Matters," *Journal of Organizational Behavior*, June 2001, pp. 425–36.

55. See L. R. Murphy, "A Review of Organizational Stress Management Research," *Journal of Organizational Behavior Management*, Fall–Winter 1986, pp. 215–27.

56. S. M. Jex and P. D. Bliese, "Efficacy Beliefs as a Moderator of the Impact of Work-Related Stressors: A Multilevel Study," *Journal of Applied Psychology*, June 1999, pp. 349–61.

57. R. Williams, *The Trusting Heart: Great News About Type A Behavior* (New York: Times Books, 1989).

58. Schuler, "Definition and Conceptualization of Stress," pp. 200–205; and Kahn and Byosiere, "Stress in Organizations," pp. 604–10.

59. See T. A. Beehr and J. E. Newman, "Job Stress, Employee Health, and Organizational Effectiveness: A Facet Analysis, Model, and Literature Review," *Personnel Psychology*, Winter 1978, pp. 665–99; and B. D. Steffy and J. W. Jones, "Workplace Stress and Indicators of Coronary-Disease Risk," *Academy of Management Journal*, September 1988, pp. 686–98.

60. B. D. Steffy and J. W. Jones, "Workplace Stress and Indicators of Coronary-Disease Risk," p. 687.

61. C. L. Cooper and J. Marshall, "Occupational Sources of Stress: A Review of the Literature Relating to Coronary Heart Disease and Mental Ill Health," *Journal of Occupational Psychology*, vol. 49, no. 1 (1976), pp. 11–28.

62. J. R. Hackman and G. R. Oldham, "Development of the Job Diagnostic Survey," *Journal of Applied Psychology*, April 1975, pp. 159–70.

63. Cited in *Fast Company*, March 2000, p. 219.

64. "Reasons for Unscheduled Absences," *Business Week Frontier*, November 8, 1999, p. F6.

65. See, for instance, J. M. Ivancevich and M. T. Matteson, *Stress and Work* (Glenview, IL: Scott, Foresman, 1981); R. D. Allen, M. A. Hitt, and C. R. Greer, "Occupational Stress and Perceived Organizational Effectiveness in Formal Groups: An Examination of Stress Level and Stress Type," *Personnel Psychology*, Summer 1982, pp. 359–70; and L. A. Muse and S. G. Harris, "The Relationship between Stress and Job Performance: Has the Inverted U Theory Had a Fair Test?" Paper presented at the Southern Management Association meeting, 1998.

66. S. E. Sullivan and R. S. Bhagat, "Organizational Stress, Job Satisfaction and Job Performance: Where Do We Go From Here?" *Journal of Management*, June 1992, pp. 361–64; and M. Westman and D. Eden, "The Inverted-U Relationship between Stress and Performance: A Field Study," *Work & Stress*, Spring 1996, pp. 165–73.

67. The following discussion has been influenced by J. E. Newman and T. A. Beehr, "Personal and Organizational Strategies for Handling Job Stress," *Personnel Psychology*, Spring 1979, pp. 1–38; J. M. Ivancevich and M. T. Matteson, "Organizational Level Stress Management Interventions: A Review and Recommendations," *Journal of Organizational Behavior Management*, Fall–Winter 1986, pp. 229–48; M. T. Matteson and J. M. Ivancevich, "Individual Stress Management Interventions: Evaluation of Techniques," *Journal of Management Psychology*, January 1987, pp. 24–30; and J. M. Ivancevich, M. T. Matteson, S. M. Freedman, and J. S. Phillips, "Worksite Stress Management Interventions," *American Psychologist*, February 1990, pp. 252–61.

68. T. H. Macan, "Time Management: Test of a Process Model," *Journal of Applied Psychology*, June 1994, pp. 381–91.

69. See, for example, G. Lawrence-Ell, *The Invisible Clock: A Practical Revolution in Finding Time for Everyone and Everything* (Seaside Park, NJ: Kingsland Hall, 2002).

70. J. Kiely and G. Hodgson, "Stress in the Prison Service: The Benefits of Exercise Programs," *Human Relations*, June 1990, pp. 551–72.

71. E. J. Forbes and R. J. Pekala, "Psychophysiological Effects of Several Stress Management Techniques," *Psychological Reports*, February 1993, pp. 19–27; and G. Smith, "Meditation, the New Balm for Corporate Stress," *Business Week*, May 10, 1993, pp. 86–87.

72. See W. A. Anthony and C. W. Anthony, *The Art of Napping at Work* (Burdett, NY: Larson Publications, 2000); J. E. Brody, "New Respect for the Nap, A Pause That Refreshes," *New York Times*, January 4, 2000, p. D7; and

"Nappers of the World, Lie Down and Be Counted!" *Training*, May 2000, p. 24.

73. S. E. Jackson, "Participation in Decision Making as a Strategy for Reducing Job-Related Strain," *Journal of Applied Psychology*, February 1983, pp. 3–19.

74. S. Greengard, "It's About Time," *Industry Week*, February 7, 2000, pp. 47–50.

75. See, for instance, M. N. Martinez, "Using Data to Create Wellness Programs That Work," *HRMagazine*, November 1999, pp. 106–109; and B. Leonard, "Health Care Costs Increase Interest in Wellness Programs," *HRMagazine*, September 2001, pp. 35–36.

76. S. Tully, "America's Healthiest Companies," *Fortune*, June 12, 1995, p. 104.

77. M. Freudenheim, "Employers Focus on Weight as Workplace Health Issue," *New York Times*, September 6, 1999, p. A11.

78. P. S. Goodman and L. B. Kurke, "Studies of Change in Organizations: A Status Report," in P. S. Goodman (ed.), *Change in Organizations* (San Francisco: Jossey-Bass, 1982), pp. 1–2.

79. R. L. Kahn and P. Byosiere, "Stress in Organizations," pp. 605–608.

The Historical Evolution of Organizational Behavior

The farther back you can look, the farther forward you're likely to see.

—W. Churchill

Why study history? U.S. Supreme Court Justice Oliver Wendell Holmes, Jr., answered this question succinctly when he said, "When I want to understand what is happening today or try to decide what will happen tomorrow, I look back." By looking back at the history of organizational behavior, you gain a great deal of insight into how the field got to where it is today. It'll help you understand, for instance, how management came to impose rules and regulations on employees, why many workers in organizations do standardized and repetitive tasks on assembly lines, and why a number of organizations in recent years have replaced their assembly lines with team-based work units. In this appendix, you'll find a brief description of how the theory and practice of organizational behavior have evolved.

So where do we start? Human beings and organized activities have been around for thousands of years, but we needn't go back beyond the eighteenth or nineteenth century to find OB's roots.

Early Practices

There is no question that hundreds of people helped to plant the "seeds" from which the OB "garden" has grown.[1] Three individuals, however, were particularly important in promoting ideas that would eventually have a major influence in shaping the direction and boundaries of OB: Adam Smith, Charles Babbage, and Robert Owen.

ADAM SMITH

Adam Smith is more typically cited by economists for his contributions to classical economic doctrine, but his discussion in *The Wealth of Nations*,[2] published in 1776, included a brilliant argument on the economic advantages that organizations and society would reap from the division of labor (also called work specialization). Smith used the pin-manufacturing industry for his examples. He noted that 10 individuals, each doing a specialized task, could produce about 48,000 pins a day among them. He proposed, however, that if each were working separately and independently, the 10 workers together would be lucky to make 10 pins in one day. If each had to draw the wire, straighten it, cut it, pound heads for each pin, sharpen the point, and solder the head to the pin shaft, it would be quite a feat to produce 10 pins a day.

Smith concluded that division of labor raised productivity by increasing each worker's skill and dexterity, by saving time that is commonly lost in changing tasks, and by encouraging the creation of labor-saving inventions and machinery. The extensive development of assembly-line production processes during the twentieth century was undoubtedly stimulated by the economic advantages of work specialization cited over two centuries ago by Adam Smith.

CHARLES BABBAGE

Charles Babbage was a British mathematics professor who expanded on the virtues of division of labor first articulated by Adam Smith. In his book *On the Economy of Machinery and Manufactures*,[3] published in 1832, Babbage added the following to Smith's list of the advantages that accrue from division of labor:

1. It reduces the time needed for learning a job.
2. It reduces the waste of material during the learning stage.
3. It allows for the attainment of high skill levels.
4. It allows a more careful matching of people's skills and physical abilities with specific tasks.

Moreover, Babbage proposed that the economies from specialization should be as relevant to doing mental work as physical labor. Today, for example, we take specialization for granted among professionals. When we have a skin rash, we go to a dermatologist. When we buy a home, we consult a lawyer who specializes in real estate. The professors you encounter in your business school classes specialize in areas such as tax accounting, entrepreneurship, marketing research, and organizational behavior. These applications of division of labor were unheard of in nineteenth-century England. But contemporary organizations around the world—in both manufacturing and service industries—make wide use of the division of labor.

ROBERT OWEN

Robert Owen was a Welsh entrepreneur who bought his first factory in 1789, at the age of 18. He is important in the history of OB because he was one of the first industrialists to recognize how the growing factory system was demeaning to workers.

Repulsed by the harsh practices he saw in factories—such as the employment of young children (many under the age of 10), 13-hour workdays, and miserable working conditions—Owen became a reformer. He chided factory owners for treating their equipment better than their employees. He criticized them for buying the best machines but then employing the cheapest labor to run them. Owen argued that money spent on improving labor was one of the best investments that business executives could make. He claimed that showing concern for employees both was profitable for management and would relieve human misery.

For his time, Owen was an idealist. What he proposed was a utopian workplace that would reduce the suffering of the working class. He was more than a hundred years ahead of his time when he argued, in 1825, for regulated hours of work for all, child labor laws, public education, company-furnished meals at work, and business involvement in community projects.[4]

The Classical Era

The classical era covered the period from about 1900 to the mid-1930s. It was during this period that the first general theories of management began to evolve. The classical contributors—who include Frederick Taylor, Henri Fayol, Max Weber, Mary Parker Follett, and Chester Barnard—laid the foundation for contemporary management practices.

SCIENTIFIC MANAGEMENT

The typical United Parcel Service (UPS) driver today makes 120 stops during his or her work shift. Every step on that driver's daily route has been carefully studied by UPS industrial engineers to maximize efficiency. Every second taken up by stoplights, traffic, detours, doorbells, walkways, stairways, and coffee breaks has been documented by UPS engineers so as to cut wasted time. It's no accident, for instance, that all UPS drivers tap their horns when they approach a stop in hopes that the customer will hurry to the door seconds sooner. It's also no accident that all UPS drivers walk to a customer's door at the brisk pace of three feet per second and knock first lest seconds be lost searching for the doorbell.

Today's UPS drivers are following principles that were laid down 90 years ago by Frederick W. Taylor in his *Principles of Scientific Management*.[5] In this book, Taylor described how the scientific method could be used to define the "one best way" for a job to be done. In this section, we review his work.

As a mechanical engineer at the Midvale and Bethlehem Steel companies in Pennsylvania, Taylor was constantly appalled at the inefficiency of workers. Employees used vastly different techniques to do the same job. They were prone to "taking it easy" on the job. Taylor believed that worker output was only about one-third of what was possible. Therefore, he set out to correct the situation by applying the scientific method to jobs on the shop floor. He spent more than two decades pursuing with a passion the "one best way" for each job to be done.

It's important to understand what Taylor saw at Midvale Steel that aroused his determination to improve the way things were done in the plant. At the time, there were no clear concepts of worker and management responsibilities. Virtually no effective work standards existed. Employees purposely worked at a slow pace. Management decisions were of the "seat-of-the-pants" nature, based on hunch and intuition. Workers were placed on jobs with little or no concern for matching their abilities and aptitudes with the tasks they were required to do. Most important, management and workers considered themselves to be in continual conflict. Rather than cooperating to their mutual benefit, they perceived their relationship as a zero-sum game—any gain by one would be at the expense of the other.

Taylor sought to create a mental revolution among both the workers and management by defining clear guidelines for improving production

TAYLOR'S FOUR PRINCIPLES OF MANAGEMENT

1. Develop a science for each element of an individual's work. (Previously, workers used approximations, derived from experience.)

2. Scientifically select and then train, teach, and develop the worker. (Previously, workers chose their own work and trained themselves as best they could.)

3. Heartily cooperate with the workers so as to ensure that all work is done in accordance with the principles of the science that has been developed. (Previously, management and workers were in continual conflict.)

4. Divide work and responsibility almost equally between management and workers. Management takes over all work for which it is better suited than the workers. (Previously, almost all the work and the greater part of the responsibility were thrown upon the workers.)

efficiency. He defined four principles of management, listed in Exhibit A-1; he argued that following these principles would result in the prosperity of both management and workers. Workers would earn more pay, and management more profits.

Probably the most widely cited example of scientific management has been Taylor's pig iron experiment.[6] The average daily output of 92-pound pigs loaded onto rail cars was 12.5 tons per worker. Taylor was convinced that by scientifically analyzing the job to determine the one best way to load pig iron, the output could be increased to between 47 and 48 tons per day.

Taylor began his experiment by looking for a physically strong subject who placed a high value on the dollar. The individual Taylor chose was a big, strong Dutch immigrant, whom he called Schmidt. Schmidt, like the other loaders, earned $1.15 a day, which even at the turn of the century, was barely enough for a person to survive on. As the following quotation from Taylor's book demonstrates, Taylor used money—the opportunity to make $1.85 a day—as the primary means to get workers like Schmidt to do exactly as they were told:

"Schmidt, are you a high-priced man?" "Vell, I don't know vat you mean." "Oh, yes you do. What I want to know is whether you are a high-priced man or not." "Vell, I don't know vat you mean." "Oh, come now,

you answer my questions. What I want to find out is whether you are a high-priced man or one of these cheap fellows here. What I know is whether you want to earn $1.85 a day or whether you are satisfied with $1.15, just the same as all those cheap fellows are getting." "Did I vant $1.85 a day? Vas dot a high-priced man? Vell, yes. I vas a high-priced man."[7]

Using money to motivate Schmidt, Taylor went about having him load the pig irons, alternating various job factors to see what impact the changes had on Schmidt's daily output. For instance, on some days Schmidt would lift the pig irons by bending his knees, while on other days he would keep his legs straight and use his back. Taylor experimented with rest periods, walking speed, carrying positions, and other variables. After a long period of scientifically trying various combinations of procedures, techniques, and tools, Taylor succeeded in obtaining the level of productivity he thought possible. By putting the right person on the job with the correct tools and equipment, by having the worker follow his instructions exactly, and by motivating the worker through the economic incentive of a significantly higher daily wage, Taylor was able to reach his 48-ton objective.

Another Taylor experiment dealt with shovel sizes. Taylor noticed that every worker in the plant used the same-sized shovel, regardless of the material he was moving. This made no sense to Taylor. If there was an optimal weight that would maximize a worker's shoveling output over an entire day, then Taylor thought the size of the shovel should vary depending on the weight of the material being moved. After extensive experimentation, Taylor found that 21 pounds was the optimal shovel capacity. To achieve this optimal weight, heavy material such as iron ore would be moved with a small-faced shovel and light material such as coke with a large-faced shovel. Based on Taylor's findings, supervisors would no longer merely tell a worker to "shovel that pile over there." Depending on the material to be moved, the supervisor would now have to determine the appropriate shovel size and assign that size to the worker. The result was, again, significant increases in worker output.

Using similar approaches in other jobs, Taylor was able to define the one best way for doing each job.[8] He could then, after selecting the right people for the job, train them to do it precisely in this one best way. To motivate workers, he favored incentive wage plans. Overall, Taylor achieved consistent improvements in productivity in the range of 200 percent or more. He reaffirmed the role of managers to plan and control and that of workers to perform as they were instructed. *The Principles of Scientific Management,* as well as papers that Taylor wrote and presented, spread his ideas not only in the United States, but also in France, Germany, Russia, and Japan. One of the biggest boosts in interest in scientific management in the United States came during a 1910 hearing on railroad rates before the Interstate Commerce Commission. Appearing before the commission, an efficiency expert claimed that railroads could save a million dollars a day (equivalent to about $18 million a day in 2003 dollars) through the application of scientific management. The early acceptance of scientific management techniques by U.S. manufacturing companies, in fact, gave them a comparative advantage over foreign firms that made U.S. manufacturing efficiency the envy of the world—at least for 50 years or so!

ADMINISTRATIVE THEORY

Administrative theory describes efforts to define the universal functions that managers perform and principles that constitute good management practice. The major contributor to administrative theory was a French industrialist named Henri Fayol.

Writing at about the same time as Taylor, Fayol proposed that all managers perform five management functions: They plan, organize, command, coordinate, and control.[9] The importance of this simple insight is underlined when we acknowledge that almost every introductory management textbook today uses these same five functions, or a very close variation of them, as a basic framework for describing what managers do.

In addition, Fayol described the practice of management as something distinct from accounting, finance, production, distribution, and other typical business functions. He argued that management was an activity common to all human undertakings in business, in government, and even in the home. He then proceeded to state 14 principles of management that could be taught in schools and universities. These principles are shown in Exhibit A-2.

EXHIBIT A-2

FAYOL'S 14 PRINCIPLES OF MANAGEMENT

1. *Division of Work.* This principle is the same as Adam Smith's "division of labor." Specialization increases output by making employees more efficient.

2. *Authority.* Managers must be able to give orders. Authority gives them this right. Along with authority, however, goes responsibility. Whenever authority is exercised, responsibility arises.

3. *Discipline.* Employees must obey and respect the rules that govern the organization. Good discipline is the result of effective leadership, a clear understanding between management and workers regarding the organization's rules, and the judicious use of penalties for infractions of the rules.

4. *Unity of Command.* Every employee should receive orders from only one superior.

5. *Unity of Direction.* Each group of organizational activities that have the same objective should be directed by one manager using one plan.

6. *Subordination of Individual Interests to the General Interests.* The interests of any one employee or group of employees should not take precedence over the interests of the organization as a whole.

7. *Remuneration.* Workers must be paid a fair wage for their services.

8. *Centralization.* Centralization refers to the degree to which subordinates are involved in decision making. Whether decision making is centralized (to management) or decentralized (to subordinates) is a question of proper proportion. The problem is to find the optimum degree of centralization for each situation.

9. *Scalar Chain.* The line of authority from top management to the lowest ranks represents the scalar chain. Communications should follow this chain. However, if following the chain creates delays, cross-communications can be allowed if agreed to by all parties and superiors are kept informed.

10. *Order.* People and materials should be in the right place at the right time.

11. *Equity.* Managers should be kind and fair to their subordinates.

12. *Stability of Tenure of Personnel.* High employee turnover is inefficient. Management should provide orderly personnel planning and ensure that replacements are available to fill vacancies.

13. *Initiative.* Employees who are allowed to originate and carry out plans will exert high levels of effort.

14. *Esprit de Corps.* Promoting team spirit will build harmony and unity within the organization.

STRUCTURAL THEORY

While Taylor was concerned with management at the shop level (or what we today would describe as the job of a supervisor) and Fayol focused on general management functions, the German sociologist Max Weber (pronounced *Vay-ber*) was developing a theory of authority structures and describing organizational activity as based on authority relations.[10] He was one of the first to look at management and organizational behavior from a structural perspective.

Weber described an ideal type of organization that he called a bureaucracy. Bureaucracy was a system characterized by division of labor, a clearly defined hierarchy, detailed rules and regulations, and impersonal relationships. Weber recognized that this "ideal bureaucracy" didn't exist in reality but, rather, represented a selective reconstruction of the real world. He meant it to be taken as a basis for theorizing about work and how work could be done in large groups. His theory became the design prototype for large organizations. The detailed features of Weber's ideal bureaucratic structure are outlined in Exhibit A-3.

EXHIBIT **A-3**

WEBER'S IDEAL BUREAUCRACY

1. *Job Specialization.* Jobs are broken down into simple, routine, and well-defined tasks.

2. *Authority Hierarchy.* Offices or positions are organized in a hierarchy, each lower one being controlled and supervised by a higher one.

3. *Formal Selection.* All organizational members are to be selected on the basis of technical qualifications demonstrated by training, education, or formal examination.

4. *Formal Rules and Regulations.* To ensure uniformity and to regulate the actions of employees, managers must depend heavily on formal organizational rules.

5. *Impersonality.* Rules and controls are applied uniformly, avoiding involvement with personalities and personal preferences of employees.

6. *Career Orientation.* Managers are professional officials rather than owners of the units they manage. They work for fixed salaries and pursue their careers within the organization.

"SOCIAL MAN" THEORY

People like Taylor, Fayol, and Weber could be faulted for forgetting that human beings are the central core of every organization and that human beings are social animals. Mary Parker Follett and Chester Barnard were two theorists who saw the importance of the social aspects of organizations. Their ideas were born late in the scientific management period but didn't achieve any large degree of recognition until the 1930s.[11]

Mary Parker Follett Mary Parker Follett was one of the earliest writers to recognize that organizations could be viewed from the perspective of individual and group behavior.[12] A transitionalist writing during the time when scientific management dominated, Follett was a social philosopher who proposed more people-oriented ideas. Her views had clear implications for organizational behavior. Follett thought that organizations should be based on a group ethic rather than on individualism. Individual potential, she argued, remained only potential until released through group association. The manager's job was to harmonize and coordinate group efforts. Managers and workers should view themselves as partners—as part of a common group. Therefore, managers should rely more on their expertise and knowledge than on the formal authority of their position to lead subordinates.

Follett's humanistic ideas have influenced the way we look at motivation, leadership, power, and authority today. In fact, much of the current emphasis in organizations on group togetherness and team effort undoubtedly has its origins in Follett's work.

Chester Barnard Like Henri Fayol, Chester Barnard was a practitioner. He joined the American Telephone and Telegraph system in 1909 and became president of New Jersey Bell in 1927. Barnard had read Weber and was influenced by his writings. But unlike Weber, who had a mechanistic and impersonal view of organizations, Barnard saw organizations as social systems that require human cooperation. He expressed his views in *The Functions of the Executive*,[13] published in 1938.

Barnard viewed organizations as made up of people who have interacting social relationships.

Managers' major roles were to communicate and to stimulate subordinates to high levels of effort. A major part of an organization's success, as Barnard saw it, depended on obtaining cooperation from its personnel. Barnard also argued that success depended on maintaining good relations with people and institutions outside the organization with whom the organization regularly interacted. By recognizing the organization's dependence on investors, suppliers, customers, and other external constituencies, Barnard introduced the idea that managers had to examine the environment and then adjust the organization to maintain a state of equilibrium. So, for instance, regardless of how efficient an organization's production might be, if management failed to ensure a continuous input of materials and supplies or to find markets for its outputs, then the organization's survival would be threatened. Much of the contemporary interest in how the environment affects organizations and their employees can be traced to ideas initially suggested by Barnard.

The Behavioral Era

The "people side" of organizations came into its own during the period we'll call the behavioral era. As we show, this era was marked by the human relations movement and the widespread application in organizations of behavioral science research. While this behavioral era really didn't begin to roll until the 1930s, three earlier events deserve brief mention because they played an important part in the application and development of organizational behavior. These are the birth of the "personnel office" around 1900; the creation of the field of industrial psychology with the publication of Hugo Münsterberg's textbook in 1913; and passing of the Wagner Act in 1935, which initiated the growth of labor unions.

THE BIRTH OF THE "PERSONNEL OFFICE"

In response to the growth of trade unionism at the turn of the century, a few firms—for example, H.J. Heinz, Colorado Fuel & Iron, and International Harvester—created the position of "welfare secretary." Welfare secretaries were supposed to assist workers by suggesting improvements in working conditions, housing, medical care, edu-

cational facilities, and recreation. These people, who were the forerunners of today's personnel or human resource management directors, acted as a buffer between the organization and its employees. The B. F. Goodrich Co. developed the first employment department in 1900, but its responsibilities consisted only of hiring. In 1902, the National Cash Register Company established the first comprehensive labor department responsible for wage administration, grievances, employment and working conditions, health conditions, recordkeeping, and worker improvement.

THE BIRTH OF INDUSTRIAL PSYCHOLOGY

Hugo Münsterberg created the field of industrial psychology with the publication of his textbook *Psychology and Industrial Efficiency*[14] in 1913. In it, he argued for the scientific study of human behavior to identify general patterns and to explain individual differences. Interestingly, Münsterberg saw a link between scientific management and industrial psychology. Both sought increased efficiency through scientific work analyses and through better alignment of individual skills and abilities with the demands of various jobs.

Münsterberg suggested the use of psychological tests to improve employee selection, the value of learning theory in the development of training methods, and the study of human behavior in order to understand what techniques are most effective for motivating workers. Much of our current knowledge of selection techniques, employee training, work design, and motivation is built on Münsterberg's work.

THE MAGNA CARTA OF LABOR

Following the stock market crash of 1929, the United States and much of the world's economy entered the Great Depression. To help relieve the effects of the depression on the U.S. labor force, President Franklin Roosevelt supported the Wagner Act, which was passed in 1935. This act recognized unions as the authorized representatives of workers, able to bargain collectively with employers in the interests of their members. The Wagner Act would prove to be the Magna Carta of labor. It legitimized the role of trade unions and encouraged rapid growth in union membership. In response to this legislation, managers in industry became much more open to finding new ways to handle their employees. Having lost the battle to keep unions out of their factories, management began to try to improve working conditions and seek better relations with its workforce. A set of studies done at Western Electric's Hawthorne plant would be the prime stimulus for the human relations movement that swept American industry from the late 1930s through the 1950s.

HUMAN RELATIONS

The essence of the human relations movement was the belief that the key to higher productivity in organizations was increasing employee satisfaction. In addition to the Hawthorne studies, three people played important roles in conveying the message of human relations: Dale Carnegie, Abraham Maslow, and Douglas McGregor. In this section, we briefly review each man's contribution. But first, we'll describe the very influential Hawthorne studies.

The Hawthorne Studies Without question, the most important contribution to the human relations movement within organizational behavior came out of the Hawthorne studies undertaken at the Western Electric Company's Hawthorne Works in Cicero, Illinois. These studies, originally begun in 1924 but eventually expanded and carried on through the early 1930s, were initially devised by Western Electric industrial engineers to examine the effect of various illumination levels on worker productivity. Control and experimental groups were established. The experimental group was presented with varying illumination intensities, while the control group worked under a constant intensity. The engineers had expected individual output to be directly related to the intensity of light. However, they found that as the light level was increased in the experimental group, output for both groups rose. To the surprise of the engineers, as the light level was dropped in the experimental group, productivity continued to increase in both groups. In fact, a productivity decrease was observed in the experimental group only when the light intensity had been reduced to that of moonlight. The engineers concluded that illumination intensity was not directly related to group productivity, but they could not explain the behavior they had witnessed.

In 1927, the Western Electric engineers asked Harvard professor Elton Mayo and his associates to join the study as consultants. Thus began a relationship that would last through 1932 and encompass numerous experiments covering the redesign of jobs, changes in the length of the work day and work week, introduction of rest periods, and individual versus group wage plans.[15] For example, one experiment was designed to evaluate the effect of a group piecework incentive pay system on group productivity. The results indicated that the incentive plan had less effect on a worker's output than did group pressure and acceptance and the concomitant security. Social norms or standards of the group, therefore, were concluded to be the key determinants of individual work behavior.

Scholars generally agree that the Hawthorne studies had a large and dramatic impact on the direction of organizational behavior and management practice. Mayo's conclusions were that behavior and sentiments were closely related, that group influences significantly affected individual behavior, that group standards established individual worker output, and that money was less a factor in determining output than were group standards, group sentiments, and security. These conclusions led to a new emphasis on the human factor in the functioning of organi-

These women were part of the experiments at the Hawthorne plant of Western Electric. The Hawthorne studies dramatized that a worker was not a machine and that scientific management's "one best way" approach had to be modified to recognize the effects of individual and group behavior.

zations and the attainment of their goals. They also led to increased paternalism by management.

The Hawthorne studies have not been without critics. Attacks have been made on their procedures, analyses of findings, and the conclusions they drew.[16] However, from a historical standpoint, it's of little importance whether the studies were academically sound or their conclusions justified. What is important is that they stimulated an interest in human factors.

Dale Carnegie   Dale Carnegie's book *How to Win Friends and Influence People*[17] was read by millions during the 1930s, 1940s, and 1950s. During this same period, tens of thousands of managers and aspiring managers attended his management speeches and seminars. So Carnegie's ideas deserve attention because of the wide audience they commanded.

Carnegie's essential theme was that the way to success was through winning the cooperation of others. He advised his audience to: (1) make others feel important through a sincere appreciation of their efforts; (2) strive to make a good first impression; (3) win people to your way of thinking by letting others do the talking, being sympathetic, and "never telling a man he is wrong"; and (4) change people by praising their good traits and giving the offender the opportunity to save face.[18]

Abraham Maslow   Few students of college age have not been exposed to the ideas of Abraham Maslow. A humanistic psychologist, Maslow proposed a theoretical hierarchy of five needs: physiological, safety, social, esteem, and self-actualization.[19] From a motivation standpoint, Maslow argued that each step in the hierarchy must be satisfied before the next can be activated, and that once a need was substantially satisfied, it no longer motivated behavior. Moreover, he believed that self-actualization—that is, achieving one's full potential—was the summit of a human being's existence. Managers who accepted Maslow's hierarchy attempted to alter their organizations and management practices to reduce barriers to employees' self-actualization.

Douglas McGregor   Douglas McGregor is best known for his formulation of two sets of assumptions—Theory X and Theory Y—about human nature.[20] Briefly, Theory X rests on an essentially negative view of people. It assumes that they have little ambition, dislike work, want to avoid responsibility, and need to be closely directed to work effectively. Theory Y, on the other hand, rests on a positive view of people. It assumes they can exercise self-direction, accept responsibility, and consider work to be as natural as rest or play. McGregor personally believed that Theory Y assumptions best captured the true nature of workers and should guide management practice. As a result, he argued that managers should free up their employees to unleash their full creative and productive potential.

BEHAVIORAL SCIENCE THEORISTS

The final category within the behavioral era encompasses a group of researchers who, as Taylor did in scientific management, relied on the scientific method for the study of organizational behavior. Unlike members of the human relations movement, the behavioral science theorists engaged in objective research of human behavior in organizations. They carefully attempted to keep their personal beliefs out of their work. They sought to develop

Abraham Maslow (1908–1970), a humanistic psychologist, gave us one of the most widely recognized theories of motivation. Maslow proposed that people possess an innate inclination to develop their potential and seek self-actualization.

rigorous research designs that could be replicated by other behavioral scientists in the hope that a science of organizational behavior could be built.

A full review of the contributions made by behavioral science theorists would cover hundreds of pages, since their work makes up a large part of today's foundations of organizational behavior. But to give you the flavor of their work, we'll briefly summarize the contributions of a few of the major theorists.

B. F. Skinner Few behavioral scientists' names are more familiar to the general public than that of B. F. Skinner. His research on operant conditioning and behavior modification had a significant effect on the design of organizational training programs and reward systems.[21]

Essentially, Skinner demonstrated that behavior is a function of its consequences. He found that people will most likely engage in a desired behavior if they are rewarded for doing so; these rewards are most effective if they immediately follow the desired response; and behavior that is not rewarded, or is punished, is less likely to be repeated.

David McClelland Psychologist David McClelland tested the strength of individual achievement moti-

Using operant conditioning chambers like those in this photo, B. F. Skinner experimented with giving food to rats and pigeons in order to test the effects of rewards on behavior.

vation by asking subjects to look at a set of somewhat ambiguous pictures and to write their own story about each picture. Based on these projective tests, McClelland found he was able to differentiate people with a high need to achieve—individuals who had a strong desire to succeed or achieve in relation to a set of standards—from people with a low need to achieve.[22] His research has been instrumental in helping organizations better match people with jobs and in redesigning jobs for high achievers so as to maximize their motivation potential. In addition, McClelland and his associates have successfully trained individuals to increase their achievement drive. For instance, in India, people who underwent achievement training worked longer hours, initiated more new business ventures, made greater investments in productive assets, employed a larger number of employees, and saw a greater increase in their gross incomes than did a similar group who did not undergo achievement training.

Fred Fiedler Leadership is one of the most important and extensively researched topics in organizational behavior. The work of Fred Fiedler on the subject is significant for its emphasis on the situational aspects of leadership as well as for its attempt to develop a comprehensive theory of leadership behavior.[23]

From the mid-1960s through the late 1970s, Fiedler's contingency model dominated leadership research. He developed a questionnaire to measure an individual's inherent leadership orientation and identified three contingency variables that, he argued, determined what type of leader behavior is most effective. In testing his model, Fiedler and his associates studied hundreds of groups. Dozens of researchers have attempted to replicate his results. Although some of the predictions from the model have not stood up well under closer analysis, Fielder's model has been a major influence on current thinking and research about leadership.

Frederick Herzberg With the possible exception of the Hawthorne studies, no single stream of research has had a greater impact on undermining the recommendations of scientific management than the work of Frederick Herzberg.[24]

Herzberg sought an answer to the question: What do individuals want from their jobs? He asked hundreds of people that question in the late 1950s, and then carefully analyzed their responses. He concluded that people preferred jobs that offered opportunities for recognition, achievement, responsibility, and growth. Managers who concerned themselves with things like company policies, employee pay, creating narrow and repetitive jobs, and developing favorable working conditions might placate their workers, but they wouldn't motivate them. According to Herzberg, if managers want to motivate their people, they should redesign jobs to allow workers to perform more and varied tasks. Much of the contemporary interest in enriching jobs and improving the quality of work life can be traced to Herzberg's research.

J. Richard Hackman and Greg Oldham   While Herzberg's conclusions were greeted with enthusiasm, the methodology he used for arriving at those conclusions was far less enthusiastically embraced. It would be the work of J. Richard Hackman and Greg Oldham in the 1970s that would provide an explanation of how job factors influence employee motivation and satisfaction, and would offer a valid framework for analyzing jobs.[25] Hackman and Oldham's research also uncovered the core job dimensions—skill variety, task identity, task significance, autonomy, and feedback—that have stood up well as guides in the design of jobs. More specifically, Hackman and Oldham found that among individuals with strong growth needs, jobs that score high on these five core dimensions lead to high employee performance and satisfaction.

OB Today: A Contingency Perspective

We've attempted to demonstrate in this appendix that the present state of organizational behavior encompasses ideas introduced dozens, and sometimes hundreds, of years ago. So don't think of one era's concepts as replacing an earlier era's; rather, view them as extensions and modifications of earlier ideas. As UPS demonstrates, many of Taylor's scientific management principles can be applied today with impressive results. Of course, that doesn't mean that those principles will work as well in other organizations. If there is anything we've learned over the past 40 years, it's that few ideas—no matter how attractive—are applicable to all organizations or to all jobs or to all types of employees. Today, organizational behavior must be studied and applied in a contingency framework.

Baseball fans know that a batter doesn't *always* try for a home run. It depends on the score, the inning, whether runners are on base, and similar contingency variables. Similarly, you can't say that students always learn more in small classes than in large ones. An extensive body of educational research tells us that contingency factors such as course content and teaching style of the instructor influence the relationship between class size and learning effectiveness. Applied to organizational behavior, contingency theory recognizes that there is no "one best way" to manage people in organizations and no single set of simple principles that can be applied universally.[26]

A contingency approach to the study of OB is intuitively logical. Why? Because organizations obviously differ in size, objectives, and environmental uncertainty. Similarly, employees differ in values, attitudes, needs, and experiences. So it would be surprising to find that there are universally applicable principles that work in *all* situations. But, of course, it's one thing to say "it all depends" and another to say *what* it all depends on.

The most popular OB topics for research investigation in recent years have been theories of motivation, leadership, work design, and job satisfaction. But while the 1960s and 1970s saw the development of new theories, the emphasis since then has been on refining existing theories, clarifying previous assumptions, and identifying relevant contingency variables. That is, researchers have been trying to identify the "what" variables and which ones are relevant for understanding various behavioral phenomena. This essentially reflects the maturing of OB as a scientific discipline. The near-term future of OB research is likely to continue to focus on fine-tuning current theories so as to better help us understand those situations in which they're most likely to be useful.

Summary

Although the seeds of organizational behavior were planted more than 200 years ago, current OB theory and practice are essentially products of the twentieth century.

Frederick Taylor's principles of scientific management were instrumental in engineering precision and standardization into people's jobs. Henri Fayol defined the universal functions that all managers perform and the principles that constitute good management practice. Max Weber developed a theory of authority structures and described organizational activity based on authority relations.

The "people side" of organizations came into its own in the 1930s, predominantly as a result of the Hawthorne studies. These studies led to a new emphasis on the human factor in organizations and increased paternalism by management. In the late 1950s, managers' attention was caught by the ideas of people like Abraham Maslow and Douglas McGregor, who proposed that organization structures and management practices had to be altered so as to bring out the full productive potential of employees. Motivation and leadership theories offered by David McClelland, Fred Fiedler, Frederick Herzberg, and other behavioral scientists during the 1960s and 1970s provided managers with still greater insights into employee behavior.

Almost all contemporary management and organizational behavior concepts are contingency-based. That is, they provide various recommendations depending on situational factors. As a maturing discipline, current OB research is emphasizing the refinement of existing theories.

Endnotes

1. See, for instance, D. A. Wren, *The Evolution of Management Thought*, 4th ed. (New York: Wiley, 1994), especially Chapters 13–18.
2. A. Smith, *An Inquiry into the Nature and Causes of the Wealth of Nations* (New York: Modern Library, 1937; originally published, 1776).
3. C. Babbage, *On the Economy of Machinery and Manufactures* (London: Charles Knight, 1832).
4. R. A. Owen, *A New View of Society* (New York: E. Bliss & White, 1825).
5. F. W. Taylor, *Principles of Scientific Management* (New York: Harper & Brothers, 1911).
6. For a review, see C. D. Wrege and R. M. Hodgetts, "Frederick W. Taylor's 1899 Pig Iron Observations: Examining Fact, Fiction, and Lessons for the New Millennium," *Academy of Management Journal*, December 2000, pp. 1283–91.
7. F. W. Taylor, *Principles of Scientific Management*, p. 44.
8. See R. Kanigel, *The One Best Way: Frederick Winslow Taylor and the Enigma of Efficiency* (New York: Penguin, 1999).
9. H. Fayol, *Industrial and General Administration* (Paris: Dunod, 1916).
10. M. Weber, *The Theory of Social and Economic Organizations*, ed. T. Parsons, trans. A. M. Henderson and T. Parsons (New York: Free Press, 1947).
11. Wren, *The Evolution of Management Thought*, Chapter 14.
12. See, for example, M. P. Follett, *The New State: Group Organization the Solution of Popular Government* (London: Longmans, Green & Co., 1918). See also, the review forum on Mary Parker Follett in *Organization*, February 1996, pp. 147–80.
13. C. I. Barnard, *The Functions of the Executive* (Cambridge, MA: Harvard University Press, 1938).
14. H. Münsterberg, *Psychology and Industrial Efficiency* (Boston: Houghton Mifflin, 1913).
15. E. Mayo, *The Human Problems of an Industrial Civilization* (New York: Macmillan, 1933); and F. J. Roethlisberger and W. J. Dickson, *Management and the Worker* (Cambridge, MA: Harvard University Press, 1939).
16. See, for example, A. Carey, "The Hawthorne Studies: A Radical Criticism," *American Sociological Review*, June 1967, pp. 403–16; R. H. Franke and J. Kaul, "The Hawthorne Experiments: First Statistical Interpretations," *American Sociological Review*, October 1978, pp. 623–43; B. Rice, "The Hawthorne Defect: Persistence of a Flawed Theory," *Psychology Today*, February 1982, pp. 70–74; J. A. Sonnenfeld, "Shedding Light on the Hawthorne Studies," *Journal of Occupational Behavior*, April 1985, pp. 111–30; and S. R. G. Jones, "Was There a Hawthorne Effect?" *American Journal of Sociology*, November 1992, pp. 451–68.
17. D. Carnegie, *How to Win Friends and Influence People* (New York: Simon & Schuster, 1936).
18. Wren, *The Evolution of Management Thought*, p. 336.
19. A. Maslow, *Motivation and Personality* (New York: Harper & Row, 1954).
20. D. McGregor, *The Human Side of Enterprise* (New York: McGraw-Hill, 1960).
21. See, for instance, B. F. Skinner, *Science and Human Behavior* (New York: Free Press, 1953); and B. F. Skinner, *Beyond Freedom and Dignity* (New York: Knopf, 1972).
22. D. C. McClelland, *The Achieving Society* (New York: Van Nostrand Reinhold, 1961); and D. C. McClelland and

D. G. Winter, *Motivating Economic Achievement* (New York: Free Press, 1969).

23. F. E. Fiedler, *A Theory of Leadership Effectiveness* (New York: McGraw-Hill, 1967).

24. F. Herzberg, B. Mausner, and B. Snyderman, *The Motivation to Work* (New York, John Wiley, 1959); and F. Herzberg, *The Managerial Choice: To Be Efficient or to Be Human,* rev. ed. (Salt Lake City: Olympus, 1982).

25. J. R. Hackman and G. R. Oldham, "Development of the Job Diagnostic Survey," *Journal of Applied Psychology*, April 1975, pp. 159–70.

26. See, for instance, J. M. Shepard and J. G. Hougland, Jr., "Contingency Theory: 'Complex Man' or 'Complex Organization'?" *Academy of Management Review*, July 1978, pp. 413–27; and H. L. Tosi, Jr., and J. W. Slocum, Jr., "Contingency Theory: Some Suggested Directions," *Journal of Management*, Spring 1984, pp. 9–26.

Research In Organizational Behavior

For every complex problem, there is a solution that is simple, neat, and wrong.

—H. L. Mencken

A number of years ago, a friend of mine was all excited because he had read about the findings from a research study that finally, once and for all, resolved the question of what it takes to make it to the top in a large corporation. I doubted there was any simple answer to this question but, not wanting to dampen his enthusiasm, I asked him to tell me of what he had read. The answer, according to my friend, was *participation in college athletics*. To say I was skeptical of his claim is a gross understatement, so I asked him to tell me more.

The study encompassed 1,700 successful senior executives at the 500 largest U.S. corporations. The researchers found that half of these executives had played varsity-level college sports.[1] My friend, who happens to be good with statistics, informed me that since fewer than 2 percent of all college students participate in intercollegiate athletics, the probability of this finding occurring by mere chance is less than one in 10 million! He concluded his analysis by telling me that, based on this research, I should encourage my management students to get into shape and to make one of the varsity teams.

My friend was somewhat perturbed when I suggested that his conclusions were likely to be flawed. These executives were all males who attended college in the 1940s and 1950s. Would his advice be meaningful to females in the 21st century? These executives also weren't your typical college students. For the most part, they had attended elite private colleges such as Princeton and Amherst, where a large proportion of the student body participates in intercollegiate sports. And these "jocks" hadn't necessarily played football or basketball; many had participated in golf, tennis, baseball, cross-country running, crew, rugby, and similar minor sports. Moreover, maybe the researchers had confused the direction of causality. That is, maybe individuals

with the motivation and ability to make it to the top of a large corporation are drawn to competitive activities like college athletics.

My friend was guilty of misusing research data. Of course, he is not alone. We are all continually bombarded with reports of experiments that link certain substances to cancer in mice and surveys that show changing attitudes toward sex among college students, for example. Many of these studies are carefully designed, with great caution taken to note the implications and limitations of the findings. But some studies are poorly designed, making their conclusions at best suspect, and at worst meaningless.

Rather than attempting to make you a researcher, the purpose of this appendix is to increase your awareness as a consumer of behavioral research. A knowledge of research methods will allow you to appreciate more fully the care in data collection that underlies the information and conclusions presented in this text. Moreover, an understanding of research methods will make you a more skilled evaluator of the OB studies you will encounter in business and professional journals. So an appreciation of behavioral research is important because (1) it's the foundation on which the theories in this text are built, and (2) it will benefit you in future years when you read reports of research and attempt to assess their value.

Purposes of Research

Research is concerned with the systematic gathering of information. Its purpose is to help us in our search for the truth. Although we will never find ultimate truth—in our case, that would be to know precisely how any person or group would behave in any organizational context—ongoing research adds to our body of OB knowledge by supporting some theories, contradicting others, and suggesting new theories to replace those that fail to gain support.

Research Terminology

Researchers have their own vocabulary for communicating among themselves and with outsiders. The following briefly defines some of the more popular terms you're likely to encounter in behavioral science studies.[2]

Variable A *variable* is any general characteristic that can be measured and that changes in either amplitude, intensity, or both. Some examples of OB variables found in this text are job satisfaction, employee productivity, work stress, ability, personality, and group norms.

Hypothesis A tentative explanation of the relationship between two or more variables is called a *hypothesis*. My friend's statement that participation in college athletics leads to a top executive position in a large corporation is an example of a hypothesis. Until confirmed by empirical research, a hypothesis remains only a tentative explanation.

Dependent Variable A *dependent variable* is a response that is affected by an independent variable. In terms of the hypothesis, it is the variable that the researcher is interested in explaining. Referring back to our opening example, the dependent variable in my friend's hypothesis was executive succession. In organizational behavior research, the most popular dependent variables are productivity, absenteeism, turnover, job satisfaction, and organizational commitment.[3]

Independent Variable An *independent variable* is the presumed cause of some change in the dependent variable. Participating in varsity athletics was the independent variable in my friend's hypothesis. Popular independent variables studied by OB researchers include intelligence, personality, job satisfaction, experience, motivation, reinforcement patterns, leadership style, reward allocations, selection methods, and organization design.

You may have noticed we said that job satisfaction is frequently used by OB researchers as both a dependent and an independent variable. This is not an error. It merely reflects that the label given to a variable depends on its place in the hypothesis. In the statement "Increases in job satisfaction lead to reduced turnover," job satisfaction is an independent variable. However, in the statement "Increases in money lead to higher job satisfaction," job satisfaction becomes a dependent variable.

Moderating Variable A *moderating variable* abates the effect of the independent variable on the dependent variable. It might also be thought of as the contingency variable: If X (independent variable), then Y (dependent variable) will occur, but only under conditions Z (moderating variable). To translate this into a real-life example, we might say that if we increase the amount of direct supervision in the work area (X), then there will be a change in worker productivity (Y), but this effect will be moderated by the complexity of the tasks being performed (Z).

Causality A hypothesis, by definition, implies a relationship. That is, it implies a presumed cause and effect. This direction of cause and effect is called *causality*. Changes in the independent variable are assumed to cause changes in the dependent variable. However, in behavioral research, it's possible to make an incorrect assumption of causality when relationships are found. For example, early behavioral scientists found a relationship between employee satisfaction and productivity. They concluded that a happy worker was a productive worker. Follow-up research has supported the relationship, but disconfirmed the direction of the arrow. The evidence more correctly suggests that high productivity leads to satisfaction rather than the other way around.

Correlation Coefficient It's one thing to know that there is a relationship between two or more variables. It's another to know the *strength* of that relationship. The term *correlation coefficient* is used to indicate that strength, and is expressed as a number between –1.00 (a perfect negative relationship) to +1.00 (a perfect positive correlation).

When two variables vary directly with one another, the correlation will be expressed as a positive number. When they vary inversely—that is, one increases as the other decreases—the correlation will be expressed as a negative number. If the two variables vary independently of each other, we say that the correlation between them is zero.

For example, a researcher might survey a group of employees to determine the satisfaction of each with his or her job. Then, using company absenteeism reports, the researcher could correlate the job satisfaction scores against individual attendance records to determine whether employees who are more satisfied with their jobs have better attendance records than their counterparts who indicated lower job satisfaction. Let's suppose the researcher found a correlation coefficient of +0.50 between satisfaction and attendance. Would that be a strong association? There is, unfortunately, no precise numerical cutoff separating strong and weak relationships. A standard statistical test would need to be applied to determine whether the relationship was a significant one.

A final point needs to be made before we move on: A correlation coefficient measures only the strength of association between two variables. A high value does *not* imply causality. The length of women's skirts and stock market prices, for instance, have long been noted to be highly correlated, but one should be careful not to infer that a causal relationship between the two exists. In this instance, the high correlation is more happenstance than predictive.

Theory   The final term we introduce in this section is *theory*. Theory describes a set of systematically interrelated concepts or hypotheses that purports to explain and predict phenomena. In OB, theories are also frequently referred to as *models*. We use the two terms interchangeably.

There are no shortages of theories in OB. For instance, we have theories to describe what motivates people, the most effective leadership styles, the best way to resolve conflicts, and how people acquire power. In some cases, we have half a dozen or more separate theories that purport to explain and predict a given phenomenon. In such cases, is one right and the others wrong? No! They tend to reflect science at work—researchers testing previous theories, modifying them, and, when appropriate, proposing new models that may prove to have higher explanatory and predictive powers. Multiple theories attempting to explain common phenomena merely attest that OB is an active discipline, still growing and evolving.

Evaluating Research

As a potential consumer of behavioral research, you should follow the dictum of *caveat emptor*—let the buyer beware! In evaluating any research study, you need to ask three questions.[4]

Is it valid? Is the study actually measuring what it claims to be measuring? A number of psychological tests have been discarded by employers in recent years because they have not been found to be valid measures of the applicants' ability to do a given job successfully. But the validity issue is relevant to all research studies. So, if you find a study that links cohesive work teams with higher productivity, you want to know how each of these variables was measured and whether it is actually measuring what it is supposed to be measuring.

Is it reliable? Reliability refers to consistency of measurement. If you were to have your height measured every day with a wooden yardstick, you'd get highly reliable results. On the other hand, if you were measured each day by an elastic tape measure, there would probably be considerable disparity between your height measurements from one day to the next. Your height, of course, doesn't change from day to day. The variability is due to the unreliability of the measuring device. So if a company asked a group of its employees to complete a reliable job satisfaction questionnaire, and then repeat the questionnaire six months later, we'd expect the results to be very similar—provided nothing changed in the interim that might significantly affect employee satisfaction.

Is it generalizable? Are the results of the research study generalizable to groups of individuals other than those who participated in the original study? Be aware, for example, of the limitations that might exist in research that uses college students as subjects. Are the findings in such studies generalizable to full-time employees in real jobs? Similarly, how generalizable to the overall work population are the results from a study that assesses job stress among 10 nuclear power plant engineers in the hamlet of Mahone Bay, Nova Scotia?

Research Design

Doing research is an exercise in trade-offs. Richness of information typically comes with reduced generalizability. The more a researcher seeks to control for confounding variables, the less realistic his or her results are likely to be. High precision, generalizability, and control almost always translate into higher costs. When researchers make choices about whom they'll study, where their research will be done, the methods they'll use to collect data, and so on, they must make some concessions. Good research designs are not perfect, but they do carefully reflect the questions being addressed. Keep these facts in mind as we review the strengths and weaknesses of five popular research designs: case studies, field surveys, laboratory experiments, field experiments, and aggregate quantitative reviews.

CASE STUDY

You pick up a copy of Soichiro Honda's autobiography. In it he describes his impoverished childhood; his decisions to open a small garage, assemble motorcycles, and eventually build automobiles; and how this led to the creation of one of the largest and most successful corporations in the world. Or you're in a business class and the instructor distributes a 50-page handout covering two companies: Wal-Mart and Kmart. The handout details the two firms' histories; describes their corporate strategies, management philosophies, and merchandising plans; and includes copies of their recent balance sheets and income statements. The instructor asks the class members to read the handout, analyze the data, and determine why Wal-Mart has been so much more successful than Kmart in recent years.

Soichiro Honda's autobiography and the Wal-Mart and Kmart handouts are case studies. Drawn from real-life situations, case studies present an in-depth analysis of one setting. They are thorough descriptions, rich in details about an individual, a group, or an organization. The primary source of information in case studies is obtained through observation, occasionally backed up by interviews and a review of records and documents.

Case studies have their drawbacks. They're open to the perceptual bias and subjective interpretations of the observer. The reader of a case is captive to what the observer/case writer chooses to include and exclude. Cases also trade off generalizability for depth of information and richness of detail. Because it's always dangerous to generalize from a sample of one, case studies make it difficult to prove or reject a hypothesis. On the other hand, you can't ignore the in-depth analysis that cases often provide. They are an excellent device for initial exploratory research and for evaluating real-life problems in organizations.

FIELD SURVEY

A lengthy questionnaire was created to assess the use of ethics policies, formal ethics structures, formalized activities such as ethics training, and executive involvement in ethics programs among billion-dollar corporations. The public affairs or corporate communications office of all *Fortune* 500 industrial firms and 500 service corporations were contacted to get the name and address of the "officer most responsible for dealing with ethics and conduct issues" in each firm. The questionnaire, with a cover letter explaining the nature of the study, was mailed to these 1,000 officers. Of the total, 254 returned a completed questionnaire, for a response rate just above 25 percent. The results of the survey found, among other things, that 77 percent had formal codes of ethics and 54 percent had a single officer specifically assigned to deal with ethics and conduct issues.[5]

The preceding study illustrates a typical field survey. A sample of respondents (in this case, 1,000 corporate officers in the largest U.S. publicly held corporations) was selected to represent a larger group that was under examination (billion-dollar U.S. business firms). The respondents were then surveyed using a questionnaire or interviewed to collect data on particular characteristics (the content and structure of ethics programs and practices) of interest to the researchers. The standardization of response items allows for data to be easily quantified, analyzed, and summarized, and for the researchers to make inferences from the representative sample about the larger population.

The field survey provides economies for doing research. It's less costly to sample a population than to obtain data from every member of that population. (There are, for instance, more than 5,000 U.S. business firms with sales in excess of a billion dollars; and since some of these are privately held and don't release financial data to the public, they are excluded from the *Fortune* list). Moreover, as the ethics study illustrates, field surveys provide an efficient way to find out how people feel about issues or how they say they behave. These data can then be easily quantified. But the field survey has a number of potential weaknesses. First, mailed questionnaires rarely obtain 100 percent returns. Low response rates call into question whether conclusions based on respondents' answers are generalizable to non-respondents. Second, the format is better at tapping respondents' attitudes and perceptions than behaviors. Third, responses can suffer from social desirability; that is, people saying what they think the researcher wants to hear. Fourth, since field surveys are designed to focus on specific issues, they're a relatively poor means of acquiring depth of information. Finally, the quality of the generalizations is largely a factor of the population chosen. Responses from executives at *Fortune* 500 firms, for instance, tell us nothing about small- or medium-sized firms or not-for-profit organizations. In summary, even a well-designed field survey trades off depth of information for breadth, generalizability, and economic efficiencies.

LABORATORY EXPERIMENT

The following study is a classic example of the laboratory experiment. A researcher, Stanley Milgram, wondered how far individuals would go in following commands. If subjects were placed in the role of a teacher in a learning experiment and told by an experimenter to administer a shock to a learner each time that learner made a mistake, would the subjects follow the commands of the experimenter? Would their willingness to comply decrease as the intensity of the shock was increased?

To test these hypotheses, Milgram hired a set of subjects. Each was led to believe that the experiment was to investigate the effect of punishment on memory. Their job was to act as teachers and administer punishment whenever the learner made a mistake on the learning test.

Punishment was administered by an electric shock. The subject sat in front of a shock generator with 30 levels of shock—beginning at zero and progressing in 15-volt increments to a high of 450 volts. The demarcations of these positions ranged from "Slight Shock" at 15 volts to "Danger: Severe Shock" at 450 volts. To increase the realism of the experiment, the subjects received a sample shock of 45 volts and saw the learner—a pleasant, mild-mannered man about 50 years old—strapped into an "electric chair" in an adjacent room. Of course, the learner was an actor, and the electric shocks were phony, but the subjects didn't know this.

Taking his seat in front of the shock generator, the subject was directed to begin at the lowest shock level and to increase the shock intensity to the next level each time the learner made a mistake or failed to respond.

When the test began, the shock intensity rose rapidly because the learner made many errors. The subject got verbal feedback from the learner: At 75 volts, the learner began to grunt and moan; at 150 volts, he demanded to be released from the experiment; at 180 volts, he cried out that he could no longer stand the pain; and at 300 volts, he insisted that he be let out, yelled about his heart condition, screamed, and then failed to respond to further questions.

Most subjects protested and, fearful they might kill the learner if the increased shocks were to bring on a heart attack, insisted they could not go on with their job. Hesitations or protests by the subject were met by the experimenter's statement, "You have no choice, you must go on! Your job is to punish the learner's mistakes." Of course, the subjects did have a choice. All they had to do was stand up and walk out.

The majority of the subjects dissented. But dissension isn't synonymous with disobedience. Sixty-two percent of the subjects increased the shock level to the maximum of 450 volts. The average level of shock administered by the remaining 38 percent was nearly 370 volts.[6]

In a laboratory experiment such as that conducted by Milgram, an artificial environment is created by the researcher. Then the researcher manipulates an independent variable under controlled conditions. Finally, since all other things are held equal, the researcher is able to conclude that any change in the dependent variable is due to the manipulation or change imposed on the independent variable. Note that, because of the controlled conditions, the researcher is able to imply causation between the independent and dependent variables.

The laboratory experiment trades off realism and generalizability for precision and control. It provides a high degree of control over variables and precise measurement of those variables. But findings from laboratory studies are often difficult to generalize to the real world of work. This is because the artificial laboratory rarely duplicates the intricacies and nuances of real organizations. In addition, many laboratory experiments deal with phenomena that cannot be reproduced or applied to real-life situations.

FIELD EXPERIMENT

The following is an example of a field experiment. The management of a large company is interested in determining the impact that a four-day workweek would have on employee absenteeism. To be more specific, management wants to know if employees working four 10-hour days have lower absence rates than similar employees working the traditional five-day week of eight hours each day. Because the company is large, it has a number of manufacturing plants that employ essentially similar workforces. Two of these are chosen for the experiment, both located in the greater Cleveland area. Obviously, it would not be appropriate to compare two similar-sized plants if one is in rural Mississippi and the other is in urban Copenhagen because factors such as national culture, transportation, and weather might be more likely to explain any differences found than changes in the number of days worked per week.

In one plant, the experiment was put into place—workers began the four-day week. At the other plant, which became the control group, no changes were made in the employees' five-day week. Absence data were gathered from the company's records at both locations for a period of 18 months. This extended time period lessened the possibility that any results would be distorted by the mere novelty of changes being implemented in the experimental plant. After 18 months, management found that absenteeism had dropped by 40 percent at the experimental plant, and by only 6 percent in the control plant. Because of the design of this study, management believed that the larger drop in absences at the experimental plant was due to the introduction of the compressed workweek.

The field experiment is similar to the laboratory experiment, except it is conducted in a real organization. The natural setting is more realistic than the laboratory setting, and this enhances validity but hinders control. In addition, unless control groups are maintained, there can be a loss of control if extraneous forces intervene—for example, an employee strike, a major layoff, or a corporate restructuring. Maybe the greatest concern with field studies has to do with organizational selection bias. Not all organizations are going to allow outside researchers to come in and study their employees and operations. This is especially true of organizations that have serious problems. Therefore, since most published studies in OB are done by outside researchers, the selection bias might work toward the publication of studies conducted almost exclusively at successful and well-managed organizations.

Our general conclusion is that, of the four research designs we've discussed, the field experiment typically provides the most valid and generalizable findings and, except for its high cost, trades off the least to get the most.[7]

Aggregate Quantitative Reviews What's the overall effect of organizational behavior modification (OB Mod) on task performance? There have been a number of field experiments that have sought to throw light on this question. Unfortunately, the wide range of effects from these various studies makes it hard to generalize.

To try to reconcile these diverse findings, two researchers reviewed all the empirical studies they could find on the impact of OB Mod on task performance over a 20 year period.[8] After discarding reports that had inadequate information, had nonquantitative data, or didn't meet all conditions associated with principles of behavioral modification, the researchers narrowed their set to 19 studies that included data on 2,818 individuals. Using an aggregating technique called *meta-analysis*, the researchers were able to synthesize the studies quantitatively and to conclude that the average person's task performance will rise from the 50th percentile to the 67th percentile after an OB Mod intervention.

The OB Mod–task performance review done by these researchers illustrates the use of meta-analysis, a quantitative form of literature review that enables researchers to look at validity findings from a comprehensive set of individual studies, and then apply a formula to them to determine if they consistently produced similar results.[9] If results prove to be consistent, it allows researchers to conclude more confidently that validity is generalizable. Meta-analysis is a means for overcoming the potentially imprecise interpretations of qualitative reviews and to synthesize variations in quantitative studies. In addition, the technique enables researchers to identify potential moderating variables between an independent and a dependent variable.

In the past 25 years, there's been a surge in the popularity of this research method. Why? It appears to offer a more objective means for doing traditional literature reviews. Although the use of meta-analysis requires researchers to make a number of judgment calls, which can introduce a considerable amount of subjectivity into the process, there is no arguing that meta-analysis reviews have now become widespread in the OB literature.

Ethics in Research

Researchers are not always tactful or candid with subjects when they do their studies. For instance, questions in field surveys may be perceived as embarrassing by respondents or as an invasion of privacy. Also, researchers in laboratory studies have been known to deceive participants about the true purpose of their experiment "because they felt deception was necessary to get honest responses."[10]

The "learning experiments" conducted by Stanley Milgram, which were conducted more than 30 years ago, have been widely criticized by psychologists on ethical grounds. He lied to subjects, telling them his study was investigating learning, when, in fact, he was concerned with obedience. The shock machine he used was a fake. Even the "learner" was an accomplice of Milgram's who had been trained to act as if he were hurt and in pain. Yet ethical lapses continue. For instance, in 2001, a professor of organizational behavior at Columbia University sent out a common letter on university letterhead to 240 New York City restaurants in which he detailed how he had eaten at this restaurant with his wife in celebration of their wedding anniversary, how he had gotten food poisoning, and that he had spent the night in his bathroom throwing up.[11] The letter closed with: "Although it is not my intention to file any reports with the Better Business Bureau or the Department of Health, I want you to understand what I went through in anticipation that you will respond accordingly. I await your response." The fictitious letter was part of the professor's study to determine how restaurants responded to complaints. But it created culinary chaos among many of the restaurant owners, managers and chefs as they reviewed menus and produce deliveries for possibly spoiled food, and questioned kitchen workers about possible lapses. A follow-up letter of apology from the university for "an egregious error in judgment by a junior faculty member" did little to offset the distress it created for those affected.

Professional associations like the American Psychological Association, the American Sociological Association, and the Academy of Management have published formal guidelines for the conduct of research. Yet the ethical debate continues. On one side are those who argue that strict ethical controls can damage the scientific validity of an experiment and cripple future research. Deception, for example, is often necessary to avoid contaminating results. Moreover, proponents of minimizing ethical controls note that few subjects have been appreciably harmed by deceptive experiments. Even in Milgram's highly manipulative experiment, only 1.3 percent of the subjects reported negative feelings about their experience. The other side of this debate focuses on the rights of participants. Those favoring strict ethical controls argue that no procedure should ever be emotionally or physically distressing to subjects, and that, as professionals, researchers are obliged to be completely honest with their subjects and to protect the subjects' privacy at all costs.

Summary

The subject of organizational behavior is composed of a large number of theories that are research based. Research studies, when cumulatively integrated, become theories, and theories are proposed and followed by research studies designed to validate them. The concepts that make up OB, therefore, are only as valid as the research that supports them.

The topics and issues in this text are for the most part research-derived. They represent the result of systematic information gathering rather than merely hunch, intuition, or opinion. This doesn't mean, of course, that we have all the answers to OB issues. Many require far more corroborating evidence. The generalizability of others is limited by the research methods used. But new information is being created and published at an accelerated rate. To keep up with the latest findings, we strongly encourage you to regularly review the latest research in organizational behavior. The more academic work can be found in journals such as the *Academy of Management Journal, Academy of Management Review, Administrative Science Quarterly, Human Relations, Journal of Applied Psychology, Journal of Management,* *Journal of Organizational Behavior,* and *Leadership Quarterly.* For more practical interpretations of OB research findings, you may want to read the *Academy of Management Executive, California Management Review, Harvard Business Review, Organizational Dynamics,* and the *Sloan Management Review.*

Endnotes

1. J. A. Byrne, "Executive Sweat," *Forbes,* May 20, 1985, pp. 198–200.
2. See D. P. Schwab, *Research Methods for Organizational Behavior* (Mahwah, NJ: Lawrence Erlbaum Associates, 1999).
3. B. M. Staw and G. R. Oldham, "Reconsidering Our Dependent Variables: A Critique and Empirical Study," *Academy of Management Journal,* December 1978, pp. 539–59; and B. M. Staw, "Organizational Behavior: A Review and Reformulation of the Field's Outcome Variables," in M. R. Rosenzweig and L. W. Porter (eds.), *Annual Review of Psychology,* vol. 35 (Palo Alto, CA: Annual Reviews, 1984), pp. 627–66.
4. R. S. Blackburn, "Experimental Design in Organizational Settings," in J. W. Lorsch (ed.), *Handbook of Organizational Behavior* (Englewood Cliffs, NJ: Prentice Hall, 1987), pp. 127–28; and F. L. Schmidt, C. Viswesvaran, D. S. Ones, "Reliability Is Not Validity and Validity Is Not Reliability," *Personnel Psychology,* Winter 2000, pp. 901–12.
5. G. R. Weaver, L. K. Trevino, and P. L. Cochran, "Corporate Ethics Practices in the Mid-1990's: An Empirical Study of the Fortune 1000," *Journal of Business Ethics,* February 1999, pp. 283–94.
6. S. Milgram, *Obedience to Authority* (New York: Harper & Row, 1974). For a critique of this research, see T. Blass, "Understanding Behavior in the Milgram Obedience Experiment: The Role of Personality, Situations, and Their Interactions," *Journal of Personality and Social Psychology,* March 1991, pp. 398–413.
7. See, for example, W. N. Kaghan, A. L. Strauss, S. R. Barley, M. Y. Brannen, and R. J. Thomas, "The Practice and Uses of Field Research in the 21st Century Organization," *Journal of Management Inquiry,* March 1999, pp. 67–81.
8. A. D. Stajkovic and F. Luthans, "A Meta-Analysis of the Effects of Organizational Behavior Modification on Task Performance, 1975–1995," *Academy of Management Journal,* October 1997, pp. 1122–49.
9. See, for example, R. A. Guzzo, S. E. Jackson, and R. A. Katzell, "Meta-Analysis Analysis," in L. L. Cummings and B. M. Staw (eds.), *Research in Organizational Behavior,* vol. 9 (Greenwich, CT: JAI Press, 1987), pp. 407–42; K. Zakzanis, "The Reliability of Meta Analytic Review," *Psychological Reports,* August 1998, pp. 215–22; C. Ostroff and D. A. Harrison, "Meta-Analysis, Level of Analysis, and Best Estimates of Population Correlations: Cautions for Interpreting Meta-Analytic Results in Organizational Behavior," *Journal of Applied Psychology,* April 1999, pp. 260–70; and R. Rosenthal and M. R. DiMatteo, "Meta-Analysis: Recent Developments in Quantitative Methods for Literature Reviews," in S. T. Fiske, D. L. Schacter, and C. Zahn-Wacher (eds.), *Annual Review of Psychology,* vol. 52 (Palo Alto, CA: Annual Reviews, 2001), pp. 59–82.
10. For more on ethical issues in research, see T. L. Beauchamp, R. R. Faden, R. J. Wallace, Jr., and L. Walters (eds.), *Ethical Issues in Social Science Research* (Baltimore, MD: Johns Hopkins University Press, 1982); and D. Baumrind, "Research Using Intentional Deception," *American Psychologist,* February 1985, pp. 165–74.
11. J. Kifner, "Scholar Sets Off Gastronomic False Alarm," *New York Times,* September 8, 2001, p. A1.

I hear and I forget. I see and I remember. I do and I understand.
—Confucius

T his section on skill-building has been added to help readers apply and use OB concepts. The 16 skills selected were chosen because of their relevance to developing competence in interpersonal skills and their linkage to one or more of the topic areas in this book.

To maximize the learning of skills, we suggest combining text content and self-assessment feedback with the skill-building modules in this section. The self-assessments are available on the CD-ROM included with this book. Exhibit SB-1 provides a matrix indicating the relevant self-assessment and skill-module for Chapters 2 through 19 in your textbook.

For each of the 16 skills, we provide the following. (1) A brief interpretation of what your self-assessment results mean. (2) A review of basic skill concepts and specific behaviors associated with developing competence in the skill. (3) A short scenario designed to provide you with an opportunity to practice the behaviors associated with the skill. (4) Several reinforcement activities to give you additional opportunities to practice and learn the behaviors associated with the skill.

Exhibit SB-1   From Knowledge to Skills

Skill-Building Chapter/Topic	Self-Assessment	Module
2. Individual Behavior	Feedback Skills (#26)	Effective Disciplining
3. Values and Attitudes	Job Satisfaction (#11)	Changing Attitudes
4. Personality and Emotions	EI Score (#20)	Reading Emotions
5. Perception and Decisions	How Creative Am I? (#8)	Creative Problem-Solving
6/7. Motivation	Personal Planning (#22)	Setting Goals
8/9. Groups and Teams	Leading a Team (#30)	Creating Effective Teams
10. Communication	Listening Skills (#25)	Active Listening
11. Basic Leadership	Leadership Style (#27)	Choosing a Leadership Style
12. Contemporary Leadership	Trusting? (#29)	Developing Trust
13. Power and Politics	Power Orientation (#31)	Becoming Politically Adept
14. Conflict and Negotiation	Conflict Style (#34)	Negotiating
15. Organization Structure	Willingness to Delegate (#40)	Delegating Authority
16. Technology and Work Design	JCM (#37)	Designing Motivating Jobs
17. HR Policies and Practices	D-M Style (#17)	Selection Interviewing
18. Organizational Culture	Right Culture? (#42)	Reading an Organization's Culture
19. Organizational Change	Response to Change (#47)	Managing Resistance to Change

---

① EFFECTIVE DISCIPLINING

Self-Assessment Interpretation

Complete the self-assessment (#26) on feedback skills. This instrument assesses how good you are at providing feedback to others.

Strong feedback skills are an important part of disciplinary actions. If your strength/weakness ratio was 6/2 or higher, you already know a considerable amount about behaviors associated with effective disciplining.

Skills Concepts and Behaviors

If an employee's performance regularly isn't up to par or if an employee consistently ignores the organization's standards and regulations, a manager may have to use discipline as a way to control behavior. What exactly is *discipline*? It's actions taken by a manager to enforce the organization's expectations, standards, and rules. The most common types of discipline problems managers have to deal with include attendance (absenteeism, tardiness, abuse of sick leave), on-the-job behaviors (failure to meet performance goals, disobedience, failure to use safety devices, alcohol or drug abuse), and dishonesty (theft, lying to managers).

The essence of effective disciplining can be summarized by the following eight behaviors.[1]

1. *Respond immediately.* The more quickly a disciplinary action follows an offense, the more likely it is that the employee will associate the discipline with the offense rather than with you as the dispenser of the discipline. It's best to begin the disciplinary process as soon as possible after you notice a violation.

2. *Provide a warning.* You have an obligation to warn an employee before initiating disciplinary action. This means that the employee must be aware of the organization's rules and accept its standards of behavior. Disciplinary action is more likely to be interpreted by employees as fair when they have received a clear warning that a given violation will lead to discipline and when they know what that discipline will be.

3. *State the problem specifically.* Give the date, time, place, individuals involved, and any mitigating circumstances surrounding the violation. Be sure to define the violation in exact terms instead of just reciting company regulations or terms from a union contract. It's not the violation of the rules per se about which you want to convey concern. It's the effect that the rule violation has on the work unit's performance. Explain why the behavior can't be continued by showing how it specifically affects the employee's job performance, the unit's effectiveness, and the employee's colleagues.

4. *Allow the employee to explain his or her position.* Regardless of what facts you have uncovered, due process demands that you give the employee the opportunity to explain his or her position. From the employee's perspective, what happened? Why did it happen? What was his or her perception of the rules, regulations, and circumstances?

5. *Keep the discussion impersonal.* Penalties should be connected with a given violation, not with the personality of the individual violator. That is, discipline should be directed at what the employee has done, not at the employee.

6. *Be consistent.* Fair treatment of employees demands that disciplinary action be consistent. If you enforce rule violations in an inconsistent manner, the rules will lose their impact, morale will decline, and employees will likely question your competence. Consistency, however, need not result in treating everyone exactly alike; doing that would ignore mitigating circumstances. It's reasonable to modify the severity of penalties to reflect the employee's past history, job performance record, and the like. But the responsibility is yours to clearly justify disciplinary actions that might appear inconsistent to employees.

7. *Take progressive action.* Choose a punishment that's appropriate to the crime. Penalties should get progressively stronger if, or when, an offense is repeated. Typically, progressive disciplinary action begins with a verbal warning and then proceeds through a written reprimand, suspension, a demotion or pay cut, and finally, in the most serious cases, dismissal.

8. *Obtain agreement on change.* Disciplining should include guidance and direction for correcting the problem. Let the employee state what he or she plans to do in the future to ensure that the violation won't be repeated.

Practicing the Skill

Read through the following scenario, then practice your skill in a role-play conducted either in front of the class or in groups of two.

You're a team leader in the customer services department at Mountain View Microbrewery. Sandy is the newest member of your 10-person team, having been there only six weeks. Sandy came to Mountain View with good recommendations from his/her previous job as a customer support representative at a car dealership. However, not long after joining your team, Sandy was late in issuing an important purchasing order. When you talked to Sandy about it, you were told it was "lost." But you discovered it in Sandy's in-box, where it had been properly placed. Then, just last week, Sandy failed to make an immediate return call to an unhappy customer who could easily have been satisfied at that point. Instead, the customer worked himself into a rage and vented his unhappiness in a letter to the company's CEO. The latest incident with Sandy came up just yesterday. As part of your company's quality-improvement program, your team members prepare periodic reports on the service they provide to each customer and turn these reports over to an upper-management team who evaluates them. Sandy didn't meet the deadline for getting his/her report into this evaluation group and you received a call from one of the team members wanting to know where this report was. Because Sandy is still on probation for another six weeks, it appears that the time has come for the two of you to talk about his/her failure to meet expected work-performance goals.

Reinforcement Activities

1. Talk with a manager at three different organizations. Ask each what guidance they've received from their organizations in disciplining employees. Have them describe specific employee discipline problems they've faced and how they've handled them.

2. Interview three of your current or past instructors. Ask them about their approaches to discipline. How do they handle late papers, cheating, excessive absenteeism, or other disciplinary problems?

2 CHANGING ATTITUDES

Self-Assessment Interpretation

Complete the self-assessment (#11) on job satisfaction. This instrument is designed to determine your general attitude about your job. Use the results to reflect on your attitudes toward your job and what, if anything, could be done to change your attitudes. This self-assessment will prepare you for thinking about how you might go about changing unfavorable attitudes that your employees might have.

Skill Concepts and Behaviors

Can you change unfavorable employee attitudes? Sometimes! It depends on who you are, the strength of the employee's attitude, the magnitude of the change, and the technique you choose to try to change the attitude.[2]

Employees are most likely to respond to change efforts made by someone who is liked, credible, and convincing. If people like you, they're more apt to identify and adopt your message. Credibility implies trust, expertise, and objectivity. So you're more likely to change an employee's attitude if that employee sees you as believable, knowledgeable about what you're talking about, and unbiased in your presentation. Finally, successful attitude change is enhanced when you present your arguments clearly and persuasively.

It's easier to change an employee's attitude if he or she isn't strongly committed to it. Conversely, the stronger the belief about the attitude, the harder it is to change it. In addition, attitudes that have been expressed publicly are more difficult to change because it requires one to admit he or she has made a mistake.

It's easier to change attitudes when that change isn't very significant. To get an employee to accept a new attitude that varies greatly from his or her current position requires more effort. It may also threaten other deeply held attitudes and create increased dissonance.

One of the most widely used techniques for bringing about attitude change is oral persuasion. The following summarizes actions you can take to be more persuasive:

1. *Use a positive, tactful tone.* Assume the person you're trying to persuade is intelligent and mature. Don't talk down to that person. Be respectful, direct, sincere, and tactful.

2. *Present strong evidence to support your position.* You need to explain *why* what you want is important. Merely saying that a request is important or urgent is not enough.

3. *Tailor your argument to the listener.* Effective persuasion demands flexibility. You have to select your argument for your specific listener. To whom are you talking? What are his or her goals, needs, interests, fears, and aspirations? What are his or her preconceived views on this subject?

4. *Use logic.* While a logical, reasoned argument is not guaranteed to persuade the subject, if you lack facts and reasons to support your argument, your persuasiveness will almost certainly be undermined.

5. *Use emotional appeals.* Presenting clear, rational, and objective evidence in support of your view is often not enough. You should also appeal to a

person's emotions. Try to reach inside the subject and understand his or her loves, hates, fears, and frustrations. Then use that information to mold what you say and how you say it.

Practicing the Skill

Form into groups of two. Person A is to choose any topic that he or she feels strongly about and state his or her position on the topic in 30 words or less. Person B's task will be to attempt to change Person A's attitude on this topic. Person B will have 10 minutes to make his or her case. When the time is up, the roles are reversed. Person B picks the topic and Person A has 10 minutes to try to change Person B's attitude.

Potential topics (you can choose *either* side of a topic) include: politics, the economy, world events, social practices, or specific management issues such as organizations should require all employees to undergo regular drug testing, there is no such thing as organizational loyalty anymore, the customer is always right, and layoffs are an indication of management failures

Reinforcement Activities

1. Try to convince a friend or relative to go with you to see a movie or play that you know the subject doesn't want to see.
2. Try to convince a friend or relative to try a different brand of toothpaste.

 # READING EMOTIONS

Self-Assessment Interpretation

Complete the self-assessment (#20) on emotional intelligence. This instrument will provide you insights into your EI score. The higher your EI score, the better you are at accurately reading others' emotions and feelings.

Skill Concepts and Behaviors

Understanding another person's felt emotions is a very difficult task. But we can learn to read others' display emotions. We do this by focusing on verbal, nonverbal, and paralinguistic cues.[3]

1. *Ask about emotions.* The easiest way to find out what someone is feeling is to ask them. Saying something as simple as "Are you OK? What's the problem?" can frequently provide you with the information to assess an individual's emotional state. But relying on a verbal response has two drawbacks. First, almost all of us conceal our emotions to some extent for privacy and to reflect social expectations. So we might be unwilling to share our true feelings. Second, even if we want to convey our feelings verbally, we may be unable to do so. Some people have difficulty understanding their own emotions and, hence, are unable to express them verbally. So, at best, verbal responses provide only partial information.
2. *Look for nonverbal cues.* You're talking with a co-worker. Does the fact that his back is rigid, his teeth clenched, and his facial muscles tight

tell you something about his emotional state? It probably should. Facial expressions, gestures, body movements, and physical distance are nonverbal cues that can provide additional insights into what a person is feeling. Facial expressions, for instance, are a window into a person's feelings. Notice differences in facial features: the height of the cheeks, the raising or lowering of the brow, the turn of the mouth, the positioning of the lips, and the configuration of muscles around the eyes. Even something as subtle as the distance at which someone chooses to position him or herself from you can convey their feelings, or lack, of intimacy, aggressiveness, repugnance, or withdrawal.
3. *Look for how things are said.* As Janet and I talked, I noticed a sharp change in the tone of her voice and the speed at which she spoke. I was tapping into the third source of information on a person's emotions—*paralanguage*. This is communication that goes beyond the specific spoken words. It includes pitch, amplitude, rate, and voice quality of speech. Paralanguage reminds us that people convey their feelings not only in *what* they say, but also in *how* they say it.

Practicing the Skill

Part A. Form groups of two. Each person is to spend a couple of minutes thinking of a time in the past when he or she was emotional about something. Examples might include being upset with a parent, sibling, or friend; being excited or disappointed about an academic or athletic achievement; being angry with someone over an insult or slight; being disgusted by something someone has said or done; or being happy because of something good that happened.

Part B. Now you'll conduct two role-plays. Each will be an interview. In the first, one person will play the interviewer and the other will play the job applicant. The job is for a summer management internship with a large retail chain. Each role play will last no longer than 10 minutes. The interviewer is to conduct a normal job interview except you are to continually rethink the emotional episode you envisioned in Part A. Try hard to convey this emotion while, at the same time, being professional in interviewing the job applicant.

Part C. Now reverse positions for the second role-play. The interviewer becomes the job applicant and vice versa. The new interviewer will conduct a nor-

mal job interview except that he or she will continually rethink the emotional episode chosen in Part A.

Part D. Spend 10 minutes deconstructing the interview, with specific attention focused on what emotion(s) you think the other was conveying? What cues did you pick up? How accurate were you in reading those cues?

Reinforcement Activities

1. Rent a video of an emotionally-laden film such as *Death of a Salesman* or *Twelve Angry Men*. Carefully watch the actors for clues to the emotions they are exhibiting. Try to determine the various emotions projected and explain how you arrived at your conclusion.
2. If you're currently working, spend a day specifically looking for emotional cues in interactions with colleagues. Did this improve communication?

 # 4 CREATIVE PROBLEM-SOLVING

Self-Assessment Interpretation

Complete the self-assessment (#8) that evaluates your creativity. This instrument will determine the degree to which you display characteristics associated with a creative personality. The following will help you to tap into more of your creative talents.

Skill Concepts and Behaviors

The uniqueness and variety of problems that managers face demand that they be able to solve problems creatively. Creativity is partly a frame of mind. You need to expand your mind's capabilities—that is, open yourself up to new ideas. Every individual has the ability to improve his or her creativity, but many people simply don't try to develop that ability.

You can be more effective at solving problems creatively if you use the following 10 suggestions.[4]

1. *Think of yourself as creative.* Research shows that if you think you can't be creative, you won't be. Believing in your ability to be creative is the first step in becoming more creative.
2. *Pay attention to your intuition.* Every individual has a subconscious mind that works well. Sometimes answers will come to you when you least expect them. Listen to that "inner voice." In fact, most creative people will keep a notepad

near their bed and write down ideas when the thoughts come to them.
3. *Move away from your comfort zone.* Every individual has a comfort zone in which certainty exists. But creativity and the known often do not mix. To be creative, you need to move away from the status quo and focus your mind on something new.
4. *Determine what you want to do.* This includes such things as taking time to understand a problem before beginning to try to resolve it, getting all the facts in mind, and trying to identify the most important facts.
5. *Think outside the box.* Use analogies whenever possible (for example, could you approach your problem like a fish out of water and look at what the fish does to cope? Or can you use the things you have to do to find your way when it's foggy to help you solve your problem?). Use different problem-solving strategies such as verbal, visual, mathematical, or theatrical. Look at your problem from a different perspective or ask yourself what someone else, like your grandmother, might do if faced with the same situation.
6. *Look for ways to do things better.* This may involve trying consciously to be original, not worrying about looking foolish, keeping an

open mind, being alert to odd or puzzling facts, thinking of unconventional ways to use objects and the environment, discarding usual or habitual ways of doing things, and striving for objectivity by being as critical of your own ideas as you would those of someone else.

7. *Find several right answers.* Being creative means continuing to look for other solutions even when you think you have solved the problem. A better, more creative solution just might be found.

8. *Believe in finding a workable solution.* Like believing in yourself, you also need to believe in your ideas. If you don't think you can find a solution, you probably won't.

9. *Brainstorm with others.* Creativity is not an isolated activity. Bouncing ideas off of others creates a synergistic effect.

10. *Turn creative ideas into action.* Coming up with creative ideas is only part of the process. Once the ideas are generated, they must be implemented. Keeping great ideas in your mind, or on papers that no one will read, does little to expand your creative abilities.

Practicing the Skill

Every time the phone rings, your stomach clenches and your palms start to sweat. And it's no wonder! As sales manager for Brinkers, a machine tool parts manufacturer, you're besieged by calls from customers who are upset about late deliveries. Your boss, Carter Hererra, acts as both production manager and sched-

uler. Every time your sales representatives negotiate a sale, it's up to Carter to determine whether production can actually meet the delivery date the customer specifies. And Carter invariably says, "No problem." The good thing about this is that you make a lot of initial sales. The bad news is that production hardly ever meets the shipment dates that Carter authorizes. And he doesn't seem to be all that concerned about the aftermath of late deliveries. He says, "Our customers know they're getting outstanding quality at a great price. Just let them try to match that anywhere. It can't be done. So even if they have to wait a couple of extra days or weeks, they're still getting the best deal they can." Somehow the customers don't see it that way. And they let you know about their unhappiness. Then it's up to you to try to soothe the relationship. You know this problem has to be taken care of, but what possible solutions are there? After all, how are you going to keep from making your manager mad or making the customers mad?

Reinforcement Activities

1. Take 20 minutes to list as many medical or health-care-related jobs as you can that begin with the letter *r* (for instance, radiologist, registered nurse). If you run out of listings before time is up, it's OK to quit early. But, try to be as creative as you can.

2. List on a piece of paper some common terms that apply to both *water* and *finance*. How many were you able to come up with?

---

⑤ SETTING GOALS

Self-Assessment Interpretation

Complete the self-assessment (#22) on personal planning. This instrument is designed to get you to think about goal setting as it relates to your school and personal life. The better you are at your personal planning and goal setting, the better qualified you'll be to help others.

Skill Concepts and Behaviors

Employees should have a clear understanding of what they're attempting to accomplish. Managers have the responsibility to see that this is done by helping employees set work goals.

You can be more effective at setting goals if you use the following eight suggestions.[5]

1. *Identify an employee's key job tasks.* Goal setting begins by defining what it is that you want your employees to accomplish. The best source for this information is each employee's job description.

2. *Establish specific and challenging goals for each key task.* Identify the level of performance expected of each employee. Specify the target toward which the employee is working.

3. *Specify the deadlines for each goal.* Putting deadlines on each goal reduces ambiguity. Deadlines, however, should not be set arbitrarily. Rather,

they need to be realistic given the tasks to be completed.

4. *Allow the employee to participate actively.* When employees participate in goal setting, they're more likely to accept the goals. However, it must be sincere participation. That is, employees must perceive that you are truly seeking their input, not just going through the motions.

5. *Prioritize goals.* When you give someone more than one goal, it's important to rank the goals in order of importance. The purpose of prioritizing is to encourage the employee to take action and expend effort on each goal in proportion to its importance.

6. *Rate goals for difficulty and importance.* Goal setting should not encourage people to choose easy goals. Instead, goals should be rated for their difficulty and importance. When goals are rated, individuals can be given credit for trying difficult goals, even if they don't fully achieve them.

7. *Build in feedback mechanisms to assess goal progress.* Feedback lets employees know whether their level of effort is sufficient to attain the goal. Feedback should be both self-generated and supervisor-generated. Feedback should also be frequent and recurring.

8. *Link rewards to goal attainment.* It's natural for employees to ask, "What's in it for me?" Linking rewards to the achievement of goals will help answer that question.

Practicing the Skill

You worked your way through college while holding down a part-time job bagging groceries at Food Town supermarket chain. You liked working in the food industry, and when you graduated, you accepted a position with Food Town as a management trainee. Three years have passed and you've gained experience in the grocery store industry and in operating a large supermarket. Several months ago, you received a promotion to store manager at one of the chain's locations. One of the things you've liked about Food Town is that it gives store managers a great deal of autonomy in running their stores. The company provides very general guidelines to its managers. Top management is concerned with the bottom line; for the most part, how you get there is up to you. Now that you're finally a store manager, you want to establish an MBO-type program in your store. You like the idea that everyone should have clear goals to work toward and then be evaluated against those goals.

Your store employs 70 people, although except for the managers, most work only 20 to 30 hours per week. You have six people reporting to you: an assistant manager; a week-end manager; and grocery, produce, meat, and bakery managers. The only highly skilled jobs belong to the butchers who have strict training and regulatory guidelines. Other less skilled jobs include cashier, shelf stocker, maintenance worker, and grocery bagger.

Specifically describe how you would go about setting goals in your new position. Include examples of goals for the jobs of butcher, cashier, and bakery manager.

Reinforcement Activities

1. Set personal and academic goals you want to achieve by the end of this college term. Prioritize and rate them for difficulty.

2. Where do you want to be in five years? Do you have specific five-year goals? Establish three goals you want to achieve in five years. Make sure these goals are specific, challenging, and measurable.

 # CREATING EFFECTIVE TEAMS

Self-Assessment Interpretation

Complete the self-assessment (#30) on leading a team. This instrument evaluates how well you diagnose team development and manage the various stages of that development. The higher your score, the better you are at creating effective teams.

Skill Concepts and Behaviors

Managers and team leaders need to be able to create effective teams. You can increase the effectiveness of your teams if you use the following nine behaviors.[6]

1. *Establish a common purpose.* An effective team needs a common purpose to which all members aspire. This purpose is a vision. It's broader than any specific goals. This common purpose provides direction, momentum, and commitment for team members.

2. *Assess team strengths and weaknesses.* Team members will have different strengths and

weaknesses. Knowing these strengths and weaknesses can help the team leader build on the strengths and compensate for the weaknesses.

3. *Develop specific individual goals.* Specific individual goals help lead team members to achieve higher performance. In addition, specific goals facilitate clear communication and help maintain the focus on getting results.

4. *Get agreement on a common approach for achieving goals.* Goals are the ends a team strives to attain. Defining and agreeing on a common approach ensures that the team is unified on the *means* for achieving those ends.

5. *Encourage acceptance of responsibility for both individual and team performance.* Successful teams make members individually and jointly accountable for the team's purpose, goals, and approach. Members understand what they are individually responsible for and what they are jointly responsible for.

6. *Build mutual trust among members.* When there is *trust,* team members believe in the integrity, character, and ability of each other. When trust is lacking, members are unable to depend on each other. Teams that lack trust tend to be short-lived.

7. *Maintain an appropriate mix of team member skills and personalities.* Team members come to the team with different skills and personalities. To perform effectively, teams need three types of skills. They need people with technical expertise, people with problem-solving and decision-making skills, and people with good interpersonal skills.

8. *Provide needed training and resources.* Team leaders need to make sure that their teams have both the training and the resources they need to accomplish their goals.

9. *Create opportunities for small achievements.* Building an effective team takes time. Team members have to learn to think and work as a team. New teams can't be expected to hit home runs every time they come to bat, especially at the beginning. Instead, team members should be encouraged to try for small achievements initially.

Practicing the Skill

You're the leader of a five-member project team that's been assigned the task of moving your engineering firm into the booming area of high-speed intercity rail construction. You and your team members have been researching the field, identifying specific business opportunities, negotiating alliances with equipment vendors, and evaluating high-speed rail experts and consultants from around the world. Throughout the process, Tonya, a highly qualified and respected engineer, has challenged a number of things you've said during team meetings and in the workplace. For example, at a meeting two weeks ago, you presented the team with a list of 10 possible high-speed rail projects and started evaluating your organization's ability to compete for them. Tonya contradicted virtually all your comments, questioned your statistics, and was quite pessimistic about the possibility of getting contracts on these projects. After this latest display of displeasure, two other group members, Bryan and Maggie, came to you and complained that Tonya's actions were damaging the team's effectiveness. You originally put Tonya on the team for her unique expertise and insight. You'd like to find a way to reach her and get the team on the right track to its fullest potential.

Reinforcement Activities

1. Interview three managers at different organizations. Ask them about their experiences in managing teams. Have each describe teams that they thought were effective and why they succeeded. Have each also describe teams that they thought were ineffective and the reasons that might have caused this.

2. Contrast a team in which you have been in which members trusted each other with another team in which members lacked trust with each other. How did these conditions develop? What were the consequences in terms of interaction patterns and performance?

7 ACTIVE LISTENING

Self-Assessment Interpretation

Complete the self-assessment (#25) on listening skills. The higher your score, the better listener you are.

Skill Concepts and Behaviors

Too many people take listening skills for granted. They confuse hearing with listening. Hearing is merely picking up sound vibrations. Listening is making sense out of what we hear; and it requires paying attention, interpreting, and remembering. Active listening is hard work and requires you to "get inside" the speaker's head in order to understand the communication from his or her point of view.

Eight specific behaviors are associated with active listening. You can be more effective at active listening if you use these behaviors.[7]

1. *Make eye contact.* We may listen with our ears, but others tend to judge whether we're really listening by looking at our eyes.

2. *Exhibit affirmative nods and appropriate facial expressions.* The effective active listener shows interest in what's being said through nonverbal signals.

3. *Avoid distracting actions or gestures.* When listening, don't look at your watch, shuffle papers, play with your pencil, or engage in similar distractions. They make the speaker feel that you're bored or uninterested.

4. *Ask questions.* The critical listener analyzes what he or she hears and asks questions. This behavior provides clarification, ensures understanding, and assures the speaker that you're really listening.

5. *Paraphrase.* Restate *in your own words* what the speaker has said. The effective active listener uses phrases such as "What I hear you saying is. . . ." or "Do you mean. . . ?" Paraphrasing is an excellent control device to check whether or not you're listening carefully and is also a control for accuracy of understanding.

6. *Avoid interrupting the speaker.* Let the speaker complete his or her thoughts before you try to respond. Don't try to second-guess where the speaker's thoughts are going.

7. *Don't overtalk.* Most of us would rather speak our own ideas than listen to what others say.

Although talking might be more fun and silence might be uncomfortable, you can't talk and listen at the same time. The good active listener recognizes this fact and doesn't overtalk.

8. *Make smooth transitions between the roles of speaker and listener.* In most work situations, you're continually shifting back and forth between the roles of speaker and listener. The effective active listener makes transitions smoothly from speaker to listener and back to speaker.

Practicing the Skill

Break into groups of two. This exercise is a debate. Person A can choose any contemporary issue. Some examples: business ethics, value of unions, stiffer college grading policies, gun control, money as a motivator. Person B then selects a position on this issue. Person A must automatically take the counterposition. The debate is to proceed for 8–10 minutes, with only one catch. Before each speaks, he or she must first summarize, in his or her own words and without notes, what the other has said. If the summary doesn't satisfy the speaker, it must be corrected until it does.

Reinforcement Activities

1. In another class—preferably one with a lecture format—practice active listening. Ask questions, paraphrase, exhibit affirming nonverbal behaviors. Then ask yourself: Was this harder for me than a normal lecture? Did it affect my note taking? Did I ask more questions? Did it improve my understanding of the lecture's content? What was the instructor's response?

2. Spend an entire day fighting your urge to talk. Listen as carefully as you can to everyone you talk to and respond as appropriately as possible to understand, not to make your own point. What, if anything, did you learn from this exercise?

8 CHOOSING AN EFFECTIVE LEADERSHIP STYLE

Self-Assessment Interpretation

Complete the self-assessment (#27) on leadership style. This instrument is designed to tap the degree to which you are task- or people-oriented. These results suggest your preferential style. But effective leadership depends on properly matching up leadership style with a situation that is congruent. By knowing your leadership tendency, you can put yourself into situations that will increase your likelihood for success.

Skill Concepts and Behaviors

Simply put, leadership style can be categorized as task- or people-oriented. Neither one is right for all situations. Although there are a number of situational variables that influence the choice of an effective leadership style, four variables seem most relevant:

1. *Task structure.* Structured tasks have procedures and rules that minimize ambiguity. The

more structured a job is, the less need there is for a leader to provide task structure.

2. *Level of stress.* Situations differ in terms of time and performance stress. High-stress situations favor leaders with experience. Low stress favors a leader's intelligence.

3. *Level of group support.* Members of close-knit and supportive groups help each other out. They can provide both task support and relationship support. So supportive groups make fewer demands on a leader.

4. *Follower characteristics.* Personal characteristics of followers—such as experience, ability, and motivation—influence which leadership style will be most effective. Employees with extensive experience, strong abilities, and high motivation don't require much task behavior. They will be more effective with a people-oriented style. Conversely, employees with little experience, marginal abilities, and low motivation will perform better when leaders exhibit task-oriented behavior.

Practicing the Skill

You are a manufacturing manager in a large electronics plant.[8] The company's management is always searching for ways to increase efficiency. They recently installed new machines and set up a new simplified work system, but to the surprise of everyone—including you—the expected increase in production was not realized. In fact, production has begun to drop, quality has fallen off, and the number of employee resignations has risen.

You don't think that there is anything wrong with the machines. You have had reports from other companies that are using them, and they confirm your opinion. You have also had representatives from the firm that built the machines go over them, and they report that the machines are operating at peak efficiency.

You know that some aspect of the new work system must be responsible for the change, but you are getting no help from your immediate team members—four first-line supervisors who report to you and who are each in charge of a section—or your supply manager. The drop in production has been variously attributed to poor training of the operators, lack of an adequate system of financial incentives, and poor morale. All of the individuals involved have deep feelings about this issue. Your team doesn't agree with you or with one another.

This morning you received a phone call from your division manager. He had just received your production figures for the past six months and was calling to express his concern. He indicated that the problem was yours to solve in any way that you think best but that he would like to know within a week what steps you plan to take.

You share your division manager's concern with the falling productivity and know that your employees are also concerned. Using your knowledge of leadership concepts, which leadership style would you choose? And why?

Reinforcement Activities

1. Think of a group or team to which you currently belong or of which you have been a part. What type of leadership style did the leader of this group appear to exhibit? Give some specific examples of the types of leadership behaviors he or she used. Evaluate the leadership style. Was it appropriate for the group? Why or why not? What would you have done differently? Why?

2. Observe two sports team (either college or professional—one that you consider successful and the other unsuccessful). What leadership styles appear to be used in these team situations? Give some specific examples of the types of leadership behaviors you observe. How would you evaluate the leadership style? Was it appropriate for the team? Why or why not? To what degree do you think leadership style influenced the team's outcomes?

9 DEVELOPING TRUST

Self-Assessment Interpretation

Complete the self-assessment (#29) on whether others see you as trusting. The higher your score, the more you're perceived as a person who can be trusted.

Skill Concepts and Behaviors

Trust plays an important role in any manager's relationships with his or her employees. Given the importance of trust, today's managers should actively seek to develop it within their work group.

You can be more effective at developing trust among your employees if you follow these eight suggestions.[9]

1. *Practice openness.* Mistrust comes as much from what people don't know as from what they do know. Openness leads to confidence and trust. So keep people informed, make the criteria on how decisions are made overtly clear, explain the rationale for your decisions, be candid about problems, and fully disclose relevant information.

2. *Be fair.* Before making decisions or taking actions, consider how others will perceive them in terms of objectivity and fairness. Give credit where credit is due, be objective and impartial in performance appraisals, and pay attention to equity perceptions in reward distributions.

3. *Speak your feelings.* Managers who convey only hard facts come across as cold and distant. If you share your feelings, others will see you as real and human. They will know who you are and their respect for you will increase.

4. *Tell the truth.* Being trustworthy means being credible. If honesty is critical to credibility, then you must be perceived as someone who tells the truth. Employees are more tolerant of hearing something "they don't want to hear" than finding out that their manager lied to them.

5. *Show consistency.* People want predictability. Mistrust comes from not knowing what to expect. Take the time to think about your values and beliefs. Then let them consistently guide your decisions. When you know your central purpose, your actions will follow accordingly, and you will project a consistency that earns trust.

6. *Fulfill your promises.* Trust requires that people believe that you are dependable. So you need to ensure that you keep your word and commitments. Promises made must be promises kept.

7. *Maintain confidences.* You trust people who are discreet and on whom you can rely. So if people make themselves vulnerable by telling you something in confidence, they need to feel assured that you won't discuss it with others or betray that confidence. If people perceive you as someone who leaks personal confidences or someone who can't be depended on, you won't be perceived as trustworthy.

8. *Demonstrate competence.* Develop the admiration and respect of others by demonstrating technical and professional ability. Pay particular attention to developing and displaying your communication, negotiation, and other interpersonal skills.

Practicing the Skill

You recently graduated from college with your degree in business administration. You've spent the past two summers working at Connecticut Mutual Insurance (CMI), filling in as an intern on a number of different jobs while employees took their vacations. You have received and accepted an offer to join CMI full time as supervisor of the policy renewal department.

CMI is a large insurance company. In the headquarters office alone, where you'll be working, there are more than 1,500 employees. The company believes strongly in the personal development of its employees. This translates into a philosophy, emanating from the top executive offices, of trust and respect for all CMI employees. The company is also regularly atop most lists of "best companies to work for," largely due to its progressive work/life programs and strong commitment to minimizing layoffs.

In your new job, you'll direct the activities of 18 policy-renewal clerks. Their jobs require little training and are highly routine. A clerk's responsibility is to ensure that renewal notices are sent on current policies, to tabulate any changes in premiums, to advise the sales division if a policy is to be canceled as a result of nonresponse to renewal notices, and to answer questions and solve problems related to renewals.

The people in your work group range in age from 19 to 62, with a median age of 25. For the most part they are high school graduates with little prior working experience. They earn between $1,850 and $2,400 a month. You will be replacing a long-time CMI employee, Jan Allison. Jan is retiring after 37 years with CMI, the past 14 spent as a policy-renewal supervisor. Because you spent a few weeks in Jan's group last summer, you're familiar with Jan's style and are acquainted with most of the department members. But people don't know you very well and are suspicious of the fact that you're fresh out of college and have little experience in the department. And the reality is that you got this job because management wanted someone with a college degree to oversee the department. Your most vocal critic is Lillian Lantz. Lillian is well into her 50s, has been a policy renewal clerk for over a dozen years, and—as the "grand old lady" of the department—carries a lot of weight with group members. You know that it'll be very hard to lead this department without Lillian's support and confidence.

Identify specific actions you will take to win the trust and support of Lillian and the rest of the department.

Reinforcement Activities

1. Keep a one-week log describing ways that your daily decisions and actions encouraged people to trust you or to not trust you. What things did you do that led to trust? What things did you do that may have led to distrust? How might you have changed your behavior so that the situations of distrust could have been situations of trust?

2. Review recent issues of a business periodical (such as *Business Week, Fortune, Forbes, Fast Company, Industry Week,* or the *Wall Street Journal*) for articles in which trust (or lack of trust) may have played a role. Find two articles and describe the situation. Explain how the person(s) involved might have used skills at developing trust to handle the situation.

10 BECOMING POLITICALLY ADEPT

Self-Assessment Interpretation

Complete the self-assessment (#31) on power orientation. This instrument is designed to compute your Machiavellian score. The higher your score, the more likely you are to be manipulative and persuasive. A high Machiavellian score also indicates a strong willingness to engage in political behaviors.

Skill Concepts and Behaviors

Forget, for a moment, the ethics of politicking and any negative impressions you might have of people who engage in organizational politics. If you want to be more politically adept in your organization, follow these eight suggestions:[10]

1. *Frame arguments in terms of organizational goals.* Effective politicking requires camouflaging your self-interest. No matter that your objective is self-serving; all the arguments you marshal in support of it must be framed in terms of the benefits that will accrue to the organization. People whose actions appear to blatantly further their own interests at the expense of the organization are almost universally denounced, are likely to lose influence, and often suffer the ultimate penalty of being expelled from the organization.

2. *Develop the right image.* If you know your organization's culture, you understand what the organization wants and values from its employee—in terms of dress, associates to cultivate and those to avoid, whether to appear to be a risk taker or risk-aversive, the preferred leadership style, the importance placed on getting along well with others, and so forth. Then you are equipped to project the appropriate image. Because the assessment of your performance isn't always a fully objective process, you need to pay attention to style as well as substance.

3. *Gain control of organizational resources.* The control of organizational resources that are scarce and important is a source of power. Knowledge and expertise are particularly effective resources to control. They make you more valuable to the organization and, therefore, more likely to gain security, advancement, and a receptive audience for your ideas.

4. *Make yourself appear indispensable.* Because we're dealing with appearances rather than objective facts, you can enhance your power by appearing to be indispensable. You don't really have *to be* indispensable as long as key people in the organization believe that you are. If the organization's prime decision makers believe there is no ready substitute for what you are giving the organization, they are likely to go to great lengths to ensure that your desires are satisfied.

5. *Be visible.* If you have a job that brings your accomplishments to the attention of others, that's great. However, if you don't have such a job, you'll want to find ways to let others in the organization know what you're doing by highlighting successes in routine reports, having satisfied customers relay their appreciation to senior executives, being seen at social functions, being active in your professional associations, and developing powerful allies who speak positively about your accomplishments. Of course, the skilled politician actively and successfully lobbies to get the projects that will increase his or her visibility.

6. *Develop powerful allies.* It helps to have powerful people on your side. Cultivate contacts with

potentially influential people above you, at your own level, and in the lower ranks. These allies often can provide you with information that's otherwise not readily available. In addition, there will be times when decisions will be made in favor of those with the greatest support. Having powerful allies can provide you with a coalition of support if and when you need it.

7. *Avoid "tainted" members.*   In almost every organization, there are fringe members whose status is questionable. Their performance and/or loyalty is suspect. Keep your distance from such individuals. Given the reality that effectiveness has a large subjective component, your own effectiveness might be called into question if you're perceived as being too closely associated with tainted members.

8. *Support your boss.*   Your immediate future is in the hands of your current boss. Because he or she evaluates your performance, you'll typically want to do whatever is necessary to have your boss on your side. You should make every effort to help your boss succeed, make her look good, support her if she is under siege, and spend the time to find out the criteria she will use to assess your effectiveness. Don't undermine your boss. And don't speak negatively of her to others.

Practicing the Skill

You used to be the star marketing manager for Hilton Electronics Corporation. But for the past year, you've been outpaced again and again by Sean, a new manager in the design department, who has been accomplishing everything expected of him and more. Meanwhile your best efforts to do your job well have been sabotaged and undercut by Maria—your and Sean's manager. For example, prior to last year's international consumer electronics show, Maria moved $30,000 from your budget to Sean's. Despite your best efforts, your marketing team couldn't complete all the marketing materials normally developed to showcase all of your organization's new products at this important industry show. And Maria has chipped away at your staff and budget ever since. Although you've been able to meet most of your goals with less staff and budget, Maria has continued to slice away resources from your group. Just last week, she eliminated two positions in your team of eight marketing specialists to make room for a new designer and some extra equipment for Sean. Maria is clearly taking away your resources while giving Sean whatever he wants and more. You think it's time to do something or soon you won't have any team or resources left.

Reinforcement Activities

1. Keep a one-week journal of your behavior describing incidences when you tried to influence others around you. Assess each incident by asking: Were you successful at these attempts to influence them? Why or why not? What could you have done differently?

2. Outline a specific action plan, based on concepts in this module, that would improve your career progression in the organization in which you currently work or an organization in which you think you would like to be employed.

11 NEGOTIATING

Self-Assessment Interpretation

Complete the self-assessment (#34) on your conflict style. The results suggest your preferred style for handling conflict. You'll want to use this information to work against your natural tendencies when the situation requires a different style. Because negotiation is a method for resolving conflicts, knowing your preferred conflict style will give you insights into how you might handle negotiations.

Skill Concepts and Behaviors

You can be more effective at negotiating if you use the following five recommended behaviors.[11]

1. *Begin with a positive overture.*   Studies on negotiation show that concessions tend to be reciprocated and lead to agreements. As a result, begin bargaining with a positive overture—perhaps a small concession—and then reciprocate the other party's concessions.

2. *Address problems, not personalities.* Concentrate on the negotiation issues, not on the personal characteristics of the individual with whom you're negotiating. When negotiations get tough, avoid the tendency to attack this person. Remember it's that person's ideas or position that you disagree with, not him or her personally. Separate the people from the problem, and don't personalize differences.

3. *Pay little attention to initial offers.* Treat an initial offer as merely a point of departure. Everyone must have an initial position. These initial offers tend to be extreme and idealistic. Treat them as such.

4. *Emphasize win–win solutions.* Inexperienced negotiators often assume that their gain must come at the expense of the other party. That needn't be the case. There are often win–win solutions. But assuming a zero-sum game means missed opportunities for trade-offs that could benefit both sides. So if conditions are supportive, look for an integrative solution. Frame options in terms of the other party's interests and look for solutions that can allow this person, as well as yourself, to declare a victory.

5. *Create an open and trusting climate.* Skilled negotiators are better listeners, ask more questions, focus their arguments more directly, are less defensive, and have learned to avoid words or phrases that can irritate the person with whom they're negotiating (such as "generous offer," "fair price," or "reasonable arrangement"). In other words, they're better at creating the open and trusting climate that is necessary for reaching a win–win settlement.

Practicing the Skill

As marketing director for Done Right, a regional home-repair chain, you've come up with a plan you believe has significant potential for future sales. Your plan involves a customer information service designed to help people make their homes more environmentally sensitive. Then based on homeowners' assessments of their homes' environmental impact, your firm will be prepared to help them deal with problems or concerns they may uncover. You're really excited about the competitive potential of this new service. You envision pamphlets, in-store appearances by environmental experts, as well as contests for consumers and school kids. After several weeks of preparations, you make your pitch to your boss, Nick Castro. You point out how the market for environmentally sensitive products is growing and how this growing demand represents the perfect opportunity for Done Right. Nick seems impressed by your presentation, but he's expressed one major concern. He thinks your workload is already too heavy. He doesn't see how you're going to have enough time to start this new service *and* still be able to look after all of your other assigned marketing duties.

Reinforcement Activities

1. Negotiate with a course instructor to raise the grade on an exam or paper on which you think you should have received a higher grade.
2. The next time you purchase a relatively expensive item (e.g., automobile, apartment lease, appliance, jewelry), negotiate a better price and gain some concessions such as an extended warranty, smaller down payment, maintenance services, or the like.

12 DELEGATING AUTHORITY

Self-Assessment Interpretation

Complete the self-assessment (#40) on willingness to delegate. This instrument taps excuses for failing to delegate and errors managers use when delegation is done improperly. The higher your score, the better your delegation skills.

Skill Concepts and Behaviors

Managers get things done through other people. Because there are limits to any manager's time and knowledge, effective managers need to understand how to delegate. *Delegation* is the assignment of authority to another person to carry out specific duties.

It allows an employee to make decisions. Delegation should not be confused with participation. In participative decision making, there's a sharing of authority. In delegation, employees make decisions on their own.

A number of actions differentiate the effective delegator from the ineffective delegator. There are five behaviors that effective delegators will use.[12]

1. *Clarify the assignment.* The place to begin is to determine *what* is to be delegated and *to whom*. You need to identify the person who's most capable of doing the task and then determine whether he or she has the time and motivation to do the task. Assuming you have a willing and able individual, it's your responsibility to provide clear information on what is being delegated, the results you expect, and any time or performance expectations you may have. Unless there's an overriding need to adhere to specific methods, you should delegate only the results expected. Get agreement on what is to be done and the results expected, but let the employee decide the best way to complete the task.

2. *Specify the employee's range of discretion.* Every act of delegation comes with constraints. Although you're delegating to an employee the authority to perform some task or tasks, you're not delegating unlimited authority. You're delegating authority to act on certain issues within certain parameters. You need to specify what those parameters are so that the employee knows, in no uncertain terms, the range of his or her discretion.

3. *Allow the employee to participate.* One of the best sources for determining how much authority will be necessary to accomplish a task is the person who will be held accountable for that task. If you allow employees to participate in determining what is delegated, how much authority is needed to get the job done, and the standards by which they'll be judged, you increase employee motivation, satisfaction, and accountability for performance.

4. *Inform others that delegation has occurred.* Delegation should not take place in a vacuum. Not only do you and the delegatee need to know specifically what has been delegated and how much authority has been given, but anyone else who may be affected by the delegation act also needs to be informed.

5. *Establish feedback channels.* The establishment of controls to monitor the employee's progress increases the likelihood that important problems will be identified early and that the task will be completed on time and to the desired specifications. Ideally, these controls should be determined at the time of the initial assignment. Agree on a specific time for the completion of the task and then set progress dates when the employee will report back on how well he or she is doing and any major problems that may have arisen. These controls can be supplemented with periodic checks to ensure that authority guidelines aren't being abused, organizational policies are being followed, proper procedures are being met, and the like.

Practicing the Skill

You're the director of research and development for a large pharmaceutical manufacturer. You have six people who report directly to you: Sue (your secretary), Dale (laboratory manager), Todd (quality standards manager), Linda (patent coordination manager), Ruben (market coordination manager), and Marjorie (senior projects manager). Dale is the most senior of the five managers and is generally acknowledged as the chief candidate to replace you if you are promoted or leave.

You have received your annual instructions from the CEO to develop next year's budget for your area. The task is relatively routine but takes quite a bit of time. In the past, you've always done the annual budget yourself. But this year, because your workload is exceptionally heavy, you've decided to try something different. You're going to assign budget preparation to one of your subordinate managers. The obvious choice is Dale. Dale has been with the company longest, is highly dependable, and, as your probable successor, is most likely to gain from the experience. The budget is due on your boss' desk in eight weeks. Last year it took you about 30 to 35 hours to complete. However, you have done a budget many times before. For a novice, it might take double that amount of time.

The budget process is generally straightforward. You start with last year's budget and modify it to reflect inflation and changes in departmental objectives. All the data that Dale will need are in your files, online, or can be obtained from your other managers.

You have just walked over to Dale's office and informed him of your decision. He seemed enthusiastic about doing the budget, but he also has a heavy workload. He told you, "I'm regularly coming in around 7 A.M. and it's unusual for me to leave before 7 P.M. For the past five weekends, I've even come in on Saturday mornings to get my work done. I can do my best to try to find time to do the budget."

Specify exactly what you would say to Dale and the actions you would take if Dale agrees to do the budget.

Reinforcement Activities

1. When watching a video of a classic movie that has examples of "managers" delegating assignments, pay explicit attention to the incidence of delegation. Was delegating done effectively? What was good about the practice? How might it have been improved? Examples of movies with delegation examples include *The Godfather*, *The Firm*, *Star Trek*, *Nine-to-Five*, and *Working Girl*.

2. The next time you have to do a group project for a class, pay explicit attention to how tasks are delegated. Does someone assume a leadership role? If so, note how closely the delegation process is followed. Is delegation different in project or study groups than in typical work groups?

13 DESIGNING MOTIVATING JOBS

Self-Assessment Interpretation

Complete the self-assessment (#37) on a job's motivating potential. This instrument indicates how motivating your job is. Use this information as a base for looking at the jobs for which you are responsible.

Skill Concepts and Behaviors

How do you enrich an employee's job? The following suggestions, based on the job characteristics model, specify the types of changes in jobs that are most likely to lead to improving their motivating potential.[13]

1. *Combine tasks.* As a manager, you should seek to take existing specialized and divided tasks and put them back together to form a new and larger module of work. This will increase skill variety and task identity.

2. *Create natural work units.* The creation of natural work units means that the tasks an employee does form an identifiable and meaningful whole. This increases employee "ownership" of the work and improves the likelihood that employees will view their work as meaningful and important rather than as irrelevant and boring.

3. *Establish client relationships.* The client is the user of the product or service that the employee works on (and may be an "internal customer" or someone outside the organization). Whenever possible, you should establish direct relationships between workers and their clients. This increases skill variety, autonomy, and feedback for the employee.

4. *Expand jobs vertically.* Vertical expansion gives employees responsibilities and control that were formerly reserved for management. It seeks to partially close the gap between the "doing" and "controlling" aspects of the job, and it increases employee autonomy.

5. *Open feedback channels.* By increasing feedback, employees not only learn how well they are performing their jobs but also whether their performance is improving, deteriorating, or remaining at a constant level. Ideally, this feedback should be received directly as the employee does the job, rather than from his or her manager on an occasional basis.

Practicing the Skill

You own and manage Sunrise Deliveries, a small freight transportation company that makes local deliveries of products for your customers. You have a total of nine employees—an administrative assistant, two warehouse personnel, and six delivery drivers.

The drivers' job is pretty straightforward. Each morning they come in at 7:30 A.M., pick up their daily schedule, and then drive off in their preloaded trucks to make their stops. They occasionally will also pick up packages and return them to the Sunrise warehouse, where they'll be unloaded and redirected by the warehouse workers.

You've become very concerned with the high turnover among your drivers. Of your current six drivers, three have been working for you less than two months and only one's tenure exceeds six months. This is frustrating because you're paying your drivers more than many of the larger delivery companies like UPS and FedEx. This employee turnover is getting expensive because you're constantly having to spend time finding and training replacements. It's also hard to develop a quality customer-service program when customers constantly see new faces. When you've asked departing drivers why they're quitting, common complaints include: "there's no room for advancement," "the job is boring," and "all we do is drive." You know that you're going to have to do something to solve this problem.

Reinforcement Activities

1. Think of the worst job you've ever had. Analyze the job according to the five dimensions identified in the job characteristics model. Redesign the job in order to make it more satisfying and motivating.

2. Spend one to three hours at various times observing employees in your college dining hall. What specific actions would you recommend to make these jobs more motivating?

 14 SELECTION INTERVIEWING

Self-Assessment Interpretation

Complete the self-assessment (#17) on decision-making style. This instrument taps your preferred style—from among directive, analytic, conceptual, and behavioral decision making. The selection interview is an important activity in which most managers will engage. The purpose of the interview is to gain information to help you make an effective decision. High emphasis in one decision-style category shows your dominant style. If your answers spread out over the four response categories, you show flexibility. Consider how your style influences the way you approach and conduct selection interviews.

Skill Concepts and Behaviors

The interview is used almost universally as part of the employee-selection process. Not many of us have ever gotten a job without having gone through one or more interviews. Interviews can be valid and reliable selection tools, but they need to be structured and well organized.

You can be an effective interviewer if you use the following seven suggestions for interviewing job candidates.[14]

1. *Review the job description and job specifications.* Prior to the interview, be sure you have reviewed pertinent information about the job. This will provide you with valuable information on which to assess the job candidate. Furthermore, knowing the relevant job requirements can help eliminate interview bias.

2. *Prepare a structured set of questions you want to ask all job applicants.* By having a set of prepared questions, you ensure that you'll get the information you want. Furthermore, by asking similar questions, you're able to better compare all candidates' answers against a common base. Choose questions that can't be answered with merely a yes or a no. Avoid leading questions that telegraph the desired response (such as "Would you say you have good interpersonal skills?") and bipolar questions that require the applicant to select an answer from only two choices (such as "Do you prefer working with people or working alone?"). Because the best predictor of future behavior is past behavior, the best questions tend to be those that focus on previous experiences that are relevant to the current job. Examples might include: "What have you done in previous jobs that demonstrates your creativity?" "On your last job, what was it that you most wanted to accomplish but didn't? Why didn't you?"

3. *Before meeting a candidate, review his or her application form and resume.* This will help you create a complete picture of the candidate in terms of what is represented on the resume or application and what the job requires. You can also begin to identify areas to explore during the interview. Areas that are not clearly defined on the resume or application but that are essential to the job need to be addressed in your discussion with the candidate.

4. *Open the interview by putting the applicant at ease and by providing a brief preview of the topics to be discussed.* Interviews are stressful for job candidates. Be friendly, and open the discussion with a few simple questions or statements that can break the ice. Once the applicant is fairly relaxed, provide a brief orientation. Preview what topics will be discussed, how long the interview will take, and explain if you'll be taking notes. Encourage the applicant to ask questions.

5. *Ask your questions and listen carefully to the candidate's answers.* Select follow-up questions that flow naturally from the answers given. Focus on the candidate's responses as they relate to information you need to ensure that the person meets your job requirements. For instance, if you feel that the applicant's response is superficial or inadequate, seek elaboration. Encourage greater response by saying, "Tell me more about that issue." To clarify information, you could say, "You said working overtime was OK *sometimes*. Can you tell me specifically when you'd be willing to work overtime?" If the applicant doesn't directly answer your question, follow up by repeating the question or paraphrasing it. Also, never underestimate the power of silence in an interview. Inexperienced interviewers often talk too much. So pause for at least a few seconds after the applicant appears to have finished an answer. Your silence encourages the applicant to continue talking.

6. *Close the interview by telling the applicant what is going to happen next.* Applicants are anxious about the status of your hiring decision. Be up front with candidates regarding others who will be interviewed and the remaining steps in the hiring process. Let the person know your time frame for making a decision. In addition, tell the applicant how you will notify him or her about your decision.

7. *Write your evaluation of the applicant while the interview is still fresh in your mind.* Don't wait until the end of the day, after interviewing several people, to write your analysis of each person. The sooner you write your impressions after an interview, the better chance you have of accurately noting what occurred in the interview and your perceptions of the candidate.

Practicing the Skill

I. Break into groups of three.
2. Take up to 10 minutes to compose five challenging job interview questions that you think would be relevant in the hiring of new college graduates for a sales-management training program at Procter & Gamble. Each new hire will spend 18 to 24 months as a sales representative, calling on retail grocery accounts. After this training period, successful performers can be expected to be promoted to the position of district sales supervisor.
3. Exchange your five questions with another group.
4. Each group should allocate one of the following roles to their three members: interviewer, applicant, and observer. The person playing the applicant should rough out a brief resume of his or her background and experience and give it to the interviewer.
5. Role-play a job interview. The interviewer should include, but not be limited to, the five questions provided by the other group.
6. After the interview, the observer should evaluate the interviewer's behaviors in terms of the previously described skill concepts.

Reinforcement Activities

I. Talk to friends who have recently experienced a job interview. Find out what kinds of questions they were asked, how they responded, and what, if anything, they learned from the experience.
2. Interview a manager about the interview process he or she uses in hiring new employees. What types of information does the manager try to get during an interview? (Be sure that as you interview this manager that you're using the suggestions for good interviewing! Although you're not "hiring" this person, you are looking for information, which is exactly what managers are looking for during a job interview.)

15 READING AN ORGANIZATION'S CULTURE

Self-Assessment Interpretation

Complete the self-assessment (#42) on identifying the right organizational culture for you. The result will suggest whether you fit better in a more formal and structured culture or a more informal and flexible one. Your success and satisfaction in an organization will be influenced by how well its culture fits your personal preference.

Skill Concepts and Behaviors

The ability to read an organization's culture can be a valuable skill. For instance, if you're looking for a job, you'll want to choose an employer whose culture is compatible with your values and in which you'll feel comfortable. If you can accurately assess a potential employer's culture before you make your job decision, you may be able to save yourself a lot of grief and reduce the likelihood of making a poor choice. Similarly, you'll undoubtedly have business transactions with numerous organizations during your professional career, such as selling a product or service, negotiating a contract, arranging a joint work project, or merely seeking out who controls certain decisions in an organization. The ability to assess another organization's culture can be a definite plus in successfully performing those pursuits.

You can be more effective at reading an organization's culture if you use the following behaviors. For the sake of simplicity, we're going to look at this skill from the perspective of a job applicant. We'll assume that you're interviewing for a job, although these skills are generalizable to many situations. Here's a list of things you can do to help learn about an organization's culture.[15]

1. *Do background work.* Get the names of former employees from friends or acquaintances, and talk with them. Also talk with members of professional trade associations to which the organization's employees belong and executive recruiters who deal with the organization. Look for clues in stories told in annual reports and other organizational literature; and check out the organization's Web sites for evidence of high turnover or recent management shake-ups.

2. *Observe the physical surroundings.* Pay attention to signs, posters, pictures, photos, style of dress, length of hair, degree of openness between offices, and office furnishings and arrangements.

3. *Make note about those with whom you met.* Whom did you meet? How did they expect to be addressed?

4. *How would you characterize the style of the people you met?* Are they formal? Casual? Serious? Jovial? Open? Reticent about providing information?

5. *Look at the organization's human resources manual.* Are there formal rules and regulations printed there? If so, how detailed are they? What do they cover?

6. *Ask questions of the people with whom you meet.* The most valid and reliable information tends to come from asking the same questions of many people (to see how closely their responses align).

Questions that will give you insights into organizational processes and practices might include: What's the background of the founders? What's the background of current senior managers? What are these managers' functional specialties, and were they promoted from within or hired from outside? How does the organization integrate new employees? Is there a formal orientation program? Are there formal employee training programs and, if so, how are they structured? How does your boss define his or her job success? How would you define fairness in terms of reward allocations? Can you identify some people here who are on the "fast track"? What do you think has put them on the fast track? Can you identify someone in the organization who seems to be considered a deviant and how has the organization responded to this person? Can you describe a decision that someone made that was well received? Can you describe a decision that didn't work out well, and what were the consequences for that decision maker? Could you describe a crisis or critical event that has occurred recently in the organization and how did top management respond?

Practicing the Skill

After spending your first three years after college graduation as a freelance graphic designer, you're looking at pursuing a job as an account executive at a graphic design firm. You feel that the scope of assignments and potential for technical training far exceed what you'd be able to do on your own, and you're looking to expand your skills and meet a brand-new set of challenges. However, you want to make sure you "fit" into the organization where you're going to be spending more than eight hours every work day. What's the best way for you to find a place where you'll be happy and where your style and personality will be appreciated?

Reinforcement Activities

1. If you're taking more than one course, assess the culture of the various classes in which you're enrolled. How do the classroom cultures differ?

2. Do some comparisons of the atmosphere or feeling you get from various organizations. Because of the number and wide variety that you'll find, it will probably be easiest for you to do this ex-

ercise using restaurants, retail stores, or banks. Based on the atmosphere that you observe, what type of organizational culture do you think these organizations might have? If you can, interview three employees at each organization for their descriptions of their organization's culture.

Self-Assessment Interpretation

Complete the self-assessment (#47) on how well you respond to turbulent change. The higher your score, the more comfortable you are with change. Not all people, of course, handle change well. Use your score to understand the type of changes that may intimidate people.

Skill Concepts and Behaviors

Managers play an important role in organizational change, often serving as change agents. However, managers may find that change is resisted by employees. After all, change represents ambiguity and uncertainty, or it threatens the status quo. How can this resistance to change be effectively managed?

You can be more effective at managing resistance to change if you use the following suggestions.[16]

1. *Assess the climate for change.* A major factor why some changes succeed and others fail is the readiness for change. Assessing the climate for change involves asking a number of questions. The more affirmative answers you get to the following questions, the more likely it is that change efforts will succeed:

    Is the sponsor of the change high up enough to have power to deal effectively with resistance? Is senior management supportive of the change and committed to it? Is there a strong sense of urgency from senior management about the need for change, and is this feeling shared by the rest of the organization? Do managers have a clear vision of how the future will look different from the present? Are there objective measures in place to evaluate the change effort, and have reward systems been explicitly designed to reinforce them? Is the specific change effort consistent with other changes going on within the organization? Are functional managers willing to sacrifice their self-interests for the good of the organization as a whole? Does management pride itself on closely monitoring changes and actions taken by competitors? Are managers and employees rewarded for taking risks, being innovative, and looking for new and better solutions? Is the organizational structure flexible? Does communication flow both down *and* up in the organization? Has the organization successfully implemented major changes in the recent past? Is employee satisfaction and trust in management high? Is there a high degree of interaction and cooperation between organizational work units? Are decisions made quickly and do decisions take into account a wide variety of suggestions?

2. *Choose an appropriate approach for managing the resistance to change.* There are six tactics that have been suggested for dealing with resistance to change. Each is designed to be appropriate for different conditions of resistance. These include *education and communication* (used when resistance comes from lack of information or inaccurate information), *participation* (used when resistance stems from people not having all the information they need or when they have the power to resist), *facilitation and support* (used when those with power will lose out in a change), *manipulation and co-optation* (used when any other tactic will not work or is too expensive), and *coercion* (used when speed is essential and change agents possess considerable power). Which one or more of these approaches will be effective depends on the source of the resistance to the change.

3. *During the time the change is being implemented and after the change is completed, communicate with employees regarding what support you may be able to provide.* Your employees need to know that you are there to support them during change efforts. Be prepared to offer the assistance that may be necessary to help your employees enact the change.

Practicing the Skill

You're the nursing supervisor at a community hospital employing both emergency room and floor nurses. Each of these teams of nurses tends to work almost exclusively with others doing the same job. In your professional reading, you've come across the concept of cross-training nursing teams and giving them more varied responsibilities, which in turn has been shown to improve patient care while at the same time lowering costs. You call the two team leaders, Sue and Scott, into your office to explain that you want the nursing teams to move to this approach. To your surprise, they're both opposed to the idea. Sue says she and the other emergency room nurses feel they're needed in the ER, where they fill the most vital role in the hospital. They work special hours when needed, do whatever tasks are required, and often work in difficult and stressful circumstances. They think the floor nurses have relatively easy jobs for the pay they receive. Scott, leader of the floor nurse team, tells you that his group believes the ER nurses lack the special training and extra experience that the floor nurses bring to the hospital. The floor nurses claim they have the heaviest responsibilities and do the most exacting work. Because they have ongoing contact with patients and families, they believe they shouldn't be called away from vital floor duties to help the ER nurses complete their tasks.

Reinforcement Activities

1. Think about changes (major and minor) that you have dealt with over the past year. Perhaps these changes involved other people and perhaps they were personal. Did you resist the change? Did others resist the change? How did you overcome your resistance or the resistance of others to the change?

2. Interview managers at three different organizations about changes they have implemented. What was their experience in implementing the change? How did they manage resistance to the change?

Endnotes

1. Based on A. Belohlav, *The Art of Disciplining Your Employees* (Upper Saddle River, NJ: Prentice Hall, 1985); R. H. Lussier, "A Discipline Model for Increasing Performance," *Supervisory Management*, August 1990, pp. 6–7; and J. J. Martocchio and T. A. Judge, "When We Don't See Eye to Eye: Discrepancies between Supervisors and Subordinates in Absence Disciplinary Decisions," *Journal of Management*, vol. 21, no. 5, 1995, pp. 251–78.

2. Based on A. Bednar and W. H. Levie, "Attitude-Change Principles," in C. Fleming and W. H. Levie, *Instructional Message Design: Principles from the Behavioral and Cognitive Sciences*, 2nd ed. (Upper Saddle River, NJ: Educational Technology Publications, 1993); and S. P. Robbins and P. L. Hunsaker, *Training in InterPersonal Skills*, 2nd ed. (Upper Saddle River, NJ: Prentice Hall, 1996), pp. 110–16.

3. Based on V. P. Richmond, J. C. McCroskey, and S. K. Payne, *Nonverbal Behavior in Interpersonal Relations*, 2nd ed. (Englewood Cliffs, NJ: Prentice Hall, 1991), pp. 117–38; and L. A. King, "Ambivalence over Emotional Expression and Reading Emotions in Situations and Faces," *Journal of Personality and Social Psychology*, March 1998, pp. 753–62.

4. Based on J. Calano and J. Salzman, "Ten Ways to Fire Up Your Creativity," *Working Woman*, July 1989, p. 94; J. V. Anderson, "Mind Mapping: A Tool for Creative Thinking," *Business Horizons*, January–February 1993, pp. 42–46; M. Loeb, "Ten Commandments for Managing Creative People," *Fortune*, January 16, 1995, pp. 135–36; and M. Henricks, "Good Thinking," *Entrepreneur*, May 1996, pp. 70–73.

5. Based on S. P. Robbins and P. L. Hunsaker, *Training in InterPersonal Skills*, pp. 54–57.

6. Based on S. P. Robbins and P. L. Hunsaker, *Training in InterPersonal Skills*, pp. 200–207.

7. Based on S. P. Robbins and P. L. Hunsaker, *Training in InterPersonal Skills*, pp. 36–39.

8. Based on V. H. Vroom, "A New Look at Managerial Decision Making," *Organizational Dynamics*, Spring 1973, pp. 66–80. With permission.

9. Based on F. Bartolome, "Nobody Trusts the Boss Completely—Now What?," *Harvard Business Review*, March–April 1989, pp. 135–42; and J. K. Butler, Jr., "Toward Understanding and Measuring Conditions of Trust: Evolution of a Condition of Trust Inventory," *Journal of Management*, September 1991, pp. 643–63.

10. Based on H. Mintzberg, *Power In and Around Organizations* (Upper Saddle River, NJ: Prentice Hall, 1983), p. 24; and S. P. Robbins and P. L. Hunsaker, *Training in InterPersonal Skills*, pp. 131–34.

11. Based on J. A. Wall, Jr., and M. W. Blum, "Negotiations," *Journal of Management*, June 1991, pp. 278–82; and J. S. Pouliot, "Eight Steps to Success in Negotiating," *Nation's Business*, April 1999, pp. 40–42.

12. Based on S. P. Robbins and P. L. Hunsaker, *Training in InterPersonal Skills*, pp. 93–95.

13. Based on J. R. Hackman, "Work Design," in J. R. Hackman and J. L. Suttle (eds.), *Improving Life at Work* (Santa Monica, CA: Goodyear, 1977), pp. 132–33.

14. Based on W. C. Donaghy, *The Interview: Skills and Applications* (Glenview, IL: Scott, Foresman, 1984), pp. 245–80; J. M. Jenks and B. L. P. Zevnik, "ABCs of Job Interviewing," *Harvard Business Review*, July–August 1989, pp. 38–42; and E. D. Pulakos and N. Schmitt, "Experience-Based and Situational Interview Questions: Studies of Validity," *Personnel Psychology*, Summer 1995, pp. 289–308.

15. Based on A. L. Wilkins, "The Culture Audit: A Tool for Understanding Organizations," *Organizational Dynamics*, Autumn 1983, pp. 24–38; H. M. Trice and J. M. Beyer, *The Culture of Work Organizations* (Upper Saddle River, NJ: Prentice Hall, 1993), pp. 358–62; H. Lancaster, "To Avoid a Job Failure, Learn the Culture of a Company First," *Wall Street Journal*, July 14, 1998, p. B1; and D. M. Cable, L. Aiman-Smith, P. W. Mulvey, and J. R. Edwards, "The Sources and Accuracy of Job Applicants' Beliefs about Organizational Culture," *Academy of Management Journal*, December 2000, pp. 1076–85.

16. Based on J. P. Kotter and L. A. Schlesinger, "Choosing Strategies for Change," *Harvard Business Review*, March–April 1979, pp. 106–14; and T. A. Stewart, "Rate Your Readiness to Change," *Fortune*, February 7, 1994, pp. 106–10.

ILLUSTRATION CREDITS

CHAPTER 1
2 Courtesy of Michael Bowser
4 David Young-Wolff/PhotoEdit
9 © Michael Okoniewski/The Image Works
15 Courtesy of Xerox
19 Carbon Five Inc
20 Richard B. Levin/© Frances M. Roberts

CHAPTER 2
36 AP/Wide World Photos
38 Steve Kagan Photography
43 Nicolette Patrick Bernhardt
49 David R. Frazier Photolibrary, Inc.
52 © Bob Daemmrich/The Image Works

CHAPTER 3
62 Microsoft Corporation/Reprinted with permission from Microsoft Corporation.
68 AP/Wide World Photos
72 AP/Wide World Photos
73 AP/Wide World Photos
75 Home Depot Inc.
81 Donna Terek Photography
83 Kent Porte/Santa Rosa Press Democrat

CHAPTER 4
92 AP/Wide World Photos
95 Mark Richards
98 Mark Richards
101 © Mark Ludak/The Image Works
105 Pool Photo/Victoria Arocho/Getty Images, Inc.
111 © Esbin-Anderson/The Image Works
111 David Young-Wolff/PhotoEdit

CHAPTER 5
122 Asquinifoto.com
127 Amy Etra/PhotoEdit
129 Photo by Gilles Mingasson/Liaison/Getty Images
131 Steve Pyke Studio
134 Mark Richards/PhotoEdit
136 AP/Wide World Photos
139 © Michael S. Yamashita/CORBIS
142 Mark Richards/PhotoEdit

CHAPTER 6
154 Insight Development Group/Photo by D.M. Photographics.
162 Michael Newman/PhotoEdit
164 Photo by Uzi Keren/Newsmakers/Getty Images
168 Photo by David McNew/Getty Images
173 AP/Wide World Photos
175 Laura Pedrick
178 SuperStock, Inc.

CHAPTER 7
188 Paulo Fridman
195 Mr. Jussi Rautavirta
199 AP/Wide World Photos
203 Chip Simmons/TimePix
205 Lambert/Getty Images, Inc.
207 © Syracuse Newspapers/C.W. McKeen/The Image Works

CHAPTER 8
218 © Ed Kashi/CORBIS
225 © Greg Girard/Contact Press Images
229 New York Times Pictures
234 Paul Rodriguez/Latin Focus Photo Agency Paul Rodriguez-Latin Focus.com
236 Mark Richards
240 Frances M.Roberts/Richard B. Levin © Frances M. Roberts. All Rights Reserved.

CHAPTER 9
256 Wes-Tex Printing
265 Courtesy of Spartech Corporation
268 Amanda Friedman
270 Honeywell
271 AP/Wide World Photos

CHAPTER 10
282 David Young-Wolff/PhotoEdit
291 Courtesy of Urbanlegends.com
297 Chris Buck Inc.
299 SuperStock, Inc.

CHAPTER 11
312 Photo by Mario Tama/Getty Images
315 Photo by Alan Dejecacion/Newsmakers/Getty Images
316 AP/Wide World Photos
319 Rose Hartman/Globe Photos, Inc.
323 Photo by Keith D. McGrew/US Army/Getty Images
324 Dan Krauss Photography
327 NASA/Johnson Space Center

CHAPTER 12
334 © Rommel Pecson/The Image Works
338 Eze Castle Software
340 AP/Wide World Photos
345 AP/Wide World Photos
351 NovaStock Image State/International Stock Photography Ltd.
353 AP/Wide World Photos
356 © Michael S. Yamashita/CORBIS

CHAPTER 13
364 Photo by Alex Wong/Newsmakers/Getty Images
366 Amilcar Getty Images/Photo by Amilcar/Liaison
370 Makoto Ishida
374 Guntmar Fritz/Masterfile Corporation
375 AFP Photo Paul J. Richards/CORBIS © AFP/CORBIS
379 Richard B. Levine/Frances M. Roberts/ © Richard B. Levine
384 Don Hogan Charles/The New York Times

CHAPTER 14
394 Photo by Jeff Christensen/Newsmaker/Getty Images
399 Bruce Ayres/Getty Images Inc.
401 Los Angeles Times Photo by Glenn Koenig
405 Republished with permission of Globe Newspaper Company, Inc.
407 Photo by © Tim Shaffer
409 REUTERS/CORBIS © Reuters NewMedia Inc./CORBIS
413 Courtesy of the American Arbitration Association

CHAPTER 15
424 © Francis Dean/The Image Works
428 Courtesy of ADP
429 Misha Gravenor Photography
434 Amy Etra/PhotoEdit
437 Chris Carroll Photography
442 © Mitch Wojnarowicz/The Image Works
445 © David Lassman/Syracuse Newspapers/ The Image Works

CHAPTER 16
454 Net Optics, Inc.
456 Courtesy of IBM
458 AP/Wide World Photos
461 Dan Lim Masterfile Corp © Dan Lim/Masterfile
469 Kristine Larsen
475 ITT Industries
477 Courtesy of Siemens

CHAPTER 17
488 Photo by Marta Nascimento/REA/Corbis SABA
491 Southwest Airlines
496 Courtesy of Buckman Laboratories
500 © Lands' End, Inc. Used with permission.
506 © Amelia Kunhardt/The Image Works
510 Jessica Brandi Lifland

CHAPTER 18
522 AP/Wide World Photos
527 Mark Richards
536 Jimmy Williams Productions
540 Olive Garden/Getty Images, Inc,
543 Tom's of Maine, Inc.

CHAPTER 19
554 Kistone Photography
558 www.corbis.com/Paul A. Souders
562 Frank Veronsky
569 Fred R. Conrad/The New York Times
573 John Manning, VP of WOW
574 Photo by Scott Nelson/Getty Images
581 © Norbert von der Groeben/The Image Works
585 Gary Tramonita/New York Times Pictures

APPENDIX A
600 Property of AT&T Archives. Reprinted with permission of AT&T.
601 Marcia Roltner/Ann Maslow Kaplan
602 Joe McNally Photography

Name Index

Page references followed by a "b" indicate boxes; "e", exhibits; "i", illustrations; and *n*, notes (lettered or numbered).

Organization Index

Page references followed by a "b" indicate boxes; "e", exhibits; "i", illustrations; and n, notes (lettered or numbered).

overestimate the influence of
internal factors when making
judgments about the behavior
of others, 126
Future orientation, 69, 70

G

Gainsharing *An incentive plan in
which improvements in group
productivity determine the
total amount of money that is
allocated,* 200
Gender, 39
   communication barriers,
    299–300
   differentiation, 69, 70e
   emotions and, 109–10
   leadership and, 349
   male competitiveness, 56
   negotiation differences,
    411–12
Globalization, 14
GLOBE studies
   cultural dimensions, 69–71
   leadership effectiveness, 357
Goal-setting theory *The theory
that specific and difficult
goals, with feedback, lead
to higher performance,*
165–67, 179, 191
Grapevine *The organization's
informal communication
network,* 290–92
Graphic rating scales *An
evaluation method in which
the evaluator rates
performance factors on an
incremental scale,* 503
Group decision making, 240
   effectiveness and efficiency,
    240–41
   e-organizations, 461–62
   groupthink and groupshift,
    241–43
   individual decision making
    compared, 240–41
   strengths, 240
   techniques, 243–45
   weaknesses, 240
Group demography *The degree to
which members of a group
share a common demographic
attribute, such as age, sex, race,
educational level, or length of
service in the organization, and*

the impact of this attribute on
turnover, 236
Group-level OB variables,
   26, 27e
Group order ranking *An
evaluation method that places
employees into a particular
classification, such as
quartiles,* 503
Groupshift *A change in decision
risk between the group's
decision and the individual
decision that members within
the group would make; can be
either toward conservatism or
greater risk,* 241–43
Group(s) *Two or more individuals,
interacting and interdependent,
who have come together to
achieve particular objectives,*
219–20, 245–47
   abilities, 225–26
   authority structures, 224
   change resistance, 561
   classification, 219–20
   cohesiveness, 237–38
   composition, 235–37
   decision making (*see* Group
    decision making)
   external conditions imposed
    on, 224–25
   five-stage group-development
    model, 220–22
   formal leadership, 226
   job design, 248
   knowledge, 225
   norms, 229–31, 232
   organization culture, 225
   organization strategy, 224
   performance evaluations and
    rewards, 224–25
   personality characteristics, 226
   power in, 372–73
   processes, 238–39
   punctuated-equilibrium model,
    222–23
   regulations, 224
   resources, 224, 225–26
   roles, 226–29
   size, 234–35
   skills, 225–26
   stages of group development,
    220–23
   status, 231–34
   structure, 226–38

   tasks, 239
   temporary groups with
    deadlines, 222–23
   types, 219–20
   work setting, 225
   Zimbardo's simulated prison,
    228–29
Groupthink *Phenomenon in which
the norm for consensus
overrides the realistic appraisal
of alternative courses of
action,* 241–43

H

Halo effect *Drawing a general
impression about an
individual on the basis of a
single characteristic,* 128
Hawthorne studies, 600–01
Heredity, 94–95
Heuristics *Judgmental shortcuts in
decision making,* 139
Hierarchy of needs theory *There
is a hierarchy of five
needs–physiological, safety,
social, esteem, and self-
actualization; as each need is
substantially satisfied, the
next need becomes dominant,*
156–57, 179
High-context cultures *Cultures
that rely heavily on nonverbal
and subtle situational cues in
communication,* 304
Higher-order needs *Needs that are
satisfied internally; social,
esteem, and self-actualization
needs,* 157
Hiring employees, 147
   interviews, 129–30, 490–92,
    493
   selection devices, 490–93, 509,
    513, 531–32, 541
   tests, 492–93
Historical precedents in decision
   making, 142–43
History of OB, 594–605
Hofstede's culture assessment
   framework, 68–69
Humane orientation, 70
Human relations, 600–01
Human relations view of conflict
   *The belief that conflict is a
natural and inevitable
outcome in any group,* 396

Human resources, 488–89
  assessment centers, 493
  career development, 496–98
  diversity (*see* Workforce diversity)
  employment interviews, 129–30, 490–92, 493
  job analysis, 489–90
  labor unions, 507–9, 514
  performance evaluations (*see* Performance evaluations)
  performance-simulation tests, 492–93
  selection devices, 490–93, 509, 513, 531–32, 541
  training and development programs (*see* Training and development programs)
  union-management interface, 507–9, 514
  work sampling, 492
  written employment tests, 492
Human skills *The ability to work with, understand, and motivate other people, both individually and in groups,* 5
Hygiene factors *Factors–such as company policy and administration, supervision, and salary–that, when adequate in a job, placate workers. When these factors are adequate, people will not be dissatisfied,* 160
Hypothesis in research, 607

I
Idea champions *Individuals who take an innovation and actively and enthusiastically promote the idea, build support, overcome resistance, and ensure that the idea is implemented,* 572
Identification-based trust *Trust based on a mutual understanding of each other's intentions and appreciation of the other's wants and desires,* 339
Illegitimate political behavior *Extreme political behavior that violates the implied rules of the game,* 375
Imitation strategy *A strategy that seeks to move into new products or new markets only after their viability has already been proven,* 441
Implicit models of organizational structure *Perceptions that people hold regarding structural variables formed by observing things around them in an unscientific fashion,* 447
Impression management *The process by which individuals attempt to control the impression others form of them,* 381
Independent variable *The presumed cause of some change in the dependent variable,* 25, 607
Individual behavior
  ability and, 40–43, 54–55
  biographical characteristics, 37–40, 54
  conflict process, 403–5
  e-organizations and, 460–61
  learning and, 43–54, 55, 56
  performance evaluations of, 500, 505
  stress (*see* Stress)
  structure of organization and, 445–46
Individualism *A national culture attribute describing the degree to which people prefer to act as individuals rather than a member of groups,* 68, 69, 70
Individual-level OB variables, 25–26, 27
Individual ranking *An evaluation method that rank-orders employees from best to worst,* 503
Informal group *A group that is neither formally structured nor organizationally determined; appears in response to the need for social contact,* 220
Information power *Power that comes from access to and control over information,* 367–68
Initiating structure *The extent to which a leader is likely to define and structure his or her role and those of subordinates in the search for goal attainment,* 316
Innovation *A new idea applied to initiating or improving a product, process, or service,* 571–72
  stimulating, 20
Innovation strategy *A strategy that emphasizes the introduction of major new products and services,* 441
Institutionalization *When an organization takes on a life of its own, apart from any of its members, and acquires immortality,* 524
Instrumental values *Preferable modes of behavior or means of achieving one's terminal values,* 64
Integrative bargaining *Negotiation that seeks one or more settlements that can create a win-win solution,* 409
Intellectual ability *The capacity to do mental activities,* 40–41, 579–80
Intentions *Decisions to act in a given way,* 401–3
Interacting groups *Typical groups, in which members interact with each other face-to-face,* 243
Interactionist view of conflict *The belief that conflict is not only a positive force in a group but that it is absolutely necessary for a group to perform effectively,* 396
Interest group *Those working together to attain a specific objective with which each is concerned,* 220
Intergroup development *OD efforts to change the attitudes, stereotypes, and perceptions that groups have of each other,* 569–70
Intermittent reinforcement *A desired behavior is reinforced often enough to make the behavior worth repeating but not every time it is demonstrated,* 49
Internals *Individuals who believe that they control what happens to them,* 98
Internet *A worldwide network of interconnected computers,* 459
Interval schedules, 49

Leadership, *(continued)*
   University of Michigan
      studies, 317
   visionary leadership, 344–45
Leading *A management function
   that includes motivating
   employees, directing others,
   selecting the most effective
   communication channels, and
   resolving conflicts,* 5
Learning *Any relatively permanent
   change in behavior that occurs
   as a result of experience,*
   43–54, 55
   education and, 56
   organizational culture, 535–38
Learning organization *An
   organization that has
   developed the continuous
   capacity to adapt and change,*
   573–74
Least-preferred co-worker (LPC)
   questionnaire *An instrument
   that purports to measure
   whether a person is task- or
   relationship-oriented,* 320
Legitimate political behavior
   Normal everyday politics, 375
Legitimate power *The power a
   person receives as a result of
   his or her position in the
   formal hierarchy of an
   organization,* 367
Lewin's three-step change model,
   564–65
Life/work balance, 20–21,
   510–11, 512
Literacy skills training, 494
LMX theory, 324–25
Locus of control *The degree to
   which people believe they are
   masters of their own fate,*
   98–99
Long-term orientation *A national
   culture attribute that
   emphasizes the future, thrift,
   and persistence,* 69
Low-context cultures *Cultures that
   rely heavily on words to
   convey meaning in
   communication,* 304
Lower-order needs *Needs that are
   satisfied externally;
   physiological and safety
   needs,* 157

Low-skilled service worker
   motivation, 207–8
Loyalty *Dissatisfaction expressed
   by passively waiting for
   conditions to improve,* 82
LPC questionnaire, 320

M

Machiavellianism *Degree to which
   an individual is pragmatic,
   maintains emotional distance,
   and believes that ends can
   justify means,* 99–100
Management, 28
   administrators, 4
   decisional roles, 5, 6
   disseminator role, 5, 6
   disturbance handlers, 5, 6
   effective *versus* successful, 7–8
   entrepreneur role, 5, 6
   figurehead role, 5, 6
   functions, 4
   information roles, 5, 6
   interpersonal roles, 5, 6
   leadership role, 5, 6
   liaison role, 5, 6
   monitor role, 5, 6
   negotiator role, 5, 6
   resource allocators, 5, 6
   roles, 4–5
   skills, 5–7
   spokesperson role, 5, 6
Management by objectives (MBO)
   *A program that encompasses
   specific goals, participatively
   set, for an explicit time period,
   with feedback on goal
   progress,* 189–91
   goal-setting theory and, 191
   practice of, 191
Management principles, 596, 597
Managerial grid *A nine-by-nine
   matrix outlining 81 different
   leadership styles,* 317, 318
Managers *Individuals who achieve
   goals through other people,* 4
Marital status, 39–40
Mass customization *Production
   processes that are flexible
   enough to create products and
   services that are individually
   tailored to individual
   customers,* 458–59
Mass production *Using division of
   labor, standardization, and

automated processes to
   manufacture products in large
   quantities,* 458
Material symbols and
   organizational culture, 537
Matrix structure *A structure that
   creates dual lines of authority
   and combines functional and
   product departmentalization,*
   435–36
MBO, 189–91
MBTI, 96–97
McClelland's theory of needs
   *Achievement, power, and
   affiliation are three important
   needs that help explain
   motivation,* 162–64
Mechanistic model *A structure
   characterized by extensive
   departmentalization, high
   formalization, a limited
   information network, and
   centralization,* 440
Mediator *A neutral third party who
   facilitates a negotiated
   solution by using reasoning,
   persuasion, and suggestions
   for alternatives,* 413
Mentally challenging work, 85
Mentor *A senior employee who
   sponsors and supports a less-
   experienced employee (a
   protégé),* 347–49
Merger barriers, 529–30
Meta-analysis, 611–12
Metamorphosis stage *The stage in the
   socialization process in which a
   new employee changes and
   adjusts to the job, work group,
   and organization,* 534–35
Model *An abstraction of reality.
   A simplified representation
   of some real-world
   phenomenon,* 22
Moderating variable, 607
Money as motivator, 180
Moods *Feelings that tend to be less
   intense than emotions and
   that lack a contextual
   stimulus,* 106
Moral leadership, 350–51
Motivating potential score *A
   predictive index suggesting the
   motivating potential in a job,*
   466–67

Motivation *The processes that account for an individual's intensity, direction, and persistence of effort toward attaining a goal,* 154–56, 178–79, 208–9
  ability and opportunity, 175, 176
  cognitive evaluation theory, 164–65
  communication and, 284
  contemporary theories of, 161–78
  contingent workers, 206–7
  creativity and, 134
  culture-bound theories, 177–78
  diversity, 207
  early theories of, 156–61, 177–78
  emotions and, 112
  employee involvement programs and, 193–99, 210
  employee recognition programs, 191–93
  e-organizations, 460–61
  equity theory, 170–73, 179, 203, 233–34
  ERG theory, 161–62, 198, 203
  expectancy theory, 173–75, 179, 201, 205
  flexible benefits, 204–5
  flow experience theory, 168–69
  goal-setting theory, 165–67, 179, 191
  hierarchy of needs theory, 156–57, 179
  intrinsic theory, 169
  laziness, 158
  low-skilled service workers, 207–8
  management by objectives, 189–91
  McClelland's theory of needs, 162–64
  money and, 180
  performance evaluations and, 499
  professionals, 206
  reinforcement theory, 167–68, 179, 193, 203
  repetitive tasks, 208
  skill-based pay plans, 202–4
  Theory X and Theory Y, 157–59, 198
  two-factor theory, 159–61
  variable pay programs, 199–201
Motor reproduction processes, 47
Multiple intelligences *Intelligence contains four subparts: cognitive, social, emotional, and cultural,* 42
Myers-Briggs Type Indicator (MBTI) *A personality test that taps four characteristics and classifies people into one of 16 personality types,* 96–97
Myth of rationality, 105

N

National culture (*see* Culture, national)
Need for achievement *The drive to excel, to achieve in relation to a set of standards, to strive to succeed,* 162
Need for affiliation *The desire for friendly and close interpersonal relationships,* 162
Need for power *The need to make others behave in a way that they would not have behaved otherwise,* 162
Negative reinforcement, 47
Neglect *Dissatisfaction expressed through allowing conditions to worsen,* 82
Negotiation *A process in which two or more parties exchange goods or services and attempt to agree on the exchange rate for them,* 407–8, 416
  bargaining strategies, 408–10
  change resistance, 562–63
  clarification and justification, 411
  closure and implementation, 411
  cultural differences, 412–13, 414
  distributive bargaining, 408–9
  gender differences, 411–12
  ground rules, 411
  integrative bargaining, 408, 409–10
  personality traits in, 411
  preparation and planning, 410–11
  problem-solving, 411
  process, 410–11
  third-party negotiations, 413–14

Nexters, 66, 67
Nominal group technique *A group decision-making method in which individual members meet face-to-face to pool their judgments in a systematic but independent fashion,* 244–45
Nonverbal communication, 288–89
Norming stage *The third stage in group development, characterized by close relationships and cohesiveness,* 221
Norms *Acceptable standards of behavior within a group that are shared by the group's members,* 229–31
  allocation of resources norms, 230
  appearance norms, 229
  classes, 229–30
  conformity, 230–31
  deviant workplace behavior, 231, 232
  performance norms, 229
  social arrangement norms, 229–30
  status and, 232

O

OB (*see* Organizational behavior (OB))
OBM, 307
OB mod *The application of reinforcement concepts to individuals in the work setting,* 51–52
OCB, 25, 27
  job satisfaction and, 82–83
OD, 566–70
Off-the-job training, 495
Ohio State studies of leadership, 316–17
Online leadership, 351–52
On-the-job training, 495
Open-book management (OBM), 307
Openness to experience *A personality dimension that characterizes someone in terms of imaginativeness, artistic, sensitivity, and intellectualism,* 97

Operant conditioning *A type of conditioning in which desired voluntary behavior leads to a reward or prevents a punishment,* 45–46

Opportunity to perform *High levels of performance are partially a function of an absence of obstacles that constrain the employee,* 175

Oral communication, 286–87

Organic model *A structure that is flat, uses cross-hierarchical and cross-functional teams, has low formalization, possesses a comprehensive information network, and relies on participative decision making,* 440

Organization *A consciously coordinated social unit, composed of two or more people, that functions on a relatively continuous basis to achieve a common goal or set of goals,* 4

Organizational behavior (OB) *A field of study that investigates the impact that individuals, groups, and structure have on behavior within organizations, for the purpose of applying such knowledge toward improving an organization's effectiveness,* 8, 28
  absolutes in, 13
  challenges and opportunities, 14–22
  contributing disciplines, 11–12
  decision-making, 135–43
  emotions and, 111–13
  e-organizations, 461–63
  globalization, 14
  group-level OB variables, 26, 27
  individual-level OB variables, 25–26, 27
  intuition *versus* systemic study of, 8–10
  model of, 22–28
  OB mod, 51–52
  organization systems level OB variables, 26, 27
  perception, 129–30, 135–43
  personality and, 98–102

structure of organization and, 445–46
  values, 71

Organizational change, 564
  action research, 565–66
  appreciative inquiry, 570
  intergroup development, 569–70
  Lewin's three-step model, 564–65
  organizational development, 566–70
  process consultation, 567–68
  sensitivity training, 567
  survey feedback, 567
  team building, 568–69

Organizational citizenship behavior (OCB) *Discretionary behavior that is not part of an employee's formal job requirements, but that nevertheless promotes the effective functioning of the organization,* 25, 27
  job satisfaction and, 82–83

Organizational commitment *The degree to which an employee identifies with a particular organization and its goals, and wishes to maintain membership in the organization,* 72–73

Organizational culture *A common perception held by the organization's members; a system of shared meaning,* 522–28, 545
  acquisition and merger barrier, 529–30
  beginning of, 531
  change barriers, 529, 546
  core values, 526
  creating and sustaining, 531–35
  customer-responsive (*see* Customer-responsive cultures)
  descriptive nature, 525
  diversity barriers, 529
  dominant cultures, 526
  encounter stage of socialization, 534
  ethical organizational cultures, 538–39
  formalization compared, 527
  formation, 531–35

functions of, 528–29
  groups and, 225
  innovation and, 571–72
  institutionalization, 524
  keeping a culture alive, 531–35
  language, 538
  learning of, 535–38
  liabilities of, 529–30
  material symbols, 537
  metamorphosis stage of socialization, 534–35
  national culture compared, 527–28
  prearrival stage of socialization, 533–34
  rituals, 536–37
  selection process, 531–32
  socialization, 532–35, 541
  spirituality and (*see* Workplace spirituality)
  stories, 535–36
  strong *versus* weak cultures, 527
  subcultures, 526
  success breeds success, 530
  top management's actions, 532
  uniform, 525–27

Organizational development (OD) *A collection of planned-change interventions, built on humanistic-democratic values, that seeks to improve organizational effectiveness and employee well-being,* 566–70

Organizational structure *How job tasks are formally divided, grouped, and coordinated,* 424–26, 446–47
  boundaryless organization, 438–39
  bureaucracy, 434, 444
  centralization, 430–31, 432, 446
  chain of command, 429
  change, 561
  customer-responsive cultures, 541
  decentralization, 430–31, 432, 446
  departmentalization, 427–29
  employee behavior and, 445–46
  environment and choice of, 443–44
  formalization, 431–33
  implicit models of, 447

matrix structure, 435–36
mechanistic model, 440
organic model, 440
simple structure design, 433–34
size of organization, 441–42
span of control, 429–30, 431, 445
strategy, 440–41
stress and, 579–80, 584–86
team structure, 436–37
technology and choice of, 442, 448
virtual organization, 437–38
work specialization, 425–27, 445
Organization systems level OB variables, 26, 27
Organizing *Determining what tasks are to be done, who is to do them, how the tasks are to be grouped, who reports to whom, and where decisions are to be made,* 5

P

Paired comparison *An evaluation method that compares each employee with every other employee and assigns a summary ranking based on the number of superior scores that the employee achieves,* 504
Participative management *A process in which subordinates share a significant degree of decision making power with their immediate superiors,* 195, 562
Path-goal theory *The theory that it is the leader's job to assist followers in attaining their goals and to provide the necessary direction and/or support to ensure that their goals are compatible with the overall objectives of the group or organization,* 325–27
Peer evaluations, 501
Perceived conflict *Awareness by one or more parties of the existence of conditions that create opportunities for conflict to arise,* 401
Perception *A process by which individuals organize and interpret their sensory impressions in order to give*

meaning to their environment, 123–24, 145–46
communication barriers, 303
ethics and decision making, 143–45
factors influencing, 124–25
individual decision making, 131–34
OB, 129–30, 135–43
organization decision making, 135–43
person, 125–30
selective, 297
shortcuts used in judging others, 127–29
Performance evaluations, 130, 498, 513–14
abolishment, 515
behaviorally anchored rating scales, 503
behaviors, 500, 505
criteria, 499–500
critical incidents, 502–3
cultural dimensions, 509–10
customer-responsive cultures, 542
decision making, 142
documentation of performance, 505
due process, 506
evaluators, 500–02, 505, 506
feedback, 506–7
forced comparisons, 503–4
graphic rating scales, 503
group order ranking, 503
groups, 224, 245–46
immediate subordinate evaluations, 501
immediate supervisor evaluations, 501
improvement suggestions, 504–6
individual ranking, 503
individual task outcomes, 500
methods, 502–4
motivation and, 499
norms, 229
paired comparison, 504
peer evaluations, 501
purpose, 498–99
selectivity, 505–6
self-evaluations, 501
teams, 267, 507
360-degree evaluations, 501–2
training evaluators, 506
traits, 500, 505
written essays, 502

Performance expectations, 130
Performance orientation, 70
Performance-reward relationship, 173
Performing stage *The fourth state in group development, when the group is fully functional,* 221
Personality-job fit theory *Identifies six personality types and proposes that the fit between personality type and occupational environment determines satisfaction and turnover,* 103–4
Personality *The sum total of ways in which an individual reacts and interacts with others,* 93–94, 114 (*see also* Personality traits)
conflict process, 400
congruent occupations and, 158
determinants, 94–95
fit with job and organization, 103–5
groups and, 226
national culture and, 102
OB influences, 98–102
teams, 265
Personality traits *Enduring characteristics that describe an individual's behavior,* 96, 115
Big Five factors, 97–98
cardinal traits, 115
Myers-Briggs, 96–97
negotiation and, 411
performance evaluations of, 500, 505
primary traits, 96, 115
secondary traits, 115
source traits, 96
Person-organization fit, 105
Person perception, 125–30
Physical ability *The capacity to do tasks demanding stamina, dexterity, strength, and similar characteristics,* 42
Physical distance, 288
Piece-rate pay plans *Workers are paid a fixed sum for each unit of production completed,* 200
Planned change *Change activities that are intentional and goal oriented,* 557–58

Training, *(continued)*
  methods, 495–96
  off-the-job training, 495
  on-the-job training, 495
  performance evaluators, 506
  problem-solving skills, 495
  teams, 270
  technical skills, 494
  types of training, 493–95
Trait theories of leadership
    *Theories that consider
    personality, social, physical, or
    intellectual traits to
    differentiate leaders from
    nonleaders,* 314–15
Transactional leaders *Leaders who
    guide or motivate their
    followers in the direction of
    established goals by clarifying
    role and task requirements,*
    343–44
Transformational leaders *Leaders
    who provide individualized
    consideration and intellectual
    stimulation, and who possess
    charisma,* 343–44
Trust *A positive expectation that
    another will not act
    opportunistically,* 336
  dimensions, 336
  leadership and, 337–38
  political behavior and, 379
  types, 338–39
Turnover *The voluntary and
    involuntary permanent
    withdrawal from an
    organization,* 24, 27, 81
Two-factor theory *Intrinsic factors
    are related to job satisfaction,
    while extrinsic factors are
    associated with
    dissatisfaction,* 159–61
Type A personality *Aggressive
    involvement in a chronic,
    incessant struggle to achieve
    more and more in less and less
    time and, if necessary, against
    the opposing efforts of other
    things or other people,* 101–2
Type B personality, 101–2

U

Uncertainty avoidance *A national
    culture attribute describing the
    extent to which a society feels
    threatened by uncertain and
    ambiguous situations and tries
    to avoid them,* 69, 70
Unconditioned response, 44
Unconditioned stimulus, 44
Unfreezing *Change efforts to
    overcome the pressures of both
    individual resistance and
    group conformity,* 564
Union-management interface,
    507–9, 514
Unity of command *A subordinate
    should have only one superior
    to whom he or she is directly
    responsible,* 429
University of Michigan studies of
    leadership, 317
Utilitarianism *Decisions are made
    to provide the greatest good
    for the greatest number,*
    143–44

V

Values *Basic convictions that a
    specific mode of conduct or
    end-state of existence is
    personally or socially preferable
    to an opposite or converse mode
    of conduct or end-state of
    existence,* 63–71, 84
Value system *A hierarchy based on
    a ranking of an individual's
    values in terms of their
    intensity,* 63–64
Variable in research, 607
Variable-interval schedule
    *Rewards are initiated after a
    fixed or constant number of
    responses,* 49, 50, 51
Variable-pay programs *A portion
    of an employee's pay is based
    on some individual and/or
    organizational measure of
    performance,* 199–201
  expectancy theory and, 201
  practice of, 201–2
Variable-ratio schedule *The
    reward varies relative to the
    behavior of the individual,*
    50, 51
Videoconferencing, 294
Virtual organization *A small, core
    organization that outsources
    major business functions,*
    437–38
Virtual teams *Teams that use
    computer technology to tie
    together physically dispersed
    members in order to achieve a
    common goal,* 261–62
Visionary leadership *The ability to
    create and articulate a realistic,
    credible, attractive vision of the
    future for an organization or
    organizational unit that grows
    out of and improves upon the
    present,* 344–45
Voice *Dissatisfaction expressed
    through active and
    constructive attempts to
    improve conditions,* 82

W

Wagner Act, 599–600
Wellness programs
    *Organizationally supported
    programs that focus on the
    employee's total physical and
    mental condition,* 585
Well pay, 53
Whistle-blowers *Individuals who
    report unethical practices by
    their employer to outsiders,* 144
Work cohorts, 66–67, 236–37
Workforce diversity *The concept
    that organizations are
    becoming more heterogeneous
    in terms of gender, race,
    ethnicity and inclusion of
    other diverse groups,* 14–16
  age, 37–39, 47, 58–59
  attitudes and, 77–78
  communication, 299–300
  decision making, 406
  emotions, 109–10
  exercise, 30–32
  force of change, 556
  gender, 39, 109–10, 299–300,
    349, 411–412
  group composition, 236
  managing, 14–16, 510–12
  marital status, 39–40
  motivation, 207
  organizational culture and, 529
  perception and, 124
  stereotyping, 129
  strategy, 29
  teams, 265, 272–73
  training, 510–12
  values, 66–67
  work design, 475
  work/life conflicts, 510–11, 512
  workplace spirituality, 544

Organizatioal Behavior, Tenth Edition
PRENTICE-HALL, INC
SINGLE PC LICENSE AGREEMENT AND LIMITED WARRANTY